"This textbook is a 'must-have' resource for those interest[ed in destination man]agement and marketing. It offers a comprehensive view on k[...] and promoting destinations, with added chapters on current issues such as sustainability, residents' wellbeing, crisis management, and e-marketing. Written in a student-friendly manner, with plenty of examples and images, the textbook is a great resource for students, academics, and practitioners."

—**Dr. Cristina Maxim,** *Senior Lecturer,*
University of West London, UK

"This book covers important topics on destination marketing and management. Prof. Morrison sheds light on the critical concepts and discusses about strategic as well as operational issues. He features useful examples, summaries and review questions in each chapter, for the benefit of his readers. I am very pleased to recommend this title to students and to aspiring practitioners."

—**Dr. Mark Anthony Camilleri,** *Associate Professor of Corporate*
Communication, University of Malta, Malta

"The performance of a destination is often judged by the way it is managed and marketed. With globalisation, digitalisation and sophistication, destinations are evolving in an unpredictable tourism environment. As such, new knowledge and up-to-date strategies are needed to survive in such an uncertain condition. In response, Alastair's third Edition on *Marketing and Managing Tourism Destinations* offers a comprehensive insight of updated management and marketing strategies to the tourism world. Enriched with 21 chapters, the book not only presents contemporary concepts from a renewed perspective, but also proposes refreshed practical examples from different parts of the world. The book adopts a unique approach; each chapter opens up with a 'warming up' and closes with a 'summing up' section. This allows readership to have a taste of the topic while aiding in a smooth digestion of the chapter. *Marketing and Managing Tourism Destinations* by Alastair Morrison is a valuable resource to the tourism community. The book will definitely delight readership in quest of knowledge on contemporary issues affecting the management and marketing of tourism destinations in the 21st century and onwards."

—**Dr. Vanessa GB Gowreesunkar,** *Associate Professor,*
Anant National University, India and Associate Editor, Emerald,
International Journal of Tourism Cities

"This book makes a very significant and valuable contribution to tourism destination marketing and management. Dr. Morrison introduces each important concept through a synthesis of the literature, diverse case studies, up-to-date data, and a variety of figures and tables. The whole book is very easy to follow and covers all the crucial aspects of this area. The real-world cases provide excellent resources for students to learn by doing and set the best examples for practitioners. It is definitely essential reading for students, instructors, scholars, and practitioners."

—**Dr. Ye (Sandy) Shen,** *Assistant Professor, Experience Industry*
Management Department, Cal Poly University, San Luis Obispo,
California, US

Marketing and Managing Tourism Destinations

Marketing and Managing Tourism Destinations is a comprehensive and integrated introductory textbook covering destination management and marketing in one volume. It focuses on how destination management is planned, implemented, and evaluated as well as the management and operations of destination management organizations (DMOs), how they conduct business, major opportunities, and challenges and issues they face to compete for the global leisure and business travel markets.

Much has changed since the publication of the second edition of this book in 2018. The COVID-19 pandemic was unpredictable at the time and has caused havoc for destinations and DMOs. The third edition includes many materials about the COVID-19 impacts and recovery from the pandemic.

This third edition has been updated to include:

- four new chapters (Chapter 2—"Destination Sustainability and Social Responsibility"; Chapter 3—"Quality of Life and Well-Being of Destination Residents"; Chapter 11—"Destination Crisis Management"; and Chapter 20—"Destination Management Performance Measurement and Management");
- new and updated international case examples to show the practical realities and approaches to managing different destinations around the world;
- coverage of contemporary topics including, for example, COVID-19, social responsibility, metaverse, mixed reality, virtual meetings, teleworking, digital nomads, viral marketing, blended travel, regenerative tourism, meaningful travel, and several others;
- a significantly improved illustration program;
- keyword lists.

It is illustrated in full color and packed with features to encourage reflection on main themes, spur critical thinking, and show theory in practice. Written by an author with many years of industry practice, university teaching, and professional training experience, this book is the essential guide to the subject for tourism, hospitality, and events students and industry practitioners alike.

Alastair M. Morrison, Ph.D., is Research Professor at the School of Management and Marketing, Greenwich Business School, University of Greenwich in London. Formerly, he was Distinguished Professor Emeritus at Purdue University, Indiana, specializing in the area of tourism and hospitality marketing. He has published approximately 350 academic articles and conference proceedings and is the author of several books on tourism marketing and development, including *Hospitality and Travel Marketing* (5th edition, 2022), *Tourism Marketing in the Age of the Consumer* (2022), and *World Tourism Cities* (2021). Prof. Morrison is the coeditor-in-chief of the *International Journal of Tourism Cities* and coeditor of *The Routledge Handbook of Tourism Cities* (2021).

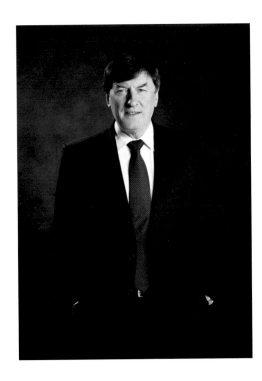

Marketing and Managing Tourism Destinations

Third Edition

Alastair M. Morrison

Routledge
Taylor & Francis Group

LONDON AND NEW YORK

Designed cover image: Alamy Stock Photo / Adam Burton

Third edition published 2024
by Routledge
4 Park Square, Milton Park, Abingdon, Oxon, OX14 4RN

and by Routledge
605 Third Avenue, New York, NY 10158

Routledge is an imprint of the Taylor & Francis Group, an informa business

First edition published by Routledge 2013
Second edition published by Routledge 2018

British Library Cataloguing-in-Publication Data
A catalogue record for this book is available from the British Library

ISBN: 978-1-032-38067-4 (hbk)
ISBN: 978-1-032-38069-8 (pbk)
ISBN: 978-1-003-34335-6 (ebk)

DOI: 10.4324/9781003343356

Typeset in Iowan Old Style
by codeMantra

Access the support material: www.routledge.com/9781032380674

To Sheng Hua (Jing), Andy, and Alick

Contents

Figures

Examples

Abbreviations

ACAT	Atlantic Canada Agreement on Tourism
ACOA	Atlantic Canada Opportunities Agency
ACVB	Atlanta Convention and Visitors Bureau
ADVICE	authority, destination, visitor, industry, community, environment
AI	artificial intelligence
AIO	activities, interests, and opinions
APA	American Psychological Association
APEC	Asia-Pacific Economic Cooperation
AR	augmented reality
ASAE	American Society of Association Executives
ASEAN	Association of South East Asian Nations
ASP	Aussie Specialist Program
ATA	Aruba Tourism Authority
ATDI	Adventure Tourism Development Index
BBM	Benefits-Based Model
BID	business improvement districts
BIE	Bureau International des Expositions
BRIC	Brazil, Russia, India, and China
BSC	Balanced Scorecard
BTI	Belle Tourism International
CAG	controller and auditor general
CAGR	compound annual growth rate
CATI	computer-assisted telephone interviewing
CBT	community-based tourism
CDME	Certified Destination Management Executive
CEO	chief executive officer
CGLCC	Canada's Gay and Lesbian Chamber of Commerce
CIA	Central Intelligence Agency
CLIA	Cruise Lines International Association

CRM	customer relationship management
CSE	Canadian Signature Experiences
CSF	critical success factors
CSR	corporate social responsibility
CTC	Canadian Tourism Commission
CVB	convention and visitors bureau
DCC	Danube Competence Center
DCT	Dubai College of Tourism
DEDP	destination experience development plan
DEI	diversity, equity, and inclusion
DET	Department of Economy and Tourism
DFA	Department of Foreign Affairs
DMAI	Destination Marketing Association International
DMAP	Destination Marketing Accreditation Program
DMC	destination management companies
DMO	destination management organization
DMP	destination management plan
DMPP	destination marketing planning process
DMS	destination marketing system
DQ	Destination Queenstown
DSR	destination social responsibility
EA	Ecotourism Australia
ECLAC	Economic Commission for Latin America and the Caribbean
ECM	European Cities Marketing
EDTEA	Economic Development, Tourism and Environmental Affairs
EIU	Economist Intelligence Unit
EMEA	Europe, Middle East and Africa
EPA	Environmental Protection Agency
ESTA	Electronic System for Travel Authorization
ETC	European Travel Commission
EV	electric vehicles
EWoM	electronic word of mouth
FCDO	Foreign, Commonwealth & Development Office
FEE	Foundation for Environmental Education
FOI	Freedom of Information
FST	Free Singapore Tour
GBA	Greater Bay Area
GBDVS	Great Britain Day Visits Survey
GBRMPA	Great Barrier Reef Marine Park Authority
GBTA	Global Business Travel Association
GBTS	Great Britain Tourism Survey
GCET	Global Code of Ethics for Tourism
GDP	gross domestic product
GHG	greenhouse gases

GMCVB	Greater Miami Convention & Visitors Bureau
GNP	gross national product
GNTB	German National Tourist Board
GPS	global positioning system
GSA	general sales agent
GSTC	Global Sustainable Tourism Council
GTW	Global Tourism Watch
HFC	Houston First Corporation
HKTB	Hong Kong Tourism Board
HMD	head-mounted displays
HTA	Hawai'i Tourism Authority
HWC	Hadrian's Wall Country
IACVB	International Association of Convention and Visitor Bureaus
IAD	internet addiction disorder
IAPCO	International Association of Professional Congress Organizers
ICCA	International Congress and Convention Association
ICT	information and communication technologies
IITTM	The Indian Institute of Tourism and Travel Management
IMC	integrated marketing communication
IMF	International Monetary Fund
INSTO	International Network of Sustainable Tourism Observatories
IoT	Internet of Things
IPS	International Passenger Survey
IQM	integrated quality management
ITA	International Trade Administration
ITC	Integrated Tourism Complex
ITSA	International Tourism Studies Association
ITU	International Telecommunication Union
IUCN	International Union for Conservation of Nature
IVS	International Visitor Survey
KPI	key performance indicator
KRA	key result area
KTO	Korea Tourism Organization
LAC	limits of acceptable change
LCC	low-cost carrier
LGBTQ	lesbian, gay, bisexual, transgender, and queer
LMX	leader–member exchange
LVCVA	Las Vegas Convention and Visitors Authority
LVEP	Local Visitor Economy Partnerships
MENA	Middle East and North Africa
MGTO	Macao Government Tourism Office
MICE	meetings, incentives, conventions/conferences exhibitions
MOT	Ministry of Tourism
MoU	memorandum of understanding

MRT	Murray Regional Tourism
NGF	National Golf Foundation
NGO	non-governmental organization
NPO	nonprofit organization
NTA	National Tourism Administration
NTCB	National Tourism Coordination Board
NTO	national tourism organizations
NVS	National Visitor Survey
NYC	New York City
ODH	Orascom Development Holding
OECD	Organisation for Economic Co-operation and Development
OIC	Organization of Islamic Cooperation
OTA	online travel agency
PATA	Pacific Area Travel Association
PCO	professional congress/conference organizer
PESTEL	political, economic, societal, technological, environmental, and legal
PHLCVB	Philadelphia Convention and Visitors Bureau
PIA	Philippine Information Agency
PIB	positioning, image, and branding
PLC	product life cycle
PNG	Papua New Guinea
PPC	pay-per-click
PPP	public–private partnerships
PPT	pro-poor tourism
PR	public relations
PRICE	planning, research, implementation, control, and evaluation
PSA	public service announcements
PTDC	Pakistan Tourism Development Corporation
Q&A	questions and answers
QTS	Quality Tourism Services
RFID	radio-frequency identification
RFP	request for proposal
ROI	return on investment
ROS	Recreation Opportunity Spectrum
RSS	Resident Sentiment Survey
RTA	regional tourism authority
RTO	regional tourism organization
RV	recreational vehicle
SAPA	social impact assessment for protected areas
SAR	Special Administrative Region
SARG	Special Administrative Region Government
SARS	Severe Acute Respiratory Syndrome
SCA	sustainable competitive advantages
SDG	Sustainable Development Goals

SEM	search engine marketing
SEO	search engine optimization
SERP	search engine report pages
SIAT	Survey of International Air Travelers
SIG	special-interest groups
SIT	special-interest travel
SITE	Society for Incentive Travel Excellence
SLTA	Saint Lucia Tourism Authority
SLTDA	Sri Lanka Tourism Development Authority
SME	small and medium-sized enterprises
SMS	short messaging services
SOP	standard operating procedures
SRI	Strategic Research and Insight
SSM	Secretariat Shopping Malaysia
STB	Singapore Tourism Board
STERG	Scottish Tourism Emergency Response Group
STO	state tourism offices
SWB	subjective well-being
SWOT	strengths, weaknesses, opportunities and threats
T&E	travel and entertainment
TA	Tourism Australia
TALC	tourism area life cycle
TAT	Tourism Authority of Thailand
TBID	tourism business improvement districts
TCC	tourism carrying capacity
TCDMG	Tourism Crisis and Disaster Management Group
TEQ	Tourism & Events Queensland
TGCSA	Tourism Grading Council of South Africa
TIA	Tourism Industry Aotearoa
TIAC	Tourism Industry Association of Canada
TIC	travel information center
TID	tourism improvement districts
TIES	The International Ecotourism Society
TKZN	Tourism KwaZulu-Natal
TMC	travel management companies
TOMM	tourism optimization management model
TOTA	Thompson Okanagan Tourism Association
TPD	tourism product development
TQoL	tourism quality of life
TRA	Tourism Research Australia
TSA	tourism satellite account
TTB	Tanzania Tourist Board
TTDI	Travel and Tourism Development Index
TTRA	Travel and Tourism Research Association

UAE	United Arab Emirates
UGC	user-generated content
UIA	Union of International Associations
UNEP	UN Environment Programme
UNESCAP	United Nations Economic and Social Commission for Asia and the Pacific
UNESCO	UN Educational, Scientific and Cultural Organization
UNWTO	United Nations World Tourism Organization
UQoL	urban quality of life
USA	United States
USP	unique selling points or propositions
USTA	US Travel Association
UTB	Uganda Tourism Board
VAMP	Visitor Activity Management Process
VCS	Visit Colorado Springs
VERP	Visitor Experience and Resource Protection
VFR	visiting friends or relatives
VIC	visitor information center
VIM	visitor impact model
VITO	Visit Indonesia tourism office
VNAT	Vietnam National Administration of Tourism
VR	virtual reality
WEF	World Economic Forum
WHS	World Heritage Site
WOM	word of mouth
WTCF	World Tourism Cities Federation
WTM	World Travel Market
WTP	willingness to pay
WTTC	World Travel and Tourism Council
WWOOF	World Wide Opportunities on Organic Farms

Preface

Before launching into the chapters, you should know why this book is required in the marketplace. Above all, the growing recognition of destination management as a distinct professional field of tourism justify this book's publication, as does the increasing acceptance of this topic as viable areas for educational and training programs, and academic research and scholarship.

Much has changed since the publication of the second edition of this book in 2018. The COVID-19 pandemic was unpredictable at the time and has caused havoc for destinations and DMOs. Four new chapters were added to reflect these changes:

- Chapter 2: "Destination Sustainability and Social Responsibility";
- Chapter 3: "Quality of Life and Well-Being of Destination Residents";
- Chapter 11: "Destination Crisis Management";
- Chapter 20: "Destination Management Performance Measurement and Management."

Research and Educational Interest in the Book's Topics

The writing of a contemporary textbook on destination management is long overdue, especially one that treats the destination marketing and destination management together as an integrated whole. One of the reasons is because university academic programs and researchers are giving more attention to destination marketing and management. Traditionally, many universities have had courses in hospitality management and fewer have been teaching travel trade or travel agency management, or event management. More recently, tourism management courses have been added, with classes in destination management or destination marketing being one element introduced within the past approximately twenty years. Figure 0.1 shows the interrelationship of these curricular areas of hospitality, travel, destination, and events. Events are portrayed as a combination of destination, travel, and hospitality. The figure also provides examples for the other intersections of destination, hospitality, and travel.

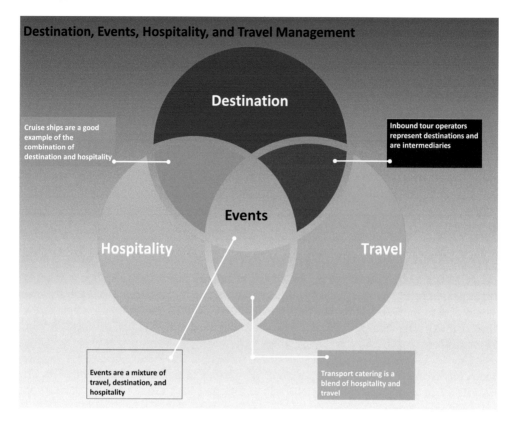

Figure 0.1 Destination Events Hospitality and Travel Management

The following data from Scopus shows that destination marketing started to enter the tourism literature in the 1980s; destination management first appeared in the 1990s (Tables 0.1 and 0.2). Both received more attention in 2000 to 2009. Most of the references to the two topics are from 2000 onwards. It is also interesting to note that destination management is catching up on destination marketing as a topic, and may overtake destination marketing from 2020 to 2029.

Table 0.1 Destination marketing

Destination marketing	Article title only	Article title, abstract, keywords
2020–2023	55	498
2010–2019	213	994
2000–2009	69	268
1990–1999	7	31
1980–1989	2	4
All	346	1,795

Source: Scopus

Table 0.2 Destination management

Destination management	Article title only	Article title, abstract, keywords
2020–2023	83	641
2010–2019	177	973
2000–2009	37	190
1990–1999	4	13
1980–1989	0	0
All	301	1,817

Scopus, author's analysis, October 2022.

The literature on destination marketing and management will be further extended with the introduction of new academic journals specifically addressing these topics. For example, Elsevier's *Journal of Destination Marketing & Management* was launched at about the same time as the publication of the first edition of this book, and the *International Journal of Tourism Cities* (Emerald and the International Tourism Studies Association) began in 2015. It can be expected that journals along similar themes will emerge in the future; for example, we may see one dedicated solely to destination leadership and governance.

It also should be recognized that there has been an explosion in the publication of many journal articles and books in related fields, including place, city, and nation branding and marketing. The journals include *Place Branding and Public Diplomacy* (2004, Palgrave) and the *Journal of Place Management and Development* (2008, Emerald). In 2002, Kotler et al. published the book *Marketing Places* (Free Press), and that became the frontrunner for a spate of new books about place and nation marketing and branding. In his book *City Branding: Theory and Cases* (2011), Keith Dinnie had the following to say about the importance of city branding:

> *City branding is a topic of significant interest to both academics and policymakers. As cities compete globally to attract tourism, investment and talent, as well as to achieve many other objectives, the concepts of brand strategy are increasingly adopted from the commercial world and applied in pursuit of urban development, regeneration and quality of life. Much of the published research into city branding originates in the disciplines of marketing and urban studies, two fields that have tended to follow parallel rather than interdisciplinary paths.*

The above quote is noteworthy because it places destinations within the scope of city branding while also suggesting that interdisciplinary approaches need to be applied in this field.

Tourism Sector Interest in the Book's Topics

There is a growing interest worldwide in the topics of destination marketing and management as more places are vying for a share of global tourism. This phenomenon is demonstrated through several different phenomena, and one of these is the expansion of professional organizations with a focus on destination marketing and management.

There are now several industry groups dedicated to this professional field, including Destinations International, located in Washington, DC; European Cities Marketing (ECM), headquartered in Dijon, France; Pacific Asia Travel Association (PATA), with its head office in Bangkok; and several others, including AACVB (Asian Association of Convention and Visitor Bureaus) and DMA West (Destination Marketing Association of the West located in California). Moreover, influential organizations, including the UN World Tourism Organization (UNWTO) (Madrid, Spain), have set up special initiatives related to destination management or marketing and are providing related technical publications, conferences, and training. The World Tourism Cities Federation (WTCF) in Beijing is also likely to attach a high priority to urban destination marketing and management.

Destinations International has approximately 600 members representing destination management organizations (DMOs) from several countries. ECM, like Destination Marketing Association International (DMAI), DMA West, and AACVB, is an organization principally dedicated to furthering the professional interests and standing of DMOs. Destinations International was founded in 1914 as the International Association of Convention Bureaus, whereas ECM's history is shorter, tracing back just more than twenty-five years. ECM has approximately 108 member cities representing most countries in Europe. DMA West is an association of DMOs in the western states and provinces of the USA and Canada, and it has around 145 members. AACVB was established in 1983 to foster regional cooperation among convention and visitor bureaus (CVBs) in Asia. The founding members were from Indonesia, Hong Kong, Malaysia, Philippines, Singapore, South Korea, and Thailand. China and Macao joined later.

The UNWTO in Madrid has a destination management and quality program and has been active in holding conferences and producing publications on destination management. The main objectives of this program are in destination competitiveness, destination quality, and destination governance. The program "is committed to respond positively to the growing need for systematic, multidisciplinary and intersectoral strategies for tourism at local, regional and national level and in particular to provide strategic guidance to reinforce the destination competitiveness and improve destination management from an efficient governance and integrated quality perspective" (UNWTO website: http://destination.unwto.org/content/about-us-4).

PATA was established in 1951 and is "internationally acclaimed for acting as a catalyst for the responsible development of travel and tourism to, from and within the Asia Pacific region" (PATA website: www.pata.org/asia-pacific-tourism-in-2015-another-record/). PATA has a diverse membership drawn from many parts of the tourism sectors and not only DMOs. Included in the membership are approximately eighty government, state and city DMOs. PATA organizes several important events and educational programs each year, and its Strategic Intelligence Centre (SIC) provides much useful research data on tourism in the Asia-Pacific region.

Pioneering Works and Programs in Destination Marketing and Management

The pioneering book on these topics was published in 1988 by Richard Gartrell, *Destination Marketing for Convention and Visitor Bureaus* (Kendall/Hunt Publishing), and it was released under the auspices of the International Association of Convention and Visitor Bureaus

(IACVB) (now Destinations International). Eric Laws published a book titled *Tourist Destination Management: Issues, Analysis and Policies* in 1995.

The introduction of the Certified Destination Management Executive (CDME) program in 1992 by the then IACVB was a watershed for the field of destination management. It recognized that destination management was not just a topic; it was more importantly a profession. The program was developed by Don Anderson at the University of Calgary in Canada and by the author while at Purdue University in the USA. Core and elective classes were offered, and the participants were senior DMO executives and managers. The four core classes are on strategic issues in destination management, destination marketing planning, destination leadership and destination advocacy and community relations. CDME focuses on upgrading the knowledge and skills of individual DMO professionals.

Later in 2004, Destinations International established a performance measurement team to begin the process of identifying DMO performance measurement benchmarks. A handbook of measures was released in 2005. Also in 2005, Destinations International released a book about destination branding called *Destination BrandScience*, co-authored by Duane Knapp and Gary Sherwin. During 2010 to 2011, Destinations International appointed a Performance Reporting Task Force, and the Task Force's efforts resulted in an updated edition of the *Standard DMO Performance Reporting: A Handbook for DMOs*. Additionally, in 2012 Destinations International produced a revised edition of the DMO Uniform System of Accounts (Standard Financial Reporting Practices for DMOs).

The Destination Marketing Accreditation Program (DMAP) was another breakthrough on the professional side of destination marketing. Destinations International has the following to say about the importance of DMAP: "The globally recognized Destination Marketing Accreditation Program (DMAP) serves as a visible industry distinction that defines quality and performance standards in destination marketing and management" (Destinations International 2023).

Unlike the CDME program, DMAP focuses on DMOs as organizations rather than on individual DMO professionals. DMAP was especially important in identifying sixteen domains for measuring the performance of a DMO (governance, finance, human resources, technology, marketing, visitor services, group services, sales, communications, membership, management and facilities, brand management, destination development, research/marketing intelligence, innovation, and stakeholder relationships).

During the first three decades of the new millennium, there was a surge in new books, academic articles and practice-oriented manuscripts on destination marketing and management. One of the most influential of the new books was *Destination Branding* (2004) by Nigel Morgan, Annette Pritchard, and Roger Pride. This new publication seemed to spur many academic researchers into doing research, writing articles, and arranging conferences around the topic of destination branding. It should be recognized that many tourism scholars beginning in the early 1970s were producing valuable research contributions on destination image and its measurement. This research undoubtedly provided a valuable platform for what was to come later about destination branding and positioning.

Another benchmark was UNWTO's *A Practical Guide to Destination Management* published in 2007. Prepared for UNWTO by TEAM Tourism Consulting of the United Kingdom (UK), this was the first practical guide on all aspects of destination management. UNWTO and the European Travel Commission (ETC) later co-sponsored two additional practical guides: *Handbook on Tourism Destination Branding* (2009, prepared by Tom Buncle) and *Handbook on Tourism Product Development* (2011, prepared by Tourism Development International).

Several related books from academic authors have been added in recent years. These have included two books by Stephen Pike: *Destination Marketing Organisations: Bridging Theory and Practice* (2005) and *Destination Marketing: An Integrated Communication Approach* (2008). Two other books were published in 2011: *Destination Marketing and Management: Theories and Applications* by Youcheng Wang and Abraham Pizam and *Managing and Marketing Tourist Destinations: Strategies to Gain a Competitive Edge* by Metin Kozak and Seyhmus Baloglu. All four of these books are welcome additions to the scholarship on destination marketing and management and offer a variety of different perspectives on the topics.

Some pioneering courses in destination management have appeared in universities in the 2000s. These include the Tourism Destination Management Certificate Program at George Washington University in the USA and the Master in Tourism Destination Management at NHTV Breda University of Applied Sciences in the Netherlands. Individual classes on either destination marketing or destination management have been introduced at universities around the world and particularly in Australia and the UK.

Generally, universities have been rather slow and hesitant to introduce individual classes and full courses on destination marketing and management. The likely reasons for this may be a viewpoint that these topics are too specialized and therefore do not warrant separate attention and that student interest in these precise topics is modest. There is certainly some validity to these viewpoints at the current time, but this may change in the next decade as destination marketing and management attract more scholars and scholarship. Because of student demand, this trend has already started with many academic programs introducing courses in event management, which arguably is just one sliver of destination management. As graduates from these event management programs increase in number and start competing in a relatively small arena, there will perhaps be a realization that universities would be better off aggregating all the components of destination management into one holistic and integrated course of study. Also, it seems likely in the future that there will be some disaggregation of the so-called tourism management programs that have awkwardly tried to span everything that falls outside of the purview of hospitality management.

Acknowledgments

My association and experiences with destination marketing and destination management span four decades, and I have been very fortunate to have been involved with these two topics at various levels across several continents as a marketer, consultant, teacher and trainer. In my numerous journeys around the world, I have learned from and been inspired by many great professionals.

I have always taught my students to be generous in sharing the credit with others and not to take credit from others when you do not deserve it. To be true to my own teaching and advising, the assistance of many other people is hereby acknowledged.

The idea for writing this book started many years ago when I was providing consulting advice for the Canadian Government Office of Tourism (now Destination Canada) and the Ontario Ministry of Industry and Tourism (now Destination Ontario). These bodies have undergone many name changes since then, but at that time we would not have called them destination management organizations, or DMOs. This was my apprenticeship period in destination management when I learned most about destination planning, research, product development, professional development and training. Much was accomplished in that time, and I had the privilege to work with some highly professional clients and mentors, including George Kibedi, Wayne Fergusson, and Bob Brock. It was also then that I had the pleasure of cooperating on tourism planning projects with Anna Pollock, who has gone on to become one of the great visionaries in destination management.

After setting up the Economic Planning Group of Canada with Gordon Phillips, David Hall and Don Anderson, I had the pleasure of participating in many more DMO projects, particularly in Ontario and the Maritime and Western Provinces.

I left Ottawa and EPG with a suitcase full of consulting reports and one great book—The Tourism System—co-authored with Robert Christie Mill, who was at our alma mater, Michigan State University, at that time. Bob is a brilliant writer and teacher as well as being a fellow Scot and graduate of the University of Strathclyde's Scottish Hotel School. The Tourism System has gone on to become a classic text in tourism and is now in its eighth edition.

After moving to Purdue University from Canada, several new avenues in destination management and destination marketing opened to me. The first one was with the UNWTO in Madrid, and this opportunity took me to many parts of the world. There were several individuals who helped me on the way to this great opportunity, and they include Carson (Kit) Jenkins of Strathclyde University in Glasgow and Don Hawkins of George Washington University. Dr. Harsha Varma at UNWTO was a valuable colleague through these years when I gained more practical experience in South and Southeast Asia, the Caribbean, Middle East, and Africa.

The second opportunity came with my continuing close working partnership with Don Anderson, who had moved to work with the University of Calgary after his successful experiences with the Calgary Convention and Tourist Bureau (now Tourism Calgary) and World Expo 1986 in Vancouver. Don is truly one of the world's greatest visionaries with respect to destination management and particularly about the advancement of the professional field. Together we worked with many great people in developing, implementing and fine-tuning the CDME program with the support of Destinations International. These people included Professors J. R. Brent Ritchie, Geoff Crouch and Lorn Sheehan at the outset. During the teaching of many core and elective courses, I got to know many wonderful and talented DMO executives who added to my knowledge of the profession. They included Rick Hughes, Joe McGrath, Elaine McLaughlin, Jim Wood, Teresa McKee Anderson, Valerie Pena, Jo Wade, Amy Vaughan, Doug Harman, Bill Talbert, Matt Carter, Maura Gast and many other truly talented DMO professionals.

The third opportunity that came my way was to go to Australia and work with Philip Pearce at James Cook University. During that time, we were fortunate to provide market research and segmentation analysis support to the Queensland Tourist and Travel Corporation (now Tourism & Events Queensland) and many other DMOs within the state. I need to thank Jonathon Day, then with QTTC and now with Purdue University, for his help in arranging this experience for me in Queensland.

A fourth opportunity that came my way was the teaching in Italy and AILUN in Sardinia and thereafter at IULM in Milan. In working with Manuela DeCarlo, Francesca d'Angella and Ruggero Sainaghi at IULM and Professor Giulio Bolacchi at AILUN, I learned much about destination marketing and management in Italy and other parts of Europe.

While at Purdue, I was also able to work with Joe O'Leary and many talented graduate students of his and my own. This was an exciting time, and we conducted many research studies on tourism consumer behavior, market segmentation analysis, special-interest travel and various other topics.

My latest adventure has taken me to the People's Republic of China, where I have conducted many marketing and consulting projects for DMOs through Belle Tourism International (BTI) Consulting at the provincial and city levels. Although at an early infancy level in China, there are many highly skilled and creative professionals in destination marketing and management, and it has been my honor to work with some of them, including Guo Minwen, Chen Meihong, Wu Bihu and Ivan Xu. I am also grateful for several opportunities that have been provided for me by PATA and especially to participate in the PATA Macao Task Force, which produced the report "Macao Tourism Positioning: Towards a World Centre of Tourism and Leisure." It was a pleasure to work with the director of the Macao Government Office of Tourism, Joao Costa Antunes, and his talented management team and my Task Force colleagues, Andrew Drysdale, Jon Hutchison, Sue Warren, Stewart Moore and Lindsay Turner.

It has also been a distinct privilege for me to work in Indonesia on destination marketing and management and in training related to the introduction of a new nationwide system of DMOs. Spanning the past ten years, it has been my pleasure to work with Wiendu Nuryanti, David Sanders, Frans Teguh, Syamsul Lussa and several others to advance destination marketing in Indonesia. The opportunity to work with Swisscontact to develop professional and higher education programs in destination management was another fantastic opportunity in Indonesia. Along with Ruedi Nuetzi, Ayu Masita and Mercya Susanto, in partnership with great people at STP Bandung (including Anang Sutono, Wisnu Rahtomo, Faisal Puksi, Haryadi Darmawan, Mita Marsongko and others) and STP Bali (Ngurah Byomantara, Yusni Wiarti, Eka Mahadewi, Micke Anggraini, Andre Hanoo, Lily Dianasari, Made Tirtawati and others), we developed some of the best and most comprehensive curricula and training materials for destination management.

My latest adventures back to the UK and the University of Greenwich is further adding to my knowledge and understanding of destination management, as is my co-editorship of the *International Journal of Tourism Cities* with Dr. J. Andres Coca-Stefaniak. My re-learning about destination management in the UK is being assisted by many great people, including Andres, Nikki MacLeod, Jithendran Kokkranikal, James Kennell (now University of Surrey), Samantha Chaperon, Ray Powell, Sven Kuenzel, Ewa Krolikowska-Adamczyk, Maria Gebbels, Michael De Domenici, Wenjie Cai, and Hai Nguyen and others at the University of Greenwich.

Last, but definitely not the least, I want to acknowledge and thank Harriet Cunningham at Routledge for her continuous help throughout this big project. She speedily read chapter drafts and returned them to me with great comments and suggestions. Also, Emma Travis at Routledge had the confidence in me to complete this third edition of *Marketing and Managing Tourism Destinations*. Thanks, Harriet and Emma.

Alastair M. Morrison, February 2023

Part I

Critical Concepts in Destination Management and Marketing

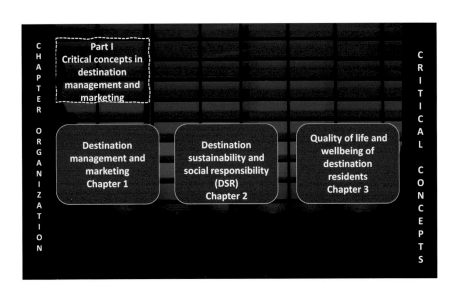

Chapter **1**

Destination Management and Marketing

Follow the roles

LEARNING OBJECTIVES

Having read this chapter, you should be able to:

1. explain the characteristics of a destination;
2. define destination management and destination marketing;
3. describe the roles of destination management;
4. differentiate between destination management and destination marketing;
5. categorize the stakeholders in destination management into groups;
6. explain the ten As of successful destinations;
7. describe the uniqueness of destination management and marketing;
8. provide a definition of destination governance and identify the strengths of the public and private sectors;
9. describe the types of DMOs at different geographic levels.

DOI: 10.4324/9781003343356-2

Warming Up

If you are new to the concepts of managing and marketing destinations, it can be confusing to read what has been written to date about them. These are two relatively new concepts in tourism and many experts have been struggling to define and differentiate them over the past thirty-five to forty years. Sometimes the concepts are used interchangeably, but although closely linked together, they are different. This book will demystify everything for you so you will truly understand destination management and destination marketing.

Destination management has become a profession requiring people with specific skills and experiences. Destination managers are a relatively new breed but their status in society is steadily increasing as destination management gains more recognition. Although relatively small in comparison to hospitality and travel management, this is an up-and-coming career field for tourism management graduates. You need to first understand destinations before you can grasp their management.

Defining a Tourism Destination

DEFINITION

Tourism destination

A tourism destination is a geographic area that attracts visitors. This is a very simple definition, although straightforward. More needs to be added so you fully understand what this book is addressing. Here are the key characteristics of a tourism destination:

- A geographic area which has an administrative boundary or boundaries: This ranges from the largest country in the world (Russia) to the smallest like Monaco and the Vatican City. States, provinces, territories, regions, counties and cities within individual countries can also be destinations.
- A place where the tourist can find overnight accommodations: These are typically hotels, but there may be many other forms of accommodation. Some of the visitors may be day-trippers (excursionists), so not all of them necessarily stay overnight.
- A destination product or mix is available for visitors: There are other facilities for tourists apart from overnight accommodations, including restaurants, entertainment and shopping areas. Most important in drawing tourists are the attractions and events. Transportation, infrastructure, welcoming services and a hospitable environment are the other elements of the destination product.
- A destination marketing effort exists: The place is marketing and branding itself to attract tourists.
- A coordinating organization structure has been created: A DMO leads and coordinates the tourism efforts of the place.
- An image exists of the place in tourists' minds: People have perceptions about what the place has to offer for tourism. These images may be accurate or inaccurate, positive or negative.
- Government agencies have introduced laws and regulations: Special laws and regulations control different aspects of tourism.

- There is a mixture of tourism stakeholders: Private-sector enterprises, government agencies, nonprofit organizations including NGOs, individuals and other entities have an interest in tourism.

Great destinations are great places to live and work as well as to visit.
(Visit England 2017)

Now that you have a basic idea about destinations, the concepts of destination management and marketing will make greater sense to you. Later in this chapter, you will get to know that there is a great variety of destinations in the world and a large number and great variety of DMOs are involved.

Destination Management and Marketing Overview

Destination Management

Destination management and destination marketing are two interrelated concepts in tourism. In fact, destination marketing is one of the functions within the broader concept of destination management. Therefore, it is important for you to first understand destination management and DMOs before moving onto the details of destination marketing.

DMOs came into being because of the need to mount a coordinated effort for planning, developing and marketing tourism destinations. The UNWTO in its publication, *A Practical Guide to Tourism Destination Management* (2007), identified four different roles of DMOs (Fig. 1.1):

1. Leading and coordinating: Leading and coordinating the efforts of all the stakeholders in tourism within the destination, the DMO is the focal organization for ensuring the appropriate use of all the elements of a destination (attractions, amenities, accessibility, human resources, image and price).
2. Marketing: Destination promotion; campaigns to drive business; unbiased information services; operation and facilitation of bookings; and customer relationship management (CRM). The DMO's marketing efforts are mainly designed to get people to visit the destination.
3. Creating a suitable environment: Planning and infrastructure; human resources development; product development; technology and systems development; and related industries and procurement. Policies, legislation and regulations are needed as a foundation for guiding and controlling tourism. This includes the DMO's policies and programs to promote sustainable tourism development within the destination.
4. Delivering on the ground: Managing the quality of tourist experiences; training and education; business advice. This means the DMO must ensure that whatever has been promised in its marketing is actually "delivered" to tourists; in other words, they get the experiences that they were promised. As Figure 1.1 indicates, the main goal is to exceed the expectations of tourists when they first arrive in the destination.

Figure 1.1 shows these four DMO roles along with the elements of a destination, according to the UNWTO. Located in a central position in the diagram, leading and coordinating is shown as being the key role of a DMO.

The following statement from the UNWTO publication clearly indicates that there is much more to destination management than just destination marketing. The very first DMOs to be created

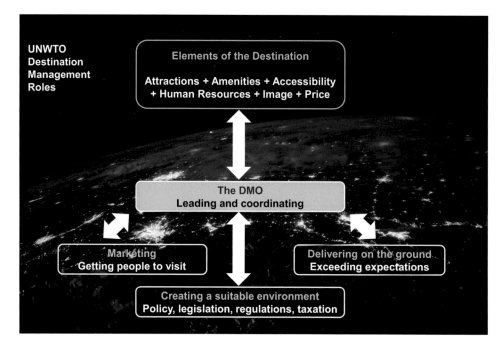

Figure 1.1 UNWTO definition of destination management roles (UNWTO 2007).

decades ago were basically promotional, sales and public relations agencies; today destination management is much broader, more professional and sophisticated. The statement mentions the need for having the "framework of a coherent strategy" and this means there needs to be an overall plan or strategy for tourism in the destination, which you will learn about in Chapter 4.

EXAMPLE 1.1

Destination Management Roles (UNWTO)

This example is a quote from UNWTO suggesting that DMOs should broaden their roles beyond marketing:

> DMOs today should not only lead on marketing, but must also be strategic leaders in destination development. This role requires them to drive and coordinate destination management activities within the framework of a coherent strategy. Promotion must attract people to visit in the first place; creating a suitable environment and quality delivery on the ground will ensure that visitors' expectations are met at the destination and that they then both recommend the destination to others and return themselves, on a future occasion.
>
> (UNWTO 2007: ix)

Learning Point

DMOs need to be doing more than just destination marketing.

UNWTO in 2019 updated these roles, saying that the fundamental DMO functions included strategic planning, formulation and implementation of tourism policy, market intelligence (research), tourism product and business development, digitalization and innovation, monitoring, crisis management, training and capacity-building, promotion, marketing and branding, and funding and fostering investments (UNWTO 2019: 13).

Another and slightly different view of the roles of the DMO in destination management was originated by Destination Consultancy Group (DCG), a US-based tourism consulting company, and adapted and expanded for this book by the author. Eight different DMO roles are identified (Fig. 1.2):

1. Planning and research: Conducting the essential planning and research needed to attain the destination vision and tourism goals.
2. Leadership, coordination, and governance: Setting the agenda for tourism and coordinating all stakeholders' efforts toward achieving that agenda.
3. Product development: Planning and ensuring the appropriate development of physical products and services for the destination.
4. Partnership and team-building: Fostering cooperation among government agencies and within the private sector and building partnership teams to reach specific goals.
5. Stakeholder relationships and involvement: Involving local community leaders and residents in tourism and monitoring resident attitudes toward tourism.
6. Visitor management: Managing the flows, impacts, and behaviors of visitors to protect resources and to enhance visitor safety, experiences and satisfaction.
7. Crisis management: Developing and implementing crisis management plans. The need for crisis management was heightened by the COVID-19 pandemic in 2020–2022.
8. Marketing, branding, and communications: Creating the destination positioning and branding, selecting the most appropriate markets and communicating about the destination.

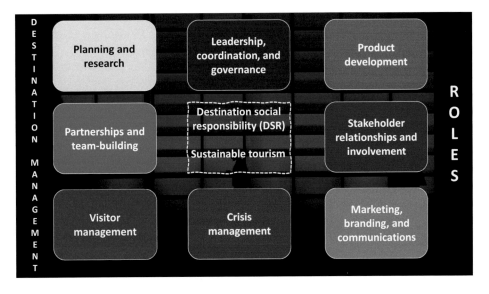

Figure 1.2 Destination management roles.

There are two similar roles in these approaches and these are leadership, coordination, and governance, and marketing. The second approach expands upon the UNWTO's two other roles of "creating a suitable environment" and "delivering on the ground." Figure 1.2 also adds, in a central position, the priorities of destination social responsibility (DSR) and sustainable tourism, which should be a focus for all DMO roles. Putting all these pieces together, the following is this book's definition of destination management and DMOs:

DEFINITIONS

Destination management

Destination management is a professional approach to guiding all of the efforts in a place that has decided to pursue tourism as an economic activity. Destination management involves coordinated and integrated management of the destination product (attractions and events, facilities, transportation, infrastructure, welcoming services and hospitable environment). DMOs are teams of tourism professionals that lead and coordinate all tourism stakeholders. DMOs' roles include planning and research; leadership, coordination, and governance; product development; partnership and team-building; community and stakeholder relationships and involvement; marketing, branding, and communications; visitor management, and crisis management. Effective destination management involves long-term tourism planning and continual monitoring and evaluation of the outcomes from tourism efforts.

Destination management organizations (DMOs)

Destination management is accomplished through specialized organizations, known as DMOs. DMOs coordinate the efforts of many stakeholders to achieve the destination's vision and goals for tourism.

Destination social responsibility (DSR)

DSR is when destinations and their DMOs take responsibility for the impacts of tourism and their actions on their communities and societies in general.

VisitEngland offers a third and slightly different definition of destination management that is more focused on sustainability and the needs of tourists and residents. All these three viewpoints (UNWTO, this book, and VisitEngland) stress the importance of coordination and balancing the needs of different groups of people.

EXAMPLE 1.2

VisitEngland Definition of Destination Management

This example suggests that DMOs must coordinate all aspects of destinations on behalf of several stakeholders.

Destination management is a process of leading, influencing and coordinating the management of all the aspects of a destination that contribute to a visitor's experience, taking account of the needs of visitors, local residents, businesses and the environment.

(VisitEngland 2012: 3)

Learning Point

DMOs must provide leadership for several stakeholders in tourism.

You might have come across the term "destination management company" or "DMC" and wondered if this is the same as a DMO. Actually, they are different types of entities, but the similarity in their names often causes great confusion. DMCs are companies that are specialists in planning and implementing meetings, incentive travel and events in particular destinations. DMOs do not usually provide these services and a DMO's roles are much broader, as you have already learned.

There are distinctive advantages of implementing the destination management concept. The UNWTO identifies the following seven of following a professional destination management approach (UNWTO 2019: 13–15):

1. establishing a competitive edge;
2. ensuring tourism sustainability;
3. avoiding overlapping and identifying gaps;
4. spreading the benefits of tourism;
5. building a tourism culture in the destination;
6. improving tourism yield;
7. building a strong and vibrant brand identity.

To sum up here, how can you differentiate between destination management and destination marketing? Destination management is the broader and more inclusive concept. It encompasses destination marketing and other activities to manage tourism in a destination.

Destination Marketing

So, what is destination marketing? Morrison (2023) describes marketing as a "continuous, sequential process through which management plans, researches, implements, controls and evaluates activities designed to meet customers' needs and wants and their own organizations' objectives." This definition stresses that marketing is a 365-days-a-year activity and that marketing should be done in a systematic fashion. Morrison also adds that the effectiveness of marketing in tourism can be greatly affected by others outside of the DMO. This holistic, multi-organization view of marketing seems well suited to DMOs who must muster the best efforts of many partner organizations and individuals to have the greatest success. Morrison's broader definition of tourism marketing is adapted and used as the foundation for the following definition of DMO marketing:

> **DEFINITION**
>
> ### Destination marketing
>
> Marketing is a continuous, sequential process through which a DMO plans, researches, implements, controls and evaluates programs aimed at satisfying travelers' needs and wants as well as the destination's and DMO's visions, goals and objectives. To be most effective, the DMO's marketing programs depend upon the efforts of many other organizations and individuals within and outside the destination. (Adapted from Morrison 2023.)

Before the concept of destination management gained widespread acceptance, there were several books and articles published on destination marketing. For example, in 1988 Richard B. Gartrell published a book called *Destination Marketing for Convention and Visitor Bureaus*.

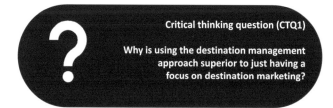

Critical thinking question (CTQ1)

Why is using the destination management approach superior to just having a focus on destination marketing?

Destination Management Roles

Earlier you learned about three definitions of destination management roles. These definitions are quite similar, but also slightly different. Now this chapter will give you a deeper understanding of destination management roles.

Planning and Research

Taking the major initiative in planning and research is a key role for destination management and a DMO. It is accurate to say that there are several destinations that do not have tourism plans, but there are many other DMOs that are very involved in tourism planning. The DMO should periodically coordinate tourism planning exercises and plans should be produced for three time frames: long-term (ten or more years), medium-term (five years); and short-term (one year).

DMOs should involve all tourism stakeholders in the planning process, including local residents. Indeed, some experts say that the planning process is just as important as the final planning document. Why? If people are invited to participate in preparing the tourism plan they are more likely to feel that their opinions have been valued and heard. So, they may develop a sense of "shared ownership" in the plan. Additionally, bringing people together who do not normally meet results in greater sharing of information and can produce more cooperation within tourism in the destination.

Plans that are not shared widely within the destination are unlikely to be very successful. The DMO should publish final tourism plan documents and ensure that all stakeholders have easy access to them. Nowadays most tourism plans are made available on DMO websites for downloading.

Tourism planning began in the 1960s and there are many countries that have achieved excellence among their DMOs in preparing tourism plans and strategies. These include, among others, Ireland, the UK, Canada, Australia and China. Plans and strategies set agendas for their destinations; for example, in June 2022, the USA released a new National Travel and Tourism Strategy containing four strategic pillars:

1. promoting the USA as a travel destination;
2. facilitating travel to and within the USA;
3. ensuring diverse, inclusive, and accessible tourism experiences;
4. fostering resilient and sustainable travel and tourism.

(Department of Commerce 2022)

Plans and strategies also set out core principles for tourism in destinations. The Greater Darwin Region in the Northern Territory of Australia in 2022 established a Destination Management Plan. Within this plan were the following principles for destination management (see Example 1.3).

EXAMPLE 1.3

The Greater Darwin Region Destination Management Plan

In this example, the Northern Territory states its destination management principles.

The Greater Darwin Region will be known for and distinguished by a distinctive identity and year-round product offerings.

- The approach to destination development will deliver benefits both for visitors and residents of the region.
- Tourism experiences in the region will be tailored to visitor expectations.
- Local values and attributes will showcase the region.
- Collaboration will drive benefits for the region.

(Tourism Northern Territory 2022)

Learning Point

DMOs should identify their basic destination management principles.

Research is a strategic investment for a DMO and usually pays rich dividends. Every DMO should have a research program and it is a good practice to prepare a plan ahead of time that indicates what research will be completed and what information will be gathered. Destination Canada has an international reputation of being outstanding at conducting tourism research.

> **EXAMPLE 1.4**
>
> ### Destination Canada: A Leading Innovator in Tourism Research
>
> This example makes the point that research is more needed due to COVID-19.
>
> > The Canadian visitor economy is facing unprecedented challenges due to the COVID-19 pandemic. We know that research is required to guide our collective response so we can make evidence-based decisions. Destination Canada regularly provides intelligence, tools and insights to our partners— equipping them to optimize their business and maximize their reach. As a result of COVID-19, this work is needed more than ever.
> >
> > (Destination Canada 2023)
>
> ### Learning Point
>
> During a crisis, there may be a need for more destination management research.

Typically, most DMOs track tourist volumes and expenditures to measure year-to-year performance and trends. More detailed tourism economic impact studies are completed by selected DMOs. Some DMOs conduct detailed visitor profile studies on a continuous basis through surveys within the destination. The Las Vegas Convention and Visitors Authority (LVCVA) surveys around 300 tourists each month in producing its annual Visitor Profile Study (LVCVA 2022).

Market data is gathered by DMOs and made available to tourism stakeholders. Tourism New Zealand, Tourism Australia, Tourism Ireland and VisitBritain are four national DMOs that do an outstanding job of sharing information on major geographic source markets.

Chapter 4 reviews destination planning, while Chapter 5 discusses destination management research.

Leadership, Coordination, and Governance

The DMO should assume the role of the leader of the tourism sector in its geographic location and coordinate the efforts of all the tourism stakeholders. For example, the Department of Tourism for South Africa says its mission is to be "leading sustainable tourism development for inclusive economic growth in South Africa" (Department of Tourism, South Africa 2022). This mission is accomplished through the following:

> **EXAMPLE 1.5**
>
> ### Department of Tourism, South Africa Mission
>
> This mission states how the national DMO in South Africa will ensure its realization.
>
> > Leading sustainable tourism development for inclusive economic growth in South Africa:

- Good corporate and cooperative governance
- Strategic partnerships and collaboration
- Innovation and knowledge management
- Effective stakeholder communications

(Department of Tourism, South Africa 2022)

Learning Point

A DMO should be clear about how it is fulfilling its mission.

This mission statement for South Africa highlights some of the main parts of a DMO's leadership and coordination role. Included are good governance, partnerships and collaboration, and stakeholder communications, for example.

The organizational purpose of the Korea Tourism Organization is "to advance tourism as a key driver for national economic growth and enhancing national welfare" (Korea Tourism Organization 2022). For many DMOs, their responsibilities go beyond economic ones as is illustrated by Tourism New Zealand:

EXAMPLE 1.6

Sustainability for Tourism New Zealand

This example clearly articulates the organizational purpose of Tourism New Zealand that has a strong emphasis on sustainability.

Tourism New Zealand's purpose is to enrich New Zealand by maximizing the contribution of visitors, we deliver this by maximizing the impact domestic and international visitors have across the four well-beings of nature, society, culture and the economy.

(Tourism New Zealand 2021)

Learning Point

Every DMO should clearly state its organizational purpose.

DMOs are the advocates, cheerleaders and champions of tourism in their areas. This is needed because tourism is often misunderstood and underestimated as an economic sector and form of business activity. There is also strong competition for local funding and the DMO needs to ensure that tourism gets its "fair share" of the available resources. DMOs build up community pride and sense of place, often by focusing on local assets and features that local residents underappreciate or do not recognize at all.

The DMO is usually the leader in tourism marketing and an innovator that other stakeholders follow. It is a main source of tourism marketing ideas and programs. The DMO tracks overall tourism trends and specific trends in tourist markets, and shares these with other stakeholders.

The DMO takes on another leadership role in helping visitors when they need information and assistance. Additionally, the DMO should promote the sustainable tourism development agenda for the destination. Destination leadership, coordination, and governance are discussed in greater detail in Chapter 6.

Product Development

The DMO's product development role relates to all aspects of the destination product. Figure 1.3 provides a comprehensive definition of the destination product that consists of the physical products, plus people, packages and programs.

Physical Products

These include attractions, facilities (hotels, restaurants, etc.), transportation and infrastructure. DMOs seldom are developers and investors in physical tourism products, but they provide insight and guidance to other stakeholders for such projects. Often DMOs have programs for identifying potential new attractions and major facilities such as resorts. For example, the Tourism Development Fund in Saudi Arabia promotes tourism development projects in six categories (tourism destinations and attractions; accommodation; food and beverages within destinations; tourism and travel services; tourism experiences and activities; and tourism retail) (Tourism Development Fund 2022).

DMOs may provide funds for conducting planning and feasibility studies on the most promising projects. Attracting investment in tourism is an activity of several DMOs and more recently this has extended into film development. Tourism New Zealand, for example, works along with the New Zealand Film Commission and Film New Zealand to attract film production, and they have been very successful in generating film tourism (Tourism New Zealand 2020).

Accessibility and the safety and security of tourists are major concerns of DMOs. Usually transportation, health and security are the responsibilities of specific agencies of government and the DMO's role is an advisory one. This is also a component of the visitor management role that is discussed in Chapter 10.

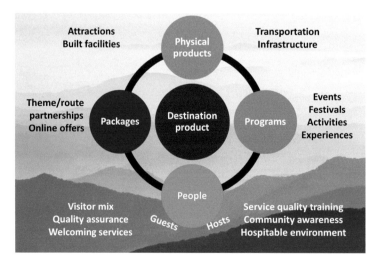

Figure 1.3 The destination product (adapted from Mill and Morrison (2012)).

EXAMPLE 1.7

The Magical Towns of Mexico

This is a great example in which the national DMO in Mexico has created a new product brand around towns across the country.

> The Pueblo Mágico (Magical Town) designation is awarded to those communities that over time have maintained their original architecture, traditions, history and culture. As well as to those that have been of great relevance to the country's history. The Pueblos Mágicos (Magical Towns) are defined as places with great symbolism and legends, they are towns whose historical importance has been fundamental for the development of history and that enhance the national identity in each of its spots. These places have a special magic that connects the visitor with our roots and traditions. With exceptional beauty, these are destinations that will most definitely captivate you.
>
> (SECTUR 2022)

Learning Point

DMOs can create new branded tourism products by creating clusters of similar places or products.

People

Human resources are extremely important to all destinations and are very much an essential part of the destination product. The interaction of hosts and guests is critical to successful destination experiences, and both sides of this interaction need to be considered by the DMO.

The visitor mix is the combination of tourist groups and individuals spending time in a destination. The DMO cannot directly and completely control the visitor mix but it can indirectly influence this through its marketing, branding, and communications. The key here is to ensure some appropriate degree of compatibility and absence of conflict among the destination's tourist markets.

Monitoring service quality and maintaining quality assurance programs are two programs that several DMOs operate. Examples of DMO quality assurance programs are Qualmark (New Zealand), Quality Tourism Services (Hong Kong), Quality Programme of Swiss Tourism, and the Tourism Grading Council of South Africa (TGCSA).

DMOs frequently arrange training programs for people involved in tourism, both within and outside of the destination. Within destinations, some DMOs offer hospitality and service quality training programs. For example, Travel Oregon has the Oregon Tourism Studios program for communities interested in tourism development, and these cover rural tourism, destination management, and tourism experiences (Travel Oregon 2022). Outside of destinations, several DMOs provide training for travel agencies and tour operators. Tourism Australia's Aussie Specialist Program is an outstanding example of training aimed at making travel companies more knowledcdgeable and skilled in selling the destination (Tourism Australia 2022).

Community awareness of tourism is very important for destinations and many DMOs recognize this and take action to build greater awareness. Grenada in the Caribbean provides a good example here.

EXAMPLE 1.8

Tourism Awareness Campaign in Grenada

This example explains how Grenada is increasing community awareness of tourism.

> Welcome to the Tourism Awareness Campaign website of the Grenada Tourism Authority. This campaign was launched in 2017 to create awareness about the benefits of tourism to Grenada, Carriacou and Petite Martinique. On this site you can find information about tourism in Grenada including statistics, our Tourism and Me Booklet, videos, audio messages, information about the environment and much more! Share this site with your family and friends.
>
> (Grenada Tourism Authority 2023)

Learning Point

It is important for DMOs to build greater awareness of tourism in their communities.

Other DMOs have special programs each year where they try to raise awareness of the size, scale, economic and other benefits of tourism. These include countries like the Philippines and many of the Caribbean nations. English Tourism Week is held in March to celebrate the positive benefits from the tourism sector (VisitBritain 2022). The National Travel and Tourism Week in May each year is organized by the US Travel Association (USTA) and celebrated by many DMOs in the USA (USTA 2022). During 2021, the World Travel and Tourism Council (WTTC) produced a video, *The Power of Travel and Tourism*, to create greater awareness of the positive effects of the sector globally (WTTC 2021).

Figure 1.4 is a graphic from Destination Canada and the Tourism Industry Association of Canada that promoted Tourism Week in 2022.

In some countries, the governments have established and operate training and educational institutions for tourism and hospitality. The Indian Institute of Tourism and Travel Management (IITTM 2022) is a stellar example of this as is the Dubai College of Tourism.

EXAMPLE 1.9

Dubai College of Tourism

This example is a case where a DMO operates a college of tourism.

> The Dubai College of Tourism (DCT) was established by Dubai's Department of Economy and Tourism to be a world-class vocational tourism college that

would drive professional excellence capability in all tourism and hospitality service personnel in Dubai.

(DCT 2022)

Learning Point

Some DMOs establish and operate colleges or polytechnics that offer curricula in tourism and hospitality management.

Packages

Most packaging in tourism is done by tour operators and travel agencies, and hotels, resorts, and airlines, but sometimes DMOs get involved as well. Some DMOs offer financial or non-financial incentives to encourage others to build new packages. Several DMOs put together packages through partnerships with their stakeholders and offer them for online sale via their

Figure 1.4 Tourism Week in Canada, 2022 (Destination Canada and the Tourism Industry Association of Canada).

websites. A great example of packaging by a DMO is the Jordan Pass developed by the Ministry of Tourism and Antiquities in Jordan (Fig. 1.5). This is a prepaid pass for two or three days including admission to several attractions and includes a waiver of tourist entry visa fees.

Figure 1.5 The Jordan Pass (Ministry of Tourism and Antiquities)

EXAMPLE 1.10

What Is the Jordan Pass?

This is an excellent example of a national DMO arranging for attractions around the country to offer attendance fees under the same brand.

> The Jordan Pass is a discount program offered by the Jordan Ministry of Tourism and Antiquities that combines a tourist visa and admission to thirty-six tourist sites across the country. The pass comes in three price levels, depending on whether you'd like to stay at Petra for one, two or three days. Costs start at JD70 (about US$98). If you buy it online before you arrive, the Jordan Pass waives visa fees of JD40 (approximately US$56) for many nationalities, making it a good bargain for even the lightest of users.
>
> (Lioy, Lonely Planet 2022)

Learning Point

DMOs can offer visitors much greater convenience by bring together various tourism sector stakeholders under a unified brand offer.

Another activity of DMOs is the creation of themed routes or itineraries where related attractions and features are linked together. This may be done just by one DMO or by several DMOs working in partnership. For example, VisitScotland with its partners created Scotland's UNESCO Trail linking its thirteen World Heritage List sites (VisitScotland 2022).

Programs

A very worthwhile endeavor for DMOs is to assist with increased programming that enhances tourist experiences within the destination. Programming includes events, festivals and individualized arranged activities and experiences for tourists. Events range from mega-events such as the Olympics, World Expo and the World Cup to smaller-scale business events. Festivals are of many varieties but they often celebrate historical and cultural aspects of local communities. Local nonprofit groups typically organize festivals and several DMOs assist them by providing grants or marketing assistance.

Individualized activities are another type of programming in which the DMO designs experiences for tourists. Historic walking tours are a great example, as are more nature-based walks and hikes. The Hong Kong Tourism Board (HKTB), for example, produces the Great Outdoors Hong Kong that is a most valuable information resource for tourists who enjoy the outdoors (HKTB 2022).

Product development is discussed in detail in Chapter 7.

Partnership and Team-Building

Effective destination management is not only in the hands of the DMO, but also requires effort by other stakeholders within the destination and partners in other places. Collaboration with other organizations and individuals is a must, especially in an era where the financial challenges are great and the competition is intense.

DMOs can achieve much more for their destinations when they work in cooperation with others. A partnership can be defined as a synergistic relationship between a DMO and other organizations or individuals, within or outside of the destination. Chapter 8 identifies the many partners and partnerships for DMOs as well as the benefits from partnering.

The Historic Highlights of Germany is a great example of a destination partnership.

EXAMPLE 1.11

Historic Highlights of Germany

This is a great example in which a national DMO has created a brand offer including its historical cities nationwide.

> The "Historic Highlights of Germany" are seventeen cities combining historical heritage with modern urban lifestyles, each making its own specific contribution to culture, business and science.
>
> (German National Tourist Board 2022)

The cities included are Aachen, Augsburg, Bonn, Erfurt, Freiburg, Heidelberg, Koblenz, Lübeck, Münster, Potsdam, Osnabrück, Regensburg, Rostock, Tübingen, Trier, Würzburg, and Wiesbaden.

Learning Point

By creating a cluster of places with a similar theme, DMOs can offer products with greater appeal to visitors.

Partnerships and team-building are the topic covered in Chapter 8.

Stakeholder Relationships and Involvement

DMOs must frequently communicate and interact with their local communities. Some would say this is a type of internal marketing and public relations for the DMO, but it is much more than that. It is extremely important that local residents are supportive of tourism and are fully aware of its contributions as an economic sector.

This is the topic for Chapter 9; however, an example is shared with you now to provide a better understanding of this role. In April and May 2022, the community residents and stakeholders in Banff, Alberta, Canada were asked to complete surveys about a proposed Tourism Master-plan for Banff (Ellis 2022).

DMOs may also do periodic surveys to gauge resident attitudes to tourism development. Tourism can have negative as well as positive effects on the lives of local residents. Traffic congestion, overcrowding at sites (overtourism), increased littering and property price inflation can be among the less positive local impacts. Community support is important for tourism development, so polling of resident attitudes is necessary and not an option.

Winning community support for tourism is dependent on: (1) the attitudes of local residents to tourism; (2) the contribution of tourism to the economic, social and cultural goals of the community; and (3) the minimization of the negative impacts of tourism on the community. A community-supported tourism management strategy brings with it political support and a warm welcome for tourists in the destination.

Visitor Management

Although DMOs may not be the main players in visitor management, it is a role that they need to share with others to protect visitors, residents, and the natural, heritage and cultural resources of their destinations. You can think of it simply as the management of visitors in different ways and mostly when they are experiencing the destination. It is the topic for Chapter 10.

There are different reasons for having visitor management programs in destinations. Figure 10.3 identifies eight of themes for destination visitor management. Among these, the main concern is for resource protection and especially within natural areas and for cultural-heritage attractions. Visitor management is of great importance for protected areas such as national and marine parks. Managing visitors has implications for the visitors as well, especially to ensure their safety and security. There are also marketing and economic reasons for considering the volumes and mixes of visitors.

Crisis Management

A crisis is an event or set of circumstances which can severely compromise or damage the marketability and reputation of a tourism business or an entire tourism destination region. A crisis is a significant threat to operations or reputations that can have negative consequences if not handled properly. In crisis management, the threat is the potential damage a crisis can inflict on a destination and DMO, their stakeholders, visitors, and the tourism sector. A crisis can create the three related threats of public safety, financial loss, and reputation loss (Swiss-contact 2016).

The COVID-19 pandemic devastated tourism worldwide and brought home the message that destinations must be better prepared in the future for crises. In recent years, tourism worldwide has experienced numerous crisis events, including terrorist attacks, natural disasters, wars, political instability, and others (Duan et al. 2022: 668). Climate change is of growing concern as a source of crises for tourism.

EXAMPLE 1.12

Climate Change and Tourism

This example is about a state tourism office actions to combat climate change.

> Still, Visit California is starting to think about global warming. "Climate change impacts California in profound ways," Ms. Beteta later wrote in an email. At a recent board meeting the group designated a board liaison, she noted, "to help navigate the industry's approach to sustainable tourism and sound practices in destination stewardship.
>
> (Levin 2021)

Learning Point

DMOs should take initiatives to deal with climate change.

Chapter 11 has a focus on crisis management.

Marketing, Branding, and Communications

This is a predominant role for many DMOs and receives a great deal of emphasis. In this book, special attention is given to destination marketing because of its great influence on effective destination management. Chapters 12–19 are devoted to marketing and markets, just a brief overview of this role is given now.

The main components of a DMO's marketing and promotion role are the following:

- Marketing planning: Following a systematic, step-by-step approach in developing marketing strategies and plans.
- Market research: Conducting the essential research, and gathering, interpreting and sharing information to make effective marketing decisions.
- Market segmentation: Dividing up tourist markets into groups that share common characteristics.
- Positioning, image, and branding: Positioning the destination in the competitive marketplace; assessing and adjusting destination image; and designing a destination branding approach.
- Marketing plan: Preparing short-term action or implementation plans to guide marketing activities.
- Integrated marketing communications: Using online and offline tools and techniques to communicate with all selected audiences.
- Marketing performance measurement: Monitoring marketing implementation and measuring the effectiveness of marketing and IMC activities.

Sometimes you will see a DMO being identified as a destination marketing organization, and this underscores the importance of destination marketing.

The Ten As of Successful Destinations

How can it be determined if a tourism destination is successful or not? And if the destination is judged to be successful, can the DMO take the sole credit for this great achievement? These are difficult questions to answer but nevertheless they should be tackled.

One answer to the first question is that the successful destinations are the ones with the most tourists. So, you will often see the "world's top destinations" identified as the ones with the most tourist arrivals according to UNWTO. These would include countries such as France, US, China, Spain, Italy and the UK. However, many will argue that this is a choice of "quantity" over "quality" and that smaller destinations are not necessarily inferior because they have fewer visitors. Additionally, these are countries and there are many more destinations and DMOs below the country level.

Some travel magazines and guidebooks publish "top destination" lists each year. For example, Lonely Planet's Ten Best in Travel 2022/Countries were (in order) the Cook Islands, Norway, Mauritius, Belize, Slovenia, Finland, Anguilla, Oman, Malawi, and Egypt. This was based on the voting of a Lonely Planet expert panel based on topicality, excitement and value (Lonely Planet 2022). TripAdvisor's Travelers' Choice 2022 Popular Destinations—World were Dubai (UAE), London (UK), Cancun (Mexico), Bali (Indonesia), Crete (Greece), Rome (Italy), Cabo San Lucas (Mexico), Istanbul (Türkiye), Paris (France), Hurghada (Egypt), Barcelona (Spain), Marrakech (Morocco), Tenerife (Spain), Corsica (France), and New Delhi (India); these were the top fifteen in the ratings followed by ten others (TripAdvisor 2022). The top ten rated "best cities to visit" in 2022 compiled by the *Telegraph* (UK) were Barcelona, Sydney, Cape Town, Lisbon, Venice, Los Angeles, Dubai, London, Vancouver, and Florence (*The Telegraph* 2022). There are many other of these "top destination" lists but just from this small collection, it is interesting to note that few destinations appeared twice on these three. But more importantly no specific and detailed criteria were given for the selections.

The Global Sustainable Tourism Council (GSTC) introduced the GSTC Criteria for Destinations in 2013 that measure how well destinations are following best practices in sustainable tourism. These criteria are divided into four sections:

1. sustainable management;
2. socioeconomic sustainability;
3. cultural sustainability;
4. environmental sustainability.

(GSTC 2021)

Based upon years of related experience, the author suggests the ten As as a useful set of attributes for judging the success of tourism destinations. Each of these ten attributes begin with the letter "A" (Fig. 1.6).

The following is a short explanation of each of the ten As' attributes:

1.   Awareness: This attribute is related to tourists' level of knowledge about the destination and is influenced by the amount and nature of the information they receive. DMO question: Is there a high level of awareness of the destination among potential tourists?

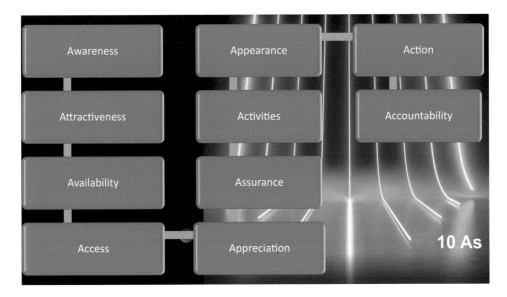

Figure 1.6 The 10 As of successful tourism destinations.

2. Attractiveness: The number and geographic scope of appeal of the destination's attractions comprise this attribute. DMO question: Does the destination offer a diversity of attractions that are appealing to tourists?
3. Availability: This attribute is determined by the ease with which bookings and reservations can be made for the destination, and the number of booking and reservation channels available. DMO question: Can bookings and reservations for the destination be made through a variety of distribution channels?
4. Access: The convenience of getting to and from the destination, as well as moving around within the destination, constitutes this attribute. DMO questions: Is there convenient access to and from the destination by all modes of transportation? Is there convenient transportation within the destination?
5. Appearance: This attribute measures the impressions that the destination makes on tourists, both when they first arrive and then throughout their stays in the destination. DMO question: Does the destination make a good first impression? Does the destination make a positive and lasting impression?
6. Activities: The extent of the array of activities and experiences available to tourists within the destination is the determinant of this attribute. DMO question: Does the destination offer a wide range of activities and experiences in which tourists want to engage?
7. Assurance: This attribute relates to the safety and security of the destination for tourists. DMO question: Is the destination clean, safe and secure?
8. Appreciation: The feeling of the levels of welcome and hospitality contribute to this attribute. DMO question: Do tourists feel welcome and receive good service in the destination?
9. Action: The availability of a long-term tourism plan and a marketing plan for tourism are some of the required actions. DMO question: Is the tourism development and marketing in the destination well planned?

10. Accountability: This attribute is about the evaluation of performance by the DMO. DMO question: Is the DMO measuring the effectiveness of its performance?

These ten attributes can be useful for all destinations, but they need to be expressed in greater detail than that shown above. Additionally, there are other criteria that could be added to this list of ten. For example, the economic contributions of tourism to the destination might also be included, as well as the degree to which the destination is following a sustainable tourism agenda, which could be called altruism.

Uniqueness of Destination Management and Marketing

Having constructed these definitions and discussed the roles of destination management and marketing, it is important to pinpoint the key differences between DMO management and marketing and for other tourism and hospitality organizations. The following differences make destination management and marketing unique.

The Lack of Control over the Quality and Quantity of Services and Products

With very few exceptions, DMOs do not own or operate the facilities, services, attractions, events, and other amenities that they represent and market (although some operate convention centers). However, this does not mean that the DMO is totally absolved from worrying about these. The quality and quantity of destination services and products greatly influence the satisfaction of visitors and the effectiveness of the DMO's programs.

The Lack of a Pricing Function

DMOs rarely get involved in pricing the services and facilities they represent; this function being performed by other tourism and hospitality organizations within the destination. Once again, although DMOs seldom do pricing themselves, they are often very concerned with the price levels in their destinations. For example, the prices of hotels and meeting/trade show facility rentals are a major concern in competitive bidding for major conventions, conferences, shows or events.

The Need to Serve the Requirements of Many Organizations

DMOs have many constituencies or stakeholders that they serve ranging from tourism businesses and government agencies to local community residents. They must balance the requirements of other organizations that may have differing priorities and objectives, and who may even be competitors. DMOs must be objective and fair in their treatment of all stakeholders.

The Need to Build Consensus among Stakeholders

The DMO is the local leader in destination management and marketing. However, it cannot fulfill this leadership role without building consensus among stakeholders for its vision, goals, strategies, objectives, plans and programs. This consensus building means selling the DMO's ideas to others in the community through formal and informal communications.

The Need to Be Sensitive to the Interests of Local Residents

DMOs not only represent tourism and hospitality organizations but also are accountable to the residents of their communities. They must be vigilant not to promote forms of tourism or developments that will undermine the environmental, social or cultural resources and values of the community. DMOs must do their utmost to involve locals in tourism and share the benefits with them.

The Need to Demonstrate Broad Economic Benefits

Most DMOs are public or quasi-public (public–private partnership, PPP) organizations. While private-sector businesses are accountable through profitability only to their owners or shareholders, DMOs are not usually profit-driven agencies. Their accountability must be demonstrated through the effective use of funds and the DMO's impact in generating additional visitor spending and employment in tourism and hospitality.

The Difficulty in Measuring Performance

DMOs have no direct sales figures at their disposal because they do not sell products and services directly to visitors. Additionally, others are involved in and responsible for bringing tourists to destinations. This means that DMOs have greater difficulty in measuring performance against their roles.

As a result of these differences, it is clear that a DMO has two distinct audiences with which it must communicate, external and internal. The external audience consists of the potential visitors to the destination, travel trade intermediaries, media companies, and others. The internal audience encompasses all the local stakeholders including the board of directors, members, industry operators, government officials and local residents. To be successful requires that a DMO communicate effectively with both the external and internal audiences; its job is not just limited to external marketing.

Stakeholders in Destination Management

This book uses the term "stakeholder" many times, and you will probably want to know what it means. Before giving the definition, you need to know that the broader view of destination management is being taken and so it is not just about the DMO's stakeholders. Stakeholders are groups and individuals that have a direct or indirect interest in the management of a destination for tourism.

DEFINITION

Destination stakeholders

Those organizations and individuals with a direct or indirect impact in the management of a destination for tourism.

Figure 1.7 shows the five main groups of stakeholders in destination management (tourists, tourism sector organizations, community, environment and government). Tourists and tourism sector organizations have a direct interest in destination management; they are directly affected by the tourism situation in the destination. The other three groups are more indirectly affected by tourism in the destination, although some of these groups and individuals are more involved with tourism than others.

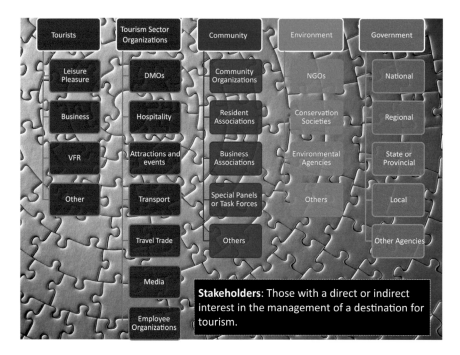

Figure 1.7 Stakeholders in destination management.

The DMO needs to be especially cognizant of all these groups of stakeholders since they all contribute in some way to the success of tourism within the destination. It is not enough to communicate and interact only with tourists and tourism sector organizations. Continuous communications are also required with government agencies, community groups and residents, and environmental groups. Consultation, involvement and participation are also needed, and especially when strategic decisions are being made about tourism. VisitEngland (2008) defines these three terms as follows:

1. Consultation: Asking for opinions and viewpoint on options, alternative strategies or programs of action.
2. Involvement: Working together with others to formulate options and strategies.
3. Participation: Facilitating stakeholders to formulate options and strategies.

The stakeholders in the DMO itself are most likely to be certain government agencies and tourism sector organizations. These parties have the most direct interest in the operations of the DMO since the strategies and programs directly affect them.

Destination Governance

Destination governance is an issue that has received more attention in destination management during the past ten years. Beritelli et al. (2007) defined destination governance as "setting and developing rules and mechanisms for a policy, as well as business strategies, by involving all the institutions and individuals." Destination governance relates to how a DMO is administered and who does the administering. It also concerns the policies, systems and processes used to ensure that all stakeholders are involved.

> **DEFINITION**
>
> **Destination governance**
>
> Destination governance is how a DMO is administered and who does the administering. Governance involves the policies, systems and processes to ensure that all stakeholders are involved and that the DMO is accountable for its results and resource usage and has a high level of transparency. Traditionally DMOs in most countries were "governed" by the public sector, meaning that they were run by government agencies with little private-sector input and involvement.

In the following section of this chapter, different types of DMOs and their governance are discussed.

Destination Management Organizations

Scattered throughout the world and spanning many different organizational sizes and types, DMOs have existed for 100-plus years. If you are a beginner, it can be really confusing to figure out exactly what is and is not a DMO. Shimasaki (2016) complains that it is like "an acronym soup on steroids" in tourism and hospitality as she deftly differentiates among DMOs, DMCs, and CVBs (convention and visitors bureaus). The author also has come across DMOs that do not realize they are DMOs. However, you will not be dropped into that thick soup of confusion.

Destination management is done by a wide variety of DMOs ranging from national to city-level organizations. The DMO types include entities at four geographic levels:

1. national;
2. state, province and territory;
3. region;
4. county and city.

Countries have different government administrative structures. For example, under the national government in Italy, there are regions and then within the regions there are provinces. In other places, it is the opposite with the regions being under states and provinces, such as in Ontario, Canada and Queensland, Australia.

Should the government administer the DMO or should the private sector or perhaps a collaboration of government and the private sector? Another difficult question to answer, but it is safe to say that in most countries it is the government that runs the DMOs. The strengths of government or the public sector in operating DMOs are considered to be:

- Governments have a mandate to do long-term, strategic planning and they are good at it.
- Destination awareness is high among governments due to their extensive responsibilities and grassroots knowledge and activities.
- Public administrators are skilled in managing complex organizations and may be better able to get financial support from government.

- Governments often provide grants and other support for small- and medium-sized enterprises.
- Public agencies may have greater powers in operating quality assurance programs.

> (Adapted from a presentation by Esencan Terzibasoglu, UNWTO, September 2011)

However, it is often argued that government agencies are very bureaucratic and slow to accomplish tasks. Other common criticisms are that they tend to be politically influenced and that key staff members are frequently changed. Governments are also considered to not be skilled at marketing.

The strengths of the private sector tend to be the opposite of the public sector and include:

- The private sector is good at implementing short-term tactics.
- Decision-making in the private sector is fast.
- The private sector is very skilled and experienced in marketing and sales approaches.
- The private sector is aware of market opportunities.
- A business management approach is followed.
- The private sector has well-developed programs for CRM.

The strongest argument against the private sector is that it is not particularly good at the long-term planning that is required for a tourism destination. Also, it can be said that the private sector is profit-motivated and may not be as concerned about community residents or the environment. The private sector may not be as able to get financial support from government agencies.

Having made these initial comments about DMO governance, the following materials describe the types of DMOs that exist around the world at the four geographic levels. As you will see, there is no single template for the organizational structure of a DMO. In fact, there is great variation in DMO types across the globe.

National DMOs

National DMOs are typically the most powerful within a country and set the overall agenda for tourism. National DMOs are set up in many different ways, and their relative power tends to be a function of how they are positioned relative to the national government.

NATIONAL TOURISM ADMINISTRATIONS AND MINISTRIES OF TOURISM

In some countries, the national DMO is called the National Tourism Administration (NTA) and performs all the DMO roles that were discussed earlier. This is the situation in Vietnam with the Vietnam National Administration of Tourism. Other countries do not explicitly use the term "NTA" but have created a separate ministry of tourism and in these cases the ministry performs all the DMO roles. This is usually an indication that tourism is considered to be a highly important economic sector for the country. Bulgaria, Cambodia, India, Jamaica, Kenya, Lebanon, Mauritius, Oman, and Trinidad and Tobago are just ten of the countries that have a ministry of tourism. Most of these are developing countries. Among the countries with dedicated tourism ministries, a good example is the Ministry of Tourism, Government of India, and a description follows.

EXAMPLE 1.13

Ministry of Tourism, India

India has a dedicated ministry of tourism.

> [The] Ministry of Tourism is the nodal agency to formulate national policies and programs for the development and promotion of tourism in the country. In the process, the Ministry consults and collaborates with other stakeholders in the sector including various Central Ministries/agencies, the State Governments/ Union Territory Administrations and the representatives of the private sector.
>
> (Ministry of Tourism, Government of India 2022)

Learning Point

Many developing countries have free-standing ministries of tourism.

Shared ministry portfolios including tourism. Some countries afford tourism a somewhat lower priority and profile, and place it along with other government entities in a shared ministerial portfolio. For example, tourism is often combined with economic development, as in the case of the Ministry of Economy, Development, and Tourism in Chile. Another popular combination is tourism and culture, with examples being the Ministry of Culture and Tourism in China, Ethiopia, Solomon Islands, and Türkiye. Sport and the arts are other portfolios often combined with tourism, including the Ministry of Tourism and Sports in Croatia and Thailand, the Ministry of Culture, Sports, and Tourism in South Korea, and the Ministry of Tourism, Arts, and Culture in Ghana and Malaysia.

In some cases, the word "tourism" does not appear in the official name of the ministry. An example of this is in New Zealand where tourism is just one of the sectors and industries within the Ministry of Business, Innovation, and Employment. In the UK, tourism, as represented by VisitBritain and VisitEngland, is under the Department for Digital, Culture, Media and Sport.

Dual National DMO Systems

Most countries have just one national DMO, but some have split the roles between two different organizations. Earlier in this chapter, the concept of coordinating all the roles of destination management was emphasized, so why create two separate organizations? The answer revolves around the destination marketing role and governments wanting to give DMOs more flexibility in conducting destination marketing. The PPP option also allows a country to harness the strengths of both the public and private sectors within the organization given the responsibility for destination marketing.

In certain countries, all roles except for destination marketing are given to the NTA. Product development, and planning and research are particularly important roles for those types of NTAs that can be found in Australia and Hong Kong Special Administrative Region (SAR), and other destinations. Australia's NTA is the Australian Trade and Investment Commission (Austrade) which reports to the Minister of Trade, Tourism, and Investment. Austrade's role is to develop policy, attract investment and provide research to grow Australia's tourism market share (Austrade 2022). Tourism Australia is the other DMO at the national level in Australia. Tourism Australia is a statutory body and is the Australian government agency responsible for attracting international visitors to Australia, both for leisure and business events (Tourism Australia 2022).

Another example of this dual DMO system is with the Tourism Commission and the HKTB. Of course, Hong Kong is not a country but a SAR of the People's Republic of China. The HKTB is the second organization in the SAR. HKTB is a government-subvented (funded) body that was founded in April 2001 under the HKTB Ordinance. HKTB does the destination marketing for Hong Kong, as well as performing other duties.

EXAMPLE 1.14

Tourism Commission, Hong Kong

Hong Kong operates a dual DMO system where the Tourism Commission assumes responsibility for policy and strategy.

> The Tourism Commission was established in May 1999 and is under the Commerce and Economic Development Bureau. It is headed by the Commissioner for Tourism who is tasked to map out government's tourism development policy and strategy; to provide a focal point for liaison with the tourism industry and to enhance coordination in developing tourism.
>
> (Tourism Commission, Hong Kong 2022)

Learning Point

The dual DMO system allows the government to maintain policy control over tourism.

These are examples of statutory bodies or "quangos" (quasi-non-governmental organizations). Traditionally, they were called commissions, boards, offices, or authorities. More recently the country names have been superseded with either "Tourism," "Visit" or "Destination" including Tourism Australia, Tourism New Zealand, VisitBritain, and Destination Canada.

One of the main advantages of these bodies is that they tend to offer a blend of public-sector and private-sector strengths. These organizations are governed by independent boards of directors drawn from government, private-sector tourism businesses, and nonprofits. They have greater management flexibility in dealing with the commercial aspects of tourism marketing and promotion. Additionally, they have closer relationships with the private sector and other non-governmental organizations (NGOs).

ROLES AND ACTIVITIES OF NATIONAL DMOS

Despite the variety of organizational structures of national DMOs, they do tend to perform similar types of roles and activities. Some of the major roles and activities of the national DMOs are as follows:

- Tourism legislation and regulations: Introduce and enforce legislation and regulations related directly to tourism. This may include the articulation of minimum standards for operating certain types of tourism businesses (accommodations; restaurants; tour guiding; travel agencies; tour operators; adventure travel, etc.).

- Tourism policymaking: Prepare overall tourism policies for their countries.
- Tourism planning and strategies: Coordinate the processes for developing country-level plans and strategies.
- Tourism development: Encourage selected types of tourism developments through financial or technical assistance.
- Tourism research: Conduct tourism research at the national level.
- Destination marketing: Implement international and domestic marketing strategies and plans.
- Education and training programs: Develop and facilitate education and training programs that increase professionalism in the country's tourism sector.
- Quality improvement and assurance: Introduce strategies and programs to improve tourism quality that in some cases involve operating quality assurance schemes.
- Sustainable tourism: Promote sustainable tourism practices in the country and operate specific programs to encourage sustainable tourism.

State, Provincial, and Territorial DMOs

Several of the larger countries in the world have governmental systems of states, provinces or territories below the national level. In these situations, DMOs are in operation at the state, provincial or territorial levels. Similar to the national level, different types of organizational structures are also found here.

Government-run DMOs

Some of these DMOs are departments or divisions of their state, provincial or territorial governments. For example, in the State of New York in the USA, the Division of Tourism is within the state government's Department of Economic Development (New York State Division of Tourism 2022). The Department of Tourism, Government of Kerala in India is another case (Department of Tourism, Kerala 2022). All of the DMOs in the provinces of China are government-operated.

Statutory Bodies and other Nonprofit Organizations (NPOs)

There has been a trend in recent times to create statutory bodies and other forms of NPOs, particularly to handle the destination marketing for states, provinces or territories. Tourism Northern Territory in Australia is an example of a statutory body (Tourism Northern Territory 2022). Visit California in the USA is an NPO classified as a (501)(C)(6) corporation (Visit California 2022).

The roles of these DMOs are similar to the national DMOs, but they place more emphasis on domestic tourism in destination marketing and on destination marketing in general. For example, Travel Alberta, the provincial DMO for Alberta, Canada describes its role as follows.

EXAMPLE 1.15

Travel Alberta, Canada

Travel Alberta's emphasis is on destination marketing.

> As a destination management organization, Travel Alberta drives the growth of the province's visitor economy, creating and promoting must-visit destinations throughout the province. We do this by helping businesses develop memorable products and experiences, marketing those products and experiences to the world, and ensuring visitors have access to them.
>
> (Travel Alberta 2022)

Learning Point

State, provincial, and territorial DMOs may have a main focus on destination marketing.

Some of these DMOs have a more extensive scope of operations than others and Tourism & Events Queensland (TEQ) in Australia is a good example.

EXAMPLE 1.16

TEQ's Primary Responsibilities

TEQ performs multiple roles.

- Marketing
- Events
- Experience design and development
- Stakeholder engagement
- Cruise, Indigenous, and nature tourism
- Education opportunities

(TEQ 2022)

Learning Point

Some state, provincial, and territorial DMOs have diversified roles.

The TEQ organization chart (Fig. 1.8) shows that it has three main groups: global marketing, events and experiences, and corporate. This organizational structure shows that TEQ is involved in destination marketing, planning and research, and product development. TEQ is also very much involved in partnerships and team-building and community relations; so in fact it covers most of the DMO roles discussed earlier.

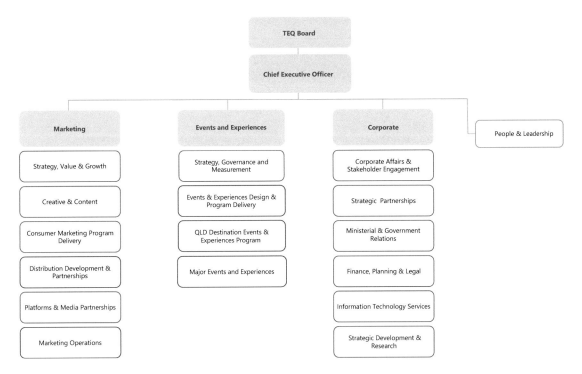

Figure 1.8 Organizational chart for Tourism and Events Queensland (TEQ 2022).

Regional DMOs

The definition of what a "region" constitutes varies from country to country and so therefore does the meaning of a regional DMO. For example, smaller-sized countries including New Zealand and Italy have regional government agencies below the national level. Larger countries such as Canada, the USA, China, Australia, and India have state, provincial or territorial government agencies below the national level and then have regions under the states, provinces, or territories.

Several countries, states and provinces have systems of regional DMOs, and these include:

- New Zealand: There are thirty-one regional tourism organizations in New Zealand (Ministry of Business, Innovation and Employment, New Zealand 2022).
- Ontario, Canada: The Province of Ontario has thirteen regional tourism organizations (Ministry of Heritage, Sport, Tourism and Culture, Ontario 2022).
- Ireland: The Republic of Ireland has eight tourism regions (Irish Tourism Industry Confederation 2018).
- Italy: There are twenty official tourism regions in Italy (Visit Prosecco Italy 2022).
- Western Australia, Australia: There are five regional tourism organizations in the state of Western Australia (Tourism Western Australia 2022).

Destination Queenstown in New Zealand is an example of a regional DMO, and the following is a description of its responsibility, mandate and role.

EXAMPLE 1.17

About Destination Queenstown, New Zealand

This is a very clear and detailed statement of what a regional tourism organization does.

Destination Queenstown is the regional tourism organization (RTO) responsible for the marketing of Queenstown as the Southern Hemisphere's premier four season lake and alpine resort. As the neutral tourism contact point for the resort, we work with local businesses, including tourism operators, the hospitality industry, accommodation providers, retailers, and service sectors to promote Queenstown as a unique destination that offers visitors truly memorable experiences. Our role is to coordinate, facilitate, motivate and develop the marketing of Queenstown.

On an international level, we work closely with Tourism New Zealand and in our long-haul markets we promote the wider Southern Lakes region alongside our neighbors Destination Fiordland and Lake Wanaka Tourism.

We are responsible for the branding and positioning of Queenstown. We have a mandate to generically promote the Queenstown District as an international visitor destination through a variety of distribution channels and we act as the neutral coordinator of initiatives and campaigns that benefit our members.

We have a core role in several areas including providing information, trade liaison and media promotion. We also coordinate the collective marketing of Queenstown—identifying, prioritizing and promoting the various visitor groups that we believe Queenstown can attract.

(Destination Queenstown 2022)

Learning Point

DMOs are sometimes not well understood, and clear statements of purpose are helpful in increasing the recognition of their roles.

Regional DMOs tend to be mainly involved in destination marketing, but in some cases they also assume other roles including planning and research and product development. In most cases, they receive funding from superior levels of government. Regional DMOs are either government-run or are structured as statutory bodies or nonprofits.

Not wanting to confuse you, it is important to know about another type of regional DMO that covers several countries, or states and provinces. There are several of these cross-border tourism regions in the world, including the Greater Mekong Subregion (Cambodia, China, Lao People's Democratic Republic, Myanmar, Thailand, and Vietnam); Danube Competence Center (Germany, Austria, Slovakia, Hungary, Croatia, Serbia, Romania, Bulgaria, Moldova, and Ukraine); and the Central America Tourism Association (Belize, Costa Rica, El Salvador, Guatemala, Honduras, Nicaragua, Panama, and Dominican Republic).

County and City DMOs

At the most local level there are county and city DMOs. These exist in most countries in the largest metropolitan areas. Glasgow in Scotland is a good example:

EXAMPLE 1.18

What Does Glasgow Life Do?

The city DMO in Glasgow, Scotland has a very broad mandate.

> Glasgow Life is a charitable organization. Our mission is to inspire the city's citizens and visitors to lead richer and more active lives through culture, sport and learning." Glasgow life is involved in the following activities:
> Sport and events: Manages indoor and outdoor sports areas.
> Museums and collections: Manages eight museums.
> Communities and libraries: Operates libraries and community facilities.
> Arts, music and cultural venues: Operates various cultural venues and manages festivals.
> Corporate services: Performs the internal administration of Glasgow Life.
> Conventions: Acts as the city's DMO.
>
> (Glasgow Life 2022)

Learning Point

City or county DMOs may operate some of the facilities that they are representing.

In some countries and especially in the USA, there are even more extensive systems of county and city DMOs. As was the case at the three other geographic levels, the county or city DMO may be run by the local government or, alternatively, it may be an NPO. The introduction of room or bed taxes in the USA at county and city levels led to a rapid expansion of the number of DMOs. Guests at hotels and other forms of accommodation pay these taxes and then part or all of the taxes collected are distributed by local governments to DMOs. In the USA, these organizations are called convention and visitors bureaus or CVBs for short. They mainly focus on destination marketing but are gradually placing greater emphasis on other destination management roles.

Careers in Destination Management and Destination Marketing

It can be very confusing and frustrating if you enter "careers in destination management" in a search engine like Google. The results you will get are mainly for destination management companies (DMCs) and not for DMOs. You will get more success when entering "careers in destination marketing" but as you already know that does not cover all of destination management.

There is such a great variety of DMOs around the world that it is difficult to talk very accurately about careers. In many countries, the DMOs are governmental agencies so the positions available are as civil servants. In other countries, the DMOs are statutory bodies and NPOs and staff are hired on a contract basis.

The Singapore Tourism Board (STB) is a statutory body that reports to the country's Ministry of Trade and Industry. In its own words, STB "champions the development of Singapore's tourism sector, one of the country's key service sectors and economic pillars, and undertakes the marketing and promotion of Singapore as a tourism destination." "Not your usual day job" is what STB promises to students and fresh graduates (Fig. 1.9), and STB describes the work as follows.

EXAMPLE 1.19

Working at the STB

This is a very positive description about careers with the STB.

> The nature of our work demands a culture and environment that is progressive, driven, energetic and fun. At STB, you will be surrounded by people who share a passion for tourism and a desire to shape and steer Singapore on the global stage. You will be inspired to dream, experiment and execute innovative ideas that will transform the tourism sector. With values that foster respect, care, collaboration and compassion, you will build lasting networks and enjoy enduring relationships both at and outside work.
>
> (STB 2019)

Learning Point

It is important for DMOs to clearly position themselves as unique employers.

Figure 1.9 Singapore Tourism Board highlights the great careers in DMOs (STB 2022).

Based on the roles of DMOs, the skills and competencies shown in Figure 1.10 seem the most suited for this career field.

DMO roles	Skills and competencies
Planning and research	· Statistics and market research · Tourism planning · Urban and regional planning
Leadership, coordination, and governance	· Leadership · Management
Product development	· Architecture and landscape architecture · Financial analysis · Urban and regional planning
Partnerships and team-building	· Management · Negotiation
Community and stakeholder relationships and involvement	· Capacity building · Community-based tourism · Management · Public relations
Marketing, branding, and communications	· Marketing · Brand management · Sales · Advertising · Public relations and journalism · Digital and social media marketing
Visitor management	· Capacity measurement · Experience design · Protected area management
Crisis management	· Crisis management communication · Crisis management planning
DMO administration	· Financial administration · Fundraising · Human resource management

Figure 1.10 Skills and competencies most suited for the DMO career field.

Hold the Printing Presses: DMOs Are Under Pressure and Need to Change

Why hold the printing presses? The simple answer is that DMOs are under growing pressure to change the ways in which they have operated for decades. Most of what you have read up until now in this first chapter has had a positive tone; however, darker clouds were surrounding DMOs in 2020–2022. Certainly, one the blackest of these clouds was the COVID-19 pandemic that decimated the budgets of many DMOs worldwide. Nevertheless, 2019 and COVID-19 did not mark the beginning of this change; it started much earlier. For example, there was a call for destination management and marketing to become more "mindful" in 2012 (Morgan 2012). More recently, destinations and DMOs have been advised to become "wiser" (Coca-Stefaniak 2021) and "smarter" (Gretzel 2022). One of the recurrent themes here is that DMOs must change from being just being "promoters" to becoming "stewards" of their destinations. A definition of destination stewardship follows.

> **DEFINITION**
>
> **Destination stewardship**
>
> "A process by which local communities, governmental agencies, NGOs, and the tourism industry take a multi-stakeholder approach to maintaining the cultural, environmental, economic, and aesthetic integrity of their country, region, or town" (Bray 2021).

One DMO that has taken heed of these needed changes is Tourism Vancouver Island in British Columbia, Canada. In April 2022, it announced that it was becoming a social enterprise and would no longer operate as a traditional DMO. You also might have noticed earlier that Glasgow Life is a charitable organization, which to date is an unusual model for DMOs although more compatible with calls to pay greater attention to the needs of local residents.

EXAMPLE 1.20

Tourism Vancouver Island Becomes a Social Enterprise

Tourism Vancouver Island (TVI) is one of the very first DMOs to change its structure into a social enterprise.

> "The travel and tourism industry has been forever changed by the pandemic," says Anthony Everett, President and Chief Executive Officer (CEO), 4VI. "Tourism Vancouver Island was a 60-year-old organization and we need to change with the times. We are making an industry-leading transition that will allow us to be Vancouver Island's respected tourism advisers known for investing profits into powering the stewardship of our destination and our home."
>
> (TVI 2022)

Learning Point

Becoming a social enterprise may allow DMOs to better serve their communities.

Some experts are arguing that DMOs have not been effective. Hay (2021), for example, suggests that the reason for being for national tourism organizations (NTOs) is "now open to question" and "they need to reinvent themselves" (Hay 2021: 182).

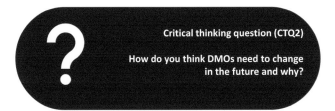

Critical thinking question (CTQ2)

How do you think DMOs need to change in the future and why?

The next two chapters reflect the growing sentiment that destination management and DMOs need to change and pay greater attention to sustainability and DSR (Chapter 2) and the well-being and quality of life of local residents (Chapter 3).

SUMMING UP

Destination management and destination marketing are two interrelated concepts that have developed in tourism over the past thirty-five to forty years. Destination management is the broader concept that encompasses destination marketing, branding, and communications and other roles. The other roles of destination management are planning and research; leadership, coordination and governance; product development; partnerships and team-building;

community and stakeholder relationships and involvement; visitor management; and crisis management.

There are many types of DMOs in the world at the national, state, provincial, territorial, regional, county, and city levels. No standardized structural template exists for a DMO, and they vary quite widely from country to country. Recently, there has been a trend for DMO governance to move from public-sector only to public–private partnerships (PPPs).

DMOs have a large variety of stakeholders with whom they must network. The fact that they need to serve the requirements of many organizations is one of the unique features of destination management and marketing. The success of a DMO is at least in part measured by how well it communicates and interacts with its stakeholders.

Successful destinations have to satisfy a variety of criteria and this book recommends the "10 As" model as a basic platform. However, there are other systems and criteria that potentially can be used for this purpose.

The field of destination management is receiving greater recognition and becoming more professional. It is a promising career field for tourism management students, although small in comparison to the hospitality management field.

The COVID-19 pandemic precipitated changes in destination management and DMOs, and these changes are expected to continue in the future. Destination stewardship, sustainability, social responsibility, and the well-being of local residents are increasing in priority.

KEYWORDS

climate change
community and stakeholder relationships and involvement
crisis management
destination governance
destination management
DMO
destination marketing

leadership, coordination, and governance
marketing, branding, and communications
overtourism
partnership and team-building
planning and research
product development

public–private partnership (PPP)
stakeholders
stewardship
sustainability
sustainable tourism
10 As
visitor management

REVIEW QUESTIONS

1. What are the key characteristics of destinations?
2. How would you define destination management?
3. What is destination marketing?
4. What are the major differences between destination management and destination marketing?
5. Who are the five groups of stakeholders in destination management?
6. What are the features that make destination management and marketing unique?
7. What are the 10 As of successful destinations?
8. What is destination governance?
9. What are the typical roles of national DMOs?
10. What are the relative benefits and weaknesses of government-run DMOs?

REFERENCES

4VI (2023) "What is 4VI," https://forvi.ca/about/

AITO The Specialist Travel Association (2022) "AITO Sustainable Tourism Guidelines. How to travel sustainably and responsibly," https://www.aito.com/sustainable-tourism/guidelines

Austrade (2022) "Supporting the Growth of Australia's Visitor Economy," www.austrade.gov.au/Australian/tourism

Beritelli, P., Bieger, T., and Laesser, C. (2007) "Destination Governance: Using Corporate Governance Theories as a Foundation for Effective Destination Management," *Journal of Travel Research*, 46 (1): 96–107.

Bray, S. (2021) "Building a Community-Centered Destination Stewardship Initiative," Center for Responsible Travel, www.responsibletravel.org/blog/community-centered-destination-stewardship

Bureau of Tourism (Palau) (2016) "Palau Responsible Tourism Policy Framework: Ensuring a pristine paradise. Palau for everyone, 2017–2021," https://www.palaugov.pw/wp-content/uploads/2017/04/Final_Palau-Responsible-Tourism-Framework1.pdf

Coca-Stefaniak, J. A. (2021) "Beyond Smart Tourism Cities: Towards a New Generation of 'Wise' Tourism Destinations," *Journal of Tourism Futures*, 7 (2): 251–258.

Department of Commerce (US) (2022) "National Travel and Tourism Strategy," https://www.trade.gov/national-travel-and-tourism-strategy

Department of Tourism, Kerala (2022) "Governmental Affairs," www.keralatourism.org/governmental-affairs

Department of Tourism, South Africa (2022) "Vision and Mission," www.tourism.gov.za/AboutNDT/Pages/Vision-and-Mission.aspx

Destination Canada (2023) "Research," https://www.destinationcanada.com/en/research

Destination Queenstown (2022) "About Us," www.queenstownnz.co.nz/about-us

Duan, J., Xie, C., and Morrison, A. M. (2022) "Tourism Crises and Impacts on Destinations: A Systematic Review of the Tourism and Hospitality Literature," *Journal of Hospitality and Tourism Research*, 46 (4): 667–695.

Dubai College of Tourism (2022) "About DCT," https://dct.ac.ae/en/about-dct

Ellis, C. (2022) "Banff Residents Invited to Have Their Say on Tourism Master Plan," *Rocky Mountain Outlook*, May 30, www.rmotoday.com/banff/banff-residents-invited-to-have-say-on-tourism-master-plan-5421770

Gartrell, R. B. (1988) *Destination Marketing for Convention and Visitor Bureaus*, Dubuque, IA: Kendall Hunt Publishing.

German National Tourist Board (2022) "Historic Highlights of Germany," www.germany.travel/en/cities-culture/historic-highlights-of-germany.html

Glasgow Life (2022) "What We Do," www.glasgowlife.org.uk/work-with-us/what-we-do

Global Sustainable Tourism Council (2022) "GSTC Criteria for Governments and Destinations," www.gstcouncil.org/for-destinations

Government Offices of Sweden (2022) "Strategy for Sustainable Tourism and a Growing Tourism Industry," https://government.se/information-material/2022/06/strategy-for-sustainabletourism-and-a-growing-tourism-industry/

Grenada Tourism Authority (2023) "Tourism Awareness Campaign," https://tac.puregrenada.com/

Gretzel, U. (2022) "The Smart DMO: A New Step in the Digital Transformation of Destination Management Organizations," *European Journal of Tourism Research*, 30. https://doi.org/10.54055/ejtr.v30i.2589

Hay, B. (2021) "The Future of National Tourism Organisations' Marketing Functions: There Is No Future?" *Journal of Tourism Futures*, 7 (2): 179–183.

Hong Kong Tourism Board (2022) "Great Outdoors Hong Kong," www.discoverhongkong.com/seasia/what-s-new/highlights/great-outdoors-hong-kong.html

Indian Institute of Tourism and Travel Management (2022) "About Us," www.iittm.ac.in/about.html

Irish Tourism Industry Confederation (2018) "Spotlight on Regionality and Tourism," www.itic.ie/spotlight-regionality-tourism/

Korea Tourism Organization (2022) "Vision and Goals," https://kto.visitkorea.or.kr/eng/overview.kto

Las Vegas Convention and Visitors Authority (2022) "2021 Las Vegas Visitor Profile Study," www.lvcva.com/stats-and-facts/visitor-profiles

Levin, R. (2021) "Can California Tourism Survive Climate Change?" *The New York Times*, October 26, www.nytimes.com/2021/10/26/travel/california-tourism-climate-change.html

Lioy, S. (2022) "How to Get the Most out of the Jordan Pass," *Lonely Planet*, www.lonelyplanet.com/articles/get-jordan-pass

Lonely Planet (2022) "Best in Travel 2022: Countries," www.lonelyplanet.com/best-in-travel/countries

Mill, R. C., and Morrison, A. M. (2012) *The Tourism System*, 7th edn, Dubuque, IA: Kendall Hunt Publishing.

Ministry of Business, Innovation and Employment, New Zealand (2022) "Regional Tourism Organisations (RTOs)," www.mbie.govt.nz/immigration-and-tourism/tourism/tourism-recovery/tourism-communities-support-recovery-and-re-set-plan/rtos

Ministry of Heritage, Sport, Tourism and Culture, Ontario (2022) "Tourism Regions," www.mtc.gov.on.ca/en/regions/regions.shtml

Ministry of Tourism and Antiquities, Jordan (2022) "The Jordan Pass," http://jordanpass.jo/

Ministry of Tourism, Government of India (2022) "Annual Report, 2021–2022," https://tourism.gov.in/media/annual-reports

Morgan, N. (2012) "Time for 'Mindful' Destination Management and Marketing," *Journal of Destination Marketing and Management*, 1: 8–9.

Morrison, A. M. (2023) *Hospitality and Travel Marketing*, 5th edn, London and New York, NY: Routledge.

New York State Division of Tourism (2022) "Contact Us," www.iloveny.com/travel-tools/contact-us

SECTUR, Mexico (2022) Pueblos Mágicos [Magical Towns], https://www.gob.mx/sectur/articulos/pueblos-magicos-206528

Shimasaki, C. (2016) "CVB, DMO, DMC: What's the difference? Destination Marketing Association International," http://blog.empowermint.com/meeting-planner-tips/cvb-dmo-dmc-whats-the-difference/

Singapore Tourism Board (STB) (2019) "Students and Fresh Graduates," www.stb.gov.sg/careers/students-and-graduates

Swisscontact (2016) "Crisis and Disaster Management for Destinations and DMOs," Bali: Swisscontact.

The Telegraph (2022) "Best Cities on Earth to Visit," https://corporate.telegraph.co.uk/2022/04/28/telegraph-travel-research-reveals-the-best-city-on-earth-to-visit

Terzibasoglu, E. (2011) "Destination Development and Marketing: A Conceptual Model," National Conference on Destination Management Organizations, Labuan Bajo, Indonesia, September 22.

Tourism and Events Queensland (2022) "What We Do," https://teq.queensland.com/au/en/industry/who-we-are/meet-the-team/executive-team

Tourism Australia (2022) "Our Organisation," www.tourism.australia.com/en/about/our-organisation.html

——— (2023) "Why Become an Aussie Specialist?" www.aussiespecialist.com/

Tourism Commission, Hong Kong (2022) "About Us," www.tourism.gov.hk/en/about-us.php

Tourism Development Fund, Saudi Arabia (2022) "Welcome to Saudi Arabia: Home to a Wealth of Opportunities," www.tdf.gov.sa/content/TDF/TDF/en/Home.html

Tourism Grading Council of South Africa (2022) "About the TGCSA," www.tourismgrading.co.za/

Tourism Industry Association of Canada (2022) "Tourism Week 2022," https://tiac-aitc.ca/tourismweek2022.html

Tourism New Zealand (2020) "Film Tourism," www.tourismnewzealand.com/markets-stats/sectors/film-tourism

——— (2021) "Sustainability," www.tourismnewzealand.com/about/sustainability/

Tourism Northern Territory (2022) Tourism NT Corporate Website. www.tourismnt.com.au

Tourism Vancouver Island (2022) "Tourism Vancouver Island Makes Industry-Leading Transition to 4VI—a Social Enterprise in Support of a Sustainable Future for Vancouver Island," https://vancouverisland.travel/2022/04/13/4vi-announcement

Tourism Western Australia (2022) "Tourism Region Fact Sheets," www.tourism.wa.gov.au/Markets-and-research/Destination-insights/Pages/Tourism-region-fact-sheets.aspx#

Travel Alberta (2022) "2022–25 Business Plan," https://industry.travelalberta.com/about/business-planning/business-plan-2022

Travel Matters (2022) "Our travel tips. A responsible tourism guide," https://www.travelmatters.co.uk/our-travel-tips

Travel Oregon (2022) "Oregon Tourism Studios," https://industry.traveloregon.com/opportunities/programs-initiatives/oregon-tourism-studios

TripAdvisor (2022) "Travelers' Choice 2022 Popular Destinations: World," www.tripadvisor.com/TravelersChoice-Destinations-cPopular

UNDP (2020) "Poverty eradication," https://sdgs.un.org/topics/poverty-eradication

United Nations (2015) "Transforming our world: The 2030 Agenda for Sustainable Development," https://sdgs.un.org/2030agenda

United Nations World Tourism Organization (2007) *A Practical Guide to Tourism Destination Management*, Madrid: United Nations World Tourism Organization.

——— (2019) "UNWTO Guidelines for Institutional Strengthening Destination Management Organizations: Preparing DMOs for New Challenges," www.e-unwto.org/doi/epdf/10.18111/9789284420841

US Travel Association (2022) "National Travel and Tourism Week," www.ustravel.org/events/national-travel-and-tourism-week

Virginia Tourism Corporation (2022) "About Virginia Tourism Corporation," www.vatc.org/about

Visit California (2022) "Let's Bring the World to California," https://industry.visitcalifornia.com/

Visit Prosecco Italy (2022) "8 Best Regions of Italy for Your Next Vacation," https://visitproseccoitaly.com/tourist-regions-of-italy/

VisitBritain (2022) "English Tourism Week 2022," www.visitbritain.org/english-tourism-week

VisitEngland (2008) "Principles for developing destination management plans," https://www.visitengland.com/sites/default/files/downloads/dm_plans_guiding_principles.pdf

——— (2012) "Principles for Developing Destination Management Plans," www.visitbritain.org/sites/default/files/vb-corporate/Documents-Library/documents/England-documents/dm_plans_guiding_principles.pdf

——— (2017) "Developing Your Destination Management Plan," www.visitbritain.org/developing-your-destination-management-plan

VisitScotland (2022) "Scotland's UNESCO Trail: The Wonders Within," www.visitscotland.com/see-do/unesco-trail/

World Travel and Tourism Council (2021) "The Power of Travel and Tourism," www.youtube.com/watch?v=9zl93vBzn18&t=82s

Chapter **2**

Destination Sustainability and Social Responsibility

People, Planet, Prosperity, Partnership, Peace

LEARNING OBJECTIVES

Having read this chapter, you should be able to:

1. describe sustainable tourism and its principles;
2. explain the certification programs available in sustainable tourism;
3. describe destination stewardship;
4. outline how social responsibility is accomplished;
5. review responsible tourism and its principles;
6. elaborate on the regenerative tourism concept;
7. explain ethical tourism and provide examples of ethical issues;
8. discuss the concepts of ecotourism, CBT, PPT, and social tourism;
9. elaborate on the meaning of greenwashing in tourism;
10. explain the doughnut economics and circular economy concepts.

DOI: 10.4324/9781003343356-3

Warming Up

Chapter 1 ended with the message that destination management and DMOs need to change and partly that means putting more emphasis on sustainable tourism and social responsibility in future. So, now you are going to hear more about these two concepts, along with destination stewardship, and plenty of examples are provided. Responsible tourism is the next topic. You will then be introduced to a newer idea known as regenerative tourism, which arrived along with the COVID-19 pandemic. The chapter also discusses ethical tourism and various ethical issues that exist within this sector. You will get to know more about ecotourism, CBT, PPT, and social tourism. Greenwashing in tourism is discussed, and the chapter ends by reviewing doughnut economics and the circular economy.

Tourism definitely does not exist in a vacuum as COVID-19 has proven. It is affected by global, regional, national, and local issues and trends. Just a small selection of the global issues include climate change and global warming, poverty, hunger, water scarcity, gender inequality, racial discrimination, human-rights abuse, environmental degradation, pollution, homelessness, domestic violence, and animal welfare.

If you take a look at Figure 1.2 again, sustainable tourism and social responsibility were placed in a central position among the roles of destination management. What does that position mean then? It means that sustainable tourism and social responsibility need to be considered and practiced in all destination management roles. For example, product development must consider potential negative impacts on the environment; destination marketing needs to meet high ethical standards; and partnership and team-building should enhance social inclusion. Now, you are going to hear about sustainable tourism.

Destination Sustainable Tourism

It is a fundamental assumption of this book that all destinations and DMOs follow the principles of sustainable tourism, so now we define the concept.

Defining Sustainable Tourism

There are countless definitions of sustainable tourism; however, the one you should know is that proposed by UNWTO.

> **DEFINITION**
>
> **Destination sustainable tourism**
>
> Within a destination this is "tourism that takes full account of its current and future economic, social and environmental impacts, addressing the needs of visitors, the industry, the environment and host communities" (UNWTO 2022a).

The key words in this definition include "current and future" and "economic, social and environmental." Destinations must ensure that current resources are maintained to be used by future generations. Economic, social, and environmental are the three pillars of sustainable development—"development which meets the needs of the present without compromising the ability of future generations to meet their own needs" (UN Brundtland Commission 1987)—and are sometimes referred to as the triple bottom line (social, environmental, economic). Who needs sustainable tourism? The answer is also in the definition—visitors, tourism industry, the environment, and communities.

Sustainable Tourism Strategies

It will help you better understand sustainable tourism if some real examples of strategies are provided from destinations. Let's start with the "Land of Smiles," the popular destination of Thailand. Tourism contributes about 20 percent of Thailand's gross domestic product (GDP), and the country wants to increase that share to 30 percent. The prime minister (Prayut) announced a new SMILE sustainable tourism strategy in 2022.

EXAMPLE 2.1

Thailand's SMILE Strategy

This example describes the main components of Thailand's sustainable tourism strategy.

   S—Sustainability in all aspects.
   M—Manpower: Boosting skills of tourism workforce to international standards.
   I—Inclusive economy: Ensuring that all sectors of the economy are included in the tourism industry.
   L—Localization: Promoting the uniqueness of communities as tourism attractions.
   E—Ecosystems: Promoting ecotourism and the local environment.
   "The SMILE strategy will help improve the country's tourism industry sustainably and ensure that we adapt to the changing world in all aspects," said Prayut.

(*The Nation* 2022)

Learning Point

DMOs should prepare strategies for sustainable tourism.

You will notice in the SMILE strategy that it not only is about sustaining the environment but also has a focus on human capital (tourism workforce skills), inclusiveness (all economic sectors), and communities (uniqueness). Thus, this strategy covers the social and economic pillars as well as the environmental.

A second example is from Sweden and cites the COVID-19 pandemic as the reason for needing a sustainable tourism strategy in the Scandinavian country. You will notice the three pillars mentioned again and the importance of addressing climate change. It also mentions clean (fossil-fuel-free) transportation and circular business models. (The circular economy is discussed later in the chapter.) The strategy places an emphasis on the development of shared knowledge.

EXAMPLE 2.2

Strategy for Sustainable Tourism in Sweden

In this example, it is explained why sustainable tourism is more important as a result of COVID-19.

> The need to continue to develop long-term, sustainable tourism and a competitive, sustainable and innovative tourism industry Sweden-wide has become very clear in the wake of the COVID-19 pandemic. The pandemic has shown how all the sectors of the tourism industry are interlinked and interdependent. Developing shared knowledge about the circumstances in which tourism operates and the need to adapt to a changing world can help to foster social, economic and environmental sustainability. Tourism must help to reduce climate impact and must not be a burden on the natural world or the environment. Fossil-free transport and circular business models need to be developed along every link in the tourism chain.
>
> (Ministry of Enterprise and Innovation [Sweden] 2022)

Learning Point

Low-carbon tourism should be part of a sustainable tourism strategy.

DEFINITIONS

Global warming

"Global warming refers to the rise in global temperatures due mainly to the increasing concentrations of greenhouse gases in the atmosphere" mainly as a result of the burning of fossil fuels (US Department of the Interior 2022).

Climate change

"Climate change refers to long-term shifts in temperatures and weather patterns. These shifts may be natural, such as through variations in the solar cycle. But since the 1800s, human activities have been the main driver of climate change, primarily due to burning fossil fuels like coal, oil and gas" (United Nations 2022).

Greenhouse gases

"Gases that trap heat in the atmosphere are called greenhouse gases." The main source of greenhouse gas is carbon dioxide (CO_2); others are methane, nitrous oxide, and fluorinated gases (US Environmental Protection Agency [EPA] 2022).

A third example is the Sustainable Tourism Plan for the city of Sedona in Arizona, USA. The plan was completed in 2019, and it was based upon public meetings and surveys of residents, businesses, and visitors (Sedona Chamber of Commerce and Tourism Bureau/City of Sedona 2019). The plan has the four strategic pillars of the environment, resident quality of life, quality of the economy, and visitor experience (Fig. 2.1).

The Sedona Tourism Sustainability Plan is excellent as it brings visitors into focus as well as the three pillars of sustainable development (environmental, social, and economic). Specific objectives and their supporting tactics are set for the environment, resident quality of life, quality of the economy, and visitor experience.

One form of sustainable tourism that you should know about is low-carbon tourism. Here is a definition of that concept.

DEFINITION

Low-carbon tourism

"Low carbon tourism is considered as a form of sustainable tourism that aims to achieve maximum tourism experience with low carbon technologies, less energy consumption, less CO_2 emission and less pollution in the process for transportation, accommodation, sightseeing and other entertainment for economic, social and environmental benefits" (Bhaktikul et al. 2021).

Figure 2.1 Strategic pillars of Sedona Sustainable Tourism Plan (Sedona Chamber of Commerce and Tourism Bureau/City of Sedona 2019).

Principles of Sustainable Tourism

UNWTO suggests the following three principles for sustainable development and tourism (UNWTO 2022a):

1. Make optimal use of environmental resources that constitute a key element in tourism development, maintaining essential ecological processes and helping to conserve natural heritage and biodiversity.
2. Respect the sociocultural authenticity of host communities, conserve their built and living cultural heritage and traditional values, and contribute to intercultural understanding and tolerance.
3. Ensure viable, long-term economic operations, providing socioeconomic benefits to all stakeholders that are fairly distributed, including stable employment and income-earning opportunities and social services to host communities, and contributing to poverty alleviation.

You will recognize that these represent the three pillars of sustainable development. As you will see later in this chapter, some organizations add visitors to this list and how they can contribute to tourism sustainability.

Now we will move on to certification programs in sustainable tourism, which gives you more specifics on sustainable tourism and how its principles are articulated in greater detail.

Certification Programs in Sustainable Tourism

There are several programs available that provide guidelines on sustainable tourism for destinations and DMOs. These programs establish standards and criteria for the sustainable tourism performance of destinations and individual businesses.

GLOBAL SUSTAINABLE TOURISM COUNCIL (GSTC)

Among the available certification programs, the GSTC Destination Criteria are the most well recognized. The criteria are in four sections (A to D) as shown in Figure 2.2.

You can see from Figure 2.2 that the criteria cover the three pillars of sustainable development plus having a section (A) on sustainable management. Many other sets of criteria and certifications have been created for sustainable tourism and you are going to learn about some of these now.

GREEN GLOBE

Based in Los Angeles, it provides certification for the sustainable operation of tourism businesses. It has a global network of auditors who inspect properties. Green Globe was established in 1997 and probably is the most highly recognized certification program in the world (apart from GSTC). The certification programs cover attractions, businesses in the supply chain (wholesale and retail), congress centers and meeting venues, cruise ships (river and ocean), golf courses, hotels and resorts, organizations, restaurants, spas and health centers, transportation (mass transportation, bus companies, limousine services, car rentals), and the travel industry (tour operators, DMCs, meetings and incentives) (Green Globe 2022). The Green Globe sustainability criteria are in four groups (cultural heritage, environmental, social economic, and sustainable management). Green Globe has 500 members in eighty countries.

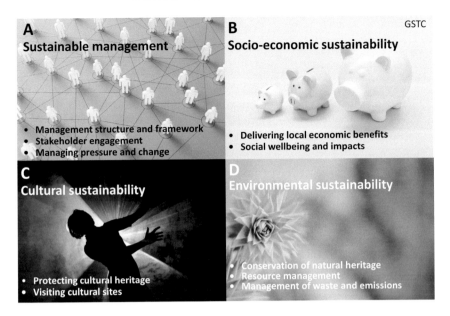

A Sustainable management
- Management structure and framework
- Stakeholder engagement
- Managing pressure and change

B Socio-economic sustainability   GSTC
- Delivering local economic benefits
- Social wellbeing and impacts

C Cultural sustainability
- Protecting cultural heritage
- Visiting cultural sites

D Environmental sustainability
- Conservation of natural heritage
- Resource management
- Management of waste and emissions

Figure 2.2 Global Sustainable Tourism Council Destination Criteria.

GREEN KEY

This program is operated by the Foundation for Environmental Education (FEE) based in Copenhagen that has existed for more than twenty-five years. FEE is a non-government NPO promoting sustainable development through ecolabeling and environmental education. It has criteria for attractions, conference centers, hotels and hostels, campsites and holiday parks, restaurants, and small accommodations. They have 3,600 certified tourism businesses in almost sixty countries around the world. FEE states that "A Green Key stands for an establishment's promise to its guests that by opting to stay with such an establishment, they are helping to make a difference on an environmental and sustainability level" (FEE 2022).

EARTHCHECK

With its head office in Brisbane, Australia, the company says, EarthCheck is "the world's leading scientific benchmarking, certification and advisory group for travel and tourism. Since 1987, we have helped businesses, communities and governments to deliver clean, safe, prosperous and healthy destinations for travelers to visit, live, work and play" (EarthCheck 2022). EarthCheck offers a diverse portfolio of services and products including certification, e.g., the EarthCheck Sustainable Destinations program. The current EarthCheck Destinations are in Portugal, Sweden, Mexico, New Zealand, Iceland, USA, and Australia.

AUDUBON INTERNATIONAL

Audubon International says it is "a global leader in environmental sustainability certifications." With its headquarters in Troy, New York, Audubon offers a number of ecolabeling certifications including programs for sanctuaries, golf courses, and lodging and hospitality properties. It has around 1,000 certified members (Audubon International 2022). Most of the members are in the USA and Canada; however, there are members in many other countries including China, Costa Rica, and the UK.

Rainforest Alliance

The Rainforest Alliance has its headquarters in New York City, USA. It works to conserve biodiversity and ensure sustainable livelihoods by transforming land-use practices, business practices and consumer behavior. It was founded in 1987 and is an NGO. The Rainforest Alliance introduced a new certification program in 2020 and the focus is on farms that produce commodities including bananas, cocoa, coffee, tea, hazelnut, and oranges. Some of the farms and plantations have lodging and other tourism facilities and services, and the Rainforest Alliance has developed the Preferred by Nature Standard for Sustainable Travel Activities (Rainforest Alliance 2022) with three sets of principles (Fig. 2.3).

You will notice that the Rainforest Alliance's tourism standards align well with the pillars of sustainable development and also with GSTC's previously mentioned Destination Criteria.

Blue Flag

The Blue Flag is a voluntary ecolabel awarded to more than 5,042 beaches and marinas in forty-eight countries in Europe, Africa, Middle East, Asia/Pacific, North and South America, and the Caribbean (Blue Flag International 2022). The Blue Flag program is owned and run by the non-government NPO the FEE. Blue Flag criteria cover beaches, marinas, and tourism boats.

EU Ecolabel

The EU Ecolabel is a "tool for tourist accommodation and campsite services to engage in a sustainable recovery, together with their staff and their customers. With the EU Ecolabel, it is possible to offer an eco-friendly and high quality alternative to conventional hotels and campsites" (One Planet Network 2021a).

There are many ecolabeling programs that are offered within specific countries or groups of countries. These include Green Tourism in the UK, Ecotourism Australia, Nordic Ecolabel, and Viabono. Based in Edinburgh, Scotland and established in 1997, Green Tourism is a not-for-profit organization that operates a sustainable certification program. It has more than 2,000 members in the UK, Ireland, and Canada (Green Tourism 2022). Ecotourism Australia is a not-for-profit organization based in Queensland and was founded in 1991. Ecotourism Australia now operates several programs: ECO certification; Climate Action; Respecting Our Culture; ECO Destination, and EcoGuide certification (Ecotourism Australia 2022a). Nordic Ecolabel has developed criteria for restaurants, hotels, conference facilities, youth hostels, and more categories (Nordic Ecolabel 2022). Viabono is an organization formed in Germany to support sustainable tourism. It covers hotels, pensions, apartments, holiday homes, farms, campsites, youth accommodation, and conference centers (Viabono 2022). A summary of these programs and their characteristics is provided in Figure 2.4.

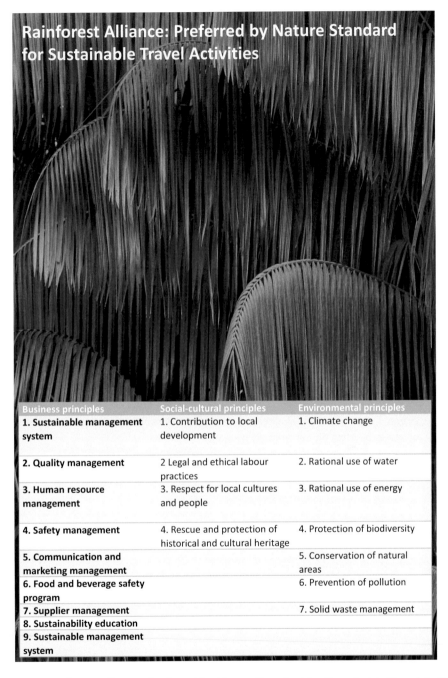

Business principles	Social-cultural principles	Environmental principles
1. Sustainable management system	1. Contribution to local development	1. Climate change
2. Quality management	2 Legal and ethical labour practices	2. Rational use of water
3. Human resource management	3. Respect for local cultures and people	3. Rational use of energy
4. Safety management	4. Rescue and protection of historical and cultural heritage	4. Protection of biodiversity
5. Communication and marketing management		5. Conservation of natural areas
6. Food and beverage safety program		6. Prevention of pollution
7. Supplier management		7. Solid waste management
8. Sustainability education		
9. Sustainable management system		

Figure 2.3 Rainforest Alliance: Preferred by Nature Standard for Sustainable Travel Activities (Rainforest Alliance 2022).

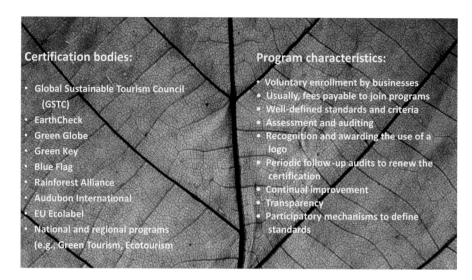

Certification bodies:

- Global Sustainable Tourism Council (GSTC)
- EarthCheck
- Green Globe
- Green Key
- Blue Flag
- Rainforest Alliance
- Audubon International
- EU Ecolabel
- National and regional programs (e.g., Green Tourism, Ecotourism

Program characteristics:

- Voluntary enrollment by businesses
- Usually, fees payable to join programs
- Well-defined standards and criteria
- Assessment and auditing
- Recognition and awarding the use of a logo
- Periodic follow-up audits to renew the certification
- Continual improvement
- Transparency
- Participatory mechanisms to define standards

Figure 2.4 Certification programs in sustainable tourism.

EXAMPLE 2.3

Green Tourism

This example provides a clear definition of green tourism.

> Green Tourism promotes greener ways for businesses and organizations to operate, by offering members advice on:
>
> - reducing energy use;
> - saving water;
> - efficient and eco-friendly waste disposal;
> - ethical buying;
> - staying local and seasonal;
> - minimizing food miles;
> - promoting biodiversity;
> - adopting a smart, sustainable outlook from top to bottom.
>
> (Green Tourism 2022)

Learning Point

Green tourism provides guidelines for tourism sector stakeholders and DMOs to operate sustainably.

You might see some people talking about green tourism (notice the lower-case letters this time). Not wanting to confuse you, this aligns with the green economy approach (discussed later) and is "small-scale tourism which involves visiting natural areas while minimizing environmental impacts" (Pintassilgo 2016).

> ### DEFINITION
>
> **Green economy**
>
> "A green economy is defined as low carbon, resource efficient and socially inclusive. In a green economy, growth in employment and income are driven by public and private investment into such economic activities, infrastructure and assets that allow reduced carbon emissions and pollution, enhanced energy and resource efficiency, and prevention of the loss of biodiversity and ecosystem services" (United Nations Environment Programme 2022).

Sustainable Tourism Organizations

There are several other organizations that are proponents of sustainable tourism and these groups also provide guidelines and criteria for sustainable tourism. You should be aware of them.

CENTER FOR RESPONSIBLE TRAVEL (CREST)

This global NPO is headquartered in Washington, DC. Its mission is "to promote responsible tourism policies and practices globally so that local communities may thrive and steward their cultural resources and biodiversity" (CREST 2022).

DESTINATION STEWARDSHIP CENTER

Located in Washington, DC, this group's mission is "to help protect the world's distinctive places by supporting wisely managed tourism and enlightened destination stewardship" (Destination Stewardship Center 2022).

GREEN DESTINATIONS

Located in Leiden, the Netherlands, it is a nonprofit foundation for sustainable destination development and recognition. Two of its programs are the Good Travel Guide and the Global Leaders Program.

SUSTAINABLE TRAVEL INTERNATIONAL

The mission of Sustainable Travel International is "to protect and conserve our planet's most vulnerable destinations by transforming tourism's impact on nature and communities" (Sustainable Travel International 2022). It is headquartered in Seattle, Washington.

THE TRAVEL FOUNDATION

This group is headquartered in Bristol, UK and says that it is an "international sustainable tourism organization dedicated to ensuring that tourism has a positive impact on destination communities. We work with governments, community groups and tourism businesses for fairer, climate-positive tourism" (The Travel Foundation 2022).

NGOs

Because of space limitations, other organizations that support sustainable development and sustainable tourism cannot be profiled in this chapter. These include NGOs, foundations, and charities such as, among many others, the World Wildlife Fund, Conservation International, International Union for Conservation of Nature (IUCN), Fairtrade International, Ocean Wise, the Nature Conservancy, and many others. Later in the chapter, you will hear about other NPOs and coalitions established to support and promote certain declarations (e.g., climate change action in tourism) and pledges.

Sustainable Development Goals

The seventeen SDGs were introduced in 2015, and the 2030 Agenda for Sustainable Development asked countries to begin efforts to achieve the seventeen SDGs over the fifteen years from 2015 to 2030. The UN says that the goals "address the needs of people in both developed and developing countries, emphasizing that no one should be left behind. Broad and ambitious in scope, the agenda addresses the three dimensions of sustainable development: social, economic, and environmental, as well as important aspects related to peace, justice and effective institutions" (United Nations 2015). Figure 2.5 displays the seventeen SDGs.

You will notice that SDG13 is climate action, and this issue has been mentioned several times already in this chapter. Not everyone shares the same level of concern for global warming and the associated climate change; some groups are more concerned than others. For example, a 2022 global survey of Generation Y and Generation Z members indicated high levels of concern for climate change (Deloitte 2022). SDG12 Responsible Consumption and Production is closely associated climate action, and almost all in Generation Y and Generation Z are making efforts to protect the environment (using recyclable or recycled paper and

Figure 2.5 United Nations Sustainable Development Goals.

plastic, using reusable mugs and utensils, buying second-hand items, and buying food that is locally or organically produced). You will also realize that most of the SDGs aim to improve the quality of life and well-being of people around the globe, and these two concepts are the focus for Chapter 3.

You might think that the SDGs apply most to the poorer parts of the world and the developing countries, and that is partially true. Later in the chapter, you will be hearing about three forms of tourism (ecotourism, CBT, and PPT) that can be particularly helpful in meeting the SDGs in less-privileged world regions.

The Tourism for SDGs platform created by UNWTO provides many examples of how tourism is contributing to goal achievement. One of the interesting examples is the Chocolala Artisan Chocolate Factory in the Dominican Republic.

EXAMPLE 2.4

Meeting the SDGs in the Dominican Republic through Chocolate

This is a great example of how the SDGs are being met in a Dominican Republic community.

> Chocolala Artisan Chocolate Factory is a society of women entrepreneurs from the community of Altamira, Puerto Plata province, in the north of the Dominican Republic, who emerged with the purpose of producing and marketing chocolates. This Women's Society was born from an Association of Mothers of Las Lajas Community who, motivated to achieve their economic autonomy to improve their quality of life, insert themselves into the local production chain and generate income to contribute to their families.
>
> (Tourism for SDGs 2022)

Learning Point

Communities can find creative ways to attain the SDGs and contribute to tourism.

Later in this chapter, the doughnut economics idea is introduced. This concept is closely aligned with the UN's SDGs.

Destination stewardship is a concept closely allied with sustainable tourism and that is the next topic to be covered.

Destination Stewardship

Stewardship is simply taking care of something and in this case it means caring for the destination.

Defining Destination Stewardship

Here are two more formal definitions of destination stewardship from leading industry bodies.

> ### DEFINITIONS
>
> **Destination stewardship**
>
> "A process by which local communities, governmental agencies, NGOs, and the tourism industry take a multi-stakeholder approach to maintain the cultural, environmental, economic, and aesthetic integrity of their country, region, or town" (GSTC 2022).
>
> "Destination stewardship is an approach that balances and meets the needs of a destination and its communities, and operates with legitimacy and consent under a participatory governance model. It requires a clear mandate, good knowledge and data and the identification of mutual interests and priorities, particularly between the public and private sectors" (WTTC 2021).

In reading these two definitions, you will get the idea about the need to form a collaborative and multi-stakeholder group to manage and guide (steward) tourism in a destination. Figure 1.7 showed all the stakeholders in destination management and destination stewardship is uniting them to sustainably manage tourism. You will also notice the mention of a "governance model" and that is another topic to which you were introduced in Chapter 1 and you will hear more in detail about in Chapter 6.

Reasons for Destination Stewardship

Figure 2.6 shows ten reasons why destination stewardship is needed. Some of these reasons require further explanation. For example, placemaking is "the planning, design, and

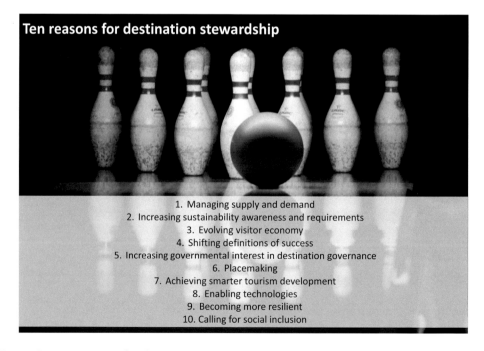

Ten reasons for destination stewardship

1. Managing supply and demand
2. Increasing sustainability awareness and requirements
3. Evolving visitor economy
4. Shifting definitions of success
5. Increasing governmental interest in destination governance
6. Placemaking
7. Achieving smarter tourism development
8. Enabling technologies
9. Becoming more resilient
10. Calling for social inclusion

Figure 2.6 Ten reasons for destination stewardship (WTTC 2021).

management of public spaces, with a focus on the use of investments and interventions to create good places to live and visit for residents and visitors, and in the process enhancing the sense of place (emotional bonds and attachment to places), identity, livability, and vibrancy, as well as the economic opportunities" (WTTC 2021: 5). The shifting definitions of success means that destinations are now placing more emphasis on the value than the volume of tourists. You will also notice the increasing priority on destination governance and social inclusion (ensuring equal opportunities for all people). A greater concern for destination resilience is a topic that is covered in detail in Chapter 11; while smarter tourism development and enabling technologies is the focus for Chapters 7 and 15. Increasing sustainability awareness and requirements (e.g., climate neutrality, green economy as defined below, and SDGs) you have already heard about in this chapter. Greater multi-stakeholder collaboration (evolving the visitor economy) and better management of the growth of tourism (managing supply and demand) are included in the reasons for stewardship as well.

Examples of Destination Stewardship

Again, a few actual examples will help this concept sink in a little more effectively. The GSTC and the Destination Stewardship Center produce regular publications on destination stewardship in which there are many successful case studies.

EXAMPLE 2.5

Destination Stewardship Cases (Vail and Azores)

These are two good case examples in which the destinations are implementing destination stewardship.

Vail, Colorado, USA

> The Vail Destination is committed to achieving climate action goals of a 50 percent reduction of GHG (greenhouse gas) emissions by 2030 and 80 percent by 2050. 100 percent of electricity used by the Town of Vail is renewable and Vail Resorts is committed to a net zero operating footprint by 2030.

Azores, Portugal

> The destination focuses on collaborative work that includes all the stakeholders of the destination, working together toward a same purpose—the sustainable development of the Azores. In this archipelago, collaboration is seen as the key for successful management.
>
> (GSTC and Destination Stewardship Center 2021)

Learning Point

Collaboration in a destination is needed for effective destination stewardship.

The Vail example emphasizes actions taken to address climate change, while for the Azores the focus is on creating more collaboration.

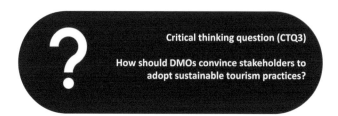

Critical thinking question (CTQ3)

How should DMOs convince stakeholders to adopt sustainable tourism practices?

Destination Social Responsibility

Defining Destination Social Responsibility

Having a willingness to share some of the responsibility for social-cultural, environmental, and economic issues and causes is the foundation of corporate social responsibility (CSR). DSR was defined in Chapter 1. In simple terms, this is about destinations and DMOs assuming and demonstrating responsibility for their actions and for tourism in general.

Practicing Destination Social Responsibility

You have heard about several examples of taking responsibility in tourism from Thailand, Sweden, USA (Sedona and Vail), and Portugal (the Azores). You also learned in Chapter 1 (Example 1.20) about Tourism Vancouver Island becoming a social enterprise called 4VI. It is noticeable that 4VI identifies the four categories of social responsibility as communities, businesses, culture, and the environment.

EXAMPLE 2.6

Four Parts of Social Responsibility at 4VI (Canada)

4VI identifies communities, businesses, culture, and environment as four pillars of social responsibility in this example.

> 4VI a social enterprise in business to ensure that travel is a force for good for Vancouver Island—forever. 4VI is contributing to an enduring, vibrant and sustainable visitor economy by delivering innovative tourism advisory services and investing profits into powering the stewardship of Vancouver Island in four pillars of social responsibility: communities, businesses, culture, and environment. 4VI is also a signatory to the Glasgow Declaration on Climate Action in Tourism.
>
> (4VI 2022)

Learning Point

It is important for a DMO to clearly identify the components of social responsibility.

4VI is a social enterprise, and it will be helpful if you know what that is. Social Enterprise UK gives this description, "By selling goods and services in the open market, social enterprises create employment and reinvest their profits back into their business or the local community. This allows them to tackle social problems, improve people's life chances, provide training and employment opportunities for those furthest from the market, support communities and help the environment" (Social Enterprise UK 2022).

Categories of Social Responsibility

Now, a closer look at the categories of social responsibility is required. 4VI identifies four categories; however, human resources need to be added to that list.

COMMUNITIES

Destinations are based on communities and not just scenery and monuments. This book advocates that destination management and DMOs must give a high priority to community relationships and involvement (Chapter 9) and the well-being and quality of life of community residents (Chapter 3).

BUSINESSES

Destinations and DMOs must carefully consider the tourism and non-tourism businesses in their communities, as well as the suppliers in the tourism value chain (discussed in Chapter 7) and travel trade intermediaries (Chapters 14, 15, and 19).

CULTURE

The safeguarding of the culture and heritage of destinations is a top priority and often forms the basis for attracting visitors.

ENVIRONMENT

Much has been said already about protecting and conserving the environments within destinations.

HUMAN RESOURCES

"Tourism is a people business" is a phrase this author frequently uses, and it is true. Responsibility must be shown to people individually and collectively. Equal opportunity, gender equality, and human rights are just three of the responsibility issues here.

EXAMPLE 2.7

Assisting with Social Projects in Communities

Destinations and DMOs can encourage business event organizers to make a positive social impact contribution to their communities, as described in this example. Several DMOs encourage meeting groups to participate in voluntary community projects. This is an example from North Carolina and the Asheville CVB.

> A community service project creates a unique team-building opportunity for your meeting attendees in Asheville. Service projects can be fun and energizing for attendees—and make a beneficial impact on the environment or residents of your host city. From river clean-ups to custom projects designed for your group at your host hotel, the Asheville CVB can connect you to the local organizations that will help you incorporate a service project in your meeting's agenda.
> (Asheville CVB 2022)

Learning Point

DMOs should be proactive in asking visitors to help with local social projects.

Before leaving the topic of social responsibility, you should not assume that this is just a good management practice. Why? CSR is needed as consumers expect companies and other organizations to embrace it, as do staff members who are keen to work for socially responsible entities. Among these people, those belonging to Generation Z particularly want organizations to practice CSR (Community Research Institute 2021).

Responsible Tourism

Another concept that is important to know about is responsible tourism.

Defining Responsible Tourism

The following is a definition of responsible tourism.

DEFINITION

Responsible tourism

Responsible tourism is about taking responsibility as a consumer or provider of tourism experiences, services, and products. Government agencies as the main policymakers for tourism play a key role in promoting responsible tourism. Third-party groups including the press and media can advocate responsible tourism and discourage practices that violate its principles.

Who needs to be responsible? Everybody directly and indirectly involved with tourism has a potential role to play—all stakeholders. This includes tourists themselves, destinations, tourism businesses, DMOs, governments, NGOs, media companies, and others. Here is a great example of implementing socially responsible tourism in Delhi, India.

EXAMPLE 2.8

The Salaam Baalak Trust City Walk, Delhi, India

This example describes how a responsible tourism project is being implemented in Delhi.

> The Salaam Baalak Trust City Walk is an English guided tour of almost two hours conducted by children who used to live in the streets of Delhi before joining our Trust. Our guides are adolescents who have been fully trained as local guides and who want to improve their communication and speaking skills. City Walk gets the children's stories heard, gives people a view of their world through their eyes.
>
> (Salaam Baalak Trust 2022)

Learning Point

Responsible tourism projects often require minimum capital investment; rather they harness the knowledge and skills of local people.

Principles of Responsible Tourism

The Cape Town Declaration on Responsible Tourism (2002) highlighted the principles of this concept (City of Cape Town, undated; The Responsible Tourism Partnership 2020). These principles are shown in Figure 2.7.

Again, you will see the principles of sustainable development and sustainable tourism woven into this declaration. Among them, involving local people in decisions that affect their lives is highly appropriate. Also, the seventh principle of responsible tourism involves what has become known as accessible tourism, a topic you will get to know more about in Chapter 7.

- Minimizes negative social, economic and environmental impacts.
- Generates greater economic benefits for local people and enhances the well-being of host communities.
- Improves working conditions and access to the industry.
- Involves local people in decisions that affect their lives and life chances.
- Makes positive contributions to the conservation of natural and cultural heritage embracing diversity.
- Provides more enjoyable experiences for tourists through more meaningful connections with local people, and a greater understanding of local cultural, social and environmental issues.
- Provides access for physically challenged people.
- Is culturally sensitive, encourages respect between tourists and hosts, and builds local pride and confidence.

Cape Town Declaration on responsible tourism

Figure 2.7 Principles of the Cape Town Declaration on responsible tourism.

You learned earlier about three sustainable tourism strategies and should know that some destinations develop responsible tourism strategies and plans. One of these is the South Pacific island nation of Palau that developed a responsible tourism policy framework. This policy was guided by six targets:

1. Responsible tourism awareness and alignment is a national priority.
2. Palau's visitor economy is responsibly managed.
3. Responsible product development attracts targeted high-value markets.
4. Palau's visitor experience is the living brand.
5. Palau's tourism industry provides improved visitor yield.
6. Palau's tourism development is community-driven.

(Palau Tourism Bureau 2016)

Responsible Consumer Travel

Responsible tourism also applies to visitors to destinations. Here, many guidelines for responsible travel are available. One of the most complete set of these guidelines is available from the UK-based AITO: The Specialist Travel Association (2022). Another is the Travel Care Code.

EXAMPLE 2.9

The Travel Care Code

The code listed in this example provides guidelines for visitors to act responsibly.

- Learn about your destination.
- Do not leave your good habits at home.
- Be a fuel efficient traveler.
- Make informed decisions.
- Be a good guest.
- Support locals.
- Dispose of waste properly.
- Protect your natural surroundings.
- Make your travel zero emissions.
- Bring your experiences home.

(Purdue Hospitality and Tourism Research Center 2018)

Learning Point

Visitors should be encouraged to behave in a responsible way within destinations.

Travelers can reduce their carbon footprints by carbon offsetting. A carbon offset negates the same amount of carbon emissions a traveler releases into the atmosphere. It is created by supporting a renewable energy source such as wind or solar, or by funding activities like tree-planting (Fleming 2019).

You now know that there is a demand and supply side to responsible tourism; travelers and destinations need to act responsibly. The evidence suggests that now—and especially as a result of COVID-19—travelers are more concerned about sustainable and responsible tourism.

EXAMPLE 2.10

Sustainable Tourism Now Is More Important to Travelers

This example provides evidence that travelers are attaching greater importance to sustainable tourism.

> An Economist Impact survey of more than 4,500 travelers in the region—across Australia, Japan, India, Malaysia, the Philippines, Singapore, South Korea, Taiwan and Thailand—shows that more than seven in ten (71.8 percent) respondents agree that COVID-19 has changed the way they think about sustainable tourism by making it more important to them.
>
> (Economist Group 2022)

Learning Point

DMOs should try to appeal more to visitors keen to support sustainable tourism.

A form of traveling that is generally considered to be more responsible is slow tourism.

DEFINITION

Slow tourism

A trip or set of trips that are purposely determined and undertaken to achieve travel motivations and goals at a slower pace and with lesser movement.

Regenerative Tourism

Regenerative tourism is a newer concept that appears to have originated around 2019 (Pollock 2019). Let us start with a definition of the concept.

Defining Regenerative Tourism

DEFINITION

Regenerative tourism

"Regenerative tourism represents a sustainable way of traveling and discovering new places. Its main goal is for visitors to have a positive impact on their holiday destination, meaning that they leave it in a better condition than how they found it. A concept that goes beyond "not damaging" the environment and that aims to actively revitalize and regenerate it, resulting in a positive cycle of impacts on local communities and economies: sustainable regeneration" (CBI Ministry of Foreign Affairs [Netherlands] 2022).

Examples of Regenerative Tourism

You will see in this definition that regenerative tourism goes one step further than sustainable tourism. Tourism leaves the destination in a "better condition" than before, not just the same as before. This applies to both the tourists and the development of tourism within destinations, as the following example of the Eden Project Qingdao reflects.

EXAMPLE 2.11

Regenerative Tourism and the Eden Project Qingdao

This example from Shandong Province, China shows how tourism projects can regenerate land damaged through industrial use.

> The project will showcase the regeneration of the site, bringing the land back in touch with its surrounding water. It will communicate the importance of water and the ongoing water challenge in a meaningful and fun way and be a positive and optimistic place for environmental and social change.
> Eden Project Qingdao is positioned on Jiaozhou Bay, surrounded by water and defined by rivers and sea. It is situated on a large area of reclaimed and environmentally damaged land originally used for salt production and then prawn breeding and is located on the confluence of two rivers.
>
> (Eden Project 2022)

Learning Point

Creative tourism development solutions can be used to regenerate polluted or damaged land areas.

Even before the regenerative tourism concept was originated, the Eden Project Cornwall was built in an abandoned former open-pit clay mine. This turned an eyesore in the country landscape into an appealing and environmentally compatible tourism attraction. The Eden Project (Cornwall) (Fig. 2.8) opened in 2001 and is run by a charitable organization operating as a social enterprise (The Valley Cornwall 2021).

> *Without travelers, there is no regenerative tourism. Mindful and respectful travelers with a desire to learn and contribute are essential cogs in the regenerative cycle.*
> *(Sheldon 2020)*

This quote talks about mindful and respectful travelers and you should know a little more about mindfulness. Basically, this means having greater awareness of a situation and our feelings. If travelers are more mindful, their experiences will be better and richer (Stankov et al. 2020).

Another example of regenerative tourism is from Copenhagen and is an innovative approach to dealing with water-based pollution in a city.

Figure 2.8 The Eden Project in Cornwall, England, is an example of regeneration through tourism.

Regenerative Tourism on Canoes in Copenhagen

This is an excellent and creative example of how tourism can be used to lessen water-body pollution in a city.

> The concept of regenerative travel has emerged as a way for the tourism industry to reimagine its role in the communities and ecosystems upon which it depends.
>
> (Schimmel 2021)

> GreenKayak is an environmental NGO that engages volunteers in the fight against environmental pollution while kayaking. We invite everyone to jump aboard a GreenKayak and paddle for free under two simple conditions—spend your time on the water collecting waste and share your experience on social media using #GreenKayak.
>
> (GreenKayak 2022)

Learning Point

DMOs can work with NGOs to create regenerative tourism activities and projects.

You should now have the idea about regenerative tourism from the definition and the two examples. Essentially, it means that tourism and tourists make a place better.

Declarations and Pledges

One of the most positive forces in destination management in the 2020s so far is the increasing level of partnering and collaboration. Several DMOs are involved in these "movements" that are often called declarations or pledges. As you will now learn these address adoption of sustainable tourism practices, environmental issues (e.g., climate change, plastic pollution), social and ethical issues (e.g., exploitation of children and animals), and the provision of authentic tourism experiences.

Tourism Declares

The COP 26 Climate Change Conference in late 2021, held in Glasgow, was the instigator for one of the most important of these declarations, now known under the label of Tourism Declares (a climate emergency).

EXAMPLE 2.13

The Glasgow Declaration: A Commitment to a Decade of Tourism Climate Action

COP 26 produced this important declaration for tourism related to climate change.

> We declare our shared commitment to unite all stakeholders in transforming tourism to deliver effective climate action. We support the global commitment to halve emissions by 2030 and reach net zero as soon as possible before 2050. We will consistently align our actions with the latest scientific recommendations, so as to ensure our approach remains consistent with a rise of no more than 1.5°C above pre-industrial levels by 2100.
>
> (One Planet Network 2021b)

Learning Point

Collective action is needed in tourism to combat climate change.

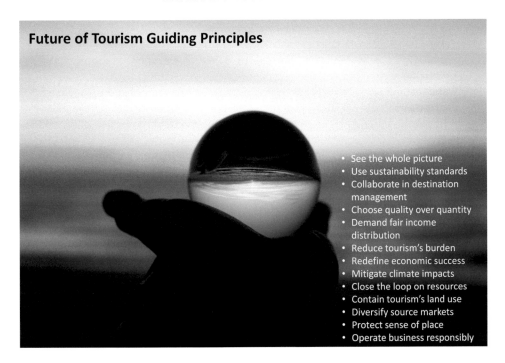

Future of Tourism Guiding Principles

- See the whole picture
- Use sustainability standards
- Collaborate in destination management
- Choose quality over quantity
- Demand fair income distribution
- Reduce tourism's burden
- Redefine economic success
- Mitigate climate impacts
- Close the loop on resources
- Contain tourism's land use
- Diversify source markets
- Protect sense of place
- Operate business responsibly

Figure 2.9 Future of Tourism Guiding Principles (2022).

Future of Tourism Coalition

The Future of Tourism Coalition (2022) is a group that has suggested a set of tourism guiding principles (Fig. 2.9). Most of these principles are already covered in this chapter; a few need more explanation. For example, diversify source markets means putting more emphasis on domestic tourism since it is likely to have greater resilience than international tourism. Closing the loop on resources suggests using reusable materials and moving away from disposable plastics.

Global Tourism Plastics Initiative

As mentioned above, the random disposal of plastic containers is a major environmental problem that adversely affects tourism, especially for oceans and other water bodies. People indiscriminately throw away plastic bottles and food containers creating major littering issues and dangers to animal welfare. During COVID-19 the random disposal of personal protective equipment (PPE) (masks, gloves, and sanitizer containers) added to this problem.

EXAMPLE 2.14

The Global Tourism Plastics Initiative

Pollution from plastics has risen to unacceptable levels in many destinations. This example describes the action taken by UNWTO to deal with this problem.

> The Global Tourism Plastics Initiative unites the tourism sector behind a common vision to address the root causes of plastic pollution. It enables businesses and governments to take concerted action, leading by example in the shift toward a circularity in the use of plastics. Developed within the framework of the Sustainable Tourism Program of the One Planet Network, a multi-stakeholder partnership to implement SDG 12 on Sustainable Consumption and Production, the Global Tourism Plastics Initiative is led by the United Nations Environment Programme and the World Tourism Organization, in collaboration with the Ellen MacArthur Foundation.
>
> (UNWTO 2020)

Learning Point

DMOs should be proactive in educating visitors and residents about plastic contamination especially in waterbodies.

Tourism Cares

Several authoritative sources state that people are increasingly looking for meaningful tourism opportunities. "Tourists are looking for an elevated travel experience that brings richness to their life, above and beyond just relaxing on a beach" (UNESCO 2020). Tourism Cares is a coalition of businesses and organizations that has a focus on delivering meaningful tourism experiences. One of its activities is producing Meaningful Travel Maps that link together tourism social enterprises.

EXAMPLE 2.15

Tourism Cares: The Meaningful Travel Map of Jordan

Greater meaningfulness and mindfulness are being recommended for tourism. This example from Jordan shows how this can be implemented on the ground.

> The map invites you to visit one of the twelve social enterprises bookable now, adding special meaning to your trip to Jordan. By offering unique and hands-on cultural experiences for travelers, each of these social enterprises is satisfying the demand from travelers seeking authentic sustainable experiences that make a difference and their need to use the power of travel to help people and places thrive.
>
> (Jordan Tourism Board 2022)

Learning Point

Meaningfulness can be encouraged by asking visitors to use social enterprises.

EPCAT International

EPCAT describes its role as coordinating "research, advocacy and action to end the sexual exploitation of children. We support the protection of children and empowerment of 122 members in 104 countries" (EPCAT International 2022). Through its group The Code, EPCAT publishes policies and guidelines on child protection, voluntourism, and orphanage tourism (The Code 2022).

DEFINITIONS

Orphanage tourism

"Orphanage tourism describes the practice of people volunteering in or visiting an orphanage whilst abroad. It can refer to any visit, from volunteering placements lasting a few months or more, to mission trips, university field trips, day trips and visits to watch dance or cultural shows which may last only an hour. On the surface, helping orphanages by giving your time or money seems like a thoughtful, charitable thing to do, but what most people don't realise is that instead of helping vulnerable children they are actually sustaining a practice which is ultimately preventing children from having what they need to develop and ensure their long-term well-being: namely, a loving family" (ReThink Orphanages 2018).

Voluntourism

"Volunteer tourism—voluntourism—is defined as organized and packaged tourist trips with a duration of a few hours to a year in which the main purpose is to volunteer. The volunteer provides their "work" within the destination free of charge" (The Code 2022).

Tourism Sustainability Commitment (New Zealand)

Several individual countries have formulated declarations, pledges, and codes of practice or ethics. New Zealand is a good example and it has the Tourism Sustainability Commitment. There are twelve specific commitments therein:

1. resilience;
2. investment;
3. innovation;
4. visitor satisfaction;
5. culture and heritage;
6. visitor engagement;
7. employer of choice;
8. community engagement;
9. sustainable supply chains;
10. restoring nature;
11. carbon reduction;
12. eliminating waste.

(Tourism Industry Aotearoa [TIA] 2022)

There are many more of these declarations and pledges for tourism, and only six of them have been described. Before leaving the topic, you should realize that participation in these initiatives is voluntary. Destinations and DMOs that join in these efforts are demonstrating social responsibility and supporting sustainable tourism. They are also behaving ethically.

Ethical Tourism

Another topic to be discussed is ethical tourism, and we start again with a definition.

Defining Ethical Tourism

> **DEFINITION**
>
> **Ethical tourism**
>
> "Ethical tourism has evolved as a term when one considers traveling to or developing tourism in a destination where ethical issues are the key driver, e.g., social injustice, human rights, animal welfare, or the environment. Ethical tourism is geared towards encouraging both the consumer and industry to avoid participation in activities that contribute or support negative ethical issues" (Travel Matters 2022).

The Global Code of Ethics for Tourism

UNWTO has developed the Global Code of Ethics for Tourism (GCET). The GCET has ten principles (articles) (Fig. 2.10) that relate to the economic, social-cultural, and environmental impacts of tourism (UNWTO 2022b). These articles are quite detailed and so we cannot fully explain them in this chapter. However, you will notice that Articles 3–5 correspond to sustainable development and sustainable tourism.

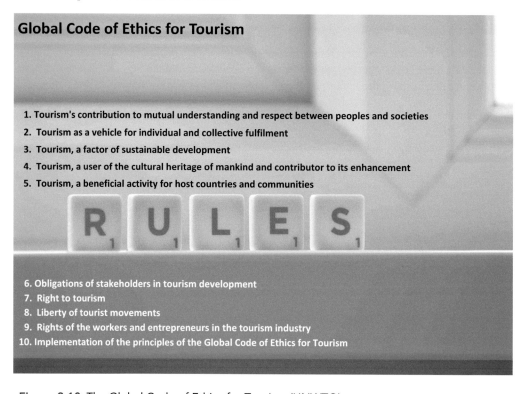

Global Code of Ethics for Tourism

1. Tourism's contribution to mutual understanding and respect between peoples and societies
2. Tourism as a vehicle for individual and collective fulfilment
3. Tourism, a factor of sustainable development
4. Tourism, a user of the cultural heritage of mankind and contributor to its enhancement
5. Tourism, a beneficial activity for host countries and communities

6. Obligations of stakeholders in tourism development
7. Right to tourism
8. Liberty of tourist movements
9. Rights of the workers and entrepreneurs in the tourism industry
10. Implementation of the principles of the Global Code of Ethics for Tourism

Figure 2.10 The Global Code of Ethics for Tourism (UNWTO).

Ethical Tourism Issues

There are two sides to ethical tourism. First, ethical tourism must be a concern of the people traveling to destinations and using tourism services: the guests. Second, ethical tourism must be practiced by tourism organizations: the hosts and all stakeholders. Certain types of tourism are considered to be unethical, such as orphanage tourism, while others are borderline cases including sex tourism, marijuana tourism, and drunk tourism. The societal acceptability of these forms of tourism are questioned.

FAIR TRADE

Sourcing products and services fairly is a demonstration of societal responsibility. Fair trade is the term given to obtaining materials produced for a reasonable price and produced under the right conditions, often from poorer countries. Tourism organizations must ensure that what they buy from their supply chains has been produced according to proper environmental standards and they want to avoid "sweatshop products" where the local labor force has been exploited.

GOVERNANCE

Transparency and accountability are two of the critical components of organizational governance. Transparency means openness in marketing and other aspects of the operations of organizations; it is the opposite of being secretive and opaque. Accountability is demonstrating that organizations are making proper use of their resources. Governance covers the policies, systems, and procedures that organizations establish for their administration. Destination governance is one of the main topics covered in Chapter 6.

HUMAN RIGHTS

Several tourism organizations and companies include human rights among their social responsibilities. The rights of women and children are receiving significant attention in tourism, and are prominent in CBT and PPT, which are discussed later. They are also being considered in child prostitution, orphanage tourism, and human trafficking. LGBTQ+ rights are receiving greater attention as cases of discriminatory treatment in tourism are coming to the public's attention. The plight of refugees fleeing war zones is another major human-rights issue today.

EXAMPLE 2.16

Tourism Supporting Refugees from Ukraine

This example shows how tourism entities can offer humanitarian assistance to refugees.

> People fleeing from Ukraine can use PKP [Polskie Koleje Państwowe] trains, Polferries and Flixbus transportation free of charge from Polish border cities to elsewhere in Poland. LOT Airlines also offers discounted tariffs for Ukrainian refugees. Uber also offers unlimited free trips between the Ukrainian border and Polish cities. Free public transport is provided in Poznan and forty-one cities of Górnośląsko-Zagłębiowska that surround Katowice, Sosnowiec, Bytom, Tychy and Gliwice. Free tickets for trains with Silesian Railways are also available free of charge.
>
> (ETC 2022)

> **Learning Point**
>
> Helping people dislocated from their homes by war and conflict is a demonstration of social responsibility.

Homelessness is another human-rights issue and a major global concern. Tourism companies are in an especially good position to help the homeless since many organizations provide food and shelter. The problems faced by homeless people expanded due to COVID-19 and caused organizations to take action. The Hospitality Against Homeless Campaign in the UK is a great example here. It aims "to bring together the hospitality industry in a focused effort to provide immediate support to homeless people across London which includes fellow hospitality industry colleagues in crisis with meals, kitchen facilities/equipment and accommodation" (Only a Pavement Away 2022).

Racism is another human-rights issue that exists in tourism. This, for example, relates to the treatment of migrant workers (Baum 2012), Indigenous peoples (Ruhanen and Whitford 2018), and international students (Brown and Jones 2013). Some authors argue that racial discrimination is rife in tourism and on the increase (Benjamin and Dillette 2021; Yu and Hyun 2021). There is also the phenomenon of online racism toward certain types of travelers and people from specific countries as well (Li et al. 2020). A brighter light has been shone on racism in society through the Black Lives Matter movement, which includes many professional athletes "taking the knee" before matches start.

Gender Inequality

This is an issue in tourism employment, and in other aspects of the tourism sector and its development (Pritchard 2014). You will have seen that gender equality is no. 5 among the SDGs and therefore it is a global issue that transcends tourism. For example, researchers have found gender inequality in tourism employment in Portugal and Spain (Costa et al. 2011; Sigüenza et al. 2013).

> *Travel and tourism have been proven to provide women with more opportunities for empowerment compared to other industries, giving the sector increased responsibility for the advancement of women.*
>
> *(The World Bank Group 2017)*

Ecotourism

Ecotourism is an approach that can make a contribution to sustainable tourism. Now, you will hear its definition.

Defining Ecotourism

> **DEFINITIONS**
>
> **Ecotourism**
>
> "Environmentally responsible visiting of relatively unspoilt natural areas, in order to enjoy and appreciate nature (and any accompanying cultural features—both past and

present), that promotes conservation, has low negative visitor impact, and provides for beneficially active socio-economic involvement of local populations" (IUCN 1996).

"Responsible travel to natural areas that conserves the environment, sustains the well-being of the local people, and involves interpretation and education" (The International Ecotourism Society [TIES] 2022).

Characteristics and Principles of Ecotourism

According to the Nature Conservancy (2015), ecotourism can be distinguished by how it emphasizes conservation, education, traveler responsibility and active community participation. True ecotourism has the following characteristics:

- conscientious, low-impact visitor behavior;
- sensitivity toward, and appreciation of, local cultures and biodiversity;
- support for local conservation efforts;
- sustainable benefits to local communities;
- local participation in decision-making;
- educational components for both the traveler and local communities.

An extensive set of ecotourism principles is suggested by the International Ecotourism Society (2022) and these are:

- Minimize physical, social, behavioral, and psychological impacts.
- Build environmental and cultural awareness and respect.
- Provide positive experiences for both visitors and hosts.
- Provide direct financial benefits for conservation.
- Generate financial benefits for both local people and private industry.
- Deliver memorable interpretative experiences to visitors that help raise sensitivity to host countries' political, environmental, and social climates.
- Design, construct and operate low-impact facilities.
- Recognize the rights and spiritual beliefs of the Indigenous people in your community and work in partnership with them to create empowerment.

A simpler set of principles of authentic ecotourism are shown in Figure 2.11.

Examples of Ecotourism

Many examples of ecotourism could be provided from around the world. However, from the author's personal experience, the Billabong Sanctuary near Townsville, Australia (Fig. 2.12) is one of the very best.

Figure 2.11 Principles of authentic ecotourism (Newsome et al. 2013).

Figure 2.12 Nature and wildlife education at the Billabong Sanctuary.

Ecotourism at the Billabong Sanctuary, Queensland, Australia

Your author has made frequent visits to the Billabong Sanctuary near Townsville, and it is a superb application of ecotourism.

> All of our staff are passionate about sharing their love of the environment. Through daily wildlife talks and feeding shows they teach our customers about Australia's unique fauna and conservation of native species. As our own contribution to this goal, the Sanctuary is involved in captive breeding programs for the endangered southern cassowary and the threatened greater bilby. Visitors leave with a better understanding of ways they can promote conservation within their own community.
>
> (Ecotourism Australia 2022b)

Learning Point

Nature-based and ecotourism can be major attractions for visitors.

Community-based Tourism

Community-based tourism (CBT) is an approach connected with sustainable tourism, and it can be defined as follows.

Defining Community-based Tourism

Community-based tourism

"Community-based tourism is tourism in which local residents (often rural, poor and economically marginalized) invite tourists to visit their communities with the provision of overnight accommodation. The residents earn income as land managers, entrepreneurs, service and produce providers, and employees. At least part of the tourist income is set aside for projects which provide benefits to the community as a whole" (Responsible Travel 2022).

Examples of Community-based Tourism

The basic idea of CBT is where communities create and operate experiences, activities, and attractions that appeal to visitors. The Nong Jia Le concept in the rural areas of China is a good CBT example. The first Nong Jia Le was started in Bie County, Chengdu, Sichuan in 1987. This has become very popular with city-dwellers wanting to escape the stresses and strains of urban living. They mostly provide local food prepared by the women of the households, and some also have overnight accommodation for guests. The concept was introduced by government as a way of creating new agricultural economic activity and stemming rural depopulation.

The key to CBT is the involvement of local people in tourism development and operations and ensuring that all or most of the profits from tourism remain in the community's hands. Many CBT projects are based partly or wholly on ecotourism (Fig. 2.13).

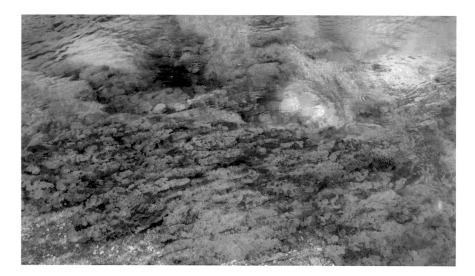

Figure 2.13 The five-colored river at Macarena de Colores, Colombia. Photo: Courtesy of BBC Travel and Dylan Baddour, 2019.

EXAMPLE 2.18

Community-Based Tourism in Colombia

Collective action has led to greater community benefits from tourism in this part of Colombia.

The Macarena de Colores project is an example of how community-based tourism can boost rural economies that rely on agriculture and natural resources. A decade ago, five counties surrounding the Serranía de La Macarena (an emerging tourist hotspot in the Meta Department) joined forces to create a tourism union. Since then, the region has experienced a spike in job creation, thanks to the year-round demand for nature guides, chefs, and other positions needed to accommodate the growing number of tourists. By weaning local economies off timber logging and cattle farming, over 1,200 acres of forests have been saved.

(Jebara 2022)

Learning Point

CBT can be beneficial when a collaborative effort is made.

Pro-poor Tourism

Reducing poverty is at the heart of the PPT approach. Eradicating extreme poverty and hunger are among the SDGs. They are SDG 1 (no poverty) and SDG 2 (zero hunger). According to UNDP (2020), in 2025 there could be 1 billion people in the world living in a condition of extreme poverty (living on an income of less than $1 per day) as conditions are worsened by the COVID-19 global pandemic.

Defining Pro-poor Tourism

A definition of PPT follows.

> ### DEFINITION
>
> **Pro-poor tourism**
>
> "Pro-poor tourism (PPT) is an approach to reduce poverty in developing nations. PPT's principal goal is to generate net benefits for poor communities. The strategy of PPT aims to increase economic stability and mitigate the negative effects of local cultures and environments. In order to do so, developing countries must apply several strategies" (The Borgen Project 2021).

Examples of Pro-poor Tourism

The Borgen Project is an NPO, located in Tacoma, Washington, that fights extreme poverty and they have an interest in PPT. The organization provides examples of PPT projects in Kenya, Lao People's Democratic Republic (PDR), Uganda (Fig. 2.14) in 2018 (Borgen Project 2018).

Figure 2.14 A deluxe "geo dome" at Byoona Amagara.

> ### EXAMPLE 2.19
>
> **Pro-poor Tourism in Uganda**
>
> This example demonstrates how tourism can be used to reduce poverty.
>
> > Byoona Amagara is a nonprofit organization that puts 100 percent of its proceeds toward various pro-poor programs. Some of the project's core initiatives include healthcare treatment, rural education and literacy, organic agriculture and indigenous forestry.
> >
> > (Borgen Project 2018)
>
> > Another great thing about Byoona Amagara is the work they do in the local community, funding and implementing various grassroots projects that support rural education, healthcare, micro-finance, and organic agriculture training for local residents. The lodge is a staff-owned, not-for-profit establishment and 100 percent of proceeds from the lodge go to support sustainable community projects.
> >
> > (Baxter 2021)
>
> **Learning Point**
>
> Poverty reduction is one of UN's SDGs and destinations in affected areas should encourage community projects with this objective.

Social Tourism

Defining Social Tourism

> ### DEFINITION
>
> **Social tourism**
>
> "Programmes, events, and activities that enable all population groups—and particularly youth, families, retirees, individuals with modest incomes, and individuals with restricted physical capacity—to enjoy tourism, while also attending to the quality of relations between visitors and host communities" (Jolin, as quoted by Social and Health Tourism 2014).

Social tourism sometimes gets called "government-subsidized" holidays, and, as such, providing for social tourism can become quite political. Parties of the left may favor implementing and supporting social tourism, while parties on the right can view it as an improper use of taxpayers' money. However, there is another perspective on social tourism and that is its potential role in regional tourism development. Within each country there are regions where tourism is underdeveloped, and social tourism may be one strategy to promote higher levels of tourism. There is also some potential in using social tourism in conjunction with PPT and CBT.

Examples of Social Tourism

The International Social Tourism Organisation (2019) provides examples of social tourism policies and programs from Belgium, Brazil, Canada, Chile (Example 2.20), Colombia, France, Germany, Hungary, Italy, Mexico, Portugal, Russia, South Korea, Spain, Switzerland, UK, and Uruguay.

EXAMPLE 2.20

Sernatur Subsidizes Travel Packages for Chilean Seniors

This example reviews an excellent social tourism initiative by the national DMO in Chile.

> Chile's national tourism organization, Sernatur, subsidizes the value of tourism packages for Chilean senior citizens in order to use tourism services in destinations prioritized by Sernatur during the low season. Strengthening the local economies of the destinations, contributing to reduce the seasonal nature of employment, developing and promoting tourism products and destinations, encouraging the development of the supply chain, and allowing seniors to enjoy the psychological and physical benefits of tourism.
>
> (International Social Tourism Organisation 2019)

Learning Point

The implementation of social tourism projects should be considered by DMOs.

Greenwashing

Defining Greenwashing

The following is a definition of greenwashing.

DEFINITION

Greenwashing

"Greenwashing is the unjustified appropriation of environmental virtue by a company, an industry, a government, a politician or even a non-government organization to create a pro-environmental image, sell a product or a policy, or to try and rehabilitate their standing with the public and decision-makers after being embroiled in controversy" (SourceWatch.org 2022).

Examples of Greenwashing in Tourism

There are undoubtedly cases in tourism where greenwashing allegations are accurate and justified; and there are situations that are debatable or even inaccurate. For tourism marketers, the most important lesson to be learned about greenwashing is not to make false or exaggerated claims related to aspects of sustainable tourism. Examples of greenwashing in tourism include:

1. promoting fake "eco" labels;
2. focusing on one positive thing and avoiding the rest;
3. using laws to pretend businesses are eco-friendly;
4. asking you to pay or do something extra for offsetting your footprint;
5. using "green" language and marketing techniques;
6. false claims that harm the surroundings;
7. promoting supposedly eco-friendly materials.

(van den Brand 2022)

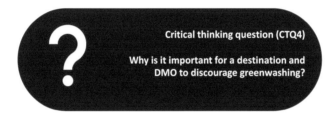

Critical thinking question (CTQ4)

Why is it important for a destination and DMO to discourage greenwashing?

Doughnut Economics and the Circular Economy

Before wrapping up this chapter, two recent economic strategy concepts need to be mentioned—doughnut economics (macroeconomic level) and the circular economy (microeconomic level). This is a case of "last but not least" as these concepts bring together much of what has been discussed in this chapter in the changing global social, economic, and environmental priorities.

Doughnut Economics

A definition of doughnut economics follows.

DEFINITION

Doughnut economics

"Doughnut Economics is a theory proposing a change of economic model as a response to humanity's major challenge of eradicating global poverty within the means of the planet's limited natural resources" (Cheung 2021).

The origination of doughnut economics is attributed to Oxford University's Kate Raworth (2017a, 2017b). Raworth argued that society should not be fixated by GDP growth anymore; there are greater and more pressing global issues now to be faced. Her concept is visualized as a doughnut shape (Fig. 2.15) where the hole is represented by shortfalls in twelve categories (many of which are addressed in the SDGs). Then there are three concentric circles, and you will see that they are similar to the three pillars of sustainable development. The innermost circle is the social foundation; next is the safe and just space for humanity, which needs to be supported by regenerative actions and fair distribution in the economy. The outer circle is the ecological ceiling or what the environment can bear. Nine overshoot environmental issues surround the ecological ceiling including climate change and various forms of pollution and environmental degradation.

Hartman and Heslinga (2022) discussed the Doughnut Destination concept and applied the Doughnut Economy Model to tourism. They identified the "overshoots" for destinations as overtourism, social uprising, displacement, CO_2 emissions, ecosystem degradation, and

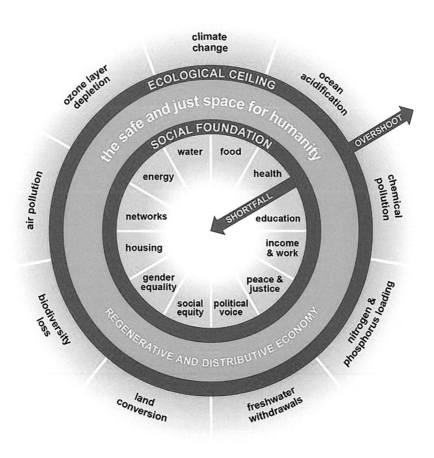

Figure 2.15 Model of the Doughnut Economy.

depletion of resources (energy, water and food). The "shortfalls" were bankruptcies, poverty, unemployment, poor working conditions, degradation of infrastructure, inaccessibility, and low visitor satisfaction. Just as Raworth had done for economists, they recommended seven ways of reframing destinations:

1. Tourism as a means: become a means of development rather than its goal.
2. Tourism embedded in a larger whole: assign greater value to connections.
3. Tourists are not rational economic people: people need to travel sustainably and give back to destinations.
4. Tourism as part of a dynamic complex system: see tourism as part of a wider system.
5. Tourism should benefit all: spread the benefits of tourism more equitably.
6. Tourism needs to be regenerative: make a destination better than it was before.
7. Tourism growth is not endless: establish limits on tourism.

Circular Economy

The circular economy is a microeconomic concept with a focus on a particular destination rather than a global concept like doughnut economics. The emphasis is on reusing resources and renewable resources in an economic system. Here is a straightforward definition of the concept.

DEFINITION

Circular economy

"A circular economy decouples economic activity from the consumption of finite resources. It is a resilient system that is good for business, people and the environment" (Ellen MacArthur Foundation 2022).

A simple example of a circular economy in tourism is destinations that have banned single-use plastics. Eight places that have done so include Aruba, Bali (Indonesia), Barbados, Chile, Costa Rica, Dominica, Koh Samet (Thailand), New Caledonia, Peru, Rwanda, and South Australia (Holiable 2019).

SUMMING UP

Much ground has been covered in this second chapter, and the author hopes you are not exhausted with all the concepts and terminology. However, knowing about them will prepare you for the chapters to come as well as showing you that destination management and DMOs are changing—some would say for the better, including your author. You will have noticed one key message throughout this chapter (we hope) and that is "quality beats quantity" in destination management.

Destinations and DMOs need to place a higher priority in the future on sustainable tourism and social responsibility. This is not only the right thing to do given the many issues worldwide, but also necessary for the survival of DMOs. It will definitely not be enough just to do destination marketing and DMOs must give greater attention to all stakeholders, especially community residents who are the focus for the next chapter. Becoming better stewards of tourism resources will be vital for future destination management and DMOs by fully embracing sound sustainable tourism practices. Consumers will increasingly favor the destinations that show excellence in sustainable tourism and stewardship; it is not just about needing to conserve and protect resources.

You should not leave this chapter thinking that destination management and DMOs have the sole responsibility for solving all ills in this world as that certainly is not true. This requires a multi-stakeholder approach that includes tourists and consumers in general. However, as the next chapter suggests, DMOs must assume a major role in enhancing the quality of life and well-being of destination residents.

Another important point is that DMOs must act as tourism leaders for their destinations, which you will hear more about in Chapter 6. They must do their part to convince stakeholders to act more responsibly. Also, they should not ascribe all the blame for negatives such as greenhouse gases to other stakeholders. Rather, they should lead a team effort to achieving net zero (when GHGs created equal GHGs removed from the atmosphere) and carbon neutrality (the same but for CO_2) goals.

KEYWORDS

accessible tourism
animal welfare
carbon footprint
carbon neutrality
carbon offsetting
circular economy
climate change
community-based tourism (CBT)
corporate social responsibility (CSR)
destination governance
destination social responsibility (DSR)
destination stewardship
doughnut economics
ecolabeling
ecotourism
ethical tourism

Generation Y
Generation Z
gender inequality
global warming
green economy
greenhouse gases (GHGs)
green tourism
greenwashing
homelessness
human rights
low-carbon tourism
meaningful tourism
mindfulness
net zero
orphanage tourism
placemaking
pro-poor tourism (PPT)
quality of life

racism
refugees
regenerative tourism
resilience
responsible tourism
sense of place
slow tourism
social enterprise
social inclusion
social tourism
sustainable development
sustainable development goals (SDGs)
sustainable tourism
triple bottom line
voluntourism
well-being

REVIEW QUESTIONS

1. What is sustainable tourism and what are its principles?
2. What are the main certification programs in sustainable tourism?
3. How would you describe destination stewardship?
4. How is DSR accomplished?
5. What is responsible tourism and its principles?
6. How would you describe regenerative tourism?
7. What are some of the ethical issues in tourism?
8. How would you explain the features of ecotourism, CBT, PPT, and social tourism?
9. What does greenwashing mean?
10. What are doughnut economics and the circular economy?

REFERENCES

AITO (2022) "AITO Sustainable Tourism Guidelines: How to Travel Sustainably and Responsibly," www.aito.com/sustainable-tourism/guidelines

Asheville Convention and Visitors Bureau (2022) "Social Responsibility," www.exploreasheville.com/meeting-planners/cvb-services/social-responsibility/

Audubon International (2022) "Certifications," https://auduboninternational.org/sustainable-communities-program

Baddour, D. (2019) "Colombia's River of Five Colours," *BBC Travel*, March 22, www.bbc.com/travel/article/20190320-colombias-river-of-five-colours

Baum, T. (2012) "Migrant Workers in the International Hotel Industry," *International Migration Paper*, 112.

Baxter, D. (2021) "Byoona Amagara: Visiting an Island Oasis on Lake Bunyonyi," *AwayGoWe Travel and Adventure*, March 23, www.awaygowe.com/lake-bunyonyi-uganda-byoona-amagara/

Benjamin, S., and Dillette, A. K. (2021) "Black Travel Movement: Systemic Racism Informing Tourism," *Annals of Tourism Research*, 88, https://doi.org/10.1016/j.annals.2021.103169.

Bhaktikul, K., Aroonsrimorakot, S., Laiphrakpam, M., and Paisantanakij, W. (2021) "Toward a Low-Carbon Tourism for Sustainable Development: A Study Based on a Royal Project for Highland Community Development in Chiang Rai, Thailand," *Environment, Development and Sustainability*, 23: 10743–10762.

Blue Flag International (2022) "About Us," www.blueflag.global/our-programme

Borgen Project (2018) "Reinvesting in Locals: The Benefits of Pro-Poor Tourism," *The Borgen Magazine*, May 16, www.borgenmagazine.com/reinvesting-in-locals-the-benefits-of-pro-poor-tourism/

Brown, L., and Jones, I. (2013) "Encounters with Racism and the International Student Experience," *Studies in Higher Education*, 38 (7): 1004–1019.

CBI Ministry of Foreign Affairs (Netherlands) (2022) "Regenerative Tourism: Moving Beyond Sustainable and Responsible Tourism," www.cbi.eu/market-information/tourism/regenerative-tourism

Center for Responsible Travel (2022) "Mission and History," www.responsibletravel.org/who-we-are/mission-history

Cheung, J. (2021) "What Is Doughnut Economics?" *Earth.org*, October 25, https://earth.org/what-is-doughnut-economics

City of Cape Town (undated) "Responsible Tourism in Cape Town," https://resource.capetown.gov.za/documentcentre/Documents/Graphics%20and%20educational%20material/Responsible_tourism_bro_web.pdf

The Code (2022) "Resources," https://thecode.org/resources/

Community Research Institute (2021) "Gen Z Favors Corporate Social Responsibility," https://communityresearchinstitute.org/679-2/

Costa, C., Carvalho, I., and Breda, Z. (2011) "Gender Inequalities in Tourism Employment: The Portuguese Case," *Revista Turismo and Desenvolvimento*, 15: 39–54.

Deloitte (2022) "The Deloitte Global 2022 Gen Z and Millennial Survey," https://www2.deloitte.com/cn/en/pages/about-deloitte/articles/genzmillennialsurvey.html

Destination Stewardship Center (2022) "For People Who Care about Places," https://destination-center.org

EarthCheck (2022) "Good for Business, Good for the Planet," https://earthcheck.org

Economist Group (2022) "Rebuilding Tourism in Asia-Pacific: A More Conscious Traveller?" https://impact.economist.com/perspectives/sites/default/files/rebuilding_tourism_apac_economist_impact_airbnb.pdf

Ecotourism Australia (2022a) "What We Do," www.ecotourism.org.au/what-we-do

——— (2022b) "Billabong Sanctuary," www.ecotourism.org.au/membership/hall-of-fame-2/billabong-sanctuary-and-bungalow-bay-koala-villagenew-membership-detail-page

Eden Project (2022) "Eden Project Qingdao, China," www.edenproject.com/new-edens/eden-project-qingdao-china

Ellen MacArthur Foundation (2022) "What Is a Circular Economy?" https://ellenmacarthurfoundation.org/topics/circular-economy-introduction/overview

EPCAT International (2022) "What We Do," https://ecpat.org/our-organisation/

European Travel Commission (2022) "European Tourism Support to the People of Ukraine," https://etc-corporate.org/european-tourism-support-to-the-people-of-ukraine

Fleming, S. (2019) "What Is Carbon Offsetting?" World Economic Forum, www.weforum.org/agenda/2019/06/what-is-carbon-offsetting

Foundation for Environmental Education (2022) "Unlocking Sustainability in the Hospitality Industry," www.greenkey.global

Future of Tourism Coalition (2022) "Guiding Principles," www.futureoftourism.org/guiding-principles

Global Sustainable Tourism Council (2022) "GSTC Criteria for Governments and Destinations," www.gstcouncil.org/for-destinations/

Global Sustainable Tourism Council and Destination Stewardship Center (2021) "Destination Stewardship Yearbook 2020–2021," www.gstcouncil.org/wp-content/uploads/Destination-Stewardship-Yearbook-2020-2021-online-ver.pdf

Green Globe (2022) "The Global Leader in Sustainable Tourism Certification," www.greenglobe.com/

Green Tourism (2022) "Helping Businesses Improve Sustainability," www.green-tourism.com/about-us

GreenKayak (2022) "Paddle for Cleaner Oceans," www.greenkayak.org/

Hartman, S., and Heslinga, J. H. (2022) "The Doughnut Destination: Applying Kate Raworth's Doughnut Economy Perspective to Rethink Tourism Destination Management," *Journal of Tourism Futures*, https://doi.org/10.1108/JTF-01-2022-0017

Holiable (2019) "Travel Plastic Free: Destinations that Have Banned Plastic," October 27, www.holiable.com/news/inspiration/plastic-free-travel

International Ecotourism Society (2022) "What Is Ecotourism?" https://ecotourism.org/what-is-ecotourism

International Social Tourism Organisation (2019) "Tourism in Actions: 20 Examples of Social Policies and Programmes around the World," www.isto.international/wp-content/uploads/2019/12/EN_Tourism-in-actions-20-examples-of-social-policies-programmes-around-the-world.pdf

International Union for Conservation of Nature (1996) "Tourism, Ecotourism and Protected areas (Hector Ceballos-Lascurain)," www.iucn.org/content/tourism-ecotourism-and-protected-areas-state-nature-based-tourism-around-world-and-guidelines-its-development

Jebara, P. (2022) "In Colombia, Community-based Tourism Is Reviving Local Economies," *Condé Nast Traveler*, www.cntraveler.com/sponsored/story/in-colombia-community-based-tourism-is-reviving-local-economies

Jordan Tourism Board (2022) "Meaningful Map of Jordan," www.myjordanjourney.com/hubfs/JTB%20Map%20Print.pdf

Li, S., Li, G., Law, R., and Paradies, Y. (2020) "Racism in Tourism Reviews," *Tourism Management*, 80. https://doi.org/10.1016/j.tourman.2020.104100.

The Nation (Thailand) (2022) "Prayut Unveils 'SMILE' Strategy for Tourism Development after COVID," June 15, www.nationthailand.com/in-focus/40016370

The Nature Conservancy (2015) (source to be confirmed; website has been revised).

Newsome, D., Moore, S. A., and Dowling, R. K. (2013) *Natural Area Tourism: Ecology, Impacts and Management*, 2nd edn, Bristol: Channel View Publications.

Nordic Ecolabel (2022) "Welcome to Nordic Ecolabelling," www.nordic-ecolabel.org

One Planet Network (2021a) "Webinar: The EU Ecolabel for Tourist Accommodations—Engaging Together in a Sustainable Recovery," www.oneplanetnetwork.org/news-and-events/webinars/webinar-eu-ecolabel-tourist-accommodations-engaging-together-sustainable

——— (2021b) "Glasgow Declaration Climate Action in Tourism," www.oneplanetnetwork.org/sites/default/files/2021-11/GlasgowDeclaration_EN_0.pdf

———(2022) "Tourism Declares Climate Emergency," www.tourismdeclares.com/

Only a Pavement Away (2022) "Hospitality against Homelessness," https://onlyapavementaway.co.uk/get-involved/events-campaigns/hospitality-against-homelessness?   /hospitality-against-homelessness

Pintassilgo, P. (2016) "Green Tourism," in J. Jafari and H. Xiao (eds), *Encyclopedia of Tourism*, Cham: Springer, pp. 405–406.

Pollock, A. (2019) "Regenerative Tourism: The Natural Maturation of Sustainability," *The Medium*, October 1, https://medium.com/activate-the-future/regenerative-tourism-the-natural-maturation-of-sustainability-26e6507d0fcb

Pritchard, A. (2014) "Gender and Feminist Perspectives in Tourism Research," in Alan A. Lew (ed.), *The Wiley Blackwell Companion to Tourism*, Hoboken, NJ: Wiley, pp. 314–324.

Purdue Tourism and Hospitality Research Center (2018) "Pledge to Travel with Care," *The Travel Care Code*, http://travelcarecode.org/thecarecode

Rainforest Alliance (2022) "Sustainable Tourism Standards and Updates," https://preferredbynature.org/certification/sustainable-tourism/sustainable-tourism-standards-updates

Raworth, K. (2017a) "Why It's Time for Doughnut Economics," *IPPR Progressive Review*, 24 (3): 216–222.

——— (2017b) *Doughnut Economics: Seven Ways to Think Like a 21st Century Economist*, White River Junction, Vt.: Chelsea Green Publishing.

Responsible Tourism Partnership (2020) "Cape Town Declaration on Responsible Tourism," https://responsibletourismpartnership.org/cape-town-declaration-on-responsible-tourism

Responsible Travel (2022) "What Is Community-Based Tourism?" www.responsibletravel.com/copy/what-is-community-based-tourism

ReThink Orphanages (2018) "Orphanage Tourism: Shedding Light on the Orphanage Scam," https://rethinkorphanages.org/problem-with-orphanage-tourism

Ruhanen, L., and Whitford, M. (2018) "Racism as an Inhibitor to the Organisational Legitimacy of Indigenous Tourism Businesses in Australia," *Current Issues in Tourism*, 21 (15): 1728–1742.

Salaam Baalak Trust (2022) "City Walk," www.salaambaalaktrust.com/city-walks.php

Schimmel, D. (2021) "Is Regenerative Travel a New Era in Tourism," February 24, Solimar International, www.solimarinternational.com/what-is-regenerative-travel-a-new-era-in-tourism/

Sedona Chamber of Commerce and Tourism Bureau and City of Sedona (2019) "Sedona Sustainable Tourism Plan: Connecting Sedona Visitors with Long-Term Destination Sustainability," https://sedonachamber.com/wp-content/uploads/2018/06/SED-STP_4-17-19-HR-UPDATE.pdf

Sheldon, P. (2020) "Regenerative Tourism 101," *Adventure Canada*, September 21, www.adventurecanada.com/regenerative-tourism-101

Sigüenza, M. C., Brotons, M., and Huete, R. (2013) "The Evolution of Gender Inequality in Tourism Employment in Spain," ROTUR, *Revista de Ocio y Turismo*, 6: 182–200.

Social and Health Tourism (2014) "Social Tourism," www.shtourism.eu/social-tourism.html

Social Enterprise UK (2022) "What's a Social Enterprise?" www.socialenterprise.org.uk/buysocial/whats-a-social-enterprise

Sourcewatch.org (2022) "Greenwashing," www.sourcewatch.org/index.php?title=Greenwashing

Stankov, U., Filimonau, V., and Vujičić, M. (2020) "A Mindful Shift: An Opportunity for Mindfulness Driven Tourism in a Post-pandemic World," *Tourism Geographies*, 22 (3): 703–712.

Sustainable Travel International (2022) "About Us," https://sustainabletravel.org/about-us

The Borgen Project (2020) "The strategy of pro-poor tourism," https://borgenproject.org/strategy-of-pro-poor-tourism/

The Travel Foundation (2022) "About Us," www.thetravelfoundation.org.uk/about-us

The Valley Cornwall (2021) "10 Facts about the Eden Project," July 23, www.thevalleycornwall.co.uk/news/6-facts-eden-project

Tourism Cares (2022) "We Believe We Can Change the World through Travel," www.tourismcares.org/

Tourism for SDGs (2022) "Chocolala: Taking Advantage of Community Resources to Make Fine Chocolates and Artisan Products and Generating Sustainable Strategies," https://tourism4sdgs.org/company_csr/chocolala-taking-advantage-of-community-resources-to-make-fine-chocolates-and-artisan-products-and-generating-sustainable-strategies

Tourism Industry Aotearoa (New Zealand) (2022) "Tourism Sustainability Commitment," Tourism-SustainabilityCommitment2020.pdf (tia.org.nz)

UN Brundtland Commission (1987) "Report of the World Commission on Environment and Development: Our Common Future," www.un-documents.net/our-common-future.pdf

United Nations (2022) "What Is Climate Change?" www.un.org/en/climatechange/what-is-climate-change

United Nations Educational, Scientific and Cultural Organization (2020) "Inspire a Positive Future by Connecting People and Nature Today," https://en.unesco.org/news/inspiring-positive-future-connecting-people-and-nature-today

United Nations Environment Programme (2022) "Green Economy," www.unep.org/regions/asia-and-pacific/regional-initiatives/supporting-resource-efficiency/green-economy

United Nations World Tourism Organization (2020) "Tourism Sector to Continue Taking Action on Plastic Pollution," www.unwto.org/news/tourism-sector-to-continue-taking-action-on-plastic-pollution

——— (2022a) "Sustainable Development," www.unwto.org/sustainable-development

———(2022b) "Global Code of Ethics for Tourism," www.unwto.org/global-code-of-ethics-for-tourism

US Department of the Interior (2022) "What Is the Difference between Global Warming and Climate Change?" www.usgs.gov/faqs/what-difference-between-global-warming-and-climate-change

US Environmental Protection Agency (2022) "Greenhouse Gas Emissions," www.epa.gov/ghgemissions/overview-greenhouse-gases

van den Brand, Y. (2022) "Examples of Greenwashing in Tourism," *Sustaying*, April 29, https://sustaying.com/greenwashing-in-tourism

Viabono (2022) "Uber uns," www.viabono.de/ueber-uns.html

World Bank Group (2017) "Women and Tourism: Designing for Inclusion," Tourism for Development Knowledge Series, https://openknowledge.worldbank.org/handle/10986/28535

World Travel and Tourism Council (2021) "Towards Destination Stewardship: Achieving Desti-
    nation Stewardship through Scenarios and a Governance Diagnostics Framework," https://
    wttc.org/Portals/0/Documents/Reports/2021/Destination-Stewardship-Framework.pdf?
    ver=2021–07–22–091804-637
Yu, M., and Hyun, S. S. (2021) "Development of Modern Racism Scale in Global Airlines: A Study
    of Asian Female Flight Attendants," *International Journal of Environmental Research and Public
    Health*, 18 (5): 2688.

Part I

Chapter **3**

Quality of Life and Well-being of Destination Residents

Locals matter! Delivering the good life for all

LEARNING OBJECTIVES

Having read this chapter, you should be able to:

1. define quality of life for destination residents;
2. identify the dimensions of quality of life;
3. describe how quality of life is measured;
4. explain the concept of well-being and its components;
5. elaborate on how to assess well-being;
6. identify aspects of tourism that tend to irritate residents;
7. elaborate on overtourism and its relationship to carrying capacity;
8. explain how resident sentiment toward tourism is measured;
9. describe what destinations should do to improve resident quality of life and well-being.

DOI: 10.4324/9781003343356-4

Warming Up

Chapter 2 introduced you to sustainable development, sustainable tourism, and social responsibility. You learned that social (along with cultural) was one of the three pillars of sustainable development and that definitely involves people including the residents of destinations. Chapter 3 connects with the previous one by emphasizing the crucial role of community residents in tourism and destination management. If you think about the banner, "Delivering the good life for all," this means that effective destination management is not only about delivering visitors, increasing GDP, revenues, and profits; it is more about spreading benefits evenly within communities and considering the expectations of all destination stakeholders including those who call the destination home.

You will no doubt guess that quality of life has material and tangible dimensions (such as money and other possessions) and non-material and intangible assessments (e.g., happiness). Tourism can and does deliver material rewards to some residents; however, it can also make some locals irritated, unhappy, and stressed. Have a look at the following quote from Wonderful Copenhagen (a DMO in Denmark) and you will get a better idea of the critical importance of residents in destination management and tourism.

EXAMPLE 3.1

Locals Are the Destination (Copenhagen)

This example argues that there is no greater attraction within a destination than the local residents.

> Locals are the destination. Locals are not a nice little sideshow, but, rather, one of the major attractions of a destination. The Little Mermaid offers no emotional or personal connection to the destination, the locals do. The delivery of an authentic destination experience depends upon the support of locals, whereas the livability and appeal of our destination—and thereby the advocacy of locals—depends on our ability to ensure a harmonious interaction between visitors and locals.
>
> (Wonderful Copenhagen 2017)

Learning Point

The contributions of local residents to the attractiveness of places need to be given a much higher priority.

To be honest with you, for many years DMOs did not pay much attention to local people as they saw their jobs as being external marketing to bring in visitors. They were rewarded for doing so as well. Long before the term "overtourism" was coined, your author was training DMO executives about community relationships (as well as marketing) as he believed locals were equally, if not more, important than visitors. The COVID-19 pandemic has accentuated the need to give locals a higher priority in destination management.

The author wanted in this chapter to provide a balanced viewpoint on the pluses and minuses from tourism for destination residents. It is hoped that this will help you to be more critical when you hear or read contents from both sides of the argument, those who would expand and those would degrow tourism. Nobody is 100 percent right!

So, this chapter begins by discussing resident quality of life since everyone in a community is affected by tourism, either directly or indirectly.

Resident Quality of Life

People often talk about quality of life, although few realize the entire and broad scope of the concept. However, destination management and DMOs must pay careful and continuous attention to resident quality of life. It is a concept about which they definitely must know.

Defining Quality of Life

Quality of life is based on people's self-assessments of quantitative and subjective aspects of their lives. Here are two more formal definitions.

DEFINITIONS

Quality of life

Destination resident satisfaction with life, and their feelings of contentment or fulfillment with experiences in the world. It is how residents view, or what they feel about, their lives (adapted from Andereck et al. 2007).

"Quality of life is broader than economic output and living standards. It includes the full range of factors influencing what people value in life beyond its material aspects. Factors potentially affecting our quality of life range from job and health status to social relationships, security and governance" (Eurostat 2022).

You will see expressions including "contentment," "fulfillment," "living standards" (standard of living), and material and non-material items in these definitions. These are fine in themselves; however, they do not comprehensively cover all the dimensions of quality of life; so, that is the next topic.

Dimensions of Quality of Life

The European Commission's Eurostat recommends that quality of life is measured by the 8 + 1 dimensions (Fig. 3.1), and they also identify twenty-five sub-dimensions (topics) (Table 3.1). Eurostat specifies how to measure each of the dimensions. Some of the sub-dimensions are measurable (quantitative) such as income and quantity of employment; others such as life satisfaction are very subjective (qualitative). Quality of life can be measured at the national, state or province, city or county level and at an individual resident level. Most of the ranking schemes that are available are at the country or city level, while tourism researchers (as you will see later) sharpen the focus to the individual resident level. The Eurostat data is published at a national level.

You will notice that in Figure 3.1 one of the dimensions is leisure and social interactions (no. 5) and it is in this activity that destination residents often encounter and interact with

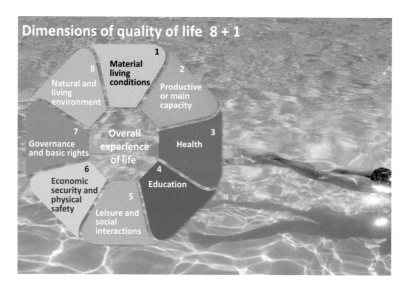

Figure 3.1 Dimensions of quality of life (Eurostat).

Table 3.1 The 8 + 1 dimensions of quality of life. Source: Eurostat (2022).

Dimensions	Topics (sub-dimensions)
1. Material living conditions	1.1. Income
	1.2. Consumption
	1.3. Material conditions
2. Productive or main capacity	2.1. Quantity of employment
	2.2. Quality of employment
	2.3. Other main activity
3. Health	3.1. Outcomes
	3.2. Drivers: healthy and unhealthy behaviors
	3.3. Access to healthcare
4. Education	4.1. Competences and skills
	4.2. Lifelong learning
	4.3. Opportunities for education
5. Leisure and social interactions	5.1. Leisure
	5.2. Social interactions
6. Economic security and physical safety	6.1 Economic security and vulnerability
	6.2. Physical and personal security
7. Governance and basic rights	7.1. Institutions and public services
	7.2. Discrimination and equal opportunities
	7.3. Active citizenship
8. Natural and living environment	8.1. Pollution (including noise)
	8.2. Access to green and recreational spaces
	8.3. Landscape and built environment
9. Overall experience of life (the +1)	9.1. Life satisfaction
	9.2. Affects
	9.3. Meaning and purpose

Source: Eurostat (2020).

visitors. Destinations and DMOs must be especially vigilant about the spaces and places where the two groups of people meet and in some cases compete for the leisure and recreational use of resources. The natural and living environment (no. 8) is another dimension, and destination residents may be concerned that having too many visitors puts excessive pressure on the natural environment and the places in which they live. You will hear more about this later as resident irritations from tourism are discussed.

You should know that there are several other approaches to measuring quality of life than that of Eurostat. One the most well known of these is WHOQOL (World Health Organization Quality of Life) (and WHOQOL-BREF) which was developed by the World Health Organization (WHO). Its measurement dimensions are called domains and include the physical, psychological, level of independence, environment, and spiritual domains (WHO 2022). WHOQOL-BREF is a shorter version of the system with four domains (physical, psychological, social relationships, and environment).

Perceived justice is another factor that appears to affect resident quality of life and levels of support for tourism. You can think about this as people's feelings of fairness in interacting with the tourism sector in their destinations. This can be divided into distributive (getting my fair share of the rewards from tourism), procedural (being treated fairly when I have problems and issues with tourism), and interactional (being shown courtesy by tourism organizations) justice (Wang et al. 2022).

Measuring Resident Quality of Life

Academic scholars have conducted many research studies to measure the quality of life of destination residents. Their findings are useful in guiding destinations and DMOs on the topics of resident quality of life and well-being. Uysal et al. (2016), in a review of quality of life and well-being research in tourism, found that it was gaining momentum in terms of scholarly contributions. This was confirmed by the author in a search of the Scopus database in July 2022 that showed 1,350 documents for a search by quality of life and tourism (and 1,465 documents for well-being and tourism). The growth in interest in tourism quality of life and well-being research is also confirmed in review studies by Hartwell et al. (2018) and Hu et al. (2022).

The first quality of life research article was published in 1987 and urged destinations to provide "improved quality of life" in the form of restaurants, shops, attractions, and entertainment (Hall 1987). Uysal et al. (2016) pointed out that tourism is generally assumed to have positive benefits for communities and residents. Chase et al. (2012), while acknowledging the potential negative quality of life impacts on residents in tourism-dependent destinations, advocated for the active engagement of local people in tourism planning and development. Weiermair and Peters (2012) suggested that there are many tourism stakeholders in destinations, including residents, and they do not necessarily perceive the positive and negative effects on quality of life in exactly the same ways.

Andereck and Nyaupane (2011) tested a new model for measuring tourism's impact on resident quality of life using a survey in Arizona. Eight TQoL (tourism quality of life) factors were identified:

1. recreation amenities;
2. community pride and awareness;
3. economic strength;
4. natural and cultural preservation;
5. community well-being;
6. way of life;

7. crime and substance abuse;
8. urban issues.

They confirmed positive TQoL influences of more jobs, better shopping, more recreation opportunities, cultural exchange, better public services, and more parks; and negative effects including more crime and traffic (Andereck and Nyaupane 2011: 258). As in previous studies, these two authors concluded that "those who have contact with tourists on a frequent basis view tourism in a much more positive light than those who do not."

DEFINITION

Community

A local "community is a collection of people who share a common territory and meet their basic physical and social needs through daily interaction with one another" (Johnson 1986: 692).

"There is no power for change greater than a community discovering what it cares about" (Wheatley 2022).

Kim et al. (2013) conducted research in Virginia with residents to determine if they perceived the economic, social, cultural, and environmental impacts of tourism. If they were aware of the impacts, the researchers also wanted to test how they affected resident sense of well-being. The results were that residents did, in fact, sense the impacts of tourism. A positive relationship was found between positive perceptions of tourism's economic impact and residents' sense of material well-being. Also, resident satisfaction with community well-being was positively correlated with feelings of the beneficial social impacts of tourism. The same was true in the relationship of positive cultural impacts and emotional well-being. Conversely, if the respondents perceived that tourism was negatively influencing the environment, their feelings of health and safety were adversely affected. Woo et al. (2015) introduced the variable of the perceived value of tourism development and found it was a determinant of sense of material and non-material life domain satisfaction.

Research on the tourism destinations of Sitges in Spain and Alghero in Sardinia, Italy, and urban quality of life was not as positive as the previously mentioned researchers (Biagi et al. 2020). There was a prevailing negative effect of tourism from the resident perspective, especially in the context of their accessibility to tourism amenities. The researchers stressed that the presence of amenities was not as important to resident quality of life perceptions as the actual accessibility to these amenities. This is indeed a very important observation as it reflects that it is the individual's assessment of how tourism affects them personally rather than everyone in the destination as a whole that truly shows the quality of life impacts.

How should we sum up this research on measuring the tourism impact on destination resident quality of life? There is agreement that quality of life should be measured by material (e.g., income and employment as in Example 3.2 from Costa Rica) and non-material factors (e.g., subjective well-being or SWB, to be discussed later). Second, not all residents perceive the quality of life effects of tourism in exactly the same way. Third, people perceive the personal (rather than general) impacts of tourism on their quality of life as being the most important.

EXAMPLE 3.2

Residents Benefit from Ecotourism in Costa Rica

This example from Costa Rica provides evidence that locals earn more from tourism.

> Ecotourism has also resulted in a rapid expansion of the job market, both at a national and local level. Residents earn almost double the monthly income in the tourism industry as compared to jobs in other industries. Local communities and schools have benefited from donations from visitors.
>
> (Garg 2022)

Learning Point

It is not always accurate to assume that local people earn less from tourism.

Do quality of life assessments by residents vary over time and according to specific destinations? These are two very good questions, and there have been attempts to answer them. A research study conducted in China found that perceived resident quality of life varied according to the tourism area life cycle (TALC) stage (covered in Chapters 4 and 7) and by geographic area (Su et al. 2022).

You are going to hear later about destination performance measurement and evaluation (Chapter 20). The measurement of resident quality of life and well-being should be included in destination performance measurement (Berbekova et al. 2022). Now, you are going to hear more about the concept of well-being.

Resident Well-being

You will often see well-being added to quality of life; however, although the two concepts are aligned, they are different. Again, it is best to start with a clear definition.

Defining Well-being

The following is a straightforward definition of well-being (there are many more complicated ones).

DEFINITION

Well-being

"Well-being is the experience of health, happiness, and prosperity. It includes having good mental health, high life satisfaction, a sense of meaning or purpose, and ability to manage stress. More generally, well-being is just feeling well" (Davis 2019).

You saw above that life satisfaction was one of the sub-dimensions of quality of life according to Eurostat, and it pops up again in the definition of well-being.

Difference between Quality of Life and Well-being

While there are overlaps between quality of life and well-being, there are more quantitative (material or measurable) measures in quality of life, while well-being is more subjective and perceptual. For example, in the above definition there is mention of a "sense of meaning" and the "ability to manage stress"; these are certainly more psychological in nature. You might be thinking then that quality of life is more about wealth, whereas well-being is more about "wellth" (if there was such a word). You are right! So, how can well-being be measured?

EXAMPLE 3.3

Emotional Closeness as a Stress Reducer in Shimla, India

This example highlights the advantages of creating a social bonding between residents and visitors.

> A very interesting study was conducted in 2021 in Himachal Pradesh and the city of Shimla. One of the findings was that the greater the emotional closeness with visitors, the less was the tourism-related stress. Resident survey respondents answered two questions about emotional closeness; "I feel close to some visitors that I have met in the city" and "I feel affection toward visitors in the city."
>
> (Gautam 2022)

Learning Point

Reducing the emotional distances between visitors and locals is highly desirable for destinations.

The Shimla example is most insightful as it suggests that if residents have greater empathy for visitors and a greater sense of closeness, this is likely to enhance their well-being. So, opportunities to involve residents with visitors should be encouraged such as engaging locals in visitor experiences.

Assessing Well-being

How can we assess the well-being of destination residents? This is a good question and a starting point as destination managers and DMOs need to track trends in resident well-being. Psychologists have been studying people's well-being for several decades and there are two major measurement approaches that are well accepted: SWB (Diener 1984; Goodman et al. 2018) and PERMA (Seligman 2011, 2018). Now, you will get an overview of these two approaches:

Subjective Well-being

Well-being is primarily subjective and about people's feelings. Figure 3.2 shows the three major components of SWB as pleasant affect, negative affect, and life satisfaction. Here affect means feelings or emotions. For example, happiness is definitely a pleasant feeling or emotion, while anger and stress are on the negative side. Destinations and DMOs can measure how happy are residents with tourism as was done in Fiji (Pratt et al. 2016). The small Himalayan country of Bhutan developed the Gross National Happiness Index (Fig. 3.3) to measure the happiness

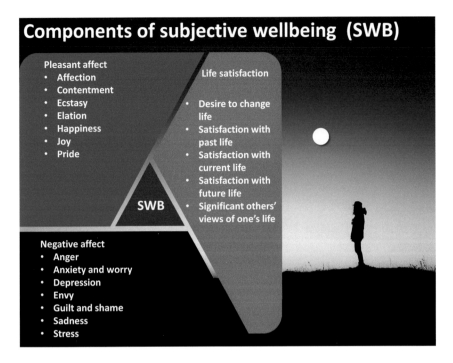

Figure 3.2 Components of subjective well-being (Diener et al. 1999).

of residents (Oxford Poverty and Human Development Initiative 2022). The discussion later about overtourism shows you that residents also can be angry and stressed with tourism in their communities, feeling their well-being is being diminished by having too many visitors.

The Gross Happiness Index has nine domains (Fig. 3.3), and there are thirty-three indicators. For example, psychological well-being includes the indicators of life satisfaction, positive emotions, negative emotions, and spirituality. There are other systems for measuring happiness and you have possibly heard of them. They include the World Happiness Report that ranks various countries. For 2022, the happiest countries were (in order) Finland, Denmark, Iceland, Switzerland, Netherlands, Luxembourg, Sweden, Norway, Israel, and New Zealand (Sustainable Development Solutions Network 2022).

PERMA

The acronym PERMA stands for positive emotions, engagement, relationships, meaning, and accomplishments (Seligman 2011). It is based on a positive psychology perspective. Positive emotions include contentment and joy, which are connected to happiness (Fig. 3.4). Engagement means that people want to do things in which they are interested and they want to be involved when things matter to them. Flow is a related concept and means when people become fully immersed in an activity. Later, you will get to know about resident empowerment in tourism and that is a form of engagement. Residents are likely to feel more valued (relationships component) when asked for their opinions (sentiment) about tourism and invited to be involved in destination management. They may derive a greater sense of meaning when being contacted about the future of tourism during a tourism planning or visioning process in the destination. Being thanked for their contributions to tourism can lead to the feeling of achievement.

Figure 3.3 Domains of the Gross Happiness Index (Oxford Poverty and Human Development Initiative).

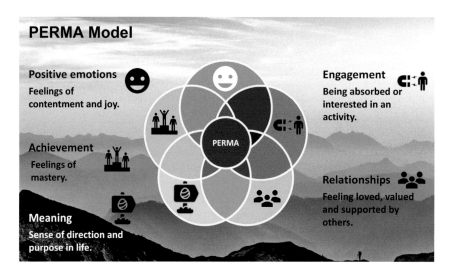

Figure 3.4 PERMA well-being model (Goodman et al. 2018).

The PERMA-Profiler is a tool for measuring well-being according to PERMA. It was developed to measure all elements of PERMA (three items per element or fifteen items total). An average for each PERMA element is calculated; the five scores are then presented to the respondent as a profile of their well-being (Bartholomaeus et al. 2020; Butler and Kern 2016). For example, the three items for engagement are:

1. How often do you become absorbed in what you are doing?
2. To what extent do you feel excited and interested in things?
3. How often do you lose track of time while doing something you enjoy?

(Butler and Kern 2016: 14)

There are several other approaches to defining well-being and one of these is the happiness pie (Brown and Rohrer 2020; Lyubomirsky et al. 2005). The three factors in the pie are the set point (genetic predisposition), intentional (volitional) activity, and life circumstances. It is argued that people can enhance their happiness through these factors and especially through the activities that they voluntarily choose to pursue.

Wellness vs. Well-being

Another concept that you will frequently hear about is wellness, and it features quite prominently in tourism as wellness tourism. What is the difference then between well-being and wellness? This is a tricky one to answer as many experts use a very broad interpretation of wellness that covers part, if not all, of what you learned about well-being. In order to remove this potential confusion, this book treats wellness as being more about the physical condition of people; while well-being is has more of a focus on emotional states (SWB and PERMA) and the interactions with other people and organizations (including DMOs). Here is a definition of wellness, which you can see is very broad in its scope.

DEFINITION

Wellness

"Wellness is an active process through which people become aware of, and make choices toward, a more successful existence."

"The National Wellness Institute promotes Six Dimensions of Wellness: Emotional, occupational, physical, social, intellectual, and spiritual" (National Wellness Institute 2022).

There is definitely a connection between well-being and wellness, although the boundaries between the two are rather hard to define. You are going to hear more about wellness tourism as a type of tourism and market segment later in this book. There is a tendency for many people to associate wellness with physical fitness and the use of spas and thermal and hot springs. However, as you saw in the wellness definition, this is a rather narrow view of the concept.

Destinations are places and now we move on to considering the effects of places on resident quality of life and well-being.

Place Attachment and Sense of Place

Do you think that place attachment is connected with resident quality of life and well-being? The author certainly does. Others also agree, "place attachment, an emotional bond that people can experience with a specific location or area, is known to increase well-being and happiness" (Scannell and Gifford 2017). The 8 + 1 dimensions of quality of life shown earlier in Table 3.1 and their sub-dimensions do not adequately demonstrate the connections between people and places, or in this case residents and their communities. So, it is important to also discuss the concepts of place attachment and sense of place. We are all attached to certain places—how about you? These could include your hometown, where you attended university, your favorite holiday destination, the home of your ancestors, and others. Here is a definition of place attachment.

> **DEFINITION**
>
> **Place attachment**
>
> "Place attachment concerns the positive emotional bonds that develop between individuals and their socio-physical environment. These attachment bonds are essential in planning for tourism development because of how tourism affects not only the appearance of local places, but also the meanings of places and the connections residents have with others and nature within the places visited by tourists" (Strzelecka et al. 2017: 61).

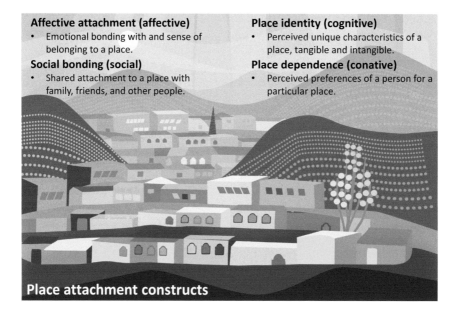

Affective attachment (affective)
- Emotional bonding with and sense of belonging to a place.

Social bonding (social)
- Shared attachment to a place with family, friends, and other people.

Place identity (cognitive)
- Perceived unique characteristics of a place, tangible and intangible.

Place dependence (conative)
- Perceived preferences of a person for a particular place.

Place attachment constructs

Figure 3.5 Place attachment constructs (Chen and Dwyer 2018).

Place attachment has the dimensions (or constructs) of cognitive attachment (place identity), affective attachment (affective attachment and social bonding), and conative attachment (place dependence) (Chen and Dwyer 2018; Scannell and Gifford 2010). Figure 3.5 provides an explanation of these four constructs.

Sense of place is a closely associated concept with place attachment and this is the meanings that people ascribe to certain places. You might think of it as the perceived personality of a community or destination. Great places to live are often great places to visit; however, great places to visit are sometimes not great places to live.

Livability is a quality often ascribed to places (mostly cities) and there are several ranking schemes that measure this it. The Global Liveability Index, published annually by the Economist Intelligence Unit (EIU), has thirty criteria (quantitative and qualitative) used in five categories (stability, healthcare, culture and environment, education, and infrastructure) to rank 173 cities globally. Ranked highest in 2022 and in order were Vienna (Austria), Copenhagen

(Denmark), Zurich (Switzerland), Calgary (Canada), Vancouver (Canada), Geneva (Switzerland), Frankfurt (Germany), Toronto (Canada), Amsterdam (Netherlands), and Osaka (Japan) and Melbourne (Australia) (tied) (EIU 2022).

The Mercer's Quality of Living Ranking was produced in its twenty-second annual edition for the year 2019. (Publication was suspended in 2020 due to the pandemic.) More than cities were ranked, and once again Vienna came out on top. The other top-ranked cities, in order, were Zurich (Switzerland), Vancouver, Munich (Germany), Auckland (New Zealand), Düsseldorf (Germany), Frankfurt (Germany), Copenhagen, Geneva (Switzerland) and Basel (Switzerland) (Mercer LLC 2022).

Since destination residents are attached in various ways to the places in which they live, they and their lifestyles can be disturbed by the presence of visitors and how visitors behave in their places. So, now we move onto factors resulting from tourism that can irritate residents.

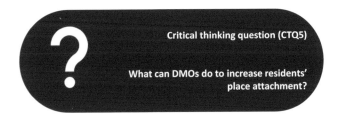

Critical thinking question (CTQ5)

What can DMOs do to increase residents' place attachment?

Resident Irritation Resulting from Tourism

What irritates or distresses destination residents about tourism in their communities? Increased traffic and crime rates have already been mentioned. There are several other irritants and destinations and DMOs must be aware of them. Gentrification of cities is one of these factors and it is being experienced in Mexico's capital city. However, let us start with the definition of gentrification.

DEFINITION

Gentrification

"Gentrification is a general term for the arrival of wealthier people in an existing urban district, a related increase in rents and property values, and changes in the district's character and culture. The term is often used negatively, suggesting the displacement of poor communities by rich outsiders. But the effects of gentrification are complex and contradictory, and its real impact varies" (PBS 2022).

The situation in Mexico City is being blamed at least partially on the impacts of the COVID-19 pandemic and an influx of remote workers ("digital nomads") from other countries.

EXAMPLE 3.4

Mexico City and Gentrification

This example suggests that digital nomads are associated with more gentrification in Mexico City.

> Many residents believe that the rate of gentrification and displacement in Mexico City is accelerating—and that the pandemic-era travel boom is partly to blame. Over the past year, the city has hosted more and more remote workers, attracting those in higher-paying jobs and fields that were previously not virtual. Furthermore, residents have complained of foreigners blatantly flouting COVID-19 safety and masking guidelines, while being negligent of cultural norms and sensitivities. The most infuriating aspect, to some locals, is how expats can be unaware of the cultural, social, and financial impact of their presence.
>
> (Nguyen 2022)

Learning Point

It is undesirable for visitors to disturb or annoy local residents and DMOs should be aware of these situations when they happen.

To be fair to digital nomads, unlike in Mexico, some destinations are trying to attract them. One example here is Mauritius (Bhutia 2022) which has launched a premium visa scheme offering long-term visas. Mauritius is not alone in making it easier for digital nomad visits; more than twenty-five countries including Brazil and the United Arab Emirates are offering special visas for digital nomads (Johanson 2022).

Another resident irritant is the rising costs and decreasing availability of housing attributed to sharing economy providers such as Airbnb and other landlords who rent out their properties to visitors on a short-term basis. This is a particularly disruptive issue in the seaside resort towns and other popular tourism destinations in the UK.

EXAMPLE 3.5

Resident Concerns on Impacts of Short-Term Holiday Lets in UK

Second homes can take housing off of the market that would otherwise be available to locals, as is suggested in this example.

> The review, launched by the Department for Culture, Media and Sport on June 29, will seek to better understand the effects of short-term holiday lets on communities across England over the past ten to fifteen years as part of the Government's Tourism Recovery Plan. The rise of apps and websites such as Airbnb has seen owners of what would otherwise be residential premises enter

the guest accommodation market, raising concerns over how this has effected local residents. The review will focus on assessing the impact the rise has had on house prices and health and safety standards.

(Wright 2022)

Learning Point

Destinations and DMOs should be aware of the impacts of second homes on local residents.

There are types of tourism that residents may feel uncomfortable with including drunk (or drinking) tourism, hen and stag tourism, birth tourism, cannabis tourism, hunting, gambling tourism, and sex tourism (Buckley 2019). Drunk, drinking, or party tourism is a phenomenon that upsets many residents. This occurs in several European cities (e.g., Budapest, Prague, Tallinn) (Pinke-Sziva et al. 2019) and in Mexican and Central American destinations (Mach et al. 2022). Some places desire high-spending visitors and thus want to limit the numbers of backpackers.

Increased traffic volumes and environmental damage caused by visitors is another complaint voiced by local residents, as evidenced in the example from Wyoming.

EXAMPLE 3.6

Resident Disdain for Tourism in Jackson, Wyoming

This example shows that local residents may grow to resent or dislike tourists when there is too much traffic and overcrowded conditions.

> Among the findings: Tourism is considered important to the local economy, but the majority of residents (53 percent) do not feel there are non-economic benefits of tourism. Only 26 percent of residents said tourism's benefits outweigh its drawbacks. Chief among the identified drawbacks are traffic, overcrowding, and the environmental impact of overcrowding.

(Robinson-Johnson 2022)

Learning Point

Destinations and DMOs should do as much as they can to reduce irritations caused by too much tourism.

The presence of an informal economy due to tourism is another factor that upsets some destination residents. Informal employment are those people engaged in tourism-related business activities without the permission of government departments and outside of government supervision, including itinerant vendors at scenic areas, unlicensed tour guides, ticket scalpers, and illegal passenger transportation (Çakmak et al. 2018). You may have encountered some of these people trying to sell you fake watches, bags, or other products.

If you recall the definition of well-being, it mentioned a person's ability to manage stress. Here, you should realize that tourism not only irritates residents, but it may also cause stress for them. A research study in Falmouth, Jamaica, measured the stress caused by a cruise port development and how locals coped with it (Jordan et al. 2015). The authors noted that the stress was particularly high among locals as they had not been consulted about the cruise port development.

A real example will help here to summarize the issues that destination residents frequently have with tourism. A survey of 500 residents of Ljubljana, Slovenia, was conducted and opinions were sought on the positive and negative aspects of tourism in the city. As you will see in Example 3.7, prices and (people) congestion were perceived to be the most problematic issues with tourism (a score of 5 was "totally agree" and 1 was "totally disagree").

EXAMPLE 3.7

Resident Opinions on Tourism Impacts on Ljubljana

This is a good example of how to determine which issues regarding tourism are of greatest concern to local residents.

Pollution (2.45)
　Tourism development destroys Ljubljana's green spaces (2.41)
　Visitors pollute Ljubljana with the rubbish that they leave behind (2.67)
　Tourism in Ljubljana causes air pollution (2.67)
　Tourism damages Ljubljana's visual and architectural image (2.06)
　Congestion (3.44)
　Tourism in Ljubljana causes congestion in public urban areas (pavements and markets) (3.55)
　Tourism in Ljubljana causes congestion in bars and shops (3.33)
　Prices (3.95)
　Because of tourism, life in Ljubljana is more expensive (3.84)
　Prices in city-center bars and restaurants are high (4.05)
　Residents' irritation (2.26)
　Tourist numbers in Ljubljana should be limited (2.57)
　In the seasonal months (June-September), there should be fewer visitors in Ljubljana (2.38)
　Life in Ljubljana (as a touristic place) is uncomfortable (2.30)
　Because of tourism, I would like to move out of Ljubljana (1.78)

(Mihalic and Kuščer 2022)

Learning Point

DMOs should regularly poll local residents about their sentiments toward tourism.

Having reviewed some of the factors that make destination residents irritated about tourism, the chapter now turns to the topics of carrying capacity and overtourism. When carrying capacity is exceeded and locals sense overtourism are two situations that destinations and DMOs want to avoid.

Carrying Capacity

The following is a very simple definition of carrying capacity.

> **DEFINITION**
>
> ### Carrying capacity
>
> "The amount of people that an area of land can support based on the amount of available resources" (Open Education Sociology Dictionary 2022).

Before the term overtourism emerged, the carrying capacity of tourism and recreation resources was recognized and measured (Bretlaender and Toth 2014: 6). There are several different forms of carrying capacity, and they are as shown in Figure 3.6.

Forms of carrying capacity

- *Physical carrying capacity*: Sites or infrastructure can no longer support the numbers of visitors.
- *Ecological carrying capacity*: Native wildlife populations are endangered due to visitor activities.
- *Economic carrying capacity*: Beneficial local activities can no longer be carried out due to tourism.
- *Social carrying capacity*: Visitors can no longer tolerate the behaviour of other visitors, or local people can no longer tolerate visitors.
- *Perceptual carrying capacity*: Visitors no longer enjoy themselves due to observable damage caused by previous visitors.
- *Environmental carrying capacity*: Environmental problems start to occur due to visitor interaction with the environment.

Figure 3.6 Forms of carrying capacity.

Please take a close look at the photograph in Figure 3.6. Would you agree that this street in Tokyo is overcrowded with people? Which forms of carrying capacity apply in this situation? Your answer might be physical carrying capacity (too many people for the space), economic carrying capacity (local residents cannot easily get to shops or move around on foot), or perceptual carrying capacity (pedestrians feel it is overcrowded). All of these answers have merit. Now with this idea of overcrowding in mind, the next topic is overtourism.

Overcrowding and Overtourism

UNWTO (2018) stated that the perceptions of overcrowding are reasons for destination resident protesting about tourism. Milano et al. (2019: 354) suggested that "the excessive growth of visitors leading to overcrowding in areas where residents suffer the consequences of temporary and seasonal tourism peaks, which have caused permanent changes to their lifestyles, denied access to amenities and damaged their general well-being." So, these authors make the connection between overcrowding and well-being and quality of life. In terms of carrying capacity, it is the social carrying capacity that is most involved here and the behavior of visitors.

UNWTO and Ipsos (2019) found 52 percent of respondents believed that tourism had a large or moderate positive impact on employment and income. However, 46 percent felt that tourism created overcrowding in their cities. Almost half (49 percent) suggested that there was a need for measures to better manage city tourism.

Academic researchers have been examining the effects of overcrowding on cities, and many journal articles and books have been published on the topic. The *International Journal of Tourism Cities* produced two special issues on overtourism: "Overtourism and the Sharing Economy" (vol. 6, no. 1 in 2020), and "Overtourism and the Marketing of Smart Tourism Destinations" (vol. 5, no. 4 in 2019). Here are two definitions of the overtourism concept.

DEFINITIONS

Overtourism

"The impact of tourism on a destination, or parts thereof, that excessively influences perceived quality of life of citizens and/or quality of visitor experiences in a negative way" (UNWTO 2018: 4).

"Destinations where hosts or guests, locals or visitors, feel that there are too many visitors and that the quality of life in the area or the quality of the experience has deteriorated unacceptably" (Goodwin 2016).

EXAMPLE 3.8

What Are the Causes of Overtourism?

This example explores the reasons why overtourism is occurring in some destinations.

An article in the *International Journal of Tourism Cities* identified the following reasons why overtourism is occurring:

- Growing visibility and popularity of destinations.
- Increasing numbers of tourists.
- Decreasing costs allowing more people to travel.
- Greater dissemination of information through social media.
- Destinations being powerless to stem inflows of visitors.
- Overdevelopment of tourism, especially in cities.
- Private sector favoring continuous growth.

(Dodds and Butler 2019)

Learning Point

There are several factors leading to overtourism.

For Germany, Namberger et al. (2019) posed the research question of overcrowding, overtourism, and local-level disturbance—how much can Munich handle? They found that local residents were most disturbed by crowds of people in the main shopping streets, Oktoberfest visitors, and football fans on match days. They identified "crowds of tourists" (e.g., football fans) and "disturbances by small groups of tourists" (e.g., stag and hen parties) to be the two main components of local level disturbances. Navarro-Ruiz et al. (2020) examined crowding caused by cruise shore excursions in Barcelona and Valencia, Spain. They found that both cities suffered from congestion in their port areas and also, especially Barcelona as the more established cruise port, the cruise excursionists put more pressure on the city's main tourist attractions. In Poland in the city of Poznan, there is a trend for residents to move out of the center city, partially at least due to changes brought about by tourism.

EXAMPLE 3.9

Why People Are Moving out of Poznan City Center (Poland)

This issue in a Polish city demonstrates how too much tourism may disturb the lives of locals.

> Taking into account the opinions expressed in the interviews, the reasons for moving to other areas of the respondents are mainly the increase in the cost of living, the disappearance of bonds between residents, noise, impact of tourism and the policy of gentrification of the city center.
>
> (Rozmiarek et al. 2022)

Learning Point

Destinations and DMOs should be aware of potential negative impacts of tourism on local residents.

UNWTO (2018) outlined a number of strategies for dealing with overtourism. These included dispersing visitors within cities, promoting time-based dispersal of visitors, stimulating new visitor itineraries and attractions, reviewing and adapting regulations, enhancing visitor segmentation, ensuring local communities benefit from tourism, creating city experiences that benefit residents and visitors, and improving city infrastructure and facilities.

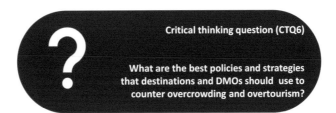

Critical thinking question (CTQ6)

What are the best policies and strategies that destinations and DMOs should use to counter overcrowding and overtourism?

Degrowth and Demarketing

Two of the ways of dealing with overcrowding and overtourism are degrowth and demarketing, both aimed at reducing tourist volumes. Demarketing means either reducing the total amount spent on destination marketing or choosing not to market to specific groups of visitors. Degrowth is a broader concept which questions the wisdom of continuing to pursue gross national product (GNP) growth and favors greater emphasis on sustainable development, environmental protection and conservation, quality of life, and well-being. Here now is a formal definition of degrowth.

DEFINITION

Degrowth

"Degrowth is an idea that critiques the global capitalist system which pursues growth at all costs, causing human exploitation and environmental destruction. The degrowth movement of activists and researchers advocates for societies that prioritize social and ecological well-being instead of corporate profits, over-production and excess consumption" (Degrowth 2022).

Some destinations are instituting measures to deal with the overtourism issue and particularly with overcrowding. These measures include: demarketing, closures, use restrictions, and pricing strategies. Bruges, Belgium, adopted demarketing by stopping its advertising to the day-trip (excursionist) market (Marcus 2019). The closure approach was demonstrated when the government of the Philippines closed the island of Boracay for six months in 2018 in order to clean up the local environment (BBC 2018). Similarly, in 2018 the government of Thailand closed down Maya Beach until 2021 (BBC 2019).

EXAMPLE 3.10

Why Do Residents Want Degrowth?

This example identifies why local residents want the growth in tourism to be reduced.

> Residents want to reclaim their lifestyle by refusing to interact with a high volume of visitors and discouraging tourists from visiting their communities. To achieve this, they call for a reduction in the number of visitors and stricter regulation of their tourism industry, as well as a slowdown in the growth of tourism (Séraphin et al. 2020).
>
> (Andriotis 2021: 5)

Learning Point

Sometimes less tourism is better for local residents.

Having restrictions on the use of entire destinations or parts of them is the third strategy for dealing with overcrowding and overtourism. For example, in 2019, Venice banned large cruise ships from docking at its historic center (Saraogi 2019). Dubrovnik in Croatia decided in 2018 to limit the number of cruise ship calls to two per day and a maximum capacity of 5,000 passengers in a move to cut down on overcrowding. This is an example of using quota systems to manage usage levels. Other places to impose restrictions on cruise ship stays include Amsterdam, Barcelona, Dublin (Ireland), and Santorini, Greece.

Pricing strategies are the fourth approach to controlling visitor numbers and for avoiding overcrowding. The Himalayan country of Bhutan famously used to cap the annual number of foreign tourists. This was changed in favor of requiring a sustainable development fee (at US$200 per person in 2022) (Tourism Council of Bhutan 2022). Adding taxes are another pricing strategy as was done by Amsterdam and Stockholm.

EXAMPLE 3.11

Venice Charges an Entrance Fee

This example may represent a future trend for popular tourism cities to charge visitors entrance fees.

> From January 16, 2023, visitors to Venice—that jewel in Italy's tourism crown—will have to pay for the privilege. It's set to become the first city in the world to require an entrance fee. The launch date was announced by Venice's councilor for tourism, Simone Venturini, at a press conference on Friday. Venturini called the new measure a "great revolution," and a solution for the overtourism problem that the lagoon city has been struggling with for decades.
>
> The cost of the ticket will range from a three-euro minimum right up to 10 euros. The price will not be fixed, but will vary according to the number of visitors: The more requests for entry, the higher the cost. The goal, explained Venturini, is not to "close the city," but to get people to book their presence to reduce the "tourist peaks." He said, "Venice is a living city and it has to stay that way."
>
> (Borghese et al. 2022)

Learning Point

Popular cities are contemplating entrance fees.

Another approach apart from these four is in providing preferential access for local residents to tourism attractions and sites, for example by offering them free admission. Requiring advance bookings or authorizations to visit is yet another strategy, with the example of the Praia das Catedrais (Cathedrals on the Beach) on the coast of Galicia, Spain, requiring a thirty-day-in-advance reservation to visit (Xunta de Galicia 2022). Creating new itineraries and guided tours to less visited areas of destinations is another suggested solution.

Just before leaving the topic of overtourism, you should not have the impression that it happens only in large, bucket-travel-list cities such as Barcelona and Venice. Unfortunately, it is also being experienced in rural areas (Butler 2020) and on small islands including Aruba (Peterson 2020) and Malta (*Malta Independent* 2022). While much of the sting of overtourism may have been taken away by COVID-19, the lesson learned is that destinations must pay greater attention to the carrying capacity of resources in its various forms. This challenge existed before the pandemic and it certainly will be there after the pandemic is defeated. Now, the impacts of that health crisis on resident–tourism relationships are discussed.

Impacts of COVID-19 Pandemic

The COVID-19 pandemic had a dramatic downward impact on visitor numbers to destinations, and some are asking if it is the solution to ending overtourism. Molz (2020) argued that COVID-19 illustrates the overdependence on tourism and the harm it brings to certain places. There is a sentiment that in the future destinations should place more emphasis on the quality of tourism and visitors and not have such a great focus on the volumes of tourists (Buckley 2020). There is also a belief that visitors should be spread out more, spatially within destinations and temporally (arriving at different times). There is growing sentiment worldwide that having too many tourists is not necessarily a good thing and that some types of tourists are not particularly welcome due to their behaviors and impacts on communities. The COVID-19 pandemic has heightened this discussion on how many and which visitors are wanted (and unwanted).

The detrimental impacts of COVID-19 on destinations that previously had loads of visitors are in some ways dividing the opinions of local residents. Kyoto in Japan is one of those places.

EXAMPLE 3.12

Kyoto Needs Foreign Tourists to Return

Having too many and having too few tourists are issues for some destinations, as in this case from Japan.

> In response (to a resident backlash), the city passed regulations that largely prevented Airbnb from operating in quiet, residential areas. It imposed a hotel tax. In the geisha entertainment quarter of Gion, a local residents' council banned photography on some private roads. Still, surveys by the city council found most local people complained of traffic jams and overcrowded buses and subways around the major attractions. All that changed almost overnight in 2020, at a time when the city was already struggling to overcome a financial crisis.
>
> (Reynolds 2022)

Learning Point

Destinations and DMOs should do their best to estimate the optimum levels of visitors.

Another interesting outcome of the pandemic was that locals became the primary (and often only) customers for local tourism businesses as there were no visitors. They were given all sorts of special deals by hotels, restaurants, and attractions. How do you think this influenced the relationships between locals and the tourism sector? There is no right answer that we have to this question for the moment. However, you probably said that this opportunity made residents more aware of what the sector has to offer and that surely must be a positive outcome. The author agrees with you. Perhaps also local people developed feelings of sympathy (sentiment) for tourism businesses. Next, the focus is on how to determine resident sentiment for tourism.

Measuring Resident Sentiment toward Tourism

You are going to hear more about resident sentiment research in Chapter 5 in the discussion on destination management research. Having a good definition of resident sentiment toward tourism is a good starting point for this topic.

DEFINITION

Resident sentiment

"Local residents' overall perceptions/views of and emotional dispositions toward tourism development, in which attitude is only one constituent part and behavior is implied" (Chen et al. 2021: 1408).

As you can see then, sentiment is about locals' views and perceptions of tourism. The definition also highlights behavior and that means that residents will act upon their sentiments. You will probably be thinking that it is essential for destinations and DMOs to have this knowledge and your author agrees. Most DMOs have not engaged in asking locals for their views. However, some DMOs have started to gather this information and several research companies have systems to measure resident sentiment, and you are going to hear about them now.

LONGWOODS INTERNATIONAL RESIDENT SENTIMENT RESEARCH

This market research company publishes resident research for the USA and Canada. Some of the results are very telling about resident involvement in tourism. For example, in 2021 American Resident Sentiment Survey, 42 percent of respondents disagreed with the statement, "Residents are consulted when major tourism development takes place in this area" (and another 26 percent were neutral) (Destinations International and Longwoods International 2022a).

TRAVELSAT© RESIDENT SENTIMENT INDEX

TCI Research based in Brussels, Belgium, operates the Resident Sentiment Index system that is applied mainly in Europe. One of the metrics calculated is the Overall Tourism Sentiment Index. For Copenhagen, it was found that "60% of the respondents in Copenhagen felt that tourism in Copenhagen generates more positive consequences than negative consequences, while 8% thought the opposite was the case. This equals a tourism sentiment index of 52%, which is 5% higher than the average of the cities included in this analysis" (TCI Research/ Wonderful Copenhagen 2019).

TOURISM SENTIMENT INDEX

This system is operated by Think! X Innovations Inc. of Vancouver, British Columbia. This Index uses a different method than the previous two by scanning and analyzing visitor comments about specific destinations on social media platforms.

EXAMPLE 3.13

Longwoods' Resident Sentiment Research

This example explains the value of resident sentiment research for destinations.

> Longwoods' newest program offering, Resident Sentiment Research, allows destinations to discover how the local community at large perceives tourism and its impacts. Increasingly, destination management must be considered a partnership between the industry and residents, to ensure that tourism

development benefits both parties and contributes to the community economically while maintaining or enhancing quality of life for its residents. Our
Resident Sentiment Research examines both practical and emerging/growing
concerns including economic development, perceived environmental impacts,
overtourism, quality of life, and many others.

(Longwoods International 2022)

For 2021, Longwoods found that 75% of Canadians agreed that "Overall, tourism is good for my province."

(Destinations International/Longwoods International 2022b)

Learning Point

Destinations and DMOs should regularly gather residents' opinions and attitudes
toward tourism.

Resident sentiment surveys can be even more precise in their questioning including asking
locals their sentiments on specific markets of visitors, e.g., foreign versus local visitors. For
example, a survey was conducted on Hong Kong resident sentiments toward visitors from
Mainland China (Chen et al. 2021).

Chapter 5 suggests that research is not a cost, rather it is an investment for the future. It definitely
is not cheap for destinations and DMOs to poll local residents; however, the payoffs can be hand-
some as listening to locals can support their quality of life and well-being. If there was such a word
as research-washing, the author would use it here. Just as with greenwashing in Chapter 2, resident
research should be conducted in good faith with sincerity, and the results must be acted upon.

Improving Resident Quality of Life and Well-being

The good life for all is the motto for this chapter. So, now the question is how can destination
management and DMOs improve resident quality of life. In multiple ways is how the author
would answer this question. Now we look into the details of doing so.

Chapter 9 is devoted to the role of community and stakeholder relationships and involvement.
It discusses how destinations and DMOs should build and maintain relationships with residents
(and other stakeholders), and how to engage with and involve locals. Paying attention and listening to the opinions of local residents is a good place to start. You have already heard in this chapter
about how to do research on resident quality of life, well-being, and sentiment toward tourism.

Beginning with Chapter 4, you are going to hear in detail about the roles of destination management and DMOs. Now, here are some examples of how residents can be engaged and involved
with each of these roles.

Planning and Research

You learned in Chapter 1 about the residents of Banff, Alberta, being asked to complete a
survey as input for a tourism masterplan. Staying in Canada, Northwest Territories Tourism
conducts resident sentiment research and in June 2021 found that 66 percent of residents
believed that the benefits of tourism outweighed the negative impacts (Government of Northwest Territories 2022).

In Chapter 4, there is a discussion of visioning processes in developing tourism plans and strategies for destinations. It is strongly recommended that these processes are participative and that local residents are involved in the visioning. You will remember from this chapter that in some of the examples local residents felt they were disregarded in the development and marketing of tourism. Visioning encourages a greater sense of shared ownership of tourism.

Leadership, Coordination, and Governance

Earlier you learned that governance was one of the dimensions of quality of life, and it appeared again in the Gross Happiness Index. This means that those responsible for destination management in communities must practice good governance, particularly through demonstrating accountability for the use of resources and being fully transparent in their operations.

Empowerment is a concept often used in leadership and human resource management and means decentralizing decision-making to give more power to the front-line employees. There is also a concept of resident empowerment in tourism. It means that locals are given or ask for a greater say (or power) in how tourism is developed, operated, and marketed in their communities (Aleshinloye et al. 2022). Chapter 2's examples of community-based and PPT are tangible demonstrations of resident empowerment, for example.

Many of the DMOs around the world are operated by government and the public sector is responsible for leading and coordinating tourism. Some of the "movements" in the management and operation of government agencies are giving residents greater access and participation in government activities. These include the ideas of open government, e-government, and new public (sector) management (making government agencies more efficient and business like and borrowing management practices from the private sector). An open government is inclusive and participatory, and allows citizens to be involved in the formulation, implementation and follow-up of public policies (UCLG 2018). E-government is the use of the Internet as a platform for exchanging information, providing services and transacting with citizens, businesses, and other arms of government (IGI Global 2022).

Product Development

It is the honest truth that many tourism developments have proceeded without any consideration of local residents. This book definitely does not support or advocate for that approach. Here are two examples of not listening to the community from Malawi and Italy.

EXAMPLE 3.14

Not Listening to the Locals (Malawi and Italy)

This example is about two situations (Malawi and Italy) where tourism development has taken place without sufficient consultation with local residents.

> The main theme that emerged was a lack of community involvement in tourism activities at the sites which has destroyed heritage assets.
>
> (Chauma and Ngwira 2022)

> Another example is in Portofino, Italy, where residents do not feel they are involved in scuba-diving tourism in a Marine Protected Area.
>
> (Scholtz and Saayman 2018)

Learning Point

It is wise for DMOs to regularly consult with local residents about tourism development and growth.

You heard about a great example of product development involving local residents in Chapter 2. This was in the Dominican Republic with the Chocolala Artisan Chocolate Factory (Example 2.4). Here is another good example that was coordinated by The Travel Foundation and the TUI Care Foundation in Croatia.

EXAMPLE 3.15

Local Involvement in Tourism Product Development in Croatia

Grassroots involvement is crucial for effective tourism development, as exemplified in this case from Croatia.

> Naturally, tourism is developed to meet the needs of tourists. However, there would be no tourism without vibrant destinations; the people, places and history that make tourists want to visit. Yet the needs of the tourist are often put in front of the needs of the destination and the people who live there. Consequently, local requirements are usually not well understood or met, and opportunities to integrate international tourism into the local economy are routinely missed... the Travel Foundation has explored how to foster more inclusive tourism development through a project in Croatia where, in partnership with the TUI Care Foundation and with cooperation from TUI Group, we trialed ways to strengthen relationships between new hotels and small businesses across two coastal village resorts on the Makarska Riviera.
>
> (The Travel Foundation 2022)

Learning Point

Local inputs into destination development must be sought by DMOs.

Partnerships and Team-building

Do you recall when we were discussing SWB and the PERMA model that there was mention of engagement, meaning, relationships, and achievement? Asking local residents to partner and join in teams is a great way to tick all of those boxes. Here is a great example from the Caribbean nation of St. Kitts in which locals are being trained to support sustainable tourism.

EXAMPLE 3.16

St. Kitts Destination Guardians

This is a great example about how to train local residents to be more supportive of sustainable tourism.

> A collaborative training workshop that raises awareness around sustainable tourism and empowers Kittitians to act as Destination Guardians who take care of their island home. At the end of the workshop, participants are asked to sign the Destination Guardian pledge and identify four concrete actions that they can commit to perform over the next year.
>
> (Sustainable Travel International 2022)

Learning Point

Educating local residents about sustainable tourism is a highly desirable initiative.

Stakeholder Relationships and Involvement

There are plenty of good applications coming up in Chapter 9 showing best practices for this role. Several destinations operate volunteer tourism ambassador programs in which locals provide travel information to visitors. One of these is Melbourne, Australia.

EXAMPLE 3.17

Melbourne's Tourism Ambassadors

Volunteering local residents can be a great assist with increasing visitor satisfaction as in the case from Australia.

> Having our bright and bubbly red coats back on our city streets will be another way we can encourage Melburnians and visitors to rediscover everything that is amazing about our city. Our volunteers have a passion for Melbourne. They're excited to return to share their local knowledge and help people make the most of their time in Melbourne. They are also looking forward to reconnecting with their fellow volunteers. Our volunteers will be back on the streets in their vibrant red coats helping people find their way, discover new attractions and access tips and hints about what to do and where to go.
>
> (City of Melbourne 2022)

Learning Point

Local volunteers can be instrumental in creating more authentic and satisfying experiences for visitors.

Marketing, Branding, and Communications

DMOs must increasingly regard residents as co-creators of marketing communications. Residents, for example, can join with DMOs in the co-creation of communication campaigns and here is an example from the USA.

EXAMPLE 3.18

What Do You Love about Your Community? (Pennsylvania)

Crowdsourcing of resident opinions is demonstrated in this example from the USA.

> The Danville (Virginia) Office of Economic Development and Tourism is conducting a survey to gather opinions for a new tourism marketing program. The survey will allow residents to voice their opinions on current local attractions and what advancements they want to see for their community in the future. "What do they love about their community? What do they want to see in their community that will drive tourism and give them a greater sense of pride for being a resident here in Danville and Pittsylvania County?" said Lisa Meriwether, tourism manager for the city of Danville and Pittsylvania County.
>
> (Shelton 2022)

Learning Point

Locals can be great sources of opinion about destination attractions, activities, and experiences.

Encouraging locals to act like visitors in their own communities is a way of sensitizing residents and making them more aware of tourism. As an example, Victoria, British Columbia in Canada, operates an annual event named Be a Tourist. The program offers discounted or free admissions to local attractions for residents (Attractions Victoria 2022).

Visitor Management

You are going to learn about the visitor management role in Chapter 11. One of the main reasons for visitor management is to ensure that visitors and their behavior are not harmful or distressing for destination residents. This chapter has highlighted some of these irresponsible behaviors and the related issues in tourism. Example 3.19 provides a list of irresponsible tourism that is proposed by Sustainable Travel.

EXAMPLE 3.19

Irresponsible Tourism

This example provides a listing of activities that destinations should discourage. Sustainable Travel has identified what it believes are examples of irresponsible tourism. Here is their list (we put it in alphabetic order, not in order of importance).

- All-inclusive resorts
- Canned hunting
- Captive animals
- Child sex tourism
- Cultural insensitivity
- Cruise liners
- Exploiting children
- Forced evictions
- Irresponsible wildlife watching
- Irresponsible hiking and biking
- Shark cage diving

(Mack 2022)

Learning Point

Destinations and DMOs should not encourage or promote certain types of tourism.

Crisis Management

Crises often affect residents as well as visitors and the tourism sector in general. How do you think the COVID-19 pandemic influenced resident views of tourism? One example here is research from Bordeaux in France. A resident survey there indicated that 58 percent had changed their opinions about tourism, with 75 percent of these people now better realizing the importance of tourism to life and the economy (Bordeaux Tourism and Congress 2022). Whether this increased positivity about tourism will be sustained remains to be seen.

It is hard to think of a place that is more associated with tourism than the islands of Hawaii. This destination has been conducting resident sentiment surveys for many years as it appreciates the value of residents to tourism and the need to determine their opinions and attitudes. The results of the 2021 survey provide a perfect ending point for Chapter 3. You will see in Example 3.20 that there is an emphasis on "managed tourism efforts" and the "quality of life benefits of tourism" for residents.

EXAMPLE 3.20

How to Improve Resident Sentiment About Tourism in Hawaii

This example underlines the importance of finding out the benefits most sought by local residents from tourism.

> Moving forward, initiatives that grow the economic and quality of life benefits of tourism, integrated with managed tourism efforts, hold the most influence for improving resident sentiment.
>
> Quality of life benefits for residents were identified as "creates shopping, restaurants and entertainment opportunities; sponsors festivals; and enhances quality of life."

> Sustainability benefits were identified as "helps preserve Native Hawaiian culture, and nature."
>
> Managed tourism efforts were defined by agreement with "feel like more effort is being made to balance economic benefits and quality of life for residents."
>
> (Hawaii Tourism Authority 2021)
>
> **Learning Point**
>
> DMOs need to find out how locals want to benefit from tourism.

SUMMING UP

Locals matter! This is the main message you should get from the third chapter. The quality of life and well-being of residents are two critical indicators that should be continuously assessed by DMOs. Another clear message in this chapter is that tourism can enhance the quality and life and well-being of local residents and conversely it can damage or diminish them—this is perhaps the greatest paradox of tourism. You have heard about the positives and negatives in this chapter, and they make it essential for destination management and DMOs to be listening to residents. You have learned about good and bad examples of tourism throughout the world and this shows that opportunities and issues with tourism are global, not just local.

Another highlight is the need for resident empowerment in tourism, or giving locals a greater say and power in destination management. Being fair and just with residents goes along with empowerment. While some DMO executives will shiver at this suggestion, it is inevitable that destination residents are playing and will want to play a greater role in tourism in the future (Ribeiro 2022). It is recommended that destination management and DMOs must consider residents when fulfilling all their roles. To overlook resident quality of life and well-being associated with any of the destination management roles will be a serious error.

Another important lesson delivered within this chapter is that destination resident well-being is better when they feel they have been consulted (in advance) and when their voices have been heard and acted upon. There are several examples in Chapter 3 in which the opinions and feelings of locals have been ignored. This causes stress for destination residents and a sense of detachment from the tourism sector. Again, it demonstrates the importance of listening to locals.

Just a cautionary note is needed here and that is that not all residents are alike. People often see things differently and that is the case with sentiment and attitudes toward tourism. Also, some residents are permanent and others may be temporary, and their perspectives can differ. DMOs need to be acutely aware of this and not use one-size-fits-all strategies. Also, not all destinations are alike and, in fact, there is a huge diversity of places across the world—what works in one place may not be successful in another location.

Delivering the good—and even better—life for all should be a motto for DMOs. All means here every stakeholder including the destination residents. In Chapters 4 to 12, you will see how DMOs can deliver on that promise.

KEYWORDS

8 + 1 dimensions
carrying capacity
co-creation
community
degrowth
demarketing
e-government
empowerment
engagement
flow
gentrification
governance
gross national happiness
   index

happiness
happiness pie
informal economy
involvement
livability
open government
overtourism
new public (sector)
   management
participative
perceived justice
PERMA
place attachment
positive psychology

quality of life
resident
resident sentiment
sense of place
shared ownership
sharing economy
standard of living
subjective well-being (SWB)
visioning
visitor management
well-being
wellness
WHOQOL

REVIEW QUESTIONS

1. How would you define quality of life in the context of destination residents?
2. What are the dimensions of quality of life?
3. How can quality of life be measured?
4. What is well-being and its components?
5. How should well-being be assessed?
6. Which aspects of tourism tend to irritate residents?
7. What is overtourism and how is it connected to carrying capacity?
8. How should resident sentiment toward tourism be measured?
9. What should destinations do to improve resident quality of life and well-being?

REFERENCES

Aleshinloye, K. D., Woosnam, K. M., Tasci, A. D. A., and Ramkissoon, H. (2022) "Antecedents and Outcomes of Resident Empowerment through Tourism," *Journal of Travel Research*, 61 (3): 656–673.

Andereck, K. A., and Nyaupane, G. P. (2011) "Exploring the Nature of Tourism and Quality of Life Perceptions among Residents," *Journal of Travel Research*, 50 (3): 248–260.

Andereck, K. L., Valentine, K. M., Vogt, C. A., and Knopf, R. C. (2007) "A Cross-cultural Analysis of Tourism and Quality of Life Perceptions," *Journal of Sustainable Tourism*, 15: 483–502.

Andriotis, K. (2021) "Introduction," in K. Andriotis (ed.), *Issues and Cases of Degrowth in Tourism*, Wallingford: CAB International, pp. 1–19.

Attractions Victoria (2022) "Discounts for Locals at Victoria's Finest Attractions," *Be a Tourist*, https://beatourist.ca

Bartholomaeus, J. D., Iasiello, M. P., Jarden, A., Burke, K. J., and van Agteren, J. (2020) "Evaluating the Psychometric Properties of the PERMA Profiler," *Journal of Well-being Assessment*, 4: 163–180.

BBC (2018) "Philippines to Temporarily Close Popular Tourist Island Boracay," www.bbc.com/news/world-asia-43650627

——— (2019) "Thailand: Tropical Bay from 'The Beach' to Close until 2021," www.bbc.com/news/world-asia-48222627

Berbekova, A., Uysal, M., and Assaf, A. G. (2022) "Toward an Assessment of Quality of Life Indicators as Measures of Destination Performance," *Journal of Travel Research*, 61 (6): 1424–1436.

Bhutia, P. D. (2022) "Mauritius Pitches Digital Nomads to Reach Goal of 1 Million Tourists in 2022," *Skift*, March 29, https://skift.com/2022/03/29/mauritius-pitches-digital-nomads-to-reach-goal-of-1-million-tourists-in-2022

Biagi, B., Ladu, M. G., Meleddu, M., and Royuela, V. (2020) "Tourism and the City: The Impact on Residents' Quality of Life," *International Journal of Tourism Research*, 22: 168–181.

Bordeaux Tourism and Congress (2022) "In the Eyes of Residents," https://agora-tourism-bordeaux.com/residents

Borghese, L., Buckley, J., and O'Hare, M. (2022) "Venice Reveals Details of Its €10 Tourist Entry Fee," *CNN Travel*, July 2, https://edition.cnn.com/travel/article/venice-entrance-fee-launch-date/index.html

Bretlaender, D., and Toth, P. (2014) "Kwanini Carrying Capacity Assessment," http://kwaninifoundation.org/wp-content/uploads/2018/10/Kwanini-Carrying-Capacity-Assessment-Study.pdf

Brown, N. J. L., and Rohrer, J. M. (2020) "Easy as (Happiness) Pie? A Critical Evaluation of a Popular Model of the Determinants of Well-being," *Journal of Happiness Studies*, 21: 1285–1301.

Buckley, J. (2019) "The Tourists Nobody Wants," *CNN Travel*, November 9, https://edition.cnn.com/travel/article/unwanted-tourist-types-overtourism/index.html

Buckley, J. (2020) "Venice Sees a New Future for Tourism Post-pandemic," *Condé Nast Traveler*, www.cntraveler.com/story/venice-sees-a-new-future-for-tourism-post-pandemic

Butler, J., and Kern, M. L. (2016) "The PERMA-Profiler: A Brief Multidimensional Measure of Flourishing," *International Journal of Well-being*, 6 (3): 1–48.

Butler, R. W. (2020) "Overtourism in Rural Areas," in H. Séraphin, T. Gladkikh, and T. Vo Thanh (eds), *Overtourism: Causes, Implications and Solutions*, Basingstoke: Palgrave Macmillan, pp. 27–43.

Çakmak, E., Lie, R., and McCabe, S. (2018) "Reframing Informal Tourism Entrepreneurial Practices: Capital and Field Relations Structuring the Informal Tourism Economy of Chiang Mai," *Annals of Tourism Research*, 72: 37–47.

Chase, L. C., Amsden, B., and Phillips, R. G. (2012) "Stakeholder Engagement in Tourism Planning and Development," in M. Uysal, R. Perdue, and M. Sirgy (eds), *Handbook of Tourism and Quality-of-Life Research*, Dordrecht: Springer, pp. 475–490.

Chauma, E. C., and Ngwira, C. (2022) "Managing a World Heritage Site in Malawi: Do Residents' Sentiments Matter?" *Journal of Heritage Tourism*, 17 (2): 142–157.

Chen, N. C., and Dwyer, L. (2018) "Residents Place Satisfaction and Place Attachment on Destination Brand-Building Behaviors: Conceptual and Empirical Differentiation," *Journal of Travel Research*, 57 (8): 1026–1041.

Chen, N., Hsu, C. H. C., and Li, X. R. (2021) "Resident Sentiment toward a Dominant Tourist Market: Scale Development and Validation," *Journal of Travel Research*, 60 (7): 1408–1425.

City of Melbourne (2022) "Warm Welcome as 'Red Coat' City Ambassadors Return," May 9, www.melbourne.vic.gov.au/news-and-media/Pages/Warm-welcome-as-%E2%80%98red-coat%E2%80%99-city-ambassadors-return.aspx

Davis, T. (2019) "What Is Well-being? Definition, Types, and Well-being Skills," *Psychology Today*, www.psychologytoday.com/gb/blog/click-here-happiness/201901/what-is-well-being-definition-types-and-well-being-skills

Degrowth (2022) "What is degrowth?" https://degrowth.info/en/degrowth-definition

Destinations International and Longwoods International (2022a) "2021 American Resident Sentiment Survey," https://longwoods-intl.com/resident-sentiment-research

———— (2022b) "Canadian Resident Sentiment towards Tourism: Highlights from the 2021 Canadian Resident Sentiment Study," https://longwoods-intl.com/resident-sentiment-research

Diener, E. (1984) "Subjective Well-being," *Psychological Bulletin*, 95 (3): 542–575.

Diener, E., Suh, E. M., Lucas, R. E., and Smith, H. L. (1999) "Subjective Well-being: Three Decades of Progress," *Psychological Bulletin*, 125 (2): 276–302.

Dodds, R., and Butler, R. (2019) "The Phenomena of Overtourism: A Review," *International Journal of Tourism Cities*, 5 (4): 519–528.

Economist Intelligence Unit (2022) "The Global Liveability Index 2022," www.eiu.com/n/campaigns/global-liveability-index-2022

Eurostat (2022) "Why Should Quality of Life Be Measured?," https://ec.europa.eu/eurostat/web/quality-of-life/data

Garg, A. (2022) "Ecotourism in Costa Rica: What You Should Know," *Tico Times*, July 3, https://ticotimes.net/2022/07/03/ecotourism-in-costa-rica-what-you-should-know

Gautam, V. (2022) "Why local residents support sustainable tourism development?," *Journal of Sustainable Tourism*, DOI: 10.1080/09669582.2022.2082449

Goodman, F. R., Disabato, D. J., Kashdan, T. B., and Kauffman, S. B. (2018) "Measuring Well-being: A Comparison of Subjective Well-being and PERMA," *Journal of Positive Psychology*, 13 (4): 321–332.

Goodwin, H. (2016) "What Is Overtourism?" Responsible Tourism Partnership, https://responsible-tourismpartnership.org/overtourism

Government of Northwest Territories (2022) "Resident Readiness Strategy," www.iti.gov.nt.ca/sites/iti/files/Resident_Readiness_Strategy_March_2022.pdf

Hall, P. (1987) "Urban Development and the Future of Tourism," *Tourism Management*, 8 (2): 129–130.

Hartwell, H., Fyall, A., Willis, C., Page, S., Ladkin, A., and Hemingway, A. (2018) "Progress in Tourism and Destination Well-being Research," *Current Issues in Tourism*, 21 (16): 1830–1892.

Hawaii Tourism Authority (2021) "Hawaii Tourism Authority (HTA) Resident Sentiment Survey 2021 Highlights," www.hawaiitourismauthority.org/media/7436/hta-resident-sentiment-spring-2021-board-presentation-062421-final.pdf

Hu, R., Li, G., Liu, A., and Chen, J. L. (2022) "Emerging Research Trends on Residents' Quality of Life in the Context of Tourism Development," *Journal of Hospitality and Tourism Research*, https://doi.org/10.1177/10963480221081382

IGI Global (2022) "What Is Electronic Government (E-government)?," www.igi-global.com/dictionary/investigating-enterprise-application-integration-adoption/9385#:~:text=E-Government

Johanson, M. (2022) "The Digital Nomad Visas Luring Workers Overseas," *BBC Worklife*, July 11, www.bbc.com/worklife/article/20220707-the-digital-nomad-visas-luring-workers-overseas

Johnson, A. (1986) "Human Arrangements," Orlando, Fla.: Harcourt Brace Jovanovich.

Jordan, E. J., Vogt, C. A., and DeShon, R. P. (2015) "A Stress and Coping Framework for Understanding Resident Responses to Tourism Development," *Tourism Management*, 48: 500–512.

Kim, K., Uysal, M., and Sirgy, J. (2013) "How Does Tourism in a Community Impact the Quality of Life of Community Residents?" *Tourism Management*, 36: 527–540.

Longwoods International (2022) "Resident Sentiment Research," https://longwoods-intl.com/resident-sentiment-research

Lyubomirsky, S., Sheldon K. M., and Schkade, D. (2005) "Pursuing Happiness: The Architecture of Sustainable Change," *Review of General Psychology*, 9 (2): 111–131.

Mach, L., Connors, J., Lechtman, B., Plante, S., and Uerling, C. (2022) "Party Tourism Impacts on Local Stakeholders," *Anatolia*, 33 (2): 222–235.

Mack, C. (2022) "Irresponsible Tourism: When It's Just Wrong," *Responsible Travel*, www.responsibletravel.com/holidays/responsible-tourism/travel-guide/irresponsible-tourism

Malta Independent (2022) "Tourism Operators Must Ensure They Do Not Negatively Impact Residential Communities—ADPD," June 19, www.independent.com.mt/articles/2022-06-19/local-news/Tourism-operators-must-ensure-they-do-not-negatively-impact-residential-communities-ADPD-6736243843

Marcus, L. (2019) "Popular Medieval Belgian Town Bruges Makes Moves to Restrict Tourism," *CNN*, www.cnn.com/travel/article/bruges-belgium-overtourism-cruise-ship-restrictions/index.html

Mercer LLC (2022) "Quality of Living City Ranking," https://mobilityexchange.mercer.com/Insights/quality-of-living-rankings

Mihalic, T., and Kuščer, K. (2022) "Can Overtourism Be Managed? Destination Management Factors Affecting Residents' Irritation and Quality of Life," *Tourism Review*, 77 (1): 16–34.

Milano, C., Novelli, M., and Cheer, J. M. (2019) "Overtourism and Tourismphobia: A Journey through Four Decades of Tourism Development, Planning and Local Concerns," *Tourism Planning and Development*, 16 (4): 353–357.

Molz, J. G. (2020) "Will COVID-19 Bring an End to Overtourism?" *World Politics Review*, www.worldpoliticsreview.com/articles/28947/will-covid-19-bring-an-end-to-overtourism

Namberger, P., Jackisch, S., Schmude, J., and Karl, M. (2019) "Overcrowding, Overtourism and Local Level Disturbance: How Much Can Munich Handle?" *Tourism Planning and Development*, 16(4), 452–472.

National Wellness Institute (2022) "The Six Dimensions of Wellness," https://nationalwellness.org/resources/six-dimensions-of-wellness/

Navarro-Ruiz, S., Casado-Díaz, A.B. and Ivars-Baidal, J. (2020) "Cruise tourism: the role of shore excursions in the overcrowding of cities," *International Journal of Tourism Cities*, 6(1), 197–214.

Nguyen, T. (2022) "Mexico City and the Pitfalls of Becoming a Remote Work Destination," *Vox*, March 30, www.vox.com/the-goods/22999722/mexico-city-pandemic-remote-work-gentrification

Open Education Sociology Dictionary (2022) "Carrying Capacity," https://sociologydictionary.org/carrying-capacity/

Oxford Poverty and Human Development Initiative (2022) "Bhutan's Gross National Happiness Index," https://ophi.org.uk/policy/gross-national-happiness-index/

PBS (2022) "What Is Gentrification," http://archive.pov.org/flagwars/what-is-gentrification

Peterson, R. R. (2020) "Over the Caribbean Top: Community Well-being and Over-Tourism in Small Island Tourism Economies," *International Journal of Community Well-Being*, https://doi.org/10.1007/s42413-020-00094-3

Pinke-Sziva, I., Smith, M., Olt, G., and Berezvai, Z. (2019) "Overtourism and the Night-time Economy: A Case Study of Budapest," *International Journal of Tourism Cities*, 5 (1): 1–16.

Pratt, S., McCabe, S., and Movono, A. (2016) "Gross Happiness of a 'Tourism' Village in Fiji," *Journal of Destination Marketing and Management*, 5: 26–35.

Reynolds, I. (2022) "Once Overcrowded Kyoto Now Longs for Foreign Tourists in Japan," Bloomberg, July 6, www.bloomberg.com/news/articles/2022-07-05/once-overcrowded-kyoto-now-longs-for-foreign-tourists-in-japan

Ribeiro, M. (2022) "Communities Move Beyond Spectator Role in Travel's Future," April 28, https://nezasa.com/blog/communities-travel-future/

Robinson-Johnson, E. (2022) "Survey Shows Jackson Residents' Disdain for Tourists," Pinedale Roundup, June 22, https://pinedaleroundup.com/article/survey-shows-jackson-residents-disdain-for-tourists

Rozmiarek, M., Malchrowicz-Mośko, E., and Kazimierczak, M. (2022) "Overtourism and the Impact of Tourist Traffic on the Daily Life of City Residents: A Case Study of Poznan," *Journal of Tourism and Cultural Change*, 20 (5): 718–734.

Saraogi, V. (2019) "Not Just Venice: Six Countries Which Have Banned Cruise Ships," *Ship Technology*, www.ship-technology.com/features/cities-who-banned-cruise-ships/

Scannell, L., and Gifford, R. (2010) "Defining Place Attachment: A Tripartite Organizing Framework," *Journal of Environmental Psychology*, 30: 1–10.

——— (2017) "The Experienced Psychological Benefits of Place Attachment," *Journal of Environmental Psychology*, 51: 256–269.

Scholtz, M., and Saayman, M. (2018) "Diving into the Consequences of Stakeholders Unheard," *European Journal of Tourism Research*, 20: 105–124.

Seligman, M. (2018) "PERMA and the Building Blocks of Well-Being," *Journal of Positive Psychology*, 13 (4): 333–335.

Seligman, M. E. P. (2011) *Flourish: A New Understanding of Happiness and Well-Being—and How to Achieve Them*, London: Nicholas Brealey.

Séraphin, H., Gladkikh, T., and Vo Thanh, T. (2020) *Overtourism Causes, Implications and Solutions*, New York: Palgrave.

Shelton, M. (2022) "Danville City and Pittsylvania County Ask Residents to Fill out Tourism Survey," Gray Media Group, June 24, www.wdbj7.com/2022/06/23/new-danville-city-pittsylvania-county-tourism-survey/

Strzelecka, M., Boley, B. B., and Woosnam, K. M. (2017) "Place Attachment and Empowerment: Do Residents Need to Be Attached to Be Empowered?" *Annals of Tourism Research*, 66: 61–73.

Su, L., Yang, X., and Swanson, S. R. (2022) "The Impact of Spatial-Temporal Variation on Tourist Destination Resident Quality of Life," *Tourism Management*, 93: 104572.

Sustainable Development Solutions Network (2022) "The World Happiness Report," https://world-happiness.report/ed/2022/

Sustainable Travel International (2022) "St Kitts Destination Guardians," https://sustainabletravel.org/destination/st-kitts/

TCI Research (2022) "The Global Standard for Measuring Residents' Sentiment Towards Tourism," https://tci-research.com/travelsat/travelsat-resident-sentiment-index/

TCI Research/Wonderful Copenhagen (2019) "Resident Sentiment Index: Are Copenhagen Residents Tourism-Supportive? 2018," www.10xcopenhagen.com/wp-content/uploads/2018/12/Resident-Sentiment-Index-2018.pdf

The Travel Foundation (2022) "Case Study: Involving Communities in Tourism Development (Makarska Riviera in Croatia)," www.thetravelfoundation.org.uk/casestudy/involving-communities-in-tourism-development/

Tourism Council of Bhutan (2022) "Bhutan Will Reopen Borders in September with Renewed Focus on Sustainability," June 29,

Tourism Sentiment Index (2022) "Essential Data for Your Destination: Real-Time Sentiment Analysis," www.sentiment-index.com/

United Cities and Local Governments (2018) "Open Governments," https://opengov.uclg.org/en/open-government

United Nations World Tourism Organization (2018) "'Overtourism'? Understanding and Managing Urban Tourism Growth Beyond Perceptions—Executive Summary," www.e-unwto.org/doi/pdf/10.18111/9789284420070

United Nations World Tourism Organization and Ipsos (2019) "Global Survey on the Perception of Residents Towards City Tourism: Impact and Measures," https://webunwto.s3-eu-west-1.amazonaws.com/imported_images/52027/unwtoispsosglobalsurveysummary.pdf

Uysal, M., Sirgy, J., Woo, E., and Kim, H. L. (2016) "Quality of Life (QOL) and Well-being Research in Tourism," *Tourism Management*, 53: 244–261.

Wang, S., Berbekova, A., and Uysal, M. (2022) "Pursuing Justice and Quality of Life: Supporting Tourism," *Tourism Management*, 89: 104446.

Weiermair, K., and Peters, M. (2012) "Quality-of-Life Values Among Stakeholders in Tourism Destinations: A Tale of Converging and Diverging Interests and Conflicts," in M. Uysal, R. Perdue, and M. Sirgy (eds), *Handbook of Tourism and Quality-of-Life Research*, Dordrecht: Springer, pp. 463–473.

Wheatley, M. J. (2022) "The Power of Community Quotes," www.ellevatenetwork.com/articles/8538-quotes-about-the-power-of-community

Wonderful Copenhagen (2017) "The End of Tourism as We Know It," http://localhood.wonderful-copenhagen.dk/

Woo, E., Kim, H., and Uysal, M. (2015) "Life Satisfaction and Support for Tourism Development," *Tourism Management*, 50: 84–97.

World Health Organization (2022) Tools and toolkits/WHOQOL/WHOQOL-BREF, www.who.int/tools/whoqol/whoqol-bref

Wright, E. (2022) "'Residents Concerned about Impact of Short-Term Holiday Lets' Says Hastings and Rye MP," *Sussex Express*, July 1, www.sussexexpress.co.uk/news/people/residents-concerned-about-impact-of-short-term-holiday-lets-says-hastings-and-rye-mp-3753096

Xunta de Galicia (2022) "Praia das Catedrais: Reserva de visita," https://ascatedrais.xunta.gal/monatr/iniciarReserva

Destination Management Roles

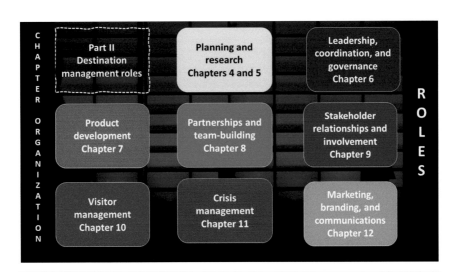

Chapter **4**

Destination Planning

The process is the plan!

LEARNING OBJECTIVES

Having read this chapter, you should be able to:

1. describe the history and influences on planning for destinations;
2. explain the benefits that come from doing long-term tourism destination planning;
3. detail the desired outcomes from completing a tourism destination plan;
4. identify the contents of a tourism destination plan;
5. elaborate on the different geographic levels for tourism destination planning;
6. explain the tourism planning process for destinations;
7. differentiate between strategic planning and visioning;
8. provide a step-by-step explanation of destination visioning;
9. pinpoint the advantages of using tourism destination planning toolkits;
10. explain the DMO roles in tourism destination planning.

DOI: 10.4324/9781003343356-6

Warming Up

In Chapters 2 and 3, you learned about sustainable development, social responsibility, and the quality of life and well-being of destination residents. Now, it is time to take a more detailed look at the roles of destination management and DMOs. The logical place to start is with destination planning (Chapter 4) and destination management research (Chapter 5).

You need to know about tourism destination planning and understand its importance. Every destination should have a long-term direction for tourism, a shared path for all stakeholders to follow for the next five, ten, or more years. Long-term (strategic) planning is the name most given to the process used to create this multi-year track to the future. The process used in tourism destination planning is crucial and particularly the people and organizations that are involved and how it is conducted—that is why our motto for this chapter is "the process is the plan."

Tourism destination planning is not a new subject, and it dates back about sixty years in the English-speaking world. So, the value and necessity of long-term planning for destinations has been accepted for many decades. However, planning for tourism is gaining even more attention as DMOs expand their roles beyond just marketing, branding, and communications, and there is greater priority being given to sustainable tourism. The COVID-19 pandemic also stimulated more planning as destinations needed to plot paths to tourism recovery.

Unfortunately, there is no standard template for conducting tourism destination planning, and practices vary from country to country, and even within countries. However, this chapter describes some common planning processes and techniques. You will get a good idea of what is involved. Planning and research is one of the roles of destination management, and it is here that a DMO starts to apply its leadership and coordinative role. If no long-term tourism destination plan exists, the DMO should take the initiative to get a planning process started. It is never too late to start planning.

Your author is an experienced tourism planner and will guide you carefully through this chapter based on his professional experiences in many countries from Canada to Vietnam. You already learned about the five-year Tourism Sustainability Plan for Sedona, Arizona, in Chapter 2 and can take a look back at that for your reference.

Before describing how a long-term direction for a destination is determined, you need to be familiar with some of the basic characteristics of tourism destination planning.

Characteristics of Tourism Destination Planning

So, now you are going to hear about the history and influences, benefits, time frames, naming, outcomes, contents, case studies, and levels of tourism destination planning.

History and Influences

Tourism destination planning as a professional activity began many years ago. It got started in countries like Ireland and France, where there was a strong belief in community long-term planning and especially in a regional context where rural areas were losing population. These earliest tourism destination plans were done by government agencies and prepared by professionals with a background in physical planning for regions and urban areas rather than tourism (Fig. 4.1). There was an emphasis on destinations' physical resources in the earliest tourism plans. Planning, in these cases, always commenced with an analysis of tourism supply and not the demand from visitors.

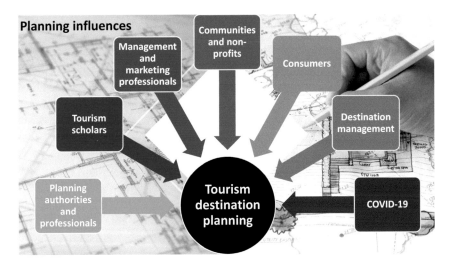

Figure 4.1 Influences on tourism destination planning.

The next influence on tourism planning was from tourism academics and professional experts. These people were mainly geographers and economists with a special interest in tourism. They included Professor Clare A. Gunn, who published the book *Tourism Planning* in 1979, and it was a watershed text for the topic (Gunn 1979). Edward Inskeep, who was a tourism planning expert with the UNWTO, made a significant contribution with his books on national and regional tourism planning (Inskeep 1991). Another important contribution was from Professor Bihu Wu in his book *Regional Tourism Planning Principles* published in 2001 and covering the tourism planning experiences in China (Wu 2001). With this influence came a greater emphasis on tourism policy and on visitor activities and flows; however, the priority remained focused on the physical resources of destinations.

Management professionals greatly influenced tourism planning, drawing especially from the fields of corporate strategic management and strategic planning. From the classic texts on strategic management, such as that from Rothaermel (2021), came the concept of SWOT (strengths, weaknesses, opportunities, threats) analysis and terms such as mission, vision, core values and guiding principles, goals, strategies, and critical success factors (CSFs). The focus was on defining a step-by-step process and emphasizing that strategic planning was a cycle to be repeated many times. Here also there was a priority on researching, analyzing and projecting external environments with the procedure of environmental scanning. This influence brought a more corporate mindset to tourism destination planning.

DEFINITION

Strategic planning

A long-term planning process typically based on an assessment of the strengths and weakness of a destination and its future prospects. The process produces goals for tourism and initiatives to achieve these goals.

More people with business management backgrounds and MBA-style educations began working for DMOs as a trend began toward PPPs and away from just public-sector governance. Marketing, public relations and sales professionals added their distinct imprints on tourism destination planning, especially in putting more emphasis on market and competitive analysis rather than just analyzing the destination's physical resources. Their influence produced more emphasis on destination marketing and the branding of destinations.

The fourth influence on tourism planning was from community planners and NPOs. Here, the focus was on the planning process and on how to get all parts of communities involved in discussing and defining future directions (you heard about this in Chapter 3). Inclusiveness and getting buy-in from all stakeholders were key features of these planning processes. The visioning process was derived from this source as an interactive planning tool that allowed many people to contribute to strategic planning. In developing countries, NGOs often play a key role in tourism planning processes. This influence meant a more active role in tourism planning for destination residents as individuals or as groups. The sustainable tourism movement, which began around the early 1980s, also highlighted the critical need to have resident and community inputs. The CBT concept got going in developing nations.

EXAMPLE 4.1

Target Market for Destination Plan Papua New Guinea

This is an example of destination planning that involved an NGO (The World Wide Fund for Nature—WWF). It was very specific about the intended target market and also who was not to be attracted to this part of the Coral Triangle.

> The target market for the project is the Nature and Adventure Travelers market. This is a psychographic market, and is broadly based on the Global Experience Seeker market identified by Tourism Australia. It prioritizes consumer personality traits, values, attitudes, interests and lifestyles rather than simple demographic data, such as age, gender or family situation. They are the most relevant market for the Coral Triangle Sustainable Nature-based Tourism Project.
>
> The Nature and Adventure Travelers market is growing and is highly interested in nature and cultural-based tourism. It is a niche, high-yield market, which suits the type of destinations included in the project while also being sympathetic to high-conservation value areas. It is important to remember these sites will not appeal to mass markets, such as the large cruise-ship market.
> (Coral Triangle Sustainable Nature-based Tourism Project, undated)

Learning Point

NGOs can be a great resource in developing destination plans and can provide guidance on the sustainable development of tourism.

Consumers are having a more significant influence on tourism destination planning in recent years, and they continue to do so. For example, their demands for greater transparency by governments and others have led to tourism destination plans becoming publicly available documents rather than being in the hands of only select people. Consumer use of the Internet and affection for using social media brought more open discussion of tourism destination planning processes and planning documents. Additionally, tourists' opinions, perceptions and expectations gathered through primary research are more valued as crucial inputs to tourism plans.

Another influence on tourism planning is from the effect of the destination management concept and its adoption in many places around the world. Destination management plans are now becoming more common.

EXAMPLE 4.2

What Is a Destination Management Plan? (VB/VE)

This example from England includes definitions of destination management and destination management plan (DMP).

> Destination management is a process of leading, influencing and coordinating the management of all the aspects of a destination that contribute to a visitor's experience, taking account of the needs of visitors, local residents, businesses and the environment. A destination management plan (DMP) is a shared statement of intent to manage a destination over a stated period of time, articulating the roles of the different stakeholders and identifying clear actions that they will take and the apportionment of resources.
>
> (VisitBritain/VisitEngland 2018)

Learning Point

DMOs should prepare plans for destination management.

Finally, the COVID-19 pandemic had a major impact on tourism destination planning. It could be said that it made most pre-existing plans invalid as the assumptions on which they were designed were no longer accurate. Also, during 2019–2022, COVID introduced great uncertainty about the future of tourism, making planning ahead more difficult. As you will see later, tourism recovery plans began to appear and planning time frames were shortened. In future, planners will have to contemplate that crises such as the pandemic may happen again.

So, tourism destination planning has evolved over the past sixty years. It is much more comprehensive and integrated than when it was first introduced in the 1960s. Tourism planning is more inclusive than before, with all stakeholders getting the opportunity to have their say on how tourism should look in the future.

Benefits

There is no doubt that every destination needs long-term tourism planning, yet not all of them have long-term plans for tourism. Essential as they might be, the DMO may be required to justify spending time and money on a long-term tourism destination planning process. Therefore, the DMO must be able to clearly articulate the benefits of long-term planning for tourism. Figure 4.2 identifies some of the key benefits of long-term planning, and then a description follows.

- Clear future directions: Long-term tourism planning produces clear overall directions for all stakeholders on how tourism will be developed and progressed in future years.
- Greater attention and emphasis for tourism: Initiating and conducting long-term planning tends to draw greater attention and focus to tourism within the destination.
- Vision and goals for tourism: Targets are set for the destination to achieve within specific time frames.
- Identification of opportunities: Specific strategies and development opportunities are identified that will enhance and improve tourism in the destination.
- Shared plan ownership: If the planning process is done openly with the involvement and contributions of all stakeholders, there will be a feeling of shared ownership in the plan.
- Implementation and evaluation guidelines: The planning process produces steps for implementation and measures for assessing the effectiveness of the plan.

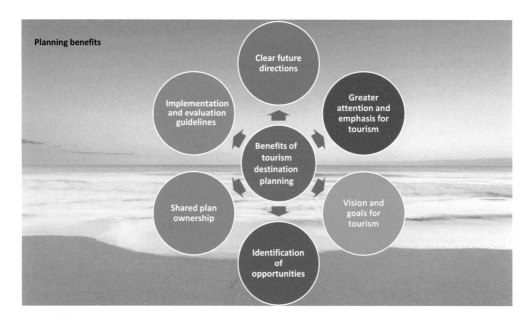

Figure 4.2 Benefits of preparing long-term plans for tourism destinations.

EXAMPLE 4.3

Goals for Tourism in Jordan

This example includes the five-year goals for tourism in Jordan.

The following KPIs were set as the goals to achieve within the Tourism Strategy 2021–2025:

- The number of tourists to return to 2019 levels by 2024

- Total receipts to recover to 2019 levels by 2023
- Direct employment in tourism to surpass 2019 figures by 2023.
(Ministry of Tourism and Antiquities [Jordan] 2021: 9)

Learning Point

It is essential that DMOs set specific medium-term goals for tourism.

Despite the many obvious benefits of long-term planning of tourism, there are many destinations that have not initiated tourism planning. Why? Probably the most important reason for this inaction is that the destinations are not attaching a high priority to tourism as an economic sector. Additionally, in some places there is a belief that the private sector can handle its own planning and there is no need for others to get involved. A third argument against doing long-term planning is that it takes too much time and costs too much money; tourism is dynamic and changing too rapidly, and often, it is assumed. A fourth reason may simply be in the perceived complexity of tourism destination planning with so many government agencies, private-sector and NPOs, and individuals involved.

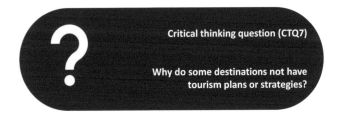

Critical thinking question (CTQ7)

Why do some destinations not have tourism plans or strategies?

Time Frames

A strategic planning process is an approach used to develop a long-term plan for a tourism destination. What then is the "long term"? In destination management practice, there is no clear agreement on how long a period a tourism plan should cover. Looking at the tourism plans and strategies that have been published over the past five to seven years, the range for long term is from up to twenty years. For example, the Malawi National Tourism Investment Master Plan has a time frame from 2022 to 2042 (Malawi Travel 2022). The Phillip Island and San Remo Visitor Economy Strategy in Australia stretches to 2035 (Destination Phillip Island 2016). These very long-term plans usually articulate a vision for tourism in the destination, such as the Mondulkiri Tourism Development Master Plan in Cambodia that envisioned the region becoming an international ecotourism destination by 2035 (Sivutha 2022).

Some tourism plans have shorter time frames than the ones for Australia, Cambodia, and Malawi. Ten-year tourism plans and strategies include the Sustainable Tourism Strategy for Spain (2020–2030) (Secretaría de Estado de Turismo (Spain) 2019), Lake Placid and North Elba Destination Management Plan 2030 in the USA (ROOST 2022), and the Sustainable Tourism Master Plan 2015–2025 for Ethiopia (Federal Democratic Republic of Ethiopia 2014). However, the trend now seems to be for shorter-duration plans of three to five years. Examples here are the Strategic Framework for Tourism in BC (2022–2024, British Columbia, Canada) (British Columbia Government 2022), the National Tourism Plan 2018–2022 from Brazil

(Organisation for Economic Co-operation and Development [OECD] 2020), and the five-year Killarney Destination and Experience Development Plan in Ireland (Fáilte Ireland 2022).

EXAMPLE 4.4

A Strategic Road Map for Lake Placid and North Elba

This is an example of a DMP from New York state, USA.

> The Lake Placid and North Elba Destination Management Plan is a strategic road map for the next 5–10 years that balances the needs of local residents, community organizations, and area businesses more effectively. Its primary aim is to establish high-level priorities, intended outcomes, and implementation strategies for the community, versus trying to solve all things for all people at a granular level.
>
> (ROOST 2022: 4)

Learning Point

DMPs should consider the needs of all stakeholders.

If tourism plans are prepared for five years or less, they are often called action plans and generally are for the next one to four years. For example, Simcoe County in Ontario, Canada was developing a Tourism Destination Development Action Plan in mid-2022 (County of Simcoe 2022). Action plans are either included within the longer-term plans or they are initiated due to previously unforeseen challenges and difficulties within the destination (such as COVID-19).

You should also know that some strategies and plans have no definite time horizons, although this is not generally considered to be very good professional practice. However, there are situations when such plans (or policies) are needed in emergency or critical situations as was the case in 2019–2022 with COVID-19. During that time period, several tourism recovery plans were developed. The UK government, for example, in June 2021 released the Tourism Recovery Plan (Department of Digital, Culture, Media and Sport 2021); the South African government issued the Tourism Sector Recovery Plan: COVID Response (Department of Tourism (South Africa) 2021); and Tourism Malaysia produced the Tourism Recovery Plan 2022 in Malaysia (Ignatius 2022).

Also, as you will find out later, DMOs develop their own operational plans and strategies that are more internally oriented and not comprehensive, destination-wide plans. These are organizational plans and strategies. For example, the Hawaii Tourism Authority (HTA) produced its Strategic Plan 2020–2025 (HTA 2020).

EXAMPLE 4.5

A Shift in Emphasis for the Hawaii Tourism Authority

Hawaii is switching its emphasis more toward enhancing resident quality of life, as stated in this example.

> What remains unchanged is HTA's mission: "To strategically manage Hawai'i tourism in a sustainable manner consistent with economic goals, cultural

values, preservation of natural resources, community desires, and visitor industry needs." This plan represents our recommitment to that mission and, significantly, shifts more emphasis to address tourism's impacts. This shift recognizes
the need for tourism to provide both a quality visitor experience and enhanced
quality of life for Hawaii's residents, which, taken together, are the necessary
ingredients for long-term success.

(HTA 2020)

Learning Point

In setting goals and objectives for tourism, DMOs should consider including the quality of life of local residents.

While the James Webb Space Telescope is helping scientists look deeper into space with
greater accuracy, the future of tourism is becoming murkier as a result of COVID-19, the war
in Europe, and other global issues. It is likely therefore that the time frames for tourism destination planning will be shorter in the years to come.

Naming

What name should be given to the tourism destination plan? That is a good question, but there
is no consistency in naming practices around the world. You can already see this from the titles
of the strategies and plans previously mentioned. The words "master plan," "plan," "strategy,"
"framework," "blueprint," and "road map" get used interchangeably. This is no doubt confusing to anybody unfamiliar with tourism destination planning, and there is a definite need for
more standardized terminology across the world.

To provide some guidelines in naming, the following three groupings of tourism plans can be
used:

1. Tourism plan or tourism master plan: A long-term plan for ten or more years.
2. Tourism strategy: A medium-term plan for five to nine years.
3. Tourism action plan: A short-term plan for two to four years.

Some tourism strategies and plans are not even titled that way but are given catchier names to
draw greater attention as well as to communicate their main themes. For example, Austria's
tourism master plan was simply called Plan T (Ministry of Sustainability and Tourism 2019).

Tying in with the theme in Chapter 2, you sharp eyes will have noticed that the label of "sustainable" is being added to the names of these plans. The Sedona Tourism Sustainability Plan
was mentioned in Chapter 2, and this chapter has cited the Sustainable Tourism Strategy for
Spain and the Sustainable Tourism Master Plan for Ethiopia.

There is a difference between planning for the destination and planning for the DMO. In
Chapter 4, the topic is planning for the destination, and planning for the DMO is discussed in
Chapters 5–12 where you learn how DMOs do planning for each of their roles. This chapter
is about the DMO jointly planning for the overall future of the destination along with all the
other tourism stakeholders.

DMOs must also prepare other plans that are more closely related to their roles and operations. For example, DMOs often produce annual corporate plans or business plans that are operating guides for the upcoming year. There may also be a community relationships and involvement plan prepared by the DMO (Chapter 9), a crisis management plan (Chapter 12), and of course, a marketing plan will be required (Chapter 10). In addition, the DMO should prepare its organization strategic plan.

Before moving on, it is important to clear up for you some potential confusion in the use of the words "strategic," "strategy," "strategies," and "strategic planning" because they have multiple meanings in tourism destination planning and practitioners tend to use them in different ways. Here is how they are used in this book:

- Strategic: This means long-term and thus planning for five or more years into the future.
- Strategy: "Tourism strategy" is used interchangeably with the term "tourism plan."
- Strategies: Selected overall programs of actions or initiatives contained in a tourism plan or strategy to achieve its stated goals.
- Strategic planning: A process emerging from the management literature that involves scanning the macro-environment (internal and external) and then defining mission, vision, core values and guiding principles, goals and strategies.

DEFINITION

Core values and guiding principles

The core values are the enduring qualities and standards that the stakeholders believe characterize the destination and that must be maintained in the future. Guiding principles govern the actions to be taken to achieve the destination's vision and long-term goals.

Outcomes

The DMO and its stakeholders must define the key goals for completing a tourism destination plan and state the desired outcomes of planning. Morrison et al. (2018) suggest that tourism planning should have at least five outcomes (Figures 4.3a and 4.3b):

1. Adapting to the unexpected: Designing contingency and crisis management plans to cope with unexpected situations.
2. Identifying alternative approaches: Pinpointing different options or scenarios for important aspects of tourism in the destination.
3. Maintaining uniqueness: Identifying the destination's unique assets and USPs (unique selling propositions) and steps to maintain and enhance them.
4. Creating the desirable: Following steps that increase the benefits of tourism.
5. Avoiding the undesirable: Anticipating potential negative impacts of tourism and taking steps to avoid them.

Adapting to the unexpected
- General economic conditions
- Energy supply and demand situation
- Values and lifestyles
- Performance of local industries
- Government legislation and regulations
- Technological advances

Identifying alternative approaches
- Marketing and branding
- Development
- Organization of tourism
- Community awareness of tourism
- Support services and activities
- Transportation and infrastructure

Maintaining uniqueness
- Local cultural and social fabric and traditions
- Local architecture and heritage
- Historical monuments and landmarks
- Local festivals, events, and activities
- Natural features and resources
- Parks and outdoor sports areas

(a)

Outcomes

Creating the desirable
- Sustainable tourism
- Climate neutrality
- High level of community awareness of the benefits of tourism
- Clear and positive image of area as a destination
- Effective organization of tourism
- High level of cooperation among tourism organizations and businesses
- Effective marketing, directional sign and travel information programs

Avoiding the undesirable
- Friction and unnecessary competition
- Hostile and unfriendly attitudes of residents towards visitors
- Damage or undesirable permanent alteration of natural features and historical resources
- Loss of cultural identities
- Loss of market share
- Stoppage of unique local events and festivals
- Overcrowding, congestion, and traffic problems
- Pollution
- High seasonality

Outcomes

(b)

Figure 4.3 The five desired outcomes of tourism destination planning.

Contents

It is important that a plan is built from a platform consisting of a clear set of long-term goals for tourism in the destination. An overall destination vision for the future needs to be articulated. A tourism destination master plan should identify the actions, roles and responsibilities, time frames, budgets, monitoring and evaluation criteria for various aspects of tourism in a destination (transportation, accommodation, activities, product development, tourism zoning, marketing, branding, and communications, institutional structures, statistics and research, legislation and regulations, and quality standards). Figure 4.4 combines the 10 As model from Chapter 1 with these aspects to produce a more detailed set of recommended topics for tourism destination plan contents.

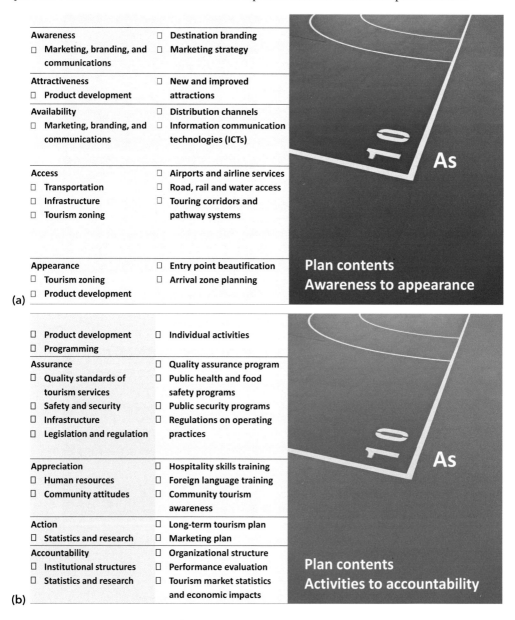

Figure 4.4 10A content areas of a tourism destination plan (awareness to appearance) and 10A content areas of a tourism destination plan (activities to accountability).

Case Studies

Now, you know what should be included in long-term tourism plans, but what in actual practice appears in completed plans? To make sure that you know what is "happening on the ground," a few examples from recently completed tourism plans for destinations are now reviewed. In truth, tourism strategies and plans come in all sizes and shapes, but the following information will give you a better feel for what they contain.

The first case study should tell you that tourism destination plans do not need to be complicated and span hundreds of pages. In fact, planning documents that are heavy to lift are hard to action and not as easily implemented. Plan T Master Plan for Tourism for Austria is just forty-four pages long (in contrast the National Tourism Development Plan for Ghana covered 362 pages). Plan T produced three clear objectives comprised on nine sub-objectives:

1. strengthening the awareness of tourism;
2. establishing a cooperation culture;
3. using digital potential;
4. designing an attractive business environment;
5. making training and labor market fit for the future;
6. keeping our livelihood sustainable;
7. creating a regional value-added for everybody;
8. further developing tourism marketing;
9. making financing and promotion more flexible.

(Ministry of Sustainability and Tourism [Austria] 2019: 16–33)

Another strength of Plan T was that it used a participatory planning process.

EXAMPLE 4.6

The Process for Plan T in Austria

Consultations of various types should be conducted in destination planning, as they were for the strategy in Austria.

> The core elements of the strategy process were nine dialogue-oriented future workshops all over Austria. Within the framework of these future workshops more than 500 persons involved in this process laid, with their ideas, proposals, measures and learning cases, the foundations for the further development of Austrian tourism.
>
> (Ministry of Sustainability and Tourism [Austria] 2019)

Learning Point

Widespread input from all stakeholders should be gathered in destination planning.

The second case is the Sedona Tourism Sustainability Plan, which you already know about. One of the impressive features of this plan that dovetails with the principles highlighted in Chapter 3 is the six resident quality of life objectives:

1. Implement new infrastructure and multi-modal solutions to facilitate visitor traffic flows and enhance access to key destinations.

2. Expand use of technology to help solve transportation challenges.
3. Deepen engagement with Sedona residents, expanding their knowledge of tourism and efforts to manage it to an effective balance.
4. Develop new sustainability-focused experiences that resonate with both Sedona residents and visitors.
5. Manage current and future accommodations in ways that increase their balance with long-term sustainability.
6. Launch initiatives that lessen tourism impacts to residents (including noise, air, and light pollution) to strengthen resident quality of life.

(Sedona Chamber of Commerce and Tourism Bureau 2019)

As with Austria's Plan T, the process used to develop the Sedona plan was participative.

EXAMPLE 4.7

The Preparation of the Sedona Tourism Sustainability Plan

Local people must be involved in destination planning as they are in Sedona.

> But concerns about being "loved to death" prompted Sedonans to undertake an extraordinary journey: the development of Arizona's first Sustainable Tourism Plan. An 18-month community conversation culminated in unanimous City Council approval of the Plan in 2019.
>
> (Sedona Arizona 2022)

Learning Point

Involving local residents in destination planning ensures that their concerns and needs are part of the process.

The Greater Darwin Region Destination Management Plan 2022 from Australia is the third case. As you can see in Example 4.8, this plan like Sedona's singles out benefits from tourism for residents.

EXAMPLE 4.8

Leading Principles for the Greater Darwin Region Destination Management Plan 2022

This example describes the underlying principles of the DMP for Northern Territory, Australia.

- The Greater Darwin region will be known for and be distinguished by a distinctive identity and year-round product offerings.
- The approach to destination development will deliver benefits both for visitors and residents of the region.

- Tourism experiences in the region will be tailored to visitor expectations.
- Local values and attributes will showcase the region.
- Collaboration will drive benefits for the region.

(Northern Territory Tourism 2022: 6)

Learning Point

There should be a clearly articulated set of principles for a destination plan.

The Darwin DMP incorporates an action plan with four priorities:

1. investment attraction;
2. strategic product packaging and marketing;
3. collaborative action;
4. capacity-building.

These three cases have different structures and contents for documents that are all called tourism destination plans. They are from three countries, and so some variation can be expected because of these political and geographic differences. However, there are common contents and themes within these tourism plan documents, including residents, product development, marketing, human resources, sustainability, and collaboration. Although this is just a small sample from among hundreds of plans, the lack of standardization in plan contents and structure is quite typical. Another feature of these three plans (please take a look at them) is their eye-catching designs and striking colors; they are anything but dull to view. Each of these three plans has strengths. By combining the strengths of these three case studies with the outline of proposed contents in Figure 4.4, the DMO has a solid foundation for structuring a comprehensive tourism destination plan.

Levels

Tourism planning for destinations is conducted at multiple levels within a country. The highest level is at the national level, with the planning process being coordinated by the country's national DMO. At the sub-national level, there can be plans for states, provinces, territories, and regions (if applicable). The local level is the third tier for tourism planning, and there can be several types of plans here depending on how local authorities are structured. In many countries, there will be counties, cities and towns, and tourism destination plans may be prepared for each of these. As mentioned in Chapter 1, some states and provinces have regional tourism setups under the sub-national level, and some countries go to the regional level right after the national level.

Under the local level, plans may be put together for specific areas such as rural communities or resorts, or districts within a city (Fig. 4.5). As you will realize in Figure 4.5, for design convenience, the local levels were not repeated for provinces, territories or regions.

The following are examples of tourism destination plans at most of these levels:

- National: 14th Five-Year Plan for Culture and Tourism, Peoples Republic of China
- State, province, territory: United States Virgin Islands Tourism Master Plan

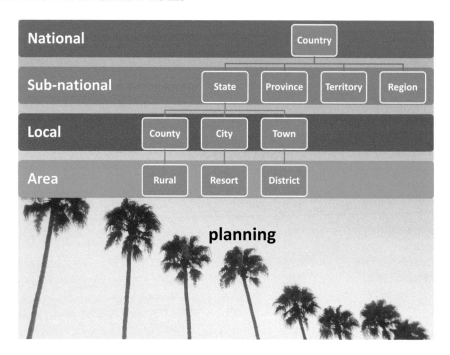

Figure 4.5 Levels of tourism destination planning.

- Region: Northern Cape Tourism Master Plan, South Africa
- County: Snohomish County Tourism Master Plan, Washington, USA
- City: Tourism Master Plan, City of Los Angeles, USA
- Town: Stony Plain Tourism Master Plan, Alberta, Canada
- District: Tourism Masterplan, Orroru Carrieton District, South Australia, Australia

You should realize that plans and strategies are also designed for multi-country regions such as the Association of South East Asian Nations (ASEAN) Tourism Strategic Plan 2016–2025 for Southeast Asia (ASEAN 2015). Places that are not geographically adjacent or connected are also included in plans and strategies defined by themes, including the Viaggio Italiano for the countries small villages and rural destinations (ENIT 2022; Hughes 2022).

In looking at the tourism destination planning practices around the world, it can be said without any doubt that some countries have more tourism plans than others. For example, many plans are found for countries such as Australia, Canada, China, Ireland, and the UK. Developing countries often have plans that are supported by UN organizations, NGOs, and multilateral development banks (e.g., the Asian Development Bank supporting the Kazakhstan plan in Example 4.11).

These then are some of the most important characteristics of tourism planning. Next, and as mentioned earlier, the process used for tourism destination strategic planning is very important, and so the following materials are devoted to this subject.

Figure 4.6 The 5Ps of tourism destination planning.

Tourism Destination Planning Process

Managing a destination means that long-term tourism planning is required, but what is the best process to employ to develop a long-term plan? Unfortunately, there is no instruction manual for organizing a long-term tourism destination planning process, and the steps followed tend to vary from plan to plan. Figure 4.6 shows the five elements present in most tourism planning processes.

Policy

It is a very good idea for all destinations to have an official tourism policy. Here is a definition of policy.

> **DEFINITION**
>
> **Tourism policy**
>
> A policy outlines the basic guidelines for tourism for the future, which may be expressed as policy goals or aims. Policies are generally formulated by national and other governments. They may be developed on a regular basis or be ad hoc when emergency or other unexpected circumstances are encountered.

For example, the South Pacific Tourism Organisation in 2021 published a policy framework for the region. The six policy focus areas were supporting prosperous and resilient economies; empowering communities; amplifying and promoting culture; accelerating climate action; protecting ecosystems; and building resilience (South Pacific Tourism Organisation 2021).

Another great example of a tourism policy is the Draft National Tourism Policy for India. It provides clear guidelines for tourism in five national missions (green tourism, digital tourism,

tourism and hospitality sector skills, DMOs, and micro, small, and medium enterprises) and ten strategic pillars:

1. visa, immigration, and customs processes;
2. a welcoming, safe, clean, and hygienic destination;
3. seamless connectivity and transportation infrastructure;
4. destination planning and development;
5. promoting investment in tourism sector;
6. marketing and promotion;
7. quality assurance and standardization;
8. research and development;
9. governance, institutional linkages, and stakeholder engagement;
10. institutional and governance framework.

EXAMPLE 4.9

The National Tourism Policy 2021 of India

Tourism policies should have clear principles, targets, and initiatives as evidenced in this example from India.

> The National Tourism Policy 2021 is part of the vision of New India on a high trajectory of growth and prosperity. The new policy is a holistic framework for sustainable and responsible growth of the tourism sector in the country. The policy is architected around five key guiding principles, five national missions and ten strategic pillars supported by an institutional and governance framework. The policy aims at improving framework conditions for tourism development in the country, supporting tourism industries, strengthening tourism support functions and developing tourism sub-sectors.
>
> (Ministry of Tourism [India] 2021)

Learning Point

Tourism policies must have clear and specific guidelines as to how they are to be implemented.

Just a further word about tourism policy before leaving the topic. Many national governments establish tourism policies, as do some state, provincial, and territorial governments. However, at lower levels and among NPOs, tourism policies are not as frequently found.

Principals

The principals are the people who coordinate the long-term planning process for tourism in the destination. The DMO will certainly want to play this role but may decide to form a steering or coordinating committee. For example, the Thompson Okanagan Tourism Association (TOTA) in British Columbia, Canada, set up an advisory steering committee to oversee the planning process for the ten-year Thompson Okanagan Regional Tourism Strategy (Thompson Okanagan Tourism Association 2018).

Independent consultants are often hired to conduct the analysis required for a long-term tourism destination plan and to facilitate the planning process. For example, your author was part of the Da Di Feng Jing (Beijing) team that prepared tourism master plans for Hangzhou (Zhejiang), Leshan (Sichuan), Xi'an (Shaanxi), and Jilin Province in China. Solimar International prepared tourism master plans for the Cayman Islands and Georgia. Roland Berger Strategy Consultants did the analyses for the Kuala Lumpur Tourism Master Plan 2015–2025 (Kuala Lumpur City Hall 2015), and Kohl & Partner (2016) assisted with preparing the National Tourism Strategy, Republic of Macedonia 2016–2020. There are consulting companies that specialize in this type of planning work. The independence and considerable experience of these consultants are the main reasons they are engaged, and this particularly happens when tourism planning is conducted in developing countries and in very large and complex destinations.

There have been some situations where long-term planning was done mainly by DMO leaders and staff members, but that is not the approach recommended in this book. Although these people may be highly capable, the active involvement of all stakeholders produces better tourism plans in which there is a sense of shared ownership.

Participants

The principals will meet and decide which organizations and individuals should be invited to participate in the long-term planning process. The invitees should represent all five groups of tourism stakeholders that were identified in Chapter 1: government, tourism sector organizations, community, environment and tourists. The input from tourists should be gathered through either surveys, focus groups or independent in-depth interviews.

There are many ways in which organizations and people can participate in tourism plan preparation. The Vancouver Tourism Master Plan in British Columbia, Canada, was developed based on 180 one-to-one interviews with stakeholders via an online survey with more than 2,100 local residents and business leaders, and two "open houses" (Resonance Consultancy 2013).

Process

The process is as important as the plan. The process is the heart of long-term tourism planning and requires great forethought about how best to accomplish the various tasks involved. Once again, there is no standardized template for a long-term tourism planning process. In actual practice, many different approaches have been used in recent years. In the following materials, five types of long-term tourism planning processes and techniques (Fig. 4.7) are described. The destination visioning process is also explained later in the chapter.

DEFINITION

Planning process

The way in which tourism planning is designed and implemented. This will include decisions on the steps to be followed, participants, time frames, and desired outputs. There may also be an overarching philosophy about how the planning is to be conducted.

1. Step-by-step planning

A process for planning involving a prescribed set of steps.

2. Meet-analyze-report-approve process

A process requiring approvals at various stages before progressing further; typical of government-led planning.

3. Strategic management and planning

Processes that include environmental scanning, SWOT, core values, vision- and mission-setting.

4. Balanced Scorecard

A performance-based approach that balances the emphasis on individual long-term goals for a destination.

5. Scenario planning

Thinking about the future for a destination and producing

Figure 4.7 Types of tourism destination planning processes.

EXAMPLE 4.10

Beneficiaries of the Nelson Tasman Destination Plan

This example from New Zealand carefully prefaces the destination plan for the Nelson Tasman region by naming the intended beneficiaries.

> This destination management plan has been prepared to improve the long-term well-being of our region and its residents by placing our environment and our community at the heart of visitor sector planning. Our aspirations for the sector extend beyond creating mutual benefits for both locals and visitors to rebuilding the sector as a resilient, sustainable and vital part of the Nelson Tasman community.
>
> (Nelson Region Development Agency [New Zealand] 2021)

Learning Point

DMOs must identify who the destination planning will benefit and in which ways.

Step-by-step Planning

One of the approaches available is a phased, or step-by-step, planning process designed specifically for tourism, with each step building upon the previous ones. Many of these process models have been developed based on actual practices in tourism destination planning. For example, Morrison et al. (2018: 139–154) recommend this approach, and there are seven steps in their tourism planning process (Fig. 4.8):

1. Background analysis
2. Detailed research and analysis
3. Synthesis and visioning
4. Goal-setting, strategy selection, and objective setting

Figure 4.8 Step-by-step tourism destination planning.

5. Plan development
6. Plan implementation and monitoring
7. Plan evaluation.

This process was developed and tested by your author when working as a planning consultant in Ontario, Canada. The following is a short description of each of the seven steps in this process.

BACKGROUND ANALYSIS

This is an analysis of the existing destination product, markets, and government policies and programs related to tourism. When these three items have been fully analyzed, the strengths, weaknesses, problems and issues of the destination are identified.

DETAILED RESEARCH AND ANALYSIS

The second step builds upon the first, and more detailed research and analysis are conducted on key aspects of tourism. These aspects include resources, activities, markets and competitors. This step produces many important findings and conclusions: for example, maps showing the locations of tourism resources and attractions, competitive strengths and weaknesses, and research results on potential markets.

SYNTHESIS AND VISIONING

In this step, position papers are prepared based on the analysis and conclusions from the previous two steps. Some of the position paper topics are product development, marketing, DMO structures, community awareness, and support services for tourism. Basically, the position papers outline the status on these aspects of tourism within the destination. Then future statements are prepared for each of these topics or aspects of tourism. These statements out-line the desired future situations for each aspect of tourism. Along with each future statement, a set of critical conditions are specified that must be met to attain them.

GOAL-SETTING, STRATEGY SELECTION, AND OBJECTIVE SETTING

Taking the position and future statements as the foundation, the fourth step begins with the statement of long-term tourism goals for the destination. These goals are set for five or more years. Once the goals have been stated, the focus then turns to identifying alternative strate-gies to meet them. For example, for a goal on product development, it is a common in spatial planning to divide up the destination into tourism zones with different functions. Finally, the strategies are selected that best fit with tourism policies and the vision for the destination. Next, shorter-term objectives are set for tourism in the destination. These objectives are for up to three years into the future and are more measurable than the goals.

PLAN DEVELOPMENT

The planning document is then prepared using the goals, selected strategies, and objectives as its basic framework. The plan details how each of the goals and objectives are going to be achieved. The programs, activities, stakeholder roles, and funding procedures are specified. The written plan is prepared in several draft versions until it receives final approval.

PLAN IMPLEMENTATION AND MONITORING

The plan is put into action, and progress is carefully monitored against the achievement of goals and objectives.

PLAN EVALUATION

When the term for the tourism plan ends, an assessment is made of the extent to which its vision, goals and objectives were attained.

EXAMPLE 4.11

Spatial Conceptual Plan for Tourism in Almaty-Bishkek Corridor, Kazakhstan

Tourism master plans often map where specific types of tourism are to be developed, as in this Kazakhstan plan.

> This tourism master plan mapped six zones in the corridor for adventure and nature tourism; cultural tourism, MICE [meetings, incentives, conferences and exhibitions]; recreational tourism; wellness and spa tourism; and winter tour-ism. Five routes associated with the Silk Road were also sketched into the conceptual plan.
>
> (Asian Development Bank 2019)

Learning Point

Plans should specify tourism development opportunities and where they are to be realized.

This step-by-step model has the advantage that it was developed based on actual success-ful experiences in tourism destination planning. It is logical and thorough in gathering and analyzing research and information directly related to tourism in the destination. However, this model does not take full advantage of the contributions from strategic management and strategic planning that are discussed below. For example, an external environment scan is not included. Additionally, it does not allow for any required government approvals (as with the meet-analyze-report-approve process, discussed next) but assumes a straight-line process for producing the plan.

EXAMPLE 4.12

Intentions of Frontenac County Destination Development Plan

This example from Ontario, Canada clearly states what a county's destination devel-opment plan is intended to achieve.

> A Destination Development Plan is a 5–10 year road map that aligns gov-ernment, economic development, community and tourism priorities. It addresses the interactions between visitors, the industry that serves them, the community that hosts them, and the environment in order to deliver a more sustainable and equitable year-round local economy. Ultimately, the plan is designed to protect and enhance the character of the destination, increase destination competitiveness and visitor spend, and optimize overall quality of life for local residents. The goal is to help ensure that everyone in the destination has an opportunity to benefit from, and contribute to, the local visitor economy.
>
> Also, the plan integrates strategic initiatives through the lens of economic, social, cultural and environmental sustainability to help ensure the plan is embraced by the community.
>
> (County of Frontenac 2022)

Learning Point

The objectives for destination planning must be clearly stated.

Meet-Analyze-Report-Approve Process

The second type of planning process is illustrated in Figure 4.9 and was the one used to pre-pare the tourism master plan for the Maldives. This process is a meet-analyze-report-approve sequence that is typical of the procedures for plans run by government agencies and involving consultants or technical assistance teams.

These processes tend to take somewhat longer because various levels of government approv-als are required before proceeding further. However, without these approvals, the plans are unlikely to be implemented successfully. This is especially important in a smaller country with a fragile environment such as the Maldives.

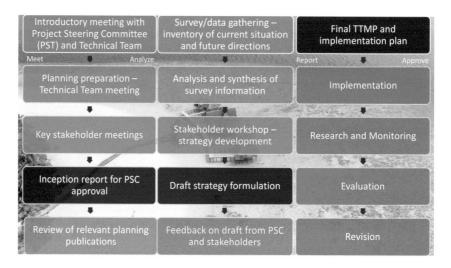

Figure 4.9 Tourism master plan process, Maldives.

Strategic Management and Planning

The third type of long-term planning process is one that follows more of the strategic management approach. As mentioned earlier, tourism planning has been greatly influenced by the concepts of strategic management and strategic planning in recent decades. These concepts have introduced the techniques of environmental scanning, SWOT analysis, and situation analysis to long-term tourism planning processes. Other ideas introduced from strategic management to tourism planning have been vision, mission and core values and guiding principles.

DEFINITION

Environmental scanning

The monitoring of internal and external environments to detect changes and trends that will affect tourism in the destination in the long term. The main emphasis in environmental scanning tends to be placed on external environments, usually called the macro-environment, and a variety of analysis approaches are used for this purpose.

Figure 4.10 shows four approaches that are used for environmental scanning.

Tourism Victoria in Australia presented the 2016 Planning Process Environment Scan in May 2015, applying the PESTEL analysis technique. This state tourism DMO stated that it is wise to start off a tourism strategy and plan with an assessment of the external factors affecting tourism.

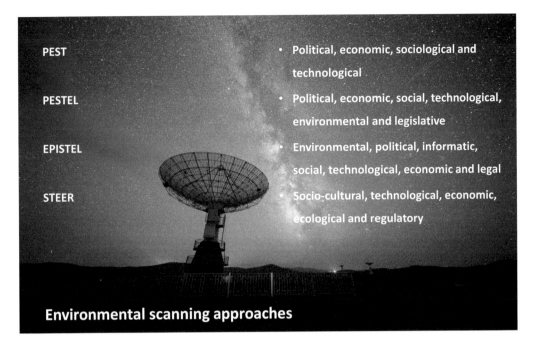

PEST
- Political, economic, sociological and technological

PESTEL
- Political, economic, social, technological, environmental and legislative

EPISTEL
- Environmental, political, informatic, social, technological, economic and legal

STEER
- Socio-cultural, technological, economic, ecological and regulatory

Environmental scanning approaches

Figure 4.10 Approaches for environmental scanning.

EXAMPLE 4.13

The Open-System Nature of Tourism

These authors argue that tourism is readily influenced by multiple external factors.

> The tourism system is not a rigid form, rather, it is dynamic and constantly changing. New concepts and phenomena such as space tourism are always arriving in tourism . . . Tourism is greatly affected by external influences such as politics, demographics, technology, war, terrorism, crime, and disease.
>
> (Morrison et al. 2018: 8)

Learning Point

Tourism's future will be affected by factors and situations that are beyond the sector's control.

Figure 4.11 shows the external trends that can affect a tourism destination and that should be analyzed in an environmental scan. A short description of each of the external trend areas in Figure 4.11 follows.

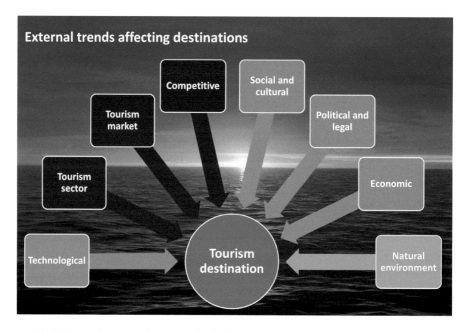

Figure 4.11 External trends affecting destinations.

SOCIAL AND CULTURAL

These trends include, for example, the increasing concern for safety and security, threat of pandemic diseases, greater desire for authentic cultural experiences, aging of the population, and increasing urbanization in developing countries.

POLITICAL AND LEGAL

Some of the trends here are the increasing security levels when traveling, greater controls on food safety, threats of terrorism, controls on tour operators, and increasing popularity of multi-country trading zones.

ECONOMIC

Trends are the fluctuations in the economic conditions of key origin countries, variations in fuel prices, changes in currency exchange rates, and greater concern with value offers.

NATURAL ENVIRONMENT

The natural environment trends are the increasing environmental awareness in society, global warming and climate change, threats of natural disasters, and movement toward sustainable tourism.

TECHNOLOGICAL

Technological trends include the increasing use of smartphones for travel information and bookings, augmented and virtual reality, artificial intelligence, growing influence of social media on tourism, and innovations in transportation modes.

TOURISM SECTOR

Tourism industry trends encompass the growth of low-cost air carriers, financial problems of some major airlines, consolidation in some sub-sectors of tourism, and globalization of brands.

TOURISM MARKET

There are many trends here, including increasing special-interest travel, more staycationing and short-break travel, higher expectations for service quality, greater concern with environmental sustainability, and impacts through travel, and new technology-enabled information and booking channels.

COMPETITIVE

Competitive trends include intensifying competition among destinations, increasing regional focus to tourism and travel, and emerging destinations getting greater market shares.

You should realize that in reviewing external trends, a destination may decide to give lesser emphasis to tourism in future, as demonstrated in the case of Oman.

EXAMPLE 4.14

Oman Will Pay Less Focus to the Tourism Sector

As shown in this example, some destinations may decide to de-emphasize tourism in their national plans.

> Oman will give tourism less focus in the 10th five-year plan (2021–2025) while adding the education sector to the main sectors for economic diversification. The Ministry of Economy announced today the six targeted sectors in the first executive plan of Oman Vision 2040. In addition to education, Oman has set even higher targets to four of the five sectors included in the previous five-year plan. These sectors are manufacturing, transport and logistics, fishery wealth and mining. As for tourism, Oman is setting a lower target of 3 percent participation in the country's Gross Domestic Product (GDP), compared to a 3.3 percent target in the 2016–2020 plan.
>
> (WAF Oman 2021)

Learning Point

Tourism has to compete with other economic sectors for resources and policy attention.

The next step is usually to prepare a SWOT analysis based on the findings and conclusions from the environmental scan about external environments. The strengths and weaknesses part of the SWOT analysis focuses on internal aspects of the destination, including the operations of its DMO. An assessment of the 10 As may be a useful starting point for the internal analysis. Environmental scanning and SWOT analysis are covered in greater detail in Chapter 5.

Part II

A large assortment of concepts and terms have come with the introduction of strategic management and strategic planning approaches to tourism planning. Unfortunately, many of these terms are used rather loosely, and this has caused much confusion. You will get a clear idea from the descriptions of terms that follow.

DEFINITION

Mission statement

A statement about an organization's purpose or its reason for being. This concept is generally not applied to a destination but to its DMO.

Mission

A DMO mission, articulated in its mission statement, describes its reason for being. It is a broad statement about the organization's business and scope, services and products, markets served and overall philosophy (Kotler 2000). The mission statement is not a goal or objective, but rather it is a clear description of what the DMO does and who it serves.

Vision statement

A statement that describes a future for a destination that is achievable and attractive and is supported by most tourism stakeholders. This concept can also be applied to the DMO itself.

Core values and guiding principles

These are enduring beliefs and principles held by tourism stakeholders about their destination. Again, this concept may also be applied to the DMO.

Goals

Broad, general results to be achieved by the destination over several years, and usually within three to five years.

Strategies

Overall actions or initiatives to be followed to achieve goals.

Critical success factors

Known as the CSFs, these are the required activities or conditions that must be met to achieve the destination's goals and vision.

There is a great amount of confusion about the difference between a vision and a mission (probably because they sound and look similar, and perhaps also due to the space program). Figure 4.12 will clear up this confusion for you. Generally, a vision applies to the destination

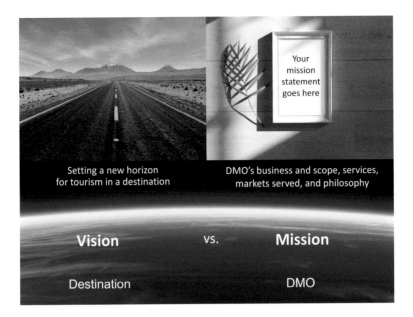

Figure 4.12 Difference between a vision and a mission.

and the mission is for the DMO. Visions are about the future; missions are more grounded in the present.

Undoubtedly, strategic management and strategic planning principles have had a major effect on tourism destination planning and have now blended with the frameworks earlier recommended by physical planners and tourism scholars. They are particularly helpful to DMOs because they have introduced more rigor into performance measurement as well as placing greater emphasis on research to support assumptions and strategy development.

Balanced Scorecard

There are more general frameworks for strategic and long-term planning than just the three described. The destination visioning approach is one of them, and it is discussed later in this chapter. Others include using the Balanced Scorecard (BSC) approach and scenario planning. The BSC was originated in 1996 by Drs. Robert Kaplan and David Norton of the Harvard Business School. The Balanced Scorecard Institute provides the following definition of this tool:

DEFINITION

Balanced Scorecard

"The Balanced Scorecard (BSC) is a strategic planning and management system. Organizations use BSCs to:

- Communicate what they are trying to accomplish
- Align the day-to-day work that everyone is doing with strategy

- Prioritize projects, products, and services

- Measure and monitor progress toward strategic targets

The name "Balanced Scorecard" comes from the idea of looking at strategic measures in addition to traditional financial measures to get a more 'balanced' view of performance" (Balanced Scorecard Institute 2022).

The original BSC has four components: (1) financial; (2) internal business process; (3) learning and growth; and (4) customers. Objectives, measures, targets, and initiatives are developed for each of these components. The BSC was designed for corporations and other types of organizations and was not originally intended for tourism destinations. However, there have been some recommendations about adapting the BSC to fit with destinations, including using the following six perspectives (Vila et al. 2010):

1. Infrastructure and resources
2. Activities and processes (tourism planning, marketing strategies, etc.)
3. Relationships (residents, tourists and visitors, and organizations)
4. Economic results
5. Social results
6. Environmental results

The BSC has been used quite often in research and planning for hospitality (Tahniyath and Said 2020). However, it has seldom been used in tourism destination planning. The BSC was used in the mid-2000s to assist Ireland West Tourism, a regional DMO, with its strategy and performance measurement (Frechtling 2006). This pioneering work was done by Dr. Douglas Frechtling of George Washington University (USA) and the Dublin Institute of Technology with financial assistance from UNWTO. This project provided many practical suggestions on how a DMO can apply the BSC approach in tourism planning for the destination and in how to measure the DMO's own performance.

Although the BSC has undoubted potential for application in destination planning, it remains a technique that needs to be more thoroughly tested and practiced. As mentioned in Chapter 1, there is no universal consensus on what constitutes a successful tourism destination, and so this represents a barrier to the implementation of the BSC for tourism destinations.

Scenario Planning

Scenario planning is another potential long-term planning technique for destinations. The following definition of scenario planning is supplied by Professor Ian Yeoman, a well-known tourism futurist:

DEFINITION

Scenario planning

"Scenario planning is the capability of organizations to understand their business environment, to think through what this means to them and then to act upon this new knowledge. Scenarios are a range of pictures and stories of the future that are constructed using drivers and trends that shape the future. Scenarios provide alternative views of the future. They identify some significant events, main actors and their motivations, and they convey how the world functions. On a practical level, it is just about crystal ball gazing and estimating the future" (Yeoman 2008).

Scenario planning involves tourism stakeholders in thinking about what the future might be for their destinations and producing different scenarios (descriptions in stories and pictures). As with the BSC, the scenario planning technique has not yet been applied often in destination planning but certainly has great potential for application in the years ahead.

EXAMPLE 4.15

VisitScotland COVID Scenario Planning

Given the uncertainty about the future due to COVID-19, scenario planning was more used by DMOs as in this example with VisitScotland.

> One valuable technique to prepare for an uncertain future is scenario planning. Scenarios are a powerful tool. They are particularly useful in the development of strategies to navigate extreme events seen recently in the world economy. Scenarios enable businesses to plot a course between the uncertainty and confusion which often strike in troubled times. When executed well, scenarios provide a range of possible situations with which to challenge and test a business plan or strategy. A scenario isn't a forecast or prediction, but a range of plausible outcomes based on available evidence. The question asked when testing your strategy should be what would I change, if anything, if this outcome happens? Scenarios will not provide all the answers, but they help to ask better questions and prepare for the unexpected. And that makes them a very valuable tool indeed.
>
> The Scottish Tourism Emergency Response Group (STERG) developed five scenarios: (1) the baseline scenario; (2) the old normal; (3) doors open; (4) long chill; and (5) five winters.
>
> (VisitScotland 2020)

Learning Point

Scenario planning allows several versions of future conditions to be described and assessed.

It is fair to say that the processes for the long-term planning of tourism destinations are still evolving, despite sixty years of practice. Planning is simpler for individual companies and organizations than for tourism destinations, which are much more complex. This is perhaps the main reason tourism planning has not yet fully matured. However, DMOs need to carefully study tourism plans that have been produced in other destinations to learn as much as they can from what has been successful elsewhere and what has not worked. There is no need for reinventing the wheel because there are several good models of tourism planning that can be followed. Moreover, the tourism planning toolkits discussed later in this chapter provide many useful tips and suggestions for a DMO's efforts at tourism planning.

Plans and Communicating about Plans

A long-term tourism plan is a written document that describes what will be done by the destination to achieve its vision, goals and objectives. Planning documents vary greatly in style and length, and they may be produced in different versions aimed at distinct audiences. Typically, a shorter document, often called an executive summary, is prepared for general distribution, and a longer, detailed report is designed for a more selective audience.

Tourism plans are written on paper, but they are not cast in stone. Communicating the essential contents of long-term tourism plans has become more important, and DMOs must pay careful attention to this task. Tourism planning processes can be long, and it may even take up to one year to prepare a plan. With so much time and effort going into the planning process and all the associated research, analysis, meetings, and discussions, it can be easy to forget that the plan is a beginning and not the end. The principals may be exhausted at the end of the planning process, but the life of the plan is just about to start then.

So how can a tourism plan be communicated in an appealing way and in a fashion that those outside of the tourism sector can also comprehend? Some plans have become the subjects of videos to expand their awareness and communication effectiveness. For example, Discover Halifax, the DMO for the city in Nova Scotia in Canada in 2021 uploaded a 4:34-minute video on its integrated tourism master plan for the region (Discover Halifax 2021). Other plans that you can find in video format include the integrated tourism master plan for Lombok, Indonesia (PUPR_BPIW 2022), and a tourism master plan for outback Murweh Shire in Queensland, Australia (Griffith University 2021).

There has also been much more effort put into designing more attractive looking plans with eye-catching images and photography. The main idea here is that tourism plans themselves need to be marketed within the destination.

Destination Visioning

Destination visioning is a long-term planning process that has gained greater popularity among DMOs from about the early 1990s. It involves a different type of process than that previously described for long-term tourism planning. Long-term planning is more prescriptive and follows a fixed, step-by-step process; visioning is more creative and dynamic, and the process is more fluid. In some ways, long-term and strategic planning start with the present and build to the future. Visioning starts with the future and then works back to the present. One definition of visioning is as follows.

DEFINITION

Vision

A vision is a clear and succinct description of what the destination should look like after it successfully implements its strategies and achieves its full potential. It is an expression by the people about what they want the destination to be—a preferred future, a word or picture of the destination the stakeholders choose to create.

The image of the horizon shown in Figure 4.12 is an excellent visual metaphor for a vision. The horizon can be seen, but we have not yet reached it. It is attainable if we follow the road ahead, just as the destination can achieve its vision if it follows the plan.

EXAMPLE 4.16

Torbay Destination Plan Vision Statement

The vision statement is a highly important outcome from destination planning as evidenced in this example from England.

> It is time to refresh and reposition the English Riviera as the UK's premier holiday resort of the future. With a unique heritage, encompassing three towns, each offering a different coastal experience, set within an exceptional natural environment, the English Riviera is so much more than the sum of its parts.
>
> Combining tradition and contemporary, we have a bright future. The English Riviera can offer the best of the seaside, outstanding seafood, exciting activities on and off the water, authentic cultural events, and experiences, and a globally significant UN Educational, Scientific and Cultural Organization (UNESCO) Global Geopark designation that runs like a golden thread through the entire visitor experience.
>
> (Torbay Council 2022)

Learning Point

Destination planning must produce a destination vision accompanied by a vision statement.

Visioning originated as a process for getting residents' input into the future directions for their communities and was later adapted for tourism destinations. Visioning processes are normally run by skilled facilitators, and there are several rounds of workshops. Task forces are also formed to deal with specific issues or topics. The following is a step-by-step process for destination visioning that was adapted from *Planning for the Future: A Handbook on Community Visioning* from the Center for Rural Pennsylvania (2006):

- Appoint a steering committee: A steering committee is appointed by the DMO and represents all stakeholders in the destination. The steering committee begins planning for the first visioning workshop. A facilitator is selected to run the visioning workshops.
- Hold first visioning workshop: The steering committee and facilitator provide an overview of the visioning process and ask participants to identify the major issues affecting tourism within the destination.
- Tally results and establish task forces: The steering committee and facilitator tally the results from the first visioning workshop. Major tourism issues are identified, and task forces are created to deal with each issue. Plans for the second visioning workshop are made.
- Hold second visioning workshop: The facilitator and steering committee review activities and progress to date. The task forces make short presentations on their specific issues, and this is followed by a general discussion of these issues. The larger group is asked to define values and guiding principles for the future of tourism in the destination.

- Hold third visioning workshop: Participants are asked to discuss what they want the destination to be like in the future. With the facilitator's help, the group drafts the vision statement for tourism in the destination.
- Hold fourth visioning workshop and celebration: This is a public unveiling of the destination vision statement and celebration among tourism stakeholders.
- Market and make the vision a reality: The steering committee and task forces present the vision statement to community groups, local government and other organizations for their approval.
- Create an action plan: Working with various other organizations and government agencies, the steering committee develops an action plan for implementing the recommendations and the elements of the vision statement.

DEFINITION

Visioning process

A participatory process for tourism destination planning, involving all stakeholders including residents. The process is usually led by experienced facilitators and conducted in several stages. The main focus is on collectively defining desirable future situations for a destination.

The destination visioning process is not as comprehensive as that described earlier for long-term tourism planning. However, it is more focused on issues and desired futures for the destination. It is more creative and less analytical than strategic planning. Although long-term strategic planning and visioning are most often viewed as alternative planning approaches, there is no reason they cannot be used together or sequentially.

EXAMPLE 4.17

The Vision Statement for Harrogate

This is a good destination vision statement for Harrogate in North Yorkshire, England.

> In 2030, the Harrogate district visitor economy has accelerated its position as a substantial driver of sustainable economic growth. Its unique position as an events destination embedded within a heritage spa town will continue to attract domestic and international visitors to the region. The result is thriving local businesses, inward investment, job creation and a vibrant way of life for our residents.
>
> (Destination Harrogate 2022)

Learning Point

Vision statements should clearly state the unique positions destinations want to attain or maintain.

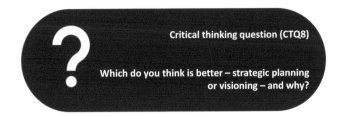

Critical thinking question (CTQ8)

Which do you think is better – strategic planning
or visioning – and why?

Tourism Planning Toolkits

To assist local communities with their tourism planning, several DMOs and other organizations have developed tourism planning toolkits. They are very helpful for guiding DMOs in implementing tourism planning. There are several of these toolkits available around the world, and they include the following: "Tourism Planning Guidelines, Western Australia, Australia" (Government of Western Australia 2014); "Developing Your Destination Management Plan, England" (VisitBritain/VisitEngland 2018); and "The Tourism Planning Toolkit for Local Government, South Africa" (Department of Tourism 2022).

The major advantage of these toolkits is that they have been built in other places based on successful tourism planning processes and techniques. Additionally, they are comprehensive in their coverage and provide useful, step-by-step instructions for DMOs to apply to their own situations. Adaptations to forms and procedures can easily be made to fit local conditions in the destination.

EXAMPLE 4.18

Future of Tourism in New Zealand

This statement grounds the future of tourism on the pillars of sustainable development.

> The future visitor economy must be regenerative and resilient. It needs to deliver net benefits across all four well-beings: social, cultural, environmental and economic.
>
> (Tourism Futures Taskforce [New Zealand] 2020)

Learning Point

Destination planning should reflect the principles of sustainable development and sustainable tourism.

Specialized Forms of Destination Planning

This chapter has focused mainly on the broader type of tourism planning for a destination, providing comprehensive coverage of all the major issues and touching upon every role of destination management. However, it must be acknowledged that there are more specialized forms of tourism planning at the destination level. Sometimes, they become components of overall plans, but at other times they are free-standing plans addressing a specific topic or reflecting a specific type of planning. They include the following:

- sustainable or responsible tourism development plans;
- spatial master plans for tourism development;
- workforce development plans or strategies.

SUSTAINABLE OR RESPONSIBLE TOURISM DEVELOPMENT PLANS

As mentioned earlier, these types of plans are becoming more numerous. They focus on sustainable tourism development principles as applied to specific geographic areas. The emphasis is on the long-term sustainability of natural, social, heritage and cultural resources. For example, they may look at the application of the principles of Agenda 21 to the destination. These types of plans are especially important in environmentally and culturally sensitive destinations, including destinations along coastlines.

Some of these plans advocate the "triple-bottom-line" approach to tourism development in which there is a balance between economic, social and environmental benefits and impacts.

SPATIAL MASTER PLANS FOR TOURISM DEVELOPMENT

These plans are physically oriented tourism plans for destinations with a focus on the proposed functions of specific geographic areas within the destination. Broadly, this can be called "tourism zoning," and the work is done by landscape architects, architects, urban planners, physical geographers and others with physical planning skills and experience. Some zones may have high potential for tourism development, whereas others may be designated as travel corridors or protected areas. These planning processes usually involve the development and design of several concept options from which a preferred alternative is selected.

WORKFORCE DEVELOPMENT PLANS OR STRATEGIES

These plans focus on tourism personnel with a view to ensuring that there will be sufficient supply and quality in the future to meet the destination's needs. The contents of these plans cover tourism workforce needs and availability, attitudes toward careers in tourism, recruitment and motivation strategies, training and education requirements, and other relevant topics.

Because people are such a crucial element to all tourism destinations, it is hard to imagine a destination planning process that would not give some emphasis to the development of human resources. As mentioned earlier, the origins of tourism planning were in the physical planning of regions and rural areas; nowadays, tourism planning has expanded to be much more comprehensive in the issues it covers and the techniques that are applied to produce plans.

EXAMPLE 4.19

National Maritime Tourism Strategy for St. Lucia

Sometimes tourism destination plans and strategies are dedicated to particular areas of tourism such as maritime or marine tourism, as here in the case of St. Lucia in the Caribbean.

The recently completed National Maritime Tourism Strategy will prioritize opportunities within Saint Lucia's Maritime Tourism portfolio. The development of the strategy spearheaded by the Maritime Tourism Committee of the Saint Lucia Tourism Authority, clearly delineates a tactical approach to leverage maritime related tourism business as well as, strategically marketing and positioning its maritime tourism product. In keeping with the vision of the Government of Saint Lucia, the Blue Economy is a central feature of this strategy.

(*St. Lucia Times* 2022)

Learning Point

Destinations often decide to develop specific plans for sub-sectors of tourism that are especially important for them.

These specialized plans may reflect issues that are of great importance to tourism in specific destinations. For example, sustainable tourism plans are especially required in highly environmentally sensitive areas and in places where local cultures and traditions are fragile and may easily be altered or damaged by tourism. Workforce strategies are needed in destinations that have shortages of personnel for tourism and where tourism growth is very rapid.

There is a whole lexicon for the different types of plans produced by urban planners and designers, land-use planners, landscape planners, and architects. Since this book has a focus on destinations, it was not considered as essential to consider these types of plans in detail. However, they are important in their own rights and destination planners should consult these plans if they are relevant to tourism.

In the chapters that follow, more detailed planning for most of the destination management roles is presented. These roles cover marketing and branding, research, product development, partnership and team-building, visitor management, community and stakeholder relationships, and crisis management. Once again, it is important to say that the DMO is demonstrating its leadership and coordination role in bringing tourism stakeholders together to prepare these plans.

Reflecting on what has happened in 2019–2022 due to COVID-19, some would say there is no point in planning tourism now. What do you think? The author disagrees with this sentiment as it overlooks one important value from planning—the process of bringing people together to reflect on the future of tourism in the destination—the process is the plan.

EXAMPLE 4.20

Recovering Tourism in Bonaire

The assumption that a "new normal" was to come post-COVID sparked many destinations into tourism recovery planning, including Bonaire in the Caribbean.

Recognizing the importance of the tourism industry for Bonaire while keeping the above in mind, we have developed this Tourism Recovery Plan as a guide to reviving Bonaire's tourism in the "new normal." While we realize that the worldwide pandemic crisis calls for a reset, we find that the main objectives of Bonaire's 2017 Strategic Tourism Masterplan (STMP) are still relevant: the plan designs a blueprint that guides and directs the Bonaire tourism sector to new heights while considering its core attributes of ocean, nature, and heritage. The main objective of the tourism master plan is for Bonaire to thrive as a destination that enhances people's quality of life.

(Bonaire Government 2021: 8)

Learning Point

Quality-of-life considerations will be a feature of most future destination planning.

Steps for Effective Destination Planning

The specific steps that a DMO should complete in tourism destination planning are shown in Figure 4.13. It is suggested that the DMO should initiate the planning process and coordinate the process through implementation, monitoring, and evaluation through to the next planning cycle.

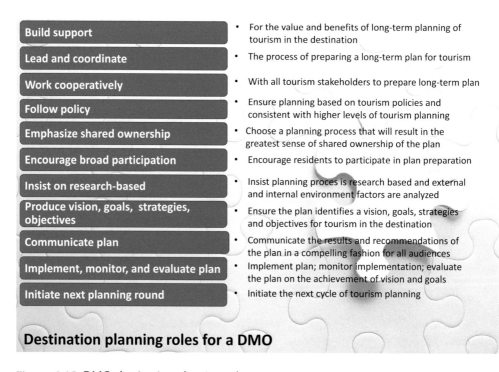

Build support	• For the value and benefits of long-term planning of tourism in the destination
Lead and coordinate	• The process of preparing a long-term plan for tourism
Work cooperatively	• With all tourism stakeholders to prepare long-term plan
Follow policy	• Ensure planning based on tourism policies and consistent with higher levels of tourism planning
Emphasize shared ownership	• Choose a planning process that will result in the greatest sense of shared ownership of the plan
Encourage broad participation	• Encourage residents to participate in plan preparation
Insist on research-based	• Insist planning process is research based and external and internal environment factors are analyzed
Produce vision, goals, strategies, objectives	• Ensure the plan identifies a vision, goals, strategies and objectives for tourism in the destination
Communicate plan	• Communicate the results and recommendations of the plan in a compelling fashion for all audiences
Implement, monitor, and evaluate plan	• Implement plan; monitor implementation; evaluate the plan on the achievement of vision and goals
Initiate next planning round	• Initiate the next cycle of tourism planning

Destination planning roles for a DMO

Figure 4.13 DMO destination planning roles.

SUMMING UP

You have learned in Chapter 4 that long-term planning for tourism within a destination is crucial, and DMOs must take a leadership and coordinative role to ensure that the planning process is as successful (and participatory) as possible. One of the major requirements of successful planning is that all stakeholders are involved because this gives the plan a sense of shared ownership.

Tourism planning has existed for around sixty years and has been subject to a variety of influences from planning authorities and professionals, tourism scholars, management and marketing professionals, communities and NPOs, consumers, and COVID-19. Done in the correct way, there are many benefits to be derived from tourism planning for destinations.

Tourism destination long-term planning processes are best achieved in a step-by-step way with each successive step building on the previous ones. Destination visioning is a more recent addition to tourism planning, and although less comprehensive in scope, it can be creative and allow for greater community resident input.

This chapter has suggested that tourism planning for destinations is still maturing and there remain many destinations around the world that are without long-term tourism destination plans. It is difficult to contemplate professional destination management without long-term planning; as the old saying goes, "Failing to plan is planning to fail."

In Chapter 5, you are going to get to know more about destination management research, the other part of the planning and research role. As you can see from this chapter, doing research is a prerequisite for tourism destination planning and plans can fail if little or no research is done.

KEYWORDS

balanced scorecard
core values and principles
COVID-19
destination management
    plan (DMP)
environmental scanning
executive summary
mission
participatory
process

scenario planning
shared ownership
strategic planning
SWOT (strengths, weak-
    nesses, opportunities,
    threats)
tourism action plan
tourism destination
    planning
tourism master plan

tourism policy
tourism recovery plans
tourism strategy
tourism zones
unique selling proposition
    (USP)
vision
visioning

REVIEW QUESTIONS

1. What have been the major influences on tourism planning over recent decades?
2. What are the major benefits that a destination will realize from initiating a tourism planning process?
3. The DMO should target which outcomes to be desired as the result of conducting tourism planning and from implementing the plan?
4. Which topics should be covered in a tourism plan for a destination?

5. At which geographic levels is tourism planning done? What are the advantages to integrating across these various geographic levels?
6. What process should be applied in tourism planning for destinations? How important is the selected process to the overall success of the planning?
7. Strategic planning and visioning are different processes. How would you describe the key differences between these two planning methods?
8. What are the advantages of using tourism planning toolkits to guide destination planning processes?
9. What are the steps in conducting a destination visioning process?
10. What roles should DMOs play in tourism planning?

REFERENCES

ASEAN (2015) "ASEAN Tourism Strategic Plan 2016–2025," www.asean.org/wp-content/uploads/2012/05/ATSP-2016-2025.pdf

Asian Development Bank (2019) "Almaty-Bishkek Economic Corridor Tourism Master Plan," www.carecprogram.org/uploads/2019-ABEC-Tourism-Master-Plan.pdf

Balanced Scorecard Institute (2022) "What Is a Balanced Scorecard?" https://balancedscorecard.org/bsc-basics-overview

Bonaire Government (2021) "Tourism Recovery Plan," www.tourismbonaire.com/includes/tourism-recover-plan.pdf

British Columbia Government (2022) "Strategic Framework for Tourism 2022–2024: A Plan for Recovery and Resilience," https://www2. gov.bc.ca/assets/gov/tourism-and-immigration/tourism-industry-resources/our-tourism-strategy/strategic_framework_for_tourism_2022_final_full_version.pdf

Center for Rural Pennsylvania (2006) *Planning for the Future: A Handbook on Community Visioning*, 3rd edn, Harrisburg, Pa.: Center for Rural Pennsylvania.

Coral Triangle Sustainable Nature-based Tourism Project (undated) "Destination Plan Papua New Guinea," https://wwfeu.awsassets.panda.org/downloads/papua_new_guinea_destination_plan_1.pdf

County of Frontenac (2022) "Frontenac Destination Development Plan," https://engagefrontenac.ca/destinationplan

County of Simcoe (2022) "Tourism Destination Development Action Plan Under Way in Simcoe County," July 12, www.simcoe.ca/CorporateCommunications/Pages/tourism-destination-development-action-plan-underway-in-simcoe-county.aspx

Department of Digital, Culture, Media and Sport (UK) (2021) "The Tourism Recovery Plan," https://assets.publishing.service.gov.uk/government/uploads/system/uploads/attachment_data/file/992974/Tourism_Recovery_Plan__Web_Accessible_.pdf

Department of Tourism (South Africa) (2021) "Tourism Sector Recovery Plan: COVID Response," www.tourism.gov.za/CurrentProjects/Pages/Tourism_Sector_Recovery_Plan.aspx

––––––– (2022) "Tourism Planning Toolkit for Local Government," https://tkp.tourism.gov.za/lg/cb/Pages/Tourism-Planning-Toolkit-for-Local-Government.aspx

Destination Harrogate (2022) "Destination Management Plan: Harrogate District, 2022–2025," https://democracy.harrogate.gov.uk/documents/s13109/Appendix%20A%20-%202022-2025%20Harrogate%20District%20Destination%20Management%20Plan.pdf

Destination Phillip Island (2016) "Phillip Island and San Remo Visitor Economy Strategy 2035," www.visitphillipisland.com.au/destination-phillipisland/our-vision

Discover Halifax (2021) "The Development of Halifax's 1st Integrated Tourism Master Plan," www.youtube.com/watch? v=qB53DVL1bzs

ENIT (2022) "Viaggio Italiano," https://viaggio.italia.it/it/

Fáilte Ireland (2022) "Fáilte Ireland Launches New Long-Term Tourism Plan for Killarney," June 21, www.failteireland.ie/Utility/News-Library/Failte-Ireland-launches-new-long-term-tourism-plan.aspx

Federal Democratic Republic of Ethiopia (2014) "Sustainable Tourism Master Plan, 2015–2025," www.tralac.org/images/docs/10510/ethiopia-sustainable-tourism-master-plan-2015-2025.pdf

Federal Ministry for Sustainability and Tourism (Austria) (2019) "Plan T: Master Plan for Tourism," https://info.bmlrt.gv.at/dam/jcr:885af4cc-c3bf-4960-9ee8-be930e6010f5/PLAN%20T%20-%20MASTER%20PLAN%20FOR%20TOURISM_Print_barrierefrei.pdf

Frechtling, D. C. (2006) "A Balanced Scorecard System for Managing Strategy and Measuring Performance of Destination Management Organizations," https://home.gwu.edu/~frechtli/material/BSCWorkingPaper4-06.pdf

Government of Western Australia (2014) "Tourism Planning Guidelines," www.wa.gov.au/system/files/2021-06/GD_tourism_planning.pdf

Griffith University (2021) "Building a Tourism Masterplan in Outback Australia," www.youtube.com/watch? v=X-fVJSXPnjQ&t=103s

Gunn, C. A. (1979) *Tourism Planning*, New York, NY: Crane Russak & Company.

Hawaii Tourism Authority (2020) "Strategic Plan 2020–2025," www.hawaiitourismauthority.org/media/4286/hta-strategic-plan-2020-2025.pdf

Hughes, R. A. (2022) "Think You Know Italy? Now It Wants You to Explore Its Hidden Attractions," July 1, www.euronews.com/travel/2022/07/01/think-you-know-italy-now-it-wants-you-to-explore-its-hidden-attractions

Ignatius, C. (2022) "Tourism Malaysia Launches Tourism Recovery Plan 2022 to Boost Domestic Tourism," *Business Today*, July 14, www.businesstoday.com.my/2022/07/14/tourism-malaysia-launches-tourism-recovery-plan-2022-to-boost-domestic-tourism

Inskeep, E. (1991) *Tourism Planning: An Integrated and Sustainable Development Approach*, New York: Wiley.

Kohl & Partner (2016) "National Tourism Strategy 2016–2020 Macedonia," http://economy.gov.mk/Upload/Documents/Kohl%20&%20Partner_Tourism%20Strategy%20Macedonia_DRAFT%20FINAL%20REPORT_16%2002%2023_E.pdf

Kotler, P. (2020) *Marketing Management: Millennium Edition*, Boston, Mass.: Pearson Custom Publishing.

Kuala Lumpur City Hall (2015) "Kuala Lumpur Tourism Master Plan 2015–2025," www.kltourismmasterplan.com

Malawi Travel (2022) "Official Launch of Malawi National Tourism Investment Master Plan," April 4, https://malawitravel.org/our-news/general/entry/official-launch-of-malawi-national-tourism-investment-master-plan.html

Ministry of Sustainability and Tourism (2019) "Plan T Master Plan," https://info.bml.gv.at/dam/jcr:885af4cc-c3bf-4960-9ee8-be930e6010f5/PLAN%20T%20-%20MASTER%20PLAN%20FOR%20TOURISM_Print_barrierefrei.pdf

Ministry of Tourism (India) (2021) "Draft National Tourism Policy," https://tourism.gov.in/sites/default/files/2022-01/Draft%20Tourism%20Policy%20ver%203%20Nov%2021%20updated.pdf

Ministry of Tourism and Antiquities (Jordan) (2021) "Tourism Strategy 2021–2025," https://procurement-notices.undp.org/view_file.cfm? doc_id=267337

Morrison, A. M., Lehto, X. Y., and Day, J. G. (2018) *The Tourism System*, 8th edn, Dubuque, Ia.: Kendall Hunt Publishing.

Nelson Region Development Agency (New Zealand) (2021) "Destination Nelson Tasman 2021–2026," www.nelsontasman.nz/assets/PDFs/Nelson-Tasman-Destination-Management-Plan-2021-2026-Compressed.pdf

Northern Territory Tourism (2022) "Greater Darwin Region Destination Management Plan 2022," www.tourismnt.com.au/research-strategies/destination-management-plans/greater-darwin-region

Organisation for Economic Co-operation and Development (2020) "OECD Tourism Trends and Policies," www.oecd-ilibrary.org/sites/222a322e-en/index.html? itemId=/content/component/222a322e-en

PUPR_BPIW (2022) "Integrated Tourism Master Plan Lombok" (in Bahasa Indonesia), www.youtube.com/watch? v=ipcslaICCgg&t=24s.

Resonance Consultancy (2013) "Participate in the Van Tourism Master Plan Survey," www.youtube.com/watch?v=UoevZaH5Jq8

ROOST (2022) "The Lake Placid and North Elba Destination Management Plan," www.roostadk.com/lake-placid-dmp

Rothaermel, F. T. (2021) *Strategic Management*, 5th edn, New York: McGraw-Hill.

St. Lucia Times (2022) "Saint Lucia Develops a Strategy for Maritime Tourism," June 25, https://stluciatimes.com/saint-lucia-develops-a-strategy-for-maritime-tourism

Secretaría de Estado de Turismo (Spain) (2019) "Sustainable Tourism Strategy for Spain 2030," https://turismo.gob.es/es-es/estrategia-turismo-sostenible/Documents/directrices-estrategia-turismo-sostenible.pdf

Sedona Arizona (2022) "The Most Beautiful Place on Earth," https://visitsedona.com/sustainable-tourism-plan

Sedona Chamber of Commerce and Tourism Bureau (2019) "Sedona Sustainable Tourism Plan," www.sedonaaz.gov/home/showpublisheddocument/40026/637042472120870000

Sivutha, N. (2022) "Mondulkiri Tourism Master Plan Launched," April 10, *Phnom Penh Post*, https://m.phnompenhpost.com/business/mondulkiri-tourism-master-plan-launched

South Pacific Tourism Organisation (2021) "Pacific 2030: Sustainable Tourism Policy Framework," https://southpacificislands.travel/wp-content/uploads/2021/07/Pacific-Sustainable-Tourism-Policy-Framework.pdf

Tahniyath, F., and Said, E. (2020) "Balanced Scorecard in the Hospitality and Tourism Industry: Past, Present and Future," *International Journal of Hospitality Management*, 91: 102656.

Thompson Okanagan Tourism Association (2018) "A Ten-Year Tourism Strategy for the Thompson Okanagan Region," https://totabc.org/resources/regional-strategy

Torbay Council (2022) "English Riviera Destination Management Plan," www.torbay.gov.uk/dmp#Vision

Tourism Futures Taskforce (New Zealand) (2020) "The Tourism Futures Taskforce Interim Report: December 2020—We Are Aotearoa," www.mbie.govt.nz/assets/the-tourism-futures-taskforce-interim-report-december-2020.pdf

Tourism Victoria (2015) "2016 Planning Process Environmental Scan," https://files.tourismvictoria.com/s3fs-public/Environmental-Scan-May-26.pdf

Vila, M., Costa, G., and Rovira, X. (2010) "The Creation and Use of Scorecards in Tourism Planning: A Spanish Example," *Tourism Management*, 31 (2): 232–239.

VisitBritain/VisitEngland (2018) "Developing Your Destination Management Plan," www.visitbritain.org/sites/default/files/vb-corporate/Documents-Library/documents/England-documents/dm_plans_guiding_principles.pdf

VisitScotland (2020) "Moment for Change: STERG Scenario Planning Toolkit," www.visitscotland.org/binaries/content/assets/dot-org/pdf/supporting-your-business/sterg/scenario-planning-toolkit.pdf

WAF Oman (2021) "Tourism Takes the Back Seat in Oman's New Five-Year Plan," https://wafoman.com/2021/01/02/tourism-takes-the-back-seat-in-omans-new-five-year-plan/?lang=en

Wu, B. (2001) *Regional Tourism Planning Principles*, Beijing: China Tourism and Travel Press.

Yeoman, I. (2008) *Tomorrow's Tourist: Scenarios and Trends*, London and New York, NY: Routledge.

Chapter 5

Destination Management Research

Research is an investment, not a cost!

LEARNING OBJECTIVES

Having read this chapter, you should be able to:

1. explain the contributions of research to destination management;
2. describe the components of a destination management research agenda and plan;
3. discuss the steps in the destination management research process and differentiate between primary and secondary research;
4. detail the procedures for analyzing existing and potential markets and for doing destination image research;
5. explain how to gather destination resident attitudes, opinions, and sentiment about tourism;
6. describe the research approaches for measuring economic impact;
7. delineate procedures for completing competitive research;
8. pinpoint the types of research projects that are done in a destination audit and to measure performance;
9. identify criteria for selecting research vendors.

DOI: 10.4324/9781003343356-7

Warming Up

Chapter 4 gave you a firm grip on destination planning and suggested that research was priceless when plotting the future. This chapter looks at the whole range of destination management research, which goes well beyond that required for planning. This is the second of two chapters on the planning and research role in destination management.

Research for destinations and tourism has exploded in the past fifty-plus years. For example, there have been many studies on consumer motivations and behaviors related to tourism as well as on people's decision-making strategies. The research on destination image has been extensive since the early 1970s. Studies on the supply side of tourism destinations are equally impressive in terms of volume and diversity. For example, there has been much research in 2020–2022 related to post-COVID recovery and to sustainable tourism in destinations.

Not everyone likes to do research, and others get bored listening to people talking about research procedures, data, and results. For some, it is a necessary evil, but there are others who have a real passion about research, including your author. No matter where you stand (or sit) on research, it is part of the foundation of professional destination management today. Then, the best place to start is to consider how research contributes to contemporary destination management.

You are in good hands with the author as he is an experienced researcher. He has spent many years designing, gathering, and analyzing research in consulting projects and for DMOs around the globe, and has done a huge amount of academic research as well.

Contributions of Research to Destination Management

Research makes an enormous contribution and is a fundamental component of professional destination management. Without research, the DMO and other stakeholders cannot make important decisions accurately or with any degree of confidence.

Figure 5.1 shows the potential research contributions and methods for each of the destination management roles ("and research" has been included in parentheses with "planning" because research contributes to all roles and not just to planning).

EXAMPLE 5.1

Research Is Integral to Everything Experience Kissimmee Does

Research comes before marketing is the key message in this example—the author agrees.

> We believe that before marketing comes research. After all, having a clear picture of industry trends, profiles, and economic data gives us the foundation for understanding who our target markets are, what they want, and how to market to them. Experience Kissimmee is continually conducting research and gathering information that helps us plan and develop our programs and campaigns. We make this research available to our industry partners to help them do the same. Event presentations, marketing and co-op information, and other research is available on PartnerNet.

> (Experience Kissimmee 2022)

Learning Point

DMOs should follow research-based marketing.

Contributions of research to destination management roles	Destination management roles	Research contributions and methods
	Destination planning (and research)	☐ Completing environmental scan ☐ Conducting SWOT analysis
	Destination leadership, coordination, and governance	☐ Estimating economic impact of tourism ☐ Documenting non-economic benefits of tourism ☐ Identifying tourism sector and stakeholder needs and issues ☐ Measuring performance
	Destination product development	☐ Preparing a destination analysis (product analysis) ☐ Analyzing successful product development in other destinations ☐ Doing project market analyses/feasibility studies ☐ Assessing customer satisfaction
	Destination partnership and team-building	☐ Studying successful partnering case studies from other destinations ☐ Measuring partnering benefits
	Destination stakeholder and community relationships and involvement	☐ Collecting resident opinions and attitudes toward tourism ☐ Gathering community input/suggestions
	Destination marketing, branding, and communications	☐ Profiling existing visitors ☐ Identifying potential visitors ☐ Determining destination image ☐ Preparing competitive analysis ☐ Analyzing marketing efficiency and effectiveness
	Destination visitor management	☐ Determining visitor impacts ☐ Monitoring visitor volumes and their dispersion ☐ Measuring visitor satisfaction ☐ Market segmentation and yield management analysis
	Destination crisis management	☐ Preparing crisis case study analysis ☐ Conducting crisis risk assessment ☐ Doing crisis preparation research

Figure 5.1 Contributions of research to destination management roles.

What about the reasons for doing destination management research and the benefits that flow to the DMO and other stakeholders? Research can be expensive to conduct, and so it often needs further justification. Morrison (2010) suggests that the five Cs (customers, competitors, confidence, credibility, and change) are the main reasons for doing tourism research. For destination management, there is a need to add three other Cs for community, continuity, and clarity. This comprises the eight Cs shown in Figure 5.2.

Here is a description of these eight Cs:

1. Customers: Helps destinations develop a detailed knowledge of visitors as well as their destination images, expectations, experiences, and satisfaction levels.
2. Competitors: Assists with identifying and assessing the relative strengths and weaknesses of competitive destinations.
3. Confidence: Reduces the perceived risks for the destination in its decision-making.
4. Credibility: Increases the credibility of the DMO as well as the claims the DMO and tourism stakeholders make in marketing, branding, and communications.
5. Change: Keeps the DMO and all tourism stakeholders updated with the constant changes in tourism and travel.
6. Community: Increases the understanding of residents' attitudes, opinions, and sentiments about tourism and its impact on their lives.
7. Continuity: Allows DMOs to track trends and variations when the same data are collected over time.
8. Clarity: Permits the destination or DMO to clear up confusion regarding particular problems or issues.

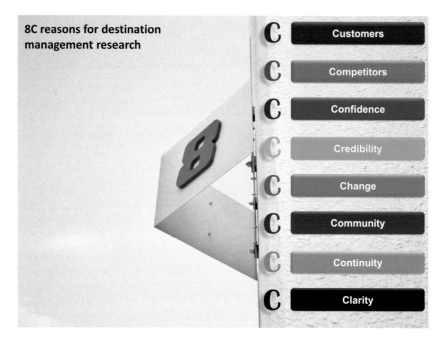

Figure 5.2 8C reasons for destination management research.

There are other reasons for conducting destination management research. The first is to demonstrate the size and importance of the tourism sector in the destination. You will get to know this later as supporting advocacy for tourism (see the definition that follows). To assess the impacts and effectiveness of funds invested in tourism by government agencies and others is a second reason. This is often called calculating the ROI (return on investment) in tourism. Third, the research that the DMO gathers helps organizations in the tourism sector to be more successful in their operations and marketing. Performance measurement is the term used here, which you will hear about later and in Chapter 20.

DEFINITIONS

Advocacy research

Research that is completed with the aim of building support for tourism in government agencies and/or within the general public. These projects frequently measure the positive impacts of tourism.

Return on investment (ROI)

The ROI is how much income or revenues are earned compared to a given investment in destination management.

Performance measurement

A process that tracks the outcomes of destination management and the performance of DMOs.

Additionally, you will remember from Chapter 4 the importance of policy in the process of tourism planning and policy research is crucial for destination management. Policy research consists of information and data that supports the formulation of tourism policies. As the quote here from Austrade about Tourism Research Australia shows, research supports government tourism policy in Australia.

EXAMPLE 5.2

About Tourism Research Australia

Australia has one of the strongest programs of tourism research worldwide.

> Tourism Research Australia (TRA) is the leading tourism economics and research body for the Australian Government. TRA provides research and analysis to support policy and industry development.
>
> (Austrade 2022)

Learning Point

It is advantageous to have a central national tourism research unit.

Developing a Destination Management Research Agenda and Plan

In every destination, there are several tourism research sponsors (those who pay for the research) and providers (those who do the research), but the focus in this chapter is on the research done by or on behalf of the DMO. What should a DMO put on its agenda for destination management research? This is a tough question to answer because it depends on the characteristics of the destination and what the strategies are within its long-term plan for tourism. However, most destination management research agendas can be divided into the three components defined below.

DEFINITIONS

Destination management research components: Ongoing research

Research projects completed and other information collected each year by the DMO.

Periodic research

Research projects and information-gathering done repeatedly by the DMO, but not each year.

As-needed research

Irregular and unexpected research projects and information-gathering required for specific opportunities, problems or issues arising in the destination.

Part II

The DMO's priority research projects are included as part of the ongoing research. This research is on matters that are expected to change every year, such as the numbers and customer mix of tourists to the destination. The DMO's marketing, branding, and communications role has a constant need for research inputs, and so much of that research is ongoing.

Important research topics where change is expected to be more gradual, such as destination image, are in the periodic research category. Other aspects that require continual research but not every year are the assessments of the destination product and human resource capacity.

As-needed research projects are completed when the need arises. For example, this might be a study on the need for a new convention and exhibition center or an analysis of an emerging market with promising potential. It is sometimes impossible to predict what research is required and when it will be needed.

Figure 5.3 shows a recommended research agenda for destination management. It consists of two sections (marketing-related and other). The marketing-related research is input to the operation of the destination marketing system (DMS), discussed in Chapter 9, and provides the data and information required for the destination marketing planning process (DMPP). The second section contains research and information needed to support the other roles of destination management.

The research items neatly fall into the two sections of Figure 5.3. However, in practice the research done in one section may also be helpful and may be drawn on in the other section. For example, many of the research projects are used as a foundation for destination planning. Additionally, some of the key performance indicator (KPI) measurements (indicators of progress toward achieving objectives) will be taken from evaluation research.

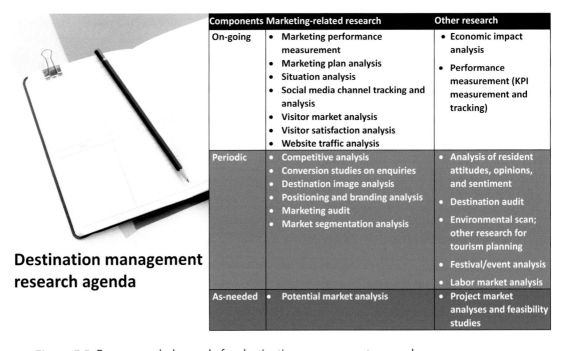

Destination management research agenda

Components	Marketing-related research	Other research
On-going	• Marketing performance measurement • Marketing plan analysis • Situation analysis • Social media channel tracking and analysis • Visitor market analysis • Visitor satisfaction analysis • Website traffic analysis	• Economic impact analysis • Performance measurement (KPI measurement and tracking)
Periodic	• Competitive analysis • Conversion studies on enquiries • Destination image analysis • Positioning and branding analysis • Marketing audit • Market segmentation analysis	• Analysis of resident attitudes, opinions, and sentiment • Destination audit • Environmental scan; other research for tourism planning • Festival/event analysis • Labor market analysis
As-needed	• Potential market analysis	• Project market analyses and feasibility studies

Figure 5.3 Recommended agenda for destination management research.

It is strongly recommended that all DMOs develop an annual research plan as well as a multi-year strategy for destination management research (Fig. 5.4). The plan should specify the research projects to be conducted; how they are to be implemented; and how the process will be managed.

Later in the chapter, the research projects done by DMOs are described in more detail. However, before moving on to discussing these projects, it is important to review two fundamentals for destination management research: the destination management research process and primary and secondary research.

How much should a DMO spend on research? Your author has been asked this question many times; alas, there is no standard research budget amount for destination management. The best approach is to follow a zero-based budgeting approach with the objective-and-task method. This means identifying all of the research projects that the DMO wants to accomplish in the next year and detailing their objectives. Then, what research designs and methods are needed to achieve these objectives and what will they cost to implement. To be very honest, some research studies can be expensive and especially when outside vendors are contracted. It is prudent for DMOs to find partners (Chapter 8) who are willing to cost-share the research costs.

Fundamentals of Destination Management Research

Nowadays, all of us are swamped by a sea of information, and DMOs are especially swimming in a huge ocean of facts and numbers. To what should the DMO give the most attention and how should the data and information be digested? The first step for the DMO is to make sure that the research that it does is accurate and reliable, and this means that it must follow the correct research process.

Figure 5.4 Destination management research plan.

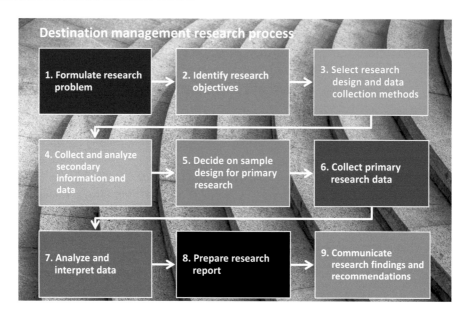

Figure 5.5 Destination management research process.

Destination Management Research Process

There is a classic research process for gathering, analyzing, and interpreting data, and it needs to be applied in destination management research projects. This process is shown in Figure 5.5 and described step-by-step after the diagram.

FORMULATE RESEARCH PROBLEM

The first step is to clearly define the research problem, which means defining the overall goal of the research. You should realize that this is not really a problem; rather, it is the situation, issue, or challenge to be investigated.

DEFINITION

Research problem

A statement of the situation, issue, or challenge to be researched. It sets an overall goal for the research.

The research problem highlights the critical items that the destination or DMO wants to get from doing a research project. For example, in 2022, Tourism Australia and Visit Northern Tasmania conducted a Responsible Tourism Survey. The research problem was how communications should be framed to educate travelers and encourage them to be responsible and respectful (*Tasmanian Times* 2022).

IDENTIFY RESEARCH OBJECTIVES

Once the overall research problem or goal has been stated, it is used to identify more detailed research objectives or questions. Here is the definition of research objectives.

DEFINITION

Research objectives

The research objectives are the specific questions that a research project must answer for the destination or DMO.

A good example of research objectives is from the New Jersey Division of Travel and Tourism and its visitor profile study.

EXAMPLE 5.3

Research Objectives of New Jersey Visitor Profile Study

Visitor profile studies should be grounded on a clear set of objectives as exemplified by New Jersey, USA.

The objectives of the study are to determine:

- Who are New Jersey's overnight leisure visitors?
- Where do New Jersey's visitors come from?
- Why do travelers visit New Jersey?
- What types of accommodations do they stay in?
- Who do they travel with?
- How long do they stay?
- What do New Jersey visitors do?
- How do New Jersey visitors rate the state?

(New Jersey Division of Travel and Tourism/MMGY Travel Intelligence 2021)

Learning Point

These are useful objectives that could be used in future visitor profile studies.

SELECT RESEARCH DESIGN AND DATA COLLECTION METHOD

The third step in the research process is to select the research design and the data collection method to meet the research objectives. Here, the research problem and objectives are like triggers because they indicate the types of data that need to be gathered. For example, if you want to get people's opinions, you need to talk with them. If you want to estimate visitor spending, a survey will be required.

There are several alternative research designs, including surveys, observations, and experiments. There are also qualitative and quantitative branches of research, which you will hear more about later. Next is the choice of a specific data collection method to fit with the selected research design. For example, for a survey research design, there are several data collection methods available, including online, mail, telephone, and face-to-face (personal interviews or intercepts). The data collection method picked will depend on several factors, including the research budget and time available to do the research project. Later, you will get to know several data collection methods used by DMOs in actual research projects.

DEFINITIONS

Qualitative research

Research projects that produce non-numerical research data through focus groups, individual depth interviews, case studies, and other non-quantitative methods.

Quantitative research

Research projects that produce numerical research data through surveys, experiments, mechanical observation, and other quantitative methods.

COLLECT AND ANALYZE SECONDARY INFORMATION

It is a good idea now to gather previously published research information related to the research problem and objectives. It can save time and money to look at secondary research information because someone may have previously completed research similar to that which the DMO is planning. For example, a DMO might be planning to investigate the market potential and characteristics of particular markets. Just as academic scholars do literature reviews, a DMO with an interest in this topic is well advised to learn from others' research. For example, the research completed by MMGY Global on accessible tourism in 2022 is a great source of information on that market.

EXAMPLE 5.4

Portrait of Travelers with Disabilities

The specific needs and requirements of particular market segments need to be researched as in this example.

The report holds many additional important insights for destination marketing organizations. When asked how travel destinations can better attract visitors with mobility disabilities, eight in ten travelers cited increased information on accessibility available prior to visiting (84 percent); infrastructure expansion and enhanced maintenance for areas such as sidewalks, ramps and mobile lifts (83 percent); and the promotion of accessible lodging options by the destination (81 percent). These travelers also cited the importance of being able to see multiple pictures of the exact room they are booking and virtual tours of places they plan to visit to determine if there are any obstacles that could make it difficult or impossible to move around with their mobility device.

(MMGY Global 2022a)

Learning Point

Market segments for destinations have differing needs and requirements that can be determined through research.

As mentioned earlier, there are now several oceans of tourism research data and information that have accumulated over the past sixty years. Some of this research is good and some not so good, but it is always worthwhile checking on what has been done before on the topic of interest to the DMO.

Decide on Sample Design for Primary Research

If the secondary, or previously published, information is insufficient or if it does not directly apply to the destination, the DMO should move forward with primary research data collection. Then, the next item to be dealt with will be the research population and the composition and size of the sample. This is a rather complex subject, and any description of sample design can quickly get into statistical theory. This is not a book about statistics; however, the DMO must be assured that the sample size is large enough to produce accurate and reliable research data results. Often, sample sizes used in research for DMOs are insufficient, and so the results they get are questionable.

Collect Primary Research Data

Using the chosen data collection method, the researchers now collect the primary data. The DMO should ensure that there are adequate quality control steps built into the data collection process. For example, this includes informing respondents of the purpose of the research being done, as in the case of Lincolnshire in England.

EXAMPLE 5.5

Lincolnshire Survey Completion Request

Crowdsourcing opinions for destination planning is demonstrated in this example from England.

> Destination Lincolnshire are conducting research to understand the best ways to support Lincolnshire's tourism and hospitality businesses, and how to grow and develop the region's visitor economy. We want to know what you think about Lincolnshire. The survey should take no more than ten minutes to complete, and your answers will go toward helping us shape the county's future. As a thank you, all completed surveys will be entered into a prize draw.
>
> (Destination Lincolnshire 2022)

Learning Point

Surveys can be used to gather resident inputs for destination planning.

ANALYZE AND INTERPRET DATA

Data analysis is a critical part of the research process, and there are many alternative ways of analyzing data. They include using statistical analysis programs such as SPSS and SAS for data entry and analysis. If the research data is qualitative (non-numerical), then other analysis techniques must be used.

The research results need to be set against the research problem (main goal) and specific research objectives that were established earlier. Every question should be addressed with the parallel data results. Said in a simpler way, the research questions must be answered.

Interpreting the results of a research project is much harder than analyzing the data, but there are a few basic questions that need to be answered. What do the research results mean for the destination? Which practical steps should be taken by the DMO and stakeholders to follow up on the research?

PREPARE RESEARCH REPORT

The results, conclusions, and recommendations of the research should then be concisely written up in a research report. It is often a good idea to produce two report versions, one that is an executive summary version and the other that contains all the results, technical details on methodology, and data tables.

COMMUNICATE RESEARCH FINDINGS AND RECOMMENDATIONS

The final step in the destination management research process is to communicate results and findings to DMO management, stakeholders, and other affected parties. This is perhaps the most critical step because it is the DMO and the tourism stakeholders that must absorb and implement programs based on the research findings. "Keep it simple" is the best advice in making these communications on research findings successful. This is often done through designing infographics. For example, Tourism Ireland uses eye-catching graphics to present facts and figures on international tourism to Ireland (Fig. 5.6).

DEFINITION

Infographic

A visual representation of research data in a colorful diagram or chart. The visual is typically shown on one page only, although sometimes infographics are longer.

A second fundamental of destination management research is the need to be able to distinguish between secondary and primary research and for DMOs to take advantage of both of these sources of information and data.

Primary and Secondary Research

The concepts of primary and secondary research were discussed during the description of the destination management research process. When does second come first? The answer is in research because secondary research information must be carefully analyzed before primary research is started. The definitions of primary and secondary research for destination management are as follows:

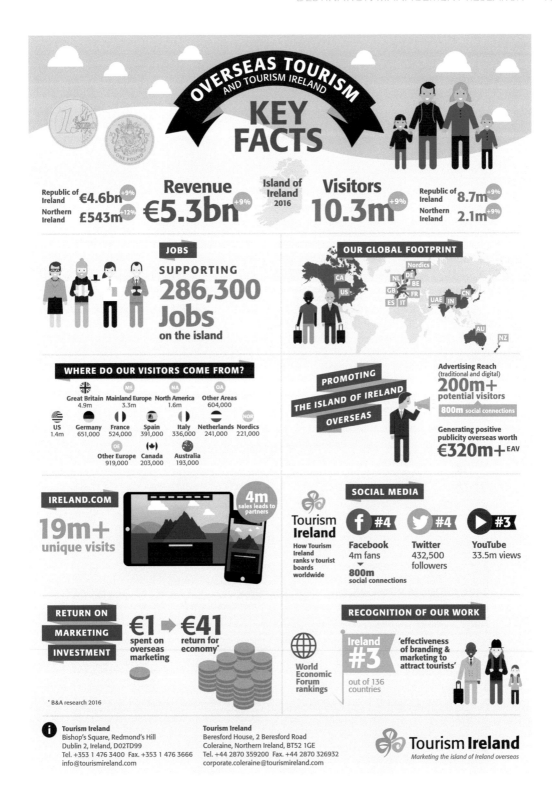

Figure 5.6 Tourism Ireland infographic.

DEFINITIONS

Secondary research

Previously gathered information, which is mostly published by organizations or persons that are not associated with the DMO. It is called secondary since someone else did the research and the DMO is a subsequent user.

Primary research

Research done by DMO staff or by research vendors commissioned by the DMO to collect data that addresses questions specific to the destination. It is "first-time" data collected for the DMO for its own specific purposes, hence the term "primary."

DMOs should use a mixture of secondary and primary research. DMO staff members can be trained where to find secondary research and how to use it. Doing primary research requires a higher level of training and education; it is often better to use a research vendor at either a private research company or an academic institution.

SECONDARY RESEARCH

There is so much secondary research information now available for destination management that it is difficult to identify and describe every source. Some of the secondary research comes from within the DMO or the destination (internal secondary), but most research is produced outside of the DMO and destination (external secondary). Figure 5.7 shows the main sources of a DMO's internal and external secondary research.

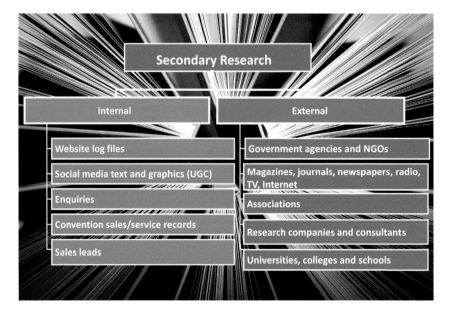

Figure 5.7 Types of internal and external secondary research.

Just so you get the idea about secondary research, think about some of the examples supplied earlier in the chapter. The 2022 survey of accessible tourism is external secondary research from a research company (MMGY Global); the data on Ireland in Figure 5.6 is external secondary research from a government agency (Tourism Ireland). Another good example is the research study produced by the ETC entitled, Europeans' Attitudes toward Responsible Travel Choices (ETC 2021). This research found that Europeans were willing to change travel patterns to reduce their carbon footprints.

Big data is a term now used to describe large quantities of secondary information or data that is usually stored on computer servers or the cloud. As the following example indicates there are three main sources of big data for destination management.

EXAMPLE 5.6

Big Data for Destination Management

This example identifies three big data categories.

> There are many big data sources available for destination management. Big data can be divided into three categories: (1) user-generated content (UGC) data; (2) device data; and (3) transaction data (Li et al. 2018).
>
> (Morrison 2022)

Learning Point

Destinations and DMOs need to make greater use of big data in the future.

UGC is one of the main sources of secondary (big) data that can be used in destination management research. Much of this is on social media platforms such as Facebook, Instagram, YouTube, and TikTok, and on review sites such as Tripadvisor. As you will already know, the information there is in the form of text, photos, and videos. For the textual data, researchers can perform content analysis either manually or using various software programs that include NVivo, ATLAS.ti, Leximancer, and several others. Your author has just completed a content analysis using Leximancer based on visitor comments on Tripadvisor about Naples, Italy.

DEFINITION

Content analysis

"Content analysis is a research tool used to determine the presence of certain words or concepts within texts or sets of texts. Researchers quantify and analyze the presence, meanings and relationships of such words and concepts, then make inferences about the messages within the texts, the writer(s), the audience, and even the culture and time of which these are a part" (Colorado State University 2022).

Device (big) data is derived mainly from smartphone use by visitors to destinations. Tracking studies using global positioning system (GPS) are one of the methods to collect such device data. Transaction data comes from purchases that visitors make and this is increasingly through cashless payment systems based on smartphones.

PRIMARY RESEARCH

Earlier there was a discussion on research design related to primary research. Figure 5.8 identifies the main primary research designs in two parts: quantitative primary research, mainly producing numerical data, and qualitative primary research, mainly generating non-numeric data. When both designs are used, this is called a mixed methods approach.

DEFINITION

Mixed methods research design

A research design that uses a combination of qualitative and quantitative methods. This allows researchers to take advantage of both approaches.

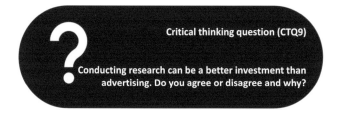

? Critical thinking question (CTQ9)

Conducting research can be a better investment than advertising. Do you agree or disagree and why?

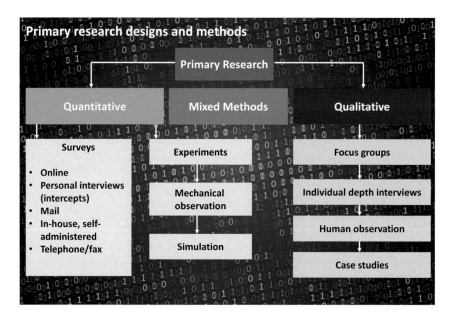

Figure 5.8 Primary research designs and methods.

1. Visitor market analysis	Profile characteristics of existing visitors
2. Potential visitor market analysis	Assess potential demand
3. Destination image analysis	Determine perceptions of destination
4. Competitive analysis	Identify competitive strengths and weaknesses
5. Resident sentiment analysis	Examine resident attitudes and opinions
6. Destination audit	Research product and management quality
7. Economic impact analysis	Estimate economic contributions of tourism
8. Performance measurement	Evaluate performance against objectives

Types of destination management research

Figure 5.9 Types of destination management research projects.

Types of Destination Management Research Projects

Now that you are familiar with these two fundamentals of destination management research—the destination management research process and secondary and primary research—it is appropriate to discuss eight types of research projects that are of special importance for DMOs and destinations. These are highlighted in Figure 5.9 along with their key outputs.

Visitor Market Analysis (Existing Visitors)

It is essential that a destination fully comprehends its portfolio of existing visitors. Primary research is needed to build this understanding of existing markets and specifically a technique that is usually called a visitor profile study. The following are the seven main steps in conducting a visitor profile study.

1. Establish study objectives, visitor characteristics, and supporting questions.
2. Define a visitor.
3. Determine data collection method.
4. Develop the survey questionnaire.
5. Determine the sample design and size.
6. Determine study schedule.
7. Analyze, interpret, report and communicate the data and results.

ESTABLISH STUDY OBJECTIVES, VISITOR CHARACTERISTICS, AND SUPPORTING QUESTIONS

Conducting a visitor profile study within a destination meets several important objectives. The visitor characteristics and supporting questions addressed are shown in Figure 5.10.

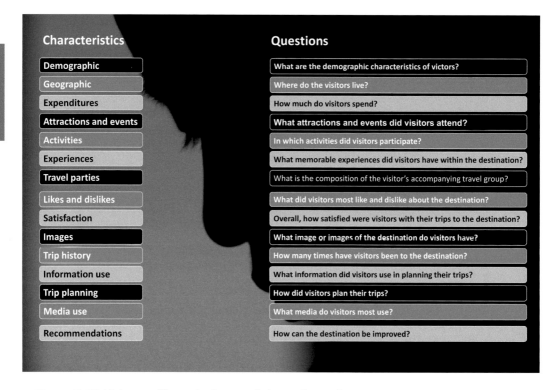

Characteristics	Questions
Demographic	What are the demographic characteristics of victors?
Geographic	Where do the visitors live?
Expenditures	How much do visitors spend?
Attractions and events	What attractions and events did visitors attend?
Activities	In which activities did visitors participate?
Experiences	What memorable experiences did visitors have within the destination?
Travel parties	What is the composition of the visitor's accompanying travel group?
Likes and dislikes	What did visitors most like and dislike about the destination?
Satisfaction	Overall, how satisfied were visitors with their trips to the destination?
Images	What image or images of the destination do visitors have?
Trip history	How many times have visitors been to the destination?
Information use	What information did visitors use in planning their trips?
Trip planning	How did visitors plan their trips?
Media use	What media do visitors most use?
Recommendations	How can the destination be improved?

Figure 5.10 Visitor profile study characteristics and questions.

DEFINE A VISITOR

A clear definition of a visitor is needed for this type of research study. Sometimes, a visitor is defined as a non-resident of the destination who stays in the destination for at least one night. Other definitions allow for visitors to include people who are non-residents but do not stay overnight in the destination. This can be especially important to places that receive a high proportion of day-trippers, or so-called excursionists. The main concern here is to exclude residents and others who are commuting every day to work in the destination. In some instances, a visitor must travel a minimum of a certain distance or be from specific geographic areas to qualify for surveying.

EXAMPLE 5.7

Definition of an International Visitor to Indonesia

This example shows that very specific definitions of who qualifies for tourism research studies are needed.

> The respondents in this survey include all identified international visitors who will leave Indonesia territory through air, sea, and land gates. The mechanism for determining respondents as international visitors are as follows:
>
> 1. Select respondents whose residence is not in Indonesia.
>
> 2. If the respondent works for wages in Indonesia, make sure that the length of stay in Indonesia is less than 365 nights.

3. If the respondent goes to school/college for more than one year, it is included in the survey coverage.

(Statistics Indonesia 2021: 14)

Learning Point

Precise quality control is required for conducting tourism research.

DETERMINE DATA COLLECTION METHOD

Visitor profile studies generally apply the survey design method, but there are now many data collection methods available for such surveys. For example, the 2021 Las Vegas Visitor Profile Study was accomplished by using face-to-face (intercept) surveys. Personal interviews are usually the most expensive and difficult way to survey existing markets, but this data collection method has distinct advantages, including there is absolute certainty that respondents (those people surveyed) visited the destination; people can recollect their destination experiences very well; and there is usually a high rate of response and completion of surveys (the refusal rate is relatively low).

EXAMPLE 5.8

Intercept Process for Las Vegas Visitor Profile Study

Visitor profile studies must gather data from people at different and key locations within the destination as in the Las Vegas study.

Visitors were intercepted in the vicinity of Las Vegas casinos, hotels, motels and at Harry Reid International Airport. To assure a random selection of visitors, different locations were utilized on each interviewing day, and interviewing was conducted at different times of the day. Upon completion of the interview, visitors were given souvenirs as "thank you's." Verification procedures were conducted throughout the project to assure accurate and valid interviewing.

(LVCVA 2022: 9)

Learning Point

Detailed procedures must be decided before launching data collection for visitor profile studies.

The personal interview method has disadvantages in addition to its higher costs. People may feel that they are being inconvenienced in being stopped and asked to complete a survey, and this is especially the case for business travelers who are often on very tight schedules. Additionally, some people may have just arrived in the destination and not yet had the full experience. Their estimates of expenditures may be more guesses than accurate facts.

Exit surveys are very popular as visitor profile studies, although they are hard to implement at destinations with multiple exit points. For example, Indonesia conducts its Passenger Exit Survey by conducting interviews with visitors at sixteen departure points around the country (Statistics Indonesia 2021). Many island destinations are ideal for exit surveys because they have very few exit points where visitors tend to congregate before leaving. These include Prince Edward Island (Canada), Jersey (Channel Islands, UK), Guam, Tasmania (Australia), and Sint Maarten (Dutch West Indies), to name just a few.

EXAMPLE 5.9

The Prince Edward Island (PEI) Visitor Exit Survey

Island destinations often find it easier to conduct exit surveys as in this Canadian example.

> A visitor exit survey is a tool used to profile visitors and estimate their impact on a destination. It can capture visitor demographics and information about their trips including their origin. Tourism PEI conducts a visitor exit survey on a four-year cycle. 8,536 surveys were completed in 2018–2019.
>
> (Tourism PEI 2020)

Learning Point

Exit surveys require full cooperation from transportation terminals and immigration and customs if at national border points.

Visitor profile studies can be completed with other data collection methods apart from personal interviews. If contact information can be gathered for visitors while they are in the destination or when they book, they can be contacted after they return home by phone, mail or email. For example, the Hawai'i Tourism Authority conducts its Visitor Satisfaction Study online (respondents are first sent an invitation by email). For the first quarter of 2022, HTA received 3,832 completed survey questionnaires in total for eight geographic areas (US and Canada) (Hawai'i Tourism Authority 2022). A major challenge with post-visit surveys is the possibility of visitors forgetting the exact details of their trips to the destination.

A second example is the National Visitor Survey conducted annually by TRA (2022). This is a study of 120,000 Australian residents that is done via telephone (less were surveyed during COVID-19). The survey has seventy questions on destinations, purpose, transportation, travel packages, sources of information about trips, activities, expenditures, accommodation, travel parties, and demographics.

With response rates usually above 50 percent and sometimes much higher, personal interviews normally produce the highest response rates and lower the risk of a non-response bias. To counterbalance this, questionnaires can be gathered more efficiently (at a lower cost) via online surveys.

EXAMPLE 5.10

Response Rate for the Jersey Passenger Exit Survey

Calculating the valid response rates for surveys is a most important procedure.

> The sample size above (2,000 interviews) represents 6.5 percent of total departing passengers on the scheduled air and sea routes in January (2020). Interviewers record the number of refusals as well as the number of self-completion questionnaires handed out in order to determine the response rate; this was 76 percent in January for the Passenger Exit Survey.
>
> (Statistics Jersey 2020)

Learning Point

The higher the response rate; the greater is the accuracy and robustness of survey data.

DEVELOP THE SURVEY QUESTIONNAIRE

The survey questionnaire should contain all the questions needed to satisfy the research objectives for the visitor profile study. However, it is important that survey questionnaires should not be lengthy because respondents get irritated when filling them out if it takes too much time. As a general rule, a questionnaire should not have more than thirty questions or take more than fifteen minutes to complete. Completing questionnaires has become easier thanks to information communication technologies, especially with the use of the Internet, smartphones, and tablets. The traditional pen-and-paper approaches are much slower in recording responses (although they still are done in some places).

You may be familiar with some online survey platforms that help researchers design and distribute questionnaires. These include Qualtrics, SurveyMonkey, Google Forms, and many others. Some are free to use, while others charge fees.

DETERMINE THE SAMPLE DESIGN AND SIZE

Here, a decision must be made about which visitors are to be surveyed and how many completed survey questionnaires are required. If several distinct groups of visitors are to be surveyed, the total sample size for the research project will be larger. For example, in the Jersey Passenger Exit Survey, 2,000 people completed questionnaires and the margin of error was 1.7 percent at the 95 percent confidence interval. The margin of error is lower as the number of surveys completed increases. But what does the margin of error mean? Here is an example for the survey in Jersey where 36 percent of the respondents said they were on business visits. Based on the sample size of 3,250 departing visitors and at a 95 percent confidence level, it can be estimated that the true percentage of business visits was from 34.3 percent to 37.7 percent (the gap is 3.4 percent, equal to twice the margin of error). The gap (3.4 percent for business visitors) would be higher if the sample size were lower.

If the personal interview method is used, decisions will also have to be made on where and when visitors are to be intercepted. Good places for intercepting visitors are at airports, ferry and bus terminals, lodging facilities, attractions, festivals/events and arts and cultural performances, shopping areas and visitor centers. The International Visitor Survey for New Zealand intercepts people at airports as they are departing the country:

DETERMINE STUDY SCHEDULE

Another question to be addressed is how many times in a year the survey is to be conducted. Of course, this will probably be dictated by the budget available for the research project, but for greater accuracy it is better to consider whether the profile of visitors varies significantly by season or even by month of the year.

In most cases, visitor profile studies are conducted only once a year, but there are some situations where surveys are completed more frequently. For example, the Las Vegas Visitor Profile Study is conducted in each month of the year. Other destinations do these studies once per quarter or once per year.

It may also be necessary to consider the day of the week and the time of day when visitor surveys are conducted. If the destination tends to get most visitors on weekends, for example, then more surveys should be completed on Saturdays and Sundays.

ANALYZE, INTERPRET, REPORT AND COMMUNICATE THE DATA AND RESULTS

As previously discussed, these steps are crucial for the success of all research projects. The example in Figure 5.6 shows that a DMO can communicate research results in a very creative and compelling way.

Potential Visitor Market Analysis

A DMO may have an interest in the future demand potential of a specific geographic market or market segment and decide to conduct research on that group. These potential market analyses can be done through either secondary research only or a primary research project. The potential markets may be completely new markets or may already be markets that are visiting the destination.

Destination Canada has a series of research studies on potential markets called the Global Tourism Watch (GTW). The potential markets for Canada from France, Germany, Japan, Mexico, the UK, and the USA were analyzed through surveys conducted in 2021. The surveys were conducted online, and the sample population for the online survey was residents of each country aged eighteen years and older who had taken an international pleasure trip staying at least one night in paid accommodation in the past three years, or with the intention to take such a trip in the next two years. For France, the sample size was 1,500 respondents, of whom 185 had recently visited Canada.

EXAMPLE 5.11

Objectives of GTW Surveys

This example from Canada describes the very clear objectives of a suite of potential visitor surveys.

- Monitor awareness, travel intentions, and other key market indicators for Canada.
- Assess perceptions of Canada and track brand performance against key competitors.

- Identify the general experiences sought by travelers, assess Canada's competitive positioning on key products and identify growth opportunities.
- Identify motivators and barriers for travel to Canada.
- Explore the role of advocacy in the tourism context.

(Destination Canada 2022)

Learning Point

Having precise goals and objectives for research projects is essential.

A second example is the analysis of CBT opportunities for Myanmar based on potential visitors from Europe (NBI Ministry of Foreign Affairs 2020). The objectives of this study were to determine the types of CBT products appealing to European visitors and how the tourism offer in Myanmar could be developed along internationally recognized sustainable tourism guidelines.

These examples demonstrate that there is a wide variety of data collection methods available for analyzing potential markets. They range from simpler secondary research analysis (European CBT visitors for Myanmar) to extensive surveys in source countries (French visitors for Canada).

Destination Image Analysis

The analysis of destination image has been a hot topic for tourism scholars since the early 1970s; however, destination image studies by DMOs have been much less frequently attempted. So much of what has been written about destination image is within tourism academic journals and conference proceedings. There is no doubt that bridging this research gap between theory and practice is desirable for destination management.

ACADEMIC DESTINATION IMAGE RESEARCH

From the academic perspective, Stepchenkova and Morrison (2008), based on the previous research by Echtner and Ritchie (1993), indicated that destination image has two main components (attributes and holistic) and three dimensions (functional, tangible, and psychological).

EXAMPLE 5.12

Destination Image Components and Dimensions

This example suggests that destination images are varied and include tangible and more intangible dimensions.

- Destination image should be envisioned as consisting of two main components, those that are attribute-based and those that are holistic.
- Each of these components of destination image contains functional, or more tangible, and psychological, or more abstract, characteristics.
- Images of destinations can also range from those based on "common" functional and psychological traits to those based on more distinctive or even unique features, events, feelings or auras.

(Echtner and Ritchie 1993)

> **Learning Point**
>
> Destination images are multidimensional.

Doing research on a destination's image attributes is normally accomplished through a survey data collection method in which respondents are asked to rank the destination on a list of predetermined attributes. You saw an example of this earlier in Destination Canada's GTW in which people were asked about their perceptions of Canada. Images can also be determined through qualitative methods, such as focus groups; in-depth interviews; and analyzing visitor blogs, destination reviews, photographs taken, and other UGC in social media.

The second main component, holistic images, are more difficult to measure because they are an overall assessment of a destination. Because they are personal opinions and vary from person to person, they cannot be measured by attribute lists. They are suited to open-ended questions to which each respondent provides unique answers. For example, in a destination image study on Brazil that was conducted in the USA, the following three open-ended questions were asked (Rezende-Parker et al. 2003):

1. What images or characteristics come to your mind when you think of Brazil?
2. What is the mood or atmosphere in Brazil?
3. Which distinctive or unique attractions can be found in Brazil?

Qualitative research data collection methods can be used to explore holistic images, including focus groups, where about eight to twelve people from the target audience are invited to attend a discussion about the destination. An experienced facilitator coordinates the focus group discussions and invites the participants to give their thoughts and opinions on a short list of open-ended questions. Then, the facilitator will get the group to reach a consensus on the most important issues within the discussion.

Measuring these two main components of destination image is not all there is to destination image research. It is also important to examine the information that causes people to form images about destinations. This image formation process is quite complex, as you are about to learn. Destination images are formed in different ways and influenced by a variety of sources of information on places, including previous visits. Gartner (1993) suggested that there are eight destination image formation agents (Fig. 5.11). They range from organic images that are formed by visiting a destination to overt induced 1, where a person notices tourism advertising by the destination. The three organic agents are the most powerful in forming destination image, and two of them are what usually gets called word of mouth (WOM).

The covert and overt induced image formation agents should constantly be tracked by the DMO. These may not be as powerful as actual visit experiences and WOM, but they can be influential, especially if the information is from a trusted and unbiased source. For example, the opinions of people on travel review sites like Tripadvisor and from influencers are often consulted in selecting destinations.

DMO Destination Image Research

On the practitioner side, DMOs conduct image research that applies directly to their destinations. For example, Longwoods International in 2021 conducted the Richmond Region Tourism: A Custom Image Perception Study on behalf of Richmond Region Tourism (North

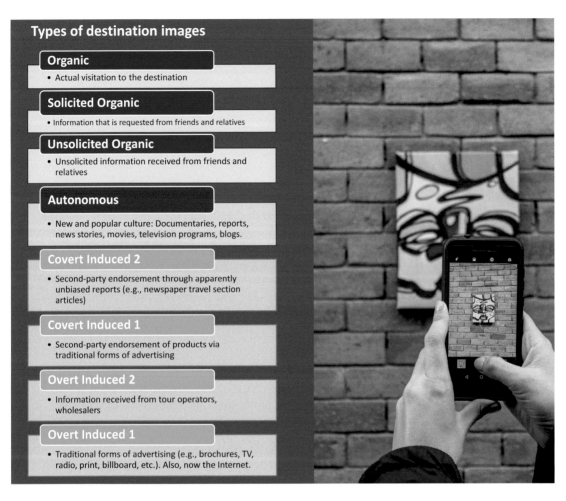

Types of destination images

Organic
- Actual visitation to the destination

Solicited Organic
- Information that is requested from friends and relatives

Unsolicited Organic
- Unsolicited information received from friends and relatives

Autonomous
- New and popular culture: Documentaries, reports, news stories, movies, television programs, blogs.

Covert Induced 2
- Second-party endorsement through apparently unbiased reports (e.g., newspaper travel section articles)

Covert Induced 1
- Second-party endorsement of products via traditional forms of advertising

Overt Induced 2
- Information received from tour operators, wholesalers

Overt Induced 1
- Traditional forms of advertising (e.g., brochures, TV, radio, print, billboard, etc.). Also, now the Internet.

Figure 5.11 Types of destination images (Gartner 1993).

Carolina, USA). Images of Richmond were more positive among those who had visited in the past two years compared to those who had not, based a survey of 1,000 people (Longwoods International 2022a).

Some DMOs do not conduct full-scale destination image studies but rather incorporate image-style questions in visitor profile and potential market studies. Of course, this saves money, and the data may be collected more frequently. For example, Tourism Northern Ireland conducts a series of Visitor Attitude Surveys that provide visitor profile characteristics as well as measuring attitudes and perceptions about various aspects of tourism experiences (Tourism Northern Ireland 2022). VisitBritain/VisitEngland produced a series of reports on destinations in England under the title of Destination Satisfaction and Perceptions. The reports "provide a summary of visitation, visitor experience, and perceptions of destinations" (VisitBritain/VisitEngland 2022). Some forty-one destinations were included in the report series.

Another practical way to assess destination image is to analyze what people are saying about the destination. This has become more popular because of the huge amount of comments being written in popular social media channels and blogs. For example, Choi et al. (2007) prepared a research study on the destination image of Macao by analyzing online content. A qualitative research design known as content analysis was applied to the online text about Macao as a destination. They found that Macao's destination image varied across five online information sources (Macao Government Tourist Office [MGTO], blogs, magazines, guides and travel trade). This type of destination image analysis is much less expensive to do when compared to visitor surveys, but it has limitations for practical application. The main drawbacks are that the content mainly represents induced image formation agents (Fig. 5.11) and the accuracy and credibility of the information are not as high as data from actual visitors.

Competitive Analysis

It is a very good idea for a destination to be constantly tracking its main competitors and what these destinations are doing. The DMO may do this informally, but periodically there is a need to do a full-blown competitive analysis study. Which competitors should be analyzed and what are the most important dimensions of these competitive destinations that should be assessed? Destination competitive sets vary according to the markets and products to be covered in the analysis. For example, the competitors for conventions and exhibitions will be different than those for pleasure or leisure travelers.

You will remember in Chapter 1 that the 10 As model of successful destinations was described and it can be used for comparisons with competitive destinations. These two sources provide a good initial list of dimensions for comparing competitive destinations.

Destination competitive analysis is another research area that has attracted great attention from tourism scholars but has not permeated the professional destination management field as deeply. Crouch (2007) divides this scholarly research into three categories:

1. diagnosing the competitive positions of specific destinations;
2. focusing on specific aspects of competitiveness, such as marketing and price competitiveness;
3. developing general models and theories of destination competitiveness.

For the third category, several models of destination competitiveness have been proposed by tourism scholars, but they have yet to be widely applied in practice. The Ritchie and Crouch (2003) model of destination competitiveness is one of the most widely accepted (Fig. 5.12) and is very comprehensive. Destination competitiveness in this model comprises five components:

1. supporting factors and resources;
2. core resources and attractors;
3. destination management;
4. destination policy, planning and development;
5. qualifying and amplifying determinants.

There is a significant divide between academics and industry practitioners with respect to destination competitiveness. While the volume of scholarly publishing on destination competitiveness is impressive, this work is rarely seen, read, or translated by DMO practitioners into management action. One main reason is differences in how academics and practitioners communicate. The Ritchie and Crouch model is extensively used by scholars and is a comprehensive portrayal of destination competitiveness; however, it may be too complex for practitioners to adopt as there are thirty-six components within it, many of which have no specific measurements or scale. It can be argued that practitioners need more simple models with clear measures.

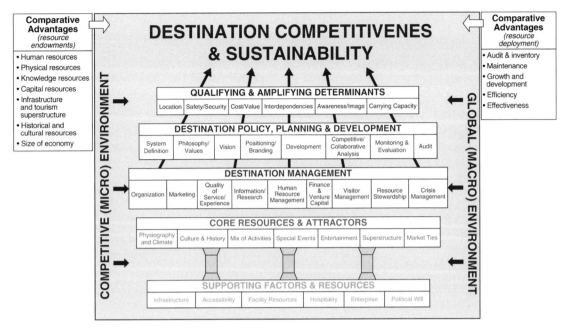

Figure 5.12 Model of destination competitiveness (Ritchie and Crouch 2003; Crouch 2007).

Models are models, and often their great complexity means that tourism practitioners find them difficult to apply in the real world. Now you will learn about applications of competitive analysis by destinations and advisory agencies. One of the most famous competitive analyses in tourism is that conducted by the World Economic Forum (WEF), based in Switzerland. The Travel and Tourism Development Index (TTDI) ranks countries according to criteria arranged in five pillars (enabling environment; travel and tourism policy and enabling conditions; infrastructure; travel and tourism demand drivers; and travel and tourism sustainability).

EXAMPLE 5.13

Top Ten TTDI Countries in 2021

This example is on a significant country tourism ranking system operated by the WEF.

> Aside from the USA (2nd), the top ten scoring countries are high-income economies in the Europe and Eurasia or Asia-Pacific regions. Japan tops the ranking, with fellow regional economies Australia and Singapore coming in 7th and 9th, respectively. Meanwhile, Italy joined the top ten (up from 12th in 2019) in 2021, while Canada slid out (10th to 13th). The remaining top ten TTDI performers are Spain (3rd), France (4th), Germany (5th), Switzerland (6th) and the UK (8th).
> (WEF 2022)

Learning Point

Benchmarking is a topic within performance measurement that is covered in Chapter 20. The TTDI is an important benchmark for national DMOs.

Resident Sentiment Analysis

Community relationships and involvement are an important destination management role and need to be supported by research on resident attitudes and opinions about tourism. Community resident support is fundamental to the sustainability of the tourism sector within a destination. You learned about this in Chapter 3.

Surprisingly, there is not much of this type of research done by DMOs, although there is a growing recognition that DMOs need to constantly pay attention to how local people perceive the tourism sector. This is another field of tourism research where scholars are doing much research but the practical application in destination management is limited.

Tourism within destinations affects residents directly and indirectly. The impacts can be positive but they can also negatively impact the lives of the people who live there. Barcelona and Venice are two popular European city destinations where there has been a backlash against too much tourism, and the small island nation of Iceland is also struggling with rapid increases in visitor numbers. Therefore, it is important to frequently gauge resident viewpoints on tourism in destination communities.

Traditionally, DMOs tended to focus most of their communications and research externally on markets, but this is not enough anymore because residents are an important internal market for the DMO and the destination. There are still many more DMO studies with a focus on visitors than on local people. Visit Flanders in Belgium completed a Resident Attitudes toward Tourism in Bruges in 2016. The good news from the survey results was that 76 percent of the residents said, "I support tourism and want to see it remain important to Bruges," and 89 percent indicated that Bruges should remain a tourist destination. In addition, 70 percent believed, "In general, the positive benefits of tourism outweigh negative impacts in Bruges." Some 81 percent felt, "Tourism in Bruges makes me proud to be a Bruges resident." Despite the overall positive attitudes and opinions, there were some reasons for concern. For example, 73 percent of residents disagreed with the statement, "I have a voice in Bruges tourism development decisions," and 43 percent said, "I want to be involved more in tourism policies and planning in Bruges" (Visit Flanders 2016). You can see that although Bruges residents were generally supportive of tourism in their city, they felt removed from the decision-making about tourism.

Another good example of resident research is the Canadian Resident Sentiment toward Tourism study prepared by Longwoods International in 2021. This research was done in cooperation with Destinations International and involved a survey of 1,000 Canadian residents. Example 5.14 provides one interesting finding from this study.

EXAMPLE 5.14

What Canadian Residents Think About Tourism

It is essential for DMOs to determine what residents think about tourism, as in this survey of Canadians.

> And Canadians credit tourism and visitors for improving the quality of life for residents in their provinces, with about half expressing this belief and less than 20 percent disagreeing with that statement. The majority believe they have

more recreational and shopping opportunities because of tourism. However, they do blame visitors for traffic and parking problems.

(Longwoods International 2021)

Learning Point

It is vital to determine if residents feel that tourism is improving their life quality or not.

Destination Audit

A destination audit is an in-depth analysis and assessment of a destination. Here is a more precise definition.

DEFINITION

Destination audit

A destination audit analyzes the current tourism situation in a destination, identifies opportunities for improvement in products and management, and evaluates future potential in terms of new developments and markets.

Known also as a destination analysis, the audit assesses the destination product, destination marketing, and organizations involved in tourism, including the DMO. Usually, a mixture of sources is used to get multiple perspectives of tourism in the destination (tourism business operators, residents, government officials, visitors). A variety of secondary and primary research methods are used to collect data and information (online searches, surveys, in-depth interviews, focus groups, mystery shopping). For greater objectivity, destination audits are sometimes carried out by consulting companies, and each firm has its own distinctive approaches. All the information and data are melded together to produce recommendations on how to improve tourism within the destination.

Providing a real example of a destination audit will help you get a better grasp on this type of research project. A destination audit was completed for a popular lakeside area in Sweden.

EXAMPLE 5.15

Destination Audit of the Eastern Coast of Lake Vättern in Sweden

As in this example, destination audits help pinpoint what needs to be enhanced or improved within destinations.

The purpose of this research was "to evaluate the current visitor experience and identify opportunities for future sustainable development in the destination." For destination marketing, one of the major recommendations of the audit was to "create a cohesive destination brand and identity, collaboration and partnerships are key especially if it is to encompass the whole lake and surrounding regions. Stay over and stay longer, visit outside the key summer months and leave no trace could be key messaging."

(Visit Östergötland 2021)

Learning Point

Destination audits should be objective and produce meaningful ideas and solutions.

The destination product part of the destination audit analyzes physical products, people, packaging, and programming. Product development is one of the roles of destination management as you learned in Chapter 1, and research must guide decisions related to all parts of the destination product. Figure 5.13 shows the specific research that can be done related to physical products, people, packaging, and programming, split by whether the focus is on the existing destination product or for expanded and new destination products.

The demand or market part of the "current situation" in a destination audit is addressed in visitor profile studies and destination image analyses as well as in gathering resident attitudes and opinions on tourism.

Visitor satisfaction and experience analysis research is a crucial important component of a destination audit because happy people tell others about their experiences and are also more likely to return.

Types of product development research	Destination product	Existing	Expanded and new
	Physical products	• Business performance surveys • Mystery shopping • Site inspections	• Product development exemplar case studies • Feasibility studies • Market analyses
	People	• Labor market analysis • Community resident analysis • Service quality audits • Visitor satisfaction analysis	• Labor needs analysis • Potential visitor analysis
	Packaging	• Surveys of package users	• Packaging exemplar case studies • Travel trade surveys
	Programming	• Festival/event participant analysis	• Festival/event exemplar case studies

Figure 5.13 Types of product development research.

Hawaii Is Tracking Visitor Satisfaction

Tracking visitor satisfaction with destinations is an extremely valuable source of information for improving tourism experiences, products, and services.

> The Visitor Satisfaction and Activity Survey is a survey of visitors who recently completed a trip to Hawai'i. As part of the survey, each respondent is asked a series of questions specific to one of the islands visited during their stay. Respondents have the opportunity to complete up to two island specific surveys.
>
> (State of Hawai'i Department of Business, Economic Development and Tourism 2022)

Learning Point

Every destination and DMO needs to measure visitor satisfaction; however, not all do.

Almost all the visitor profile studies discussed earlier contain one or more questions about visitor satisfaction. Although they may not be investing in full-scale visitor satisfaction studies, these DMOs are still constantly tracking the satisfaction levels of their visitors.

Festival and event research is widespread and even has two academic journals (*Event Management* and *International Journal of Event and Festival Management*). Again, this is a very popular field of research for tourism scholars but gets much less attention from DMOs. However, some destinations conduct research to profile visitors to their biggest festivals and events and to estimate impacts. For example, the impacts of festivals in Edinburgh, Scotland, are being measured. In 2020, a very interesting research study—Edinburgh Festivals: Inspiring Creativity in Pupils—was completed. Overall, it was found that Edinburgh Festivals were actively engaging with local schools and have a positive influence on the creativity of schoolchildren.

Research on Edinburgh Festivals' Engagement with Local Schools

This is an outstanding example of performance measurement by festivals in the Scottish capital.

> Festivals are engaging with the vast majority of Edinburgh's schools, and together have a substantial year-round cultural offer for schools, covering all aspects of creative learning. It is clear that through their work with schools, festivals are successfully engaging with areas of the city and communities that would otherwise tend not to participate in their programs. Further research is

continuing to better understand the needs and priorities of all schools, and to gain new insights into potential barriers to engagement with festivals.

(EdinburghFestivalsCity.com 2022)

Learning Point

Research on the engagement of various markets with events and festivals should be conducted.

The assessment of destination quality levels is a branch of product development research that some DMOs undertake and consider it to be of great importance. You will learn more about this in Chapter 7, which is devoted to the DMO product development role. The most popular research methods and techniques are discussed in greater detail there.

There is another type of analysis that is also often called a destination audit, although it is not the same as you have just learned. This is an audit of a DMO and its effectiveness. The City of Scottsdale, Arizona carried out an audit of Experience Scottsdale, the DMO that has a contract to provides destination marketing services for the city government (City of Scottsdale 2022). This is a topic that will be picked up again in Chapter 6 (related to transparency and governance) and in Chapter 20 (related to performance measurement and evaluation).

Economic Impact Analysis

The measurement of the economic impact of tourism has been an important research topic for destinations for at least the past forty-five years, and many approaches have been used. Many "tourism multiplier" studies were conducted in the earliest period and demonstrated that the spending and employment in the tourism sector have a ripple effect in other economic sectors of the destination. Tourism Vancouver Island's Dynamic Connections graphic (Fig. 5.14) does a great job in displaying this effect.

Several countries have now introduced tourism satellite accounts (TSAs), including Australia, Ireland, New Zealand, South Africa, the UK, and the USA. TSAs show the impacts of tourism on GDP as well as how tourism affects other sectors of the economy. A short description of the South Africa's TSA is provided in Example 5.18.

EXAMPLE 5.18

The TSAs in South Africa

This example describes how South Africa measures the economic impact of tourism through Satellite Accounting.

The Tourism Satellite Accounts (TSA) give an overview of the role that tourism plays in South Africa and provide information on tourism's contribution to the South African economy both in terms of expenditure and employment. The TSA for South Africa is compiled and published by Statistics South Africa (Stats SA) according to the framework (Tourism Satellite Account: Recommended

Methodological Framework (TSA: RMF)) developed by the United Nations World Tourism Organization (UNWTO).

(Department of Tourism [South Africa] 2022)

Learning Point

Tourism satellite accounting is increasingly being accepted as the best way to measure economic impact.

Figure 5.14 The ripple effect of tourism.

To give you a clearer idea of the outputs of a TSA, some results for tourism in New Zealand will be helpful. Tourism directly contributed $8.5 billion to New Zealand's GDP (April 2020 to March 2021), the equivalent of 2.9 percent of GDP. Due to the effects of the COVID-19 pandemic, that was a decrease of 47.5 percent over the previous year. Unfortunately, the number of overseas visitors fell by 98.6 percent (Ministry of Business, Innovation and Employment [New Zealand] 2021).

DMOs can also check secondary sources for economic impact and expenditure data. Globally, major sources of data on economic impact and tourist spending are the WTTC and UNWTO. WTTC

Part II

publishes regular economic impact reports for many countries (WTTC 2022). UNWTO publishes the most comprehensive and authoritative statistics on international tourism arrivals and spending (UNWTO 2022). The OECD is another useful source of these data (OECD 2022). At a regional level, the ETC and PATA are important generators of these data (ETC 2022; PATA 2022).

There are many ways to do economic impact analysis research for destinations, and this discussion has been short. However, the topic of economic impacts is discussed in greater detail in Chapter 6. It suffices to say here that economic impact research data are vital for proving the relative value of tourism as an economic sector of the destination (advocacy research).

Performance Measurement

Performance measurement and reporting are important tasks that a DMO needs to accomplish with great professionalism. What are the main reasons for doing evaluation research and why should the DMO make an investment in this branch of research? There are internal and external reasons for conducting evaluation research, and they are shown in Figure 5.15.

Measuring and reporting the DMO's performance require many research inputs. DMOs around the world are increasingly being closely scrutinized and asked to demonstrate their accountability for the funds with which they have been entrusted.

A DMO's performance needs to be measured by its effectiveness in accomplishing the roles that it has been assigned. You will remember from Chapter 1 that there are eight roles that DMOs can play, and a DMO should have specific objectives for each role. We can also call these roles the KRAs, or key result areas. For each KRA (or role), KPIs are established. KPIs are specific measurements, or metrics (Fig. 5.16).

Some DMOs adopt KPIs established by other agencies or companies to assess their tourism performance. For 2019, as an example, the Ministry of Tourism in Saudi Arabia reported that the country had climbed up by ten places in the WEF's TTDI (Ministry of Tourism [Saudi Arabia] 2022).

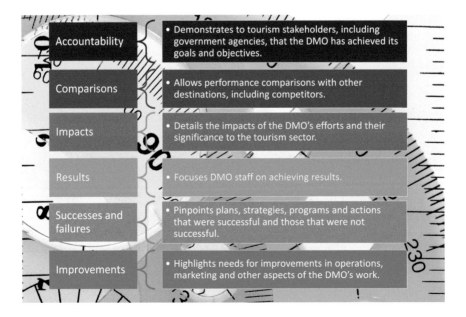

Figure 5.15 Reasons for DMO performance measurement.

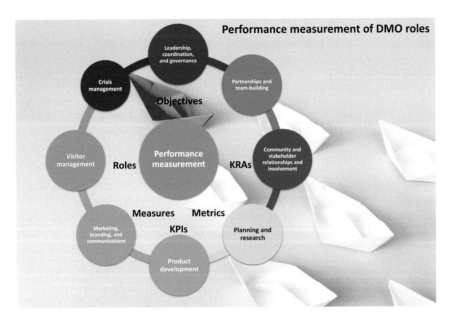

Figure 5.16 Performance measurement of DMO roles.

Destinations International has produced a set of standard performance measures for DMOs. Activity, performance and productivity measures are specified for five performance reporting areas, and the ROI of the DMO is also estimated:

1. DMO convention sales performance reporting;
2. DMO travel trade sales performance reporting;
3. DMO marketing and communications performance reporting;
4. DMO membership performance reporting;
5. DMO visitor information center performance reporting;
6. DMO ROI.

EXAMPLE 5.19

Standard DMO Performance Reporting

This system is discussed more in Chapters 19 and 20. It was a very valuable and meaningful initiative by Destinations International on behalf of DMOs.

> With the adoption of standard DMO performance reporting techniques, the DMO community has recognized benchmarks to utilize in order to assess its internal performance over time as well as provide meaningful comparisons to other DMOs. Most importantly, with ever-growing accountability and scrutiny from its stakeholders, the utilization of industry standards re-enforces confidence in DMO operating and reporting practices.
>
> (Destinations International 2011)

Learning Point

DMOs need more benchmarks for performance measurement.

Many companies and NPOs are required to prepare annual reports of performance and these can also be classified as a type of evaluation research. What types of research are done to complete these reports to share with shareholders and/or stakeholders? You are right if you answered that annual reports quote secondary research information, and that this comes from internal (e.g., financial statements) and external (e.g., published tourism statistics) sources.

There are certainly other analysis topics and types of research projects that can be done by DMOs. However, eight of the most prominent analysis topics have been described in the foregoing materials. Next, there is a need to discuss some of the organizational details to get research done smoothly.

You are probably curious about whether every DMO does these research studies on a consistent basis. From the author's experience, the answer is definitely in the negative. Unfortunately, DMOs do not yet give a high enough priority to destination management research and need to do more in the future.

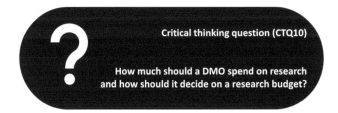

?

Critical thinking question (CTQ10)

How much should a DMO spend on research and how should it decide on a research budget?

DMO Research Departments and Staff

Not all DMOs have full-time research staff, but there are many that do. Some even have their own research departments. It is quite normal for national-level DMOs to have research officers, and they are also found in most state, provincial, and territorial DMOs. Some well-funded city DMOs, including Las Vegas, have their own research departments. Research departments at DMOs are typically small, with most ranging from one to five full-time staff members. Although the number of positions is limited, careers in doing research at DMOs are interesting, rich and rewarding. People with a good background in tourism management and statistical analysis skills are especially well suited for these positions.

EXAMPLE 5.20

Research Department at Ministry of Tourism, Israel

It is rare to find much information on DMO research units and having this information from Israel is most useful.

The Statistics, Research and Information Management Department is mainly occupied with the following subjects:

- collecting, optimizing and analyzing data regarding the tourism industry in Israel;
- regular reports regarding tourism in Israel, including tourist entry, tourist accommodation and new relevant researches regarding tourism;

- promoting surveys and studies regarding tourism, including an annual survey of incoming tourists in Israel;
- various processing work on survey data;
- management of a library containing around 8,000 items, including books, articles and journals;
- work with international organizations (OECD, UNWTO, EUROSTAT, INROUTE).

(Ministry of Tourism [Israel] 2022)

Learning Point

DMOs need to be more involved with research.

As in the case of the Ministry of Tourism in Israel, many DMOs keep track of basic statistics on numbers of visitors and their trends. For national-level DMOs, this task is easier for international visitors as they have to pass through immigration. Estimating numbers of visitors for domestic travel and at other geographic levels is not as straightforward, and often accuracy is lacking. Having good visitor profile and economic impact analyses provides a better foundation for such estimation.

Because of staff capability limitations, outsourcing to research vendors is very popular among DMOs, and several research companies have developed specialties in conducting tourism research. You have heard about two of these companies in this chapter, Longwoods International and MMGY (Longwoods International 2022b; MMGY 2022b), and there are many others. The DMO needs to develop requests for proposals (RFPs) and vendor selection criteria for its outsourced research projects. Figure 5.17 presents a model (RESPECT U) developed by the author for research vendor selection.

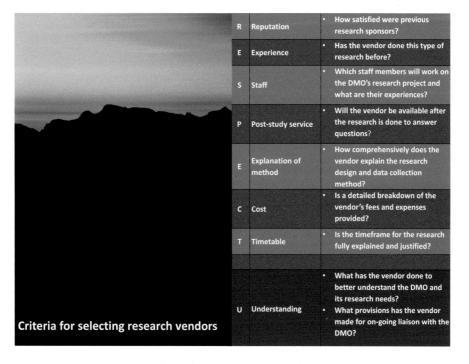

R	Reputation	• How satisfied were previous research sponsors?
E	Experience	• Has the vendor done this type of research before?
S	Staff	• Which staff members will work on the DMO's research project and what are their experiences?
P	Post-study service	• Will the vendor be available after the research is done to answer questions?
E	Explanation of method	• How comprehensively does the vendor explain the research design and data collection method?
C	Cost	• Is a detailed breakdown of the vendor's fees and expenses provided?
T	Timetable	• Is the timeframe for the research fully explained and justified?
U	Understanding	• What has the vendor done to better understand the DMO and its research needs? • What provisions has the vendor made for on-going liaison with the DMO?

Criteria for selecting research vendors

Figure 5.17 RESPECT U criteria for selecting research vendors.

Steps for Effective Destination Management Research

In a summary format, the specific steps for a DMO to accomplish its research role are to:

- prepare a research agenda and plan for destination management research for the next year and three to five years ahead;
- ensure that research contributes to all the destination management roles;
- describe which analysis topics, research designs, and data collection methods will be selected from the available portfolios;
- clearly articulate the rationale and expected benefits of the research contemplated in the agenda and plans;
- prepare a research budget estimate and include it in the research plan;
- implement the research agenda and plan;
- communicate research results to all tourism stakeholders and to other parts of the local community as required;
- evaluate the research plan.

SUMMING UP

The main message in Chapter 5 that you have learned is that destination management research needs to be viewed as an investment in the future rather than an expense in the present. Research is a critical component of professional destination management and contributes to all destination management roles. A DMO should establish a research agenda, covering ongoing, periodic and as-needed research, and prepare an annual research plan and budget as well as a multi-year strategy for destination management research.

Customers, competitors, confidence, credibility, change, community, continuity, and clarity—the eight Cs—are the eight main reasons for doing destination management research. Other reasons for destination management research include demonstrating the size and importance of the tourism sector in the destination, assessing the impacts and effectiveness of funds invested in tourism by government agencies and other sources, guiding tourism policy decisions, and helping organizations in the tourism sector to be more successful in their operations and marketing through performance measurement and benchmarking.

When doing destination management research, it is important to follow the classic research process. Primary and secondary research data and information are used together in many research projects. Before starting any original or primary research for its own purposes, the DMO should carefully scan what others have previously published.

The DMO should select from among a portfolio of analysis topics based on its own and the destination's research needs—on existing and potential markets, destination image, resident sentiment toward tourism, destination product auditing, economic impact, competitor strengths and weaknesses, and performance effectiveness.

Now you have learned about the two parts of the planning (Chapter 4) and research (Chapter 5) role in destination management. The next topic to be covered is the leadership, coordination, and governance role. As you found out early in this chapter, research makes a major contribution to leadership, coordination, and governance. Two of the specific contributions are in producing advocacy research data and in measuring the performance of destination management.

A parting comment from the author is still needed. Although he has a great passion for research, it is not the solution to every problem and issue in destination management. Also, research projects can be done with great accuracy and excellence; however, the research is only as good as how well it is interpreted and acted upon. Research reports that just sit on shelves or hard disks are of little use unless they are actioned.

KEYWORDS

advocacy research
annual reports
as-needed research
big data
competitive analysis
content analysis
destination audit
destination quality levels
economic impact analysis
eight Cs
holistic images
image attributes
infographics
intercepts
key performance indicator (KPI)
key result area (KRA)

margin of error
methodology
ongoing research
organic images
performance measurement
periodic research
policy research
potential market analysis
primary research data
qualitative
quantitative
questionnaire
request for proposal (RFP)
research agenda
research budget
research plan
research problem

research process
research objectives
research vendors
resident sentiment analysis
return on investment (ROI)
sample design
secondary research information
survey platforms
tourism satellite account (TSA)
tracking studies
user-generated content (UGC)
visitor profile study

REVIEW QUESTIONS

1. What are the contributions of research for each of the roles of destination management?
2. What are the components of a destination management research agenda and a destination management research plan?
3. Which steps are followed in the destination management research process?
4. How are secondary and primary research data and information different?
5. How are existing and potential visitors analyzed?
6. How are destination images measured?
7. How important is it to determine resident sentiments about tourism and how is this research accomplished?
8. What is a destination audit and how can destination product research help to improve the destination product?
9. How do destinations measure the economic impact of tourism?
10. How important is competitive analysis for a destination and how is the analysis done?
11. Why is it important for a DMO to do performance measurement?
12. Which criteria should be used to select research vendors?

REFERENCES

Austrade (2022) "About tourism research. Tourism Research Australia," https://www.austrade. gov.au/australian/tourism/news-research-and-publications/research#:~:text=Tourism%20 Research%20Australia%20%28TRA%29%20is%20a%20professionally%20independent,and%20 to%20inform%20industry%E2%80%99s%20operational%20and%20investment%20decisions

CBI Ministry of Foreign Affairs (Netherlands) (2020) "What Are the European Opportunities for Community-Based Tourism Products in Myanmar?" www.cbi.eu/market-information/tourism/ myanmar-0/what-are-european-opportunities-community-based-tourism

Choi, S., Lehto, X. Y., and Morrison, A. M. (2007) "Destination Image Representation on the Web: Content Analysis of Macao Travel Related Websites," *Tourism Management*, 28 (1): 118–129.

City of Scottsdale (2022) "Destination Marketing Contract, Audit Report No. 2206," www.scotts-daleaz.gov/news/destination-marketing-contract-audit-no-2206

Colorado State University (2022) "Using Content Analysis," https://writing.colostate.edu/guides/ guide.cfm? guideid=61

Crouch, G. I. (2007) *Modelling Destination Competitiveness: A Survey and Analysis of the Impact of Competitiveness*, Queensland, Australia: CRC for Sustainable Tourism.

Department of Tourism (South Africa) (2022) "Tourism Satellite Accounts (TSA)," https://tkp. tourism.gov.za/Research/Statistical/Pages/sataccount.aspx#:~:text=Tourism%20Satellite%20 Accounts%20%28TSA%29%20%E2%80%8BThe%20Tourism%20Satellite%20Accounts, economy%20both%20in%20terms%20of%20expenditure%20and%20employment

Destination Canada (2022) "Global Tourism Watch," www.destinationcanada.com/en/global-tourism-watch

Destination Lincolnshire (2022) "Destination Lincolnshire: Take Part in Our Survey," www.visitlin-coln.com/blog/take-part-in-our-survey

Destination Marketing Association International (2011) *Standard DMO Performance Reporting: A Handbook for Destination Marketing Organizations (DMOs)*. Washington, DC: DMAI.

Echtner, C. M., and Ritchie, J. R. B. (1993) "The Measurement of Destination Image: An Empirical Assessment," *Journal of Travel Research*, 31 (4): 3–13.

EdinburghFestivalsCity.com (2020) "Edinburgh Festivals Inspiring Creativity in Pupils," https:// www.edinburghfestivalcity.com/assets/000/004/675/Edinburgh_Festivals_Inspiring_Creativity_ in_Pupils_-_February_2020_original.pdf?1582289261

European Travel Commission (2021) "Europeans' Attitudes towards Responsible Travel Choices," https://etc-corporate.org/reports/europeans-attitudes-towards-responsible-travel-choices

——— (2022) "Research," https://etc-corporate.org/research

Experience Kissimmee (2022) "Partner Resources," www.experiencekissimmee.com/partners/ partner-resources

Gartner, W. C. (1993) "Image Formation Process," in M. Uysal and D. Fesenmaier (eds.), *Communication and Channel Systems in Tourism Marketing*, New York, NY: Haworth Press, pp. 191–215.

Hawai'i Tourism Authority (2022) "Visitor Satisfaction Study Q1 2022," www.hawaiitourismauthority. org/media/9543/2022_q1_dbedt_vsat_report-final.pdf

Las Vegas Convention and Visitors Authority (2022) "Las Vegas Visitor Profile Study 2021," https:// assets.simpleviewcms.com/simpleview/image/upload/v1/clients/lasvegas/2021_Las_Vegas_ Visitor_Profile_Study_6fb123b2-d75e-4dd6-875b-eb33acd00541.pdf

Li, J., Xu, L., Tang, L., Wang, S., and Li, L. (2018) "Big Data in Tourism Research: A Literature Review," *Tourism Management*, 68: 301–323.

Longwoods International (2021) "Canadian Resident Sentiment towards Tourism: Highlights from the 2021 Canadian Resident Sentiment Study," https://longwoods-intl.com/ resident-sentiment-research

——— (2022a) "Richmond Region Tourism: A Custom Image Perception Study—A Customer Success Story," https://longwoods-intl.com/news-press-release/richmond-region-tourism-custom-image-perception-study

——— (2022b) "Our Services," https://longwoods-intl.com/what-we-do

Ministry of Business, Innovation and Employment (New Zealand) (2021) "Tourism Satellite Account for Year Ended March 2021 Released," https://teic.mbie.govt.nz/teiccategories/ resources/2021/12/10/stats-nz-tourism-satellite-account-2021-released/#:~:text=Tourism%20 satellite%20account%3A%20Year%20ended%20March%202021%20includes,   the%20official% 20tourism%20satellite%20account%20%28TSA%29%20time%20series

Ministry of Tourism (Israel) (2022) "Statistics, Research and Knowledge Management Department," www.gov.il/en/Departments/Units/statistics_and_research

Ministry of Tourism (Saudi Arabia) (2022) "Saudi Arabia Jumps 10 Places in Global Tourism Ranking," https://mt.gov.sa/en/mediaCenter/News/MainNews/Pages/news-02-25-05-22.aspx

MMGY Global (2022a) "Portrait of Travelers with Disabilities: Mobility and Accessibility," August 2, www.mmgyglobal.com/news/portrait-of-travelers-with-disabilities

——— (2022b) "Research: We Know What They're Thinking," www.mmgy.com/services/research-data

Morrison, A. M. (2010) *Hospitality and Travel Marketing*, 4th edn, Clifton Park, New York: Cengage Delmar.

——— (2022) *Hospitality and Travel Marketing*, 5th edn, London and New York, NY: Routledge.

New Jersey Division of Travel and Tourism and MMGY Travel Intelligence (2021) "New Jersey Overnight Leisure Visitor Profile, Q4 2020–Q3 2021," https://visitnj.org/sites/default/files/FY2021_New_Jersey_Visitor_Profile_Overnight_Leisure_Report.pdf

Organisation for Economic Co-operation and Development (2022) "Tourism," www.oecd.org/cfe/tourism

Pacific Asia Travel Association (2022) "Industry Data," www.pata.org/research-industry-data

Rezende-Parker, A. M., Morrison, A. M., and Ismail, J. A. (2003) "Dazed and Confused? An Exploratory Study of the Destination Image of Brazil," *Journal of Vacation Marketing*, 9 (3): 243–259.

Ritchie, J. R. B., and Crouch, G. I. (2003) *The Competitive Destination: A Sustainable Tourism Perspective*, Wallingford: CABI.

State of Hawai'i Department of Business, Economic Development and Tourism (2022) "Visitor Satisfaction Study Q1 2022," https://files.hawaii.gov/dbedt/visitor/vsat/VSAT-2022-1st-qrt%20report.pdf

Statistics Indonesia (2021) "Statistics of Expenditure of International Visitors," www.bps.go.id/publication/2021/10/20/edd8fc78594be9545eacc2c1/statistik-pengeluaran-wisatawan-mancanegara-2020.html

Statistics Jersey (2020) "Passenger Exit Survey, January 2020," www.gov.je/government/pages/statesreports.aspx?reportid=5240#:~:text=From%20January%202020%2C%20Statistics%20Jersey%20has%20been%20undertaking,   and%20profile%20of%20tourism%20visits%20to%20the%20Island

Stepchenkova, S., and Morrison, A. M. (2008) "Russia's Destination Image among American Pleasure Travelers: Revisiting Echtner and Ritchie," *Tourism Management*, 29 (3): 548–560.

Tasmanian Times (2022) "Responsible Tourism Survey," May 6, https://tasmaniantimes.com/2022/05/responsible-tourism-survey

Tourism Ireland (2022) "Overseas Tourism and Tourism Ireland: Key Facts," www.tourismireland.com/Research/Overseas-Tourism-and-Tourism-Ireland-Key-Facts

Tourism Northern Ireland (2022) "Visitor Attitude Surveys," www.tourismni.com/industry-insights/visitor-attitude-surveys

Tourism PEI (2020) "PEI Visitor Exit Survey Overall Results," www.tourismpei.com/sites/default/files/2022-03/ExitSurveyOverallResults2019.pdf

Tourism Research Australia (2022) "National Visitor Survey Methodology," www.tra.gov.au/Domestic/national-visitor-survey-methodology

United Nations World Tourism Organization (2022) "Statistics," www.unwto.org/statistics

VisitBritain/VisitEngland (2022) "Destination Satisfaction and Perceptions," www.visitbritain.org/destination-satisfaction-and-perceptions

Visit Flanders (2016) "Resident Attitudes Towards Tourism in Bruges," https://toerismevlaanderen.be/sites/default/files/assets/documents_KENNIS/onderzoeken/2017-01-25_Resident-survey-Bruges-2016_global-Report.pdf

Visit Östergötland (2021) "Destination Development: Östra Vättern 2021—Pre-study Analysis and Recommendations for Sustainable Development of the Eastern Coast of Lake Vättern," www.regionostergotland.se/contentassets/ef4fc7f3088d45cb9ad8f8f3ac343cf9/sustainable_destination_audit_vattern.pdf

World Economic Forum (2022) "Travel and Tourism Development Index 2021: Rebuilding for a Sustainable and Resilient Future," https://www3.weforum.org/docs/WEF_Travel_Tourism_Development_2021.pdf

World Travel and Tourism Council (2022) "Economic Impact Reports," https://wttc.org/Research/Economic-Impact

Chapter **6**

Destination Leadership, Coordination, and Governance

Lead by example

DOI: 10.4324/9781003343356-8

Warming Up

You have just heard about destination planning and research in Chapters 4 and 5. Now, you are going to get to know about the second destination management role involving leadership, coordination, and governance. This role is done more effectively if preceded by good planning and research.

Destination leadership, coordination, and governance is a crucial role of destination management. DMOs must be the leaders for the tourism sector, and this chapter tells you about their leadership functions. For DMOs to provide effective leadership, they must themselves employ great leaders who provide the vision and set the positive examples for DMO staff, tourism sector stakeholders, local community residents, partners, and others. You will learn that there are many leadership theories and concepts and that DMO leaders can have different traits, styles, and approaches. However, a service orientation and a participative philosophy to decision-making are best suited for the people who head up DMOs. Leaders and DMOs must abide by certain ethical standards as well.

Coordination is a word that is often used but seldom defined in enough detail. As a starting point, you can think of it as bringing people together so they communicate openly and frequently and synchronize their activities. However, the tourism sector is diverse, and there is a tendency to find a silo effect based on insufficient knowledge and information, distrust, and a lack of shared interests. DMOs must demolish the silos and encourage more communication, cooperation, and collaboration.

Destination governance has become a hot topic and especially among tourism academics. Two prominent academic journals (*Journal of Sustainable Tourism* and *Tourism Review*) had special issues on tourism governance in 2011 and 2010, respectively. An edited book, *Tourism Destination Governance: Practice, Theory and Issues*, was published in 2011 (Laws et al. 2011). However, reading some of this recent literature can be confusing because people tend to use the word "governance" in different ways. You get a more practical approach to destination governance covering all its dimensions in Chapter 6. Special attention is given to the two interrelated dimensions of accountability and transparency. Demonstrating performance effectiveness by setting and measuring results is another dimension of destination governance, and guidelines on doing this are provided. Structure and power are also dimensions of destination governance, and so this chapter discusses DMO organizational structures, funding levels and funding mechanisms. Details are provided about the operation of boards of directors, and the functions of bylaws are discussed.

You are in good hands again for this chapter as the author served on the board of directors of a US DMO for several years. He also trained DMO executives for around fifteen years and got to know much about their leadership, coordination, and governance approaches.

Definitions of Destination Leadership, Coordination, and Governance

In Chapter 1, leadership and coordination were said to be setting the agenda for tourism and coordinating all stakeholders' efforts toward achieving that agenda. Here are more formal definitions of destination leadership and coordination:

> ### DEFINITIONS
>
> **Destination leadership**
>
> The visionary direction of the organization and all its staff by qualified and experienced destination management professionals. DMO leaders must act as the chief representatives and advocates of tourism within their communities, generating interest, enthusiasm, and involvement for DMO programs and activities.
>
> **Destination coordination**
>
> The DMO coordinator convinces groups and individuals to work together harmoniously and in an organized way for achieving specific goals or objectives. This involves the DMO working as the coordinator of tourism sector stakeholders and local community residents.

Destination Leadership

DMOs must assume a leadership role for the tourism sector in their destinations and so must their senior executives. In fact, it is rather a unique situation because the DMO executives must be leaders of their own organizations and champions of the tourism sector for their destinations. This does not necessarily apply to other organizations and companies. The importance of the DMO leadership role is accentuated in communities where tourism is not given a high priority and the benefits of tourism are not well understood.

Leadership Functions of DMOs

What functions must a DMO fulfill to demonstrate its leadership? The eight destination management leadership functions that the DMO must perform are shown in Figure 6.1.

A more detailed description of these eight key destination leadership functions now follows.

Setting the Tourism Agenda

The DMO should set the agenda for tourism and coordinate all tourism stakeholder efforts toward achieving it. Of course, you now know from the previous chapters that the DMO does not and should not do the agenda setting on its own. It needs to do this with the active involvement and input from tourism stakeholders and local community residents within the destination.

Setting the agenda means defining a long-term vision for tourism and engaging the tourism sector in long-range planning. The visionary function of the DMO is one of the key requirements for its leadership.

Guiding and Coordinating Tourism Sector Stakeholders

The DMO needs to guide and coordinate the efforts of tourism sector stakeholders. This is a difficult task given the diversity of stakeholders and their varying opinions and viewpoints on tourism. The coaching function of the DMO is to bring all the team together to focus on a shared set of goals and objectives.

Figure 6.1 Destination management leadership functions.

Championing Tourism

Tourism is generally not well understood and is under-appreciated as an economic sector. It is often afforded the role of a "second-class citizen" when compared to manufacturing, agriculture and even mining. It does not always get the respect it deserves. The championing function of the DMO is to continuously communicate and confirm the positive contributions to their destinations. Another name for this function is advocacy, which you learned about in Chapter 5.

EXAMPLE 6.1

USTA Sets Up the Sustainable Travel Coalition

This example demonstrates how an organization advocates for sustainable travel by creating collaboration among tourism sector stakeholders.

> US Travel's new Sustainable Travel Coalition will focus on developing and advancing the strategies that will enable a more sustainable future, bridging the travel, transportation and technology sectors to foster alignment and cooperation that generates meaningful progress on this issue. With nearly sixty members, the Sustainable Travel Coalition will serve as a forum to inform US Travel of the pulse of sustainability issues and concerns at their organizations and in their destinations, share current obstacles or those on the horizon.
>
> (USTA 2022)

Learning Point

Advocacy coalitions build on the synergy created by partners working together.

Educating and Researching about Tourism

By conducting research and keeping up to date about tourism, the DMO is a source of data, information and facts for tourism sector stakeholders and local community residents. DMO management and staff should continuously participate in training and professional development because tourism is a dynamic and fast-changing economic sector. The scholar–teacher function of the DMO makes everybody in the destination better understand tourism and the trends in the sector and its markets.

Leading Tourism Marketing, Branding, and Communications

The DMO is the body entrusted with marketing, branding, and communications for the destination as a whole. It needs to set the directions for tourism sector stakeholders to follow and provide partnering opportunities to achieve marketing goals and objectives. The DMO should develop the destination positioning and branding approaches that provide a communications platform for all involved in tourism. The communicator function of DMOs increases awareness and brings in more visitors to the destination.

Hosting Visitors

The DMO serves visitors in many ways, especially in providing information about tourism in the destination. It must be active in visitor management, including taking steps to ensure the safety and security of visitors and their ease of movement within the destination. The visitor host function of the DMO enhances the satisfaction and experiences of people who come to the destination on business or for leisure.

Maintaining Tourism Quality Standards

The DMO must participate in the setting and monitoring of tourism quality standards. It must ensure that quality standards match with the positioning and branding of the destination. The quality controller function of the DMO enhances the experiences of visitors in the destination and makes them want to return and recommend.

Stewarding Resources

The DMO must advocate a sustainable approach to tourism development as you learned about in Chapter 2. The DMO must also be a careful steward of the funds and other resources with which it is provided. The steward function of the DMO means that resources are used prudently and that natural and cultural resources are preserved for future destinations.

All eight functions are important, and it is difficult to say which should be given the highest priority. Certainly, being visionary is one of the most important in leadership of all types, and this applies to DMOs as well. Of course, being accountable requires that the DMO is a good steward of resources, and so this is also a high priority leadership role. Leading tourism marketing, branding, and communications is essential, as are quality assurance and visitor hosting and management.

The advent of the COVID-19 pandemic may have created a ninth leadership role for destination management and DMOs and your author calls this the minesweeper function. You can think of this as being the early warning system that detects future crises for the destination and preparing stakeholders and partners for the challenges ahead.

Destination Leadership Styles

To be honest, the leaders of DMOs tend to often change for political reasons, voluntary departures, dismissals, and other reasons. DMO leaders with five or more years of tenure are quite hard to find. For destinations, this is unfortunate because leadership continuity is much more desirable for achieving visions and long-term tourism strategies and frequent turnover causes discontinuity and can lead to unnecessary changes to a DMO's programs and activities. However, a long debate on this issue is not needed in this book; you should just be aware of the phenomenon.

The leadership style of DMO leaders influences the way the organization behaves and how it interacts with tourism sector stakeholders and local community residents. So what are the ideal leadership styles for DMO leaders? There have been so many books and articles written about leadership styles that it is difficult to know where to start answering this question. Northouse's (2021) textbook provides a great account of the many theories and concepts in leadership, but it does not directly discuss destination management leadership. The book describes the trait, skills, behavioral and situational approaches; path-goal and leader–member exchange (LMX) theories; and transformational, authentic, servant, and adaptive leadership. Although all ten of these leadership paradigms have their merits, this chapter will not give you a detailed treatment of each one. Rather, Figure 6.2 provides you a quick snapshot of these approaches.

Back to the question, then, about what types of leadership suit destination management. The best place to start is with the roles of destination management, which first appear in Chapter 1. The earlier chapters emphasize the need for having a clear destination vision to set the agenda for the longer term in tourism. Hankinson (2007), in his article about destination branding, listed strong, visionary leadership as one of the guiding principles. So the ability to lead the

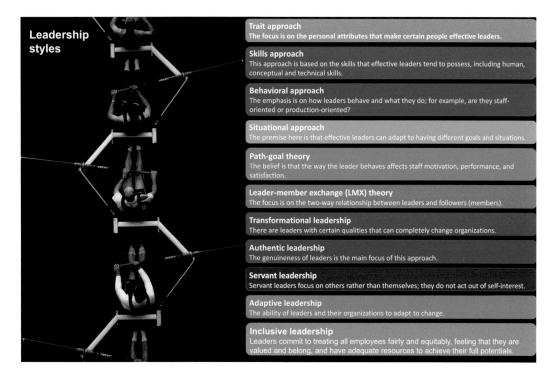

Leadership styles

Trait approach
The focus is on the personal attributes that make certain people effective leaders.

Skills approach
This approach is based on the skills that effective leaders tend to possess, including human, conceptual and technical skills.

Behavioral approach
The emphasis is on how leaders behave and what they do; for example, are they staff-oriented or production-oriented?

Situational approach
The premise here is that effective leaders can adapt to having different goals and situations.

Path-goal theory
The belief is that the way the leader behaves affects staff motivation, performance, and satisfaction.

Leader-member exchange (LMX) theory
The focus is on the two-way relationship between leaders and followers (members).

Transformational leadership
There are leaders with certain qualities that can completely change organizations.

Authentic leadership
The genuineness of leaders is the main focus of this approach.

Servant leadership
Servant leaders focus on others rather than themselves; they do not act out of self-interest.

Adaptive leadership
The ability of leaders and their organizations to adapt to change.

Inclusive leadership
Leaders commit to treating all employees fairly and equitably, feeling that they are valued and belong, and have adequate resources to achieve their full potentials.

Figure 6.2 Destination leadership styles (Northouse 2021).

tourism sector toward a shared vision is one important skill for a DMO leader. Of course, there is more to visionary leaders than just having a vision, and this has been highlighted by many previous authors, including Westley and Mintzberg (1989). They viewed visionary leadership as a psychological gift that only certain people have.

Coordination, partnerships and team-building (Chapter 8), and community and stakeholder relationships and involvement (Chapter 9) are DMO roles that require strong interpersonal and networking skills. Bringing different parties together to focus on product development (Chapter 7) and destination marketing, branding, and communications (Chapter 10), initiatives requires a similar skill set, as also do visitor management (Chapter 11) and crisis management (Chapter 12). To be successful, DMO leaders must be outstanding communicators and presenters and have exceptional abilities to listen.

EXAMPLE 6.2

Command-and-Control Leaders Need Not Apply

This example suggests that the command-and-control (military-style) leadership does not fit well for DMOs.

> Coming from the military, this is an authoritative and top-down style of leadership that is often found in highly bureaucratic organizations, including many government agencies. Power and privilege is given to the leaders, and decision-making is not participative. This "leadership by the book" style is not well suited for destination management and DMOs, but it is found in some places.
>
> Liz Ryan, writing in *Forbes* (2016), titled her piece, "Command-and-Control Management Is for Dinosaurs." So, if a DMO wants to avoid becoming a prehistoric animal, it should not hire command-and-control leaders.
>
> (Ryan 2016)

Learning Point

Autocratic leaders are not needed in destination management.

As you have seen, DMOs have a diverse set of stakeholders with whom they must work. The stakeholders often have widely divergent opinions and interests, but still DMO leaders must guide them toward a consensus. This requires flexibility and the willingness to allow debate and participation in decision-making.

DEFINITION

Servant leadership

"A philosophy and set of practices that enriches the lives of individuals, builds better organizations and ultimately creates a more just and caring world" (Greenleaf Center for Service Leadership 2022).

"A servant leader focuses on the growth and well-being of employees and other stakeholders in their organization. Servant leaders seek to help the people they serve grow as individuals" (Purdue Global 2020).

You see from Figure 6.2 that there are many leadership styles. One of those that can fit with DMO situations is servant leadership, which was introduced as a concept by Greenleaf (1977). Servant leaders focus on others rather than on themselves, and they are not motivated by self-interest. The primary objective is to serve and meet the needs of others. Servant leaders help other people develop, provide vision, and gain the trust and credibility of others (Stone 2003). Figure 6.3 shows the twenty attributes of servant leadership based on a literature review by Russell and Stone (2002). The nine functional attributes are the ones most often found in the literature on service leadership. The accompanying attributes complement the functional attributes and are prerequisites to effective service leadership.

Some of the attributes in Figure 6.3 may not be as instantly recognizable as others; so here are some explanations. Modeling means leading by example and by behavior. Pioneering means taking the initiative and showing the way for others to follow. Stewardship is managing the properties or business affairs of other persons.

LMX theory is another approach that is favored in tourism and hospitality and a definition follows:

DEFINITION

Leader–member exchange (LMX) theory

"A dyadic, relational approach to leadership that assumes that (a) leaders develop exchange relationships with each one of their subordinates and (b) the quality of these leader–member exchange (LMX) relationships affects subordinates' responsibility, influence over decisions, access to resources, and performance. Those group members who are linked to the leader by a strongly positive LMX relationship are part of the unit's ingroup, whereas those who have a low-quality LMX relationship are relegated to the outgroup" (American Psychological Association [APA] 2022)

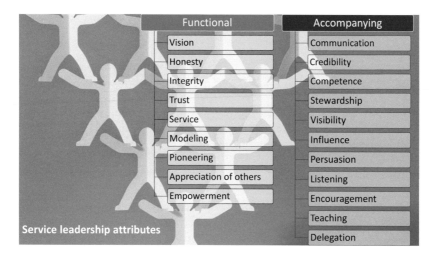

Figure 6.3 Attributes of servant leadership (Russell and Stone 2002, p. 154).

LMX applies to how DMO leaders interact with individuals within and outside of their organizations. The positive aspects of these one-on-one relationships are critical for effective destination management; however, the idea of there being "outgroups" is not a good one for destination management.

Are you looking at Figure 6.2 and saying to yourself—"surely DMO leaders must be inclusive, authentic, adaptive, and transformational as well?" You are indeed very perceptive and smart. The author agrees with you and especially with everything that destinations have endured in 2020–2022 with the COVID-19 pandemic, when DMOs had to adapt and transform as business sources declined and markets changed. Perhaps, it is better to say then that a blending of the various leadership styles shown in Figure 6.2 is more appropriate for destination management and DMOs.

EXAMPLE 6.3

Tourism Industry Transformation Plan for New Zealand

This example highlights the formation of a leadership team in New Zealand to advise on the pandemic recovery.

> The Leadership Group has met five times since late 2021 to discuss workforce problems and opportunities, analyze the root causes of these problems, and think about future trends that will impact on the tourism workforce. Coming out of these conversations, we have suggested a package of actions that we think will help address the problems and harness the opportunities.
> (Ministry of Business, Innovation and Employment [New Zealand] 2022: 5)

Learning Point

Often, groupings of leaders effectively deal with complex DMO problems and issues.

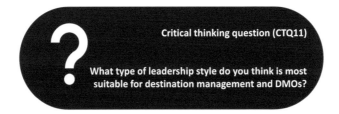

? Critical thinking question (CTQ11)

What type of leadership style do you think is most suitable for destination management and DMOs?

Corporate Social Responsibility (CSR)

You learned about CSR in Chapter 2. Having a willingness to share some of the responsibility for social-cultural, environmental and economic issues and causes is behind the concept of CSR. The nine aspects of CSR shown in Figure 6.4 are briefly defined below:

1. Impact: The positive environmental, social and cultural influences of an organization and its leaders.
2. Ethics: The policies and practices of an organization and its leaders related to important or controversial issues.
3. Partnership: The actions taken by an organization and its leaders to cooperate and collaborate with others in achieving social responsibility goals.

4. Drive: The level of initiative taken by an organization and its leaders to fulfill social responsibility.
5. Growth: The organization's and leaders' vision for growth with a sustainable development perspective.
6. Integrity: The organization's and leaders' ability to act with honesty and consistency in doing the right things.
7. Sensitivity: The organization's and leaders' responses to social, cultural, environmental and economic issues and problems.
8. Contribution: The organization's and leaders' financial and non-financial contributions to addressing and solving social, cultural and environmental problems and challenges.
9. Goals: The social responsibility targets of an organization and its leaders for the short, medium and long terms.

DMO leaders must also act ethically and according to certain standards and these are the next topics for discussion.

Ethical Leadership Practices and DMO Standards

DMOs and their leaders must behave ethically, and how they conduct business and interact with others is closely connected to leadership. You should be familiar with several codes of ethics that apply to all DMOs and know about ethical business practices in general. Also, you will know from the discussion of DMO boards of directors that some DMOs also have their own codes of conduct.

This review of ethical leadership practices and standards begins with a discussion of three systems that apply on an international level.

Global Code of Ethics for Tourism

The Global Code of Ethics for Tourism was introduced in 1999 by the UNWTO. Their overall purpose is to guide all involved in tourism development, including governments, the tourism

Aspects of corporate social responsibility

Figure 6.4 Aspects of CSR with icons.

sector, communities and visitors, "to help maximise the sector's benefits while minimising its potentially negative impact on the environment, cultural heritage and societies across the globe" (UNWTO 2022). There are ten articles (topics) in this code of ethics, and they were shown earlier in Figure 2.9.

Global Sustainable Tourism Destination Criteria (GSTC)

You already heard about the Global Sustainable Tourism Council and their criteria in Chapter 2 and Figure 2.2. These criteria are designed for the following purposes (Global Sustainable Tourism Council 2022):

- Serve as basic guidelines for destinations that wish to become more sustainable.
- Help consumers identify sound sustainable tourism destinations.
- Serve as a common denominator for information media to recognize destinations and inform the public regarding their sustainability.
- Help certification and other voluntary destination level programs ensure that their standards meet a broadly accepted baseline.
- Offer governmental, non-governmental, and private-sector programs a starting point for developing sustainable tourism requirements.
- Serve as basic guidelines for education and training bodies, such as hotel schools and universities.

Destination Marketing Accreditation Program (DMAP) Standards

The DMAP is a "globally recognized accreditation serving as a visible industry distinction that defines quality and performance standards in destination marketing and management" (Destinations International 2022). There were around 200 DMOs that had received DMAP accreditation in 2022 according to information published on Destinations International's website. Figure 6.5 shows the seventeen standard areas for the DMAP accreditation and you can see that these cover much more than marketing. These standards apply to DMOs as organizations rather than to individual DMO leaders.

❑ Governance
❑ Strategic planning
❑ Stakeholder engagement and advocacy
❑ Finance
❑ Human resources
❑ Management and operations
❑ Technology
❑ Research and marketing intelligence
❑ Brand management
❑ Marketing
❑ Communications
❑ Sales and services
❑ Visitor services
❑ Membership and partnerships
❑ Destination development
❑ Volunteer relations
❑ Aspirational

Figure 6.5 Destination Marketing Accreditation Program standards (Destinations International 2020).

In addition to these worldwide codes and criteria, individual DMOs can have their rules on business ethics and conduct. The following is an example from the Visit Hagerstown Convention and Visitors Bureau in Maryland in the USA:

EXAMPLE 6.4

Visit Hagerstown Convention and Visitors Bureau's (CVB's) Code of Business Practices

This example from Maryland, USA, shows how a DMO can create its own code of business practice.

- Accountability. To provide value and high standards, offering a safe and family-friendly destination, and abide by all City, State and Federal laws.
- Professionalism. To consistently honor all commitments and ensure customer satisfaction through courteous and respectful business practices.
- Excellence. To strive for excellence, providing value in quality products and exceptional service.
- Responsiveness. To handle all inquiries, requests, transactions and complaints promptly with dignity and fairness.

(Visit Hagerstown 2022)

Learning Point

It is advisable that DMOs follow guidelines for good conduct.

You will hear more about ethical codes in the discussion on governance and boards of directors.

Destination Coordination

Moving on now to the second major topic in Chapter 6, destination coordination. Critics often say that the tourism sector suffers from of a lack of it; however, they seldom offer any practical solutions. You need to know precisely what destination coordination is, and the best place to start is to tell you the symptoms of a lack of coordination within a destination and a DMO. The following are the symptoms and signs of insufficient coordination:

- Delays in making decisions and acting: If there are many groups involved and their actions are not well coordinated, it takes longer to accomplish tasks.
- Duplication of effort and redundant activities: When groups work independently and do not coordinate their efforts, there is a danger they overlap and do similar things.
- Lack of communications: When groups work separately without adequate coordination, the communications tend to be weaker.
- Lack of integration: When groups coordinate and work together, the integration of effort creates synergies.

> **EXAMPLE 6.5**
>
> **Fragmentation of DMOs in the UK**
>
> This example is a quote from an assessment of the DMOs in England. It suggests the need for a more uniform template for structuring and funding DMOs.
>
> > The current landscape in England is a complicated patchwork quilt, with each DMO managed and led in different ways. They can be limited companies, a team in a local authority, a business investment district, or a community interest company. Their funding models are also diverse and often opaque—some entirely private, some entirely public, some a mix of the two. There is fragmentation across the landscape, as well as geographical overlap, duplication, distorted priorities and competition when there should be alignment. While a bit of variation is fine, the unstructured nature of the landscape is ultimately hard to get your head around. There was an overriding call throughout the review and from all parties for a degree of coherence. Everyone wanted a simplified structure with clear channels of communication between DMOs and national government, a clear definition as to what a DMO is and what it should do and a common understanding of expectations, roles and priorities.
> >
> > (Department of Digital, Culture, Media and Society 2021)
>
> **Learning Point**
>
> Fragmentation among DMOs makes their coordination more difficult.

The term "fragmentation" is often used to describe the tourism sector, and it is often said that DMOs are also fragmented. What does this mean? You should know first that fragmentation refers to a lack of sufficient coordination in a system. Fragmented means that the system is broken into many (sometimes small) parts that are not adequately connected (such as the DMOs in England).

The Silo Effect

Silos are structures found on farms to store grain. They are towers built from cement or metal to protect what is contained inside from spoilage by outside elements and are isolated from other silos. Silos are often used as a metaphor for unhealthy competition among and lack of integration of departments or units within organizations. *The Silo Effect* is the title of a 2015 book by Gillian Tett that reviews this tendency and how organizations can deal with it. Figure 6.6 has an image of a farm silo and a quote from Barnett (2015) based on a review of Tett's book.

The silo effect not only occurs within individual organizations as described by Tett; it also exists in the relationships of different organizations in communities, among governmental agencies, and within economic sectors such as tourism. Rivalries cause turf wars to happen when organizations feel their responsibilities or spheres of influence are being encroached

Narrow-mindedness, institutional bias, and rampant interdepartmental rivalries. Silos are a metaphor for business structures that prevent the corporate whole from being greater than the sum of its parts (Barnett, 2015).

Figure 6.6 The silo effect in organizations (Barnett 2015).

upon by others. Struggles for autonomy, control, and power lead to various parties becoming isolated and protective of their domains (just as silos protect their crops). There is also a danger of DMOs becoming siloed from their communities and residents. These situations indicate a lack of a shared vision and goals and an absence of adequate coordination of efforts.

There are pathways to coordination as illustrated in the six dichotomies illustrated in Figure 6.7. The diagram in Figure 6.7 deserves some explanation. The desirable conditions for the tourism sector in a destination are that it is coordinated, collaborative, united, interdependent, and harmonious, and all this depends on a strong sense of trust among the stakeholders. The other sides of the two-way arrows are undesirable states (disorganized, competitive, fragmented, independent, discordant, and distrust). The positive ends of the arrows all point toward the pathway to a well-coordinated tourism sector.

The Four Cs

The silo effect suggests that organizational barriers make cooperation and collaboration difficult within tourism and individual destinations. Three Cs are often cited as coordination, cooperation, and collaboration (Fig. 6.8). Communication is the foundation for the three Cs, and so it can be said that there are four Cs as shown in Figure 6.8.

The DMO can apply the four Cs process in the following ways:

- Communication: The DMO encourages tourism sector stakeholders, government agencies, and local communities to share ideas, opinions and information and provides several opportunities and venues for these exchanges.

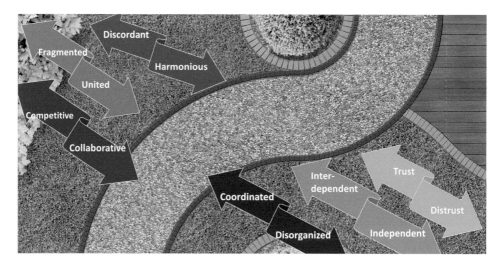

Figure 6.7 Pathways to effective destination coordination.

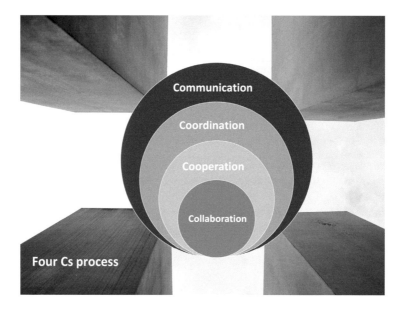

Figure 6.8 The four Cs process.

- Coordination: The DMO leads various parties within the destination to co-develop a shared vision and goals, to harmoniously integrate activities and programs, to co-create products and visitor experiences, and to have frequent communications.
- Cooperation: The DMO provides programs and opportunities for organizations to work together and with the DMO.
- Collaboration: With the support of the DMO, organizations share assets and produce new and creative outcomes that would not happen if working separately.

Lack of Sufficient Coordination during COVID-19 (WTTC)

During crises, there is a greater need for coordination during the response and recovery stages as highlighted in this example about the WTTC initiative.

> The World Travel and Tourism Council (WTTC) today publishes a new report on best practices and support for governments for the introduction of a common "Digital Travel Portal," to allow safe, stress-free travel, which would reduce delays at airports. The COVID-19 pandemic highlighted a lack of global coordination as governments introduced a constant patchwork of digital and paper requirements. WTTC is calling for alignment to build resilience and ensure there is a clear global system focused on an individual's health status that does not bring international travel to a standstill, which throughout the pandemic caused serious economic damage.
>
> (WTTC 2022)

Learning Point

Better coordination among government agencies, DMOs, and tourism sector stakeholders is required when major crises occur.

Coordination Functions of DMOs

Now, you know that DMOs must break down the barriers (or silos) that inhibit cooperation and collaboration and that the four Cs is a process that they should employ in doing so. Leadership and coordination are closely connected, and a DMO that cannot effectively lead will not be a successful coordinator (and vice versa). In fact, coordination is a key role of DMOs worldwide in bringing together many parties directly and indirectly involved in tourism. DMOs must apply coordination to all eight destination management roles.

The overall DMO coordination functions and the coordination functions for the eight destination management roles are briefly described below.

OVERALL COORDINATION FUNCTIONS

DMOs must perform six overall coordination functions for their destinations as shown in Figure 6.9a. Together, these can be described as convincing everyone to pursue the same vision and goals for tourism.

PLANNING AND RESEARCH COORDINATION FUNCTIONS

As you learned in Chapter 4, much coordination is required to effectively complete tourism destination planning because there are multiple groups of principals and participants involved in the planning process (Fig. 6.9b). Additionally, when conducting research, there are often several parties working together, and their efforts need to be coordinated.

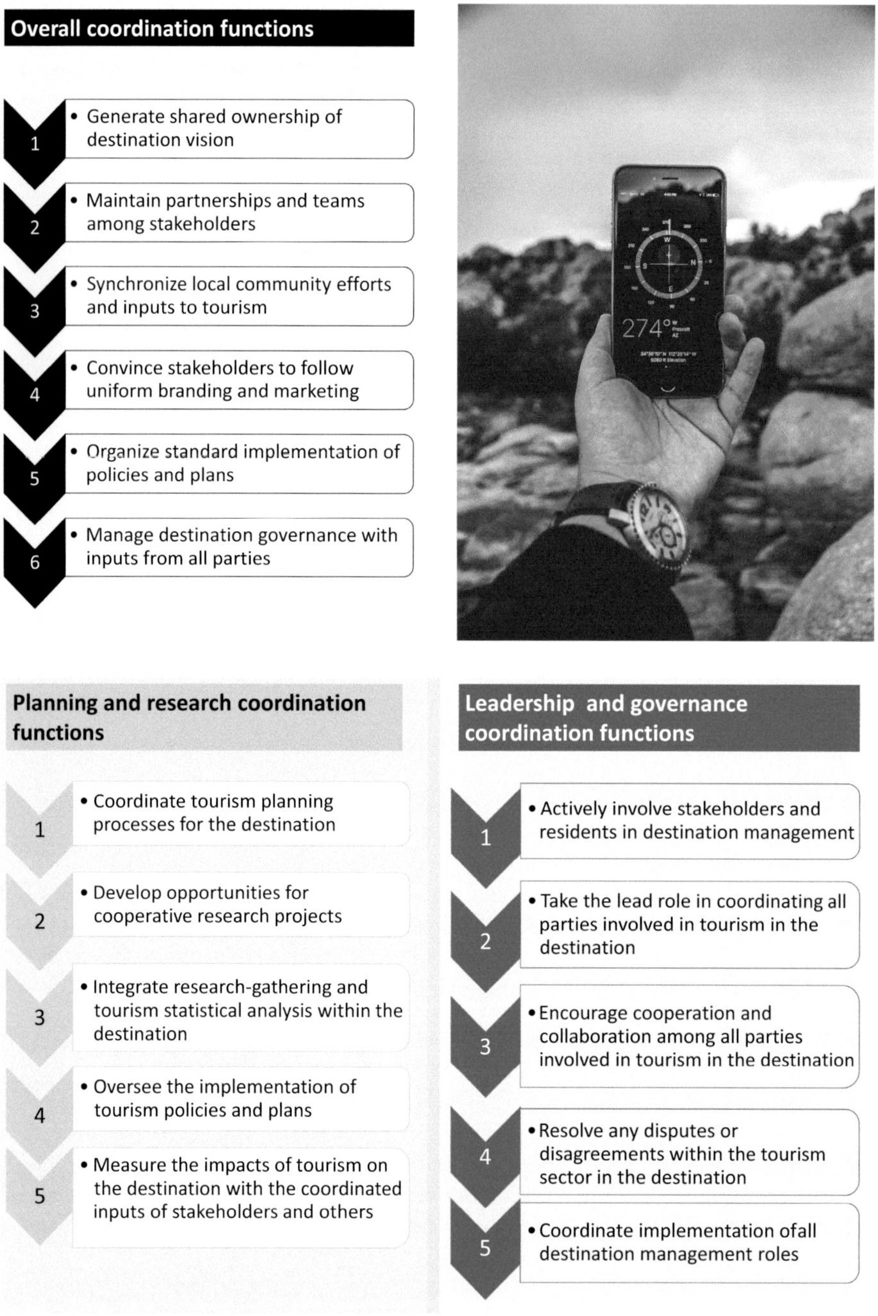

Overall coordination functions

1 • Generate shared ownership of destination vision

2 • Maintain partnerships and teams among stakeholders

3 • Synchronize local community efforts and inputs to tourism

4 • Convince stakeholders to follow uniform branding and marketing

5 • Organize standard implementation of policies and plans

6 • Manage destination governance with inputs from all parties

274°

Planning and research coordination functions

1 • Coordinate tourism planning processes for the destination

2 • Develop opportunities for cooperative research projects

3 • Integrate research-gathering and tourism statistical analysis within the destination

4 • Oversee the implementation of tourism policies and plans

5 • Measure the impacts of tourism on the destination with the coordinated inputs of stakeholders and others

Leadership and governance coordination functions

1 • Actively involve stakeholders and residents in destination management

2 • Take the lead role in coordinating all parties involved in tourism in the destination

3 • Encourage cooperation and collaboration among all parties involved in tourism in the destination

4 • Resolve any disputes or disagreements within the tourism sector in the destination

5 • Coordinate implementation of all destination management roles

Figure 6.9 (a) Overall coordination functions. (b) Planning and research and leadership and coordination functions.

LEADERSHIP AND GOVERNANCE COORDINATION FUNCTIONS

Leadership requires coordination of individuals and groups for it to be effective. Figure 6.9b shows five leadership coordination functions.

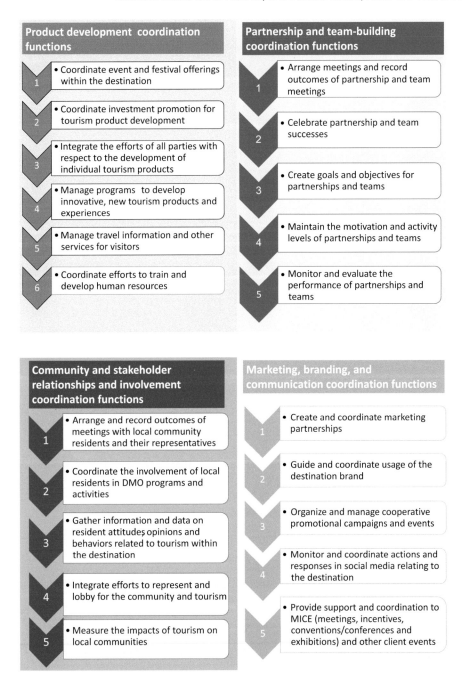

Figure 6.9 (c) Product development and partnership and team-building coordination functions. (d) Stakeholder relationships and involvement and marketing, branding, and communications coordination functions.

PRODUCT DEVELOPMENT COORDINATION FUNCTIONS

There are many players in tourism development, within and outside of destinations. Again, DMOs play a pivotal role in bringing these people together through five specific activities.

Part II

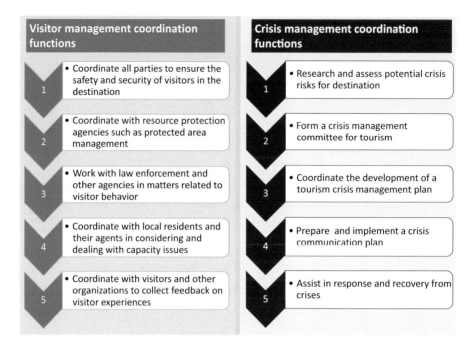

Figure 6.9 (e) Visitor management and marketing crisis management coordination functions.

Figure 6.9c shows six product development coordination functions for DMOs. A good example here is the Experiencias de Barrio (neighborhood experiences) program coordinated by the Secretary of Tourism, Government of Mexico City (Secretaría de Turismo, Government of Mexico City 2022).

PARTNERSHIPS AND TEAM-BUILDING COORDINATION FUNCTIONS

DMOs should be involved in five specific coordination activities in performing their partnership and team-building role (Fig. 6.9c).

COMMUNITY AND STAKEHOLDER RELATIONSHIPS AND INVOLVEMENT COORDINATION FUNCTIONS

The community and stakeholder relationships and involvement role of DMOs requires considerable levels of coordination. The five activities here for DMOs are listed in Figure 6.9d.

MARKETING, BRANDING, AND COMMUNICATIONS COORDINATION FUNCTIONS

Marketing and promotion require a high level of coordination to work best. As the destination marketing leader, the DMO should be responsible for the five coordination functions in Figure 6.9d.

VISITOR MANAGEMENT COORDINATION FUNCTIONS

Many organizations in addition to DMOs have an interest in different aspects of visitor management; so this is a role requiring a high level of coordination. Five specific visitor management coordination functions for DMOs are identified in Figure 6.9e.

CRISIS MANAGEMENT COORDINATION FUNCTIONS

Figure 6.9e identifies five crisis management functions for a DMO. The two main ones are forming a tourism crisis management committee and, with that group, preparing a crisis management plan.

EXAMPLE 6.7

Crisis Management Plan for Aqaba, Jordan

This example argues that organizations must be crisis prepared.

> Crisis preparedness is critical for survival and an organization's ability to man-age crises effectively will largely depend on their crisis preparation efforts. Research has shown that preparedness reduces the number of incidents. Cri-sis prepared companies report one-third fewer emergencies than crisis prone ones, according to the Harvard Business Journal. Crisis prepared organizations also stay in business longer and fare better financially. The average return on assets is double the average return of crisis prone companies. Preparedness affects an organization's reputation, as well.
>
> (United States Agency for International Development 2014)

Learning Point

DMOs should have crisis management plans.

Destination Governance

What is destination governance, and how does the concept relate to the roles of a DMO? If you look it up in a dictionary, it will be described as the act of governing. You might then ask, is that not what governments do? Yes, of course, governments do govern, but now the concept is much broader and includes corporate governance and NPO governance (Fig. 6.12). A definition of governance from UNESCAP (2009) is shown below, and it emphasizes how decisions are made and implemented.

UNESCAP identified eight characteristics of good governance, and these are shown in Figure 6.10. It should be noted that these are broad characteristics of good governance and were not intended to specifically reflect the governance of DMOs. Accountability and transparency are discussed in detail later, but the other six characteristics require a short description of how they can be applied to DMOs:

1. Responsive: The DMO and its processes respond to stakeholders within a reasonable time.
2. Equitable and inclusive: All groups of stakeholders as well as community residents have an input to the DMO's policies, plans, strategies, programs and activities. The DMO does not delib-erately exclude any stakeholder or resident group from its operations and communications.
3. Effective and efficient: The DMO sets and meets its goals and objectives. It is not wasteful in its use of resources. The DMO has internal controls to manage and monitor how resources are used.
4. Follows the rule of law: The DMO follows all the applicable laws and has no discriminatory practices.

5. Participatory: Every stakeholder group and type of individual has an equal opportunity to participate in the activities of the DMO.
6. Consensus-oriented: The DMO works to coordinate all the tourism stakeholders in the destination and builds consensus on the most important tourism issues and opportunities.

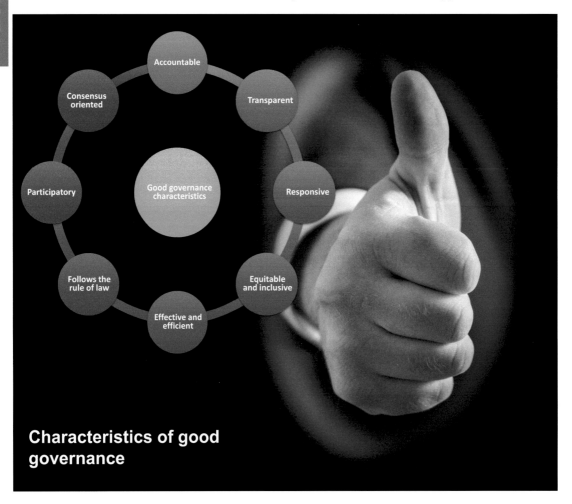

Characteristics of good governance

Figure 6.10 Characteristics of good governance (UNESCAP 2009).

EXAMPLE 6.8

UNESCAP Definition of Governance

This example provides a good, basic definition of governance by a United Nations agency.

The concept of "governance" is not new. It is as old as human civilization. Simply put "governance" means: the process of decision-making and the process by which decisions are implemented (or not implemented). Governance can be used in several contexts such as corporate governance, international governance, national governance and local governance.

(UNESCAP 2009)

Learning Point

Governance is the about the decision-making processes within organizations.

Based on these materials, the following definition of destination governance is used in this book. The focus of the definition is on who administers the DMO and how it is administered and on the accountability and transparency that is demonstrated by the DMO in its operations. You already saw this definition in Chapter 1.

DEFINITION

Destination governance

Destination governance is how a DMO is administered and who does the administering. Governance involves the policies, systems and processes to ensure that all stakeholders are involved and that the DMO is accountable for its results and resource usage and has a high level of transparency.

Dimensions of Governance

The characteristics of good governance in the UNESCAP model are shown in Figure 6.10. These are being accountable, transparent, responsive, equitable and inclusive, effective and efficient, following the rule of law, participatory, and consensus-oriented.

A review of the literature on governance by Ruhanen et al. (2010) revealed dimensions of governance that were cited the most often and six of the top ones are shown in Figure 6.11. Accountability and transparency were the most frequently identified dimensions. Involvement in the UNESCAP model of good governance is similar to the concept of an organization being participatory, and effectiveness is found in both Figures 6.10 and 6.11. The structure and power dimensions were not specifically included in the UNESCAP characteristics.

EXAMPLE 6.9

Tourism Australia Board and Governance

This example highlights the importance of accountability, structure, risk management, and strategy for effective DMO governance.

Tourism Australia is governed by a board of directors who report to the Federal Minister for Tourism. The main role of the board is to determine

Tourism Australia policy and ensure that the organization performs in a proper and efficient manner.

The board's charter includes the following responsibilities: "Accountability for monitoring Tourism Australia's business" and "ensuring good corporate governance, including effective risk management, legal compliance, strategic direction and appropriate organizational structure of Tourism Australia."

(Tourism Australia 2022a, 2022b, 2022c)

Learning Point

DMO boards of directors must be given clear requirements for organizational governance.

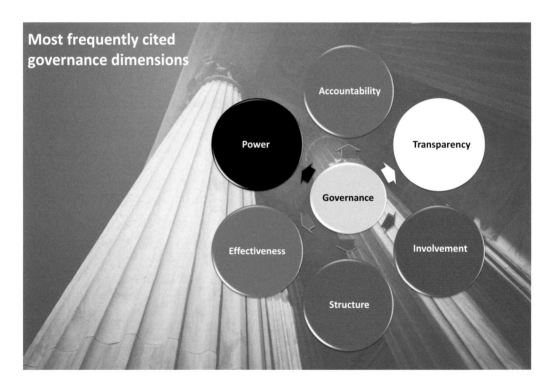

Figure 6.11 Most frequently cited governance dimensions (Ruhanen et al. 2010, pp. 9–10).

Accountability

Accountability is one of the core dimensions of destination governance, and DMOs are increasingly being held accountable for their activities and use of resources. It is not a new concept in destination management, having been discussed since at least 1990 by academic scholars, including Perdue and Pitegoff (1990). However, the scope of the accountability concept has expanded from just destination marketing, branding, and communications to now include all aspects of destination management and all DMO activities. It is best to start with a definition of accountability as it applies to a DMO.

> **DEFINITION**
>
> **Accountability**
>
> The obligation of a DMO to justify and account for its programs and activities; and to accept responsibility for results. The DMO must disclose these results in a transparent manner and take responsibility for the use of all resources with which it has been entrusted.

This definition places the obligation on DMOs to account for what they do and take the full responsibility for their actions and results. You can see that the following actions are required of the DMO to prove accountability:

JUSTIFYING PROGRAMS AND ACTIVITIES

The DMO must explain why it is proposing to implement specific programs and activities for an upcoming cycle of business operations. This means that the DMO must reveal its assumptions and facts based upon research that has been completed. Typically, this is accomplished by preparing plans for each of the destination management roles and then making presentations of these in different ways, sometimes through public meetings.

MEASURING RESULTS FROM PROGRAM AND ACTIVITY IMPLEMENTATION

The DMO must first specify the results it intends to achieve from specific programs and activities. Here is where the DMO uses KRAs and KPIs (Fig. 6.16), which were discussed earlier in Chapter 5. The DMO must then measure the results from the implementation of the programs and activities.

DISCLOSING RESULTS

The DMO cannot keep the results secret but must disclose them in the way that it is required by its legal constitution. If the DMO is governmental, it may be subject to open public records, and thus any resident can request to see all of its records. Many developed countries have enacted freedom of information laws that apply to national, state, provincial and territorial government agencies and give the public access to documents, data and other information from governments. Disclosure is related to the concept of transparency that is discussed in this chapter as another dimension of destination governance. By disclosing details of its decision-making and other information, a DMO is also demonstrating its transparency.

ACCEPTING RESPONSIBILITY FOR RESULTS

The DMO must take full responsibility for the actual results of specific programs and activities. If the results that the DMO expected were not achieved, the DMO must explain why it did not perform up to the standard that it set for itself.

ASSUMING RESPONSIBILITY FOR RESOURCE USE

The DMO must account for its use of all resources and especially for the budget that was consumed. The accounting for the use of funding is done through the preparation of audited financial statements. Many DMOs produce annual reports that provide an overall summary of results as well as looking ahead to future operating cycles.

Maintaining and measuring accountability are other topics that are of great significance for destination management. Some DMOs maintain accountability by developing internal control systems, including setting up internal audit departments or having an audit committee. For example, the HKTB has an audit committee that checks the adequacy of internal controls and effectiveness and efficiency of HKTB operations.

EXAMPLE 6.10

Audit Committee of the HKTB

Chapter 20 is about performance measurement and having and audit committee, as in the HKTB example, increases the probability of greater efficiency and effectiveness.

> This committee provides advice to the board on the adequacy of internal controls and the effectiveness and efficiency of the HKTB's operations, and is authorized to investigate any activities within its terms of reference. It reviews and endorses the annual audit plan to ensure adequate audit coverage of critical operations, reviews findings, recommendations and the implementation of actions arising from internal audit and other relevant authorities. It also reviews the annual audited financial statements before submission to the board. The committee meets three times a year, and extraordinary meetings can be convened if necessary. It comprises a chairman and six members from the board, with the director, Internal Audit acting as committee secretary.
>
> (HKTB 2021: 77)

Learning Point

DMOs must have systems of internal control.

Measuring accountability may be done periodically by having an independent audit carried out on the DMO. Normally, these independent audits are done by consultants with vast experience in the operations of DMOs. These types of audits are often quite critical of DMOs and traumatic for senior executives. One audit conducted in 2006 in the USA found that over $1.5 million had been misappropriated from the DMO. Another US audit found that the DMO was not sufficiently involving stakeholders and especially the local government.

Transparency

Another dimension of destination governance is that there must be transparency to the DMO and its operations. In everyday use, transparent means an object that you can see through; in a destination management context, it can be defined as follows.

DEFINITION

Transparency

Transparency means openness in operations and communications.

Tourism stakeholders in the destination should be able to see what the DMO is doing and understand its decision-making. Being transparent is the opposite of keeping business matters hidden and secret. The following is an example of how Visit Colorado Springs (VCS) aspires to be transparent.

EXAMPLE 6.11

Transparency at Visit Colorado Springs

This is an excellent example of how a DMO describes what it does and the reasons for doing so. VCS is almost detailing its mission so that the local community better knows why it exists.

> Visit Colorado Springs is a private, nonprofit 501(c)(6) trade organization that provides information and inspiration to people thinking of traveling to the Pikes Peak region. Our funding is provided by both public and private sources. We are committed to complete transparency in how we are funded, how we allocate these funds, how we operate and the results that we achieve. Tourism promotion is a tool that helps our local community by putting people to work and making this a great place to live—it's likely that someone in your family or one of your neighbors directly benefits from the tourism industry. And the entire community benefits indirectly. Tourism promotion is an investment in our community and our people. The work of Visit Colorado Springs puts people to work and provides economic opportunity. Tourism promotion is funded largely by those who visit and not the people that live here. We thank the community and our local, state and nationally elected officials for their ongoing support as we provide this important public service.
>
> (VCS 2022)

Learning Point

DMOs must be operated with full transparency.

As you can see, the accountability and transparency dimensions of destination governance are closely linked. For a DMO to be accountable, it must practice transparency. The DMO must show how it has used money and other resources and must reveal its results. What specifically must a DMO do to be a transparent organization? The following are some of the key steps required for DMO transparency:

HOLDING PUBLIC MEETINGS

One of the ways to demonstrate openness is to hold public meetings at which the DMO reveals its past results and planned programs and activities. A good example of this is the annual press conference organized each year by the Macao Government Tourist Office (MGTO). Several hundred people attend this event to hear about MGTO's future priorities and plans.

> ### EXAMPLE 6.12
>
> **Annual Press Conference of MGTO**
>
> Reporting is a component of performance measurement and management for a DMO. This is a very good example of reporting from Macao.
>
> > The Macao Government Tourism Office (MGTO) is to host its Annual Press Conference on 10 February. During the event, officials from MGTO will give a summary of last year's activities and of the 2020 performance of Macao's tourism sector, which was negatively impacted by the COVID-19 pandemic. The office will also announce during the press conference the marketing and promotional programs for 2021.
> >
> > (MGTO 2021)
>
> **Learning Point**
>
> DMOs should periodically share their operating results within their destinations.

Making Financial Results Available

Budgets and financial statements are made available. Many DMOs do this by publishing an annual report that contains the financial data; others make budgets and financial statements available on their websites.

Providing Records from Meetings

Agendas and minutes are kept for all formal meetings and are available for perusal. Some DMOs open their board meetings to the public, and this enhances transparency.

Publishing All Policies, Plans, and Strategies

This means that such documents must be located in a place for all to view. Many DMOs accomplish this by making documents available for download on their websites.

Revealing DMO Salary Information

Salary levels are often a contentious issue with DMOs, especially those at senior management levels. To be transparent, DMOs should make salary information available.

A good example of such transparency is the LVCVA in the USA. On its business website, LVCVA provides a wide range of information and data that demonstrate its transparency. Board of directors' meeting agendas and minutes are available for reading and downloading (LVCVA 2022a). The mission and purpose of LVCVA are provided and so is a detailed description of the organization, its fourteen-person board and operating departments. LVCVA explains its purchasing policies and information on the status of bids it has authorized. Very detailed financial information is provided on the website, including a financial status report, comprehensive annual financial reports, popular annual financial reports, annual budgets and quarterly budgets, and statistical reports. The salary bands for all staff are published in these financial materials (LVCVA 2022b).

Transparency on the travel expenses of DMO staff members is a consideration as well because these expenses often cause controversy. Some DMOs open the books on these travel expenses, and Tourism New Zealand is one of them. It makes all the travel expenses of its chief executive available for viewing on its corporate website (Tourism New Zealand 2022). Destination Canada makes public the total value of the travel and hospitality expenses of all its senior officers (Destination Canada 2021).

Accountability and transparency are two complementary dimensions of governance and rather like two sides of the same coin. There can be no doubt that DMOs will be the subject of more intense scrutiny in the future, and so learning more about being accountable and transparent is a must.

DMO Organizational Structures, Boards, and Bylaws

This book's definition of destination governance states that it is how a DMO is administered and who does the administering. More specifically, it is about how decisions are made by the DMO and who makes them. Therefore, the way that the DMO is organized and the checks and balances that are built into DMO policies, systems and procedures have a major impact on destination governance.

Power and Influence

Figure 6.11 identified structure and power as two other dimensions of governance. How a DMO is structured and how it makes important decisions are the most important issues here. Power is a concept that comes more from political science and political governance, but it is also an important issue for corporate governance. For example, if a DMO is a separate tourism ministry and has a high level of funding, it has more power and influence than if tourism is just one of several units within a ministry and its budget is low.

If tourism is the major economic sector within a destination, it is likely that its DMO will have more power and influence. For example, in places like the Bahamas and the Maldives, where tourism predominates, you would expect their DMOs to have strength and influence. However, these types of situations are unique and rather rare on a worldwide basis. Most economies are quite diversified, and normally tourism represents only a small proportion of their GDPs.

It also needs to be remembered from Chapter 1 that DMOs do not have direct control over the products in the destination that they are representing, and so they need to collaborate and coordinate with tourism sector stakeholders and borrow power from this association with tourism operators and other supporting organizations.

Organizational Structures

How DMOs are organized is fundamental to their governance. There is a huge variety of organizational structures for DMOs around the world, and there is certainly not one template for how to organize these specialized entities. DMOs range from government-operated tourism ministries or departments to ones that are purely private-sector-funded and sometimes through business associations. There are considerable variations in structures from country to country and based upon the unique legislation in individual jurisdictions.

Figure 6.12 shows the three major organizational structure approaches for DMOs as government (public sector) NPO (e.g., as a PPP), and private sector. For the latter approach, several

DMOs emerged from chambers of commerce, and some are still attached to their chambers. For nonprofits and where tourism is at a very early stage of development, NGOs may create and run DMOs. This is currently the situation in Indonesia, where Swisscontact is operating DMOs in Flores, Tanjung Puting, Toraja, and Wakatobi (Swisscontact 2018).

According to the UNWTO and the ETC, NTOs in developing countries tend to be 100 percent funded by government and part of government. In developed countries, NTOs tend to be PPPs with a combination of public- and private-sector governance.

EXAMPLE 6.13

Pakistan's NTO Coordinates a Response to COVID-19

As suggested in Example 6.6, greater coordination of effort is required when the tourism sector encounters a major crisis. This example demonstrated how this was accomplished in Pakistan during the pandemic.

> This document presents the strategies and action plan for the containment of the threat posed by COVID-19 to Pakistan's tourism industry. Immediate steps are required to protect jobs, facilitate business and restore the confidence of local and international visitors which was built before the outbreak. The National Tourism Coordination Board (NTCB) and its implementing body, Pakistan Tourism Development Corporation, is working closely with federal government, provincial tourism departments and private-sector organizations to develop a coordinated and comprehensive response.
>
> (National Tourism Coordination Board [Pakistan] 2022)

Learning Point

Various levels of DMOs within a country need to cooperate to deal with major crises.

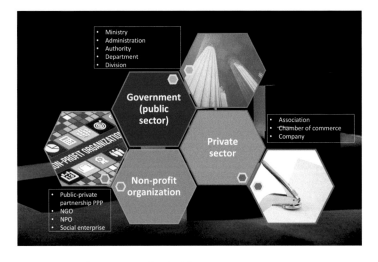

Figure 6.12 Organizational structures for DMOs.

The MGTO is an example of a government-operated DMO, and its organization chart is shown in Figure 6.13. MGTO is a unit under the Secretariat for Social Affairs and Culture of the Macao SAR government. It has a director, two deputy directors, seven departments and twelve divisions. The departments and divisions are organized by functions and roles. For example, there is a destination marketing department (marketing and integrated marketing communications [IMC]) and a tourism product and events department (product development). The communication and external relations department handles relations within the local community and externally. Because this is a purely governmental unit, it does not have a board of directors; instead, it is under the direct administration of the Secretariat.

Tourism and Events Queensland (TEQ) is a state-level DMO in Australia and provides another type of structural model. TEQ is a statutory body created with the Tourism & Events Queensland Act 2012, and that Act describes TEQ's powers and functions. TEQ is governed by a nine-member board, and the board members are appointed by the governor and are responsible to the Minister of Tourism and Major Events in the Queensland government. One of the board members is the director general of the Department of Innovation, Tourism Industry Development and the Commonwealth Games, a state government agency. The CEO of TEQ

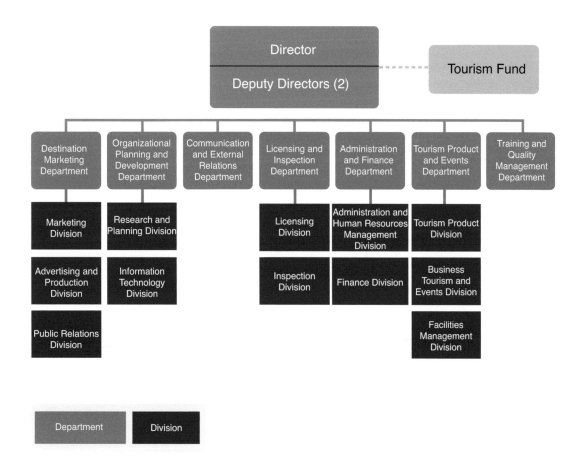

Figure 6.13 Organization chart for the Macao Government Tourist Office (MGTO 2022).

reports to the board. The organization chart for TEQ is shown in Figure 1.8. The structure below the TEQ's CEO is quite different from that under the director of MGTO. There are three departments (marketing, events and experiences, and corporate affairs, corporate services), and people and leadership is a fourth identified unit. TEQ operates several international offices (Tourism and Events Queensland 2022).

What is the best organizational structure to guarantee effective governance of a DMO? This may be the hardest question to answer in this entire book. There also is not much research that has been done that critically evaluates the effectiveness of different DMO organizational structures. Most of the materials that exist just describe different types of DMOs and do not attempt a deeper analysis or classification. From the examples, you can see that there is great diversity in organizational structures. However, governments play the key role in operating or at least funding most DMOs. There is a trend toward more PPPs in the more advanced economies.

Boards of Directors

For the DMOs that are not wholly operated by government agencies, the most common structure is for a CEO or executive director to be hired and for this DMO leader to work with a board of directors. This is the preferred structure for the growing number of PPPs in destination management. It is typical with this type of structure that the board must approve all DMO expenditures above a specified level.

Chapter 9 discusses DMO relations with boards of directors and reviews board composition; board member recruitment, selection, orientation and motivation; board member conduct; board size and members' terms of office; and board performance assessment. There are many other aspects and issues for DMOs in dealing with boards of directors to ensure more effective governance.

Again, it needs to be reiterated that many DMOs are NPOs and board members are not compensated for the time they spend at meetings or any other time they dedicate to DMO affairs. Therefore, the motivation and management of DMO board members is difficult and challenging.

How many meetings to schedule for boards of directors seems like a trivial matter, but in fact it is very important to the DMO's governance. If boards meet too infrequently, they may be just rubber-stamping the decisions of the CEO and senior management of the DMO and may not be able to keep up with what is going on within the CVB. Bill Geist in his books believes that when boards meet quarterly (four times per year), this is not frequent enough for them to effectively govern the DMO. He strongly recommends that boards of directors meet monthly, especially when the DMOs are locally based (Geist 2004, 2017).

Who sets the agenda for boards of directors' meetings? This is another seemingly innocuous matter, but again it is an issue that needs to be given great thought. Geist (2004, 2017) recommends that the chairperson of the board should prepare the agendas for meetings, perhaps with some assistance from the leader of the DMO. However, he suggests that the DMO should not be wholly entrusted with writing the board meeting agendas.

The culture created for boards of directors is another important matter as well as how board meetings are conducted. The board chairperson is the key in the development of the board culture and must ensure that divergent views are encouraged and valued at board meetings.

Motivating board members is a high priority for NPOs, and this responsibility falls again to the board chairperson, who should request the assistance of the DMO executive and other senior management staff. Geist (2004, 2017) and others recommend giving visibility to board members in their communities as the main basis for motivation. This means getting favorable publicity and exposure for board members in local media channels and commending them for their contributions to the DMO and the tourism sector in general.

BYLAWS

Many DMOs are created by acts of legislation and must abide by the conditions specified therein. In addition, most DMOs have bylaws that specify in detail how the DMO is to be operated and the most important policies and procedures. Bylaws are the rules that govern the internal operations of a DMO. They are normally established when the DMO first begins operations and may be changed (amended) by subsequent boards of directors. For example, Destination Canada, which is a Crown Corporation, has bylaws that were set in 2001 and amended several times, most recently in 2012. There are three bylaws that govern Destination Canada, and these are shown in Figure 6.14. These bylaws contain specific instructions and conditions for the management of Destination Canada, including about the composition of the board of

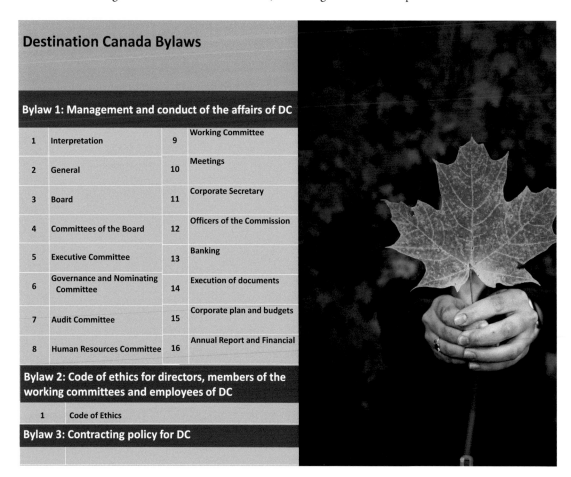

Destination Canada Bylaws

Bylaw 1: Management and conduct of the affairs of DC

1	Interpretation	9	Working Committee
2	General	10	Meetings
3	Board	11	Corporate Secretary
4	Committees of the Board	12	Officers of the Commission
5	Executive Committee	13	Banking
6	Governance and Nominating Committee	14	Execution of documents
7	Audit Committee	15	Corporate plan and budgets
8	Human Resources Committee	16	Annual Report and Financial

Bylaw 2: Code of ethics for directors, members of the working committees and employees of DC

1	Code of Ethics

Bylaw 3: Contracting policy for DC

Figure 6.14 Bylaws of Destination Canada (Destination Canada 2022a).

directors and the sub-committees of the board. For example, the bylaws specify that there should not be more than twelve board members. The bylaws also dictate rules about meetings and reports that must be prepared.

The enforcement of DMO bylaws is important to DMO governance to ensure that the internal rules are strictly followed. The question then becomes who should enforce these bylaws? In the real word, bylaws are often forgotten and neglected by organizations, unless they have particularly meticulous board members or DMO staff. Dealing with bylaws and changing them is often viewed as a chore that few board members want to deal with. However, bylaws are critical to DMO governance. It is recommended that the board chairperson should take responsibility for this matter and that the bylaws are reviewed in at least one board meeting per year.

BOARD FUNCTIONS

The bylaws specify the major functions and objectives of boards of directors. Some of the typical functions of boards are to:

- approve the annual budget of the DMO, including expected sources of funding and planned expenditures;
- assist the DMO with its programs and activities when necessary;
- govern the DMO in the manner described in the bylaws;
- monitor the finances of the DMO;
- provide overall direction and oversight for DMO operations;
- monitor and review the annual performance of the DMO;
- monitor and review the performance of the CEO or executive director;
- periodically review and amend where necessary the bylaws of the DMO;
- represent the DMO and the tourism sector within the destination.

BOARD COMMITTEES

Most boards of directors have committees to deal with specific matters, and these are smaller groups of board members with usually not more than six people. Permanent committees created by bylaws are known as standing committees, and these often include an executive committee, a finance committee and a governance or audit committee. Committees created for a short-term period and not included in the bylaws are most often called *ad hoc* committees.

BOARD OFFICERS

Once again, according to bylaws, several board officer positions are specified. Most boards have at least four officers, including the chairperson, vice-chairperson, treasurer and secretary. The bylaws specify how officers are to be selected and the terms of their office.

DMO Funding

There are many different funding formulas for DMOs, and it can also be said that there is great variation in the budget levels of DMOs. Figure 6.15 shows the potential sources of funding and revenues for DMOs.

Funding sources for DMOs

Figure 6.15 Funding sources for DMOs.

The funding of DMOs is a topic that always seems to draw much public debate. Funding levels certainly affect the power and influence of DMOs, especially within the tourism sector itself. DMOs with low funding levels struggle to be influential; those with high budgets can lead from the front because they have adequate resources to take fresh initiatives and help other partners. However, the situation is complicated by the fact that DMOs seldom control their own destinies in terms of long-term funding. Their budget levels can vary from year to year based on external factors and the decisions of other actors. You will know perhaps that many DMO budgets were slashed during the COVID-19 pandemic in 2020–2022, and some case examples follow.

How a DMO is funded has a great influence on its governance. There is an old saying that "he or she that pays the piper calls the tune," and that means that those providing most of the funding tend to play a major role in destination governance. In many countries, DMO funding comes directly from government. For example, VisitBritain/VisitEngland received £45.39 million for 2022 through grant-in-aid from the Department of Digital, Culture, Media and Sport (VisitBritain/VisitEngland 2022). Tourism Australia received AUD 191.9 million from government appropriations for 2020/2021. The Singapore Tourism Board received SGD 419.54 million in 2022 from government grant funding (Ministry of Finance [Singapore] 2022). The federal government in Canada provided annual support of CAD 96.2 million for the operations of Destination Canada in 2021 (Destination Canada 2022b).

A report prepared by the UNWTO and the ETC (2010) was based on a survey of sixty-two NTOs around the world. They found that three-quarters (75 percent) of the NTOs received more than two-thirds of their income from the central government.

A unique DMO funding formula has been developed in the USA through the introduction of local taxes on rooms. These are called bed taxes or hotel occupancy taxes. These are user-pay taxes, meaning that guests pay the taxes as a percentage on top of their room costs. According to Destinations International (2022), 73 percent of its DMO members receive funding through occupancy taxes on hotels.

The LVCVA is the CVB with the largest budget in the USA at $398 million for fiscal 2022–2023 (O'Connor 2022). (You will notice that is more than the national DMOs in Australia, Canada,

Singapore, and the UK receive from governments.) The LVCVA gets a majority of its funding through room taxes and gaming fees. The LVCVA operates the Las Vegas Convention Center and the Cashman Center, and so it has an additional source of revenue from rentals at these properties.

There have been mixed fortunes for DMO funding in different places in recent times; some DMO budgets have been slashed, and others have been increased. Generally, these DMO funding cuts are attributed to overall governmental budgetary problems. The issue for government-run and government-funded DMOs is they have their budgets set annually and the budget levels fluctuate from year to year. In addition, they are usually not able to carry forward surpluses from one year to the next. This is certainly not a situation that is favorable for stable DMO governance. During COVID-19 in 2020–2022, budgets were cut for those DMOs that are dependent on room and other user taxes.

Some DMOs have been experiencing recent declines in funding because of COVID-19 and adverse economic conditions, and the resulting impacts on the tourism sector. This has been especially so for those DMOs that depend mainly on room taxes because their revenues decreased as hotel occupancies declined.

EXAMPLE 6.14

Pandemic Hits State Tourism Taxes (USA)

DMOs that depend on user-pay taxes suffer when there are major downturns in business volumes, as they did in the USA during COVID-19. This is a topic covered in Chapter 20.

> In 2019, tourism generated $180 billion in tax revenues for federal, state and local governments. During the pandemic's early days, tourism-reliant states were hit hard by declining revenues. Hawaii initially projected $300 million in lost tax collections and 6,000 jobs. New York City lost $1.2 billion in tax revenue. Nevada faced a bleak economic outlook when visitor spending declined by 52.2 percent from the previous year. While traditional tourist destinations faced massive losses, rural areas across America saw an uptick in travelers.
> (National Conference of State Legislatures [USA] 2022)

Learning Point

DMOs are in jeopardy when they rely mostly on user-pay taxes.

Figure 6.15 provided a summary of the major funding mechanisms and sources for DMOs. You should not assume that every DMO receives funds from all six sources listed in Figure 6.15; rather, these are a set of potential funding sources. There are certain other funding sources in addition to those shown in Figure 6.15 that DMOs are increasingly considering as traditional funding is threatened. These include revenues from the operation of events and festivals, sales of printed and digital collateral materials (e.g., guides, maps, videos), sales of souvenirs and other local merchandise, and private-sector sponsorships. For example, Göteborg & Co., in Sweden and the Singapore Tourism Board receive part of their revenues from operating events.

Indonesia's Tourism Funding Slashed as a Result of COVID-19

It is somewhat inevitable that higher levels of government will cut (public-sector) DMO budgets during a major crisis, as in the case of Indonesia.

> Indonesia's Ministry of Tourism and Creative Economy will be putting destination marketing campaigns on hold after its annual budget was slashed by 41.3 per cent to 2.02 trillion rupiah (US$140 million) from 4.9 trillion rupiah, as the government redirects funding to fight COVID-19. The budget cut will affect some international marketing programs, as well as the income of Visit Indonesia Tourism Offices, the country's overseas tourism marketing representatives.
>
> (Hudoyo 2021)

Learning Point

Governments have a tendency to reduce DMO funding during national and global crises.

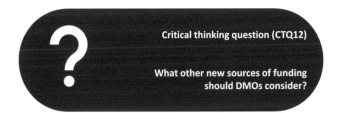

Critical thinking question (CTQ12)

What other new sources of funding should DMOs consider?

Measuring DMO Effectiveness

Ensuring the efficiency and effectiveness of operations is another dimension of destination governance. In demonstrating it is accountable, a DMO must prove that it has been efficient and effective in the use of resources. Efficiency usually means doing things at the lowest possible cost, and effectiveness measures the degree of success in attaining goals and objectives. Part of the task in ensuring efficiency is through day-to-day management of the DMO and through the application of an internal control system.

However, measuring effectiveness is about measuring results, and you already know that DMO accountability includes projecting results and then measuring results. The projected results should be based upon specific plans that the DMO has prepared (e.g., marketing plan, community relationship and involvement plan, product development plan, etc.). They need to be justified by research that the DMO has conducted or other credible information and assumptions. These must not be guesstimates based upon personal opinions. It is also assumed that the projected results prepared by the DMO and its staff will be reviewed and approved by the governing body, and this most often is a board of directors.

> ### EXAMPLE 6.16
>
> ### England to Get New DMO Accreditation System
>
> Accreditation systems have to potential to increase standardization of DMO operating practices. This is desirable in England where there is great fragmentation among DMOs.
>
> > A new accreditation system will be introduced over the 2022–2023 financial year, with VisitEngland receiving new funding to develop and administer the scheme. By creating a new national portfolio of accredited, high-performing Local Visitor Economy Partnerships we will reduce fragmentation and bring coherence to the DMO landscape, helping actors across the private and public sector. We are proposing to change the name of DMOs to Local Visitor Economy Partnerships to capture the wider strategic focus on the visitor economy and the breadth of activity and relationships they will establish to support the local visitor economy.
> >
> > (Department of Digital, Culture, Media and Sport, UK 2022)
>
> ### Learning Point
>
> Accreditation systems for DMOs are desirable and can be effective.

DMOs nowadays express results in KPIs within KRAs. This topic was discussed earlier in Chapter 5 in the discussion of measuring effectiveness. Figure 6.16 displays an overall framework for measuring DMO effectiveness using the eight destination management roles as the KRAs.

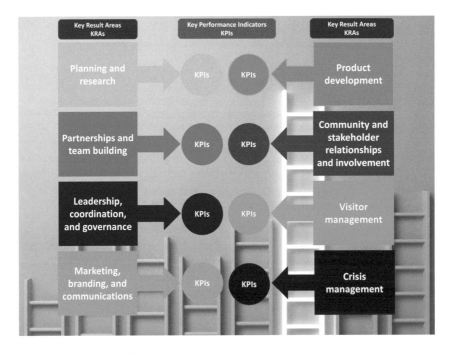

Figure 6.16 KPIs and KRAs for destination management.

As you can see in Figure 6.16, KPIs are developed for each destination management role, and this is one of the options open to setting KPIs for a DMO. In actual practice, DMOs usually have specific initiatives that have been identified within each destination management role, and the KPIs are tied to these initiatives. The initiatives will have been developed within a corporate or business plan, marketing plan, community relationship and involvement plan, long-term tourism plan or other planning documents.

Tourism Australia provides a real-life example of successfully setting and measuring KPIs, having set these for three areas: (1) grow demand; (2) industry recovery; and (3) corporate (Tourism Australia 2022c). The specific criteria for Tourism Australia's KPIs for 2021–2025 are in four parts for the first two of these areas:

1. grow visitor expenditure;
2. improve brand metrics;
3. drive industry recovery;
4. rebuild business events pipeline.

EXAMPLE 6.17

South African Tourism Does Well on Its KPIs

DMOs should have KPIs and periodically report on them as in this example from South Africa.

> SA Tourism presented its 2019/20 Annual Report achieving twenty-three out of thirty-seven KPIs, with significant progress on four and ten unachieved. Some failures could be attributed to the COVID-19 pandemic and the travel restrictions that ensued.
>
> (Parliamentary Monitoring Group [South Africa] 2021)

Learning Point

DMOs should at least once per year report on their performance against KPIs.

DMOs and their trade associations have recognized the need to demonstrate accountability and to measure their performance. An outstanding example is the work done by Destinations International on the *Standard DMO Performance Reporting Handbook* (Destinations Marketing Association International 2011). You will remember this system was discussed in Chapter 5.

Before leaving this discussion on DMO effectiveness, you should be aware of one controversial issue. Can DMOs claim to be solely responsible for the numbers of visitors who come to the destinations and their spending? This is hotly debated, and truthfully there is no precise evidence to say that a DMO can or cannot make this claim. However, it is most unlikely that a DMO can take 100 percent of the credit because there are other influential parties including airlines, hotels and resorts, attractions, travel trade, and the media. It is most prudent for a DMO not to over-exaggerate its influence on visitor volumes and better to acknowledge that the DMO played a major role but with the assistance of others. Additionally, DMOs should do research and information-gathering to identify those visitors who were drawn specifically because of the DMO's marketing, branding, and communications efforts.

Involvement

Figures 6.10 and 6.11 identified involvement as one of the dimensions of governance. The idea of involvement is strongly associated with political governance and the desirability of citizen involvement. However, the concept still has application to corporate governance and to destination management.

It is important that DMOs encourage involvement in their affairs and that they are open to inputs, especially from tourism stakeholders and community residents. This topic is discussed extensively in Chapters 8 and 9. Chapter 8 discusses building involvement with the DMO through partnerships and team-building. Chapter 9 reviews many ways to involve local community residents and tourism sector stakeholders in DMO programs and activities.

Göteborg & Co. (2022) in Sweden provides an outstanding case study in encouraging the involvement of other entities in strategic efforts, as evidenced by its cluster organization and Tourism Forum.

EXAMPLE 6.18

Collaboration and Involvement at Göteborg & Co.

There are often many entities involved directly or indirectly with tourism. In this example from Sweden, the structure encourages the integration and engagement of such multiple entities.

> Göteborg & Co. is owned by the City of Gothenburg and is the parent company for the cluster Tourism, Culture and Events—with the subsidiaries Liseberg AB, Got Event AB, Stadsteatern i Göteborg AB and Göteborg & Co. The company is organized into five departments. The board is appointed by the city council. Collaboration with the private business community takes place via the Tourism Industry Forum where representatives from the hospitality industry in the Gothenburg region participate.
>
> (Göteborg & Co. 2022)

Learning Point

Coordination of multi-organization effort is needed in tourism.

Risk Management

Effective destination governance includes giving adequate attention to risk management. As mentioned earlier, DMOs are exposed to different types of risks, some of which are internal to their own operations and others that affect tourism within their destinations. CBI Ministry of Foreign Affairs (Netherlands) (2020) suggests that destinations face threats such as the 2020 global coronavirus pandemic, natural disasters such as earthquakes and floods, political unrest, and terrorist attacks. For risks to destinations through natural and other disasters, some DMOs have prepared tourism crisis management plans.

DEFINITION

Risk management

The tourism risk management process is concerned with identifying and analyzing the risks ("the chance of something happening that will have an impact upon objectives") to a destination or organization and deciding what can and should be done about them (Asia-Pacific Economic Cooperation [APEC] 2006).

The Tourism Council of Bhutan (2021) has prepared a disaster management and contingency plan for the tourism sector.

EXAMPLE 6.19

Bhutan's Disaster Management and Contingency Plan for the Tourism Sector

Bhutan is highly dependent on tourism; however, it is also highly vulnerable to crises and disasters. Being prepared with a plan for such adverse events is a priority for the nation.

> Today, tourism is one of the key economic sectors contributing significantly to the socioeconomic development process, but also remains vulnerable due to natural and man-made hazards given the geological conditions of the country. With its growing importance to the national economy, any disruption to the tourism sector could significantly undermine business competitiveness and sustainable development. It is, therefore, critical to put in place measures to enhance preparedness and safety in the tourism sector.
>
> (Tourism Council of Bhutan 2021: 4)

Learning Point

DMOs are advised to prepare for encounters with crises and disasters.

DMOs face risks other than crises, and these result directly from and within their operations. These include fraud and misappropriation of funds by the DMO's staff members. They also face risks if part of their funding is used inappropriately for personal rather than business purposes. In addition, there are risks from the major projects and other initiatives of the DMO. Tourism Australia (2022b) defines risk as uncertainties that can negatively affect the achievement of a DMO's objective, and identifies three types of risks (strategic, project, and operational):

EXAMPLE 6.20

Risk Management Policy and Procedure at Tourism Australia

Tourism Australia, in this example, identifies the risks to which it is potentially exposed.

> Risk is the effect of uncertainty on objectives and risk management is the adoption of consistent processes within a comprehensive framework to ensure that risk is managed effectively, efficiently and coherently across an organization.
>
> Risks can have an impact on the achievement of objectives at all levels of the organization. Those risks associated with the high-level objectives, strategies and policies — and ultimately the mission of the organization — are often referred to as strategic risks. At the implementation or operations level, risks are often referred to as project risks (which could impact on the delivery and success of projects) or operational risks (associated with people, systems, and processes)."
>
> (Tourism Australia 2022b: 1–2)

Learning Point

DMOs need to be fully aware of all of the risks they might encounter and to plan for dealing with these risks.

The audit and finance committee of Tourism Australia's board of directors oversees its risk management policies and procedures. In addition to strategic, project, and operational risk, Tourism Australia also identifies other categories of potential risks to achieving its objectives as political, brand and reputation, legal and regulatory, financial, work health and safety, and information.

Ensuring adequate insurance coverage is one of the ways to manage risk at DMOs, as is DMO management planning ahead and anticipating what risks might be present in their programs and activities.

Steps for Effective Destination Leadership, Coordination, and Governance

The specific steps to be taken for a DMO to accomplish its destination leadership, coordination, and governance roles are to:

- perform the leadership and coordination roles that are expected of DMOs;
- take all the steps necessary to demonstrate the accountability of the DMO;
- ensure that the operations and decision-making of the DMO have transparency;
- if applicable, ensure that the board of directors conducts its functions effectively and follows the rules specified in the DMO's bylaws;
- be a good steward of the funds and other resources with which the DMO is entrusted;
- have an internal control system and other policies and procedures to ensure the efficiency of DMO operations;
- measure the effectiveness of the DMO's programs and activities by estimating results and then calculating the degree of attainment of these results;
- identify KRAs and KPIs;
- encourage the involvement of tourism stakeholders and community residents in the DMO's programs and activities;
- implement a risk management program.

SUMMING UP

DMOs need to be leaders of the tourism sector in their destinations. The major leadership roles of DMOs are to be visionaries, coaches, champions, scholar-teachers, communicators, visitor hosts, quality controllers, and stewards. DMOs and their leaders may adopt different leadership styles. Servant leadership is one style that seems very well suited for destination management. DMO leaders also must be adaptive, authentic, inclusive, and transformational, and have mutually beneficial two-way relationships with stakeholders at the individual level.

Coordination accompanies leadership as an important role for DMOs in breaking down the silos that can exist in the tourism sector and within their communities. DMOs must encourage cooperation and collaboration among parties and ensure a free flow of communications.

Destination governance is a concept that is receiving increasing attention. This is how a DMO is administered and who does the administering. Governance involves the policies, systems, and processes to ensure that all stakeholders are involved and that the DMO is accountable for its results and resource usage and has a high level of transparency.

Two of the key dimensions of destination governance are accountability and transparency. Accountability is the obligation of a DMO to justify and account for its programs and activities and to accept responsibility for results. The DMO must disclose these results in a transparent manner and take responsibility for the use of all resources with which it has been entrusted. Transparency means openness in operations and communications. The tourism stakeholders in the destination should be able to see what the DMO is doing and understand its decision-making.

There are many different types of organizational structures for DMOs. However, PPPs with independent boards of directors are becoming more of the norm. The operation of boards of directors affects governance, and board chairpersons have a key role to play in ensuring that boards function effectively. Bylaws set out the rules for boards of directors, and they must be checked periodically to guarantee compliance.

The funding of DMOs in many places in the world has been under threat from government budget deficits and downturns in tourism business levels. Several DMOs are looking for new ways to earn revenues in the face of significant cost cutting.

The effectiveness of DMO operations needs to be measured, and this is done mainly through defining KRAs and setting KPIs. KPIs need to be set for all of the destination management roles and not just for marketing, branding, and communications.

Risk management is another dimension of effective destination governance. The DMO in particular must ensure that it is fully protected from all potential risks and some that may even threaten its future existence.

KEYWORDS

accountability	bylaws	coordination
adaptive leadership	championing function	corporate social responsibility (CSR)
advocacy	coaching function	
agendas	collaboration	destination management leadership functions
annual report	communication	
authentic leadership	communicator function	disclosure
board of directors	cooperation	effectiveness

efficiency
fragmentation
funding
governance
inclusive leadership
internal control
involvement
leader–member exchange
 (LMX) theory
leadership

leadership style
minesweeper function
minutes
modeling
pioneering
quality controller function
risk management
scholar–teacher function
servant leadership
silo effect

steward function
stewardship
structure
transformational
 leadership
transparency
user-pay taxes
visionary function
visitor host function

REVIEW QUESTIONS

1. What are the major leadership roles that DMOs should assume within their destinations?
2. How should DMOs effectively coordinate the activities of other parties?
3. How would you define destination governance?
4. What are the main dimensions of destination governance?
5. What are accountability and transparency, and which actions does a DMO need to take to prove it is being accountable and transparent?
6. How do DMO organizational structures affect destination governance?
7. What are the different funding mechanisms and sources that are used for DMOs?
8. What have been some of the recent trends in the funding of DMOs?
9. What steps should a DMO take to measure its effectiveness?
10. Why is it important for a DMO to plan for risk management, and what are some of the risks that might be encountered?

REFERENCES

American Psychological Association (2022) "Leader-Member Exchange Theory (LMX Theory)," https://dictionary.apa.org/leader-member-exchange-theory

Asia-Pacific Economic Cooperation (2006) "Introduction to Risk Management in Tourism: Participant's Workbook," www.apec.org/docs/default-source/publications/2007/4/tourism-risk-management-an-authoritative-guide-to-managing-crisis-in-tourism-december-2006/toc/introduction-instructors-guide.pdf?sfvrsn=46c4896b_1

Barnett, P. (2015) "Breaking Bad Barriers," www.strategy-business.com/article/00382?gko=5df7f

CBI Ministry of Foreign Affairs (2020) "How to Manage Risk in Tourism?" www.cbi.eu/market-information/tourism/how-manage-risks-tourism/

Department of Digital, Culture, Media and Sport (2021) "The de Bois Review: An Independent Review of Destination Management Organisations in England," https://assets.publishing.service.gov.uk/government/uploads/system/uploads/attachment_data/file/1011664/2585-C_The_de_Bois_Review_ACCESSIBLE__for_publication_.pdf

Department of Digital, Culture, Media and Sport, UK (2022) "Government Response to the Independent Review of Destination Management Organisations in England," July 20, www.gov.uk/government/publications/government-response-to-the-independent-review-of-destination-management-organisations-in-england

Destination Canada (2021) "Disclosure of Travel and Hospitality Expenses," www.destinationcanada.com/sites/default/files/archive/1546-Proactive%20Disclosure%20-%20Travel%20and%20Hospitality%20Expenses%20-%20December%202021/12%202021%20SMC%20Disclosure.pdf

——— (2022a) "Corporate Governance," www.destinationcanada.com/en/corporate-governance

—— (2022b) "Building the Tourism of Tomorrow: 2021 Annual Report," www.destinationcanada.com/sites/default/files/archive/1613-Destination%20Canada%20Annual%20Report%20-%202021/2021%20Annual%20Report.pdf

Destination Marketing Association International (2011) *Standard DMO Performance Reporting. A Handbook for Destination Marketing Organizations (DMOs)*. Washington, DC: DMAI.

Destinations International (2011) "Standard DMO Performance Reporting," https://destinationsinternational.org/sites/default/master/files/pdfs_Dest_Intl_2011_Performance_Reporting_Handbook.pdf

—— (2020) "DMAP Standards," https://destinationsinternational.org/destination-marketing-accreditation-program-dmap

—— (2022) "Destination Organization Performance Reporting," https://destinationsinternational.org

Geist, B. (2004) *Destination Leadership for Boards*, Miami Shores, Fla.: Neverland Publishing.

—— (2017) *Destination Leadership*, Miami Shores, Fla.: Neverland Publishing.

Global Sustainable Tourism Council (2022) "GSTC Destination Criteria," www.gstcouncil.org/gstc-criteria/gstc-destination-criteria

Göteborg & Co (2022) "Organization," https://goteborgco.se/om-goteborgco/organisation

Greenleaf, R. K. (1977) *Servant Leadership: A Journey into the Nature of Legitimate Power and Greatness*, Mahwah, NJ: Paulist Press.

Greenleaf Center for Servant Leadership (2022) "What Is Servant Leadership?" www.greenleaf.org/what-is-servant-leadership

Hankinson, G. (2007) "The Management of Destination Brands: Five Guiding Principles Based on the Recent Developments in Corporate Branding Theory," *Brand Management*, 14 (3): 240–254.

Hong Kong Tourism Board (2021) "Corporate Information," www.discoverhongkong.com/eng/about-hktb/annual-report/annual-report-20202021/about-us.html

Hudoyo, M. (2021) "COVID-19 Slashes Indonesia's Tourism Budget by 41%," *TTG Asia*, August 25, www.ttgasia.com/2021/08/25/covid-19-slashes-indonesias-tourism-budget-by-41

Las Vegas Convention and Visitors Authority (2022a) "Board of Directors Meetings," www.lvcva.com/who-we-are/board-of-directors/schedule-and-minutes/

—— (2022b) "Funding and Finance," www.lvcva.com/funding-finance

Laws, E., Richins, H., Agrusa, J., and Scott, N. (eds.) (2011) *Tourism Destination Governance*, Wallingford: CABI.

Macao Government Tourism Office (2021) "MGTO to Hold Annual Press Conference This Month," https://mtt.macaotourism.gov.mo/2021/02/mgto-to-hold-annual-press-conference-this-month

——(2022) "About Us," www.macaotourism.gov.mo/en/about-us

Ministry of Business, Innovation and Employment, New Zealand (2022) "Tourism Industry Transformation Plan: He Mahere Tiaki Kaimahi Draft Better Work Action Plan," www.mbie.govt.nz/dmsdocument/23385-he-mahere-tiaki-kaimahi-draft-better-work-action-plan

Ministry of Finance, Singapore (2022) "Head V. Ministry of Trade and Industry," www.mof.gov.sg/docs/librariesprovider3/budget2022/download/pdf/49-mti-2022.pdf

National Conference of State Legislatures (USA) (2022) "Travel Is Taxing in More Ways Than One," www.ncsl.org/research/fiscal-policy/travel-is-taxing-in-more-ways-than-one.aspx

National Tourism Coordination Board (Pakistan) (2022) "Strategy to Help Mitigate the Impact of COVID-19 on Pakistan's Tourism Industry," https://tourism.gov.pk/publications/strat_covid.pdf

Northouse, P. G. (2021) *Leadership: Theory and Practice*, 9th edn, Thousand Oaks, Calif.: SAGE.

O'Connor, D. (2022) "Las Vegas Visitors Authority Approves Record $398m Budget," *Casino.org*, May 25, www.casino.org/news/las-vegas-visitors-authority-approves-record-398m-budget

Parliamentary Monitoring Group (South Africa) (2021) "South African Tourism 2019/20 Annual Report," https://pmg.org.za/committee-meeting/32330/#:~:text=SA%20Tourism%20achieved%2023%20out%20of%2037%20KPIs%2C, Plan%202019%2F20%20was%20presented%3A%20Programme%201%3A%20Corporate%20Support

Perdue, R. R., and Pitegoff, B. E. (1990) "Methods of Accountability Research for Destination Marketing," *Journal of Travel Research*, 28 (4): 45–49.

Purdue Global (2020) "What Is Servant Leadership?" www.purdueglobal.edu/blog/business/what-is-servant-leadership

Ruhanen, L., Scott, N., and Tkaczynski, A. (2010) "Governance: A Review and Synthesis of the Literature," *Tourism Review*, 65 (4): 4–16.

Russell, R. F., and Stone, A. G. (2002) "A Review of Servant Leadership Attributes: Developing a Practical Model," *Leadership and Organization Development Journal*, 23 (3): 145–157.

Ryan, L. (2016) "Command-and-Control Management Is for Dinosaurs," Forbes, www.forbes.com/sites/lizryan/2016/02/26/command-and-control-management-is-for-dinosaurs/?sh=1ae3ecbf24ed

Secretaría de Turismo, Government of Mexico City (2022) "Experiencias de Barrio," www.turismo.cdmx.gob.mx/storage/app/media/banner2020/2catalogo-de-experiencias-de-barrio-2020-sectur.pdf

Stone, A. G. (2003) "Transformational Versus Servant Leadership: A Difference in Leader Focus," School of Leadership Studies, Regent University.

Swisscontact (2018) "Tourism Development for Selected Destinations in Indonesia," www.swisscontact.org/en/country/indonesia/projects/projects-indonesia/project/-/show/tourism-development-for-selected-destinations-in-indonesia.html

Tett, G. (2015) *The Silo Effect: The Peril of Expertise and the Promise of Breaking Down barriers.* New York, NY: Simon & Schuster.

Tourism Australia (2022a) "Our Board," www.tourism.australia.com/en/about/our-organisation/our-board.html

——— (2022b) "Risk Management Policy and Procedure," www.tourism.australia.com/content/dam/assets/document/1/6/x/6/p/2002561.pdf#:~:text=Tourism%20Australia%20is%20also%20committed%20to%20ensuring%20that,   a%20competitor%20and%2For%20%20benefit%20to%20Tourism%20Australia%29

——— (2022c) "Corporate Plan 2021/22–2024/25," www.tourism.australia.com/content/dam/digital/corporate/documents/corporate-plan-fy22-aug-21.pdf

Tourism Council of Bhutan (2021) "Disaster Management and Contingency Plan for the Tourism Sector," www.tourism.gov.bt/uploads/attachment_files/tcb_exUruay2_DMCP%20for%20tourism%20sector%20(2021-2026).pdf

Tourism and Events Queensland (2022) "Who We Are?" https://teq.queensland.com/au/en/industry/who-we-are

Tourism New Zealand (2022) "Chief Executive Expenses," www.tourismnewzealand.com/about-us/corporate-responsibility

United Nations Economic and Social Commission for Asia and the Pacific (2009) *What Is Good Governance?* Bangkok: United Nations Economic and Social Commission for Asia and the Pacific. www.unescap.org/resources/what-good-governance

United Nations World Tourism Organization (2022) "Global Code of Ethics for Tourism," http://ethics.unwto.org/en/content/global-code-ethics-tourism

United Nations World Tourism Organization and European Travel Commission (2010) *Budgets of National Tourism Organizations 2008–2009*, Madrid: United Nations World Tourism Organization.

United States Agency for International Development (2014) "C5 Crisis Management and Communication Plan," https://pdf.usaid.gov/pdf_docs/PA00KCP8.pdf

US Travel Association (2022) "Sustainable Travel Coalition," www.ustravel.org/programs/sustainable-travel-coalition

VisitBritain/VisitEngland (2022) "Annual Report and Accounts for the Year Ended 31 March 2022," www.visitbritain.org/sites/default/files/vb-corporate/Documents-Library/documents/transparency/e02757318_hc_400_visitbritain_visitengland_ara_21-22_web_accessible.pdf

Visit Colorado Springs (2022) "Transparency," www.visitcos.com/about-us/transparency

Visit Hagerstown (2022) "Code of Business Practices," www.visithagerstown.com/members/code-of-business-practices

Westley, F. and Mintzberg, H. (1989) "Visionary leadership and strategic management," *Strategic Management Journal*, 10(S1), 17–32.

World Travel and Tourism Council (2022) "WTTC Publishes Report on Digital Travel Post COVID," https://wttc.org/News-Article/WTTC-publishes-report-on-Digital-Travel-post-COVID

Chapter **7**

Destination Product Development

Be principled

LEARNING OBJECTIVES

Having read this chapter, you should be able to:

1. define the destination product and identify its components;
2. discuss the principles of destination product development;
3. explain the TALC model and how it impacts destination product development;
4. describe the continuum of DMO involvement in product development;
5. differentiate between hard and soft product development and explain the importance of destination quality;
6. elaborate on product development strategy models for destinations;
7. describe the development of accessible tourism, visitor information centers (VICs), signage, and interpretation;
8. elaborate on the types of strategies and programs that a DMO can offer to enhance human resource development;
9. explain the roles and benefits of packaging and programming;
10. define experience design and identify the characteristics of effectively crafted visitor experiences.

DOI: 10.4324/9781003343356-9

Warming Up

Now that you have learned about planning and research, and leadership, coordination, and governance, it is time to hear about how they are applied to make better destinations. Product development benefits from the careful long-term planning and solid research that were discussed in Chapters 4 and 5. Visionary leadership is also crucial to effective product development, as covered in Chapter 6.

Chapter 1 introduced the concept of the destination product as consisting of physical products, people, packages, and programs. Historically, destination product development was a role that many DMOs gave a low priority because they focused most attention on marketing, branding, and communications. However, with intensifying competition among destinations and the knowledge that customer satisfaction and the presentation and quality of products and services are also important parts of destination marketing, DMOs started to take a more active role in product development.

There are many parts of the world where tourism is underdeveloped and product development there has an equal or higher priority than destination marketing, branding, and communications (see Example 7.2 on Lao PDR). Even in countries that have advanced economies, TPD is used as a tool of regional economic development. Tourism development strategies or plans are prepared to guide product development in these countries and regions.

DMOs have different levels of involvement ranging from being a bystander to becoming a partner in development. The level of involvement is affected by the destination's stage in the TALC and the unique local circumstances and characteristics.

There are approximately 200 country destinations in the world with many sub-regions, and so it is difficult to describe a common template for destination product development. However, there are some guiding principles for product development, and you will learn about them after the destination product and its components are defined.

Your author has been a tourism development adviser for many years and has consulted for destinations in different countries including Australia, Canada, China, Indonesia, Trinidad and Tobago, USA, and others. In Chapter 7, the contents reflect his global experiences in destination product development.

Definition and Components of the Destination Product

You will want to know first what the destination product is and what its components are. These are topics that have sparked great debate among tourism scholars since at least the 1970s. The conversations among academics have been interesting, but unfortunately DMOs have found little practical value in their propositions and research findings. This gap between theory and practice needs to be bridged in the future.

In developing this book's approach to defining the destination product and its components, the contributions of several prominent tourism scholars were considered. Middleton (1989) argued that from the standpoint of a potential customer considering any form of tourist visit, the product may be defined as a bundle or package of tangible and intangible components, based on the activities available at a destination. The package is perceived by the tourist as an experience, available at a price. This is a useful definition because it says that the destination product has both tangible and intangible components, and this is certainly true. Also, it highlights the importance of activities and experiences to tourists.

Smith (1994) suggested that the generic tourism product consisted of five elements: (1) the physical plant, (2) service, (3) hospitality, (4) freedom of choice, and (5) involvement. Freedom of choice and involvement are factors related to tourists: that there is some choice of product available to them in the destination and that the tourists are themselves involved in the experiences they have purchased. Smith also described a tourism production process of primary inputs (resources), intermediate inputs (facilities), intermediate outputs (services), and final outputs (experiences). This was another valuable definition and confirmed Middleton's identification of tangible (physical plant) and intangible (service and hospitality) components. There was again an emphasis on tourists' involvement in experiences.

Ritchie and Crouch (2003) in their model of destination competitiveness (Figure 5.12) provided another view on the destination product consisting of the two levels of core resources and attractions (physiography and climate, culture and history, mix of activities, special events, entertainment, superstructure, and market ties) and supporting factors and resources (infrastructure, accessibility, facilitating resources, hospitality, enterprise, and political will). This was a much more detailed description of the destination product and extended the definition to include stakeholder support and entrepreneurial capacity.

Murphy et al. (2000), using data on visitors to Victoria in British Columbia, Canada, found that two aspects of the destination product, namely environment and infrastructure, influenced tourists' perceptions of the quality and value of Victoria as a destination. Environment comprised the attributes of pleasant climate, attractive scenery, clean city, heritage ambiance and friendly people, and infrastructure included good food, interesting attractions and good hotels. You will note that this is not the definition of infrastructure as used in this book.

So there are at least two important perspectives on what constitutes the destination product: (1) how the customer views and perceives the product within the destination; and (2) the product itself with its tangible and intangible components. The DMO can indirectly influence the customers' product perceptions through marketing, branding, and communications and steps taken to improve product and service quality. The DMO does not usually have direct control over the product itself but rather must rely on tourism stakeholders to make product improvements and changes.

Reflecting the second of these perspectives, Mill and Morrison (2012) referred to the destination product as the destination mix or a blending of interdependent elements. All elements need to be present to produce satisfying experiences for tourists. The five elements are attractions and events, facilities, infrastructure, transportation, and hospitality resources.

Morrison (2010) suggested three extensions to product in McCarthy's traditional marketing mix (four Ps) to better fit with the tourism sector and what the sector offers for customers. These three product extensions were people, packaging, and programming (Fig. 7.1). Blending Mill and Morrison's (2012) and Morrison's (2010) concepts produces the destination product model shown in Figure 1.3. This admittedly does not cover all the elements, especially those on the consumers' side or the support from local stakeholders, but it is a practical and understandable solution to defining the destination product. Here, then, is this book's definition of the destination product:

DEFINITION

Destination product

The destination product is an interdependent mixture of tangible and intangible components comprising physical products, people, packages, and programs. The interaction of the hosts and guests within the destination is an important dimension of the destination product.

Figure 7.1 Product extensions in destination development.

Despite its simplicity, this definition provides a practical foundation for a DMO to determine what to include in its product development role. The four destination product components are items over which, in partnership with tourism stakeholders and others, the DMO can exert some direct control.

Before discussing the DMO product development role in detail, it is important for you to know a little more about the principles for destination product development and the TALC.

Principles of Destination Product Development

The DMO, in consultation with tourism stakeholders and community residents, must identify a set of basic principles for destination product development. This is an important sub-role in product development for the DMO.

EXAMPLE 7.1

What It Will Be Like in 2032

Having a vision of the destination's future should guide product development as shown in this example from Australia.

> Queensland will be world-renowned for life-changing experiences that sustain, enhance and regenerate our environment and authentically immerse visitors in our Indigenous cultures and tropical lifestyle.
>
> (Department of Tourism, Innovation and Sport, Queensland 2022)

Learning Point

The destination vision sets fundamental principles for product development.

Guiding Principles for Destination Development

Guiding principles are values and requirements that steer the direction of tourism development in a destination for the longer term. The destination should not deviate from these principles. The following is a list of principles for destination product development that was adapted from the UNWTO and ETC *Handbook on Tourism Product Development* (2011):

- Appropriate scale: Development is large enough to have a significant positive impact on the tourism sector but not so big that it causes problems for other stakeholders, the environment or the destination's economy.
- Authenticity: Authenticity requires that development be a true and authentic reflection of the destination and its history, culture, and peoples.
- Community support: Community residents are not opposed to the development and support its proceeding (as you learned in Chapter 3).
- Competitive differentiation: Development is substantially different from what is found in competitive destinations.
- Creativity and innovation: Development is a one-of-a-kind in its category or at least demonstrates new features that are innovative in the tourism sector.
- Destination vision: Development is consistent with the destination vision and preferably actively contributes to its realization (as in the Queensland, Australia and Lao PDR examples).
- Integration: Development integrates well with the existing destination product.
- Market need and feasibility: The market need and economic feasibility of the development have been proven.
- Positioning: Development fits with the destination positioning and branding approaches.
- Sustainability: Development does not harm the environment or the social and cultural fabric of the destination.
- Tourism stakeholder support: Stakeholders, particularly those within the tourism sector, support the development.
- USPs: Development reflects or takes advantage of the identified USPs of the destination.

EXAMPLE 7.2

Vision for the Lao Tourism Development Plan

This Lao PDR plan specifies how tourism development will reflect the country's unique resources.

> The 2021–2025 Lao Tourism Development Plan aims to develop, promote and manage cultural, historical and agricultural tourism to a high standard in a green and sustainable manner to enable regional and international integration and become a leading economic driver that will help lift people out of poverty in accordance with the government policies.
> (Ministry of Information, Culture and Tourism (Lao PDR) 2021)

Learning Point

Tourism product development should emphasize a destination's USPs.

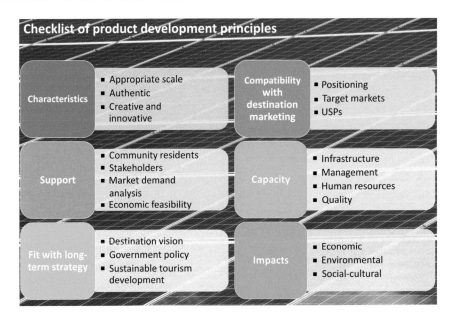

Figure 7.2 Checklist of principles of destination product development.

Figure 7.2 shows a categorization of these principles into four groups (characteristics, support, fit with long-term strategy, and compatibility with destination marketing), and two additional groups are added, capacity and impact.

Sustainable Tourism Development

The importance of the environment to the destination product has already been mentioned. Sustainable tourism development has emerged as the broad concept for ensuring that tourism grows in a fashion that does not permanently damage the environment, society and the culture of the destination. You learned about the concept in Chapter 2.

The DMO should be a catalyst and champion for sustainability within its destination. There are many sustainable tourism criteria and models now available for destinations to follow. They include the Global Sustainable Tourism Destination Criteria (Global Sustainable Tourism Council 2022) and many guidelines on encouraging low-carbon tourism practices (Scott et al. 2016; Zhang and Zhang 2018). One of the specific initiatives that the DMO can take is to design a sustainable tourism development charter or code of ethics for the destination. This charter or code spells out the guiding principles for sustainability in tourism within the destination.

EXAMPLE 7.3

Low-Carbon Tourism Measures in China

Low-carbon tourism is a strategy for addressing climate change. This example describes the low-carbon tourism initiatives in China.

Several concrete countermeasures in transportation and accommodation could effectively reduce CO_2 emissions while simultaneously avoiding the high costs imposed on the tourism industry by a carbon tax. These countermeasures include the development of bio-energy and the use of low-carbon materials in the aviation industry, investment in new energy vehicles for transport via road, popularization of low-carbon materials, energy saving and water conservation, and other low-carbon management measures that could be used in the hotel industry. To further popularize low-carbon technologies, the Chinese tourism industry should also be required to advocate voluntary CO_2 emissions reductions, thus helping a low-carbon attitude to become part of the tourism enterprise culture.

(Zhang and Zhang 2018: 28)

Learning Point

Low-carbon tourism needs to be given a higher future priority.

The DMO should also encourage tourism operators to follow green practices and accomplish this in various ways, including offering related education and training. Other techniques include informing operators of best practices in sustainability program applications and establishing special award programs for those operators in the destination that demonstrate leadership in sustainable development practices. The basic approach envisaged for the sustainable development of tourism is the triple bottom line (Fig. 7.3) through which a balancing of economic, social and environmental goals are achieved.

It is worthwhile noting here that sustainable tourism is not only an issue related to product development, but it also impinges on the DMO's relationship with community residents and has implications for destination marketing, branding, and communications. Local residents want to be assured that tourism is sustainable and that it will not adversely affect cherished natural, heritage and cultural resources. Moreover, there is an increasing number of tourists who are environmentally conscious (Castro 2022), and a portion of these people will prefer destinations that adopt sustainable or responsible tourism practices. Finally, sustainable

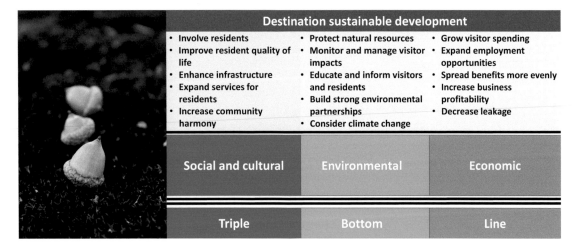

Figure 7.3 The triple-bottom-line approach to destination sustainable development.

tourism development is an area for collaboration among tourism stakeholders, and so it is discussed again in Chapter 8 on partnerships and team-building.

EXAMPLE 7.4

Consumers Are More Aware of Negative Environmental Impacts of Tourism

This example provides evidence of consumers becoming more knowledgeable about how tourism damages the environment.

> A recent Technavio report revealed that consumers are becoming increasingly aware of the negative environmental impacts of tourism, which is spurring a demand for sustainable tourism. In fact, the sustainable tourism market is growing al a compound annual growth rate of 9.72 percent and is expected to register an incremental growth of $235.21 billion between 2020 and 2025, according to the report.
>
> (Castro 2022)

Learning Point

DMOs should engage with visitors and residents to jointly find solutions reduce environmental damage from tourism.

Tourism Area Life Cycle

The TALC concept is of great relevance for a DMO's product development role. TALC is like the product life cycle (PLC) concept that encompasses the stages of introduction, growth, maturity, and decline. The PLC was introduced by Joel Dean and is well accepted among management experts and scholars as a foundational principle, especially those specializing in marketing (Dean 1950).

Although the TALC model has had its critics among scholars, it has stood the test of time over the forty-plus years since the first article was published about it in 1980. The originator of the TALC model, Professor Richard Butler (2011), defines TALC and explains its basic purpose as follows:

DEFINITION

Tourism area life cycle (TALC)

"The Tourism Area Life Cycle is a process describing how a destination starts off slowly with visitor numbers limited by the facilities and access. As the destination attracts more visitors, amenities are improved and visitor numbers grow rapidly towards and sometimes beyond the carrying capacity of the destination. The purpose of the model was to draw attention to the dynamic nature of destinations and propose a generalised process of development and potential decline which could be avoided by appropriate interventions (of planning, management and development), or as suggested in the title of the article, the management of resources" (Butler 2011).

The title of Butler's 1980 article in *Canadian Geographer* was "The Concept of the Tourist Area Life-Cycle of Evolution: Implications for Management of Resources." You should especially note in Butler's statement of the TALC model's purpose the idea that management and development (as well as planning) interventions will help in avoiding a decline in the life cycle of an area. Stated in a simpler way, the destination needs to anticipate a decline and deal with this through destination planning, management, and development. So, here is one of the parts of the DMO's product development role: determining where the destination is located along the TALC model.

Before leaving this topic and moving on, it is best to mention one serious criticism of the TALC model, which is that the model of a destination is too general and many destinations have sub-products at different stages of their life cycles. For example, Malaysia has had tropical beach resorts for many years, but the recent introduction of medical tourism facilities and services is a new part of the country's destination product. China has offered culture- and history-based travel for more than three decades, but the introduction of wine tourism in Shandong and Ningxia Provinces is a fresh initiative. British Columbia is well known for its spectacular natural scenery and winter sports, but mountain biking is a relatively new addition to its tourism product portfolio (David Nairne & Associates 2014). Butler (2011) acknowledges this point and agrees that destinations may be experiencing several cycles at different stages of development and that the TALC is an aggregate model made up of several life cycles. Therefore, the DMO needs to pay heed to this extension of the TALC model and not blindly follow the single-cycle assumption.

EXAMPLE 7.5

Tourism Development Plan for Drakenstein, South Africa

It is advisable for DMOs to prepare tourism development plans as described in this example from South Africa.

> The purpose of this Tourism Development Plan is to ensure that the destination is adequately prepared to become a global premier destination in the tourism space through facilitating an enabling environment to develop key components in the overall tourism value chain. These components include:

- Tourism product development
- Development of cultural and heritage tourism
- Enhancing the existing destination marketing activities
- Tourism infrastructure development
- Tourism skills development.

(Drakenstein Municipality 2018)

Learning Point

Tourism development plans are valuable for destinations.

DMO Involvement in Product Development

How do DMOs participate in product development on the ground? As you will see, there is no standard formula for DMOs in accomplishing this role.

DMO Product Development Roles

How should the DMO get involved in product development and what are the sub-roles that it should perform? This varies across the many destinations and DMOs in the world, but there is a continuum of involvement (Fig. 7.4) ranging from being a bystander to becoming a partner in product development. The following is a description of the four approaches for a DMO:

1. Bystander: The DMO as a bystander watches on as other tourism stakeholders do the product development. The argument for non-involvement is usually that if private-sector companies in the tourism sector can take care of product development, there is no need for the DMO to get involved.
2. Facilitator: The DMO as a facilitator provides a basic level of information and advice for tourism stakeholders, developers, and investors who wish to engage in product development, such as in the Northwest Territories' Tourism Product Development Workbook.
3. Instigator: The DMO as an instigator takes an active role in identifying opportunities for product development and finds strategies to realize these opportunities.
4. Partner: The DMO as a partner is not only an instigator, but makes a financial, staff or other resource investment in product development, usually along with other tourism stakeholders.

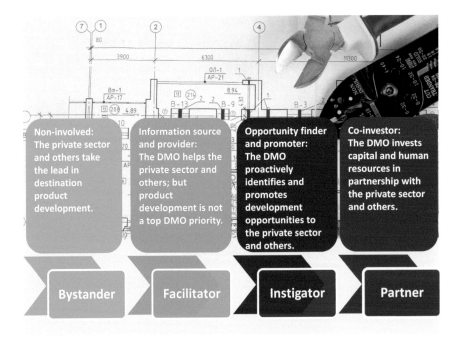

Figure 7.4 Continuum of DMO involvement in product development.

Tourism Product Development Workbook, Northwest Territories

This example from Canada demonstrates a proactive DMO approach to destination product development.

> In this workbook, you will learn how to develop a product based on the different types of visitors, their motivations for travel, their travel values, and their countries of origin. You will also learn about CBT, Indigenous tourism, and ecotourism for a tourism industry that remains equitable and sustainable for everyone involved. You will also complete activities that will help bring you closer to developing your own tourism product.
>
> (Government of Northwest Territories, undated)

Learning Point

DMOs should provide advice to tourism sector stakeholders on product development.

The bystander position is one of non-engagement in destination product development, and presumably the DMO has a 100 percent focus on marketing, branding, and communications or has another reason for not assuming this role. The other three active roles of facilitator, instigator, and partner need some further discussion and clarification. Figure 7.5 provides more details on the specific tasks DMOs perform as facilitators, instigators, and partners. For a newly emerging place that needs a higher level of product development, it could be expected that the DMO's role would be the most proactive (acting and being results oriented) and the DMO may be willing to be a partner in product developments. Where the destination is more mature (but not in a decline stage of the TALC) or where there are concerns about the environmental, social

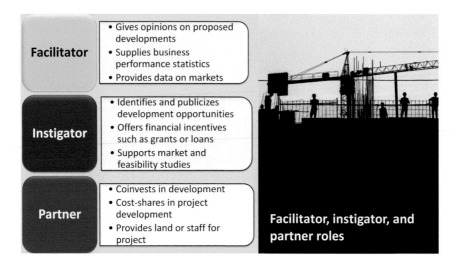

Facilitator
- Gives opinions on proposed developments
- Supplies business performance statistics
- Provides data on markets

Instigator
- Identifies and publicizes development opportunities
- Offers financial incentives such as grants or loans
- Supports market and feasibility studies

Partner
- Coinvests in development
- Cost-shares in project development
- Provides land or staff for project

Facilitator, instigator, and partner roles

Figure 7.5 Facilitator, instigator, and partner roles in product development.

and cultural impacts of tourism, the DMO might be the least proactive and is more likely to be a facilitator.

The information below from the State of Georgia in the USA is a good example of a DMO working as a facilitator and an instigator. The examples for Drakenstein in South Africa and the Northwest Territories in Canada (Examples 7.5 and 7.6) are other good examples.

EXAMPLE 7.7

Tourism Product Development Team, Georgia, US

This US example is a great case study in guiding destination product development.

> The product development team assists private for-profit, nonprofit and governmental clients by analyzing their product development goals and objectives and providing organizational assistance. The product development team works in concert with the nine Regional Tourism Project Managers to provide technical assistance and in turn direct the client toward Georgia's various state agencies with their respective financial and technical assistance resources. The team works to develop and nurture partnerships to effect change and positively impact Georgia's visitor industry. The Office of Product Development assists communities and tourism partners in giving new life to existing resources and in fostering new tourism products within communities. This is done by delivering technical assistance and financial resources in hopes of creating new opportunities/markets for Georgia tourism products through strategic partnerships, packaging and marketing. The tourism product development (TPD) team works to increase Georgia's TPD portfolio and creating opportunities to introduce new audiences to Georgia's amazing variety of sites and attractions.
>
> (Georgia Department of Economic Development 2022)

Learning Point

Having a product development team within a DMO will produce more effective results for the destination.

Product Development Variations by Types of Destinations

You should also realize that not all destinations are the same and therefore the DMO's role in product development varies because of the special circumstances of the country or region. In certain circumstances, a DMO is compelled to get involved in destination product development and cannot be a bystander, especially in a newly emerging destination and where environmental protection is crucial.

The *Handbook on Tourism Product Development* (2011), prepared on behalf of the UNWTO and the ETC, identified the following varieties of destinations; the author supplies the examples:

- Mature destinations: Many of the seacoast beach resorts of Spain, Portugal, Italy, Türkiye, and Greece are in this category. These may be approaching the decline stage in the

TALC, and so a greater emphasis needs to be given to diversification and new product development.

- Newly emerging destinations: The People's Republic of China is one of the best examples here because its tourism development is rapid now. Saudi Arabia, Indonesia, South Africa, and Sri Lanka are others that might fit. Again, DMOs need to be very proactive in product development in these situations.

- Centrally planned economies: China is a great example here again, and its government-run DMOs are highly proactive in destination product development, especially for new physical products.

- Destinations with fragile environments and endangered species: Included here would be destinations such as Antarctica, the Galápagos Islands, and Komodo in Indonesia. It might be expected here that DMOs would not be instigators of new product development but rather be involved in more of a resource conservation role.

- Countries with perception problems in international markets: Destinations such as Ukraine, Iraq, Afghanistan, Syria, Venezuela, and Iran fit in this category. DMOs may be more concerned with marketing communications to counterbalance negative perceptions rather than focusing on new product development.

- Destinations with a dominant product: Las Vegas with its many casinos fits into this group. Parts of East and Southern Africa also belong, with their reliance on safaris and wildlife viewing. Product diversification may be a strategy here, requiring the DMO to take an active role in product development.

- Destinations with a major tourism development opportunity: Countries with large populations and rapidly growing economies such as the BRICS (Brazil, Russia, India, China and South Africa) grouping are in this category. These situations justify DMOs being proactive in TPD.

- Destinations specializing in sports, adventure or activity tourism: New Zealand and Nepal are good case examples here. In addition to adding new and fresh experiences, the DMO must assure that measures are in place to ensure the safety of people participating in high-adrenaline and physically demanding activities.

- Historic cities: Athens, Beijing, Bruges, Budapest, Cairo, Istanbul, Prague, Rome, Venice, and Vienna are just a few of these great historic cities. Many of them are under huge pressure from tourism, and the capacity of their historic and heritage resources is finite and limited. Here, the DMOs must produce visitor management strategies to protect and conserve their precious resources.

Figure 7.6 groups destinations into six categories in line with what you have just learned.

Hard and Soft Tourism Product Development

Another way of looking at the DMO role in product development is to consider the two aspects of hard and soft development. Hard product development in tourism means building physical products such as attractions, hotels, roads, transport terminals, travel information centers, tourism schools or colleges, and festival or event performance areas (Fig. 7.7). Generally, these initiatives fit into the physical products component of the destination product, but there are situations when physical structures are needed to support people and programming projects.

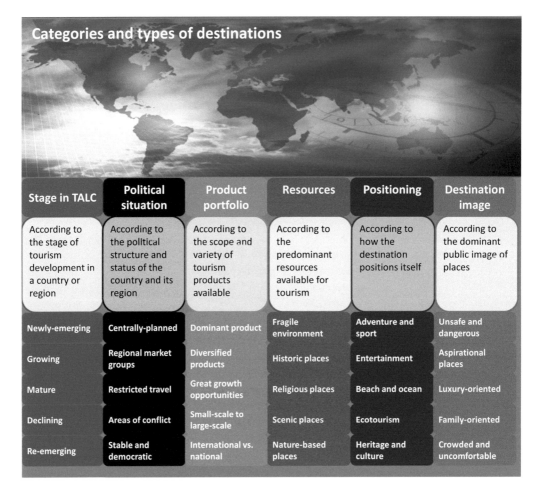

Stage in TALC	Political situation	Product portfolio	Resources	Positioning	Destination image
According to the stage of tourism development in a country or region	According to the political structure and status of the country and its region	According to the scope and variety of tourism products available	According to the predominant resources available for tourism	According to how the destination positions itself	According to the dominant public image of places
Newly-emerging	Centrally-planned	Dominant product	Fragile environment	Adventure and sport	Unsafe and dangerous
Growing	Regional market groups	Diversified products	Historic places	Entertainment	Aspirational places
Mature	Restricted travel	Great growth opportunities	Religious places	Beach and ocean	Luxury-oriented
Declining	Areas of conflict	Small-scale to large-scale	Scenic places	Ecotourism	Family-oriented
Re-emerging	Stable and democratic	International vs. national	Nature-based places	Heritage and culture	Crowded and uncomfortable

Figure 7.6 Categories and types of destinations.

Soft product development in tourism encompasses things that do not leave a long-term imprint on the physical landscape of the destination, including preparing workforce development strategies, conducting education and training programs, designing packages, creating themed itineraries or driving tours, operating quality assurance programs, providing interpretation services, and setting up product clubs. Generally, these activities fall within the people, packaging, and programming components of the destination product.

DEFINITION

Product club

"A product club is a partnership comprised of participants often from small and medium-sized businesses that have a common vision for the development of a specific product or niche market" (Plummer et al. 2005; Telfer 2002).

"Sustainable tourism has to put quality over quantity, be careful with natural resources and act socially acceptable" (Kühhas 2019).

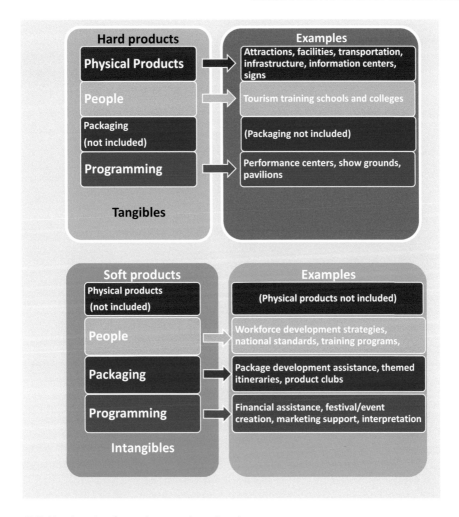

Figure 7.7 Hard and soft tourism product development.

Destination Quality

The notion of the hard and soft sides of the product inevitably leads to a discussion of desti-nation quality. The argument is often made that it is not the physical structures or their size that truly matters to customers; what is more important is their quality and the quality of the service provided by staff as well as the hospitality and welcome given by local community residents. There will probably never be a winner in this argument over quality versus quantity. More important for the destination and the DMO is to determine the dimensions of quality and to have programs to manage these dimensions. Koch (2004) suggested that quality in tourism had three main dimensions: hardware (physical products), software (services and informa-tion), and the environment (Fig. 7.8). This model of quality in tourism was based on earlier work by Professor Felizitas Romeiss-Stracke (1995).

This viewpoint of the quality of tourism in a destination again adds the condition of the envi-ronment into the destination product. There are three parts within the environment dimension: landscape (and landscaping too), resource consumption (sustainable use), and freedom from or lack of pollution. The software dimension consists of service and hospitality, as previously

Figure 7.8 Dimensions of destination quality (Koch 2004).

mentioned. However, information is a third part of software, and as you can imagine, this includes information provided within the destination and information distribution elsewhere, including in the online world. The hardware dimension represents the physical products in the destination and has three parts: facilities (what they provide), functions (what they do for customers), and aesthetics (how they look).

Managing quality is an important sub-role of destination product development because this undoubtedly affects the tourist experience. The European Commission publication (2003), *A Manual for Evaluating the Quality Performance of Tourist Destinations and Services,* lists ten reasons and benefits for a DMO and its stakeholders for managing destination quality (Fig. 7.9).

Figure 7.9 Reasons for and benefits from managing quality (European Commission 2003).

How, then, can the DMO implement a quality management program? One of the recommended ways of doing this is by adopting an integrated quality management (IQM) approach. IQM for destinations reflects the multidimensional nature of tourism quality. IQM combines four key elements in its approach (European Commission 2003):

1. Tourist satisfaction: Regularly monitoring tourists' satisfaction levels with the products and services in the destination.
2. Local tourism industry satisfaction: Evaluating the quality of jobs and the careers of employees in the tourism sector and the well-being of local tourism enterprises.
3. Local people's quality of life: Finding out what residents think of the effects of tourism.
4. Environmental quality: Measuring the positive or negative impacts of tourism on the environment, including natural, cultural, and human-made assets.

What should the DMO's specific roles be with respect to destination quality? The following represents a range of activities in which the DMO can engage to manage destination quality levels:

- Control quality through mandatory licensing or registration programs.
- Regularly inspect tourism operations to check quality levels.
- Introduce quality assurance programs that guarantee approved businesses meet certain standards.
- Initiate award programs for excellence in tourism quality.
- Provide advice or financial incentives for businesses to upgrade quality levels.
- Offer training programs to improve tourism workforce skills and knowledge.
- Continuously measure tourist and tourism stakeholder satisfaction levels.
- Establish parameters for environmental quality and resident life quality and periodically measure these parameters.

Figure 7.10 summarizes the actions that can be taken to manage quality within a destination.

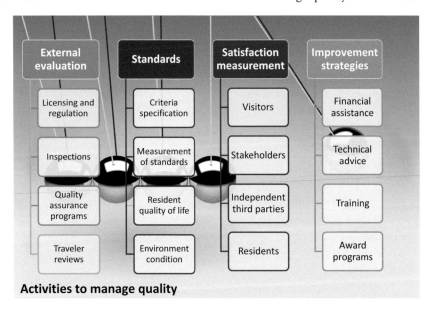

Figure 7.10 Actions to manage quality in a destination.

An outstanding example of an awards program is TidyTowns, which was introduced in Ireland in 1958 by its DMO (now Fáilte Ireland).

EXAMPLE 7.8

SuperValu TidyTowns, Ireland

This excellent and long-standing awards program in Ireland encourages towns to improve their visual and other quality standards.

> The national SuperValu TidyTowns competition is an annual contest organized by the Department of Rural and Community Development. The competition is supported by the title sponsor SuperValu and many other agencies. The competition involves participating areas being rated on all aspects of their local environment and prizes awarded to the best under many different categories. The overall winner is "Ireland's Tidiest Town" which is announced at a national ceremony in September each year.
>
> (Department of Rural and Community Development 2022)

Learning Point

DMOs should consider recognizing places and businesses that demonstrate high levels of quality.

Product Development Strategy Models

There are many general models for product development in management textbooks, but they do not fit as well with tourism destinations because they are mainly for manufactured products and IT start-ups. However, there are some useful models that can be applied by DMOs, and you will get a brief description of five of them now:

1. the Ansoff Matrix;
2. the destination product function model;
3. the tourism value chain model;
4. the new product development process;
5. the tourism product portfolio approach.

Ansoff Matrix: Product/Market Expansion Grid

There is a general product development strategy model that can be applied to destinations and has already been used in tourism. The Ansoff Matrix is a simple model, and it identifies four destination product development strategies in a two-by-two matrix (Fig. 7.11).

MARKET PENETRATION

Market penetration strategy means that the destination adjusts the product to attract a higher volume from existing markets; hence, existing markets, existing product. Another way of implementing this strategy is to try to get existing markets to return to the destination more often, and this is accomplished through destination marketing, branding, and communications programs.

Market penetration is the least risky of the four strategies because no long-term changes are being made to physical products. This is basically a change in destination marketing, branding, and communications approaches.

MARKET DEVELOPMENT

The existing destination product is used, but the market development strategy is to attract new markets to use the product. For example, the tropical southern island of Hainan Province in China decided some years back on a strategy to attract holidaymakers from Russia to its beach resorts. The strategy has worked very well. Another example from China is the opening of the Shanghai Disney Resort in 2016, an existing product for Disney in a theme park resort and a new market in terms of the city of Shanghai and Mainland China.

Again, this is not a particularly risky strategy because it is just adding new target markets to the destination's marketing strategy. However, there is greater marketing investment required than with the market penetration strategy.

PRODUCT DEVELOPMENT

The destination adds new products for existing markets in the product development strategy. The construction of the Kai Tak cruise terminal in Hong Kong, which opened in 2013, is a good case study here. Hong Kong was already attracting cruise ships, but the reconstruction of the runway of the old Hong Kong airport allows two mega-cruise ships to berth at Kai Tak. This is a riskier strategy than the first two because new product development is required. However, the market demand for the new product already exists.

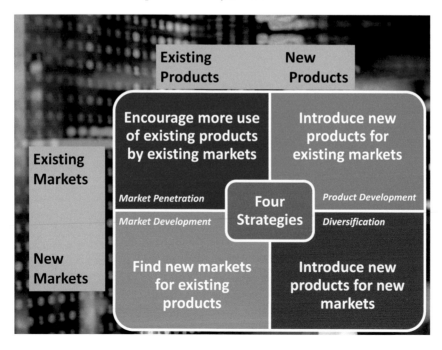

Figure 7.11 Ansoff Matrix (Ansoff 1987).

DIVERSIFICATION

The destination introduces new products and uses them to pursue new markets. The addition of integrated resort developments such as casinos on Sentosa Island in Singapore is an example. The casinos were a new product for Singapore, and gaming customers were a new market. The diversification strategy is the riskiest of the four strategies. New product development is needed, and the markets at which they are aimed are not proven. Additionally, there must be more marketing investment because new markets are being targeted.

EXAMPLE 7.9

Development of Hawana Salalah in Oman

This example shows how Oman is diversifying its product offerings to visitors.

> Hawana Salalah, the largest [integrated tourism complex] in the country, is situated in Dhofar. Built and operated by internationally acclaimed builder of fully integrated towns, Muriya, a joint venture between Oman Tourism Development Company (OMRAN) and Orascom Development Holding, Hawana Salalah currently features 1,200 hotel rooms spread across luxurious four- and five-star beachfront hotels. This is in addition to a marina surrounded by cafes, shops and restaurants, Oman's first aqua park, as well as freehold residential properties available to own by all nationalities, and hotels ready to welcome visitors for the Khareef season. In collaboration with Muriya, local and international tour operators have been able to add year-round flights into Salalah Airport from France, Germany, Italy, Poland, Slovakia and the Czech Republic as part of package holidays. With tourism once more picking up pace, in the first six months of 2022 alone, Hawana Salalah welcomed 30,532 visitors.
>
> (Muriya 2022)

Learning Point

Destinations with more diversified portfolios of attractions, activities, and experiences are likely to be more resilient.

Destination Product Function Model

Another practical model for product development is to consider projects by their function within the destination. The destination product function model has the following six component product categories, shown in Figure 7.12.

Now, here is more of a detailed description of these six product categories.

FLAGSHIP PRODUCTS

You should think of flagships as the core attractions or draws of destinations. They can be powerful enough to be a primary reason for people to visit a place. Included are historic attractions, such as the Great Wall and Terracotta Warriors in China, Angkor Wat in Cambodia,

Flagship
- Core products for destinations
- Influence image of destination
- Terra Cotta Warriors and Horses for Xi'an, China

Hub
- Central and strategic locations
- "Jumping-off" points
- Dubai for the Arabian Gulf

Cluster
- Themed groupings of attractions
- Groupings create "critical mass"
- Wineries for Margaret River, Western Australia

Circuit
- Linked attractions in a circular or trail configuration
- Visitors circulate from point to point
- The Cabot Trail for Cape Breton Island, Canada

Event or festival
- Portray local culture and other destination aspects
- Helpful in extending products and seasons
- Edinburgh Festivals for Scotland

Support
- Demand is derived from attractions and events
- Accommodation properties, food and dining, entertainment, and shopping are included
- Galleria Vittorio Emanuele shopping for Milan, Italy

Figure 7.12 Destination product function model.

and the Colosseum in Rome. One-of-a-kind natural features, such as the Grand Canyon in the USA, the Galápagos Islands in Ecuador, and Uluru (Ayers Rock) in the Northern Territory of Australia are also flagship products. Human-made cultural and entertainment attractions can be flagships, and examples include the Rijksmuseum in Amsterdam, Sydney Opera House in Australia, and the London Eye in the UK. These days some call these bucket list places to visit.

Moriarty (2014) says flagships play a major role in defining the tourism product of a region, and you can certainly think of some cases of this phenomenon. What about the theme parks in Orlando and the casino resorts in Las Vegas, both leading US destinations with an emphasis on entertainment?

TOURISM HUB DEVELOPMENTS

Hubs are central or strategically located places within destinations, which are the major arrival and departure points for people's trips. Some of these hubs owe part of their success to the airlines, including Dubai in the United Arab Emirates. Other places are jumping off points to major attractions, such as Cairns in North Queensland, Australia, for the Great Barrier Reef and Calgary in Alberta, Canada, as a gateway to the Canadian Rockies.

PRODUCT CLUSTERS

This is where attractions are grouped within a destination according to a unifying theme. Examples of clusters are the wineries in the Margaret River area in Western Australia, the filming locations of Outlander in Scotland, and the art district of Santa Fe, New Mexico, in the USA. By combining venues with a similar theme, clusters increase the appeal of the destination as well as the scope and scale of the attractions. Technically, this can be called agglomeration.

EXAMPLE 7.10

Mexico's Pueblo Mágico Cluster

This example describes how Mexico is implementing a clustering approach.

> The Pueblo Mágico (Magical Town) designation is awarded to those communities that over time have maintained their original architecture, traditions, history and culture as well as to those that have been of great relevance to the country's history. The Pueblos Mágicos (Magical Towns) are defined as places with great symbolism and legends, they are towns whose historical importance has been fundamental for the development of history and that enhance the national identity in each of its spots. These places have a special magic that connects the visitor with our roots and traditions. With exceptional beauty, these are destinations that will most definitely captivate you. Currently throughout the territory there are 132 Pueblos Mágicos, whose attractions generate great admiration among domestic and foreign visitors from all around the world.
>
> (Secretariat of Tourism, Mexico 2022)

Learning Point

Product clustering can enhance a destination's market appeal.

CIRCUITS

These are routes along which visitors travel to experience places and attractions that are usually linked by a common interest or topic. Sometimes called themed routes or trails, they include places such as the Cabot Trail on Cape Breton Island, Nova Scotia, Canada, where the emphasis is on scenery; the Buddhist Circuit in India, with a focus on religion and religious buildings; the Agatha Christie Literary Trail on the English Riviera; and the European Route of Historical Thermal Towns, which features health and heritage.

Using the term "circuits" implies that visitors move around but not always necessarily in a circular pattern. For example, people traveling on the Silk Road in China and Central Asian countries normally go in just one direction and do not retrace their steps to the departure point.

EXAMPLE 7.11

The City Visitor Trail, London

This example describes the development of a walking trail in London.

The features of this trail are:

- A paper map (A2) describing the best walking routes between the City's top attractions, with suggested stops along the way for lunch, a spot of retail therapy and the odd insider tip about a feature of a building or the streetscape itself.
- Six themed routes: City Highlights; Law and literature; London stories, London people; Culture vultures, Market mile; and Skyscrapers and sculpture'—all of which are quicker to follow than any public transport option and the map was cleverly gridded to tell the user exactly how long a walk will take.
- An audio app (for iPhone or Android) through which visitors can hear stories about what they are seeing from the mouths of those that know the attractions best, be that a Beefeater at the Tower of London, or a choirboy at one of the City's churches.
- A children's map with stickers and plenty of activities to engage families.

(VisitEngland, undated)

Learning Point

Walking trails are popular with visitors to cities.

EVENTS AND FESTIVALS

You will learn more later in this chapter about events and festivals as an application of programming. These products perform multiple functions that include offsetting seasonality, increasing community involvement, and attracting new target markets to destinations.

SUPPORTING PRODUCTS

The preceding five types of products create a need and visitor demand for other developments that function in a supportive way. Supporting products include accommodation, food and dining, entertainment and shopping facilities located within destinations or between places.

Tourism Value Chain Model

A third model that can be strategic in guiding destination development is the tourism value chain. This is a mapping of visitors' experiences and all the transactions associated with these experiences before, during, and after trips. This model is often used to trace the spread and impact of tourism in economies and particularly in lesser-developed nations. A partial tourism value chain is shown in Figure 7.13.

The model in Figure 7.13 shows that the tourism products straddle visitor origins and destinations and there are multiple players that provide services and physical products. The players or suppliers are grouped into sub-sectors, including distribution, transportation, accommodation, food and entertainment, attractions and events, and tours and travel. With six categories and

Part II

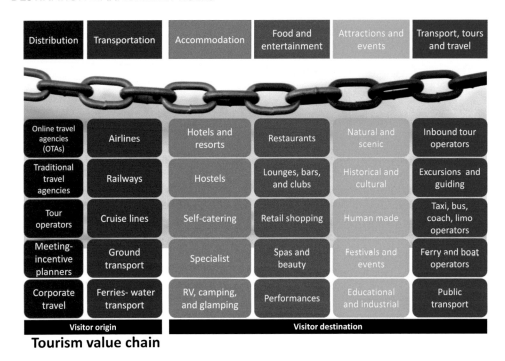

Figure 7.13 A partial tourism value chain (adapted from Christian et al. 2011).

thirty sub-groupings, this value chain may seem impressive, but it is more complex and elaborate than that shown in Figure 7.13. The UNWTO (2013) has charted a more complete tourism value chain that adds policies and planning, goods and services supplies, utilities, and support institutions to the tourism industries that are pictured in Figure 7.13.

EXAMPLE 7.12

Tourism Value Chain as a Process

The meaning of the tourism value chain is explained in this example.

> Adding value is a process that covers the entire creation of a product, from raw material extraction to consumption by end customers. Ideally in fact, it continues beyond this to include the recycling, upgrading or reuse of a product (circular economy). The value chain describes this process in which each activity creates value, uses resources and is in turn connected to other activities. The object being considered in a value chain is always a product or service.
>
> (GIZ 2020)

Learning Point

DMOs should be aware of the value chain architecture in tourism in their destinations.

Another reason that the value chain figures in destination development is in corporate expansion, growth and branding strategies. For financial, quality or marketing reasons, large companies decide to operate in different parts of the tourism value chain. Here, the German travel company giant, the TUI Group, is a good example. This company uses horizontal (several tour operators) and vertical integration (hotels and airlines) strategies.

New Product Development Process

The new product development process is a fourth model that can be applied to destinations. A model of the process is shown in Figure 7.14.

A brief description of these eight steps in new product development is given below:

1. Preliminary market research: Surveys or focus groups are conducted with potential or existing visitors to identify gaps in the products or services that they need. This is often supplemented with interviewing tourism experts and selected stakeholders.
2. Idea generation: This involves brainstorming (group problem solving to generate creative ideas) using the data from the first step to pinpoint creative and innovative ideas that will fill the gaps in consumers' needs and requirements.
3. Idea screening: The best ideas from the second step are retained and evaluated against a set of criteria through idea screening. The criteria include the principles for destination product development mentioned earlier. Also, the destination's capability and capacity for offering the new product or service needs to be considered.
4. Concept development: The idea that passes the screening in the third step with the highest rating is then put into concept development. Planners and consultants may assist in developing conceptual plans and drawings and recommending the scale and content of the product or service.
5. Business strategy: A business model is developed for the launching of the new product or service. Normally, this is detailed in a written business plan for the new venture. This plan includes information on the product-service features, target markets, organizational structure, financing, and positioning and branding. A market study or economic feasibility analysis will also be part of this step.

Figure 7.14 New product development process.

6. Marketing plan: A marketing plan is then prepared that implements the business strategy. The document includes a rationale, an implementation plan, and an executive summary.
7. Market test: The seventh step involves a test market of the new product or service. This is very hard to do with destination products and services because many physical products (such as resorts and attractions) need to be completely built out and cannot be test-marketed. However, it may be possible with new services to evaluate them on a limited basis before their full introduction.
8. Product launch: The last step is the full-scale introduction of the new product or service. Typically, with many physical products a soft opening precedes the full product launch.

EXAMPLE 7.13

Tower Walk 100, Kuala Lumpur, Malaysia

This example describes a new attraction in Malaysia.

> The Tower Walk 100 is the newest attraction at Menara Kuala Lumpur that recently opened its doors to the public on 27th November 2021. The "100" in the name indicates that you are over 100 feet (30.48 meter) above the ground! If you don't mind the height, you can try to walk through the glass-transparent platform with an audible crack that will be heard as you step onto it. (But don't worry, those are just sound effects!)
>
> (Tourism Malaysia 2022)

Learning Point

DMOs should announce the opening of exciting new tourism development projects.

Tourism Product Portfolio Approach

The tourism product portfolio approach identifies all the assets within a destination in fine detail (Morrison 2022). This supplies a checklist for those involved in tourism. Using the checklist, important assets are not overlooked in tourism marketing, branding, and communications, and product development. Figure 7.15 shows twenty items in the destination product portfolio, ranging alphabetically from accommodation to resident support and friendliness.

Now that five basic strategies and principles of destination product development have been reviewed and you know about the importance of destination quality, this chapter turns to how the DMO performs its role for each of the physical and intangible components of the destination product.

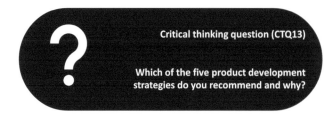

? Critical thinking question (CTQ13)

Which of the five product development strategies do you recommend and why?

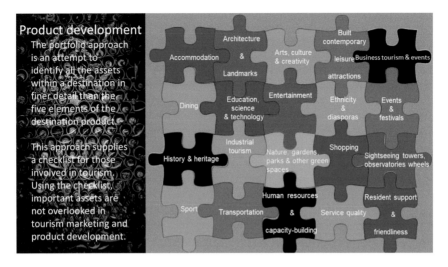

Figure 7.15 Portfolio approach to destination product development.

Physical (Hard) Product Development

Physical or tangible products are what first come to mind when people talk about tourism development or destination product development, but as you already know there is more to the destination product than just physical structures. What are the various types of physical products and how should they be assessed?

Types of Destination Physical Product Developments

This discussion was opened briefly in Chapter 1. The destination's physical products include attractions, facilities, infrastructure, transportation, and certain other supportive facilities and amenities (Fig. 7.16).

ATTRACTIONS AND EVENTS

These are critical to the tourism sector because they draw visitors to the destination. Swarbrooke and Page (2015) identify four categories of attractions:

1. features within the natural environment;
2. human-made buildings, structures and sites that were designed for a purpose other than attracting visitors, such as for religious worship, but which now attract substantial numbers of visitors who use them as leisure amenities;
3. human-made buildings, structures and sites that are designed to attract visitors and are purpose-built to accommodate their needs, such as theme parks;
4. special events.

BUILT FACILITIES

Generally (but not always), built facilities play a supportive role to attractions and events. The three major categories of facilities are accommodations, food and beverage facilities, and retail outlets of different types. These are mostly built facilities and operated by the private sector.

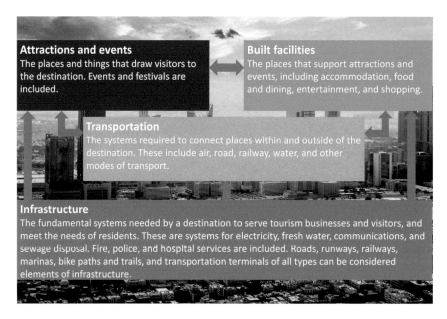

Attractions and events
The places and things that draw visitors to the destination. Events and festivals are included.

Built facilities
The places that support attractions and events, including accommodation, food and dining, entertainment, and shopping.

Transportation
The systems required to connect places within and outside of the destination. These include air, road, railway, water, and other modes of transport.

Infrastructure
The fundamental systems needed by a destination to serve tourism businesses and visitors, and meet the needs of residents. These are systems for electricity, fresh water, communications, and sewage disposal. Fire, police, and hospital services are included. Roads, runways, railways, marinas, bike paths and trails, and transportation terminals of all types can be considered elements of infrastructure.

Figure 7.16 Main types of physical products.

There are certain other facilities that support the destination product, including VICs and venues for conventions, exhibitions, and meetings. Some events and festivals require physical structures and spaces. Interpretive and directional signs and displays are also critical in tourism destinations.

INFRASTRUCTURE

This is a term that has a huge range of definitions, but there is one classic meaning in tourism, which is that infrastructure includes roads, utilities, water supply, sewerage, and other basic physical systems to support the destination and its community. These are essential for the tourism sector but often require a substantial initial investment.

TRANSPORTATION

Access to a destination is crucial, and so the development of transportation services is crucial in product development. As with infrastructure, the investment in transportation facilities is substantial and tends to be mainly done by governments. Typically, the DMO plays an advisory role on transportation planning and strategies.

Analysis of Physical Product Developments

All physical product opportunities need to be thoroughly researched and analyzed, and the DMO can play a role in ensuring that this is accomplished. Figure 7.17 shows the main parts of a new project analysis.

- Site evaluation: Site evaluation considers the physical characteristics of the site and its accessibility.

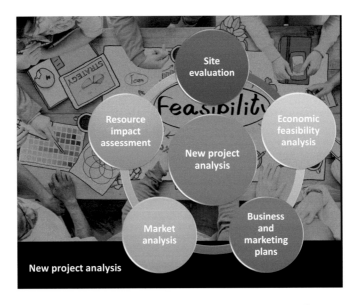

Figure 7.17 Main parts of a new destination development project analysis.

- Resource impact assessment: The environmental, social and cultural impacts of the project are analyzed in a resource impact assessment.
- Market analysis: The market potential of the project is assessed in this step—will there be enough demand?
- Economic feasibility analysis: The profitability and ROI in the project are estimated.
- Business and marketing plan preparation: A marketing plan for the project and a broader business plan are prepared.

Information Provision and Information Centers

The DMO should consider tourism information as being part of the destination product, particularly if it operates one or more travel or VICs. According to *A Practical Guide to Tourism Destination Management* published by UNWTO (2007), "the visitor information centre is the showcase for the destination and must set the standard in terms of quality, integrity and customer care which other industry operators can follow." VICs, then, are a sort of destination product showcase that merchandises all the components of tourism.

VICs perform multiple roles for the destination and tourism stakeholders, and these include the following:

- Encouraging higher per capita spending: Many VICs try to upsell their destinations, encouraging tourists to spend more money on their trips.
- Handling requests for pre-visit information: Often, people contact VICs for information prior to leaving for the destination. The VIC responds to information requests received by phone, social media, email, mail or fax.
- Interpreting local history, culture and nature: VICs include displays or show videos that interpret the most important tourism-related resources of the destination.

- Making bookings: Many VICs make bookings for accommodations, attractions, entertainment shows, local tours, and transportation. Typically, the VIC earns a commission on these bookings.
- Merchandising hub for tourism stakeholders: VICs are places where tourism stakeholders can publicize their products and services.
- Providing information during visits: This is the traditional role of VICs, and tourists expect them to provide accurate, detailed and up-to-date information on all aspects of the destination.
- Recommending itineraries: VIC staff can recommend customized itineraries based on people's interests and time constraints.
- Selling travel-related literature and local souvenirs: Many VICs include retail operations where tourists can buy maps, guidebooks, DVDs, clothing and local souvenirs.

The Visit York Information Centre in England is a good case study of a VIC. This state-of-the-art VIC was opened in May 2010 and welcomed 400,000 people in its first year of operations. Located in a nineteenth-century historic building, the center offers the full range of services as identified above. VIC staff members, who have multilingual capabilities, provide services including ticket sales for attractions, tours and concerts; accommodation and some transportation bookings; and personal itinerary planning. There is a shop in the VIC where gifts, souvenirs, and local produce can be bought. Large digital screens show videos of what to see and do in York and other parts of Yorkshire (Visit York 2022). Another good example is the Discover Greenwich Visitor Centre in England. This VIC is in a historic building and contains many displays of information about Maritime Greenwich and a shop (Discover Greenwich 2022).

There are now many different varieties of VICs, ranging from the full-service VIC playing all the roles described above to kiosks with no VIC staff present.

"Successful visitor centers know people don't come to their destination to visit a visitor center" (White 2022). DMO websites, plus related social media sites, are now the major providers of information about destinations. Are these a part of the destination product? Some would argue that they are not and that these online information channels are part of destination marketing, branding, and communications. However, there are other ways of looking at this. Websites and social media sites reflect the destination and in some ways they function like virtual VICs, albeit without the human touch. It can also be argued that these online channels are becoming more like virtual destinations where Internet users can experience the places online. In later chapters about the markets for destinations, there are in-depth materials about destination websites and social media sites. It suffices to say here that there is a good case for including these online tools within the concept of the destination product.

With the rapidly expanding use of mobile phones, and especially smartphones, several DMOs have developed applications (apps) that can be downloaded and used on these devices as well as tablets.

Accessible Tourism

Another aspect of the destination product that requires the DMO's attention is in the provision of accessible tourism. The European Commission provides this definition of accessible tourism:

Accessible tourism

"Accessible tourism is about making it easy for everyone to enjoy tourism experiences. Making tourism more accessible is not only a social responsibility—there is also a compelling business case for improving accessibility as it can boost the competitiveness of tourism in Europe.

Evidence shows that making basic adjustments to a facility, providing accurate information, and understanding the needs of disabled people can result in increased visitor numbers. Improving the accessibility of tourism services increases their quality and the enjoyment of all tourists. It also improves the quality of life in local communities" (European Commission 2022).

There are different roles that DMOs should play in improving the accessibility within their destinations. VisitEngland (undated) offers the Top Ten Tips for Inclusive Tourism as follows:

1. Train all staff in disability awareness and ensure they are familiar with accessible facilities, services and equipment available.
2. Always welcome assistance dogs.
3. Ask all your customers if they require any assistance with evacuation in an emergency. Record any specific arrangements.
4. Ensure your website meets accessibility standards and all written communications with customers are available in accessible formats.
5. Provide accessible ways for disabled customers to give feedback, acting and responding promptly to comments.
6. Provide sufficient accessible parking spaces.
7. Include images of disabled people in your marketing.
8. Appoint an Accessibility Champion and encourage accessibility ambassadors.
9. Ensure emergency pull-cords hang to the floor and are regularly tested.
10. Provide a detailed and accurate Accessibility Guide to promote your accessibility.

Although one visualizes people using wheelchairs, it is important that you know that accessible tourism is not just for people with mobility challenges:

It's Not Just About Wheelchair Access

This example provides a broader definition of accessibility needs.

Too often we tend to equate disability and accessibility with mobility impairments and those using wheelchairs. However, only 8 percent of disabled people use a wheelchair so, while they shouldn't be ignored, we should remember those with other types of impairments. Very few people who are partially sighted, have a hearing impairment and walk with a stick would describe themselves as disabled but they are likely to have accessibility needs. And don't forget, not all disabilities are visible and obvious such as diabetes, asthma, heart conditions, allergies and food intolerances.

(VisitEngland, undated)

Learning Point

Destinations must consider all accessibility needs and requirements.

Tourism Signage

Signs of different varieties are very much a part of the destination product. This is sometimes overlooked by DMOs and not given the attention that it deserves. However, signs are of importance to destinations and tourism operations that rely most heavily on motorists and drive markets. They are also important within urban and rural areas to direct people to attractions and sites and other tourism facilities, often called wayfinding.

There are three major categories within tourism signage: (1) welcome signs; (2) directional signs; and (3) interpretive signs. The roles of interpretive signs have already been discussed, but directional signs have not yet been covered. It can be said that the use of directional signs in most jurisdictions is usually strictly controlled by government agencies and especially those regulating transportation. The DMO role is typically to work in collaboration with transportation agencies to ensure that there is adequate tourism directional signage and to lobby for this signage program to be distinctive and attractive (if possible). For example, the brown-and-white tourism signs in the UK are very distinctive.

Do signs (or the lack of them) affect tourist experiences and satisfaction levels in destinations? There is no accurate, worldwide statistic that says so, but from the results of many visitor profile studies in a range of destinations, tourists often complain about getting lost or not finding what they wanted to see because of inadequate directional signage. What can the DMO do to resolve these sorts of issues? Although this is a difficult question to answer because of the need for inter-agency coordination, the DMO can at least make the tourism sector aware of the signage policy within the destination.

EXAMPLE 7.15

Queensland Tourism and Transport Strategy

This Australian example is a great case study in inter-agency cooperation and joint planning.

Significant work has already been done across individual transport modes and the strategy aims to build on these achievements. This strategy addresses the immediate future while also providing a framework for long-term tourism growth. It includes a mix of aspirational and future focused outcomes to guide government and industry efforts, balanced with activities that can make a meaningful difference in the short term. This strategy takes a holistic view of tourism and transport, placing visitor needs front and center, to ensure we can achieve the vision of providing an exceptional journey for every visitor. The vision will be achieved through strengthening partnerships across all levels of government and with industry.

(Department of Tourism, Innovation and Sport, Queensland 2016)

Learning Point

The alignment of destination product development and transportation strategy is critical for destinations.

Of course, there is another side to the topic of signs and especially those along roads. This is the aesthetic impacts of signs and their influence on tourists' perceptions of the place and its environment. For example, the DMO surely wants to avoid an ugly and unsightly proliferation of signs at its entry points. (Remember about first impressions in the 10 As?)

Intangible (Soft) Product Development

You are now going to get to know more about selected types of intangible or soft product development, beginning with human resources.

Human Resource Development (People)

Destinations especially as a result of the COVID-19 pandemic face major human resources development challenges. Destinations and their DMOs need to get involved in tourism human resources development.

EXAMPLE 7.16

Tourism Jobs Remain Unfilled in the UK

Staff shortages in the UK have resulted from the COVID-19 pandemic.

A new analysis of staff shortages by the World Travel & Tourism Council (WTTC) has revealed 205,000 tourism jobs across the UK predicted to remain unfilled by the end of this year. The UK alone is predicted to see a shortfall of around 12 percent, with one in eight job vacancies left unfilled.

(Willis 2021)

Learning Point

Tourism staff retention is crucial to destination success.

People are an exceptionally important component of the destination product because of the personal service provided and the overall feeling of hospitality and welcome. Having sufficient numbers of staff with the right skills, knowledge and attitudes is essential for the proper functioning of the destination product. Many destinations and DMOs recognize this and play an active role in human resources development.

TOURISM WORKFORCE DEVELOPMENT STRATEGIES

Several destinations have developed specific strategies or plans for tourism human resources, and these tend to be called workforce development strategies or plans. These include several states and provinces in Australia, Canada and the USA as well as destinations in New Zealand, South Africa and the UK.

TOURISM WORKFORCE STANDARDS AND EDUCATION AND TRAINING PROGRAMS

Another initiative that can be taken is to establish systems of standards for jobs within the tourism sector. These systems identify the skills and knowledge required for specific job positions. Often, these are competency-based models, and a complete training curriculum is developed. For example, the ASEAN has developed a Mutual Recognition Arrangement on Tourism Professionals (ASEAN 2018). These competencies are for hotel services (front office, housekeeping, food production, food and beverage service) and travel services (travel agencies and tour operation). Tourism HR Canada has created the Emerit Skills Training and Certification program, which covers several occupations in tourism. This training is based on National Occupational Standards (Tourism HR Canada 2022).

The CDME program is operated by Destinations International in Washington, DC. This is a very important program because the focus is on destination management. This training program is for senior executives and managers in DMOs. To earn the CDME designation, DMO professionals must take certain core and elective courses, complete papers on the core courses and pass a final comprehensive exam.

EXAMPLE 7.17

Certified Destination Management Executive

The CDME program has made an important contribution to increasing professionalism in destination management.

> The Certified Destination Management Executive (CDME) is the tourism industry's highest individual educational achievement. The CDME program prepares senior executives to thrive in a constantly changing environment. The program focus is on vision, leadership, productivity and implementing business strategies. Start or continue your professional journey, advance your career, and enhance your industry knowledge, skills and professional credibility.
>
> (Destinations International 2022)

Learning Point

More programs and initiatives are needed to increase professional standards in DMOs and destination management.

MENTORING PROGRAMS

Some DMOs have created mentoring programs where they team up seasoned entrepreneurs, managers or supervisors with colleagues who want to learn more about specific tasks.

TRAVEL TRADE STAFF EDUCATION PROGRAMS

These programs are aimed at training people in travel agencies and tour operating companies in source markets. The Aussie Specialist Program (ASP) operated by Tourism Australia is an outstanding case study.

EXAMPLE 7.18

The Aussie Specialist Program (ASP)

This is the Gold Standard for training travel trade partners about destinations.

> Voted the best travel agent training program in the world for the quality of its content, ease of use and the impact it has on our agents' businesses. Decades of research understanding how people learn has informed the design of the program. A combination of self-paced learning is supported with informal instructor led learning, group webinars and deeper.
>
> (Tourism Australia 2022)

Learning Point

Destinations need to constantly be building awareness within travel trade organizations and staff.

Package Development

Packaging in tourism is unique, and there is no other economic sector that has anything quite like it. There are professional companies such as tour operators, incentive travel companies and travel agencies that specialize in packaging. Resorts, hotels, airlines, cruise line companies, attractions and other tourism stakeholders also develop packages. Before discussing the DMO's roles here, there are some basics to be covered first about the roles and benefits of packaging in tourism.

Roles of Packaging

New tourism packages do not usually require that a new physical product be developed. However, packages attract tourists to destinations, and so they are a very powerful part of the destination product.

Tourism packages combine several travel and hospitality offers together at a single price. Packages play a very important role in tourism because the capacity of different components of the destination product is fixed. Packaging plays the following specific roles:

- Uniting tourism stakeholders' product and service offers: Packaging is a great demonstration of partnerships and collaboration in tourism. It brings together different businesses and other organizations into an integrated offer.

- Smoothing out business cycles: Packages are used to build business at times when demand is in a down-cycle. Doing this tends to improve the profitability of tourism businesses as well as reducing seasonality in destinations.
- Diversifying market segments: Packages can be developed and customized for specific market segments, allowing the destination and tourism stakeholders to diversify marketing strategies.
- Consolidating the destination product: Packaging brings together components of the destination product in a convenient format for buyers.
- Providing value: Packages offer distinct value to buyers and extend the value perceptions of the destination.

BENEFITS OF PACKAGES

Packages are popular among tourists mainly because of their convenience and value. They are also popular among operators in the tourism sector. The major benefits of packaging for customers and the tourism sector are shown in Figure 7.18.

DMO ROLES IN PACKAGING

DMOs can perform three distinct roles related to new package development:

1. Provide training for tourism operators on how to develop effective packages.
2. Encourage tourism stakeholders to develop new packages with marketing or financial assistance.
3. Create new packages themselves and either offer the packages for sale directly to the public or find tourism stakeholders to do the distribution and sales.

Visitor benefits of packages	Destination benefits of packages
❏ Ability to budget for trips	❏ Added appeal to specific markets
❏ Added value	❏ Attraction of new target markets
❏ Assurance of consistent quality	❏ Easier business forecasting
❏ Convenience	❏ Increased business in off-peak
❏ Satisfaction of special interests	❏ Increased customer satisfaction
	❏ Increased efficiency
	❏ Partnering opportunities

Benefits of packaging and programming

Visitor benefits of Programs	Destination benefits of programs
❏ Active participation in experiences	❏ Attraction of special-interest markets
❏ Added excitement	❏ Destination image enhancement
❏ Greater aesthetic/personal fulfillment	❏ Increased economic impact
❏ Increased learning and understanding	❏ Increased length of stay and per capita spend
❏ Increased trip satisfaction	❏ Increased tourist satisfaction
❏ More entertainment	❏ New marketing initiatives
❏ Richer experiences of destination	❏ Reduction of seasonality
❏ Satisfaction of special interests	❏ Stakeholder partnering opportunities

Figure 7.18 Benefits of packaging and programming.

As an example of the first role, the Government of Northwest Territories, Industry, Tourism and Investment (2018) in Canada has developed a self-guided workbook, *Product Packaging,* for tourism operators for designing effective packages. For the second role, several destinations encourage package development through financial incentive schemes.

The Bihar State Tourism Development Corporation (2022) in India provides a case study for the third DMO packaging role. This DMO has itself created ready-made packages that are based on itinerary circuits related to Buddhism and the Sikh and Jain religions. DMOs usually play this most proactive packaging role when there is no private-sector interest in creating and offering packages.

Two other roles that the DMO can play that are related to packaging and programming are designing thematic itineraries, routes or trails, and assisting in the establishment of product clubs. These concepts are both represented in the Wine Routes of Spain (Turespaña 2022), which is a series of themed itineraries that represent several product clubs in different parts of the country. Product clubs are discussed in more detail in Chapter 8 because they are a form of partnership as well as a packaging of experiences.

The creation of themed driving tours is another form of packaging and programming done by certain DMOs. The Elkhart County Convention and Visitors Bureau (2022) in Indiana in the USA has created the Heritage Trail Driving Tour and supports this with a map and an audio podcast that are available from its website.

Program Development

Programming is a crucial component of the destination product; it is sometimes done within packaging but often separately. There are different varieties of programming ranging from huge mega-events to teaching one individual visitor how to scuba dive. The following are the roles and benefits of programming.

ROLES OF PROGRAMMING

Programming plays multiple roles for a tourism destination:

- Enhancing experiences of tourists: Programming creates new activities and experiences in which tourists engage.
- Increasing economic impact of tourism: New or expanded events and festivals can create significant incremental economic benefits for destinations.
- Increasing tourist spending and length of stay: Programming encourages people to stay longer, and if they stay longer, they spend more money in the destination.
- Informing and educating tourists: Programming, and especially interpretation, provides tourists with a deeper understanding of the destination and its resources. Later, you will hear more about interpretation.
- Involving tourists in experiences: Nowadays, more people like to participate and be actively involved in their destination experiences, and programming does exactly that.
- Satisfying special interests: Programs can be developed to satisfy all sorts of special interests, from architecture to zoology.

BENEFITS OF PROGRAMMING

The benefits from programming are profound if well planned and executed. The major benefits of programming for tourists and the destination are illustrated in Figure 7.18.

DMO Roles in Programming

As with packaging, there are several roles that a DMO can perform to support programming development. For example, the DMO can encourage the development of new events or festivals or the expansion of existing ones through providing financial assistance. Often, this financial assistance is to help cover marketing expenses or programming enhancements and is not for physical product development.

A second potential role is where the DMO creates a new festival or event, and usually this is done with the assistance of tourism stakeholders. The HKTB introduced the Hong Kong Wine and Dine Festival in 2009, and it has been staged every year since then (HKTB 2022).

A third potential DMO programming role is to encourage tourism stakeholders to develop activities and experiences for tourists. The Canadian Signature Experiences (CSE) introduced by Destination Canada (then the Canadian Tourism Commission) in 2011 is an excellent demonstration of this role. When launched, the CSE included forty-eight experiences offered by tourism businesses (now they are in the hundreds), and research showed that these experiences were attractive to high-spending international travelers to Canada. As you will realize, arranging these experiences for tourists is a form of programming (Destination Canada 2022). There is a huge variety of programmed experiences in the CSE, ranging from viewing grizzly bears in British Columbia to cruising among icebergs off Newfoundland and Labrador. Destination Canada actively markets the CSE through social media, web marketing, and travel trade relationships.

A fourth role related to programming is usually performed only by the DMOs in very large cities along with their national and state/provincial DMOs. This role is in bidding for major events that have a potentially huge impact on destinations. These events include the mega-hallmark events such as the summer and winter Olympic Games, the World Expo and football's World Cup. Although the DMOs are only one part of the bid teams, they have an influential role in selling their destinations and ensuring that holding these events has a long-lasting positive impact (legacy) on tourism within their destinations.

A fifth programming role of DMOs relates to the provision of interpretation. This is such an important topic that a separate heading has been assigned to it here.

Interpretation

Interpretation is fundamentally important in tourism, although it does not attract the same attention as glitzy new resorts, theme parks and other major physical product developments within destinations. Interpretation is a product type that combines both the intangible (for example, tour guides making presentations) and tangible (interpretive signs).

Freeman Tilden, a US scholar, provided one of the very first definitions of interpretation.

DEFINITION

Interpretation by Freeman Tilden

"Interpretation is the work of revealing, to such visitors as desire the service, something of the beauty and wonder, the inspiration and spiritual meaning that lies behind what the visitor can with his senses perceive" (Tilden 1977).

Interpretation is helping people understand more deeply what they are seeing and experiencing in the destination. Interpretation can be done in many ways, including through physical products, such as displays, signs and audio-visual materials including augmented and virtual reality, or it can be done by people, such as tour guides, through oral interpretation. Before discussing how the DMO can be involved with interpretive services, the primary roles and benefits of interpretation are discussed.

ROLES AND BENEFITS OF INTERPRETATION

Interpretation began at places like national parks and heritage-cultural sites but is now much more pervasive in tourism. Some of the key roles and main benefits of interpretation are the following:

- Communicating issues and concerns: Interpretation can be used to make visitors aware of major issues and concerns on the sustainability of the resources they are viewing and experiencing.
- Deepening understanding: Interpretation deepens tourists' understanding and appreciation for specific aspects of a destination, including its history, culture and natural environment.
- Encouraging appropriate visitor behaviors: Especially at sensitive natural and heritage-cultural sites, interpretation is used to put across an appropriate code of behavior while enjoying the experience.
- Enhancing visitor satisfaction and experiences: Interpretation involves visitors with their experiences and done well increases their satisfaction levels and the quality of experiences.
- Entertaining: Interpretation can be designed to be engaging and entertaining and may include some element of audience participation.
- Informing tourists: Interpretation informs and educates tourists about the destination.
- Managing visitors: Interpretation can be used as a visitor management technique by controlling the flows of people at an attraction or site.
- Presenting content: Interpretation is a set of presentation techniques for delivering content to tourists about specific resources within a destination.

DMO ROLES IN THE PROVISION OF INTERPRETATION

Because DMOs traditionally have not been involved in the operation of sites and attractions, they have not historically played an active role in the provision of interpretation. It is also true that other governmental agencies have had a stronger focus on interpretation, including those responsible for parks, museums and other heritage and cultural sites and facilities. However, with the increasing interest in product development, DMOs are now paying greater attention to interpretation.

Some real-life examples from tourism will help you better understand how DMOs are increasingly engaging with interpretation. One role is for the DMO to produce materials or how-to guides that assist others in providing interpretive services. Fáilte Ireland (2022), for example, produced a manual named *Sharing Our Stories* to help heritage sites improve visitor experiences through more effective interpretation.

A second role is for the DMO to engage in or encourage the training of professional tour guides who provide oral interpretation. Indeed, in some countries the national DMOs have licensing programs for tour guides so that they can control the quality of guiding and human oral interpretation. You might think this happens only in developing countries such as Belize or Indonesia, but that is not true because places such as Washington, DC, New York City and Singapore have tour guide licensing programs.

Many DMOs operate ambassador or volunteer programs in which they recruit local people to guide or in other ways help visitors in their community. Bermuda is a good example here with its Bermuda Tourism Ambassadors program, but there are many other similar programs world-wide (Bermuda Tourism Authority 2022).

A fourth role is for DMOs to provide financial assistance to produce materials that assist with interpretation. For example, several DMOs have matching grant programs where they share production costs equally for such items as videos that can be used as part of interpretive presentations. The Colorado Tourism Office (2022) in the USA is an example here with its Marketing Matching Grant Program.

So these are four specific roles that the DMO can play in providing interpretation and in encouraging others to do so more professionally. There is no doubt that DMOs will become even more involved with interpretation in the future as more of them realize the value of enriching the experiences of tourists.

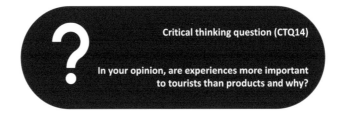

? Critical thinking question (CTQ14)

In your opinion, are experiences more important to tourists than products and why?

Experience Design

The design of experiences is a hot topic in destination management, and the following statement from Destination Canada (and the Canadian Tourism Commission [CTC]) explains why.

DEFINITION

Experiential travel

"Experiences are the new 'currency' that differentiates tourism businesses and destinations around the world. They are expanding the ways travellers can engage with people, places and cultures" (Destination Canada 2018).

"Experiential travel engages visitors in a series of memorable travel activities, that are inherently personal. It involves all senses, and makes connections on a physical, emotional, spiritual, social or intellectual level. It is travel designed to engage visitors with the locals, set the stage for conversations, tap the senses and celebrate what is unique in Canada" (CTC 2011).

The essence of visitor experiences is that, done right, they benefit visitors and destinations; in other words, they are a win-win proposition. For destinations, this is an opportunity to involve residents in tourism to tell their stories to visitors. In so doing, no investment in physical products may be needed. The experiences add another dimension to destinations' product offerings and can diversify their appeal to visitors. As the Destination Canada statement suggests, experiences make places unique and differentiate destinations from competitors. For visitors, experiences are engaging, educational and entertaining and deepen their appreciation and understanding of destinations. They increase the memorability of destinations that people visit.

The inspiration for the great interest among destinations in experiences is usually attributed to publications in the *Harvard Business Review* by Pine and Gilmore (1998, 2011). Although these two scholars certainly lit the fuse of curiosity in memorable tourism experiences, you should know that this branch of programming began in the 1940s and 1950s with places like Disneyland (1955) and Plimoth Patuxet Museums (1947) in the USA. If you scan the Destination Canada statement above, the term engage is included, and it is a key word in implementing experience design. Experience design is a technique for engaging visitors with the people, culture and environments of destinations.

Engaging visitors means that they need to actively participate in their experiences and not just be onlookers. The experiences must be authentic and involving local people in the delivery is a good way to ensure that. Visitor learning of different types is often an intended educational outcome of experience design.

Experiences can entertain visitors as is well illustrated in a case study from Indonesia. Saung Angklung Udjo (2022) is a community-based attraction in Bandung, where visitors learn about the traditional Javanese bamboo musical instrument, the *angklung*. In addition to watching music and dance performances by local children and adults, visitors get the opportunity to play the *angklung* themselves (and do it successfully). This is truly a memory that does not dim with time.

Experience design is crafting how the visitor will interact with the local people, culture and traditions, and natural environment of the destination.

Figure 7.19 provides the author's viewpoint on the essential characteristics of effective visitor experiences, arranged by the AEIOU concept. No, this is not about learning the English vowels; it is just an easy way for you to remember fifteen features of experiences.

Figure 7.19 Characteristics of visitor experiences in the AEIOU concept.

EXAMPLE 7.19

What Is a Maid Cafe in Japan?

This example highlights a trend in the experiences wanted especially by younger travelers.

> Maid cafes are a kind of cosplay-themed cafe in which the staff (typically women) are dressed up in maid outfits and serve customers. They are a fun, carefree entertainment spot where the customer is put on a pedestal. Unlike typical cafes, where customers might buy a drink and rest for a while, maid cafes charge an entry fee (usually 500–700 yen) per person, plus food or beverage charges. Photographs with the maid staff are also typically available for a minor charge.
>
> (Live Japan 2022)

Learning Point

Cosplay is a growing experience trend in tourism.

Steps in Effective Product Development

In summary, the specific steps for a DMO to accomplish for its product development role are to:

- determine the destination's position on the TALC and identify individual sub-product cycles within that;
- decide on the dimensions of tourism quality within the destination and introduce a tourism quality management program;
- in consultation with tourism stakeholders and community residents, identify a set of basic principles for destination product development, including sustainable tourism approaches and practices;
- prepare a TPD strategy as a component of the overall destination plan;
- identify opportunities and needs for new physical product developments within the destination;
- develop a comprehensive visitor information provision strategy incorporating VIC facilities and online information sources;
- advise and assist tourism operators and other tourism stakeholders to achieve a higher level of accessible tourism;
- work collaboratively with transportation and other regulatory agencies to ensure an adequate program of tourism directional signage;
- work collaboratively with other tourism stakeholders to develop a tourism workforce development strategy and support this with the appropriate standards and education and training programs;
- encourage the development of a wider assortment of packaging and programming offers within the destination that appeal to identified market trends and needs;
- assist stakeholders in crafting visitor experiences that are highly memorable;
- create specific programs to increase the quality of interpretation in the destination.

EXAMPLE 7.20

Digital Nomad Villages in Portugal and Brazil

This example uncovers the trend of catering to the growing legions of digital nomads.

> The company behind Europe's first "digital nomad village" in Madeira, an autonomous region of Portugal, is now taking the project to Brazil. A pilot project first being revealed to Skift will open in Pipa, in the country's northeastern state of Rio Grande do Norte, on November 1 and run at least until the end of April. Like most destinations during the pandemic, Madeira faced a slump in tourism. As a result, the regional government backed digital community NomadX's village concept in the small town of Ponta do Sol.
>
> (Parsons 2022)

Learning Point

DMOs and their destinations should carefully be tracking emerging societal trends.

SUMMING UP

DMOs are becoming more involved in destination product development as the competition for visitors intensifies. There is also greater recognition that destination marketing, branding, and communications and product development are closely intertwined and that those involved in destination marketing should have an interest and involvement in product development.

Scholars have offered many definitions of the tourism product. For this book's purposes, the destination product is defined as an interdependent mixture of tangible and intangible components comprising physical products, people, packages, and programs. In assessing a destination's product, it is important to determine its position along the TALC.

DMOs vary in their levels of involvement in product development from non-engagement (bystanders) to being partners in development. They can also be facilitators or instigators of product development. Involvement depends to some extent on the TALC stage and the circumstances of the destination. No matter the situation, the DMO and tourism stakeholders should prepare a set of principles for destination product development. DMOs should play the key role in encouraging the implementation of sustainable tourism practices within their destinations. Product development should be guided by the principles of sustainable tourism so that the destination product will remain intact for future generations to enjoy.

Ansoff's Matrix provides a useful model for destination product development. The four specific strategies (market penetration, market development, product development and diversification) can be contemplated by most destinations in future planning for tourism.

Destination quality is critical for destinations, and all dimensions of quality (hardware, software, and environment) need to be managed. Significant benefits accrue to those destinations that make a concerted effort to manage quality. An IQM approach is recommended for destinations.

There are different types of physical product developments that can take place in a destination. New project analysis should be done professionally and include a site evaluation, resource impact assessment, market analysis, financial feasibility analysis and the preparation of business and marketing plans.

Visitor information can also be considered as part of the destination product, and VICs play a key role here. Online information and mobile phone apps should be viewed as additional elements of the information products supplied by destinations.

There are some aspects of the destination product that often do not get adequate attention from DMOs. These include accessible tourism and tourism signage. Because these items are integral to the tourist experience, they require a higher priority and a proactive involvement from DMOs.

All destinations are facing serious challenges with respect to human resource availability and quality. DMOs can make significant contributions to meeting these challenges by working with tourism stakeholders to prepare workforce development strategies, develop national standards for tourism occupations, and design education and training programs.

Packaging and programming play several key roles for destinations and offer significant benefits for customers and for the destination. DMOs should play an active role in encouraging innovative packaging and programming among the tourism stakeholders in their destinations. The development of interpretation and visitor experiences are a high priority for DMOs.

KEYWORDS

accessible tourism
Ansoff Matrix
authenticity
brainstorming
built facilities
business model
business plan
bystanders
capacity
circuits
clusters
concept development
destination competitiveness
destination product
destination product function
    model
destination quality
diversification strategy
economic feasibility analysis
events and festivals
experience design
facilitators
flagships
guiding principles

hubs
human resources
idea screening
impact
information
infrastructure
instigators
integrated quality
    management (IQM)
interpretation
low-carbon tourism
market development
    strategy
market penetration strategy
market study
memorable tourism
    experiences (MTEs)
new product development
    process
packaging
partners
proactive
product clubs

product development
    strategy
product launch
product life cycle (PLC)
programming
resource impact
    assessment
site evaluation
supporting products
sustainable tourism
test market
tourism area life cycle
    (TALC)
tourism product
tourism product portfolio
    approach
tourism signage
tourism value chain model
transportation
triple bottom line
visitor information center
    (VIC)
wayfinding

REVIEW QUESTIONS

1. What is the definition of the destination product and what are its components?
2. Which principles should be articulated to guide product development within a destination?
3. What are the stages of the TALC model and how do these stages impact the product development role of a DMO?
4. The levels of involvement of DMOs in product development vary significantly. Can you explain the continuum of involvement indicating the roles that a DMO can play?
5. What is the difference between hard and soft product development and what are the dimensions of destination quality?
6. Which product strategy models can be applied in destinations?
7. What is involved in the development of accessible tourism, VICs, signage, and interpretation?
8. Which types of strategies and programs can a DMO offer to enhance human resource development?
9. What are the roles and benefits of packaging and programming in tourism?
10. What is experience design and what are the characteristics of well-crafted visitor experiences?

REFERENCES

Ansoff, H. I. (1987) *Corporate Strategy*, New York, NY: McGraw-Hill.

ASEAN (2018) *Mutual Recognition Arrangement on Tourism Professionals*, 2nd edn, https://asean.org/wp-content/uploads/2012/05/ASEAN-MRA-TP-Handbook-2nd-Edition-2018.pdf#:~:text=ASEAN%20Common%20Competency%20Standards%20for%20Tourism%20Professionals%20refers, AEC%20ASEAN%20Economic%20Community%20amS%20ASEAN%20Member%20States

Bermuda Tourism Authority (2022) "Bermuda Tourism Ambassadors," www.gotobermuda.com/bta/tourism-ambassadors

Bihar State Tourism Development Corporation (2022) "Travel with BSTDC," http://bstdc.bihar.gov.in/

Butler, R. W. (1980) "The Concept of the Tourist Area Life Cycle of Evolution: Implications for Management of Resources," *Canadian Geographer*, 24 (1): 5–12.

——— (2011) *Tourism Area Life Cycle: Contemporary Tourism Reviews*, Oxford: Goodfellow.

Canadian Tourism Commission (2011) *Experiences: A Toolkit for Partners of the CTC*, 2nd edn. http://publications.gc.ca/collections/collection_2011/ic/Iu86-19-2011-eng.pdf

Castro, M. (2022) "The Secret Behind Ecological Developments That Meet New Sustainable Tourism Standards," July 21, www.forbes.com/sites/forbesbusinesscouncil/2022/07/21/the-secret-behind-ecological-developments-that-meet-new-sustainable-tourism-standards/?sh=62df70f37144

Christian, M., Fernandez-Stark, K., Ahmed, G., and Gereffi, G. (2011) "The Tourism Global Value Chain: Economic Upgrading and Workforce Development," https://gvcc.duke.edu/wp-content/uploads/2011-11-11_CGGC_Ex.Summary_Tourism-Global-Value-Chain.pdf

Colorado Tourism Office (2022) "Tourism Marketing Matching Grant," https://oedit.colorado.gov/tourism-marketing-matching-grant

David Nairne & Associates (2014) "Northern BC Mountain Bike Recreation Tourism Development Strategy," https://naturetrailssociety.com/wp-content/uploads/2015/04/MBTA-Northern-BC-Mountain-Bike-Recreation-Tourism-Development-Strategy-12042014.pdf

Dean, J. (1950) "Pricing Policies for New Products," *Harvard Business Review*, 28 (6): 45–54.

Department of Rural and Community Development, Ireland (2022) "SuperValu TidyTowns," www.tidytowns.ie/competition/

Department of Tourism, Innovation and Sport, Queensland (2022) "Towards 2032: Reshaping Queensland's Visitor Economy to Welcome the World," www.dtis.qld.gov.au/__data/assets/pdf_file/0004/1626448/towards-2032-reshaping-queenslands-visitor-economy.pdf

Destination Canada (2018) "Signature Experiences," www.destinationcanada.com/en/programs

——— (2022) "Canadian Signature Experiences," https://travel.destinationcanada.com/canadian-signature-experiences

Destinations International (2022) "Certified Destination Management Executive (CDME) Credential," https://destinationsinternational.org/cdme

Discover Greenwich (2022) "Discover Greenwich," https://greenwichhistory.org/discover-greenwich/

Drakenstein Municipality (2019) "Tourism Development Plan," http://drakenstein.gov.za/sites/dw/DocumentLibrary/Tourism_Development_Plan_20190930_final.pdf

Elkhart County Convention and Visitors Bureau (2022) "Heritage Trail," www.visitelkhartcounty.com/things-to-do/heritage-trail/

European Commission (2003) "A Manual for Evaluating the Quality Performance of Tourist Destinations and Services," https://op.europa.eu/en/publication-detail/-/publication/d6a1c97f-3080-4eed-8e22-d30766542ab6

European Commission (2022) "Accessible Tourism," https://single-market-economy.ec.europa.eu/sectors/tourism/offer/accessible-tourism_en

Fáilte Ireland (2022) *Sharing Our Stories*, www.failteireland.ie/FailteIreland/media/WebsiteStructure/Documents/2_Develop_Your_Business/3_Marketing_Toolkit/5_Cultural_Tourism/Heritage_Interpretation_Manual.pdf

Georgia Department of Economic Development (2022) "Tourism Product Development Team," www.georgia.org/product-development-team

GIZ (Deutsche Gesellschaft für Internationale Zusammenarbeit GmbH) (2020) "The Tourism Value Chain: Analysis and Practical Approaches for Development Cooperation Projects," www.switch-asia.eu/site/assets/files/2460/giz_tourism_value_chains_en.pdf

Global Sustainable Tourism Council (2022) "GSTC Destination Criteria," www.gstcouncil.org/gstc-criteria/gstc-destination-criteria/

Government of Northwest Territories (2018) Tourism Product Packaging, www.iti.gov.nt.ca/en/services/ressources-de-formation-en-tourisme/tourism-product-packaging

Government of Northwest Territories (undated) "Tourism Product Development," www.iti.gov.nt.ca/en/services/ressources-de-formation-en-tourisme/tourism-product-development

Hong Kong Tourism Board (2022) Hong Kong Wine and Dine Festival, www.discoverhongkong.com/eng/what-s-new/events/dhk-highlighted-events/hong-kong-wine-and-dine-festival.html

Koch, K. (2004) *Quality Offensive in Swiss Tourism. European Seminar-Workshop on Tourism Quality Systems*, Vilnius: UNWTO.

Kühhas, C. (2019) "Quality before Quantity—Also in Tourism!" www.nf-int.org/en/presse/presseaussendungen/quality-quantity-also-tourism#:~:text=Sustainable%20tourism%20has%20to%20put%20quality%20over%20quantity%2C,not%20all%20fun%20and%20games%E2%80%9D%2C%20explains%20Cornelia%20K%C3%BChhas

Live Japan (2020) "5 Maid Cafes in Tokyo You Won't Want to Miss," http://livejapan.com/en/in-tokyo/in-pref-tokyo/in-akihabara/article-a0000048/

Ministry of Information, Culture and Tourism, Lao PDR (2021) "Tourism Development Plan Lao PDR 2021–2025," https://laos-dmn.com/e-library/lao-pdr-tourism-development-plan-2021-2025_mict_english_draft/#:~:text=The%20five-year%20tourism%20development%20plan%20for%20the%20Lao, plan%20for%202021-2025%20and%20the%20vision%20to%202030.

Middleton, V. T. C. (1989) "Tourist Product," in S. F. Witt and L. Moutinho (eds.), *Tourism Marketing and Management Handbook*, Hemel Hempstead: Prentice Hall, pp. 337–340.

Mill, R. C., and Morrison, A. M. (2012) *The Tourism System*, 7th edn, Dubuque, IA: Kendall Hunt.

Moriarty, K. (2014) "Tourism Product Development and Good Marketing Practices," Ministry of Culture, Sports and Tourism, Vietnam National Administration of Tourism, Hanoi.

Morrison, A. M. (2010) *Hospitality and Travel Marketing*, 4th edn, Clifton Park, NY: Cengage Delmar.

——— (2022) *Tourism Marketing in the Age of the Consumer*, London and New York, NY: Routledge.

Muriya (2022) "Destination Dhofar: The Tropical Side of Oman, Cision by PR Newswire," August 15, www.prnewswire.com/ae/news-releases/destination-dhofar-the-tropical-side-of-oman-883040313.html

Murphy, P., Pritchard, M. P., and Smith, B. (2000) "The Destination Product and Its Impact on Traveller Perceptions," *Tourism Management*, 21 (1): 43–52.

Parsons, M. (2022) "Behind Brazil's Plan to Launch South America's First Digital Nomad Village," *Skift*, August 5, http://skift.com/2022/08/05/behind-brazils-plan-to-launch-south-americas-first-digital-nomad-village/

Pine B. J., and Gilmore J. H. (1998) "Welcome to the Experience Economy," *Harvard Business Review*, 76 (4): 97–105.

——— (2011) *The Experience Economy*, Boston, Mass.: Harvard Business Review Press.

Plummer, R., Telfer, D., Hashimoto, A., and Summers, R. (2005) "Beer Tourism in Canada Along the Waterloo-Wellington Ale Trail," *Tourism Management*, 26 (3): 447–458.

Queensland Government (2016) "Queensland Tourism and Transport Strategy," https://www.tmr.qld.gov.au/About-us/Corporate-information/Publications/Queensland-Tourism-and-Transport-Strategy.aspx

Ritchie, J. R. B., and Crouch, G. I. (2003) *The Competitive Destination: A Sustainable Tourism Perspective*, Wallingford: CABI.

Romeiss-Stracke, F. (1995) *Service-Qualität im Tourismus*, Munich: ADAC.

Saung Angklung Udjo (2022) "Welcome to Saung Angklung Udjo," http://angklung-udjo.co.id

Scott, D., Gössling, S., Hall, C. M., and Peeters, P. (2016) "Can Tourism Be Part of the Decarbonized Global Economy? The Costs and Risks of Alternate Carbon Reduction Policy Pathways," *Journal of Sustainable Tourism*, 24 (1): 52–72.

Secretariat of Tourism, Mexico (2022) "Pueblos Mágicos," http://www.visitmexico.com/en/types-of-tourism-in-mexico/pueblos-magicos-magical-towns

Smith, S. L. J. (1994) "The Tourism Product," *Annals of Tourism Research*, 21 (3): 582–595.

Swarbrooke, J., and Page, S. J. (2015) *The Development and Management of Visitor Attractions*, 2nd edn, London and New York, NY: Routledge.

Telfer, D. J. (2002) "Canadian Tourism Commission's Product Clubs," in E. Laws (ed.), *Tourism Marketing: Quality and Service Management Perspectives*, London: Continuum International Publishers, pp. 126–139.

Tilden, F. (1957) *Interpreting our heritage*. Chapel Hill, NC: University of North Carolina Press.

Tourism Australia (2022) "Why Become an Aussie Specialist?" www.aussiespecialist.com/en-us

Tourism HR Canada (2022) "Emerit Skills Training and Certification," http://tourismhr.ca/programs-and-services/emerit-skills-training-and-certification/

Tourism Malaysia (2022) "Tower Walk 100: The Newest Attraction in Kuala Lumpur!" www.malaysia.travel/explore/tower-walk-100-the-newest-attraction-in-kuala-lumpur

Turespaña (2022) "Spain's Wine Routes," www.spain.info/en/topic/wine-routes-spain/

United Nations World Tourism Organization (2007) "A Practical Guide to Tourism Destination Management," www.unwto.org/global/publication/practical-guide-tourism-destination-management

——— (2013) "Aid for Trade and Value Chains in Tourism," www.e-unwto.org/doi/epdf/10.18111/9789284415977

United Nations World Tourism Organization and European Travel Commission (2011) *Handbook on Tourism Product Development*, Madrid: UNWTO.

VisitEngland (undated) "Top 10 Tips on Inclusive Tourism," www.visitbritain.org/sites/default/files/vb-corporate/business-hub/resources/top_10_tips_inclusive_tourism_2.pdf

Visit York (2022) "Visitor Information," www.visityork.org/visitor-information

White, R. (2021) "12 Things Successful Visitor Centres Do Differently," https://tourismeschool.com/blog/12-things-successful-visitor-centres-do-differently/

Willis, E. (2021) "WTTC: Labour Shortages Hitting UK Tourism Trade," *Traveller-news.space*, December 29, https://traveller-news.space/2021/organisations-operators/wttc-labour-shortages-hitting-uk-tourism-trade/

Zhang, J., and Zhang, Y. (2018) "Carbon Tax, Tourism CO_2 Emissions and Economic Welfare," *Annals of Tourism Research*, 69: 18–30.

Chapter **8**

Destination Partnership and Team-Building

Together everyone achieves more

LEARNING OBJECTIVES

Having read this chapter, you should be able to:

1. define the terms destination partnership and destination team-building;
2. discuss how partnerships contribute to the accomplishment of the roles of destination management;
3. describe the relationship between destination governance and destination partnerships;
4. explain the benefits of destination partnerships;
5. discuss the potential partners for a DMO and how a DMO identifies them;
6. explain the concept of PPPs and their advantages;
7. elaborate on the barriers and challenges in forming destination partnerships;
8. identify the types of partnerships into which DMOs can enter;
9. describe the ingredients of a successful destination partnership;
10. explain how a DMO performs as a destination team-builder.

DOI: 10.4324/9781003343356-10

Warming Up

You have heard repeatedly about partnerships, cooperation, and collaboration in Chapters 1–7 and perhaps you are wondering why. One reason is because tourism is such a fertile field for partnerships, cooperation, and collaborations of all types. This is because it is unusual for one company, government agency, or other type of organization to control all the stages in the tourism value chain (to which you were introduced in Chapter 7 and shown in Figure 7.13), whereas visitors expect destination offers to be integrated (or seamless).

Tourism stakeholders are increasingly recognizing the positive synergies that result from working together rather than separately. As destinations enter new markets, they need to build fresh relationships because DMOs are lacking in local marketing, branding, and communication experiences and contacts. Joining together to achieve a faster and more comprehensive recovery from the harsh impacts of the COVID-19 pandemic provided an even greater incentive for partnering (UNWTO 2020).

There are many different benefits that result from destination partnerships, and it is worthwhile for DMOs to invest in cooperation and collaboration. However, partnering is not for everyone, and there are barriers and challenges to building new partnerships. Finding the right partners is a critical decision for a DMO. This chapter explains the steps for identifying partners and building partnerships that produce synergies for everybody.

A DMO's partners are those organizations and individuals which have the same or similar goals. Most DMOs have limited resources, especially finances, and partnering is a good way to extend the impact of these resources by teaming up with others. It is important that a DMO is proactive (ready in advance) for creating destination partnerships and does not just wait to join partnerships assembled by other organizations. In this chapter, you will learn how a DMO sets up a destination partnership planning team and the steps that this team follows to form cooperative agreements with partners.

Team-building is another aspect of this destination management role and includes proactive efforts by DMOs to build, support, and maintain teams of people and organizations to implement specific strategies, programs or actions. Just like in any sports team, the DMO may act as the captain or the coach and needs to get the best out of all the team players. Partnership and team-building is not a trivial role for DMOs today, although they traditionally put most emphasis on marketing, branding, and communications.

Your author has been involved in establishing several partnerships and teams. One of the partnerships was between and industry association (Destinations International) and universities (University of Calgary and Purdue University) in creating the CDME credential. He fully understands the benefits and steps involved with building partnerships. As a former football player and coach, and company CEO, he also knows a great deal about teams and team-building.

Definitions of Destination Partnership and Team-Building

Partnership and team-building are crucial to effective destination management. However, before moving ahead, you need to know the definitions of the two key concepts.

Destination Partnership

You heard about the partnership concept in Chapters 1 and 3. In this chapter, all the potential DMO relationships with other parties are identified and explained. Just to be sure, here is the definition of a destination partnership.

> **DEFINITION**
>
> **Destination partnership**
>
> A partnership is a synergistic relationship between a DMO and other organizations or individuals within or outside of the destination.

Giving you a great example will surely make for a good start. If you have ever had to wait in an airport for six or more hours and wished you could have escaped to explore the place more, an example from Singapore provides a great partnership model. In 2017, the Singapore Tourism Board, Changi International Airport, and Singapore Airlines signed a three-year partnership agreement to increase the tourism appeal and increase visitor traffic. Occupying three different spots on the tourism value chain, the three partners committed to spend $34 million on destination marketing and product development. Later, the three organizations signed a two-year extension to that agreement (Singapore Tourism Board 2019). Part of this joint effort involved working together on the Free Singapore Tour.

> **EXAMPLE 8.1**
>
> **Free Singapore Tour**
>
> An airport, an airline, and a DMO partnered to create this great experience for people flying into Singapore.
>
> > Be enthralled by the sights, sound and colors of Singapore during your transit. Take a walk through history at the Merlion Park. Experience a multi-sensory buzz in vibrant Chinatown or bustling Kampong Glam. Enjoy a panoramic view of the city, with a backdrop of the Singapore Flyer and Gardens by the Bay.
> >
> > (Singapore Airlines 2022)
>
> **Learning Point**
>
> When partners share the same goal, significant synergy can be achieved.

In the Singapore case, a DMO (Singapore Tourism), an airport (Changi International Airport), and an airline (Singapore Airlines) created an opportunity out of what can be a less than pleasant experience while also demonstrating collaboration along the tourism value chain (Fig. 7.13). The Free Singapore Tour options include a heritage tour and a city tour, each lasting two and a half hours, and they can be pre-booked through a travel agent or Singapore Airlines office. Then, transportation is provided through Singapore Airlines or another airline to Changi International Airport. Also in transportation are the tour buses used for the excursions. Accommodation and food and beverages are not currently included in the Free Singapore Tours, but tourism attractions are. The Free Singapore Tours are also included in leisure excursions and tours. Although DMOs usually appear in the value chain only as operators of VICs, in this case the Singapore Tourism Board is a co-organizer of a tour excursion.

There are several other terms and concepts associated with partnership, and as Figure 8.1 illustrates, they include creating win-win (all partners gain and benefit) situations and coordination, cooperation, collaboration, and teamwork. Alliance or strategic alliance are terms also used but not shown on Figure 8.1.

What are synergy and synergistic relationships? There is an enormous range of definitions of synergy, but the concept is best summed up as "the whole is greater than the sum of the parts." A more formal description of synergy is that when two or more entities work together, they achieve more than they could individually and separately. Another view is that when collaborating, organizations or individuals can do things that they could not do on their own.

DEFINITION

Synergistic relationship

A synergistic relationship for a DMO is a deliberate, cooperative arrangement that produces benefits for the DMO and its partners that would not be achieved without working together. This results from the pooling of effort and resources, either financial or non-financial, or both.

As some say, synergistic relationships are where one plus one equals more than two (Fig. 8.1)!

The coordination-cooperation-collaboration concept (the three Cs) shown in Figure 8.1 is attributable to Dr. Mark Elliott of Collabforge, a strategy consulting company based in Australia (Collabforge 2022). This is a concept mainly applied to describe partnering in supply or value chains. Coordination is the preliminary and lowest level of partnering; collaboration is the highest and usually means that the partners invest assets to co-create something. Do you remember the discussion of the 4Cs in Chapter 6? The fourth C there was communication (Fig. 6.8) that is a foundation for the 3Cs. A fifth C, creativity, is added in Figure 8.1 as partnerships are typically a spark for innovation. Communication is the foundation for partnerships and teams, and it expands and improves as groups working in tandem move toward collaboration. Also, creativity tends to grow as partnerships move from just coordinating their activities to collaborating with each other.

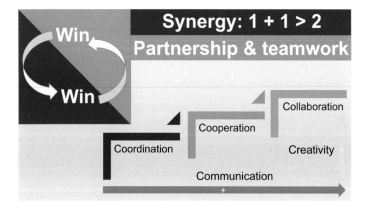

Figure 8.1 Synergy, partnerships, and teamwork and the Cs.

Figure 8.2 Cliffs of Moher on the Wild Atlantic Way.

DMOs cannot effectively perform all the roles of destination management without the assistance of tourism stakeholders and partners outside of the destination—they must communicate, coordinate, cooperate, collaborate, and be creative in so doing. Partnering with others is essential in today's business climate where DMO budgets are shrinking but competition is intensifying. Moreover, DMOs get more done and accomplished when they communicate, coordinate, cooperate, and collaborate with others.

The creation of the Wild Atlantic Way by Fáilte Ireland and its partners is a great example of collaboration (Fig. 8.2). This beautiful 2,600-kilometer driving trail along the west coast of Ireland was co-created by Fáilte Ireland and its partners and did not exist before it was launched in 2014. Do you remember the discussion of circuits in Chapter 7? The Wild Atlantic Way is a great case study of the circuit product function.

EXAMPLE 8.2

The Wild Atlantic Way: Ireland's Spectacular Coastal Route

This is an outstanding example of creating a great regional tourism brand based upon cooperation among many entities and people.

The Wild Atlantic Way, 1,600 miles (2,600 km) in length, is one of the longest defined coastal routes in the world. It winds its way all along the Irish west coast from the Inishowen Peninsula in the north down to the picturesque town of Kinsale, County Cork, in the south. This route from start to finish unfolds the wonders of nature, the power of the ocean and its imprint on the west coast of Ireland, and the stunning countryside in all its diversity. Enchanting villages are nestled along the coast as well as ancient monuments—their origins having long sunk into the mists of oblivion dot the landscape. Behind every bend on this magical coastal road a new delight awaits.

(Fáilte Ireland 2022)

Learning Point

Circuits and trails are a grew way to build partnerships.

You might come across the terms "strategic partnerships" and "strategic alliances" when you read about tourism and some specific parts of the tourism sector, including airlines. Here, the meaning of strategic is long-term and the partners agree (often in writing) to work together for three or more years. The Star Alliance (Star Alliance 2022), Oneworld Alliance (Oneworld Alliance 2022), and SkyTeam Alliance (SkyTeam 2022) demonstrate the highest levels of commitment in partnerships and are an example of collaboration on a global scale by major airlines. Mentioned later, the BestCities Global Alliance is an example of worldwide DMO collaboration.

Destination Team-building

Some partnerships are the result of team-building by the DMO, and this is a demonstration of the leadership, coordination, and governance role in destination management that you learned about in Chapter 6. There are so many diverse tourism stakeholders in a destination that the DMO often must be proactive in bringing groups of different organizations and people together to deal with specific issues or opportunities. Here, then, is the definition of destination team-building:

DEFINITION

Destination team-building

Team-building represents proactive efforts by DMOs to build, support, and maintain teams of people and organizations to implement specific strategies, programs or actions.

As you will realize, the concepts of destination partnership and team-building are linked; in fact, it is a bit hard to say where one stops and the other begins. Through team-building, a DMO creates new partnerships, but the DMO can also join partnership teams organized by others.

Destination Management Role Contributions of Partnerships

Before getting into the specific benefits of destination partnerships, you need to know about the broad scope of partnering in destination management. When partnering was first discussed in tourism, this was mainly in the context of marketing, branding, and communications (Palmer and Bejou 1995). Today, it is recognized that partnerships and collaboration can make a valuable contribution to all destination management roles. Here are some examples to prove this point:

DESTINATION PLANNING

The process for preparing plans and strategies must be collaborative, as you already learned in Chapter 4. Many real-life examples could be provided here, but one will suffice. In preparing the Tourism Master Plan for Vancouver (Tourism Vancouver 2018), many local residents and businesses provided their opinions through a survey.

DESTINATION MANAGEMENT RESEARCH

Destination research is sometimes co-sponsored by DMOs and others that have an interest in the results (Chapter 5). The Great Britain Tourism Survey (GBTS) (VisitBritain 2022) is an outstanding partnership case for destination research. GBTS is jointly sponsored by three national tourist boards in the UK: VisitEngland, VisitScotland and Visit Wales, in cooperation with VisitBritain.

LEADERSHIP, COORDINATION, AND GOVERNANCE

Partnering and team-building are coordination tools that DMOs can use to bring parties together. An example of a DMOs showing leadership through partnering is the cooperation among five Mexican states in the Yucatán Peninsula.

EXAMPLE 8.3

The Mundo Maya Region in Mexico

Partnering based on shared historical and cultural heritage is exemplified in this case from Mexico.

> Five Mexican states are drawing on their Mayan heritage to form a tourism alliance designed to attract more visitors and help improve local living standards. Collectively found in south-eastern Mexico, the "Mundo Maya Region" states include the Yucatán, Quintana Roo, Chiapas, Tabasco and Campeche. The agreement will facilitate cooperation between governments, the private sector, and local communities to "strengthen tourism and promote social integration, the feeling of identity, and contribute to better economic conditions for the inhabitants of the region by promoting a constant flow of regional, national and international visitors."
>
> (Travel Industry Today 2020)

Learning Point

A strong theme can be the basis for an excellent destination partnership.

PRODUCT DEVELOPMENT

Chapter 7 cited several examples of partnerships related to product development (such as in product clubs and circuits), and there are many potential avenues of cooperation in developing destinations. The Experience Mekong Collection in Southeast Asia is a group of small businesses, working under the same brand umbrella, that emphasize responsible tourism experiences across several countries (Cambodia, China, Lao PDR, Myanmar, Thailand, Vietnam) (Experience Mekong Collection 2022).

PARTNERING AND TEAM-BUILDING

Well, that is the name of this chapter. This role certainly involves partnering and team-building, and you get many examples on the pages to follow. How about an innovative example here to keep your interest? Popular TV series in the UK, *Line of Duty* and *Shetland*, are having a positive impact on tourism in Belfast, Northern Ireland, and Shetland respectively (VisitBelfast 2022; VisitScotland 2022). The DMOs and local tour companies are encouraging more people to visit and to see the filming locations for the TV series.

COMMUNITY AND STAKEHOLDER RELATIONSHIPS AND INVOLVEMENT

DMOs are active in developing partnerships and teams within communities and among stakeholders. The Tourism Diversity Matters initiative in the USA is a great case study here. Several diversity, equity, and inclusion programs have been developed by this partnership that includes DMOs from certain cities.

VISITOR MANAGEMENT

Partnerships are needed, along with great teamwork, to manage and care for visitors within destinations. Several DMOs are working with Airbnb to improve services for those working remotely, also known as digital nomads. These include DMOs in Argentina, Australia, Austria, Colombia, Dubai, France, Indonesia, Italy, Malta, Mexico, Portugal, South Africa, Spain, and the USA (Airbnb 2022).

CRISIS MANAGEMENT

You already heard in Chapter 2 about the Glasgow Declaration on Climate Change Action (UNWTO 2021) and this is a great demonstration of partnering to deal with a crisis. Several DMOs were among the initial signatories to this Declaration.

MARKETING, BRANDING, AND COMMUNICATIONS

Partnership is identified as one of the eight Ps of destination marketing, branding, and communications (Chapter 12), and cooperative marketing has been very strong in tourism for many years. A good example here is the partnership between Manchester United and Visit Malta, and the football club will market the destination to its fan base (Manchester United 2022).

The main point of this discussion, along with the examples, was to communicate that destination partnerships are pervasive and can be used as strategies to fulfill all roles of destination management.

Partnerships and Destination Governance

Destination governance is a sub-topic of Chapter 6, and you should know that there is a relationship between destination partnerships and destination governance. Achieving effective destination governance is a major reason for partnerships. Do you remember the discussions on engagement and inclusion as dimensions of governance in Chapter 6?

Some DMOs were established with a specific mandate to collaborate with others in the tourism sector and partnering is not optional for these entities. Brand USA is a case study on a DMO built for collaboration:

EXAMPLE 8.4

Brand USA: A DMO Built to Collaborate

Brand USA was created with the basic notion that it would be a partnership composed on many players from the private and public sectors.

> As one of the best levers for driving economic growth, international travel to the USA supports more than 1 million American jobs and benefits virtually every sector of the US economy. The international segment of the travel economy is especially high-value because visitors from abroad on average spend more time and money and visit more destinations than domestic travelers. Since its founding, Brand USA has worked with thousands of partner organizations to invite the world to explore the exceptional, diverse, and virtually limitless travel experiences and destinations available in the United States of America.
>
> (Brand USA 2022)

Learning Point

Strong brands have the support of multiple partners.

There are also certain instances where government agencies agree to have various DMOs collaborate, and Australia provides one example (Australian Government 2005). The document *Achievement by Partnerships: Tourism Collaboration Intergovernmental Arrangement* spells out how all the tourism ministries at the national, state and territorial levels will collaborate and coordinate tourism activities and build stronger partnerships. This arrangement was based on specific principles for collaboration and cooperation, shown in the example.

EXAMPLE 8.5

Principles and Processes for Collaboration and Cooperation

This example shows how Australia tries to coordinate the activities and programs of multiple DMOs.

The Australian governmental tourism agencies agreed on the following principles:

- Consult with each other on matters of shared interest and benefit.
- Minimize duplication.
- Align and mutually reinforce tourism promotional messages where appropriate.
- Explore opportunities for collaborative funding.
- Strengthen existing collaborative arrangements.
- Avoid cost-shifting.
- Recognize and respect the roles of tourism agencies in all jurisdictions, including their relationships with key stakeholders.

(Australian Government 2005)

Learning Point

It is crucial that DMOs avoid duplicating what other DMOs are doing.

Cost-shifting usually means that when one party under-pays for services; other parties have to put in more than their shares. This example from Australia exposes you to another perspective on the need for partnering. Again, this is more of a destination governance perspective, and avoiding the duplication of effort and redundancy of programs and actions is a key reason for forming closer partnerships. Better communications among partners is another justification.

There is a need for partnerships based on the characteristics of tourism, and some agencies are compelled to engage in them. In addition, some government agencies agree to coordinate their tourism activities for better governance reasons. However, as you will see, there are also many other benefits that accrue from partnerships to DMOs and destinations.

Some partnerships are mandated by governments and this is an arrangement about which you should also be aware. The Greater Bay Area (GBA) in China is an example of a region that was designated by government.

EXAMPLE 8.6

What Is the GBA?

Some partnerships are created by senior governments as policy initiatives as in the case of the GBA.

The Guangdong-Hong Kong-Macao Greater Bay Area (Greater Bay Area) comprises the two SARs of Hong Kong and Macao, and the nine municipalities of Guangzhou, Shenzhen, Zhuhai, Foshan, Huizhou, Dongguan, Zhongshan, Jiangmen and Zhaoqing in Guangdong Province. The total area is around 56,000 km². Based on the latest figures provided by the Guangdong Province, the Hong Kong Special Administrative Region Government (SARG) and the Macao SARG, the total population in the Greater Bay Area is over 86 million and the GDP is USD 1,668.8 billion in 2020. The development of the Greater Bay Area is accorded the status of key strategic planning in the country's development blueprint, having great significance in the country's implementation of innovation-driven development and commitment to reform and opening up. The objectives are to further deepen cooperation among Guangdong, Hong Kong and Macao, fully leverage the composite advantages of the three places, facilitate in-depth integration within the region, and promote coordinated regional economic development, with a view to developing an international first-class bay area ideal for living, working and traveling.

(Constitutional and Mainland Affairs Bureau, Hong Kong 2018)

Learning Point

DMOs that are located close to each other and that share key resources (e.g., a bay) should consider forming partnerships.

Benefits of Destination Partnerships

Destinations and their DMOs can enjoy profound benefits from being involved in destination partnerships. In fact, in some of the more advanced tourism destinations, including Denmark, there is recognition that tourism has entered a new era of collaboration and that partnering is no longer optional for DMOs.

EXAMPLE 8.7

Getting Things Done through Others

This example stresses that DMOs should not act alone; it is more effective to work with and through others.

As an official Destination Management Organization (DMO), our official destination recommendations are no longer sought after. Rather than promoting to others, we need to promote through others [author's emphasis]. We anticipate a task that we will share with many, in which we will take the lead on developing and managing the destination by enabling others to build experiences based on that one thing that sets us apart and yet pulls us together: our shared sense of localhood.

(Wonderful Copenhagen 2017)

Learning Point

Working with local residents is essential for DMOs.

Five significant partnership benefits as more budget, shared information, greater expertise, increased market appeal, and shared facilities. This is just a short list, and there are many other benefits of destination partnerships as you will see.

ACCESSING CUSTOMER DATABASES

The usage of a partner's proprietary customer databases can be a powerful advantage of cooperation. Mastercard in 2022 announced a three-year partnership with the Kenya Tourism Board (Mastercard 2022).

EXAMPLE 8.8

Mastercard Partners with Kenya Tourism Board

Credit card companies can be great partners for DMOs as shown in this example from Kenya.

> The aim of the memorandum of understanding (MoU) is to drive growth of tourism numbers into Kenya by leveraging various Mastercard channels, including its Priceless.com platform. The MoU also includes increasing transparency on tourism trends, anonymized traveler profiles and economic impact through Mastercard's Data Insights capabilities, which will enable Kenya Tourism Board to plan, execute and improve its campaign reports. Mastercard will also explore a loyalty and rewards program to boost tourism and enhance the impact of destination marketing efforts, including campaign planning and execution.
> (Mastercard 2022)

Learning Point

DMOs should seek out non-traditional partners as well as working together with traditional types of partners.

ACCESSING NEW MARKETS

A partnership may provide new geographic markets or other new target markets for the DMO or promise increased access to certain markets. The Tourism Authority of Thailand and Wego, the largest online travel platform in the Middle East and North Africa (MENA), agreed to a new partnership in 2022 that will increase the marketing of Thailand in the MENA region (Wego 2022).

BETTER SERVING CUSTOMER NEEDS

When DMOs and other tourism stakeholders pool facilities, services and other resources, this often better serves tourist needs. The Cities Destination Alliance (European Cities Marketing) (2022), for example, provides great convenience to tourists in its partner cities through the distribution of City Cards. This requires the cooperation and collaboration of many tourism stakeholders in the participating cities.

ENHANCING IMAGE

Associating with other destinations and their DMOs can enhance customers' perceptions and the positioning of destinations. The BestCities Global Alliance (www.bestcities.net) is an outstanding application of partnering that gives all participants an enhanced image within a specific market segment, business events. The twelve city DMOs belonging to the alliance are

Berlin, Cape Town, Copenhagen, Dubai, Dublin, Guadalajara, Houston, Madrid, Melbourne, Singapore, Tokyo, and Vancouver.

Expanding Social Responsibility

Partnering with others often expands DMO CSR efforts. Richmond Region Tourism in Virginia, USA created a partnership with VisitAble to provide educational programs to enhance accessible tourism (RVAHub.com 2022).

Increasing Budgets

Often, when the DMO agrees to cooperate with others, the total budget amount for all the partners is increased through the pooling of funds. In addition to the amount being greater for all, the partners may be able to do things that they could not do on their own. The European Quartet is a great case study of mutual benefit through long-term cooperation in tourism. The four countries (Czech Republic, Hungary, Poland, and Slovakia), for example, have booths at major travel shows and exhibitions, which they might not be able to afford by themselves. This has meant that all the DMOs can reach out to long-haul markets, such as China, because the pooled budget is large enough to allow them to do so.

Increasing Market Appeal

When the DMO works with others with similar interests in certain markets, the result is usually an increased appeal to these people. The City of Athens in Greece though the Athens Development and Destination Management Agency signed a partnership agreement in 2021 with the International Association of Professional Congress Organizers (IAPCO). This will increase the market appeal of Athens to meeting planners and the MICE markets (Sustain Europe 2021).

Increasing Pool of Expertise

A partnership may be formed because the DMO and the other partners have expertise that the other partners need to pursue the tasks that their cooperation involves. A good example is the Meetings Mean Business Coalition (2022), an initiative set up by the USTA to showcase the great economic and non-economic benefits of meetings and events. This pools the expertise of many people and organizations involved in holding and hosting business meetings, trade shows, incentive travel, exhibitions, conferences and conventions to more effectively communicate their benefits to people and communities. A coalition is a temporary alliance for collective action.

Sharing Facilities

If the DMO teams up with other organizations, this may help each partner to afford certain physical facilities. For example, DMOs that share office space in foreign countries find this more affordable than leasing and operating their own stand-alone offices. Also, many DMOs share booth spaces at travel shows and exhibitions.

Sharing Information

Most destination partnerships result in a great deal of sharing of information among the participants.

EXAMPLE 8.9

The European Quartet Joint Marketing

This is a partnership that your author truly admires, having seen it operating in China. Here, four countries have united under one theme and banner.

> The Czech Republic, Hungary, Poland and Slovakia have joined together to promote tourism to the four Central European sovereign states, to overseas visitors. The promotional name for this joint marketing initiative by the national tourism head offices, is the European Quartet. The Quartet, otherwise known as the Visegrad Four (V4), has been working together to ensure long-term success in fields of common interest, through continued and reinforced internal cooperation. The Visegrad initiative is an expression of the effort to develop the region of Central Europe within the wider framework of Europe-wide integration. All four countries share both historical roots and cultural traditions. At the same time however, each of the member countries has its own unique identity, be this in the field of architecture, art, religion, folklore and traditions or landscape. It is because of these unique characteristics that visitors to the V4 region are surprised to find new and intriguing surprises at every step of their journey and are most certainly not bored. The Visegrad area offers several unique UNESCO monuments, world famous spas, authentically preserved historical towns and places of stunning natural beauty.
>
> (Czech Tourism 2018)

Learning Point

By aggregating similar resources, DMOs in partnerships may gain more.

Ten distinct destination partnerships benefits have now been identified and described, and there may be more. However, these benefits are substantial enough to prove the great power in destination partnerships. Now, you need to know who the potential partners for a DMO are.

Destination Partners

Five types of destination partners are customers, other DMOs, organizations in related businesses, organizations in non-related businesses, and digital alliances. However, you should know this is just the tip of the iceberg when it comes to the assortment of potential partners that a DMO needs to consider. You will figure this out from the examples earlier in this chapter. The following is an extended list and description of potential destination partners.

E-collaborators

When the Internet started being used by DMOs around 1995, this new tool brought with it many novel ways of partnering online. Mentioned already in Chapter 1, the Historic Highlights of Germany have a website showcasing seventeen of the historic cities (German National Tourist Board 2022).

You heard earlier about the BestCities Global Alliance, which also includes an impressive, shared website. Other online partnership applications include reciprocal hyperlinking of partner websites (each partner provides a hot link to the other partner websites) and shared social media sites.

EDUCATION AND TRAINING INSTITUTIONS

There has been significant expansion around the world in tourism and hospitality education as well as in training and professional development programs in destination management. DMOs sometimes find it advantageous to work with academic institutions and suppliers of training to implement human resources development and research projects. UNWTO has established the International Network of Sustainable Tourism Observatories (INSTOs) at thirty-two locations around the world. These are located in Argentina, Australia, Brazil, Canada, China, Colombia, Croatia, Greece, Guatemala, Indonesia, Italy, Mexico, Portugal, Spain, and the USA (UNWTO 2022a). They involve DMOs along with universities and research institutes.

EXISTING AND POTENTIAL TOURISTS

DMOs can develop programs to build closer relationships with existing tourists. An interesting application is in Australia where the Great Barrier Reef Marine Park Authority (GBRMPA) is crowdsourcing information from divers and snorkelers on the reef's conditions. In GBRMPA's Eye on the reef program, visitors are encouraged to share their photos through a smartphone app, especially those of coral bleaching incidents and marine animals (GBRMPA 2022).

GOVERNMENT AGENCIES

DMOs often see the benefits in working closely with government agencies, whether or not they themselves are governmental agencies. The collaboration and cooperation among government tourism agencies in Australia has already been mentioned. In Chapter 7, the linkages of DMOs with transportation agencies on tourism signage programs are another example. A case on an even grander scale is the Silk Road Tourism initiative that is being coordinated by UNWTO. This initiative brings together the national DMOs from thirty-four member states, from Japan in the east to Spain in the west. It also involves other tourism stakeholders along the route of the Silk Road (UNWTO 2022b). The key stakeholders in this Silk Road partnership are shown in Figure 8.3.

LOCAL COMMUNITY RESIDENTS

DMOs often recruit residents to be ambassadors or volunteers to assist visitors to their communities, and this is a form of partnership with local people. The Greeters and City Champions program operated by Visit Brighton in England is an outstanding case in DMOs partnering with locals.

EXAMPLE 8.10

Visit Brighton's Greeters and City Champions

This is a great example from the south coast of the UK of partnering with local residents to provide needed information services for visitors.

> Visitors to Brighton sign up to be welcomed by a Visit Brighton Greeter who spends about two hours with them sharing their knowledge of the classic British

seaside resort community. City Champions are on street volunteers providing a friendly welcome to visitors and offer them information and advice to help them get the most out of their stay.

(Visit Brighton 2022)

Learning Point

Local volunteers have the potential of being great partners for DMOs.

The Bermuda Ambassadors program was mentioned in Chapter 7. There are also many tourism ambassador programs in US cities and counties and there is Certified Tourism Ambassador™ credential and certification program (Ambassador Institute 2022).

MEDIA COMPANIES

DMOs often work with different types of media companies to accomplish various destination management roles and particularly those related to marketing, branding, and communications. *National Geographic*, for example, under its geotourism concept, partners with DMOs in North America and worldwide to produce maps, websites, and other materials that promote sustainable tourism (*National Geographic* 2022).

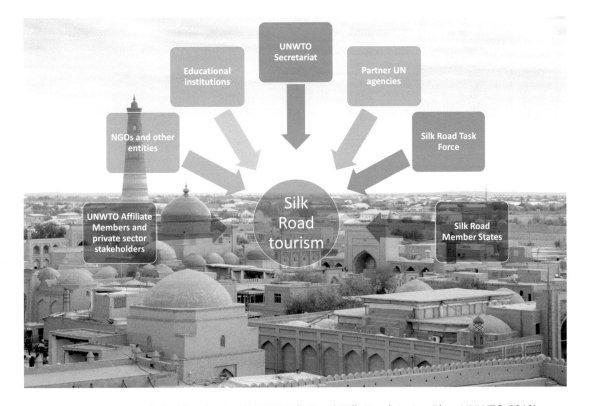

Figure 8.3 Key stakeholders in the UNWTO Silk Road (Silk Road Action Plan; UNWTO 2019).

NONPROFIT ORGANIZATIONS

DMOs can find good partners among NPOs when they need to address specific issues and challenges. Tourism Cares is one such organization that partners with DMOs across the globe.

EXAMPLE 8.11

Tourism Cares and the Meaningful Map of Colombia

This example shows how tourism social enterprises can be partnered and offer visitors more meaningful travel experiences.

> The Meaningful Map of Colombia was created in collaboration with Tourism Cares and ProColombia as part of our 2021 Global Summit to highlight and connect social enterprises throughout the country of Colombia to the greater travel trade. The map invites you to explore social enterprises bookable now, offering unique and hands-on cultural experiences for travelers. Each of these social enterprises is satisfying the demand from travelers seeking authentic sustainable experiences that make a difference and their need to use the power of travel to help people and places thrive.
>
> (Tourism Cares 2022)

Learning Point

Clusters or circuits of meaningful creative experiences can be created.

NON-TOURISM COMPANIES

Automobile companies, banks, credit cards, sporting equipment and goods manufacturers, sport teams, and food processing and technology suppliers are just a small sample of these potential partners. Great Wall Motor (Thailand), a producer of electric vehicles, joined with the Tourism Authority of Thailand in an effort to boost sustainable tourism in the country (Koumelis 2022).

OTHER DMOs

This is possibly the most popular type of partnership because DMOs tend to understand each other's goals and priorities very well and they are in frequent contact with one another. Many countries and some states and provinces have associations of DMOs, and their members work together on joint initiatives. Near the time of writing, Jamaica and the Cayman Islands were discussing how to partner to promote multi-destination travel (Travelweek Group 2022), and Indonesia and Singapore were likewise talking about how to develop a twin destination (Boey 2022).

TOURISM SECTOR ASSOCIATIONS

DMOs often work in partnership with tourism sector associations because they share similar goals. You heard about the Tourism Diversity Matters initiative in the USA earlier in this chapter and that is a good example here. Destinations International and European Cities Marketing are associations that represent DMOs.

TOURISM SECTOR EMPLOYEES

DMOs can partner with people working in the tourism sector and not just with their bosses. This often happens when DMOs have booths at tourism and travel exhibitions, and DMO staff from various organizations volunteer to work together in them.

TOURISM STAKEHOLDERS

Most DMOs work very closely with the tourism sectors in their destinations and create partnerships of various types. Membership programs are operated by many DMOs, especially in the USA, and these are a type of partnership. Other DMOs appoint advisory boards partly or wholly from the tourism sector, and this is another example of partnering.

TRANSPORTATION COMPANIES

An example given before was of a DMO (Singapore Tourism Board) working cooperatively with an airline (Singapore Airlines) and an airport operator (Changi International Airport).

TRAVEL TRADE

Many mutually beneficial partnerships occur between DMOs and companies in the travel trade, including traditional travel agencies, online travel agencies (OTAs), tour operators, destination management companies, meeting and event planners, incentive travel planners and others. Earlier, you heard about the agreement between Wego and the Tourism Authority of Thailand for the MENA region.

EXAMPLE 8.12

Qatar Specialist Program

Travel trade staff and companies are often productive partners for DMOs. It makes sense to keep them aware and informed about what the destination has to offer.

> Qatar Tourism has launched a new, interactive online training course—Qatar Specialist Program—designed to enhance its global travel trade partners' knowledge of Qatar's diverse product offering and provide a recognized qualification for its global travel trade partners. The program, which uses the latest technologies in digital learning, replaces the current Tawash program and supports Qatar's mission to become a leader in Service Excellence. Available in eleven languages, Qatar Specialist Programme equips trade partners with the relevant knowledge and tools to promote and sell Qatar internationally more effectively.
>
> (Travel Agent Central 2022)

Learning Point

Travel agent specialist programs can be highly beneficial for DMOs.

These, then, are fourteen potential partners for DMOs, and there could be more. The main point is that a DMO has many potential partners that it can call upon for collaboration and cooperation. Figure 8.4 provides a composite picture of destination partnership benefits and destination partners. You will see that there are twenty-five blocks in this matrix of benefits and partners, and only one of these is the DMO itself. Once again, you will see there is great potential for a DMO in destination partnering.

Identifying Destination Partners

How does a DMO find the right partners? This is a matching process, and the key is to find other organizations or individuals with the same or similar goals or objectives to the DMOs. Another key is that the partners share an interest in a specific tourist market, or they want to tackle a specific issue, challenge or problem in tourism that the DMO also wants to address. This could be to advocate a sustainable tourism development agenda for the destination, to make local people more aware of tourism, to improve destination quality, or many other situations best worked on together as a team.

There must be willingness on both sides to work together, and all partners must have a win-win mentality. Mutual trust is another prerequisite. Partners must also be comfortable with the idea of interdependence and be able to accept change. It is much better if partners have a future orientation rather than an orientation to the past.

Apart from these general conditions required for collaboration, there are other ways of identifying potential partners. Finding a common ground is the key step here. This is accomplished through recognizing shared resources, including geographic features, history and heritage, cultures, and transportation linkages. The following are some examples based on the sharing of specific characteristics:

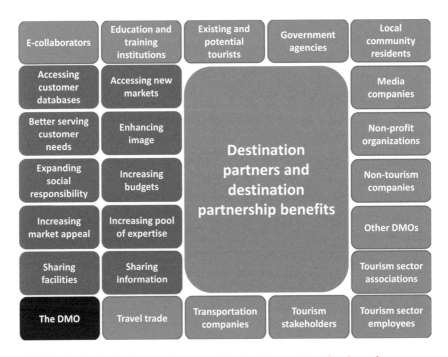

Figure 8.4 Matrix of destination partners and destination partnership benefits.

CULTURES AND TRADITIONS

The European Quartet of the Czech Republic, Hungary, Poland and Slovakia is an example of four countries that have shared cultural traditions, including a rich history of music. Another good case study is the Greater Shangri-La region of China, which includes the strong Tibetan ethnic cultures in Qinghai, Sichuan and Yunnan Provinces and Tibet itself. Mundo Maya in Mexico is another case here.

GEOGRAPHIC FEATURES

These include mountain ranges; seas, rivers and lakes; coastlines; climate; and other physical geographic characteristics. A good example is the Baltic Sea Tourism Forum (2022) that has its offices in Rostock, Germany.

EXAMPLE 8.13

Aims of the Baltic Sea Tourism Forum

This is an example of a regional tourism partnership in which the partners share common goals and objectives,

- Support a sustainable and balanced development of tourism and voice the interest of the tourism industry in the Baltic Sea region
- Strengthen the sustainable and responsible cooperation of all Baltic Sea region countries and exploit the existing international development potential more efficiently
- Provide and secure a permanent platform for information and know-how exchange with the Baltic Sea Tourism Forum at its core for continuous collaboration on the basis of a multilevel process
- Position the Baltic Sea as a coherent travel destination on the global tourism market and promote the area as an attractive, safe and natural destination for international tourists.

(Baltic Sea Tourism Forum 2022)

Learning Point

Regional tourism partnerships represent a trend that is expanding worldwide.

GEOGRAPHIC LOCATIONS

A shared geographic location is one of the primary motivations for destination partnerships, especially where there are adjoining political boundaries. The cooperation, through the Caribbean Tourism Organization (headquartered in Barbados), among the countries of the Caribbean, is just one example of destination marketing, branding, and communications and product development for a shared geographic region (Caribbean Tourism Organization 2022).

HISTORY AND HERITAGE

Partners may be found where there is a shared history of heritage through the presence of people, human-made structures, historic trails or routes, or events from the past. The trail to

Figure 8.5 The distinctive direction symbol on the Camino de Santiago de Compostela in Burgos, Spain.

Santiago de Compostela (Camino de Santiago de Compostela, Fig. 8.5) that follows the Way of St. James through parts of France and Spain is an excellent example (UNESCO 2022a). There are numerous other examples of historic tourism trails, including the Trail of Tears in the USA (National Park Service 2022a); the Abraham Path in Egypt, Jordan, Israel, and Palestine (Abraham Path Initiative 2022); the Ancient Tea Horse Road in China (Pang 2022).

Places sharing human-made historic structures often find ways to form destination partnerships, and examples include Hadrian's Wall in England and the Great Wall and the Grand Canal in China (UNESCO 2022b, 2022c, 2022d). Destinations that were all touched by famous people in history provide another reason for collaboration. Argentina, Bolivia, and Cuba have joined together to form a tourism trail based on the revolutionary, Che Guevara (BoliviaBella. com). This was made popular by the movie *Motorcycle Diaries*, released in 2004, and is about the epic journey of Che and his friend, Alberto Granado.

EXAMPLE 8.14

Hadrian's Wall Country

Partnering based on shared historic structures is exemplified in this UK example.

Hadrian's Wall Country is the brand used to promote the Hadrian's Wall World Heritage Site as a tourist destination. The Hadrian's Wall Country brand was researched and developed by the Hadrian's Wall Tourism Partnership and launched in 2002. The Hadrian's Wall Trust reviewed and adapted the brand logo in 2007, developing a suite of sub-brands for the bus, railway line, walking, cycling, local produce and guidance on their use. The Hadrian's Wall Country brand recognizes the wider landscape and cultural context of Hadrian's Wall. Hadrian's Wall Country is defined as an area ten miles north and south of the line of Hadrian's Wall itself and ten miles inland from the Cumbrian coast. Uniquely for a heritage site, traveling and movement are key parts of the Hadrian's Wall experience.

The vision for Hadrian's Wall Country (HWC) is a wide network of interconnected and distinctive interpretation and activity offers. These will help to position HWC as a multifaceted destination in which the outstanding natural and cultural landscape contributes significantly to the visitor experience and understanding of the Hadrian's Wall World Heritage Site. This in turn will help to establish a desire in visitors and local people to visit multiple locations and to make repeat visits.

(Hadrian's Wall Country 2022)

Learning Point

A strong and shared historic theme can be an excellent foundation for destination partnering.

INDUSTRIAL CHARACTERISTICS

A shared industrial heritage is another reason for places to link up together. The Malt Whisky Trail (2022) in Scotland is a fine case study. The European Route of Industrial Heritage (2022) is another example on a larger scale and covers more than thirty countries.

TRANSPORTATION ROUTES

This is another popular reason for destinations grouping together, and there are many examples worldwide. Route 66 in the USA is one of the most famous of these (National Park Service 2022b). The extensive canal systems of Europe also link many destinations.

You learned about the concept of circuits in Chapter 7. You will hear more later about themed routes and itineraries as a type of destination partnership, and many DMOs have been very active in creating these destination product offers for tourists.

Figure 8.6 provides a visual illustration of how a DMO can identify potential partners by looking at similarities in resources, location, markets, and challenges and problems. You should also realize that there are occasions when a DMO wants to find partners based on dissimilarities, when it needs partners that have resources or expertise that it does not have. In these situations, the desired result is a rounding out of the partnership team.

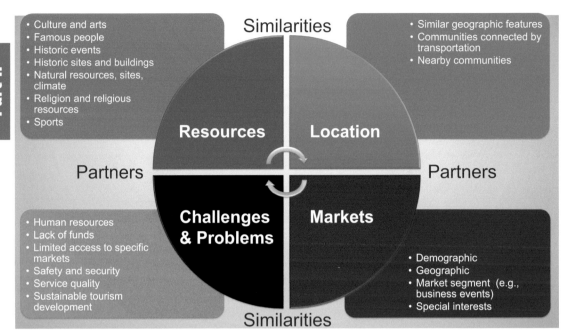

Figure 8.6 Destination partner identification wheel.

EXAMPLE 8.15

Danube Competence Center

Another regional tourism partnership is featured in this example among places located along the Danube River.

> The Danube Competence Center (DCC), based in Belgrade, is a Danube focused association of tourism actors for a sustainable and competitive destination Danube. The association's main task is to build and support networks of tourism stakeholders by enhancing transnational cooperation through various tourism development and promotional activities while implementing and promoting a unique tourism brand for a competitive European Danube region. As an association of members from the public, private and non-governmental sectors of ten Danube related countries (Germany, Austria, Slovakia, Hungary, Croatia, Serbia, Romania, Bulgaria, Moldova and Ukraine), the DCC contributes to the development of a sustainable tourism sector in the entire Danube region by initiating and implementing relevant projects, building the capacities of the tourism stakeholders and defining and promoting high-quality standards of tourism services and products.
>
> (DCC 2022)

Learning Point

Regional tourism partnerships focus partners' attention on shared opportunities and concerns.

Public–Private Partnerships in Destination Management

PPPs are becoming a popular way to structure DMOs and to accomplish specific projects within destinations. Chapter 1 introduced this topic by explaining the strengths and weaknesses of government (public-sector) and company (private-sector) operations. Both have their respective advantages and disadvantages. Figure 8.7 gives you a quick perspective of a PPP and shows that they are formed when governments and the private sector see that they have shared goals and interests. This triggers the co-investment of funds, assets and human resources into a PPP. The assets can include buildings, equipment and intellectual properties, such as brands. The results from co-investing and co-creating the PPP produce outputs that each side desires.

Tourism Australia and TEQ (both constituted as statutory bodies) are good examples of this formula of blending together the strengths of the two sectors (Tourism Australia 2022; TEQ 2022). These organizations are established through special statutes, or decrees of national, state, provincial, or territorial governments. They are administered by boards of directors selected from government agencies and the private sector. It can be said that they are at arm's length from the government but are also not fully in the private sector. You heard about this topic in Chapter 6, under destination governance, and a detailed description is not needed here. The main point to be made is that many DMOs today are themselves a partnership of government and private-sector organizations.

Barriers and Challenges for Destination Partnerships

There are some limitations to the concept of destination partnerships, and you need to be aware of them. The main barriers and challenges regarding the development and operation of destination partnerships are as follows:

High Turnover Rate of Principals

People tend to move from position to position quite quickly in the tourism sector. Thus, the original principals who formed the partnership may leave and be replaced by others who do not have the same enthusiasm for working together in the same way. Thus, the DMO must think about the sustainability of each new partnership and ensure that the partnership will continue even after staff departures.

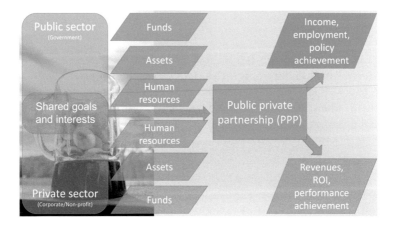

Figure 8.7 Public–private partnership process.

Huge Diversity of the Tourism Sector

The tourism sector is very diverse, involving many government agencies, private-sector companies, nonprofits and others. In addition, geography and cultures, even within the same country, tend to separate people and their ideas about how to proceed with tourism initiatives. It is extremely difficult to coordinate such a complex variety of entities and therefore to form effective partnerships.

Imperfect Information Communications

There are many success stories and best practices in destination partnering, and this chapter has revealed several of them. However, because of difficulties in communications, the sharing of these case studies is seldom very widespread in tourism.

Independence and Self-interest

The tourism sector is composed of many small and medium-sized enterprises, and their owners tend to have a strong sense of independence. They may be unwilling to cooperate or share information. Apart from this, there are people who act only out of self-interest, and they tend not to make very good team players in a partnership.

Lack of Adequate Funds

Funding can be a huge barrier to destination partnerships. There may be willingness to partner but not enough money to create and operate the partnership's initiatives.

Long-Term Payoffs

Sometimes partnerships take years rather than months to produce tangible benefits. Partners looking for short-term paybacks may not have the patience to remain in the collaboration for several years.

Measurement Difficulties

As with many programs in tourism, it is often difficult to measure the results of destination partnerships.

Sub-sector Differences

Tourism is composed of many sub-sectors, and often there is some friction among them: for example, between airlines and travel agencies. This may result in a lack of mutual trust and an unwillingness to coordinate and cooperate. Often, in tourism there is something called the silo effect (Tett 2015), when different parties isolate themselves and do not effectively coordinate their actions (you learned about the silo effect in Chapter 6).

Uneven Partner Benefits

Not all partners receive equal benefits from a destination partnership, and this may not be acceptable for some of the partners. The Collaborations and Partnerships Issue Work Team for the preparation of the Michigan Tourism Strategic Plan in the USA had this to say about the distribution of partnering benefits.

Mutual Benefit Does Not Mean Equal Benefit

This example is a cautionary note—not everyone in destination partnerships benefits exactly to the same degree.

> There is also a mindset challenge operating within this sphere [tourism]. While the value of collaborating can be in its ability to generate "win-win" results, industry members need to recognize and accept the fact that "mutual benefit" does not necessarily mean "equal benefit." It must also be recognized that the benefits from collaboration may be direct or indirect and may be immediate or realized over a longer period of time.
>
> (Collaborations and Partnerships Issue Work Team 2006)

Learning Point

Benefits from destination partnerships can be uneven and require years to be fully realized.

Figure 8.8 Challenges of building destination partnerships.

Figure 8.8 shows that these challenges and barriers to destination partnerships can be divided into two groups. The tourism sector challenges result from the features of tourism; the process challenges are because of difficulties in implementing partnerships.

Therefore, what looks easy may not in reality be that straightforward. There are many barriers and challenges on the way to establishing a great destination partnership. In reality, destination partnerships often succeed because of the passion of a few of the principals to make them work and to sustain the enthusiasm that is always there at the very beginning.

Destination Partnership Types

There is an enormous variety of types of destination partnerships. Some are short-term and are not repeated; others are long-term (strategic), and the cooperation spans several years.

Figure 8.9 Twelve types of destination partnerships.

Partnerships can be one-shot propositions covering just one activity or initiative, or they can be multifaceted and involve several activities. Figure 8.9 displays twelve opportunities for destination partnerships, and these are described in greater detail below.

COOPERATIVE PROMOTIONS (CO-OPS)

These are the most common types of partnerships found in tourism and involve collaboration in destination marketing, branding, and communications. Most often, co-ops are done as part of advertising campaigns, but they occur across all types of IMC. The DMO for the Northern Territory in Australia (Tourism NT) says that cooperating with them allows tourism sector operators to target people who have already decided to visit or intend to visit Australia's "Top End" (Northern Territory Tourism 2022).

CUSTOMER CARE

There are many good examples where DMOs arrange customer care training for operators in the tourism sector and other tourism stakeholders. For example, several DMOs in the UK offer the Welcome to Excellence training course to improve the service levels of staff in the tourism sector (Welcome to Excellence 2022). Visit Raleigh in North Carolina, USA, arranges quarterly classes on Customer Care for the Hospitality Industry (Visit Raleigh 2022).

DMO ORGANIZATIONAL STRUCTURES

Often, DMOs are established that are partnerships in themselves. For example, the Tourism Partnership of Niagara in Ontario, Canada, is a regional tourism organization that represents Niagara Falls Tourism, Tourism Niagara-on-the-Lake, City of St. Catharines Department of Economic Development and Tourism, Twenty Valley Tourism Association, and Niagara's South Coast Tourism Association (Tourism Partnership of Niagara 2022).

EVENT AND FESTIVAL SPONSORSHIPS

DMOs often seek sponsorships for business and sporting events as well as other types of events and festivals. There are so many potential case studies here that it is hard to pick one. However, the Qingdao International Beer Festival (China Discovery 2022) in Shandong Province, China, is an interesting one to discuss briefly. It was started by the Tsingtao Brewery Co. Ltd., and they are still its main sponsors. However, it has grown to be so big and popular that there are many other partners now involved, including the local DMO.

PRODUCT CLUBS

Product clubs may be formed with or without the intervention of a DMO, but in several cases DMOs have been involved in creating these partnerships of tourism stakeholders. You learned about product clubs in Chapter 7 and the Wine Routes of Spain is a good example (Turespaña 2022).

PROFESSIONAL DEVELOPMENT, EDUCATION AND TRAINING

Many DMOs get involved in partnerships that provide professional development and training programs or that lend support to other forms of tourism education. In fact, they are a major thrust of DMOs and their associations. These partnerships occur in almost every destination because DMOs recognize that training and education are continuously needed in the tourism sector because of the high rate of labor turnover. The CDME credential training is mentioned in several places in this book and is offered by Destinations International (Destinations International 2022).

SPONSORED RESEARCH

DMOs pool funds with others to do specific research projects. For example, several state tourism offices and CVBs buy custom reports from the Survey of International Air Travelers conducted each year by the US Department of Commerce's International Trade Administration [ITA] (ITA 2022).

STRATEGIC MARKETING CONSORTIA

These are long-term agreements between DMOs and other partners to conduct marketing, branding, and communications over several years. You have already heard about several of these including the Baltic Sea Tourism Forum, Caribbean Tourism Organization, European Quartet, and Tourism Mekong. Another two are the DCC based in Belgrade, Serbia (DCC 2022) and Travel South USA (Travel South USA 2022).

SUSTAINABLE TOURISM

There is a growing interest worldwide in sustainable tourism development. DMOs and their partners are getting more involved in joint programs related to sustainable tourism. In this chapter, you learned about the Tourism Cares effort in Colombia and UNWTO's network of sustainable tourism observatories.

THEMED ROUTES, CIRCUITS OR ITINERARIES

You have already heard about UNWTO's Silk Road and the Wine Routes of Spain, and these are great examples of touring routes linked by a common theme. Another outstanding example is much more than just a themed itinerary, and it has become a DMO partnership known as HWC (HWC 2022). This is the area surrounding Hadrian's Wall in Northern England (Fig. 8.10).

Figure 8.10 Hadrian's Wall Country, a great DMO collaboration.

TOURISM ADVOCACY

This means helping to communicate the benefits of tourism and its contributions to the economy and society. A great example of tourism advocacy is on the website of the Wisconsin Department of Tourism in the USA. The site contains detailed information on the significant economic impacts of tourism on the state (Wisconsin Department of Tourism 2022).

WEBSITES AND SOCIAL MEDIA

This is where a DMO partners with others to develop a website or sites on popular social media channels. For example, the website of Destination Napoleon (European Federation of Napoleonic Cities 2022) provides tourism information for many cities in Europe that were associated with Napoleon Bonaparte.

EXAMPLE 8.17

Getting Involved in Cooperative Marketing in Australia's Northern Territory

Most DMOs are involved in cooperative marketing as in this case from Australia.

> Tourism NT builds the territory's destination appeal through a range of media and marketing activities including familiarizations, training sessions, trade events and cooperative marketing. We work closely with local operators and key trade partners around Australia to ensure you are armed with the

knowledge and enthusiasm to engage the end customer, enabling them to better convert consumer desire into actual visitation.

(Northern Territory Tourism 2022)

Learning Point

All partners gain from cooperative marketing.

Ingredients of Successful Destination Partnerships

What steps can a DMO take to make sure a destination partnership is successful? It is very difficult to generalize in answering this question because partnerships are so diverse. However, there are some basic ingredients needed, and several authors have discussed them. For example, in her famous article, "Collaborative Advantage: The Art of Alliance," Rosabeth M. Kanter of the Harvard Business School (1994) identified the eight Is of partnership development, which she argued were the basic ingredients of successful partnerships:

1. Individual excellence: The partners are strong and have something to contribute to the collaboration.
2. Importance: The partnership fits with the goals and strategies of the partners.
3. Interdependence: The partners need each other, and they have complementary resources, skills and experiences.
4. Investment: The partners invest in each other.
5. Information: The partners share information and communications are open.
6. Integration: The partners create linkages and shared ways of doing things.
7. Institutionalization: The partnership is given a formal status, for example, with a contract or a MoU.
8. Integrity: Mutual trust is increased because partners behave in an honorable way toward each other.

A successful destination partnership, like a good marriage, is one that lasts. A few good examples will help to make this point sink in more deeply. For almost three decades, there has been joint marketing of the provinces of New Brunswick, Newfoundland and Labrador, Nova Scotia, and Prince Edward Island. It is a great example of a PPP because governmental DMOs and provincial tourism associations cost-share the partnership. The government of Canada contributes through the Atlantic Canada Opportunities Agency, and the four provincial governments also put funds into the pool.

EXAMPLE 8.18

The Atlantic Canada Agreement on Tourism (ACAT)

This is an example of a long-standing tourism partnership in Eastern Canada.

The ACAT drives growth in the sector by promoting travel to Atlantic Canada through research-driven marketing campaigns and activities in key international markets such as the USA, the UK, Germany, as well as to select markets within Canada. The ACAT markets Atlantic Canada with major consumer advertising campaigns, travel trade programs and media relations activities.

(ACAT Secretariat 2022)

Learning Point

It makes great sense when visitors go to multiple destinations within a region for their DMOs to collaborate.

Another tourism partnership of adjoining destinations is known as Borderless Borders and is formed by the three East African countries of Kenya, Rwanda and Uganda (East Africa Tourism Platform 2022).

A third example of a destination partnership is among the Vanilla Islands in the Indian Ocean. This organization was created in 2010 to market the islands of Comoros, Madagascar, Mauritius (Fig. 8.11), Mayotte, Réunion, and Seychelles as quality, world-class destinations. One of the ingredients of the success of this partnership is the common branding approach.

EXAMPLE 8.19

Where Vanilla Is Certainly Not Vanilla

Smaller island destinations can gain greater market strength by joining together with nearby islands under a common theme and branding, as with the Vanilla Islands.

The Vanilla Islands are a marketing grouping. It is a partnership of six island nations of Indian Ocean islands: Comoros (island country); La Réunion (French territory); Madagascar (the largest island); Mauritius (island country); Mayotte (French territory); Seychelles (island country). The organization is working like a tourism board for all these islands. It operates like a link between the

Figure 8.11 Mauritius, one of the Vanilla Islands.

tourist offices, the official tourism authorities and the private sector. A win-win approach is searching in the activities: increase the number of visitors, provide the tools for better efficiency, promote quality standards and services. The Vanilla Islands are working in cooperation with the existing tourism structures.

(Vanilla Islands 2022)

Learning Point

Vanilla is not bland in this case—rather it is a brand uniting a group of DMOs that share similar resources, opportunities, and constraints.

Having looked at these three case studies from Canada, Africa, and the Indian Ocean, you can see they share common ingredients. First, they have unanimous or at least widespread support from all the adjoining jurisdictions covered. Second, all partners share a desire to market and develop the entire destination. Third, the participants share a common interest, either in similar markets or in a similar style of tourism development.

It is also instructive to consider why destination partnerships fail; this alerts partnership planners on what to avoid or how to anticipate potential major problems. These include a lack of time and investment in the destination partnership, changes in priorities, insufficient communications, unrealistic timetables or time frames, unrealistic expectations of partnership benefits, and a lack of detailed partnership planning.

Destination Partnership-Building Steps

A destination and its DMO should take a proactive approach to partnership-building rather than always waiting for others to invite them to join their collaborations. Planning of partnerships is needed just as much as it is for overall destination planning (Chapter 4), destination marketing, branding, and communications (Chapter 12), destination research (Chapter 5), and destination product development (Chapter 7).

Figure 8.12 shows the steps reflecting this proactive approach to destination partnership-building. A description of each of these steps now follows:

1. Form a destination partnership planning team: A team dedicated to partnership-building is put together consisting of DMO staff and tourism stakeholders. The composition of the team depends on the types of partnerships to be pursued.
2. Review partnership needs and desired benefits: The team identifies partnership needs across all the roles of destination management and attaches priorities to these roles and their respective needs. The benefits desired from specific partnership needs are articulated as well.
3. Set partnership goals: The team establishes goals, in quantitative terms if possible, for the priority partnership proposals.
4. Identify potential partners: The team searches for potential partners using a set of partner selection criteria that it has established.
5. Prepare a draft written partnership proposal: The team writes up a partnership proposal that is shared with potential partners.

Steps in building destination partnerships

11. Evaluate the results of the partnership

10. Appoint partnership leadership team

9. Prepare a contract or MOU

8. Modify proposal and move toward consensus

7. Commence discussions with partners

6. Appoint a partnership leader

5. Prepare a draft written partnership proposal

4. Identify potential partners

3. Set partnership goals

2. Review partnership needs and desired benefits

1. Form partnership planning team

Figure 8.12 Steps in building destination partnerships.

6. Appoint a partnership leader: For each individual partnership, the team appoints a partnership leader.
7. Commence discussions with most appropriate partners: The team selects the most appropriate partners and begins discussions with them using the partnership proposal as an outline for the talks.
8. Modify proposal as necessary and move toward consensus: Several rounds of discussions may be required, and the partnership proposal may need a few drafts. It is also possible that agreement may not be reached and the discussions are ended. However, assuming the talks remain positive, the team should work toward reaching a consensus with its potential partners.
9. Prepare a contract or MoU: A formal agreement is prepared specifying the duties and responsibilities of all parties involved in the destination partnership. The agreement includes rules about opting out of the partnership agreement and conditions that will lead to its dissolution.
10. Appoint partnership leadership team: After the signing of the agreement, all partners signing appoint a leader and a deputy leader from their respective teams.
11. Evaluate the results of the partnership: Periodically, the results from the partnership against the goals and desired benefits are measured.

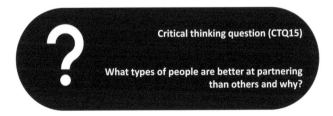

?

Critical thinking question (CTQ15)

What types of people are better at partnering than others and why?

Destination Team-building

The second part of this destination management role is team-building, which is so important to the success of DMOs. You first need to know what is meant by a team and the benefits from building destination management teams.

Team Definition and Benefits

DMOs must build their own (internal) teams and surround and align themselves with other (external) teams to be most effective. What, then, is a team in the context of marketing and managing tourism destinations? Here is this book's definition of such a team:

DEFINITION

Team

A small number of people, assembled by a DMO, who have complementary skills and a common purpose, performance objectives and approach, for which they are mutually accountable. (Adapted from Herriot and Pemberton 1999.)

You might wonder about the benefits of forming teams as opposed to going it alone. Figure 8.13 shows an old business saying (source unknown) about the essence and desired results of teams. The lesson here is that there is more to be gained for DMOs from working in a team approach than trying to do everything themselves.

Characteristics of High-Performing, Effective Teams

How do DMOs build high-performing teams, then? Much is written on this in the management and organization development fields. Figure 8.14 provides some guidelines for building effective teams by showing their characteristics. This begins from a platform or foundation of participative leadership, where the DMO leaders invite input from staff and stakeholders on important decisions. This style of leadership builds support for teams by creating a positive environment and open communications, which are accompanied by a willingness to coordinate activities with a cooperative spirit. Teams that are supported by participative leaders have codes of values that include welcoming complementary skills and balanced participation, where diversity is valued and conflict is managed. High-performing teams establish practices to achieve success, including having clear objectives, accountability and well-defined roles, with frequent communication and simplified decision-making.

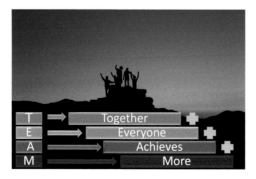

Figure 8.13 TEAM: Together Everyone Achieves More.

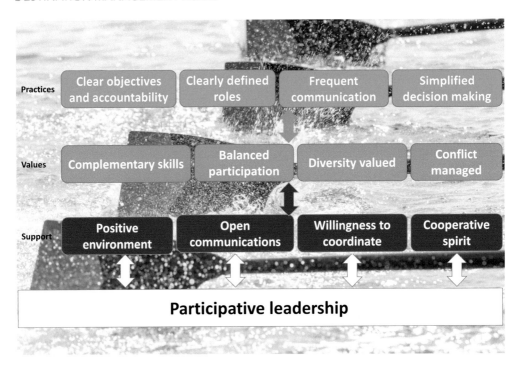

Figure 8.14 Characteristics of high-performing and effective teams (Ebb Associates Inc. 1999, in Biech 2007: 14).

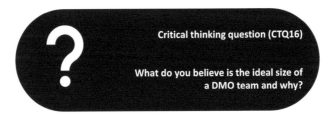

? Critical thinking question (CTQ16)

What do you believe is the ideal size of a DMO team and why?

Teamwork

If you hear about teams, you usually will notice that teamwork is often mentioned. Successful athletes and sports personalities almost always praise their team-mates and attribute success to team effort. Great teamwork is a hallmark feature of effective destination teams, and the quote below sums up the teamwork concept very nicely: "Teamwork is the ability to work together toward a common vision. The ability to direct individual accomplishments toward organizational objectives" (Andrew Carnegie).

Having a shared vision, goals or objectives is a key to teamwork. Winning is normally the vision that guides sports teams, and their coaches set up team formations to win (or not to lose).

EXAMPLE 8.20

Spurs and the Korea Tourism Organization Team Up

Football and tourism can mix well as shown in this example of a partnership spanning from Northeast Asia to North London.

Through the new partnership, Korea Tourism Organization messaging will run on digital advertising boards during games at Tottenham Hotspur Stadium. The partnership will also see both parties collaborate on content and promotion of Korean tourism for our visit in July 2022. We are currently the most watched and best-supported overseas football team in South Korea and home to two of the country's most loved players, Heung-Min Son and So-hyun Cho, who are Men's and Women's national team captains respectively.

(Tottenham Hotspur 2022)

Learning Point

Football is becoming a more lucrative venue for DMO partnerships.

Types of Teams in Destination Management and Marketing

Building partnerships with people and groups outside of the destination is a form of team-building, and you have heard much about that in this chapter. However, team-building is also used by DMOs to build internal partnerships within the DMO and the destination, and this is part of the leadership, coordination, and governance role.

Team-building is a topic that is also discussed in Chapters 6 and 9 because it is related to community and stakeholder relationships and destination governance. DMOs with a strong orientation toward community and stakeholder relationships and involvement are the most effective at team-building.

Teams can be either ad hoc (temporary and single purpose) or more permanent. As an example of the first type of (temporary) team, the mayor of San Antonio, Texas, in the USA formed a task force in 2015 to determine whether the government-run DMO should be converted into an NPO (Bailey 2015). Permanent teams include departments, divisions or units within DMOs. For example, the Virginia Beach Convention and Visitors Bureau in the USA tells meeting planners to "meet the team" in referring to the DMO's Convention Sales, Marketing and Service Team (Virginia Beach Convention and Visitors Bureau 2022).

DMOs assemble different teams to handle specific tasks, as you can see from the two examples previously discussed. Here are other specific team-building examples:

- Advisory teams: These are groups of tourism stakeholders who provide ongoing advice to DMOs, and they may meet regularly.
- Board of directors: You will hear much more about DMO boards of directors in Chapter 9 and you already had some information on them in Chapter 6. They are teams of people appointed or elected for a set number of years per the bylaws of DMOs.
- Committees: People selected from a larger group to form committees that focus on a specific function or issue.
- Crisis management teams: Teams that are either formed to plan for crisis situations that may occur in the destination or that are appointed to deal with specific crises that have occurred. You will learn much more about these teams in Chapter 11.
- Festival and event teams: Groups formed to plan or help at festivals or events, including at business events.
- Panels: A group of customers or experts who provide information or advice on specific topics or questions.

- Planning teams: Again, usually these are teams of local stakeholders formed when the DMO and destination are preparing plans.
- Research teams: Groups that share an interest in tourism research, information and market trends for the destination. These people may be from hotels and attractions as well as from the DMO, and they freely share information among themselves. Sometimes, they are joined by academic researchers and people from market research firms.
- Sales teams: Teams of sales directors and managers from hotels, attractions, transport companies and other organizations. Sometimes, these teams are used for sales blitzes, which are attempts to find new customers and tourists for the destinations.
- SIGs (special-interest groups): Teams that normally form on a voluntary basis because the members have a common interest. You might also see another version of SIG as a strategic implementation group.
- Steering committees: Here another word for steering could be guiding because steering committees guide a destination or DMO in making decisions or forming strategies. As an example, there is a steering committee for the preparation of Maui Nui Destination Management Action Plan in Hawai'i (Hawai'i Tourism Authority 2022).
- Task forces: You heard earlier about the task force appointed in San Antonio, Texas, to deliberate on the best structure for the DMO. These are teams assigned to perform specific tasks.
- Tourism advocacy teams: Groups of people who assist the DMO in communicating about the positive economic and other benefits of tourism within the destination.
- Tourism ambassador and welcoming teams: This has been mentioned several times already. These are teams of local tourism stakeholders and residents who welcome guests and provide travel information and advice.

Not all teams and partnerships work out and are successful. You probably already know this; however, the chapter cannot be closed out without some mention of the darker side of partnerships and teams. In the previous issue of this book, there was an example about the cooperation between China and South Korea hosting a joint website to encourage tourism to and between the two neighboring countries. Fast-forward to 2017, and the Chinese government's objection to the installation of the THAAD anti-missile defense system by the USA in South Korea is attributed to a sharp decline in Chinese visitors to South Korea (Macfarlane 2017). The website is gone. Also in 2017, United Airlines cut its previous partnerships with several airlines in the Middle East, claiming they were competing unfairly by taking government subsidies (Summers 2017). You will quickly gather from these two examples in tourism that politics and government policies can wreck partnerships and teams.

But politics are not the only reason teams and partnerships become ineffective. Douglas McGregor (2006) wrote a classic management book in 1960 in which he identified the characteristics of effective and ineffective teams. Here are some of characteristics of ineffective teams from McGregor's work and from Katzenbach and Smith (2015):

- Unclear or confused goals: The team does not have clear goals, or team members are confused about what the goals are.
- Uneven contributions: A few people do most of the work, whereas others are disinterested and do not engage.
- Poor listening: Team members do not listen to each other or ignore what others are saying.

- Poor conflict resolution: If disputes arise, they are not dealt with effectively.
- Faulty decision-making: Decision-making is complicated, or decisions are made too quickly or slowly.
- Autocratic leadership: The team leader is very controlling and does not invite much participation from other team members. You learned about this command-and-control leadership style in Chapter 6.
- Inadequate accountability: Teams do not adequately measure their performance.
- Unclear roles and disorganized actions: Nobody on the team knows what they should be doing, and things are accomplished in a disorganized way.

Rather than ending this chapter on a sour note, you should now have a very good understanding of the importance and opportunities for partnership and team-building in destination management and marketing.

Steps in Effective Destination Partnerships and Team-Building

The specific steps for a DMO to accomplish its partnership and team-building role are to:

- provide accurate information to tourism stakeholders about destination partnerships and build enthusiasm for partnering;
- appoint a destination partnership planning team from DMO staff and tourism stakeholders;
- pinpoint highest-priority partnering needs and the likely benefits that will result from addressing these needs through partnerships;
- identify partnership opportunities by type and potential partners;
- prepare destination partnership proposals for sharing with potential partners;
- engage in discussions with potential partners and negotiate cooperative agreements;
- prepare written agreements, either as contracts or MOUs;
- participate in partnerships;
- evaluate the results and benefits resulting from each destination partnership in which the DMO participates;
- build teams within the destination to achieve specific tasks;
- communicate and celebrate the positive results of destination partnerships and team activities.

SUMMING UP

Destination partnerships are very popular in tourism and fit well with an economic sector that is so diverse. A destination partnership is a synergistic relationship between a DMO and other organizations or individuals within or outside of the destination. The real power of destination partnerships is that they can be applied to all destination management roles and they are not exclusively for marketing, branding, and communications. DMOs are discovering that when they recruit the help of others, more tends to get accomplished.

A wide assortment of benefits result from destination partnerships, including increasing budgets, sharing information, increasing pool of expertise, increasing market appeal, sharing facilities, better serving customer needs, accessing customer databases, accessing new markets, enhancing image, and expanding social responsibility. DMOs have many potential partners in government and the private sector and among NPOs and individuals with an interest in tourism.

PPPs in destination management have become more widespread as more destinations realize the synergies of blending government with private enterprise. There is a definite trend of more DMOs changing from being exclusively run by governments to being jointly administered by both the public and private sectors.

Although the potential benefits from destination partnerships are substantial, there are many barriers and challenges to setting up such cooperation and collaborations. Lack of adequate financial resources, communication problems, uneven benefit distribution and unwillingness to cooperate are just a few of the roadblocks to destination partnerships.

There are many types of destination partnerships across the world today. They last all the way from a single day to several years or decades. Cooperative promotions, customer care programs, DMO organizational structures, event and festival sponsorships, product clubs, professional development/education/training, sponsored research, strategic marketing consortia, sustainable tourism initiatives, themed routes, tourism advocacy, and shared websites and social media are the main types of destination partnerships.

Successful destination partnerships tend to have certain common ingredients. They have widespread support from all partners that share the same or similar goals or interests. The partners want to focus on specific markets and see the wisdom of joining forces to appeal to these markets. They are willing to make an investment in each other and share information freely.

DMOs should be proactive in destination partnership-building, and there is a set of steps they should follow, including appointing partnership planning teams. It is best to put partnership agreements in writing and have all parties sign them.

Team-building is an important sub-role of destination management, and DMOs are frequently called upon to assemble different teams within their communities. Teams are either short-term or long-term, and they are assembled to address specific issues or tasks that the DMO has in completing its destination management roles.

Partnership and team-building are not exactly the same concepts, although they are very intertwined.

KEYWORDS

advisory boards	creativity	silo effect
coalition	interdependence	statutory bodies
co-create	MoU (memorandum of	steering committees
collaboration	understanding)	synergy
committees	multi-destination travel	team-building
communication	mutual trust	teamwork
cooperation	partnership	tourism value chain
cooperative marketing	public–private partnership	win-win
(co-ops)	(PPP)	
coordination	proactive	

REVIEW QUESTIONS

1. What are the definitions for destination partnership and destination team-building?
2. How does partnering help a DMO to accomplish all roles of destination management?
3. What is the relationship between destination governance and destination partnerships?
4. What are the benefits of destination partnerships?
5. Who are a DMO's potential partners and how should a DMO identify them?
6. PPPs are becoming more popular in destination management and marketing. What are the reasons behind this trend?
7. What are the major barriers and challenges to the formation of destination partnerships?
8. What are the types of destination partnerships available to DMOs?
9. What are the main ingredients of successful destination partnerships?
10. How does a DMO perform as a builder of teams?

REFERENCES

Abraham Path Initiative (2022) "The Abraham Path Cultural Route," http://abrahampath.org

ACAT Secretariat (2022) "About the ACAT," https://acat-etra.ca

Airbnb (2022) "Airbnb Expands Destination Partnerships to Make Living and Working Anywhere," https://news.airbnb.com/20-destinations-supporting-remote-work/#:~:text=Airbnb%20has %20today%20announced%20it%20will%20partner%20with, including%20Bali%2C%20the%20 Canary%20Islands%20and%20the%20Caribbean

Ambassador Institute (2022) "CTA Community," www.ctanetwork.com

Australian Government (2005) "Achievement by Partnerships: Tourism Collaboration Intergovern-mental Arrangement," https://federation.gov.au/sites/default/files/about/agreements/Tourism-Collaboration-Intergovernmental-Arrangement-2005.pdf

Bailey, S. W. (2015) "Mayor's CVB Task Force Calls for New Nonprofit to Market San Antonio," www.bizjournals.com/sanantonio/news/2015/12/10/mayor-s-cvb-task-force-calls-for-creating-new.html

Baltic Sea Tourism Forum (2022) "Baltic Sea Tourism Forum," https://bstc.eu/bstf

BestCities Global Alliance (2022) "About Us," www.bestcities.net/about-us

Biech, E. (ed.) (2007) *The Pfeiffer Book of Successful Team-Building Tools: Best of the Annuals*, 2nd edn, New York, NY: Pfeiffer/Wiley.

Boey, C. (2022) "Indonesia to Start Talks with Singapore for Twin Destination Partnership," *TTG Asia*, June 14, www.ttgasia.com/2022/06/14/indonesia-to-start-talks-with-singapore-for-twin-destination-partnership/#:~:text=Indonesia%20is%20proposing%20to%20work%20with%20 Singapore%20on, hub%20position%20to%20help%20revive%20its%20tourism%20industry

BoliviaBella.com (2022) "Ruta del Che Guevara in Bolivia," www.boliviabella.com/ruta-del-che.html

Brand USA (2022) "About: Who We Are," www.thebrandusa.com/about/whoweare

Caribbean Tourism Organization (2022) "CTO News," www.onecaribbean.org/media/cto-news/

China Discovery (2022) "Qingdao International Beer Festival," www.chinadiscovery.com/shandong/qingdao/qingdao-beer-festival.html

Cities Destination Alliance (European Cities Marketing) (2022) "Through Branding Campaign, ECM Members Join Forces and Benchmark More Than 4.5 Million City Cards," www.europeancities-marketing.com/branding-campaign-ecm-members-join-forces-benchmark-4-5-million-city-cards

Collaborations and Partnerships Issue Work Team (2006) "Michigan Strategic Tourism Plan: Collaboration and Partnership IWT Report to the Council."

Collabforge (2022) "The 3Cs: Coordination, Cooperation, Collaboration," https://collabforge.com/the-3cs-coordination-cooperation-collaboration

Constitutional and Mainland Affairs Bureau, Hong Kong (2018) "What Is the Greater Bay Area?" www.bayarea.gov.hk/en/about/overview.html

Czech Tourism (2018) "About Discovery Central Europe," http://discover-ce.eu/about-us

Danube Competence Center (2022) "About DCC," https://danubecc.org/about-dcc/

Destinations International (2022) "Certified Destination Management Executive (CDME) Credential," https://destinationsinternational.org/cdme

East Africa Tourism Platform (2022) "East Africa Tourism Platform," https://ea-tourism.org/

European Federation of Napoleonic Cities (2022) "Napoleonic Cities," www.destination-napoleon.eu/villes-napoleoniennes/?lang=en

European Route of Industrial Heritage (2022) "Welcome to the European Route of Industrial Heritage," www.erih.net

Experience Mekong Collection (2022) "Experience Mekong Collection," www.experiencemekong.com/

Fáilte Ireland (2022) "Ireland's West Coast: The Wild Atlantic Way—Ireland's Spectacular Coastal Route," www.thewildatlanticway.com

German National Tourist Board (2022) "Historic Highlights of Germany," www.germany.travel/en/cities-culture/historic-highlights-of-germany.html

Great Barrier Reef Marine Park Authority, Australia (2022) "Eye on the Reef," www.barrierreefaustralia.com/info/sustainability/eye-on-reef/#:~:text=Through%20the%20Great%20Barrier%20Reef%20Marine%20Park%20Authority%E2%80%99s,on%20Reef%20health%2C%20the%20marine%20life%20and%20incidents

Hadrian's Wall Country (2022) "About," https://hadrianswallcountry.co.uk/about

Hawai'i Tourism Authority (2022) "Steering Committee," www.hawaiitourismauthority.org/what-we-do/hta-programs/destination-management-action-plans/maui-nui/steering-committee/

Herriot, P., and Pemberton, C. (1999) "Teams: Old Myths and a New Model," in J. Billsberry (ed.), *The Effective Manager: Perspectives and Illustrations*, Thousand Oaks, CA: SAGE.

International Trade Administration (USA) (2022) "Survey of International Air Travelers (SIAT)," www.trade.gov/survey-international-air-travelers-siat

Kanter, R. M. (1994) "Collaborative Advantage: The Art of Alliances," *Harvard Business Review*, 72 (4): 96–108.

Katzenbach, J. R., and Smith, D. K. (2015) *The Wisdom of Teams: Creating the High-Performance Organization*, Boston, Mass.: Harvard Business Review Press.

Koumelis, T. (2022) "Great Wall Motor Partners with Tourism Authority of Thailand to Promote Ecotourism and New-Energy Vehicles While Restoring and Driving Thailand's Economic Growth," *TravelDailyNews Asia*, August 17, www.traveldailynews.asia/great-wall-motor-partners-with-tourism-authority-of-thailand

McGregor, D. (2006) *The Human Side of Enterprise,* New York, NY: McGraw-Hill Education.

Macfarlane, A. (2017) "China is crushing Korea's tourism industry," http://money.cnn.com/2017/04/26/news/Chinese-tourism-south-korea/index.html?iid=hp-toplead.intl

Malt Whisky Trail (2022) "Malt Whisky Trail," http://maltwhiskytrail.com/

Manchester United (2022) "Visit Malta, Official Global Partner of Manchester United," www.manutd.com/en/partners/global/visit-malta

Mastercard (2022) "Mastercard Announces MoU with Kenya Tourism Board (KTB) to Help Boost Tourism," June 20, www.mastercard.com/news/eemea/en/newsroom/press-releases/press-releases/en/2022/june/mastercard-announces-mou-with-kenya-tourism-board-ktb-to-help-boost-tourism

Meetings Mean Business Coalition (2022) "Our Coalition," www.meetingsmeanbusiness.com/about

National Geographic (2022) "Geotourism," www.nationalgeographic.com/maps/topic/geotourism

National Park Service (USA) (2022a) "Trail of Tears," www.nps.gov/trte/index.htm

—— (2022b) "Travel Route 66," www.nps.gov/subjects/travelroute66/index.htm

Northern Territory Tourism (Tourism NT) (2022) "Get Involved," www.tourismnt.com.au/marketing/get-involved

Oneworld Alliance (2022) "Oneworld Member Airlines," www.oneworld.com/members

Palmer, A., and Bejou, D. (1995) "Tourism Destination Marketing Alliances," *Annals of Tourism Research*, 22 (3): 616–629.

Pang, K. (2022) "The Ancient Tea Horse Road," www.chinahighlights.com/travelguide/special-report/tea-horse-road/#:~:text=The%20Ancient%20Tea%20Horse%20Road%20%20%2028in%20China%2029%29%20was, pathway%20was%20called%20the%20Tea%20Horse%20Road.%20Features

RVAHub.com (2022) "Richmond Region Tourism Partners with VisitAble to Offer Disability Awareness Education to Local Hospitality Community," https://rvahub.com/2022/08/11/rich-mond-region-tourism-partners-with-visitable-to-offer-disability-awareness-education-to-local-hospitality-community

Singapore Airlines (2022) "Free Singapore Tour," www.singaporeair.com/en_UK/us/plan-travel/privileges/free-singapore-tour/

Singapore Tourism Board (2019) "SIA, CAG, STB Strengthen Commitment to Tourism with Largest Partnership to Date," www.stb.gov.sg/content/stb/en/media-centre/media-releases/sia-cag-stb-strengthen-commitment-to-tourism-with-largest-partnership-to-date.html

SkyTeam Alliance (2022) "About," www.skyteam.com/en/about

Star Alliance (2022) "About," www.staralliance.com/en/about

Summers, B. (2017) "United Ends Cooperation Agreements with 5 Middle East Airlines," *Skift*, https://skift.com/2017/04/28/united-ends-cooperation-agreements-with-5-middle-east-airlines

Sustain Europe (2021) "New Destination Partnership Between City of Athens and IAPCO," November 30, www.sustaineurope.com/new-destination-partnership-between-the-city-of-athens-iapco-20211130.html

Tett, G. (2015) *The Silo Effect: The Perils of Expertise and the Promise of Breaking Down Barriers*, New York, NY: Simon & Schuster.

Tottenham Hotspur (2022) "Tottenham Hotspur Announces Partnership with Korea Tourism Organisation," www.tottenhamhotspur.com/news/2022/may/tottenham-hotspur-announces-partnership-with-korea-tourism-organisation

Tourism Australia (2022) "Our Organisation," www.tourism.australia.com/en/about/our-organisation.html

Tourism Cares (2022) "The Meaningful Map of Colombia," www.tourismcares.org/programs/colombia-map

Tourism Diversity Matters (2022) "Tourism Diversity Matters," https://tourismdiversitymatters.org/about

Tourism and Events Queensland (2022) "Who We Are," https://teq.queensland.com/au/en/industry/who-we-are

Tourism Partnership of Niagara (2022) "Boards and Committees," www.visitniagaracanada.com/board-committees/

Tourism Vancouver (2018) "Vancouver Tourism Master Plan," www.tourismvancouver.com/about/tourism-master-plan

Travel Agent Central (2022) "Qatar Tourism launches Specialist Program to upskill trade partners," https://www.travelagentcentral.com/destinations/qatar-tourism-launches-qatar-specialist-program-upskill-global-travel-trade-partners

Travel Industry Today (2020) "MUNDA MAYA: Mexican States Unite to Tout Tourism," August 17, https://travelindustrytoday.com/munda-mayamexican-states-unite-to-tout-tourism

Travel South USA (2022) "The Official Regional Destination Marketing Organization of the Southern USA," https://industry.travelsouthusa.com/

Travelweek Group (2022) "Jamaica, Cayman Islands Team Up for Multidestination Tourism, Airlift and More," Travelweek.ca, August 11, www.travelweek.ca/news/jamaica-cayman-islands-team-up-for-multi-destination-tourism-airlift-and-more

Turespaña (2022) "Spain's Wine Routes," www.spain.info/en/topic/wine-routes-spain/

United Nations Educational, Scientific and Cultural Organization (2022a) "Routes of Santiago de Compostela: Camino Francés and Routes of Northern Spain," http://whc.unesco.org/en/list/669

——— (2022b) "The Grand Canal," https://whc.unesco.org/en/list/1443

——— (2022c) "The Great Wall," https://whc.unesco.org/en/list/438

—— (2022d) "Hadrian's Wall," https://whc.unesco.org/en/list/430

United Nations World Tourism Organization (2019) "Silk Road Action Plan Update: Re-defining Cooperation Along the Historic Routes," https://webunwto.s3.eu-west-1.amazonaws.com/imported_images/50120/patrick_.pdf

—— (2020) "Secretary-General's Policy Brief on Tourism and COVID-19," www.unwto.org/tourism-and-covid-19-unprecedented-economic-impacts

—— (2021) "Tourism Unites Behind the Glasgow Declaration on Climate Action at COP26," www.unwto.org/news/tourism-unites-behind-the-glasgow-declaration-on-climate-action-at-cop26

—— (2022a) "World Tourism Organization International Network of Sustainable Tourism Observatories (INSTO)," http://insto.unwto.org/observatories

—— (2022b) "Silk Road," www.unwto.org/silk-road

Vanilla Islands (2022) "Vanilla Islands of Indian Ocean," www.vanilla-islands.org/en

Virginia Beach Convention and Visitors Bureau (2022) "Meet the Team," www.visitvirginiabeach.com/meetings/meet-the-team

VisitBelfast (2022) "Line of Duty Tour," https://visitbelfast.com/partners/line-of-duty-tour

VisitBrighton (2022) "Greeters and City Champions," www.visitbrighton.com/plan-your-visit/visitor-information/greeters-and-city-champions

VisitBritain (2022) "GB Tourism Survey (Domestic Overnight Tourism): Latest Results," www.visitbritain.org/great-britain-tourism-survey-latest-monthly-overnight-data

Visit Raleigh (2022) "'Customer Care for the Hospitality Industry' Classes," www.visitraleigh.com/partners/customer-care class

VisitScotland (2022) "Shetland TV Tour: On the Trail of Jimmy Perez," www.visitscotland.com/info/tours/shetland-tv-tour-on-the-trail-of-jimmy-perez-00c8b47a

Wego (2022) "Wego: New Partnership with Tourism Authority of Thailand to Drive Tourism from MENA," *Cision PR Newswire*, July 21, www.prnewswire.com/news-releases/wego-new-partnership-with-tourism-authority-of-thailand-to-drive-tourism-from-mena-301590377.html

Welcome to Excellence (2022) "High Impact Customer Service Training Courses," www.welcometoexcellence.co.uk/

Wisconsin Department of Tourism (2022) "Economic Impact," www.industry.travelwisconsin.com/research/economic-impact/#main-content

Wonderful Copenhagen (2017) "The End of Tourism as We Know It," http://localhood.wonderfulcopenhagen.dk/

Chapter  **9**

Destination Stakeholder Relationships and Involvement

Be connected

LEARNING OBJECTIVES

Having read this chapter, you should be able to:

1. define the term stakeholder;

2. describe the tourism sector stakeholders in a destination;

3. elaborate upon the activities a DMO uses to maintain positive relationships with tourism sector stakeholders;

4. describe DMO membership programs and membership activities and benefits;

5. explain the considerations with DMO boards of directors;

6. explain the importance of community relationships and involvement to destination management;

7. describe the reasons and benefits of having positive relationships with local residents;

8. discuss the activities included in managing the relationships and involvement of local residents;

9. review the main concerns with government relationships and relationships with the environment.

DOI: 10.4324/9781003343356-11

Warming Up

In Chapter 8, you were introduced to relationship building with various partners and working with teams of different types. In this chapter, the focus is on the relationships with stakeholders (tourism sector stakeholders, community, government, environment, and tourists).

Your author always says that "DMOs have many bosses," and that is a very accurate statement based on his experiences worldwide. You are first going to learn about the entire stakeholder landscape for destination management and you will see it has many parts and great complexity. Then, you will hear a little, but not too much, about stakeholder theory. After that all of the stakeholder categories are discussed and how DMOs engage with them. The discussion about tourists is left for later chapters; tourism sector stakeholders, local residents, government, the environment, and others are the focus in Chapter 9.

Stakeholder Landscape for Destination Management

Figure 1.7 in Chapter 1 identified five categories of destination stakeholders. These are shown again in Figure 9.1, which represents the stakeholder landscape for destination management.

Stakeholder landscape for destination management

Stakeholder categories	Stakeholder types	Stakeholder concerns, issues, activities	Stakeholder images
Tourism sector stakeholders	DMOs, hospitality, attractions and events, transport, travel trade, media, employee organizations, associations	Profitability, growth, development, competition, innovation, support, advocacy, professional development	
Community	Community organizations, resident associations, business associations, special panels and task forces, others	Quality of life, wellbeing, sentiment, employment, housing, neighborhood quality, support, hospitality, usage	
Government	National, regional, state, provincial, territorial, local, other agencies	Policies, laws, regulations, support, restrictions, standards	
Environment	Protected areas, NGOs, conservation societies, environmental agencies, others	Protection, conservation, environmental awareness, cleanliness, lack of pollution	
Tourists	Leisure/pleasure, business, VFR, personal, other	Needs, wants, motives, expectations, experiences, satisfaction, loyalty, recommendations	

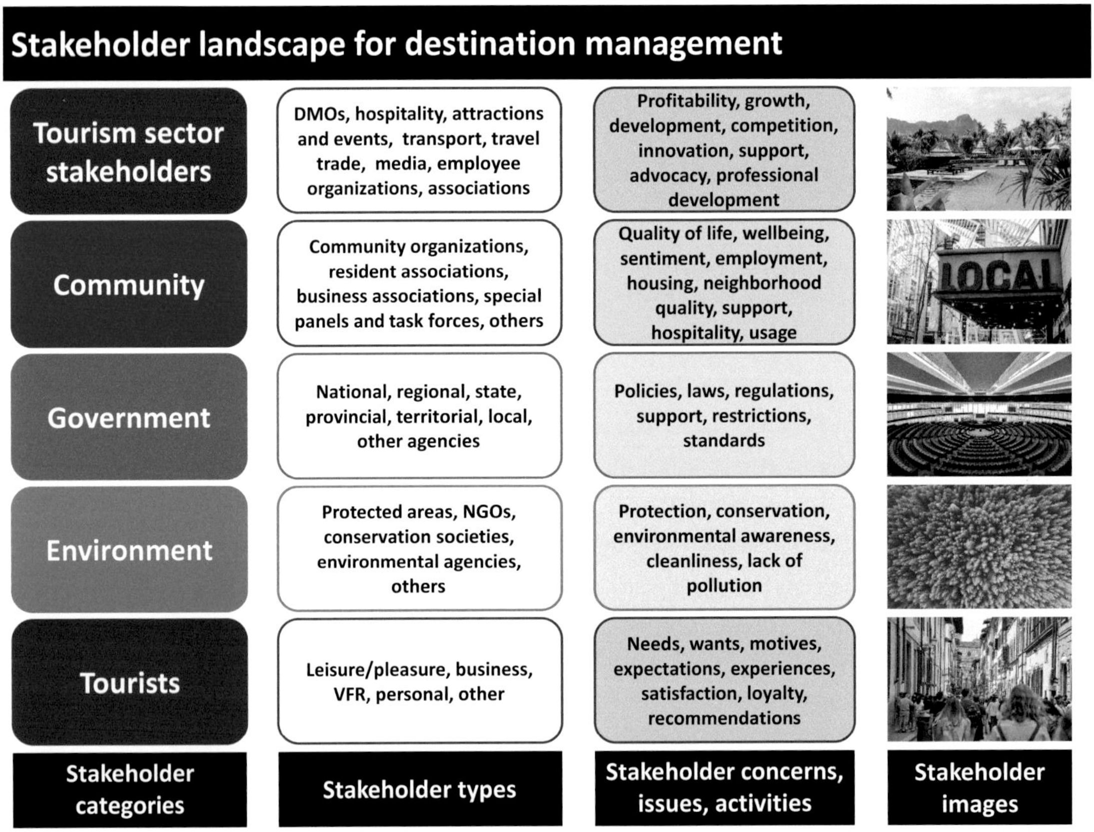

Figure 9.1 Stakeholder landscape for destination management.

In the third column of Figure 9.1, you can see the main concerns, issues, and activities of each stakeholder category. The DMO must be familiar with these as they are the foundation for building stakeholder relationships. You will hear more about these throughout this chapter.

Figure 9.2 is another model of stakeholders in tourism called the VICE model (visitors, industry [and government], community and the environment), and this highlights where DMOs must build relationships and encourage involvement. The VICE model for destination management relationships suggests the following:

- Visitors: Every destination must welcome, involve, and satisfy visitors.
- Industry and government: In a successful destination, the industry (tourism sector) must be prosperous and profitable. Government agencies should be effective in implementing tourism policies.
- Community: Tourism and DMOs must engage with and benefit local residents.
- Environment: The environment must be protected and enhanced.

Your author has adapted the VICE model into the ADVICE (authority, destination, visitor, industry, community, environment) model for visitor management, which you will learn about in the next chapter.

Stakeholder Relationships and Involvement

Destinations contain a wide variety of stakeholders, which are groups and individuals that can affect or be affected by the outcomes of destination management. The tourism sector stakeholders are those most directly involved with tourism. The DMO's relationships with tourism sector stakeholders are vital to its effectiveness. The DMO must build a strong destination tourism team from these stakeholders and have their complete support.

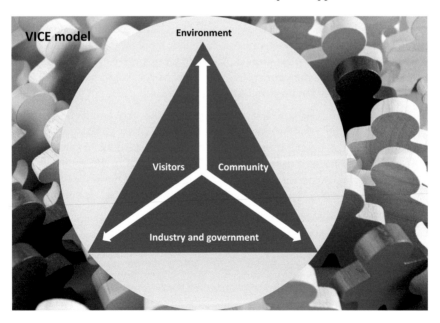

Figure 9.2 The VICE model for destination management relationships (TRREC 2006).

Chapter 1 identified five groups of stakeholders in tourism management: tourists, tourism sector organizations, community, environment, and government. Chapter 3 discussed the quality of life and well-being of local residents (community); visitors are covered in later chapters (Chapters 10, 16–19). The chapter now focuses on stakeholder organizations, and it begins with a discussion of stakeholder theory and then follows with an identification of the different types of stakeholders found within destinations.

Stakeholders and Stakeholder Theory

Because this chapter is talking about stakeholders, you might want to know exactly what stakeholder means and what the basic theory is behind the concept of stakeholders. This concept of stakeholders has its origins in organizational theory and corporate management. It is attributed to R. Edward Freeman and his book, *Strategic Management: A Stakeholder Approach* (1984). Freeman's definition of a stakeholder was "any group or individual that can affect or is affected by the achievement of a corporation's purpose." In the case of this book, corporation needs to be replaced by DMO. Freeman's basic argument was that there were many more groups and individuals who had a stake in corporations than just its employees and shareholders. This is certainly very true of tourism and destination management because there are many groups and individuals involved, and many groups and individuals are affected by tourism within a destination.

DEFINITION

Destination stakeholders

Those organizations and individuals with a direct or indirect impact in the management of a destination for tourism.

For stakeholder theory as applied to corporations, Donaldson and Preston (1995) identified eight stakeholder groups: investors, customers, suppliers, employees, communities, trade associations, governments, and political groups. All these groups exist in a destination, although the DMO itself does not have the same types of investors as does a corporation. However, those providing the DMO with its funding can be considered the equivalent of investors.

There are many academic papers and practitioner books about stakeholder theory and approaches to stakeholder relationships and involvement. These publications highlight that all are not equal among an organizations' stakeholders; some stakeholders are more important than others. Organizations need to analyze and map stakeholders to determine how to manage their relationships and engage with different stakeholder groups. One of the most popular tools to use for this mapping is the Mendelow Power-Interest Matrix, which is shown in Figure 9.3.

DMOs need to prioritize stakeholders within the destination. The situations vary from destination to destination; however, it is likely that the tourism sector stakeholders will be in the top-right box in Figure 9.3 because they have a high interest in destination management and may also be highly influential or powerful.

Another relationship management strategy suggested for different groups of stakeholders is to contrast the potential for cooperation with the potential to threaten. Savage et al. (1991) suggested a classification of stakeholders based upon their potential to cooperate and potential to threaten the organization, shown in Figure 9.4.

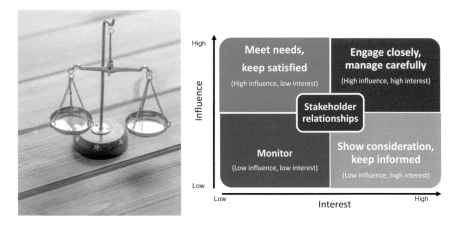

Figure 9.3 The Mendelow Power-Interest Matrix (Mendelow 1991).

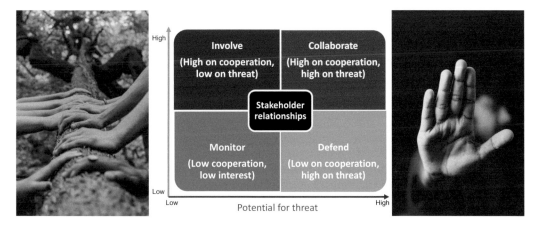

Figure 9.4 The potential to cooperate–potential to threaten matrix (Savage et al. 1991).

The four stakeholder relationship management strategies recommended based on Figure 9.4 are:

- Collaborative: Stakeholders with high potential to cooperate and with high potential to threaten.
- Involvement: Stakeholders with high potential to cooperate and low potential to threaten.
- Defensive: Stakeholders with high potential to threaten and low potential to cooperate.
- Monitoring: Stakeholders with low potential to threaten and low potential to cooperate.

This means that DMOs should focus on organizations and individuals who have a high potential for cooperation and do not engage as extensively with those where there is a low potential to cooperate.

Next, the need to "be connected" with each stakeholder category is discussed, beginning with tourism sector stakeholders.

Tourism Sector Stakeholders

Figure 9.5 shows the main tourism sector stakeholder types and a brief description of each of these eight tourism sector stakeholder groups is provided below:

1. Attractions: Natural and human-made attractions. These can be private-sector operations or run by government agencies or NPOs.
2. Events and festivals: The organizers of significant events and festivals held regularly in the local community. Once more, these may be private-sector operations or run by government agencies or NPOs.
3. Convention and meeting venues: Convention and exhibition centers.
4. Hotels and other accommodations: Hotels, resorts and specialist accommodations.
5. Restaurants and other food services: Restaurants, banquet halls, catering companies.
6. Transport: Motor coach, taxi, ferry, train and other transport companies.
7. Travel trade: Destination management companies, OTAs, travel agencies, tour operators, guides, meeting planners, incentive planners.
8. Media: Newspapers, magazines, TV and radio stations, and online media.

There are trade associations representing some or all of these sub-sectors of tourism. For example, there are associations for hotels, restaurant and food services, and attractions. These are also included under the definition of tourism sector stakeholders.

Some DMOs, and especially those that operate at a geographic level below a state, province or territory, have membership programs that are optional for tourism sector stakeholders. This is especially the case at city, county and regional levels (that are not governmentally administered regions). This in many cases introduces two distinct categories of tourism sector stakeholders for the DMO: members and non-members.

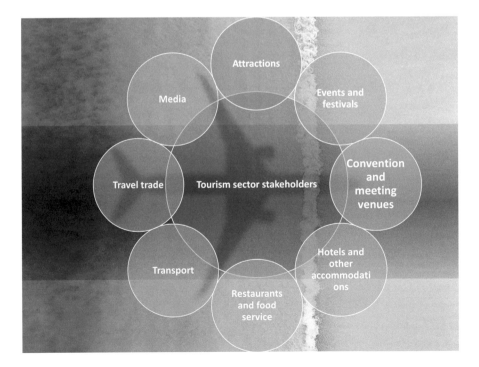

Figure 9.5 Tourism-sector stakeholders.

Another layer of complexity is introduced in stakeholder relationships if the DMO has a board of directors or an advisory board or committee of some type. These two concepts are not the same because a board of directors governs the DMO, but an advisory board/committee is there to provide advice and does not have direct power over the DMO and its executives. DMOs with boards of directors are becoming more common around the world, but they are particularly found in certain countries, and the USA is one of these. Ford et al. (2011) found more than 93 percent of CVBs in the USA have a governance structure that includes a board of directors. With the worldwide trend toward PPP DMOs, more of them are being run by boards of directors.

For DMOs with boards of directors, those stakeholders on the board are especially important. Additionally, it is reasonable to expect that members will be given a higher priority than non-members. You will hear much more about this later.

The sources of financial support for DMOs vary from country to country and sometimes by province and state as well. If the DMO is government-run and gets all its funding from government, then all tourism sector stakeholders should have equal priority. There are other situations in which DMOs are mainly funded through user-pay taxes, most commonly through taxes on rooms and entertainment. This may or may not influence these DMOs to give greater attention to the sources of the tax revenues (e.g., hotels, casinos, restaurants, etc.).

Figure 9.1 indicated that the main concerns, issues, and activities for tourism sector stakeholders were profitability, growth, development, competition, innovation, support, advocacy, and professional development. They expect DMOs to foster a healthy and sustainable business environment as a foundation for profitability, growth, and development. These stakeholders want DMOs to effectively counter competitors, and to be innovative and creative in so doing. Tourism sector stakeholders look for a mutually supportive relationship with DMOs and for DMOs to be strong advocates of tourism. Also, there is a need for DMOs to actively improve tourism through professional development and educational programs. You will appreciate that DMOs need to deliver on these expectations.

EXAMPLE 9.1

Sector Stakeholders Build Awareness of Tourism in Costa Rica

Tourism sector stakeholders can be powerful advocates for destinations as in this example from Costa Rica. Ticos is a nickname for people from Costa Rica.

> Sometimes, it is the sector stakeholders that are advocates of tourism as in this case from Costa Rica in Central America. "I depend on tourism is the name of the campaign launched by the group of Costa Rican tourism businessmen in order to educate and raise awareness among the population about the importance of tourism for the country. The campaign that began two months ago has been reinforced with videos that educate the national population on the importance that all Ticos depend on tourism, emphasizing that this is a chain, generating work for many people."
>
> (*The Costa Rica News* 2022)

Learning Point

DMOs and tourism sector stakeholders should join together to advocate on behalf of destinations.

Relationships with and Involvement of Tourism Sector Stakeholders

DMOs are transitioning from being just destination marketing organizations to becoming destination management organizations. Part of this new management responsibility is the relationship management and involvement of tourism sector stakeholders, and DMOs need to hone their skills in building and maintaining these contacts. Once again, it is much better for the DMO to approach this in a professional way and prepare a plan for how it will handle stakeholder relationships and involvement. A range of specific activities should be included (Fig. 9.6). DMOs are expected to provide leadership and coordination for the tourism sector, but they do not have this function with respect to local residents.

A description of these activities is now provided:

LEADING AND COORDINATING STAKEHOLDERS

Leadership, coordination, and governance is one of the roles of destination management. One of the sub-roles is for the DMO to be a coordinator of groups and individuals within the destination, including tourism sector stakeholders. Then, what is a coordinator, and what does coordination involve? For the purposes of this book, the following definition of coordination is used:

DEFINITION

Destination coordination

The coordinator convinces groups and individuals to work together harmoniously and in an organized way for achieving specific goals or objectives. Mainly, this involves the DMO working as the coordinator of tourism sector stakeholders.

1. Leading and coordinating stakeholders
2. Listening to stakeholders
3. Analyzing stakeholder opinions
4. Involving and engaging with stakeholders
5. Communicating with stakeholders
6. Informing stakeholders on programs and activities
7. Representing stakeholders
8. Celebrating successes with stakeholders
9. Evaluating stakeholder relationships and involvement

STAKEHOLDER

Relationships and involvement activities

Figure 9.6 Tourism-sector stakeholder relationship and involvement activities.

An example of coordination is when DMOs work with tourism stakeholders in arranging familiarization tours ("fams") for the travel trade and media within the destination. For example, Tourism Malaysia arranged a familiarization trip in 2022 for travel agents from Japan (*TTR Weekly* 2022).

Many DMOs have convention or business events services departments that coordinate the logistics for events with tourism stakeholders and others. London & Partners, the Mayor of London's official promotional agency, says "We've helped to build world-class events for thousands of delegates. We've supported international congresses, conventions and conference teams to deliver successful and inspiring events at scale" (London & Partners 2022). The Cape Town and Western Cape Convention Bureau in South Africa offers the following meeting and event services:

EXAMPLE 9.2

Cape Town and Western Cape Convention Bureau Services

Chapter 19 describes business event markets that are the main target for many DMOs. This example from South Africa indicates the types of services that DMOs can offer business event organizers.

> Our mandate is to secure meetings and conferences, and as a government agency we do not charge for any of our services. We can help you with the following:

- pre- and post-bid assistance
- review bid or event requirements
- assess financial requirements
- source and suggest suitable venues and service providers
- where applicable, apply for funding
- identify suitable legacy programs
- conference and meeting bid production and presentation
- conference and meeting bid promotion support material
- site inspection (flight arrangements on application)
- convention planning support
- introductions to service suppliers
- business sector introduction and creating networking opportunities (if applicable)
- public relations support and building attendance
- destination weblinks for conference websites and assistance in marketing events
- on-site event services
- facilitate visitor information booths
- welcome banners
- post-event servicing and evaluation
- BestCities network introduction.

(Cape Town and Western Cape Convention Bureau 2022)

Learning Point

DMOs are major providers of services for business event planners.

DMOs coordinate marketing, branding, and communications efforts of different types. The Department of Tourism in the Philippines coordinated the development of the Colors of Mindanao with the collaboration of five regional offices (Cebu Daily News 2022).

Some DMOs coordinate festivals and events in their communities. The MGTO organizes the annual Macao International Fireworks Display Contest (Fig. 9.7). Teams from various countries compete in this spectacular event held on the waterfront in Macao (MGTO 2022).

These are good examples of DMOs coordinating tourism sector stakeholders. What about leading and leadership, then? This is a topic that was discussed in detail in Chapter 6, but of course, it can be said now that there are many facets of leadership. Undoubtedly, DMOs and their executives need to be accepted as leaders by tourism sector stakeholders and must therefore earn the respect of many people. Apart from requiring personal charisma, DMOs need to be visionary and strategic in thinking and planning to be viewed as leaders. The leadership role is reinforced if DMOs are successful in gathering all the resources they need to operate successfully and if they can prove that these resources have been used effectively.

Listening to Stakeholders

DMOs must always keep the channels of communication open for listening to stakeholders' suggestions, issues and concerns. Some DMOs and their executives make a point of regularly visiting tourism stakeholders at their offices or places of business to hear stakeholders' ideas and share the latest news about the DMO's activities and successes. This is an excellent way of demonstrating that the DMO is actively listening to stakeholders. One executive of a large DMO (Rossi Ralenkotter, LVCVA) said this about the importance of listening:

Figure 9.7 Macao Government Tourist Office coordinates the Macao International Fireworks Display Contest.

EXAMPLE 9.3

The Importance of Being a Good Listener

Your author is a great supporter of this principle that is a quote from a former leader of a major US DMO.

> First and foremost, be a good listener. This helps you understand what someone really wants or what the real issue is. I spend a great deal of my time just listening to people . . . whether it's clients and stakeholders telling me about an issue or how I can help my staff by offering solutions.
>
> (Destinations International 2014)

Learning Point

You will often learn more from listening than from speaking.

Analyzing Stakeholders' Opinions

The DMO should periodically gauge the sentiments of stakeholders about the status of the tourism sector and major issues and challenges that they face in the future. One outstanding example of this activity is the Tourism Barometer survey conducted by Fáilte Ireland:

EXAMPLE 9.4

Fáilte Ireland Tourism Barometer

This example shows how a DMO keeps updated on progress in its tourism sector.

> The Fáilte Ireland Tourism Barometer is a survey of tourism businesses designed to provide insight into tourism performance for the year to date and prospects for the remainder of the year/for the following year.
>
> "Fáilte Ireland designed a questionnaire which was set up online by Strategic Research and Insight, an independent research agency. Fáilte Ireland distributed the survey link to its trade database on 10th May 2022."
>
> 732 valid responses were received.
>
> (Fáilte Ireland 2022)

Learning Point

DMOs should regularly poll tourism sector stakeholder opinions.

A second example is from Northern Territory Tourism (NT) in Australia (2022). Tourism NT surveys operators online four times per year in what it calls the Industry Sentiment Poll. The information gathered from research on stakeholders is valuable for the DMO in gauging stakeholders' feelings and sentiments about the current conditions and prospects for the tourism sector. This is also useful in tracking recent trends occurring in local tourism. It can be an early warning system for the DMO about emerging problems and issues in tourism. Moreover, it demonstrates to tourism sector stakeholders that the DMO highly values their opinions and input.

Involving and Engaging with Stakeholders

Chapter 8 discussed the team-building activities of DMOs, and one of the main goals of these efforts is to involve tourism sector stakeholders and create a greater sense of teamwork. The following eight types of teams were identified: advisory, crisis management, festival and event, planning, research, sales, tourism advocacy, and tourism ambassador and welcoming teams.

A common way to get tourism sector stakeholders involved with DMOs is to invite them to be partners or members. Tourism Vancouver Island in Canada requires online registration by its stakeholders, who receive the following benefits:

EXAMPLE 9.5

Tourism Vancouver Island Stakeholder Program

Stakeholder may be a better name than a member if this example is the right approach.

> Organizations taking the stakeholder route fund themselves through pay-per-play initiatives such as cooperative marketing programs and other promotional initiatives that allow stakeholders to effectively target regional, national and international travel consumers in affordable fashion.
>
> (Tourism Vancouver Island 2022)

Learning Point

Mutual benefits are generated through membership ("stakeholdership") programs.

Communicating with Stakeholders

The DMO must constantly keep in touch with tourism sector stakeholders and therefore needs to find the right channels to do so. Websites are now one of the most popular ways to communicate with stakeholders, but social media and printed materials like newsletters are also used. Some DMOs create members-only sections of their websites, whereas others have separate, dedicated websites for tourism sector stakeholders.

Many DMOs have decided to save trees and go paperless with e-newsletters, and this also helps increase the reach of the DMO news. By asking website visitors to sign up to receive e-newsletters, DMOs can build larger databases.

Another more formal way to ensure ongoing communications is by setting up advisory boards, councils or committees that give frequent input to DMOs and destinations. For example, in Germany there is the Advisory Council for Tourism Matters at the Federal Ministry for Economic Affairs and Energy.

A second case study is the Tourism Advisory Council of the Arizona Office of Tourism (2022) in the USA. The council has fifteen members who are appointed by the governor for terms of five years. It has representatives from recreational and tourist attractions, lodging, restaurant and food services, and transportation industries as well as other tourism businesses and the general public. The council assists and advises the director of the Arizona Office of Tourism in preparing the budget and establishing policies and programs that promote and develop tourism for Arizona.

Informing Stakeholders on Programs and Activities

Providing relevant information and data to tourism sector stakeholders encourages more professional and better informed decision-making. Once again, DMO websites are one of the best tools because much information can be placed there and accessed at the convenience of tourism sector stakeholders. An interesting example here is the PartnerNet website operated by the HKTB. By signing up, partners can access a great amount of up-to-date information and research on tourism in Hong Kong (HKTB 2022a).

Representing Stakeholders

The DMO is the most important representative for all the tourism sector stakeholders in a destination. The stakeholders may also belong to trade associations, but the DMO is the only body that represents tourism as a whole. For example, the DMO can periodically present the tourism sector's most pressing issues to leaders in government to ensure that these officials are aware of the issues and will consider taking steps to deal with them. An example of this is the National Tourism Day celebrated in India each January.

EXAMPLE 9.6

National Tourism Day in India

Many DMOs find the occasions to celebrate the tourism sector including India.

> Not many people know that January 25 is celebrated as National Tourism Day in India. It is a day that has been marked by the Indian government in order to promote tourism within the country. It's a day dedicated to educating people about the importance of tourism and the role it plays in the Indian economy. It is perhaps the best day to know how amazing a country India is when it comes to travel and tourism. Many of us dream of visiting alluring destinations abroad without considering how much there is to see in our own country.
>
> (Merala 2020)

Learning Point

DMOs are the voice of the tourism sector.

Another good example, which is both representing and listening, is with Visit Greenland, a national DMO. Most DMOs have visual image or media libraries, which are of great help to stakeholders and partners. In this way, DMOs are representing stakeholders by collecting and distributing tourism photography. Visit Greenland is a small DMO, and staff members were spending significant time in posting to photo-sharing sites and sending large photos to stakeholders and partners via Dropbox.com. Users were also finding it difficult to choose and find new images and gave this feedback to Visit Greenland. A solution was found to this problem in working with PhotoShelter for Brands, and now accessing the visual media library is much more convenient (Visit Greenland 2022).

Celebrating Successes with Stakeholders

It is important that the DMO and tourism sector stakeholders together celebrate the success stories of tourism within their destinations. This builds a sense of pride and excitement and reinforces the feelings of belonging to a vital sector of the economy.

One of the most popular types of activities that DMOs implement to achieve this purpose is tourism awards programs. Almost every destination in the world has these types of awards programs, and it is difficult to pick out specific examples. The Tourism Authority of Thailand (TAT) has run such a program every two years since 1996; it is used to reward best practices in the Thai tourism sector and to encourage tourism operators to strive for higher levels of professional standards. The three award categories for 2021 were attractions, accommodation establishments, and health and wellness enterprises. TAT also uses the awards program for promotional purposes and feels that it increases the credibility of Thai tourism among domestic and international visitors (Tourism Authority of Thailand 2021).

Evaluating Stakeholder Relationships and Involvement

The evaluation of performance in improving and enhancing stakeholder relationships and involvement is the final activity. Here are some good questions to include in this evaluation:

- How satisfied are stakeholders with their current levels of business?
- What do stakeholders see as the destination's current strengths and weaknesses?
- What are the major current issues in tourism from the stakeholder viewpoint?
- What do stakeholders expect the future trends in tourism in the destination to be?
- How satisfied are stakeholders with the DMO's marketing, branding, and communications programs?
- How satisfied are stakeholders with the DMO?
- How well respected is the DMO within the destination?

Figure 9.8 provides a summary diagram of the activities that should be included in the plan for stakeholder relationships and involvement.

There are two groups among tourism stakeholders that have special importance for DMOs. These are members and boards of directors, and now you will get to know more about interacting with these two groups of people. All the previously mentioned stakeholder activities apply to DMO members and boards; however, certain specific initiatives are required because these people have closer relationships with DMOs and their governance.

Relationships with DMO Members

Many non-governmental DMOs, including PPPs, operate membership programs, and the relationships with members require special attention. One estimate from Destinations International

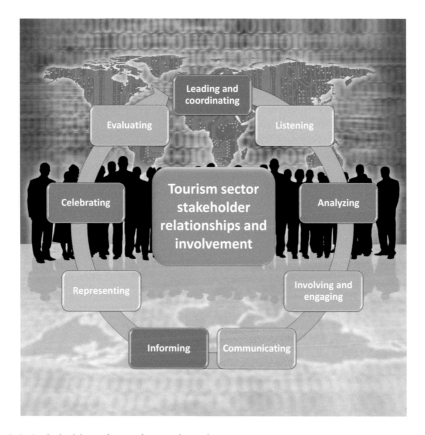

Figure 9.8 Stakeholder relationship and involvement activities.

is that 50 percent of DMOs operate membership programs and the other 50 percent are funded wholly by government.

What are the reasons for DMOs having membership programs (Fig. 9.9)? The willingness of stakeholders to belong as members confirms the relevancy and legitimacy of DMOs in their destinations. Moreover, DMOs use their membership numbers as an indicator of their influence and approval among stakeholders, as demonstrated in the following example for Cumbria Tourism in England.

EXAMPLE 9.7

Membership Benefits from Cumbria Tourism in England

Cumbria Tourism in this example clearly communicates its membership program benefits.

Cumbria Tourism is the official DMO for an important tourism county in northern England that includes the Lake District, Hadrian's Wall and the Pennines. It proudly announces on its website that it has many members and provides several reasons for joining:

- "We promote the Lake District, Cumbria as a leading destination to national and international visitors and offer a range of promotional activity for members of Cumbria Tourism to buy into.
- We offer specialist business and marketing advice and can visit you at your business. As a member you would also get access to legal and business development helplines.
- We work with suppliers and corporate businesses to negotiate discounts and savings on key services that underpin your business."

Cumbria Tourism also describes its print marketing, digital marketing, research, and events, and the benefits members can derive from these programs.

(Cumbria Tourism 2022)

Learning Point

DMOs depend on members for funding and also as a source for their credibility.

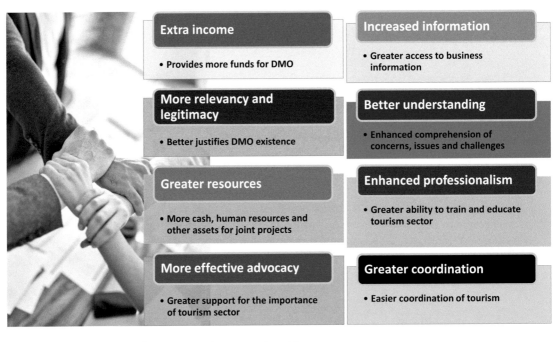

Extra income
- Provides more funds for DMO

Increased information
- Greater access to business information

More relevancy and legitimacy
- Better justifies DMO existence

Better understanding
- Enhanced comprehension of concerns, issues and challenges

Greater resources
- More cash, human resources and other assets for joint projects

Enhanced professionalism
- Greater ability to train and educate tourism sector

More effective advocacy
- Greater support for the importance of tourism sector

Greater coordination
- Easier coordination of tourism

Figure 9.9 Reasons for DMOs to have membership programs.

Membership fees represent a significant income source for many DMOs, and this is another reason for having membership programs. By uniting with members, DMOs can achieve and accomplish more, by co-investing financial, human and other assets in joint activities and projects (a form of co-creation). Joining hands with members is more impressive in advocating for the importance of the tourism sector. Closer relationships with members give DMOs greater access to business information on the tourism sector and a better feel for the pulse of tourism and its trends. Also, by being in closer and regular contact with members, DMOs have a much better understanding of the tourism sector's concerns, issues and challenges. DMOs can invest in their members through professional development, education and training and eventually increase the levels of professionalism in the tourism sector. It becomes easier for a DMO to coordinate when it has members who are cooperative and communicative and adopt similar standards.

Highly professional membership programs are a characteristic of effective DMOs. There are specific activities associated with successful membership programs, and these are listed in Figure 9.10.

Structuring Membership Benefits and Services

Members will join DMOs if they perceive there to be value in belonging. Therefore, DMOs must offer members meaningful and significant benefits and services to entice them to join. Generally, for DMOs, these benefits are business oriented and fall under the heading of marketing, branding, and communications; however, advocacy, professional development, training and education, and research information are becoming increasingly important.

DEFINITION

Advocacy

Programs and activities undertaken by DMOs or the tourism sector to influence public opinion or the policies and decisions of political, economic, or social institutions. This is often supported by advocacy research released in publications or presentations of various types.

DMO member relationships and involvement

1. Structuring membership benefits and services
2. Defining membership categories and setting fees
3. Staffing the membership function
4. Recruiting members
5. Serving members
6. Retaining members
7. Rewarding and awarding members
8. Evaluating member relationships and involvement

Figure 9.10 DMO membership activities.

The sharing of sales leads for potential business events is a typical benefit offered by city-based DMOs, especially where there is an emphasis on attracting conventions, meetings and other events. Figure 9.11 provides a list of potential DMO membership benefits (in alphabetical order):

- Access to research findings: Chapter 5 discussed the various types of research that DMOs conduct. Sometimes, DMOs limit the access to the findings to members or offer reduced prices for purchasing reports or data by members and charge non-members significantly more.
- Advocacy: Representing the interests of members in dealing with governmental agencies and other entities is an essential membership role for DMOs. They need to be the champions for the concerns and issues of members and ensure that the voice of the tourism sector is heard in the policy setting and budgeting of governments.
- Award programs: DMOs frequently operate award programs that are available to members. These operate on an annual basis, and there is a nomination and selection process.
- Discount programs: Some DMOs arrange for members to receive price reductions on the purchase of specific products and services, using the DMOs' bulk purchasing power. A specific example here is for exhibiting at tourism fairs and exhibitions.
- Familiarization tour participation ("fams"): DMOs frequently organize trips for travel trade and media people to sample the destination. It is very advantageous for a tourism operation to get exposure on these tours. Members are normally given preference for inclusion in familiarization tour itineraries.
- Leads and referrals: Members receive leads and referrals from DMOs for meeting planners and travel trade professionals who have shown an interest in the destination.
- Media exposure assistance: DMOs often help their members to get publicity in the media (traditional and online).
- Networking: Meeting and getting to know other members and DMO staff—networking—is a significant benefit because many tourism stakeholders need to work together to get business or solve problems of mutual interest.
- Professional development, training and education: Chapter 7 explained the types of educational and professional development programs being organized by DMOs and gave several examples. Normally, DMO members can participate in these programs free of charge or at reduced rates.
- Publication listings and descriptions: DMOs produce several publications each year, and members are listed in these free of charge. These typically include visitor guides, meeting planner guides, and calendars of events.
- Receipt of DMO materials: Members receive supplies of DMO publications as well as getting the DMO's own newsletter.
- Recognition: The DMO issues physical or digital certificates, stickers and other display materials that validate membership of the destination's official tourism body. Official membership lists are available online or in hard copy verifying memberships. Belonging to the DMO may be required to apply for government grants or other sources of support.
- VIC information distribution: Members can have their printed materials displayed and distributed at VICs operated by DMOs.
- Website and social media listings and descriptions: DMOs often list and describe the members on their official tourism websites, and this gives members outstanding online exposure.

The Greater Miami Convention and Visitors Bureau in Florida provides an excellent case study in offering cooperative marketing opportunities:

- Access to research findings
- Advocacy
- Award programs
- Discount programs
- Familiarization tour participation
- Leads and referrals
- Media exposure assistance
- Networking
- Professional development, training and education
- Publication listings and descriptions
- Receipt of DMO materials
- Recognition
- Visitor information center information distribution
- Website and social media listings and descriptions

BENEFITS

DMO membership benefits

Figure 9.11 Benefits from DMO memberships.

EXAMPLE 9.8

Cooperative Marketing Opportunities with the Greater Miami Convention and Visitors Bureau

This large US city DMO has an active membership program described in the example.

> The Greater Miami Convention and Visitors Bureau (GMCVB) does a great job of presenting cooperative marketing opportunities to tourism sector stakeholders. In the GMCVB document, Digital and Print Advertising Opportunities 2021–2022, these opportunities are:
>
> - Digital advertising on MiamiandBeach.com
> - Digital advertising on Miami Insider e-newsletter
> - Digital advertising in sponsored email
> - GMCVB "Partner of the Week" opportunity
> - Travel trade sales events
> - Miami Temptations programs
>
> (GMCVB 2022)

Learning Point

DMOs must be very clear and specific about membership benefits.

Defining Membership Categories and Setting Fees

DMOs often have different membership categories, and member benefits vary for each category. This is usually done in a classification by tourism sector stakeholder type (e.g., hotels, attractions, restaurants, etc.), but there are other approaches that accord to the scope of the benefits that a member desires.

Although some DMOs have free memberships, most charge for membership, and this represents a source of income. However, membership programs seldom if ever represent a major source of funding for DMOs. More important for the DMO is the bonding that is formed with members and the members' support for the organization and its programs and activities. The general appeal in getting tourism stakeholders to join is to work together with the DMO to grow the tourism sector in the destination.

Staffing the Membership Function

Members are important to DMOs and organizational sustainability for the long term, and so member relationships are frequently assigned to a team of staff in a dedicated membership department. DMOs may also have membership committees of their boards of directors.

The Philadelphia Convention and Visitors Bureau (PHLCVB) in the USA has the PHLCVB Partnership Program.

EXAMPLE 9.9

PHLCVB Partnership Program

Memberships become partnerships in Philadelphia—again like the name stakeholder, the name partner communicates a higher level of engagement with the DMO.

> By partnering with the PHLCVB, partners can dynamically market their organizations and services to meeting professionals, overseas leisure visitors, business travelers and convention attendees. In addition to supporting our partners' marketing efforts through extensive marketing and promotional benefits, the program provides partners the opportunity to grow, connect and build their business connections through education and networking events. As well, partners will have access to the latest research and industry trends designed to help them not only weather the current business climate but grow their businesses.
>
> (Philadelphia Convention and Visitors Bureau 2022)

Learning Point

It may be better for DMOs to market partnerships rather than memberships.

Recruiting Members

DMOs must constantly be searching for new members. The most likely membership pools for DMOs are the tourism sector stakeholders; however, the entire tourism value chain needs to be considered in membership drives. Additionally, seemingly unrelated companies and organizations may join for CSR and promotional reasons. The DMO membership recruitment net must be cast widely.

There is an assortment of tools and techniques for DMO member recruitment. These include asking existing members to refer potential new members. Using social media and websites to draw people to sign up online for memberships is now a very popular recruitment technique.

EXAMPLE 9.10

Destination Gold Coast (DGC) Recruits Members Online

Being part of a bigger team is one the main benefits communicated through this Australian DMO membership program.

> As a member, you will have the opportunity to receive advocacy through the peak tourism body for the Gold Coast, the potential to be involved with cooperative marketing efforts, invitations to industry-run training events as well as information and advice on marketing best practice and government funding opportunities. You will gain a connection to the tourism industry through networking and introductions as well as insights into industry research and qualified data. We look forward to working with you and having you as a part of our DGC team.
>
> (Destination Gold Coast 2022)

Learning Point

DMOs should emphasize the team-building and teamwork aspects of their membership programs.

Networking and member recruitment events and face-to-face, telephone and email membership sales can also be used. Public speaking by DMO executives and staff also helps to uncover potential members, as does frequent blogging and e-newsletters.

Serving Members

The support of members is crucial to all DMOs that have membership programs, and so continuously delivering meaningful member services is key. Primarily, this involves delivering all the benefits described above and shown in Figure 9.11.

Frequent communications that demonstrate the relevancy of the DMO are also a key to serving members. Apart from keeping in touch through newsletters, special member events organized by DMOs are important to cementing relationships. These range from monthly business or networking meetings to more elaborate annual conferences and tourism banquets. Being available to handle questions and inquiries from members is an essential part of this service, as is always listening for members' issues, concerns and business trends.

Retaining Members

As with all membership organizations, it is often very hard work to retain members year after year, and DMOs must continue to deliver high value and maintain frequent member communications if they want to stay relevant. It would not be unusual, for example, for a DMO to lose 10 percent to 20 percent of its members annually and mostly for reasons beyond the DMO's control, such as business ownership changes and closures.

Sending advance notice of membership fees coming due and offering discounts on early fee renewal payments are common techniques that promote retention. However, personalized approaches are usually more effective in reminding and convincing members to renew, such as phone calls and personal letters or e-mails from DMO executives. Quantifying the individual benefits that a specific member received for their current year's membership fees can be especially persuasive.

Rewarding and Awarding Members

Celebrating successes is mentioned beforehand as an activity in fostering tourism sector stakeholder relationships and involvement, and this is especially important in the recognition of DMO members. Award programs operated by DMOs are often the hallmark efforts in the acknowledgment of the excellence and contributions of outstanding members.

Apart from these grander celebrations, DMOs must do all that they can to provide recognition for all members. Badge of honor initiatives, such as issuing membership recognition certifications, online seals and physical decals, provide members with proof of belonging that they can use to build credibility with visitors and others.

Evaluating Member Relationships and Involvement

Gathering members' opinions on a frequent basis is essential for a membership-based DMO. This, for example, can be accomplished through conducting an annual DMO member survey that could include questions such as the following:

- Why did you decide to become a member of the DMO?
- How valuable do you think your membership has been?
- Why have you decided to continue your membership with the DMO?
- How important to you are the individual benefits offered by the DMO?
- How effective are the DMO's communications with its members?
- How satisfied are you with the DMO's marketing, branding, and communications efforts?
- In which DMO activities did you participate in the last year?
- How satisfied are you with the DMO?
- How well respected is the DMO within the destination?
- Which programs or activities should the DMO add that will increase the value of your belonging?

Relationships with DMO Boards of Directors

It can be said that without doubt the stakeholders on boards of directors take on great significance for DMOs and their executives because boards often have direct power over the DMOs and their executives. Boards of directors were explained in Chapters 6 and 7 because they provide leadership and are directly involved in destination governance. However, in this chapter you learn about some of the basic considerations for boards and their relationships with DMOs. Figure 9.12 provides a list of many of the most important considerations for board of director relationships. Each of these board relationship considerations are now discussed.

Board Composition

The way that DMO boards of directors are created varies greatly across the world, and it is difficult to generalize about their composition. The main differences lie in the legal status of the DMO. Boards range from ones in which all the members are appointed through a strict procedure set by government (over which the DMO has little control) to situations where the DMO can more freely elect most board members subject to certain conditions. For example, if the DMO is a NPO at a city or local level, it usually has more freedom to select board members.

VisitBritain has all its members being appointed by specific government agencies in the UK. The board includes the chairman of VisitBritain and four board members appointed by the secretary of state for Digital, Culture, Media and Sport and three other people in an Observer status. England, Northern Ireland, Scotland and Wales are all represented as well (VisitBritain 2022).

Another example of an externally appointed board is for Tourism Australia. There is a Tourism Australia Board Charter that spells out all the rules and policies for the board (Tourism Australia 2022). In this case, the federal minister responsible for tourism appoints eight of the members of this nine-person board, and the ninth member is the managing director of Tourism Australia. VisitBritain and Tourism Australia are statutory bodies that were established by special pieces of legislation in the UK and Australia, respectively. In these situations, the DMO itself has little if any control over board composition.

Board Size

Boards of directors vary in size from under ten to thirty or more. As you previously saw, Visit-Britain (2022) has a board of eight people (five voting and three non-voting), and Tourism Australia (2022) also has a nine-person board. The LVCVA has fourteen board members (LVCVA 2022); the HKTB has nineteen (HKTB 2022b); while New Orleans & Company has more than

Figure 9.12 Considerations for DMO board of director relationships.

twenty board members (BIZ New Orleans 2020). So it is hard to recommend an ideal size for a board, and indeed there are two contradictory considerations. The board of directors needs to be small enough to make decision-making more convenient and easier to coordinate. However, the board must be large enough to represent all the tourism sector stakeholders within the destination. Generally, boards with twenty or more people are difficult to manage and coordinate, whereas boards of fewer than ten people are unlikely to represent all the tourism sector stakeholders within the destination. In actual practice, most boards of directors have between ten and nineteen members.

Board Member Recruitment and Selection

From what has just been said, you can see that some DMOs can choose board members, whereas others must accept boards that others, typically governments and specific politicians, select. So for the first group of DMOs, board member recruitment and selection is a very important issue.

Ford et al. (2011) indicate that many DMOs in North America and especially in the USA are NPOs, and they recruit board members who can help the DMO access important resources and provide specific types of expertise. As mentioned earlier, the DMO must also determine which stakeholder groups are the most important (or salient) and ensure that these stakeholder groups are represented on the board of directors. For example, where DMOs are being funded through user taxes that are collected and distributed by local governments, it is important to have local government representation on boards. As Sheehan and Ritchie (2005) found, it is very helpful to have representatives from hotels and hotel associations and attractions and attraction associations because DMOs work very closely with these tourism sector stakeholders.

Board Orientation

Preparing board members for their tasks through proper orientation needs to be given a high priority. Again, it cannot be assumed that all people understand what DMOs do and what their priorities are. Board member orientations should cover topics including the destination and DMO vision, DMO mission, DMO business and marketing plan, expectations of board members and board code of conduct.

Board Member Motivation

Unlike corporate boards, the boards of directors of many (but not all) DMOs are unpaid and essentially are volunteering their time and services. This is an important consideration in the DMO–board relationship because the DMO must find non-financial means to motivate and reward volunteer board members. This is one of the greatest challenges for DMOs and especially those that are NPOs that are not statutory bodies. Nowadays, people have so many demands on their time, and it is difficult to motivate them when there is no monetary compensation. The responsibility for board member motivation falls mainly to DMO executives, and success depends on the strength and quality of the relationships that executives build and maintain with board members.

Board Member Conduct

Board members make decisions that involve the use of the DMO's resources. Therefore, it is common for DMOs to have codes of conduct and stated policies regarding conflicts of interest that the board must follow. Tourism Nova Scotia (2022) in Canada provides a good example of a code of conduct for their DMO board of directors, which also applies to all employees. This code includes requirements on loyalty, corporate opportunities, confidential information and conflict of interest.

DEFINITION

Conflict of interest

"A conflict of interest arises when a director or employee's private or personal interest supersedes or competes with his or her official duties with TNS [Tourism Nova Scotia]. This could arise from an actual, potential or perceived conflict of interest of a financial or other nature. Directors and employees must avoid not only actual conflict, but the potential for conflict and perceived conflicts" (Tourism Nova Scotia 2022).

Board Members' Terms of Office

The terms of office of board members are another important consideration for DMOs. Generally, appointments to DMO boards are for two or three years and may be renewable for one additional term. Most DMOs with boards have a member rotation pattern such that there is an overlap in lengths of term so that there is more continuity. In other words, they try to avoid situations where board members are all new at the same time.

Board Performance Assessment

Boards need to assess their overall performance each year to ensure that they are achieving their purposes. In addition, the performance of every individual board member should be assessed and feedback provided to them. In their excellent article about nonprofit CVB boards, Ford et al. (2011) suggested five basic propositions:

1. A nonprofit board that has directors representing critical or key stakeholder groups will be more successful than one that is less representative.
2. Nonprofits that take the time and effort to ensure proper board composition, size and term of office will be more effective than those that are less successful.
3. More successful nonprofits' executives are more likely to provide a formal orientation program for board members than those who are less successful.
4. Providing the rewards that motivate each board member will increase the likelihood that the board member will be more engaged in the activities and mission of the organization.
5. Boards and board members whose performances are evaluated annually will be more effective in helping a CVB to understand its future selection needs more than performance that is evaluated less often.

EXAMPLE 9.11

Irving (Texas) CVB Board of Directors

This Texas example describes how the DMO's board of directors operates.

A department of the City of Irving, the Convention and Visitors Bureau reports to a board of directors appointed by the Irving City Council. Board terms are two-year commitments; appointees may serve a maximum of three consecutive terms. The board of directors makes recommendations to the City Council about convention facilities, assists with attracting visitors to the city and hires the executive director; it is a policymaking board. Board member "job descriptions" have been offered by the board and business development committee. Annually, board members conduct a self-evaluation.

(Irving Convention and Visitors Bureau 2022)

Learning Point

Clear operating guidelines and procedures must be established for DMO boards.

Critical thinking question (CTQ17)

Is it wise for a DMO to pay greater attention to some tourism sector stakeholders. Why or why not?

As you can see, DMOs need to give special attention to the needs of their members and boards of directors. It is especially critical that DMOs have the support of these two groups. Farley (2019) suggested that there is an academic knowledge gap on the role of DMO board relations and your author definitely agrees. More research is needed on this topic.

Relationships with Community Residents

Figure 9.1 suggests that the main concerns, issues, and activities of local residents are quality of life, well-being, sentiment, employment, housing, neighborhood quality, support, hospitality, and usage. You learned about quality of life and well-being in Chapter 3 and also about the importance of regularly analyzing resident sentiment (attitudes and opinions) about tourism in their communities. Residents are concerned about having good employment opportunities and housing, and that quality is maintained in their neighborhoods. DMOs and the tourism sector hope that residents will be supportive of tourism, create an environment of hospitality and welcome for visitors, and also patronize tourism businesses.

Community Resident Relationships and Involvement

You already know that in the past, DMOs focused much of their attention on marketing, branding, and communications and these efforts were directed at people living outside of their destinations. There was a tendency to neglect the people in the destination and especially local residents. DMO leaders thought they would be judged on the results of external marketing, and most emphasis was put there.

Things have changed, and if DMOs ignore residents, they do so at their own peril. Local community support of and involvement in tourism are essential. As the leaders and coordinators for the tourism sector, DMOs must reach out and get the broad support of their communities. One of the ways to accomplish this in a professional fashion is to prepare a specific plan, and you will hear about the types of activities in such a plan.

One of the dominant themes in this chapter is the need for ongoing communications with the local community and for actively involving residents. Above all, the DMO must recognize that it has external markets (tourists) and internal markets (residents and tourism sector stakeholders) to serve and needs the support and involvement of both to be successful.

The word "community" is a very broad term and includes everyone who lives and works in the destination. However, for the purposes of this chapter, two specific groups are identified and discussed. Local residents are the people who permanently live in the destination; they may work in the tourism sector, but usually most residents are not involved in tourism. Also included are their elected representatives, community and interest groups and non-tourism businesses.

Importance of Community Relationships and Involvement

Encouraging community relationships and involvement is one of the roles of destination management. As you read in Chapters 1 and 3, DMOs need to have ongoing communications and interactions within local communities. Local residents must support tourism and fully comprehend its economic (and non-economic) contributions. This point was well highlighted in a study of twenty-five Canadian destinations by Bornhorst et al. (2010):

EXAMPLE 9.12

Importance of Community Relationship Management

This example based on a research study confirms the importance of community relationships for DMOs.

> A compelling finding in this study for practitioners is the number of responses highlighting the importance of relationship management within the destination by the DMO. If DMO executives cannot effectively manage relationships within the destination, specific resource inputs (such as funding) from both the private and public sector may become impaired, thus threatening the very existence of the organization.
>
> (Bornhorst et al. 2010)

Learning Point

DMO success and survival can hinge of the quality of community relationships.

Bornhorst et al. (2010) separately identified the success determinants of the DMO and the destination. They defined three sets of factors:

1. input variables (resources to the DMO and products to the destination);
2. process variables (marketing, community support, suppliers/other organization relations, and operations [management/services]);

3. performance variables (ROI for DMO, visitor numbers and visitor experience for the destination).

Figure 9.13 shows the process variables and highlights the influence of community relationships and involvement on the success of the DMO and the destination. The DMO needs community resident support, and tourism in the destination also requires the backing of locals. You will also notice from Figure 9.13 that marketing is another determinant of DMO and destination success.

For the DMO, there are two other success determinants: relationships with suppliers and other organizations and operations (management/services). The first of these is what this chapter refers to as tourism sector stakeholder relations. The second is the operational activities of the DMO, which in the Canadian study, were mainly marketing and management and to a lesser extent, service and product development.

You will remember from the discussion of the destination product in Chapters 1 and 7 that the feeling of welcome from residents was viewed as being important to the success of tourism. If residents do not support tourism or their relationship with the DMO is not good, they may be unfriendly toward tourists. Again, it is recommended that DMOs fulfill this destination management role by being proactive rather than waiting for opportunities to engage with and involve the local community.

Having community support is the major desired outcome from the community relationship role of destination management, but there is a longer list of reasons and potential benefits that result from building and maintaining closer relationships with local residents (Fig. 9.14). Here is a description of these eight community resident roles:

- Residents are potential customers of the tourism sector.
- Residents interact and share local facilities and services with tourists.

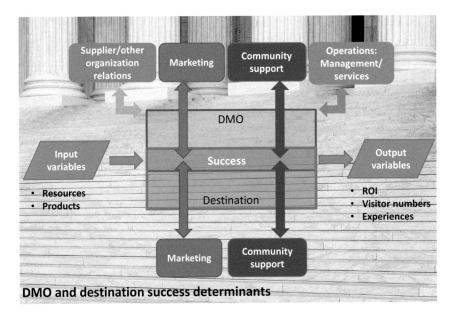

Figure 9.13 Determinants of DMO and destination success (Bornhorst et al. 2010).

- Residents can give tourists an unforgettable experience of welcome (and unfortunately, the other way as well).
- Residents take their friends and relatives to local attractions, restaurants, shops and other tourism venues.
- Residents vote, and political leaders are concerned about their opinions.
- Residents write about their communities on paper and in blogs and microblogs. It is much better for tourism if they do so in a positive way.
- The local community is a labor pool for the tourism sector; if residents positively perceive tourism, they may be more willing to work in the sector.
- Tourists often ask local people for directions and advice on what to do and see and where to eat in the community.

Community roles in destinations

Potential customers	• Residents spend money at tourism businesses	Share facilities	• Residents share spaces with visitors
VFR influencers	• Residents bring friends and relatives to tourism businesses	Provide welcome	• Residents can provide a strong welcome
Voters in elections	• Residents vote for their favorite local politicians	Information providers	• Residents give directions and information
Labor pool	• Residents work in tourism businesses	Content sharers	• Residents post blogs and reviews

Figure 9.14 Community roles in destinations.

EXAMPLE 9.13

Palau Plans to Become World's First Carbon Neutral Destination

This is an example of a small country that has ambitious goals in dealing with climate change.

> With climate change a very real threat to Palau's existence, Sustainable Travel International is implementing a project in partnership with Slow Food and the

Palau Bureau of Tourism to help the archipelago become the world's first car-bon neutral destination. The project will combat climate change and boost community resilience by:

- neutralizing tourism's carbon footprint;
- improving the livelihoods of local food producers;
- increasing local food security;
- empowering women to participate more fully in the tourism value chain;
- conserving coastal ecosystems that act as carbon sinks;
- reducing food waste and building a circular economy.

(Sustainable Travel International 2022)

Learning Point

DMOs should be more active in promoting the low-carbon economy.

All this discussion underscores the crucial importance of community relationships and involvement to the DMO and the tourism sector in general. The next section, therefore, discusses how community relationships and involvement should be planned.

Community Relationship and Involvement Planning

Some DMOs prepare annual community relationship and involvement plans; others include this as a component of marketing or business plans. This demonstrates a professional commitment by DMOs to engage with and involve their communities. What specific activities should be included in such a plan? The nine priority activities that the planning should cover are shown in Figure 9.15 and then explained.

Analyzing Community Residents' Attitudes and Perceptions

The DMO periodically needs to do research on community residents' perceptions of tourism within the destination. This was previewed in Chapters 3 and 5 with research study examples from several destinations. It is critical to determine how residents feel about tourism, and academic scholars have contributed many studies from different viewpoints since around the mid-1980s. You already learned about this research in Chapters 3 and 5. These were studies by tourism scholars rather than by DMOs. However, there seems to be some consensus forming from these research studies. Residents generally acknowledge that there are positives and negatives to tourism and that if their overall assessment of tourism is positive, they will be supportive. Educating residents about tourism and making them more aware of both the positive and negative impacts appears to be the best way forward for destinations and DMOs in the future.

Recent (and pre-COVID) developments in prominent European cities suggest that a back-lash against tourism occurs when there is overcrowding and competition for use of places and resources and when property values escalate because of tourism. With these concerns growing in Europe and other popular destinations along with the threats of terrorism where tourists congregate, it is now even more important that DMOs listen to and communicate with residents.

Figure 9.15 Priority activities in community relationship and involvement planning.

Communicating with the local community

The DMO must find ways and open more channels to maintain an ongoing dialog with the local community. DMOs do this through a combination of social media, websites and more traditional channels, such as open houses and other resident events and media publicity. For example, you may never have heard of Cabarrus County in North Carolina in the USA, but its DMO's communication with residents reflects a powerful message. The Cabarrus County Convention and Visitors Bureau (2022) delivers the message through its website that each local household saves an average of $115 in state and local taxes in 2020 (it was more before the pandemic) because of tourism.

The most important part of this communications is simply telling local people about what the DMO has done and is doing. It cannot be assumed that every local resident knows about the DMO and fully comprehends what a DMO does. So raising the visibility of the DMO needs to be a goal of local community communications.

Educating the Community

It cannot be assumed that residents know what the tourism sector encompasses or how tourism benefits the community. Only those who work in the tourism sector and have studied tourism management truly understand tourism. It is not wrong to say that most uninformed people tend to underestimate the positive impacts of tourism. Thus, it is not only important to regularly communicate with residents, but an ongoing effort to educate them about tourism is also needed.

There are many good examples around the world of DMOs developing materials and implementing programs to educate their communities about tourism. For example, the MoTCE in Indonesia began a tourism awareness campaign in July 2022. Another good case study is from Grenada in the Caribbean and its awareness campaign.

EXAMPLE 9.14

Grenada Tourism Awareness Campaign

Grenada educates its residents about tourism in this example.

> Welcome to the tourism awareness campaign website of the Grenada Tourism Authority. This campaign was launched in 2017 to create awareness about the benefits of tourism to Grenada, Carriacou and Petite Martinique. On this site you can find information about tourism in Grenada including statistics, our Tourism and Me Booklet, videos, audio messages, information about the environment and much more! Share this site with your family and friends.
>
> The Tourism and Me Booklet is both a physical and digital book for children which comprises of; what is tourism, who is a tourist, careers in tourism, crossword puzzles and games, multiple-choice questions, a tourism pledge and so much more.
>
> (Grenada Tourism Authority 2022)

Learning Point

Greater resident support may result from higher awareness levels of tourism.

Many community tourism education efforts are targeted at the general public, meaning all local residents. Others are more precisely targeted, as is the tourism awareness program in Jordan. The Ministry of Tourism in Jordan announced a national plan to raise the awareness of tourism in early 2017. Working in partnership with Jordan's government education ministries and the Jordan Tour Guides Association, this plan is intended to reach five million Jordanian students in the next five years (*Jordan Times* 2017).

Involving and Engaging with the Community

Educating communities increases residents' knowledge and comprehension about tourism; however, participation deepens understanding and commitment. Involving and engaging residents in tourism can be more effective and longer lasting than only telling them why tourism is important. Just to make sure that you are not confused here, involving means "doing something to" and engaging is "doing something with" local community residents. Looking around the world, there is a huge range of involvement and engagement from DMO events for residents to CBT, in which it is the communities themselves that run tourism.

One type of involvement strategy is to give local community residents samples of what is on offer free of charge or at a much-reduced price for a short time. A great example here is the Residents' Festival in York, England (Visit York 2022). During a weekend, the residents of York are given free admission to local attractions and special discount rates at restaurants (Fig. 9.16).

Figure 9.16 Jorvik Viking Centre, York, England.

The York Residents' Festival, England

This is a great example of involving local people in tourism.

> Organized by Make It York, this annual festival is our way of saying a HUGE "thank you" for the warm welcome you give to York's 8.4 million visitors.
>
> (Make it York 2022)

> York Residents' Festival is returning this January with over seventy attractions, events and offers. Taking place predominantly over the weekend of 29th–30th January, some offers are extended for up to a week exclusively for York residents. Major attractions in the city will be offering free entry to York residents, including York Minster, JORVIK Viking Centre, York Castle Museum and Merchant Adventurer's Hall. For theater lovers, there'll be exclusive behind the scenes tour available to book at York Theatre Royal, Grand Opera House and Joseph Rowntree Theatre.
>
> (Turner-Chaplin 2022)

Learning Point

Giving locals samples of tourism is a great way to build support and awareness of the sector.

Another set of great examples here are the Be a Tourist in Your Own Town programs that take place in selected cities in Canada and the USA. Several destinations in British Columbia, for example, organize these events annually including Victoria and Kelowna. These are community-wide programs that are designed to get local people to try out local tourism attractions, restaurants and other destination facilities and services. In so doing and after having a first-hand experience, residents have a better and more accurate understanding of tourism in their hometowns. They are more likely to recommend places to friends, relatives and others if they have been there themselves. When they encounter visitors who ask them for advice, they are also in a much better position to say where to go and what to do.

A third outstanding case study is from New York City and NYC & Company's See Your City program. This initiative encourages New Yorkers to explore the city's five boroughs and neighborhoods.

EXAMPLE 9.16

See Your City of NYC

Larger cities benefit from promoting specific neighborhoods as has happened in New York City.

> NYC & Company asked for help inspiring travel to under-the-radar NYC neighborhoods. Bellweather's founding partners, Emily Lessard and Louis Lee, created the See Your City brand and campaign, now beloved by locals and visitors alike. The vibrant brand identity reframes lesser-known NYC neighborhoods as exotic travel destinations, pairing beautiful images with humorous copywriting and local content. We also created the social media strategy, which integrates See Your City Social Media Ambassadors and user-generated images throughout. The branding for the campaign combines passport- and stamp-inspired logos, a vibrant color palette, and bold typography. These bold brand graphics are combined with humorous and snarky copywriting, seen in the tagline: "For some it's the trip of a lifetime, for you it's just a subway ride away." The brand voice is carried through all of the elements and is crucial for the campaign to connect with discerning locals.
>
> (Bellweather 2022)

Learning Point

Neighborhood marketing has great potential for city tourism destinations.

Theme years are another type of strategy for generating greater resident involvement in tourism. Scotland has organized several theme years, including 2022—Year of Stories, 2021—Year of Coasts and Waters, and 2018—Year of Young People (VisitScotland 2022). Ireland staged The Gathering in 2013, and it was highly successful (Fáilte Ireland 2013).

Listening to the Community

The DMO should always have open channels of communication to the community and not just when a formal research study of resident perceptions is being conducted. There are also certain key times at which listening becomes particularly important and strategic. When the destination is engaged in the preparation of a long-term plan for tourism, this is one of these special occasions when the voices of community residents need to be heard. In Chapters 2 and 4, you heard about how locals were involved in the preparation of the Sedona Tourism Sustainability Plan in Arizona.

When major tourism development projects are being considered is another vital time to get community resident input. Residents may have concerns about the environmental, social and cultural impacts of projects, and these opinions should be gathered and included in the project assessment. Sometimes, resident opinions on large tourism development projects spontaneously emerge, such as with the proposed reclamation project of Benoa Bay in Bali, Indonesia (Langenheim 2016). The luxury resort development faced stiff resident opposition because of potential environmental damage from land reclamation.

Lobbying for Tourism

Interacting with the elected representatives of political parties and government officials is crucial for DMOs and for tourism in any destination. At least some part of this effort is called lobbying; this means trying to influence or persuade public officials to support, think or even vote in a certain way. Generally, for tourism these are attempts to convince politicians to be more supportive of the sector.

This can be accomplished in different ways, as can be seen from some examples. The Tourism Works for Florida partnership in the USA arranges a Florida Tourism Day where DMO executives meet with state legislators in the state capital of Tallahassee and discuss the challenges that they are facing in tourism. In some cases, DMOs will engage the services of professional lobbyists to assist them in gaining more influence on government legislators. These are specialized public relations professionals who have built strong relationships with politicians and the political parties in their communities. This is especially important when the DMO funding is coming mainly from government or there are proposed changes to legislation that will significantly affect DMO operations or tourism in the destination.

Gaining Community Support

Various types of partnering with community residents and community groups were discussed in Chapter 8, including local ambassador programs. Another example is the City of Melbourne in Australia that has a volunteer program and recruits city ambassadors and volunteers for two VICs. The requirements for volunteering are the following: passionate about Melbourne, customer service focused, computer literate, available for one four-hour shift (either morning or afternoon) each week for a minimum of one year, team players who love engaging with people, flexible and willing to assist with additional shifts when needed, keen to participate in ongoing learning and training, and ability to demonstrate commitment to their values (City of Melbourne 2022).

These volunteer programs are aimed at individual residents, but there are other efforts that address entire communities. These efforts are often implemented to focus community attention on service quality or the hospitality levels in the destination. The goal is to raise overall community awareness and support for an initiative. An interesting example here is the Sapta Pesona code developed for tourism in Indonesia. With a logo like a sun (Fig. 9.17), the seven rays beaming from it are each representative.

Figure 9.17 The Sapta Pesona code for tourism in Indonesia. Source: http://sinartejo. blogspot.com/2016/08/pelajari-7-sapta-pesona-sebelum.html.

Representing Tourism in the Destination

DMOs must be the champions and cheerleaders for tourism in their destinations. This is a demonstration of the leadership, coordination, and governance role of destination management. The DMO must be the official representative of tourism in the community and assume all the duties that this involves.

As previously mentioned, the first part of this role is to continuously educate the local community about the positive impacts of tourism. A second part is being a team leader for the tourism stakeholders within the destination and keeping their enthusiasm for tourism always at a high level. The third part is to be a defender or protector of tourism when the sector is the subject of unfair or ill-informed criticism.

Gretzel et al. (2006) organized a forum of DMO executives in the USA to discuss the future challenges facing DMOs. One of the conclusions from this forum was that DMOs must establish themselves as "local experts, the "go-to" people, or the "information clearing house" for tourism in their communities. DMOs also should be perceived as valuable partners when major development projects were being contemplated locally. These are attributes of a leader and key representative of an economic sector in a community, and a DMO must have these attributes.

Evaluating Community Relationships and Involvement

DMOs must regularly assess their relationships with their communities and the extent of involvement of local community residents. This should be accomplished through research, and approaches to gathering the information and data were already discussed.

With the intensity of competition for tourist markets, DMOs are under increasing pressure to show excellent performance in completing their destination marketing, branding, and communications role. So in reality, it is difficult for DMOs to devote time and energy to local community relations because there is constant pressure and stress to deal with external marketing. This has implications for DMO staffing because steps must be taken to ensure that community relations activities are not neglected. Some DMOs deal with this by appointing specific staff members to coordinate and monitor the implementation of community relations initiatives. Some DMOs go even further and have a separate division or department to look after community relations.

Figure 9.18 summarizes the nine priority activities that go into community relations planning for destination management, and it is called the community resident engagement wheel. The background visual is used to communicate that DMOs need grassroots support from local community residents. As you learned at the outset of this chapter, community resident relations are a new endeavor for many DMOs, but it is now crucial that they get fully involved and view this role as being just as important as destination marketing and promotion.

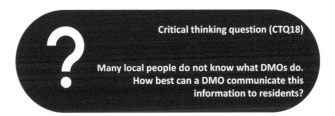

Critical thinking question (CTQ18)

Many local people do not know what DMOs do. How best can a DMO communicate this information to residents?

Relationships with Government

Government agencies at various levels have a significant influence on destinations and DMOs. As you know from Chapter 6, governments are a major source of funding for most DMOs. In

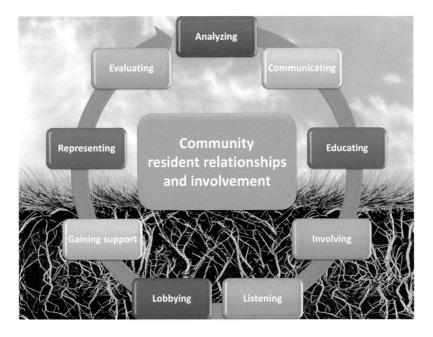

Figure 9.18 The community resident engagement wheel for destination management.

Figure 9.1, you can see that policies, laws, regulations, support, restrictions, and standards were the concerns, issues, and activities identified for governments. Destinations and DMOs are influenced by government policies, laws, regulations, standards, and restrictions. You are well aware of how government restrictions on travel during COVID-19 adversely affected tourism globally. Conversely, the funding and other support from government agencies are highly beneficial for DMOs and destinations.

Government Relationships and Involvement

Earlier in the chapter, you heard about lobbying for tourism as well as the concept of advocacy. Here is a more formal definition of lobbying.

DEFINITION

Lobbying

"Lobbying, the oral or written communication with a public official to influence legislation, policy or administrative decisions, often focuses on the legislative branch at the national and sub-national levels. However, it also takes place in the executive branch, for example, to influence the adoption of regulations or the design of projects and contracts. Consequently, the term public officials include civil and public servants, employees and holders of public office in the executive and legislative branches, whether elected or appointed" (Organisation for Economic Cooperation and Development 2022: 7).

There are several purposes of building and maintaining good relationships with governments, elected officials, and civil servants. These include influencing government policy and decision-making, spurring governments to take action, educating lawmakers and government officials, and obtaining financial and other support.

EXAMPLE 9.17

Cabarrus County Holds a Legislative Reception

Engaging with government and politicians is extremely important for DMOs as the public sector is usually a major source of funding.

> As part of their efforts to advocate for the hospitality and tourism industry, the Cabarrus County Convention and Visitors Bureau [CCCVB] hosted a legislative reception at Charlotte Motor Speedway prior to the 63rd running of the Coca-Cola 600 on Sunday, May 29. With the goal of showcasing the significant economic impact of Cabarrus County's tourism industry, the CCCVB invited state and local elected officials to join them in Concord for the crown jewel event. Just before the green flag dropped, the reception provided the opportunity for Cabarrus County's hospitality and tourism leaders including

the CVB's board of directors to connect with representatives and highlight the industry's impact first-hand.

(WBTV News 2022)

Learning Point

Holding relevant events for public sector officials can be instrumental in building closer relationships with DMOs.

You should not get the idea that government relations is all about DMOs lobbying the public sector; it certainly is much more than that. Many DMOs are branches or departments of governments and, in this case, inter-agency relationships and coordination is a topmost priority, as shown in the example from Mexico. Governments also are in many cases advocates of tourism as you saw demonstrated in the tourism awareness campaign of the MoTCE in Indonesia.

EXAMPLE 9.18

Mexico Creates a Tourism Diplomacy Council

In this example, a country is shown to be using its foreign missions to market tourism.

Foreign Secretary Marcelo Ebrard and Tourism Secretary Miguel Torruco presided over the inauguration of the Tourism Diplomacy Council today in the Foreign Ministry. The council, created to improve the competitiveness of the country's tourism, will make recommendations on the planning, design and implementation of strategies to promote Mexico internationally. The Council will be comprised of Mexico's diplomatic staff abroad, twenty-eight well-known business executives and other experts committed to national tourism. This is a joint undertaking. The tourism ministry is responsible for the content of Mexico's tourism policy, while the Foreign Ministry's embassies and consulates will help promote Mexico in international tourism markets.

(Government of Mexico 2019)

Learning Point

Foreign embassies and consulates of countries can be of great assistance in marketing inbound tourism.

Relationships with the Environment

Chapter 7 indicated that the environment is a dimension of destination quality and natural environments play a major role in attracting visitors to places around the globe. Figure 9.1 shows that the major concerns and issues with the environment as a stakeholder are protection, conservation, environmental awareness, cleanliness, and the lack of pollution. You will remember that Chapter 2 reviewed destination sustainability and social responsibility and part of this was about the relationships among destinations, DMOs, and the environment.

One of the major roles of DMOs here is to build a greater sense of environmental awareness and to encourage tourism sector stakeholders, residents, and tourists to act responsibly in terms of protecting the environment. You can see this responsibility expressed in the example from Tourism New Zealand.

EXAMPLE 9.19

Responsibility at Tourism New Zealand

New Zealand sets an example for other countries in its concerns for the environment.

> To ensure tourism gives back more than it takes, we target high-quality visitors from key markets. Once here, it's important our visitors have a great experience, so we also guide them on traveling safely and caring for our home, people and culture. We want to ensure that tourism contributes across four well-being pillars:
>
> - Economy: The tourism economy thrives and grows adding incremental value to the New Zealand economy and its assets.
> - Nature: Tourism restores, maintains and nourishes the environment for the intergenerational benefit of New Zealand.
> - Culture: The tourism story and experience preserve and enhance our values, culture and heritage, the makeup of our identity.
> - Society: People in and part of tourism communities thrive through jobs, shared knowledge, and physical and mental well-being.
>
> (Tourism New Zealand 2022)

Learning Point

DMOs must show great concern for the environment and treat it as a prime stakeholder of the destination.

Relationships with Tourists

The main concerns, issues, and actions of tourists are their needs, wants, motives, expectations, experiences, satisfaction, loyalty, and recommendations (Fig. 9.1). These topics are the focus for Chapter 16 on consumer behavior and Chapters 17–19 on specific markets.

Relationships with Other Stakeholders

Have we missed any stakeholders in this chapter? Your sharp mind and eyes will have noticed that there has been no discussion of those who work for DMOs, nor of companies outside of tourism. DMO staff members are crucial stakeholders in destination management as you can imagine. Your author has had the honor of working with and knowing hundreds of DMO staff members. He has been hugely impressed by their passion and enthusiasm for their communities. However, since this is not a book on human resources management, it does not delve deeply into that topic.

EXAMPLE 9.20

DMO Staff—Passionate Local Experts

This example stresses the importance of the skills and knowledge of DMO staff.

> An important, and frequently cited strength of the current set of English DMOs, is the local knowledge and expertise that DMO staff possess. DMOs know their destinations, their brand and their tourism "offer" better than anyone else and are passionate about and committed to selling it to consumers whenever they get the chance. They can "story tell" about their destination, tying together its key strengths to develop an appealing brand that at its best can appeal to a wide range of visitors (domestic and international), tourism businesses and other regional players.
> (Department for Digital, Culture, Media and Sport 2021)

Learning Point

DMO staff are hugely important to destination and DMO success.

Chapter 6 included examples of DMOs working in partnership with entities that were not tourism sector stakeholders. You might recall, for example, that the TAT had entered into a partnership with a manufacturer of electric vehicles and many other examples could be cited.

Steps in Effective Stakeholder Relationships and Involvement

The specific steps a DMO must take to accomplish its stakeholder relationship and involvement role are to:

- prepare an annual stakeholder relationships and involvement plan;
- champion tourism and build excitement and enthusiasm for the sector within the destination, especially among tourism sector stakeholders;
- communicate regularly and openly with tourism sector stakeholders and local residents;
- convince tourism stakeholders to work together harmoniously and in an organized way to achieve the destination's goals and objectives;
- educate local residents to better understand tourism and its positive and negative effects;
- if applicable, provide meaningful benefits to DMO members and maintain frequent communications with members;
- invite the active participation and involvement of local residents and tourism sector stakeholders in the programs and activities of the DMO;
- lobby with people in government to ensure that tourism receives an adequate share of resources;
- provide information and data to tourism sector stakeholders to allow them to operate more professionally and profitably;
- if applicable, recruit, select, orient, motivate and assess board members;
- represent tourism within the destination in all matters that are likely to have a significant impact on the sector stakeholders from within their communities.

SUMMING UP

Stakeholder relationships and involvement are becoming a more important role of destination management as DMOs increasingly recognize that they must have the support of tourism sector stakeholders and local residents. This is putting much more pressure on DMOs not only to perform at a high level in external markets but also to be outstanding at building and maintaining relationships at home.

It is strongly recommended that a DMO prepare an annual stakeholder relationships and involvement plan that details how it proposes to interact with tourism sector stakeholders, locals, government agencies, and others. Destination stakeholders can be defined as any group or individual who can affect or is affected by the achievement of the DMO's goals and objectives and by the results of the tourism sector in general. These stakeholders include the tourism sector and local residents. The tourism sector stakeholders include attractions, events and festivals, convention and meeting venues, hotels and other accommodations, restaurants and other food services, transport, travel trade and media.

The portion of the stakeholder relationships and involvement plan dedicated to tourism sector stakeholders should encompass nine activities: leading and coordinating, listening, analyzing, involving and engaging, communicating, informing, representing, celebrating and evaluating. The portion of the plan dedicated to local residents should cover at least nine potential activities: analyzing, communicating, educating, involving, listening, lobbying (government), getting support, representing and evaluating.

Many DMOs operate membership programs, and they must ensure that members receive meaningful benefits for joining and continuously renewing their membership. Most of the member benefits provided by DMOs relate to the marketing, branding, and communications of members' businesses.

Boards of directors play an extremely crucial role for many DMOs around the world. The relationships between board members and the DMO can directly affect the DMO's effectiveness and credibility within the destination. The key issues and considerations relative to DMOs include board composition; board member recruitment, selection, orientation and motivation; codes of conduct and conflict of interest guidelines; board size and member terms of office; and board performance assessment.

The support of local residents is crucial to tourism and destination management success. As with tourism sector stakeholders, there is a set of specific steps in building and maintaining positive relationships within local areas and this is called the community resident engagement wheel.

Government relations and relationships with the environment must be given a high priority in destination management. The connections with tourists, DMO staff, and non-tourism companies and entities are also of great importance and must be built into the stakeholder relationships and involvement plan.

KEYWORDS

advocacy
board of directors
co-creation
codes of conduct

community resident engagement wheel
conflict of interest
engaging

familiarization tours
inter-agency relationships
involving
lobbying

membership programs
networking
professional development
public relations
relationship management

stakeholder landscape
stakeholder relationships
 and involvement plan
stakeholders
stakeholder theory

statutory bodies
theme years
tourism awards programs
tourism awareness
vice model

REVIEW QUESTIONS

1. How is the term "stakeholder" defined and how should a DMO determine which stakeholders are the most important?
2. Who are the tourism sector stakeholders within a destination?
3. How should a DMO maintain positive relationships with tourism sector stakeholders?
4. How do DMOs operate membership programs and what are the program benefits?
5. What are the most important considerations for the relationships between boards of directors and DMOs?
6. Why are community relationships and involvement important to destination management?
7. What are the reasons and benefits of having positive relationships with local residents?
8. What types of actions and initiatives should be included for managing relationships with local residents?
9. What are the main concerns in managing relationships with government and the environment?

REFERENCES

Arizona Office of Tourism (2022) "Tourism Advisory Council," https://tourism.az.gov/tourism-advisory-council

Bellweather (2022) "A Surprising Tourism Campaign That Reframes the Lesser-Known as Exotic," https://bellweather.agency/case-studies/see-your-city-marketing-and-advertising

BIZ New Orleans (2020) "New Orleans & Company Announces 2020 Board," www.bizneworleans.com/new-orleans-company-announces-2020-board

Bornhorst, T., Ritchie, J. R. B., and Sheehan, L. (2010) "Determinants of Tourism Success for DMOs and Destinations: An Empirical Examination of Stakeholders' Perspectives," *Tourism Management*, 31 (5): 572–589.

Cabarrus County Convention and Visitors Bureau (2022) "Who We Are," www.cabcocvb.com

Cape Town and Western Cape Convention Bureau (2022) "How We Can Help," www.wesgro.co.za/convention-bureau/how-we-can-help

Cebu Daily News (2022) "DOT Promotes Mindanao as Key Tourist Destination with Colorful New Brand," May 26, https://cebudailynews.inquirer.net/442093/dot-promotes-mindanao-as-key-tourist-destination-with-colorful-new-brand

City of Melbourne (2022) "City Ambassadors," www.visitmelbourne.com/regions/melbourne/practical-information/visitor-information-centres/city-ambassadors

Costa Rica News (2022) "Tourism Entrepreneurs in Costa Rica Continue to Reinforce Their Campaign 'Depending on Tourism'," August 19, https://thecostaricanews.com/tourism-entrepreneurs-in-costa-rica-continue-to-reinforce-their-campaign-depending-on-tourism

Cumbria Tourism (2022) "Join Us: Why Join Cumbria Tourism?" www.cumbriatourism.org/join-us/

Department for Digital, Culture, Media and Sport (UK) (2021) "The de Bois Review: An Independent Review of Destination Management Organisations in England," https://assets.publishing.service.

gov.uk/government/uploads/system/uploads/attachment_data/file/1011664/2585C_The_de_ Bois_Review_ACCESSIBLE__for_publication_.pdf

Destination Gold Coast (2022) "Destination Gold Coast Membership," www.destinationgoldcoast. com/membership

Destinations International (2014) "Hall of Fame 2014 Inductee: Rossi Ralenkotter," https://destinationsinternational.org/general-information/destinations-international-hall-fame

Donaldson, T., and Preston, L. E. (1995) "The Stakeholder Theory of the Modern Corporation: Concepts, Evidence and Implications," *Academy of Management Review*, 20 (1): 65–91.

Fáilte Ireland (2013) "The Gathering Ireland 2013: Final Report," www.failteireland.ie/FailteIreland/media/WebsiteStructure/Documents/eZine/TheGathering_FinalReport_JimMiley_December2013.pdf

—— (2022) "Tourism Barometer," May, www.failteireland.ie/FailteIreland/media/WebsiteStructure/Documents/3_Research_Insights/tourism-barometer-may-2022.pdf

Farley, J. (2019) "A Stakeholder Approach for Destination Management Organisations," in M. A. Camilleri (ed.), *The Branding of Tourist Destinations: Theoretical and Empirical Insights*, Bingley: Emerald Publishing, pp. 43–60.

Federal Ministry for Economic Affairs and Climate Action (Germany) (2022) "Tourism Advisory Board," www.bmwk.de/Redaktion/EN/Artikel/Ministry/advisory-boards-04-tourism-advisory. html

Ford, R. C., Gresock, A. R., and Peeper, W. C. (2011) "Board Composition and CVB Effectiveness: Engaging Stakeholders That Can Matter," *Tourism Review*, 66 (4): 4–17.

Freeman, R. E. (1984) *Strategic Management: A Stakeholder Approach*, Boston, Mass.: Pitman.

Government of Mexico (2019) "SECTUR, SRE Inaugurate Tourism Diplomacy Board to Promote Mexico Abroad," www.gob.mx/sre/en/articulos/sectur-sre-inaugurate-tourism-diplomacy-board-to-promote-mexico-abroad-208595

Greater Miami & Miami Beach Convention & Visitors Bureau (2021) *Digital and Print Advertising Opportunities 2021–2022*. Miami: GMCVB.

Grenada Tourism Authority (2022) "Tourism Awareness Campaign," https://tac.puregrenada.com/

Gretzel, U., Fesenmaier, D. F., Formica, S., and O'Leary, J. T. (2006) "Searching for the Future: Challenges Faced by Destination Marketing Organizations," *Journal of Travel Research*, 45 (2): 116–126.

Hong Kong Tourism Board (2022a) "PartnerNet," https://partnernet.hktb.com/en/home/index.html

—— (2022b) "Structure and Management," www.discoverhongkong.com/eng/hktb/about/management.html

Irving Convention and Visitors Bureau (2022) "Board of Directors," www.irvingtexas.com/about-us/board-of-directors/

Jordan Times (2017) "Tourism Ministry Raising Awareness of Sector's Role, Opportunities," www. jordantimes.com/news/local/tourism-ministry-raising-awareness-sector%E2%80%99s-role-opportunities%E2%80%99

Langenheim, J. (2016) "Mounting Opposition to Bali Mass Tourism Project," *The Guardian*, www. theguardian.com/environment/the-coral-triangle/2016/mar/22/mounting-opposition-to-bali-mass-tourism-project

Las Vegas Convention and Visitors Authority (2022) "Board of Directors," www.lvcva.com/who-we-are/board-of-directors/

London & Partners (2022) "About Us," www.conventionbureau.london/about-us

Macao Government Tourism Office (2022) "Macao International Fireworks Display Contest," https:// fireworks.macaotourism.gov.mo/

Make It York (2022) "York Residents' Festival 2022," www.visityork.org/residents-festival

Mendelow, A. (1991) "Proceedings of the Second International Conference on Information Systems, Cambridge, Massachusetts."

Merala, D. (2020) "National Tourism Day in India: Did You Know These Facts about Your Own Country?" January 20, www.india.com/travel/articles/national-tourism-day-in-india-did-you-know-these-facts-about-your-own-country-3230664/

Northern Territory Tourism (2022) "Industry Sentiment," www.tourismnt.com.au/research-strategies/research/industry-sentiment

Organisation for Economic Cooperation and Development (2022) "Recommendation of the Council on Principles for Transparency and Integrity in Lobbying," https://legalinstruments.oecd.org/en/instruments/OECD-LEGAL-0379

Philadelphia Convention and Visitors Bureau (2022) "PHLCVB Partnership Program," www.discoverphl.com/partnership/

Savage, G., Nix, T., Whitehead, C., and Blair, J. (1991) "Strategies for Assessing and Managing Organizational Stakeholders," *Academy of Management Executives*, 5 (2): 51–75.

Sheehan, L., and Ritchie, J. R. B. (2005) "Destination Stakeholders: Exploring Identity and Salience," *Annals of Tourism Research*, 32 (3): 711–734.

Sustainable Travel International (2022) "Palau Carbon Neutral Destination Program," https://sustainabletravel.org/project/palau-carbon-neutral-tourism-destination

Tourism Australia (2022) "Our Board," www.tourism.australia.com/en/about/our-organisation/our-board.html

Tourism Authority of Thailand (2021) "Thailand Tourism Awards 2021 Honours 185 Thai Tourism Enterprises," www.tatnews.org/2021/10/thailand-tourism-awards-2021-honours-185-thai-tourism-enterprises/

Tourism New Zealand (2022) "What We Do," www.tourismnewzealand.com/about-us/what-we-do/

Tourism Nova Scotia (2022) "Code of Conduct," https://tourismns.ca/sites/default/files/2017-01/TNS%20Code%20of%20Conduct.pdf

Tourism Recreation Research and Education Centre (2006) *Tourism Planning Toolkit for Local Government*, Lincoln: Lincoln University.

TTR Weekly (2022) "Japanese Agents and Media Visit Malaysia," August 23, www.ttrweekly.com/site/2022/08/japanese-agents-and-media-visit-malaysia/

Turner-Chaplin, N. (2022) "York Resident's Festival 2022: Over 70 Attractions and Offers," https://bestthingstodoinyork.co.uk/york-residents-festival

VisitBritain (2022) "Our Team," www.visitbritain.org/our-team

Visit Greenland (2022) "Greenland Photo Database," https://visitgreenland.photoshelter.com/index

VisitScotland (2022) "Scotland's Theme Years," www.visitscotland.com/about/themed-years/

Visit York (2022) "York Residents' Festival 2022," www.visityork.org/residents-festival

WBTV News (2022) "Cabarrus County CVB Showcases Importance of Tourism with Legislative Reception at Coca-Cola 600," www.wbtv.com/2022/06/07/cabarrus-county-cvb-showcases-importance-tourism-with-legislative-reception-coca-cola-600/

Chapter **10**

Visitor Management

Caring about visitors

DOI: 10.4324/9781003343356-12

Warming Up

Visitor management is not a traditional role for DMOs to play. In fact, DMOs historically were just concerned with bringing visitors to destinations, and other parties looked after guests when they arrived. DMOs were evaluated on how many visitors showed up and how much they spent. However, this narrow view of DMO engagement with visitors is changing as tourism matures in many places around the world. Bringing more visitors to certain destinations is not necessarily all positive, both for the visitors themselves and for the people who live in the communities. It may also put too much pressure on natural and cultural-heritage resources. For example, overcrowding at favored spots irks many visitors and can cause resentment among residents. Although DMOs may not be the main players in all aspects of visitor management, such as within national parks and other protected areas, it is a role that they need to share with others to protect visitors, residents and the natural, heritage and cultural assets of destinations.

This chapter on visitor management was added after the first edition of *Marketing and Managing Tourism Destinations*. The author acknowledges the encouragement from Indonesian and Swiss colleagues to have this new chapter in the second edition. The COVID-19 pandemic further justified having a chapter on visitor management as there was greater focus in 2020–2022 on people's safety and security. The third edition has an additional chapter (Chapter 11) on crisis management, which further extends the focus on visitor management.

Definition of Visitor Management

You can think of it simply as the management of visitors in different ways and mostly when they are experiencing the destination. Some pre-planning and aftercare are required as well for visitor management. The following is this book's definition for visitor management.

DEFINITION

Visitor management

Managing the flows, impacts, and behaviors of visitors to protect resources and to enhance visitor safety and security, experiences, and satisfaction. There is also a strategic dimension to visitor management with respect to the visitor segments and yield that destinations desire.

The ADVICE Model for a Visitor Management Program

You will now want to know the components of a visitor management program for a destination, so let's move on to that topic. Figure 10.1 provides an image of the ADVICE model, which shows that visitors to destinations interact with various organizations, the environment, and local communities. These interactions must be planned for in a visitor management program. It may not be obvious from the model in Figure 10.1 that visitor interactions occur before, during, and after trips; in fact, they do.

The diagram in Figure 10.1 was created by the author; however, you should know about another helpful model applied in tourism destination planning known as the VICE (visitor, industry, community, environment) model (you learned about it in Chapter 9). Lincoln University

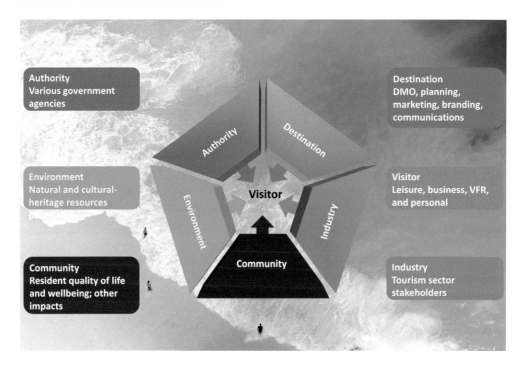

Authority
Various government
agencies

Destination
DMO, planning,
marketing, branding,
communications

Environment
Natural and cultural-
heritage resources

Visitor
Leisure, business, VFR,
and personal

Community
Resident quality of life
and wellbeing; other
impacts

Industry
Tourism sector
stakeholders

Figure 10.1 The ADVICE model for visitor management.

with the Ministry of Economic Development in New Zealand developed the VICE model. The authors indicated that successful and sustainable tourism required welcoming, involving, and satisfying visitors (V), achieving a profitable and prosperous industry (I), engaging and benefiting the hosts (C), and protecting and enhancing the local environment (E) (Tourism Recreation Research and Education Centre (2006).

Following are brief descriptions of the six parts of the ADVICE model:

Authority

Visitors have contact with various government agencies beginning from the trip planning stage (e.g., visa issuance authorities) until they exit destinations (e.g., tax and immigration agencies). While within destinations, visitors may interact with resource protection bodies of government (e.g., in national parks) and with law enforcement agencies.

Destination

DMOs, representing the destination, have several roles that involve direct and indirect engagement with visitors. Visitors are part of the focus for tourism destination planning and research, marketing planning, destination branding, IMC, product development, and information provision. DMOs are concerned about creating satisfied visitors as well as assuring that they are safe and secure within their destinations and receive good service and memorable experiences.

Visitor

Of course, visitors are the core focus for visitor management and the ADVICE model. However, you should understand that visitors also interact with other visitors within the destination as well as sharing information on social media and in other ways (WOM and electronic word of mouth [eWoM]).

Industry

Tourism sector stakeholders play an important role in serving visitors and in creating experiences for them. In fact, when in destinations, visitors may have the greatest contact with hotels, restaurants, attractions, tour operators, and transport providers.

Community

Visitors have an impact on residents' quality of life directly and indirectly. Overcrowding may affect resident access to places and traffic congestion can restrict their everyday movements (Fig. 10.2). Property values may be pushed upward and become too expensive for locals. Traditional neighborhoods disappear with gentrification (arrival of wealthier people in an urban district, a related increase in rents and property values, and changes in the district's character and culture, Chapter 3 definition). However, residents also benefit in different ways from the positive economic impacts of tourism, including having better infrastructure and public amenities.

Figure 10.2 Overcrowding and selfie-taking at the Trevi Fountain in Rome.

EXAMPLE 10.1

Gentrification Causing Resentment in Portugal

This example discusses gentrification in California and Portugal and how it is irritating local residents.

> But resentment of newcomers is growing. Angelenos (people from Los Angeles) can't always escape—and sometimes are at the root of—questions over gentrification, income disparities and immigration. The phrase "expat" itself has become loaded in Lisbon, a city that attracts tens of thousands of working-class immigrants from Brazil, Ukraine, Romania and India. In Facebook groups and cafe meetups, well-to-do Westerners debate over how to define themselves. On the streets, Portuguese activists have protested against evictions and skyrocketing rents caused in part by foreigners with banks that count in dollars and pounds.
>
> (Kaleem 2022)

Learning Point

DMOs need to be aware of the levels of gentrification in their communities and to gather resident sentiment on the issue.

Environment

The natural and cultural-heritage environments of destinations are normally the core of the visitor experience. However, these resources are often fragile and can be irreparably damaged or transformed through visitor use. The natural environments of destinations often pose physical dangers for visitors based upon the activities in which they participate and from crises and natural disasters (see Figures 10.14 and 10.15, for example).

Reasons for Visitor Management

The interactions of the six elements in the ADVICE model are the foundation for the components of a visitor management program for a destination and DMO. For example, the interactions of visitors and environments require resource protection, safety, crisis and disaster management, and interpretation and education programs. The contacts among visitors and with the tourism sector require quality standards and codes of behavior and, again, safety programs.

These interactions provide the reasons for having visitor management programs in destinations in which DMOs engage. Figure 10.3 identifies eight reasons for destination visitor management. Among these, one major concern is for resource protection and especially within natural areas and for cultural-heritage attractions. For example, visitor management is of great importance for protected areas, such as national and marine parks. Managing visitors has implications for the visitors as well, especially to ensure their safety, security, and enjoyment. There are also marketing, branding, and communications and economic reasons for considering the volumes and mixes of visitors. Now follows a brief description of each of the reasons in Figure 10.3.

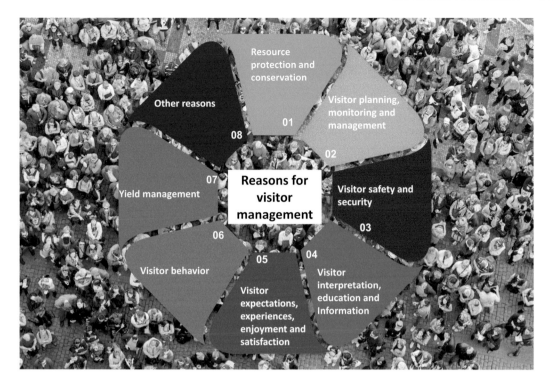

Figure 10.3 Reasons for visitor management.

Resource Protection and Conservation

Resource protection is a principal reason visitor management is required in destinations. Worldwide experiences with tourism demonstrate that visitors cause damage to natural and cultural-heritage resources and globalize traditional lifestyles. It is paradoxical but true that visitors can undermine the sustainability of resources, but they are at the same time an agent for sustainable tourism (Fig. 10.4). The direction of impacts depends on visitor characteristics and how visitors are managed at vulnerable sites. It is important to realize that DMOs and protected area managers often have dissimilar policies, priorities and goals; however, it is important to harmonize these differences.

EXAMPLE 10.2

Management Plan for Banff National Park of Canada

This example discusses the new management plan in a popular Canadian protected area.

Some strategies—such as those addressing climate change, moving people sustainably, and strengthening Indigenous relations—are new to this plan, while others—such as those for conserving resources, managing development, and providing true-to-place experiences—advance the direction established in previous plans.

(Parks Canada 2022)

Learning Point

Resource protection and conservation are crucial in protected areas.

As you can see in the example from Banff National Park in Alberta, Canada, the park authority is concerned about climate change as well as visitors circulating in a sustainable way.

Visitor Planning, Monitoring, and Management

Planning, monitoring, and managing visitor flows is another reason for visitor management. New smart tourism technologies are assisting in visitor flow identification. Smartphone and in-vehicle GPS technologies are helping DMOs to track visitor flows. They are also assisting visitors to have more enjoyable destination experiences by accessing real-time, location-based information. This is often called SoLoMo (social-local-mobile) marketing by DMOs and the tourism sector (Knopf 2016). Visitor flow management is important for destinations as well as for individual sites and attractions to avoid overcrowding and unsafe and unpleasant visitor experiences.

Figure 10.4 Beach clean-up in Indonesia.

> **DEFINITION**
>
> **Smart tourism destination**
>
> "A smart destination is a geographical space (which can range from a neighborhood to a network of cities) where tourism development is planned and executed based on technological infrastructure, allowing local sustainable development while providing quality of the experiences for visitors and quality of life for locals" (Bettini 2018).

One way in which destinations are becoming smarter is through tracking visitor movements. This is a topic you already heard about in Chapter 5 in the discussion on tracking studies. The Disney theme parks have been using tracking for several years through special wristbands and smartphone apps (Disneyland Resort 2022). For guests, the real-time information they get from the apps can make visits more convenient and enjoyable; the theme parks accumulate big data on visitor movements and can also spot overcrowded situations.

> **EXAMPLE 10.3**
>
> **Visitor Tracking**
>
> You learned in Chapter 5 that tracking studies using GPS are one of the methods to collect device data. Tracking visitor movements within destinations is reviewed in this example.
>
>> Using GPS and mobile phones data allows for studying tourism more precisely and efficiently because these data have better spatial and temporal accuracy, the follow-up periods are longer, they allow researchers to follow tourists during their whole visit and the collection and processing of big amounts of digital data are easier than with conventional data. However, the use of space-time information always raises moral and legal issues related to the protection of personal data and the privacy of the subjects being tracked.
>>
>> (Padrón-Ávila and Hernández-Martín 2020: 93)
>
> **Learning Point**
>
> Technology is allowing DMOs to know more about visitor movement patterns.

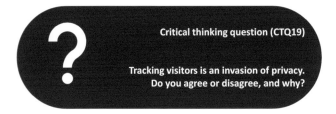

?

Critical thinking question (CTQ19)

Tracking visitors is an invasion of privacy.
Do you agree or disagree, and why?

Visitor Safety and Security

Visitor management must not be just supply and resource oriented. Resources need to be protected, but so do visitors. Destinations and their DMOs must consider demand-side issues and potential problems that visitors might encounter during their stays. Visitor management systems and procedures must assure the safety and security of visitors within destinations and at individual sites and attractions. Destinations that are perceived as unsafe have challenges in attracting visitors. Visitors need to be protected from physical dangers through their activity participation as well as from health risks, criminal and terrorist threats.

EXAMPLE 10.4

Sri Lanka's Safe and Secure Program for Tourism

Sri Lanka's health program during COVID-19 is discussed in this example.

> The "Safe and Secure" certificate is being awarded to tourism establishments and service providers that have been audited by KPMG an Independent Auditing firm and met the requirements of the COVID-19 Health Protocol. The certificate comes with a unique QR code. The certified service providers should display the certificates or a copy in the common areas so that it could be easily accessed by international and domestic guests.
>
> (Sri Lanka Tourism Promotion Bureau 2022)

Learning Point

During the pandemic, it was important that visitors were given safety information and protected from the virus.

Visitor Interpretation, Education, and Information

The imparting of visitor interpretation, education, and information is an important program of visitor management. Although some visitors do not want or expect to be educated while on holiday or business, increasing their knowledge can enhance enjoyment and make destination experiences more authentic and memorable. Authenticity is defined below. Also, with the trend toward more responsible tourism and special-interest travel, the educational role of destinations is becoming increasingly critical. For protected areas like national parks, education through interpretation is an especially crucial role for management in putting across the principles of resource protection and conservation.

DEFINITION

Authentic tourism experiences

Experiences that visitors perceive to be true, accurate, appropriate, and respectful regarding a geographic area, culture or lifestyle, nature and heritage, products and services, and other aspects of a destination.

Visitor Expectations, Experiences, Enjoyment, and Satisfaction

Visitor enjoyment should be enhanced but without damaging or compromising natural and cultural-heritage resources. Overcrowding and visitor incompatibility that can spoil destination experiences and their occurrence need to be addressed. People's enjoyment can be adversely affected by the behavior of other visitors and, in some instances, by aggressive local vendors and other local people. Enjoyment can also be enriched through visitor education and professional interpretation programs.

Visitor Behavior

The behavior of individual visitors and of groups of visitors is another concern for destinations and DMOs. Visitors may misbehave in ways that offend residents and other visitors or cause harm to natural and cultural-heritage resources. They may engage in excessive drinking or illegal activities, such as drug taking, sex tourism, and shoplifting. Borderline ethical activities such as forced shopping by tour operators and travel agencies may also cause problems for destinations (McMillan 2016).

EXAMPLE 10.5

South Africa Says "No" to Wild Animal Interaction

Human interactions with wild creatures is not necessarily beneficial for them. This example reviews this issue in South Africa.

> It's important that wildlife should remain and roam freely in their natural habitat and not be confined to small spaces in so-called sanctuaries or parks that promote cub petting and rehabilitation centers. As eager holiday makers, everyone would like an adventure. However, sometimes that perception of adventure comes in the form of animal interaction and tourists flood to animal-petting centers. These centers mislead visitors to believe that they're promoting conservation and sadly, this is not the case.
>
> (South African Tourism 2022)

Learning Point

It is beneficial for animals and destinations to restrict their interactions with humans.

Yield Management

This is the strategic dimension highlighted in the definition of visitor management. Many destinations, for economic reasons mainly, are concerned with the yields of certain target markets and specific types or groups of visitors. For example, destinations may prefer to attract high-yielding luxury travelers and discourage perceived low-yielding markets, such as backpackers. Yield is measured by per capita spending per day in destinations. There are confounding factors in such measurements, however. These include seasonality of demand, length of stay, economic leakage, and use extent of specific resources. For example, backpackers may stay longer and spend more than other visitors for their entire trips.

EXAMPLE 10.6

Seeking a Higher Yield on the Galápagos

Areas of pristine nature must ensure that visitor volumes are not so high that they damage the precious resources on which they are based.

> Visitors currently pay a $100 (£81) fee to enter the Galápagos National Park, which funds its activities. Its director, Danny Rueda-Cordova, says this may be increased to refocus on low-number/high-yield tourism. He says visitor numbers fell from a record 270,000 in 2019 to half that in 2021 at the peak of the pandemic. Because most of them were Ecuadorians (who just pay a $6/£4.90 entry fee), revenues fell, affecting funding.
>
> (Stratton 2022)

Learning Point

Lower volumes of higher-yield visitors can provide a sounder funding base for protected areas as well as furthering conservation and protection goals.

Other Reasons

There are other reasons for visitor management that include, for example, research on various aspects of the visitor experience that contributes to the enhancement of destination products. Monitoring online UGC from visitors is important as well. Past visitors and DMOs can co-create contents that convince other people to visit destinations.

Benefits from Visitor Management

Why has visitor management not been on the radar of DMOs in the past? This is an interesting question for you to contemplate. You should see that there is a close connection between visitor management and sustainable tourism (the triple bottom line). Adding the visitor management role for DMOs reflects the transition from just destination marketing, branding, and communications to the broader scope of destination management. Without visitor management, there are potential risks, dangers and costs for destinations and DMOs. On the positive side, significant benefits result from well-orchestrated visitor management programs, and Figure 10.5 highlights six of these benefits for destinations and DMOs.

The following is a brief review of the six benefits from visitor management shown in Figure 10.5:

1. Improved and expanded interpretation and information.
2. More community and stakeholder involvement.
3. Greater harmony with local residents.
4. Increased visitor safety and enjoyment.
5. Better resource protection and conservation.
6. Higher economic yield.

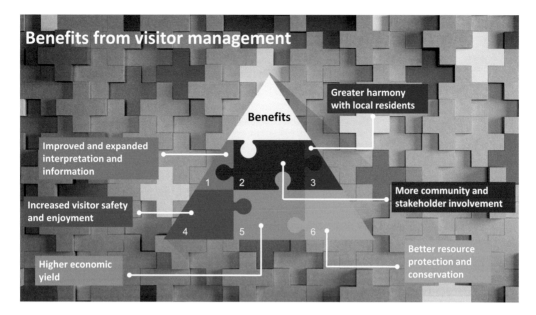

Figure 10.5 Benefits of visitor management.

Improved and Expanded Interpretation and Information

Destinations should do all that they can to create meaningful and memorable experiences for visitors so they do not just go home with suntans and a few extra kilos. Interpretation is particularly important at nature areas and within cultural-heritage attractions to give visitors a greater appreciation and knowledge of their surroundings. Interpretation should transmit important messages about environmental conservation and intercultural harmony and understanding. This can be done, for example, by using augmented reality viewed on apps on visitor smartphones, as in Uist Unearthed in Scotland.

EXAMPLE 10.7

Uist Unearthed in Scotland's Outer Hebrides

Augmented reality can improve interpretation services at historic sites as in this case from the Scottish Highlands.

> The app presents users with stunning, life-sized digital reconstructions of sites as they might have looked, using augmented reality (AR). This technology allows digital information (such as text, images, 3D models, or audio) to be projected over your normal scope of vision, enhancing it with new details. Through the app, long-vanished settlements spring to life once more, enabling visitors to experience these sites in a new light. Uist Unearthed uses location-triggered technology and AR alignments, alongside animation, photography, 3D models, and audio, to create a truly unique offering in the heritage interpretation field.
>
> (*Current Archaeology* 2022)

> **Learning Point**
>
> AR can deepen and improve visitor experiences at attractions.

More Community and Stakeholder Involvement

Visitor management provides several opportunities to involve local residents and tourism sector stakeholders. For example, residents should be involved in resource protection and conservation efforts. Also, the interactions of visitors and residents are of great importance to destinations. Resident awareness education and training are critical to ensuring friendly and positive encounters. The assistance of tourism sector stakeholders in visitor safety programs is essential, and they play a key role in enhancing visitor enjoyment and satisfaction.

Greater Harmony with Local Residents

As evidenced in the overtourism concept, residents may become resentful of the intrusions of visitors and visitors' impacts on their ways of living (such as with the overcrowding demonstrated in Figure 10.2). Thus, it is essential that residents are involved and have a strong say in visitor management programs. Participation in decision-making and the sharing of the economic benefits from tourism are crucial to harmonious relationships between residents and visitors. Education and information-sharing about tourism help residents to better understand visitors and their behaviors.

> **DEFINITION**
>
> **Overtourism**
>
> "Destinations where hosts or guests, locals or visitors, feel that there are too many visitors and that the quality of life in the area or the quality of the experience has deteriorated unacceptably. It is the opposite of responsible tourism which is about using tourism to make better places to live in and better places to visit. Often both visitors and guests experience the deterioration concurrently" (Responsible Tourism Partnership 2022).

Many visitors are seeking meaningful and authentic interactions with local people, and these interchanges should be encouraged by DMOs and tourism sector stakeholders.

Increased Visitor Safety and Enjoyment

Visitors must be assured of a high level of personal safety and security. Several players are involved, including local law enforcement authorities, DMOs, and tourism sector stakeholders, including transportation providers, local residents, travel agencies and tour operators, and visitors themselves. This is partly accomplished through visitor and tourism sector stakeholder education and by regulations, monitoring, and enforcement. Planning ahead to protect visitors and residents from crises and disasters is another aspect of assuring safety (discussed in Chapter 11).

Effective visitor management systems and procedures create greater visitor enjoyment and satisfaction. Visitor management programs that focus on visitors' whole experiences within destinations are required and DMOs are instrumental in developing such programs. The coordination of many players within destinations is required to deliver greater visitor enjoyment and satisfaction.

Higher Economic Yield

Destinations have choices in terms of the types of visitors that they most want to attract. It is preferable to have visitors who spend more and who are also sensitive to the environment and resource protection. Although destinations seldom can have full control over who visits, techniques such as yield management along with solid market research assist with increasing economic yield.

EXAMPLE 10.8

"Rubbish Tourism" Unwanted in Swiss Village

Unfortunately, some tourists create more waste for smaller places rather than in injecting more money, as in this example from Switzerland.

> Fans of the South Korean television series *Crash Landing on You* are flocking to Switzerland from all around Asia. The influx is more than the village of Iseltwald can bear and has sparked a backlash from locals and tourism officials.
> The Bönigen-Iseltwald Tourism office acknowledges that these residents' statements are "unfortunately true." "There has been no particular increase in the village's tourism income as a result of the series. We only spent money on disposing of the waste. We are currently discussing with the local municipality to find a solution," the office said. This would include how to benefit financially from the new tourists.
>
> (Ono and James 2022)

Learning Point

Smaller villages and towns must be especially careful about levels and types of visitors.

Better Resource Protection and Conservation

Planning for visitors and managing and monitoring their behavior produces many beneficial outcomes for the protection of natural environments and cultural heritage. These benefits include more protection of specific ecosystems; increased control of harmful economic activities, such as uncontrolled hunting and fishing; reinvestment of visitor expenditures into research and better conservation programs; and greater understanding among visitors and residents of environmental issues.

EXAMPLE 10.9

Conservation Passports in Mexico

This example reviews how Mexico has created a source of income that is used for conservation purposes in protected areas. The National Commission of Natural Protected Areas in Mexico (CONANP) issues Conservation Passports.

> The Mexican Comisión Nacional de Áreas Naturales Protegidas (CONANP) governs the protected biospheres of Mexico and requires visitors who are in these areas for any recreational activities to purchase either a Biosphere Bracelet that is good for one day's use, or an annual Conservation Passport, valid for one year.
>
> (Government of Mexico 2022)

> The price has increased for 2022. The cost is US$80 plus an additional US$10 processing fee. Part of the fees that go to CONANP support conservation efforts and community development. The Conservation Passport now allows you to access any protected area in Mexico except for Revillagigedo National Park and the Isla Guadalupe Biosphere Reserve.
>
> (Discover Baja Travel Club 2022)

Learning Point

A user-pay strategy can be applied to protect and conserve natural resources.

Components of a Visitor Management Program

Now you know what visitor management is and the reasons for and potential benefits from visitor management programs. You are also familiar with the ADVICE model and the interactions that visitors have with destinations. Then, it is time to dig deeper into a visitor management program, which should encompass these nine components that closely correspond with the reasons for visitor management in Figure 10.3 and the potential benefits in Figure 10.5:

- Resource protection and conservation.
- Visitor planning, monitoring, and management.
- Visitor safety and security.
- Crisis and disaster management.
- Visitor interpretation, education, and information.
- Visitor expectations, experiences, enjoyment, and satisfaction.
- Visitor behavior.
- Yield management.
- Other visitor management efforts.

EXAMPLE 10.10

Zoning of the Great Barrier Reef Marine Park

If you visit the Great Barrier Reef Marine Park, you will be impressed by how well it is organized into zones (as has been your author).

> Zoning helps to manage and protect the values of the Marine Park that people enjoy. Each zone has different rules for the activities that are allowed, the activities that are prohibited, and the activities that require a permit. Zones may also place restrictions on how some activities are conducted. Zoning maps are tools to help you get to know the zones. Before heading out on the water make sure you have a zoning map, know the zones and what's allowed there.
>
> (GBRMPA 2022)

Learning Point

Zoning strategies in protected areas are essential to ensure the sustainability of natural resources.

Resource Protection and Conservation

Many destinations worldwide rely on their natural and cultural-heritage resources to attract visitors. Protecting and conserving these resources is crucial to sustaining tourism for the long term. To enable protection and conservation requires measuring the impacts of visitors on resources and their surrounding communities.

There is a long tradition of visitor management practices with respect to the use of natural environments and especially for protected areas. In that context, visitor management relies on managing visitors through regulating numbers, group size, and length of stay; providing information and education; and enforcing regulations (Newsome et al. 2013: 241). This definition is mainly about the demand perspective of managing visitors; however, visitor management also affects the management of resources on which visitors have impacts. The visitor management for natural areas, as well as for cultural-heritage resources, has demand and supply impacts, strategies, and actions.

Protected areas are set up by government authorities to protect and conserve resources and involve both natural areas and cultural-heritage buildings and sites. Establishing these areas prevents the deterioration of the resources. Preventing or minimizing negative impacts of tourism is one of the factors in the establishment of protected areas (Mason 2008). There are widely accepted ways for categorizing protected areas, and these schemes are important for destination management. Among these, the UNESCO World Heritage List and IUCN's protected area categories are the best-known worldwide. Here first is a widely accepted definition of a protected area.

DEFINITION

Protected area

"A protected area is a clearly defined geographical space, recognized, dedicated and managed, through legal or other effective means, to achieve the long term conservation of nature with associated ecosystem services and cultural values" (IUCN 2022).

In 1972, various international bodies united to draw up the World Heritage Convention. It was designed as a way for international cooperation to occur to protect cultural and natural places of outstanding universal value so that future generations would enjoy them as we do now. To be included on the World Heritage List, sites must be of outstanding universal value and meet at least one out of ten selection criteria. The World Heritage List includes cultural sites, natural sites, and mixed (cultural and natural) sites. There were 1,157 sites in the list in March 2023 (UNESCO 2023). The IUCN classifications (Fig. 10.6) include seven categories of protected areas (IUCN 2022).

You learned earlier that visitor management should reflect the principles of sustainable tourism. Therefore, three impact perspectives must be adopted—environmental (planet), social-cultural (people) and economic (profit) according to the triple-bottom-line concept of sustainable development. It is insufficient just to look at the environmental impacts of tourism.

You should know that visitors have both positive and negative impacts on resources and the communities within which they are located. There are several research studies and books that highlight the negative environmental effects of visitor use of natural and protected areas. Buckley and Pannell (1990) cited soil erosion and compaction, damage to vegetation, disturbance to wildlife, water pollution, vandalism, and noise from increasing visitor use of national parks and conservation reserves in Australia. Newsome et al. (2013) classified visitor impacts resulting from trampling and wear, access roads and trails, use of built facilities and camping areas, use of water edges, and effects on wildlife habitats.

Social-cultural impacts from visitors can be less obvious than environmental and more difficult to measure. For protected areas, the International Institute for Environment and Development

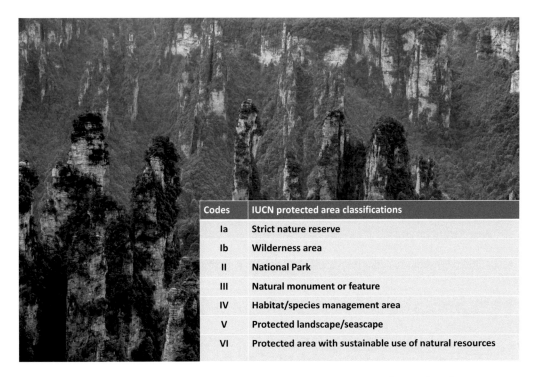

Codes	IUCN protected area classifications
Ia	Strict nature reserve
Ib	Wilderness area
II	National Park
III	Natural monument or feature
IV	Habitat/species management area
V	Protected landscape/seascape
VI	Protected area with sustainable use of natural resources

Figure 10.6 International Union for Conservation of Nature protected area classifications.

(2022) recommends the SAPA (social impact assessment for protected areas) process. The focus of SAPA is on the positive and negative impacts on the well-being of communities. Well-being is divided into three parts:

1. Material well-being (physical requirements of life, such as income, wealth, assets or physical health, and the ecosystem provided by the physical environment).
2. Relational well-being (social interactions, collective actions, and the relationships involved in the generation and maintenance of social, political and cultural identities).
3. Subjective well-being (cultural values, norms and belief systems; notions of self; individual and shared hopes, fears and aspirations; expressed levels of satisfaction or dissatisfaction; trust; and confidence).

Visitors create economic impacts for destinations, as you already know. The research approaches to measuring economic impacts were reviewed in Chapter 5. There are several methods available to estimate economic impacts but the direct expenditures approach is the most popular as well as being relatively simpler to apply. The direct expenditure value is an estimate of total visitor expenditures for a given time and usually one year. The indirect and induced effects or impacts can also be estimated, but this is more difficult to do because it requires more sophisticated research methodologies.

Visitor Planning, Monitoring, and Management

Although not all visitor-related opportunities, challenges, and issues are predictable in advance, visitor planning is crucial for effective destination management. Why is visitor planning so needed? Recent trends in tourism and society have accentuated the need for visitor management planning in destinations. The reasons for visitor planning include but are not limited to those shown in Figure 10.7.

You have already learned about tourism destination planning in Chapter 4. Visitor planning should follow a similar basic process, which covers the functions of planning, research,

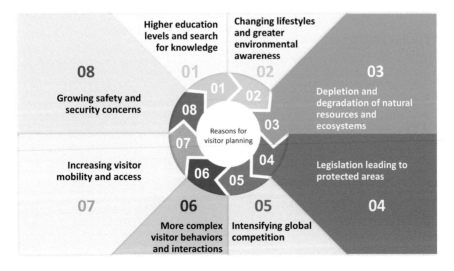

Figure 10.7 Reasons for visitor planning.

implementation, control, and evaluation. In this case, the word "monitoring" equates to control and evaluation in visitor planning.

It is recommended that DMOs should lead the visitor planning process in their destinations. There should be significant and meaningful involvement for local residents and tourism sector stakeholders. The following materials deal with visitor management planning primarily in natural areas and with the purpose of resource protection and conservation. However, the principles and processes can be applied to destinations in general. In this context, the major focus is on managing visitor impacts and particularly to reduce potential negative impacts on natural environments. Several visitor planning processes and techniques are available, including the following eight:

1. Carrying capacity (or tourism carrying capacity, TCC)
2. Recreation Opportunity Spectrum (ROS)
3. Limits of Acceptable Change (LAC)
4. Visitor Activity Management Process (VAMP)
5. Visitor Impact Model (VIM)
6. Visitor Experience and Resource Protection (VERP)
7. Tourism Optimization Management Model (TOMM)
8. Benefits-Based Model (BBM)

CARRYING CAPACITY

Carrying capacity as applied to tourism emerged as a concept in the 1960s. Carrying capacity is the maximum level of (visitor) use an area can sustain (Newsome et al. 2013). The carrying capacity concept is widely acknowledged in recreation and tourism. However, some experts suggest that the carrying capacity concept has failed to produce practical results and is insufficient on its own as a visitor planning approach. Carrying capacity is not one-dimensional; rather there are six forms of carrying capacity that can be studied and measured or evaluated (Fig. 10.8).

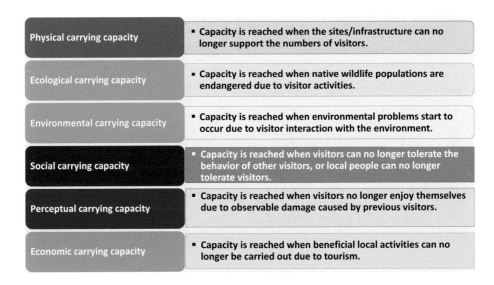

Physical carrying capacity	▪ Capacity is reached when the sites/infrastructure can no longer support the numbers of visitors.
Ecological carrying capacity	▪ Capacity is reached when native wildlife populations are endangered due to visitor activities.
Environmental carrying capacity	▪ Capacity is reached when environmental problems start to occur due to visitor interaction with the environment.
Social carrying capacity	▪ Capacity is reached when visitors can no longer tolerate the behavior of other visitors, or local people can no longer tolerate visitors.
Perceptual carrying capacity	▪ Capacity is reached when visitors no longer enjoy themselves due to observable damage caused by previous visitors.
Economic carrying capacity	▪ Capacity is reached when beneficial local activities can no longer be carried out due to tourism.

Figure 10.8 Forms of carrying capacity (Bretlaender and Toth 2014: 6).

You can equate social carrying capacity with the overtourism concept defined earlier. Residents can become less tolerant if they perceive there to be too many visitors—the social carrying capacity has been exceeded. TCC is the tourism carrying capacity of a destination or a specific area within a destination. The conceptual diagram in Figure 10.9 shows that sustainable tourism development is located mid-range within the measurement of TCC.

In practical terms, carrying capacity has proven difficult to apply and especially to large areas, such as an entire resort area or city destination. This dilemma about carrying capacity forced organizations and planning experts to find other visitor planning approaches.

DEFINITION

Demarketing of tourism

You saw the definition of degrowth in Chapter 3. Here now is a definition of demarketing: "Demarketing is generally recognized as that aspect of marketing that aims at discouraging customers in general or a certain class of customers in particular on either a temporary or permanent basis and has been increasingly posited as a potential tool to degrow tourism and improve its overall sustainability, particularly as a result of so-called overtourism" (Hall and Wood 2021).

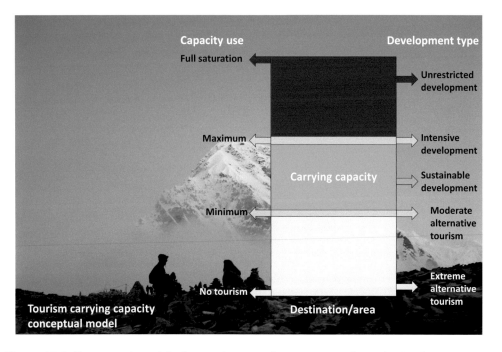

Figure 10.9 Conceptual model of a carrying capacity assessment for a destination or an area (UNEP 1999).

RECREATION OPPORTUNITY SPECTRUM

ROS is a classification system that identifies and determines the diversity of recreation opportunities within a protected area or other natural area. The range of opportunities is from primitive to urban (Fig. 10.10).

LIMITS OF ACCEPTABLE CHANGE

The LAC planning system was developed in the USA. It is a carrying capacity–based approach designed for recreational use of national parks and wilderness protected areas. There are nine steps in implementing LAC, and it starts with identifying issues and concerns and involves zoning approaches (Fig. 10.11). For example, LAC was applied to identify resource and social

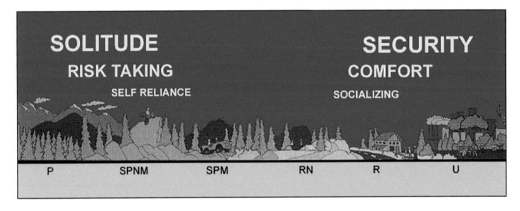

Figure 10.10 Recreational Opportunity Spectrum (US Forest Service 2022a).

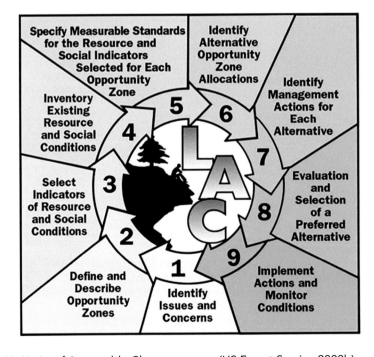

Figure 10.11 Limits of Acceptable Change process (US Forest Service 2022b).

indicators and standards for managing snorkeling in the Koh Chang National Marine Park in Thailand. This was done because of concerns with the impacts of tourists on the park's coral reefs. The indicators developed were coral mortality, diversity, and vulnerability to trampling and the number of other snorkelers. Because of LAC, a standard of thirty to thirty-five snorkelers was established, and zones and management actions were determined for different areas based upon intensity of use and coral vulnerability.

Visitor Activity Management Process

VAMP is a visitor management procedure developed and applied by Parks Canada, which defines it as follows:

DEFINITION

VAMP

"A decision making framework used by Parks Canada to contribute to the preparation, integration and implementation of the public opportunity portion of management plans and service plans. This framework applies to both new and existing parks, historic sites or canals and assists in: identifying opportunities and assessing public needs related to public understanding, appreciation and enjoyment; visitor activities planning, definition of levels of service, and operation of facilities; and evaluation of effectiveness in providing service to the public consistent with the Parks Canada mandate" (Parks Canada 2017a).

Basically, VAMP tries to match visitor interests with the educational and outdoor recreation opportunities in a protected area. VAMP has been used to set up a national park and assess the impacts of cross-country skiing and for interpretation planning in Canada (Newsome et al. 2013).

Visitor Impact Model

VIM focuses on visitor impacts with the purpose of keeping these within acceptable ranges. The VIM process identifies the probable causes of impacts to do more research and monitoring on these effects. In an application of VIM to the Jenolan Caves in New South Wales, Australia, issues were found with near-capacity vehicle parking, vehicle-pedestrian conflicts, overcrowding above and below ground, and hydrological disturbance in the caves from above-ground developments (Newsome et al. 2013). With such impacts and their probable causes pinpointed, management strategies for remedying them were prepared and implemented.

Visitor Experience and Resource Protection

VERP was developed by the US National Park Service to address concerns about the carrying capacities of the country's national parks. As with LAC, it identifies the appropriate visitor experiences for various areas within parks. VERP was applied in the Arches National Park in Utah in the USA and identified its potential management zones as pedestrian, hiker, backcountry, primitive, motorized sightseeing, motorized rural, semi-primitive motorized, sensitive resource protection, and developed.

TOURISM OPTIMIZATION MANAGEMENT MODEL

TOMM is a planning approach that was developed in Australia and was based on LAC (Fig. 10.12). The rationale behind the TOMM framework is that if all people directly or indirectly related with tourism are well informed of the internal goals and state of each of them, they will be more engaged with achieving those goals. A fundamental part of this approach is the community engagement through community consultation during the planning stage and as broad distribution of information during the rest of the process (Manidis Roberts Consultants 1997). TOMM, for example, has been applied in South Australia (Kangaroo Island) and in British Columbia (Clayoquot Sound).

BENEFITS-BASED MODEL

BBM is an approach to visitor planning that focuses decision-making on understanding and managing for outcomes of visitor engagement. These outcomes are a result of managerial actions in providing specific attributes of settings, certain visitor-held attributes (such as previous experience, norms and expectations) and visitor interaction with attributes during a recreational engagement (McCool et al. 2007). BBM determines the benefits the public wants from sites/lands and then reports on the extent to which these benefits have been achieved (Newsome et al. 2013). The BBM process has been widely used in Canada and the USA. From the area and community perspectives, the potential outcomes are social benefits accruing to communities, economic benefits to local communities resulting from managerial investments in recreation settings, increased protection to cultural and natural heritage values, recreation opportunities, and negative consequences. The psychological benefits that visitors experience from protected area recreational engagement include, among others, learning about and appreciating nature, appreciating scenery, stress release, solitude, being with family or friends, challenge, adventure, humility, independence, and freedom (McCool et al. 2007).

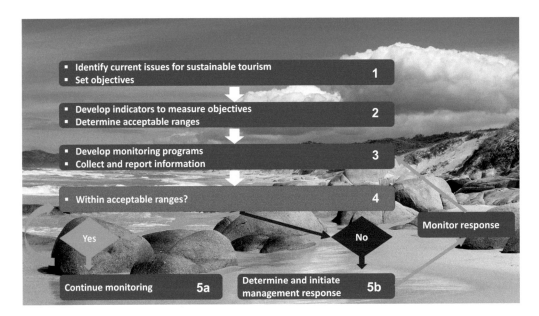

Figure 10.12 Tourism Optimization Management Model (Bakker et al. 2015: 9; Manidis Roberts Consultants 1997).

You can see that several of these visitor planning procedures and techniques were designed for the management of visitor recreation activities in protected areas rather than for larger destinations. However, many of the processes are applicable and can be applied to destinations.

Visitor planning needs to be followed up with visitor monitoring and managing. Here are the definitions of these terms.

DEFINITIONS

Monitoring visitors

Monitoring is the systematic collection, analysis, and interpretation of visitor data and its integration into destination management strategies and actions.

Managing visitors

Managing visitors involves implementing strategies and actions that protect and conserve natural and cultural-heritage resources; ensure visitor safety, enhance visitor enjoyment and satisfaction; increase community participation and economic benefits; and reduce the negative impacts of tourism while growing the positives from tourism.

Monitoring visitors involves observing visitors and their behaviors and counting visitor numbers. Monitoring assists with several aspects of visitor management and is an essential function. Monitoring should be a continuous, day-to-day activity and is required to check the progress with the implementation of the visitor management plan. There are numerous reasons for monitoring and managing visitor flows and volumes, and these are shown in Figure 10.13.

Resource protection and conservation	• Control or regulate visitor numbers • Determine areas of overuse
Visitor flow monitoring	• Detect bottlenecks and lengthy queues • Avoid overcrowding • Disperse visitors
Visitor safety	• Control crowds • Observe participation in activities • Detect dangerous situations
Visitor education and information	• Deliver information on rules and regulations • Provide interpretation
Visitor enjoyment and satisfaction	• Determine visitor satisfaction • Manage visitor numbers to ensure greater enjoyment
Visitor behavior	• Observe behaviors of individuals and groups • Remind visitors of required conduct • Resolve undesirable behavior
Yield management	• Track visitor expenditures (revenues) • Determine return on investment (ROI)
Other reasons	• Suggest points of interest through smartphones • Determine visitor profile characteristics

Figure 10.13 Reasons for visitor monitoring and management.

There are different types of data and information that need to be collected related to visitors, including numbers of visitors, visitor profile characteristics, behavior patterns, expenditures, and satisfaction levels. There are many systems, techniques and technologies for monitoring visitors, such as automatic or electronic counters, human observation, still and video photography, smartphone tracking, visitor interviews and surveys, and UGC analysis. Do you remember learning about visitor profile studies in Chapter 5?

There are different strategies and actions for managing visitors within destinations. Newsome et al. (2013) divide these into site management (supply) and visitor management (demand) approaches. Site management actions might include relocating facilities to improve visitor flows or reduce crowding. Regulating visitor use by restricting numbers is an example of a visitor management approach.

Visitor Safety and Security

Destination management must give careful attention to visitor safety because it is an increasing concern among tourists and affects destination choices. Visitors are becoming increasingly concerned with safety and security as they travel the world, especially as a result of the COVID-19 pandemic. Therefore, DMOs must pay attention to visitor safety and have programs to address this issue, both in everyday situations and for when crises and disasters occur (the topic in Chapter 11). Destinations and DMOs must identify all potential dangers and threats that visitors may encounter.

Perceived and real safety are two aspects of this issue that DMOs must consider. Perceived safety is the level of safety that visitors feel is present in a specific destination; their perceptions may not be accurate, but they still affect destination selection. Real safety is the actual safety that visitors experience within a destination. It is the duty and responsibility of destinations to inform visitors of all potential dangers. Because DMOs are on the ground, they can gather the most accurate and updated information on safety and security issues and should immediately pass this information along to potential visitors and visitors already within the destination. This results in better informed visitors who will be more mindful of the potential threats to their safety.

Destinations need to monitor foreign government's travel advisories, noting particularly any recent updates. It is especially important to check the accuracy of these advisories and to verify that potential dangers and threats to visitors still exist or have passed. Travel advisories can become outdated, and it is advisable for DMOs to use their websites and social media pages on Facebook, Instagram, and Twitter, for example, to provide the real-time current conditions within the destination.

EXAMPLE 10.11

Travel Advisories Issued by Ireland

Travel advisories are designed to protect the safety of citizens when they are traveling to particular places.

> Irish holidaymakers wishing to go abroad to a select few countries are being advised by the Department of Foreign Affairs (DFA) to exercise a "high degree

of caution" when traveling. Recent heatwaves have led to outbreaks of wild-fires across Spain. Currently, there is an alert for high temperatures across the country with most areas expected to exceed 40°C once again. The Spanish government is also asking for "maximum precaution" to avoid forest fires. People in Spain are being urged to avoid throwing cigarettes, rubbish and, especially, glass bottles. Wildfires and seismic activity in Portugal are also highlighted with the DFA saying: "The regional government of the Azores continues to report significant levels of seismic activity around São Jorge island which may indicate a risk of earthquakes or volcanic eruption." The DFA is advising tourists to monitor the news and to follow the instructions from local authorities in both countries in relation to wildfires and seismic activity.

(White 2022)

Learning Point

Government travel advisories are an essential part of the safety system for outbound travelers.

There are physical risks and dangers for tourists within all destinations, and these are perhaps more prevalent at protected areas because of the topography and the presence of animals (Fig. 10.14). Advance information supplemented with warning signs and staff observation and supervision must be provided to help visitors avoid such physical dangers. People with health or physical problems should be advised not to participate.

Dangers are also present in specific visitor activities (Figures 10.14 and 10.15). Even in a typical theme park, visitors face dangers. However, some dangers and risks are self-selected by visitors and especially by those choosing adventure tourism and extreme sports. Legislation and regulation along with enforcement of these codes are required to approve and license tour operators offering adventure travel. Visitors also need to be given warnings of the dangers involved in their participation.

Sometimes, consumer trends and fashions bring about new dangers when traveling. For example, the use of selfie sticks to take photos using smartphones is very popular. This practice is widespread at major tourism sightseeing spots (Fig. 10.2) and attractions but poses potential dangers to the visitors themselves and other visitors and to the upkeep and maintenance of facilities. Because of the potential damage from selfie sticks and the reduction in the quality of visitor experiences, several famous museums have completely banned their use. DMOs and tourism businesses have a duty to inform visitors of the potential dangers from using selfie sticks, and they may decide to prohibit their use.

Overcrowding occurs at popular tourism spots and at special occasions like festivals and events. Although tolerable at times, overcrowding generally detracts from visitors' enjoyment and can spoil their experiences. Unfortunately, overcrowding becomes dangerous and deadly when people stampede or crush. Destination managers must be vigilant about overcrowding situations and seek to avoid them. DMOs and tourism businesses must inform visitors of potential dangers from overcrowding and implement policies and procedures to lessen the negative impacts of too many visitors at the one time. A good way of doing this is to tell visitors about

Figure 10.14 Dangerous walk at Mount Hua (Huashan) in Shaanxi Province, China.

Figure 10.15 Rock climbing on Kalymnos Island, Greece.

where and when peak crowding occurs and to make suggestions for visiting at off-peak periods or for following alternate visiting patterns.

Apart from the dangers from overcrowding, there are other potential dangers in the interactions of visitors themselves and with other people in the destination. These include the HIV/AIDS dangers from sex tourism and the potential of fighting and other violence. Accidents can also happen involving visitors that can be fatal, such as with visitors driving in unfamiliar conditions and with vehicles to which they are unaccustomed.

Food safety is a huge global challenge and especially so in developing countries where there is significant poverty. Food poisoning is a common complaint in tourism, and in a small proportion of cases can become life-threatening or even deadly.

EXAMPLE 10.12

New Safety Standards in the Caribbean

Travelers are becoming more concerned about safety within destinations and the tourism sector is responding with new safety programs, as in the Caribbean.

> The standards, which are to be issued in the coming months, provide international best practice in seven areas—food and safety sanitation, water treatment management and efficiency, sewage treatment and management, solid waste management, energy management and efficiency, integrated test management, and environmental management system—all for the tourism industry.
>
> (*Barbados Today* 2022)

Learning Point

Destinations must assure the safety of visitors within their areas and have specific programs to ensure visitor protection.

Visitor safety is a responsibility shared by the destination and the DMO along with tourism sector stakeholders and the visitors themselves. For destination managers, including those in protected areas, an important role is to inform and educate visitors and tourism sector stakeholders about safety through various methods. There are a variety of approaches that destination managers should use to ensure high levels of visitor safety. These include legislation and regulations; enforcement (inspections and special tourist police forces) (Sri Lanka Police 2022); visitor safety announcements; visitor safety brochures; education, information and interpretation; and visitor safety signage.

EXAMPLE 10.13

Tourist Police Assistance in South Korea

This example describes the tourist police system that is being used in South Korea.

> Tourist police assistance is available to international visitors at major tourist attractions, not only to prevent crime, but also to provide tour information and resolve any inconvenient issues. If you experience any misconduct or discrimination as a tourist, ask for help from the officers wearing navy jackets and black berets.
>
> (Korea Tourism Organization 2022)

Learning Point

The presence of tourist police can alleviate people's fears of traveling within those destinations.

Crisis and Disaster Management

Chapter 11 provides a detailed description of destination crisis management. It can be said here, however, that crises are happening more often in tourism and are becoming a greater concern in visitor and destination management.

EXAMPLE 10.14

Crises in Tourism Are Occurring More Frequently

It is unfortunate that crises are happening more regularly in tourism.

> Recently, global tourism has experienced numerous crisis events, including terrorist attacks, natural disasters, wars, political instability, economic recessions, disease outbreaks, and biosafety and food safety threats. With the expansion of tourism worldwide and industrial growth, crises occur more frequently.
>
> (Duan et al. 2022: 668)

Learning Point

Destinations must be prepared with crisis management plans.

Visitor Interpretation, Education, and Information

Chapter 7 on destination product development has already given you a definition of interpretation (Tilden 1957) and described interpretation's roles and benefits. Also, that chapter explained the DMO's role in the provision of interpretation.

DMOs are major tourism information providers and need to play a strong role in educating visitors about the resources within their areas. The delivery of information is not only critical to ensuring visitor safety but also serves destination marketing, branding, and communications purposes. Interpretation is an important visitor management tool because it informs and educates people. For example, interpretation not only educates but also transmits important messages about environmental and societal issues, such as climate change and global warming, deforestation, loss of wildlife habitats, and coral reef and coastal erosion. The knowledge gained through interpretation is not only very meaningful to visitors; it can also greatly enhance their enjoyment and experiences within destinations. Effective interpretation should adhere to certain principles and these are highlighted in Figure 10.16.

There are many techniques for DMOs and others to deliver interpretation including the following:

VISITOR, INTERPRETIVE OR NATURE CENTERS

These centers are a primary venue for interpretation in destinations and at specific sites. They must be well planned to fully engage visitors and not just be for accommodation bookings, ticket sales, and administrative offices. You already have learned about the roles of VICs in Chapter 7.

Figure 10.16 Principles for effective interpretation (Newsome et al. 2013: 296–300).

Tour Guiding

Tour guiding is one of the most effective ways to deliver interpretation within destinations. Guiding can be very powerful and effective if done right. Tour guides can respond to visitor needs and questions. Guides can engage and actively involve visitors. Guiding provides an opportunity to involve local community experts in interpretation. Proper training is required, and guides may have to be controlled through licensing.

Self-Guided Itineraries, Trails, and Maps

Some visitors prefer to strike out on their own without the services of guides. Self-guided itineraries and trails are always available and allow visitors to proceed at their own pace. Handheld or smartphone maps can be provided to help with self-navigation. Self-guiding systems must be supported by good directional and interpretive signs, and there may be certain problems in maintaining these signs because of weathering and vandalism. This interpretation is widely used in protected areas worldwide and is popular with visitors who enjoy the independence and freedom of discovering things on their own.

Interpretive Signage

Interpretive signage is vitally important within destinations and at specific attractions and sites. They help visitors better understand what they are viewing. Designing and maintaining interpretive signs are major challenges. In addition to providing multiple language translations of the information, most signs are outdoors, and so they suffer from weathering and may also be vandalized. Destination managers must constantly be checking the conditions of interpretive signs to ensure their continuing quality.

Viewing Platforms, Telescopes, and Hides

Scenic and wildlife viewing is an important activity and viewing platforms, hides, and telescopes are needed. Platforms and telescopes are also found at many scenic spots within destinations to provide better viewing and viewpoints. Some viewing platforms are spectacular attractions themselves, for example, the Columbia Icefield Skywalk in Jasper National Park, Canada (Fig. 10.17).

Brochures, Maps, Posters, and Printed Guides

Printed materials are frequently used for visitor interpretation. Their advantages are portability and relatively low cost. Disadvantages include the need for updating and foreign language translations, potentially poor reproduction quality and contribution to waste and littering. Now, it is more ecological to provide this information via websites or apps for use on smartphones and tablets while on-site or off-site.

Smartphone and Tablet Apps

Visitors are increasingly using their smartphones and other devices to access destination information before, during, and after trips (Fig. 10.18). Destinations are responding by creating apps that can be downloaded for use on phones. Apps can be frequently updated and provide an ecologically oriented alternative to printed versions of interpretation materials. They also allow more interactivity and can incorporate AR and virtual reality.

Figure 10.17 Visitors on the Columbia Icefield Skywalk, Alberta, Canada.

Figure 10.18 Apps such as maps being used for directions.

EXAMPLE 10.15

Virtual Reality for Visitors to Snowdonia, Wales

Virtual reality can be applied to enhance visitor experiences as within this national park in Wales.

> Visitors to Snowdonia National Park will be able to experience the area and connect with it in a new way, leading the way in adventure innovation. Fly Snowdon, developed by Frontgrid the adventure innovation specialist has opened to the public, pioneering the benefits that virtual tourism can bring to real world places. The three games that make up the Fly Snowdon series all have different learning outcomes. "Snowdon Navigator" looks to orientate people in the environment and allows them to experience it in a totally new way, exploring the destination from the sky. "Snowdon by Night" highlights the beauty of the area at night, with the national park being one of the UK's Dark Skies Reserves, teaching people about the constellations and ways to consider reducing light pollution. "Snowdon Peak Challenge," encourages flyers to explore the three mountain ranges, showing that Snowdonia National Park is not just about Mt. Snowdon itself and looking to inspire people to visit other parts of the park.
>
> (RLI 2022)

Learning Point

Virtual tourism experiences can lead to greater visitor enjoyment while also extending interpretive services.

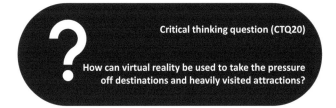

? Critical thinking question (CTQ20)

How can virtual reality be used to take the pressure off destinations and heavily visited attractions?

VIDEOS

Videos are highly versatile and useful in providing information and interpretation to groups of people as well as through multiple online channels. Video content is thought to be more persuasive and communicates at more of an emotional level in putting across environmental messages and issues. The use of music, movement, and high-quality photography is another advantage of videos. However, like printed materials, videos quickly become outdated, and they are relatively costly to produce at a high quality. Great videos require skilled directors and producers who know their audiences well.

WEBSITES AND SOCIAL MEDIA

Websites and social media are very effective for sharing information with potential and current visitors.

Visitor Expectations, Experiences, Enjoyment, and Satisfaction

Expectations, experiences, enjoyment, and satisfaction are linked together. Visitors arrive at their destinations full of expectations about what they will experience there. Destination managers should do all that they can through visitor research to develop a full understanding of visitor expectations.

Visitor Expectations

When people select a destination, they have prior expectations of how it will perform when compared to their ideal levels of performance. This has been the focus for much research in service quality. Figure 10.19 of the Expectation Confirmation (Disconfirmation) Theory shows the relationship between visitor expectations and satisfaction based on the destination's actual performance during a trip.

Destination Perceived Performance

Visitor perceptions of a destination's performance relative to their prior expectations affects their trip satisfaction levels. Destination managers must be very concerned about this performance, which in practical terms is difficult to manage. Continual auditing or assessment of destination performance is required.

Visitor Experiences

This is a newer mindset that now is shared by many destination managers. Unfortunately, others have too much of a product orientation. There are four phases to visitor experiences, as shown in the consumer journey diagram you will see later in Chapter 16. DMOs must adopt a holistic approach to ensuring the best experiences for their visitors and, as such, need to realize that there are several—and not just one—phases of visitor experiences. DMOs need to be active during all four phases of visitors' experiences by providing real-time and updated information to them. This can be best accomplished by establishing one-to-one communications through

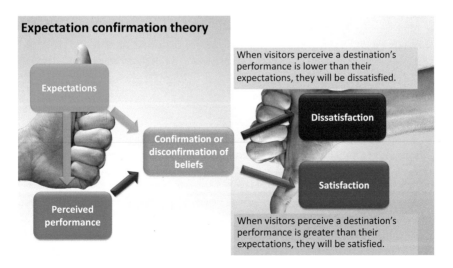

Figure 10.19 Expectation Confirmation (Disconfirmation) Theory (Oliver 1980).

social media channels and email. For example, when visitors are within destinations, information on things to do and places to eat can be shared to visitors' smartphones. When visitors have returned home, a simple thank you can be sent to them via online channels.

EXAMPLE 10.16

Deep Dive Dubai Offers a New Visitor Experience

Innovative experiences such as this one in Dubai can add significantly to the visitor appeal of destinations.

> Those who love free-falling into mysterious watery terrains can now put their skills to the test at Deep Dive Dubai—the only facility in the world where you can dive to depths of 60 meters, which is 15 meters deeper than any other space, not to mention four times bigger. Located in Dubai's Nad Al Sheba neighborhood, the Deep Dive Dubai pool has been verified by Guinness World Records as the world's deepest swimming pool and holds 14 million liters of water, the equivalent of six Olympic-sized pools. To try it out you need to book in advance and it's only open to those aged ten years and above for the scuba. Built to resemble a vast sunken city, this eerie hole in the heart of the desert is equipped with fifty-six cameras to ensure visitor safety along with state-of-the-art lighting and sound systems.
>
> (Procter 2022)

Learning Point

Destinations should be continuously searching for new visitor experiences that add to and diversify their attractiveness.

Visitor Enjoyment

Visitors must enjoy their experiences within the destination, and destination managers need to know whether visitors had enjoyable experiences. This can be accomplished through questions on a visitor survey. For example, Parks Canada determined that in 2015–2016, 95 percent of the visitors to its national parks enjoyed their visits, and 82 percent considered the experiences meaningful (Parks Canada 2017b).

Visitor Satisfaction

Satisfying visitors must be a topmost goal for destination managers, and they should periodically measure visitor satisfaction. Satisfaction affects visitors' willingness to recommend the destination and the intention to return. It also influences what visitors communicate in social media (UGC) and through other channels. Just meeting expectations does not guarantee that visitors will leave their destinations satisfied. Destination managers should conduct regular visitor surveys to measure satisfaction levels.

Visitor Behavior

Managing visitor behavior is a complex and difficult task for destination managers, but this should start with a thorough understanding of tourist consumer behavior, which is the topic in Chapter 16. It is especially important for DMOs to understand visitor motivations and why people are selecting their destinations. People's motivations for travel vary, and their behaviors are influenced by these motivations and by those with whom they travel (if they are not solo travelers). Visitors encounter people they did not know before—locals and other visitors—and the interactions with these people influence their behaviors. Visitors find themselves in unfamiliar environments and may need to adjust their behaviors to comply with local norms—some visitors are better than others at adjusting their behaviors.

In addition to understanding tourist consumer behavior, destination managers must decide how to handle visitor behavior while the visitors are present. Some constraints on visitor behavior are required in all destinations. The most difficult situation for destination managers is dealing with inappropriate or disruptive visitor behavior. Certain groups of visitors have gained notoriety for bad behavior, for example, visiting football fans. However, it is essential that DMOs and tourism sector stakeholders avoid stereotyping any group of visitors.

There are different approaches that destinations can use to manage visitor behavior:

Rules or House Rules

Good examples of these are found with museums and other heritage buildings and sites. For example, people are not allowed to bring selfie sticks into the collection exhibition areas of the Louvre Museum in Paris (Musée du Louvre 2022).

EXAMPLE 10.17

Rules on Photography within the Louvre, Paris

There have to be clear rules on photography in museums and other sites that can potentially be damaged by the activity.

> You can take photos and videos in the permanent collections if they are for personal use. However, you are not allowed to use selfie sticks, flash or lighting. In the temporary exhibition galleries, it may be prohibited to take photos or videos of certain works.
>
> (Musée du Louvre 2022)

Learning Point

Many museums and other attractions have introduced rules related to photo- and video-taking to protect resources (and people).

Codes of Conduct

Several destinations have introduced codes of conduct that they ask visitors to follow. Chile and Kerala, India are just two examples. Generally, these codes stress responsible tourism guidelines while urging an understanding of local traditions and lifestyles. For example, the Chile Conduct for the Responsible Tourist (SERNATUR, Chile 2022) asks visitors to:

- value local traditions and customs;
- support the local economy;

- respect the environment;
- be careful when visiting wilderness, heritage, archaeological and other areas that seem fragile and/or valuable;
- be an informed and respectful traveler.

EXAMPLE 10.18

Kerala Code of Ethics for Travelers

This is an excellent visitor ethics code that has been developed for Kerala in India.

- Do an in-depth research on the customs and practices of God's Own Country before you plan your visit
- Appreciate the culture of the land and its tradition
- Be polite to the native people and appreciate their habits
- Learn a few basic words of greetings and polite phrases in the native language before your visit
- Respect the diverse religious and social customs of Kerala
- Observe the local laws and codes of the land
- Try to actively involve yourself in the cultural and environmental concerns of Kerala and cooperate accordingly
- Avoid trying to purchase or own things which are not legally permissible or might be protected
- Do not force entry into prohibited or restricted areas that will disrupt the ecology or the cultural sentiments of the land
- Conserve energy by minimizing the use of fans, lights, geysers etc. whenever not required
- Avoid overuse, wastage and pollution of water, contributing to the global conservation of water resources
- Avoid littering public places and ensure that waste is disposed only in bins earmarked for the purpose.

(Kerala Tourism [India] 2022)

Learning Point

Rules and guidelines for responsible visitor behavior are helpful for destinations and also can assure visitors of better travel experiences.

MONITORING BEHAVIOR

Destination managers should be monitoring the behavior of visitors but without this being obtrusive and spoiling people's experiences. Monitoring can be in the form of human supervision and observation or through using video cameras. For example, supervision may be required for resource protection or safety reasons while visitors are on trails in protected areas or when participating in adventure sports. Cameras in public areas, such as restaurants, shopping areas and hotels, are common and record visitor behavior.

REGULATIONS

It is necessary in some situations to constrain visitor behavior by introducing certain laws and regulations. For example, visitors may be limited to a certain number, such as for the climb of Mount Everest (Fig. 10.9). There may be laws and regulations prohibiting photography or for removing plants and flowers, shells and corals, rocks and stones.

POLICE ENFORCEMENT

The ultimate step in controlling visitor behavior is through law enforcement, and unfortunately, this is not too uncommon in many destinations. Police should deal with visitors who are drunk and disorderly; involved in illegal activities, such as narcotics and sex tourism; or guilty of shoplifting, assault, vandalism or other crimes.

There are several alternative ways to manage visitor behavior, and they range from inviting voluntary behaviors through codes of conduct to enforcing visitor behavior through police intervention. Destination managers have a key role to play in clearly communicating model and acceptable behaviors to visitors in the pre-trip and within-destination phases of travel. Codes of responsible tourism behavior are particularly important and should be developed by all destinations to suit the specific local circumstances.

Yield Management

Yield management was popularized among airlines and later adopted by hotels as revenue management. Unlike airlines and hotels, yield or revenue management is more difficult to apply to destinations for two main reasons. Destinations and DMOs usually have no inventory under their direct control to sell to visitors. Thus, they have no direct income generated from visitors. Rather, yield management for destinations focuses on the expenditures of visitors.

DEFINITION

Destination yield management

Yield management is a process that a destination applies to maximize visitor expenditures within a given time period. This process involves consideration of market segments, pricing levels, seasons and time periods, and economic conditions.

Destination yield management requires the involvement of DMOs along with their tourism sector stakeholders. The components of destination yield management are shown in Figure 10.20.

The following are short explanations of the yield management components depicted in Figure 10.20:

- Visitor markets: a destination's target markets have differing spending propensities.
- Segmentation: the destination must segment its markets and estimate segment spending potentials.
- Economic conditions: fluctuating economic conditions will affect markets and spending levels.
- Prices: the rates charged by hotels, admission prices, and other stakeholders' pricing levels.

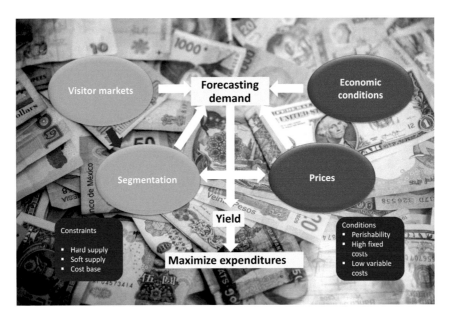

Figure 10.20 Destination yield management components (HOSPA and Jones 2017: 8).

- Forecasting demand: future visitor numbers and the market breakdown must be projected.
- Yield: the proportion of achieved expenditures to potential total expenditures.
- Maximize expenditures: the goal of destination yield management is to maximize visitor expenditures.
- Constraints: factors that limit expenditure creation in a destination, including the physical capacity of resources.
- Conditions: general factors in tourism that affect expenditure creation, including perishability and types of costs.

EXAMPLE 10.19

More "Quality Tourism" Wanted for Southeast Asia

Destinations are becoming increasingly conscious and concerned about the yields from specific types of visitors.

These objectives are directing the discussion toward "quality tourism." Various interpretations are voiced by political leaders. These include high-quality tourism (Indonesia), high-yield tourists (Malaysia), high-end tourists (Cambodia), and high-value, low-impact tourism (Thailand). The goal is the same, to augment average visitor spend. The result of this ongoing quest to monetize inbound tourism will be an increase in the overall cost of travel in Southeast Asia. This will impact international and domestic tourists.

(Bowerman 2022)

Learning Point

Quality tourism is more preferable than quantity (or mass) tourism.

HOSPA and Jones (2017) provides a simple and easy to understand version of destination yield management, expressed as five rights: selling the right destination products and experiences, to the right customers, at the right times, for the right prices and through the right channels. Yield management is not an accidental thing that automatically happens in a destination; rather, it is a strategic approach to visitor management. Thus, applying the five rights to destinations means having the following:

1. Right products and experiences: DMOs must select to market the products and experiences with the greatest expenditure potential.
2. Right customers: The target markets with the greatest expenditure-generating potential must be selected.
3. Right times: Approaches need to be varied by season and time of year and according to economic conditions.
4. Right prices: Excessive discounting and other price-cutting approaches are to be avoided and full cost-recovery guaranteed.
5. Right channels: Distribution channels that deliver the highest prices should be chosen over those that require deep discounts.

Many destinations around the world aspire to attract high-spending visitors. So, for example, they want to discourage low-yield visitors, such as youthful backpackers, and encourage high-yield visitors, such as luxury seekers. However, backpackers stay much longer than other tourists and may even spend more for their entire trips. The export content of serving specific markets must also be considered. For example, luxury seekers may stay in resorts that repatriate much of their profits to other countries. Thus, differentiating between high- and low-yielding visitors is not as simple as it seems but requires a more sophisticated analysis of many factors.

DMOs should set up yield management teams composed of people with differing skills and knowledge, including destination marketing, branding, and communication, market research and forecasting, managerial accounting, hotel revenue management, airline yield management, attractions, retail shopping and restaurants, and inbound tour operators and travel agencies.

Other Visitor Management Efforts

There are other visitor management efforts in which DMOs should engage. Many of these activities relate to the destination marketing, branding, and communications, planning and research, and product development roles of DMOs. For example, as you will learn in Chapters 12–15, DMOs need to track and analyze UGC online and mainly on social media. Also, the co-creation of online contents provides a great opportunity for DMOs to interact with visitors. DMOs should on occasion seek advice for past and potential visitors as well as gathering research data from people. The emergence of the metaverse is another reason why destinations and DMOs need to become more engaged in visitor management.

EXAMPLE 10.20

The Metaverse Will Transform the Tourism Industry

The metaverse is expected to have a significant effect on how people gather and use information about destinations.

The metaverse can also help and improve tourism-related businesses:

- Virtual tours of hotels, museums, convention centers and destinations, even more immersive, inclusive and realistic, easily enjoyed from home.
- Inspections or simulations of the physical hotel experience before the event date. In fact, the user could anticipate the experience of the stay by viewing the room, common areas, and surroundings before booking.
- Event organizers could view room setup options and choose the best one in minutes.

(Canzani 2022)

Learning Point

Destinations must quickly get prepared for much wider visitor use of metaverse.

Steps in Effective Visitor Management

For the most effective visitor management, DMOs need to do the following:

- Prepare a plan incorporating all the components of visitor management.
- Work in harmony with resource protection agencies.
- Develop strategies and approaches for visitor planning, monitoring, and management.
- Assess the current levels of safety and security for visitors within the destination.
- Implement approaches to ensure greater safety and security for visitors.
- Assess all potential risks of crises and disasters in the destination and develop a crisis and management plan (Chapter 11).
- Establish codes for visitor behavior, especially related to sustainable and responsible tourism.
- Apply yield management to the destination.
- Build a yield management team.

SUMMING UP

Although visitor management is not a traditional role, it is now essential that DMOs recognize this responsibility. The ADVICE model indicates the interactions that visitors have within destinations and where visitor management is required. The benefits to be gained from effective visitor management are improved and expanded interpretation and information, more community and stakeholder involvement, greater harmony with residents, increased visitor safety and enjoyment, higher economic yield, and better resource protection and conservation.

There are several processes that can be used for visitor planning, monitoring, and management, several of which were designed for recreation in protected areas. These include TCC, ROS, LAC, VAMP, VIM, VERP, TOMM, and the BBM.

Visitor safety and security are becoming increasingly critical for destinations, even more so as a result of COVID-19. Safety has both perceived and real dimensions from a visitor perspective. Visitors will temporarily or permanently avoid destinations that they perceive to be unsafe. DMOs must anticipate all potential dangers that visitors face and take steps to reduce these. Every DMO should develop a crisis management plan.

In today's highly competitive tourism marketplace, destinations must exceed visitor expectations or risk having dissatisfied customers. Expectations, experiences, enjoyment, and satisfaction are linked concepts, and DMOs need to conduct research with visitors to fully understand how their destinations are performing.

DMOs should apply various techniques of interpretation to inform and educate visitors about their destinations. Apart from the educational aspect, interpretation can increase visitor enjoyment and enhance destination experiences. Also, it is a vehicle for communicating important messages about the natural environment, heritage and culture.

Visitor behavior needs to be monitored and in some cases, regulated and controlled. Rules and codes of conduct should be developed, especially to encourage responsible tourism behaviors among visitors.

Yield management techniques should be applied to destinations to maximize the beneficial economic impacts of tourism. This involves making choices among different market segments and considering pricing levels and seasonality.

Other visitor management efforts correspond to the DMO roles of marketing, branding and communications, planning and research, and product development. For example, gathering and analyzing visitor UGC is important in shaping marketing programs as well as determining visitor satisfaction levels with destinations.

KEYWORDS

ADVICE model
augmented reality (AR)
authenticity
benefits-based model (BBM)
carrying capacity
co-create
codes of conduct
degrowth
demarketing
ecological carrying
    capacity
economic carrying capacity
environmental carrying
    capacity
food safety
gentrification
impacts
interpretation

limits of acceptable change
    (LAC)
memorable experiences
metaverse
monitoring
overcrowding
overtourism
perceived safety
perceptual carrying capacity
physical carrying capacity
real safety
recreation opportunity spec-
    trum (ROS)
responsible tourism
selfie sticks
social carrying capacity
smart tourism
sustainable tourism

tourism carrying capacity
    (TCC)
tourism optimization man-
    agement model (TOMM)
tracking
travel advisories
triple bottom line
virtual reality
visitor activity management
    process (VAMP)
visitor experience and
    resource protection
    (VERP)
visitor impact model
    (VIM)
visitor management
visitor planning processes
yield management

REVIEW QUESTIONS

1. How would you define visitor management?
2. What are the elements of the ADVICE model?
3. What are the reasons for and benefits from visitor management?
4. How would you describe resource protection and conservation from the visitor management perspective?
5. What are the procedures involved in visitor planning, monitoring, and management?
6. How can destinations and DMOs plan to assure visitors of greater safety?
7. Why are visitor interpretation, education, and information important?
8. What steps should DMOs take to enhance visitor experiences, enjoyment, and satisfaction?
9. Why do DMOs need to be concerned about visitor behavior?
10. How should destinations apply yield management and for what purpose?

REFERENCES

Bakker, M., Daniels, J., Ellermann, U., Hödl, C., and Solis-Sosa, R. (2015) "An Integrated Management Framework for the Clayoquot Sound Biosphere Reserve: An Application of TOMM in the Pacific Northwest," University of Natural Resources and Applied Life Sciences, Vienna, Simon Fraser University.

Barbados Today (2022) "New Safety Standards for Tourism Industry," March 5, https://barbadostoday.bb/2022/03/05/new-safety-standards-for-tourism-industry

Bettini, J. (2018) "Smart Destinations: Quality Tourism for Visitors and Sustainable Development for Residents," Inter-American Development Bank, https://blogs.iadb.org/sostenibilidad/en/smart-destinations-quality-tourism-for-visitors-and-sustainable-development-for-residents

Bowerman, G. (2022) "Raising the Cost of Tourism in South East Asia," Asia Media Centre, August 10, www.asiamediacentre.org.nz/features/raising-the-cost-of-tourism-in-south-east-asia

Bretlaender, D., and Toth, P. (2014) "Kwanini Carrying Capacity Assessment (Pemba, Tanzania)," www.themantaresort.com/files/ccs.pdf

Buckley, R., and Pannell, J. (1990) "Environmental Impacts of Tourism and Recreation in National Parks and Conservation Reserves," *Journal of Tourism Studies*, 1 (1): 24–32.

Canzani, M. (2022) "The Metaverse Will Transform the Tourism Industry," *The Cryptonomist*, August 13, https://en.cryptonomist.ch/2022/08/13/metaverse-transform-tourism-industry

Current Archaeology (2022) "Uist Unearthed: Hebridean Archaeology Goes Virtual," *The Past*, August 3, https://the-past.com/feature/uist-unearthed-hebridean-archaeology-goes-virtual

Discover Baja Travel Club (2022) "Conservation Passports," https://www.discoverbaja.com/go/conservation-passports/

Disneyland Resort (2022) "The Official Mobile App for the Disneyland Resort Puts the Magic at Your Fingertips," https://disneyland.disney.go.com/guest-services/download-disneyland-mobile-app/

Duan, J., Xie, C. W., and Morrison, A. M. (2022) "Tourism Crises and Impacts on Destinations: A Systematic Review of the Tourism and Hospitality Literature," *Journal of Hospitality and Tourism Research*, 46 (4): 667–695.

Government of Mexico (2022) "Pasaporte de la Conservación," https://pasaportedelaconservacion.conanp.gob.mx/vistas/inicio.php

Green Barrier Reef Marine Park Authority (Australia) (2022) "How Marine Park Zoning Works," www2.gbrmpa.gov.au/access/zoning/how-it-works

Hall, C. M., and Wood, K. J. (2021) "Demarketing Tourism for Sustainability: Degrowing Tourism or Moving the Deckchairs on the *Titanic*?" *Sustainability*, 13: 1585.

HOSPA and Jones, P. A. (ed.) (2017) *Revenue Management*, 2nd edn, Bournemouth: Wentworth Jones.

International Institute for Environment and Development (2022) "Assessing Social Impacts of Protected and Conserved Areas," www.iied.org/assessing-social-impacts-protected-areas

International Union for Conservation of Nature (2022) "Protected Areas and Land Use," www.iucn.org/theme/protected-areas/about

Kaleem, J. (2022) "Welcome to Portugal, the New Expat Haven. Californians, Please Go Home," *Los Angeles Times*, May 12, www.latimes.com/world-nation/story/2022-05-12/california-expats-portugal-relocation-lisbon

Kerala Tourism (India) (2022) "Code of Ethics for Travellers and Tour Operators," www.keralatourism.org/guidelines/index.html

Knopf, L. (2016) "What Is SoLoMo and Why Is It Important?" *Optimistic*, March 2. www.optimistics.co.uk/blog/what-solomo-and-why-it-important#.WpdonOhubn0

Korea Tourism Organization (2018) "Tourist Police," https://english.visitkorea.or.kr/enu/TRV/TV_ENG_3_3.jsp

McCool, S. F, Clark, R. N., and Stankey, G. (2007) "An Assessment of Frameworks Useful for Public Land Recreation Planning," US Forest Service, www.fs.usda.gov/treesearch/pubs/26955

McMillan, A. F. (2016) "China Cracks Down on Forced Shopping and Cheap Tours," TheStreet, November 25, https://realmoney.thestreet.com/articles/11/25/2016/china-cracks-down-forced-shopping-and-cheap-tours

Manidis Roberts Consultants (1997) *Developing a Tourism Optimisation Management Model (TOMM): A Model to Monitor and Manage Tourism on Kangaroo Island, South Australia: Final Report*, Surry Hills, NSW, Australia.

Mason, P. (2008) *Tourism Impacts, Planning and Management*, 2nd edn, London and New York, NY: Routledge.

Musée du Louvre (2022) "Museum Rules," www.louvre.fr/en/visit/museum-rules

Newsome, D., Moore, S. A., and Dowling, R. K. (2013) *Natural Area Tourism: Ecology, Impacts and Management*, 2nd edn, Bristol: Channel View.

Oliver R. L. (1980) "A Cognitive Model of the Antecedents and Consequences of Satisfaction Decisions," *Journal of Marketing Research*, 17 (4): 460–469.

Ono, R., and James, H. (2022) "Fans of Netflix Series Disrupt Peaceful Swiss Village," swissinfo.ch, August 27, https://www.swissinfo.ch/eng/business/fans-of-netflix-series-disrupt-peaceful-swiss-village/47851764

Padrón-Ávila, H., and Hernández-Martín, R. (2020) "Tourist Tracking Techniques as a Tool to Understand and Manage Tourism Flows," in H. Séraphin, T. Gladkikh, and T. Vo Thanh (eds), *Overtourism: Causes, Implications and Solutions*, Basingstoke: Palgrave Macmillan, pp. 89–105.

Parks Canada (2017a) "Visitor Activity Management Process (VAMP)," www.pc.gc.ca/en/docs/pc/poli/princip/gloss#v

——— (2017b) "2015–2016 Departmental Performance Report," www.pc.gc.ca/en/docs/pc/rpts/rmr-dpr/03312016#sec03-p4

——— (2022) "Banff National Park of Canada Management Plan 2022," www.pc.gc.ca/en/pn-np/ab/banff/info/gestion-management/involved/plan/plan-2022

Procter, E. (2022) "A Sunken City and an Instagrammer's Dream: Dubai's New Water Attractions Tap into Revenge Tourism Trend," CNBC, August 23, www.cnbc.com/2022/08/23/dubais-water-attractions-tap-into-revenge-tourism-trend.html

Responsible Tourism Partnership (2022) "Overtourism," http://responsibletourismpartnership.org/overtourism

Retail & Leisure International (2022) "The UK's First Location Based Flying Experience in VR, Fly Mt Snowdon Opens at Adventure Parc Snowdonia," www.rli.uk.com/the-uks-first-location-based-flying-experience-in-vr-fly-mt-snowdon-opens-at-adventure-parc-snowdonia

SERNATUR, Chile (2022) "Sustainable Travel," www.chilesustentable.travel

South African Tourism (2022) "Say NO to Animal Interaction," www.southafrica.net/gl/en/travel/article/say-no-to-animal-interaction

Sri Lanka Police (2022) "Tourist Police," www.police.lk/index.php/item/50-tourist-police

Sri Lanka Tourism Promotion Bureau (2022) "Safe and Secure Certificate," https://srilanka.travel/safe-and-secure

Stratton, M. (2022) "How New Initiatives Are Protecting the Galápagos for Future Generations," August 26, *National Geographic*, www.nationalgeographic.co.uk/travel/2022/08/how-new-initiatives-are-protecting-the-galapagos-for-future-generations

Tilden, F. (1957) *Interpreting Our Heritage: Principles and Practices for Parks, Museums, and Heritage Places*, Chapel Hill, NC: University of North Carolina Press.

Tourism Recreation Research and Education Centre (2006) *Tourism Planning Toolkit for Local Government*, Lincoln: Lincoln University.

United Nations Educational, Scientific and Cultural Organization (2022) "World Heritage List," http://whc.unesco.org/en/list

United Nations Environment Programme (1999) "Carrying Capacity Assessment for Tourism Development: Coastal Area Management Programme (CAMP) FUKA-MATROUH—Egypt," https://iczmplatform.org/storage/documents/xxnSWbLStRM7QQQdnjsHx3jPfSNMb2U8zm6Gza4z.pdf

US Forest Service (2022a) "ROS Primer and Field Guide," www.fs.usda.gov/Internet/FSE_DOCUMENTS/stelprdb5335339.pdf

—— (2022b) "Limits of Acceptable Change," www.fs.usda.gov/detail/dbnf/home/?cid=stelprdb5346360

White, J. (2022) "Irish Tourist Safety Advice in 2022 with Spain and Portugal Considered 'High Risk'," *Irish Mirror*, August 4, www.irishmirror.ie/news/irish-news/irish-tourist-safety-advice-2022-27639958

Chapter **11**

Destination Crisis Management

Be prepared, endure, and prosper

LEARNING OBJECTIVES

Having read this chapter, you should be able to:

1. define crises and disasters;
2. identify the categories of crises and disasters;
3. explain why destinations are susceptible to crises and disasters;
4. describe how crises and disasters impact tourism;
5. identify the stages of a crisis or disaster;
6. elaborate on crisis management planning;
7. describe the steps in crisis communications strategy and planning;
8. explain the concept of risk management;
9. describe how destinations can increase their resilience to crises and disasters;
10. explain the recovery process from crises and disasters.

DOI: 10.4324/9781003343356-13

Warming Up

You are probably well aware of crises as a result of the COVID-19 pandemic. The news during 2020, 2021, and 2022 was full of stories on how COVID decimated travel and tourism worldwide. Can you think of other crises or disasters that damaged or are hurting tourism? There are plenty of them, and it was not difficult to find examples for this chapter.

You will learn in this chapter that destinations and DMOs need to be prepared for crisis and disasters since they inevitably happen in tourism. The main lesson you will get is that it is wrong to wait until bad things occur; it is much better to be proactive and anticipate crises and disasters. Destinations and DMOs also need to endure these events and be resilient, and plot clever and innovative recovery strategies to prosper in the future.

The chapter begins with clear definitions of crises and disasters and then discusses their categories and sub-categories. It explains why tourism and destinations are so prone to experiencing negative outcomes as a result of crises and disasters, and how these events tend to impact the sector. Next, the stages of crises and disasters are identified.

Chapter 11 concludes with sharing important information about the management of crises and disasters. What do destinations and DMOs do when faced with significant crises and disasters? The topics are crisis management planning, crisis communications strategy and planning, risk management, and resilience-building and recovery. It emphasizes the importance of being truthful and consistent in crisis communications. Some crisis communication failures in tourism are highlighted.

Your author was asked to develop and deliver a training program on crisis management in Indonesia. This was a great experience for him and he learned much from participants who had gone through major crises and disasters in their destinations. As the co-editor-in-chief of the *International Journal of Tourism Cities*, he has been guest editor for special issues on terrorism, overtourism, and COVID-19 impacts. Preparing several research articles about crises and crisis management has also increased the author's knowledge of these topics. As usual, the author wants to give you a practical account of crisis management based upon these experiences, rather than loading this chapter with theoretical concepts (of which there are many). Also, as you will soon see, the contents have a global perspective with examples from many different countries. Crises and disasters know no geographic boundaries and we hope that you too will recognize the need to look at these important topics with a world view.

In writing this chapter, the author has considered how destinations and DMOs deal with the crises and disasters that affect them. However, you should be aware from Chapters 2 and 3 that DMOs need to practice social responsibility and that means they must try to share in helping others to solve their problems. For example, poverty might not exist in the destination, but it does in other places. Homelessness is not necessarily a result of tourism; however, DMOs can contribute to its alleviation. We hope you get the point here.

Definitions of Crises and Disasters

It is always good to start with clear definitions of the main topics in a chapter. You might be wondering also about the difference between a crisis and a disaster—you will get the answer later. Here are the working definitions for the two terms.

DEFINITIONS

Crisis

A crisis is an event or circumstances that severely compromise or damage the demand, tourism sector, marketability, and reputation of a tourism destination.

Disasters

"Disasters are serious disruptions to the functioning of a community that exceed its capacity to cope using its own resources. Disasters can be caused by natural, human-made and technological hazards, as well as various factors that influence the exposure and vulnerability of a community" (International Federation of Red Cross and Red Crescent Societies 2022).

One important point made in the definition of disasters is that they are not just natural ones. Historically, the disasters at Bhopal, India (1984) (*Business Standard* 2022) and Chernobyl, Ukraine (1986) (International Atomic Energy Agency 2022) were human-made; when Hurricane Sandy hit New York City in 2015 that was a natural disaster (Gibbens 2019).

Disasters tend to occur in specific destinations (the earthquakes in Christchurch, New Zealand, in 2010 and 2011) or geographic regions (e.g., the Indian Ocean tsunami in 2004) and result in significant losses of lives and injuries, as well as physical devastation of buildings and infrastructure. Normally, the causes of disasters are clearly identifiable. Many crises are more broad-ranging and may not result in physical damage or significant deaths and injuries (e.g., energy shortages).

When the second edition of this book was published in 2018, there was no suggestion that a major global crisis lay ahead for the tourism sector that would be a game-changer. Of course, that was COVID-19 and its emergence shows how unexpected crises and disasters can be. The result was that globally 2020 was the worst year ever for the tourism sector.

EXAMPLE 11.1

2020 Was Worst Year in Tourism History

After many years of continuous growth, tourism experienced a huge global downturn in 2020.

> While few industries have been spared by the impact of the COVID-19 pandemic over the past two years, even fewer have been hit as hard as the tourism sector. After "the worst year in tourism history," international tourist arrivals increased by just 5 percent in 2021, as travel restrictions remained in place for protracted periods in many parts of the world. International tourist arrivals once again fell more than one billion short of pre-pandemic levels, keeping the industry at levels last seen in the late 1980s.
>
> (Richter 2022)

Part II

> **Learning Point**
>
> The tourism sector has gone through unprecedented change in the past three years.

COVID-19 can be classified as a health safety crisis as was SARS (Severe Acute Respiratory Syndrome) that occurred earlier in 2002–2003. Now, you will hear about all the categories of crises and disasters.

Categories of Crises and Disasters

Crises can result from external (not limited to the destination itself) and internal (within-destination and/or DMO) forces. External crises generally cannot be completely controlled by the destination or DMO; internal crises have the potential of being managed and resolved. Tourism has been affected by many crises and disasters, most of which were beyond the control of destinations and DMOs. Crises and disasters can be classified into seven different categories:

1. natural disasters;
2. security crises;
3. economic and financial crises;
4. health safety crises;
5. environmental safety crises;
6. accidents and calamities;
7. public opinion crises.

(Duan et al. 2022; Figure 11.1)

The following are some sub-categories of these crises and disasters (Duan et al. 2022; Fotiou 2012; Ritchie and Roser 2021; Rossell et al. 2020).

Figure 11.1 Categories of crises and disasters (Duan et al. 2022, p. 676).

NATURAL DISASTERS

Avalanches, climate change impacts (e.g., drought), cyclones, earthquakes, floods, hailstorms, hurricanes, landslides, storms, tornadoes, tsunamis, typhoons, volcanoes, wildfires and bushfires. The flooding in Pakistan and the Australian wildfires are cases reflecting these types of disasters. The situation in Pakistan in 2022 was attributed to the effects of climate change.

EXAMPLE 11.2

Climate Change Negatively Affects Pakistan's Tourism

Climate change is deeply and adversely impacting tourism in several countries including Pakistan.

> "Tourism had begun growing in Pakistan and especially in Lahore at the end of the last decade. But then COVID-19 struck," Adil said. While the global tourism industry was jolted by the coronavirus pandemic, it was yet another knockout punch for Pakistan, which had only just begun its recovery. Despite the country's relative success in countering COVID-19, the pandemic also brought a climate wake-up call for Lahore.
>
> (Shahid 2022)

Learning Point

Destinations must become more proactive in dealing with issues caused by climate change.

SECURITY CRISES

Crime, civil and social unrest, harassment, political instability, refugee crises, regional conflicts, terrorism, wars. 9/11 fits into this category as does the conflict in Ukraine with Russia.

ECONOMIC AND FINANCIAL CRISES

Cost of living crises, devaluations, energy crises, export declines, foreign exchange shortages and rate fluctuations, high rates of inflation, labor shortages, productivity declines, recessions, stock market crashes, unemployment. The cost of living and energy crises being experienced in Europe and the UK at the time of writing are examples.

EXAMPLE 11.3

Cost of Living Crisis in Europe

At the time of writing, Europe was experiencing a major cost of living crisis.

> The Eurozone's tourism boom, aided by the single currency's fall against the dollar, is one bright spot in a region that economists are increasingly concerned will fall into recession over the second half of this year. But by the time the weather cools European businesses and consumers will face more economic

pressure. The war in Ukraine has left the region's factories, barely recovered from the pandemic, facing fresh supply-chain woes. Germany's more manufacturing-dependent economy stagnated in the second quarter, missing analysts' expectations of a slight expansion and highlighting how grave the situation is for northern economies that can rely less on hospitality.

Russia's invasion and doubts over Moscow's willingness to keep gas flowing to Europe has triggered a surge in households' energy costs, which are up by 40 percent over the past twelve months, while food costs are up by 10 per cent over the same period, leading to the worst cost of living crisis in decades.

(Kazim et al. 2022)

Learning Point

Cost of living crises inevitably have a knock-on (negative) impact on tourism.

HEALTH SAFETY CRISES

Animal epidemics, human epidemics and pandemics, food safety and foodborne diseases, plagues, plant epidemics, transmissible and contagious diseases. You already know that COVID-19 fits here, as does bovine foot-and-mouth disease.

ENVIRONMENTAL SAFETY CRISES

Air pollution and air quality crises, cold waves, coral bleaching, deforestation, heatwaves, insect infestations, land erosion, global warming/climate change, noise pollution, nuclear disasters, oil and gas spills, plastic disposal pollution, soil pollution, traffic congestion, water-body pollution. On a global scale, climate change is one of the root causes of these crises.

ACCIDENTS AND CALAMITIES

Air, rail, road, and water accidents; operational accidents; toxic material releases. The nuclear disasters at Chernobyl (Ukraine) and Fukushima (Japan) are examples.

PUBLIC OPINION CRISES

Boycotts, petitions, and protests; improper and unethical conduct; scandals. You are going to hear later about the boycott of travel to Hong Kong by citizens of Mainland China as an example of a public opinion crisis.

When does a problem situation get labeled as a crisis? The answer to this question is rather elusive; however, let us think about it together. The topic of this chapter is about public crises rather than personal (individual) ones. So, when a problem situation is publicized in the traditional or social media, it is in the first stages of becoming a crisis. Then, if the situation receives widespread media and netizen coverage—and is called a crisis in these media—it is further on its way to being a crisis. A good example here is the overtourism concept that went from a mention in a *Skift* article in 2016 (Ali 2018) to a full-blown worldwide crisis by 2019. Some crises are very deep-rooted and are more insidious. One of these not mentioned so far in the sub-categories is racism. Your author sees racism as a social crisis affecting tourism and destinations (and society in general), and other experts agree (Goodwin 2020; Temblador 2020).

The anti-Asian backlash that accompanied COVID-19 is an example of racial discrimination in tourism (Wassler and Talarico 2021; Zheng et al. 2020). Homelessness is another global social issue that seems to be under the radar as a crisis and is not often mentioned in connection with tourism and destinations (Chambers 2014).

This list of crises and disasters is long and intimidating. What do you think of this extensive inventory of crises and disasters? The more worrying aspect is that all of these can impact tourism and destinations. Are these crises or disasters separate or do they connect to each other? This is a good question and the answer is that that they can occur in clusters and some are antecedents (come before) others. The example about Cuba demonstrates this point.

EXAMPLE 11.4

Cuba's Tourism Impacted by Several Crises

Coping with simultaneous, multiple crises is demonstrated here in Cuba's case.

> On top of an energy crisis, Cuba has suffered repeated shocks to its vital tourism industry this year. Western sanctions on Russia after its February invasion of Ukraine restricted a flow of visitors to the island. An explosion caused by a gas leak ripped through a top luxury hotel in the capital just before it was due to reopen in May, killing dozens.
>
> (Wicary and Bloomburg 2022)

Learning Point

Many destinations are having to deal with multiple crises that are extenuating the negative effects on tourism.

Why do you think tourism experiences so many crises and disasters? It would be interesting to listen to your answers. There are several reasons and next we are going to discuss why tourism is so susceptible to crises and disasters.

Susceptibility of Destinations to Crises and Disasters

The COVID-19 pandemic proved to all how vulnerable tourism is to crises and disasters. Ask yourself, why is it so? The answer is about the level of susceptibility to crisis and disaster impacts.

General Susceptibility in Tourism

Tourism destinations need to be especially well prepared and vigilant concerning potential crises and disasters. This is because tourism is highly susceptible and prone to the adverse impacts of these events. Tourism is an open system that can be affected and influenced by a variety of external sources, for example:

- Financial crises affect people's ability to travel.
- Political crises and civil unrest may deter tourists from traveling to specific destinations, e.g., the conflict in Ukraine described in the example.

- Tourists travel to destinations that are more prone to disasters, such as coastal and mountainous areas.
- Accidents and disasters happen when tourists are using modes of transportation.
- Tourists often engage in activities that are dangerous.
- Tourists have become a favored target of terrorists.

The openness of tourism makes the sector fragile to influence by external factors. You will learn about the PESTEL framework in this book and that is the acronym for political, economic, societal, technological, environmental, and legal factors that affect tourism. The PESTEL factors can positively or negatively affect destinations.

Specific Susceptibility

Are some geographic areas and destinations more susceptible to crises and disasters than others? If you answered in the positive, you are definitely correct. For example, countries bordering on the conflict in Ukraine were more likely to be negatively affected than ones further away from the war. The UNWTO has produced a report on the impacts of the war.

EXAMPLE 11.5

Impact of Russia–Ukraine Conflict on International Tourism

Military conflicts have immediate negative impacts on tourism that spread into nearby regions.

> The military offensive risks hampering the return of confidence to global travel. The US and Asian source markets could be particularly impacted, especially regarding travel to Europe, as these markets are historically more risk averse.
>
> The destinations most impacted so far (aside from Russia and Ukraine) are the Republic of Moldova with a 69 percent drop in flights since 24 February (compared to 2019 levels), Slovenia (–42 percent), Latvia (–38 percent) and Finland (–36 percent) according to data from Eurocontrol. Russian bookings of outbound flights also plunged in late February and early March but have since rebounded according to data from Forwardkeys.
>
> (UNWTO 2022)

Learning Point

War and tourism do not mix well.

Some countries and states are more likely to experience natural disasters than others due to their locations or geographic characteristics. California is prone to earthquakes as are parts of New Zealand. Florida, Louisiana, and Caribbean areas are often in the paths of hurricanes, while cyclones and typhoons regularly hit the northeast of Australia and the Philippines, Taiwan, and the East Coast of China. Indonesia is known for being on the Ring of Fire and experiences volcanic eruptions as well as earthquakes. You can probably think of many more examples.

Then there are parts of the world that suffer more from security crises including the Middle East, and parts of Africa and Latin America. Rescue.org (2022) lists Sudan, Somalia, Democratic Republic of Congo, South Sudan, Nigeria, and Ethiopia, all in Africa, as places with major political and other issues; Syria, Yemen, and Afghanistan are others named that are more associated with the Middle East. You can imagine that these are destinations most travelers will avoid rather than being attracted to them. Myanmar in Southeast Asia is another country listed by Rescue.org. Lebanon is another country that seems to be plagued by continual security crises and so much so that the tourism sector is appealing for help from Lebanese living abroad.

EXAMPLE 11.6

Lebanon Faces Economic and Energy Crises

Some destinations suffer from recurring crises and find recovery to be especially difficult. (Note: A diaspora represents people who originated from a particular country and now live in other countries.)

> Lebanon, facing rampant power cuts and skyrocketing inflation, relies on the diaspora for hard currency. Rampant power cuts over the past year, a more than 1,000 percent increase in the price of food, and a Lebanese pound that has lost more than 90 percent of its value against the dollar in three years are just a few of the many factors that make operating a business expensive.
>
> (Chehayeb 2022)

Learning Point

In times of major crises, destinations may turn to their diasporas for help and assistance.

You will recall from Chapter 2 the discussion of the United Nation's Sustainable Development Goals, also known as the SDGs. The SDGs correspond to major global issues and crises and these are shown in Figure 11.2.

You will see in Figure 11.2 that climate change is identified as a major global crisis. Environment crises on land (SDG15) and below water (SDG15) and with fresh water supplies (SDG6) are another three of the global crises. Gender quality is specified as a global issue (SDG5), as are poverty (SDG1) and energy (SDG7). It is not hard to see the connections between these issues and crises and disasters that are affecting destinations including, for example, the influence of climate change on wildfires (D'Amore 2020), drought (Drought. gov 2022), rising levels of oceans (McConnell 2022), deforestation (Šergo et al. 2014), polar icecap reductions (Wang et al. 2020), and coral bleaching (Great Barrier Reef Foundation 2022).

The United Nations in a recent report talked about the "cascading" of global crises and how this is making the achievement of the SDGs more difficult.

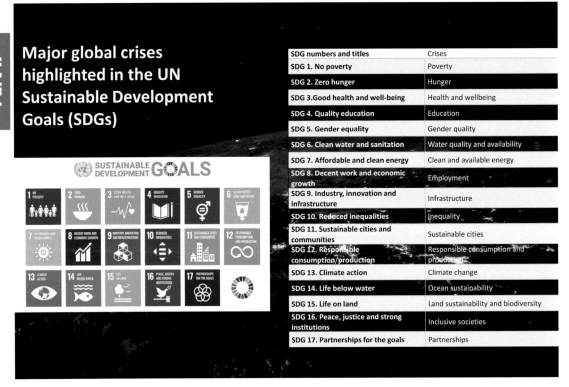

Major global crises highlighted in the UN Sustainable Development Goals (SDGs)

SDG numbers and titles	Crises
SDG 1. No poverty	Poverty
SDG 2. Zero hunger	Hunger
SDG 3.Good health and well-being	Health and wellbeing
SDG 4. Quality education	Education
SDG 5. Gender equality	Gender quality
SDG 6. Clean water and sanitation	Water quality and availability
SDG 7. Affordable and clean energy	Clean and available energy
SDG 8. Decent work and economic growth	Employment
SDG 9. Industry, innovation and infrastructure	Infrastructure
SDG 10. Reduced inequalities	Inequality
SDG 11. Sustainable cities and communities	Sustainable cities
SDG 12. Responsible consumption/production	Responsible consumption and production
SDG 13. Climate action	Climate change
SDG 14. Life below water	Ocean sustainability
SDG 15. Life on land	Land sustainability and biodiversity
SDG 16. Peace, justice and strong institutions	Inclusive societies
SDG 17. Partnerships for the goals	Partnerships

Figure 11.2 Sustainable Development Goals (SDGs) and related global crises.

EXAMPLE 11.7

Cascading Global Crises

Multiple crises are challenging the achievement of the SDGs.

> The climate crisis, the COVID-19 pandemic and an increased number of conflicts around the world have placed the seventeen SDGs in jeopardy, according to *The Sustainable Development Goals Report* 2022, released by the United Nations today. The report highlights the severity and magnitude of the challenges before us, with these cascading and intersecting crises creating spin-off impacts on food and nutrition, health, education, the environment, and peace and security, and affecting all the SDGs, the blueprint for more resilient, peaceful and equal societies.
>
> (United Nations 2022)

Learning Point

Crises such as COVID-19 may divert attention away from the SDGs.

Now, you know that there are multiple crises and disasters that are influencing tourism. In which ways do crises and disasters affect tourism and destinations? This is the next topic for our discussion.

Impacts of Crises and Disasters on Tourism

Crises and disasters impact the demand and supply sides of tourism, as well as influencing the economic, social-cultural, and natural environments that affect destinations. What are the impacts then? Taking COVID-19 as an example, your author noted the following impacts in keynote presentations in 2022 at the conferences of the Tourism Sciences Society of Korea and the International Tourism Studies Association (Morrison 2022a, 2022b):

- Changes in demand levels: The pandemic decreased international travel; however, domestic tourism grew (Freed 2021).
- Changes in forms of tourism: Staycationing (traveling closer to home in your own country) increased as did various slow tourism activities. There were greater preferences for ecotourism, food tourism, and luxury travel (Sung et al. 2021; Wen et al. 2020).
- Changes in values and behaviors: People became more environmentally responsible (*Economist* 2022) and traveled closer to home and in smaller groups.
- Job layoffs and temporary and permanent business closures: On the supply side, with no patronage many business had to lay off or furlough staff to save on operating costs. Eventually, this had a knock-on effect that some have called the "great resignation" (Chugh 2021). The tourism sector in the UK is one example of where people are choosing not to return to their former jobs in hospitality and travel.

EXAMPLE 11.8

Tourism Job Crisis in UK

The global pandemic has been a human resource catastrophe for tourism and hospitality.

> Almost 130,000 travel and tourism jobs in the UK remain unfilled with many establishments struggling to find staff following the COVID pandemic. The World Travel & Tourism Council (WTTC) has warned the sector's recovery is at serious risk with one in fourteen openings expected to remain vacant.
> Restaurants and hotels are struggling to find staff but the UK government, unlike countries such as Portugal, is refusing to allow temporary workers in from overseas. The UK's hotel, entertainment, and aviation industries are forecast to be the worst affected, facing unfulfilled vacancies of 18 percent (one in six), 12 percent (one in eight), and 11 percent (one in nine), respectively.
>
> (Gibbons 2022)

Learning Point

Destinations and tourism and hospitality employers must develop new strategies to enhance the appeal of employment and careers in the sector.

The WTTC and Rescue.org (2022) quantified the economic impacts of crises and disasters on travel and tourism. They identified specific impacts as lost arrivals and lost visitor spending, and considered health crises (foot-and-mouth in the UK, Ebola in Sierra Leone, SARS in Hong Kong, Zika virus in Brazil and Miami), natural disasters (hurricane in Puerto Rico, drought in Cape Town), terrorism (Bali, Brussels, London, and Madrid), and political turmoil (MENA, Thailand). They considered ninety different crisis and disaster events in their analysis and found that impacts varied according to geographic location and for specific events. It was especially significant that civil unrest and political turmoil had the greatest and most long-lasting negative impacts, while acts of terrorism had the lowest adverse economic damage and most short-lived impacts.

Other analyses give further support to the notion that impacts vary according to individual countries and regions. For example, the Organization of Islamic Cooperation (OIC) (2017) found differences among its member countries; the Economic Commission for Latin America and the Caribbean (2020) noted differing impacts of COVID-19 on tourism in these regions.

The impacts of a crisis on a destination can be at the macro, meso, or micro levels. A macro-level impact is the most comprehensive and affects all in the destination. The meso-level is the effect on a specific sector such as tourism. The impacts on individual people and business is the micro level (Duan et al. 2022). The COVID-19 pandemic had a macro-level impact on tourism and other economic sectors worldwide. The second-home ownership issue in North Wales featured in the example is more of a meso-level impact; while a food poisoning incident on a cruise ship is at a micro level. The situation in North Wales is more of a public opinion crisis, with commentators saying it is causing anti-English feelings among residents (hence the xenophobia or dislike of outsiders or foreigners). These feelings are common around the world about second-home owners and it is not a situation just limited to Wales and England.

EXAMPLE 11.9

Second-Home Ownership Causing Problems in North Wales

Second-home ownership can cause resentment among residents of this type of visitor.

> Attempts to limit the sale of second homes, to tackle a housing crisis in tourism hotspots, are not exclusive to Wales: similar efforts are being made across England where local communities are being overwhelmed by wealthy visitors.
> Neither is Wales alone in consulting on a tourism tax, which is already commonplace in many parts of Europe and beyond. Critics say efforts to curb overtourism in these places cannot simply be ascribed to xenophobia. Instead, they are genuine attempts to tackle issues causing widespread social turmoil.
>
> (Forgrave 2022)

Learning Point

Although a long-running issue, this is approaching crisis levels in popular destinations.

Do crises and disasters, when they affect several countries, impact these countries to the same degree? The answer is "no" as some countries and destinations will be affected more than others. The World Bank Group (2020) did an analysis on a country-by-country basis on vulnerability in the face of the COVID-19 pandemic. The resulting report indicated that level of economic tourism dependency (percentage of GDP), income levels (low, medium, high), and major origin markets influenced the resilience and recovery capabilities of individual nations.

Are the outcomes of crises and disasters all negative for the tourism sector and destinations? That is an intriguing question—what are your thoughts on the answer? Some say that COVID-19 reduced overtourism and pollution, and returned environments to more like their natural states. Another interesting example is the light pollution crisis and the opportunity it has given for places with dark sky viewing.

EXAMPLE 11.10

Are There Pros and Cons to Certain Crises? Bright and Dark Skies

Dark sky tourism is experiencing an upward trend as light pollution becomes more severe.

Is it possible that apart from the negative effects, crises may produce opportunities or benefits for specific destinations? That's an intriguing question, is it not? For example, travel restrictions during COVID-19 reduced overcrowding and pollution levels at popular destinations. Here is another interesting example involving the light pollution crisis.

"Light pollution, the excessive or inappropriate use of outdoor artificial light, is affecting human health, wildlife behavior, and our ability to observe stars and other celestial objects" (National Geographic 2022).

"The Lowell Observatory in Flagstçaff, Arizona is just one of many to witness how the light pollution that seems to be encroaching everywhere has fed a growing genre of tourism. There are now travelers going to great lengths to see our increasingly rare, genuinely dark night skies. The observatory now sees 100,000 visitors a year" (Park 2018).

Learning Point

Crises in some cases benefit particular destinations by creating more demand for what they have to offer.

Stages in Crises and Disasters

Crises and disasters go through predictable stages from the perspective of a destination. Figure 11.3 shows six stages as suggested by Faulkner (2001). This model was slightly modified by Morrison and Maxim (2022) to show the before, during, and after stages.

Nowadays with social media, communications about crises and disasters are much more rapid and deeper in their content. The public opinion crisis that occurred in Mainland China after the demonstrations in Hong Kong is a good example of the power and influence of social media during a crisis or disaster.

Figure 11.3 Stages of a crisis or disaster (Faulkner 2001).

EXAMPLE 11.11

Public Opinion Crisis in Mainland China Due to Occupy Central in Hong Kong

Civil disturbances may cause resentment of destinations among potential visitors as in this case with Hong Kong. This example about Hong Kong shows how a security crisis can transform into a public opinion crisis through the spread of information on social media. Occupy Central was a civil disobedience event in Hong Kong that began in September 2014 and lasted almost eighty days. The movement was not well appreciated by many netizens in Mainland China.

> Within the secondary crisis communication, especially of Occupy Central on Weibo, more and more negative emotions toward Hong Kong were displayed, along with the intentional behavior of a tourism boycott. These showed a strong reluctance to travel to Hong Kong, as for example, one suggesting "Only those who have nothing to do will go to Hong Kong.'"
>
> (Luo and Zhai 2017: 160)

Learning Point

Public opinion backlashes occur more quickly and more extensive due to opinions shared on social media platforms.

Given the inevitability that crises and disasters will occur and influence destinations, there is a need for proactive planning and that is the next topic for discussion. The broader topic of crisis management planning is our starting point.

Crisis Management Planning

Every destination should prepare a tourism crisis management plan, but not every place has one. This is one element of the planning and research role of DMOs (Chapters 4 and 5); it is also a demonstration of leadership and requires a high level of coordination (Chapter 6). It calls for dedicated partnerships and team-building (Chapter 8), and participation from tourism sector stakeholders and local residents (Chapter 9). You might be wondering why some destinations do not have these plans—and that is something that bewilders even your author. These plans are seen more often in destinations that are prone to crisis, such as Florida and Louisiana in the southern US; other places are less likely to have them.

Two priority actions for destination crisis and disaster management are forming a special group to coordinate the tourism crisis and disaster management and planning and tasking this group initially with preparing a crisis management plan for the destination.

The 4Rs are widely considered to be four essential parts of a crisis and disaster management plan and are described in Figure 11.4. PATA published a booklet in 2003 to make the tourism sector more aware of and better prepared for crises and disasters: *Crisis: It Won't Happen to Us!* The booklet introduced the four Rs concept and suggested steps to be included for reduction, readiness, response, and recovery. The PATA booklet did not specifically address DMOs' roles in crisis and disaster management; however, your book has adapted the basic approach to DMOs. From the tourism perspective, the DMO must take a lead role in getting the destination better prepared for potential crises or disasters that will affect tourism.

You now need to know a little about each of the four Rs, starting with reduction and readiness, which are the two pre-crisis steps in the four Rs procedure.

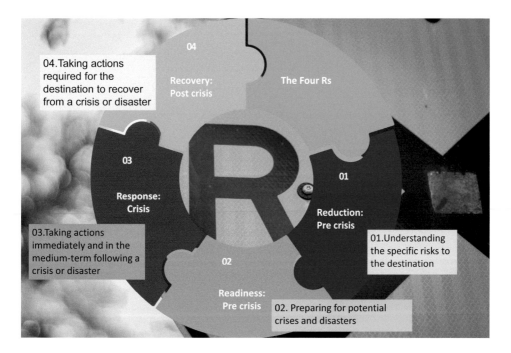

Figure 11.4 The 4Rs for crisis management planning.

An example is provided of a crisis management plan for the Murray Region of Australia. This region follows the Murray River through New South Wales and Victoria. The example is especially useful in describing the objectives of the crisis management plan.

EXAMPLE 11.12

The Murray Regional Tourism Crisis Management Plan

This Australian example demonstrates how a destination should prepare for encounters with crises.

> The Murray Regional Tourism (MRT) Crisis Management Plan has been developed so that in the event of a crisis, MRT can take a proactive stance and quickly and effectively respond to ensure that impacts on the tourism industry are minimized. The purpose of this plan is to provide MRT with an effective crisis management plan that may be enacted in the event of a tourism-related crisis within the Murray Region. It focuses on the three major phases of crisis management; planning, execution and recovery. The plan aims to:
>
> - minimize confusion among visitors about the crisis event, and support their safety;
> - increase understanding of the tourism industry's needs among stakeholders who are making decisions in response to the crisis, such as the emergency services agencies;
> - minimize misinformation in the media;
> - reduce booking cancelations and loss of business;
> - help to protect the region's brand/reputation;
> - increase the resilience of tourism operators to manage their business successfully through a crisis;
> - rapidly restore visitor confidence.
>
> (MRT Board [Australia] 2022)

Learning Point

All destinations must have crisis management plans.

Reduction: Pre-crisis

The basic purposes of the reduction stage are to lessen the risks associated with crises and to lower potential negative impacts. Mainly this stage involves identifying the potential risks and analyzing them in detail. Sometimes this is referred to as preparedness or prevention. There are four specific steps that should be coordinated by the DMO for the reduction of risk:

1. Forming a tourism crisis and disaster management group (TCDMG).
2. Building greater awareness of crises and disasters.
3. Generating political awareness and support.
4. Developing standard operating procedures (SOPs).

The first and critical step is for the DMO to establish a TCDMG. Group members should include DMO senior managers, key tourism sector stakeholders, local community leaders, emergency services officials, and others. The onset of major crises and disasters stretch a DMO's human resources beyond their limits. Therefore, it is common for DMOs to set up volunteer groups from tourism sector stakeholders and others in the community that assist in the efforts to handle crises and disasters. Volunteers need to be trained in advance of such events and prepared to perform specific tasks and roles.

The TCDMG's work begins with conducting an analysis of crises and disasters that might occur in the destination. Included in this analysis should be the following:

1. existing crisis and disaster management plans and programs;
2. potential environmental, political, economic, and other crises and disasters;
3. existing relationships with local and international media;
4. potential DMO hazards.

Government or political support is crucial, especially because crises and disasters usually affect much more than tourism. The DMO must make government leaders and officials aware of how crises and disasters negatively impact tourism and the scope and extent of their effects. They should request financial and other forms of support from government to help the destination deal with crises and disasters. Additionally, the support of emergency management agencies is needed.

The DMO should develop SOPs that help it and the destination avoid crises and hazards. These include items like conflict of interest guidelines (for DMO staff and boards of directors); competitive bidding procedures by tender; fire, hurricane, and other evacuation drills; external DMO audits; and other preventive procedures.

Readiness: Pre-crisis

The second stage is getting the destination and DMO ready for crises in general as well as for specific types of crises and disasters. DMOs must assess the potential exposure to crises and disasters and develop strategic, tactical, and communications plans. After the TCDMG has prepared the risk analysis in the reduction stage, a crisis management plan should be developed. The plan should be structured around the four Rs framework. The functions of the crisis management plan include:

- describing plan activation procedures;
- allocating roles and responsibilities;
- identifying control and coordination mechanisms;
- setting SOPs;
- specifying information requirements;
- establishing communication channels and methods;
- describing crisis communication strategies.

A crisis communications strategy should be developed now and be ready for activation during the next (response) stage. A media spokesperson should be appointed and a dark website (not yet online) be developed for launching when a crisis or disaster happens. Crisis communications are covered in greater detail in the next part of this chapter.

Another step here is considering health and safety measures. For the DMO, this means creating a network of organizations and professionals who will assist in crises and disasters, including law enforcement, fire departments, emergency services, ambulance and medical support.

The inclusion of a crisis and disaster management component in tourism destination plans is another step in the readiness stage. This is often overlooked in actual practice because these plans tend to focus on product development and marketing, branding, and communications. Several agencies have produced handbooks, manuals, and frameworks to help destinations to be readier for crises and disasters, and British Columbia, Canada is one of these. Victoria, Australia is another destination that offers an excellent set of guidelines (Business Victoria 2022).

EXAMPLE 11.13

British Columbia Tourism Emergency Management Framework

This Canadian province has got ready to deal with crises and emergencies affecting tourism.

Mitigation

The tourism sector continues to build resilience to support business continuity, crisis communications and post-disaster marketing in the face of disaster events.

Preparedness

Tourism agencies and industry are ready to respond to emergency events and support emergency agencies and visitors, and visitors' needs are integrated into emergency management plans.

Response

The Tourism Emergency Response Plan is ready to activate in support of emergency agencies to ensure the safety and well-being of visitors and maintain the reputation of BC as a safe and desirable destination.

Recovery

The economic impact of emergencies on the visitor economy is reduced.
(Ministry of Tourism, Arts, Culture and Sport, British Columbia 2022)

Learning Point

Planning ahead is the best way to deal with the potential impacts of crises.

Response: During Crisis

The third stage, response, occurs during a crisis. This means taking actions immediately and in the weeks following a crisis or disaster in a destination. This stage can be the most chaotic if the previous two stages have not been fully completed. The crisis communications strategy should be triggered right away; however, the priority must be on preserving lives and tourism properties. All emergency response procedures that were developed previously are put into action. The crisis communications plan is implemented, and all affected parties in the destination are informed. DMO staff members should be trained to help where they are most needed and assist the local emergency management agencies.

The tourism sector and DMOs are well suited to provide certain types of humanitarian aid to affected visitors, residents, and staff. For example, a DMO should assist by providing meals and food supplies, transportation and temporary accommodation. From a previously arranged crisis center, the DMO also must be a major source of accurate and up-to-date information on the situation.

It is important that the DMO begin gathering accurate and up-to-date information and data about the crisis or disaster. The types of information to be gathered include the cause and impacts of the crisis or disaster, the cost of the damage caused, and potential legal and political issues. The DMO's communications during this response stage are critical as the following case example of Visit Florida clearly shows.

EXAMPLE 11.14

The Deepwater Horizon Oil Spill

This is a "textbook case" in how to deal with a major disaster.

> The *Deepwater Horizon* oil spill occurred in April 2010 and was the largest marine oil spill in the history of the world, resulting from the explosion of the oil rig, *Deepwater Horizon*, located south of the coast of Louisiana in the Gulf of Mexico. The oil spill affected beaches in Louisiana and Alabama and in the northwest of Florida. Although the oil spill spread to a small portion of the beaches of Florida and none on its Atlantic coastline, there was a public perception that the disaster was more extensive. Also, the incident happened at a time when many people were planning their summer holidays, and so the timing was not favorable for Florida's tourism. In other words, the DMO had to respond and communicate to clear up doubts and misperceptions about the oil spill's damage. Visit Florida's disaster communications were extensive and successful. They included consumer advertising, social media, three websites, live webcam broadcasts, oil spill research, webinars with associated Power-Point presentations, FAQs for tourism sector stakeholders, corporate blogs, marketing response updates and the issuance of palm cards to consumers and the media (see below). Visit Florida's communication efforts because of this disaster spanned from April to August 2010.

Visit Florida Consumer Palm Cards

> Florida has 825 miles of beautiful beaches. Some areas have been impacted, but most of Florida beaches are unaffected and you can count on us to keep providing you accurate, real-time information to make your vacation decisions.
>
> (Visit Florida 2010)

Learning Point

DMOs must act decisively and extensively in the aftermath of a major natural disaster.

The *Deepwater Horizon* case study demonstrates the importance of a DMO in clarifying the geographical extent of a crisis. With the BP rig disaster many were assuming that the spill was affecting all of Florida's beaches, and that was not the case. A similar situation was experienced with the outbreak of Ebola in the west of Africa. Many consumers wrongfully assumed that Ebola was everywhere in Africa and therefore DMOs in unaffected countries had to correct these beliefs.

Recovery: After Crisis

The recovery stage comes after the crisis has passed. It involves taking actions required for the destination to recover from a crisis or disaster. Four steps are recommended:

1. Measuring effectiveness of crisis and disaster management planning.
2. Preparing a business continuity plan.
3. Dealing with human resource issues.
4. Debriefing.

You are going to hear more about recovery later in this chapter. Figure 11.5 provides a summary of the steps involved in crisis management planning covering the 4Rs.

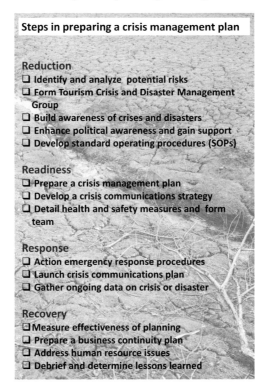

Steps in preparing a crisis management plan

Reduction
- ❑ Identify and analyze potential risks
- ❑ Form Tourism Crisis and Disaster Management Group
- ❑ Build awareness of crises and disasters
- ❑ Enhance political awareness and gain support
- ❑ Develop standard operating procedures (SOPs)

Readiness
- ❑ Prepare a crisis management plan
- ❑ Develop a crisis communications strategy
- ❑ Detail health and safety measures and form team

Response
- ❑ Action emergency response procedures
- ❑ Launch crisis communications plan
- ❑ Gather ongoing data on crisis or disaster

Recovery
- ❑ Measure effectiveness of planning
- ❑ Prepare a business continuity plan
- ❑ Address human resource issues
- ❑ Debrief and determine lessons learned

Figure 11.5 Steps in preparing a crisis management plan.

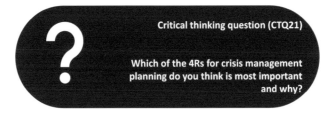

Critical thinking question (CTQ21)

Which of the 4Rs for crisis management planning do you think is most important and why?

Crisis Communications

You can see that a crisis communications strategy and plan was included in crisis management planning. The experts agree that communications by a destination and its DMO are vital when a crisis or disaster is encountered. Here then is our definition of crisis communications.

DEFINITION

Crisis communications

Crisis communications is the process, once a crisis has started, of minimizing its negative consequences for the destination and tourism sector stakeholders. It requires immediate decisions and countermeasures using all communication tools to influence and steer situations in as positive a direction as possible.

Once again, planning crisis communications ahead is much better than waiting for events to happen. The development of a crisis communications plan is strongly recommended.

Purposes of a Crisis Communications Plan

The purpose of preparing a crisis communication plan is to minimize the negative impact of a crisis on stakeholders including visitors, staff, residents, and the destination's tourism sector. This is achieved by proactively providing accurate and timely information so that people can make more informed decisions about visiting the destination and moving around within it. The example from Raleigh, North Carolina highlights the purposes of a crisis communication plan.

EXAMPLE 11.15

The Greater Raleigh CVB Crisis Communication Plan

This example reviews the crisis communication plan of a DMO in the USA.

> Imagine you are in an unfamiliar city during an emergency situation. Do you try to go home? Do you stay in your hotel? What does a visitor need to know during a crisis? What information can the Greater Raleigh CVB provide to our hospitality partners that may make a bad situation more tolerable?
>
> The GRCVB crisis communication plan is designed to relay information specific to the needs of visitors and/or our hospitality partners in the event of a crisis. The CVB plan will only take effect when a situation has the potential to be threatening to visitors, to a hospitality partner business or to the Bureau itself. The plan is also intended to reflect the professionalism and dedication of the staff of the GRCVB and our commitment to all of our constituents. We will continue to develop the plan and add new tactics to communicate with our partners and the public as accurately and quickly as possible.
>
> (GRCVB 2022)

> **Learning Point**
>
> DMOs should have crisis communication plans ready to launch when a crisis or disaster occurs.

Contents of a Crisis Communications Plan

You already know what goes into a crisis management plan and now the contents of a crisis communications plan are detailed. You can think of this as being a "mini marketing plan" like the overall marketing plan described later in Chapter 12. The following is a description of the steps involved (Fig. 11.6).

ASSESS COMMUNICATIONS RISKS

The risks of highest likelihood crises or disasters are identified and analyzed. Here, it must be assumed that not all these events are alike, nor do they carry exactly the same risks. Apart from the human and physical risks that accompany many crises and disasters, a destination faces damage to its image and reputation as you will see in the example about Japan and the Fukushima disaster.

FORM A CRISIS COMMUNICATIONS TEAM

A specific team needs to be formed for crisis communications. The team should be drawn from the DMO and its stakeholders. Normally, the senior executive of the DMO and key marketing, branding, and communications staff members will be selected to serve. The roles and responsibilities of each team member need to be specified. A spokesperson must be appointed and this should be a person who is not camera-shy and has experience in dealing with the media.

DEVELOP CRISIS COMMUNICATION OBJECTIVES

The crisis communications plan should be founded upon a specific set of objectives. The Greater Raleigh plan has the overall objective "to relay information specific to the needs of visitors and/or our hospitality partners in the event of a crisis."

IDENTIFY CRISIS COMMUNICATIONS TARGET GROUPS

An overall marketing plan has specific target markets; likewise, a crisis communications plan is not random, rather it addresses specific target groups (Fig. 11.7). Ideally, these groups span all the stakeholders that you learned about in Chapters 1 and 9 and that are shown in Figures 1.7 and 9.5. Usually, the communications team pools their suggestions on contact lists of specific people to receive the crisis communications information (e.g., media, tourism sector stakeholders, travel trade intermediaries, associations, government agencies, influencers).

Embassies and consulates are included in Figure 11.7, and this requires greater explanation. Foreign governments issue travel advisories for their citizens planning to travel to foreign countries. For example, the UK government says this about travel to Afghanistan: "The Foreign, Commonwealth and Development Office advises against all travel to Afghanistan. If you choose to travel or stay in Afghanistan, you should keep a low profile. There is a heightened risk of detention of British nationals" (Gov.uk 2022). You will know that this is

Figure 11.6 Steps in crisis communications strategy and planning.

Figure 11.7 Crisis communication target groups.

an extreme case; however, it probably will convince many Britons not to travel to Afghanistan. Travel advisories should be carefully check during crisis communications planning. You should also be aware that these sources of travel advice are thought by some to be politically biased (Deep and Johnston 2017) and others feels they are out of date and too geographically expansive.

One of the initial tasks of the team is to draft official statements about the crisis or disaster and supporting stories. Expected questions and answers should also be prepared along with tips for dealing with the media. Selected photography is needed to accompany the statements and stories prepared by the crisis communications team. Specific branding approaches may also be incorporated in the team's strategy. Later you are going to hear about I AM IN NEPAL NOW #NepalNOW #stillsmiling that was used by tourism agencies when Nepal was recovering from a devastating earthquake.

DETAIL THE CRISIS INTEGRATED MARKETING COMMUNICATIONS (IMC)

Chapter 14 reviews the IMC approach in detail and it must be followed when communicating about a crisis or disaster. Consistency among the messages transmitted is particularly important in crisis communications. Figure 11.8 shows the six components of IMC (e-marketing, advertising, sales, sales promotion, merchandising, and public relations and publicity). Public relations and publicity and e-marketing are especially crucial today when communicating information about destination crises and disasters. Press conferences or media briefings are common and reflect traditional public relations and publicity efforts. Social media is now the carrier of most crisis communications.

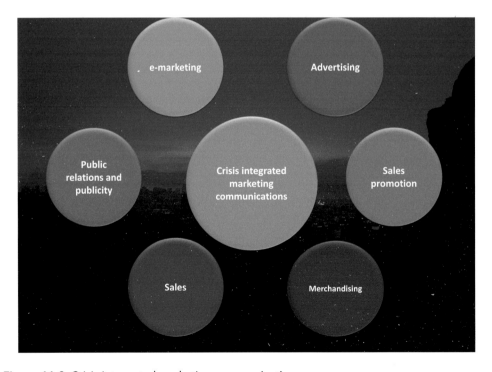

Figure 11.8 Crisis integrated marketing communications.

EXAMPLE 11.16

Foreign Exchange Crisis Affects Tourism in Sri Lanka

As in the case of Sri Lanka, developing countries are more susceptible to economic crises.

> Sri Lanka, a popular destination for holidaymakers, should be teeming with tourists at this time of year. Instead, an unprecedented economic crisis and political turmoil have all but wreaked its tourism with about 40 percent of the pre-bookings being canceled recently.
> Tourism accounts for about 5 percent of Sri Lanka's GDP, with Britain, India, and China being the main markets. Sri Lanka is facing its worst foreign exchange crisis after the COVID-19 pandemic hit the island nation's earnings from tourism and remittances. According to the Sri Lanka Tourism Development Authority, the number of tourist arrivals decreased by 60 percent in June.
> (Press Trust of India 2022)

Learning Point

Severe economic crises can destabilize the images of the countries in which they happen.

There are several golden rules as to how a destination or DMO should deliver information about these events. The first rule is to always tell the truth and to tell it first (Cramer 2015; Hennes Communications 2022). The four pillars of crisis communications must be honesty, transparency, accountability, and consistency (Dearnell 2018). These correspond with the dimensions of governance that were among the topics in Chapter 6. In this chapter, you hear about a crisis communications failure when government officials were not totally truthful in their initial responses on cruise boat drownings in Thailand.

Implement the Crisis Communications Plan

The plan should be triggered as soon as a crisis or disaster is evident. News travels at lightning speed these days with social media, so the immediacy of a communications response is critical. The media will become suspicious if destinations do not rapidly respond and communicate about a crisis or disaster.

Not all of the crisis communications can be scripted in advance, as media channels and netizens will continuously be adding and uploading stories and comments about the destination. The example on Sri Lanka is a good case in this respect; the story originating from India is largely negative about the situation in Sri Lanka. It is incumbent on destinations and DMOs to publish counter-arguments to stories like this that tend to paint all of Sri Lanka with the same brush. Just as in the Nepali case, "good news" stories should be penned and distributed by DMOs to offset the damage from negative publicity.

Monitor the Plan's Implementation

Crises and disasters, and public and media opinions on them, evolve quickly, and it is essential to track what is being said about the events. There are primary communications or stories in traditional and online media; and secondary communications that includes comments and shares on social media platforms. You heard about content analysis in Chapter 5 and that is a tool that is especially helpful in analyzing the text in primary and secondary communications. Photographs and other graphics must also be collected and analyzed. Time-stamping of contents is vital to be able to track how the external communications evolve and for how long they last.

MEASURE AND EVALUATE PLAN'S SUCCESS

When the crisis or disaster comes to an end, the crisis communications team should assess the extent to which the plan's objectives were achieved and what were the major things learned in the process of communications.

EXAMPLE 11.17

Reputational Damage for Japan

Crises can rapidly undermine the positive images of destinations as in this example about Japan.

> The reputation of Japan as a safe and secure destination has crumbled down and been washed away by the earthquake and tsunami in March. People who have never experienced an earthquake would be terrified to visit Japan where you cannot tell when and where another earthquake will hit you. Furthermore, the accident at the Fukushima Daiich Nuclear Power Plant and the wide spread of radiation have accumulated the unsafe impression of Japan. The myth of safe food in Japan also fell to pieces as the vegetables, tea leaves, seafood, milk and even beef produced in Japan was found to be contaminated by radiation.
>
> (Takamatsu 2011)

Learning Point

DMOs must carefully manage the reputations of their destinations and take corrective action when required.

Crisis Communication Media Targets, Channels, and Tools

Chapter 12 will introduce you to destination marketing, branding, and communications. Chapter 13 focuses on destination positioning, image, and branding (PIB) and Chapter 14 is on destination IMC. All three chapters closely connect with crisis communications, as it is a special form of marketing, branding, and communications.

Crisis communications must follow an IMC process using the six components depicted in Figure 11.6. You will get the definitions and detailed descriptions of these components in Chapter 14. For now, it needs to be said that all communications on a crisis or disaster must be consistent.

As in overall destination marketing and branding, the groups to be targeted in crisis communications must be carefully selected and well understood. Figure 11.7 identifies four groupings—residents and visitors; media; travel trade, associations, and other organizations; and governmental agencies and DMOs.

Crisis Communication Failures

You should not get the impression that all crisis communications efforts are successful as that is definitely not the case. Just giving you one specific example from tourism will prove this point. More than forty Chinese tourists drowned in a cruise boating accident involving two vessels sailing off of Phuket, Thailand in July 2018. One senior official in the Thai government blamed the sinkings on Chinese tour operators who had not followed the country's safety rules (Reuters 2018). This caused a severe backlash from Chinese citizens on social media due to inaccurate statements and misleading crisis information from Thai officials (Xie et al. 2022). There are important implications for crisis communications from this case study. First, destinations and DMOs should not be too quick in ascribing blame to other external parties or factors. Second, it is better to tell the whole truth backed up with accurate and verified facts on situations. Another communications failure, also in Southeast Asia, happened with the disappearance of Malaysia Airlines MH370. Media reporters and public relations experts agreed that the airline and government officials bungled the communications about this accident (Banu 2014; Tilley 2014).

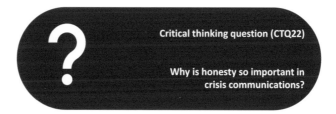

Critical thinking question (CTQ22)

Why is honesty so important in crisis communications?

Risk Management

Destinations and DMOs must implement risk management processes to reduce the impacts of crises and disasters. The following is a definition of risk management.

DEFINITION

Risk management

"The tourism risk management process is concerned with identifying and analyzing the risks ('the chance of something happening that will have an impact upon objectives') to a destination or organization and deciding what can and should be done about them" (APEC 2015).

Figure 11.9 is an image of a step-by-step risk management process that consists of five steps.

1. Establish context: This is deciding on the background of the risk situation. Who are the stakeholders most likely to be affected by a crisis or disaster? What are the major strengths

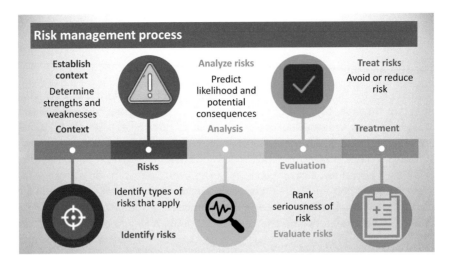

Figure 11.9 Risk management process (CBI 2020).

and weaknesses of the destination that decrease or increase the potential negative influences of these events?

2. Identify risks: This step involves determining the types of risks to which a destination is most susceptible. Are they natural disasters, security crises, health safety crises, environmental safety crises, or economic and financial crises?

3. Analyze risks: The likelihood and potential outcomes of the most likely crises and disasters are estimated in this analysis step.

4. Evaluate risks: This is an assessment of the seriousness of risks for a destination.

5. Treat risks: How will the destination deal with the risks is the focus for this step.

Resilience and Recovery

Especially in the aftermath of the COVID-19 pandemic, destinations are being urged to become more resilient. The following is a definition of the term "resilience."

DEFINITION

Resilience

"Resilience is the ability of a system to reduce the chances of a crisis occurring, mitigate the impacts of a crisis, and recover its essential structures and functions quickly. The speed of recovery from a crisis (or stress event) will depend on different forms of capital (social, political, economic) built up in the phases before the event" (OIC 2017: 2).

In the above definition, mitigation means to decrease the gravity or seriousness of the impacts of a crisis or disaster on tourism in a destination.

The WTTC and Rescue.org (2022) offer a non-academic and practical definition of resilience as "specific things destinations can do, and are already doing, to learn from recent and ongoing stress and shock events, to prepare for the next catastrophic event, and to ensure the long-term sustainability of their evolving tourism activities." You can think of resilience as the capability to bounce back more rapidly and effectively from adversity.

EXAMPLE 11.18

Tourism Resilience Varies by Country

Not every destination shares the same resilience level as other places as explained in this example.

> The broader economic impacts of the slump in travel and tourism on individual countries and destinations will vary depending on their economic dependence on tourism and their resilience, as well as the dynamics of demand in their key source markets. The global economic and pandemic uncertainty is therefore a key limiting factor for both source markets and destinations. Countries that are highly dependent on tourism include many small island countries, as well as lower and lower-middle income countries with many people employed by travel and tourism. The resilience of destinations is conditioned by factors such as the local policy environment, public health policies, ICT readiness, government policies for tourism, and the extent of tourist service infrastructure.
>
> (World Bank Group 2020)

Learning Point

DMOs and destinations should take steps to increase tourism sector resilience.

Four Rs of Resilience

How specifically does a destination become more resilient? First and foremost, a destination must learn from its previous experiences with crises and disasters. Then, there are another 4Rs associated with the resilience concept—robustness, redundancy, resourcefulness, and rapidity. Robustness is the capability to resist crises and disasters without significant damage. Destinations with broader portfolios of customer markets and diverse product offerings are likely to be more robust. Redundancy is the extent to which the system performs a backup in case of a loss or failure. You can think of this as having the proverbial "Plan B" or a default mode. Resourcefulness is the ability to assess the challenges and deploy the right resources. Having crisis management and communications plans ready to deploy on short notice is a demonstration of resourcefulness. Rapidity is the ability to alleviate losses and restore operations on time (Bruneau et al. 2003). Again, having action plans ready to implement will quicken responses.

The recovery by Nepal is a good case study on resilience and about how effective communications can contribute to recovery in tourism.

EXAMPLE 11.19

Post-Earthquake Recovery of Tourism in Nepal

This is a success story from Nepal in how to deal with the impacts of a major natural disaster.

> Following the earthquake in Nepal in 2015, when 9,000 people lost their lives and more than 800 monuments were damaged, the nation's image suffered from negative international reporting and tourist arrivals fell by more than one-third in the year, from 790,000 in 2014 to 539,000 in 2015. However, the Nepal Tourism Recovery action group quickly launched the I AM IN NEPAL NOW #NepalNOW #stillsmiling social media campaign to counter the vast numbers of negative stories circulating on the Internet. The campaign encouraged international visitors to Nepal to post images of themselves holding placards featuring the slogan.
>
> The campaign and positive stories on the accompanying website, nepal-NOW, generated a significant amount of positive coverage and, alongside rebuilding, rebranding and additional communications, helped to stimulate tourism growth. By the end of 2018, tourist arrivals had exceeded 1 million for the first time, with the country welcoming 1.2 million arrivals.
>
> (CBI 2020)

Learning Point

Crisis communication strategies and campaigns can help destinations recover from major crises and disasters.

The Nepal case study shows that destinations and DMOs need to counter negative publicity in the media and communicate "alternative realities." This is absolutely vital since some reporting tends to be inaccurate or exaggerates the negative, while there is also the possibility of fake news.

Recovery Communications

It was mentioned earlier that tourism sector stakeholders were among the groups to be targeted in the crisis communications plan. Part of these communications should deal with what is being done to recover from adverse situations and this has been especially needed during the COVID-19 pandemic. The national DMO for South Africa, for example, produced a COVID-19 recovery plan that contained seven initiatives that included stimulating domestic tourism and executing a new global international marketing program (South African Tourism 2021). Another example here is the joint effort (Enpact program) by the TUI Care Foundation, GIZ, and the Federal Ministry for Economic Cooperation (Germany) to assist in small tourism business recovery in Egypt, Kenya, Mexico, South Africa, and Tunisia (Enpact 2022).

Recovery Times

A question often asked for this topic is how long does it take for a destination to recover from a crisis or disaster. What do you think is the correct answer? It is not as simple as it seems. The WTTC, in partnership with Rescue.org, has looked into this and produced some useful results.

Recovery Times for Crises and Disasters

It is useful to be aware about recovery times from crises and disasters and this example provides some relevant metrics.

> Among the cases with evident impact, terrorism cases had the lowest recovery time at 11.5 months on average, with the recovery time ranging from as little as 2 months to a maximum forty-two months. Civil unrest and political instability cases had the highest recovery time at 22.2 months on average, with a range between 10 and 44.9 months. Disease cases had average recovery times of 19.4 months, with a range between 10 and 34.9 months. Recovery from natural disasters took 16.2 months on average. Natural disasters had the greatest range of recovery time, from just one month to ninety-three months. This is due to the wide variation in the severity of natural disaster events within our case examples.
>
> (WTTC and Rescue.org 2022: 9)

Learning Point

DMOs need to be aware of recovery times for crises and disasters.

Recovery times therefore depend on the category of crisis and disasters. Some tend to be more protracted and insidious in nature including political turmoil and civil unrest. An example here is Venezuela, which was plagued with economic and political problems even before the COVID-19 pandemic (Froyd 2018). Tunisia is another nation that is struggling; "the main challenge that Tunisian tourism is facing today is the image of the country being unsafe. Until this image is changed positively, the sector will continue to suffer weakness" (OIC 2017: 92). There also may be a "lightning does not strike twice" mentality with events such as terrorism and in highly popular destinations like Paris. Although not proven yet by research, these consumer opinions may be why these destinations bounce back more quickly from adversity.

SUMMING UP

Unfortunately, destinations are highly susceptible to crisis and disasters, and they are negatively impacted by many situations beyond their control. The inevitability of crises and disasters means that DMOs and tourism sector stakeholders must get prepared to act before it is too late to do anything.

There are several categories of crises and disasters including natural disasters, security crises, economic and financial crises, health safety crises, environmental safety crises, accidents and calamities, and public opinion crises. They may occur separately or be experienced at the same time.

Every destination should prepare a crisis management plan. Here, the four Rs is a process used for crisis management planning, consisting of reduction, readiness, response, and recovery. Effective communications and teamwork are essential to crisis and disaster management for destinations. A crisis communications plan should be prepared and follow the procedures and principles discussed in later chapters on marketing, branding, and communications.

Resilience and recovery are two significant topics in the management of crises and disasters. Resilience concerns the destination's ability to withstand a crisis or disaster and return to a normal or improved state. There are four Rs here too: robustness, redundancy, resourcefulness, and rapidity. The return journey from a crisis or disaster is the recovery phase that can span months or years.

The author hopes that you have learned not to view all crises and disasters, and all destinations, in the same way. Many differences are highlighted in this chapter and anomalies and enigmatic situations including where crises and disasters have helped certain destinations. There are no surefire, one-size-fits-all explanations and outcomes for the topics and situations in this chapter.

While the outcomes of most crises and disasters are negative, they are events that provide opportunities for DMOs to be true leaders and champions for the tourism sector. DMOs in so doing can integrate several roles including planning and research (e.g., risk assessment), partnership and team-building (e.g., forming a TCDMG and crisis communications team), stakeholder relationships and involvement (e.g., creating a crisis management plan), and marketing, branding, and communications (e.g., crisis communications).

Be prepared, endure, and prosper was the banner headline for Chapter 11. You have learned that destinations and DMOs must prepare crisis management and crisis communications plans, and be involved with risk management. That is being prepared for crises and disasters as destination management professionals. Endure signifies being resilient and patient until crises and disasters are over—this is certainly the case in terms of COVID-19. Crisis management must be a continuous, long-term activity for DMOs and not just a short-term activity. Prosper implies a successful recovery from crises and disasters. Destinations must become more robust and resourceful to guarantee brighter futures.

Next up are the chapters on destination marketing, branding, and communications. It is the last of the eight destination management roles to be discussed in this book, but it is definitely not the least!

KEYWORDS

accidents and calamities
accountability
consistency
crisis
crisis communications
crisis communications
    plan
crisis management plan
disaster
economic and financial
    crises
emergency management
    agencies
environmental safety crises

external crises
fake news
four Rs for crisis manage-
    ment planning
four Rs of resilience
health safety crises
honesty
immediacy
internal crises
macro
meso
micro
mitigation
natural disasters

open system (nature of
    tourism)
PESTEL
preparedness
prodromal
public opinion crises
rapidity
readiness
recovery
reduction
redundancy
resilience
resourcefulness
response

risk	sustainable development	transparency
risk management	goals (SDGs)	travel advisories
robustness	tourism crisis and disas-	
security crises	ter management group	
standard operating	(TCDMG)	
procedures (SOPs)	tourism dependency	

REVIEW QUESTIONS

1. What are the definitions of a crisis and a disaster?
2. What are the categories or crises and disasters?
3. How do crises and disasters affect tourism?
4. Why are destinations susceptible to crises and disasters?
5. What are the stages of a crisis or disaster?
6. How should a crisis management plan be developed?
7. What steps should be followed in a crisis communications plan?
8. What does destination risk management entail?
9. How can a destination build up its resilience to crises and disasters?
10. What should destinations do to recover from crises and disasters?

REFERENCES

Ali, R. (2018) "The Genesis of Overtourism: Why We Came Up with the Term and What's Happened Since," *Skift*, August 14, https://skift.com/2018/08/14/the-genesis-of-overtourism-why-we-came-up-with-the-term-and-whats-happened-since/

Asia-Pacific Economic Cooperation (2015) "Introduction to Risk Management in Tourism: Participant Workbook," https://sustain.pata.org/wp-content/uploads/2015/02/Introduction-Participants-English.pdf

Banu, Z. (2014) "MH370 Communications Disaster Lays Bare Malaysia's Incompetence," *South China Morning Post*, March 28, www.scmp.com/comment/insight-opinion/article/1459099/mh370-communications-disaster-lays-bare-malaysias

Bruneau, M., Chang, S. E., Eguchi, R. T., Lee, G. C., O'Rourke, T. D., Reinhorn, A. M., Shinozuka, M., Tierney, K., Wallace, W. A., and von Winterfeldt, D. (2003) "A Framework to Quantitatively Assess and Enhance the Seismic Resilience of Communities," *Earthquake Spectra*, 19 (4): 733–752.

Business Standard (2022) "What Was Bhopal Gas Tragedy?" www.business-standard.com/about/what-is-bhopal-gas-tragedy

Business Victoria (2022) "Tourism Crisis Management Guide," https://business.vic.gov.au/business-information/tourism-industry-resources/tourism-crisis-management-guide

CBI Ministry of Foreign Affairs (Netherlands) (2020) "How to Manage Risks in Tourism?" www.cbi.eu/market-information/tourism/how-manage-risks-tourism

Chambers, J. (2014) "How Are Tourism and Homelessness Related?" National Coalition for the Homeless, https://nationalhomeless.org/tourism-homelessness-related/

Chehayeb, K. (2022) "Desperate for Diaspora: Lebanon Begs for a Tourism Cash Injection," *Al Jazeera*, June 27, www.aljazeera.com/news/2022/6/27/desperate-for-diaspora-lebanon-begs-for-tourism-cash-injection

Chugh, A. (2021) "What Is 'the Great Resignation'? An Expert Explains," *World Economic Forum*, November 29, www.weforum.org/agenda/2021/11/what-is-the-great-resignation-and-what-can-we-learn-from-it/

Cramer, B. (2015) "Crisis Communications: Tell the Truth, and Show Your Humanity," International Bridge, Tunnel and Turnpike Association, November 3, www.ibtta.org/blog/crisis-communications-tell-truth-and-show-your-humanity#

D'Amore, R. (2020) "Australia Wildfires Fan Fears of 'Detrimental' Impact to Tourism Industry," *Global News*, January 7, https://globalnews.ca/news/6376952/australia-fires-tourism-economy/

Dearnell, A. (2018) "The Key to Successful Crisis Communications: Show Up," *Forbes*, September 18, www.forbes.com/sites/adriandearnell/2018/09/18/crisis-communications-show-up/?sh=3db0fe31738b

Deep, A., and Johnston, C. S. (2017) "Travel Advisories: Destabilising Diplomacy in Disguise," *Journal of Policy Research in Tourism, Leisure and Events*, 9 (1): 82–99.

Drought.gov (2022) "Recreation and Tourism," www.drought.gov/sectors/recreation-and-tourism

Duan, J., Xie, C. W., and Morrison, A. M. (2022) "Tourism Crises and Impacts on Destinations: A Systematic Review of the Tourism and Hospitality Literature," *Journal of Hospitality and Tourism Research*, 46 (4): 667–695.

Economic Commission for Latin America and the Caribbean (2020) "The Impact of the COVID-19 Pandemic on the Tourism Sector in Latin America and the Caribbean, and Options for a Sustainable and Resilient Recovery," www.cepal.org/en/publications/46502-impact-covid-19-pandemic-tourism-sector-latin-america-and-caribbean-and-options

Economist (2022) "Rebuilding Tourism in Asia-Pacific: A More Conscious Traveller?" https://impact.economist.com/perspectives/sites/default/files/rebuilding_tourism_apac_economist_impact_airbnb.pdf

Enpact (2022) "Tourism Recovery Program," https://enpact.org/entrepreneurial-support/empowering-entrepreneurship-initiative/tourism-recovery-programme/#/

Faulkner, B. (2001) "Towards a Framework for Tourism Disaster Management," *Tourism Management*, 22 (2): 135–147.

Forgrave, A. (2022) "Tourism Tax and Second Homes Unleashed 'Vile Tsunami of Anti-English Hatred' in Wales," *Daily Post*, August 27, www.dailypost.co.uk/news/north-wales-news/tourism-tax-second-homes-unleashed-24867518

Fotiou, S. (2012) "Disaster Risk Management in Tourism Destinations," www.slideshare.net/fotiou/risk-management-in-tourism-destinations

Freed, J. (2021) "Asia Tourism Reopens with Big-Spending Chinese Stuck at Home," *Reuters*, November 5, www.reuters.com/world/asia-pacific/asia-tourism-reopens-with-big-spending-chinese-stuck-home-2021-11-03/

Froyd, J. N. (2018) "Tourism in Venezuela Decreasing Every Day," *Tourism Review News*, October 8, www.tourism-review.com/tourism-in-venezuela-is-going-down-news10772

Gibbens, S. (2019) "Hurricane Sandy, Explained," *National Geographic*, February 12, www.national-geographic.com/environment/article/hurricane-sandy

Gibbons, B. (2022) "Travel and Tourism Jobs Crisis with 130,000 Vacancies Unfilled in Pandemic Aftermath," August 1, www.business-live.co.uk/economic-development/travel-tourism-jobs-crisis-130000-24638914

Goodwin, H. (2020) "Racism in Tourism," Responsible Tourism Partnership, July 29, https://responsibletourismpartnership.org/racism-in-tourism/

Gov.uk (2022) "Foreign Travel Advice: Afghanistan," www.gov.uk/foreign-travel-advice/afghanistan

Great Barrier Reef Foundation (2022) "What Is Coral Bleaching?" www.barrierreef.org/the-reef/threats/coral-bleaching

Greater Raleigh Convention and Visitors Bureau (2019) "Crisis communication plan," https://assets.simpleviewinc.com/simpleview/image/upload/v1/clients/raleigh/GRCVB_Crisis_Communication_Plan_abridged_bd4d771b-26fc-4584-94e2-b6896fb97b46.pdf

Hennes Communications (2022) "Tell the Truth and Tell It First," www.crisiscommunications.com/tell-the-truth-tell-it-first

International Atomic Energy Agency (2022) "FAQs: What Caused the Chernobyl Accident?" www.iaea.org/newscenter/focus/chernobyl/faqs

International Federation of Red Cross and Red Crescent Societies (undated) "What Is a Disaster?" www.ifrc.org/what-disaster#

Kazim, A., Quinio, A., and Wise, P. (2022) "Summer Tourism Brightens Eurozone Economy but Cost of Living Crisis Casts Shadow," *Financial Times*, July 31, www.ft.com/content/04e61d8c-3663-4aeb-9785-098741744172

Luo, Q., and Zhai, X. (2017) "'I Will Never Go to Hong Kong Again!' How the Secondary Crisis Communication of 'Occupy Central' on Weibo Shifted to a Tourism Boycott," *Tourism Management*, 62: 159–172.

Ministry of Tourism, Arts, Culture and Sport (British Columbia) (2022) "British Columbia Tourism Emergency Management Framework," www2.gov.bc.ca/assets/gov/tourism-and-immigration/tourism-industry-resources/tourism_emergency_management_framework_may_2022_final.pdf

Morrison, A. M. (2022a) "Towards a New Normal in Tourism," Presentation to the 91st TOSOK (Tourism Sciences Society of Korea) International Tourism Conference, February.

——— (2022b) "Tourism Marketing in the Age of the Consumer," Presentation to the 9th Biennial ITSA (International Tourism Studies Association) Conference, July 27.

Morrison, A. M., and Maxim, C. (2022) *World Tourism Cities*, London and New York, NY: Routledge.

Murray Regional Tourism Board (Australia) (2022) "Crisis Management Plan," www.murrayregional-tourism.com.au/research-resources/strategies-plans/crisis-management-plan/

National Geographic (2022) "Light Pollution," https://education.nationalgeographic.org/resource/light-pollution

Organization of Islamic Cooperation (2017) "Risk and Crisis Management in Tourism Sector: Recovery from Crisis in the OIC Member Countries," www.sbb.gov.tr/wp-content/uploads/2021/02/Risk_and_Crisis_Management_in_Tourism_Sector.pdf

Pacific Asia Travel Association (2003) *Crisis: It Won't Happen to Us! Expect the Unexpected, Be Prepared*, Bangkok: Pacific Asia Travel Association.

Park, M. Y. (2018) "In Search of Dark Skies: How Light Pollution Is Spurring a New Tourism Industry," *The Points Guy*, June 13, https://thepointsguy.com/news/dark-skies-how-light-pollution-spurred-a-new-tourism-industry/

Press Trust of India (2022) "Sri Lanka Economic Crisis: Lucrative Tourism Industry Bears Major Brunt," *Outlook*, July 15, www.outlookindia.com/business/sri-lanka-economic-crisis-lucrative-tourism-industry-bears-major-brunt-news-209455

Rescue.org (2022) "Watchlist 2022: The Top 10 Crises the World Can't Ignore in 2022," www.rescue.org/article/top-10-crises-world-cant-ignore-2022

Reuters (2018) "Death Toll in Thai Tourist Boat Disaster Rises to 44," Reuters, July 10, www.reuters.com/article/us-thailand-boat-accident-idUSKBN1K00GA

Richter, F. (2022) "International Travel Levels Tipped to Soar Again in 2022," World Economic Forum and Statista, June 30, www.weforum.org/agenda/2022/06/international-travel-2022-covid19-tourism/

Ritchie, H., and Roser, M. (2021) "Natural Disasters," https://ourworldindata.org/natural-disasters

Rossell, J., Becken, S., and Santana-Gallego, M. (2020) "The Effects of Natural Disasters on International Tourism: A Global Analysis," *Tourism Management*, 79. doi:10.1016/j.tourman.2020.104080

Šergo, Z., Peršurić, A. S. I., and Matošević, I. (2014) "The Influence of Tourism on Deforestation and Biodiversity," *Academica Turistica*, 7 (2): 153–168.

Shahid, K. W. (2022) "Pakistan's Tourism Industry Rocked by Climate Change," *Al Jazeera*, June 5, www.aljazeera.com/news/2022/6/5/pakistans-tourism-industry-rocked-by-climate-change

South African Tourism (2021) "Tourism Sector Recovery Plan: Covid-19 Response," www.gov.za/sites/default/files/gcis_document/202008/tourismrecoveryplan.pdf

Sung, Y.-A., Kim, K.-W., and Kwon, H.-J. (2021) "Big Data Analysis of Korean Travelers' Behavior in the Post-COVID-19 Era," *Sustainability*, 13 (1): 310.

Takamatsu, M. (2011) "Tourism Crisis Management as Business Continuity Plan 1," JTB Tourism Research & Consulting Co., September 1, www.tourism.jp/en/tourism-database/insights/2011/09/tourism-crisis-management-1/

Temblador, A. (2020) "How the Travel Industry Can Do Its Part in the Fight Against Racism," *Travel Pulse*, June 2, www.travelpulse.com/news/features/how-the-travel-industry-can-do-its-part-in-the-fight-against-racism.html

Tilley, J. (2014) "Analysis: Malaysia Airline's Mishandled Response to the MH370 Crisis," *PR Week*, www.prweek.com/article/1286333/analysis-malaysia-airlines-mishandled-response-mh370-crisis

United Nations (2022) "The Sustainable Development Goals Report 2022," https://unstats.un.org/sdgs/report/2022/The-Sustainable-Development-Goals-Report-2022.pdf

United Nations World Tourism Organization (2022) "Impact of the Russian Offensive in Ukraine on International Tourism," www.unwto.org/impact-russian-offensive-in-ukraine-on-tourism

Visit Florida (2010) "Visit Florida Deepwater Horizon Crisis Response," www.visitflorida.org/media/4132/deepwatertimeline.pdf

Wang, S., Mu, Y., Zhang, X., and Jia, X. (2020) "Polar Tourism and Environment Change: Opportunity, Impact and Adaption," *Polar Science*.

Wassler, P., and Talarico, C. (2021) "Sociocultural Impacts of COVID-19: A Social Representations Perspective," *Tourism Management Perspectives*, 38. https://doi.org/10.1016/j.tmp.2021.100813.

Wen, J., Kozak, M., Yang, S., and Liu, F. (2020) "COVID-19: Potential Effects on Chinese Citizens' Lifestyle and Travel," *Tourism Review*, 76 (1): 74–87.

Wicary, S. and Bloomberg (2022) "Cuba's Energy Crisis and Crippling Tourism Industry Is Causing the Biggest Exodus to the US in Decades," *Fortune*, August 17, https://fortune.com/2022/08/17/cuba-energy-crisis-tourism-indsutry-biggest-exodus-us-decades/

World Bank Group (2020) "Rebuilding Tourism Competitiveness: Tourism Response, Recovery and Resilience to the COVID-19 Crisis," https://openknowledge.worldbank.org/bitstream/handle/10986/34348/Rebuilding-Tourism-Competitiveness-Tourism-response-recovery-and-resilience-to-the-COVID-19-crisis.pdf?sequence=5

World Travel and Tourism Council and Rescue.org (2022) "Enhancing Resilience to Drive Sustainability in Destinations," https://wttc.org/Portals/0/Documents/Reports/2022/WTTCxICF-Enhancing_Resilience-Sustainable_Destinations.pdf?ver=2022-06-13-213556-57

Xie, C., Zhang, J., Huang, Q., Chen, Y., and Morrison, A. M. (2022) "An Analysis of User-Generated Crisis Frames: Online Public Responses to a Tourism Crisis," *Tourism Management Perspectives*, 41. https://doi.org/10.1016/j.tmp.2021.100931.

Zheng, Y., Goh, E., and Wen, J. (2020) "The Effects of Misleading Media Reports about COVID-19 on Chinese Tourists' Mental Health: A Perspective Article," *Anatolia*, 31 (2): 337–340.

Chapter **12**

Planning Marketing, Branding, and Communications

Getting the message across

LEARNING OBJECTIVES

Having read this chapter, you should be able to:

1. explain the key destination marketing professional principles;
2. describe the different levels of goals and objectives in the DMP;
3. differentiate between a vision and a mission;
4. detail the components of the PRICE model;
5. provide an explanation of the steps in the DMS;
6. describe the contents of a destination marketing plan;
7. explain each of the 8Ps of destination marketing, branding, and communications;
8. elaborate on the evaluation of DMO marketing performance.

DOI: 10.4324/9781003343356-14

Warming Up

You have just learned about crisis management in Chapter 11, and crises and disasters are often triggers for new or intensified destination marketing, branding, and communications.

Destination marketing, branding, and communications are some of the most important DMO tasks. The planning of destination marketing takes on a high priority for a DMO, and this planning must be done professionally, systematically, and thoroughly. Marketing, branding, and communications are expensive, and so making the right choices of which markets to target and how to communicate with them most effectively is crucial. Competition among destinations is intense; therefore, there is a constant need to stand out from the crowd.

Destination marketing, branding, and communications are dynamic, and they require a high level of creativity and innovation. Although marketing, branding, and communications are constantly changing, they must be based on a scientific approach using solid research and systematic procedures known to produce the most effective results. This chapter explains the marketing planning process as a systematic approach for accomplishing the DMO's marketing, branding, and communications role.

There are many career professionals engaged in destination marketing, branding, and communications around the world. It can be said that without doubt they have a passion about their work because of its challenges and ever-changing nature. More recently, social media have enlivened destination marketing, branding, and communications and attracted a new breed of professionals with content creation and storytelling skills. The arrival of AI, AR and VR, and the metaverse will hasten this trend further.

Your author has had a long career consulting on destination marketing, teaching and training the subject, and writing books and articles on it. He has been fortunate that this has taken him to around fifty countries to provide marketing and product development advice. His companies have prepared several destination marketing strategies and plans, IMC campaigns, branding and positioning approaches, websites and videos. These experiences are the foundation for this chapter.

Definitions of Marketing, Branding, and Integrated Marketing Communications

This chapter is the beginning of the discussion of the marketing, branding, and communications role in destination management. Here are the definitions of these three terms.

DEFINITIONS

Destination marketing

Marketing is a continuous, sequential process through which a DMO plans, researches, implements, controls and evaluates programs aimed at satisfying traveler's needs and wants as well as the destination's and DMO's visions, goals and objectives. To be most effective, the DMO's marketing programs depend upon the efforts of many other organizations and individuals within and outside the destination. (Adapted from Morrison 2022.)

Destination branding

The steps taken by a DMO, in collaboration with its stakeholders, to develop and communicate an identity and personality for its destination, which are different from those of all competing destinations.

Destination IMC

IMC is the coordination and integration of all of a DMO's external communications and promotions to increase their effectiveness and consistency. This is much superior to using each IMC component separately and independently.

You will easily find other definitions of destination marketing online. For example, Tremento (2018) says destination marketing is "the advertising of a location with the objective to increase the amount of visitors to this place." Your author disagrees with this definition as it is incomplete and outdated, and does not reflect everything involved in today's marketing of destinations. Destination marketing, branding, and communications are not just advertising. Also, DMOs may not want to increase the numbers of visitors; in fact, some want to decrease visitor volumes (with degrowth or demarketing strategies). Be careful what you read, and be even more careful about what you believe.

Destination Marketing Principles

It is best to start with the basics on marketing before getting into the details of planning. Contemporary destination marketing, branding, and communications are founded on four key professional principles that apply to all DMOs.

Marketing Concept and Customer Orientation

The first principle of modern marketing, branding, and communications is that success is based mainly on the continuing satisfaction of the customer's needs and wants—this is known as the marketing concept and reflects a customer orientation (Fig. 12.1). For a DMO, this principle raises an important question: who are the DMO's customers? The first and most instinctive answer would be the people who travel to the destination for business, pleasure, visiting friends or relatives (VFR), and other reasons. However, a DMO has many other audiences, including tourism sector stakeholders, government officials, and local residents. You will remember that these stakeholders were identified and discussed in Chapters 1 and 9. In some ways, they are also customers of the DMO.

Destination Life Cycle

The PLC is another widely accepted principle of marketing. The notion here is that every product in time goes through the four stages of introduction, growth, maturity, and decline. The overall PLC model has been converted into a destination life cycle concept. Butler (1980) described a TALC with seven stages, consisting of exploration, involvement, development, consolidation, stagnation, decline and rejuvenation (Fig. 12.2).

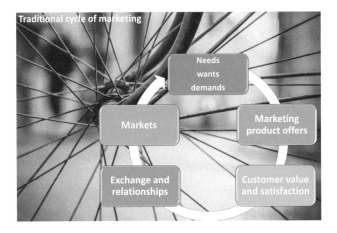

Figure 12.1 Traditional cycle of marketing.

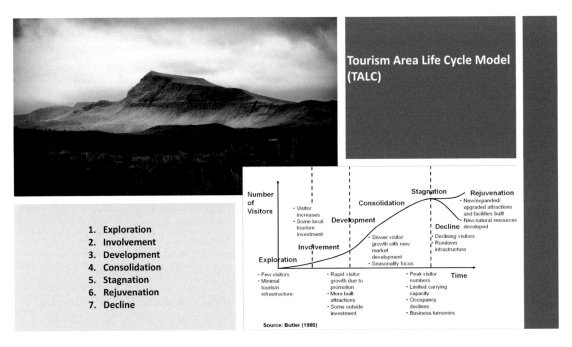

Figure 12.2 Tourism area life cycle model (Butler 1980: 5–12). This material is reproduced with permission of John Wiley & Sons, Inc.

Market Segmentation

Greater marketing, branding, and communications success follows from pursuing specific groups of tourists (target markets) rather than trying to appeal to the mass market. Moreover, it is wasteful for a DMO to go after everyone in the market. The DMO needs to decide how it will divide pleasure and business tourists into groups (market segmentation analysis) and select target markets from among these available groups. Chapters 17–19 review three major target markets—domestic leisure and VFR travel markets (Chapter 17), international pleasure and leisure travel markets (Chapter 18), and business travel and business event markets (Chapter 19).

Marketing Mix

All destination marketers have a toolbox of techniques to use in appealing to customers. These tools have come to be known as the Ps of marketing, which McCarthy (1960) first designated as the four Ps of marketing, which are product, price, place, and promotion. Several authors have argued that the traditional four Ps do not fit as well with tourism and destinations as they do for physical products. Morrison (2022) adds four additional Ps (packaging, programming, partnership, and people) to address the unique aspects of marketing tourism and destinations. You will hear more about these eight Ps of destination marketing, branding, and communications later in this chapter.

Planning Marketing, Branding, and Communications

Planning is not haphazard but rather requires a systematic, step-by-step approach. The DMP is one template that can be used. This is a tried-and-tested process that the author pioneered and has used extensively over the past thirty years with DMOs in several countries.

Planning Process

Every DMO needs to plan its destination marketing, branding, and communications, and it is important to think of this planning as consisting of long-term (strategic) and short-term (tactical) time dimensions. The strategic dimension is defined as three to five years or further into the future, and the tactical dimension is one to two years ahead. A core part of the planning process is the creation of a time-ordered hierarchy of goals and objectives. Figure 12.3 shows this hierarchy, which includes the destination vision, DMO vision, destination marketing goals, and destination marketing objectives. A description of these four follows the figure. There are also core values and guiding principles.

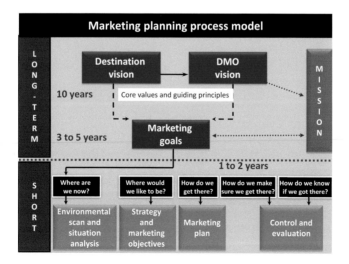

Figure 12.3 Destination marketing planning (DMP) process model.

Destination Vision

Every DMO's destination marketing, branding, and communications efforts should be driven by a set of explicitly articulated goals. These goals should be established to achieve the destination vision, which is identified through a planning process known as visioning, where the outcome is the definition of a super long-term goal for the destination.

DEFINITION

Destination vision statement

A destination vision statement is a concise, desired word picture of the destination at some point in the future. It is a verbal image of the destination that local people aspire for it to become. The vision provides a clear focus on what the destination will strive to be. This sets the overall direction for marketing, branding, and communications and the development of the destination in the upcoming years.

The destination vision should be articulated in a vision statement. Ritchie (1993) suggests that the destination visioning process should be completed in three stages: (1) envisioning an image of the desired future destination state, which (2) when effectively communicated to those responsible (3) serves to empower these people so they can enact the vision. The following is an example of a vision statement from Tourism Australia.

EXAMPLE 12.1

Tourism Australia's Vision Statement

This is a short vision statement; nevertheless, it clearly indicates what Tourism Australia aspires to achieve in the future.

> Our vision is to make Australia the most desirable (first-time visitors) and memorable (attracting repeat visitors) destination on earth—because this underpins everything we do at Tourism Australia.
>
> (Tourism Australia 2022)

Learning Point

"Most desirable" and "memorable" are the keywords in this vision statement. It clearly indicates the markets—first-time and repeat visitors.

Visit Greenland provide a good second example of a vision. As you can see in this one, the emphasis is on adventure tourism and sustainable development. Greenland is an island country that is part of the Kingdom of Denmark.

Visit Greenland's Vision

The strengths of this vision are the emphasis on sustainable development and the focus on Greenland becoming a sought-after adventure tourism destination. The earlier parts sound more like a mission to the author.

> We help create economic growth, jobs and the sustainable development of our community by making Greenland an internationally known and sought-after adventure destination with a focus on quality, safety and sustainability.
>
> (Visit Greenland 2021)

Learning Point

The emphasis on adventure tourism is key part of this vision and makes it clear what Visit Greenland is aspiring to do.

DMO Vision

The destination vision statement creates a pathway for future marketing action. However, the prime responsibility and accountability for achieving the destination vision are given to the officially recognized DMO. The next step is for the DMO to define its own vision for the future that will set it on the right course to achieving the destination vision in cooperation with its internal and external stakeholders.

The DMO vision statement should be more concrete than the destination vision statement because the DMO will be accountable for achieving this vision. It is helpful to think of the destination and DMO visions as being the super long-term goals from which all the other marketing, branding, and communications goals and objectives flow. Some DMO vision statements are quite short and simple, as in the Aruba example.

The Aruba DMO Vision

The Aruba Tourism Authority (ATA) aspires to be the most innovative and creative DMO in the Caribbean (by the way, DMMO is destination marketing and management organization). It is a laudable aspiration; however, measuring it might be difficult.

> The ATA will become the most innovative and creative DMMO in the Caribbean.
>
> (ATA 2022)

Learning Point

DMO vision statements should make the organizations stretch to improve in specific ways in the future. It is better if DMO visions are connected in some way to the destination vision.

Core Values or Guiding Principles

Core values and guiding principles should be articulated that support the destination vision. These are the definitions of the two terms.

DEFINITIONS

Core values

Beliefs and values commonly shared within a particular destination that underpin what is most important to people and reflect how they want tourism to be implemented and how stakeholders are expected to behave.

Guiding principles

These are principles that set standards for decision-making and behavior in support of the achievement of the decision-making.

For example, a destination may decide that sustainable development is a core value. A guiding principle might be that all stakeholders will be involved and engaged when important decisions are being made about tourism. The following is an example of the values of a regional DMO in Australia.

EXAMPLE 12.4

Values of Tourism Tropical North Queensland

It is vital that core values and guiding principles are articulated when preparing destination and DMO visions. This is a very good example for northeastern Australia. Tourism Tropical North Queensland specifies its values in great detail on its website.

> Tourism Tropical North Queensland, as the regional tourism organization, brings together the industry and the community to drive the value of the visitor economy through destination marketing. COVID-19 has created global uncertainty around the future of travel and tourism that we must respond to as a collective to support local businesses and retain local jobs.

Values

- Professionalism, e.g., behaving in a fair, logical and consistent manner.
- Leadership, e.g., demonstrating active listening by allowing someone to speak without interrupting and listening to what's being said and providing a meaningful reply to ideas and opinions.
- Collaboration, e.g., a willingness to work together as a team.
- Respect, e.g., having respect for diversity by embracing differences in talents, strengths and weaknesses.
- Creativity, e.g., encouraging creativity to develop fresh ideas.

(Tourism Tropical North Queensland 2022)

Learning Point

A destination vision must be underpinned by core values and guiding principles for the destination and DMO.

DEFINITIONS

Goals

Goals are medium-term (three to five years) measurable results that the DMO wants to achieve.

Objectives

Objectives are short-term (one to two years) measurable results that the DMO wants to achieve.

Destination Marketing, Branding, and Communications Goals

These goals are like stepping-stones on the DMO's path to realizing the destination and DMO visions. They are longer-term (three to five years) measurable results that the DMO wants to achieve for its destination marketing, branding, and communications. It is best if the goals are target market, time specific, and state an intended result in a quantified format, but not all goals exactly fit these criteria. For example, it is becoming more common now for destinations to express goals in numerical terms as in the case of the Korea Tourism Organization.

EXAMPLE 12.5

Korea Tourism Organization Goals

The Korea Tourism Organization has set for 2026 for each of its core values that are digital innovation, industrial growth, interregional cooperation, global competitiveness, and public satisfaction. The vision is "to advance tourism as a key driver for economic growth and enhancing national welfare."

> Number of tourism digital data used: 850,000
> Identifying and supporting tourism businesses: 4,325 companies
> Number of domestic visitors at tourism sites: 270 million
> Market attractiveness of Korea as a travel destination: 85 points
> Public evaluation: highest rank.

(Korea Tourism Organization 2022)

Learning Point

It is crucial to connect visions with core values and goals.

Some destinations express these goals without specific quantitative measures. The following example shows the cases of this from Prague (Czech Republic) and Estonia.

EXAMPLE 12.6

Prague's Tourism Marketing Goals

This is very clever set of marketing goals for a city. The emphasis on image is useful as are the specific ways of increasing visitor yield and return visits. The author would classify these as goals rather than objectives.

Through the implementation of our marketing strategy, we seek to achieve the following objectives:

- Increase average spend per visitor
- Increase overnights
- Increase arrivals or, in some markets, recover declining arrivals
- Motivate repeat visits
- Improve off-season arrivals in some target groups
- Bolster interest in visiting areas outside of the immediate historical center
- Improve Prague's image with domestic visitors, combat negative stereotypes
- Promote Prague as a convention destination via partnership with the Prague Convention Bureau.

(Prague City Tourism 2022)

Learning Point

It is vital to be explicit in setting goals for a DMO—what exactly will the DMO try to achieve?

EXAMPLE 12.7

Estonian Tourism Board Strategic Goals

Sometimes simpler strategies work much better than complex ones. This may be especially true for smaller DMOs. Estonia's four goals are clear and have a focus on yield.

Visit Estonia is made up of more than thirty people with a mission. We work in three teams, one that looks after the end consumer, one that interacts with the travel trade, and one that deals with development questions. We work closely together to give our home country an advantage it deserves. We operate as flexibly and creatively as possible. We react to fast-changing situations in the world of travel and adapt accordingly. Our strategy is made up of the following goals:

- Encourage first visits from long-haul markets and repeated visits from closer target markets.

- Increase visits outside peak season.
- Prolong the duration of stay.
- Expand the customer base to include a wider segment—different ages and interests, more demanding and higher-paying travelers.

(Estonian Tourism Board 2022)

Learning Point

Keep it simple if you can—plans are more likely to succeed that way.

The DMO is not alone in achieving the goals but rather must rely on the efforts of its private- and public-sector partners within and outside the destination.

Destination Marketing, Branding, and Communications Objectives

Objectives are short-term (usually one to two years) measurable results that the DMO wants to achieve. These objectives must be based on the goals and be interim steps toward achieving these goals. As with the goals, objectives should if possible be target market, time specific, and indicate a quantified result. It should be realized here that many DMOs have objectives but have not derived these through a visioning process and goal-setting. Objectives are often set as part of the annual process of developing a marketing plan. Although objectives are essential foundations for a marketing plan, they are more effective when derived from a long-term visioning process and goal-setting. The objectives for Brand USA for 2022 are shown in Example 12.8:

EXAMPLE 12.8

Brand USA Objectives

Brand USA set four objectives for 2022. They also specified measures for judging the success of each objective. The emphasis was on recovery from the effects of COVID-19.

1. Help the US travel and tourism sector recovery by driving international visitation and spending to the USA on a market-by-market basis as conditions warrant.

2. Help US travel and tourism industry stakeholders reengage international markets.

3. Integrate critical themes into Brand USA recovery campaign and content efforts.

4. Maintain sound financial management and corporate governance.

(Brand USA 2021: 12)

Learning Point

It is important to set measures for judging the success of each objective.

DMO Mission

On the right side of Figure 12.3, you will see the term "mission." It is placed there as the mission is not a goal or objective. You should also know that the mission applies to the DMO and not to the destination. Here is the definition of the DMO mission.

> **DEFINITION**
>
> **DMO mission**
>
> The DMO mission, articulated in its mission statement, describes its reason for being. It is a broad statement about the organization's business and scope, services and products, markets served and overall philosophy (adapted from Kotler et al. 2017).

Again, you should realize that the mission statement is not a goal or objective, but rather it is a clear description of what the DMO does and whom it serves. DMO mission statements are sometimes confused with vision statements and goals, but these are three quite different concepts. In fact, the DMO's mission statement should be derived from the destination and DMO vision statements and be consistent with the goals. Figure 12.4 makes clear the distinction between a destination vision and a DMO mission.

An example is provided of the mission statement of Wonderful Copenhagen, the DMO for the capital city of Denmark.

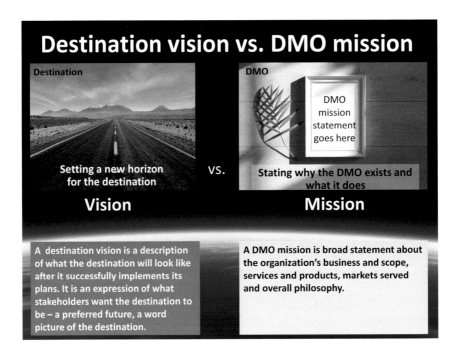

Figure 12.4 Difference between a destination vision and a DMO mission.

Wonderful Copenhagen's Mission

Wonderful Copenhagen does not say the following is its mission; however, the author classifies it as a DMO mission. Note the use of "official tourism organization" and the clear statement of the aim of this DMO.

> Wonderful Copenhagen is the official tourism organization of the Capital Region of Denmark, working to promote and develop both business and leisure tourism. The aim of Wonderful Copenhagen is to drive tourism development in a sustainable direction. Working together with hundreds of public and private partners, the organization's key focus areas are attracting new congresses, meetings, events, cruise visitors and airline routes; as well as promoting Copenhagen; and developing city tourism, cultural tourism, new markets and knowledge.
>
> (Wonderful Copenhagen 2022)

Learning Point

A DMO mission statement—as with this one—must clearly say what it does and who it serves.

Another DMO mission—this one at a provincial level—is shown in the example for Tourism KwaZulu-Natal in South Africa.

Mission of Tourism KwaZulu-Natal (TKZN)

This is a clear statement of what TKZN. You should note the emphasis on strategic marketing and tourism development in this South African province.

> TKZN is responsible for the development, promotion and marketing of tourism into and within the province. Our mission is to initiate, facilitate, coordinate and implement strategic tourism marketing and demand-driven tourism development programs; to grow tourism, transform the province's tourism sector and provide economic benefits to all stakeholders.
>
> TKZN is overseen by the Department of Economic Development, Tourism and Environmental Affairs in South Africa.
>
> (TKZN 2022)

Learning Point

This mission statement emphasizes that the DMO works to benefit all stakeholders through program initiation, facilitation, coordination, and implementation.

The author has seen examples of destination mission statements and some of them were rather humorous. Apart from being a pointless exercise, you should know that destinations are not organizations, so missions do not fit. Also, these statements are not needed if there are already visions, goals, and objectives for destinations.

It was decided to use the terms "vision," "goals," and "objectives" in this book. However, many different terms are used by DMOs. For example, the terms "initiatives," "strategic initiatives," "strategies," or "priorities" are sometimes applied in place of goals. The word "objective" is often replaced with "action" or "tactic." Essentially, the meanings are the same, but the choice of terminology is the difference.

DMOs do not (and should not) just pluck their visions, goals, and objectives from the air. You should understand that there are specific techniques and processes DMOs use to define them, including visioning and environmental scanning, completing situation analyses, marketing strategy selection, PIB (positioning, image, and branding) projects, and marketing plans. Additionally, visions, goals, and objectives must be consistent with the DMO mission statement and roles, and core values and guiding principles.

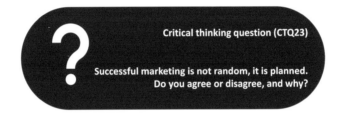

Critical thinking question (CTQ23)

Successful marketing is not random, it is planned.
Do you agree or disagree, and why?

The Destination Marketing System and the PRICE model

A more detailed description is now provided of how a DMO develops its marketing, branding, and communications activities and programs. The destination marketing goals trigger the rest of the planning process because the goals are the connection between the long-term and short-term dimensions (Fig. 12.3). The PRICE model suggested by Morrison (2022) provides a logical sequence for the remaining elements of the planning process. The PRICE model is derived from the DMS (Fig. 12.5), which involves answering five questions in a sequence of steps:

1. Where are we now?
2. Where would we like to be?
3. How do we get there?
4. How do we make sure that we get there?
5. How do we know if we got there?

The PRICE model (Fig. 12.6) identifies the key destination marketing, branding, and communications functions as planning (P), research (R), implementation (I), control (C) and evaluation (E). The DMO's planning and research tasks are accomplished by answering the first two DMS questions (Where are we now? Where would we like to be?) by doing research-based planning and then analyzing the resulting information to develop a strategy and objectives. DMOs must make choices among alternative types of activities and programs. A conscious effort in planning is needed to make the right choices. For planning to be as effective as possible, research must be done and then analyzed before making the choice of a future strategy and the supporting activities and programs.

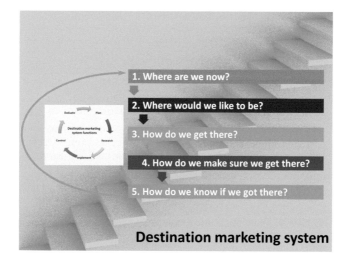

Figure 12.5 Destination marketing system.

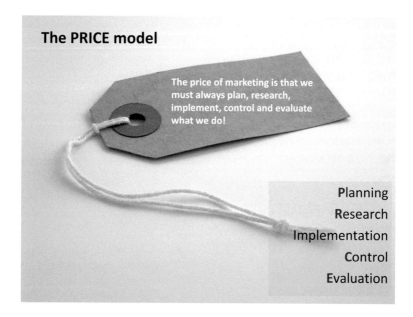

Figure 12.6 PRICE model for destination marketing, branding, and communications.

The objectives are developed based on the selected strategy and are the main guides for specifying the activities and programs. The accomplishment of the selected strategy and objectives is articulated and described in a written format in a marketing plan, which is implemented by the DMO (How do we get there?).

Then, the implementation of the marketing plan is evaluated in two stages: (1) formative evaluation, through monitoring and controlling progress toward the objectives (How do we make sure we get there?), and (2) summative evaluation, through performance measurement at the end of the marketing plan period (How do we know if we got there?). A more contemporary name for evaluation commonly used by DMOs is demonstrating accountability for the money and other resources expended in implementing a marketing plan.

Each DMS step and marketing function in the planning process involves using specific techniques and concepts to achieve the objectives. The steps, functions, techniques, and concepts are identified in Figure 12.7.

Every DMO is faced with a huge array of marketing, branding, and communications choices. Some of the most crucial of these decisions include which tourists to try to attract (target markets), which services and products should be developed and communicated (destination product) and what image of the destination should be communicated (destination PIB). Rather than making quick and arbitrary decisions, a careful and thoughtful approach of research-based planning must be followed to make the best choices. This approach is now described in the five DMS steps.

Where Are We Now? (Planning and Research)

Figure 12.8 shows the inputs and outputs of the first step in the DMS (Where are we now?). When beginning a new cycle of planning, the DMO starts with its mandate to attain the destination vision, DMO vision, and goals along with the lessons it has learned from implementing the DMO's previous marketing plans from the summative evaluation step (DMS step 5).

The DMO identifies and assesses strengths, weaknesses, trends, challenges, opportunities, and threats as they relate to its marketing goals and the destination vision. This involves using an environmental scan and situation analysis. Often, when combined, they are referred to as a SWOT analysis. These should not merely be academic exercises but must yield practical ideas for marketing implementation. The Newport Beach & Company case is an example. There were a total of sixteen cells in this analysis (four audiences by four SWOT dimensions); however, Example 12.11 only shows four of the sixteen.

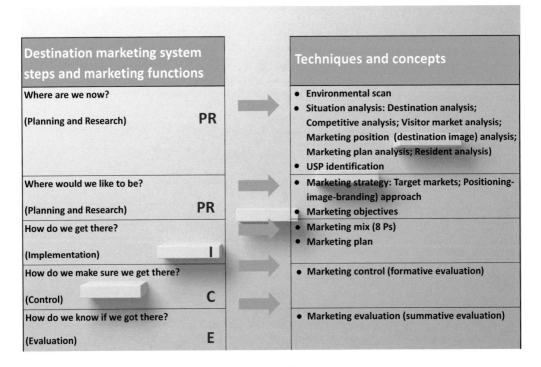

Figure 12.7 Destination marketing system steps, functions, techniques, and concepts.

Inputs	DMS Step 1	Outputs
• Destination vision and DMO vision • Marketing goals • Performance, conclusions and recommendations from previous marketing plan (DMS Step 5)	**Where are we now?** **PLANNING AND RESEARCH** PR_{ICE}	• Environmental scan (challenges, opportunities, and threats in the marketing environment) • Situation analysis (destination analysis, visitor market profile, competitive analysis, marketing position and plan analysis, resident analysis) • Strengths and weaknesses of the destination and the DMO • Unique selling propositions (USPs)
Inputs	DMS Step 2	Outputs
• Environmental scan (trends, challenges, opportunities, and threats) • Situation analysis (strengths and weaknesses) • USPs	**Where would we like to be?** **PLANNING AND RESEARCH** PR_{ICE}	• Market segmentation analysis • Target markets • Positioning-image-branding approach • Marketing objectives

Figure 12.8 Destination marketing system Steps 1 and 2.

EXAMPLE 12.11

Newport Beach and Company SWOT Analysis

This is a great case study in how to complete a SWOT analysis. In fact, this DMO does SWOT analyses for each of its four audiences—leisure traveler, meeting planner, local community, corporate—and this is rather unusual.

Strengths
- Corporate audience
- Committed staff, executive committee and board of directors
- Strong city council and city staff
- Accredited destination marketing organization (eight years with distinction)
- Certified Destination Management Executive (CDME) team
- Industry leaders
- Small but mighty marketing and sales experts
- Innovative community-marketing organization model, strong company core values, benefits, educational opportunities, team spirit, office space, company events and collaboration resulting in amazing work productivity, results and achievements
- Premier destination product
- Ten-year Tourism Business Improvement District and Transient Occupancy Tax contracts with the city of Newport Beach
- Appealing office infrastructure, environment and scenic location

- Visit California, a marketing powerhouse that leads and sets the agenda for all DMOs in the state

Weaknesses
- Leisure traveler
- Traveler patterns
- Short length of stay
- High rate of day-trip versus overnight
- Low winter occupancy
- Limited beachfront hotels
- Parking and public transportation options
- Limited in-city attractions
- Limited national/international awareness

Opportunities
- Meeting planner audience
- Expansion of corporate end-users in Southern California region
- Onboarding and continued engagement with new and existing TBID partners
- Increased customer awareness of destination location for meetings
- Expanded airlift/direct flights (John Wayne Airport, Long Beach Airport)
- Broadening exposure for our high-end hotels, now including VEA Newport beach, a Marriott Resort and spa and Pendry Integrated marketing campaign targeting luxury audience leveraging all industry partnerships
- Enhanced incentives for third parties

Threats
- Local community audience
- Sharing economy
- Economic and political uncertainty/instability
- COVID-19: variants, vaccines, state/federal mandates
- Hurdles to international access into the USA: Laptop/travel bans, visa access
- US international perception/image
- Online sourcing platforms make it easy to circumvent Newport Beach
- Natural weather-related disasters
- California "fire season"
- Third-party commission structures
- Limited capacities at attractions and tourism/hospitality
- Business incidents going viral on social media causing negative sentiment/"cancel culture" toward destination or local businesses
- Supply-chain crisis impacting tourism-related resources

(Newport Beach & Company 2022)

Learning Point

It is better to consider SWOT in the context of the destination's different target markets, as in this case example.

Environmental Scan

An environmental scan pinpoints trends and the potential challenges, opportunities and threats in the marketing environment. The environmental factors to be analyzed include the political situation and economic conditions, social and cultural patterns, technological advances, environmental changes, and legislation and regulation (PESTEL). For each of these factors, the six questions shown in Figure 12.9 should be answered.

Situation Analysis

Next, the DMO identifies the strengths and weaknesses of the destination and the DMO's internal strengths and weaknesses. An effective DMO is constantly taking inventory of its destination's and the DMO's strengths and weaknesses. The DMO's traditional ways of marketing are forever being challenged to see whether there is a better way of doing things.

The six techniques in completing a DMO situation analysis are shown in Figure 12.10 and then described.

Destination Analysis

A destination analysis (also sometimes called a product or product development analysis) is a careful assessment of the strengths and weaknesses of the destination, ideally based on input from a variety of sources within and outside the destination. More recently, this process has become known as a destination audit and may be completed by an independent consulting or research company on the DMO's behalf.

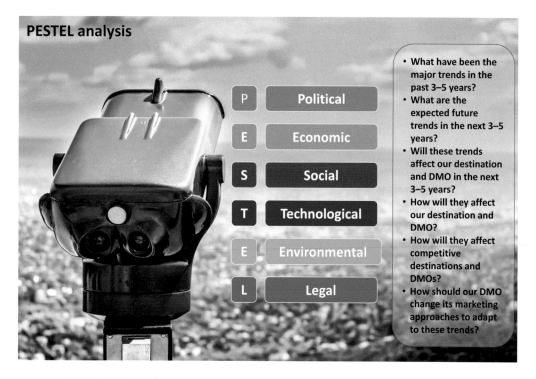

Figure 12.9 PESTEL analysis.

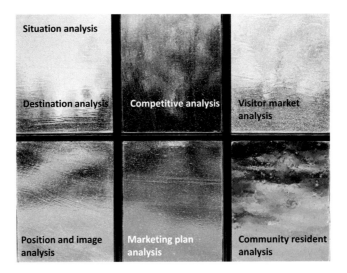

Figure 12.10 Situation analysis.

DEFINITION

Destination audit

A comprehensive and systematic assessment of the strengths and weaknesses of a destination, often conducted by an independent third party. Tangible and intangible aspects are evaluated through a variety of research techniques.

This audit normally analyzes the destination (product development assessment), marketing, branding, and communications programs (marketing assessment), and the DMO and its local partners (organization assessment). A variety of sources are polled through different types of research inquiries, including a visitor survey, secret or mystery shopping within the destination, and personal interviews with community and tourism leaders. Recommendations are provided on needed improvements by the tourism sector and the community/local area within the destination for future marketing, branding, and communications, and for the DMO and sector associations.

The DMO should develop a set of criteria for analyzing the destination. The ten As model described in Chapter 1 is one set of suggested criteria for assessing the many dimensions of a destination.

Competitive Analysis

A competitive analysis is another important element in destination marketing planning and research, but surprisingly is not something that DMOs tend to do well. Often, this is a result of inadequate or inaccurate definitions of the destination's competitive set or sets. Most destinations' competitors vary by target market, and therefore it is best to divide the competitive analysis in that way. For example, a destination may have a different set of competitors for business conventions and meetings than it has for individual pleasure travelers.

The DMO's marketing and sales team should have a good feel for the closest competitors, but the best source is visitors themselves. Asking the destination's visitors in surveys to pinpoint other destinations that they considered for their trips is one way to tackle this. Another option is to use a focus group approach in which past or potential visitors reach a consensus on the destination's closest competitors. Secondary sources of research information may also be helpful in shedding light on the most popular destinations for specific visitor market segments.

Visitor Market Analysis

Every DMO should have a detailed visitor market profile at its disposal. Some DMOs do this research on a monthly or quarterly basis every year, whereas others conduct visitor profile studies only once every two or three years. Unfortunately, there are many DMOs that have never developed a detailed profile of their visitors through a research study. The categories of information that should be provided by a visitor profile analysis were highlighted earlier in Figure 5.10.

An outstanding example of conducting a visitor profile study within a city destination is the research done by the LVCVA.

EXAMPLE 12.12

Las Vegas Visitor Profile Study

This is a model for a visitor profile study that can be conducted for a destination. Visitors are interviewed each month.

> The Las Vegas Visitor Profile Study is reported annually, to provide an ongoing assessment of the Las Vegas visitor and trends in visitor behavior over time, based on ongoing intercept surveys of travelers to Las Vegas. Due to the COVID-19 pandemic no report was issued in 2020.
>
> More specifically, the Las Vegas Visitor Profile aims to:
>
> - Compare 2021 Las Vegas visitors with pre-pandemic visitors from 2016–2019.
> - Provide a profile of Las Vegas visitors in terms of socio-demographic and behavioral characteristics.
> - Monitor trends in visitor behavior and visitor characteristics.
> - Supply detailed information on the vacation and gaming habits of different visitor groups, particularly gaming and non-gaming expenditures.
> - Allow the identification of market segments and potential target markets.
> - Provide a basis for calculating the economic impact of different visitor groups.
> - Determine visitor satisfaction levels.
>
> (LVCVA 2022)

Learning Point

Having credible and consistent visitor profile data is a key for effective destination marketing, branding, and communications.

Marketing Position (Destination Image) Analysis

Every destination needs to understand its image or position in the minds of past and potential visitors. Unfortunately, although DMO practitioners acknowledge its importance, image research for specific destinations is done infrequently and seldom with great rigor and accuracy. You heard about how to do a destination image analysis in Chapter 5.

EXAMPLE 12.13

Britain's Image Abroad

Destinations must be concerned about their overall images in source markets. In this example, VisitBritain reports on the results of a panel survey that reveal perceptions of Britain as a destination.

> The Anholt-Ipsos Nation Brands Index is an annual online study among 60,000 consumers in twenty panel countries around the world. Respondents score sixty nations on a raft of attributes including some relating to tourism, culture and people as well as those relating to exports, governance and immigration. Respondents are representative of the online population in each market.
>
> Looking at the dimensions relevant for tourism, the UK ranked sixth out of sixty nations for tourism and fourth for culture. Within these dimensions the UK ranked highest for contemporary culture, sport, historic buildings/monuments and vibrant city life. Within other dimensions, education qualifications, having a close friend from the UK and willingness to live and work in the UK were held in high regard as well. Attributes such as natural beauty, welcome and behaving responsibly to protect the environment were ranked lowest in 2021.
>
> (VisitBritain 2022)

Learning Point

Image studies frequently show positive as well as less positive perceptions of destinations. DMOs must carefully consider how these results will affect future marketing, branding, and communications.

Marketing Plan Analysis

The marketing plan analysis involves an objective assessment of the DMO's past marketing plans. This is done mainly by evaluating and measuring the effectiveness and results for the previous marketing plan. The summative evaluation of the last period's performance against marketing objectives must answer three key questions in the RAN framework (Fig. 12.11).

Community Resident Analysis

Residents and their well-being and quality of life was the topic in Chapter 3. Some destinations conduct research on community resident attitudes or sentiments about tourism in their communities. This is especially important when tourism represents a very large part of the local economy and affects residents' everyday lives.

Figure 12.11 RAN framework for marketing plan analysis.

Hawai'i provides a very good example of this kind of situation where tourism is a very dominant economic force. The HTA conducts a regular resident sentiment survey to monitor residents' attitudes to tourism on the islands and how people's sentiments are changing. The survey's objectives are identified in the example.

EXAMPLE 12.14

Hawai'i Resident Sentiment Survey

The Resident Sentiment Survey conducted in Hawai'i is a model for other destinations to follow. The state realizes that resident support is critical to its tourism sector and they have conducted this research for more than twenty years.

Resident sentiment toward Hawai'i's visitor industry is vital to maintaining Responsible and Regenerative Growth in the industry and in the state's economy overall. The Resident Sentiment Survey (RSS) has been conducted nineteen times since 1999, and the current survey was conducted by Omnitrak Group, Inc. The primary objectives of the RSS research are:

- to track key resident attitudes toward tourism in Hawai'i over time;
- to identify perceived positive and negative impacts of the visitor industry on local residents;
- to identify for the visitor industry and HTA, issues or concerns regarding tourism expressed by residents;
- to explore resident perceptions on ideas to "manage" or mitigate the negative impacts associated with tourism.

(HTA 2022)

Learning Point

It is important to ask about negative impacts of tourism as well as positive ones. Also, to determine resident issues and concerns relative to tourism is crucial.

Unique Selling Points or Propositions (USP) Identification

The major outcome of all these analyses is a clearer understanding of how the destination is different from competitive destinations and how this will be reflected in the marketing strategy. According to Porter (1996), competitive strategy is about being different, and the DMO must identify these differences early in its marketing planning. Sometimes, these differences are referred to as USPs, sustainable competitive advantages or differential-distinct competitive advantages. Adapting Barney's (1991) work, a sustainable competitive advantage for a destination and its DMO would mean having the assets and/or skills that meet the following conditions:

- They are valuable to visitors.
- They are rare among the destination's current and potential competitors.
- They must be imperfectly imitable (cannot be easily copied).
- There are no strategically equivalent substitutes for the assets or skills.

Output Summary for DMS Step 1

When Step 1 of the DMS is finished by the DMO, it will have a completed environmental scan and situation analysis. The strengths and weaknesses of the destination and DMO will be known. Additionally, the destination's unique USPs will have been identified (Fig. 12.12).

Figure 12.12 Output summary for DMS Steps 1 and 2.

When beginning DMS Step 2, the DMO has several inputs to use for deciding on its marketing strategy and objectives:

- The trends, opportunities, challenges and threats presented in the external environment: How to take advantage or adapt to these in future marketing strategies and plans.
- The major issues resulting from the destination and competitive analyses: How to change in the future to deal with these issues.
- The characteristics and feedback from visitor research: How to respond to visitor feedback and changes in tourists.
- The assessment of marketing position and previous marketing plan: How to improve positioning, branding, and marketing plan.
- The attitudes of residents toward tourism: What needs to be done to address residents' concerns with the operations of the tourism sector?
- The statement of USPs: How to apply and communicate USPs more effectively in the future.

EXAMPLE 12.15

Berlin Citizens' Advisory Council

It is becoming increasingly important for DMOs to give local residents a voice in shaping destination marketing, branding, and communications, and in tourism planning and development. This is an outstanding example of how to accomplish this.

> In Berlin, locals will have a formal voice into the development of tourism in their city under a new initiative called the Citizens' Advisory Council. They will have an opportunity to preserve their city's authenticity and character as it emerges as one of Europe's most popular tourist destinations.
>
> Under the initiative, two selected representatives from each of Berlin's twelve districts will form an independent council that will meet four times a year and advise tourism officials on how to develop tourism for the city sustainably. The council application process ends in October.
>
> (Habtemariam 2022)

Learning Point

This is a novel approach to ensuring that local residents are involved in the decision-making on the future of tourism in their city. It will offer a greater guarantee of authenticity in Berlin's tourism.

Where Would We Like to Be? (Planning and Research)

The DMO's marketing strategy and objectives are developed in the second DMS step (Fig. 12.8). These should be based on the strengths, weaknesses, trends, challenges, opportunities, and threats identified in the first DMS step. The DMO considers several options with respect to target markets and destination PIB approaches before choosing what it considers the ideal strategy for the upcoming marketing period. PIB is the topic covered in Chapter 13.

Figure 12.13 shows the marketing strategy stages in the left column and the steps that DMO marketers must complete are listed in the middle column; the right column indicates the outcomes that result from the completion of the steps.

Marketing Strategy

The DMO's marketing strategy is a combination of the selected target markets and the PIB approach.

VISITOR MARKET SEGMENTATION ANALYSIS

As you learned in Chapter 1, market segmentation is one of the key professional principles of marketing and an extremely important step in selecting a marketing strategy. Each of the DMO's major markets should first be subjected to a visitor market segmentation analysis. Morrison (2022) describes this process as one of dividing the visitor market into groups that share common characteristics.

The most widely accepted practice in destination marketing is to begin by dividing markets by geographic origin and by broad trip purpose into business and pleasure/personal travelers. The following sets of segmentation criteria may be used to divide up overall markets:

- Trip purpose: Defining the market segment by the visitor's main purpose of the trip, with four main divisions: business meetings and conventions; pleasure, vacation or leisure; VFRs; and personal.
- Geography: Describing markets by place of residence.
- Socio-demographics: Profiling tourists according to census-style characteristics, such as age, education, occupation, income, and household composition.

Marketing strategy stages, steps, and outcomes

Marketing strategy stages	Steps	Outcomes
Where would we like to be?	PR = Planning and Research	
Visitor market segmentation analysis	→ Divide the market into segments	• Market segments available
Target market selection	→ Develop criteria for selecting target markets → Select target markets	• Single target market, concentrated, full-coverage or undifferentiated?

Positioning-image-branding (PIB) approach development	→ Select positioning, image and branding:
	  ○ Overall positioning and image
	  ○ Positioning and image for each selected target market
	→ Destination branding
		• Specific product features, benefits/problem solution/needs, specific usage occasions, against another product or product class dissociation?

Marketing objective-setting	→ Write marketing objectives for each selected target market	• Marketing objectives that are target-market specific, results-oriented, quantitative and time-specific

Figure 12.13 Stages, steps, and outcomes in destination marketing strategy.

- Psychographics: Dividing up visitors by their psychological orientations; lifestyles; or activities, interests, and opinions.
- Behavior: Differentiating among groups of visitors based on past purchasing and travel behaviors or future travel purchase intentions.
- Product-related: Using some aspect of the product to define the market segment, such as ski slopes and alpine skiers, golf courses and golfers, reefs and scuba divers, or spa-goers.
- Channel of distribution (business-to-business, or B2B): Applying different criteria, specific travel trade intermediaries are divided into sub-groups. For example, this might include defining travel agent markets by geographic area or commission volume level. Tour operators might also be defined geographically or by specialty or destinations served.

TARGET MARKET SELECTION

Having divided up its markets, the DMO must now select from among the market segments. To do this effectively, the DMO must have a set of criteria to evaluate the relative merits of each market segment. The potential criteria and some possible ways of measuring or evaluating them are as follows:

SEGMENT SIZE, GROWTH AND SALES POTENTIAL

Segment size can be measured in number of visitors, total expenditures within the destination or daily expenditure per visitor, which is often referred to as the segment's yield. The rate of growth in a visitor market segment can be calculated in percentage terms in recent years and may then be compared to the rate of that segment's growth in competitive destinations.

COMPETITION AND SEGMENT STRUCTURAL ATTRACTIVENESS

Here, measures of the competitiveness for each segment and the relative power of buyers (visitors), travel trade intermediaries and sellers (DMOs, transportation providers, attractions, hotels and other suppliers) are evaluated.

DESTINATION VISION AND DMO'S VISION AND MARKETING GOALS

The appropriateness of market segment should be gauged against the destination vision and DMO vision and marketing goals.

SERVICEABILITY

The degree of match between the segment's needs/benefits sought and the destination product is determined. Additionally, the DMO must decide whether the destination has the managerial, financial and other resources and skills required to effectively tap into and service the market. For example, this would be the case if medical tourism were being considered by a DMO.

COSTS

The additional investment required to break into the target market or to significantly increase market share.

PIB APPROACH DEVELOPMENT

The DMO must decide in its marketing strategy how to position the destination in the minds of potential visitors and among its competitors. The DMO must also decide how to brand the destination given the selected positioning and images that reflect this positioning. The PIB approach is the combination of positioning, image, and branding.

POSITIONING AND IMAGE COMMUNICATION

The DMO must select a positioning approach to communicate an image of the destination to people within its selected target markets. Al Ries and Jack Trout (2001) introduced the positioning concept to the world in 1981 in their classic book, *Positioning: The Battle for Your Mind.* The following definition provides a clear picture of what positioning involves.

DEFINITION

Destination positioning

The steps taken by a DMO, in collaboration with its stakeholders, to identify and communicate a unique destination image to people within its target markets. Therefore, positioning is how the destination decides to make itself unique among competing destinations from the tourist's perspective.

Positioning by the DMO should be done in a series of steps, and Morrison (2022) suggests using the following five Ds of positioning:

1. Documenting: This step involves doing research with past and potential visitors to determine which benefits they are seeking in visiting the destination.
2. Deciding: The second step is accomplished in two stages: (1) determining what images past visitors and non-visitors have of the destination (perceived image); and (2) deciding what image the DMO wants visitors to have of the destination (desired image).
3. Differentiating: Positioning communicates the differences between the destination and competitors. Positioning is performed in two stages: (1) determining which destinations are in the competitive set (from the competitive analysis); and (2) pinpointing the factors and USPs, especially as these relate to the desired visitor benefits, which can be used to make the destination appear different from competitive destinations.
4. Designing: Fourth, the DMO must decide how it is going to communicate the select positioning or image to potential visitors within its target markets. The DMO must also make sure the destination product supports the selected approach to positioning.
5. Delivering: The DMO must implement and monitor the chosen approach to positioning. In Chapter 1, this was referred to as delivering on the ground.

The DMO should develop a destination positioning statement that expresses the differences and uniqueness of the place.

Destination Branding

The concepts of destination PIB are closely linked, with branding being used to support the selected positioning approach in communicating the desired destination image. Shaoxing, an ancient city in Zhejiang Province, China, provides an excellent example of destination positioning and branding. Shaoxing's DMO has been using the phrase Shaoxing, Vintage China as its positioning statement, which was created by your author and his company, BTI Consulting. The city's five USPs are shown Figure 12.14 along with the reasoning for using the word vintage. You should know that Shaoxing is world famous for its distinctive yellow rice wine (hence the vintage).

Another outstanding example of positioning and branding is Virginia's approach, Virginia Is for Lovers®.

Figure 12.14 Shaoxing, Vintage China.

EXAMPLE 12.16

Virginia Is for Lovers®

This must be one of the longest-running campaigns in the history of tourism. Its success possibly comes from its flexibility in application plus the underlying positive message of love. There is such great temptation to swap campaigns with the rapid pace of change that Virginia deserves great praise for maintaining consistency over six decades.

> Virginia is for Lovers® was created in 1969, fifty years ago, and has become one of the most beloved and well-known slogans in the world. While it has meant a lot of different things to a lot of different people, one thing hasn't changed—the LOVE. Celebrate 50 Years of LOVE when you visit participating cities and counties all across the state. You'll find everything from special lovers lagers at breweries and lovers blends at wineries, 1969 inspired meals and

prices at restaurants, special 50 Years of Love events, annual events with 1969 themes, contests, giveaways, and much more. Find an experience below and discover why Virginia is for Lovers.

(Virginia Tourism Corporation 2022)

Learning Point

This campaign demonstrated the value of being consistent in communications.

Marketing Objectives

Specific short-term objectives are set for each target market. These objectives serve as guidelines for the activities and programs included in the DMO's marketing plan. An example of the objectives of Brand USA was provided earlier in this chapter.

Output Summary for DMS Step 2

On completion of DMS Step 2, the DMO will have (Fig. 12.12):

- a set of identified target markets—what are the priority groups of tourists to be targeted?
- positioning and destination branding approaches: how to communicate the destination's uniqueness;
- the marketing objectives for the next marketing plan—what do we need to accomplish in the period ahead?

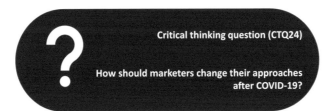

Critical thinking question (CTQ24)

How should marketers change their approaches after COVID-19?

EXAMPLE 12.17

Malaysia's New Tourism Marketing Plan

Tourism Malaysia launched a new five-year marketing plan in 2022—it could be classified as a strategic market plan. In the plan, eight specific goals were identified, associated with the domestic market, international recovery, health and safety, digitalization, and innovation.

Tourism Malaysia's domestic and international tourism promotion efforts have been strongly impacted by the outbreak of the COVID-19 pandemic. Generally, this marketing plan focuses on the domestic market, international recovery, health and safety, digitalization, and innovation. It aims to:

- emphasize more on the domestic market;
- focus on creative and digital marketing;
- enhance mix promotion;
- shift product-based promotion to emotional and sentiment-based promotion;
- build trust and confidence;
- convert the support and lead product;
- move from mass market to customized market;
- strengthen Malaysia's tourism branding—"Malaysia Truly Asia".

(Tourism Malaysia 2022: 11)

Learning Point

Following a major crisis, it is necessary for a DMO to refocus and recalibrate its marketing strategy, as in this case with Tourism Malaysia.

How Do We Get There? (Implementation)

The third element of the DMS is the selection of a marketing mix and the development and implementation of a marketing plan (Fig. 12.15). This is one of the most detailed and time-consuming stages in destination marketing and its planning (Fig. 12.16). DMOs usually divide

Inputs	DMS Step 3	Outputs
• Selected target markets • Positioning-image-branding approach • Marketing objectives	**How do we get there?** **IMPLEMENTATION** PR**I**CE	• Marketing mix selection (8 Ps) • Marketing plan • Marketing budget • Marketing plan timetable or schedule • Assignment of responsibilities • Control and evaluation procedures and measurements • Marketing implementation
Inputs	**DMS Step 4**	**Outputs**
• Marketing objectives • Marketing plan (8 Ps) and activities and programs • Marketing plan timetable • Marketing plan implementation responsibilities • Marketing budget	**How do we make sure we get there?** **CONTROL** PRI**C**E	• Progress reports (formative evaluations) • Marketing plan modifications
Inputs	**DMS Step 5**	**Outputs**
• Marketing objectives • Progress reports (formative evaluations) • Marketing plan modifications	**How do we know if we get there?** **EVALUATION** PRIC**E**	• Marketing effectiveness or performance measures • Changes required in next marketing plan

Figure 12.15 DMS Steps 3 to 5.

Marketing plan stages, steps, and outcomes

Marketing plan stages	Steps	Outcomes
How do we get there?	I = Implementation	
Marketing mix selection	➔ Decide on how the 8 Ps are to be used to achieve the marketing objectives for each selected target market	☐ Use of product, partnership, people, packaging, programming, place, promotion and pricing
Marketing plan development	➔ Write a plan including executive summary, marketing plan rationale and implementation plan	☐ Written marketing plan
Marketing budget development	➔ Prepare the marketing budget per the marketing objectives and the activities and programs to achieve them	☐ Marketing budget
Marketing plan timetable or schedule	➔ Prepare a month-by-month timetable showing when each activity and program will be implemented	☐ Month-by-month timetable
Assignment of implementation responsibilities	➔ Allocate responsibilities to different marketing departments and between DMO and its partners	☐ Responsibility assignments
Control and evaluation procedures and measurements	➔ Specify how the implementation of the marketing plan will be tracked and evaluated	☐ Control and evaluation procedures and measures
Marketing plan implementation	➔ Implement the marketing plan per the specifications in the written documents	☐ Implementation of specific activities and programs

Figure 12.16 Stages and steps in destination marketing plan.

up the preparation of their marketing plans by the divisions or units within their organizational structures. For example, one group might handle business tourism, conventions and exhibitions, and another group will focus on pleasure or leisure travelers.

Marketing Mix Selection

The marketing mix is one of the key professional principles of marketing. The DMO has eight principal weapons within its marketing mix toolbox for achieving the marketing objectives for each target market (product, price, place, promotion, packaging, programming, partnership, and people) (Fig. 12.17). Each of the eight Ps are described below.

Product

A DMO does not have a specific product or service to sell to potential visitors. However, there can be no doubt that the DMO represents the destination as a whole and the destination is what it markets. Morrison et al. (2018) describe all the components of what a destination offers to visitors as the destination product. The five components of the destination product are:

1. Attractions and events
2. Built facilities (hotels, resorts, other lodging; food and beverages; convention and exhibition centers; shopping; and other)
3. Transportation

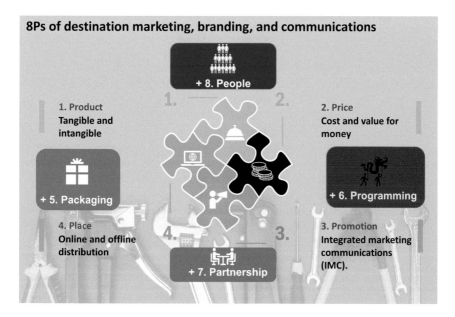

Figure 12.17 Eight Ps of destination marketing, branding, and communications.

4. Infrastructure
5. Service quality and friendliness.

The attractions and events play the key role, representing the unique assets that draw people to the destination.

As discussed in Chapter 1, the destination product is multidimensional. It includes physical products (attractions, facilities, transportation, infrastructure) but also has a human dimension (people). The people dimension includes both the hosts (hospitality resources) and the guests (tourists). The destination also offers many packages and arranges events and festivals (programming).

A DMO must be concerned about the quality of experiences that visitors are having within the destination because this impacts satisfaction levels, word-of-mouth recommendations and repeat visit intentions. Many DMOs have become involved in developing service and hospitality training programs, with a particular emphasis on front-line employees.

A destination audit can be very useful in evaluating the physical and qualitative aspects of the destination product. One specific qualitative measurement technique that is increasingly being used is mystery shopping. This is a form of participant observation where the researchers act as customers or potential customers to monitor the quality of processes and procedures used in the delivery of a service (Wilson 1998).

EXAMPLE 12.18

Killarney Tourism to Emphasize Visitor Experiences

Destinations are shifting to put a greater priority on visitor experiences. Fáilte Ireland has prepared a Destination Experience Development Plan for Killarney.

Killarney town situated in Killarney National Park in County Kerry in the Southwest of Ireland, at the feet of the McGillicuddy Reeks mountain range. Killarney has been Ireland's premiere destination for tourists for centuries, drawn by the town's charming architecture; amenities and heritage sites; a welcoming place where the people are genuinely friendly and helpful, with a diverse range of hospitality and accommodation options and the town's proximity to the National Park, its wildlife, lakes and mountains.

The Killarney KDEDP is a destination development plan designed to build on a new collective vision for tourism in Killarney. It is designed to enhance the way in which visitors experience the town while maximizing its role as the principal exploration base for the wider Kerry tourism economy. This plan has been developed through collaboration and consultation. The plan will provide a destination development focus for the next five years, harnessing existing strategic plans and examining new projects to create a world-class destination.

(Fáilte Ireland 2022)

Learning Point

Greater focus must be put on developing experiences for visitors within destinations.

PRICE

With respect to price, the DMO can act more as a price influencer than a price setter. Above all the DMO must recognize that price is a multifaceted concept. In the private sector, it is a major determinant of profitability. Prices also tend to attract certain markets and repel others. A destination where the prices are high may earn a reputation of being exclusive or luxury oriented, whereas a destination with low prices can be viewed as a place for mass tourism. Additionally, price levels influence value-for-money perceptions.

PLACE

Place represents distribution and the online and traditional travel trade channels the DMO uses to draw visitors to the destination. The DMO can market directly to potential visitors (direct distribution) or indirectly through travel trade intermediaries (indirect distribution). Today, much of the distribution in tourism is done online.

PROMOTION

Promotion—now called IMC—has been a traditional activity of DMOs, with most organizations placing the greatest emphasis on advertising and sales (personal selling). The IMC components include e-marketing, advertising, personal selling (sales), public relations, sales promotion, and merchandising. Now, DMOs are heavily involved with e-marketing and especially with promotion through websites, email, smartphones and social media. All promotions are types of communications, and it is essential that a DMO integrates promotions so that they are consistent. You will learn more in detail about IMC in Chapter 14 and e-marketing is the topic for Chapter 15.

You will often see the word "campaign" used to describe a specific set of IMC efforts. It will probably help if you have a definition of this concept.

Campaign

A campaign is a specific and planned set of IMC activities that is usually named and is implemented for a short- or medium-term period of time. Campaigns are normally designed and implemented by creative agencies on behalf of destinations and DMOs.

PACKAGING

Packaging in tourism is very different from product packaging and is a key tool for the DMO in customizing the destination product for specific target markets. Additionally, packaging is important in helping the destination to smooth out seasonal (peak and valley) patterns of visitor volumes. Packaging is the combination of related and complementary hospitality and tourism services and facilities into a single-price offering (Morrison 2022).

PROGRAMMING

There are many opportunities for destinations to arrange special activities or programs that are attractive to visitors. A festival is one of the best examples of programming in tourism. Packaging and programming when combined can be very powerful in convincing people to visit a destination or a tourism business.

PARTNERSHIP

DMOs have been involved in building marketing partnerships for many years, but the recent decades have seen an increasing emphasis on tapping into the power of combining forces with other players. You learned about many great partnerships in Chapter 8.

PEOPLE

There is no question that tourism is a people-intensive business and that personal service encounters within a destination have a great impact on the visitor's experience and satisfaction.

EXAMPLE 12.19

Vanuatu Domestic Marketing Strategy

COVID-19 caused many DMOs to give greater emphasis to domestic travelers. This is an example in which the Vanuatu Tourism Office created a new marketing strategy for the domestic market in the South Pacific nation.

> The Vanuatu Tourism Office is excited to release our Domestic Tourism Marketing Strategy 2021–2023. This new strategy is just another way that VTO is Answering the Call of Vanuatu. One of the few positives to emerge from the global COVID-19 pandemic is the opportunity that it has given VTO to be able to trial a domestic tourism marketing campaign, Sapotem Lokol Turisim.

VTO have been trialing this campaign to encourage more Ni-Vanuatu and expatriate residents to experience more of what Vanuatu has to offer. We live in one of the most stunningly beautiful countries on earth, but sometimes, we take this fact for granted, and forget to take the time to go in our own country.

With VTO's trial Sapotem Lokol Turisim campaign, many more people are realizing this. The campaign has built on the strong consumer sentiment that exists in the community for supporting local business through this difficult time

The Domestic Tourism Marketing Strategy has three goals:

1. Provide short-term revenue streams for the tourism industry while borders are closed;

2. Encourage the domestic market to make a habit of using tourism businesses as part of their everyday lives;

3. Encourage the domestic market to see more of Vanuatu, and drive dispersal of domestic tourists to businesses beyond Efate.

(Vanuatu Tourism 2022)

Learning Point

Enduring and dealing with major crises often leads to innovation in destination marketing, branding, and communications. This may involve shifting priorities among target markets.

Marketing Plan Development

A marketing plan is a written document that describes the activities and programs that the DMO will use to accomplish its marketing objectives. This document should include an executive summary, marketing plan rationale, and implementation plan (Fig. 12.18).

Figure 12.18 Steps in developing a marketing plan.

EXECUTIVE SUMMARY

This is a summary in a few pages of the key highlights and major initiatives outlined in the marketing plan. It is called an executive summary partly because it can be read quickly and conveniently by DMO leaders and other busy stakeholders.

MARKETING PLAN RATIONALE

This is where the DMO explains the reasons and assumptions behind its choices of activities and programs. It also explains the selected marketing strategy and lists the marketing objectives. The marketing plan rationale covers the first two DMS steps (Where are we now? Where would we like to be?); it summarizes the results of the planning and research done to prepare the marketing plan. The contents of the marketing plan rationale are:

- environmental scan and situation analysis highlights;
- USPs;
- marketing strategy;
- marketing objectives.

EXAMPLE 12.20

British Columbia Is Investing in Iconics

British Columbia is using place branding to build tourism around iconic routes and places within the province. The strategy is intended to provide a greater spread of tourism geographically and seasonally. Indigenous tourism is a major element of this effort.

> We are competing fiercely to differentiate British Columbia from other destinations and position the province as one of the most extraordinary places to visit on earth.
>
> We want BC's remarkable destinations to be recognized alongside other wonders of the world. Through new and compelling place brands, we can disperse our visitors to more places in the province, at more times of the year. BC's natural beauty is truly unique. With a diversity of Indigenous cultures, raw wilderness, rugged coastlines, vibrant cities, and welcoming people—when paired with strong and emotive place brands—they are compelling reasons to explore the province far and wide.
>
> (Destination British Columbia 2022)

Learning Point

Branding can be a powerful tool for differentiating a destination from competitors. Routes and iconic locations can be effectively branded.

IMPLEMENTATION PLAN

The implementation plan is the most detailed and longest part of the marketing plan. It describes in detail how each of the eight Ps (marketing mix) will be used for each target market to achieve that market's objectives for the upcoming period. The contents of the implementation plan are as follows:

- marketing objectives;
- activities and programs (marketing mix, or eight Ps);
- marketing budget;
- timetable or schedule;
- assignment of responsibilities;
- control and evaluation procedures and measures.

The marketing plans are written for internal purposes to guide marketing, but they are also used to inform stakeholders and partners.

Marketing Budget Development

Once the DMO has determined the activities and programs (tasks) that it will use for each target market, it should develop the marketing budget to go along with the marketing plan. The best approach to doing this is with the objective-and-task budgeting method. This method builds the marketing budget from the bottom up, starting with the objectives, the activities and programs to achieve each objective, and the estimated costs of implementing each activity and program. The marketing budget should be detailed out by expense category and month.

Marketing Plan Timetable or Schedule

A month-by-month timetable should be developed showing when each activity and program will be implemented. Usually, it is necessary to divide the timetable by target market or according to the marketing department that is responsible for each target market. For example, the marketing plan timetable may be sub-divided into month-by-month schedules for the following target markets and audiences:

- business meetings, conventions, and exhibitions and incentive travel;
- leisure tourism/pleasure travel;
- digital marketing/social media;
- travel agents and tour operators;
- travel exhibitions/fairs;
- festivals and events;
- local community/residents;
- media or press;
- other target markets/audiences.

Assignment of Implementation Responsibilities

It is very important to indicate who has the responsibility for implementing each activity and program. There should be an assignment of responsibilities to each marketing department as well as an indication of what the DMO will do and what it expects its partners and other stakeholders to accomplish. The assignment of responsibilities depends on how the DMO marketing department or division is structured. However, internationally, it is common to find the following units:

- convention/meeting sales and service;
- leisure tourism/pleasure travel (independent travelers);
- group travel;
- sports marketing;
- public relations and communications;
- tourism development;
- administration and accounting.

Control and Evaluation Procedures and Measurements

The marketing plan must include specific control and evaluation procedures and measurements for the remaining two DMS steps. Particularly important here is the identification of evaluation measures or metrics, milestones and performance standards.

- Evaluation measures or metrics: The activities and programs that will be measured and the units of measurement (how the activities and programs will be measured).
- Milestones: The dates at which measures will be taken or calculated (e.g., monthly, bimonthly, every quarter, every six months).
- Performance standards: The range of acceptable performance (e.g., the quantified target for an objective plus or minus a certain percentage).

Marketing Plan Implementation

The DMO now uses the marketing plan as a guide for implementing its selected marketing activities and programs. The marketing budget, timetable and assignment of implementation responsibilities are key tools for guiding the marketing plan implementation.

Output Summary for DMS Step 3

The major outputs from Step 3 are the marketing mix selection and the written marketing plan (Fig. 12.19).

HOW DO WE MAKE SURE WE GET THERE? (CONTROL OR FORMATIVE EVALUATION)

The last two DMS steps are both types of marketing evaluation:

- Control or formative evaluation: measuring progress while the marketing plan is being implemented.
- Evaluation or summative evaluation: measuring after the marketing plan has been completed.

Unfortunately, these are two highly important steps that DMOs often neglect or they just do partially. Control and evaluation among DMOs is quite incomplete and mostly focused

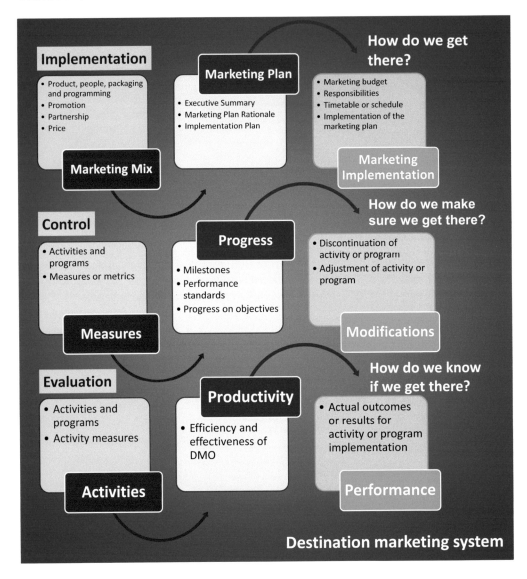

Figure 12.19 Output summary for DMS Steps 3–5.

on measuring activities rather than productivity and performance. Also, it is common to see DMOs keeping track of numbers of visitors and expenditures, but nothing else. Although it is essential for a DMO to measure these factors, the DMO cannot itself take full credit for these results.

The DMO monitors its progress in implementing the marketing plan during the formative evaluation step (control) of the DMS (Fig. 12.19). There are four measures, or metrics, which can be used in DMO evaluation:

1. Activities: The destination marketing activities and programs identified in the marketing plan. The completion of these activities and programs is one type of measure. For example,

the DMO held a festival or forum, attended a travel exhibition or fair, launched a new website or completed a familiarization tour.

2. Activity measures: These are quantitative measures of activities when there is more than one instance or occasion. For example, the DMO exhibited at eight different travel exhibitions or fairs.

3. Productivity measures: These are measures of the efficiency and effectiveness of the DMO in using its financial, human and other resources. For example, how many people came to the DMO's booth during a travel exhibition or fair?

4. Performance measures: These are the actual outcomes or results from implementing the activities and programs contained in the marketing plan.

Output Summary for DMS Step 4

Step 4 takes place as the marketing plan is being completed and involves tracking the progress of plan implementation, especially the degree to which the marketing objectives are being achieved (Fig. 12.19). If the progress on a specific activity or program is very poor, the DMO may consider discontinuing it or making a corrective adjustment in the activity or program.

HOW DO WE KNOW IF WE GOT THERE? (EVALUATION, SUMMATIVE EVALUATION)

When the marketing plan is completed, a thorough evaluation should be conducted.

DMOs are increasingly being asked to demonstrate their marketing effectiveness and performance, thereby showing their accountability for the funds that are invested in marketing activities and programs. Chapter 20 discusses destination performance measurement and evaluation.

Faulkner (1997) defined evaluation as "a systematic process for objectively assessing an organization's (or program's) performance." He suggested the following three criteria for evaluating a DMO's performance:

1. Appropriateness: the extent to which the DMO's objectives and priorities match the needs of its stakeholders.
2. Effectiveness: the extent to which the DMO achieves its marketing goals and objectives.
3. Efficiency: the extent to which the DMO's marketing program outcomes are achieved at a reasonable cost and within a reasonable time frame.

Output Summary for DMS Step 5

When the marketing plan is completed, the DMO evaluates the results and produces measures of activities, productivity, and performance (Fig. 12.19).

Steps for Effective Planning of Marketing, Branding, and Communications

The specific steps that DMOs must complete in destination marketing planning are as follows:

- Develop a destination vision and DMO vision.
- Prepare a set of three- to five-year destination marketing goals.

- Write a DMO mission statement.
- Prepare an environmental scan.
- Develop a situation analysis.
- Conduct market and marketing research to support decisions.
- Identify the destination's USPs.
- Conduct market segmentation analysis.
- Select target markets.
- Write a destination positioning statement.
- Create a destination branding approach.
- Prepare a set of marketing objectives.
- Write a marketing plan.
- Monitor the implementation of the marketing plan and report on progress (control).
- Evaluate the effectiveness of the marketing plan and measure the DMO's performance.

SUMMING UP

Marketing has been the mainstay activity of destinations and DMOs for more than 100 years. However, it has progressed from just sales and advertising to a broader, more sophisticated and professional role for DMOs. Destination branding has become an integral part of marketing, which you will hear more about in Chapter 13. Promotion has morphed to IMC where all communications are consistent and supportive of each other. Communications are moving more into the online world and new technologies (e.g., AI, AR, VR, and metaverse) are providing greater scope for marketing and branding destination product development is receiving greater attention and being meshed more closely with marketing, branding, and communications.

Marketing, branding, and communications remains one of the most important roles of a DMO, requiring careful, step-by-step planning. The DMP is an approach that has proved to be effective in practice. This involves developing a hierarchy of goals and objectives, including a destination vision, DMO vision, marketing goals and marketing objectives, and core values and guiding principles. A DMO mission also needs to be written, although it is not a goal or objective.

You have seen in many of the examples cited in Chapter 12 that DMOs are changing (pivoting) marketing, branding, and communications in the aftermath of COVID-19. They are being forced to reevaluate previous approaches and to introduce new strategies and plans to adapt to different realities.

Part III of this book which follows delves in greater depth into branding and IMC. Chapter 13 covers PIB; Chapter 14 discusses IMC; and Chapter 15 reviews e-marketing.

KEYWORDS

accountability
campaign
control
core values
customer orientation

destination audit
destination marketing
 system (DMS)
destination vision
DMO vision

eight Ps of destination
 marketing, branding, and
 communications
environmental scan
evaluation

executive summary
formative evaluation
four Ps of marketing
guiding principles
hierarchy of goals and
    objectives
implementation
implementation plan
long-term
market segmentation
marketing concept
marketing control

marketing evaluation
marketing goals
marketing mix
marketing objectives
marketing plan
marketing plan rationale
marketing strategy
mission
mission statement
planning
price model
product life cycle (PLC)

research
short-term
situation analysis
summative evaluation
SWOT
target market
tourism area life cycle
    (TALC)
vision statement
visioning

REVIEW QUESTIONS

1. What are the key destination marketing professional principles?
2. Which five questions comprise the DMS?
3. What are the management functions represented by each of the letters in the PRICE model?
4. Which time frames are specified within the DMP?
5. What is the difference between a DMO vision and a DMO mission?
6. What are the three parts included in a destination marketing plan?
7. What are the eight Ps of destination marketing, branding, and communications, and which steps does each of them involve?
8. How are destination marketing control and evaluation accomplished?

REFERENCES

Aruba Tourism Authority (2022) "Aruba Tourism Authority," www.aruba.com/us/organization/aruba-tourism-authority

Barney, J. (1991) "Firm Resources and Sustained Competitive Advantage," *Journal of Management*, 17 (1): 99–120.

Butler, R. W. (1980) "The Concept of the Tourist Area Life Cycle of Evolution: Implications for Management of Resources," *Canadian Geographer*, 24 (1): 5–12.

Destination British Columbia (2022) "Invest in Iconics Strategy," www.destinationbc.ca/invest-in-iconics-strategy/

Estonian Tourism Board (2022) "About Visit Estonia/Estonian Tourism Board," www.visitestonia.com/en/forthetrade/estonian-tourist-board

Fáilte Ireland (2022) "Killarney Destination and Experience Development," www.failteireland.ie/killarneydedp.aspx

Faulkner, W. (1997) "A Model for the Evaluation of National Tourism Destination Marketing Programs," *Journal of Travel Research*, 35 (3): 23–32.

Habtemariam, D. (2022) "Berlin Gives Local Residents a Say in Tourism Planning," *Skift*, August 31, https://skift.com/2022/08/31/berlin-gives-local-residents-a-say-in-tourism-planning-with-new-council/

Hawaii Tourism Authority (2022) "Resident Sentiment Survey Spring 2022 Highlights," www.hawaiitourismauthority.org/media/9744/dbedt-resident-sentiment-spring-2022-hta-board-presentation-accessible.pdf

Kotler, P., Armstrong, G., and Opresnik, M. O. (2017) *Principles of Marketing*, 17th edn, Harlow: Pearson.

Korea Tourism Organization (2022) "Vision and Goals," https://kto.visitkorea.or.kr/eng/overview.kto

Las Vegas Convention and Visitors Authority (2022) "Las Vegas Visitor Profile Study 2021," https://assets.simpleviewcms.com/simpleview/image/upload/v1/clients/lasvegas/2021_Las_Vegas_Visitor_Profile_Study_6fb123b2-d75e-4dd6-875b-eb33acd00541.pdf

McCarthy, E. J. (1960) *Basic Marketing: A Managerial Approach*, Homewood, Ill.: Irwin.

Morrison, A. M. (2022) *Hospitality and Travel Marketing*, London and New York, NY: Routledge.

Morrison, A. M., Lehto, X. Y., and Day, J. G. (2018) *The Tourism System*, 8th edn, Dubuque, IA: Kendall Hunt.

Newport Beach & Company (2022) "Newport Beach & Company Destination Business Plan, Fiscal Years 2023 and 2024," www.visitnewportbeach.com/about/marketingplan/

Porter, M. E. (1996) "What Is Strategy?" *Harvard Business Review*, November–December, 61–78.

Prague City Tourism (2022) "Prague City Tourism Marketing Objectives," www.praguecity-tourism.cz/en/our-services/marketing-/prague-city-tourism-marketing-objectives

Ries, A., and Trout, J. (2001) *Positioning: The Battle for Your Mind*, 20th anniversary edn, New York: McGraw-Hill.

Ritchie, J. R. B. (1993) "Crafting a Destination Vision: Putting the Process of Resident Responsive Tourism into Practice," *Tourism Management*, 14 (5): 379–389.

Tourism Australia (2022) "Our Vision," www.tourism.australia.com/en/about/our-organisation/our-vision.html

Tourism KwaZulu-Natal (2022) "KZN Has It All," https://zulu.org.za/corporate/

Tourism Malaysia (2022) "Tourism Malaysia Marketing Plan 2022–2026," www.tourism.gov.my/activities/view/tm-marketing-plan-2022-2026

Tourism Tropical North Queensland (2022) "TTNQ Strategic Direction 2022/2023," https://tourism.tropicalnorthqueensland.org.au/what-we-do/purpose/

Tremento (2018) "What Is Destination Marketing and How Do You Use It?" https://tremento.com/destination-marketing-how-to-use/

Virginia Tourism Corporation (2022) "Virginia Is for Lovers," www.virginia.org/plan-your-trip/virginia-is-for-lovers/

VisitBritain (2022) "Britain's Image Overseas," www.visitbritain.org/britain%E2%80%99s-image-overseas

Visit Greenland (2021) "Towards More Tourism: Visit Greenland's Marketing and Market Development Strategy, 2021–2024," https://traveltrade.visitgreenland.com/wp-content/uploads/2021/02/Strategi-EN-feb2021.pdf

Wilson, A. M. (1998) "The Role of Mystery Shopping in the Measurement of Service Performance," *Managing Service Quality*, 8 (6): 414–420.

Wonderful Copenhagen (2022) "Wonderful Copenhagen: About Us," www.wonderfulcopenhagen.com/wonderful-copenhagen/about-us/wonderful-copenhagen

Destination Marketing, Branding, and Communications

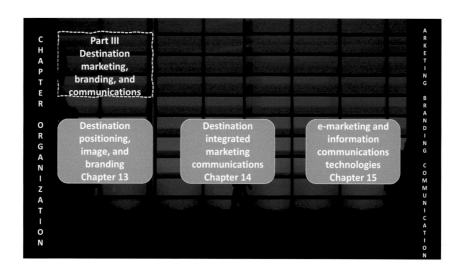

Chapter **13**

Destination Positioning, Image, and Branding

Perception is everything

DOI: 10.4324/9781003343356-16

Warming Up

You heard about destination PIB as part of the discussion of destination marketing planning in Chapter 12. Although they were briefly introduced there, these are such critical concepts that you need to have a more in-depth explanation of how they are practiced in destination management.

Destination branding has been one of the hottest topics among destination marketers and tourism academic scholars since the late 1990s. In 1998, the Travel and Tourism Research Association held its annual conference under the theme of Branding the Travel Market, and J. R. Brent Ritchie and Robin Ritchie (1998) were also advocating a more rigorous and well-planned approach to the branding of tourism destinations. Thanks to pioneering work by Morgan et al. (2002) and their book on the topic, destination branding finally attained a high professional status in tourism and became better understood and appreciated. Other useful books and handbooks followed, including a book on branding smaller cities by Baker (2007), *The Handbook on Tourism Destination Branding* by the ETC and UNWTO (2009), and a book on city branding by Dinnie (2011).

Of course, there was a sort of branding for destinations that existed before these pioneers made their contributions, but this was mainly within the world of advertising agencies, and thus its focus was on slogans, logos, and TV commercials. Not much thought was given to destination image research or to consensus-based approaches involving tourism sector stakeholders and residents for building destination brands. Moreover, the destination brand was something communicated only in advertising; it was not a promise to be delivered and experienced in the destination. The brand tended to change each time a new advertising agency was appointed.

EXAMPLE 13.1

The Power of Logos and Slogans Is Overrated

Several top experts in place and destination branding believe that the power and contribution of logos and slogans is overrated. For example, Robert Govers said the following about logos and slogans that are attached to places.

> The contribution that logos and slogans can make to the management of places as brands is rather limited.

> - Logos and slogans seem to be ascribed with powers that they do not possess, diverting focus, resources and effort from what actually is important in place branding.
> - As places already have (more often than not meaningful) names and landmarks, the amount of time and investment generally spent on designing logos and slogans as opposed to actual reputation management for places, seems to be a waste.

> (Govers 2013)

Learning Point

Brands are much more than a logo and a slogan.

Destination branding is surely not yet an exact science, but it has progressed in its understanding and applications by leaps and bounds over the past thirty years. The destination branding topic now is often considered within the concepts of place branding and even nation or country branding, and these broader perspectives are helping to further deepen the understanding of destination branding.

There are many tourism destination brands in the world; some are outstanding and some are not so good. This chapter explains a systematic, step-by-step process to develop a long-term destination brand. You will see that this is not a how-to description of the ways to develop logos and slogans, but rather, it is a research-based and stakeholder-involved process.

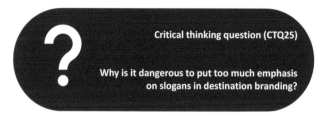

Critical thinking question (CTQ25)

Why is it dangerous to put too much emphasis on slogans in destination branding?

As you learned in Chapter 12, your author and his colleagues have developed positioning and branding approaches for several destinations. This has been a tremendous learning experience and the results are reflected in this chapter. It would be easy to fill out the pages of this chapter with accounts of many of the theories about branding; however, your author resisted that temptation in favor of giving you practical insights into PIB.

Definitions of Destination Positioning, Image, and Branding

Here are our definitions of the three key terms.

DEFINITIONS

Destination positioning

The steps taken by a destination management organization (DMO), in collaboration with its stakeholders, to identify and communicate a unique destination image to people within its target markets. Positioning is how the destination decides to make itself unique among competing destinations from the tourist's perspective.

Destination image

The mental pictures people have in their minds of specific tourism destinations. These images are formed from multiple sources of information. Destination images are difficult to change in the short term.

Destination branding

The steps taken by a DMO, in collaboration with its stakeholders, to develop and communicate an identity and personality for its destination, which are different from those of all competing destinations.

EXAMPLE 13.2

Bravery Is Ukraine's Brand

Most reasonable people would describe the people of Ukraine as being brave to take on the might of Russia in an armed conflict. Bravery is possibly a personality characteristic that will be ascribed to the Ukraine for many years to come. Now it has become the nation's brand.

> Bravery is our brand: Executives from the Ukrainian advertising agency Banda first pitched the idea for Ukraine's Bravery Campaign to the government shortly after Russia invaded in February 2022. Based in Kyiv and Los Angeles, the agency had already worked before the war on government-sponsored campaigns, marketing Ukraine as a tourism and investment destination.
>
> Ukraine is the first country to launch an official nation branding campaign in the midst of war. For the first time, brand communication is a key part of a country's response to a military invasion. The campaign attempts to transform an intangible value, like bravery, into an asset that can be converted into real military, economic, and moral support.
>
> (Kaneva 2022)

Learning Point

Although born from adversity, this branding approach is highly believable in the current environment. Believability and authenticity are two critical factors for destination branding success.

Positioning, Imaging, Branding (PIB) Approach

In Chapter 12 when discussing marketing strategy, the PIB approach was introduced. You learned that the concepts of destination PIB were closely intertwined, as shown in Figure 13.1. DMO marketing strategies must specify who the destination's target markets are and how destinations are to be positioned (what images are to be created) in the minds of potential visitors within these target markets. DMOs need to consider how to make their destinations unique within their competitive sets. Additionally, DMOs must determine the existing destination images that people have within their markets using the research techniques discussed in Chapter 5. Then, DMOs must decide how to brand destinations given their selected positioning approaches and the types of images that support this positioning.

As illustrated in Figure 13.1, there are two-way feedback links between each pairing of these concepts. Destination positioning impacts destination branding, but it also is intended to affect destination image. Tourists' actual destination images should influence both destination positioning and destination branding. Destination branding is a marketing strategy approach intended to have a positive effect on destination image; its results will also impact on future destination positioning decisions. It is best to view the relationship among these three concepts as a cycle or system rather than as a step-by-step, linear process. You should realize that this is not a static model, but rather, it is dynamic and evolving over time. It is worth knowing that destination image is the hardest of the three concepts to change quickly; tourists' images of places may take several years to modify.

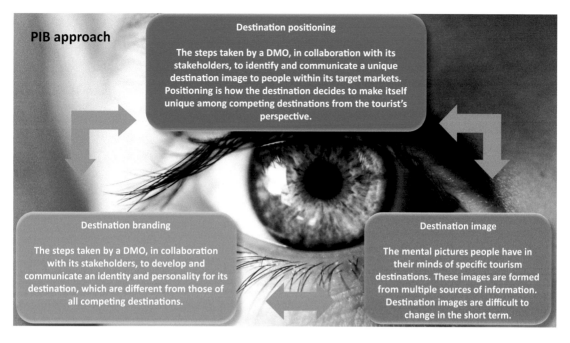

PIB approach

Destination positioning

The steps taken by a DMO, in collaboration with its stakeholders, to identify and communicate a unique destination image to people within its target markets. Positioning is how the destination decides to make itself unique among competing destinations from the tourist's perspective.

Destination branding

The steps taken by a DMO, in collaboration with its stakeholders, to develop and communicate an identity and personality for its destination, which are different from those of all competing destinations.

Destination image

The mental pictures people have in their minds of specific tourism destinations. These images are formed from multiple sources of information. Destination images are difficult to change in the short term.

Figure 13.1 Destination positioning-image-branding: The PIB approach.

To ensure that you have a complete understanding of these three interconnected concepts, their definitions are placed within the contexts of tourism destinations and destination marketing and shown in Figure 13.1. Here are the definitions of brand identity and brand personality.

DEFINITIONS

Brand identity

This has two meanings. First, it is the perception of a brand in the tourism marketplace that is based on its positioning and brand personality. The second is the visual design of the brand, which normally includes a logo and some words and symbols.

Brand personality

The outward characteristics of the brand is sometimes associated with human traits.

Because you may not know immediately what brand personality means in the destination branding definition, the case of the Queensland brand is explained in the example.

EXAMPLE 13.3

Queensland's Destination Brand Personality

A brand personality is how our destination brands are portrayed, based on human characteristics.

Real: Authentic, inclusive, caring
Dynamic: Discovery, exploration, ever-moving
Optimistic: Confident, honest, assured
Enchanting: Charming, endearing, welcoming.

(Tourism & Events Queensland 2022)

Learning Point

A destination brand personality makes the place seem more human.

You can see from the three definitions in Figure 13.1 that two of the concepts, positioning and branding, are determined by DMOs. Destination images are under the control of the tourists and are how they perceive destinations. There are two types of images in these definitions: the images or perceptions that tourists have in their minds about destinations and the desired images (positioning) that DMOs want them to have.

DMOs must decide on the desired destination images (positioning) and the identity and personality (branding) for their destinations. This sounds quite simple and straightforward, but as you will soon see, these are difficult tasks for DMOs to accomplish and much more complex than branding consumer goods. Developing a destination brand can be time-consuming and expensive, and so it is vital to fully understand why it is important to design a destination brand. Additionally, the potential benefits to the destination and its marketing and to residents and tourists need to be recognized.

Importance and Benefits of Destination Branding

Why is branding so important in destination marketing, and what are its specific benefits to destinations and tourists? Why have so many books, handbooks, articles, and blogs been written on this topic? Blain et al. (2005) identified three reasons for the importance of destination branding.

Enhancing Destination Image

Branding clarifies and potentially improves the image of the destination among potential travelers. For example, the classic case of 100% Pure New Zealand enhanced the image of New Zealand as a natural, clean, and environmentally sensitive destination. The Incredible!ndia branding fundamentally changed and improved the image of India as a tourism destination (Fig. 13.2).

Figure 13.2 Incredible India destination branding.

EXAMPLE 13.4

India Is Incredible

Having visited India more than five times, your author can attest that it is an incredible destination—incredible sights, incredible hospitality, incredible food, incredible culture and many more incredibles.

> Portraying the beauty of India as an attractive tourist destination by highlighting its rich culture and glorious history, Incredible!ndia is an international tourism campaign that has been run by the Government of India since 2002. The campaign was conceptualized by Shri Amitabh Kant, the then Joint Secretary to Tourism Department. Indian actor Shri Aamir Khan was commissioned to endorse the campaign, titled "Atithi Devo Bhava," which is Sanskrit translation for "Guests are like God." Atithi Devo Bhava was aimed at creating awareness about the effects of tourism and sensitizing the local population about the preservation of India's heritage, culture, and hospitality. In 2017, veteran actor Shri Amitabh Bachchan and actress Smt. Priyanka Chopra were chosen as the new brand ambassadors for the Incredible!ndia campaign.
>
> The Incredible!ndia Logo was conceptualized by Shri Amitabh Kant, along with his counterparts. The exclamation mark in the logo forms the letter "I" of India and was used creatively across several visuals, which compliments the concept behind the word "Incredible."
>
> (Presentations.gov.in 2022)

Learning Point

Many destinations have tried to copy India's "one-liner" brand with plenty of interesting adjectives. They have definitely not had as much success as India. Believability is at the core of Incredible!ndia's recognition.

Reinforcing Unique Image or Personality

Branding can reinforce what potential travelers already perceive about the destination in terms of a unique image or personality. For example, Las Vegas has a reputation of being a sort of adult vacation playground; so, the branding around the theme of What happens here, stays here® (LVCVA 2022) reinforces this image.

EXAMPLE 13.5

Adult Freedom in Las Vegas

The LVCVA reinforces the image of the destination with its tagline, What happens here, stays here®. This is very memorable and has received numerous awards. As with Malaysia Truly Asia, it has also stood the test of time.

Brand research and analytics confirmed that what motivated people to choose Las Vegas over other locales was the opportunity to cut loose, have fun and do things they wouldn't do back home. The overall mystique of Vegas was universal, but rooted in individual imagination and triggered by emotion. The heart of the new brand was adult freedom. The campaign, centered around the now-iconic tagline, What happens here, stays here®, taps into a fundamental truth about human behavior and aligns with the core of the Vegas brand.

The campaign began with a series of television and print ads, a new website and an intensive PR campaign. Television spots were produced along with supporting print and a redesigned website. Each ad was engineered to reach a different target audience based on age, demographics and various behaviors. PR coverage for the new effort was secured across the big media outlets such as *USA Today*, *The Wall Street Journal*, *The New York Times*, CNN, NPR, *Sports Illustrated* and *Advertising Age*. Although the campaign has passed its 15-year anniversary, we continue to keep it contemporary and relevant, with evolving disciplines and tactics. These included creating custom microsites that gave visitors the tools to change their identity and become their Vegas persona; changing wallscapes that revealed Vegas stories over time; using projection media at events like the Super Bowl; and securing numerous media partnerships with networks and shows such as *Jimmy Kimmel Live*.

(LVCVA 2022)

Learning Point

A brand and its associated slogan or tagline must ring true for the destination. This is certainly achieved for Las Vegas.

Assisting in Measuring Achievements

DMOs with destination brands find it easier to measure results through research. They have a definite concept that can be reviewed and discussed with consumers and can track changes in perceptions and attitudes over time. Some other aspects of the importance of destination branding are as follows.

ARTICULATING AMBITION, RAISING EXPECTATIONS AND MAKING A QUALITY PROMISE

A successful destination brand has ambition, raises expectations, and makes a promise to the visitor. Kotler and Gartner (2002) agree that brands offer consumers a promise of value. Having ambition means putting into words and images what the destination wants to be; the desired identity and personality of the destination are made more concrete and less vague. Raising expectations is two sided: the DMO and tourism stakeholders raise their sights on what will be achieved through destination branding, and tourists increase their expectations of the experiences and quality that they will receive within the destination.

DIFFERENTIATING DESTINATION AMONG COMPETITORS

An effective brand makes the destination stand out among its competitors, and this is one of the most important purposes of destination branding. Some of the leading experts in place branding refer to this process as creating a competitive identity.

The specific benefits of destination branding for tourists have been identified by Clarke (2000) and others and include the following:

LOWERING RISKS IN DECISION-MAKING

Destination brands give consumers more confidence in their choices of holidays and destinations. This lowers their perceived risks because they have a clearer idea of what to expect.

REDUCING IMPACT OF INTANGIBILITY

Tourism is an experience good and is intangible at the time when a trip purchase decision is being made. Destination branding provides clues and cues to potential tourists that help to reduce the impact of intangibility.

CONVEYING GREATER CONSISTENCY

If the destination branding is widely applied in the destination, this creates greater consistency in brand implementation across multiple tourism sector stakeholders and continuously over several years.

For DMOs and destinations, the benefits of destination branding follow (Clarke 2000; Baker 2007).

FACILITATING PRECISE MARKET SEGMENTATION

Branding forces destinations and DMOs to think very clearly about their audiences and to take aim at specific segments of the market.

INTEGRATING STAKEHOLDER EFFORTS

A destination brand provides a platform and a focus for tourism sector stakeholders to work together toward a mutually beneficial outcome.

GENERATING INCREASED RESPECT, RECOGNITION, LOYALTY AND RENOWN

A place can gain more respect, recognition and renown from having an outstanding destination brand. For example, the Malaysia Truly Asia branding has helped Malaysia earn greater respect and recognition as a tourism destination. The example shows how Tourism Malaysia defines the Truly Asia concept.

EXAMPLE 13.6

The Malaysia Truly Asia Brand

This brand has existed since 1999 and it has obviously been successful for Malaysia. The multicultural nature of Malaysia makes this brand believable.

> Malaysia, Truly Asia captures and defines the essence of the country's unique diversity. It sums up the distinctiveness and allure of Malaysia that make it an exceptional tourist destination.

> There is only one place where all the colors, flavors, sounds and sights of Asia come together—Malaysia. No other country has Asia's three major races, Malay, Chinese, Indian, plus various other ethnic groups in large numbers. Nowhere is there such exciting diversity of cultures, festivals, traditions and customs, offering myriad experiences. No other country is Truly Asia as Malaysia.
>
> (Tourism Malaysia 2021)

Learning Point

The memorability of a brand is critical to its success and the rhyming nature of Malaysia's destination brand is a great example of memorability.

CORRECTING INACCURATE PERCEPTIONS

Sometimes, people within the destination itself have outdated and inaccurate perceptions of their own place. Negative attitudes often exist internally, and the process of destination branding should counter this pessimism with fresh new ideas and accurate market and competitive information. For example, the Philippines Department of Tourism in 2022 launched a new destination branding approach for Mindanao to dispel perceptions that it was a dangerous place to visit.

EXAMPLE 13.7

Colors of Mindanao Branding Approach

Branding is sometimes used to counter negative images of certain destinations. Negative media news stories can darken destination images, while new branding campaigns communicate the positive aspects of these places.

> The Tourism Department has launched a new campaign focusing on the diverse attractions of Mindanao, the southern Philippine islands that have long been saddled with a sweeping perception of bandits and lawlessness.
>
> (BusinessWorld 2022)

> The Colors of Mindanao aims to show the world that the island has more to offer in terms of tourist spots, culinary dishes, and culture. It also seeks to remove the stigma brought by a previous reporting of unfortunate events, safety concerns, and wars that made an impression of a chaotic island.
>
> (Philippine Information Agency (PIA) 2022)

Learning Point

This branding approach emphasizes the colorfulness, diversity, and harmony that is a true reflection of Mindanao as a destination.

INCREASING TOURISM'S ECONOMIC BENEFITS

Effective destination branding should, with continued implementation over several years, improve stakeholders' incomes and profits and increase tax revenues for government.

ENHANCING COMMUNITY PRIDE AND ADVOCACY

Good brands make local people feel a greater sense of pride in the places where they live. This also helps to increase community support and advocacy for tourism.

EXPANDING THE PRIMARY MARKET FOR ALL TO SHARE

Expanding the size of the pie (or primary market) potentially gives stakeholders a larger share rather than having to rely on lowering prices to get a share of a smaller pie. These fifteen reasons for the importance of destination branding are listed in Figure 13.3 in a summary format.

When a DMO is introducing a new destination brand to stakeholders and residents, it should clearly articulate the importance of the brand. For example, Tourism Northern Ireland insisted that its new brand "reflects who we are."

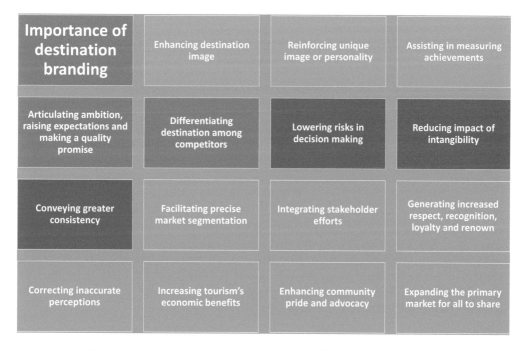

Figure 13.3 Reasons for importance of destination branding.

EXAMPLE 13.8

Embrace a Giant Spirit in Northern Ireland

This may have come from the famous Giant's Causeway in Antrim County; however, it admirably reflects the spirit of endurance of Northern Ireland and its people.

> The Northern Ireland Embrace a Giant Spirit brand reflects who we are. It encompasses that "can do" attitude and the spirit of our communities pulling together and supporting each other through challenging times. It is based on

what our visitors have fed back time and again, and encompasses our desire to share our country, culture and passion for life. The most important asset in our brand armory is our people. That warmth of welcome and humor is integral to our brand promise.

Our new brand was launched to the world in November 2019 and now more than ever it will be fundamental to attracting visitors back to Northern Ireland. It will transform how prospective visitors think of our destination on the island of Ireland and internationally. Over the next ten years, the Embrace a Giant Spirit brand will benefit Northern Ireland, by once again:

- increasing our domestic and international reputation as an attractive holiday destination;
- building the number of visitors who come here from international and local destinations;
- increasing the length of time visitors stay away from home;
- increasing the amount of money visitors spend;
- supporting the growth of our small, medium and larger sized tourism businesses.

(Tourism Northern Ireland 2022)

Learning Point

Enhancing community pride can be an outcome of effective destination branding. Tourism Northern Ireland undoubtedly generated pride in the Embrace a Giant Spirit brand.

Branding is critical and strategic to the marketing of tourism destinations, and it has many potential benefits. Now that the importance of destination branding has received much greater recognition in the past thirty years, highly professional procedures and practices are available to DMOs. However, destination branding faces a set of daunting challenges that need to be confronted and overcome. These challenges are now discussed.

Challenges of Destination Branding

Destination branding is very challenging in practical terms, and branding is difficult to accomplish and maintain over long time periods. Yet the world's best destination brands have been around for decades. Eight specific challenges are listed in Figure 13.4 and described in more detail below. These challenges reflect the added complexities of branding tourism destinations.

Destinations Are a Mix of Different Products and Services

Unlike physical products that have finite and known characteristics, tourism destinations are complex and variable. They are not single products but rather an amalgam of products and services under different ownerships. You learned about the destination product concept in Chapters 1 and 7, and it has several dimensions, including attractions and events, built facilities, transportation, infrastructure, and service quality and friendliness. All these quite different elements need to be integrated under one brand.

- Mix of different products and services
- Lack of total control over product
- Requires a team effort
- Needs a long-term commitment
- Tourism is an experience good
- Lack of sufficient funding
- Political influences
- Subject to public discussion and criticism

Challenges of destination branding

Figure 13.4 Challenges of destination branding.

DMOs Do Not Have Total Control over the Destination Product That Is Being Branded

DMOs do not own or manage the products and services that are covered under the destination branding. Other companies and organizations are responsible for delivering the destination brand. A diverse range of tourism sector and other stakeholders are involved; their quality standards may vary quite widely. This is a very different situation than that experienced by a company because a company has total control over product quality and brand delivery. It is much more challenging for a DMO that must rely on the quality and experiences delivered by multiple tourism sector stakeholders. Moreover, the DMO usually has no direct power or control over stakeholders but can act only in an advisory capacity.

Requires a Team Effort

A DMO should not do destination branding on its own; in fact, it requires a team effort. The team should include tourism sector stakeholders and others in the community who can make useful contributions. Past and potential tourists should also be recruited for the team and provide their valuable inputs. Figure 13.5 shows that four major groups of people are involved in developing and using the destination brand: tourism sector stakeholders, community residents, the DMO, and tourists. It takes a team effort to achieve destination branding success.

Of course, there will be others on the destination branding team. These will include a tourism destination branding consulting company and a creative design company. These professionals will work along with the DMO's marketing department, especially for the development of the brand strategy and brand identity design.

Needs a Long-Term Commitment

The *Slovenia Times* (2010) likened destination branding to a relay race, in which the baton is passed from person to person until the finish line is reached. What a great metaphor that is

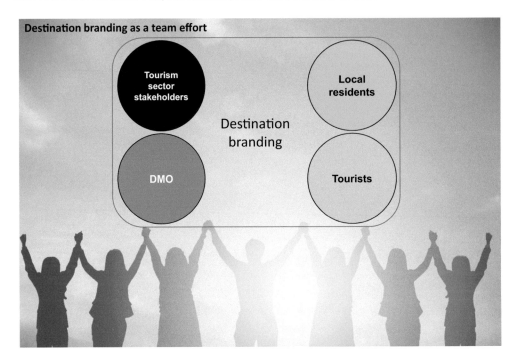

Figure 13.5 Team effort and players for destination branding.

because destination branding needs a long-term commitment and may not produce immediate results. Also, the players may change at the DMO and within the destination, but destination branding must continue its course. The challenges are to be patient and to ensure that the continuity of destination branding is maintained. The Virginia Is for Lovers® destination branding is an outstanding example of a state DMO making a long-term commitment to a destination branding approach, which you heard about in Chapter 12 (Virginia Tourism Corporation 2022).

Tourism Is an Experience Good

Tourism is not bought and consumed like physical products; tourism and destinations are experience goods. The quality of destinations cannot truly be observed and assessed in advance; destinations must be experienced to determine their real quality. So, tourism destinations cannot be tried on or tried out before booking them to see whether they fit the tourist's needs and wants. This level of uncertainty about the destination experience makes branding more challenging.

You will see the word "experience" used repeatedly throughout this chapter and in many of the destination branding examples. This is not accidental, but rather, it mirrors the need to promise and deliver the experiences that tourists most desire in destinations.

Lack of Sufficient Funding to Support Destination Branding Efforts

The biggest DMOs around the world can afford to do destination branding because their marketing budgets are large enough. However, many small and medium-sized DMOs find it difficult to produce the funds to hire branding consultant specialists and to pay for the approaches and materials that the consultants recommend.

What does destination branding usually cost? This is an extremely difficult question to answer because the costs vary widely from destination to destination. You will see some figures quoted in the examples in this chapter, and they vary from $100,000 to over one million US dollars. Of course, the costs vary according to what is included in the estimates. The minimum cost would be for the fees and expenses of hiring an expert consulting organization in destination branding, and presumably this would not be much less than $100,000 and could also be significantly higher than this.

Political Influences May Be Felt

Destinations are places, and places have governments with political leaders. Politicians are very sensitive about the images of the places within their jurisdiction. If a powerful politician does not personally like a suggested destination branding approach, it might not get the approval of government. For example, a new Always Natural destination branding was developed for the Maldives at a cost reported to be around $100,000. However, with the political crisis and change of government there, the political leaders opted to have another new destination brand.

In fact, this is one of the real threats to the longevity of a destination brand. When political parties and leaders change, as they do frequently, there is a tendency to want to sweep clean all that was done by previous administrations. Weak destination brands that do not have the complete support of stakeholders are in grave danger of being scrapped and replaced. Outstanding brands that are deeply embedded in consumers' minds and wholeheartedly embraced by stakeholders have a much better chance of surviving a political house-cleaning.

Brands and Destination Advertising Are Subject to Public Discussion and Criticism

Everybody is a tourism expert. Because almost everybody travels and becomes a tourist themselves, they all have opinions about how to put across the images of the places where they live. Reporters and editors in the media also like to talk and write about local tourism branding and advertising approaches. Therefore, destination brands often become the topic of widespread debate in the local media. This can be a difficult process for a DMO to manage because some opinions may be misinformed but still influential.

EXAMPLE 13.9

Destination Brands Can Be Hard To Fully Deliver Upon

Launched in 1999, the 100% Pure New Zealand branding is considered as one of the very best national tourism destination branding efforts of all time. However, the 100 percent part makes it hard to deliver upon.

> In New Zealand's Southern Alps, braided rivers radiate turquoise from the glacial flows coming off snow-capped mountains. Breath-taking vistas like these have provided the backdrop for Hollywood epics like Lord of the Rings and

underpin one of the world's most recognized tourism campaigns, 100% Pure New Zealand.

But behind New Zealand's clean and green image is a dirty truth—its freshwater rivers are among the most polluted in the developed world. Last year, a government report found nearly 60 percent of the country's rivers carry pollution above acceptable levels, with 95 to 99 percent of rivers in pastoral, urban and non-native forested areas contaminated.

(Melhem 2021)

Learning Point

This is a great destination branding approach by Tourism New Zealand. Realistically, however, it is difficult to deliver 100 percent on such a promise.

With the introduction of worldwide communications through social media networks, there is now much more public scrutiny and discussion of destination brands. For example, when the Philippine Department of Tourism (2018) launched its new brand with the slogan, "It's more fun in the Philippines," many observers in cyberspace noted this was the same slogan as was used in Switzerland decades before. The previous campaign, Pilipinas Kay Ganda, was short-lived and drew huge criticism from netizens. One of the criticisms came within one week after its launch when bloggers noticed the logo was strikingly like the logo for Poland's tourism (Galarpe 2010).

The Tourism Australia advertising campaign, "So where the bloody hell are you?" was withdrawn amid widespread criticism online and offline. Non-English speakers could not understand what was meant by the phrase, and some countries banned the advertisements, deeming them to be too risqué (Malkin 2010).

These are just a few examples of what can happen after a tourism destination brand goes public in today's instant communication society. As you will see later in this chapter, it is much better to take more time and reveal preliminary ideas for the brand identity to tourism sector stakeholders and test them with consumers.

Many destination brands are failures, and you should know some of the reasons they are not effective and get scrapped. The reasons place and destination brands fail are shown in Figure 13.6 with some adaptation. To the right of this figure, there is a quote saying that sometimes, one must fail to eventually achieve success, and this does happen with destination branding.

Before starting to discuss how to do destination branding, it is good for you to first know about what makes an effective destination brand. It is important to have some basic criteria for what constitutes a good destination brand before starting the process of developing a new brand. This provides benchmarks against which the destination brand can be compared to ensure that it meets certain standards.

Characteristics of a Good Destination Brand

Based upon successful experiences around the world in the past forty to fifty years, effective destination brands have certain shared characteristics:

Destination branding failures

- Lack of clear objectives
- Too much emphasis on promotion
- Short-term perspective
- Politically motivated
- Complexity not appreciated
- No consensus established
- Inadequate funding
- Not enough attention to implementation details
- Insufficient management and evaluation of implementation

Figure 13.6 Reasons for destination branding failures.

Attractive

Although a destination brand is not only visual; it is important that its visual elements be attractive and appealing to people in the target markets. For example, the destination brand logo for Spain's tourism is beautiful in its design and color scheme and was created by the famous Spanish painter, Joan Miró (Fig. 13.7).

Figure 13.7 Spanish destination branding approach.

EXAMPLE 13.10

Sol de Miró: Spain's Destination Brand

Spain's brand image is perhaps one of the most artistic ever used by a destination. Joan Miró used the sun as a central feature of his masterpiece and that is certainly something one associates with Spain's tourism.

The ministry offered to pay Miró for the design, but Miró refused to accept payment, saying, "for the King and for the government it's all free." Before the Sol de Miró, most countries used their flag on tourist posters, and not a single other country had ever used an abstract design for a logo. The logo was first used in Europe and then in the USA. It also became a well-known symbol in Spain, and its impact was powerful. In just five years, the Spanish tourism industry doubled its income.

(Surovek Gallery 2022)

Learning Point

Yes, we must be honest that we said logos were overrated, and this is still true. Here is an exception, however.

Communicates Destination Quality and Experiences

As an experience good, an effective destination brand puts across the types of experiences that tourists will have as well as promising a certain level of quality. Some destinations define their value proposition to be delivered in visitor experiences. For example, Raleigh, North Carolina, in the USA, clearly states the benefits of its destination brand that are to be experienced by visitors.

EXAMPLE 13.11

Greater Raleigh Brand Promise and Proposition

This example from North Carolina demonstrates how a DMO defines what visitors can expect and the experiences they will leave with when they depart Raleigh.

Destination brand promise

"Visitors to Raleigh will depart feeling enriched by what they have experienced in this Southern capital city, thanks to Raleigh's smart and passionate residents who are shaping the growth of the historic city's emerging creative businesses, innovative festivals and food establishments, passionate music and sports scenes and modern cultural experiences."

Destination brand proposition

"Visitors to Raleigh will leave feeling enriched and energized by their experiences—whether dining/food, event/festival, music or sports experiences—thanks to the investment made into this historic capital city by a smart, passionate, inventive local population."

(Greater Raleigh Convention and Visitors Bureau 2022)

Learning Point

A DMO should be clear about the experiences that visitors should expect.

Consistent with Positioning

The destination brand must convey the desired image that has been selected. For example, an eco-oriented tourism destination like Costa Rica is well advised to use a good deal of green in its communications supporting the destination branding. Bloom Consulting and Placematters analyzed the national branding of Costa Rica in 2017 and found that it has maintained its "prominent positioning as a natural tourism destination" (Arias 2017).

Expresses the Destination's Personality

The tone projected by the destination brand fits well with the character of the place. For example, Destination British Columbia in Canada identifies the attributes of the province as strong, free-spirited, adventurous, open and generous (Destination British Columbia 2022: 8).

Is Supported by Marketing Activities

A good destination brand is the foundation for and supported by effective IMC campaigns. You will learn all about how this is done in Chapter 14.

Memorable

A good destination brand is not easily forgotten. For example, how many of us can forget, I Love New York? Many people think this is the brand of New York City, but it was introduced by the state DMO on Valentine's Day 1977. This memorable brand has been a huge benefit to tourism in the state of New York and New York City. This is also a characteristic of the Malaysia, Truly Asia brand.

Simple

It is better that a destination brand not be too complex because consumers may not be able to interpret what is meant by the brand. Many of the truly successful destination brands of the past decades, including I Love New York and 100 percent Pure New Zealand, are the essence of simplicity. In contrast, the failed brands include many that were too hard to interpret and understand.

Market Tested

A good destination brand has been market tested in a preliminary form with a representative group of people in the intended target markets. It also has been given the stamp of approval by tourism sector stakeholders.

Transportable to the Web and Social Media

You will hear about IMC in Chapters 14 and 15, and it is a real bonus if the destination branding can yield some text or an expression that can be transported to the Web as a domain name. For example, the Vanilla Islands groups together Comoros, Madagascar, Mauritius, Mayotte, Réunion and Seychelles in the Indian Ocean. The regional brand name is easily used on the Web and in social media (e.g., #vanillaislands) (Vanilla Islands 2022). Another great example is Business Iceland's (2022) Inspired by Iceland branding approach.

Unique

Being different is one of the keys to the success of destination branding, and this means standing out among competitors. Netherlands Board of Tourism and Conventions (NBTC) Holland Marketing (2022), for example, defines Holland as the open-minded country. If that is not unique enough, which country do you associate with the color of orange?

EXAMPLE 13.12

The Dutch DNA and NL Passions

Open-mindedness is in the Dutch DNA and NBTC sees this as part of the country's brand identity. We might say that the NL Passions are the USPs for tourism.

Dutch DNA

The stories and experiences that we introduce are rooted in our DNA, i.e., our country's identity. Research shows that the Dutch are internationally known as open-minded people. A combination of three core values is what makes our country distinctive and unique:

- Open
- Inclusive
- Inventive

NL Passions

NL Passions are the physical elements that make our country unique and that generate interest with international visitors:

- Water (landscape)
- Flowers
- The Coast
- Dutch masters and art
- Traditional Netherlands and heritage
- New Netherlands and creative sector
- Bicycles.

(NBTC 2022)

Learning Point

Being distinctive is a key requirement of an effective destination positioning and branding. The Netherlands stands out in this regard with its unique DNA and NL Passions backed with the distinctive orange coloring.

Well Accepted by All Stakeholders

The destination brand must have acceptance of the stakeholders within the destination and especially the tourism sector stakeholders. If stakeholders oppose the destination brand or are not particularly impressed by it, it has a low probability of succeeding.

Classic Concepts in Branding

Branding is one of those topics in management and marketing that is a real alphabet soup of terminology; there are so many concepts thrown about that it confuses even the experts. So that you will not be confused, some of the classic concepts in branding are defined below.

Brand equity

Aaker (1991) defined brand equity as having five elements: Brand loyalty, brand awareness, perceived quality, brand associations, and other proprietary brand assets. Brand equity is the total accumulated value or worth of a brand.

Brand essence

The main or core characteristics or values that are the main platform for the brand's competitive identity.

Brand identity

Brand identity was defined earlier.

Brand positioning

The image of the brand in the minds of customers and potential customers.

Brand personality

Brand personality was defined earlier.

Brand promise

The expectations that customers have of the brand based upon what they have seen in marketing communications.

The Swisstainable concept provides a good example of the brand promise concept.

EXAMPLE 13.13

Swisstainable Is Part of Switzerland's Brand Promise

This is a clever play on words to place sustainability in a prominent position within the destination branding for Switzerland.

> Switzerland as a travel destination differentiates itself through sustainability. We want to draw on our strengths to clearly differentiate ourselves from the competition. In 2019, we refocused our brand. Our promise—"Our Nature Energises You"—calls for a consistent focus on sustainability. We offer our guests authentic and rich naturalness, and live by this with our values of originality, reliability and safety.
>
> By fusing together, the terms "Swiss" and "sustainable," we are signaling an independent and, above all, Switzerland-specific sustainability strategy. In

our communications, we resolve the play on words in a clear and comprehensible manner with the claim "Excellence in Sustainability." In this way, we emphasize our pioneering role and our ambitious vision.

(Switzerland Tourism 2021)

Learning Point

It can be advantageous if a destination can associate its brand with a major global trend and movement; in this case, Switzerland with sustainable development.

Steps in Destination Branding

In Chapter 12, you learned about the destination marketing planning system, and destination branding falls within the second step that addresses the question of where would we like to be? As Figure 13.8 illustrates, there are four parts in this process. The first part of destination branding is the situation analysis, consisting of destination analysis (or destination audit), competitive analysis, market analysis, destination image analysis (or marketing position analysis), resident analysis, and analysis of past marketing programs. The destination image analysis determines the existing perceptions of the destination among past and potential tourists.

Before starting the description of the brand development process, you might be curious about how long it takes to develop a destination brand. Unfortunately, there are no industry averages for this. Travel Alberta's (Remember to Breathe) (Singh 2017) destination branding for the province was eighteen months in development. The new destination brand for the nearby state of Montana took almost a year to develop. These examples show that destination brand development can be time-consuming and can take more than a year from the basic research to the brand launch. Having said this, there are no doubt some cases where destination brands

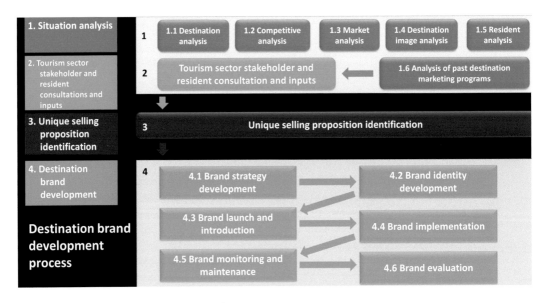

Figure 13.8 Destination brand development process.

have been designed in less than a year, but as you will see now, it is hard to believe that all the following steps can be accomplished that quickly.

Situation Analysis

Chapter 12 explained how a situation analysis is done as a step in developing a marketing plan. The different parts (destination, competitive, market, destination image, resident, and past marketing programs) of the situation analysis also provide rich and necessary information for destination branding. There is no doubt that these analyses can be very time consuming but they should not be skipped over in developing a destination brand. Just doing one or two quick focus groups with a few handfuls of people is not sufficient, although it happens quite often in brand-building.

Potential tourists are the main audience for a new destination brand. Therefore, the development of the destination branding should be based on a thorough understanding of these people and what they want to experience within the destination. The brand must be built to resonate with customers and not just to reflect what is available in the destination. This means that research needs to be conducted on the current images of the destination among people within the target markets.

A good case study here is the market research that preceded the development of the Shaoxing Vintage China destination branding in Zhejiang Province, China. BTI Consulting conducted extensive research with consumers in China and abroad to provide the support for brand development. Consumer surveys were conducted in Japan, South Korea, Macao, and Taiwan as well as in several cities in China (Shanghai, Beijing, Guangzhou, Hangzhou, Nanjing, Suzhou, Wuxi, and Wenzhou). A travel agency survey was completed in Hong Kong. Respondents were asked about their awareness of the existing major attractions in Shaoxing. The two items in which there were the highest levels of awareness were Shaoxing yellow rice wine and Lu Xun, a famous Chinese contemporary writer who lived in Shaoxing and wrote about life in the city. Respondents were also asked which activities and experiences they most wanted to engage in when traveling to China and Shaoxing. Meetings were held with tourism sector stakeholders in Shaoxing, and after this analysis, the Shaoxing Vintage China destination branding was developed for international tourist markets (Fig. 12.14).

A second example of a research-based approach to destination branding comes from Glasgow in Scotland. Glasgow City Marketing Bureau began the research in February 2013 by interviewing fifty of the city's leaders. After this, in March and April, the opinions of Glasgow residents were collected via postcards and collection boxes at sixty locations within the city. In addition, potential visitor opinions were gathered online from 1,500 people in forty-two countries. The consensus on the question of What makes Glasgow great? was that it was the people living in the city. After this, the new brand was created as PEOPLE MAKE GLASGOW (capital letters used) (Glasgow City Marketing 2022).

Tourism Sector Stakeholder and Resident Consultations and Inputs

Input should be gathered from tourism sector stakeholders and residents on their suggestions about the image and positioning of the destination as you just heard about for Glasgow. Stakeholders and residents should be asked to express what they see as being the most unique features of the destination. Stakeholders' and residents' opinions cannot and should not be taken as a substitute for those of tourists; however, there is no point in having a destination branding that they do not support. Additionally, it is essential that tourism sector stakeholders adopt the destination brand and use it in their own marketing and promotional programs.

As an example, the Montana Office of Tourism and Business Development in the USA conducted eight meetings across the state and received input from more than 350 stakeholders (Destination Analysts 2016). The input from stakeholders was placed against the results of consumer focus groups in developing the most relevant and believable attributes of the Montana brand.

EXAMPLE 13.14

Unbranding? Nebraska. Honestly, It's Not for Everyone

Destination branding must stand out and sometimes that is done with quirky approaches, as in that used by Nebraska Tourism (Fig. 13.9).

Figure 13.9 Tourism Nebraska advertising campaign.

Two years after its launch, Ricks said the campaign put Nebraska's tourist amenities on the map. In the year the campaign launched, the website had an increase of 180,000 visitors. The message spread so fast that in December, the reach or number of people who possibly could have heard the campaign's messages was 884 million people, according to Ricks (state tourism Director). Besides communication successes, the campaign also brought more visitors into Nebraska. Ricks said lodging tax income broke previous records in 2018 and 2019, and in those two years, overnight visitors in Nebraska increased by 300,000. Before those two years, it took ten years to increase visitors by that amount.

The campaign's playful attitude was based on stereotypes that hold Nebraska's tourism industry back, Ricks said. The team decided to debunk these stereotypes one by one, noting that the Great Plains are anything but plain and connecting Nebraska's reputation of being "fly-over country" with the magnificent sandhill crane migration. "This self-deprecating humor that evolved out of it got people's attention," Ricks said.

(Champion 2021)

Learning Point

Nebraska differentiated itself from competitors by employing an unusual approach in its branding and communications. It worked.

Unique Selling Proposition Identification

The destination's unique selling propositions (USPs) are one of the most critical inputs to destination branding because these USPs articulate what is truly different in the place when compared to competitors. For example, in the Shaoxing case discussed in Chapter 12 and above, six USPs were identified: (1) Shaoxing yellow rice wine, (2) ancient canal city, (3) celebrities, (4) nature, (5) artistic impression, and (6) beauty and love. The visual expressions of four of these USPs were illustrated in Figure 12.14. The Shaoxing yellow rice wine is shown in the containers in each of the four images.

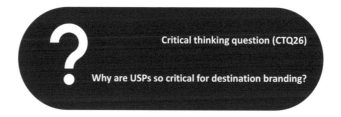

A trend now is to express USPs as brand pillars or experience pillars, as in the case of Queensland, Australia. For São Paulo, these are unexpected and unforgettable experiences, diverse cultures, contemporary society, and communities (São Paulo Turismo 2022). The Northern Cape Tourism Authority in South Africa expresses its three brand pillars as: (1) real culture, (2) extreme adventure, and (3) experience nature (Northern Cape Tourism Authority 2022).

EXAMPLE 13.15

Destination DNA

A destination brand should reflect the true uniqueness of a place, which we can call its DNA.

From my own experience, a successful destination brand is based on the uniqueness of the place and not what makes it like other destinations. This

> uniqueness is the destination's DNA rather than a slogan or a logo, and by DNA, I mean the "destination's non-imitable assets" [Fig. 13.10].
>
> (Morrison 2014)

Learning Point

The essence of a place—its DNA—is what truly makes it different from competitors.

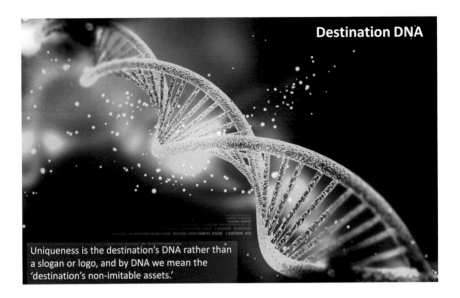

Figure 13.10 A destination's non-imitable assets are its DNA.

Destination Brand Development

Destination brand development comprises six sequential steps as shown in Figure 13.8. This is much like a micro version of the destination marketing planning process described in Chapter 12.

BRANDING STRATEGY DEVELOPMENT

Branding strategy represents the approaches used to develop the destination brand, and the following questions need to be answered in this step:

- Why does the destination need a new tourism brand? A clear rationale or reasoning behind starting the process of developing a new brand must be given.
- What are the objectives for the destination branding? A set of specific destination branding objectives must be articulated. As shown in Figure 13.6, the lack of specific objectives is a cause of destination brand failures.
- What image will the new destination brand communicate? The way the destination will be positioned in the new brand must be explained.
- Who are the targets for the destination brand? The target markets to which the new destination brand will be communicated must be identified and described.

- How will the new destination brand look? A basic and general idea of the new destination brand needs to be developed.

The starting point for designing a destination brand is the development of branding objectives: What is it that the destination brand is expected to achieve and by when? *The Handbook on Tourism Destination Branding* prepared by the ETC and UNWTO (2009) suggested a set of destination branding objectives, and these were adapted for this book and are shown in the example.

EXAMPLE 13.16

Destination Branding Objectives

These are four suggested branding objectives that could apply to any destination. You should look back at Figure 13.3 to see other potential branding objectives.

1. To differentiate the destination from competitors.
2. To increase awareness, recognition and memorability of the destination over time among potential visitors.
3. To create a positive image of the destination that makes people responsive to the DMO's marketing messages and therefore more likely to visit.
4. To give the destination a strong and compelling brand identity.

(ETC and UNWTO 2009)

Learning Point

Differentiation is a key objective for destination branding.

The next stage in branding strategy development is deciding on the brand positioning. Destination positioning has already been defined in this chapter as the image that the destination wants to create in the minds of people within its target markets. You might say these are the perceptions that it wishes people to have about the destination. In 2016, for example, Vienna Tourism in Austria introduced a new destination brand positioned according to visitors experiencing personal moments of enjoyment in the city (Vienna Tourism 2018). Norway's brand is based on a positioning around nature and is expressed as Norway. Powered by Nature (Innovation Norway 2022). The country's USPs are spectacular fjords, coast and natural phenomena, fresh seafood and coastal specialties, thriving coastal culture, and nature-based activities.

The branding strategy must be aligned with the destination's market segmentation strategy and be crafted for the target markets that have been selected. It is likely that the destination brand will have to be adapted and applied differently for dissimilar target markets, although it is most desirable that there is consistency among the different applications. Visit Greenland (2019) surveyed international visitors in several of its destinations in 2012. Based on the visitors' responses, it developed a unique segmentation scheme using two key factors, interest focus (culture, culture and nature, nature, and personal challenge) and engagement level (observation, interaction, and total immersion). Forming a matrix of the two factors, eleven segments were identified. Visit Greenland's destination brand fits with all these market segments, and different photographic approaches are used to appeal to the various groups.

Based upon the situation analysis results and the inputs from stakeholders and residents along with the branding objectives and positioning and marketing segmentation strategy, the DMO then prepares a brief or written summary document, which is the foundation for the creative development. This gives a basic and general picture in words about how the new destination brand should feel and look.

EXAMPLE 13.17

Co-branding Football and a Country's Tourism

When two brands come together, synergy can be achieved. In this case, Rwanda achieves greater recognition by sponsoring Arsenal in the English Premier League and Paris Saint-Germain in Ligue 1 of France.

> Visit Rwanda is Arsenal Football Club's official Tourism Partner and its first shirt sleeve partner. The Visit Rwanda logo features on the left sleeve of all AFC [Arsenal Football Club] teams for the duration of the exciting, three-year partnership. The Arsenal shirt is seen 35 million times a day globally and AFC is one of the most watched teams around the world, enabling Visit Rwanda to be seen in football-loving nations around the world and helping its drive to be an even more successful tourism and investment destination.
>
> Visit Rwanda is proud to be a Premium Partner of Paris Saint-Germain Football Club. For three seasons, the Paris Saint-Germain community and the world will have a unique opportunity to experience Rwanda's breath-taking beauty, creative culture, innovative environment, and modern and distinctive Made in Rwanda products through unprecedented and creative communications. The partnership will also convey Rwanda's openness to welcome business partnerships from France and across the world.
>
> (Visit Rwanda 2022)

Learning Point

Brands can enhance their impact on the market by co-branding with well-known organizations or products.

The Montana Office of Tourism and Business Development (2022) identified the following three brand pillars to guide its branding process. The first pillar was its strongest characteristic, which it called its ace card, or differentiator:

1. More spectacular unspoiled nature than anywhere else in the lower forty-eight (the ace card, or differentiator).
2. Vibrant and charming small towns that serve as gateways to our natural wonders (the surprise card, or mitigator).
3. Breath-taking experiences by day and relaxing hospitality at night (card that ties the hand together, or brand builder).

BRAND IDENTITY DEVELOPMENT

Brand identity is the creative stage of destination brand development. Here, the brief or summary document is interpreted into a creative strategy that can encompass a new logo, color scheme and other visual image (VI) guidelines; slogan (or strapline); musical score and other elements.

The wording and the typography are extremely important elements of brand identity. Two of the most highly commended destination brands attest to this point. Launched in 1999, 100% Pure New Zealand has undoubtedly been the world champion of destination branding. Set on a black background when it was first introduced, this destination branding by Tourism New Zealand set the standard for others to follow. Another highly acclaimed brand is very simple (two words) but conveys so much meaning about tourism in a vast country. Incredible!ndia was launched in 2002 and has been hugely beneficial to tourism in India (WEF 2017). Another great example is I AMSTERDAM (Fig. 13.11), the branding used by Amsterdam & Partners (2019).

Although beautiful logos are not destination brands, it really helps if the logo is highly attractive and memorable. A great example here is the logo developed by the famous Catalan painter Joan Miró in 1982 for Tourism Spain (2018). The colors used with the brand identity can be very crucial. For example, NBTC in the Netherlands uses orange in the destination logo and accompanying elements.

The brand promise reflects the expectations that tourists have, based upon what is contained in the DMO's marketing communications and how the communications are delivered.

Figure 13.11 I AMSTERDAM destination brand.

BRAND LAUNCH AND INTRODUCTION

The brand launch is when a new destination brand is revealed to the public for the first time. Normally, this is done with some pomp and ceremony and is a major public relations event in the destination. For example, the Passion Made Possible destination brand was launched by the Singapore Tourism Board in August 2017 and introduced in various international markets thereafter (Singapore Tourism Board 2022).

It is dangerous to put the principal focus on a new logo in launching a destination brand. Again, a destination brand is much more than just a logo, but if the DMO focuses on the logo in the launch, others will also focus on it. It seems that many DMOs are not listening to this advice, and their launches are mainly for presenting new tourism logos and slogans.

EXAMPLE 13.18

Uganda Launches New Destination Brand

This is an example of a new destination brand launch by Uganda in East Africa. You will notice the use of the terms brand promise and brand identity.

> As the world starts to recover from the effects of the pandemic and opening up borders and skies to global tourism, Uganda, has refreshed its tourism destination brand promise, with the unveiling of a new brand identity that promises both domestic, regional and global tourists, an adventure of a lifetime.
>
> The new brand—Explore Uganda, The Pearl of Africa—draws upon Uganda's global reputation as one of the most endowed destinations, famous for its thousands of plant and wildlife attractions, as well as vast and beautiful landscapes, temperate climate, warm people, and cultural diversity.
>
> The brand identity—Explore Uganda, The Pearl of Africa—was unveiled on Friday, 21st January 2022, by the country's president, H. E. Yoweri Kaguta Museveni in Kampala, Uganda's capital city. The president was assisted by Col. Rtd Tom Butime, Hon Martin Bahinduka Mugarra and Ms. Doreen Katusiime, the Cabinet, State Minister and Permanent Secretary for Tourism, Wildlife and Antiquities, respectively. The brand was developed by Uganda Tourism Board (UTB), Uganda's tourism marketing and regulatory agency. The UTB Chief Executive Officer, Ms. Lilly Ajarova and her Deputy, Mr. Bradford Ochieng; and the Board Chairman, Hon. Daudi Migereko together with board members, hosted the unveiling, held at the Kololo Ceremonial Grounds.
>
> (UTB 2022)

Learning Point

There will be fanfare accompanying a destination brand launch with political and tourism leaders invited to give speeches. These events build excitement for new destination brands.

The brand launch above all needs to relay information on the research that was done with consumers and explain how stakeholders' input was collected and integrated. In fact, the whole brand story must be related to the audience. Some DMOs refer to the entire process as a destination branding journey, and that indeed is a very good metaphor because the launch should be more like a starting point than an ending to the journey. If the logo and slogan are perceived as being the final product of the destination branding process, that is not the impression to be communicated in a brand launch. You just need to consider the longevity of the world's most successful destination brands to realize that the life span of a good brand will be ten or more years. Even if the brand takes two years to develop, it will have many more years ahead of it. Thus, the logo and slogans may be modified in the future, but the basic ideas underpinning the destination branding will not.

After the launch, tourism sector stakeholders will be anxious to get going with the new destination brand. The DMO needs to develop a variety of materials for the introduction of the brand and the use of the brand internally and by tourism sector stakeholders. These materials include the following items:

- Brand manual: A brand manual (or playbook) is a complete guide to the new destination brand and explains how and why it was developed and how it is to be implemented. This is sometimes called the brand story (Knapp and Sherwin 2005). You will hear about some outstanding examples soon.
- Photo library or gallery: Photographs and videos are tremendously important in destination communications, and they are even more critical in supporting the images of the destination brand.
- Style manual: Guidelines on how and how not to use the brand logo and a color palette and directions on how to apply the brand.

EXAMPLE 13.19

Ottawa's Brand Playbooks for Different Audiences

This is an outstanding example of a DMO preparing stakeholders to develop content for specific audiences that interprets the destination branding.

> Ottawa Tourism developed four Ottawa Contents Playbooks for visitors, citizens, businesses, and students. It also called these brand storybooks that described the brand development process and provided guidelines on using the brand.
> "This brand storybook is written using the combined knowledge gained from previous steps in our city identity and branding process:
>
> - Place DNA
> - Brand framework
> - Brand themes
> - Brand storybook.
>
> The brand storybook emphasizes storytelling about Ottawa:
> Stories are at the heart of a city brand. They directly affect a city's reputation. Storytelling has a powerful influence on what people think about a place, how much affinity they feel, how desirable it is and how memorable

their experiences are. As perceptions change, so does behavior. Stories that resonate can literally shape cities.

(Ottawa Tourism and Convention Authority 2022)

Learning Point

The DMO should encourage tourism sector stakeholders and other audiences to deliver the brand in communications in the form of storytelling. In this example, Ottawa Tourism prompts this form of communications with content guidelines.

The brand introduction includes steps taken by the DMO to educate tourism sector stakeholders on the new destination brand. This is not just the launch event but a concerted campaign to make stakeholders aware of the reasons for the brand and how to use it. There are different ways to accomplish this; one is to prepare a brand book or manual providing all the details on the destination brand. Destination Canada's brand playbook is a great example here (Destination Canada 2022). The Destination Brand Guidelines provided by Cumbria Tourism (2018) in England is another excellent case study.

Several DMOs have designed special training programs, including seminars and workshops (see the Calgary, Alberta example), which present their new destination brands to tourism sector stakeholders. These programs are supplemented with information and materials on DMOs' websites that explain the branding in greater detail and are always there for reference purposes.

It is also very helpful in introducing and communicating a brand if it can be expressed in a visual representation that captures the main features of the brand. A great case study is the branding of Greenland, which invites you to Be a Pioneer (Visit Greenland 2019).

EXAMPLE 13.20

Living the Brand of Calgary

This is an example of brand culturalization, which means introducing a new brand throughout a destination. The brand is fully explained to tourism sector stakeholders, local residents, and others. In Calgary's case, this was accomplished through a series of workshops.

To help partners across all sectors strategically align with Calgary's new destination brand model, Living the Brand workshops were hosted. In the workshop presentation the brand essence (daring and undaunted) and brand personality (confident, energetic, engaging and kind) of Calgary are expressed.

In Calgary we nourish our communities through ideas, cultures and experiences because we are driven by big dreams and determined to make a contribution. We are daring and undaunted when it comes to our goals. Seen as confident, energetic, engaging and kind, Calgary is big enough to be lively and connected enough to feel intimate. We get it done. Together.

(Tourism Calgary 2019)

> **Learning Point**
>
> This is a case study in how to do destination branding the right way. Sharing the brand with all constituents is essential.

Brand Implementation

Instead of saying brand implementation, this could have been titled living the brand. Knapp and Sherwin (2005) call this process brand culturalization, or the road map for how the destination will deliver the brand promise. Once the destination brand is launched and introduced, it must be embedded within the destination and appear in every communication and interaction with tourists and potential tourists. Embedded in the destination means that the brand must be practiced; it is not a vague concept that just appears on paper or in a video. Remember that the brand is a promise and a promise builds expectations of what will be experienced in the destination. Therefore, every service encounter with tourism staff and residents, the ways in which tourism sector stakeholders deliver the experiences, and all the marketing that is done by stakeholders must support and enhance the destination brand. Ensuring the consistency of the message delivered within the destination is critical to effective destination branding.

Brand implementation also involves incorporating a new destination brand in all the DMO's marketing and IMC programs and activities. Chapters 14 and 15 discuss how this is accomplished, and so it is unnecessary to go into detail here about IMC using traditional (offline) and information and communication technology (online) channels. It just needs to be said that the destination branding must be reflected in all the DMO's communications and that it be always consistently applied.

A brief example of brand incorporation is provided here and follows on from one of the previous examples. The Shaoxing Vintage China destination brand was implemented in the development of a new English-language website, and thereafter several other language versions were developed (Japanese, Korean, Spanish and German). An event was created for a group of foreign expatriates living in nearby Shanghai and was staged just before the 2,500th anniversary of the city. The event was called the 25 @ 100 percent Vintage Shaoxing Experiences, and it generated much positive publicity for Shaoxing. The participants at the event kept diaries of their experiences, and many photos were taken of their trips within Shaoxing. These were later used in the production of an English guidebook, Experience Vintage Shaoxing. As you can see, these were a well-integrated set of marketing and IMC activities to implement a new destination brand.

Brand Monitoring and Maintenance

It is very important that the performance of the brand is monitored and maintained. Brand monitoring implies tracking the implementation of destination branding and assessing the progress toward the achievement of objectives. This monitoring can be accomplished using a variety of research techniques, including content analysis of travel blogs and consumer destination reviews (qualitative), surveys (visitor profile surveys, post-visit surveys, and random surveys of visitors and non-visitors) (quantitative), and focus groups (qualitative). The items to be measured here include awareness and recall of the brand, impact on intentions to visit the destination, and image of the destination.

The DMO acts as the brand guardian, making sure that the initial excitement from the launching of the new brand is maintained over the long term, which will be years rather than months. As such, the DMO must monitor how tourism sector stakeholders are applying the brand in their marketing and operations and make suggestions on how usage can be enhanced. This is one part of the task of brand maintenance.

There are other brand maintenance tasks that occur in the lifetime of good and long-lasting destination brands. Usually, these are not major repair jobs but the fine-tuning of aspects of the brand identity to keep up with contemporary design trends and changes in market priorities and customer expectations. For example, although the tourism brand logo for Spain has remained the same since 1982, the words accompanying it have been changed.

BRAND EVALUATION

The true test of the effectiveness of a destination brand is whether it achieves its objectives. Here again, solid research is needed to conclusively determine whether the destination branding impacted the target market as intended. Winning awards for excellent destination branding is nice and makes for great publicity; however, awards do not prove that destination brands have achieved their objectives. The types of research that should be completed are like those mentioned previously for brand monitoring.

There are several universal questions that should be addressed in any destination brand evaluation, and these include the following:

- Did the brand increase the levels of awareness of the destination in target markets?
- Did the brand increase intentions to visit the destination in target markets?
- Did the brand improve the destination's image among people in the target markets?
- Did the brand create a unique competitive identity for the destination?
- Was the brand an instrumental factor in increasing tourist volumes and expenditures in the destination?
- Does the brand have a high level of recall and memorability among people within the target markets?

These are good questions, and there are undoubtedly others that can be addressed in brand evaluation. The results of the evaluation are critical and especially if another new destination branding cycle is being contemplated.

These types of brand evaluation research supply an excellent platform for brand reassessment. The research for Montana included interviews with tourism stakeholders, an online survey of 6,250 potential visitors from key markets in the USA and Canada, in-depth interviews with potential visitors and focus groups of potential visitors in key markets. This research confirmed that potential visitors perceived the state as having unique scenic beauty and unspoiled natural assets.

Steps in Effective Destination Positioning, Image, and Branding

Here is what a DMO must accomplish to do destination PIB effectively:

- Determine the images of the destination among past and potential visitors.
- Develop a positioning approach, corresponding to the destination's USPs.
- Carefully document the reasons for needing a new destination brand, noting why the previous destination brand is to be discontinued.

- Conduct a situation analysis.
- Obtain input from tourism sector stakeholders on the destination brand.
- Identify the destination's USPs.
- Develop a destination brand strategy, including objectives, positioning, and target markets.
- Write a summary as the basis for the creative development of the brand.
- Work with vendors for brand identity development.
- Launch the new destination brand.
- Introduce the new destination brand to the market and tourism sector stakeholders.
- Implement the brand in marketing communications and within the destination.
- Monitor and maintain the brand.
- Evaluate the brand.

SUMMING UP

Destination branding has become a hot topic in tourism during the past thirty years. This is an element of destination marketing strategy, and its perceived importance has increased as destination competitiveness has intensified worldwide. There is a trio of interrelated concepts that work together in this aspect of destination marketing strategy: destination positioning, destination image, and destination branding.

Destination branding is important in several ways but particularly in establishing a place's competitive identity and communicating what makes it unique among all destination choices. Many benefits are created for destinations and tourists through effective destination branding. Above all, effective destination branding makes places stand out among competitors, and as a result, the destinations draw more tourists than they did before the brands were launched.

Branding tourism destinations is very challenging given the diversity of the destination product and the experience good characteristic of tourism. Destination branding often requires time to be successful, and so patience is required as well as continual investment in the brand. The classic success stories in tourism destination branding have withstood the test of time and have been in place for ten to more than forty years. These include Virginia is for Lovers®, I Love New York®, 100% Pure New Zealand, Incredible!ndia, and Malaysia Truly Asia. Many destinations tend to chop and change approaches very often, and this is a clue that they are not following the principles of professional destination branding. Instead, they are on a never-ending search for the perfect slogan and logo.

The past thirty years have brought great professionalism and flair into destination branding. However, political interference often gets in the way of excellent destination branding and spoils the continuity of professional branding efforts. Also, destination marketers often face a barrage of criticism online, although some of this is deserved, it must be said. The best advice for DMOs is to invest in solid research to prove the value and contributions of their destination brands and to continue to keep tourism sector stakeholders and residents informed and on their side.

Brand development starts with a situation analysis that provides the facts, figures and conclusions for the rest of the process. This includes analyses of the destination, competitors, market, destination image, residents and past marketing programs. Then, there are consultations with tourism sector stakeholders and local residents to get their vital inputs into the destination branding process. The third step is to identify the destination's USPs that make it different from competitors.

The actual development of the destination brand takes place in six steps: brand strategy development, brand identity development, brand launch and introduction, brand implementation, brand monitoring and maintenance, and brand evaluation. A brand is not just a logo and a slogan; in fact, it is a promise that the destination makes to potential visitors about the experiences they will have. So, delivering on the brand is not just about marketing and IMC; it involves the service quality in the destination and how tourism sector stakeholders deliver experiences. If a brand is not actually lived in the destination, then it is not truly a destination brand.

Chapters 14 and 15 explain how destination positioning and branding approaches are communicated. The concept of IMC is explained there in greater detail.

KEYWORDS

brand culturalization
brand development process
brand equity
brand essence
brand evaluation
brand identity
brand implementation
brand introduction
brand launch
brand maintenance
brand manual
brand monitoring

brand personality
brand pillars
brand positioning
brand promise
brand strategy
branding objectives
branding strategy
brief
co-branding
competitive identity
destination brand
    development

destination branding
destination image
destination positioning
experience goods
logo
nation or country branding
place branding
recall
slogan
unique selling propositions
    (USPs)

REVIEW QUESTIONS

1. Destination PIB are interconnected concepts. How are these three concepts interrelated, and in what ways do they impact each other?
2. Why is destination branding important?
3. What are the benefits that can accrue to destinations and tourists from destination branding?
4. What are the major challenges involved with doing destination branding?
5. Why do destination brands sometimes fail?
6. What are the characteristics of a good destination brand?
7. What are the steps involved in destination brand development?
8. Which items are included in a destination brand strategy?
9. How would you describe the brand promise?
10. How long should a destination brand last? Please explain your reasoning based on actual practice.

REFERENCES

Aaker, D. A. (1991) *Managing Brand Equity: Capitalizing on the Value of a Brand Name*, New York, NY: The Free Press.

Amsterdam & Partners (2019) "Brand Manual I AMSTERDAM," www.iamsterdam.com/media/pdf/corporate/i-amsterdam-brand-manual-en.pdf?la=en

Arias, L. (2017) "Costa Rica's Country Brand Is the Fastest Growing in the Americas," *The Tico Times*, July 7, www.ticotimes.net/2017/07/07/country-brand-costa-rica

Baker, B. (2007) *Destination Branding for Small Cities: The Essentials for Successful Place Branding*, Tualatin, Oreg.: Creative Leap Books.

Belle Tourism International Consulting (2008) *International Tourism Marketing Implementation Plan for Shaoxing*, Shanghai: Belle Tourism International Consulting.

Blain, C., Levy, S. E., and Ritchie, J. R. B. (2005) "Destination Branding: Insights and Practices from Destination Management Organizations," *Journal of Travel Research*, 43 (4): 328–338.

Business Iceland (2022) "Inspired by Iceland," www.inspiredbyiceland.com/about/

BusinessWorld (2022) "Rebranding Mindanao: DoT Highlights Ecotours, Farms, and Halal in New Campaign," May 3, www.bworldonline.com/editors-picks/2022/05/03/446218/rebranding-mindanao-dot-highlights-ecotours-farms-and-halal-in-new-campaign/

Champion, M. (2021) "'Nebraska. Honestly, It's Not for Everyone' Campaign Grows State Tourism," Nebraska News Service, May 7, https://nebraskanewsservice.net/state/nebraska-honestly-its-not-for-everyone-campaign-grows-state-tourism/

Clarke, J. (2000) "Tourism Brands: An Exploratory Study of the Brands Box Model," *Journal of Vacation Marketing*, 6 (4): 329–345.

Cumbria Tourism (2018) "Destination Brand Guidelines: The Lake District Cumbria," www.cumbria-tourism.org/wp-content/uploads/2015/07/brand-guidelines.pdf

Destination Analysts (2016) "Montana Destination Brand Research Study: Report of Findings," https://brand.mt.gov/_shared/Marketing/docs/brand-research.pdf

Destination British Columbia (2022) "BC's Destination Brand Guidelines," www.destinationbc.ca/learning-centre/bcs-destination-brand/

Destination Canada (2022) "Our Playbook," https://brand.destinationcanada.com/en

Dinnie, K. (2011) *City Branding: Theory and Cases*, Basingstoke: Palgrave Macmillan.

European Travel Commission and United Nations World Tourism Organization (2009) *Handbook on Tourism Destination Branding*, Madrid: ETC/UNWTO.

Galarpe, K. (2010) "'Pilipinas Kay Ganda' Logo Lifted from Poland Logo?" http://news.abs-cbn.com/lifestyle/11/18/10/pilipinas-kay-ganda-logo-lifted-poland-logo

Glasgow City Marketing (2022) "About Glasgow Life," https://peoplemakeglasgow.com/about-us

Govers, R. (2013) "Why Place Branding Is Not About Logos and Slogans," *Place Branding and Public Diplomacy*, 9 (2): 71–75.

Greater Raleigh Convention and Visitors Bureau (2022) "What Is GRCVB?" https://res.cloudinary.com/simpleview/image/upload/v1/clients/raleigh/New_Hospitality_Employee_Orientation_v02_6758d203-ecce-4a81-82b5-37dee35a13d9.pdf

Innovation Norway (2022) "How Norway Is Promoting Sustainability in Tourism," www.theexplorer.no/stories/tourism/how-norway-is-promoting-sustainability-in-tourism/

Kaneva, N. (2022) "With 'Bravery' as Its New Brand, Ukraine Is Turning Advertising into a Weapon," Fast Company, August 22, www.fastcompany.com/90780875/with-bravery-as-its-new-brand-ukraine-is-turning-advertising-into-a-weapon

Knapp, D., and Sherwin, G. (2005) *Destination Brand Science*, Washington, DC: Destinations International (DMAI).

Kotler, P., and Gartner, D. (2002) "Country as a Brand, Product and Beyond: A Place Marketing and Brand Management Perspective," *The Journal of Brand Management*, 9 (4/5): 249–261.

Las Vegas Convention and Visitors Authority (2022) "What Happens Here, Stays Here®," www.lvcva.com/destination-marketing/advertising-campaigns/what-happens-here-stays-here/

Malkin, B. (2010) "Australia Drops Controversial Tourism Campaign for 'Safer' Slogan," *The Telegraph*, March 31, www.telegraph.co.uk/news/worldnews/australiaandthepacific/australia/7540023/Australia-drops-controversial-tourism-campaign-for-safer-slogan.html

Melhem, Y. B. (2021) "New Zealand's Troubled Waters," *ABC News*, March 17, www.abc.net.au/news/2021-03-16/new-zealand-rivers-pollution-100-per-cent-pure/13236174

Montana Office of Tourism and Business Development (2022) "Discovering the Montana brand," http://brand.mt.gov/_shared/Marketing/docs/discovering-the-montana-brand.pdf

Morgan, N., Pritchard, A., and Pride, R. (2002) *Destination Branding: Creating the Unique Destination Proposition*, London: Routledge.

Morrison, A. M. (2014) "A Slogan Is Not the DNA of a Destination," www.researchgate.net/publication/261995674_A_slogan_is_not_the_DNA_of_a_destination

Netherlands Board of Tourism and Conventions (2022) "Destination Netherlands: The Dutch DNA," www.nbtc.nl/en/site/destination-netherlands/dutch-dna.htm

Northern Cape Tourism Authority (2022) "Our Brand Pillars," www.experiencenortherncape.com/corporate/pages/our-brand-pillars

Ottawa Tourism and Convention Authority (2022) "Welcome to Canada in One City," https://otta-watourism.ca/en/canadainonecity

Philippine Information Agency (2022) "DOT Launches 'Colors of Mindanao' Campaign," May 7, https://pia.gov.ph/news/2022/05/07/dot-launches-colors-of-mindanao-campaign

Philippine Department of Tourism (2018) "Introducing the Philippines," https://itsmorefuninthephilippines.co.uk/

Presentations.gov.in (2022) "Incredible!ndia," https://presentations.gov.in/logos/incredible-india-eng/

Ritchie, J. R. B., and Ritchie, R. J. B. (1998) "The Branding of Tourism Destinations: Past Achievements and Future Challenges," Annual Congress of the International Association of Scientific Experts in Tourism, Marrakech, Morocco.

São Paulo Turismo (2021) "São Paulo Brand Book," https://dorve.com/wp-content/uploads/2021/05/BRANDBOOK-SAO-PAULO.pdf

Singapore Tourism Board (2022) "About Passion Made Possible," www.visitsingapore.com/about-passion-made-possible/

Singh, H. (2017) "Travel Alberta Takes a Breath of Fresh Content," Strategy, October 4, http://strategyonline.ca/2017/10/04/travel-alberta-takes-a-breath-of-fresh-content/

Slovenia Times (2010) "The Relay Race of Destination Branding," November 5.

Surovek Gallery (2022) "Joan Miró: The Power of the Sol de Miró," https://surovekgallery.com/joan-miro/

Switzerland Tourism (2021) "Swisstainable," www.stnet.ch/app/uploads/2021/02/Swisstainable_Strategie_E.pdf

Tourism and Events Queensland (2022) "Queensland Brand Playbook," https://teq.queensland.com/content/dam/teq/corporate/corporate-searchable-assets/industry/what-we-do/marketing/Brandplaybook.pdf

Tourism Calgary (2019) "Living the Brand Workshop, Winter and Spring 2019," www.visitcalgary.com/sites/default/files/2020-11/Living_the_%20Brand_%20_Workshop_%20Presentation_%20and_%20Activities%20%281%29.pdf

Tourism Malaysia (2021) "Malaysia Truly Asia," www.tourism.gov.my/campaigns/view/malaysia-truly-asia

Tourism Northern Ireland (2022) "Embrace a giant spirit," https://www.tourismni.com/business-guidance/sector/mice-travel-trade/mice-and-travel-trade-trends-and-opportunities/northern-ireland---embrace-a-giant-spirit/

Uganda Tourism Board (2022) "A New Dawn for Uganda's Tourism As a New Destination Brand Is Launched," https://utb.go.ug/press-releases/new-dawn-uganda%E2%80%99s-tourism-new-destination-brand-launched

Vanilla Islands (2022) "Vanilla Islands of Indian Ocean," www.vanilla-islands.org/en/

Vienna Tourism (2018) "New Brand Identity for Vienna as a Tourist Destination: Now. Forever," https://b2b.wien.info/en/press-media-services/new-brand#Brand-Manual

Virginia Tourism Corporation (2022) "Virginia Is for Lovers," www.virginia.org/plan-your-trip/virginia-is-for-lovers/

Visit Greenland (2019) "The Brand of Greenland," https://traveltrade.visitgreenland.com/the-brand-of-greenland/#top

Visit Rwanda (2022) "Partnerships," www.visitrwanda.com/

World Economic Forum (2017) "Incredible!ndia 2.0: India's $20 Billion Tourism Opportunity," www3.weforum.org/docs/White_Paper_Incredible_India_2_0_final_.pdf

Chapter 14

Destination Integrated Marketing Communications

Communicating

DOI: 10.4324/9781003343356-17

9. review the concept of theme and event years as a basis for DMO IMC;

10. discuss the steps involved in the planning, implementation, and evaluation of an IMC campaign.

Warming Up

Marketing, branding, and communications represent one of the eight roles of destination management as you learned about in Chapter 1. Chapter 12 provided an in-depth description of destination marketing planning and briefly touched upon IMC; Chapter 13 reviewed destination PIB and also mentioned IMC. Chapters 14 and 15 elaborate on destination IMC and explain its components. Promotion, one of the eight Ps in the marketing mix, is a traditional activity of DMOs, with most organizations historically putting the greatest emphasis on advertising and sales (personal selling). Public relations and publicity, sales promotion, and merchandising are the three other traditional components.

DMOs are now making heavy use of ICTs in e-marketing. Sometimes also referred to as digital, online, or interactive marketing, these technologies include websites, email, social media, blogging and vlogging, mobile phones and smartphones, AR and VR, artificial intelligence, and several others. E-marketing is covered in detail in Chapter 15.

A definition of IMC is provided, and the six major IMC components are explained. The roles and functions of each IMC component are described, and how their effectiveness is measured. The chapter also reviews some overall specific approaches for destination marketing and IMC, including crowdsourcing, films and movies, and theme and event years.

Your author has had great experiences in designing IMC campaigns and enjoys the creative challenges involved. He would be the first person to tell you that not all destination IMC is great; that would cover up the many mistakes that are made. Just as you learned about destination brands, IMC campaigns also often get publicly criticized by media people, politicians, and ordinary citizens. Criticism is usually accompanied by quotes about the high costs of IMC campaigns. You will hear about several negative cases and criticisms of IMC in Chapter 14.

EXAMPLE 14.1

Campaign Draws Sharp Criticism

IMC campaigns are intended to be widely viewed and read. With this amount of openness, inevitably they can receive a mixture of praise and criticism. This example from Fiji shows a quote from a media company (*Skift*) article that is highly critical of the DMO's campaign, arguing that it has colonialist overtones and does not adequately show the local people and their culture.

> What happens when an all-white leadership team—tourism board, ad agency, production company and actress—comes together to design the tourism marketing campaign for an Indigenous archipelago?
>   You get Fiji's new "Open for Happiness" video—a shocking visual display of colonial tropes, in a narrative that centers the needs of the privileged tourist,

portrays the country's host communities and culture as a mere backdrop, and sells the stereotype of a "happy Indigenous" brown island as "paradise."

(Girma 2021)

Learning Point

Advertising and other IMC efforts should be carefully pretested, not only with the potential audience but also with local residents of the destination.

Definition of Integrated Marketing Communications

The concept of IMC was briefly discussed in Chapter 12. The basic idea behind IMC is that DMO promotions are types of communications and it is essential that DMOs integrate all types, making sure that they are consistent.

> **DEFINITION**
>
> **Integrated marketing communications**
>
> Integrated marketing communications, or IMC, is the coordination and integration of all of a DMO's external communications and promotions to increase their effectiveness and consistency. This is much superior to using each IMC component separately and independently.

Components of Integrated Marketing Communications

IMC for DMOs has six major components (Fig. 14.1).

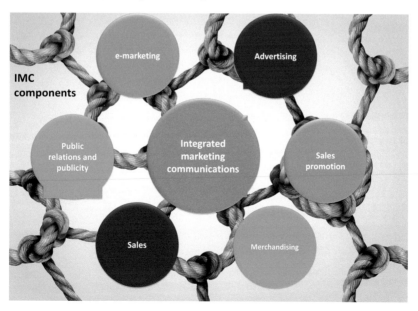

Figure 14.1 Components of integrated marketing communication.

Definitions of these six components are provided below:

> ### DEFINITIONS
>
> #### e-marketing
>
> The use of digital-format ICTs to liaise with various audiences, to provide information, and to promote destinations.
>
> #### Advertising
>
> The placement of persuasive messages by a DMO in any of the mass media or other venues to remind, inform, or persuade potential pleasure travelers, business event planners, travel trade companies, and others to consider the destination for future trips.
>
> #### Sales
>
> Sales or personal selling involves communications between DMO sales staff and prospective customers (prospects). These communications can be face-to-face, by telephone, short messaging services (SMS), email or messaging and virtual meeting program (e.g., Zoom, MS Teams, Skype, WhatsApp, WeChat, Line), or through other online services.
>
> #### Public relations and publicity
>
> All programs and activities that a DMO initiates or participates in with the purpose of maintaining or improving its relationship with other organizations and individuals, externally and internally. Publicity is a PR technique involving non-paid communications of information about destinations or DMOs.
>
> #### Sales promotion
>
> Approaches used by DMOs to give short-term inducements for people to visit and special communication methods and techniques not included in other promotional components.
>
> #### Merchandising
>
> Retail merchandising materials and point-of-purchase advertising done by DMOs in places such as VICs, transportation terminals, attractions, and accommodations.

Benefits of Integrated Marketing Communications

DMOs that follow the IMC approach realize significant benefits, and six of the most important of these benefits are as follows:

1. Greater consistency in communication messages.
2. Added impact because messages are repeated.
3. Reflects different customer buying-process stages.

4. More effectively puts across positioning and branding approaches.
5. Better accommodates different consumer learning styles.
6. Components complement and support each other.

Greater Consistency in Communication Messages

Greater consistency in DMO communications is the major benefit from using IMC. You heard about how the Netherlands always uses orange in Chapter 13. Switzerland also consistently uses one color, red, in its communications and always features that distinctive cross that is also on its national flag. In 2022, Switzerland Tourism launched the "Follow Roger Federer around Switzerland" campaign. There was plenty of red used in that IMC campaign as the tennis great toured around his home country.

EXAMPLE 14.2

Switzerland Tourism and Roger Federer

This is a technique called a celebrity testimonial, here in the person of tennis great, Roger Federer, whose homeland is Switzerland.

> Just as it is with the Grand Slam in tennis, so it is with the Grand Tour of Switzerland—exceptional. At more than 1,000 miles in length, this unique route encompasses all of Switzerland's most enthralling highlights—deep blue lakes, majestic mountains, vibrant cities and picturesque villages. Roger Federer is our guide for this remarkable road trip, presenting his own personal favorite route sections.
>
> (Switzerland Tourism 2022)

Learning Point

Testimonials from famous people, including sporting legends, create greater curiosity about destinations and drive additional visits.

Added Impact Because Messages Are Repeated

One message from a DMO may not get to the intended receiver. However, if the same or a similar message is passed through multiple channels, there is a much greater probability that it will get to the target successfully. More importantly, if the receiver gets the same message from multiple channels, the messages reinforce each other and are more effective collectively. The repetition of the DMO's messages makes it likelier that they will be recalled and remembered by individual people.

Reflects Different Customer Buying-Process Stages

You will learn later about consumer buying-process stages in Chapter 16. One of the most accepted of these buying-stage models has seven sequences: need recognition, information search, pre-purchase evaluation, purchase, consumption, evaluation, and remembering and sharing. Past research has shown that different IMC elements work better at specific buying-process stages; for example, advertising is more influential in the need recognition stage, but sales and sales promotion are more powerful at the purchase stage. Because the DMO's audience will have people spread across all the buying-process stages, it is better for the DMO to be simultaneously using all the IMC components and not just one of them.

More Effectively Puts Across Positioning and Branding Approaches

Using all IMC components in a consistent way more convincingly communicates the destination's chosen positioning and branding approaches. Each component has individual advantages for expressing images and branding. Some are highly visual, including videos, advertising, social media and websites, and so they are good at visually communicating these concepts. PR and publicity and sales rely more on words and text, and so they convey more in-depth explanations about the image and branding of destinations.

EXAMPLE 14.3

Western Australia's Walking on a Dream Campaign

This is a great example of a multi-component IMC program to support a new campaign. You must see the great video that is part of this campaign.

> The Walking on a Dream campaign showcases the state's natural tourism attractions, following local performers Rika Hamaguchi and Ian Wilkes, on a dreamlike journey as they interact with the magical and wonderous locations.
> The ad features a reimagined version of electronic band Empire of the Sun's hit song, "Walking on a Dream." Brimming with magic, special effects and a dreamlike storyline, the aim is to promote Western Australia as a unique holiday destination within the fiercely competitive global travel marketplace.
> The $15 million campaign, which includes TV, print, radio, digital and social activity, will underpin the brand's marketing activities for the next five years. It is supported by WA Government's $195 million Reconnect WA package, which aims to boost visitor numbers, infrastructure and jobs in tourism and related sectors.
>
> (Long 2022)

Learning Point

A dramatic campaign like Walking on a Dream needs to appeal to all the senses at an emotional level. Visual and auditory IMC components are essential in these communications.

Better Accommodates Different Consumer Learning Styles

Different people have unique learning styles. Some people learn best by reading text on printed materials or online. Others find it easier to absorb facts and knowledge by listening to people speaking. Still others prefer to see visuals to make their learning more effective. The IMC components vary in their use of text, visuals and spoken narratives, and so when used together by the DMO, they will accommodate all different consumer learning styles.

Components Complement and Support Each Other

Each IMC component has its unique strengths and weaknesses. For example, advertising is not particularly good at closing the sale, which means getting the customer to make the purchase. However, sales and sales promotions tend to be much more effective in convincing people to make buying decisions. The weakness of one IMC component (advertising) is compensated for by using other IMC components (sales or sales promotions)—they are complementary.

The impact of this IMC can be extended even further into what is called viral marketing. With viral marketing the original message is spread even further by other people. During 2014, a video appeared with the title of I Hate Thailand, and with that name, everyone thought it surely could not have been produced by a DMO.

EXAMPLE 14.4

Reverse Psychology and Viral Marketing: I Hate Thailand

Watched 4.7 million times on YouTube since its uploading in 2014, this is about a British tourist, James, who loses all his money on a first trip to Thailand. He makes good friends, finds his wallet was stolen by monkeys, and ends up staying in Thailand. What a great story! Later the Tourism Authority of Thailand (2015) took credit for the video, and it went on to win several marketing awards.

> It's been a bad year for tourism in Thailand, and at first glance it looked like a new YouTube video was adding to the misery. The video called I Hate Thailand drew more than one million views within days of being posted.
>
> It comes after the country's image was battered by a military coup in May and the brutal murders of two British tourists on an idyllic beach on the island of Koh Tao in September.
>
> (Hutchinson 2014; Tourism Authority of Thailand 2015)

Learning Point

This is an example of doing the unexpected with IMC. Some might call it guerrilla marketing, while it certainly was an effort that went viral. The approach taken by Nebraska and discussed in Chapter 13 is another example of a DMO doing something that was quite unexpected.

DEFINITIONS

Guerrilla marketing

Guerrilla marketing is doing something unconventional or unexpected, and normally it involves an IMC approach or activity not usually practiced by competitors. Originally, it was thought of as being a low-cost activity producing high revenue and profit levels.

Viral marketing

A technique in which consumers are asked or encouraged to share information on a destination on social media channels. In other words, the information is spread online.

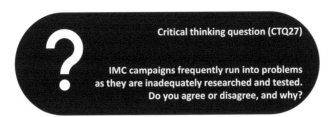

Critical thinking question (CTQ27)

IMC campaigns frequently run into problems as they are inadequately researched and tested. Do you agree or disagree, and why?

E-marketing

This section has been labeled as e-marketing, but it could have been called online or interactive marketing or given some other fancy name. Getting past the naming issue, what is really involved here is the DMO working with all forms of ICTs that use digital formats.

Chapter 15 reviews these channels and techniques in detail and highlights the strategic importance of DMO websites and social media as platforms for connecting with other ICTs. e-marketing has definitely become much more critical for the overall success of destination marketing, branding, and communications. Here is a very brief overview of the items in Figure 14.2.

WEBSITES

Websites are now unquestionably the principal communications platform for most DMOs along with social media. Many DMOs have websites in multiple languages as well as sites designed for specific audiences, for example, consumer and corporate sites.

EMAIL

Email does not get the same attention as social media and websites, but it is essential for online communications and is also a marketing and communications channel. It is used by salespersons in DMOs and also to respond to people who request information either via email or on DMO social media and websites. In addition, sometimes, DMOs conduct IMC campaigns solely using email.

SOCIAL MEDIA

The most popular of the social media platforms include Facebook, Instagram, TikTok, and YouTube, but there are hundreds of them. Most DMOs have established their own pages on the major social media platforms.

TRAVELER REVIEW SITES

Traveler review sites are websites in which travelers provide their comments on hotels, restaurants, attractions, destinations, and other travel-related offers. The most famous site is Tripadvisor.

BLOGGING AND VLOGGING

Web logs, or simply blogs, are a hobby for some and a profession for others (the influencers). DMOs study these blogs to get feedback about their destinations. Moreover, many DMOs are writing their own blogs and distributing them through their websites and social network platforms. Vlogs are videotaped versions of blogs.

SMARTPHONES

There are now billions of smartphones and mobile phones around the world, and these phones are becoming increasingly important for destination marketing, branding, and communications. Several DMOs have developed travel guides and other apps for smartphones that can be downloaded free of charge.

OTHER ICTS

These include augmented and virtual reality, GPS, geo-tagging, podcasts, smart cards, virtual visitor guides and brochures, Google Maps and Google Earth, e-book readers, wikis, and others.

ONLINE ADVERTISING

Although not shown in Figure 14.2, online advertising does fit into e-marketing as well. It is discussed later and involves the use of banner/display advertising and keywords. Placements are made on search engines and social media platforms.

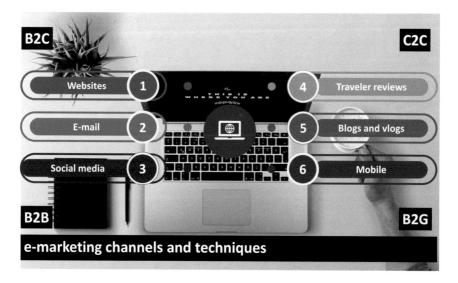

Figure 14.2 E-marketing channels and techniques. B2C: business-to-consumer; B2B: business-to-business; B2G: business-to-government; C2C: consumer-to-consumer.

EXAMPLE 14.5

If You Seek: New Zealand Tourism Campaign

This example reflects the power and flexibility of e-marketing in communicating New Zealand's 2022 campaign. It is much easier to have convincing storytelling online with vivid and emotion-stimulating videos and films.

Tourism New Zealand unveiled its first global campaign in two years—if you seek—the country's invitation to international visitors who seek more through extraordinary travel. Launched in core visitor markets such as Australia and the USA, IF YOU SEEK invites audiences to explore Aotearoa New Zealand via unexpected and alluring glimpses of the destination's people and places.

"There is intense competition as destinations compete to capture the imaginations of travelers. Because of our size and location, New Zealand will have to work hard to encourage visitation post-COVID with international visitor numbers taking years to build up and Kiwis now having the option of traveling overseas," Tourism New Zealand CEO René de Monchy said.

A suite of eighteen short films showcases New Zealand's distinct local culture, generosity and famed natural beauty—suggesting Aotearoa New Zealand is reserved for the inquisitive traveler, in quest of authenticity and discovery.

In accompaniment to the eighteen videos, a 60" manifesto film further summons seekers to explore Aotearoa New Zealand with numerous cutdowns and iterations to make IF YOU SEEK accessible across paid, owned, earned and trade channels. An immersive digital experience extends the campaign through Tourism New Zealand's owned environment IF YOU SEEK mini experiences, providing viewers with more to seek and entice them to book.

(McKay 2022)

Learning Point

Destination marketing campaigns are seldom one-dimensional today. This campaign although mainly communicated online is backed by public relations and advertising to announce its launch.

There has been a very strong trend toward DMOs placing greater emphasis on e-marketing in recent years and correspondingly making less use of some of the traditional IMC components. For example, Destinations International (2018) found that DMOs allocated 40 percent to online and 60 percent to offline communications in 2017 and that online share is higher now. This is a trend that is sweeping through most DMOs, and was accelerated due to staffing challenges during the COVID-19 pandemic. It is likely that DMOs will be devoting more than 50 percent of their communication budgets to e-marketing.

Another indicator of this trend is the many DMOs now with their own departments, units and staff looking after their website and social media site maintenance and communications and other digital marketing efforts. This is a clear sign of the growing importance of digital marketing for DMOs. For example, Destination DC in the USA has a Social Media Manager, Content Manager, Digital Content Manager, Content Specialist, and Videographer (Destination DC 2022).

Measuring the Effectiveness of E-marketing

Generally, e-marketing is one of the most measurable of the IMC components because ICTs maintain a footprint of interactions. Figure 14.3 identifies some of the performance metrics (measures) that can be applied to the main e-marketing channels and techniques. For example, log-file analyzer programs can be used to track and analyze all the traffic to DMOs' websites, providing data on numbers of users, favorite pages, time spent on each page and on the website in total, and many other useful statistics. Additionally, all the major social media platforms maintain their own special sets of statistics, and so it is easy to measure their traffic.

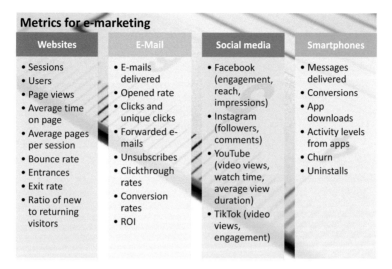

Metrics for e-marketing

Websites	E-Mail	Social media	Smartphones
• Sessions • Users • Page views • Average time on page • Average pages per session • Bounce rate • Entrances • Exit rate • Ratio of new to returning visitors	• E-mails delivered • Opened rate • Clicks and unique clicks • Forwarded e-mails • Unsubscribes • Clickthrough rates • Conversion rates • ROI	• Facebook (engagement, reach, impressions) • Instagram (followers, comments) • YouTube (video views, watch time, average view duration) • TikTok (video views, engagement)	• Messages delivered • Conversions • App downloads • Activity levels from apps • Churn • Uninstalls

Figure 14.3 Metrics for e-marketing.

EXAMPLE 14.6

Co-op E-marketing as a Path to Destination Recovery

It is simpler to cooperate in e-marketing than in traditional ways. This example recommends that DMOs engage more in co-op e-marketing.

> But even at a time of great difficulty for destination marketing, solutions are starting to emerge. One of the most promising strategies for destinations looking to engage travelers during this unprecedented period is a strategy called co-op marketing. Using co-op marketing destinations pool marketing budgets and messaging with local tourism partners, helping them to more easily scale marketing campaigns, help resource-constrained tourism businesses tap into larger marketing efforts, and offer new opportunities to more easily experiment with campaign messaging, communication channels, and engagement tactics.
>
> Best of all, today's digital-first co-op marketing strategies represent a dramatic step forward for destinations and their partners. Even though co-op marketing has existing for many years, today's digitally driven co-op platforms help provide real-time performance data to partners, allow detailed customization of campaign goals for each partner, and make it easier for destinations to oversee campaign strategy to ensure consistency.
>
> (Skift and Sojern 2020)

Learning Point

It should be easier for destinations and DMOs to form partnerships online through e-marketing campaigns.

Advertising

The advertising of destinations has existed for decades and remains a major component of many DMOs' IMC campaigns. Destination advertising tends to be quite expensive, and for some DMOs, it occupies a significant share of the total IMC budget. It is difficult (and can be misleading) to quote statistics about how much DMOs spend on advertising as the amounts vary so much across the globe and by size of the organizations. You will see some figures for specific campaigns mentioned in this chapter (e.g., AUD15 million for Western Australia's campaign). London was reported to be spending £6 million on a domestic advertising campaign in 2021 (Choat 2021). The LVCVA reported advertising expenditures of $52 million in 2021 (much lower than in 2019 and 2020) (LVCVA 2021: 9). At the national level, Tourism Australia (2022a) in 2020/21 devoted 58.3 percent (AUD 89.7 million) of its total supplier expenses of AUD 154 million to advertising; 23.5 percent was spent on employees. Brand USA reported spending $14.3 million on advertising and media in 2021 (Brand USA 2022: 41). Although these figures can in no way be taken as representative of all DMOs in the world, they demonstrate that destination advertising expenditures are significant.

Importance of Advertising for Destinations

How important is advertising to tourism destinations? This is a difficult question to answer because there is some variation in importance according to different destinations. The variation is impacted partly by the TALC, of which you learned about in Chapters 7 and 12. For example, advertising can be instrumental in building destination awareness in the early stages of the TALC and, again, be crucial in more mature destinations that are facing intense competition. In the intermediate stages, advertising may not be as important as other IMC components.

Some people have argued that advertising a destination is not that effective in bringing people in and that advertising budgets can be cut and nothing much will happen. However, the case of Colorado in the USA provides evidence of what transpires when a DMO completely stops IMC. This case is carefully documented by Dr. Bill Siegel, CEO of Longwoods International of Toronto, Canada (2011). The Government of Colorado made the unprecedented decision in 1993 to stop advertising state tourism; this later resulted in a significant plunge in tourist arrivals and expenditures. Colorado is a well-established and popular tourism destination and is beautiful with much to offer tourists. It is not a new destination and is more toward the mature stages of the TALC. Some might say, therefore, that Colorado does not need to heavily advertise itself for tourism. Based on this actual experience, however, this was not the case, and a cessation of destination advertising corresponded with a significant decline in tourism.

Roles of Advertising

Destination advertising plays three major roles for DMOs:

1. Informing
2. Persuading
3. Reminding.

INFORMING

Informing is the very basic value level of destination advertising in making markets aware of destinations and their tourism products. New and emerging destinations tend to suffer from a lack of market awareness, and advertising, especially in the traditional mass media and online, is how to get their messages out to thousands or even millions of people.

PERSUADING

When destinations are mature and facing close substitutes, they must be more concerned that advertising is persuading. Many destinations around the globe find themselves in this situation now particularly as a result of COVID-19, and the creativity in their advertisements is at a premium.

EXAMPLE 14.7

Creative Destination Advertising by Madhya Pradesh

Creative approaches to advertising get people's attention and are remembered. One video produced by the Madhya Pradesh Tourism Board in India is bursting with creativity, yet it features no human actors (and is not in English). Rather, it uses toys as the characters and sets. With the title of MP Mein Dil Hua Bache Sa, the one-minute video has 5.8 million views on YouTube (in March 2023).

> Relive the fun, carefree times of childhood in Madhya Pradesh! Shape-shifting marble mountains to ship-like historic monuments and a lot more, will make you too sing MP Mein Dil Hua Bache Sa. Madhya Pradesh triggers your curiosity, enthusiasm and sense of wonder. From marble crocodiles to monuments from outer space, it has a lot to bring out the child within you! The film uses customized toys made out of tin and painted in the MP art form (Gondha) to showcase different locations, culture, people, dresses, wildlife, textile, womenfolk, markets, marble mountains, forts, and religion. It uses a cot with a rotating dice on it which includes pictures of different places of the state.
>
> (Campaigns of the World 2016)

Learning Point

Although you may not speak the language of this video ad, its creativity is obvious and draws your attention to Madhya Pradesh and its tourism attractions. The ad was done by Ogilvy and Mather.

REMINDING

For some audiences, DMOs need to do advertising as a reminder of the destination, and typically, this means the advertising is toward people who have already visited. It is frequently used in domestic tourism marketing campaigns where the audience is already quite familiar with the destinations, and reminding people can be effective.

EXAMPLE 14.8

Scotland Is Calling

Sometimes DMOs need to remind potential visitors about how special their destinations are. This became even more crucial post-COVID. In this example, VisitScotland reminds people about the uniqueness of the nation.

> We've launched a global marketing campaign to keep Scotland front of mind for potential visitors as they make their future travel plans. Scotland is Calling is aimed specifically at overseas visitors who, research suggests, spend longer planning and researching their trips. It will form a strategically timed global rollout to key markets—critical to helping to build back Scottish tourism sustainably—to support the long-term recovery of the country's tourism and events industry from the impacts of COVID-19 and subsequent restrictions.
>
> In 2019, prior to the pandemic, Scotland welcomed 3.5 million international visitors who generated 43 percent of the total tourism spend that year. Re-engaging with international visitors now aims to benefit Scotland against competitor destinations.
>
> Scotland is Calling will also be rolled out across the UK to support the domestic market recovery and extend the visitor season through autumn and winter. The campaign aims to appeal to the hearts and minds of future visitors, inviting them to enjoy Scotland's world-class food and drink, events, film and culture. Targeted consumer content will feature on digital channels, social media and through publishing partnerships. We'll also engage with travel media through educational activity to help industry develop sustainable and responsible travel itineraries.
>
> The £6.5 million marketing campaign, coupled with the £1.5 million fund, supports Scotland's brand positioning as a welcoming, inclusive and progressive nation with content telling Scotland's story as a responsible destination where you can slow down, recharge, escape and enjoy immersive and sustainable tourism experiences.
>
> (VisitScotland 2021)

Learning Point

IMC is not a one-time effort; audiences need to be continuously reminded about destinations and their unique offerings.

Advertising tends to be one of the more expensive of the IMC components along with sales where a sales staff must be maintained. Just one quick cost example will prove this point for you. The 2022 national rates for *Travel + Leisure* magazine had a rate base of 950,000; this means that *Travel + Leisure* guarantees that the circulation of the magazine will be 950,000 copies. If a DMO decided to place a four-color ad just once in the *Travel + Leisure* print magazine version, the 2022 rate was $192,200 (*Travel + Leisure* 2022). *Travel + Leisure* also has digital and tablet versions of its publications.

Advertising Media Alternatives

DMOs are faced with a choice of several advertising media alternatives and must weigh up their costs and relative advantages. These include television, radio, magazines, newspapers, and outdoor and transit, and online advertising. Advertising of destinations tends to work best in color rather than black and white, and it is better if the ads are large rather than small. Magazines are therefore a favored place for destination advertising because of their quality and because they tend to be read in a relaxed way. Outdoor and transit advertising are also very popular because of the large size and potential visual impact along with their ability to be viewed by commuters and other passing traffic. The introduction of smartphones and tablets, especially iPads, has provided an exciting set of new advertising opportunities for traditional magazine publishers as well as for distributing the traditional destination printed visitor guides. In addition, magazine publishers, such as *Travel + Leisure*, have social media sites and allow DMOs to advertise in channels such as Facebook, Twitter, Instagram, and Pinterest.

The other favorite is television advertising, which adds so many more dimensions to the still advertisements placed in magazines and on outdoor and transit venues. Good examples here are the advertising done by Egypt and Saudi Arabia in 2021 and 2022. Saudi Arabia's Welcome to Saudi Arabia ad shows many beautiful destinations in the kingdom, while Egypt's Follow the Sun encourages cold-weather dwellers to enjoy its sunshine (Best Destination 2021; *Daily News Egypt* 2022; Experience Egypt 2022).

Recently, DMOs have been doing much more online advertising to catch the attention of the ever-expanding number of Internet users around the world. There are several formats for this type of online advertising, including display or banner advertising and using keywords in search engines and paying on a pay-per-click (PPC) basis. Google AdWords is one of the most popular PPC options (Google 2022).

Banner advertisements are ads that are embedded on website pages, and they are often animated to draw the user's attention. When the page is opened and the ad appears, this is called an impression, which means the ad is potentially viewed. If the user clicks on the ad, that is called a click-through. The other option is to use keywords, for example, on major search engines. For example, on Google's AdWords are keywords chosen by advertisers. When users of the search engine enter one of the advertiser's keywords, their AdWords will appear at the top of the list of search results.

Online advertising is a part of e-marketing, which is discussed later in this chapter as well as in the next chapter. DMOs are increasingly allocating more of their budgets to e-marketing. One of the major advantages of e-marketing, including online advertising, is the measurability of its results, and measuring advertising effectiveness is the next topic for discussion.

Measuring the Effectiveness of Advertising

Measuring advertising effectiveness has traditionally presented challenges to marketers. In the past, some DMOs have claimed that all the tourists came to their destination as a result of the DMO's advertising and other IMC. This is a dangerous claim for a DMO to make and quite unrealistic as well. The leading professional associations of DMOs, including Destinations International, strongly warn against such exaggerated claims.

A Strong Caution from Destinations International

There is nothing wrong with a DMO reporting on visitor volumes and spending. However, it is dangerous if the DMO implies that these outcomes were solely as a result of its efforts (and no one else's).

> The ultimate measure of marketing productivity is the number of individuals whose visit to the destination was clearly and significantly generated by the DMO's marketing efforts. DMOs are strongly cautioned against using their destination's total number of visitors as it is extremely unlikely that the DMO generated each and every visitor to its destination.
>
> (Destinations International 2012: 29)

Learning Point

It is better for a DMO to share the credit for success among all its shareholders.

Your author has also cautioned against DMOs taking too much of the credit for visitor volumes and expenditures in a blog on LinkedIn (Fig. 14.4). His main point, as detailed subsequently, is that there can be a significant proportion of visitors who are not influenced by DMO IMC programs.

A DMO should never take all the credit for the number of
visitors and their spending in the destination!

Figure 14.4 A warning for DMOs.

Statistics Can Hide the Real Facts

DMOs should realize that there are visitors to their communities who are there for reasons other than seeing the destination's IMC programs. Statistics should be carefully checked to separate out those visitors that the DMO may have influenced.

It is naïve for DMOs to think that their marketing and promotions generate all or a major portion of visitor demand. There is so much complexity in how people select destinations these days, and multiple influencing factors within and outside of tourism.

Hidden among those visitor statistics may be a significant proportion of business travel that is not in any way associated with or affected by the DMO's marketing and promotions. Of course, DMOs are heavily involved in pursuing business (MICE) events, but there's usually much more to business travel than these affairs.

(Morrison 2016)

Learning Point

Not all visitors to destinations arrive as a result of DMO communications programs.

One of the traditional methods for measuring advertising effectiveness was to conduct conversion studies. These studies were used for direct-response advertising campaigns in which people were asked to telephone a certain number, mail in a request for more information or click on a link online. Samples of people who responded were drawn, and the researchers determined what percentages of those who inquired went to the destination later. This percentage was called the conversion rate on the advertising. Undoubtedly, this is a useful advertising effectiveness research technique and has been widely applied by DMOs, but it has a major flaw. It tends to overestimate the number of tourists who come due to advertising because some people have already decided to visit before seeing the advertisements. Another type of research on advertising is called advertising tracking and is done by market research companies while the advertising campaign is underway.

Sales (Personal Selling)

Personal selling or sales is very important for certain DMOs, especially those that have a strong focus on attracting business events. This is certainly the case in the USA where most of the DMOs are called convention and visitors bureaus, with the word convention coming first, which indicates that business events are their topmost priority.

Roles of Sales (Personal Selling)

Personal selling by DMOs plays several distinct roles:

- Communicating with travel trade, associations, corporations, and other groups: Some communications in tourism need a personal touch and require more direct contact with potential clients. This is certainly so for industrial (B2B) buying, where people are making large purchases on behalf of an association, company or other group.
- Providing detailed and up-to-date information to event planners and travel trade: It is important to keep business event planners and travel trade companies updated on new developments in the destination. This is the case at travel shows and exhibitions where sales persons dispense much detailed information at their booths.
- Maintaining a personal relationship with key clients: Sales is very much about one-to-one relationships between salespersons and their clients and prospects. Making sales calls on clients and keeping in touch with them in other ways maintain these important personal relationships.

- Identifying decision-makers, decision processes and qualified buyers: Part of the sales activity is called prospecting, which means finding and qualifying organizations and people who can buy.
- Gathering information on competitors: Sales team members often gather information on competitive destinations through their communications with clients and prospects.

An example of a DMO sales organization is the Houston First Corporation (HFC) in Texas in the USA. The Visit Houston (2022) website of HFC indicates that it has nineteen sales staff. So, there is a significant investment in sales at this DMO, including a senior vice president of sales.

Typically, DMOs that have sales departments divide up staff according to geographic territories and, sometimes, also by type or size of business event. Special training is required for this type of work in DMOs, and sales management approaches are applied. For example, the senior sales executive will develop a sales plan for each year with the input of all the sales team. Team members may be assigned sales quotas based on this plan. Given the relatively high costs of maintaining sales teams and support for their sales efforts, the measurement of sales performance is critical for DMOs. The following materials discuss the types of performance reporting approaches that can be used.

Measuring the Effectiveness of Sales

The results of sales activities are more easily tracked than advertising and can more directly be attributed to the work of DMOs and their sales staff teams. Figure 14.5 shows Destinations

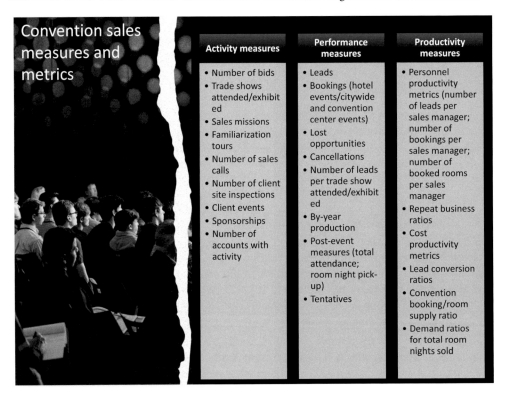

Convention sales measures and metrics	Activity measures	Performance measures	Productivity measures
	• Number of bids • Trade shows attended/exhibited • Sales missions • Familiarization tours • Number of sales calls • Number of client site inspections • Client events • Sponsorships • Number of accounts with activity	• Leads • Bookings (hotel events/citywide and convention center events) • Lost opportunities • Cancellations • Number of leads per trade show attended/exhibited • By-year production • Post-event measures (total attendance; room night pick-up) • Tentatives	• Personnel productivity metrics (number of leads per sales manager; number of bookings per sales manager; number of booked rooms per sales manager • Repeat business ratios • Cost productivity metrics • Lead conversion ratios • Convention booking/room supply ratio • Demand ratios for total room nights sold

Figure 14.5 Activity measures, performance measures and productivity metrics for DMO convention sales (Destinations International 2012: 7–12).

International's (2012) recommendations for measuring the effectiveness of DMO sales efforts aimed at generating conventions (business events), consisting of activity measures, productivity measures, and performance measures. As you can see, sales performance is primarily measured by leads (prospective conventions for the destination) and bookings (actual conventions held in the destination). Destinations International also recommends travel trade sales performance reporting procedures that include activity measures, performance measures and productivity metrics. In the case of travel trade sales, the performance measures are expressed in only leads and bookings.

Public Relations and Publicity

You already know about some aspects of a DMO's public relations efforts from the discussion of stakeholder and community relationships and involvement in Chapter 9. It is crucial for DMOs to maintain and enhance these at-home connections with local residents, the tourism sector and other stakeholders.

EXAMPLE 14.11

Seychelles Unveils Refreshed Branding at Ceremony

You learned in Chapter 13 about the need to periodically refresh long-running destination brands. This is an example of a public relations event in which Tourism Seychelles revealed their refreshed brand.

> Seychelles' tourism industry players were shown on Wednesday the archipelago's "modernized" brand with newly infused "energy," in a bid to remain on the same level with competitors in the field. The refreshed logo still maintains elements of the initial shape representative of important Seychelles icons, from palm trees and flowers to endemic birds like the Paradise Flycatcher and the Tropicbird—but with a modern twist.
> The facelift to Seychelles as a tourism destination cost the western Indian Ocean island state £30,000 ($34,469) or SCR 452,000. The Union—a company based in Glasgow, Scotland, which initially worked on the complete rebranding of the Seychelles islands' marketing sixteen years ago—was chosen to carry out the tweaks on the new logo.
>
> (Seychelles News Agency 2022)

Learning Point

Public events such as this create greater awareness and build excitement for new marketing and branding initiatives.

Roles of Public Relations and Publicity

PR and publicity serve three major roles for a DMO:

1. Maintaining a positive public presence: The DMO wants to ensure that the destination has a positive image externally and within the destination as well. This component is called

public relations because the DMO has several publics with whom it interacts. Figure 14.6 identifies the internal publics and external publics with which DMOs must maintain positive relationships.

2. Enhancing effectiveness of other IMC components: Getting publicity enhances and extends the effects of other IMC components. For example, the It's more fun in the Philippines attracted significant media attention, and this has augmented the positive impacts of IMC.

3. Handling negative publicity: A destination can receive negative publicity for several reasons, including natural disasters, acts of terrorism, or outbreaks of serious illnesses. You heard earlier in the chapter about the criticisms of destination marketing in Fiji. The DMO must handle these situations tactfully and in the best interests of the destination.

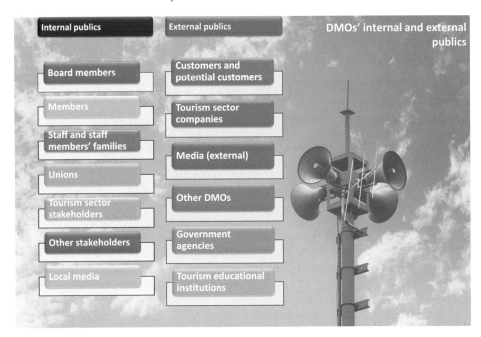

Figure 14.6 DMOs' internal and external publics.

EXAMPLE 14.12

DMO Marketing Gets Criticized

This is an example in which a DMO attracted negative publicity after an official government audit. While the DMO has to deal with the adverse news in the press, it must also make improvements in its marketing, branding, and communications practices.

> The Controller and Auditor General report has revealed the Tanzania Tourist Board weaknesses in promoting and marketing the country's tourism products. The weaknesses include slow adaptation of technological changes, failure to effectively harness regional market and potentials as well as inadequate capacity to promote and market the products. Others are the shortage of promotion

and marketing tools and technology, lack of promotion and marketing destination experts, budgetary constraints and shortages of processing staff.

(The Citizen 2022)

Learning Point

DMOs are often open to public scrutiny and this may include critiques of how they conduct marketing, branding, and communications. They must be prepared to accept and deal with criticism.

The media relations portion of this IMC is particularly important because the media, or press, is the source of publicity. Here, the DMO may attend media tradeshows, organize media missions, conduct media familiarization tours, visit media contacts, prepare press releases, participate in media interviews, and handle media inquiries. Most DMOs prepare newsletters and public service announcements, and these are within public relations and publicity.

As Figure 14.6 shows, the internal publics are those within the DMO and the destination. The DMO has staff members, and it may also be partly unionized. Many DMOs have boards of directors, and some have membership programs. The stakeholders outside of the DMO include the tourism sector stakeholders, other stakeholders, and local media.

The external stakeholders are outside of the destination, and two of the most important ones are customers/potential customers and the media (press). Tourism sector companies include airlines, travel trade companies, hotel and resort companies, and others with connections to the destination. Other DMOs, including competitors, government agencies, and tourism educational institutions, are the remaining external publics.

As was mentioned in Chapter 12, DMOs in the past did not pay as much attention to their internal publics as they devoted to their external publics. This has changed drastically in recent times as DMOs have begun to develop a greater appreciation of the value of having solid support and backing within their destinations.

Measuring the Effectiveness of Public Relations and Publicity

Some of the outcomes of public relations are quite difficult to measure; however, there are traditional ways of measuring the publicity generated by a DMO for its destination. Usually, this is accomplished by measuring the placements or stories about the destination that result from the DMO's own public relations efforts or those initiated by the media. News in the form of press releases prepared by DMOs are commonly the major source of publicity coverage. DMOs track publicity by where it occurs (e.g., domestic vs. international) and in which media the stories appear (e.g., television, radio, newspaper, magazine, online, etc.).

In addition to counting the number of stories in the media, DMOs will estimate the number of impressions (e.g., the circulation of a magazine) and advertising equivalency value of these stories. DMOs may do the tracking of publicity coverage themselves or may outsource this to specialized companies that are typically called media clipping services. BurrellesLuce (2022) and Cision (2022) are two of the most famous of these companies in North America.

EXAMPLE 14.13

IMC for Troubled Places

You learned about destination crisis management in Chapter 11. It is hard enough to communicate about places that enjoy relative peaceful environments; however, what about destinations that are perceived as being troubled? In this example, a few of these destinations are mentioned.

Colombia:

While security measures have certainly boosted tourism, especially local tourism, it was also essential for the authorities to transform the image of a country, considered for decades as dangerous and inaccessible, and all the more so to attract international tourists. As highlighted in the UNWTO report "Colombia, back on the map of world tourism" (UNWTO 2009), the country was well known to the public at the time, and communications efforts had to focus more on correcting a distorted image rather than on the creation of an image.

(Guilland and Naef 2019)

Dominican Republic:

A slew of US tourists deaths have occurred under mysterious circumstances in the Dominican Republic in recent weeks. Three occurred in May at the same chain of resorts, the Bahia Principe, within days of each other. Another two occurred at the Hard Rock Hotel and Casino in Punta Cana months apart. A sixth occurred in June 2018. The Ministry of Tourism has been quick to point out that the rate of tourist incidences in 2018 was just 1.4 in every 100,000 visitors. It added that it is committed to ensuring the "highest industry standards are met so that all tourists are safe when visiting".

(*Spinks* 2019)

Papua New Guinea (PNG):

This study found that key challenges for tourism growth in PNG are high crime rates, negative media publicity, systematic corruption and a lack of competition in the airline sector. Despite these challenges, PNG has tourism potential that can be developed and marketed to international and domestic tourists.

(Sumb 2020)

Learning Point

DMOs must acknowledge the challenges they face in troubled places and develop IMC campaigns that emphasize positive aspects of their destinations as well as correcting inaccurate and exaggerated media coverage.

Sales Promotion and Merchandising

Sales promotions and merchandising are often closely connected, and so they have been grouped together for this discussion. These techniques are generally used tactically, meaning that they are used in the short term for specific purposes, like attracting more tourists in the off-season.

Roles of Sales Promotion and Merchandising

Sales promotions and merchandising perform several specific roles for DMOs. These roles are not necessarily met by other IMC components. For example, sales promotion really means to promote sales, and that usually implies providing a short-term inducement to buy. The following are several specific roles of sales promotions and merchandising:

- Getting people to come to the destination for the first time: Inviting people to visit the destination for the very first time may be the goal of a sales promotion campaign. Offering some sort of incentive to the first-time visitor or having an invitation extended by a past visitor are two ways to achieve this.
- Increasing off-peak demand: Getting tourists to come at off-peak times is one of the most frequent applications of sales promotions. Often, this is done using discounted prices (price-offs) that are incorporated into packages.
- Increasing demand in periods that coincide with major events, vacations or special occasions: Another very popular time to introduce sales promotions is in the time periods leading up to major events, holidays and other special occasions.
- Encouraging travel trade intermediaries to make a special effort to sell the destination: Travel agencies and tour operators are very important sources of business for many destinations. Planners of business events are another highly influential group and especially for city tourism destinations.
- Helping sales staff get business from prospects: Some DMOs have sales staffs, and most of these are positioned to generate new demand from business events or travel trade companies. These sales staff are given a variety of audio-visual materials that help them in making sales, such as apps, videos, photo libraries, PowerPoint presentations, guides, and brochures.
- Facilitating travel trade intermediary marketing: DMOs provide materials to travel agencies, tour operators, business event planners, and other travel trade companies that help them with their marketing. These include posters, visitor guides and brochures, and videos.

Types of Sales Promotion and Merchandising

There are many types of sales promotion and merchandising techniques available to destination marketers. These fall into two main categories: special communication methods and special offers. Figure 14.7 identifies most of the techniques that fall into these two categories.

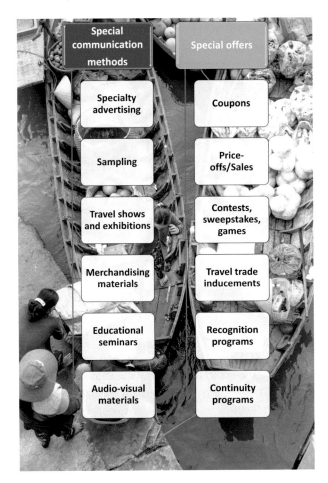

Figure 14.7 Sales promotion and merchandising techniques.

The following is a brief description of the techniques within these two categories of sales promotions and merchandising.

SPECIAL OFFERS

Some of these sales promotion techniques give tourists a value offer so that they will make a purchase in the short term, including coupons and price-offs, or sales. Contests, sweepstakes and games create excitement and encourage people to take immediate action. In 2022, New Brunswick, Canada ran a contest where the winners won free trips to the province.

EXAMPLE 14.14

New Brunswick Gone-Aways Contest

This is an example of a DMO using a sales promotion technique. The contest is aimed at the visiting friends and relatives travel market. This is an appropriate communications effort given the long separation of family and friends during the COVID-19 pandemic.

The government is offering up a five-day, four-night vacation for three of the winner's favorite "gone-aways" to come back home to "reconnect with them and New Brunswick."

According to the rules, entrants must live in New Brunswick and have a valid New Brunswick driver's license. The prize package includes three round-trip plane tickets from anywhere in Canada, car rental, hotels and meals. The services of a travel agent are also covered in order to help plan the whole trip, including activities.

(Urquhart 2022)

Learning Point

Contests are useful in motivating potential travelers to think about visiting certain destinations. They may encourage people to take action more quickly than they otherwise would have done.

TRAVEL TRADE INDUCEMENTS

These typically involve some type of commission paid to travel agencies or discounts offered on services and facilities within the destination.

RECOGNITION PROGRAMS

These are promotional approaches that recognize travel trade companies, other organizations or individual tourists for their past contributions or demonstrated interest level in destinations. An example of a type of recognition program is a combination of a special communication method and a special offer. The Aussie Specialist Program offered by Tourism Australia (2022b) is a very good example.

CONTINUITY PROGRAMS

These programs are sales promotions in which people must continue to make repeated purchases, sometimes over a long period of time. If they do not, their status levels within the programs will be lower. Frequent-flyer and frequent-guest programs are continuity recognition programs. There have not yet been many applications of continuity programs by DMOs.

SPECIAL COMMUNICATION METHODS

This is a sort of catch-all for methods that do not exactly fit into other IMC components, and it also includes all the merchandising techniques. As the name suggests, these are special ways to communicate with potential tourists, travel trade companies, and planners of business events. Within this category are several approaches that are commonly used by DMOs, including exhibiting at travel shows and exhibitions, arranging familiarization tours and site inspections, designing posters, and arranging educational seminars and workshops.

SPECIALTY ADVERTISING

Specialty advertising involves the preparation of many types of items bearing the name and/or brand mark of the destination. These items are most often given away as gifts and usually in conjunction with sales, sales promotion, and public relations events and programs, and activities. These include T-shirts, cups and other containers, logo bags, books and diaries, desk ornaments, and many other items.

SAMPLING

For DMOs, sampling typically means inviting people to visit the destination to see what it has to offer. There are two main sampling formats: familiarization tours and site investigations. Familiarization tours are arranged for influencers, travel agents, tour operators, travel writers, and media companies.

EXAMPLE 14.15

Can a Familiarization Trip Be Virtual?

The COVID-19 pandemic severely restricted the ability of destinations to organize familiarization trips or tours. This example shows how one DMO creatively used technology to offer a virtual familiarization trip. The author suggests you read more about this case study.

> In the age of COVID-19, how are you showcasing your destination to the media, meeting planners, and travel agents? Some destination marketing organizations, like Tempe Tourism, are turning to virtual familiarization trips (FAM) to stay top of mind with these audiences and creatively market their destinations.
>
> (Manoukian 2021)

Learning Point

Sales promotions and e-marketing can be effectively twinned to give the travel trade, media, and consumers virtual touring experiences of destinations.

Communicating with influencers is taking on a higher priority with DMOs. Marketing @ Millionmetrics (2017) suggests that social media influencers are of increasing importance to DMOs in positively affecting the images and intentions of their followers. Gretzel (2017) indicates that a significant proportion of followers make purchases based on the experiences and recommendations of social media influencers. This is a topic that is picked up again in Chapter 15.

Site inspections are conducted by associations, companies, and other organizations that are seriously considering the destination as a place for a future event, such as a convention, an exhibition, a trade show, or some other type of meeting. These meeting planners are especially interested in viewing the hotels that they may be using and the venues for events, such as convention and exhibition centers. It is common for DMOs to pay for all the costs of the site inspection team while they are in the destination.

Many major travel shows and exhibitions are held around the world each year and they attract numerous DMOs to exhibit. Some of the largest of these international events are shown in Figure 14.8.

- ITB Berlin, Germany
- World Travel Market, London, England
- The Motivation Show, Chicago, USA
- Salon Mondial du Tourisme, Paris, France
- BIT, Milan, Italy
- Arabian Travel Market, Dubai
- MITT, Moscow, Russia
- Rendez-vous Canada
- China International Travel Market, Shanghai/Kunming, China.

Figure 14.8 A selection of the world's largest travel shows and exhibitions.

Most of these shows and exhibitions are operated by private companies, and DMOs pay fees based upon their exhibit space and locations at the events. However, in some cases the shows are actually run by the DMOs themselves, and the objective is to showcase the destinations and tourism stakeholders within their jurisdictions. These include Rendez-vous Canada, operated by Destination Canada (2022), and the China International Travel Mart, run by the Ministry of Culture and Tourism (China) (2022).

DMOs produce many merchandising materials for display and distribution in a variety of places. These materials include printed visitor guides, maps and a variety of brochures as well as posters. Although DMOs do not necessarily operate shops (some do), they often have VICs and brochure material distribution points at local hotels, attractions and transportation terminals. DMOs also distribute much literature at travel shows and exhibitions. These materials are often called printed collateral by DMOs.

Educational seminars can be very effective sales promotion tools for DMOs, especially when directed at travel agencies and tour operators in key origins of tourists. The Ireland Specialists program is a good example of a successful educational initiative by a DMO (Trade Ireland 2022).

EXAMPLE 14.16

Ireland Specialists

DMOs need to deepen the knowledge about their destinations within travel trade organizations and their staff members. Educating travel agents and tour operator product development specialists is the key activity here.

Benefits of becoming an Ireland specialist:

- Improve your earning potential by selling Ireland as a destination

- The ability to promote yourself as an Ireland expert to your customers
- Receive a Gold or Silver Ireland Specialist Certificate.

(Trade Ireland 2022)

Learning Point

Programs like the Ireland Specialists are win-win situations for DMOs and travel trade companies.

DMOs produce many audio-visual materials that are used in various ways for communication purposes. These include printed collateral materials, videos, USB flash drives, photo galleries, podcasts, PowerPoint presentations, and others. The audio-visual materials are utilized at travel shows and exhibitions and by sales representatives in making presentations to prospective customers. The materials are also made available to media companies for their use in publicity coverage. Materials are given to business event organizers to help them generate greater attendance and participation. Some of the materials are made available to individual tourists; for example, videos can be viewed on YouTube or TikTok, and photo galleries can be perused on Instagram or other photo-sharing sites.

Measuring the Effectiveness of Sales Promotion and Merchandising

Measuring the effectiveness of some of the special-offer sales promotions is quite straightforward and involves calculating the percentages of people who received the offers who actually purchased or booked the offers. Some of the special communications can also be measured, whereas others are difficult to measure. For example, leads resulting from exhibiting at travel shows and exhibitions can be tracked, and participants in familiarization tours and site investigations and at educational seminars and workshops can be counted.

For some of the special communication methods, it is much more difficult to assess the exact impacts of posters, printed collateral, merchandising materials, and specialty advertising items that are offered as gifts. These may be noticed and appreciated, but no immediate action is taken or response given after exposure to the materials.

EXAMPLE 14.17

Crowdsourcing Resident Opinions on Tourism

Crowdsourcing can be applied in market and marketing research; in this case, the Christchurch DMO is asking locals about tourism in their area.

> What does Christchurch mean to you? What makes us unique?
> How do we talk about ourselves? What about how others talk about us?
> How do we attract visitors? And what kind of visitors do we want to attract?
> These are some of the questions that ChristchurchNZ is seeking answers to with a major piece of work now underway. We have been asked by the Ministry

of Business, Innovation and Employment to produce two destination management plans (DMPs), one for Greater Christchurch (including Selwyn, Waima-
kariri and parts of Mid Canterbury) and one for Banks Peninsula. Of course,
Banks Peninsula is technically part of Christchurch City but, as a destination, a
rugged, sparsely populated peninsula with significant cruise visitation is a very
different proposition than New Zealand's second city.

(Adams 2022)

Learning Point

It is crucial to get local resident input when planning IMC and choosing target markets.

Crowdsourcing and Content Co-creation

Connected with e-marketing, you should be aware of one promotional technique called crowdsourcing, which is associated with the use of social media. The definition of crowdsourcing
is to outsource a task to a group (crowd) of people, in this case, to individuals outside of the
DMO. Crowdsourcing has been used by several DMOs in recent years, and Tourism Australia,
Destination Canada, and Tourism New Zealand are examples. Under one scenario, basically
what happens is the DMO invites local people to upload written materials and photos of their
favorite places, experiences and activities in the destination. This falls within what is called
content co-creation, meaning that consumers and DMOs jointly contribute text and visual
materials. Tourism Australia used this approach in their campaign. There's nothing like Australia. The crowd that helped in response to Tourism Australia's request was quite large. Apart
from the benefits to IMC campaigns, these initiatives involve local community residents with
tourism and the DMO, and that is very positive. Additionally, tourists get truly authentic experiences that have been fully vetted by locals. This can be called a win-win-win proposition.

Another scenario is to invite a smaller group of selected outsiders to help in building communication campaigns. BTI Consulting invited twenty-five foreign expatriates for a weekend in the
ancient city of Shaoxing in Zhejiang Province, China. With the sponsorship and assistance of the
local DMO, Shaoxing Tourism Commission, the participants were involved in authentic local
experiences, such as being an apprentice Chinese opera singer or cooking a famous local-recipe
tofu dish. The expats were asked to keep diaries of their experiences and take photos and videos.
BTI collected these, and they were later used as part of an English guidebook for Shaoxing.

Another variation on crowdsourcing is to ask for proposals for new products or services from
people with expertise and knowledge. Füller et al. (2016) refer to these approaches as idea
contest platforms. For example, the Singapore Tourism Board launched an initiative called the
Tourism Accelerator program.

EXAMPLE 14.18

Singapore Tourism Accelerator Program

In this example, the DMO is seeking innovative technology start-up entrepreneurs. It
appears to be an application of crowdsourcing in the B2B environment.

The Singapore Tourism Accelerator is a highly selective, equity-free four-month program for the world's most promising technology start-ups or pre-scaleups that can power the travel and tourism industry. The Accelerator is organized by the Singapore Tourism Board (STB) and its appointed corporate innovation partner, Ravel Innovation. We are looking for the very best in innovation and are particularly interested in companies that are developing solutions to future-proof the travel and tourism industry and help tourism companies thrive amidst the challenges brought about by COVID-19. Whether you already have some traction in the industry, or are looking to apply your solution to the industry for the first time, we want to hear from you.

The selected companies will gain unparalleled access to work with some of Asia's and the world's most important industry players. They will learn in a series of capacity-building intensive workshops, including sessions to scope potential pilots, while preparing and executing on their pilots with selected industry partners.

(STB 2022)

Learning Point

DMOs should make efforts to spur innovation in tourism within their destinations. Finding creative entrepreneurs and start-up companies is part of these efforts.

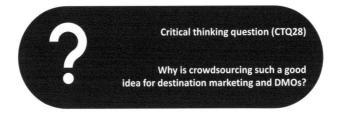

? Critical thinking question (CTQ28)

Why is crowdsourcing such a good idea for destination marketing and DMOs?

Theme Year and Event Marketing

Several national DMOs have adopted a strategy of consistently having theme years to heighten the interest of tourists in visiting their countries. VisitScotland's (2022) Homecoming Scotland 2009 and 2014 and The Gathering Ireland (Fáilte Ireland 2013) are good examples of years with a specific theme.

However, this practice originated from and is most popular in Asia, with China, Indonesia, Malaysia, and Thailand being four of the countries that use this strategy most frequently. The Tourism Authority of Thailand began its Visit Thailand years in 1987. This first theme year in Thailand had a significantly positive impact on inbound international tourism. It also attracted the attention of other destinations in Southeast Asia, and they decided to try out a similar strategy.

Movie and Film Development

Movie-, film- and TV-induced or screen tourism has really caught the attention of destination marketers and tourism scholars in the past decades. This has been because people like to visit the places where famous movies and films were shot. Two of the most discussed case studies here are *Lord of the Rings* for New Zealand and *Braveheart* for Scotland, but there are many more examples. Since then, popular TV series, including *Game of Thrones*, *Downton Abbey*, and *Outlander*, have attracted many fans to their filming locations.

You might wonder what this topic is doing in a chapter about IMC, and indeed you should know. Some destinations have recognized this phenomenon and used movies and films as part of their promotions. Other destinations have gone even further and put tourism development and marketing together with film development and marketing, knowing the synergies that can occur between the two.

Rajasthan in India is a spectacular destination, which has attracted several Indian and foreign movie productions. Some popular international movies filmed in Rajasthan include *The Best Exotic Marigold Hotel*, *The Darjeeling Limited*, and *The Dark Knight Rises*.

EXAMPLE 14.19

Screen Tourism in Britain

There is no doubt that Britain is a great location for filming given its history and heritage along with the varied scenery and landscapes. It is also the place of many famous people and legends. The tourism effects of screen tourism are well recognized by British DMOs.

> Why do people decide to visit the UK? Is it to see the landmarks such as Big Ben and Buckingham Palace, etc.? What about to attend the world-renowned events such as the Edinburgh Festival or Glastonbury? Both of these reasons attract 100s of thousands of tourists every year, but there's another less well-known reason which is doing a great job of attracting visitors, and it's called screen tourism.
>
> This terms relates to the act of going out and visiting the sets and locations used in some of the pop culture's most famous films and TV shows. And it's turning out to be a very lucrative stream of tourist revenue. The latest figures estimate that inbound tourists spent just under £600 million in film-related tourism, with popular destinations associated with TV shows seeing substantial increases in visitor numbers.
>
> (Morris 2019)

> VisitBritain provides a long list of movies and TV series filmed in Britain including *Harry Potter*, *James Bond*, *The Theory of Everything*, *Pride and Prejudice*, *Miss Potter*, *Love Actually*, *Braveheart*, *The Queen*, *The King's Speech*, *Bridget Jones*, and others.
>
> (VisitBritain 2022)

Learning Point

Popular firms and TV series attract visitors to destinations. They are worthwhile including in the IMC campaigns for places.

Steps in Effective Planning of Integrated Marketing Communications

IMC needs to be carefully planned, and there is a definite sequence of events that should be followed. The following is a brief description of the steps for planning a specific IMC campaign.

SET IMC CAMPAIGN OBJECTIVES

It is very important to begin by setting clear and measurable objectives for the IMC campaign. These objectives, for example, may be to increase tourist numbers and tourism spending from the intended audience by specific amounts or percentages.

ESTIMATE A TENTATIVE IMC CAMPAIGN BUDGET

The DMO needs to prepare a preliminary budget estimate for the IMC campaign bearing in mind the funds it has available for marketing and promotion.

CONSIDER PARTNERSHIP MODEL AND POTENTIAL PARTNERS

The DMO should identify potential partners who share similar objectives and might be interested in participating as a co-sponsor of the IMC campaign. Potential partnership models also need to be identified. Negotiations with these potential partners should take place.

EXAMPLE 14.20

Cooperative Marketing in British Columbia

Chapter 8 discussed partnerships in tourism and cooperative marketing is a powerful partnership tool for DMOs. British Columbia provides an excellent example of this approach.

> Destination BC has operated its Co-op Program since 2015. Funding requests must be for a minimum of $20,000, to a maximum of $250,000, per year.
>
> **Purpose of the Co-op Program**
> To enable groups that share common interests and common marketing goals, that align with provincial tourism priorities, to leverage both private and public funds in order to achieve greater marketing impact in driving tourism revenue.
> To drive industry collaboration, align industry marketing efforts to provincial and regional strategies, and to connect industry to the provincial destination brand, building brand equity through all province-funded marketing initiatives.
>
> (Destination British Columbia 2022)

Learning Point

DMOs can augment the effectiveness of their IMC by inviting tourism sector stakeholders to join them in cooperative marketing.

Determine Mix of IMC Components

The DMO determines which components of IMC will be used in the campaign and how these will be interconnected. The DMO also needs to decide when and how often components will be used and in which sequences if appropriate.

Design and Test IMC Campaign

A theme and creative approach are chosen reflecting a specific communication message idea or ideas. Proposed materials should be pretested by showing them to members of the intended audience and getting their feedback and suggestions. Materials should be revised accordingly.

Prepare Final IMC Campaign

The IMC materials for the campaign are finalized based on the pre-test and prepared in a finished format.

Develop a Final IMC Budget

The tentative budget is reviewed and revised into a final IMC budget based on the finished format materials and their placements.

Launch, Maintain, and Monitor IMC Campaign

The IMC campaign is implemented, and it is likely that the DMO or its vendors (e.g., advertising, PR or digital marketing consultants) will have to be involved, especially if there is a component for the social network sites that involves interacting with people that respond to the IMC campaign.

Measure and Evaluate Results of IMC Campaign

The results of the IMC campaign are measured and compared to the objectives that were set in the first step.

SUMMING UP

IMC is the coordination and integration of all of a DMO's communications and promotions to increase their effectiveness and consistency. Using IMC helps DMOs overcome some of the communications challenges because messages are repeated in different formats and media channels. E-marketing, advertising, sales, public relations and publicity, sales promotion and merchandising are the components of IMC. Campaigns involve some combination of the six components.

E-marketing using ICTs is now being given much greater emphasis by DMOs. The most important techniques and venues include websites, email, social network sites, traveler review sites, blogging and mobile phones. Crowdsourcing is a relatively new promotional technique that often involves digital communications and is where the DMO outsources some of the responsibility for a promotion to a group of people.

Advertising can be very expensive for DMOs, especially if placed on television or in leading travel magazines. Because of its high costs, destination advertising has attracted criticism in many parts of the world, but media advertising remains an important component of IMC for many DMOs. A case study in Colorado in the USA clearly underscored the dangers of closing down a destination's advertising campaigns. Because of its high costs, it is particularly important that destination advertising is tracked and its effectiveness measured. Advertising plays three major roles for DMOs: informing, persuading and reminding. The traditional media for destination advertising were television, radio, magazines, newspapers, outdoor and transit. In recent times, DMOs have made greater use of online advertising.

Sales or personal selling is of great importance for many DMOs and especially those that place strong emphasis on attracting business events. Among the most important of the sales roles is to appeal to and win group business from associations, corporations and the travel trade.

Public relations and publicity involve developing and maintaining positive relationships with all of the DMO's publics. All DMOs have both internal publics (within the destination) and external publics (outside of the destination). Publicity is sometimes called free advertising but it usually has some costs because the DMO must keep the media informed about key events and stories that are taking place within the destination.

Sales promotion and merchandising are two closely connected IMC components. These are techniques that are used tactically and for short periods of time. There are two categories, special offers and special communication methods. Sampling (familiarization tours and site investigations) and exhibiting at travel shows and exhibitions are two techniques that are especially important for DMOs.

Popular films, movies and TV series have been instrumental in generating significant tourism increases for the destinations in which they have been shot. In some places, the responsibilities for tourism development and marketing and film development and marketing have been combined into one agency; in other words, the DMO and film commission have been integrated.

An IMC campaign needs to be carefully planned and should follow a distinct sequence. The IMC plan should always start with the setting of objectives and end with the measurement of results.

KEYWORDS

activity measures	conversion studies	mobile
advertising	crowdsourcing	movie-, film- and tv-induced
advertising tracking	email	or screen tourism
banner advertisements	e-marketing	negative publicity
blogs and vlogs	external publics	online advertising
bookings	familiarization trips or tours	pay-per-click (PPC)
closing the sale	(FAMs)	performance measures
collateral (brochures, maps,	guerrilla marketing	performance metrics
posters, visitor guides)	influencers	personal selling
complementary	informing	persuading
consistency	integrated marketing com-	positioning and branding
consumer buying-process	munications (IMC)	approaches
stages	internal publics	productivity measures
content co-creation	leads	prospecting
contests, sweepstakes and	learning styles	publicity
games	media relations	public relations
continuity programs	merchandising	recognition programs

reminding	smartphones	theme years
repetition	social media	traveler review sites
sales	special communication	travel shows and
sales promotion	methods	exhibitions
sampling	special offers	travel trade inducements
site investigations or	specialty	viral marketing
inspections	advertising	websites

REVIEW QUESTIONS

1. What is the definition of IMC, and what are its components and benefits?
2. What are the major e-marketing channels and techniques?
3. Why is advertising important for destinations, and what are advertising's three main roles for a DMO?
4. What roles do sales or personal selling perform for DMOs?
5. What are the roles played by sales promotion and merchandising?
6. What are the roles of public relations and publicity?
7. What is crowdsourcing, and how can it be applied in IMC by DMOs?
8. Theme and event years have been used by several countries as a tourism marketing strategy. Why are these theme/event years a good platform for IMC?
9. How are tourism and film/movie development interrelated, and how can they benefit each other in terms of both marketing and development?
10. What are the steps involved in planning IMC?

REFERENCES

Adams, A. (2022) "What Does Christchurch Mean to You? Have Your Say on Our Own Tourist Destination," *New Zealand Herald*, September 14, www.nzherald.co.nz/nz/what-does-christchurch-mean-to-you-have-your-say-on-our-own-tourist-destination/NTJLHSTIUK7YB3LS4ONIUEZ574/

Best Destination (2021) "Welcome to Saudi Tourism Saudi Arabia," www.youtube.com/watch?v=kDqTPT1SQbU

Brand USA (2022) "FY 2021 Annual Report," www.thebrandusa.com/system/files/BrandUSA_FY21_Annual_Report%20%281%29.pdf

BurrellesLuce (2022) "Media Reporting," www.burrellesluce.info/

Campaigns of the World (2016) "Madhya Pradesh Tourism Latest Ad Campaign: MP Mein Dil Hua Bache Sa," June 18, https://campaignsoftheworld.com/tv/madhya-pradesh-tourism-latest-ad-campaign-mp-mein-dil-hua-bache-sa/

Choat, I. (2021) "London Tourism Gets £6m Boost with New Advertising Campaign," *The Guardian*, May 10, www.theguardian.com/travel/2021/may/10/london-tourism-gets-6m-boost-with-new-advertising-campaign

Cision (2022) "Know Whom Your Campaign Is Reaching, Who's Talking About You and What They're Saying," www.cision.com/us/products/analytics/

The Citizen (2022) "Tanzania Tourism Board's Failure to Promote and Market Destinations Exposed," April 16, www.thecitizen.co.tz/tanzania/news/national/tanzania-tourism-board-s-failure-to-promote-and-market-destinations-exposed-3784474

Daily News Egypt (2022) "'Follow the Sun' Campaign Named Best Tourism Ad in May," https://dailynewsegypt.com/2022/06/08/follow-the-sun-campaign-named-best-tourism-ad-in-may/

Destination British Columbia (2022) "Co-op Marketing," https://blog.hellobc.com/what-we-do/funding-sources/co-op-marketing/

Destination Canada (2022) "RVC+ 2022 Toronto, Ontario," www.rendezvouscanada.ca/

Destination DC (2022) "Meet the Destination DC Team," https://washington.org/DC-information/meet-destination-dc-team

Destinations International (2012) "Standard DMO Performance Reporting: A Handbook for Destination Marketing Organizations (DMOs)," https://destinationsinternational.org/sites/default/master/files/pdfs_Dest_Intl_2011_Performance_Reporting_Handbook.pdf

Destinations International (2018) "Organization and Financial Profile," https://destinationsinternational.org/organization-and-financial-profile-study

Experience Egypt (2022) "Follow the Sun," www.youtube.com/watch?v=noSCcFlAJPw

Fáilte Ireland (2013) "The Gathering Ireland Final Report," www.failteireland.ie/FailteIreland/media/WebsiteStructure/Documents/eZine/TheGathering_FinalReport_JimMiley_December2013.pdf

Füller, J., Hutter, K., and Koch, G. (2016) "Crowdsourcing in Tourism: From Idea Generation to Merchandising User-Generated Souvenirs," in R. Egger, I. Gula, and D. Walcher (eds), *Open Tourism: Open Innovation, Crowdsourcing and Co-Creation Challenging the Tourism Industry*, Berlin: Springer-Verlag, pp. 277–289.

Girma, L. L. (2021) "Tourism Fiji's Shameless New Campaign Is a Reminder for Marketers Everywhere," *Skift*, December 7, https://skift.com/2021/12/07/tourism-fijis-shameless-new-campaign-is-a-reminder-for-marketers-everywhere/

Google (2023) "Google Adwords," https://ads.google.com/intl/en_uk/home/

Gretzel, U. (2017) "Influencer Marketing in Travel and Tourism," in M. Sigala and U. Gretzel (eds.), *Advances in Social Media for Travel, Hospitality and Tourism: New Perspectives, Practice and Cases*, London and New York, NY: Routledge.

Guilland, M.-L., and Naef, P. (2019) "Tourism Challenges Facing Peacebuilding in Colombia," *VIA Tourism Review*, 15. https://doi.org/10.4000/viatourism.4046

Houston First Corporation (2022) "Sales Staff," www.visithoustontexas.com/about-us/sales/

Hutchinson, J. (2014) "I Hate Thailand Video Goes Viral . . . but It's Designed to ATTRACT Visitors to the Country Using 'Reverse Psychology' to Restore Country's Tarnished Image," *Daily Mail*, November 26, www.dailymail.co.uk/travel/travel_news/article-2850005/I-Hate-Thailand-video-goes-viral.html

Las Vegas Convention and Visitors Authority (2021) "Comprehensive Annual Financial Report," https://assets.simpleviewcms.com/simpleview/image/upload/v1/clients/lasvegas/ACFR_FY_2021_71844e23-87b3-4465-be14-c4496e04cbaa.pdf

Long, D. (2022) "WA Tourism Showcases Dreamy Magic to Entice Visitors," *The Drum*, September 9, www.thedrum.com/news/2022/09/09/wa-tourism-showcases-dreamy-magic-entice-visitors

McKay, R. O. (2022) "Tourism New Zealand Seeks to Attract 'High-Quality Visitors' in New Campaign," *Travel Weekly*, August 18, www.travelweekly.com.au/article/tourism-new-zealand-seeks-to-attract-high-quality-visitors-in-new-campaign/

Manoukian, J. (2021) "How Tempe Arizona Ran a Virtual Multi-Stop FAM Trip," *CrowdRiff*, https://crowdriff.com/resources/blog/tempe-tourism-virtual-fam

Marketing @ Millionmetrics (2017) "The Power of Social Influencers in Destination Marketing," September 26, www.millionmetrics.com/influencers-destination-marketing/

Ministry of Culture and Tourism (China) (2022) "China International Travel Mart," www.citm.com.cn/

Morris, J. (2019) "Screen Tourism: How Much Money Is This Tourism Trend Making in the UK?" *Tourism Review*, October 24, www.tourism-review.com/film-related-inbound-tourism-in-uk-news11231

Morrison, A. M. (2016) "Taking Too Much Credit—a Cardinal Sin of Destination Marketing?" www.linkedin.com/pulse/taking-too-much-credit-cardinal-sin-destination-morrison-ph-d-/

Seychelles News Agency (2022) "Seychelles' Tourism Officials 'Refresh' Country Brand Ahead of Paris Tourism Fair," www.seychellesnewsagency.com/articles/17361/Seychelles+tourism+officials+refresh+country+brand+ahead+of+Paris+tourism+fair

Siegel, B. (2011) *What Happens When You Stop Marketing? The Rise and Fall of Colorado Tourism*, Toronto: Longwoods International.

Singapore Tourism Board (2022) "Singapore Tourism Accelerator," www.stb.gov.sg/content/stb/en/trade-events-and-resources/Singapore-Tourism-Accelerator.html

Skift and Sojern (2020) "Co-op Marketing for Destinations: The Path Forward for COVID-19 Recovery," https://skift.com/insight/skift-trend-report-co-op-marketing-for-destinations/

Spinks, R. (2019) "Dominican Republic Counters Negative Publicity After US Tourist Deaths," *Skift*, June 13, https://skift.com/2019/06/13/dominican-republic-counters-negative-publicity-after-u-s-tourist-deaths/

Sumb, A. (2020) "Developing Papua New Guinea's Tourism Sector," Department of Pacific Affairs (Acton, Australian Capital Territory), Working Paper 2020/3, https://openresearch-repository.anu.edu.au/bitstream/1885/203231/1/DPA%20Working%20Paper%2020203%20Sumb.pdf

Switzerland Tourism (2022) "With Roger Federer on the Grand Tour of Switzerland," www.myswitzerland.com/en-us/experiences/experience-tour/grand-tour-of-switzerland/with-rogerfedereron-the-grand-tourofswitzerland/

Tourism Australia (2022a) "Annual Report 2020/2021," www.tourism.australia.com/content/dam/digital/corporate/documents/ta-annual-report-fy21.pdf

——— (2022b) "About the Program," www.aussiespecialist.com/en/why-register/about-the-program.html

Tourism Authority of Thailand (2015) "TAT Viral Sensation Video 'I Hate Thailand' Wins Social Media Award at AdFest 2015," www.tatnews.org/tat-viral-sensation-video-i-hate-thailand-wins-social-media-award-at-adfest-2015/

Trade Ireland (2022) "Welcome to Ireland Specialists," https://trade.ireland.com/en-ie/training/ireland-specialist

Travel + Leisure (2022) "Travel + Leisure Media Kit 2022," www.meredith.com/Travel-and-Leisure-Media-Kit.pdf

Urquhart, M. (2022) "N.B. Tourism Contest Targets 'Gone-Aways' with Promise of Free Holiday Back Home," *CBC News*, May 31, www.cbc.ca/news/canada/new-brunswick/tourism-campaign-targets-former-nbers-1.6471243

VisitBritain (2022) "Britain on Film," www.visitbritain.com/gb/en/britain-film

VisitScotland (2021) "Scotland Is Calling," www.visitscotland.org/news/2021/scotland-is-calling-launch

——— (2022) "Scotland's Themed Years," www.visitscotland.com/about/themed-years/

Chapter **15**

E-marketing and ICTs

Spreading the online word

DOI: 10.4324/9781003343356-18

Warming Up

Where do you get information and news? Your answer is probably online as around 70 percent of the world's population are using the Internet. That percentage goes up to around 75 percent for Generation Z (born 1997–2012), as more younger people are online. Other figures are higher still; one statistic from the Pew Research Center indicating that in the USA, 99 percent of people aged 18–29 used the Internet in 2021 (Pew Research Center 2021). Perhaps it might surprise you even more that 75 percent of those aged sixty-five and over were also using the Internet.

With such pervasive use of the Internet, the marketing, branding, and communications of destinations is increasingly moving online and making use of varied technologies. This chapter continues the discussion from Chapter 14 on IMC in describing e-marketing for DMOs. Thereafter, the broader topic of ICT is explained.

Your author has developed websites and website evaluation systems for destinations including the WebEVAL and I AM OUTSTANDING models. He has also been involved in the production of destination videos, the administration of social media pages, and in research on robots in tourism. These experiences are integrated into this chapter. Once again, practical insights are offered rather than theoretical, and negative as well as positive aspects of e-marketing are highlighted.

Definition and Increasing Importance of E-marketing

ICTs have had a major impact on the tourism sector during the past thirty-five years. The impacts began in the early 1990s and are accelerating more quickly now. The destination marketing, branding, and communications role of destination management was the first to feel the effects of ICT innovations, but the impacts have now spread to all other destination management roles.

The introduction of the Internet especially had a huge impact on destination management and on visitors. It has affected how people search for information about destinations and plan trips. The Internet changed how people book travel and spawned a new breed of intermediaries, OTAs. For DMOs, the Internet along with social media have become the major information dissemination and e-marketing channels.

Social media have opened a new world of dialog among people, including conversations about destinations. DMOs have joined these conversations by building their own sites on major social media platforms. The main advantages of social media for destinations are in content co-creation and the stimulation of eWoM recommendations. Blogging and vlogging have become popular among consumers and DMOs. Blogs serve multiple purposes and have distinct advantages for DMOs. Smartphones are numerous around the world, and their use has had a significant effect on tourism and destinations. The number of travel and tourism applications (apps) for smartphones has grown rapidly, and there are thousands of them.

A simple definition of e-marketing for DMOs follows:

DEFINITION

E-marketing

The use of digital-format ICTs by DMOs to liaise with various audiences, to provide information, and to market and brand destinations.

The following example provides a succinct explanation of the value and major trends in e-marketing.

EXAMPLE 15.1

What Is the Value of E-Marketing for Destinations?

These are some great insights on e-marketing from a leading tourism consulting firm, Solimar International. The article cites three advantages and four trends in DMO e-marketing.

What is the value of digital destination marketing?

1. From local to global
2. Focused targeting
3. Improved measurability

What are the top digital marketing trends to inspire a DMO's strategy in 2022?

1. Everything must be mobile, mobile, mobile
2. Content is king
3. Go virtual
4. The power of video in destination marketing

(Elmes-Bosshard 2022)

Learning Point

The value of e-marketing is already considerable, and it is going to increase further in the future.

The value of digital destination marketing is significant. It enables DMOs to promote products and services to a more targeted audience, it affords the use of cost-effective channels to reach wider geographic markets, and it helps to enrich content. All of these combined drives success for the destination.

Functions of Digital Media for Visitors

Digital media have become much more than an information source for visitors. People use websites, social media platforms, mobile phone apps, and other digital media for multiple reasons and purposes. TEAM Tourism Consulting of the UK identified twelve reasons for and functions in using digital media (Fig. 15.1) (UNWTO and ETC 2007). Travelers are using digital media at all stages of the trip cycle beginning with dreaming and ending with recollecting. For example, videos are viewed when people are considering destinations to visit, and blogs or vlogs are composed to remember the trips to these destinations. The stages of travelers' trip cycles are briefly described as follows:

- Dreaming, enthusing, and informing: Before booking their trips, online contents are used for dreaming, enthusing, and informing people about potential destinations.

- Planning, selecting, and booking: When people make the decision to travel, they use online sources for trip planning and selecting destinations. People may also book trips online.

- Traveling, visiting, and enjoying: People may refer to online information, especially on mobile phones and smartphones, when traveling within the destination and for visiting and enjoying places of interest.

- Repeating, recommending, and recollecting: People may want to go back to the destination, and so they revisit online content sources. They may recommend platforms, apps, and destinations to relatives and friends. In addition, they may return online just to remember the details of their trips.

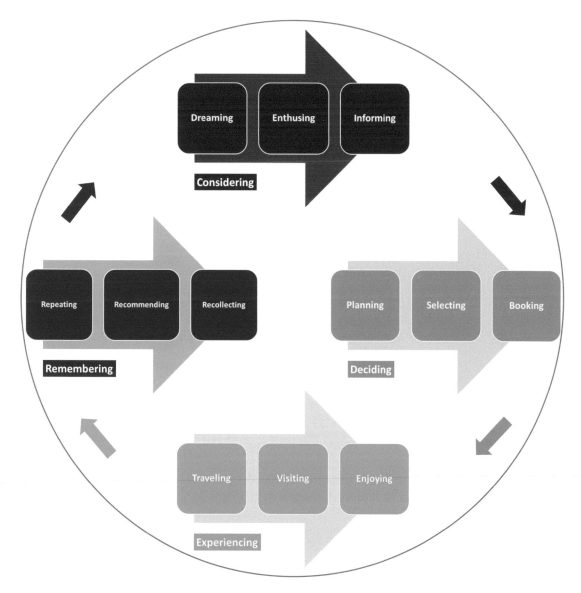

Figure 15.1 Consumer reasons for and functions in using DMO online contents (UNWTO and European Travel Commission 2007).

There are many destinations that do not have high awareness levels and e-marketing can provide the means to being considered by more consumers, as in the case of Namibia in Southwest Africa.

EXAMPLE 15.2

Namibia Launches Digital Marketing Campaign

Many people do not know much about Namibia—some do not even know where it is located. Destinations that are not top of mind places for travel must do more to get noticed and online is a great place to do that.

> Namibia on Wednesday launched a tourism digital marketing campaign to rebuild consumer confidence and drive travel recovery post-COVID.
>
> "Namibia as a tourism destination is competing with the rest of the world; online presence is regarded as tourism infrastructure," Shifeta (Minister of Environment, Forestry and Tourism) said, adding that "just as websites are essential, social media presence is a must and for Namibia to be properly represented online, the industry should be empowered and encouraged to engage more online to create a powerful tourism profile of the country."
>
> (Xia 2022)

Learning Point

Apart from the benefits of e-marketing, DMOs must compete with others online and cannot afford not to be present there.

When planning the design of websites, social media pages and apps, DMOs need to be sure to provide for all these potential customer reasons and purposes. There are supply requirements (DMO and tourism sector stakeholder) and demand (visitor) requirements to DMO digital media, and both must be blended together for the most effective marketing. It is not surprising that some DMOs have multiple online platforms and channels that are segmented by audience and allow different types of interactions with visitors. DMOs also must continuously track the trends in consumer online behavior, as the national DMO in Mexico is doing.

EXAMPLE 15.3

Domestic Tourism in Mexico Changes as a Result of COVID-19

How did the COVID-19 pandemic affect traveler's use of online travel sources? This example from Mexico indicates that their domestic tourists made greater use of the Internet then.

> The new normal and social distancing measures have modified travel trends and while it poses great challenges for the tourism industry, the need to travel remains a fundamental activity.

During the month of January, travel-related searches have rebounded, due to the long periods of isolation in which we have lived and the undeniable importance of human mobility. According to data obtained by visitmexico. com, Mexico's official tourism promotion website, the behavior of Mexican travelers during the first month of 2021 shows an increase in internet searches for tourist routes, highways and Magical Towns. These preferences respond to factors such as the proximity of destinations, the possibility of traveling in your own car, avoiding crowds, as well as visiting places with open spaces and carrying out outdoor activities.

(Secretaría de Turismo del Gobierno de México 2021)

Learning Point

COVID-19 may have accelerated the growth in the use of online travel sources for information and booking.

Main Components of E-marketing

Chapter 14 identified e-marketing as one of the components of IMC. Figure 14.2 identified six channels and techniques of e-marketing (websites, email, social media, traveler review sites, blogs and vlogs, and mobile), but there are other areas of e-marketing and ICTs that are reviewed in this chapter. This electronic-assisted marketing has rapidly become the most important form of marketing and the major IMC tool for many DMOs around the world.

For travelers, the Internet is the most important information source and trip planning tool. The Internet is more than a source of information, a partner for travelers and a tool for DMOs and the tourism sector; it has become an entertainment venue to gain knowledge and have hands-on experiences. One of the best ways to effectively use the Internet is through the creation

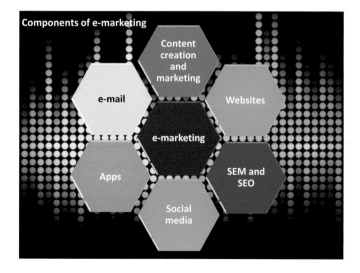

Figure 15.2 Main components of e-marketing.

of interactive and informative websites, social media pages, and apps. Figure 15.2 shows the major components of e-marketing for DMOs.

Each of the six major e-marketing components shown in Figure 15.2 is now discussed.

Content Creation and Marketing

Content is at the heart of DMO e-marketing (as the Solimar International example suggested), and this is not just a one-sided proposition. DMOs and consumers interactively create content on multiple platforms that include social media and websites. The assembling and communication of this information is often called content curation in the digital sphere (Fig. 15.3). The three major sources of digital content for DMOs include DMO-developed, user-generated (UGC), and co-created content.

Content creation

Figure 15.3 Content creation in e-marketing.

DEFINITION

Content marketing

Content marketing is a strategic marketing approach focused on creating and distributing valuable, relevant, and consistent content to attract and retain a clearly defined audience—and, ultimately, to drive profitable customer action (Content Marketing Institute 2022).

DMOs must curate all types of content and put the emphasis on presenting information that conveys the experiences that visitors can have in their destinations. For destinations, video and still photography are critical to communicating these experiences; your tour of DMO content starts there, before moving onto information based on text.

VIDEO

Destination videos have always been important; however, in e-marketing they are becoming even more critical for success. The flexibility and ability to show the thrills and emotions of travel experiences make videos a prime content format for DMOs. A good measure of the appeal of destination videos is the 40 million views on YouTube of one Incredible!ndia video (Incredible!ndia 2018). Not all videos are so successful, and they depend on quality production, themes and contents, and distribution.

EXAMPLE 15.4

The Rise of Video Marketing

Well-designed and professionally produced videos can be expensive. That is true, however, video marketing is becoming one of the most powerful techniques in destination IMC. The statistics in this example attest to the high use of video marketing.

Video continues to be used by an overwhelming majority of businesses.

- 86 percent of businesses use video as a marketing tool.
- Why don't some marketers use video?
- 23 percent of non-video marketers don't use video for marketing as they lack time.
- 16 percent of non-video marketers don't use video for marketing as they don't know where to start with creating video.
- 13 percent of non-video marketers say they don't use video for marketing as they don't feel it's needed.
- 10 percent of non-video marketers don't use video for marketing because it's too expensive.

(wyzowl 2022)

- 88 percent of video marketers say they've generated a positive ROI.
- 93 percent of marketers have landed new customers through social media videos.
- Video marketing can generate up to 66 percent more qualified leads per year.
- Those who use video marketing can boost their brand awareness by 54 percent.
- Videos have increased sales for 80 percent of video marketers.
- By 2022, it's estimated that a whopping 82 percent of global internet traffic will come from video streaming and downloads—an 88 percent increase from just four years ago. The takeaway? There is virtually limitless potential in the future of video marketing.

(Volume Nine 2021)

Learning Point

It is hard to think of a place that is serious about tourism that does not have a destination video. Videos are essential for destination marketing, branding, and communications.

360-degree video provides eye-catching images of destinations while giving viewers a feeling of physically being there. The use of drones for video and still photography is also adding another creative dimension to these images.

> ### EXAMPLE 15.5
>
> **Vietnam's 360-Degree Video Tours of Cities**
>
> Not many people are familiar with Hanoi, Da Nang, Nha Trang, Da Lat, and Hoh Chih Minh City as tourism destinations. Having 360-degree videos online allows people to explore these cities and decide whether they want to visit.
>
> > Vietnam's cities are treasure troves for explorers. Love eating? There's virtually no end to the secret stalls and new variations on Vietnamese dishes you thought you knew. Enjoy a hushed walk in a hidden pagoda? You won't believe the worlds that are tucked away right in the heart of town. Just here for a good time? Countless speakeasies and rooftop bars are waiting for you to check out (and check in on Instagram). We could go on, but the best way to get a sense of Vietnam's urban hubs is to see them for yourself. Plan your future trips with the interactive 360-degree tours below.
> >
> > (Vietnam Tourism 2022)
>
> **Learning Point**
>
> Sampling destinations is very difficult and videos make them more realistic and better understood.

PHOTOGRAPHY

Images through photos have always been important for the visual communication of destinations. Their significance increased in Web 1.0 (around 1990) and the introduction of destination websites and became even more pronounced in the Web 2.0 era (around 2005) of social media. These include images taken by professional photographers for DMOs or stock photography companies (e.g., Shutterstock, iStock, and Getty), selfies and other photos taken by visitors, and photos from tourism sector stakeholders and local residents.

Why are videos and still photos so critical to the effectiveness of DMO e-marketing? You may guess that the answer is that photos better demonstrate what destinations offer. That, however, is only partly right. The rest of the answer is that people are more likely to share photos.

TEXT

The most traditional content on destinations is the written word. Although recently being overshadowed by photos and videos, many people still enjoy reading about places online and offline. Engaging writing is at a premium in DMO websites, social networking platforms, blogs and microblogs, e-mails and chats, and so on.

Storytelling is of greater significance to destinations now, and all stories must be well written. DMOs must themselves write engaging stories as well as helping others to prepare stories in words and with visual images.

Blogs and Vlogs

The blogs and vlogs (blogs including videos) about destinations have had a significant impact on destination marketing and management. Blogs appear in many different places on the Internet and are developed by many different types of authors. For DMOs, there four important sources of blogs/vlogs: DMO-developed, consumer, influencer, and tourism sector stakeholders.

DMO-Developed

Many DMOs put together blogs, and in certain ways these replace some of the traditional types of press or news releases. Some DMOs write their own blogs and share them through their websites or social networks. Monterey in California is one example with its Blog Monterey page (Monterey County Convention and Visitors Bureau 2022). The usual format for DMO blogs is to have staff members and other local experts prepare the written materials. This is not really a completely new activity for DMOs, but the online venue is a new place for distributing stories.

Blogs have not received as much attention as social media platforms, but blogging is continuously attracting more writers and readers. Schmallegger and Carson (2008) analyzed how DMOs and tourism businesses were using blogs and found there were five main applications:

1. Communication: B2C (business-to-consumer) or corporate blogs are being increasingly used by DMOs; B2B (business-to-business) blogs are also prepared by DMOs to communicate with tourism sector stakeholders, travel trade companies, meeting and event planners, and other businesses.
2. IMC: DMOs often consider blogging to be a less expensive form of IMC than traditional advertising. However, blogs need to provide added value to potential visitors and cannot be too commercial. Some DMOs have turned to sponsored bloggers (influencers) to meet this challenge.
3. Product distribution: This means using blogs to create online bookings, but this suffers from the same challenges as promotions in blogs. It can make the DMO blogs look more commercial and less objective.
4. Management: Blogs can be very useful in customer relationship management (CRM) and in monitoring the image and reputation of the destination.
5. Research: Most of the blogging activity around the world is C2C (consumer to consumer). This massive store of text and graphics is a highly valuable source of research information for tourism academic scholars and tourism practitioners, including DMOs.

Schmallegger and Carson (2008) also identified four major advantages of blogs over other types of content, including in comparison with website content:

1. relatively easy to update;
2. flexible in structure;
3. encouraging interaction between authors and reader;
4. allowing people who would not otherwise have the opportunity to exchange information.

Consumer

Many travelers prepare blogs or vlogs about the places they have visited (Fig. 15.4). Several social networking and review sites allow for the posting of blogs and vlogs. These include

Selfie-taking, selfie-sticks, blogging and vlogging

Figure 15.4 Selfie-taking, selfie sticks, blogging and vlogging.

Facebook, YouTube, Instagram, TikTok, TripAdvisor, and many more. Also, there are specialized travel and tourism blog sites to which people contribute blogs on their travel experiences, such as Travel Blog (www.travelblog.org/), Travellerspoint (www.travellerspoint.com/), TravelArk (www.travelark.org/), and OffExploring (www.offexploring.com/).

Microblogging came after blogging as more people began using their mobile phones and smartphones to communicate shorter pieces of information to other groups of people. Whereas blogs average more than 1,000 words, microblogs are limited in character length, such as the 280-character limit for Twitter. Sina Weibo is a highly popular microblogging platform in China.

Influencers

Influencers or social influencers are a group of professional or semi-professional travel writers who frequently prepare blogs and vlogs. They play an important role as a source of information and inspiration for those who follow them. You can find numerous lists and rankings of these influencers, which to some extent depend on where they upload content. Influencers can be useful marketing allies for destinations; however, DMOs must be selective in choosing with whom to partner.

Tourism Sector Stakeholders

Blogs prepared in the tourism sector and especially by stakeholders represent critical content for DMOs.

User-Generated Content (UGC)

One of the core concept understandings of e-marketing is the generation of UGC on destinations and how DMOs can use UGC in a variety of ways. For example, UGC can provide significant positive WOM for a destination as well as being a valuable repository of research information and feedback. Consumers are making significant use of UGC in gathering travel information and making trip decisions.

Co-created Content

Co-creation is an initiative taken by a DMO to develop content together with visitors, potential visitors, and local residents. This content usually revolves around the travel experiences within the destination.

The other e-marketing components depend on the quality and quantity of content that the DMO curates. They are the platforms for distributing and presenting digital contents, which consumers receive and can view on a variety of devices, including smartphones, tablets, laptops and PCs. The discussion of the other five e-marketing components begins with DMO websites.

Websites

Websites must offer online users a wide array of information while seeming to be personalized for just one visitor. The information provided must span from what the destination is, why it should be visited and what should be visited, to all other components of the experience. DMOs count on the Internet for its ability to communicate with existing and potential customers whether they are nearby or on the other side of the world. Geographic boundaries do not exist online, and when the Internet is used well, it is a highly individualized and targeted medium. The ideal destination website increases awareness and curiosity; therefore, it attracts more visitors.

Major Roles and Marketing Functions of DMO Websites

Destination websites have existed since around 1994, and they have become much more than information channels. Circumstances have changed greatly since then, and websites are just part of integrated e-marketing communications that also include social media, phone apps, and email. Today, websites play multiple roles, of which there are at least nine (Fig. 15.5).

The destination information source role of DMO websites is still a critical function because people use them for trip planning and selecting destinations. For example, research done by BTI Consulting in China indicated that websites and the Internet were the top source of information for international visitors when planning their trips to China. Attractive, informative, and engaging websites in multiple languages are a must have for DMOs that are pursuing international visitors.

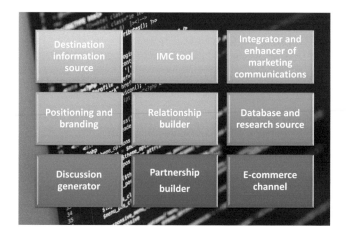

Figure 15.5 **Roles of websites.**

DMO websites have become increasingly important as marketing tools and in engaging in communications with travelers. A majority of the nine roles relate to some aspect of destination marketing, branding, and communications. One way of thinking about the multiple roles of a DMO website is to regard it as the hub of communications with potential visitors and other audiences. The website is a place where everyone can go for information and advice on the destination. It is also where the DMO talks one-to-one with individual potential visitors and others. The following is a more detailed description of the nine roles of DMO websites:

1. Provide information on the destination.
2. Promote destination product and services.
3. Support and enhance traditional IMC.
4. Communicate destination positioning and branding.
5. Build relationships with visitors and travel trade.
6. Engage travelers in discussions via the social media.
7. Generate visitor databases and research.
8. Encourage destination partnerships.
9. Allow bookings and reservations (e-commerce).

PROVIDE INFORMATION ON THE DESTINATION

When DMOs first started introducing websites, they were like electronic brochures (e-brochures) packed with information about the destinations. They were not very interactive and did not include many features. Nowadays, the information is provided in a much more attractive way with considerable scope for interactivity.

PROMOTE DESTINATION PRODUCT AND SERVICES

Websites are the global shop window for promoting destinations. With great photography, colors, sounds, and interactivity, websites allow for a highly convincing and appealing presentation of destinations.

SUPPORT AND ENHANCE TRADITIONAL IMC

Websites provide support to the traditional IMC components, including public relations and publicity, advertising, sales, sales promotions and merchandising. These all now work together as IMCs built upon an online platform. For example, websites have become the major venue for posting the news releases of DMOs as well as the place to first introduce major new IMC campaigns. The example from County Clare, Ireland is a good demonstration of using websites and social media to deliver a contest.

EXAMPLE 15.6

Digital Marketing Campaign Competition by County Clare

The flexibility of combining e-marketing with traditional IMC components—in this case a sales promotion—is shown in this example from Ireland. To get 34,000 entries for this contest was a great outcome. This is also a good case study in partnering.

A digital tourism marketing campaign offering a five-day getaway break to County Clare has attracted more than 34,000 entries from across the USA and

Canada. Hosted by the Cliffs of Moher Experience and supported by Tourism Ireland, Aer Lingus and Clare tourism operators, the Epic Trip competition targeted the North American market and reached an audience of 3.4 million people via Cliffs of Moher Experience social media channels.

"The success of this digital marketing campaign is the result of a collaborative effort involving Aer Lingus and Tourism Ireland and is evidence that an inter-agency digital marketing campaign can be very effective at capturing a wider audience," stated Geraldine Enright, Director of the Cliffs of Moher Experience.

(Cliffs of Moher Experience 2022)

Learning Point

E-marketing can be successfully combined with traditional IMC components.

COMMUNICATE DESTINATION POSITIONING AND BRANDING

Websites reflect the image that the DMO wants to create for the destination and support the chosen approach to branding the place. The outstanding visual qualities and interactivity of websites make for convincing image presentations.

BUILD RELATIONSHIPS WITH VISITORS AND TRAVEL TRADE

People sign up on websites to receive more information as well as more details on their travel interests. Databases of individuals (B2C) and travel trade (B2B) are built through sign-ups at websites and social media pages and then used to maintain ongoing contacts.

ENGAGE TRAVELERS IN DISCUSSIONS VIA THE SOCIAL MEDIA

The social media channels provide a platform for DMOs to place information content and to engage in conversations and discussions with potential visitors.

GENERATE VISITOR DATABASES AND RESEARCH

Websites can be used to conduct online surveys and to build databases of people who register. This can be a low-cost alternative to gathering research data when compared to traditional offline methods.

ENCOURAGE DESTINATION PARTNERSHIPS

Websites are a great tool for partnerships with tourism sector stakeholders and other organizations with which the DMO has established collaboration.

EXAMPLE 15.7

Singapore Partners with Traveloka and Trans Digital Media

The online world makes it easier to form partnerships between DMOs and digital travel companies. In this case, the STB created these partnerships to boost inbound travel from Indonesia.

Singapore is gearing up to welcome visitors from Indonesia with its Singa-poReimagine recovery campaign to get visitors to reignite their passion for travel through fresh and innovative experiences in Singapore. To drive visita-tion, the STB partners, through two Memoranda of Cooperation, with lifestyle super app Traveloka and Trans Digital Media to signal the start of the year-long rollout of joint tactical campaigns.

(Traveloka 2022)

Learning Point

DMOs must carefully study each inbound market and determine which digital travel companies are influential.

ALLOW BOOKINGS AND RESERVATIONS (E-COMMERCE)

Several DMO websites allow bookings and reservations to be made at hotels, attractions and other stakeholder locations.

DMO websites are an essential part of marketing strategy and marketing plan implementation. Indeed, some experts say websites are the most important part of destination marketing, brand-ing, and communications. There are at least ten marketing functions of DMO websites (Fig. 15.6).

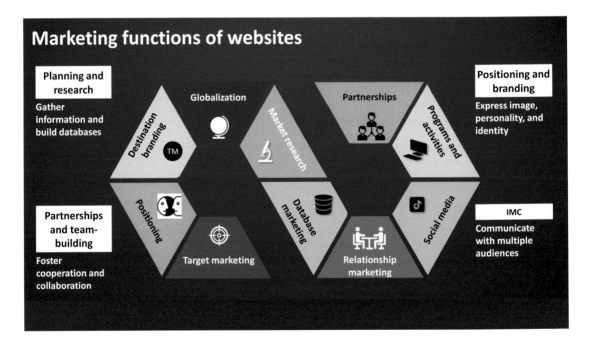

Figure 15.6 Marketing functions of websites.

1. Target marketing: For marketing strategy, official destination websites play a role in target marketing, destination positioning and branding. Often, there are different parts of DMO websites for individual target markets, or separate websites are designed for individual markets (see Example 15.9).

2. Positioning: A DMO website can be used to visually demonstrate the image that the destination has decided to communicate. For example, using predominantly green colors can give an image of an eco- or nature-based destination (e.g., www.visitcostarica.com/en, https://discoverdominica.com/en/home).

3. Destination branding: The destination branding approach selected by the DMO can be reflected in its websites (e.g., www.incredibleindia.org/content/incredible-india-v2/en.html). Depicting images and colors that reflect the branding reinforces brand adoption and equity.

4. Globalization: Websites allow DMOs and destinations to reach out globally and build awareness around the world. To do this, DMO websites must be in multiple languages as well as being reflective of the cultural differences among countries. You will hear more about this later.

5. Market research: Websites are great not only for providing information to customers but also for gathering information from customers. Market research data are collected through online surveys and feedback forms.

6. Relationship marketing: Information that customers enter about themselves is built into databases and used to create closer relationships with them. Websites support DMOs' CRM efforts.

7. Social media: Social media platforms are places where customers discuss aspects of the destination and thereby provide valuable intelligence for the DMO. This application is discussed in greater detail later in this chapter.

8. Marketing programs and activities: Websites are venues for implementing all types of marketing activities and programs (using the eight Ps discussed in Chapter 12). Websites are also a key element in IMC.

9. Partnerships: The online environment is a great place for building partnerships. In Chapter 8, several examples were provided of online partnerships and e-collaborators, including the BestCities Global Alliance (www.bestcities.net/).

Characteristics of Effective Destination Websites

What are the characteristics of the world's best DMO websites? To demonstrate these characteristics, the I AM OUTSTANDING model is introduced and explained in detail (Fig. 15.7). There are fourteen important characteristics of excellent international DMO websites and taken one by one they spell out I AM OUTSTANDING. They reflect website features that are not only important to customers but are also critical to effective DMO marketing communications. There are undoubtedly other features of great DMO websites, but these fourteen are among the most important for a successful Internet presence.

I = INTERNATIONAL

The website of VisitDenmark (www.visitdenmark.com) has nine language versions. Most of the major countries of Europe are covered, and Chinese is also available. The VisitBritain

I = International

A = Address website
   users as individuals

M = Monitored or
   constantly evaluated
   and improved

O = Outstanding, award-winning
U = Up-to-date
T = Targeted
S = Social media
T = Telephone versions
A = Attractive
N = Networked
D = Dynamic
I = Integrated
N = Niche markets
G = Great contents

I AM OUTSTANDING

Figure 15.7 I AM OUTSTANDING framework.

holiday site (www.visitbritain.com) is available in eighteen language/country versions. These include five country versions of English. The foreign languages include Chinese, Japanese, Arabic, and many European tongues. The Tourism Australia site (www.australia.com) has sixteen country and language versions, including several English-language versions.

A = ADDRESS

The great DMO websites treat website users as individuals and allow personalization of the website experience. Myswitzerland.com (www.myswitzerland.com/en/home.html) is a great example of addressing travelers as individuals (Switzerland Tourism 2022). People planning to visit the country can book hotels, look at expert tips and get recommendations for different types of activities on trips to Switzerland. The HKTB's website (www.discoverhongkong.com) is full of contents that provide interactive experiences for travelers. The website offers Traveller Essentials that include mobile apps and e-guidebooks (HKTB 2022).

M = MONITORED

Excellent international DMO websites are always being constantly checked, evaluated and updated by their owners; evaluation is constant. There are many tools and indicators available to assess DMO websites, and these should be applied continuously. These tools include log-file analysis software programs and website user surveys. Many DMOs, for example, use Google Analytics to evaluate their website traffic.

O = OUTSTANDING

Great DMO websites often win awards or some other recognition. Some of the website award and recognition programs are the Webby Awards (www.webbyawards.com), the PATA Gold Awards (www.pata.org/pata-gold-awards), HSMAI Adrian Awards (www.adrianawards.com/), World Travel Awards (www.worldtravelawards.com/), WebAwards (www.webaward.org/); Interactive Media Awards (https://interactivemediaawards.com/) and others. There are also ratings by online sources, including Skift (Fig. 15.8) and by tourism consultants. The ten best-designed tourism websites in the world in 2022, as judged by Skift, are shown in Figure 15.8.

U = UPDATED OR UP TO DATE

The excellent international DMO websites are updated frequently and therefore are current. They include timely information and never appear out of date. The destination website for New

Destination	DMO	Domain
1. Iceland	Visit Iceland (Icelandic Tourism Board)	https://www.visiticeland.com/
2. California, USA	Visit California	https://www.visitcalifornia.com/
3. Zurich, Switzerland	Zürich Tourismus	https://www.zuerich.com/en
3. Brazil	Embratur	https://www.visitbrasil.com/en/
5. New York City, USA	NYC & Company	https://www.nycgo.com/
6. Finland	Visit Finland (Business Finland Oy)	https://www.visitfinland.com/en/
7. Australia	Tourism Australia	https://www.australia.com/
8. Peru	PROMPERÚ	https://www.peru.travel/en
9. Italy	ENIT	https://www.italia.it/en
10. Greenland	Visit Greenland	https://visitgreenland.com/

Figure 15.8 Best-designed DMO websites for 2022 (Skift 2022).

York City illustrates a good case study of introducing timeliness. New York City is famous for its Broadway (www.nycgo.com/broadway) and off-Broadway shows and other live performance events. The site is frequently updated to include information on the current shows and events, and so it always has a fresh content look and feel.

Here are more details on the Icelandic website that was voted the best in class for 2022.

EXAMPLE 15.8

Iceland Has the Best-Designed Tourism Website in 2022

Skift does a great job in identifying the best tourism websites and Iceland definitely has one of the best ones. The review highlights that the Icelandic website is uncomplicated and easy to navigate, while being convenient to view on a phone.

> The clean-cut and minimalistic nature of Nordic graphic design works well to communicate visual appeal, send concise messages with clarity (or humor), and entice further curiosity with minimal effort, especially in the website world. Visit Iceland leads our list with a transitional homepage display, decorated with background images that hover along the page as they overlap and interact with the text on the screen, making the website feel inviting and alive.
>
> As users scroll further down, the website displays excellent examples of utilizing the organized nature of drop-down menus and vertically moving lists. With a clean white background and bold capitalized black font, readers are able to quickly catch sight of what they want to read, without feeling overwhelmed by options. Blog articles of potential itineraries and Iceland travel tips are also organized in a format reminiscent of YouTube, integrated with carousel elements that are easy to view via mobile phone.
>
> (Ha 2022)

Learning Point

Not only large countries with huge DMOs can have great websites, as this example proves. Of course, the spectacular and unique scenery of Iceland make its visual images very appealing; however, it is the website design that delivers success.

T = TARGETED

The great international websites segment information according to major target markets. The Paris website (https://en.convention.parisinfo.com/) is aimed at the business events markets and has its own unique website domain name. It describes all the meeting venues in the great French city. An online request for proposal is included. The Jamaica Tourist Board has devoted part of its website (www.visitjamaica.com/weddings-and-honeymoons) to the wedding and honeymoon market.

S = SOCIAL MEDIA

All the excellent international websites are closely integrated with social media channels. The most successful DMOs are making frequent use of popular social media channels. Tourism

Australia is one of the DMOs considered to be making outstanding use of social media. Its international English website (www.australia.com/en) has links to Facebook, Twitter, Instagram, YouTube, and Pinterest; the Chinese site also is linked to Sina Weibo, WeChat, and Douyin. Tourism Australia's Facebook site (www.facebook.com/SeeAustralia) has over eight million likes and 8.3 million followers (see Figure 15.9 for more statistics on Tourism Australia social media programs).

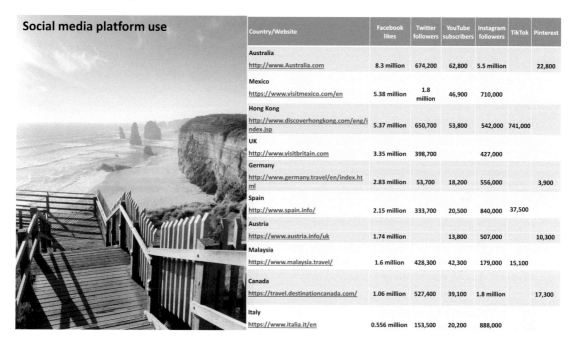

Social media platform use

Country/Website	Facebook likes	Twitter followers	YouTube subscribers	Instagram followers	TikTok	Pinterest
Australia http://www.Australia.com	8.3 million	674,200	62,800	5.5 million		22,800
Mexico https://www.visitmexico.com/en	5.38 million	1.8 million	46,900	710,000		
Hong Kong http://www.discoverhongkong.com/eng/index.jsp	5.37 million	650,700	53,800	542,000	741,000	
UK http://www.visitbritain.com	3.35 million	398,700		427,000		
Germany http://www.germany.travel/en/index.html	2.83 million	53,700	18,200	556,000		3,900
Spain http://www.spain.info/	2.15 million	333,700	20,500	840,000	37,500	
Austria https://www.austria.info/uk	1.74 million		13,800	507,000		10,300
Malaysia https://www.malaysia.travel/	1.6 million	428,300	42,300	179,000	15,100	
Canada https://travel.destinationcanada.com/	1.06 million	527,400	39,100	1.8 million		17,300
Italy https://www.italia.it/en	0.556 million	153,500	20,200	888,000		

Figure 15.9 Social-media platform use based on data for destinations' social-media sites (September 2022).

T = TELEPHONE READY

There has been huge growth in the use of smartphones. Many DMOs have developed mobile phone versions of their website materials as well as downloadable phone applications (apps).

A = ATTRACTIVE

Bold photography and colors and eye-catching headlines make these sites stand out. Several of the websites listed in Figure 15.8 are highly attractive. For example, spectacular videos greet you on the front pages of Visit Iceland and Visit Greenland (https://visitgreenland.com/).

N = NETWORKED

Great DMOs often partner with others in Internet marketing. Berlin, Cape Town, Copenhagen, Dubai, Dublin, Guadalajara, Houston, Madrid, Melbourne, Singapore, Tokyo and Vancouver have joined forces to create a website, BestCities Global Alliance (www.bestcities.net), to gain a larger share of international business events markets. This is a great example of cooperation among top-class cities that have decided it is better to work together than always being competitors. The four provinces of Atlantic Canada (New Brunswick, Newfoundland

and Labrador, Nova Scotia, and Prince Edward Island) along with Destination Canada have partnered together for marketing in the USA and internationally through the Atlantic Canada Agreement on Tourism (www.actp-ptca.ca/). The states in the southeast of the USA have had a long-standing cooperation in tourism promotion that has been extended into e-marketing, Travel South (https://travelsouth.visittheusa.com/).

D = Dynamic

The outstanding international DMO websites have compelling interactive features. The 360-degree videos described the Vietnam cities example is a good demonstration of interactivity.

I = Integrated

The best websites of international DMOs are part of carefully crafted and multi-element IMC programs. Promote Iceland's Inspired by Iceland campaign is a wonderful example of this integration among the DMO websites and various social media. The website (www.inspiredbyiceland.com/) has links to Facebook, Twitter, YouTube, and Instagram. All sites carry the Inspired by Iceland branding and reflect this in a consistent way.

N = Niche Markets

The outstanding international websites often pick out good potential niche, or special-interest, markets and appeal directly to them. Belgium is famous for chocolate, and Wallonia Belgium Tourism includes a section for chocolate lovers on its website (http://walloniabelgiumtourism.co.uk/en-gb/3/i-love/food-and-drink/experiences/chocolate).

G = Great Contents

This is a hallmark of excellent DMO websites, but giving obvious and convenient ways of accessing these great contents is also very important. The Argentinean DMO website provides excellent contents in a well-organized manner for the 5,000-kilometer Road 40 that runs from the north to the south of this South American country.

It can be fairly said that these effective international websites resemble the most glossy, modern magazines. They are sophisticated and eye-catching and creative as well. They are often the essence of simplicity while being deep in content and highly potent as marketing tools. The I AM OUTSTANDING model identifies fourteen important characteristics and features of excellent DMO websites. The following summary explains and connects these aspects of effective DMO websites.

Aspects of Effective Websites

RECOGNIZED FOR EXCELLENCE

The world's most effective DMO websites often win awards or gain some other type of recognition for excellence.

ADDRESS TRAVELERS AS INDIVIDUALS AND ARE DYNAMIC

The effective international DMO websites treat website users as individuals and allow for personalization. Dynamic, interactive features are included to provide each user with an individualized experience.

GLOBAL, ATTRACTIVE AND CONTAIN GREAT CONTENTS

The effective DMO websites have multiple foreign language versions and make other adjustments to fit the cultures of originating regions. With bold photography and colors and eye-catching headlines, they stand out and attract users. They have great, in-depth contents with obvious and convenient ways of accessing the detailed information.

TARGETED AND APPEAL TO NICHE, OR SPECIAL-INTEREST, MARKETS

Effective DMO websites are target marketing tools and provide contents for different segments of the market. Many of them address markets with specialized travel interests and give these customers the unique information that they are seeking online. Here is an example in which the Costa Rican national DMO is targeting a specific market (digital nomads).

EXAMPLE 15.9

Costa Rica Creates Website for Digital Nomads

This initiative demonstrates the flexibility of destination websites. The digital nomad market has developed recently and is growing. The DMO in Costa Rica has noticed that and prepared a page especially for this market on its main destination website.

> The Costa Rican Tourism Institute (ICT) developed a specialized microsite for digital nomads within the Visit Costa Rica website. The specific information for digital nomads can be found by clicking on the top banner and "Things to do." According to the ICT, this website aims to provide all foreigners who define themselves as digital nomads and wish to come to Costa Rica to telework, explore and live unique tourist experiences with the necessary information to prepare for their trip.
>
> This page is dedicated entirely to digital nomads. It contains all the information regarding the requirements, benefits, a step-by-step guide to obtaining the issuance of migratory documents, data on the medical services policy, details for a future visa renewal, and other relevant information.
>
> In addition, the site has a direct link to the General Directorate of Immigration website, where those interested can find the forms that must be completed, as well as the link to download the regulations of Law 10.008, known as the "Digital Nomads Law."
>
> (Costa Rica Tourism Board 2022; Fernandez 2022)

Learning Point

It is important to customize a website for specific markets that have unique expectations and requirements of a destination.

UP TO DATE AND MONITORED

The excellent international DMO websites are updated frequently and are very current. They are constantly being watched, evaluated and improved.

Have Smartphone Applications Available

The great DMO websites have responded to the smartphone trend and have developed mobile phone applications that can be downloaded from their websites.

Use Social Media Channels and Generate User Content

The most successful DMOs have been making extensive use of popular social media channels for several years. They encourage users to provide their own contents in words, photos or videos and then use some of these materials in DMO promotions and share it with other potential visitors.

Are Part of IMCs

The best websites of international DMOs are part of carefully crafted and multi-component IMC programs. Each online and offline component fits together well, and they all reinforce each other.

Networked with Partners and Partner Sites

Great DMOs recognize the value of cooperation and often partner with others in Internet marketing. Sometimes, they work together with other nearby DMOs to form regional websites that create greater online exposure for all partners.

Websites as DMO Platforms

There was a time when websites were stand-alone marketing and communication tools, but that has changed greatly over the past twenty years. DMO websites now provide a platform for connecting with other ICTs and applications and for informing and communicating with DMOs' audiences. For example, some DMO websites incorporate virtual communities where interested people discuss various aspects and features of destinations and recollect their trips for others to read and enjoy. Many people write blogs within these communities. Additionally, most DMO websites link site visitors to the most popular social network sites, such as Facebook, YouTube and Instagram. Increasingly, websites are including download information for DMO apps for smartphones. DMO websites now provide many types of downloads that offer a variety of communication tools for potential visitors. A website is no longer just a website for a DMO but rather an online location to interconnect with various audiences using an integrated set of ICTs.

Intranets and Extranets

Intranets are proprietary websites (portals or gateways) that give employees access to an organization's proprietary information. These websites are suitable for large DMOs that may have hundreds of employees. One commonly used intranet platform in organizations is SharePoint (Microsoft).

Extranets are important in B2B marketing. One research study based on a tour operator's extranet (used by travel agencies) measured the six criteria dimensions of usefulness, relative advantage, entertainment, ease of use, response time, and trust (Caber et al. 2013).

Search Engine Marketing and Optimization

The traditional way for people to find DMO websites was through search engines. Because Google has by far the largest market share, it is common to hear people suggesting Google it to access a specific website. According to one much-used source, Google commands around 92 percent of the market among search engine companies (Oberlo 2022). The next three search engines in terms of market share are Bing (Microsoft), Yahoo!, YANDEX, and Baidu.

Search Engine Marketing (SEM)

SEM involves DMOs in promoting the visibility of their websites on search engines with the objective of appearing on more search engine report pages. This is usually accomplished through paid advertising on the search engines. Search engine advertising can be done on a PPC basis in which the sponsor pays only when users click on the ads. The pricing system used for Google AdWords is at https://ads.google.com/home/pricing/, for example.

Search Engine Optimization (SEO)

SEO represents the steps that DMOs take to ensure that their sites are relevant and important to potential visitors and other audiences. The purpose of SEO is to get destinations listed early and frequently in Google and other search engine searches by potential visitors. There are many techniques that site designers use in SEO involving frequently used keywords, adding keywords to sites' meta data, and interlinking pages within sites and with external sites.

Social Media

Since around 2003 to 2004, social media have had a major influence on destinations and DMOs. Now, most DMOs are active in the social media and are using them for information dissemination, communications and marketing purposes. Social networking sites are many and varied and offer differing features for users. However, most of what you saw already in Figures 15.5 and 15.6 for websites also applies to DMO social media sites.

A scan of the websites of some leading DMOs around the world shows you that many of them have established sites on Facebook, Instagram, TikTok, Twitter, and YouTube. Figure 15.9 illustrates the channels used by these country destinations in the world, and almost all are using these four social media channels. Pinterest, Weibo, and WeChat are quite popular as well. Among the Facebook sites, Australia, Mexico and Hong Kong have the most likes. For Twitter followers, Mexico has the largest number, followed by Australia and Hong Kong. Australia has the most YouTube subscribers, followed by Hong Kong and Mexico. Australia and Canada have the largest numbers of followers on Instagram. The TikTok statistics are incomplete; however, it appears that Hong Kong leads on this platform.

The following is basic information on eighteen of the most popular social network sites and apps for mobile phones. Most of the user statistics are from Datareportal (2022):

1. Facebook (Meta): Started in 2004 and in 2022 had 2.934 billion monthly active users. As shown later in Figure 15.14, many of the Facebook users are outside of North America.
2. YouTube: YouTube was launched in 2005 and in 2022 that it had 2.5 billion monthly active users. India has the most YouTube users at 467 million. YouTube is a Google subsidiary.
3. WhatsApp: This is a mobile messaging app that has 2 billion monthly active users.
4. Instagram: Instagram was launched in October 2010 and since then has had a rapid growth in popularity with 1.44 billion monthly active users in July 2022. Instagram was purchased by Facebook (Meta) in 2012.

5. WeChat: Hugely popular in China, this is a mobile phone chat app that is like WhatsApp, LINE, and Facebook Messenger. Owned by Tencent Holdings, it had 1.288 billion active user accounts in 2022.
6. TikTok: TikTok has 1.02 billion users. It was first introduced as Douyin in China in 2016. It specializes in displaying short-form videos.
7. Facebook Messenger: It has reportedly over a billion users.
8. LinkedIn: This business networking site has approximately 850 million members in 200 countries (LinkedIn 2022).
9. Telegram: Monthly active users for Telegram are approximately 600 million in 2022.
10. Snapchat: This is an increasingly popular service in which users exchange selfies, videos and stories and engage in chats. In 2022, Snapchat had 617 million users.
11. Douyin: The Chinese equivalent of TikTok, it had around 613 million daily active users in 2022.
12. Kuaishou: Had around 598 monthly active users in 2022.
13. Sina Weibo: This is a microblogging site with the users mainly in China. Sina Weibo had 582 million monthly active users in 2022.
14. QQ: This is an instant messaging software service that is owned by Tencent with its users mainly residing in China. In 2022, QQ had 564 million monthly active users.
15. Twitter: Launched in 2006, Twitter is the one of the world's most popular microblogging platforms. There are microblogging sites (called Weibo) in China that have more users than Twitter. In 2022, Twitter had 486 million monthly active users.
16. Pinterest: Introduced in 2011, Pinterest (2017) now has 433 million monthly active users. It is an image bookmarking system on which users "pin" photos and other images in specific categories.
17. Reddit: Has around 430 million monthly active users.
18. Quora: Has approximately 300 million monthly active users.

Other popular social media platforms include Teams, LINE (South Korea and East-Southeast Asia), Vimeo, Dailymotion (France), Tumblr, and VK (Russia).

There are thousands of other social network services and mobile phone apps and far too many to cover in this chapter. However, you should know that other services not described are popular in certain countries but not much used in English-speaking communities. For example, VK is a popular social media service in Russia; however, it is not used as much in the English-speaking world. It has around 100 million monthly active users. Kakao Talk is a much-used mobile chat app in South Korea. China has many social network sites and mobile apps that are primarily based on the use of Mandarin, including Xiaohongshu.

Social networks media platforms offer are a great array of online venues for DMOs to distribute information and communicate with others. There are many activities in which DMOs can engage; some of the most important of these are identified below:

- Building and maintaining communities of interest: Social networks tend to build communities that share similar interests. For DMOs, the goal is to build communities that have an interest in their specific destinations.
- Collecting UGC: This is a very important function of social media sites for DMOs because people post their blogs, comments, videos and photographs of trips to destinations.
- Displaying photography and videos: Some of the social media channels are designed specifically for displaying visual materials: for example, YouTube and TikTok (for videos) and Instagram (for photographs).

- Distributing topical news stories: The social networks are a great place for DMOs to push out news stories about their destinations. This is done through websites but can be more effective when distributing to communities of people who have indicated an interest in the destination.
- Emphasizing current events and campaigns: The social networks are very timely, and people are constantly checking them. Placing upcoming events and new promotional programs here gives a freshness to the information.
- Encouraging word-of-mouth recommendations: This is another of the most important functions of social networks for DMOs. The positive recommendations of past visitors may influence others to go to the destinations.
- Getting feedback: The DMO can request feedback in several ways from people using social networks. Some DMOs conduct polls and place research surveys on social networks.

The use of social networks is growing in importance among DMOs. Consumers are increasingly accessing social media through mobile phones and smartphones, and apps for these phones are the next component of e-marketing.

Apps

More people are using mobile phones and tablets to access the Internet and all sorts of digital media. The sales of PCs, laptops and notebooks are not growing as rapidly as for smartphones. According to the Pew Research Center (2022), 85 percent of US residents owned smartphones in 2021 compared to only 35 percent in 2011. The demand for mobile phone apps is increasing along with these purchasing and usage trends. There were 2.65 million apps (for Android) in the Google Play Store in June 2022 and 3.79 million in the Apple App Store (for iOS) in March 2022 (Statista 2022a, 2022b).

They might be called by different names in different places, including cell phones, hand phones, mobile phones or mobiles, but there is little doubt about the huge impact these devices have had on society worldwide. These cellular phones and networks got started around 1978 to 1979 in the USA and Japan. Digital mobile phones were introduced in the early 1990s. With this scenario, the emphasis in DMO communications and marketing is switching more toward mobile phones and smartphones. This trend is already evident with the proliferation of DMO visitor guide apps and the development of apps for popular travel guidebooks, including Lonely Planet and the Rough Guides, and for traveler review sites, including Tripadvisor.com.

Mobile phones and smartphones are used at all stages of the travel cycle of consumers (Fig. 15.1), from dreaming to recollecting. Although there are no comprehensive worldwide data yet on the use of mobile phones and smartphones for accessing travel information when traveling, this is undoubtedly on a steep upwards trend.

Traditionally, DMOs printed and distributed paper-based visitor guides, which often accompanied visitors on trips. Now, most destinations have either launched mobile versions of their websites or developed native apps for smartphones. Peres et al. (2011) say that apps are an emerging technology and they have promising potential because of several advantages for visitors and DMOs:

- Visitors are better able to utilize their time in the destination by not having to physically go to get information (e.g., at VICs).
- Visitors can access information anywhere and anytime.
- Time saving may mean that visitors spend more in the destination.

- DMOs can provide more information and a greater variety of information.
- Tourist loyalty to the destination may be increased.
- DMOs can monitor visitors' experiences.
- DMOs can more directly influence the information available to visitors.

Many DMOs have developed apps for smartphones, and they are very handy tools to have on a mobile phone or tablet when traveling within destinations but also before going and when planning trips. i Tour Seoul—The Official Travel Guide to Seoul, developed by the Seoul Tourism Organization in South Korea, is a great example (https://english.visitseoul.net/website-Info-article/i-Tour-Seoul-Smartphone-Application_/650). It can be downloaded from the Apple App Store and Google Play.

Smart tourism is the term used when ICTs are being used in assisting visitors in wayfinding and improving their overall experiences and enjoyment in destinations, like the i Tour Seoul app docs. The Hamburg Tourism App offers suggestions as to what you can do next as you are walking down a specific street (Hamburg Tourismus GmbH 2018), www.hamburg.com/useful-information/11900814/hamburg-app/.

Tablet computers, or simply tablets, have a flat touch screen and are highly portable and convenient. Although the Apple iPad, considered to be a post-PC tablet, may be the best-known of these, there are many other brands and models on the market as well. Around 53 percent of US adults owned tablet computers in 2021 (Statista and Thomas Alsop 2022). Because of their portability, they have become very popular with travelers, and so this has put pressure on DMOs to communicate with and provide applications for these devices. With larger screens than smartphones have, tablets are better for viewing documents and photos. Therefore, some DMOs have produced tablet-ready visitor guides, and these are very appealing when viewed.

The curating of apps on their destinations is another useful role for DMOs to play. With the steady proliferation of travel and tourism apps, consumers are faced with choices on which apps to select for trips.

Email

Email marketing is the online equivalent of direct mail, and it should be used primarily to help build and enhance relationships with potential and past visitors. Its major advantages are often said to be the ease of use and low cost of communicating in this way online. Added to that, almost everyone who uses the Internet has an email address. According to a survey by Adestra (2017), 84 percent of owners used their smartphones for receiving and sending personal e-mails, and 34 percent used them for business e-mails.

DMOs and their staff members are using mobile messaging and conferencing apps to communicate with potential and past business event and other visitors; they are not just relying on email. Some of the most popular of these apps were mentioned earlier, and they include WhatsApp, WeChat, Facebook Messenger, Telegram, LINE and others.

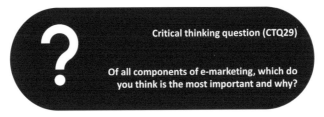

Critical thinking question (CTQ29)

Of all components of e-marketing, which do you think is the most important and why?

Other Components of E-marketing

There are other activities in which DMOs engage in their e-marketing apart from these six main components. These are now briefly discussed.

Traveler Review Sites

Traveler review sites are websites that include assessments by people who have visited destinations, hotels, attractions and restaurants or used other travel services and facilities. Tripadvisor is the most used among these websites. The main appeal of these websites is the perceived objectivity of the reviews for people who are considering going to the destination or using a specific tourism operation.

Tripadvisor has over 490 million unique visitors every month and around 1 billion reviews and opinions by travelers (Tripadvisor 2022). Other traveler reviews are found in a variety of sites, including the sites of traditional travel guidebook publishing companies. For example, Lonely Planet (2018) has the Thorn Tree forum, which is an online discussion group for travelers with over 1 million members. Frommer's (2018) operates several forums on its website, and these are broken down into different regions of the world. Rough Guides (2018) also operates a travel community but on its Facebook site and through other social networks. Fodor's Travel (www.fodors.com/community/) has several forums on its website, and these are mainly organized by geographic region. Travel guidebooks are trusted for their objectivity and lack of commercial ties to destinations and tourism businesses, and this extends to their online forums and discussion groups.

Recent surveys of traveler review sites indicate that most consumers find the reviews to be credible and useful. Using these sites also appears to be growing in popularity. However, you should be aware that there has been some criticism of these sites. The main lesson here for DMOs is that there must be a willingness to accept both positive and negative reviews by past visitors.

Some of the reviews that are included on these sites are very brief comments, whereas others are more extensive and can be classified as blogs.

EXAMPLE 15.10

About Tripadvisor

A majority of people consult Tripadvisor when planning trips. It is essential that DMOs monitor the reviews about their destinations and tourism sector stakeholder businesses.

> Tripadvisor, the world's largest travel guidance platform, helps hundreds of millions of people each month become better travelers, from planning to booking to taking a trip. Travelers across the globe use the Tripadvisor site and app to discover where to stay, what to do and where to eat based on guidance from those who have been there before. With more than 1 billion reviews and opinions of nearly 8 million businesses, travelers turn to Tripadvisor to find deals on accommodations, book experiences, reserve tables at delicious

restaurants and discover great places nearby. As a travel guidance company available in forty-three markets and twenty-two languages, Tripadvisor makes planning easy no matter the trip type.

(Tripadvisor 2022)

Learning Point

Tripadvisor can provide DMOs with a "report card" on their destinations. It is a great source of UGC and needs to be continually tracked.

Podcasts

Podcasts are short digital audio or video files that are made available on websites and social media. For example, some DMOs are using podcasts to deliver timely short videos that are coordinated with upcoming events or festivals. One of the potential advantages of podcasting is that it can be done at a relatively low cost and within a short time period. Destination Melbourne in Australia is one city DMO that is using podcasting. According to its podcast page, "The Destination Melbourne podcast brings you interviews with some of the brightest minds in the Melbourne visitor industry" (https://destination.melbourne/news/podcast). There are also some services that offer collections of podcasts. For example, Player FM (https://player.fm/podcasts/Tourism) provides a wide selection of tourism podcasts from which to choose.

Short Messaging Services (SMS)

Tourism destinations have been using SMS for some time now. One of the applications of SMS is to allow mobile phone users to request destination information with their prior permission. Text Local (2017) conducted an analysis of mobile phone usage in the UK in 2016 and found that there were just over 79 million active devices, 80 percent of which were smartphones. They estimated that around 13.4 million holidaymakers had opted in (or given permission) to receive SMS messages from the tourism sector. Another application used with driving and walking tourism is to push out SMS to people's devices when entering and moving about destinations. This system is widely used by DMOs and attractions in Mainland China, for example.

Virtual Visitor Guides and Brochures

Sometimes called interactive guides, these are online visitor guides that have the appearance of a real visitor guide, and people flip over the pages as they would with a real guide. Of course, these save paper, and the photo quality is very good and sharp when viewed online. They also do not have to be delivered to the door of potential visitors or printed out from PDF files. Users can quickly navigate to the guide sections in which they are most interested without having to flip many pages. Another advantage is that these are searchable and can contain embedded videos. Links to the DMO's website are hyperlinked into these guides as well.

As the title suggests, shorter visitor brochures can also be published online in this format. These brochures have the same advantages as virtual guides, but an added benefit is that they can be updated more frequently without wasting an existing stock of printed brochures.

Big Data Analysis

There are great opportunities in today's digital society for DMOs to use large data sets for guiding marketing and other management decisions. These data are both numerical (quantitative) and non-numerical (qualitative, including text and photos). UGC from social network systems represents one of the most significant sources of big data that can be mined by DMOs.

Performance Evaluation of DMO E-marketing

The constant evaluation of e-marketing efforts is essential. Figure 11.12 provides a comprehensive set of criteria and metrics for measuring the performance of websites, email, social media and mobile marketing. There are also systems and techniques available for assessing specific e-marketing components. For example, DMO WebEVAL® is a system developed by BTI Consulting to evaluate websites (Fig. 15.10). This system is a comprehensive tool used to measure the effectiveness and quality of DMO websites. In addition, it also provides useful guidelines for developing websites and testing their performance. The system is designed to detect weaknesses that can be improved upon and strengths that can be accentuated. WebEVAL uses four perspectives for DMO website evaluation:

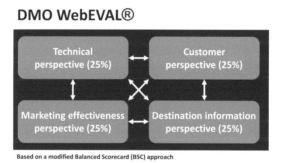

Figure 15.10 The DMO WebEVAL® system (BTI Consulting 2022).

1. Technical perspective: Is the website free from technical problems, and does it have good link popularity? Some of the specific technical criteria are download time, browser compatibility, spelling and use of HTML.
2. Customer perspective: How user-friendly and attractive is the website for travelers? The criteria include site accessibility, site navigation, visual attractiveness, ease of contact and currency of information.
3. Marketing effectiveness perspective: How effective is the website in marketing, positioning and branding the destination? The marketing effectiveness criteria comprise globalization, market segmentation and targeting, positioning and branding, tangibilizing products, marketing research, relationship and database marketing, partnerships and value adding.
4. Destination information perspective: Does the website provide the complete range of information that travelers, travel trade, media and others expect from a DMO? These criteria include destination product information; general travel information; and information for meeting planners, media/press and travel trade.

EXAMPLE 15.11

Digital Skills Accelerator for Tourism Program in New South Wales

It is insufficient for just the DMO to improve its e-marketing skills and capacity. To be most effective, tourism sector stakeholders must also upgrade their professional abilities to conduct e-marketing. This example describes how New South Wales is helping operators to do so.

> Digital innovation is crucial to success in the contemporary tourism landscape. Helping businesses in the visitor economy to improve their digital competency is a key pillar of the NSW Government's Visitor Economy Strategy 2030, which aims to make NSW the premier visitor economy of the Asia-Pacific.
> In addition to a customized digital health check report, successful applicants will also receive two, one-hour consultation sessions with a digital adviser and access to a course library to help improve their knowledge and digital skills.
> (New South Wales Government 2022)

Learning Point

DMOs and their tourism sector stakeholders are highly interdependent. Everyone needs to upskill in e-marketing.

ICT Definition and History

Having reviewed e-marketing, it is important to give you a more complete picture of ICTs. E-marketing is technology based and reliant on ICTs. These technologies include the Internet, social media and networks, smartphones, laptops and tablets, GPS and many others. Providing access alone does not do justice to the many roles and functions that ICTs play. ICTs allow people to interact with the information, with other users and with DMOs. The following is a more complete definition of ICTs.

DEFINITION

ICTs

ICT is an umbrella name that covers communication devices or applications (radio, television, cameras, mobile phones, computer and network hardware and software, satellite systems, etc.) as well as their associated services and applications, including video conferencing, distance education, cloud computing, Wi-Fi, and augmented and virtual reality.

Brief Recent History of ICTs

One of the first major ICT waves came around 1993 with the development of HTML and the World Wide Web. DMOs started developing websites around 1994 to 1995. The second wave was the introduction of e-commerce into tourism very soon after destinations started using the Internet. The third wave, mobile commerce (m-commerce), came right on the heels of e-commerce around 1997. The fourth wave was the so-called Web 2.0, or the use of social media online, with the first social network site being launched in 1997. However, the most popular social media sites started around 2003 to 2004. The fifth wave came with the introduction of smartphones, the earliest versions appearing in 2002. The Apple iPhone was introduced in 2007. Mobile broadband Internet access began around 2007.

Figure 15.11 includes data from the International Telecommunication Union (ITU 2022) on the use of the main types of ICT across the world. These data show the number of subscriptions per 100 inhabitants, and mobile-cellular telephone subscriptions have the highest penetration rate, followed by active mobile broadband. ITU estimated that there were 8.65 billion mobile-cellular subscriptions in 2021 and a global adoption rate of 109.9 percent. ITU found the overall adoption rate of the Internet was 62.5 percent in 2021.

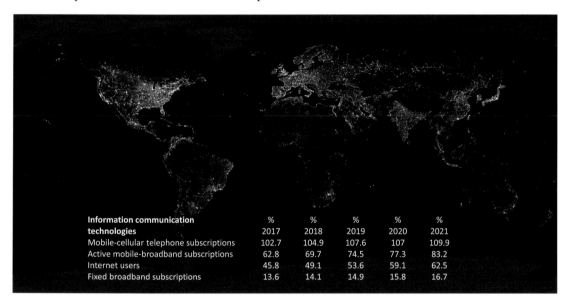

Information communication technologies	% 2017	% 2018	% 2019	% 2020	% 2021
Mobile-cellular telephone subscriptions	102.7	104.9	107.6	107	109.9
Active mobile-broadband subscriptions	62.8	69.7	74.5	77.3	83.2
Internet users	45.8	49.1	53.6	59.1	62.5
Fixed broadband subscriptions	13.6	14.1	14.9	15.8	16.7

Figure 15.11 Growth in the adoption of ICTs (ITU 2022).

Internet Usage

There were almost 5.5 billion Internet users in the world in 2022 (Fig. 15.12), and that was 40 percent higher than the Internet population in 2017. Europe has emerged as the second-largest Internet market and Africa is third, with Latin America and the Caribbean in fourth place. The highest market penetration rates of the Internet are in North America, Europe, and the Middle East. Asia is the leading region with 67.8 percent of all the world's Internet users. There are almost three billion Internet users in Asia. However, the market penetration of Internet users is only 67.8 percent in Asia. There is potential in the future for growing the Internet user market in Asia, as there is in Africa as well.

China is the leading internet user market in the world at 1.01 billion, followed by India (833.7 million), USA (312.3 million), Indonesia (212.4 million), Brazil (178.1 million), and Nigeria (154.3 million) (Miniwatts Marketing Group 2022). It is notable that several developing countries are among the top twenty in terms of Internet users (Fig. 15.13).

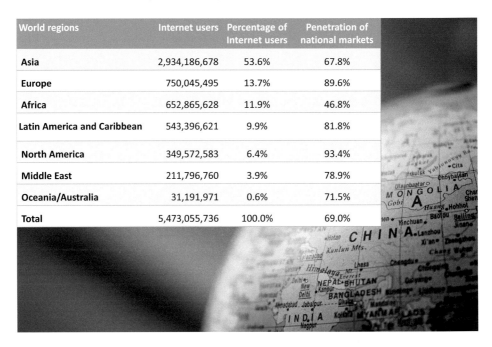

World regions	Internet users	Percentage of Internet users	Penetration of national markets
Asia	2,934,186,678	53.6%	67.8%
Europe	750,045,495	13.7%	89.6%
Africa	652,865,628	11.9%	46.8%
Latin America and Caribbean	543,396,621	9.9%	81.8%
North America	349,572,583	6.4%	93.4%
Middle East	211,796,760	3.9%	78.9%
Oceania/Australia	31,191,971	0.6%	71.5%
Total	5,473,055,736	100.0%	69.0%

Figure 15.12 World internet population, July 31, 2022 (Miniwatts Marketing Group 2022).

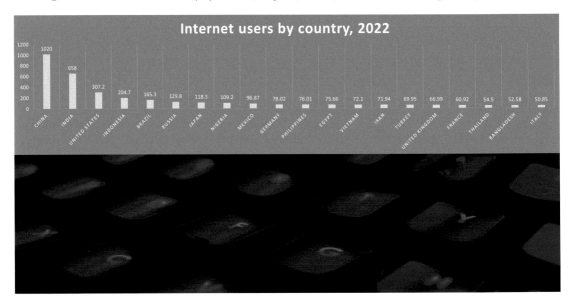

Figure 15.13 Countries with the most internet users (Statista 2022).

Facebook is the world's largest social networking site in terms of users with 2.93 billion monthly active users in August 2022 (Datareportal 2022). Interestingly when you look at Figure 15.14, you will see that India has the most Facebook users, and the USA is second. Indonesia, Brazil, and Mexico round out the top five countries in Facebook users.

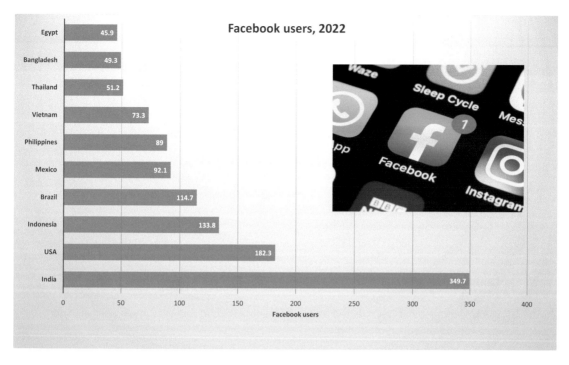

Figure 15.14 Facebook users, 2022 (Datareportal 2022).

EXAMPLE 15.12

The Swedish Number: Viral Marketing

You could also call this guerrilla marketing as it was a very unusual and unexpected approach to marketing tourism to a country. After it was initiated, this effort went viral and as you will see almost 200,000 phone calls were received.

> To encourage more tourism to Sweden, the Swedish Tourist Association created what turned out to be an incredibly innovative viral marketing campaign: The Swedish number +46 771 793 336.
>
> (FancyCrave 2002)

> The first country in the world with its own phone number. Get connected to a random Swede and talk about anything. Two hundred and fifty years ago, in 1766, Sweden became the first country in the world to introduce a constitutional law to abolish censorship. To honor this anniversary, Sweden is now the first country in the world to introduce its own phone number. Call today and get connected to a random Swede, anywhere in Sweden and talk about anything you want.
>
> (Swedish Tourist Association 2022)

> They have received a total of 197,678 incoming calls, which has totaled a call duration of 367 days. It's not just effective in the USA though, which accounts for 32 percent of the calls, as they've received calls from 190 different countries.
>
> (FancyCrave 2022)
>
> What's happened in a little more than two months is 30,000 volunteers have signed up and fielded nearly 180,000 calls. The Swede volunteers don't have a script or talking points. They are encouraged to just have a conversation with the callers. Most volunteers report that some of the calls aren't specifically about tourism at all, but they talk about issues like politics and racism, and other callers are just lonely . . . This unique marketing campaign shows us that the human connection and word-of-mouth advertising is still some of the best marketing your dollars can buy.
>
> (Goodman 2016)

Learning Point

Doing what is most unexpected in destination marketing can be a huge success and lead to a communication going viral.

Traveler ICTs

Following is a brief overview of ICTs that are being used by travelers.

Global Positioning System (GPS)

GPS has multiple applications in tourism destinations. A standard feature in most cars for getting directions to places, GPS is also now a function available on smartphones. As you read earlier, GPS technology on phones is being used by DMOs, including Seoul apps for wayfinding and for letting users know what is near their current locations. There are many other more generic mapping apps that allow people to find their way around in destinations using mobile phones because this also can be done with purpose-designed, handheld GPS devices.

Geo-tagging

Geo-tagging uses GPS technology to add specific geographic location data to a photo, video, blog or another type of digital file. This is entirely feasible now with smartphones that have built-in cameras and GPS functions. Geo-tagged photos are popular in photo-sharing social media networks because they allow users to see exactly where photos were taken. Geo-tagging is being used by DMOs in interactive mapping and the placement of geo-coded photos on these maps.

Cashless Payment Systems and Smart Cards

Consumer payments without using cash or physical credit cards (digital payments) are rapidly becoming more prevalent. This convenience is especially popular in Asia, including China,

Hong Kong, Singapore and India. Again, this trend is being enabled by the widespread ownership of mobile phones and smartphones. Extensions to popular messaging apps and systems such as PayPal are accelerating this trend.

Smart cards have been available for several years for travel on public transportation systems in major cities around the world. However, their use is expanding to other parts of tourism, including paying admission fees at attractions, restaurants and shopping. The traditional smart cards have embedded integrated circuits that are recognized by special reader devices hooked up to computers. Now, these smart cards can be downloaded into smartphones, and the phone is used for scanning rather than a card. This technology is being used in several urban public transportation systems. Smartphone boarding passes are another similar application where airline passengers have their phone screens scanned.

Travel—Google, Google Maps and Google Earth

Google introduced the Google Trips app (https://get.google.com/trips/) in 2016 and now has a suite of useful apps for travelers. There are several mapping tools available on the Internet that can be useful for DMOs, and two of the prime ones are Google Maps and Google Earth.

The National Geographic Society based in the USA also has some great online maps (https://mapmaker.nationalgeographic.org/) as well as an app for viewing maps on smartphones. Several DMOs are using prominent mapping sources like these to provide directions to visitors. They are also trying to embed more sites within their destinations on the maps and some of these, with geo-coded photos.

Internet of Things (IoT)

The IoT will greatly enhance the value of 5G networks. IoT means connecting everything to the Internet. More technically, Atzori et al. (2010) say that IoT takes things that are around us "such as radio-frequency identification tags, sensors, actuators, mobile phones, etc. through unique addressing schemes, which are able to interact with each other and cooperate with their neighbours." Xia et al. (2012) describe the IoT as the networked interconnection of everyday objects.

Videoconferencing

Videoconferencing has existed for many years and many thought it would never replace face-to-face meetings—then along came the COVID-19 pandemic and things dramatically changed as people could not physically congregate together. Applications such as Zoom and Teams became very popular in 2020 to 2022. Virtual meetings (all participants online) and hybrid meetings (some meeting in person, some online) were common during this time period.

Some people like online meetings while others prefer to meet in person. Much has been written, therefore, about the advantages and disadvantages of virtual meetings. On the positive side, lower costs, greater accessibility, increased safety, and sharing of information are often cited. The lack of human interaction is the most mentioned drawback. Inhibiting creativity is another criticism of virtual meetings, as the example explains.

EXAMPLE 15.13

Videoconferencing Inhibits Creative Ideas

The COVID-19 pandemic forced most meetings to be held online via platforms such as Zoom and Teams. This example explains the results of a research study showing that videoconferencing stifles creative ideas.

> In a laboratory study and a field experiment across five countries (in Europe, the Middle East and South Asia), we show that videoconferencing inhibits the production of creative ideas. By contrast, when it comes to selecting which idea to pursue, we find no evidence that videoconferencing groups are less effective (and preliminary evidence that they may be more effective) than in-person groups. Departing from previous theories that focus on how oral and written technologies limit the synchronicity and extent of information exchanged, we find that our effects are driven by differences in the physical nature of videoconferencing and in-person interactions. Specifically, using eye-gaze and recall measures, as well as latent semantic analysis, we demonstrate that videoconferencing hampers idea generation because it focuses communicators on a screen, which prompts a narrower cognitive focus. Our results suggest that virtual interaction comes with a cognitive cost for creative idea generation.
>
> (Brucks and Levav 2022)

Learning Point

While more research is needed to support these findings, this study highlights that not all the outcomes of virtual meetings are positive.

Wikis

Wikis are websites on which the contents are contributed by online communities of people. Theoretically, any user can add, modify or delete content on the wiki, but that basic concept has been modified by some wikis to give more control over the content. Wikipedia is probably the best-known wiki. There are several wikis that exist for tourism, travel and hospitality, but DMOs do not seem to make much use of this ICT application at present.

Recent ICT Innovations

There are many other ICTs available that are being applied in tourism destinations or have the potential to be used. Indeed, there are almost too many to write about, and the focus of this chapter has been on e-marketing applying the main ICTs. There are ICTs that are being applied within specific types of tourism businesses, such as in hotels and restaurants, but the author decided not to review these in detail. However, there are a few additional ICTs that need to be discussed briefly so that you have a more complete picture of their usage within destinations in general.

Augmented Reality (AR)

AR is an ICT application involving the use of smartphones. AR uses visitors' existing environments and overlays virtual information on top of them (Reality Technologies 2016). It is done by users pointing phone or tablet cameras at specific attractions, points of interest and other locations and then computer software overlaying images, icons or information on the images in their camera screens (Fig. 15.15).

Figure 15.15 AR superimposes information on a visitor's tablet.

DEFINITION

Augmented reality (AR)

AR is the enhancement of a real-world environment using layers of computer-generated images through a device (usually a smartphone or tablet) (Yung and Khoo-Lattimore 2019).

AR can be used to enhance the interpretation at sightseeing spots or at specific attractions such as museums and art galleries. For example, in the camera screens of smartphones, the original structure of buildings can be superimposed upon the ruins at which visitors are pointing. This use of ICTs can be very helpful in fulfilling at least some of the roles of interpretation that are discussed in Chapter 7.

Virtual Reality (VR)

Earlier in this chapter, you heard about how several destinations are using 360-degree video as a form of virtual reality (VR). As the following definition shows, VR takes people to artificial environments (Fig. 15.16).

Figure 15.16 VR can transport people to the destinations they want to visit.

DEFINITION

Virtual reality (VR)

VR is the use of a computer-generated 3D environment, that the user can navigate and interact with, resulting in real-time simulation of one or more of the user's five senses (Yung and Khoo-Lattimore 2019).

VR, as demonstrated by 360-degree video, allows people to sample destinations by viewing and imagining tourism experiences. VR headsets (Fig. 15.16) are another way of taking people to their desired destinations.

EXAMPLE 15.14

Germany Turns to VR Tourism

During the COVID-19 pandemic, many DMOs began to offer virtual travel experiences. This was intended to help in the recovery post-COVID as well as offering more people the opportunity to sample destinations.

In this environment, a number of countries have stepped up VR marketing efforts to prepare for the gradual recovery of their tourism industries. Among the most prominent is Germany, which has unveiled a number of immersive projects to highlight the country's potential as a travel destination.

In 360-degree videos designed to be seen on Oculus Rift headsets, for example, the German National Tourist Board (GNTB) has taken viewers on trips across the country, as well as to parts of its Baltic and North Sea coasts. Another set of videos—for the Microsoft Hololens—includes views of six of the country's most famous castles and palaces. "Digital applications cannot, and are not intended to, replace the experience of real-world travel," GNTB chief executive Petra Hedorfer told the BBC.

(Debusmann Jr 2020)

Learning Point

VR tourism has a promising future, although it is not an entire substitute for real travel experiences. It has great potential for destination marketing, branding, and communications in the years to come.

Metaverse

The metaverse is a new technology that is as yet not widely applied by destinations and DMOs. However, it is expected to be widely used in the future. Here is a definition.

DEFINITION

Metaverse

It is a collective virtual space, created by the convergence of virtually enhanced physical and digital reality. In other words, it is device-independent and is not owned by a single vendor. It is an independent virtual economy, enabled by digital currencies and nonfungible tokens (NFTs). A Metaverse represents a combinatorial innovation, as it requires multiple technologies and trends to function. Contributing tech capabilities include AR, flexible work styles, head-mounted displays, an AR cloud, the IoT, 5G, AI and spatial technologies (Gupta 2022).

There are not yet many DMOs that are using the metaverse; however, one example is given where it is being applied in Atlanta, Georgia.

EXAMPLE 15.15

Atlanta Meta World

The metaverse is in the very early stages of application to destination management. The DMO in Atlanta, Georgia is one of the pioneers of this new technology.

> Exploring Digital, a Cobb County-based media and virtual reality experiences company, is behind the groundbreaking creation and launch of Atlanta Meta World—the country's first visually realistic virtual world representation of a built environment for Atlanta Convention and Visitors Bureau (ACVB). This new technology was unveiled last month at the American Society of Association Executives' annual meeting in Nashville, Tennessee.
>
> Atlanta Meta World is a photo-realistic representation of an existing destination where users can select an avatar and navigate the virtual experience, interacting with other users in real time. Atlanta Meta World is accessible through a browser, making the world available to anyone with a computer and internet connection without the need for a VR headset.
>
> Atlanta Meta World is a digital twin of Centennial Olympic Park and the structures within the park, including ACVB's visitor information center where all Meta World experiences begin. The 22-acre greenspace on Georgia World Congress Center's campus lies in the heart of downtown Atlanta, surrounded by attractions, hotels and restaurants. Currently, visitors to Atlanta Meta World can explore the many areas of the park by running, walking and even flying overhead. As Atlanta Meta World expands with the possible addition of surrounding venues, visitors will be able to facilitate virtual walkthroughs of those locations.
>
> (Gol 2022)

Learning Point

The metaverse has great potential for destinations in creating virtual environments in which potential visitors can explore, participate, and interact.

Artificial Intelligence (AI)

DEFINITION

Artificial intelligence (AI)

In the simplest terms, AI which stands for artificial intelligence refers to systems or machines that mimic human intelligence to perform tasks and can iteratively improve themselves based on the information they collect. AI manifests in a number of forms (including chatbots, intelligent assistants, and recommendation engines) (Oracle 2022).

AI is getting machines to simulate aspects of human intelligence and provide services for visitors planning to or engaging in travel and tourism (Fig. 12.17). Driverless cars are an example of this AI technology that is on the horizon. However, there are many other AI applications relating to information provision that have potential for destinations. AI personal and digital assistants are being increasingly used to provide information for customers across a wide variety of industries.

Challenges and Issues

Despite the widespread usage of e-marketing and ICTs, there are challenges and issues that need to be mentioned before closing out Chapter 15. These include human resource challenges in having adequate competencies and skills in performing e-marketing; data security and privacy issues; fake news potential; and user overuse and online addiction. Globally, there is also the issue of a digital divide in terms of dissimilar levels of accessibility to the Internet and other ICTs (ITU 2022, pp. 23–26).

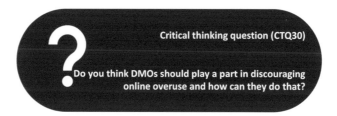

Critical thinking question (CTQ30)

Do you think DMOs should play a part in discouraging online overuse and how can they do that?

Human Resource Challenges

The introduction of new technologies and platforms is rapid; however, reskilling and upskilling of people to use them often cannot keep pace with the rate of change. A recent independent review of DMOs in England highlights this problem.

EXAMPLE 15.16

Digital Skills Are Low across England's Tourism Sector

There is a tendency to think that e-marketing skills are topnotch especially in highly developed countries such as the UK. However, an independent review of DMOs in England found quite the contrary as this example shows.

> The issue of skills within DMOs is also exacerbated by current funding models. This is of particular concern in relation to digital skills, a key emerging area that the tourism sector must make the most of if England is to remain competitive. Digital skills and knowledge are low in general across the tourism sector, and are not helped by DMO staff themselves lacking the expertise and the resources to help support businesses and upskill them. I lost count of the number of times I was told that DMO websites were "poor" and I got a sense many DMOs were not sufficiently equipped to embrace opportunities like the online business-to-business platform TXGB or marketing via mediums such as

TikTok. Furthermore, if a DMO does not know what it's annual budget is going to be at the start of the year, it stands to reason it is going to struggle to attract and maintain skilled staff.

(Department for Digital, Culture, Media and Sport 2021: 47)

Learning Point

There is still a considerable amount to be done to upgrade DMO e-marketing skills to acceptable levels overall.

This issue of a lack of human capacity is exacerbated in poorer, less-developed countries where use and adoption rates of ICTs are lower. This is highlighted in the example about Cambodia.

EXAMPLE 15.17

Some Countries Need to Catch Up with E-Marketing

The adoption and use of e-marketing among the world's DMOs is not even. Some DMOs are much further advanced and sophisticated in their applications of ICTs. Cambodia is one the countries that needs to catch up with other destinations.

On the digital marketing front, the country has a lot of work to do. The prime minister acknowledged the lack of "a functioning marketing and promotions that are based on international practices" as an ongoing weakness to be addressed in his roadmap.

"There is no independent tourism board in Cambodia as it stands," said Nick Ray. The country has the Cambodia Tourism Federation and Cambodian Association of Travel Agents [both didn't respond to media inquiries], but none of them are tasked with marketing or a budget, said Hanuman Travel Product Director Nick Ray. Businesses can promote themselves, but you need a coordinated campaign or a large umbrella to sit under," Ray said "That's where we are a bit lacking. We don't have that strategic vision like you have coming from the tourism authority in Thailand and the budget to back it up."

The lack of digital marketing could be one reason why Angkor Wat remains the country's selling point. An "over reliance on Angkor for tourism marketing" was one of the weaknesses of the tourism sector listed by the prime minister in his roadmap.

(Habtemariam 2022)

Learning Point

It is difficult for a destination to launch effective e-marketing unless there is a strong DMO to coordinate the effort.

Given these human resource capacity issues, what can be done to solve them? One of the answers is for government agencies and DMOs to provide training or other forms of advice. You learned earlier about how the Government of New South Wales in Australia introduced a program to provide advice on technology use within the visitor economy. A second example is from British Columbia, Canada where Destination British Columbia arranges a Tourism Digital Academy (Destination British Columbia 2022). UNWTO has also introduced the Digital Futures Programme as profiled in the example.

EXAMPLE 15.18

UNWTO Digital Futures Programme

The rapid adaptation to e-marketing requires upskilling of many people in DMOs and among tourism sector stakeholders. It has created a major need for related training and education. While larger companies and organizations have the resources to adapt, smaller- and medium-size entities struggle to increase their capacities.

> UNWTO Digital Futures seeks to accelerate economic recovery of the tourism sector by scaling up innovative small and medium-sized enterprises (SMEs) to unleash digital technologies to create jobs and enhance future resilience in the linkages of the tourism value chain post-COVID-19.
>
> While the health crisis was a harsh reality for many SMEs, it also created incredible opportunities for those that could innovate and take advantage of the expansive reach of digital channels. According to an analysis by Mastercard Test and Learn®, digitally enabled SMEs saw a 5.0 percent increase in customer spending and a 4.5 percent increase in transactions compared to their peers.
>
> The UNWTO Digital Futures Programme recognizes that SMEs are at the forefront of economic recovery and aims to support their digital transformation journey by facilitating the diffusion of relevant technologies to SMEs in the tourism value chain.

(UNWTO 2022)

Learning Point

The move toward e-marketing has created human resource capacity issues and challenges.

You have learned in this chapter about proactive e-marketing in IMC; however, there is another side to this set of activities. At times, DMOs must adopt a defensive posture in dealing with negative publicity. Technology is accelerating the pace and geographic spread of information. Viral marketing can work wonders for destinations; negative viral news can be highly detrimental. Among this news, is that classified as fake (intentional) and misinformed (not fake but still damaging). The example from Manila in the Philippines highlights the dangers of fake news.

EXAMPLE 15.19

Fake News Adversely Impacts Philippine Tourism

This is an example in which even local residents are guilty of spreading fake news.

> Authorities on Tuesday appealed to the public to stop spreading fake news about baggage pilferage at the Ninoy Aquino International Airport, saying the bad publicity would affect the tourism industry in the country.
>
> Transportation Secretary Arthur Tugade also urged the public to be more responsible in sharing posts on social media about baggage theft and other accusations involving airport workers. Tugade acknowledged that incidents in the past had left a dent on the integrity and honesty of airport officials and personnel, but he said sharing non-verified posts would only make things worse.
>
> (Zurbano 2018)

Learning Point

Destinations and DMOs must be vigilant in tracking news and online stories that may have a negative impact on tourism. Corrective action and communications should be rapidly implemented.

Another serious issue connected with e-marketing is the overuse of the Internet by a small, although significant, portion of the population. The example discusses the problem of Internet Addiction Disorder (IAD).

EXAMPLE 15.20

Internet Addiction Disorder (IAD)

Destinations and DMOs are definitely not going on their own be able to tackle and solve this social. However, they should be aware of it and, if appropriate, warn against excessive use of the Internet.

> Internet addiction disorder (IAD) is a type of behavioral addiction that involves compulsive Internet use. People with an Internet addiction may have underlying mental health or substance use issues that may require specialized addiction treatment.
>
> While not officially recognized as a disorder in the USA, compulsive Internet use is believed to be fairly common, affecting an estimated 1.5 to 8.2 percent of people in North America.
>
> (AddictionResource.net 2022)

Learning Point

This is an example of taking social responsibility in dealing with a societal problem.

Steps in Effective E-marketing

For the most effective e-marketing, DMOs need to do the following:

- Gather and curate content for use in various e-marketing efforts.
- Continuously track travel blog and vlog sites. Provide feedback and comments when required.
- Use blogging to provide ongoing information and stories on the destination.
- Design and maintain effective websites, including continual evaluation of these websites.
- Establish and maintain pages on the most popular social media platforms.
- Develop apps for the most popular smartphones and tablet devices.
- Make effective use of email and messaging apps for communications with potential visitors, stakeholders, and others.
- Continuously track comments about the destination and tourism stakeholder operations on traveler review sites. Provide feedback and comments when required.
- Consider using other e-marketing tools, including traveler review sites, podcasts, SMS, virtual guidebooks and brochures, and big data analysis.
- Keep updated on the introduction of new ICTs in tourism and related fields.

SUMMING UP

E-marketing is becoming the most important way to communicate about destinations. The six main components of DMO e-marketing are content creation, websites, SEM and optimization, social media, apps, and email marketing. The Internet has become the most important venue for destination marketing, branding, and communications as well as being the consumer's first-choice place to search for information on destinations.

Digital media perform different functions for travelers through their trip cycles. The reasons and purposes for using DMO digital media can be divided into four stages:

1. Dreaming-enthusing-informing.
2. Planning-selecting-booking.
3. Traveling-visiting-enjoying.
4. Repeating-recommending-recollecting.

Curating different types of digital content is the foundation of effective DMO e-marketing. This content is a combination of DMO-developed content and UGC. Video and still photography along with text are the main formats of content. Videos are becoming increasingly important and more interactive as demonstrated by 360-degree presentations.

Blogging and vlogging are popular among consumers, and travel is one of the most discussed themes for people to write about online. Most of the activity is C2C communications about travel trip experiences. DMOs are using blogs for five purposes: communication, promotion, product distribution, management, and research.

Effective DMO websites have several specific characteristics and the I AM OUTSTANDING model expresses fourteen of these (international, address website users as individuals, monitored or constantly evaluated and improved, outstanding/award winning, up-to-date, targeted, social media, telephone versions, attractive, networked, dynamic, integrated, niche markets and great contents). SEM and SEO enhance the visibility and relevancy of DMO websites. This is particularly important for Google, which has the largest share of searches.

Most DMOs are now heavily engaged in using social media platforms and especially the most popular ones, including Facebook, YouTube, Instagram, and Twitter. The major activities of DMOs in using social network sites include building and maintaining communities of interest, collecting UGC, displaying photography and videos, distributing topical news stories, emphasizing current events and campaigns, encouraging word-of-mouth recommendations and getting feedback.

Mobile phones and smartphones are being used extensively in travel and tourism with multiple applications. Guides are one of the major apps being developed by DMOs for visitors to access on mobile phones, smartphones and tablets.

Email marketing can be accomplished quickly and at a relatively low cost, producing a good ROI for DMOs. However, visitors should give their permission to opt in to receive e-mails from destinations.

Other e-marketing activities in which DMOs may engage include traveler review sites, podcasts, SMS, virtual visitor guides and brochures, and big data analysis.

Various ICTs support the e-marketing of DMOs, with the Internet being the primary platform. Consumers have many ICTs available to them for trip planning and while traveling, such as GPS; geo-tagging; cashless payment systems and smart cards; Google Trips, Google Maps and Google Earth; e-readers and wikis. More recent ICT technologies that are being introduced into destination marketing and management include AR, VR, metaverse, and AI.

KEYWORDS

- 360-degree video
- artificial intelligence (AI)
- augmented reality (AR)
- big data
- blogs
- content curation
- content marketing
- customer relationship management (CRM)
- digital divide
- drones
- email
- e-marketing
- extranet
- fake news
- global positioning system (GPS)
- hybrid meetings
- influencers
- information communications technologies (ICTS)
- internet
- internet of things (IoT)
- intranet
- metaverse
- microblogging
- online addiction
- online travel agencies (OTAs)
- podcasts
- security and privacy issues
- smart cards
- smart tourism
- short message service (SMS)
- social media
- storytelling
- traveler review sites
- user-generated content (UGC)
- video
- videoconferencing
- video marketing
- viral marketing
- virtual meetings
- virtual reality (VR)
- vlogs
- websites

REVIEW QUESTIONS

1. Why is e-marketing now so important for DMOs?
2. What are the major components of e-marketing?
3. What types of digital content do DMOs need to curate?
4. What are the major roles, marketing functions, and characteristics of effective DMO websites?

5. Why do DMOs need to be involved in SEM and SEO, and what is involved in these activities?
6. Why are social media so important for DMOs?
7. Why are apps now so important for DMOs and destination marketing?
8. How should DMO e-marketing performance be evaluated?
9. Which ICTs are enjoying the greatest growth in recent times?
10. What are the potential applications of AR, VR, metaverse, and AI to destination marketing?

REFERENCES

AddictionResource.net (2022) "Internet addiction: Causes, effects, and treatments," https://www.addictionresource.net/behavioral-addictions/internet/#:~:text=Internet%20addiction%20disorder%20%28IAD%29%20is%20a%20type%20of,adults%20in%20the%20United%20States%20use%20the%20Internet

Adestra (2017) "Consumer Digital Usage & Behavior Study," https://www.adestra.com/resources/2017-consumer-digital-usage-behavior-study/

Atzori, L., Iera, A., and Morabito, G. (2010) "The Internet of Things: A Survey," *Computer Networks*, 54 (15): 2787–2805.

Belle Tourism International Consulting (2022) *DMO WebEVAL*, Shanghai: Belle Tourism International Consulting.

Brucks, M. S., and Levav, J. (2022) "Virtual communication curbs creative idea generation," *Nature*, 605(7908), 108–112.

Caber, M., Albayrak, T., and Loiacono, E. T. (2013) "The Classification of Extranet Attributes in Terms of Their Asymmetric Influences on Overall User Satisfaction: An Introduction to Asymmetric Impact-Performance Analysis," *Journal of Travel Research*, 52 (1): 106–116.

Cliffs of Moher Experience (2022) "Digital Tourism Campaign Targets North American Market," www.cliffsofmoher.ie/digital-tourism-campaign-targets-north-american-market/

Content Marketing Institute (2022) "What Is Content Marketing?" https://contentmarketinginstitute.com/what-is-content-marketing/

Costa Rica Tourism Board (2022) "Live, Work and Explore in Costa Rica," www.visitcostarica.com/en/costa-rica/digital-nomads

Datareportal (2022) "Global Social Media Statistics," https://datareportal.com/social-media-users

Debusmann Jr., B. (2020) "Coronavirus: Is Virtual Reality Tourism About to Take Off?" BBC, October 30, www.bbc.com/news/business-54658147

Department for Digital, Culture, Media and Sport (UK) (2021) "The de Bois Review: An Independent Review of Destination Management Organisations in England," https://assets.publishing.service.gov.uk/government/uploads/system/uploads/attachment_data/file/1011664/2585-C_The_de_Bois_Review_ACCESSIBLE__for_publication_.pdf#

Destination British Columbia (2022) "Tourism Digital Academy," www.destinationbc.ca/learning-centre/tourism-digital-academy/

Elmes-Bosshard, L. (2022) "What Is the Value of Digital Destination Marketing?" *Solimar International*, May 24, www.solimarinternational.com/what-is-the-value-of-digital-destination-marketing/

FancyCrave (2022) "3 Examples of Viral Marketing in Tourism," https://fancycrave.com/viral-marketing-in-tourism/

Fernandez, I. (2022) "Costa Rica Tourism Institute Starts Website for Digital Nomads," *Tico Times*, July 26, https://ticotimes.net/2022/07/26/costa-rica-tourism-institute-starts-website-for-digital-nomads

Frommers (2018) "Forums," https://www.frommers.com/forums

Gol, S. (2022) "Exploring Digital Launches First Metaverse World for One of the Country's Largest Destination Marketing Organizations," *Marietta Daily Journal*, September 15, www.mdjonline.com/pressrelease/exploring-digital-launches-first-metaverse-world-for-one-of-the-country-s-largest-destination-marketing/article_ec316704-343f-11ed-8368-1bb595e3e9e0.html

Goodman, M. (2016) "Call Me Maybe . . . The Viral Marketing Power of Word of Mouth," www.linkedin.com/pulse/call-me-maybethe-viral-marketing-power-word-mouth-melinda-goodman?trk=articles_directory

Gupta, A. (2022) "What Is a Metaverse?" Gartner, www.gartner.com/en/articles/what-is-a-metaverse

Ha, M. A. (2022) "The 10 Best-Designed Tourism Websites in the World 2022," *Skift*, June 15, https://skift.com/2022/06/15/the-10-best-designed-tourism-websites-in-the-world-2022/

Habtemariam, D. (2022) "Cambodia's Long Overdue Effort to Digitize Its Tourism Industry," *Skift*, September 6, https://skift.com/2022/09/06/cambodias-long-overdue-effort-to-digitize-its-tourism-industry/

Hong Kong Tourism Board (2023) "Hello," https://www.discoverhongkong.com/uk/index.html

Incredible!ndia (2018) "The Maharani of Manhattan," www.youtube.com/watch?v=djjl_6n4ef0

International Telecommunication Union (2021) "Measuring Digital Development: Facts and Figures 2021," www.itu.int/en/ITU-D/Statistics/Documents/facts/FactsFigures2021.pdf

——— (2022) "Global Connectivity Report 2022," www.itu.int/itu-d/reports/statistics/global-connectivity-report-2022/

LinkedIn (2022) "About LinkedIn," https://about.linkedin.com/

Lonely Planet (2018) "Thorn Tree forum," https://www.lonelyplanet.com/thorntree/welcome

Miniwatts Marketing Group (2022) "Internet world Stats," www.internetworldstats.com/stats.htm

Monterey County Convention and Visitors Bureau (2022) "Blog Monterey," www.seemonterey.com/blog/

New South Wales Government (2022) "Free Program Accelerates Digital Skills in NSW Visitor Economy," May 11, www.nsw.gov.au/enterprise-investment-trade/media-releases/digital-skills-tourism

Oberlo (2022) "Search Engine Market Share in 2022," www.oberlo.com/statistics/search-engine-market-share

Oracle (2022) "What Is AI? Learn about Artificial Intelligence, www.oracle.com/artificial-intelligence/what-is-ai/

Peres, R., Correia, A., and Moital, M. (2011) "The Indicators of Intention to Adopt Mobile Electronic Tourist Guides," *Journal of Hospitality and Tourism Technology*, 2 (2): 120–138.

Pew Research Center (2021) "Internet/Broadband Fact Sheet," www.pewresearch.org/internet/fact-sheet/internet-broadband/

Pinterest (2017) "175 million people discovering new possibilities on Pinterest," https://business.pinterest.com/en/blog/175-million-people-discovering-new-possibilities-on-pinterest

Reality Technologies (2016) "Augmented Reality," http://www.realitytechnologies.com/augmented-reality

Rough Guides (2018) "Escape the everyday with Rough Guides," https://www.roughguides.com/

Secretaría de Turismo del Gobierno de México (2021) "Travel Preferences of Internet Users in 2021 According to Visitmexico.com," www.visitmexico.com/en/blog/preferencias-de-viaje-de-los-internautas-en-este-2021-segun-visitmexicocom

Schmallegger, D., and Carson, D. (2008) "Blogs in Tourism: Changing Approaches to Information Exchange," *Journal of Vacation Marketing*, 14 (2): 99–110.

Skift (2022) "The 10 Best Designed Tourism Websites in the World 2022," https://skift.com/2022/06/15/the-10-best-designed-tourism-websites-in-the-world-2022/

Statista (2023) "Countries with the highest number of internet users 2023," https://www.statista.com/statistics/262966/number-of-internet-users-in-selected-countries/

Statista and L. Ceci (2022a) "Google Play: Number of Available Apps 2009–2022," July 27, www.statista.com/statistics/266210/number-of-available-applications-in-the-google-play-store/

——— (2022b) "Number of Active Apps from the Apple App Store 2008–2022," May 17, www.statista.com/statistics/268251/number-of-apps-in-the-itunes-app-store-since-2008/

Statista and Thomas Alsop (2022) "Tablet Ownership Among US Adults 2010–2021," February 14, www.statista.com/statistics/756045/tablet-owners-among-us-adults/

Swedish Tourist Association (2022) "The Swedish Number," www.theswedishnumber.com/

Switzerland Tourism (2023) "We need Switzerland," https://www.myswitzerland.com/en/

Text Local (2018) "The State of SMS," https://www.textlocal.com/blog/2017/05/26/6-sms-marketing-ideas-for-travel-and-tourism-businesses/

Travel Blog (2022) "Travel Blog," www.travelblog.org/

Travellerspoint (2022) "Our Travel Community," www.travellerspoint.com/

Traveloka (2022) "Singapore Tourism Board Partners Traveloka and Trans Digital Media to Welcome Indonesian Travellers to Singapore as Part of the SingapoReimagine Recovery Campaign," May 25, https://sg.finance.yahoo.com/news/singapore-tourism-board-partners-traveloka-023000197.html

Tripadvisor (2022) "Tripadvisor Is the World's Largest Travel Site," https://ir.tripadvisor.com/investor-relations

UNWTO (2022) "UNWTO Digital Futures Programme for small and medium-sized enterprise (SMEs)," https://www.unwto.org/digitalfutures#:~:text=UNWTO%20Digital%20Futures%20is%20a%20platform%20where%20SMEs,workforce%20and%20be%20successful%20in%20the%20new%20normal

UNWTO and European Travel Commission (2007) "A practical guide to tourism destination management," https://www.unwto.org/global/publication/practical-guide-tourism-destination-management

Vietnam Tourism (2022) "Vietnam City in 360°," https://vietnam.travel/things-to-do/vietnam-360-degrees

Volume Nine (2021) "2021 Video Marketing Stats Brands Shouldn't Ignore," www.v9digital.com/insights/2021-video-marketing-stats/

Wyzowl (2022) "Video Marketing Statistics 2022," www.wyzowl.com/video-marketing-statistics/

Xia, H. (2022) "Namibia Launches Digital Campaign to Promote Tourism," *Xinhuanet*, August 11, https://english.news.cn/20220811/9b17ac800a92417ea4cdc99fe94d56ea/c.html

Xia, F., Yang, L. T., Wang, L., and Vinel, A. (2012) "Internet of Things," *International Journal of Communication Systems*, 25: 1101–1102.

Yung, R., and Khoo-Lattimore, C. (2019) "New Realities: A Systematic Literature Review on Virtual Reality and Augmented Reality in Tourism Research," *Current Issues in Tourism*, 22 (17): 2056–2081.

Zurbano, J. E. (2018) "Fake News Affects Tourism," *ManilaStandard.net*, February 6, www.manilastandard.net/news/top-stories/258091/fake-news-affects-tourism.html

Destination Markets and Trends

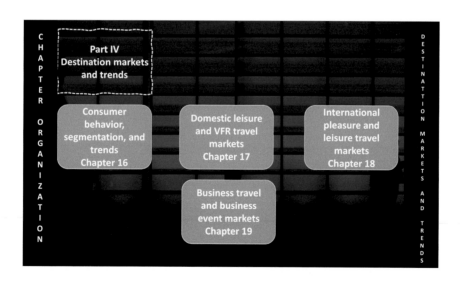

Chapter **16**

Consumer Behavior, Segmentation, and Market Trends

Knowing the customer

LEARNING OBJECTIVES

Having read this chapter, you should be able to:

1. describe motivations for visiting destinations for leisure trips;

2. explain the factors that affect the selection of destinations;

3. explain the process by which destination images are formed and how destination images impact destination selection;

4. review the process of travel purchase behavior, and pinpoint the different stages that travelers tend to go through;

5. elaborate on market segmentation for destinations and the main ways of classifying people into distinct groups;

6. review the recent market trends in tourism.

Warming Up

How did the COVID-19 pandemic affect how and where you traveled? If you are like the author, you traveled much less and closer to home. Did your interests change and did some things become more or less important on your trips? Were you more cautious about what you did when

DOI: 10.4324/9781003343356-20

leaving home? Why are we asking all these questions? The answer is that the questions relate to consumer travel behavior and how it was affected by the pandemic. While the health scare is less in some countries, the imprints of COVID-19 still linger on in the world. This is a lesson in how external environments affect tourism and the attitudes and behaviors of people when they travel.

Chapter 16 begins the four-chapter review in Part IV of destination markets and trends. It covers consumer travel behaviors and gives you an overview of how people tend to make decisions about destinations, including their motives, selection criteria, perceptions of destinations, and purchasing stages. It is fascinating to know how complex these processes can be.

The chapter begins by briefly reviewing motivational theories that have been proposed for tourism, leisure, and recreation. Although there is no consensus among competing theories, there seems to be some agreement that there are two sides to motivation in pleasure/leisure travel: push (internal to tourists) and pull (destination product and marketing) factors.

There are a variety of factors that influence people when selecting destinations for their trips. These are discussed, and a model of destination selection is reviewed. The formulation of people's destination images is also discussed, and a model is described of image formation.

Market segmentation is discussed, and criteria for dividing up markets are explained. Trip purpose and geography have traditionally been used by DMOs to segment markets, but more sophisticated approaches are now being applied by destinations.

The chapter ends by reviewing some of the predominant market trends that are impacting destinations. These trends result from changes in demographics, countries of origin, trip purposes, trip planning and travel arrangements, psychographics and lifestyles, special interests, and uses of technology. The implications of these trends for destinations and DMOs are identified.

Your author has had a long-term interest in consumer behavior and market segmentation in tourism. Several research studies have been completed and the results are reflected in Chapter 16.

Motivations for Travel

Before starting this discussion, you should know that the focus of this chapter is on what is usually called leisure, or pleasure, travel and not on business travel. The motivations for leisure and business travel are quite different. Business travel is motivated by organizational and career needs and priorities, whereas pleasure/leisure travel is based on personal needs and wants. There is less freedom and flexibility in selecting the destinations for business travel than for leisure travel. The motivations for business travel are reviewed in Chapter 19. Here are our definitions of motivation, needs, and wants:

DEFINITIONS

Motivation

Inner drives that customers have that cause them to take action to satisfy their needs.

Needs

Gaps between what customers have and what they would like to have.

Wants

Needs of which customers are aware.

Academic scholars have put forward several theories and approaches to explain why people decide to travel for vacations and holidays. John Crompton, Graham Dann, Seppo Iso-Ahola, and Philip Pearce are four of the most famous of these scholars, but there are several others who have attempted to explain tourist motivations. Some scholars have adapted general models of human motivation to tourism, including the theories advanced by Abraham Maslow, Frederick Herzberg (1964), and others. There is no consensus among scholars on what motivates pleasure/leisure travel, and so what follows is a review of the approaches that appear to be the most accepted.

Mill and Morrison (2012) suggest that an analysis of the travel literature indicates that travel motivations can fit into Maslow's (1943) hierarchy of needs model, which consists of:

- Survival: hunger, thirst, rest, activity.
- Safety: security, freedom from fear and anxiety.
- Belonging and love: affection, giving and receiving love.
- Esteem: self-esteem and esteem from others.
- Self-actualization: personal self-fulfillment.

These are arranged in a hierarchy, and lower-level needs (survival, safety) require more immediate attention and satisfaction before people turn to taking care of higher-level needs. Although the application of Maslow's theory to tourist motivations has gained acceptance, some scholars have judged it to be inadequate in dealing with the special situation of destinations.

EXAMPLE 16.1

Camping Market in China Growing Rapidly

This trend in China is a result of the COVID-19 pandemic in which people are favoring the outdoors and avoiding crowds. Camping is also quite underdeveloped in China when compared with other major countries.

In China, camping and outdoor activities are booming. The popularity of camping reflects a long-term rise in interest in outdoor sports and activities, as well as a trend toward short-haul and local travel driven by the pandemic. The budding industry presents a host of new opportunities in the outdoor activity industries.

Camping has become one of the hottest new trends in China's travel industry. Domestic travel companies have reported a surge in searches for camping during recent holidays, and sales of camping equipment are growing at triple-digit rates. The trend reflects a new direction for the travel industry, as consumers move away from traditional tour groups and COVID-19 restrictions make short-haul nature breaks more attractive to city folks. It also signals an increasing interest in outdoor activities and sports, opening up a range of new possibilities for travel companies that specialize in outdoor tours.

The market is red-hot but also has considerable room to grow. According to the US camping association Kampground, the participation rate of Americans in outdoor activity is over 50 percent. In China, it remains at under 10 percent. As living standards continue to rise and younger generations yearn for a return to nature, outdoor activities and sports are expected to continue on their upward trajectory, presenting an exciting new growth market for investors.

(Huld 2022)

Learning Point

COVID-19 caused travelers to be more concerned about health safety. This trend in China shows the reactions of consumers to the virus threat.

Dann's (1977) push–pull theory is one of the most accepted among the more specific explanations of tourist motivation (Fig. 16.1). The push factors are within individuals themselves as people act to take care of certain internal drives such as the need for escape (Fig. 16.2). The pull factors are the products and marketing by destinations that attract people to visit (Fig. 16.3). DMOs and tourism sector stakeholders have the most control over the pull factors, although they cannot totally orchestrate how people form images of their destinations.

What comes first, push or pull? Generally, it is accepted that the push factors start the process of motivating a person to travel, and the pull factors make them select a specific destination or business within the destination. Klenosky (2002) said that the push factors are related to needs and wants and include the need for escape, rest and relaxation, adventure, prestige, health and fitness, and social interaction. Lee et al. (2002) suggested that push factors determine whether to go, and pull factors determine where to go (Fig. 16.1). The diagram in Figure 16.1 shows that vacation destination choices are impacted by internal motivational driving forces (push) and destination attributes (pull). The two-way arrow between the push and pull factors suggests that there is an interaction between the two factors as people are making their travel decisions. This model also

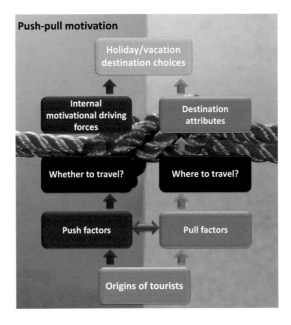

Figure 16.1 Push and pull tourist motivation factors (Lee et al. 2002, p. 93).

Figure 16.2 Some people travel to satisfy inner needs, such as to do yoga.

implies that the push and pull factors vary according to the origins of tourists, and this may be because of economic, sociocultural, and geographic (e.g., location and climate) differences.

Another model with good acceptance is that of Iso-Ahola, who proposed a social psychological model of tourism motivation (Iso-Ahola 1980, 1982, 1983, 1989). He suggested there were two main motives in leisure (including tourism) and these were seeking intrinsic rewards and escaping the everyday environment. These motives can exist simultaneously, and both have personal (psychological) and interpersonal (social) elements (Snepenger et al. 2006). Iso-Ahola proposed four dimensions: (1) personal seeking, (2) personal escape, (3) interpersonal seeking, and (4) interpersonal escape.

Crompton (1979), based upon unstructured, in-depth interviews with respondents in Texas and Massachusetts, found two categories of motives for travel: socio-psychological and cultural. The seven socio-psychological motives were as follows:

Figure 16.3 The lure of Machu Picchu pulls many international tourists from around the world.

1. Escape from a perceived mundane environment: getting away from the place of residence and from home and job environments.
2. Exploration and evaluation of self: having the opportunity to reevaluate and discover more about oneself or acting out one's self-images.
3. Relaxation: taking more time to enjoy activities of interest within the destination.
4. Prestige: increasing one's social status through traveling to certain destinations or businesses.

5. Regression: doing things that are inconceivable in a person's usual lifestyle.
6. Enhancement of kinship relationships: enhancing and enriching family relationships through traveling to and experiencing destinations together.
7. Facilitation of social interaction: meeting new people in different locations.

There were two cultural motives: novelty and education. According to Dann's model, the socio-psychological motives could be classified as push factors and the cultural motives as pull factors.

EXAMPLE 16.2

What Is a Flashpacker?

Here are three alternate definitions of the term "flashpacker." This is a market that is acknowledged to be growing. Some say it reflects the maturing of the backpacker.

> Someone who travels like a backpacker but with a bigger budget; usually any-where from their mid-twenties to mid-forties, seeking adventure and new experiences, and have a bigger travel budget, usually from an established career.
>
> (Flashpacker Headquarters 2022)

> Flashpacking has an association of more disposable income while traveling and has been defined simply as backpacking with a bigger budget. Flash-packer can be thought of as backpacking with flash, or style.
>
> (Nomads World 2017)

> Similar to the common backpacker in that they also travel alone or in pairs rather than using tours, and carry the eponymous trekking pack; however, they typically are in their thirties and forties with enough income to stay in guesthouses instead of dorm rooms. They stay for shorter periods of time and are willing to pay for the fastest or most comfortable means of transportation (but not exclusively). These travelers might be former backpackers who aren't going to argue over the price of a beer, but still aren't traveling in luxury.
>
> (*Urban Dictionary* 2022)

Learning Point

It could be said that flashpackers are flash (stylish) and splash (the cash). Toting back-packs rather than suitcases seems to be the preferred way of transporting clothes and belongings.

Another tourist motivation theory is the travel career approach proposed by Philip Pearce (1982). This approach proposes that the motivation to travel changes with the amount of travel experience that individual tourists have accumulated. Pearce and Lee (2005) found that experiencing different cultures and being close to nature were more important motivating factors for experienced travelers. Less-experienced travelers placed a higher priority on stimulation, personal development, relationship (security), self-actualization, nostalgia, romance, and recognition. These scholars also found that there was a core set of four motivation factors for all tourists: escape, relaxation, relationship enhancement, and self-development.

Beard and Ragheb (1983) developed the leisure motivation scale containing four types of motives that were derived from Maslow's hierarchy of needs theory. These were as follows:

1. Intellectual: engaging in mental activities while traveling, including learning, exploring, discovering, thinking, and imagining.
2. Social: seeking friendship and social esteem from others through traveling.
3. Complete mastery: showing mastery, usually of physical activities, by meeting certain challenges or competition.
4. Stimulus avoidance: escaping and getting away from overstimulating life situations.

Other academic scholars have produced typologies of tourist motivations by placing the motives from various research studies and theories into categories. Swarbrooke and Horner (1999) suggested there were six categories of motivators in tourism:

1. Cultural: sightseeing, experiencing new cultures.
2. Physical: relaxation, sun, exercise and health, sex.
3. Emotional: nostalgia, romance, adventure, escapism, fantasy, spiritual fulfillment.
4. Tourist: status, exclusivity, fashionability, obtaining a good deal, ostentatious spending opportunities.
5. Personal development: increased knowledge, learning a new skill.
6. Personal: VFR, making new friends, need to satisfy others, search for economy if on limited income.

Mill and Morrison (2012) developed a set of motives and referenced actions/desires from the tourism research literature and placed these within Maslow's hierarchy of needs dimensions. These are shown in Figure 16.4.

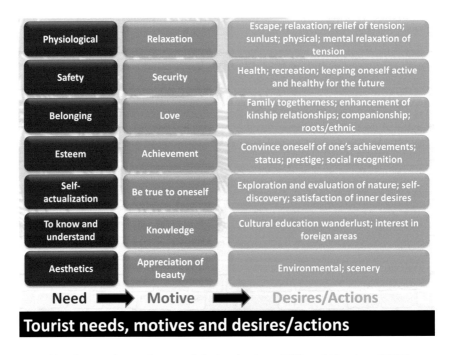

Figure 16.4 Tourist needs, motives, and desires/actions (Mill and Morrison 2012).

This is not a book solely dedicated to consumer behavior in tourism; however, this discussion of tourist motivations should have given you a taste of the complexity of this topic. You should realize that there are many reasons people travel on vacations or holidays to destinations. DMOs need to conduct research to determine the motives for pleasure/leisure travel to their specific destinations. Above all, those who are doing destination marketing, branding, and communications must realize that people's motivations vary greatly, even if they are from the same geographic origins or have similar socio-demographic characteristics.

Destination Selection

People are faced with a wide array of potential destinations for their trips. They can travel locally, regionally, nationally (domestically), and internationally. How do they select their destinations? Once again, the process of destination choice or selection has been a popular topic among tourism academic researchers. They have offered an assortment of choice models that have proven useful in understanding why people pick certain destinations.

From these models, the factors that have been found to affect destination selection include the following:

- Socio-psychological (personal): According to Um and Crompton (1990), these internal inputs include the personal characteristics, motives, values, and attitudes of the tourist. As you saw earlier, these characteristics are linked closely with people's motives for pleasure/leisure travel.
- Situational factors: the constraints that individuals or families have in terms of available time and financial resources to travel.
- Interpersonal (social): the influence of family members, other relatives, friends, business associates, opinion leaders, and others.
- Awareness levels: Tourists must be aware of destinations to consider them for pleasure/leisure travel trips. People have awareness sets and evoked sets of destinations (Um and Crompton 1990). The awareness set includes all the places that a person has thought or dreamed about going (Fig. 16.5). The evoked set is a smaller group of destinations from the awareness set that are feasible for a specific trip based on situational and other factors.
- Destination images: These are the perceptions that people have of specific destinations. These images are discussed in more detail in the next section of this chapter. You also heard about destination images in Chapters 4 and 13.
- Destination products: The destination products offered by alternative destinations may be influential and especially the specific attractions, events, experiences, and activities that they offer tourists.
- Marketing and IMC: the messages and images transmitted by DMOs and tourism sector stakeholders through a variety of channels.
- Information search: The process of searching for information on evoked set destinations and the information gathered may influence decisions. For example, people may develop more favorable or less favorable perceptions of destinations in reading travel blogs and traveler review sites.

- Past experience in visiting: The past history of visits to specific destinations. It is generally accepted that previous visitors to a destination have a higher probability of visiting than those who have not yet visited.
- Geographic origins and cultures: Tourist statistics clearly indicate that travel destinations vary by geographic origin and by people's cultural backgrounds.

DEFINITION

Perception

The mental process consumers employ using their five senses—sight, hearing, taste, touch, and smell—to size up destinations and their communications.

Figure 16.5 Paris is in many people's awareness sets as a destination they want to visit.

Some of these factors are external to the people making the destination selection, including the interpersonal factors, destination products, and marketing and IMC campaigns. The others are internal factors, including the particular circumstances of people, their socio-psychological characteristics and past travel behaviors, and cognitive processes (e.g., awareness levels and destination images).

Moscardo et al. (1996) proposed a model integrating the theories relating to these internal and external factors. This activities model of destination choice recognized the contributions of four fields of tourism research (Gilbert and Cooper 1991):

1. tourist motivation theories and research;
2. destination image research;
3. destination choice model research;
4. market segmentation research.

The activities model of destination choice suggested tourists' desired activities, experiences and benefits linked motivation with destination choice; this is shown in Figure 16.6.

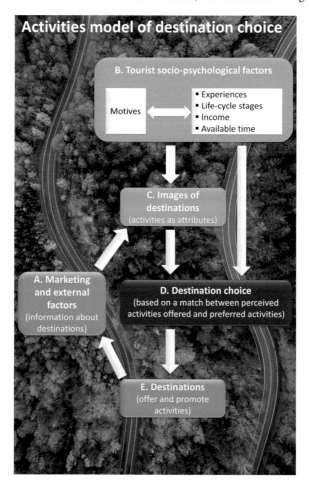

Figure 16.6 Activities model of destination choice (Moscardo et al. 1996).

The five components of the model (A to E) are briefly described below:

A. Marketing and external factors: all the information about destinations' activities and experiences from marketing and IMC, and interpersonal sources.
B. Tourist socio-psychological factors: motives, socio-demographic characteristics, and situational factors of tourists.

C. Images of destinations: tourists' perceptions of the activities and experiences as destination attributes of specific places.

D. Destination choice: the choice of destination based on the best match between tourists' preferred activities/experiences and the perceived activities/experiences at specific places.

E. Destinations: the activities and experiences offered by destinations. This is the destination product, as defined earlier in Chapter 7.

The Influence of Destination Images

The topic of people's images of destinations has been introduced already, and destination image has been a favorite research subject for tourism academic scholars since at least the early 1970s. It is difficult indeed to summarize all the research that has been done on this topic. Pike (2002) reviewed 142 papers that had been published on destination image from 1973 to 2002, and there have been many others that have appeared in the twenty-plus years since then.

Chapter 5 reviewed the use of research to measure and assess destination images. You learned in that chapter about attributes and holistic images as defined by Echtner and Ritchie (1993). Chapter 5 also showed that destination images are formed in various ways and influenced by a variety of sources of information on places, including previous visits. Eight destination image formation agents suggested by Gartner (1993) were discussed and shown in Figure 5.11. These were divided into three groups of information: organic, autonomous, and induced.

Beerli and Martin (2004) tested a proposed model of the formation of destination images, and this is shown in Figure 16.7. Most of the terms in this model have already been introduced in this chapter, but affective and cognitive images require more explanation. Affective images are people's feelings about destinations; as such they are subjective. Cognitive images are based

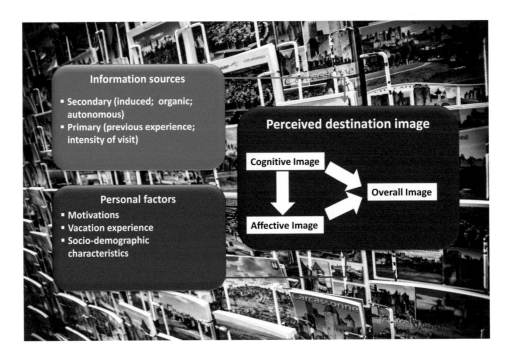

Figure 16.7 Model of the formation of destination images (Beerli and Martin 2004, p. 112).

on people's knowledge of a destination and an evaluation of the destination's attributes. Figure 5.11 provided the definitions of induced organic and autonomous images.

The model in Figure 16.7 suggests that perceived destination images are formed through the combined effects of information sources and personal factors. The information sources are organized according to Gartner's (1993) classification and divided into primary (previous visits to the destination) and secondary. The personal factors include motivations (as discussed earlier), vacation experience (as per Pearce's travel career concept) and socio-demographic characteristics of tourists. The overall image of a destination is formed from two components: the cognitive and affective images.

Several previous tourism research studies have shown that destination images directly influence the choice of tourism destinations. For example, Chen and Tsai (2007) conducted a visitor survey in southern Taiwan and found that destination image directly impacted the selection of the destination. In addition, they concluded that destination image affected the after-decision-making behaviors of tourists.

This discussion once again highlights how influential images are in the selection of destinations. Therefore, as suggested in Chapter 5, it is crucial that DMOs conduct research to determine the existing images of their destinations. In addition, although it may require a long-term commitment of resources, DMOs must position the images of their destinations in an optimum way, through both marketing communications and attention to service quality and other aspects of the destination product.

Travel Purchase Behavior Process

People go through several stages in planning travel to the destination, experiencing the destination, and after returning home from the destination. You may remember the twelve stages of the customer cycle from Chapter 15 and that is just one of the many models suggested for travel purchasing behavior. A more classic model is shown in Figure 16.8 and consists of seven sequential stages (Morrison 2022). A quick note on the model is that the seventh step is traditionally named as divestment, but that label was judged inappropriate for destination experiences. The title of remembering and sharing was substituted.

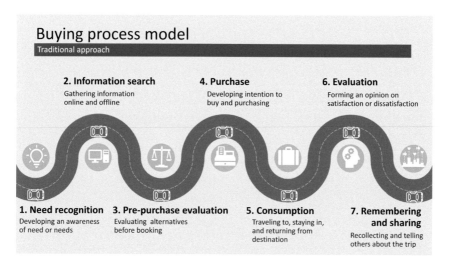

Figure 16.8 Model of the travel purchase behavior process.

Need Recognition

The travel purchase process begins when people become aware of needs (need recognition) that they feel going on holiday or vacation will satisfy. Usually, this awareness is triggered by one or more of a variety of stimuli from three main sources (personal, interpersonal, and commercial). The needs are recognized when the stimulus is strong enough.

COMMERCIAL

DMOs and their marketing and IMC campaigns represent the commercial sources; these DMO messages are intended to make people recognize their needs to travel. It is better for these communications therefore to focus on customer needs and desires rather than being purely about the features of destinations.

INTERPERSONAL

It is recognized that WOM is more powerful in influencing people than commercial information. It has been verified in study after study that interpersonal information and recommendations are heavily relied upon in tourism because of their objectivity and credibility. Interpersonal sources include family members and friends, business associates, and opinion leaders (including influencers). Chapter 15 mentioned new breeds of interpersonal sources on social media platforms, and this might be called eWoM. This may not be as powerful and believable information and advice as real WOM, but it seems to be significantly more credible than commercial information.

PERSONAL

Personal (internal) drives to deal with need deficiencies are the third source that can trigger need recognition. You have heard these described as the push factors earlier in this chapter.

People may recognize need deficiencies because of the combined impact of several sources and stimuli. In fact, it may require a combination of two or three of these factors to get people started on their search for information.

Search for Information

The second stage in the travel purchase process is an active search for information. Once people become aware of needs, they tend to begin looking for information on destinations, products and services that they feel will satisfy those needs. When people recognize needs, these become wants; if wants exist, people usually start an information search. There are three main sources of information available:

1. destination-dominated information;
2. interpersonal and third-party information;
3. internal sources.

DESTINATION-DOMINATED INFORMATION

These information sources are the marketing and IMC campaigns by DMOs and other tourism sector stakeholders. Websites and social media platforms are the major sources for finding information about destinations, but there are also the other elements of DMO IMC campaigns (advertising, sales, public relations and publicity, sales promotion, and merchandising) described in Chapters 14 and 15.

INTERPERSONAL AND THIRD-PARTY INFORMATION

The interpersonal sources include family, friends, business associates, and opinion leaders; they are the word-of-mouth sources. Independent, third-party and objective assessments can be gathered from travel guidebooks, such as Lonely Planet, the Rough Guides, Frommer's, Fodor's, and others. Government and independent rating systems like the famous Michelin scheme also are available for helping with decision-making. Traveler review sites like Tripadvisor and the travel blogs and vlogs of other people are also included in this category of information.

INTERNAL SOURCES

This is the information about places stored in people's own memories. It includes past travel experiences in going to places and their memories of destination IMC campaigns. Importantly, these also encompass people's perceptions or images of specific destinations.

As mentioned earlier, Um and Crompton (1990) suggested that all people have an awareness set of places that they would like to visit. People may also become aware of other desirable destinations during information searches. Not all the available destinations will be considered. Lack of awareness, perception of places not being affordable, previous bad experiences, and negative word-of-mouth information will eliminate some destinations. The final list is the evoked set, the alternative destinations selected for further consideration.

EXAMPLE 16.3

Increasing Concern for Safety and Security

This survey was conducted pre-COVID; however, it still shows the high level of safety concerns with traveling. These perceptions of risk were elevated during the pandemic.

> Terrorism is no longer a primary concern. This year, more than two-thirds (69 percent) of respondents ranked crime atop their three greatest traveling threats, followed by health and medical issues (67 percent) and then terrorism (41 percent). Less than one-quarter (22 percent) of respondents ranked terrorism as their number one threat, with 33 percent of respondents ranking health and medical issues as their top concern. In 2018, 40 percent of respondents ranked terrorism as the greatest threat to their travel.
>
> Much like last year, 48 percent of respondents will do more research when it comes to their travel safety concerns, while 30 percent will do nothing at all and 25 percent will prepare themselves for a possible crisis.
>
> (Global Rescue 2019)

Learning Point

Destinations and DMOs must do their best to reduce fears of travel by offering factual information about potential risks and what is done to ensure traveler safety and security.

Pre-purchase Evaluation of Alternatives

The next stage is assessing the short-listed evoked set destinations using objective and subjective criteria developed by the potential traveler. Some people are very careful and organized in their trip planning and write things down on paper or in their computers and smartphones; others just do the work in their heads. Objective criteria include airfares, destination products, activities and experiences, hotel and other prices, and destination locations. Subjective criteria are intangible items, such as people's perceived images of destinations.

Purchase

People have now determined which destination best meets their criteria. They develop a definite intention to book their trips to the destination, but the decision-making process may still be incomplete. Whether they buy can still be influenced by other factors. They may want to talk over their choices with family members, friends, and other interpersonal sources. Social media platforms may be checked to confirm selections. Information or opinions might be found that lead to questioning the destination choice. This may cause a postponement of the purchase or a complete re-evaluation of the decision. Additionally, situational factors may change, including employment and financial circumstances, leading to a delay in the purchase decision.

Perceived risk is another factor that may delay purchases or cause them to be postponed. Pleasure/leisure travel to destinations represents the purchase of an experience good. Destinations are booked sight unseen if the person has not visited them before. These decisions therefore involve an above-average level of risks. The risks are financial (will my money be well spent at the destination?), psychological (will going to the destination improve my self-image?), or social (will my friends and family think more of me after I have been to the destination?). If the risks are considered too great or the rewards perceived to be too low, people do something to correct the situation. They may postpone purchases, search for more information or choose a better-known or more familiar destination. Risk can also be reduced by continually returning to the same destinations. DMOs must design their IMC campaigns and information services to reduce these perceived risks.

You should also realize that picking a destination is not the only decision that needs to be made. In fact, there are numerous other sub-decisions that must be taken before the final purchase is made. These include when to travel, how to pay, how and where to make bookings, how long to stay, how much to spend, how to get there, what routes to take and what to do at the destination. If the decision maker is not a solo traveler, these decisions can be complicated and involve several people (e.g., in a family, the parents and children).

Cognitive dissonance is a psychological state that some people feel after making a booking. They may be unsettled or unsure as to whether they have made the best decision. The intensity of dissonance increases with the importance and value of the purchase. For example, dissonance may be higher for a long-haul trip than travel to a more familiar domestic destination. Here, it is the job of the tourism sector stakeholders and the DMO to do all that they can to reassure people that they have made good decisions.

Consumption

This stage is the experiences that people have within the destination. For the DMO, the priority is to ensure that the destination meets or exceeds expectations and that visitors leave very satisfied. This is difficult for the DMO to accomplish because they do not control the products and services consumed by tourists; these are delivered primarily by tourism sector stakeholders. As suggested in Chapter 7, the DMO should have a quality assurance program in place to provide a better guarantee of satisfaction for tourists.

In the model proposed by Moscardo et al. (1996) (Fig. 16.6), tourists expect that the activities, experiences, and benefits they will receive in the destinations of their choice will match their preferences. If this expectation is not realized, there will be dissatisfaction with the destination. Therefore, the DMO must pay attention to this issue and ensure that the activities, experiences, and benefits are available and delivered at a level that meets or exceeds expectations.

Post-consumption Evaluation

When tourists are on their way back from the destination or have returned home, they will evaluate their destination experiences against their expectations. Expectations are based on the information they received from destination-dominated sources (DMO and tourism sector stakeholder IMC campaigns) and interpersonal and third-party sources (family, friends, business associates, opinion leaders, travel blogs, traveler review sites). If expectations are met or exceeded, they are most likely to be satisfied with the destination. If not, they are more than likely to be dissatisfied. The golden rule for the DMO and its stakeholders is never to promise more than can be delivered.

With social media platforms, it has become much more convenient for people to write about their good and bad experiences with traveling. DMOs need to be vigilant in tracking such commentaries online and responding when they deem it to be appropriate.

When people are satisfied with destinations, the dividends are significant. Satisfied tourists are more likely to be repeat visitors (with greater destination loyalty). They have experienced the destinations and know that their expectations were met and the experiences were delivered as anticipated. By telling friends, relatives, and associates about positive destination experiences they will influence others to visit through word-of-mouth recommendations.

However, dissatisfied tourists are less likely to be repeat visitors, and they will tell others, thereby discouraging other people from visiting the destination. Information from interpersonal sources carries more weight for people than destination-dominated sources. Therefore, DMOs must be especially concerned about having dissatisfied tourists.

Remembering and Sharing

Based just upon the huge number of travel blogs/vlogs and vacation/holiday photographs posted on social media platforms, many people like to remember and share their travel and destination experiences (Fig. 16.9). DMOs and tourism sector stakeholders should do all they can to encourage this tendency to reminisce and tell others about travel experiences. Providing online communities on their websites and pages on social media platforms for comments are two ways to accomplish this.

People derive great enjoyment from this last stage of the travel purchase behavior process, but last in this case is not the least important. For DMOs, these are a great source of credible testimonials that can be shown to people considering traveling to their destinations.

Figure 16.9 People like to share their travel experiences online.

Destination Market Segmentation

Chapter 12 introduced the market segmentation concept as part of marketing strategy and as the foundation for selecting the approaches to destination positioning and branding. Most DMOs carefully select their priority target markets to make more effective use of their resources and to generate the best return on investment.

There are several ways that DMOs can divide up markets, and many of these segmentation approaches are shown in Figure 16.10. Your author likes to use metaphors while teaching, and Figure 16.10 is a visual metaphor. What do you see in the image? Indeed, there are eight slices

Destination market segmentation approaches

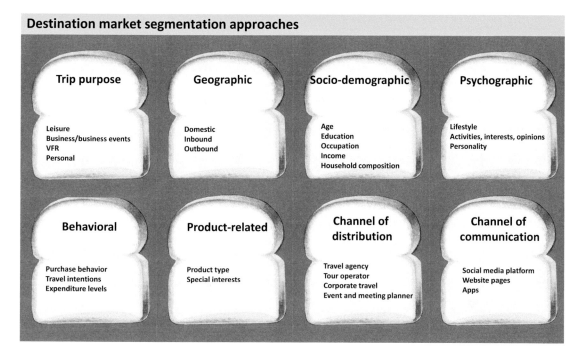

Figure 16.10 Destination market segmentation approaches.

of bread. What has that go to do with destination market segmentation? Market segmentation is about slicing up a market to form dissimilar groups. What do you do when making a sandwich from slices of bread? Of course, you know that involves putting two or more slices together. Each slice in Figure 16.10 is a market segmentation approach. An example is shown later of VisitScotland using several segmentation approaches together.

EXAMPLE 16.4

Sandwiching Segmentation Approaches in the UK

Can you sandwich together different destination market segmentation approaches? Of course, that can be done and here is an example from VisitScotland. This is a combination of a tripographic (an overnight stay), a socio-demographic classification (life stages), trip purpose, and geography (country and region of residence). That is a quadruple-decker sandwich of approaches!

This short report provides bite-size insight into overall trends in domestic overnight tourism by examining the traveling behavior in different "life stages" (based on age and children in the household) between 2017 and 2019:

- Pre-nesters: aged 16–34, no children
- Families: aged 16–54, with children
- Older independents: aged 35–54, no children
- Empty nesters: aged over 55

Empty nesters travel the most in Scotland generating 37 percent of all overnight travel and 38 percent of domestic travel spend. At 3.6 nights per trip, their average length of stay is the highest of all life stages.

Visitors from all life stages travel to go on a holiday (56 percent of all visits). The second most important reason to make an overnight trip is to visit friends and relatives (28 percent), followed by business trips (14 percent).

Roughly half of all overnight trips in Scotland were taken by residents of Scotland (50.6 percent) and the other by residents of England and Wales (49.4 percent).

(VisitScotland 2020)

Learning Point

Destination market segment approaches when used together give marketers greater precision in defining their customers.

As mentioned in Chapter 12, the most widely accepted practice in destination marketing is to begin by dividing markets by geographic origin and trip purpose.

Trip Purpose

The four principal trip-purpose divisions are leisure travel, VFR, business travel and business events, and personal travel (Fig. 16.11). For a destination, there are three geographic

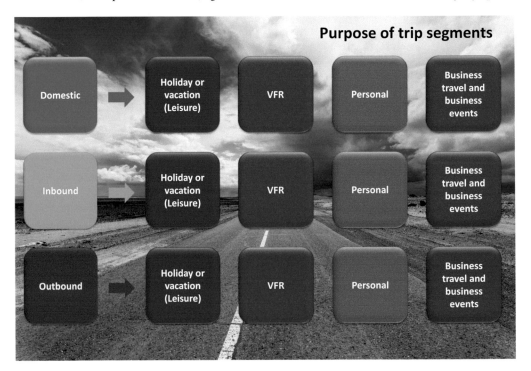

Figure 16.11 Purpose of trip segments.

dimensions of these markets: domestic, inbound, and outbound. It is reasonable to assume that the motives for these four trip purposes are different. Earlier in this chapter, you learned about the many potential motives for leisure travel.

Research has shown that VFR travel is more diverse than might initially be thought. People with this trip purpose share some of the same motives as pleasure/leisure travelers, but interpersonal motives are stronger. The VFR travel market is discussed in more detail in Chapter 17 in the context of domestic travel.

Business travel is often the largest market for certain destinations and especially for major cities. This segment is very diverse and includes normal business travel as well as travel related to business events. Hankinson (2005) defined the latter as travel associated with attendance at MICE events.

EXAMPLE 16.5

Business Travel Has Changed Forever

Business travel is a critical component of the market for many destinations. Since 2019, this trip-purpose segment has experienced disruptions and changes. This example describes some of the changes.

> At a *New York Times* event back in November 2020, Bill Gates sent a chill through the travel industry when he predicted that more than 50 percent of business travel and more than 30 percent of days worked in offices would go away permanently.
>
> Flash forward sixteen months and Gates' assessment is now accepted, more or less, both inside and outside the travel industry. "The pandemic has led to extensive use of videoconferencing and virtual meetings, and many companies expect virtual work to persist over the long term," concluded the US Bureau of Labor Statistics in a February 2022 report forecasting employment demand in various industries. The labor bureau predicted that many types of business trips would be replaced by virtual meetings, though some in-person trips—for instance, sales pitches and trade conferences—would return to pre-pandemic normal.
>
> (Kelleher 2022)

Learning Point

Some destinations will have to consider what to do to compensate for less business travel.

Personal travel can be a very significant market for destinations. People travel for a variety of other purposes beyond leisure, VFR, and business travel and business events. These are mostly for personal reasons, including medical, educational, job search, and legal advice travel.

Geographic

Geographic markets are defined by place of residence or source of origin, and this is one of the most common ways to define the markets for destinations. Often, the following terminology is used to classify geographic markets into their broadest categories (Fig. 16.11):

- Domestic travel: travel by the residents of a country within their own country.
- Inbound travel: travel into a country by the residents of foreign nations.
- Outbound travel: travel by the residents of a country to places outside of their own country.

EXAMPLE 16.6

Domestic Travel Increases in the Asia-Pacific Region

From a research study by Mastercard, the results highlight the strong trend toward more domestic travel.

> With people increasingly relying on domestic modes of transportation, particularly cars, for mobility during the pandemic, the spending on auto rentals and tolls consistently exceeded 2019 levels throughout the past two years. Domestic ground travel has seen a robust demand in many Asia-Pacific markets where road trips have retained their appeal. Fuel spending has steadily increased in Singapore, Hong Kong, the Philippines, and Australia, while public transportation and cruise lines have also firmly stepped back onto the road to recovery, after an initial slow start due to restrictions surrounding group travel.
>
> (Davitt 2022)

Learning Point

The trend toward greater domestic travel was accelerated by the COVID-19 pandemic when international travel was severely restricted.

Domestic travel markets are discussed in Chapter 17, international inbound markets are covered in Chapter 18, and business travel and business events are reviewed in Chapter 19. Domestic travel grew significantly in 2020 to 2022 as highlighted in the example.

Socio-demographic

Socio-demographics are characteristics such as age, education, occupation, income, and household composition. Traditionally, these characteristics were much used by DMOs in market segmentation analyses, and they are still used to profile tourists. The age-cohort and generational classification that you will hear about later in this chapter is a good example.

EXAMPLE 16.7

Representativeness in Gender Marketing

The following example argues that the images of women used in destination advertising are not representative and this is certainly the truth.

> So many destinations and brands are guilty of exclusively featuring thin, white, young women in their content. Yes, these are women, but most definitely not representative of all women. Prioritize featuring diverse women in your content; think about race, age, ability, size, gender expression, and every other form of intersectionality. Representation is not only an important first step when combating inequality, it's also good for business.
>
> (Mack 2022)

Learning Point

It is important that destination marketers use images that are representative of all types of women (and men).

One DMO that is using socio-demographics is Tourism Australia in its targeting of the youth market.

EXAMPLE 16.8

The Importance of Youth Travel

Younger travelers are taking on greater importance around the world and Australia is one country that has a tradition of having specific programs to attract this market through, for example, the Working Holiday Maker.

> The youth sector is vital to Australian tourism. The youth market contributes 27 percent of all visitor arrivals to Australia and 45 percent of all visitor spend. There were 2.4 million youth visitors to Australia in 2019 who spent $20 billion.
>
> The Working Holiday Maker program allows young adults from eligible partner countries to work in Australia while having an extended holiday. Working holiday makers tend to stay longer, spend more and disperse more widely throughout the country than most other target segments. They have a higher-than-average length of stay and propensity to combine work, visiting friends and family, and holiday/leisure experiences.
>
> (Tourism Australia 2022a)

Learning Point

It is advisable for destinations and DMOs to give special consideration to youth markets due to generational changes.

If you look online and read travel trade journals and newspapers, you will also undoubtedly come across the term "luxury travel," and this usually involves wealthy people and those with very high incomes. The luxury travel market is discussed in more detail in Chapter 17.

Household composition segmentation is also very popular and much discussed in travel trade publications and among DMOs as well. Within these groups, the family travel market is a popular target. The family market is an especially important factor in domestic tourism as discussed in Chapter 17.

Several tourism research studies have shown that the combination of age, income level, and education has a strong influence on travel behaviors and spending. However, in recent times, several DMOs have moved away from using socio-demographic characteristics for identifying and describing their target markets.

Psychographic

Market researcher Stanley Plog (2002) popularized the concept of using psychographics to divide up tourist markets. He called these personality profiles, which involves dividing up people by their psychological orientations, lifestyles or AIOs (activities-interests-opinions).

DEFINITION

Lifestyle

The way people live based on their attitudes, interests, and opinions.

Destination Canada is one of the DMOs that has moved to a more sophisticated market segmentation approach, based more on personality than socio-demographic characteristics.

EXAMPLE 16.9

Canada's Explorer Quotient

This example is one of the very best applications of psychographic segmentation for a destination. It explains the strength of this approach when compared to others.

> EQ is a market segmentation system based on the science of psychographics. Environics Research Group, a globally respected player in social values and consumer research, developed EQ for Destination Canada, to apply sophisticated, values-based segmentation specifically for the travel market. Psychographics is an evolution of the traditional field of demographics. Instead of just breaking travelers into groups based on age, income, gender, family status or education level—all of which is useful information—psychographics looks deeper at people's social values and views of the world. EQ breaks each geographic market down into different psychographic groups, called Explorer Types. Each type is identified by particular characteristics stemming from social and travel values, travel motivations, and behaviors.
>
> (Destination Canada 2022)

Learning Point

This is a model approach for other destinations to emulate.

The example from Destination Canada is an outstanding case study in applying psychographic segmentation to tourist markets. The Destination Canada system has identified ten groups of travelers within its international inbound markets. The free spirits, cultural explorers, and authentic experiencers are the three segments that Destination Canada considers to be its core global markets. A short description of the ten groups is shown in Figure 16.12. An image of a person likely to be a free spirit visiting Canada is shown in Figure 16.13.

Destination Canada EQ segments

Free spirits	*Personal history explorers*
Highly social and open-minded. Their enthusiasm for life extends to their outlook on travel. Experimental and adventurous, they indulge in high-end experiences that are shared with others.	• Primarily defined by their desire to connect to their own cultural roots – and do so by traveling in comfort, style and security.
Cultural explorers	*Rejuvenators*
Defined by their love of constant travel and continuous opportunities to embrace, discover and immerse themselves in the culture, people and settings of the places they visit.	Family-oriented people who travel with others to escape form the stresses of everyday life to get pampered and indulge themselves.
Authentic experiencers	*Gentle explorers*
Typically understated travelers looking for authentic, tangible engagement with destinations they seek, with a particular interest in understanding the history of the places they visit.	Primarily defined by their reluctance to venture far beyond the comfort of home and travel 'on condition,' demanding the very best and most comfortable environments for themselves when they must do so.
No-hassle travelers	*Cultural history buffs*
Extroverted, flashy people who seek secure group travel, allowing them to be pampered in luxurious surroundings while seeing all the main sights of a destination.	Defined by their focused interest in the history, culture and natural surroundings of the places they visit. They are driven to learn everything about a culture, in the company of other like-minded people.
Social samplers	*Aspiring escapists*
Defined by their affinity for traveling in groups, as well as by the idea that time is limited while traveling, thus they show a preference for focusing on 'must-see' attractions.	Stressed about life in general and more apprehensive about traveling – but if travel offers sufficient comfort and safety, they may be tempted to leave the comforts of home to escape.

Figures 16.12 Destination Canada's psychographic market segmentation system—Explorer Quotient (Destination Canada 2022).

Figures 16.13 A free spirit exploring Canada by canoe.

Behavioral

This approach involves dividing tourists into groups based upon their actual purchasing and travel behaviors or future travel purchase intentions. One of the most important behavioral distinctions for destinations is repeat visitors versus those visiting for the first time.

EXAMPLE 16.10

The Importance of Repeat Visitors

Returning visitors are vital to many destination's survival and sustainability. It seems that more effort is put into attracting first-time visitors. This example concerns Hawaii advocates giving more emphasis to the repeat visitor.

In 2019, statewide, repeat visitors accounted for 68 percent of all arrivals, a number that had been rising. Did you know that on average a return visitor to Hawaii has been back to the islands more than seven times?

Guests that return provide airlines, accommodations, and almost everyone with a regular income stream. Thus, the loyalty of returning guests has made them a cherished asset, especially since they tend to also be the brand advocates for Hawaii. They become influencers with a broad reach across social media, and in comments on websites such as Beat of Hawaii. Return guests are said to spend more because they already value Hawaii and know it meets or exceeds their expectations. They're also more likely to accept paid upgrades and ancillary options for the same reason. It's easier to manage expectations with return visitors who simply know what's reasonable.

(Beat of Hawaii 2022)

Learning Point

Repeat visitors should not be neglected by destinations and DMOs.

Related to the repeat visitation concept are the theories of variety seeking and novelty seeking. These theories are somewhat similar and suggest that people behave in such a way to get the right balance between familiarity and variety/novelty. Some tourists prefer a high level of familiarity, and so they may return to the same destination several times. Others are more likely to switch their destinations because they desire more variety and novelty for their tourism experiences.

Product-related

Destinations may have certain products that will focus DMOs' attention on specific segments with the highest interest levels in using these products. For example, Travel Oregon in the USA has placed an emphasis on cycling, those who enjoy it and where there are bike trails. An Oregon Scenic Bikeways system is available and is described in the example.

EXAMPLE 16.11

Oregon Scenic Bikeways

This is a growing market and can be of great benefit to rural areas. Long-distance cycling is normally defined as covering a route of 100 miles or more (161 kilometers).

Scenic Bikeway routes are the best bike rides in Oregon and showcase beautiful scenery, state history and local communities. They run past state parks on paved paths and roads, cross mountain passes and high deserts. The

Oregon Scenic Bikeway program is the first of its kind in the country. The routes are nominated by locals and selected by Oregon State Parks. Bikeways are official state-designated routes with printable maps, GPS and on-road signage.

(Oregon State Parks 2022)

Cycling routes are relatively inexpensive to plan for and develop, they can directly generate jobs if route construction is needed and they can indirectly support jobs in local communities through the expenditures of cyclists and their support crews.

(Depew and Smith 2020)

Learning Point

Oregon is a beautiful state in which to travel and its Scenic Bikeway system is a model for other destinations to follow.

The inventory of such products is very long, and so only an indicative list of eleven products and their markets is provided in Figure 16.14.

Products	Images	Market segments
Alpine or downhill ski slopes		Skiers and snowboarders
Casinos		People who like to gamble

Equestrian facilities		Horse owners and riders
Golf courses		Golfers
Reefs and shipwrecks		Scuba divers and snorkellers
Religious structures, sites and legends		Believers
Health, wellness and spa facilities		Medical tourists/spa-goers

Marinas for yachts and other watercrafts	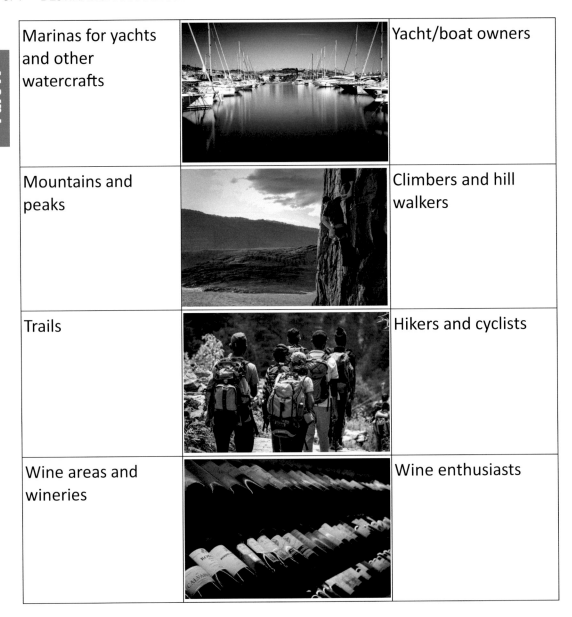	Yacht/boat owners
Mountains and peaks		Climbers and hill walkers
Trails		Hikers and cyclists
Wine areas and wineries		Wine enthusiasts

Figures 16.14 Product-related segmentation and markets.

Product-related segmentation can be practiced at various geographic levels. At a national level, for example, the Belize Tourism Board (2022) promotes to a range of special interests, from archaeology to snorkeling.

The Importance of Visitor Activities: Belize

Belize is a small country; however, it has a wonderful and diverse range of activities to offer visitors. These are presented very well on its consumer website at www.travelbelize.org/. Activities listed include archaeology, Belize Barrier Reef, birding, canoeing, caving, fishing, hiking, horseback riding, kayaking, sailing, scuba-diving, and snorkeling.

Archaeology

The mysteries of Maya without the traps of tourism: With only a small percentage of our ancient Maya temples uncovered, it's not uncommon to come across ancient pieces of pottery or hear that a distant hill is actually a temple. Whether you want to explore for an afternoon, a day or a week, the ancient Maya sites are well worth it. All sites are managed by the Institute of Archaeology and have interpretive centers, as well as trained guides to show you around. From Caracol and Cerros to Lamanai and little villages and forest areas, pretty much anywhere you go here, you'll find ancient Maya temples.

Scuba-diving and snorkeling

The Belize Barrier Reef turned 10,000 years old on June 8, 2022, and Belize is celebrating the longevity of this natural wonder by pledging to continue preserving it for generations today and those to come. The second-largest barrier reef in the world, it extends the full length of our nation, forming an enormous lagoon along our coast and protecting our shores from large waves, even during extreme weather. This also creates an ideal habitat for a wide variety of oceanic creatures, from rock-like living coral to endangered sea turtles to over 500 species of fish in every color of the rainbow.

(Belize Tourism Board 2022)

Learning Point

Travelers think about what they can do in particular destinations. It is crucial to tell them what activities and products are on offer.

On the other end of the scale at the city level, Buenos Aires, Argentina, proudly communicates that it is the birthplace of tango dancing (Buenos Aires Cuidad 2022). Naples in Italy has gained UNESCO recognition for the art of making Neapolitan pizza and markets this to visitors (Visit Naples 2022).

The increasing popularity of pursuing special interests and hobbies when traveling has made product-related segmentation a more viable alternative for certain DMOs. This point is reviewed in more detail later as well as in Chapters 17 and 18.

Channel of Distribution

This type of segmentation is used in business travel and in marketing to travel trade intermediaries. Business travel market segmentation is discussed in Chapter 19. For travel trade intermediaries, tour operators can be classified geographically or by specialty or destinations served. Travel agencies may also be targeted by geographic origin markets for the destination. Another common approach is to focus on tour operators and travel agencies that have already sent tourists to destinations. Specialized agencies, such as cruise-only agencies and those with a focus on special interests, may be identified and targeted by DMOs. OTAs versus traditional (brick-and-mortar) agencies is another type of channel of distribution segmentation.

Channel of Communication

Channel of communication segmentation means dividing people according to the platform for communication. This is becoming an increasingly popular approach as there is so much UGC online. With great quantities of UGC available, channel of communication segmentation will be more used by destinations and DMOs in the future.

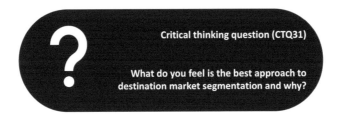

Critical thinking question (CTQ31)

What do you feel is the best approach to destination market segmentation and why?

Market Trends

Tourism markets are dynamic and undergoing constant change. The motivations and desires for specific destination experiences vary over time. Therefore, you should know about the major market trends, and this part of Chapter 16 describes these trends.

Statistics on tourist arrivals are not enough when a DMO is engaged in highly competitive marketplaces. DMOs must dig deeper to develop a more detailed understanding of markets. DMOs need to go behind the statistics to know how and why tourists are changing. Winning marketing strategies frequently are a result of using good market research results in an appropriate and creative way. It is especially important for DMOs to know the latest trends in markets according to the eight factors shown in Figure 16.15.

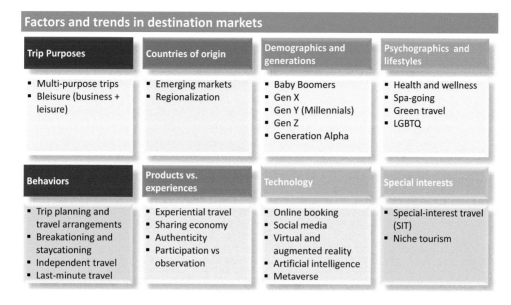

Figure 16.15 Factors and trends in destination markets.

Unfortunately, some DMOs are not engaging in this level of market analysis. Perhaps this is because DMOs do not feel the need to invest in market research on consumers that still represent a small proportion of total tourism demand. This may be especially so for the emerging markets in international tourism. However, as international tourist arrivals have plummeted recently, these research data are becoming more valuable because competition among destinations is intensifying.

Trip Purposes

Although trip purposes have tended to be enduring over many decades, external forces and especially tough economic conditions, socio-demographic changes, and shifting lifestyles have been reshaping them. The combinations of multiple trip purposes in one trip have been a noticeable trend.

MULTIPURPOSE TRIPS

Most destinations neatly divide markets into leisure, VFR, business travel/business events, and personal travel segments. However, this apportionment of the market is not totally accurate, and the distinctions between the four segments are becoming blurred. Increasingly, people are pursuing multiple trip purposes. Time poverty is a factor influencing this trend, as is the desire for experiential travel and greater authenticity.

EXAMPLE 16.13

Experiential Travel on the Rise

People are traveling more to participate in experiences that are authentic and meaningful. This example mentions experiences being offered in Kerala, India.

The bucket list is what has given birth to the concept of experiential travel as there is no other joy than striking off a particular travel trend on one's bucket list. For instance, Kerala has recently started its Caravan Tours providing travel services for travelers to trip around Kerala on their own accord in fully furnished vans, including beds, kitchens, and amenities that are commonly found in hotels. In short, travelers would travel with the hotel. How can something like this not be a part of a bucket list?

However, tourists and travelers no longer want to simply cross items off their bucket lists. As authenticity has become a guiding concept, people want to seek out experiences that will enhance, develop, and energize them as a person, while allowing them to spend time connecting with locals to help establish an emotional connection rather than just staring out the window of a tourist bus.

(Chittilapilly 2022)

Learning Point

Travelers are looking for more authentic and unique experiences in their destinations. This can be called experiential travel.

Bleisure

This is the combination of business and leisure when traveling. It is a long-term trend rather than a new one; however, it is gaining recognition and seems to be expanding as new generations of business travelers become more predominant. The bleisure trend is discussed in more detail in Chapter 19.

Research shows that long-haul destinations experience higher levels of multipurpose travel trips. This is particularly important for destinations considering inbound business tourism from Europe, North America, Australia, New Zealand and other long-haul origin countries. For the highly desirable travel destinations in people's awareness sets, those taking business trips may seriously consider bringing family members or friends along with them.

Countries of Origin

DMOs interested in attracting international tourists are constantly tracking the trends in the major countries of opportunity. In 2021, the five countries with the greatest expenditures on international tourism were in order China, USA, Germany, France, and UK (Statista 2022). However, some other countries are moving up the world rankings very rapidly, so DMOs should not overlook the emerging markets.

Much of the international travel in the world is done within distinct geographic regions. For example, most of international arrivals in Europe and Asia are regional, Europeans within Europe and Asians within Asia. This trend is likely to strengthen in the future and especially within regional blocs such as ASEAN.

Demographics and Generations

All eyes in tourism are currently fixed on three generational cohorts (people born between certain defined years): Generations X, Y, and Z. A fourth group is the Baby Boomers. These age-group cohorts span about fifty-five years from 1946 to 2000, and they represent the bulk of the decision-making tourism consumers in the world. The children of Generation X and Generation Y (Millennials) are known as Generation Z.

Baby Boomers

The populations in most Western and some Asia-Pacific countries like Australia, Japan, New Zealand and South Korea are aging. The largest group of older consumers is known as the Baby Boomers, and these people were born between 1946 and 1964. There were an estimated 205 million Baby Boomers worldwide in 2021 (Living Your Senior Life 2022).

Older age groups are more willing to travel than previous generations and are interested in active and adventurous travel experiences. ElderTreks (Small Group Exotic Adventures for Travelers 50 Plus) (2022) is a good example of a tourism company that has done a great job in attracting the adventurous Baby Boomers. The company, based in Canada near Toronto, was established in 1987 and offers active holiday tours in over 100 country destinations around the world.

Generation X

GenXers are people in the age group that followed the Baby Boomers. They were born from 1965 to around 1979 and are also sometimes called the Baby Busters. GenXers are known to be very independent thinkers and more adventurous and tougher to please than the Baby Boomers when traveling. GenXers make extensive use of websites and social media platforms to find travel information and make bookings. They especially like using social media, including Facebook, Twitter and various blog sites and discussion forums. Being in the age range from 35 to 50, GenXers often have children and travel as families.

Generation Y

These are people born from around 1980 to 2000; they are also sometimes called Millennials, Echo Boomers or the Net Generation. This generation really likes to travel. Many Millennials reject traditional achievements, placing a much higher importance on intangible, life-enriching moments, such as travel (Global Blue 2018).

Millennials represent the largest generation, making up 31.5 percent of the world's population (Condor Ferries 2022). The same source says, "they are reshaping how travel works by focusing on experiences and culture, solo travel, planning their own itineraries, ignoring cheap stock content, and drawing their decision and influence from social media or UGC. What's more, all of these new travel trends are done directly on their smartphone, from research to booking."

Generation Z

These are the children mainly of Generation X and the grandchildren of the Baby Boomers. They are defined as those born after 1995. This is a market almost of the same size as the Millennials and the one that will eventually take over from them. It is the generation that grew up with social media, smartphones and tablets, and so they are the most adept in online buying. They are likelier than other generations to take an activity-based vacation (e.g., skiing or hiking), or travel for a special event (e.g., concert, festival, sports) or a party (Expedia Group 2018).

Generation Alpha

This is group born between 2013 and 2025 and after Generation Z. They are influenced by their Millennial parents (Generation Y) and Generation Z role models, and this rising cohort is characterized by their strong ethics and values (Wunderman Thompson 2019).

Behaviors

There is no doubting that travel behaviors are changing and DMOs need to keep up with these shifts.

TRIP PLANNING AND ARRANGEMENTS

Hu and Morrison (2002) used the terms "tripography" and "tripographics" to describe the characteristics of the travel trips to destinations that people arrange. There have been some definite trends in both trip planning and the resulting tripographics in recent years. One of these trends has been the increased popularity of multigenerational travel, which is discussed in Chapter 17 in the context of domestic tourism.

BREAKATIONING AND STAYCATIONING

With the pressures of modern society and work, many people have the money to travel, but they do not have enough free time to take the long vacations that previous generations did. These people can be called cash rich, but time poor. The recently difficult economic times in many developed countries and the pandemic have accentuated this phenomenon, which has resulted in more frequent and shorter-duration trips being taken by these busy people.

The types of trips made by these travelers are called short breaks or breakations (mixture of breaks and vacations). Staycationing when used in tourism means staying in your own country for holidays or vacations and not traveling abroad.

EXAMPLE 16.14

Staycationing in Indonesia

Staycationing became much more popular since 2019. Indonesia is one destination that capitalized on this trend in its growing domestic travel market.

> Staycations are expected to see a surge in popularity, following the reopening of some tourist destinations in Indonesia, a research and consultancy firm has stated. Inventure predicted that with the current travel restrictions in place, local travelers would be the segment that boosts the Indonesian tourism sector.
>
> (Eloksari 2020)

> Wego's survey of post-pandemic vacation trends conducted on Indonesian travelers revealed staycation as one of the most desired types of trip. Around 26 percent of respondents expressed their interest to have a staycation when the situation improves and more restrictions are eased.
>
> (Wego Travel 2020)

Learning Point

Staycationing is here to stay and is a solid market to develop within domestic tourism.

These are not particularly positive trends for long-haul destinations, but they benefit destinations and countries within a specific country or region. Therefore, they are good news for domestic travel and for international markets that are close to countries of origin.

INDEPENDENT TRAVEL

During the past thirty years, there has been a significant increase in the popularity of independent travel. Sometimes, this is referred to as free independent travel, or FIT for short. However, there are two somewhat different meanings to the term independent travel. The first is when a person travels alone without any companions; the second is when the person travels with others but is not part of an organized group tour with a fixed itinerary.

Let's start with the first definition of independent travel, people traveling alone without travel companions. Solo independent travelers tend to be younger, and some are what are commonly referred to as backpackers. These may be gap year Millennial travelers, for example. However, older singles may also be traveling alone and can even be from among the Baby Boomers.

It is important to know that independent travelers do not use tour companies and they may also not work with traditional travel agencies. Instead, they rely heavily on information from websites and social media platforms and independent travel guidebooks such as Lonely Planet, the Rough Guides and Frommer's. To communicate with independent travelers, the key information channels that must be used are social media and guidebooks; independent travelers will not be as effectively reached through the travel trade intermediaries.

LAST-MINUTE TRAVEL

The increasing propensity for short breaks and the growing availability of online deals are two main factors fueling last-minute travel. Another ingredient in this equation is the use of smartphones for travel bookings. Several OTAs are active in last-minute travel, including last-minutetravel.com and booking.com.

PRODUCTS VERSUS EXPERIENCES

Travelers today are more concerned about collecting unique experiences than about buying products. This is becoming known as experiential travel and most often means a deeper involvement with the destination, its hosts and culture.

EXPERIENTIAL TRAVEL

Pine and Gilmore (1999) introduced the concept of the experience economy, and since then there is more of a focus on the unique experiences that people can have within destinations compared to physical products. Tourism Australia has established the Signature Experiences of Australia program to meet these needs.

EXAMPLE 16.15

Signature Experiences of Australia

Some countries, including Australia and Canada, are featuring specific experiences to be had in their destinations. These are based on the growing demand for experiential travel and are a good template for partnerships and building community involvement in tourism.

The program seeks to connect with travelers who are specifically seeking out destinations that can deliver memorable experiences closely aligned to their own specific interests. It is designed to grow visitation and attract high-value tourists who are willing to travel to Australia to follow their passions.

Signature Experiences of Australia currently comprises wineries, luxury lodges, golf courses, guided walks, Aboriginal guided experiences, fishing adventures, wildlife encounters, and cultural attractions. In each case Tourism Australia has partnered with select industry collectives that have a compelling marketing proposition and share a common goal and vision.

(Tourism Australia 2022b)

Learning Point

It is good to think about marketing, branding, and communicating experiences rather than always promoting places and products.

SHARING ECONOMY

The sharing economy creates peer-to-peer models, usually supported by online platforms, for accommodations, transportation, tours, dining, and other types of tourism facilities and services. Use of the sharing economy is particularly popular with Millennials.

EXAMPLE 16.16

The Sharing Economy

The impacts of sharing economy providers on destinations are controversial. Many are critical of the negative impacts on traditional tourism sector stakeholders and the contribution to overtourism. Others feel that the sharing economy has given consumers greater freedom of choice. This example provides a quote from Europe that appears to be balanced and appropriate on this issue.

The "sharing economy is undoubtedly an added value for our cities and economies, it is also a great way for visitors to engage with the locals—to get the real and authentic city experience delivered by real people, living real lives. We urge key players to do their utmost to play with local rules in order to make the pie bigger, i.e., increase the total number of visitors to some destinations, attracted by what sharing economy platforms offer there. However, up to now, the growth of the tourism sharing economy has largely happened with engagement of every other stakeholder group except governmental authorities. If managed properly, the sharing economy can be a tool that can prove highly cost-effective, provide opportunities for deeper citizen engagement and offer considerable rewards on environmental impact too," concluded the ECM President.

(de Delàs 2022)

> ## Learning Point
>
> There are many sides to every issue affecting destinations. It is important to have a balanced view of sharing economy providers.

AUTHENTICITY

Authenticity is connected to the sharing economy trend because people perceive that using sharing economy providers gives them more authentic local experiences in destinations. It is related to the growing consumer demand for experiential travel as well.

PARTICIPATION VERSUS OBSERVATION

In the past, many people who traveled were rather passive, choosing to observe destinations through sightseeing or by laying on a beach soaking up the sun. These surely still exist; however, there is a trend for more people wanting to have active participation in what they do when traveling. By doing more, these travelers have deeper and more authentic encounters with their destinations. This relates to the search for authenticity and more experiential travel.

Psychographics and Lifestyles

People have been changing the ways they live, and this has spilled over to destinations. These changes have, for example, spurred the increased popularity of spas and health/wellness tourism and environmentally sensitive travel and tourism.

HEALTH AND WELLNESS

Consumers are increasingly concerned about health and wellness, and this affects both their everyday lives and how they travel. While traveling, some want to maintain their fitness levels or just stay active and to ensure they keep with their dietary regimens. Others desire to use travel to improve their well-being or lifestyle habits.

This trend has had numerous impacts on tourism and destinations, including the increasing popularity of spas and medical and fitness resorts; more active vacation and holiday products, including soft and hard adventure; health-oriented menus, including vegetarian meal options; and greater preference levels for green travel destinations, such as New Zealand, Costa Rica and Australia.

SPA-GOING

The stress in consumers' daily lives is creating a need for pampering, and spas are a way to escape pressures and get re-energized. Moreover, people of all genders are seeking different ways of looking and feeling younger.

Spas have been popular at least since the Roman times, but today's spas have much greater variety and sophistication. Today's spas can be divided into two main groups: beauty, health care and retreat spas; and natural hot springs spas. There is also a distinction between day spas (people do not stay overnight at the property) and resort/hotel spas (people stay overnight).

Thai Square Spa (2022) supplies the following top ten reasons for going to a spa, but there are undoubtedly others:

1. relaxation and stress management;
2. detox;
3. lose weight;
4. improved self-esteem and confidence;
5. improved circulation and blood pressure;
6. anti-aging and skin benefits;
7. manage pain;
8. improved sleep patterns and breathing;
9. getting inspired;
10. connecting with loved ones.

GREEN TRAVEL

Consumers are showing increasing concern for the environment, and this is extending into the travel trips that they take. As a result, the demand for nature-based and ecotourism destinations and packages is growing.

People who place a special emphasis on eco-friendly destinations and practices are sometimes called green travelers. Destinations such as Costa Rica, Belize, Australia and New Zealand, to name just a few, have had outstanding success with ecotourism and other types of nature-based tourism.

EXAMPLE 16.17

More Socially and Environmentally Conscious Travel

Several studies and reports, including this one from American Express, suggest that post-pandemic, people are more concerned about sustainability when they travel.

> Travelers are focused on engaging in positive practices, including wellness activities, giving back to communities, protecting the environment, and more. Travelers are now spending more time thinking through who and what they are traveling for, with 78 percent of respondents wanting to have a positive impact on the community they are visiting.
>
> (American Express Travel 2022)

Learning Point

The trend toward more sustainable and responsible travel will continue to grow.

LGBTQ+

The lesbian, gay, bisexual, transgender, and queer (LGBTQ) market is a mainstream segment of tourism. UNWTO estimated this market generated 35 million international overnight visitors in 2015 (UNWTO 2017). Another source says it is a $211 billion market globally (Stone

2021). A survey by CMI (Community Marketing and Insights 2019) showed US LGBTs are avid international travelers, with 79 percent having passports (compared to about 50 percent on average).

Many major destinations consider LGBTQs to be an important market with great potential. For example, Vienna in Austria has a dedicated website page for this market (Vienna Tourist Board 2022). Some destinations are very popular with LGBTQ tourists, and it is not surprising that they also do a great job of marketing to this market segment. They include San Francisco, New York and Montreal in North America; Amsterdam in Europe; and Sydney in Australia. San Francisco is one of the best-known areas in the world for LGBTQ (Visit California 2022).

EXAMPLE 16.18

The Canadian LGBTQ+ Travel Market

Globally, the LGBTQ travel market is huge; however, it is yet to be fully understood by destinations and DMOs. This example from Canada points out how diverse this market is.

> Before starting to actively target the LGBT+ travel market, it is essential that destinations, tourism businesses and industry stakeholders have an understanding of the diversity of the LGBT+ travel market and their requirements and preferences. Although the actual size of the population that identifies as LGBT+ is unknown, it is estimated that in North America, there are close to 30 million LGBT+ people (6–8 percent of the total population). The total value of spending by the North American LGBT+ consumer market is estimated at $750 billion USD, with tourism spending estimated to be more than $70 billion USD (according to research conducted in 2016 by World Travel Market and Out Now). Overall, Canadian LGBT+ travelers have income levels that mirror that of the general population, but only 30 percent have one or more children living in their household, which generally results in higher discretionary income. On average, Canadian LGBT+ travelers spend $1,855 per trip compared to $265 per trip for the general traveling public—which is seven times higher.
>   Based on CGLCC's [Canada's Gay and Lesbian Chamber of Commerce's] research, we have developed niche archetypes or profiles for common Canadian LGBT+ travelers and their preferences (encompassing activity preferences and some data regarding their demographics across LGBTQ+ communities— safety-conscious travelers, metropolitan foodies, practical lodging travelers, frequent travelers, value travelers, cultural explorers, and influence-driven travelers).
>
> (CGLCC 2020)

Learning Point

It is crucial that destinations understand the diversity and complexity within segments of the travel market.

Technology

Chapter 15 provided an in-depth discussion of ICTs and how DMOs are using these channels and tools. People are increasingly making use of various technologies in selecting and booking destinations as well as during and after their visits to destinations.

ONLINE BOOKING

There were 5.473 billion Internet users in the world on June 30, 2022 (Miniwatts Marketing Group 2022). Asia is the biggest regional market with 2.934 billion, or more than half of the users. However, Internet penetration is highest in North America, Europe, and Latin America and the Caribbean. Therefore, in terms of reaching and communicating with potential tourists, the Internet and social media are now the most important channels for DMOs to use. e-marketing is part of the application of ICTs and has several components that were covered in Chapter 15. Because tourists are increasingly using the Internet and smartphones to get travel and tourism information and to make bookings, every DMO needs to develop an integrated e-marketing communications strategy. For DMOs, this means having effective websites in multiple languages; initiating multilingual email marketing communication programs; making extensive use of social media platforms, blogging, vlogging, and discussion groups; providing apps and other information services through smartphones; and implementing other e-marketing components.

SOCIAL MEDIA

There is no doubt that social media platforms on the Internet are drawing in billions of people around the world. This has had a huge impact on the volume and types of information available about destinations. Additionally, it has significantly affected how DMOs are marketing to domestic and international tourists.

Through blogs, microblogs, and vlogs, consumers themselves have become travel writers and critics. For many people, blogging and vlogging are not only ways to communicate with others, but it has also become a pastime or hobby. For DMOs, blogs are a good source of information about tourists' satisfaction and experiences in their destinations. Social media marketing is now a vital part of destination marketing, and almost all international DMOs are heavily engaged.

EXAMPLE 16.19

Moving to the Metaverse

Technology is constantly evolving and influencing consumers and tourism. The move to the metaverse could be one of the strongest technological trend in coming years.

> Physical and virtual worlds collided last year. With strict social distancing requirements, consumers learned how to stay connected, forming new online communities that offer a range of interactivity, from livestreaming to gaming. Social networks are advancing their capabilities, and in some cases, acquiring tech start-ups, to enter The Metaverse Movement. The constant stream of content and ability to go viral on video-dominant social platforms like TikTok and YouTube showcase the influence of community-based networks.

Now, online socialization is the preferred form of entertainment for many consumers, particularly younger generations, who spend more time playing games on mobile, desktop and AR/VR headsets. During The Metaverse Movement, consumers will outfit their avatars to explore virtual worlds alongside users from across the globe. The prevalence of shared, 3D virtual spaces will characterize a future rendition of the Internet.

(Euromonitor International 2022)

Learning Point

Destination marketers must get more involved with the metaverse as this is a strong trend among consumers.

Virtual and Augmented Reality

VR technology is thought to have great potential for destination marketing, and it is already being applied by several destinations. AR is another branch of technology that has caught on in destinations in conjunction with smartphone use. Pointing smartphones with AR apps super-imposes information or images on the images on the phone screen. You learned about VR and AR in Chapter 15.

Artificial Intelligence

This topic is discussed in Chapter 19 in the context of business travel and business events. AI is being used via chatbots by travel agencies to assist clients to make travel bookings. It is also being used by airlines to help customers choose their ideal holiday destinations. Robots are increasingly being tried out or introduced to perform roles in hospitality and tourism.

Special Interests

Another predominant trend has been niche marketing, or appealing to tourists who have special interests when they travel:

Special-Interest Travel (SIT)

SIT has been one of the hottest trends in tourism in recent times. The main reason behind this trend has been that consumers' interests today have become much more diverse than before. Some of the SIT segments that have emerged include those shown later in Figure 17.10. There are many other activities than those shown in that figure. An excellent source of information on SIT markets is Boomers Bucket List Travel (2022). Boomers Bucket List Travel (Specialty Travel Index) has information on ninety travel activities worldwide.

Niche Tourism

This means that destinations and private-sector companies decide to focus on niche (smaller and more specialized) markets, activities, and interests in tourism. They develop special knowledge, skills and experiences to serve particular visitors and conduct niche marketing communications. For example, places associated with popular movies and TV series often mount campaigns to appeal to their fans. *Game of Thrones* fans can visit filming sites in Ireland, Croatia, and Iceland and can imagine the scenes from this popular HBO series (Lazzarus 2020). Literary tourists like to go to places associated with their favorite authors and the books that they wrote.

EXAMPLE 16.20

The Glamping Experience

Glamping is short for (more) glamorous camping. This example quotes the results from a research study conducted in the USA and Canada on plans to go on glamping trips post-COVID.

> Glamping is an increasingly popular and accessible modern form of camping. To address current and future impacts of COVID-19 on glamping, 2,926 active leisure travelers in the USA and Canada were surveyed. Respondents were asked about post-COVID-19 glamping trip plans and hotel/resort trip plans for comparison. Results indicate more active leisure travelers have plans to take glamping trips (45.9 percent) after COVID-19 when permissible than hotel/resort trips (24.7 percent). The results highlight that the broad accessibility of glamping make it a viable leisure travel alternative during and after the pandemic.
>
> (Craig and Karabas 2021, p. 251)

Learning Point

Glamping is a type of tourism that will grow in the future due to its increasing attractiveness to consumers as well as the opportunities to travel more sustainably.

Many more pages could have been written about consumer behavior, segmentation, and market trends. In fact, entire books have been written on each of these topics. However, space was limited in this book, and the intention was to give you a broad overview on the topics. Many other theories and models could have been introduced and discussed, but the preferred route was to give you a straightforward and practical introduction to consumer travel behavior and not to lose you in the intricacies of complex models. A major message that it is hoped you take away from this information is that all travelers are different. To treat people as if they are the same is unlikely to be a winning strategy for a destination!

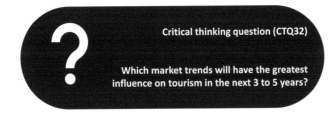

? Critical thinking question (CTQ32)

Which market trends will have the greatest influence on tourism in the next 3 to 5 years?

Implications for Destinations and DMOs

With respect to consumer behavior, segmentation, and trends, it is recommended that DMOs take the following actions:

- Use research to better understand the reasons tourists visit their destinations (note: it is often hard to find out people's underlying motives).
- Find out which sources of information tourists used in planning trips to the destination.
- Conduct destination image research among past visitors and non-visitors.
- Develop marketing/product strategies for consumers according to all stages in the tourism purchase process.
- Analyze the online reviews and comments about their destinations; respond to reviews/comments when appropriate.
- Develop special marketing and incentive programs for past visitors to encourage repeat visits.
- Segment markets scientifically based upon data that have been generated from visitor profile and other studies.
- Constantly track market trends and consider ways to capitalize on these trends in the future.
- Regularly share recent market trends and segmentation approaches with tourism sector stakeholders.

SUMMING UP

Why do people travel to destinations for leisure reasons? This has been a topic of academic debate for many decades, and several competing theories have been proffered. Among these, Dann's push–pull theory appears to have gained the greatest acceptance. The push factors are internal drives that vary from person to person; the pull factors are destinations' products and marketing communications.

There is a set of factors that influence tourists' choice of destinations. These include socio-psychological (personal), situational factors, interpersonal (social), awareness levels, destination images, destination products, IMC campaigns, information search, past visitation, and geographic origins and cultures.

One of the powerful factors affecting the selection of destinations is the images that people have of the places. This has been the focus of many research studies for 45-plus years, and many image measurement models have been suggested by academics. People form images of destinations based upon multiple sources of information. They are also influenced by personal factors.

People tend to go through several distinct stages in planning travel, experiencing the destination, and after returning home. One travel purchase behavior process model has tourists passing through seven sequential steps: need recognition, search for information, pre-purchase evaluation of alternatives, purchase, consumption (within-destination), post-consumption evaluation, and remembering and sharing. For DMOs, it is worth emphasizing that their job does not finish after the purchase or booking has been made. They also need to play an active role in the last three of the seven steps.

Market segmentation is important for destinations in more sharply focusing their attention on specific groups of travelers. Today, there is really no concept of a mass market, and indeed, tourism has become more of a one-to-one phenomenon. There are eight main variables that can be used to segment tourism markets: trip purpose, geography, socio-demographics, psychographics, behavior, product-related, channel of distribution, and channel of communication. These can be applied separately or in combinations.

DMOs need to constantly stay on top of market trends because consumers and their behaviors are changing more quickly than before. It is especially important to keep a focus on market trends caused by changes in trip purposes, countries of origin, demographics and generations, psychographics and lifestyles, travel behaviors, products versus experiences, technology uses, and special interests.

KEYWORDS

activities model of destination choice
affective images
AIOs (activities-interests-opinions)
autonomous
awareness set
baby boomers
business travel
buying process
choice models
cognitive dissonance
cognitive images
COVID-19
destination image
destination selection
domestic travel
electronic word of mouth (EWoM)
evoked set
experience good
experiential travel
family travel market

flashpacking
gender marketing
generation alpha
Generation X
Generation Y
Generation Z
glamping
hierarchy of needs
inbound
independent travel
induced
international travel
last-minute travel
lifestyles
luxury travel
market segmentation
meetings, conferences, exhibitions and incentives (MICE)
metaverse
motivation
need recognition
novelty seeking

objective criteria
organic images
origin (geographic)
outbound
perceived risk
perception
personal travel
psychographics
purchase decision
purpose of trip
push–pull theory
search for information
socio-demographics
special interests
staycations
subjective criteria
travel career approach
travel purchase process
tripography
variety seeking
VFR travel
word of mouth (WOM)

REVIEW QUESTIONS

1. How does the push and pull theory explain why people travel?
2. What are the main factors that influence tourists in selecting destinations?
3. How do people's images or perceptions of destinations affect their decisions on where to travel?
4. What are the stages that people tend to go through when purchasing, consuming, and recalling trips to destinations?
5. How can tourist markets be divided into groups that share common characteristics?
6. How have recent market trends affected tourism?

REFERENCES

American Express Travel (2022) "2022 Global Travel Trends Report," www.americanexpress.com/en-us/travel/discover/get-inspired/global-travel-trends

Beard, J. G., and Ragheb, M. G. (1983) "Measuring Leisure Motivation," *Journal of Leisure Research*, 15 (3): 219–228.

Beat of Hawaii (2022) "Why Hawaii's Repeat Visitors Aren't Returning – Does Anyone Care?" https://beatofhawaii.com/why-hawaiis-repeat-visitors-arent-returning-does-anyone-care/

Beerli, A., and Martin, J. D. (2004) "Factors Influencing Destination Image," *Annals of Tourism Research*, 31 (3): 657–681.

Belize Tourism Board (2022) "Small Country, Big Adventure: Things to Do," www.travelbelize.org/things-to-do/

Boomers Bucket List Travel (2022) "The Comprehensive Resource for Boomers' Travel Adventures," https://boomersbucketlisttravel.com/

Buenos Aires Cuidad (2022) "Tango," https://turismo.buenosaires.gob.ar/en/agrupador-noticias/tango?gclid=EAIaIQobChMI1IyF85Kx-glVkNKWCh0RMA5gEAAYASAAEgKaC_D_BwE

Canada's LGBT+ Chamber of Commerce (2020) "An LGBT+ Travel Market Guide and Tourism Development Toolkit," www.cglcc.ca/wp-content/uploads/2021/01/CGLCC_Travel_Market_Guide_2020-EN.pdf

Chen, C.-F., and Tsai, D. C. (2007) "How Do Destination Image and Evaluative Factors Affect Behavioral Intentions?" *Tourism Management*, 28 (4): 1115–1122.

Chittilapilly, A. K. (2022) "Rise of Experiential Travel and Its Impact on Tours and Activities," ET HospitalityWorld.com, August 24, https://hospitality.economictimes.indiatimes.com/news/speaking-heads/rise-of-experiential-travel-and-its-impact-on-tours-and-activities/93748196

Community Marketing and Insights (2019) "24th Annual LGBTQ Tourism and Hospitality Survey US," https://cmi.info/

Condor Ferries (2022) "Millennials Travel Statistics and Trends 2020–2021," www.condorferries.co.uk/millennials-travel-statistics-trends

Craig, C. A., and Karabas, I. (2021) "Glamping After the Coronavirus Pandemic," *Tourism and Hospitality Research*, 21 (2): 251–256.

Crompton, J. L. (1979) "Motivations for Pleasure Vacation," *Annals of Tourism Research*, 6 (4): 408–424.

Dann, G. (1977) "Anomie, Ego-Enhancement and Tourism," *Annals of Tourism Research*, 4 (4): 184–194.

Davitt, D. (2022) "Mastercard Report Outlines Latest Travel Trends in Resurgent Asia Pacific Market," *The Moodie Davitt Report*, May 18, www.moodiedavittreport.com/mastercard-report-outlines-latest-travel-trends-in-resurgent-asia-pacific-market/

de Delàs (2022) "European Cities Welcome the Sharing Economy and Collectively Claim for Adaptation to Local Legislation," City Destination Alliance, https://citydestinationsalliance.eu/european-cities-welcome-sharing-economy-collectively-claim-adaptation-local-legislation/

Depew, E., and Smith, J. W. (2020) "Long-Distance Cycling Routes: Economic Impacts, Best Practices, and Marketing Strategies," Institute of Outdoor Recreation and Tourism, Utah State University, https://extension.usu.edu/iort/files/Long-distance_cycling_routes.pdf

Destination Canada (2022) "Tools-Explorer Quotient," www.destinationcanada.com/en/tools

Echtner, C. M., and Ritchie, J. R. B. (1993) "The Measurement of Destination Image: An Empirical Assessment," *Journal of Travel Research*, 31 (4): 3–13.

ElderTreks (2022) "Small Group Exotic Adventures for Travelers 50 Plus," www.eldertreks.com/

Eloksari, E. A. (2020) "Demand for Staycations to Surge As Tourist Destinations Reopen," *The Jakarta Post*, August 7, www.thejakartapost.com/news/2020/08/07/demand-for-staycations-to-surge-as-tourist-destinations-reopen.html

Euromonitor International (2022) "Top 10 Global Consumer Trends 2022," https://go.euromonitor.com/white-paper-EC-2022-Top-10-Global-Consumer-Trends.html

Expedia Group (2018) "Gen Z Travelers: More Open to Influence and Inspiration Than Other Generations," https://advertising.expedia.com/about/press-releases/gen-z-travelers-more-open-to-influence-and-inspiration-than-other-generations/

Flashpackers Headquarters (2022) "Flashpacker Defined! The Evolution of the Backpacker," http://flashpackerhq.com/flashpacker-defined/

Gartner, W. C. (1993) "Image Formation Process," in M. Uysal and D. Fesenmaier (eds), *Communication and Channel Systems in Tourism Marketing*, New York, NY: Haworth Press, pp. 191–215.

Gilbert, D. C., and Cooper, C. P. (1991) "An Examination of the Consumer Behavior Process Related to Tourism," *Progress in Tourism, Recreation and Hospitality Management*, 3: 78–106.

Global Blue (2018) "Millennials: The New Travellers," www.globalblue.com/corporate/market-insights/millennials-the-new-travellers#slide1

Global Rescue (2019) "Survey Finds 87 Percent of Travelers Have Travel Safety Concerns," March 14, www.globalrescue.com/common/blog/detail/Survey-Finds-87-Percent-of-Travelers-Have-Travel-Safety-Concerns

Hankinson, G. (2005) "Destination Brand Images: A Business Tourism Perspective," *Journal of Services Marketing*, 19 (1): 24–32.

Herzberg, F. (1964) "The Motivation-Hygiene Concept and Problems of Manpower," *Personnel Administration*, 27 (1): 3–7.

Hu, B., and Morrison, A. M. (2002) "Tripography: Can Destination Use Patterns Enhance Understanding of the VFR Market?" *Journal of Vacation Marketing*, 8 (3): 201–220.

Huld, A. (2022) "Camping and Outdoor Activity: Tapping into China's Hottest New Travel Trend," *China Briefing*, August 10, www.china-briefing.com/news/china-camping-and-outdoor-activity-tapping-into-the-new-travel-trend/

Iso-Ahola, S. E. (1980) *The Social Psychology of Leisure and Recreation*, Dubuque, IA: Brown.

—— (1982) "Toward a Social Psychological Theory of Tourism Motivation: A Rejoinder," *Annals of Tourism Research*, 9 (2): 256–262.

—— (1983) "Towards a Social Psychology of Recreational Travel," *Leisure Studies*, 2 (1): 45–56.

—— (1989) "Motivation for Leisure," in E. L. Jackson and T. L. Burton (eds), *Understanding Leisure and Recreation: Mapping the Past, Charting the Future*, State College, Pa.: Venture Publishing.

Kelleher, S. R. (2022) "How COVID Changed Business Travel Forever," *Forbes*, March 12, www.forbes.com/sites/suzannerowankelleher/2022/03/12/covid-changed-business-travel/?sh=7dff32af53a0

Klenosky, D. (2002) "The 'Pull' of Tourism Destinations: A Means-End Investigation," *Journal of Travel Research*, 40 (4): 385–395.

Lazzarus, L. (2020) "How 'Game of Thrones' Affected Tourism in This Country (and the Locals Are Not Happy)," *The Travel*, February 26, www.thetravel.com/game-of-thrones-affected-tourism/

Lee, G., O'Leary, J. T., Lee, S. H., and Morrison, A. M. (2002) "Comparison and Contrast of Push and Pull Motivational Effects on Trip Behavior: An Application of a Multinomial Logistic Regression Model," *Tourism Analysis*, 7 (2): 89–104.

Living Your Senior Life (2022) "All About Baby Boomers: The Facts, the Stats, and the Trends," https://livingyourseniorlife.com/all-about-baby-boomers

Mack, C. (2022) "How to Champion Gender Equality in Tourism Marketing," GLP Films, www.glpfilms.com/news/gender-equality-tourism-marketing

Maslow, A. H. (1943) "A Theory of Human Motivation," *Psychological Review*, 50 (4): 370–396.

Mill, R. C., and Morrison, A. M. (2012) *The Tourism System*, 7th edn, Dubuque, IA: Kendall Hunt.

Miniwatts Marketing Group (2022) "World Internet Usage and Population Statistics," www.internetworldstats.com/stats.htm

Morrison, A. M. (2022) *Hospitality and Travel Marketing*, 5th edn, London and New York, NY: Routledge.

Moscardo, G. M., Morrison, A. M., Pearce, P. L., Lang, C., and O'Leary, J. T. (1996) "Understanding Vacation Destination Choice through Travel Motivation and Activities," *Journal of Vacation Marketing*, 2 (2): 109–122.

Nomads World (2017) "Flashpacker or Backpacker? What Type of Traveler Are You?" https://nomadsworld.com/what-type-of-traveler-are-you/

Oregon State Parks (2022) "Scenic Bikeways," https://stateparks.oregon.gov/index.cfm?do=things-to-do.scenic-bikeways

Pearce, P. L. (1982) *The Social Psychology of Tourist Behavior*, Oxford: Pergamon Press.

Pearce, P. L., and Lee, U.-I. (2005) "Developing the Travel Career Approach to Tourist Motivation," *Journal of Travel Research*, 43 (3): 226–237.

Pike, S. D. (2002) "Destination Image Analysis: A Review of 142 Papers from 1973–2000," *Tourism Management*, 23 (5): 541–549.

Pine, B. J., and Gilmore, J. H. (1999) *The Experience Economy: Work Is Theatre and Every Business Is a Stage*, Cambridge, Mass.: Harvard Business Press.

Plog, S. C. (2002) "The Power of Psychographics and the Concept of Venturesomeness," *Journal of Travel Research*, 40 (3): 244–251.

Snepenger, D., King, J., Marshall, E., and Uysal, M. (2006) "Modeling Iso-Ahola's Motivation Theory in the Tourism Context," *Journal of Travel Research*, 45 (2): 140–149.

Statista (2022) "Countries with the Highest Outbound Tourism Expenditure Worldwide from 2019 to 2021," www.statista.com/statistics/273127/countries-with-the-highest-expenditure-in-international-tourism/

Stone, M. (2021) "Hotels and Travel Businesses That Aren't Openly Welcoming to LGBTQ Visitors Are Missing Out on a $211 Billion Market," *Insider*, June 30, www.businessinsider.com/cost-of-inequity-lgbtq-travel-market-growing-but-barriers-remain-2021-6

Swarbrooke, J., and Horner, S. (1999) *Consumer Behavior in Tourism*, Oxford: Butterworth–Heinemann.

Thai Square Spa (2022) "Top 10 Reasons to Visit a Spa," https://thaisquarespa.com/blog/top-10-reasons-to-visit-a-spa/

Tourism Australia (2022a) "The Youth Sector," www.tourism.australia.com/en/markets-and-stats/industry-sectors/youth.html

Tourism Australia (2022b) "Signature Experiences of Australia," www.tourism.australia.com/en/about/our-programs/signature-experiences-of-australia.html

Um, S., and Crompton, J. L. (1990) "Attitude Determinants in Destination Choice," *Annals of Tourism Research*, 17 (3): 432–448.

United Nations World Tourism Organization (2017) "Second Global Report on LGBT Tourism," www.unwto.org/archive/global/press-release/2017-05-06/unwto-releases-2nd-global-report-lgbt-tourism

Urban Dictionary (2022) "Flashpacker," www.urbandictionary.com/define.php?term=Flashpacker

Vienna Tourist Board (2022) "For LGBT," www.wien.info/en/all-of-vienna/gay-lesbian

Visit California (2022) "LGBTQ travel in San Francisco," www.visitcalifornia.com/in/attraction/lgbt-travel-san-francisco

Visit Naples (2022) "The Art of Pizza Makers Becomes a UNESCO World Heritage," www.visitnaples.eu/en/neapolitanity/flavours-of-naples/the-art-of-pizza-makers-becomes-a-unesco-world-heritage

VisitScotland (2020) "Domestic Overnight Trip Profile," www.visitscotland.org/binaries/content/assets/dot-org/pdf/research-papers-2/uk-visitors/domestic-overnight-trip-profile-2017-19.pdf

Wego Travel (2020) "Staycation Interest in Bandung and Yogyakarta Keeps Surging As Domestic Tourism Reopened," September 11, https://blog.wego.com/staycation-interest-in-bandung-yogyakarta-surging/

Wunderman Thompson (2019) "Generation Alpha: Preparing for the Future Consumer," www.wundermanthompson.com/insight/generation-alpha-2019

17

Domestic Leisure and VFR Travel Markets

Staying at home

LEARNING OBJECTIVES

Having read this chapter, you should be able to:

1. explain the benefits of domestic tourism;

2. discuss the size and importance of domestic tourism in selected countries and compare the domestic and international tourism contributions;

3. elaborate upon the recent trends and prospects for domestic tourism;

4. review the major challenges in the marketing and development of domestic tourism;

5. describe major segments of domestic tourism including the family, multigenerational, drive tourism, and luxury travel markets;

6. examine the VFR market and explain its importance for domestic tourism;

7. pinpoint the reasons the positive impacts of the VFR market are sometimes underestimated;

8. discuss a systematic, step-by-step approach to the marketing, branding, and communications of domestic tourism;

9. describe successful domestic tourism marketing campaigns.

DOI: 10.4324/9781003343356-21

Warming Up

You already know that international tourism collapsed in 2019–2020 with the onset of COVID-19. Many people could not even leave their homes and working from there was common. Teleworking and online shopping became the norm (Shah et al. 2022). When restrictions were eased a little, people traveled locally and to nearby places in their own countries—this was domestic travel. Reading Chapter 16, you learned about some of the key trends including stay-cationing close to home and greater levels of concern for health safety.

Before the pandemic, domestic travel sustained the tourism sector in many countries and not international tourism. You might think of it as the staple food or bread-and-butter market for many DMOs and tourism sector stakeholders. Although domestic tourism may not hold the same glamour for some destinations as international tourism, it is hugely important to many parts of the world. Moreover, many local people say they want to discover their own countries first before venturing abroad. Often, tourism industry associations are keen to advocate the merits of domestic tourism, as in the case of New Zealand.

EXAMPLE 17.1

Domestic Tourism Is the Foundation

In many countries, domestic tourism is much larger than international and New Zealand is one case of this. This example outlines the policy position on domestic tourism of Tourism Industry Aotearoa (TIA), the country's major tourism trade association.

> Domestic tourism activity provides the "foundation" tourism demand (pre-COVID approaching 60 percent of total spend) and thereby enables international tourism products and services to exist. TIA has long championed the importance of domestic tourism and will continue to do so. When borders were closed by the pandemic, domestic tourism's importance has been elevated to being an essential industry lifeline. TIA supports a continuation of Tourism NZ's 2020 mandate to promote domestic tourism, along with a national discussion on the nature of the policy, insight and marketing support domestic tourism needs to deliver sustainable social, cultural, and economic benefits.
>
> (TIA 2022)

Learning Point

The size and contribution of domestic tourism should never be underestimated.

The status of domestic tourism varies across the world. In advanced-economy countries of Europe, North America, and the Asia-Pacific, domestic tourism is mature, with decades of development, marketing, branding, and communications. With large middle classes and reasonably high household incomes, most people can afford to travel within their own countries for leisure purposes.

The situation is not the same in the poorer, developing countries, and indeed, domestic tourism is a new concept to some of these nations. Several of these countries are experiencing high rates of economic growth and personal disposable incomes, and so domestic tourism is starting to boom. China, India, and Indonesia are good examples of places where domestic tourism is on a sharp upward trend. There are many benefits of developing domestic tourism within a destination; there are also limitations.

VFR travel is closely linked with leisure travel, and it is significant in both domestic and international tourism. Usually, VFR travel is more important in domestic tourism, and thus it is discussed in this chapter. Despite its size and importance, the value of VFR travel is often underestimated and undervalued. There are no plausible reasons for any DMO to ignore this important market.

Chapter 17 begins with a definition of domestic tourism and identifies its benefits. Then the size and importance of domestic tourism is reviewed, with examples from around the world supplied. Limitations of domestic travel are also mentioned. The trends and prospects for domestic tourism are discussed, and issues and challenges are highlighted. Governments started providing incentives to stimulate domestic travel during the COVID-19 pandemic in 2020–2022 and these initiatives are described. Thereafter, the factors stimulating domestic travel are considered. The remainder of the chapter is devoted to explaining domestic tourism market segments including the VFR travel market.

Your author has for many years been a strong proponent of domestic travel and VFR. He has written extensively about VFR travel, admonishing DMOs for ignoring this important demand source and not trying to fully investigate its potential. He has championed domestic tourism, being one of the first authors to devote entire book chapters to this market. While it was difficult to find reports and articles about domestic travel for the first and second editions of this book, that changed dramatically with COVID-19—in 2022 there were plenty of sources as destinations had to rely much more heavily on locals!

Definition of Domestic Tourism

Here now is a definition of domestic tourism.

DEFINITION

Domestic tourism

Tourism can be regarded as a social, cultural and economic phenomenon related to the movement of people outside their usual place of residence. Domestic tourism comprises the activities of a resident visitor within the country of reference (OECD 2022).

Benefits of Domestic Tourism

Many countries in the world, particularly the lower GDP nations, have had a strong orientation toward generating foreign currencies through international tourism development and marketing. Domestic tourism for these countries has had a much lower priority. This has not necessarily been the case in developed economies, where domestic tourism has had a mainstay status and is well recognized and appreciated. Domestic tourism offers significant economic, social, and cultural benefits for tourism in a country.

EXAMPLE 17.2

The Economic Importance of Domestic Tourism

This example reveals the importance of domestic tourism in major economies. Some of the numbers are surprisingly high.

> Domestic travel is the main driving force of travel and tourism in major economies. In fact, in twenty-two countries of the thirty-one countries analyzed, domestic tourism accounted for at least 50 percent of the total travel and tourism spending, with Brazil ranking first with 94 percent of spending coming from domestic tourists. Brazil is followed by India, Germany, China and Argentina each with 87 percent. Japan, Mexico, the UK and the USA also enjoyed significant levels of domestic spending—all at 80 percent or more of travel and tourism's internal spending.
>
> (WTTC 2018)

Learning Point

While more attention is often focused on international tourism, domestic tourism is a more significant economic force in many cases.

Some of the benefits that have been attributed to domestic tourism are identified in Figure 17.1 and described later.

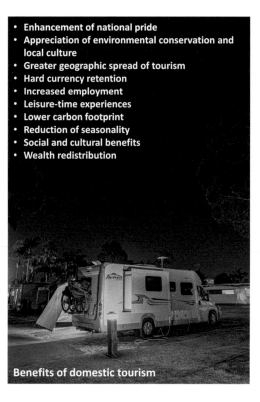

- Enhancement of national pride
- Appreciation of environmental conservation and local culture
- Greater geographic spread of tourism
- Hard currency retention
- Increased employment
- Leisure-time experiences
- Lower carbon footprint
- Reduction of seasonality
- Social and cultural benefits
- Wealth redistribution

Benefits of domestic tourism

Figure 17.1 Benefits of domestic tourism.

Enhancement of National Pride

This means creating more pride and ambassadorship for one's own country through enhanced understanding, experience and appreciation of all that it offers (Trenchard 2020). Residents may become better tourism ambassadors for their regions and countries if they have traveled and experienced the country more extensively.

Greater Appreciation of Environmental Conservation and Local Culture

This means better educating local people so they develop a deeper awareness of the natural and cultural resources of their countries. They attach a higher value to these resources after experiencing them at first hand.

Greater Geographic Spread of Tourism

Travelers are dispersed across and deeper into the destination, stretching tourism activity and attractions beyond the main cities. People leave heavily populated urban areas and visit the countryside, rural, and resort locations. This is facilitated by drive tourism, including using recreational vehicles (Fig. 17.1).

EXAMPLE 17.3

Drive Tourism (Queensland)

Driving around one's own state, province, or country has always been a popular leisure travel activity. This is particularly important for large destinations such as Queensland, Australia in this example.

> Queensland's drive tourism market consists of visitors who travel for leisure and use a vehicle to reach their destination. This includes both day trips and overnight trips to one or more destinations. Drive tourism is important for Queensland as it encourages visitors to:
>
> - travel beyond the major tourism destinations
> - stopover in small towns
> - spend money at local businesses
> - drive tourism presents valuable opportunities for businesses, and contributes financially to many rural and regional communities.
>
> (Business Queensland 2022a)

Learning Point

Drive tourism is a large market in many countries and spreads tourism around a nation and allows domestic and international travelers discover large and small communities.

Hard Currency Retention

Hard currency is retained that would otherwise leave the country in the form of outbound travel expenditures in foreign destinations.

Increased Employment

Domestic tourism generates more jobs for local people in the tourism sector (both direct and indirect) because of greater and ongoing tourism activity.

Leisure-Time Experiences

Domestic tourism enables residents who have growing disposable incomes to participate in productive and satisfying experiences during their leisure time. As you learned in Chapter 2, there are also social tourism opportunities in domestic travel. Social tourism was defined as "programs, events, and activities that enable all population groups—and particularly youth, families, retirees, individuals with modest incomes, and individuals with restricted physical capacity—to enjoy tourism, while also attending to the quality of relations between visitors and host communities."

Lower Carbon Footprint

Traveling domestically may have a lower carbon footprint than traveling to other parts of the world when air travel is required.

Reduction of Seasonality

Domestic travel creates year-round tourism activity and lessens the valleys in seasonality curves, enabling tourism operators to operate longer (Gan 2020).

Social and Cultural Benefits

Domestic travel delivers social and cultural benefits to residents who might not otherwise be able to experience the cultural and natural richness of their own nations.

Wealth Redistribution

Domestic tourism redistributes wealth within a country's boundaries. For example, people from the cities go to rural and poorer areas of a country and spend money in these more economically depressed regions.

While these benefits are substantial, are there are any limitations that come along with domestic tourism? There certainly are, is the answer to that question. One of the main limitations is that domestic tourism does not generate foreign currency earnings for a country. Also, it is argued that domestic tourism contributes to global warming through emissions of greenhouse gases, just as does international tourism. It is also suggested that domestic visitors do not spend as much as foreigners and they tend to be less wealthy. Smaller, less-developed countries may have lower domestic population levels and many citizens without the financial means to travel.

Size and Importance of Domestic Tourism

Indicators of the relative economic importance of domestic tourism are demonstrated in Figure 17.2. This shows statistical estimates by the WTTC (2022) of the contributions of domestic versus foreign visitor spending by country.

Part IV

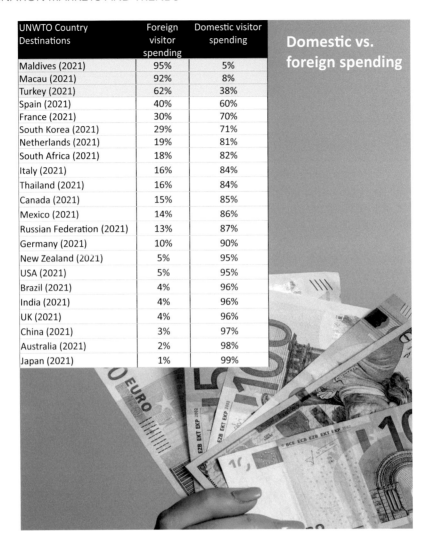

UNWTO Country Destinations	Foreign visitor spending	Domestic visitor spending
Maldives (2021)	95%	5%
Macau (2021)	92%	8%
Turkey (2021)	62%	38%
Spain (2021)	40%	60%
France (2021)	30%	70%
South Korea (2021)	29%	71%
Netherlands (2021)	19%	81%
South Africa (2021)	18%	82%
Italy (2021)	16%	84%
Thailand (2021)	16%	84%
Canada (2021)	15%	85%
Mexico (2021)	14%	86%
Russian Federation (2021)	13%	87%
Germany (2021)	10%	90%
New Zealand (2021)	5%	95%
USA (2021)	5%	95%
Brazil (2021)	4%	96%
India (2021)	4%	96%
UK (2021)	4%	96%
China (2021)	3%	97%
Australia (2021)	2%	98%
Japan (2021)	1%	99%

Domestic vs. foreign spending

Figure 17.2 Domestic vs. foreign spending on tourism (World Travel & Tourism Council 2022).

Overall, the WTTC (2022) estimated that domestic visitor spending contributed 85 percent to travel and tourism's total spending in 2021, 5.7 times greater than foreign visitor spending.

EXAMPLE 17.4

Eighty-Five Percent Share of Total Spending in 2021

There is an astonishing statistic in this example with an estimated 85 percent of total tourism spending in the world coming from domestic tourism, up 13 percent over 2019. Undoubtedly, this was mainly due to the travel restrictions during the COVID-19 pandemic.

Global Travel and Tourism's recovery was supported more by the rise in the spending by domestic visitors than revenues from international visitors. Travel and Tourism domestic spending recovered strongly—by 31.4 percent globally—whereas spending by international visitors recovered by only 3.8 percent as travel restrictions for foreign visitors remained in place across many countries. As a result, domestic spending's share of total Travel and Tourism spending increased from 72 percent in 2019 to 85 percent in 2021. Travel and Tourism business spending and leisure spending grew at 30.9 percent and 25.1 percent respectively.

(WTTC 2022)

Learning Point

The economic importance of domestic tourism has grown significantly in recent years.

Now, you will hear some facts about domestic tourism in individual countries.

China

In the world's most populated countries, the potential domestic travel markets are vast. For example, China's domestic travel market is huge and involves billions of people moving about the country. There were 3.25 billion domestic tourist trips in China in 2021 (China Travel News 2022). Trips were less in the first half of 2022 due to lockdowns in major cities in the enforcement of the zero-COVID policy. There are massive movements of people at the time of major national holidays and especially at the Spring Festival (Chinese New Year), May Day Holiday, and National Day Golden Week.

India

The Market Research Division of the Ministry of Tourism in India (Ministry of Tourism, [India] 2022) found there were 2.36 billion domestic tourist visits to the states and union territories of India in 2019. Due to the pandemic, the volume dropped to around 610 million in 2020. The top five states in terms of number of domestic tourist visits during 2020 were Tamil Nadu, Uttar Pradesh, Karnataka, Andhra Pradesh, and Telangana.

USA

The USTA (2022) estimated that US residents spent $751 billion in 2021 on domestic leisure travel. International inbound spending in the USA was around 5 percent of domestic, at $40 billion. Domestic business travel spending equaled approximately 16 percent of domestic leisure travel spending.

Canada

Statistics Canada (2022) estimated that Canadians made 202.3 million person-trips within Canada in 2021. Most of these trips were to destinations in Ontario and Quebec. Around 42.5 percent of these domestic trips were for holiday, leisure or recreation, and 35 percent were for VFR.

Mexico

According to the Secretaría de Turismo (2021), there were 27.93 million domestic arrivals to hotel rooms in Mexico in 2020 compared to 10.28 million international arrivals.

European Union

For the European Union (EU), domestic tourism represented 72.7 percent of all the holiday trips taken by Europeans in 2019 according to Eurostat (2022).

Germany

Within the EU, the German domestic travel market is the largest.

EXAMPLE 17.5

Germany Has Europe's Largest Domestic Travel Market

We often think of Germans as the globetrotters who reach all parts of the world in their travels. As this example highlights, however, domestic tourism in Germany is substantial and increasing.

> Travel warnings and quarantine obligations have been dropped for many popular holiday destinations in Germany, with demand for stay-at-home holidays providing a boon to landlords, hoteliers and guests alike. The challenges faced by the tourism sector over the past year have been assuaged by rising vaccination levels and the sharp decline in COVID-19 incidence rates, making holidays in Germany a real possibility once more.
>
> The German travel and tourism markets possess tremendous potential for both tour operators and travel agencies. Germans are known for their "travel bug," whether on vacation or in the office, and they spend plenty of time on both domestic and international trips. According to Eurostat, Germany is the biggest domestic tourism market within Europe with an average of four nights that a German annually spends in German hotels.
>
> (German Trade and Invest 2022)

Learning Point

There are huge domestic travel markets in major countries. In crisis times, these markets become even more crucial for destinations and tourism sector stakeholders.

UK

There were 122.8 million domestic trips taken in the UK in 2019, about 49 percent were for holiday purposes, 35 percent for VFR, and 13 percent for business (VisitBritain and Kantar 2022a).

Australia

Australians made 85.8 million overnight trips within Australia in the year ending June 2022 (Tourism Research Australia 2022). This was 24 percent less than in the previous year.

Most domestic overnight trips in Australia were taken in New South Wales, Queensland, and Victoria.

South Africa

Domestic visitors contributed 73 percent of total tourism expenditures of R451.5 billion in South Africa in 2019 (Statistics South Africa 2022). There were 6 million domestic trips taken in 2021 compared to 15 million in 2020 (South African Tourism 2022). The most popular destinations were Eastern Cape, KwaZulu, and Gauteng.

Although many of these numbers are not directly comparable because of differences in definitions of trips and visits, they clearly underline the magnitude of domestic tourism in the selected countries.

Often, we look too far, sometimes the answer is closer than we think.

The author asks that you read this part carefully—it was included in the previous edition of this book that was published in 2018, pre-COVID. Although the main point may already be made about the critical importance of domestic tourism in several top destinations, there is a follow-on point that also requires some emphasis, and you need to know about it. You learned in Chapter 11 about the susceptibility of domestic and international tourism to crises, and this has been demonstrated with 9/11 (2001), SARS (2003), and the worldwide economic problems in 2007 to 2009. When crises such as these are encountered, inbound international tourism is particularly affected and can drop precipitously. What are the potential solutions for destinations that rely heavily on tourism? The answer has been to focus marketing, branding, and communications closer to home and especially on domestic leisure travelers. In some ways, domestic tourism provides an insurance policy for times when international tourism experiences a downturn; therefore, domestic tourism should never be neglected or given an inferior status in national tourism. Now, having read that passage, do you think the author was right? What he said was definitely the experience with the COVID-19 pandemic in 2020–2022.

As a final postscript to this discussion, there are some destinations in the world where international tourism is massively important to their economies and where domestic tourism is minimal. For example, 74.6 percent of Aruba's and 78.9 percent of the Maldives' total exports in 2020 were from international tourism (World Bank 2022). You saw in Figure 17.2, the high proportions of foreign tourism spending for the Maldives (95 percent) and Macau (92 percent). The figure for Aruba was 89 percent.

Domestic tourism is the primary and sometimes exclusive focus of many DMOs around the world. These DMOs pay very little attention to international tourism marketing, branding, and communications, leaving this task to higher-level DMOs within their countries. This is true of many of the CVBs operating in the USA and of many regional tourism associations around the world.

Trends and Prospects for Domestic Tourism

What are the principal trends that have been impacting domestic tourism, and what are the prospects for this very important branch of the tourism sector? Chapter 16 highlighted seven overall trends that have been occurring in tourism worldwide, and most of these have affected domestic tourism:

1. Demographics: There are five generational markets—Baby Boomers, Generation X, Generation Y (Millennials), Generation Z, and Generation Alpha. There is more travel by and attention being paid to Gens Y and Z.

2. Trip purposes: There are more multipurpose trips, bleisure (business plus leisure), and short-break vacations/holidays. City breaks are included here and these typically involve stays of two to four nights in urban centers.

3. Trip planning and travel arrangements: There is more independent and solo travel, and last-minute travel is on the increase.

4. Psychographics and lifestyles: There are increases in health and wellness trips, spa usage, green travel, and the LGBTQ+ travel market.

5. Special interests: There is more interest among consumers in adventure, cruises, casino gaming, culinary, cultural, dark tourism, nature-based and ecotourism, health and wellness, heritage/historic, industrial, religious, voluntourism, and wine tourism.

6. Technology uses: There is greater searching and booking travel online, and use of social media platforms.

7. Use of sharing economy providers' services: There is greater use of services such as Airbnb and Uber.

Added to this mixture of influential factors are the recessionary or poorer economic conditions in many developed countries, with the main effects being experienced in 2007 to 2009 and its aftermath. Another factor has been the relative pricing levels within domestic versus outbound tourism destinations. In some cases, domestic prices have risen to much higher levels than available in the outbound destinations. Additionally, the development of low-cost carrier (LCC) airlines on international routes has encouraged more outbound tourism, and this has particularly been the case in Europe and the Asia-Pacific region.

Without wanting to be too repetitive here, some of these trends will be briefly mentioned again in the context of their impacts on domestic tourism:

- Demographics: The changing demographic structures in society are affecting domestic tourism. Later in this chapter, you will hear about multigenerational domestic travel, one of the outcomes of demographic changes. The Millennial influence is another topic about which you will hear.

- Multi-purposing travel trips: This trend has clearly helped domestic tourism destinations in many countries. In the tougher economic times and because of time poverty, people have been increasingly combining business and leisure trip purposes; this is the so-called bleisure trend.

- Psychographics and lifestyles: Domestic tourism is experiencing the impacts of changes in psychographics and lifestyles. One of the trends noted here is the growth in green travelers; these people are concerned about environmental protection and conservation.

- Short-break holidays (breakations and staycations): The trend toward taking shorter holidays favors places close to the residences of tourists and is not beneficial for long-haul destinations. Breakations refers to short-duration holidays at home and abroad. For example, the Office for National Statistics (2017) in the UK finds that "In the last twenty years, UK tourists have turned their backs on traditional two-week holidays in favor of short breaks and week-long trips." Staycations is a term used in some countries, including the UK and Canada, when residents decide to take holidays in their own countries.

- SIT: The trend toward more SIT applies both to domestic and international tourism. This topic is discussed later in this chapter as well as in Chapter 13 and 15. Figure 17.9 provides a listing of thirty SIT options.

- Technology uses: The effects of ICTs on tourism are universal and pervasively impacting domestic tourism. For example, domestic travelers are now relying most heavily on social media platforms and websites to gather information on destinations.

- Trip planning and travel arrangements: Trips are being planned on shorter time frames than before, and last-minute travel arrangements are gaining in popularity in domestic and international tourism.
- Use of sharing economy providers' services: Airbnb and Uber launched in 2008 and 2009, respectively, and since then have had a major impact on domestic tourism.

Although there has been strong growth in domestic travel in several countries (including China, India, and Indonesia), other countries have noted a softness in demand and even declines in domestic tourism prior to COVID-19 (including Australia, New Zealand, South Africa, and the UK). This negative trend in domestic tourism is attributed mainly to the relative costs of foreign versus domestic travel, the global economic problems in 2008 and 2009, and the impact these problems had on residents of the nations that were most affected.

EXAMPLE 17.6

How Domestic Tourism Creates Hospitality Demand

This example is about the United Arab Emirates (UAE) and was prepared by hospitality consulting firm, CBRE. It describes four forms of domestic demand for hotels and resorts.

Daycations: Use of a hotel room for the day. Limited creation of demand for hotels due to the short nature of the stay. Popular with resorts in the higher end of the market.

Staycations: Hotel overnight stay in the guest's place of residence. Some demand created for hotels as staycations can last a few nights. Popular mostly with resorts in the higher end of the market.

Getaways: Short overnight stay within the country. Creates some level of demand for hotels and can be used to fill properties during low occupancy days for instance. Can potentially target all market segments.

Holidays: "Standard" holidays taken within the UAE. Creates the most demand for hotels due to the length of the stay. Can benefit properties in all market segments.

(Trenchard 2020)

Learning Point

Locals can be a viable source of business for hotels and resorts. Hospitality property operators need to be creative in preparing these offers to serve domestic travelers.

The COVID-19 outbreak, commencing at the end of 2019, changed everything. The prospects for the expansion of domestic tourism are bright. Domestic travel is expanding more rapidly than international. In addition, there are sixteen countries in the world with populations of over 100 million in 2022 (Central Intelligence Agency [CIA] 2022). In all these countries, the potential for future expansion of domestic tourism is significant, although some will be hampered by low per capita incomes and other unique local constraints and conditions.

Countries with high growth rates in real GDP are particularly primed for domestic tourism growth, including Vietnam, China, Philippines, Kenya, and Indonesia. Other countries such as the USA, UK, and Japan are experiencing poorer economic conditions, and domestic tourism will grow more modestly.

Despite the favorable conditions in many countries for domestic tourism in the future, there are issues and challenges that will be encountered, and these are now reviewed.

Issues and Challenges for Domestic Tourism

Domestic tourism faces some overall issues as well as some specific challenges in development, marketing, branding, and communications.

Whose Responsibility Is Domestic Tourism?

Generally, there is an acceptance that the official national DMO should do the destination marketing, branding, and communications for its country abroad. The consensus is not as strong on who should market, brand, and communicate about domestic tourism. This issue is further complicated by the fact that in many countries, residents travel mainly within their own states, provinces or territories. The question then becomes, why not have the states, provinces or territories and cities market domestic tourism because they are the major beneficiaries? It is a good question because every state, province and territory has an official DMO as well as many city-/county-level DMOs and sometimes, also regional tourism organizations or regional tourism authorities. Indeed, these sub-national DMOs are generally very active in domestic tourism marketing, branding, and communications. However, there is still a need for a national tourism office to promote the concept of domestic tourism within a country.

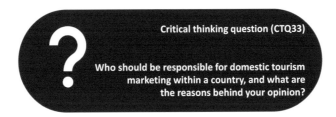

Critical thinking question (CTQ33)

Who should be responsible for domestic tourism marketing within a country, and what are the reasons behind your opinion?

Competition between Domestic and International Tourism and Tourists

In several ways, domestic and international tourism are competing. At one level, they are competing for increasingly scarce government tourism resources to support the tourism sector. At another level, domestic and international tourism are competing for business from the residents of a given country. The relative price levels and convenience of travel are key factors in who wins this competition.

There are varying tendencies among the citizens of different countries to take holidays at home (domestic) and travel outbound (international), and this is well demonstrated for Europe. For example, more trips by residents (fifteen years and older) of Belgium were taken outside of their country in 2019 than by French residents (Eurostat 2022).

Another aspect of competition comprises situations when domestic and international tourists are mixed together at tourism attractions and facilities within a specific country. In most cases, this blending of the two markets is good for tourism and presents no visitor management problems. However, there are a few situations where the differing behaviors and expectations can cause some tension between the two groups. For example, some international visitors to famous sites in China are disturbed and put off by the large numbers of domestic tourist groups who do not tend to follow the same manners and rules of etiquette to which they are accustomed in their home countries.

Impacts of Currency Rate Fluctuations

Changes in currency exchange rates can have a significant influence on tourist volumes, including those for domestic tourism. For example, when a country's currency is stronger, the buying power of its citizens when traveling abroad increases. The USA provides a good example of this currency rate exchange issue, with the strengthening of the US dollar in 2012 to 2015. This was expected to have a positive impact on outbound US tourism to Mexico and Canada (WTTC 2016). These types of challenges are impossible for the tourism sector to deal with on its own and reflect the susceptibility of tourism to forces and crises outside of its own realm.

Is a Day Tripper a Tourist?

Often, a significant portion of domestic travel involves day trips where there are no overnight stays in the destinations. UNWTO says there are tourists and excursionists, and excursionists are temporary visitors who stay less than twenty-four hours in a destination. This is a particularly important point in counting international tourist arrivals at very busy cross-border points between two countries. Counting excursionists as international tourist arrivals is discouraged by UNWTO for the sake of uniformity of counting around the world.

However, in a domestic tourism situation, is it as necessary to make this distinction between overnight tourists and day-trippers? This is not just an important point for market researchers, but it also has implications for product development, marketing, and the management of visitor attractions. In some cases, there seems to be a type of resentment against day visitors whereby they are perceived as low spenders when compared to "real" tourists. Data from The Great Britain Day Visitor 2019 annual report, however, indicate that day visitors have a significant economic impact. For 2019, residents of Great Britain took 1.653 billion domestic Tourism Day Visits and around £67 billion was spent during these visits (VisitBritain 2022).

EXAMPLE 17.7

Day-Trip Activities in Great Britain

The Great Britain Day Visits Survey (GBDVS) identifies fifteen activities for day-tripping in England, Scotland, and Wales. The most popular single activity was visiting friends and family for leisure.

> This report provides the main results of GBDVS 2019 including estimates of the total volume and expenditure of Tourism Day Visits and the main results regarding activities undertaken, destination type, transport types used, money spent during visits and the profile of visitors. Results are provided at an overall GB level and individually for visits taken to destinations in England, Scotland and Wales.

- Visited friends or family for leisure (24 percent of all trips)
- Went out for a meal (11 percent)
- "Special" shopping for items that you do not regularly buy (7 percent)
- Went on a night out to a bar, pub and/or club (7 percent)
- Undertook outdoor leisure activities such as walking, cycling, golf (7 percent)
- Went out for entertainment to a cinema, concert or theater (6 percent)
- Went on general days out/to explore an area (6 percent)
- Watched live sporting event (not on TV) (5 percent)
- Went to visitor attractions such as a historic house, garden, theme park, museum, zoo (5 percent)
- Took part in other leisure activities such as hobbies, evening classes (outside of your home) (3 percent)
- Went to a special public event such as a festival, exhibition (3 percent)
- Took part in sports, including exercise classes, going to the gym (2 percent)
- Went to a special event of a personal nature such as a wedding, graduation, christening (2 percent)
- Went on day trips/excursions for another leisure purpose not mentioned above (2 percent)
- Went on days out to a beauty/health centre/spa (1 percent)

"Trips" are classified as trips or journeys away from the respondent's place of residence, not being an activity, which is undertaken "very regularly" and has lasted at three hours (including travel) and less than a day, taken by adults aged sixteen and over and accompanying children aged up to fifteen.

(VisitBritain 2022)

Learning Point

Day-trippers (excursionists) participate in a wide variety of activities while outside their places of residence.

Some destinations have decided that day-trippers, or day visitors, are important and need attention from the DMO as well. For example, the USTA defines a person-trip as a trip by one person away from home overnight in paid accommodations or on a day or overnight trip to places 50 miles or more (one-way) away from home. This type of definition for domestic tourism based on the distance traveled is a fair and reasonable way to consider the day-visitor market.

Unfortunately, it is difficult to compare day visitors across different countries because the definitions vary. For example, Tourism Research Australia (2021) defines day visitors as shown in the example.

EXAMPLE 17.8

Tourism Research Australia's Definition of Day Visitors

A day-visitor in Australia is defined by distance traveled and trip duration. Also, trips have to be for non-work or school purposes.

Day visitors are those who travel for a round-trip distance of at least 50 kilometers, are away from home for at least four hours and do not spend a night away from home. Same day travel as part of overnight travel is excluded, as is routine travel such as commuting between work/school and home.

(Tourism Research Australia 2021)

Learning Point

Definitions of day trips vary from country to country making comparisons difficult, if not impossible.

You can see these definitions are different for VisitBritain (three hours including travel), the USTA (50 miles from home), and Tourism Research Australia (four-hour trip and a 50-kilometer round trip).

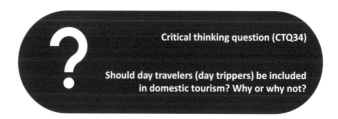

Critical thinking question (CTQ34)

Should day travelers (day trippers) be included in domestic tourism? Why or why not?

Slower Development of Tourism for Domestic Markets

In some countries, domestic tourism has been neglected in favor of product development, marketing, branding, and communications for international tourists. This has been a practical decision based on the desire to earn more in foreign currencies and to take advantage of the potentially higher spending power of foreign tourists. Facilities developed for international tourists may be priced at levels that are too high for residents, and this may lead to some resentment among residents as well as excluding them from buying.

Providing Incentives for Domestic Travel

Without much international tourism in 2020–2022, many governments turned their attention to domestic travelers to sustain tourism and promote its recovery. UNWTO found that these initiatives fell into five categories (UNWTO 2020a). Here are some examples of the programs.

Financial

Italy introduced the Holiday Bonus (Bonus Vacanze) scheme that targeted lower-income households. It provided up to €500 for eligible holidays (*Local IT* 2021). Several countries, including South Korea, provided coupons that could be used in qualifying tourism and hospitality businesses (Korea.net 2022).

Marketing and IMC

Some destinations launched new IMC campaigns to encourage greater domestic travel. These included France and its Cette été je visite La France campaign (France.fr 2022). Argentina had the Promocioná tu destino to generate new ideas about how to promote domestic destinations (Ministerio de Turismo y Deportes 2022).

Product Development and Partnerships

Paraguay improved the city center infrastructure in Asunción. The MGTO partnered with travel trade groups to offer discounts on tours for locals in the Macao Ready Go! Local tours program (MGTO 2021).

Market Intelligence

The Department of Tourism in the Philippines conducted an online survey with residents about domestic travel (Department of Tourism [Philippines] 2021).

Capacity-Building and Training

In 2020, the Costa Rica Institute of Tourism launched on online platform, ICT Capacita. The online courses, talks, and webinars were designed for entrepreneurs and partners in the tourism sector. The objective was to provide training in different topics to improve business management, quality, and contents (Instituto Costarricense de Turismo 2020).

EXAMPLE 17.9

Japan Domestic Travel Subsidy Program

Several countries introduced subsidy and discount programs to stimulate domestic travel in 2020–2022. This example is about Japan that had two consecutive programs, Go To Travel and National Travel Discount.

> Japan will run a new domestic tourism subsidy program from October 11 to late December (2022) as part of efforts to spur domestic tourism and revive the coronavirus-hit economy, tourism minister Tetsuo Saito said Monday. The National Travel Discount will provide the equivalent of up to ¥11,000 ($77) in discounts and coupons per traveler per day, which can be used for meals, shopping and accommodation expenses.
>
> The National Travel Discount program, which is available to Japan residents only, comes in the wake of the Go To Travel subsidy program and expands on similar existing programs operating at the prefectural level.
>
> (*Japan Times* 2022)

Learning Point

When tourism is reduced, governments should think about providing incentives to stimulate domestic travel.

Factors Influencing Domestic Tourism

What factors influence domestic travel flows and characteristics? You learned in Chapter 16 that consumers are influenced by personal and interpersonal factors (including UGC, WoM, and eWoM), and by commercial messages from destinations and DMOs. They are also affected by various external environmental trends and events such as in the economy and as a result of crises such as COVID-19. The following six factors were identified by RAND Europe in research on behalf of the UK Government (Phillips 2021):

1. Economic factors: High domestic travel prices deter domestic tourism.
2. Activities and specific destination-related attributes: These influence where people travel and the level of domestic tourism.
3. Demographic characteristics: Households with lower education levels and with children present are more likely to travel domestically.
4. Environmental attitudes: People with more environmentally friendly attitudes are positively inclined toward domestic holidays (Fig. 17.3).
5. Weather: Climate influences decisions to take domestic holidays or travel abroad.
6. Transport infrastructure: Good transport connectivity and improved accessibility are positively associated with domestic travel.

Figure 17.3 People are engaging in more environmentally friendly activities including hiking.

Domestic Tourism Market Segments

There are different ways in which domestic travel market segments can be described. They are usually divided by geographic origin and then into pleasure/leisure or holiday travel, VFR, business travel, and other.

As you know from Chapter 16, there are at least eight ways to form segments of destination markets (trip purpose, geography, socio-demographics, psychographics, behavior, product-related, channel of distribution, and channel of communication). All these segmentation approaches can be applied to domestic tourists. In this chapter, part of the focus is on trip-purpose segments, pleasure/leisure/holiday travel and VFR; business travel is discussed in Chapter 19.

Because there are nearly 200 countries in the world, it is very difficult to deal with geographic origin segmentation; as a result, that topic is not discussed here, although picked up in Chapter 18. The focus is now placed on socio-demographic, product-related, and psychographic segmentation (Fig. 17.4), beginning with the family travel market.

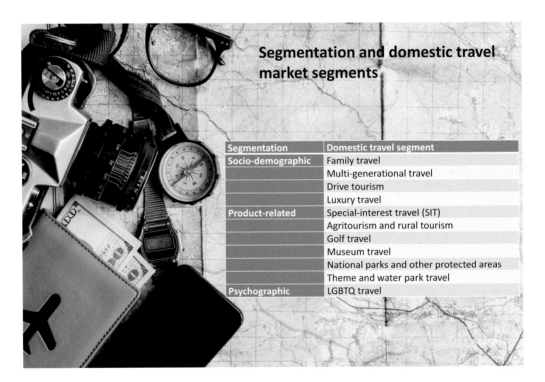

Segmentation and domestic travel market segments

Segmentation	Domestic travel segment
Socio-demographic	Family travel
	Multi-generational travel
	Drive tourism
	Luxury travel
Product-related	Special-interest travel (SIT)
	Agritourism and rural tourism
	Golf travel
	Museum travel
	National parks and other protected areas
	Theme and water park travel
Psychographic	LGBTQ travel

Figure 17.4 Segmentation and domestic travel market segments.

Some of these markets have entire books discussing them; e.g., family tourism (Schänzel et al. 2012); drive tourism (Carson et al. 2002; Prideaux and Carson 2011); and golf tourism (Hudson and Hudson 2014). Given the space limitations, only snapshot summaries can be provided in this book.

Socio-demographic Segmentation Approach

FAMILY TRAVEL MARKET

> **DEFINITION**
>
> **Family travel market**
>
> Travel by adults, including grandparents and great-grandparents, with children.

Families traveling with children represent a significant proportion of most domestic tourism markets (Fig. 17.5). For example, a survey conducted in the USA in 2020 determined that although parents express concern with traveling, a majority (85 percent) anticipate traveling domestically in the next twelve months (Marriott 2020).

Figure 17.5 Beach areas like Bondi in Sydney, Australia, are magnets for families and other visitors.

As well as going to beaches and the seaside, camping is a highly popular activity for families in many countries. You heard about the glamping trend in Chapter 16, and that is extending the appeal of traditional camping. Camping trips are made to commercial campgrounds and recreational vehicle (RV) parks, national, state, county, and local parks. Earlier in this chapter, you learned about the growth in camping in China.

Families have several decision-makers (parents and children), and there are several vacation/holiday sub-decisions, as was mentioned in Chapter 16. From the research that has been completed on family vacation decision-making, it appears quite clear that the female head of household (mother) plays the key role.

EXAMPLE 17.10

The Power of Women in Travel

The female role in travel decision-making is significant, including for families. This example provides some impressive statistics to confirm this.

> Today, 56 percent of leisure travelers are women, and over the past five years, they have steadily held this majority stake. Women make close to 85 percent of all travel decisions: where to go, when to fly, where to stay, what to see. Of affluent travelers with annual incomes upwards of $250,000, women also account for 54 percent, according to MMGY Global, an advertising agency specializing in travel, tourism, and hospitality. In total, women represent 60 percent of the wealth in the USA, and they notch 58 percent of all online sales. Importantly, women also live longer than men and outnumber them in a crucial travel bracket—retirees—making them an investment that yields greater, and longer, returns.
>
> (LaGrave 2021)

Learning Point

Women are the major travel decision-makers in families.

Many destination marketers are targeting the family travel market, often with very creative programming. For example, a resort in Batam, Indonesia, staged the Family Bonding Staycation program in June 2017 (Jakarta Globe 2017). Thirty-eight families from nearby Singapore participated in the program, in which they worked on cooking Indonesian dishes.

The demographic characteristics of families are changing and the circumstances in family life were altered in 2020–2022 due to the COVID-19 pandemic. More teleworking (or telecommuting) and online shopping were earlier mentioned; many households were also forced into the home schooling of children during lockdowns.

MULTIGENERATIONAL TRAVEL MARKET

Some experts regard multigenerational travel as one of the hottest growth markets in leisure travel and particularly for domestic tourism. Here is our definition of this segment.

DEFINITION

Multigenerational travel

Multigenerational (3G) travel is a trip party that includes three or more generations: for example, grandparents, parents and children (Fig. 17.6).

Figure 17.6 A multigenerational trip in Hong Kong.

Some travel companies have set up offers to cater to multigenerational travel. Tauck Tours (2022) is one of them with their Tauck Bridges program for family travel. This program includes travel for families for graduations, celebrations, and reunions.

EXAMPLE 17.11

Tauck Tours and Multigenerational Travel

Tauck Tours are one of the leading tour operators in the USA. They are demonstrating leadership in the sector by specifically catering to multigenerational travelers. This example explains the company's Tauck Bridges journeys.

> Travel should be life-changing, eye-opening, exciting—and engaging for kids, teens, parents and grandparents alike. Our vacations designed just for families have been created to spark a passion, inspire a sense of wonder, and enrich understanding—and when these experiences are shared with loved ones and other families, they bring you closer together. Whether on a land journey, river cruise or small ship cruise, we take care of every detail so you can do, see, and be together as a family . . . making every moment count and memories that will last forever.

> Our Tauck Bridges journeys are designed to create new and deeper connections that last by allowing multigenerational families to grow closer to each other as they explore faraway places together . . . making new friends along the way. Insider experiences, custom-designed hands-on activities, and authentic local color all add to the fun . . . not to mention our best in class team of family-oriented tour directors, guides, and experts. Easy, effortless and one upfront price . . . we take care of the little things, so you don't miss out on the big things.
>
> (Tauck Tours 2022)

Learning Point

Bringing families closer together is one of the outcomes of multigenerational travel.

VisitEngland carried out the Multi-Gen Visitor Research study covering eight international markets (VisitEngland 2019). Some 62 percent visitors of from the eight international markets and the UK domestic audience had either taken a multigenerational trip or would consider one; 25–30 percent of the total market in France, China, Germany, the UAE, and the UK had actually taken one in the previous three years.

The influence of Millennials as well as the desires of Baby Boomers are sparking the growth of multigenerational travel. The Millennials are avid travelers and get very involved in planning trips, especially online. The Baby Boomers are increasingly wanting to spend time with their families. 3G travel satisfies the needs of Baby Boomers and younger generations.

EXAMPLE 17.12

Multigenerational Home Living

It is common for three generations to live together in some countries, including China. However, this was traditionally not the case in developed countries. That is changing and there is more multigenerational home living, as this example for the USA demonstrates.

> Multigenerational living has grown sharply in the USA over the past five decades and shows no sign of peaking. When asked why they share their home with relatives, Americans often give practical reasons related to finances or family caregiving. But the experience also has an emotional component. About a quarter of adults in multigenerational homes say it is stressful all or most of the time, and more than twice that share say it is mostly or always rewarding. These experiences with multigenerational living vary by demographic group, especially by age and income, according to a Pew Research Center survey conducted in October 2021.
>
> (Cohn et al. 2022)

Multigenerational living—that is, living in a household that includes two or more adult generations, typically consisting of those ages twenty-five and older—has increased among all age groups over the past five decades. But the increase has been fastest among adults ages twenty-five to thirty-four. In 1971, similar shares of adults across age groups lived in a multigenerational household, but by 2021, young adults were far more likely than older Americans to have this type of living arrangement.

(Fry 2022)

Learning Point

Greater multigenerational home living will positively influence multigenerational travel.

Drive Tourism

You heard earlier in this chapter about the importance of drive tourism to Queensland, Australia. This form of traveling around has existed for at least seventy-five years in some developed countries (Prideaux 2020). In rapidly developing countries where incomes are increasing, drive tourism is also growing; an example being in Xinjiang Province of China (Qu et al. 2018).

DEFINITION

Drive tourism

The use of an owned or rented vehicle (including RVs) to visit destinations outside of the usual place of residence, either for one or more days or for a day excursion. Typically, the vehicle is driven by one or more persons within the traveling group.

Drive or self-drive tourism is a popular way for families and multigenerational groups to travel together. It allows people to visit multiple destinations on one trip. A study of drive tourism also suggested that it was a means for dealing with social distancing requirements during the pandemic (Hattingh 2022).

You learned about circuits and trails in Chapter 7 as one of the functional approaches to product development for destinations. Examples such as the Wild Atlantic Way in Ireland and the Cabot Trail in Canada have been discussed, and these are themed routes specifically created for drive tourism. Drive tourism allows people to reach more places in a country and this can be beneficial for local communities (there can be environmental and social-cultural costs as well).

The RV market is a part of drive tourism. It is a significant market in some countries; for example, 11 percent of the households own RVs in the USA (Condor Ferries 2022). As highlighted in the example, traveling by RV is popular among Millennials.

EXAMPLE 17.13

Profile of RV Ownership

There is a tendency to assume that RV owners are seniors; however, as this example shows, that is not accurate. Younger generations are also showing enthusiasm for buying and using RVs.

> The study found RV ownership has increased over 62 percent in the past twenty years with a record 11.2 million RV owning households, split almost equally between those over and under the age of fifty-five, with significant growth among 18–34-year-olds, who now make up 22 percent of the market. Additionally, an incredible 9.6 million households intend to buy an RV within the next five years. Among current RV owners who plan to buy another RV in the next five years, the numbers for Millennials and Gen Zers stand out, with 84 percent of 18–34-year-olds planning to buy another RV, with a 78 percent preferring to buy a new model.
>
> While the median annual usage for current RV owners remains steady at twenty days, people intending to buy an RV plan to use their RV a median of twenty-five days per year. This increase is indicative of the changing attitudes toward remote work and the ability for more people to be able to work from a destination more frequently than traditional vacation days afforded in the past.
>
> (RV Industry Association 2022)

Learning Point

The ownership and use of recreational vehicles is diversifying in terms of socio-demographic characteristics.

Although this chapter is not on international tourism, you should know that the renting of RVs by foreigners to explore countries including Australia, New Zealand, and the USA is becoming more popular.

LUXURY TRAVEL MARKET

Luxury travel is partly socio-demographic and partly lifestyle in nature. The luxury travel market is a segment of domestic and international tourism markets that has a hierarchy of needs, depicted in Figure 17.7. These special needs are over and above those in Maslow's hierarchy of needs, which was discussed in Chapter 16.

There are many articles written about luxury travelers, but precious few statistics have ever been published on their numbers and characteristics. It is easier to identify the tourism products they prefer, such as first-class air travel, luxury yacht trips (Fig. 17.8), and the top five-star hotels and resorts, like Aman, Shangri-La, and Banyan Tree. Although much of luxury travel is generated by people from Europe and North America, this market is growing more rapidly in other places, including China and India.

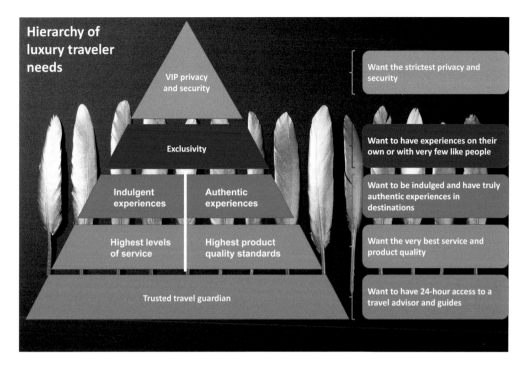

Figure 17.7 Hierarchy of luxury traveler needs (Amadeus 2017).

Figure 17.8 Unique experience of traveling on a luxury yacht.

Product-Related Segmentation Approach

SIT MARKETS

SIT markets are usually drawn to destinations by specific types of destination products (Fig. 17.9); for example, golfers go to destinations that have courses they want to play, scuba divers go to ocean areas where they can see reefs or shipwrecks, and those who want to gamble seek out casino destinations (see Figure 16.14). Therefore, SIT is closely aligned with product-related segmentation. However, there is also a human side to SIT because it reflects the psychographics and lifestyles of specific people.

Domestic tourism has experienced an increase in SIT markets. In Chapter 18, fifteen market segments with growth potential are identified and briefly described. All fifteen segments are significant and growing as part of the domestic tourism in many countries. Because the fifteen SIT segments are described in Chapter 18, they are not elaborated upon in this chapter. Obviously, a list of fifteen items does not cover every possible SIT activity that can take place in a country.

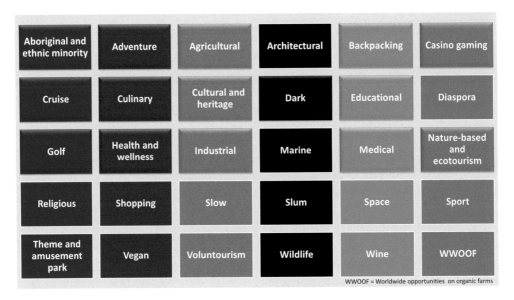

Aboriginal and ethnic minority	Adventure	Agricultural	Architectural	Backpacking	Casino gaming
Cruise	Culinary	Cultural and heritage	Dark	Educational	Diaspora
Golf	Health and wellness	Industrial	Marine	Medical	Nature-based and ecotourism
Religious	Shopping	Slow	Slum	Space	Sport
Theme and amusement park	Vegan	Voluntourism	Wildlife	Wine	WWOOF

WWOOF = Worldwide opportunities on organic farms

Figure 17.9 Thirty special interests that are important in domestic and international travel.

AGRITOURISM AND RURAL TOURISM MARKET

> **DEFINITION**
>
> **Agritourism**
>
> "A subset of rural tourism which encompasses recreational experiences involving visits to rural settings or rural environments for the purpose of participating in or experiencing activities, events or attractions not readily available in urbanized areas" (Rogerson and Rogerson 2014).

Another SIT category is agritourism, also sometimes called agrotourism or agricultural tourism. Traditionally associated with Europe, agritourism has spread throughout the world to the Americas, Australia, New Zealand, Africa, and Asia. Agritourism remains a strong attraction in Europe; for example, Italy had 23,615 agritourism farms in 2018, all licensed by government, and many offer overnight accommodation (Gismondi et al. 2021). Rural tourism and agritourism have experienced rapid growth throughout Asia as well. In the 1990s, a very popular agritourism concept was introduced in China, known as *nong jia le* (happy farm family homes). Usually, these farms provide meals based on farm produce and some also provide overnight accommodation.

EXAMPLE 17.14

Rural Tourism Boom in China

China has a huge domestic travel market. Due to international travel restrictions, the trend in 2020–2022 was for more Chinese residents to travel to rural areas in order to avoid crowded conditions in cities and threats of infection. This travel was also facilitated by an excellent and expanding high-speed rail system in China.

> China is in the middle of a boom in rural tourism as city-dwellers escape the country's rapidly expanding urban centers to head out to small communities, farms and orchards for a taste of the simple life. And the Chinese government couldn't be more pleased.
>
> China has one of the largest domestic tourism markets in the world. The Ministry of Culture and Tourism estimated there will be more than four billion trips made across China in 2021, a market worth just over $500 billion.
>
> With international tourism all but impossible due to the ongoing pandemic and quarantine restrictions, a demand for domestic alternatives isn't surprising—especially as China is home to fifty-five UNESCO World Heritage Sites.
>
> (Westcott and Wang 2021)

Learning Point

Travel to rural areas increases as domestic travel grows.

Agritourism has been especially popular in domestic tourism because it allows urban dwellers to experience a simpler lifestyle at a reasonable cost. Magnini (2017), in studying the economic impact of agritourism on the state of Virginia in the USA, found six reasons people were attracted:

1. bonding with family or friends;
2. educational/experiencing something new;
3. enjoying the outdoors;
4. fun/entertainment;

5. live close by/passing through/visiting friends or family in the area;
6. purchasing good food, beer, cider, and/or wine.

The motivations for farm businesses to engage in agritourism in Virginia were to generate additional income, market farm products, and share a lifestyle or way of living with others. In addition, agritourism is important in sustaining the livelihoods of farm families and keeping them on the land.

Agritourism is now particularly well developed in North America. The Oregon Tourism Commission (2017) produced an excellent practical resource, *The Oregon Agritourism Handbook*, which includes a comprehensive list of potential agritourism activities, which are summarized in Figure 17.10.

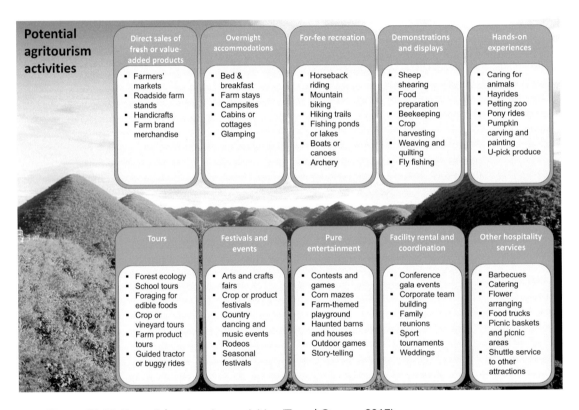

Figure 17.10 Potential agritourism activities (Travel Oregon 2017).

As well as the specific activities that agritourism can offer, agricultural landscapes can be beautiful in themselves and draw domestic and international tourists for sightseeing. There are numerous examples around the world, including the cherry blossom orchards of Japan, the terraced rice paddies of Bali, the tea hills of Sri Lanka and India, the rapeseed fields of China and the UK, the tulip fields of the Netherlands, and the lavender fields of France and other countries (Fig. 17.11).

Figure 17.11 Lavender fields in bloom are highly attractive to visitors.

Another more recent offer within agritourism is WWOOFing, and Example 17.15 provides a description of this concept.

What Is WWOOFing?

Domestic travelers are becoming more environmentally conscious. Locations practicing organic agriculture are becoming increasingly popular for leisure travel trips, in close proximity to cities and further afield. WWOOFing is a trend that has emerged in agritourism.

WWOOF comes in as a movement that aims to join organic farmers and growers with volunteers in an effort to increase cultural understanding. It's all about constructing a global community. Here's all about WWOOF.

WWOOFing stands for "World Wide Opportunities on Organic Farms." The volunteer or "WWOOFer," gets the opportunity to spend time in an organic farm, learn what it's like, how it works and what sustainable agriculture is all about. During your stay in the farm, you don't have to pay for board or lodging. It is not a monetary exchange program.

> WWOOF is an educational program and it offers the visitors/WWOOFers the chance to learn what WWOOFing is about. It is all about learning how to farm, taking part in the organic agriculture program and learning the culture. WWOOFing is a worldwide movement, and WWOOF-USA® Host Farm Directory has more than 2,000 organic farms all over the nation. Agritourism is rising in popularity.
>
> (Federation of WWOOF Organisations 2022)

Learning Point

WWOOF represents an intersection of two major consumer trends—greater concern for the environment and for health and wellness.

Golf Travel Market

> **DEFINITION**
>
> ### Golf tourism
>
> Golf tourism is the term used to describe trips undertaken by persons for which the main purpose is to play golf. Golf may also be pursued as a secondary activity (for example, someone on a beach holiday playing a round during their vacation). This type of activity is more difficult to measure, and while it can be important for the golf courses themselves it has little significance for tour operators (Caribbean Tourism Organization 2022).

Some think golf is a subset of sport tourism. However, golf tourism is a popular mode of travel in both domestic and international tourism and requires separate attention by destination managers. Golf tourism includes trips or holidays in which the main purpose is to play golf. In the broader definition of domestic travel, these trips include those by day visitors. Golf is also played as a secondary activity on many holidays.

The R&A (2022) finds there were 38,081 golf facilities in the world in 2021. The most golf courses are in the USA, followed by Japan, UK, Canada, and Australia (Moore 2022). The golf market is large in several developed countries (Fig. 17.12). For example, the National Golf Foundation (NGF 2022) estimated that there were 37.5 million golfers in the USA in 2021. The NGF indicated that 25.1 million of these golfers played on courses, and the remaining 12.4 million engaged in off-course activities such as driving ranges. The European Golf Association has 4.32 million registered golfers with the largest numbers being in England, Germany, Sweden, Netherlands, and France (European Golf Association 2022).

Kim and Ritchie (2012) completed a study on the motivations of Korean golfers for golf tourism. Using Dann's push and pull theory of motivation, they found five push factors (business opportunity, benefits, learning and challenging, escape/relax, and social interaction/kinship factors). The pull factors of destinations were natural environment, golfing-related availability and accessibility, golf resort/course facilities and services, tourism attractions, tourism facilities and services, nightlife and entertainment, and price and ease of access.

Figure 17.12 Golfing vacations are popular in domestic tourism.

Several destinations consider golf tourism to be a priority and have developed long-term strategies for market and product development. These include Victoria, Australia (Visit Victoria 2018), New Zealand (Golf NZ 2022), and Scotland (VisitScotland 2022). The objectives of the Victoria strategy are to:

- leverage the hosting of major international golf events to position the Melbourne Sandbelt as one of the top five golf destinations in the world;
- capitalize on Melbourne's position as a world-class golf destination to disperse visitation to Victoria's premier golf regions (Mornington Peninsula, Bellarine Peninsulas and the Murray River) and to other locations with unique golf tourism experiences;
- establish Melbourne as Australia's Home of Golf, a year-round destination for the best golf experiences;
- position Victoria's premier golf regions as top travel destinations with year-round appeal for domestic and international visitors.

Scotland, in 2022, also released the new Scottish Golf Tourism and Visitor Strategy (VisitScotland 2022).

A great example of a domestic golf tourism destination that is also an excellent partnership example is the Robert Trent Jones Golf Trail (2022) in Alabama in the USA. It joins together eleven sites (twenty-six courses) with 468 holes of golf. The first course was completed in 1992, with all the courses being designed by one of the world's most famous golf course designer, Robert Trent Jones. Hundreds of thousand rounds of golf are played on the trail each year, and it has become an attraction for international golfers as well.

Museum Travel Market

Visiting museums is a highly important feature of domestic tourism, although technically it is a component of cultural and heritage tourism. The museum travel market is substantial. The total combined attendance of the top-twenty museums worldwide was 22.4 million in 2020 (Themed Entertainment Association 2020). These include, among others, the National Air and Space Museum (Washington, DC, USA), Palace Museum (Beijing, PR China), Louvre (Paris, France), National Museum of Natural History (Washington, DC, USA), Metropolitan Museum of Art (New York, USA), British Museum (London, UK), Shanghai Science and Technology Museum (PR China), National Gallery (London, UK), and Vatican Museums (Vatican City). For cities such as Washington, Beijing, London, and Paris, museums are a key draw for domestic and international tourists.

Museums are having to adapt to changes in demand and supply, including the adoption of the latest innovations in technology such as augmented and virtual reality. They are having to do more marketing and programming to attract and provide experiences for tourists, residents, and traditional markets (Fig. 17.13).

Figure 17.13 Museums and galleries play an important role in domestic tourism.

National Parks and Other Protected Areas

National parks and other protected areas play a major role in domestic tourism. The USA as the birthplace of national park systems has a huge volume of park visits.

EXAMPLE 17.16

Visits to US National Parks in 2021

National parks are highly popular with domestic travelers for various forms of outdoor recreation and sightseeing. The USA had the first national parks. This example provides visitor statistics for 2021.

> 297,115,406 recreation visits
> 1,356,657,749 recreation visitor hours
> 12,745,455 overnight stays (recreation + non-recreation)
> Three parks had more than ten million recreation visits: Blue Ridge Parkway, Great Smoky Mountains National Park, and Golden Gate National Recreation Area.
> Eleven parks had more than five million recreation visits, which is up from seven parks in 2020 and equal to the number of parks in 2019.
> Seventy-three parks had more than 1 million recreation visits (19 percent of reporting parks), which is up from sixty in 2020 and down from eighty parks in 2019.
> Nineteen national parks had more than 1 million recreation visits (30 percent of national parks)
> 25 percent of total recreation visits occurred in the top eight most-visited parks (2 percent of all parks in the National Park System).
>
> (National Park Service [US] 2022)

Learning Point

National parks are a source of pride for citizens as well as a strategy for environmental protection and conservation. In some countries, including the USA, they are major destinations for domestic travel.

Within national parks and other protected areas, visitors can engage in a wide array of outdoor recreation activities, including sightseeing, camping, walking and hiking, cycling, canoeing, bird and other wildlife viewing, nature and environmental education, caving, and many others.

Theme and Water Park Travel Markets

The segment of the domestic tourism market visiting theme parks is substantial in many countries (Fig. 17.14). According to the 2020 Theme Index and Museum Index from Themed Entertainment Association (2020), the top twenty-five theme parks in the world had a combined annual attendance of 83.3 million in 2020. The figure for 2019 was 253.7 million. The top twenty theme parks in North America had combined attendances of 44.3 million, the top twenty in Asia-Pacific had 59.5 million, the top twenty in Europe, the Middle East and Africa had 22.2 million, and the top ten parks in Mexico, South and Central America had 4.3 million. The audiences for theme parks, although much less after 2019, are huge, and a large proportion of the attendances result from domestic tourism.

Figure 17.14 Most theme parks have strong regional demand within their countries.

Water parks are also becoming more important in domestic tourism (Fig. 17.15). The top sixty water parks worldwide had a combined total attendance of 23 million in 2020 (Themed Entertainment Association 2020). The Chimelong Water Park in Guangzhou, PR China, had the largest annual attendance at 3.0 million.

Figure 17.15 Having a great time at a water park in Germany.

OTHER LEISURE MARKET SEGMENTATION APPROACHES

The market approaches described above have focused on the travel party compositions (e.g., families and multigenerational groups), products offered (e.g., agritourism, golf, theme and water parks, museums, national parks and other protected areas), and psychographics. There are other ways to segment domestic markets. Chapter 16 describes demographic profiles of visitors, and Chapter 18 discusses country of origin or geographic source segmentation.

There are many other segments of domestic tourism and a myriad of activities in which people can engage. Most of these are in the list in Figure 17.9 and fifteen of them are described in Chapter 18, since they can be experienced abroad and at home:

- adventure tourism;
- casino gaming;
- cruise tourism;
- culinary or food tourism;
- cultural and heritage tourism;

- dark tourism;
- health and wellness tourism;
- industrial tourism;
- medical tourism;
- nature-based tourism and ecotourism;
- religious tourism;
- shopping tourism;
- sport tourism;
- voluntourism;
- wine tourism.

There are still others beyond these fifteen including diaspora tourism (CBI 2020a), SAVE (Scientific, Academic, Volunteering and Educational) travel (CBI 2020b), and walking tourism (CBI 2021). You also heard about the importance of cycling tourism in Chapter 16.

A significant portion of domestic tourism is VFR travel and that is the next topic for discussion.

Psychographic Segmentation Approach

It has already been mentioned that some the discussed market segments partially are based on psychographics and lifestyles, including luxury and multigenerational travel, and WWOOF-ing. You will hear in Chapter 18 about another of these segments in health and wellness travel.

LGBTQ Travel

LGBTQ is a large and expanding market for domestic travel. One estimate for Europe is that this market represents 5.9 percent of the total travel market (CBI 2020c). The same source defines LGBTQ tourism as "the tourism products and services created with special attention for the LGBTQ (lesbian, gay, bisexual, transgender and queer or questioning) community." This is not a homogenous market as there are variations in ages, marital status, and whether they have children.

It is essential that this market be shown respect and the UNWTO (2017: 81) makes the following specific recommendations:

- Protect individuals from homophobic and transphobic violence.
- Prevent torture and cruel, inhuman and degrading treatment.
- Repeal laws criminalizing homosexuality and transgender people.
- Prohibit discrimination based on sexual orientation and gender identity.
- Safeguard freedom of expression, association and peaceful assembly for all LGBTQ people.

There are a variety of travel characteristics for this market, including a preference for urban destinations and overall, a higher propensity to travel. Destinations that are more open and LGBTQ-friendly tend to be the more successful.

Visiting Friends and Relatives (VFR) Market

> **DEFINITION**
>
> **VFR travel market**
>
> Travel to visit family, friends, or both in places outside the normal area of residence. This may be a main trip purpose or an activity undertaken along with another main trip purpose. These can be day visits or for several days, and may involve staying with family and friends or in commercial accommodation.

The VFR travel market represents a significant proportion of domestic tourism in many countries. Evidence from around the world indicates that VFR ranges from 30 percent to 50 percent of domestic travel. Earlier in this chapter, you learned that 35 percent of all overnight trips in the UK in 2019 were for VFR (VisitBritain/Kantar 2022) and it was also 35 percent for Canadians in 2021 (Statistics Canada 2022). For the EU, the figure was 33.3 percent of all trips (Eurostat 2022). For 2019, the National Visitor Survey in Australia estimated that 34 percent of all overnight domestic trips had a VFR purpose (Tourism Research Australia 2020). The importance of VFR travel increased during the COVID-19 era.

Figure 17.16 Children's visits to grandparents' homes is one important reason for VFR travel.

EXAMPLE 17.17

VFR Instrumental to Post-Pandemic Travel Recovery

This example provides evidence that VFR will gain market share in 2020 and beyond. Survey results for 2020, 2021, and 2022 support this assumption as VFR travel grew more rapidly.

> In 2019, VFR was the second-most typically taken travel type (46 percent) by global respondents, according to GlobalData's Q3 2019 consumer survey—beaten out solely by "sun and beach getaways" (58 percent). The degree to which VFR dominates the travel landscape also depends upon the source market. In the USA, 53 percent of travelers are making this type of trip their first priority. In Australia, 52 percent of respondents indicated the same, and the same figure came in at 49 percent in Canada, 64 percent in India and 60 percent in Saudi Arabia.
>
> (Baratti 2021)

Learning Point

The VFR travel market will increase in relative importance post-pandemic.

Because VFR is such a significant element of domestic and international tourism, it is described in more detail in this chapter. A special issue of the *Journal of Tourism Studies* in 1995 was a watershed event for research on the VFR market. Guest editors Joseph T. O'Leary and your author bemoaned the lack of respect that was given to VFRs by the tourism sector (Morrison and O'Leary 1995). Later in 2015, another milestone was reached with the publication of *VFR Travel Research: International Perspectives* edited by Elisa Zentveld (Backer) and Brian King. Subsequently, the *International Journal of Tourism Research* (vol. 19, no. 4, July/August 2017) published a special issue with the title of "VFR Travel: Is It Still Underestimated?" with Elisa Zentveld (Backer) and your author as guest editors.

EXAMPLE 17.18

VFR Still Seeking More Respect

Your author wrote the article, "The VFR—Visiting Friends and Relatives—Market: Desperately Seeking Respect," with Prof. J. T. O'Leary in 1995. Twenty-two years later, in this example, Elisa Zentveld and your author stated that VFR travel still lacked adequate recognition.

> In 1995, the first VFR special issue stated that VFR travel is desperately seeking respect. These editors feel that while, more than two decades later, it is still seeking more respect, it has certainly gained much respect over those

decades. And while still underestimated to some degree, industry and aca-
deme have learned much particularly in the last decade.
> (Morrison and O'Leary 1995; Zentveld (Backer) and Morrison 2017)

Learning Point

Destinations and DMOs need to attach a higher priority and give greater recognition
to VFR travel.

Although this book classifies VFR and leisure travel as two different trip-purpose segments,
there is some overlap between the two concepts. Moscardo et al. (2000) used an empirical
research study to prove that the VFR market was not one large homogeneous group but rather
was composed of multiple sub-segments. These researchers pointed out that there was a difference between VFR as a trip purpose and VFR as an activity. Five factors were defined that
differentiated VFRs:

1. Type (VFR as a primary motivation or trip purpose vs. VFR as an activity);
2. Scope (domestic vs. international);
3. Range (short-haul vs. long-haul);
4. Accommodation used (accommodated with friends/relatives vs. not accommodated with
   friends/relatives);
5. Focus of visit (visit friends vs. visit relatives vs. visit friends and visit relatives) (Fig. 17.17).

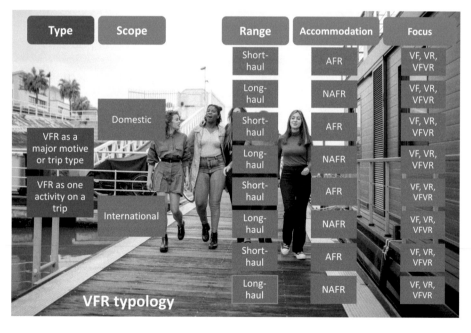

Figure 17.17 VFR typology (Moscardo et al. 2000, p. 252). VFR: visiting friends and
relatives; AFR: accommodated solely with friends and/or relatives; NAFR:
accommodated at least one night in commercial accommodation; VF: visit
friends; VR: visit relatives; VFVR: visiting both friends and relatives.

The importance of VFR is often underestimated for a variety of reasons. Elisa Zentveld (Backer) (2009) of Federation University in Australia says this is mainly because VFRs have not been as deeply researched as other types of tourists.

EXAMPLE 17.19

Well-Known, But Not Known Well

The quote in this example argues that many people know about the existence of VFR; however, it is under-researched and its characteristics are therefore not well understood.

> In comparison to its size, there has been little research into VFR travelers, their motivations, behaviors and characteristics, and the factors that influence their choices. This has led to their lack of recognition as a market segment and an assumption that they contribute little to local economies and tourism industries. While VFR travel is one of the largest and most significant forms of travel, "VFR travel remains well-known but not known well."
>
> (Zentveld (Backer) 2009: 18)

Learning Point

There is a need for more research to be done on the VFR travel market.

The first reason is that there is an assumption that VFRs only stay at the homes of friends and relatives and do not use hotels or other commercial accommodation. However, research has proven that this assumption is inaccurate because some VFRs do use commercial accommodation. Based on research conducted on the Sunshine Coast of Australia, Zentveld (Backer) (2010) found that 26 percent of VFRs stayed in commercial accommodation, and she classified them as CVFRs. Braunlich and Nadkarni (1995) also reached a similar conclusion based upon research in the USA. They found that over one-fifth of the VFR travelers in the East North Central Census region were hotel users.

The second reason is that the expenditures by VFRs and their hosts in a destinations' tourism sector are often assumed to be modest. However, several research studies have proven that this too is inaccurate. Some of the research suggests that VFRs outspend other domestic tourists in certain categories of expenditures (but not for lodging).

Another apparent reason VFRs tend to be neglected is that some DMOs feel they cannot influence these people to travel to their destinations. The assumption is made that VFRs are most influenced by word of mouth and invitations from their friends and relatives. In fact, this is an erroneous assumption because many VFRs plan trips the same way as do other tourists. Additionally, DMOs can promote the idea of VFR travel to local community residents; you learned in Chapter 14 about the contest used by the DMO in New Brunswick, Canada.

There are several DMOs that have realized the value of the VFR market, and they have implemented special marketing, branding, and communications programs aimed specifically at locals and VFRs. In Chapter 9, you heard about the York Resident's Festival in England and that is a good example.

Domestic Leisure Travel and VFR Marketing, Branding, and Communications Procedures

Almost every DMO should prepare a marketing strategy and plan for domestic tourism and its component market segments. Typically, these strategies and plans are focused on specific geographic regions and cities within the home country. It is recommended that the DMS model as reviewed in Chapter 12 is followed for the marketing, branding, and communications of domestic tourism.

Where Are We Now?

A situation analysis should be completed each year that identifies the destination's strengths, weaknesses, and marketing opportunities for domestic tourism. Conducting a situation analysis was discussed in detail in Chapter 12, and so there is no need to repeat that discussion here. However, it is important to emphasize that the DMO should conduct a thorough market analysis of domestic tourism as a foundation for developing a marketing strategy and plan for domestic leisure and VFR travelers. This task is easier in countries that have regular national surveys of domestic travelers and is much more difficult in places where no such data are available.

EXAMPLE 17.20

National Visitor Survey, Australia

Australia has a very comprehensive survey of residents, which is described in this example. As you can see, the sample size is large.

The National Visitor Survey (NVS) commenced in 1998 to provide an official measure of travel by Australian residents. Each year, interviews are conducted with 120,000 residents aged 15 years and over. COVID-19 has impacted the target sample size. Respondents are interviewed through a computer-assisted telephone interviewing system with phone numbers selected using random digit dialing.

The survey runs continuously with interviews taking place on each weekday and on weekends (excluding national public holidays). Residents classified as "in scope" for interviewing include those who:

- are aged fifteen years and over who have their usual address in Australia;
- have lived at their contact address for at least three months;
- live in a private dwelling.

Respondents interviewed in the NVS are randomly sampled to be representative of the Australian population.

(Tourism Research Australia 2022)

Learning Point

Decisions by DMOs and tourism sector stakeholders are made easier when there is good and regular data on markets.

The Great Britain Tourism Survey (GBTS) and GBDVS are conducted annually in the UK. Some 100,000 face-to-face interviews are done for the GBTS. For the GBDVS, 35,000 adults are surveyed online (VisitBritain 2022).

Survey data like these in Australia and the UK provide a solid foundation for domestic tourism marketing, branding, and communications. Without such data, DMOs are left to guess about domestic markets based on anecdotal evidence that may or may not be accurate. Countries such as Australia, Canada, New Zealand, the UK, and the USA are setting a great example for other nations with their continuing surveys of domestic travelers. There are still some countries that do not have such comprehensive data available on a regular basis for DMO marketers, and China and Russia are two of these.

The major outcomes of the domestic tourism situation analysis should be an articulation of the destination's strengths and weaknesses and unique selling propositions vis-à-vis domestic tourism.

Where Would We Like to Be?

The second step in domestic marketing, branding, and communications is to select target markets and then develop a PIB approach for domestic leisure and VFR travelers. As you know from Chapters 12 and 13, this is part of the development of the marketing strategy.

The biggest source market for Queensland, Australia is the domestic market (Business Queensland 2022b). The state DMO, Tourism & Events Queensland (2021), develops a domestic marketing strategy and in 2021 used the Good to Go IMC campaign. A good second example of developing a planned approach and strategy for domestic tourism is the island nation of Vanuatu. In its *Domestic Tourism Marketing Strategy 2021–2023*, the three goals are to:

1. provide short-term revenue streams for the tourism industry while borders are closed;
2. encourage the domestic market to make a habit of using tourism businesses as part of their everyday lives;
3. encourage the domestic market to see more of Vanuatu, and drive dispersal of domestic tourists to businesses beyond Efate (a popular island tourism destination).

(Vanuatu Tourism Office 2021)

Just as in Vanuatu's case, marketing goals and objectives for domestic tourism need to be specified by the DMO as the platform for building the domestic tourism marketing plan.

How Do We Get There?

The third step is to develop a marketing plan that meets the objectives for the domestic marketing by using the eight Ps (as described in Chapter 12). The eight Ps are covered in an IMC campaign.

An interesting past campaign is by Tourism Australia called No Leave No Life (Alphawest and Tourism Australia, undated; Traveller 2022). This campaign was based on the knowledge that Australian's were stockpiling their holiday leave entitlements. The No Leave No Life campaign not only targeted employees but also their companies. The message was simple: If you do not take holidays, it is not good for you and not good for your employers either. Australians had stockpiled a staggering total of 129 million days of leave entitlement (unused holiday time). A special website was created for the campaign, and it included a number of employer tools. In these materials, five program benefits were identified:

1. It helps reduce your financial liability.
2. It helps you attract and take care of employees.
3. It increases productivity.
4. It provides a framework for discussion.
5. It encourages executives to lead by example.

Other countries have recently initiated domestic tourism marketing campaigns including Slovenia with My Slovenia and VisitBritain/VisitEngland with Escape the Everyday (Slovenian Tourist Board 2022; VisitBritain/VisitEngland 2022).

How Do We Make Sure We Get There?

Domestic tourism marketing, branding, and communications need to be carefully monitored during their implementation to ensure that they are on track to achieving objectives. Periodic checks should be made at least every quarter to see whether the preliminary results are satisfactory or changes need to be made in the implementation of programs and activities.

How Do We Know If We Got There?

The DMO must demonstrate its accountability by evaluating the results and outcomes from its domestic tourism marketing, branding, and communications. This is the topic that is discussed in detail in Chapter 20.

SUMMING UP

Domestic tourism is a mainstay of the tourism sectors in many parts of the world, particularly in the developed nations. It is less important in the developing world, but domestic tourism is rapidly expanding in some of these countries and notably in China, India, and Indonesia. Unfortunately, domestic tourism is often given a second-class status compared to international tourism. The COVID-19 pandemic dramatically changed this as destinations scrambled to replace international tourism business.

The benefits of domestic tourism are significant albeit somewhat less well recognized than the advantages of international tourism. It is more dispersed within a country than international tourism and tends to be less seasonal. Residents can have a first-hand experience of the natural and cultural resources of their own countries. Domestic tourism enhances national pride and has social and cultural benefits. Residents also become more effective ambassadors for domestic destinations.

There are several significant issues and challenges in the development, marketing, branding, and communications of domestic tourism. The first issue is to whom the responsibility for domestic tourism should be assigned. Another issue is the competition between domestic and international tourism, and this has several levels: for example, competition for increasingly scarce government funding, domestic versus outbound destination competition for local resident travel, and behavioral conflicts between local and international tourists. Another issue with domestic tourism—and it is also present in international tourism—is whether day visitors (day-trippers or excursionists) should be included. There are parts of the tourism sector that believe only overnight visitors should be classified as tourists. However, day visitors have a major positive economic impact on several destinations, and many destinations include them within domestic tourism.

The future growth potential for domestic tourism varies by country, but overall, the prospects are positive and particularly in the countries with the highest populations. Factors such as growing household incomes and increases in vehicle ownership will spur domestic tourism in developing countries.

The trends and influences on domestic tourism have included changes in demographics, trip purposes, trip planning and travel arrangements, psychographics and lifestyles, special interests, technology uses, recessionary or poorer economic conditions in many developed countries, relative pricing levels within domestic versus outbound tourism destinations, and the development of LCC airlines.

There are several market segments in domestic tourism that are significant and enjoying growth. These include family travel, multigenerational travel, drive tourism, luxury travel, SIT, agritourism, golf tourism, trips to national parks and other protected areas, travel to theme and water parks, and museums.

The DMS should be followed in developing and implementing a marketing strategy and plan for domestic tourism. As a top priority, the DMO must have in-depth research data on the characteristics of domestic tourists and use these data in forming its approach to market segmentation. The DMO needs to select domestic tourism target markets and a PIB approach to communicate with and attract these tourists. Several DMOs design and implement IMC campaigns for their domestic markets.

The VFR market is significant in domestic tourism, but it is often underestimated and has not been as deeply researched as other market segments. DMOs often do not engage in VFR marketing, branding, and communications because of erroneous assumptions about VFRs. These mistaken assumptions are that VFRs never use commercial accommodations, VFRs do not spend as much money as other tourists, and DMOs cannot influence VFRs to travel to their destinations.

KEYWORDS

agritourism
bleisure
breakations
camping
carbon footprint
city breaks
circuits and trails
currency exchange rates
cycling tourism
day trips
diaspora tourism
domestic travel or tourism
drive tourism
excursionists
family travel market
foreign currencies

golf tourism
green travelers
home schooling
last-minute travel
LGBTQ tourism
lockdowns
luxury travel market
museum travel
   market
multigenerational (3G)
   travel
national parks
national surveys
online shopping
outdoor recreation
recreational vehicle (RV)

redistributing wealth
SAVE travel
seasonality
social distancing
social tourism
special-interest travel (SIT)
   markets
staycations
teleworking
   (telecommuting)
theme and water park travel
   markets
themed routes
visiting friends and relatives
   (VFR)
WWOOFing

REVIEW QUESTIONS

1. What are the benefits of domestic tourism?
2. How large is the domestic travel market and how important is domestic tourism to certain countries?
3. What have been the recent trends and what are the future prospects for domestic tourism?
4. What are the major challenges with domestic tourism?
5. What are some of the major segments of domestic tourism?
6. What are some of the reasons for underestimating the contributions of VFRs to the tourism sector?
7. How important is the VFR market in domestic tourism?
8. How should domestic tourism be systematically marketed, branded, and communicated?
9. Why is it difficult to effectively market, brand, and communicated domestic tourism without in-depth research data on domestic travelers and their segmentation?
10. What have been some of the domestic tourism marketing and IMC campaigns in recent times?

REFERENCES

Alphawest and Tourism Australia (undated) "No Leave, No Life Case Study," www.tourism.australia.com/content/dam/assets/document/1/6/x/7/n/2002595.pdf

Amadeus (2017) "Shaping the Future of Luxury Travel: Future Traveller Tribes 2030," www.amadeus.com/documents/future-traveller-tribes-2030/luxury-travel/shaping-the-future-of-luxury-travel-report.pdf

Baratti, L. (2021) "Visiting Friends, Relatives Will Power Post-Pandemic Travel," *Travel Pulse*, August 13, www.travelpulse.com/news/features/visiting-friends-relatives-will-power-post-pandemic-travel.html

Braunlich, C. G., and Nadkarni, N. (1995) "The Importance of the VFR market to the Hotel Industry," *Journal of Tourism Studies*, 6 (1): 38–47.

Business Queensland (2022a) "Drive Tourism," www.business.qld.gov.au/industries/hospitality-tourism-sport/tourism/qld/drive

——— (2022b) "Queensland Tourism Markets," www.business.qld.gov.au/industries/hospitality-tourism-sport/tourism/qld/data/markets

Caribbean Tourism Organization (2022) "Golf," www.onecaribbean.org/content/files/Golf.pdf

Carson, D., Waller, I., and Scott, N. (2002) "Drive Tourism: Up the Wall and Around the Bend," *CRC Sustainable Tourism*, https://sustain.pata.org/wp-content/uploads/2015/02/DriveTourism_v4.pdf

CBI (Netherlands) (2020a) "Entering the European Market for Diaspora Tourism," www.cbi.eu/market-information/tourism/diaspora-tourism/market-entry

——— (2020b) "Entering the European Market for SAVE Travel Products," www.cbi.eu/market-information/tourism/save-tourism/market-entry

——— (2020c) "The European Market Potential for LGBTQ Tourism," www.cbi.eu/market-information/tourism/lgbtq-tourism/market-potential

——— (2021) "Entering the European Market for Walking Tourism Products," www.cbi.eu/market-information/tourism/walking-tourism/market-entry

Central Intelligence Agency (2022) "The World Factbook: Country Comparisons, Population," www.cia.gov/the-world-factbook/field/population/country-comparison

China Travel News (2022) "China Tourism Academy: 2022 Domestic Travel Revenue Will Recover to 70% of Pre-Pandemic Level," January 26, www.chinatravelnews.com/article/150254

Cohn, D., Horowitz, J. M., Minkin, R., Fry, R., and Hurst, K. (2022) "Financial Issues Top the List of Reasons US Adults Live in Multigenerational Homes," Pew Research Center, March 24, www.pewresearch.org/social-trends/2022/03/24/financial-issues-top-the-list-of-reasons-u-s-adults-live-in-multigenerational-homes/

Condor Ferries (2022) "RV Statistics 2020–2021," www.condorferries.co.uk/rv-statistics

Department of Tourism (Philippines) (2021) "Relaxed and Standard Health Protocols, Personalized Trips Key to Tourism Recovery, Says Latest Philippine Travel Survey," February 17, http://tourism.gov.ph/news_features/PhilippineTravelSurvey.aspx

European Golf Association (2022) "Golf in Europe: Number of Registered Players," www.ega-golf.ch/content/golf-europe-number-registered-players

Eurostat (2022) "Tourism Statistics: Characteristics of Tourism Trips," https://ec.europa.eu/eurostat/statistics-explained/index.php?title=Tourism_statistics_-_characteristics_of_tourism_trips#Europeans_prefer_trips_inside_their_own_country_of_residence

Federation of WWOOF Organisations (2022) "What Is WWOOF?" https://wwoof.net/

France.fr (2022) "#CetÉtéJeVisiteLaFrance," www.france.fr/fr/campagne/cetetejevisitelafrance

Fry, R. (2022) "Young Adults in US Are Much More Likely Than 50 Years Ago to Be Living in a Multigenerational Household," Pew Research Center, July 20, www.pewresearch.org/fact-tank/2022/07/20/young-adults-in-u-s-are-much-more-likely-than-50-years-ago-to-be-living-in-a-multigenerational-household/

Gan, S. (2020) "The Rise of Domestic Tourism in 2020 and How to Leverage Data to Increase Tourism in Your City," Airbtics, https://airbtics.com/rise-of-domestic-tourism-2020-2021/

Germany Trade and Invest (2022) "Tourism & Leisure: A Place for Business and Pleasure," https://www.gtai.de/en/invest/industries/consumer-industries/tourism-leisure#:~:text=Germans%20are%20known%20for%20their%20%E2%80%9Ctravel%20bug%E2%80%9D%2C%20whether,that%20a%20German%20annually%20spends%20in%20German%20hotels

Gismondi, R., Magliocchi, M. G., Oropallo, F., and Truglia, F. G. (2021) "Integration of Agritourism Farms' Microdata: Economic Analysis and Impact Assessment of the COVID-19 Effects," *Rivista di Statistica Ufficiale*, N1/2021, www.istat.it/it/files//2021/05/RSU-1_2021_Article-4.pdf

Golf NZ (2022) "Golf New Zealand Strategic Plan, 2020–2025," www.golf.co.nz/strategic-plan

Hattingh, L. (2022) "Going Out-There: A Literature Review on Drive Tourism within the South African Context," *African Journal of Hospitality, Tourism and Leisure*, 11: 595–616.

Hudson, S., and Hudson, L. (2014) *Golf Tourism*, 2nd edn, Oxford: Goodfellow.

Instituto Costarricense de Turismo (2020) "ICT estrena plataforma digital de capacitación para trabajadores y empresarios turísticos," May 29, www.ict.go.cr/es/noticias-destacadas-2/1709-ict-estrena-plataforma-digital-de-capacitacion-para-trabajadores-y-empresarios-turisticos.html

Jakarta Globe (2017) "Family Tourism in Batam," http://jakartaglobe.id/features/family-tourism-batam/

Japan Times (2022) "Japan to Run New Domestic Travel Subsidy Program through Late December," September 26, www.japantimes.co.jp/news/2022/09/26/national/japan-run-new-domestic-travel-subsidy-program-late-december/

Kim, J. H., and Ritchie, B. W. (2012) "Motivation-Based Typology: An Empirical Study of Golf Tourists," *Journal of Hospitality and Tourism Research*, 36 (2): 251–280.

Korea.net (2022) "Gov't Offers 1M Discount Coupons for Domestic Lodging Facilities," April 7, www.korea.net/NewsFocus/FoodTravel/view?articleId=212942

LaGrave, K. (2021) "The Power of Women in Travel," *AFAR*, www.afar.com/magazine/the-power-of-women-in-travel

Local IT (2021) "Italy's €500 'Holiday Bonus' Is Set to Return for Summer 2021," www.thelocal.it/20210429/italys-e500-holiday-bonus-is-set-to-return-for-summer-2021/

Macao Government Tourism Office (2021) "Inspired by 'Macao Ready Go! Local Tours,' Tourism Operators Launch New Products," https://mtt.macaotourism.gov.mo/en/2021/02/inspired-by-macao-ready-go-local-tours-tourism-operators-launch-new-products/index.html

Magnini, V. P. (2017) "The Economic and Fiscal Impacts of Agritourism in Virginia," Virginia Tech, Pamplin College of Business.

Marriott (2020) "Family Travel Planning," Marriott Bonvoy Bold from Chase Survey, https://familytravel.org/wp-content/uploads/2021/01/2020-Family-Travel-Planning-Survey-Chase-Marriott-Bonvoy-Bold.pdf

Ministry of Tourism (India) (2022) "Tourism Statistics," https://tourism.gov.in/sites/default/files/202204/India%20Tourism%20Statistics%202021.pdf

Ministerio de Turismo y Deportes (Argentina) (2022) "Promocioná tu destino," www.argentina.gob.ar/turismoydeportes/promociona-tu-destino

Moore, C. (2022) "Which Country Has the Most Golf Courses? (All the Stats!)," *Golfah*, https://golfah.com/which-country-has-the-most-golf-courses/

Morrison, A. M., and O'Leary, J. (1995) "The VFR Market: Desperately Seeking Respect," *Journal of Tourism Studies*, 6 (1): 1–5.

Moscardo, G., Pearce, P., Morrison, A. M., Green, D., and O'Leary, J. T. (2000) "Developing a Typology for Understanding Visiting Friends and Relatives Markets," *Journal of Travel Research*, 38 (3): 251–259.

National Golf Foundation (2022) "Golf Industry Facts," www.ngf.org/golf-industry-research/

National Park Service (US) (2022) "About Us: Visitation Numbers," www.nps.gov/aboutus/visitation-numbers.htm

Office for National Statistics (UK) (2017) "Holidays in the 1990s and Now," www.ons.gov.uk/peoplepopulationandcommunity/leisureandtourism/articles/holidaysinthe1990sandnow/2017-08-07

Oregon Tourism Commission (2017) "Checklist: Type of Agritourism Activities," http://industry.traveloregon.com/industry-resources/toolkits/welcome-oregon-agritourism-handbook/consider-agritourism/

Organisation for Economic Co-operation and Development (2022) "OECD Tourism Statistics," https://www.oecd-ilibrary.org/economics/data/oecd-tourism-statistics/domestic-tourism_beb70251-en

Philipps, W. D. (2021) "Understanding the Reasons for Domestic Tourism," RAND Europe, www.rand.org/randeurope/research/projects/understanding-the-reasons-for-domestic-tourism.html

Prideaux, B. (2020) "Drive and car tourism: a perspective article," *Tourism Review*, 75(1), 109–112.

Prideaux, B., and Carson, D. (eds.) (2011) *Drive Tourism: Trends and Emerging Markets*, London and New York, NY: Routledge.

Qu, H., Hsu, C., Li, M., and Shu, B. (2018) "Self-Drive Tourism Attributes: Influences on Satisfaction and Behavioural Intention," *Asia Pacific Journal of Tourism Research*, 23 (4): 395–407.

Robert Trent Jones Golf Trail (2022) "Explore the Trail," www.rtjgolf.com/trail/

Rogerson, C. M., and Rogerson, J. M. (2014) "Agritourism and Local Economic Development in South Africa," *Bulletin of Geography, Socio-economic Series*, 26: 93–106.

RV Industry Association (2023) "Go RVing RV Owner Demographic Profile," https://www.rvia.org/go-rving-rv-owner-demographic-profile

Schänzel, H. A., Yeoman, I., and Backer, E. (eds) (2012) *Family Tourism: Multidisciplinary Perspectives*, Bristol: Channel View.

Secretaría de Turismo (Mexico) (2021) "Results of Tourism Activity, December 2020," http://datatur.sectur.gob.mx/RAT/RAT-2020-12(EN).pdf

Shah, H., Carrel, A. L., and Le, H. T. K. (2022) "Impacts of Teleworking and Online Shopping on Travel: A Tour-Based Analysis," *Transportation*, https://doi.org/10.1007/s11116-022-10321-9

Slovenian Tourist Board (2022) "Presentation of the My Slovenia Promotional Campaign," www.slovenia.info/en/business/my-slovenia-promotional-campaign

South African Tourism (2022) "Domestic Tourism Report," www.southafrica.net/gl/en/corporate/page/domestic-tourism-report

Statistics Canada (2022) "Travel by Canadian Residents in Canada and Abroad by Trip Purpose," www150.statcan.gc.ca/t1/tbl1/en/tv.action?pid=2410004501&pickMembers%5B0%5D=1.2&pickMembers%5B1%5D=2.1&cubeTimeFrame.startMonth=01&cubeTimeFrame.startYear=2021&cubeTimeFrame.endMonth=01&cubeTimeFrame.endYear=2022&referencePeriods=20210101%2C20220101

Statistics South Africa (2022) "Tourism in South Africa: A Pre-COVID-19 Benchmark," www.statssa.gov.za/?p=14992

Tauck Tours (2022) "Multi-generational Travel," www.tauck.com/guest-travel/multi-generational-travel

Themed Entertainment Association (2020) "TEA/AECOM 2020 Theme Index and Museum Index: The Global Attractions Attendance Report," https://aecom.com/wp-content/uploads/documents/reports/AECOM-Theme-Index-2020.pdf

Tourism and Events Queensland (2021) "The Six Months Ahead: Teq's Domestic Marketing Strategy, https://teq.queensland.com/au/en/news-and-media/queensland-news/2021/the-six-months-ahead—teq-s-domestic-marketing-strategy

Tourism Industry Aotearoa (2022) "Policy Positions—Industry Issues—Domestic Tourism," https://www.tia.org.nz/advocacy/policy-positions-industry-issues/domestic-tourism/

Tourism Research Australia (2020) "Visiting Friends and Relatives," www.tra.gov.au/search.aspx?moduleid=11599&multisite=false&keywords=visiting%20friends%20and%20relatives

———— (2022) "National Visitor Survey Results June 2022," www.tra.gov.au/data-and-research/reports/national-visitor-survey-results/national-visitor-survey-results

Traveller (2022) "No Leave, No Life? No Interest," www.traveller.com.au/no-leave-no-life-no-interest-g131

Travel Oregon (2017) "Checklist: Type of Agritourism Activities," http://industry.traveloregon.com/industry-resources/toolkits/welcome-oregon-agritourism-handbook/consider-agritourism/

Trenchard, B. (2020) "The Significant Benefits of Domestic Tourism," CBRE, www.cbre.ae/en/about-cbre/blog/Benefits-of-domestic-tourism?article=80c30b12-3c3f-4122-bf82-e4fd4970714e&feedid=6e27a567-89a2-4a3e-9b0e-55180a5cd95d

United Nations World Tourism Organization (2017) "Second Global Report on LGBT Tourism," www.e-unwto.org/doi/book/10.18111/9789284418619

———— (2020) "Understanding Domestic Tourism and Seizing Its Opportunities," www.e-unwto.org/doi/book/10.18111/9789284422111

US Travel Association (2022) "US Travel Answer Sheet," www.ustravel.org/sites/default/files/2022-05/ust-data-master.pdf

Vanuatu Tourism Office (2021) "Domestic Tourism Marketing Strategy 2021–2023," https://images.impartmedia.com/vanuatu.travel/article/VTO-Domestic-Tourism-Marketing-Strategy_2021-2023.pdf

VisitBritain (2022) "About GBTS and GBDVs," www.visitbritain.org/about-gbts-and-gbdvs

VisitBritain and Kantar (2022a) "The GB Tourist 2019 Annual Report," www.visitbritain.org/sites/default/files/vb-corporate/gb_tourist_annual_report_2019_final.pdf

———— (2022b) "GB Day Visits Survey: Latest Results," www.visitbritain.org/gb-day-visits-survey-latest-results

VisitBritain and VisitEngland (2022) "Be Part of Our Domestic Marketing Campaign: Escape the Everyday," www.visitbritain.org/be-part-our-domestic-marketing-campaign-escape-everyday

VisitEngland (2019) "Multi-Gen Visitor Research Report," www.visitbritain.org/multi-generational-travel

VisitScotland (2022) "New Scottish Golf Tourism and Visitor Strategy Launched," August 19, www.visitscotland.org/news/2022/golf-strategy-launched

Visit Victoria (2018) "Victoria's Golf Tourism Strategy 2018–2023," https://corporate.visitvictoria.com/news/golf-tourism-strategy-a-hole-in-one-for-victoria

Westcott, B., and Wang, S. (2021) "China Is Experiencing a Rural Tourism Boom Amid the COVID-19 Pandemic," CNN, May 12, www.cnn.com/travel/article/china-rural-tourism-pandemic-cmb-intl-hnk/index.html

World Bank (2022) "International Tourism, Receipts (% of Total Exports), https://data.worldbank.org/indicator/ST.INT.RCPT.XP.ZS

World Travel and Tourism Council (2016) "The Effect of Exchange Rate Trends on Travel and Tourism Performance," https://medium.com/@WTTC/the-effect-of-exchange-rate-trends-on-travel-tourism-performance-8a74b3fb1233

———— (2018) "Domestic Tourism Importance and Economic Impact," https://sp.wttc.org/Portals/0/Documents/Reports/2018/Domestic%20Tourism-Importance%20Economic%20Impact-Dec%2018.pdf?ver=2021-02-25-182514-683

———— (2022) "Travel and Tourism Economic Impact 2022," https://wttc.org/Portals/0/Documents/Reports/2022/EIR2022-Global%20Trends.pdf

Zentveld (Backer), E. (2009) "VFR Travel: An Assessment of VFR Versus Non-VFR Travellers," Southern Cross University, https://researchportal.scu.edu.au/discovery/fulldisplay/alma991012821911902368/61SCU_INST: Research Repository

———— (2010) "Opportunities for Commercial Accommodation in VFR," *International Journal of Tourism Research*, 12 (4): 334–354.

Zentveld (Backer), E., and Morrison, A. M. (2017) "The Value and Contributions of VFR to Destinations and Destination Marketing," in E. Backer and B. King (eds), *VFR Travel Research: International Perspectives*, Bristol: Channel View, pp. 13–27.

Part IV

18

International Pleasure and Leisure Travel Markets

Going abroad

> ## LEARNING OBJECTIVES
>
> Having read this chapter, you should be able to:
>
> 1. indicate the size of the global international tourist market and the distribution of tourist arrivals by region and for leading destination countries;
>
> 2. elaborate on the trends and prospects for international tourist arrivals;
>
> 3. discuss the major challenges involved with inbound international tourism to destinations;
>
> 4. identify and profile the emerging geographic origin markets;
>
> 5. describe selected market segments that have growth potential;
>
> 6. explain a procedure for marketing, branding, and communications for international pleasure and leisure travel markets.

Warming Up

You know that international tourism was decimated in 2020 and 2021 as a result of the COVID-19 pandemic. You learned in Chapter 17 that domestic tourism to a large extent replaced

DOI: 10.4324/9781003343356-22

international tourism. A modest recovery in international tourism was experienced in 2022 and 2023. Despite the recent adversity, international tourism remains lucrative for many destinations and may experience a brighter future.

Destinations are normally very keen to attract international visitors, for both economic and political prestige reasons. Domestic travel is often seen as not being as appealing as inbound tourism, and politicians tend to talk more about the numbers of international tourists to their countries and the economic benefits they generate. The rationale for this is rather simple: international tourists inject new money into a country's economy; domestic tourists recycle money within a national economy. This argument tends to be quite unfair to domestic tourism because it has major beneficial impacts on various regions within countries. However, from a macro perspective, there is truth to this argument.

International tourism was experiencing a long-term growth trend until COVID-19 hit, although there were some short-term downturns pre-pandemic caused by economic and other crises. Regionally, Asia-Pacific was gaining market share, and Europe's proportion of total worldwide tourist arrivals was declining.

Marketing, branding, and communications for international pleasure and leisure markets has a unique set of challenges. The openness of the tourism sector to the influences of external factors is great, and tourism is particularly vulnerable to economic and political dislocations, natural disasters, and health and security crises.

For international tourism, every DMO needs a marketing strategy: this is a clear and well-justified set of country origin markets upon which the DMO will focus its marketing, branding, and communications. A general marketing approach for international tourism using the DMS is explained in this chapter.

Chapter 18 begins by discussing the size and scope of international tourism and recent trends. The future prospects and major challenges for international tourism are discussed. The topic of emerging markets is the next subject reviewed. Fifteen market segments with growth potential are profiled in snapshot summaries. The chapter ends by outlining a systematic approach to the marketing, branding, and communications for international tourism.

Your author has had several opportunities to advise on marketing, branding, and communications for international tourism. At a national level, he developed strategies for international marketing for Indonesia and Vietnam; as well as preparing international marketing plans for several destinations in China including Jiangsu and Sichuan Provinces and the cities of Hangzhou and Shaoxing in Zhejiang Province, and Shanghai.

Size of the International Tourist Market

The most comprehensive worldwide statistics of tourist numbers are maintained by the UNWTO in Madrid, Spain. This section begins by reviewing recent statistics from UNWTO, starting with the total arrivals by region and then for the top destination countries. You should realize when viewing these statistics that they include other trip purposes in addition to pleasure/leisure travel. The UNWTO does provide a breakdown by trip purpose on a worldwide basis, but it does not exactly match this book's definition. For 2019, UNWTO estimates that leisure, recreation and holidays were 55 percent of all international tourist arrivals; business and professional travel represented 11 percent. The remaining 28 percent was for VFR, health, religion, and other, and 6 percent for not specified (UNWTO 2020a).

Total Arrivals by Region

UNWTO estimated there were 415 million international tourist arrivals worldwide in 2021, up by 4 percent over 2020 (UNWTO 2022a). In the first seven months of 2022, arrivals had improved to 57 percent of the levels in 2019 (pre-pandemic) (they fell by 73 percent in 2020). Europe received the highest proportion of these arrivals, at 49.9 percent (Fig. 18.1). Asia and the Pacific had the second-largest share, at 25 percent, and the Americas had 16.1 percent. The Middle East and Africa each had 4.3 percent and 4.7 percent, respectively, of the total arrivals.

Country destinations (inbound)	2019 arrivals	2020 arrivals
France	90.9	41.7
Italy	64.5	25.2
Mexico	45.0	24.8
U.S.	79.4	19.5
Spain	83.5	18.9
Turkey	51.2	15.9
Austria	31.9	15.1
Germany	39.6	12.5
U.K.	39.4	10.7
China	65.7	8.0
Hungary	16.9	7.4
Greece	31.4	7.4
Netherlands	20.1	7.3
UAE	21.6	7.2
Russia	24 4	6 4

International tourist arrivals

Figure 18.1 Top country destinations by total arrivals.

Total Arrivals by Destination Country

According to the UNWTO's 2020 figures, France was the top destination in the world, followed by Italy and Mexico (Fig. 18.1). The USA and Spain were in the fourth and fifth places. China has been steadily climbing the world ranks before 2020; however, that trend abruptly ended in 2020.

When considering the international tourist figures for individual countries, there is variation in origin markets. Ten examples are shown below of the top origins for individual countries.

1. Australia: (1) New Zealand; (2) India; (3) UK; (4) Singapore; (5) USA (Tourism Australia 2022).
2. Canada: (1) USA; (2) UK; (3) France; (4) China; (5) Germany (Destination BC 2021).
3. Germany: (1) Netherlands; (2) Switzerland; (3) Poland; (4) Austria; (5) Denmark; (6) UK; (7) USA; (8) Belgium; (9) France; (10) Italy (German National Tourist Board 2021).
4. Italy: (1) France; (2) Germany; (3) Switzerland; (4) Austria; (5) UK (Banca D'Italia 2021).
5. Malaysia: (1) Thailand; (2) Singapore; (3) Indonesia; (4) China; (5) India; (6) Japan; (7) South Korea; (8) UK; (9) Philippines; (10) Pakistan (Tourism Malaysia 2022a).
6. New Zealand: (1) Australia; (2) UK; (3) USA; (4) Cook Islands; (5) Vanuatu; (6) Samoa; (7) China; (8) India; (9) Singapore; (10) Thailand (Statistics New Zealand 2022).
7. Spain: (1) France; (2) Germany; (3) UK; (4) Netherlands; (5) Nordic countries; (6) Belgium; (7) Portugal (National Statistics Institute [Spain] 2022).

8. Türkiye: (1) Russia; (2) Germany; (3) Ukraine; (4) Bulgaria; (5) Iran; (6) Iraq; (7) Netherlands; (8) France; (9) Poland; (10) Romania (Ministry of Culture and Tourism [Türkiye] 2022).

9. UK: (1) Ireland; (2) France; (3) USA; (4) Spain; (5) Germany; (6) Netherlands; (7) Poland; (8) Italy; (9) Gulf Cooperation Council (GCC); (10) Romania (VisitBritain 2022a).

10. USA: (1) Mexico; (2) Canada; (3) Colombia; (4) UK; (5) India; (6) Ecuador; (7) Dominican Republic; (8) Peru; (9) Argentina; (10) Guatemala (US Department of Commerce 2022).

Although this is only a small selection of countries, there are some noticeable differences and similarities in sources. In most cases, nearby and adjacent countries represent the main sources of international tourists and this was particularly true during the COVID-19 pandemic.

International Tourism Expenditures by Country

Which countries' residents spend the most on international tourism? Figure 18.2 provides the answer. China was at the top of the table in 2021, followed by the USA and Germany. France and UK were in fourth and fifth positions, respectively.

In addition to the total spending by the residents of a country, DMOs must also consider factors related to the yield of the market. Yield can be expressed in different ways, but typically it means the trip per capita expenditures or daily average expenditures in the destination. For example, the UK's top three markets in terms of total inbound visits in 2021 were Ireland (708,000), France (667,000), and the USA (663,000); however, the USA was the top-yielding

Highest-spending outbound markets	2021 $ Billions
China	105.7
U.S.	56.9
Germany	48.2
France	34.8
U.K.	24.3
UAE	21.8
South Korea	16.7
Italy	15.0
Belgium	14.7
India	12.6
Spain	12.2
Russia	11.4
Switzerland	11.2
Qatar	10.0
Netherlands	9.9

Figure 18.2 Highest-spending outbound markets.

of these markets with total spending of £783 million compared to £294 million for Ireland and £420 million for France (VisitBritain 2022a). This means a US visitor was more valuable to the British economy than a visitor from Ireland or France.

The seasonality or distribution of expenditures over the twelve months of the year is another important issue when assessing the yield from different country markets. If the spending from a specific country market tends to be concentrated in a destination's off-peak season, the DMO may decide that the yield from that market is more valuable and attractive.

The import content required to serve specific country markets must also be considered. Serving certain countries may require the importation of foodstuffs from their countries, resulting in a leakage from the local economy. They may also stay in hotels and resorts owned by companies and travel with branches of travel trade companies from their home countries. Economic leakage from the local destination's economy should be considered when yield levels are being estimated.

Trends and Prospects for International Tourism

The long-term trend was for international tourism to be increasing up to the end of 2019. In fact, worldwide tourism arrivals had grown from 528 million in 1995 to 1.5 billion in 2019 (UNWTO 2020b). There were three years from 1995 to 2011 where international tourism arrivals declined: 2000, 2003, and 2009. The prospects for international tourism are hard to predict in the post-COVID era, although a recovery was being experienced in 2022 and 2023.

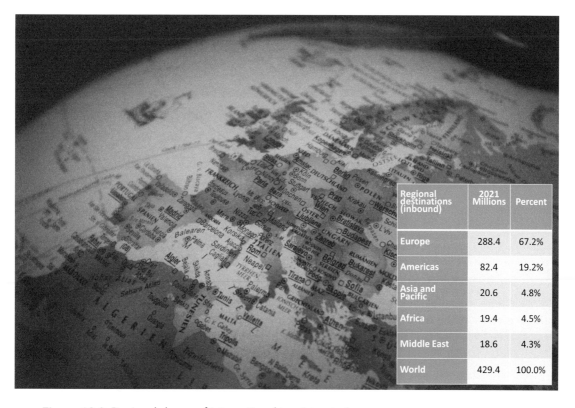

Regional destinations (inbound)	2021 Millions	Percent
Europe	288.4	67.2%
Americas	82.4	19.2%
Asia and Pacific	20.6	4.8%
Africa	19.4	4.5%
Middle East	18.6	4.3%
World	429.4	100.0%

Figure 18.3 Regional shares of international tourist arrivals.

Regional market shares changed in 2021, with Europe and the Americas commanding a combined total of 86.4 percent (Fig. 18.3). The share of the Asia-Pacific region fell significantly to 4.8 percent.

EXAMPLE 18.1

Five Hundred Thousand Free Airline Tickets from Hong Kong

Chapter 14 introduced you to the guerrilla marketing concept. This example is an unprecedented campaign by Hong Kong to give away free airline tickets to recover from the catastrophic effects of COVID-19.

> Hong Kong has a plan to get visitors back to its shores as the pandemic recedes: free airline tickets. The Hong Kong Tourism Board plans to give away 500,000 airline tickets, worth the equivalent of HK$2 billion ($254.8 million) once the city-states remaining coronavirus restrictions are lifted, per the BBC.
>
> "Once the government announces it will remove all COVID-19 restrictions for inbound travelers, we'll roll out the advertising campaigns for the free air tickets," Dane Cheng, Executive Director of the Hong Kong Tourism Board, told the BBC.
>
> Hong Kong's government introduced strict travel rules in response to the outbreak of the coronavirus pandemic. They included requiring anyone entering the city-state to quarantine for two weeks in hotels.
>
> (Jones 2022)

Learning Point

When circumstances are exceptionally difficult, DMOs may consider approaches that have no precedent and seem daring.

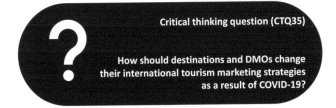

? Critical thinking question (CTQ35)

How should destinations and DMOs change their international tourism marketing strategies as a result of COVID-19?

Challenges for International Travel

Marketing, branding, and communicating for international pleasure and leisure travel markets presents a unique set of challenges, most of which are not found with domestic tourism. The scale and complexity of international markets is perhaps the most serious challenge.

Where to Focus Marketing and Promotion?

The world is so large with so many countries, that the major challenge for DMOs is where to market, brand, and communicate their destinations. They obviously cannot afford to be marketing in every country of the world, and choices must be made about where to focus effort to produce the best ROI. One of the most obvious solutions to this challenge is to focus on the markets that are presently generating the most tourists, and this type of strategy is the most popular, especially for those DMOs with limited resources. Destination Canada operates in its traditional top nine inbound markets (Australia, China, France, Germany, Japan, Mexico, South Korea, UK, USA) (Destination Canada 2022). Brand USA is targeting thirteen countries that traditionally produce a majority of the inbound tourism to the country: Australia, Belgium, Brazil, Canada, China, France, Germany, India, Italy, Japan, Mexico, South Korea, and the UK (Brand USA 2022a). Smaller countries and states, provinces and cities may have a more restricted set of international market targets.

It is a simple task for a destination to pick out its top international origin markets by visitor volume and spending but more difficult to decide upon other markets with significant future growth potential. The example describes a scorecard that Brand USA plans to use to select international origin markets.

EXAMPLE 18.2

Brand USA Market Scorecard

Brand USA announced in 2022 that it would pioneer a new market scorecard to justify its selection of country origin markets to be targeted. The scorecard is described in this example.

> As the world begins to emerge from the pandemic, Brand USA will pioneer a market scoring system based on standardized measures of opportunity across all major current Brand USA markets and potential future markets. The new scorecard will also factor in a series of analyses to determine market potential in relationship to costs and risks. The scorecard will include approximately thirty indicators distributed across key categories such as travel market size, spending power, growth prospects, ROI, and potential responsiveness of each market.
>   The measures to be included are market size; country size; growth; headroom; sentiment; alignment; purchasing power; visitor value; affordability; presence; risks; and accessibility.
>   The scorecard will cover up to thirty international markets and will be updatable with new data as global and market conditions evolve.
>
> (Brand USA 2022b)

Learning Point

DMOs should use a multi-factor set of criteria to objectively determine the potential value of country-of-origin inbound markets.

Some academic scholars have suggested other ways to select international target markets. SooCheong Jang and his co-researchers (Jang et al. 2004a, 2004b) recommended a portfolio approach in which the risks and rewards from each market are calculated and balanced. The unique contribution of these works is in the assessment of market risks in addition to rewards and in suggesting that DMOs need to balance the risk and rewards to derive the optimum scenarios for country market selections.

Balance of Payment Deficits

There are several countries that have balance of payment deficits for tourism. This means that their own residents spend more for tourism in other countries than international tourists spend in their countries. Having such a deficit is not a good long-term situation for a country's tourism sector.

What can a country do that has a deficit in its balance of payments in tourism? There are three main strategy options: (1) attract more international visitors (2) convince residents to holiday or vacation at home rather than going abroad (encourage more domestic travel); and (3) change the proportions of international tourist country sources. The third strategy may not be as obvious to you, and so a little further explanation is given. Often, destinations have positive tourism balances with certain countries but run deficits with others.

One example of a country that has had a deficit turned into a surplus in tourism is the USA. The so-called "travel gap" was a huge economic issue for decades in the USA. It became so bad that one of their presidents asked people to not travel as much abroad.

Marketing and Promotion Challenges

To market effectively at an international level, a DMO needs the authority to do so and must have adequate financial and human resources to carry out the mandate. The USA represents an interesting case study here again because up until 2012 it did not have such a body with the official mandate and budget to market, brand, and communicate for international tourism. After much lobbying by the tourism sector and demonstrating that the US share of world tourism dropped from 2000 to 2010, the federal government passed the Travel Promotion Act of 2010. A new body was created, Brand USA, and for its fiscal year of 2022, it had budgeted expenses of $76.9 million (Brand USA 2021) for marketing the country abroad by means of tourism private-sector contributions plus a share of the fees from the countries in the Visa Waiver Program and the Electronic System for Travel Authorization.

Another major marketing challenge is in adapting approaches and campaigns for different languages and cultures. For example, DMO websites must be translated into several languages, and great care must also be taken in adapting to the varied cultural nuances among countries. Many countries have their own social network sites, and adjustments must also be made for these.

Susceptibility to Crises

The trends for worldwide international tourism discussed earlier and in Chapter 11 clearly prove that tourism is quite susceptible to major crises that can cause declines in tourist movements and expenditures, albeit short-term in duration (except for the effects of the COVID-19 pandemic).

Tourism is an open-system economic sector, and therefore it can be rapidly and extensively affected by developments and incidents in external environments.

Although not necessarily a crisis, fluctuations in currency exchange rates can have a major impact on inbound tourism. If a destination's currency rate increases versus inbound origin countries' currencies, this may have a negative impact on arrivals; if the rate falls, a positive impact may be experienced.

A Global Recession on the Horizon

This example is a warning from the World Bank that a global economic recession will occur soon. Such a recession would have a negative effect on international travel.

> Since the beginning of the year, a rapid deterioration of growth prospects coupled with rising inflation and tightening financing conditions, has ignited a debate about the possibility of a global recession—a contraction in global per capita GDP.
>
> Consensus forecasts for global growth in 2022 and 2023 have been downgraded significantly since the beginning of the year. Although these forecasts do not point to a global recession in 2022–2023, experience from earlier recessions suggests that at least two developments—which either have already materialized in recent months or may be underway—heighten the likelihood of a global recession in the near future.
>
> (World Bank 2022)

Learning Point

Destinations and DMOs should be aware and should prepare for future economic conditions in the world.

Uneven Distribution of Tourists

It is common for international tourists to flock to the most popular destinations within countries, whereas other regions in the countries receive very few of them. A good example here is the distribution of international visitors to the UK. There were 43 percent of inbound visits to London, but there were only 9 percent to Scotland and 3 percent to Wales (VisitBritain 2022b).

In geographically larger countries than the UK, including Australia, Canada, China and Russia, this phenomenon is even more pronounced because tourists cannot possibly visit all the destinations within these nations in a short space of time. For Australia in 2021–2022, 50.6 percent of international tourists visited New South Wales, 36.1 percent went to Victoria, and 25.3 percent went to Queensland. However, the percentages were much lower for other parts of Australia: 10.7 percent for Western Australia, 5.1 percent for South Australia, 2.9 percent for Northern Territory, 3.4 percent for Australian Capital Territory, and 2.8 percent for Tasmania (Tourism Research Australia 2022).

This is a difficult challenge to deal with because it tends to be market-driven and thus hard to change. A DMO that represents an entire country cannot show favoritism to a region that attracts a below-average share of international tourists. However, the national DMO can encourage local DMOs to become more aggressive in marketing, branding, and communicating for international tourism and try to convince travel agencies and tour operators to provide more products for international markets.

Another challenge for individual countries and regions are the travel advisories issued by foreign governments over which these destinations have no control. The example of the US travel advisory for Russia in 2022 contains severe warnings about travel between the two countries.

EXAMPLE 18.4

Travel Advisory for Russia

This example reflects a severe warning to US citizens that it is better not to travel to Russia during its conflict with Ukraine. Although some people may ignore this advice, most would take it seriously and not travel to Russia.

> Do not travel to Russia due to the unprovoked and unjustified invasion of Ukraine by Russian military forces, the potential for harassment against US citizens by Russian government security officials, the singling out of US citizens in Russia by Russian government security officials including for detention, the arbitrary enforcement of local law, limited flights into and out of Russia, the embassy's limited ability to assist US citizens in Russia, COVID-19-related restrictions, and terrorism. US citizens residing or traveling in Russia should depart Russia immediately. Exercise increased caution due to wrongful detentions.
>
> US citizens should note that US credit and debit cards no longer work in Russia, and options to electronically transfer funds from the USA are extremely limited as a result of sanctions imposed on Russian banks. There are reports of cash shortages within Russia.
>
> (US Department of State 2022)

Learning Point

Travel advisories can curtail travel to certain countries and regions.

Emerging International Travel Markets

The term "emerging markets" is used by many DMOs around the world, and usually, these markets are defined by geography. When designated in this way, emerging means that these geographic origin markets are growing at above-average rates when compared to the world mean value. The four BRIC (Brazil, Russia, India, and China) are commonly pinpointed as being among the most promising emerging markets.

Brazil

With a population estimated at 217.2 million in 2022, Brazil is the seventh most populated nation in the world. Brazil's GDP in 2020 was around $3 trillion and $14,100 per capita. Brazil's real GDP is the eighth highest in the world (CIA 2022a).

According to UNWTO estimates, the Brazilian outbound market was in 21st place in terms of international tourism expenditures in 2019 ($17.6 billion). Brazilians made an estimated 11.6 million outbound trips in 2019 (VisitBritain 2022c). A majority (68.2 percent) of the international trips by Brazilians are to Europe (GlobalData 2022).

Russia

Russia is the ninth most populated country in the world with 142 million people in 2022. The GDP of Russia in 2020 was $3.875 trillion and $26,500 per capita (CIA 2022b). The Russian outbound market ranked sixth in the world in international tourism expenditures in 2019 at $36.2 billion. VisitBritain (2022d) reported that there were 31.1 million outbound trips from Russia in 2019. Russians' favorite destinations include Türkiye and Spain.

With the Russian invasion of the Ukraine in February 2022 and the international sanctions that ensued, it is unlikely that Russian outbound travel will continue to grow as it did up until 2019. The banning of Russian airline and banking operations was a part of these sanctions.

India

India is the second most populous nation in the world with 1.39 billion people. Its GDP was estimated at $8.4 trillion in 2020 but only $6,100 per capita (CIA 2022c).

The Indian outbound market was in fifteenth place in 2019 in terms of expenditures. There were 21.8 million outbound trips from India in 2019 according to VisitBritain (2022e). The most-visited destination is the UAE.

EXAMPLE 18.5

Anti-Asian Issues Discouraging Travel to USA

This example reports on a disturbing trend in which people are reluctant to travel to a particular country due to feeling unwelcomed and fearing high crime rates.

> This month, Morning Consult published a study on this exact trend. Their findings, based on a survey of 1,000 adults, showed that "a plurality of Chinese have little to no interest in US travel," with violence and anti-Asian discrimination both cited as factors.
>
> According to Morning Consult's data, 22 percent of Mainland Chinese respondents are "not interested at all" in visiting the USA, with an additional 23 percent saying they are "not that interested."
>
> Of the survey respondents, 57 percent say that violent crime is a primary reason they don't want to go to the USA, while 52 percent cite terrorism, 36 percent say petty crime, and 44 percent say they are concerned about anti-China bias by locals.
>
> (Marcus and Toh 2022)

Learning Point

Destinations and DMOs must take a more active role in educating citizens not to discriminate against visitors based on national or ethnic origin.

China

The People's Republic of China is the world's most populated country with 1.41 billion people in 2022. China's GDP was $23 trillion in 2020 and $16,400 per capita (CIA 2022d). It had the largest real GDP in the world in 2020.

The Chinese outbound market ranked first in 2019 in terms of international tourism expenditures ($254.6 billion) (VisitBritain 2022f). The outbound market from Mainland China was growing rapidly up to and including 2019. However, due to the outbreak of COVID-19 and the strict restrictions on outbound international travel, there were large declines in outbound tourism from China in 2020–2022.

EXAMPLE 18.6

Chinese Outbound Travel Status

This example highlights the downturn in Chinese outbound tourism in 2020–2022. There is a prediction that it will start growing again in 2023.

> As more countries open their borders to international tourism, the absence of Chinese visitors is causing more than a little economic pain. From Phuket to Paris, major tourist destinations have relied on an average of 150 million Chinese travelers spending up to US$255 billion yearly on sightseeing. Now three years into the COVID-19 pandemic, many of these destinations are starting to realize that it will be a while till the Chinese tourists return. Some analysts believe that this could impose serious economic consequences on affected countries.
>
> Despite the rest of the world moving toward an endemic approach to the virus, China continues to implement a zero-COVID policy. As of August 2022, China has a quarantine system in place for inbound travelers as well as rigorous measures that get promptly activated in case of outbreaks. Yet, it is precisely such measures that allow Chinese tourists to feel safer when traveling across provinces and have fueled the growth of the country's domestic tourism industry.
>
> According to recent forecasts, a "strong wave" of outbound travel from China will start up again in 2023, returning to its pre-pandemic levels by 2024. Such predictions are backed by plans announced by the country's aviation regulator, which has issued a five-year development plan, with a strong focus on expanding domestic flights and restoring international air travel by 2025.
>
> (Interesse 2022)

Learning Point

Never put all of your eggs in one basket—an old saying that suggests that many destinations were becoming too dependent on Chinese travelers pre-COVID.

There is also a destination-specific way of defining emerging markets, and you should be aware of that as well. For example, a single destination may have a unique situation where certain origin markets have above-average growth but overall growth in that market is not as high.

EXAMPLE 18.7

Thailand to Target Central Asia

Emerging markets must be continuously tracked as the economic and political circumstances in specific countries are fluid. In this example, Thailand spotted the market potential from Central Asia.

The Tourism and Sports Ministry of Thailand is looking to new markets in Central Asia, particularly Kazakhstan and Uzbekistan, as post-COVID trends show strong demand for international tourism. Minister Phiphat Ratchakitprakan said Central Asia has potential as a new market for inbound tourism because of short flight times of no more than seven and a half hours.

The Ministry's market analysis showed that travelers from this region have high demand to travel internationally after the pandemic. In particular, Kazakhstan and Uzbekistan have higher potential for economic growth than other nations in the region.

(Vietnam Investment Review 2022)

Learning Point

It is essential that destinations and DMOs frequently reevaluate their portfolios of inbound tourism markets.

International Travel Market Segments with Growth Potential

In addition to looking at markets by geographic origin and trip purpose, the markets can also be analyzed in greater detail by interests, activities, and desired experiences. Within each country of origin and trip purpose market, there is great variety in motivations and what people want to do on their trips.

There are international tourism market segments that have been demonstrating growth potential in recent years, and these include several of the SIT markets that were identified in Chapter 17 (Fig. 17.9). In briefly reviewing fifteen of these market segments (Fig. 18.4), although they are found in both domestic and international pleasure and leisure travel; here, they are discussed in the context of international tourism. There are very few accurate estimates on the size of these markets on a worldwide basis, and the discussion that follows is mainly descriptive. The following accounts are just snapshots of these market segments, and much more could be said about each of them.

- Casino gaming
- Cruise tourism
- Culinary or food tourism
- Cultural and heritage tourism
- Dark tourism
- Health and wellness tourism
- Industrial tourism
- Medical tourism
- Nature-based tourism and ecotourism
- Religious tourism
- Shopping tourism
- Sport tourism
- Voluntourism
- Wine tourism

International travel market segments with growth potential

Figure 18.4 Market segments with growth potential.

Adventure Tourism

> ### DEFINITION
>
> **Adventure tourism**
>
> "Adventure tourism is a tourism trip that includes at least two of the following three elements—physical activity, natural environment, and cultural immersion. It often involves risk and some skill from the tourist" (CBI 2021a).

Generally, adventure tourism is divided into hard and soft adventure, based upon the physical demands and potential risks involved. Mountain and rock climbing are considered a hard adventure activity, while most types of camping are soft adventure activities.

Destinations with rich and spectacular natural resources tend to be the most popular destinations for adventure tourism. According to the 2020 Adventure Tourism Development Index (Adventure Travel Trade Association 2020), the top ten adventure tourism destinations in developed countries were Iceland, Switzerland, New Zealand, Germany, Norway, Finland,

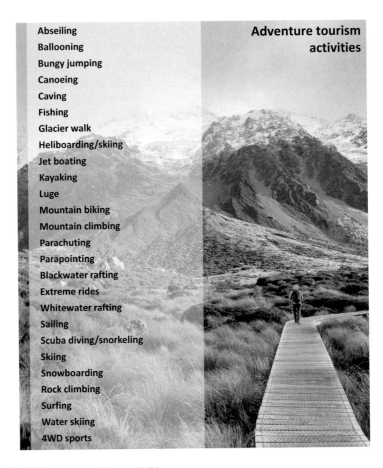

Adventure tourism activities

Abseiling
Ballooning
Bungy jumping
Canoeing
Caving
Fishing
Glacier walk
Heliboarding/skiing
Jet boating
Kayaking
Luge
Mountain biking
Mountain climbing
Parachuting
Parapointing
Blackwater rafting
Extreme rides
Whitewater rafting
Sailing
Scuba diving/snorkeling
Skiing
Snowboarding
Rock climbing
Surfing
Water skiing
4WD sports

Figures 18.5 Adventure tourism activities.

Sweden, Canada, Australia, and Denmark. The top ten for developing countries were Czech Republic, Chile, Slovak Republic, Slovenia, Israel, Estonia, Poland, Bulgaria, Romania, and Costa Rica. Among these twenty destinations, New Zealand stands out as a place that has done an outstanding job of building and marketing adventure tourism. Figure 18.5 shows the adventure tourism activities that can be enjoyed in New Zealand.

Just to make sure you understand this idea, these fifteen markets do sometimes overlap; they are not mutually exclusive. Take, for example, a safari trip to Africa (Fig. 18.6). Is this adventure tourism or is it wildlife tourism? Some might say that it is also a type of nature-based tourism. Also, culinary and wine tourism are often experienced together.

Figures 18.6 Safari tourism in Africa.

EXAMPLE 18.8

Nautical Tourism

All recreational and sport activities that take place on or in oceans are part of nautical tourism. This includes sailing and yachting, scuba-diving and snorkeling, sea canoeing, and other activities. Technically, it could also encompass cruise tourism. This example describes the growth of sailing tourism in Europe.

> Nautical tourism is defined as nautical recreational marinas and activities or more specifically as a "poly-functional tourist activity with a strong maritime

component" (Luković 2013: 401), in which sailboat-based activities are a key component.

The nautical tourism sector in Europe creates 234,000 jobs and generates €28 billion in revenue each year. Thirty-six million citizens of the European Union regularly participate in boating activities, keeping about six million vessels in European waters. As one of the fastest-growing sectors in European tourism, sailing has experienced continuous growth over the past thirty years.

(Luković 2013; Shen et al. 2023)

Learning Point

Sailing tourism is an increasingly important market segment for European maritime destinations.

Casino Gaming

DEFINITION

Casino gaming

The definition of a casino is quite broad. It can include everything from racetracks and restaurants to casinos and hotels. Some even hold entertainment events. While the word casino is derived from Italian, the term can mean any building (vessel or other mode of transportation) where people can gamble (Lannen Designs 2022).

Author addendum: In this book, casino gaming involves travel away from the normal place of residence. Vessels include cruise ships and riverboats.

Casino gaming is booming around the globe and being introduced in places where this activity was previously illegal. Although destinations such as Monte Carlo have always been associated with casinos, other destinations have drawn more attention recently. These include Las Vegas and Atlantic City in the USA, Macau SAR in China, Singapore, South Korea, the Philippines, and several others.

The international star of casino development in the past twenty years has been Macau (Fig. 18.7). In 2021, the total gaming revenues in Macau were around $10.8 billion (O'Connor 2022). Macau's gaming revenues in 2021 were 73 percent lower than in 2019 (*Macao News* 2022). Nevada's total casino revenues were $13.45 billion in 2021, including Las Vegas (Tang 2022). The Nevada figure was higher than in 2019 and 71 percent greater than in 2020 (University of Las Vegas Gaming Research Center 2022). These results reflect the trends you learned about in Chapter 17. Macau and its gaming are heavily dependent on international visitors; Nevada and Las Vegas mainly serve domestic travelers. South Korea has experienced significant growth in casino development and revenues, although results were severely affected in 2020 and 2021 by the COVID-19 pandemic (CGR Asia 2022). As part of its so-called integrated resort developments on Sentosa Island, Singapore introduced two casinos in 2010 (Marina Bay Sands and Resort World Sentosa). However, the total revenues for the casinos in Singapore are low in comparison to those in Macau and South Korea. Other Asian countries are opening up to casino gaming, including Vietnam, the Philippines, and Japan.

Figure 18.7 Casinos are developing rapidly and especially in Asia.

Casino gaming has expanded rapidly in the USA, although most of the gaming revenues are being earned from US residents rather than from international tourists. According to the American Gaming Association (2021), consumer spending on casino gaming in 2020 was $29.98 billion, with thirty states that allow casinos.

It is also worth mentioning the overlap between cruise tourism and casino gaming. Cruise ships and riverboats have become popular casino venues, particularly in places where gambling is not allowed on land. This trend has been evident in both the USA and Hong Kong.

EXAMPLE 18.9

Responsible Gaming

Gambling can become addictive and it is incumbent on casinos to advocate responsible gaming. They must also make sure that minors do not participate. This example is a part of the American Gaming Association's responsible gaming policy for casino operators.

Casino gambling including sports betting advertising and marketing will not:

- contain images, symbols, celebrity/entertainer endorsements and/or language designed to appeal specifically to children and minors;

- feature anyone who is or appears to be below the legal age to participate in gambling or sports betting activity or imply that underage persons engage in casino gambling or sports betting;
- depart from contemporary standards of good taste that apply to all commercial messaging, as suits the context of the message or the medium utilized;
- be placed with such intensity and frequency that they represent saturation of that medium or become excessive;
- contain claims or representations that gambling activity will guarantee an individual's social, financial or personal success;
- be placed before any audience where most of the audience is ordinarily expected to be below the legal age to participate in gambling or sports betting activity;
- imply or suggest any illegal activity of any kind.

(American Gaming Association 2022)

Learning Point

Responsible gaming policy and procedures are essential in casino gaming.

Cruise Tourism

DEFINITION

Cruise tourism

A luxurious form of traveling, involving an all-inclusive holiday on a cruise ship of at least 48 hours, according to specific itinerary, in which the cruise ship calls at several ports or cities (Research Center for Coastal Tourism, n.d.).

Cruising enjoyed significant growth in past decades until the COVID-19 pandemic and is an important source of demand for destinations in the Caribbean (Fig. 18.8), Mediterranean, and other maritime and riverfront destinations. Cruise tourism has been fast gaining in popularity, and its volume has been steadily increasing. However, the capsizing of the *Costa Concordia* off Italy and resulting passenger deaths as well as some well-publicized onboard food poisoning incidents led to some public concern about this mode of international pleasure and leisure travel, as did allegations about ocean pollution by cruise ships.

The major destination for cruise tourism in the world is the Caribbean, and the markets for Caribbean cruise tourism are primarily from North America. The Cruise Lines International Association (CLIA) estimated the demand for cruising increased 62 percent from 2005 to 2015. However, the 2021 worldwide cruise market was 4.75 million, down from 29.7 million in 2019

Figure 18.8 Cruises take people to many beautiful destinations in floating resorts.

(CLIA 2022a). Around 80 percent of the demand is from North America and Western Europe. Mainland China was emerging as major source of cruise passengers prior to COVID-19.

The most popular length of cruises is four to seven days (66 percent in 2021), and passengers are very satisfied after experiencing this type of tourism. A majority of passengers say they will definitely or probably book cruises as their next vacations (CLIA 2022b). Some 85 percent of Millennials, for example, say they will cruise again in the future. Although the Caribbean and the Mediterranean are the two main hubs of cruise tourism, other regions are experiencing growth and investing more in this market segment. One of these growth regions is in the Asia-Pacific.

Culinary Tourism

> **DEFINITION**
>
> **Culinary tourism**
>
> Any tourism experience in which a person learns about, appreciates, consumes or indulges in food and drink that reflects the local cuisine, heritage, or culture of a place (Ontario Culinary Tourism Alliance 2022).

This form of tourism is called either culinary tourism or gastronomic tourism, or even food tourism. Several DMOs have developed culinary tourism strategies or plans for their destinations, and this is a great idea where there is a rich food and wine tradition. Slovenia has developed the Taste Slovenia initiative, of which the three marketing goals are: raising international visibility, ensuring sustainability, and creating higher added value (Slovenian Tourist Board 2018).

Although every tourist has to eat while visiting a destination, culinary tourism transforms the food and local wines and their preparation into an attraction and, sometimes, also an event. CBI (2021b) identifies the examples of culinary tourism activities shown in Figure 18.9.

L'Assiette de Pays in France is a great example of cooperation among restaurants to feature regionally distinctive cuisine. This program was established in 1997 and is now operating in Aquitaine, Brittany, Languedoc-Roussillon and Normandy (L'Assiette de Pays 2022). Another example that has been developed into a culinary tourism route is La Route des Saveurs de Charlevoix in Quebec, Canada (Tourisme Charlevoix 2022).

- Cooking with locals
- Foraging for ingredients
- Cooking workshops
- Participating in the local harvest
- Eating at locals' homes
- Visiting wineries, distilleries
- Eating at local restaurants
- Visiting farms, orchards
- Eating street food
- Visiting markets, fairs, festivals
- Food and drink tours and trails
- Testing sessions of wines, beers, spirits

Culinary tourism activities

Figure 18.9 Eating food at city markets is very popular worldwide.

Catalonia Aspires to Become a World-Leading Gastronomy and Wine Tourism Destination

This example is about a Spanish destination that wants to put more emphasis on the unique food and wines produced by its agricultural sector.

> A €12 million investment by the Catalonia Tourist Board aims to establish the Spanish region as a leading destination for wine and gastronomy tourism. The "unprecedented" spend will allow Catalonia to accelerate the development of its wine and food industry in three years rather than taking a decade. The tourist board estimates that travelers interested in wine and food tourism tend to spend 3.5 times more when visiting Catalonia.
>
> The regional government will create infrastructure to bring new specialist activities across Catalonia and consolidate its position as a top leading wine and gastro-destination and be among the top eight ranking in Europe. The drive comes as part of a strategy to diversify the tourism offering and help drive visitors outside the shoulder season and contribute to spreading travel throughout the territory in line with a sustainable tourist model.
>
> (Davies 2022)

Learning Point

People are looking for novel and quality experiences that involve food and wine. Destinations with these rich agricultural resources need to take advantage of this trend.

Cultural and Heritage Tourism

Cultural tourism

A type of tourism activity in which the visitor's essential motivation is to learn, discover, experience and consume the tangible and intangible cultural attractions/products in a tourism destination. These attractions/products relate to a set of distinctive material, intellectual, spiritual and emotional features of a society that encompasses arts and architecture, historical and cultural heritage, culinary heritage, literature, music, creative industries and the living cultures with their lifestyles, value systems, beliefs and traditions (UNWTO 2022b).

Heritage tourism

The National Trust for Historic Preservation in the USA defines heritage tourism as "traveling to experience the places, artifacts, and activities that authentically represent the stories and people of the past and present. It includes visitation to cultural, historic, and natural resources" (Partners for Livable Communities 2014).

Many other definitions of cultural tourism have been proposed, and it tends to be associated with heritage and historic tourism. Fáilte Ireland (2022) says cultural and heritage tourism is the full range of experiences visitors can enjoy, which make a destination distinctive—the lifestyle, the heritage, the arts, the people. Cultural tourism is a mixture of history and traditional and modern-day culture.

Cultural and heritage tourism is of great importance to many destinations around the world. For example, the UNESCO World Heritage List in 2023 included 1,157 properties spread throughout 167 countries of the world that are the globe's most significant cultural and natural treasures (Fig. 18.10). Some 900 of these properties were classified as cultural, 218 as natural

Figure 18.10 Visiting the World Heritage List site of Petra, Jordan.

and thirty-nine as mixed (cultural and natural) (UNESCO 2022a). For example, the Tower of London (UK), Route of Santiago de Compostela (Spain), and the Great Wall (China) are cultural properties; the Great Barrier Reef (Australia) and the Canadian Rocky Mountain Parks are natural properties. These 1,000-plus properties are representatives of tangible heritage, but there is also intangible heritage. UNESCO maintains a list of intangible cultural heritage and this includes traditions or living expressions inherited from our ancestors and passed on to our descendants, such as oral traditions, performing arts, social practices, rituals, festive events, knowledge and practices concerning nature and the universe or the knowledge and skills to produce traditional crafts (UNESCO 2022b). For example, Chinese acupuncture and calligraphy are on the intangible culture list, as is Spain's flamenco dancing.

There are many significant cultural and heritage and historical tourism sites and resources that are not transcribed on the World Heritage List, but they are still visited and enjoyed by international tourists.

For several destinations, scholars and experts have tried to describe cultural and heritage tourists and the activities they prefer. Often, these profiles have been based on the involvement of people with the places they are visiting or the cultural performances they are experiencing. For example, Choose Chicago (2014) believes the cultural traveler considers the destination attributes shown in Figure 18.11 to be important or very important.

Indigenous tourism is steadily growing in certain countries including Australia and Canada, and it is a subset of cultural tourism.

Cultural traveler destination attributes

- Aquariums and zoos
- Architecture or historical buildings
- Art museums
- Churches or attractions of religious significance
- Cultural events or festivals
- Gardens or parks
- Historic sites and attractions
- Live music
- Natural history or science-related museums and attractions
- Theatre or the performing arts
- Unique, off-the-beaten-path arts or cultural activities or attractions

Figure 18.11 Cultural traveler destination attributes.

EXAMPLE 18.11

Indigenous Tourism

Indigenous tourism is growing and receiving a much higher priority from governments and DMOs. This example highlights the positives and potential negatives of Indigenous tourism.

> The large influx of tourists visiting native destinations can often dominate natural resources. In 2018, it was reported that 7.2 million visitors were expected to engage in Indigenous tourism experiences between 2019 and 2020 in Canada. Tourism Australia also revealed that the number of international visitors taking part in Indigenous tourism-related activities had risen by 40 percent since 2013. It is clear that such experiences are now highly coveted. To ensure that these figures incite positive change, the implementation of Indigenous tourism should follow the principles of sustainable development and resource management. However, this is often not the case. Tourism in Indigenous areas, especially rural Indigenous areas can produce undesirable impacts such as pollution, littering, damage to the natural environment and degradation of local ecological habitats.
>
> (It's Your Planet 2022)

Learning Point

Indigenous tourism should be developed in a sustainable way.

Dark Tourism

DEFINITIONS

Dark tourism

Dark tourism may be referred to as the act of travel to sites associated with death, suffering and the seemingly macabre (Stone 2006: 146). Tarlow (2005: 48) identifies dark tourism as visitations to places where tragedies or historically noteworthy death has occurred and that continue to impact our lives.

Some people seem to have a fascination with traveling to places that are associated with death, suffering, atrocity, tragedy or crime (Light 2017). A few examples here might bring this concept into clearer focus for you. Some of the most famous dark tourism sites include Ground Zero (New York City) (Fig. 18.12), Auschwitz concentration camp (Poland), and the Pont de l'Alma road tunnel in Paris, where Princess Diana died. Stone (2006) divides dark tourism destinations and products into the seven categories shown in Figure 18.12.

Dark tourism product and destination categories

- Dark fun factories (e.g., Schloss Dracula at Erlebnispark Strasswalchen near Salzburg, Austria, and the London Dungeon)
- Dark exhibitions (e.g., Tuol Sleng Genocide Museum in Phnom Penh, Cambodia)
- Dark dungeons (e.g., Port Arthur in Tasmania, Australia)
- Dark resting places (e.g., various cemeteries, including the World War I and World War II cemeteries in Europe)
- Dark shrines (e.g., the Hiroshima Peace Site in Japan and the Nanjing Massacre Memorial Hall in Jiangsu, China)
- Dark conflict sites (e.g., Normandy landings and battlefields)
- Dark of genocide (e.g., Auschwitz in Poland)

Figure 18.12 Dark tourism products and destinations—Ground Zero.

A research study on dark tourism in Lithuania called this phenomenon heritage that hurts, and this sometimes seems to be an apt description (Isaac and Budrytė-Ausiejienė 2015). For example, visiting the site in Sichuan, China, shown in Figure 18.13, can take a huge emotional toll on people as they try to imagine the tragedy at the school that collapsed.

Figure 18.13 Earthquake disaster memorial in Ying Xiu, Sichuan Province, China.

There has been a vigorous debate among scholars about what constitutes dark tourism, but not much research has been done on the characteristics and behaviors of the tourists who consume it. Additionally, not much work has been done on how to market dark tourism.

Health and Wellness Tourism

> **DEFINITION**
>
> **Wellness tourism**
>
> An emerging market segment directed not only for those who pursue solely thermal treatments but also for those seeking illness prevention, physical improvement and spiritual balance or even for those eager for cultural and relaxation programs (Costa et al. 2015).

There has been a great spurt in interest in health and wellness tourism as people are becoming more concerned about their fitness and overall health. There are many traditional spas around the world that have relied on the healing qualities of their natural spring waters (Fig. 18.14). Places like Bath in England, Baden-Baden in Germany, and Carlsbad (Karlovy Vary) in the Czech Republic are among the most famous for these sorts of experiences.

Figure 18.14 Relaxing and enjoying the mineral benefits of the Blue Lagoon in Iceland is an example of wellness tourism.

According to Smith and Puczkó (2009), there are many definitions of health and wellness tourism, and they tend to vary by country and region of the world. These authors define five types of health tourism:

1. holistic (wellness);
2. leisure and recreation (wellness);
3. medical (wellness);
4. medical (therapeutic);
5. medical (surgery).

EXAMPLE 18.12

Cycle or Bike Tourism

This example highlights the growth in cycle tourism and emphasizes its potential contribution to wellness and health, and to sustainable destinations.

With a new appreciation for the outdoors following extended lockdown periods, biking not only offers individuals treasured freedom but it adds to the list of sustainable habits that our global community needs to be adopting. The value that people are placing on this privilege of being in nature, is evident with the unprecedented bike shortage that is currently plaguing the whole world. Predicted to continue well into 2021, and potentially as far as 2022, the sheer demand for bikes in recent times has caused a massive rethink of the international supply chain as suppliers cater to interest.

Prior to 2020, the cycle tourism sector in Europe alone was valued at €44 billion. Although numbers are not yet out on the current state of the niche, the fact that biking falls into the health and wellness sector, has many sub-sectors, appeals to young and old along with experienced and inexperienced riders, we anticipate further growth for this sector. Having stood the test of time over the years and proving to be extremely resilient during an international pandemic, bike tourism ticks all of the boxes for a niche that is set to thrive in coming years.

(Tourwriter 2022)

Learning Point

Cycle or bike tourism is a growth market. Destinations should increase their accessibility and experiences for cyclists.

Medical tourism is discussed below under a separate category. Smith and Puczkó define holistic wellness as incorporating spiritual, yoga and meditation, and new age experiences. Wellness leisure and recreation includes beauty treatments, pampering, and sports and fitness. The upwards trend in the use of spas at numerous types of locations (day spas, airports, hotels and resorts, cruise ships, etc.) is included in this market segment.

Industrial Tourism

DEFINITION

Industrial tourism

Industrial tourism is where people visit the sites or buildings of existing or former industries. These include tours of factories, mines, farms and orchards, docklands, and other current or heritage industries.

The Fundidora Industrial Park in Mexico (Fig. 18.15) is an excellent case study of converting a disused industrial site into a significant leisure and tourism attraction. Another successful industrial tourism attraction is the Dole Plantation in Hawai'i, in the USA. The focus at the Dole Plantation is on the production of pineapples, and one of the key attractions is the world's largest and longest pineapple garden maze. The Guinness Storehouse® in Dublin, Ireland, is a third great industrial tourism case study.

Figure 18.15 The Fundidora Industrial Park in Monterrey, Mexico, is a great example of an attraction based on industrial heritage.

EXAMPLE 18.13

How to Turn a Steel Plant into a Tourist Attraction

This is a great example of creating an educational and tourism facility out of a disused industrial plant.

> The foundry closed in 1986 and in 1988 its transformation to a new use commenced. Fundidora Park [Fig. 18.15] was declared an Industrial Archaeological Museum Site by the state government in 2001. The structure housing Horno Alto No. 3 became a science and technology center managed by a nonprofit organization known as horno3. It is an educational facility that showcases the origin of the industrialization and modernization of Mexico and the important role of the foundry in this venture.
>
> (World Monuments Fund 2017)

Learning Point

Before tearing down industrial structures, it is worthwhile to consider their regeneration into tourism attractions and/or educational or community facilities.

Medical Tourism

> ### DEFINITION
>
> **Medical tourism**
>
> Medical tourism is the term commonly used to describe international travel for the purpose of receiving medical care. Medical tourists may pursue medical care abroad for a variety of reasons, such as decreased cost, a recommendation from friends or family, the opportunity to combine medical care with a vacation destination, a preference for care from providers who share the traveler's culture, or to receive a procedure or therapy not available in their country of residence. Medical tourism is a worldwide, multibillion-dollar market that continues to grow (Benowitz and Gaines 2019).

Medical tourism is where people leave their own countries for medical treatment or surgery in other countries. The Medical Tourism Association (2022) offers another definition of where

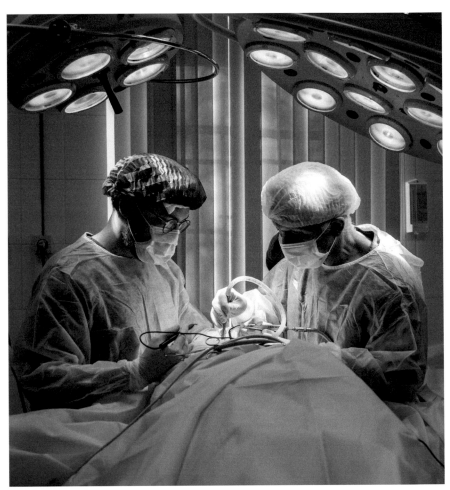

Figure 18.16 Medical procedure in progress.

people who live in one country travel to another country to receive medical, dental and surgical care while at the same time receiving equal to or greater care than they would have in their own country, and are traveling for medical care because of affordability, better access to care or a higher level of quality of care (Fig. 18.16).

This has been a popular trend because the medical costs are lower but the standards of medical care are still high. Some of the top medical tourism destinations in the world include Hungary, India, Malaysia, Singapore, South Korea, Thailand, and Ukraine. The medical treatments sought in different places vary. For example, some destinations are famous for cosmetic surgery, and others are known for dentistry, including some Central European countries.

Nature-Based Tourism and Ecotourism

DEFINITION

Ecotourism

"Responsible travel to natural areas that conserves the environment, sustains the well-being of the local people, and involves interpretation and education." The society also suggests that education applies to both visitors and tourism staff and that ecotourism is "about uniting conservation, communities, and sustainable travel" (TIES 2015).

TIES recommends that ecotourism should follow the eight principles shown in Figure 18.17.

- Minimize physical, social, behavioral and psychological impacts
- Build environmental and cultural awareness and respect
- Provide positive experiences for both visitors and hosts
- Provide direct financial benefits for conservation
- Generate financial benefits for both local people and private industry
- Deliver memorable interpretative experiences to visitors that help raise sensitivity to host countries' political, environmental and social climates
- Design, construct and operate low-impact facilities
- Recognize the rights and spiritual beliefs of Indigenous people in communities and work in partnership with them to create empowerment

Figure 18.17 Principles of ecotourism (TIES).

Nature-based tourism is a broader concept than ecotourism and it means that visitors are attracted by some aspect of nature. This may involve viewing landscapes and beautiful scenery (Fig. 18.18), as well as watching wildlife including bird-watching. Safaris also can be placed in nature tourism as can be whale-watching.

Figure 18.18 Ecotourism includes visits to areas of outstanding natural beauty.

EXAMPLE 18.14

Bird-Watching Tourism

Bird-watching is a specific component of nature-based tourism. This example identifies the requirements of birders in terms of destinations. These travelers tend to be well-educated and with higher incomes, making them a lucrative market for destinations.

The presence of interesting bird life is the key requirement for a bird-watching destination and it is important that you know about the resident bird life in your region. An iconic species will help to bring your destination to the fore-front of the birding community and will attract large numbers of casual birders with an interest in native bird life. An endemic species (which means it is only found in a particular region/area/country) will attract the enthusiastic and hard-core bird watcher who wants to tick a bird or birds off his or her list. Migratory species are also appealing, particularly those in large numbers. However, the behavior of these birds is usually seasonal. The presence of large numbers of identifiable species are appealing to European tour operators as they will help "sell" their bird-watching holidays.

South America, Asia and Africa are all excellent destinations for bird-watching. The biodiversity within these regions make exceptional habitats for vast numbers of bird species . . . Colombia, Peru and Brazil have the highest bird diversity in the world, while Indonesia has the greatest number of endemic species.

(CBI 2021b)

Learning Point

Bird-watching as a hobby and leisure activity is increasing. It is incumbent on destinations and DMOs to carefully assess the potential of this market segment.

Not all tourism is ecotourism because some is based on culture and heritage. It is also true that not all that is offered as being ecotourism is genuine. The greenwashing concept (fake ecotourism) was discussed in Chapter 2.

Religious Tourism

DEFINITION

Religious tourism

Religious and spiritual tourism refers to travel for religious or spiritual purposes, such as undertaking a pilgrimage and visiting sacred sites. Also known as sacred or faith tourism, it is one of the oldest forms of tourism. Religious tourism is a niche within the segment of cultural tourism, comprising four specialist niches: pilgrimages, visiting sacred sites, church, mosque and temple tourism, and travel for the purpose of mission or worship (CBI 2020a).

Religious tourism is one of the oldest forms of travel. People with a religious trip-related purpose are a significant part of the inbound international tourism for several countries, including Saudi Arabia, Italy, Portugal, Spain, Croatia, India, Sri Lanka, and several others. Additionally, many other international tourists visit religious sites and buildings. Religious tourism in fact comes in many formats and includes the activities shown in Figure 18.19.

Rinschede (1992) divided religious tourism into two parts: short-term and long-term. Short-term religious tourism is mainly local and regional travel to pilgrimage sites or to participate in a religious celebration, religious conference or church meeting. Long-term religious tourism involves national or international travel for several days or weeks. These destinations include major religious pilgrimage sites, such as Mecca (Saudi Arabia), the Vatican City in Rome, Benares (India), Jerusalem (Israel), Lourdes (France), Fátima (Portugal), Guadalupe (Mexico), and Santiago de Compostela (Spain).

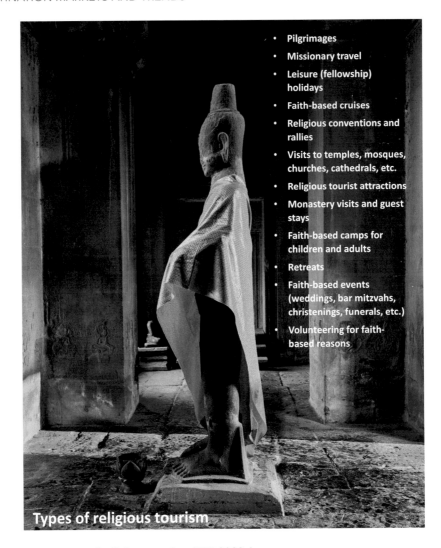

- Pilgrimages
- Missionary travel
- Leisure (fellowship) holidays
- Faith-based cruises
- Religious conventions and rallies
- Visits to temples, mosques, churches, cathedrals, etc.
- Religious tourist attractions
- Monastery visits and guest stays
- Faith-based camps for children and adults
- Retreats
- Faith-based events (weddings, bar mitzvahs, christenings, funerals, etc.)
- Volunteering for faith-based reasons

Types of religious tourism

Figure 18.19 Types of religious tourism (CBI 2020a).

Shopping Tourism

> **DEFINITION**
>
> **Shopping tourism**
>
> A contemporary form of tourism fostered by individuals for whom purchasing goods outside of their usual environment is a determining factor in their decision to travel. This description treats shopping more as a motivation for travel than as an incidental activity (UNWTO 2014).

Shopping is an activity in which most international pleasure and leisure tourists engage and greatly enjoy. However, there is a difference between shopping as one of several activities engaged in when traveling and shopping as the principal purpose and reason for a trip. When people travel to places like the Mall of America (Bloomington, Minnesota, USA), West Edmonton Mall (Edmonton, Alberta, Canada), and the Dubai Mall or to duty-free shopping zones, their main desired travel experience might be the shopping. Apart from shopping in modern structures like these malls, visitors also enjoy visiting storied department stores, such as Harrod's in London, and outdoor and indoor markets (Fig. 18.20).

Figure 18.20 Craft and souvenir markets are popular with international tourists.

Noticing this tendency for serious shopping, several places around the world have been aggressively promoting themselves as shopping destinations for international tourists, including Malaysia.

EXAMPLE 18.15

Shopping Tourism in Malaysia

Malaysia is one destination country that has for at least two decades made a concerted effort to develop and market shopping tourism. This example explains the reasons for establishing the Secretariat Shopping Malaysia (SSM).

Secretariat Shopping Malaysia (SSM) was established by Tourism Malaysia in 2002 with the vision of streamlining all efforts in developing the shopping sector of Malaysia's tourism economy. As the promotion arm of Tourism Malaysia, SSM's mission is to promote Malaysia as a world-class shopping destination to overseas and domestic tourists. SSM plays three major roles which are in line with its efforts to boost the local tourism and retail industries by increasing tourist arrivals and tourists' spending. First, SSM plans marketing campaigns, shopping events and activities to highlight shopping experiences to tourists. Second, SSM forms strategic partnerships and creates marketing initiatives with domestic and international trade and shopping industry players. Third, SSM facilitates and coordinates shopping-related government policies as well as private-public sector initiatives that promote the country as one of the world's best shopping destinations.

(Tourism Malaysia 2022b)

Learning Point

Shopping is a major destination attraction and activity. Destinations and DMOs should develop specific plans and strategies for shopping tourism.

Shopping tourism can be classified as leisure shopping, and there are three distinctive environments for leisure shopping: ambient shopping (typical shopping at a mall), magnet leisure in a new-generation shopping mall (such as the Mall of America), and heritage-destination leisure (shopping in historic areas) (Timothy 2005).

Not all shoppers have the same behaviors, and that is the case for all these special-interest markets. There was great focus on the buying of luxury goods by Chinese outbound tourists prior to COVID-19. Another concept that attracts specific customers is outlet shopping where famous branded goods are sold at discounted prices. Some of the most famous of these are the Dubai Outlet Mall, Bicester Village (UK), and Sawgrass Mills (US).

Sport Tourism

DEFINITION

Sport tourism

A social, economic and cultural phenomenon arising from the unique interaction of activity, people and place (Weed and Bull 2004). It is tourism associated with professional and amateur sport.

Tourism associated with both professional and amateur sport is a market that is receiving increasing attention from DMOs. Several DMOs have created sport tourism departments to plan for and capture a larger share of this blossoming aspect of tourism. UNWTO (2016) identifies the following sport-related reasons people travel:

- to actively participate in a sport or sporting event, individually or as part of a team;
- self-development or enhanced training for sport as an individual or as a team;
- watching sport as a spectator or supporter of a team, a sport or a sporting event;
- visiting sites and places associated with the history, heritage, culture of a sport or a sporting legend;
- to improve their health and well-being through a sporting activity.

Therefore, sport tourism is a very broad concept that offers a wide spectrum of opportunities for destinations. These opportunities range from mega sporting events like the Olympics and the World Cup to amateur sports tournaments and everything in between. CBI (2020b) specify eight specific sport tourism activities plus sport tourism trips and these are listed in Figure 18.21. Destination British Columbia (2013) identifies the fourteen types of sports events shown in Figure 18.21.

Sport activities:
Sport tourism trips
Running
Golf
Ski
Cycling
Water sports
Diving
Fishing
Adrenaline sports

Sport events:
Megaevents
Games
Championships
Tournaments
Training camps
Development courses
Conferences
Professional sports
Cause related
Media events
Showcases
Spectator events
Created sport events
One-off events

Types of sport tourism activities and events

Figure 18.21 Types of sport tourism activities and events.

One tournament type of sport event that is becoming very popular among destinations is the marathon. Marathons can attract thousands of runners.

EXAMPLE 18.16

Marathons and Tourism

Marathons are an increasingly important part of sport tourism. This example describes the benefits of marathons to runners and destinations.

> The idea of marathon tourism makes running far more interesting and motivating. Apart from the competition, it becomes an experience of a lifetime as the runner gets to explore the surroundings on a run. This freedom of venturing through different and new places while still under harsh training and physical strain has pushed the number of participants in multiple and international marathons more than the local and straightforward ones. Often, marathon tourism is termed as tourism with benefits as it keeps a check on physical fitness while facilitating an adventurous exposure of new places.
>
> (Gupta 2019)

Learning Point

Marathoning is a unique way to discover a destination, as well as being a great opportunity to capitalize on sport tourism.

Voluntourism

DEFINITION

Voluntourism

The term "voluntourism" is a combination of the words "volunteer" and "tourism." It is also sometimes referred to as volunteer travel or volunteer vacation. Voluntourism is a form of tourism in which travelers participate in voluntary work, typically for a charity. Voluntourists range in age and come from all over the world (Dubay 2021).

The *Oxford Dictionary* defines voluntourism as a form of tourism in which travelers participate in voluntary work, typically for a charity. The volunteering is done with the desire to help others. People who engage in voluntourism are on holiday, but they also want to help local destinations through volunteer elements within their trips. They feel good by giving something back to local communities and believe they get a more authentic cultural exchange.

This is a concept that particularly attracts younger travelers and that takes place in developing countries. It may or may not be related to religious or charitable organizations. There are also medical and dental missions whereby doctors and dentists travel to less-privileged places to offer services free of charge.

Figure 18.22 Volunteering for beach clean-up in Bali, Indonesia.

There is significant controversy and criticism surrounding some aspects of voluntourism, especially that which is being called orphanage tourism in countries such as Cambodia and Myanmar. You learned about this concept in Chapter 2.

EXAMPLE 18.17

Best Practices in Voluntourism

There are many justifiable criticisms of volunteering while traveling internationally. This example provides two cases of best practices in voluntourism.

> Homestay programs in Thailand gives tourists the opportunity of living in a small Thai village, helping to host visitors, making meals, doing laundry, and growing produce.
>
> (CBI 2020a)

> The homestay participant must provide tutor or classroom conversational English up to fifteen hours a week to help family members (and their students if family member is a teacher) to improve their English. A timetable will be worked out between the tutor and host family upon arrival. The rest of the tutor's time is considered free time and can be spent as he or she pleases.
>
> (Xploreasia.org 2022)

> La Choza Chula, in Guatemala, runs turtle and mangrove tours, cooking classes, homestay programs, cultural immersion programs, volunteer programs. They also offer weekly English classes for their guides, funded the construction of a library, set up a mobile library, and built a computer lab and a secondary school.
>
> (CBI 2020a)

> La Choza Chula is a social enterprise seeking to ensure local communities and the environment benefit from the growing tourism of El Paredón, Guatemala. We work to provide education, enterprise and employment opportunities for the people of El Paredón, promoting positive impact from tourism on the local community, and improving human and environmental well-being. Our local tours and products ensure that the local community benefits from the growing tourism in the area as well as providing support for our projects.
>
> (La Choza Chula 2022)

Learning Point

There are genuine programs for voluntourism. It is important for participants to carefully check program details and determine the reputation of providers.

Wine Tourism

Wine tourism

Wine tourism involves visits to vineyards, wineries, wine festivals and wine shows for which grape wine tasting and/or experiencing the attributes of a grape wine region are the prime motivating factors for visitors (Hall and Mitchell 2000). Getz and Brown (2006) add that there are three perspectives on wine tourism: the wine producers, DMOs, and consumers.

Wine tourism has become very popular in many parts of the world, including North and South America, Europe, South Africa, Australia (Fig. 18.23), and New Zealand.

Figure 18.23 Tasting different wines at wineries is an important experience in wine tourism.

As seen around the world, wine production can be the core around which tourism destinations are built. Wine is also an important component of culinary tourism and a part of the food culture of places.

In Chapters 7 and 8, you learned about the wine tourism product clubs and the Wine Routes of Spain from the perspective of creating destination partnerships.

Other International Tourism Growth Markets

The fifteen markets previously discussed are defined by the destination product and the specific activities and experiences travelers are seeking. There are several other growth markets that follow different segmentation characteristics. Given space limitations, the focus will be on a sample of two of these—diaspora tourism and solo travelers.

Diaspora Tourism

DEFINITION

Diaspora tourism

Diaspora tourism refers to the travel of people in a diaspora to their ancestral homelands in search of their roots or to feel connected to their personal heritage (Huang et al. 2013).

Diaspora tourism is connected with emigration, whether voluntary or forced (Li et al. 2020). For many of those returning to their roots in West Africa, the departure from there was a result of slavery (Dillette 2020); for those returning to the UK and Ireland, the journeys may be more nostalgic for visiting the "old country." Most commentators on this phenomenon say it is a market that is expanding, although precise statistics are lacking on visitor volumes. The example provided explains the potential in diaspora tourism and the offers that are possible.

EXAMPLE 18.18

Diaspora Tourism: Searching for One's Roots

Searching for one's ancestral roots is becoming a stronger motivation for international travel. This example provides background information on this form of travel known as diaspora tourism.

> Diaspora populations can help to open markets for new tourism destinations and goods produced in and associated with the culture of their countries of origin. Tourists from the diaspora are more likely than most international tourists to have or make connections with the local economy, staying in locally owned, smaller accommodations (or with relatives), eating in local restaurants, buying goods from local vendors, and so forth—rather than staying in foreign-owned tourist enclaves with little connection to their surroundings.

The many forms of diaspora tourism include medical tourism, business-related tourism, heritage (or "roots") tourism, exposure or "birthright" tours, education tourism, VIP tours, and peak experience tours. Not all forms are aimed exclusively at the diaspora, but many are pursued by country-of-origin governments as part of their efforts to bind the diaspora more closely to the homeland. Each of these forms has the potential to contribute to development, by attracting investors, volunteers, philanthropists, or consumers from the diaspora.

(Newland and Taylor 2010)

Learning Point

Destinations and DMOs should reach out to emigrant populations and their families with invitations to return to their homelands.

Solo Travelers

DEFINITION

Solo traveler

A solo traveler is a person who embarks on a journey, either long or short, in which they are both physically and emotionally away from the people and the culture with which they are familiar (solotravel365).

Solo travel is partly driven by the fact that an increasing share of the population in developed countries lives in single-person households (Laesser et al. 2016).

Another market segment that appears to be in the growth process is solo tourism. You should know that this is not the same as independent travel, which is more about how travel is booked. It means when a person goes places without companions.

EXAMPLE 18.19

The Solo Tourism Market

Going it all alone when traveling internationally is a growth trend in tourism. This example provides two perspectives on solo travel.

Traveling solo can be one of the most exciting, liberating and eye-opening experiences, no matter your age. It offers ample opportunity for self-reflection and growth with the joy of boundless freedom. It can also be daunting, especially if you've never traveled solo before.

(Lonely Planet 2022)

> The market for solo tourism products in Europe is booming. The number of singles is growing, as is the number of people that travel solo by choice. They increasingly tend to visit developing countries, seeking adventures, relaxation, solitude or connection. Self-development and unique experiences are important aspects of solo travel. Personal guided tours are especially popular.
>
> (CBI 2018)

Learning Point

Most destinations are set up to cater to pairs or larger groups of people. There is now a need to give greater attention in product development and marketing, branding, and communications to the solo traveler.

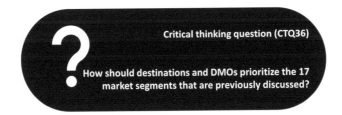

? Critical thinking question (CTQ36)

How should destinations and DMOs prioritize the 17 market segments that are previously discussed?

International Pleasure/Leisure Travel Marketing, Branding, and Communications Procedures

The DMS model was described in Chapter 12. It is recommended that this model is followed when marketing to international pleasure and leisure travel markets. The five questions in the model should be applied to each origin country that is being targeted (Morrison 2022).

Where Are We Now?

What is the existing situation in the market that is being considered? The DMO needs to analyze the recent past history of visits from this market as part of a market analysis. Several DMOs do this very professionally and share their summary results with tourism sector stakeholders as part of a series of market profiles. These DMOs include the National Travel and Tourism Office (USA), Tourism Australia, Tourism Ireland, Tourism New Zealand, VisitBritain and others. Figure 18.24 shows the content that market analyses by origin country should include.

It can be very helpful here if the DMO has conducted a survey of previous visitors from the country of origin because this provides more in-depth information on what people do and what they most like and dislike about the destination. Having more detailed information like this better informs the subsequent marketing strategy and plan for that country of origin.

Some countries conduct regular international visitor surveys, usually on an annual basis, and their results provide a good foundation for future marketing. Australia, for example, has the International Visitor Survey (IVS), which has an impressive number of respondents. The Australian IVS contains questions regarding the following: Usual place of residence; repeat visitation; group tours; travel party; sources for obtaining information about Australia; purpose of visit and places visited; transportation and accommodation; activities; expenditures; and demographics.

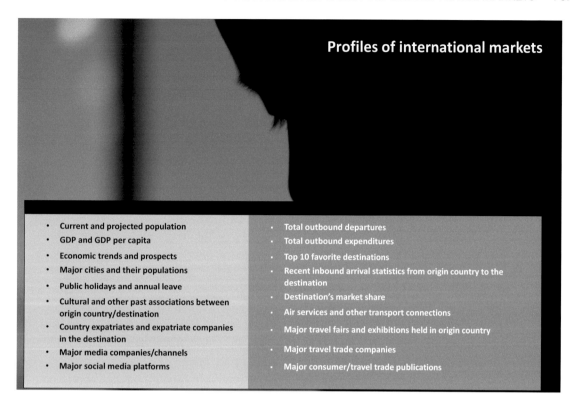

Profiles of international markets

- Current and projected population
- GDP and GDP per capita
- Economic trends and prospects
- Major cities and their populations
- Public holidays and annual leave
- Cultural and other past associations between origin country/destination
- Country expatriates and expatriate companies in the destination
- Major media companies/channels
- Major social media platforms

- Total outbound departures
- Total outbound expenditures
- Top 10 favorite destinations
- Recent inbound arrival statistics from origin country to the destination
- Destination's market share
- Air services and other transport connections
- Major travel fairs and exhibitions held in origin country
- Major travel trade companies
- Major consumer/travel trade publications

Figure 18.24 Profiles of international markets.

EXAMPLE 18.20

The Survey of International Air Travelers, USA

The survey program discussed in this example is one of the most long-running in the world.

The Survey of International Air Travelers (SIAT) is an ongoing primary research program which gathers statistical data about air passenger travelers in US—overseas and US—Mexican markets. Survey data provides information on passenger trip planning, travel patterns, demographics and spending for two separate populations—non-US residents traveling to the USA and US residents traveling from the USA. The Survey has been conducted on a monthly basis continuously since January 1983. Survey data, which can be used to analyze specific visitor segments, is a source of information for planners, marketers, and policymakers.

The paper-based survey instrument is available in twelve languages including: Arabic, Chinese, English, French, German, Italian, Japanese, Korean, Polish, Portuguese, Russian and Spanish. An English version e-Survey and other electronic versions of the survey instrument have been tested over time and so far, the paper version of the questionnaire still obtains more responses than any other version. Questions are grouped into the relative categories: travel planning, trip data including origin-destination(s), trip expenditures, choice factors and passenger demographics.

(ITA 2022)

Learning Point

It is essential that destinations and DMOs have accurate and robust information on their international visitors.

New Zealand has an IVS, which is a sample survey of international visitors to New Zealand aged fifteen years or older (Ministry of Business, Innovation and Employment 2022). In the UK, the Office for National Statistics (2022) conducts the International Passenger Survey. Between 700,000 and 800,000 interviews are conducted a year. You learned about Destination Canada's Global Tourism Watch survey program in Chapter 5.

Of course, surveys such as these tend to be somewhat expensive and not all DMOs can afford to do them, especially on a regular basis. Most often then, DMOs must rely on secondary data sources. For example, some DMOs use the FutureBrand Country Brand Index (FutureBrand 2022) for information on other countries' perceptions.

Where Would We Like to Be?

To complete this step, DMOs must develop a marketing strategy that allocates priorities and sets goals for each market. In addition to target country selection, the international marketing strategy must also encompass a destination PIB approach. Here, there are two options available: a global approach, which does not significantly vary by country, or an individualized approach, where the PIB is customized for each market or each region.

How Do We Get There?

A mini marketing plan should be designed for each international market to guide the implementation of marketing, branding, and communications. These plans should be based on specific objectives for each market and detail how the eight Ps will be applied (product, price, place, promotion, packaging, programming, partnership and people).

PRODUCT

It is important to have information on the activities and experiences most desired by the tourists from each origin country. This chapter has discussed several tourism product categories that appear to have increasing appeal for international tourists. You heard about seventeen market segments with growth potential for domestic and international tourism; these segments are based on different aspects of the tourism product.

Certain slight adjustments to normally delivered products may be needed to meet the requirements of international tourists. Food and dietary restrictions are an obvious example here, and DMOs should educate tourism sector stakeholders about the product modifications needed for specific origin markets and according to religious and traditional requirements.

PRICE

Price levels and value for money are undoubtedly very important decision attributes for international tourists. However, DMOs seldom are directly involved in setting prices for tourism products within their destinations.

PLACE

As mentioned in Chapter 12, place in tourism means the distribution channels that DMOs use. These channels include online distribution, which comprises such things as websites, social media platforms, OTAs and smartphones, and traditional distribution channels through travel trade companies, such as travel agencies and tour operators.

Using the available distribution channels is exceptionally important for marketing to international pleasure and leisure tourists. This is because traditional consumer IMC methods, such as advertising, can be very expensive when conducted in foreign countries, particularly if the ROI is considered.

SALES PROMOTION

Different types of sales promotions are most often used in marketing to international pleasure and leisure tourists. Having booths at travel shows and exhibitions in origin countries is a very common approach because it is a very efficient way to meet with the travel trades and consumers. Road shows or promotional seminars/workshops are other favored approaches. Typically, these events are for travel trade companies and representatives of the media.

Familiarization tours, or fams, are another very popular approach in the marketing for international pleasure and leisure tourists. They give influential people a first-hand view and experience with the destination that they can pass along to potential tourists.

Travel agent training and certification programs are a great way to develop an influential group of travel professionals to help sell destinations. The Aussie Specialist Program, operated by Tourism Australia, was mentioned in Chapter 7 as an outstanding example of such training (Tourism Australia 2021).

PACKAGING

A significant proportion of inbound tourists buy packaged vacations/holidays, and others are on pre-arranged itineraries. These are usually designed and operated by travel trade companies, hotels and resorts, airlines and other tourism sector stakeholders and are not a DMO responsibility. However, the DMO should act in an advisory role in encouraging other players to develop the most appropriate packages and tours for inbound international tourists.

Sometimes, DMOs must play a regulation and control role with inbound tours and packages to protect international guests and ensure their satisfaction. There have been several instances with the Chinese inbound market where unscrupulous tour operators and their guides have been forcing their customers to shop in specific stores and insisting that they spend large amounts of money (this is called forced shopping).

PROGRAMMING

Many of the seventeen market segments discussed in this chapter require elements of programming to provide interpretation, activities and participatory experiences for international tourists. Adventure tourism requires experienced guides and instructors, sport tourism may require that tournaments be organized, and voluntourism needs special program development.

Additionally, destinations may create events and festivals mainly for international markets. For example, The Great Singapore Sale is from the end of May to the end of July and is designed to attract shoppers from around the world to hunt for bargains (Wong 2022).

PARTNERSHIP

Partnering is an essential for marketing internationally because a DMO is unlikely to be successful on its own. The partners may include airlines flying between the origin country and the destination, other DMOs, and major hotels and attractions in the destination.

PEOPLE

Human resources are another extremely important consideration when catering to international pleasure and leisure tourists. For example, it may be essential to have staff members who are completely fluent in the language of the origin country as well as being very familiar with the country's culture and traditions.

The training of guides may be essential to ensure that inbound tourists have an enjoyable and hassle-free stay in the destination and extract the maximum value from the sites they see and the shopping in which they engage.

How Do We Make Sure We Get There?

The marketing, branding, and communications for each international market must be carefully monitored to ensure that they remain on track. In Chapter 12, you learned about the concepts of destination marketing control and evaluation. For each international market, DMOs will have specific activities and programs identified in their respective mini marketing plans. The completion of these activities and programs is one type of control measure (e.g., if the DMO arranges a fam or attends a travel exhibition or fair).

As well as having activity tracking, DMOs must also have productivity and performance measures. The productivity measures show the efficiency and effectiveness of the DMO in using resources (e.g., how many people came on fams to the destination or attended the DMO's seminars or workshops). The performance measures are the actual outcomes or results from implementing the activities and programs for each international market.

How Do We Know If We Got There?

A careful assessment of marketing performance must be completed for each international market. Here, it is essential that DMOs define KRAs and KPIs for each market.

Many national DMOs have offices abroad in their major focus countries, and these offices become an important element of DMO operations. There are several models for establishing these offices, and the first one is to operate the offices with full-time staff of the DMO. The second model is not to have any full-time staff but rather to work with a vendor or contractor known as a representative or general sales agent (GSA). The third model is for a DMO to have a combination of self-operated and representative offices. A fourth model is to have just a consular or embassy unit or attaché with the responsibility of tourism as well as other commercial and trade activities.

SUMMING UP

Unfortunately, the long-term growth trend in international tourism came to an abrupt halt in 2020. Despite the growth potential, tourism remains highly susceptible to negative impacts from various types of crises, as well demonstrated by the effects of COVID-19 in 2020–2022.

There are several unique challenges for international tourism and in marketing, branding, and communications for international leisure and pleasure travel markets. From the broader perspective, balance of payments in tourism deficits is an issue for several countries, and the uneven distribution of international tourists within a host country destination is a second concern. Another major challenge is in selecting which origin countries to target. Many DMOs consider the yields of various origin countries in determining their market strategies.

Outbound markets, including Brazil, Russia, India, and China (the BRICs), are expanding at an above-average pace and attracting the attention of more DMOs. These four nations are among the top ten most populated countries and are experiencing significant economic growth that is stimulating outbound travel.

Not all international tourists are alike, and in fact they may be looking for different types of experiences within destinations. Certain specific market segments have demonstrated strong growth and are expected to continue to have good future potential for destinations. A growing proportion of international tourists are visiting destinations to pursue special interests and specific forms of tourism (adventure, casino gaming, cruise, culinary, cultural-heritage, dark, nature-based and ecotourism, health and wellness, industrial, medical, religion, shopping, sports, volunteering, and wine tourism). Diaspora tourism and solo travel are also expanding.

It is recommended that DMOs follow the DMS when marketing, branding, and communicating internationally. The operation of DMO offices in other countries is an important part of the international tourism marketing role.

KEYWORDS

adventure tourism
balance of payment deficits
bird-watching tourism
casino gaming
crises
cruise tourism
culinary or food tourism
currency exchange rates
cycling or bike tourism
cultural and heritage
   tourism
dark tourism
diaspora tourism
diving tourism
economic leakage
emerging markets
food tourism

gastronomic tourism
greenwashing
hard and soft adventure
health and wellness tourism
import content
indigenous tourism
industrial tourism
intangible heritage
marathons
market segments
medical tourism
nature-based tourism and
   ecotourism
nautical tourism
orphanage tourism
outlet shopping
religious tourism

representative or general
   sales agent (GSA)
responsible gaming
return on investment
   (ROI)
roots tourism
seasonality
shopping tourism
solo travelers
sport events
sport tourism
tangible heritage
travel advisories
voluntourism
wildlife tourism
wine tourism
yield

REVIEW QUESTIONS

1. What have been the trends in international tourism arrivals in recent years?
2. What are the prospects for international tourism for the next five to ten years?
3. What are the major challenges facing DMOs in the international marketing, branding, and communications for pleasure and leisure travel?
4. Which geographic origin markets are emerging, and why have they earned this designation?
5. Which market segments have shown substantial growth potential in recent years?
6. What are the procedures that DMOs need to follow in marketing, branding, and communications for international pleasure and leisure tourists?

REFERENCES

Adventure Travel Trade Association (2020) "ATDI 2020 Released: Iceland and Czech Republic Score Top Marks for Adventure Tourism Competitiveness in 2020," www.adventuretravelnews. com/atdi-2020-released-iceland-and-czech-republic-score-top-marks-for-adventure-tourism-competitiveness-in-2020

American Gaming Association (2021) "State of the States 2021: The AGA Survey of the Commercial Casino Industry," www.americangaming.org/wp-content/uploads/2021/05/AGA-2021-State-of-the-States_FINALweb-150ppi.pdf

American Gaming Association (2022) "Responsible Gaming Code of Conduct," www.americangaming.org/responsibility-old/member-code-of-conduct/

L'Assiette de Pays (2022) Assiette de Pays, https://gastronomie.tourisme64. com/bonnes-tables/assiette-de-pays/

Banca D'Italia (2021) "Survey on International Tourism," www.bancaditalia.it/pubblicazioni/indagine-turismo-internazionale/2021-indagine-turismo-internazionale/en_statistiche_ITI_18062021.pdf?language_id=1

Benowitz, I., and Gaines, J. (2019) "Medical Tourism, CDC Yellow Book (Center for Disease Control)," https://wwwnc.cdc.gov/travel/yellowbook/2020/travel-for-work-other-reasons/medical-tourism

Brand USA (2021) "FY 2022 Objectives and Business Plan," www.thebrandusa.com/system/files/FY2022%20Objectives%20and%20Business%20Plan%20FINAL_0.pdf

——— (2022a) "Market Information," www.thebrandusa.com/resources/market-information

——— (2022b) "Restoring Brand USA Act Funding Plan May 2022," www.thebrandusa.com/system/files/Restoring_BrandUSA_Act_Funding_Plan_May_2022.pdf

CBI, Netherlands (2018) "What Are the Opportunities for Solo Tourism from Europe?" www.cbi.eu/market-information/tourism/solo-tourism

——— (2020a) "The European Market Potential for SAVE Tourism," www.cbi.eu/market-information/tourism/save-tourism/market-potential

——— (2020b) "The European Market for Sports Tourism," www.cbi.eu/market-information/tourism/sport-tourism/market-potential

——— (2021a) "Entering the European Market for Food Tourism Products," www.cbi.eu/market-information/tourism/food-tourism/market-entry

——— (2021b) "The European Market Potential for Adventure Tourism," www.cbi.eu/market-information/tourism/adventure-tourism/adventure-tourism/market-potential

Central Intelligence Agency (2022a) "The World Factbook: Brazil," www.cia.gov/the-world-factbook/countries/brazil/

——— (2022b) "The World Factbook: Russia," www.cia.gov/the-world-factbook/countries/russia/

——— (2022c) "The World Factbook: India," www.cia.gov/the-world-factbook/countries/india/

——— (2022d) "The World Factbook: China," www.cia.gov/the-world-factbook/countries/china/

CGR Asia (2022) S. Korea 2021 Casino Rev Up 13pct Y-O-Y Due to Kangwon Land," January 29, www.ggrasia.com/s-korea-2021-casino-rev-up-13pct-y-o-y-due-to-kangwon-land/

Choose Chicago (2014) "Promoting Chicago's Cultural Assets: A Cultural Tourism Strategy for Chicago," www.choosechicago.com/about-us/cultural-tourism/

Costa, C., Quintela, J., and Mendes, J. (2015) "Health and Wellness Tourism: A Strategic Plan for Tourism and Thermalism Valorization of São Pedro do Sul," in M. Peris-Ortiz and J. Álvarez-García (eds), *Health and Wellness Tourism: Emergence of a New Market Segment*, Cham: Springer, pp. 21–31.

Cruise Lines International Association (2022a) "2021 Global Market Report," https://cruising.org/-/media/clia-media/research/2022/2021-1r-clia-001-overview-global.ashx

——— (2022b) "2022 State of the Cruise Industry Outlook," https://cruising.org/-/media/clia-media/research/2022/clia-state-of-the-cruise-industry-2022_updated.ashx

Davies, P. (2022) "Catalonia to Spend €12 Million on Food and Wine Tourism Promotion," *Travel Weekly*, September 8, https://travelweekly.co.uk/news/tourism/catalonia-to-spend-e12-million-on-food-and-wine-tourism-promotion

Destination British Columbia (2013) "Tourism Business Essentials: Sport Tourism," www.destinationbc.ca/getattachment/programs/guides-workshops-and-webinars/guides/tourism-business-essentials-guides/tbe-guide-sport-tourism-jun2013_2.pdf.aspx

——— (2021) "International Visitor Arrivals," www.destinationbc.ca/content/uploads/2021/09/International-Visitor-Arrivals-July-2021.pdf

Destination Canada (2022) "Markets," www.destinationcanada.com/en/markets

Dillette, A. (2020) "Roots Tourism: A Second Wave of Double Consciousness for African Americans," *Journal of Sustainable Tourism*, 29 (2–3): 412–427.

Dole Plantation (2022) "Welcome to Dole Plantation," www.doleplantation.com/

Dubay, A. (2021) "Voluntourism: The Good and the Bad," World Vision Canada, www.worldvision.ca/stories/voluntourism-the-good-and-the-bad

Fáilte Ireland (2022) "Sharing Our Stories," www.failteireland.ie/FailteIreland/media/WebsiteStructure/Documents/2_Develop_Your_Business/3_Marketing_Toolkit/5_Cultural_Tourism/Heritage_Interpretation_Manual.pdf

FutureBrand (2022) "FutureBrand Country Index," www.futurebrand.com/country-brand-index

German National Tourist Board (2021) "2020 Facts and Figures," www.germany.travel/media/redaktion/pdf/ueber_uns/2021/DZT_ZahlenFlyer2021_EN.pdf

Getz, D., and Brown, G. (2006) "Critical Success Factors for Wine Tourism Regions: A Demand Analysis," *Tourism Management*, 27 (1): 146–158.

GlobalData (2022) "The Brazilian Market Is Increasingly Valuable, but Tourists Defy Travel Trends, Says Globaldata," July 28, www.globaldata.com/media/travel-tourism/brazilian-market-increasingly-valuable-tourists-defy-travel-trends-says-globaldata/

Guinness Storehouse Limited (2022) "Welcome to the Home of Guinness," www.guinness-storehouse.com/en

Gupta, R. (2019) "TravelHer: Five Reasons Why Marathon Tourism Is Becoming Popular," shethepeople.tv, www.shethepeople.tv/travellers/five-reasons-marathon-tourism-popular/

Hall, C. M., and Mitchell, R. (2000) "Wine Tourism in the Mediterranean: A Tool for Restructuring and Development," *Thunderbird International Business Review*, 42 (4): 445–465.

Huang, W.-J., Haller, W. J., and Ramshaw, G. P. (2013) "Diaspora Tourism and Homeland Attachment: An Exploratory Analysis," *Tourism Analysis*, 18: 285–296.

Interesse, G. (2022) "Tourism in China: 2022 Trends and Investment Opportunities," *China Briefing*, August 9, www.china-briefing.com/news/chinese-tourism-2022-trends-and-opportunities/

International Trade Administration (USA) (2022) "Survey of International Air Travelers (SIAT)," www.trade.gov/survey-international-air-travelers-siat

Isaac, R., and Budrytė-Ausiejienė, L. (2015) "Interpreting the Emotions of Visitors: A Study of Visitor Comment Books at the Grūtas Park Museum, Lithuania," *Scandinavian Journal of Hospitality and Tourism*, 15 (4): 400–424.

It's Your Planet (2022) "Indigenous and Cultural Tourism," https://itsyourplanet.org/travellers/indigenous-and-cultural-tourism/

Jang, S., Morrison, A. M., and O'Leary, J. T. (2004a) "A Procedure for Target Market Selection in Tourism," *Journal of Travel and Tourism Marketing*, 16 (1): 17–31.

———— (2004b) "The Tourism Efficient Frontier: An Approach to Selecting the Most Efficient Travel Segments," *Journal of Travel and Tourism Marketing*, 16 (4): 33–46.

Jones, S. (2022) "Hong Kong Is Giving Away 500,000 Free Airline Tickets to Tempt Tourists Back, Following the Pandemic Travel Slump, Reports Say," *Insider*, October 6, www.businessinsider.com/hong-kong-giving-away-500000-free-airline-tickets-2022-10

La Choza Chula (2022) "We Are La Choza Chula," https://lachozachula.org/

Laesser, C., Beritelli, P., and Riklin, T. (2016) "Solo Travel: Explorative Insights from a Mature Market (Switzerland)," *Travel and Tourism Research Association: Advancing Tourism Research Globally*, 57, https://scholarworks.umass.edu/ttra/2007/Presented_Papers/57

Lannen Designs (2022) "The Definition of a Casino," https://lannendesigns.com/the-definition-of-a-casino/

Li, T. E., McKercher, B., and Chan, E. T. H. (2020) "Towards a Conceptual Framework for Diaspora Tourism," *Current Issues in Tourism*, 23 (17): 2109–2126.

Light, D. (2017) "Progress in Dark Tourism and Thanatourism Research: An Uneasy Relationship with Heritage Tourism," *Tourism Management*, 61: 275–301.

Lonely Planet (2022) "Considering a Solo Trip? Here Are the 20 Things You Need to Know Before You Go," www.lonelyplanet.com/articles/20-tips-for-traveling-solo

Luković, T. (2013) "Nautical Tourism," Wallingford: CABI International.

Macao News (2022) "Gross Gaming Revenue Hits Mop 86.86 Billion in 2021," January 1, https://macaonews.org/gaming/gross-gaming-revenue-hits-mop-86-86-billion-in-2021/

Marcus, L., and Toh, M. (2022) "Anti-Asian Hate Crimes Are Scaring Chinese Travelers Away from the US," *CNN Travel*, September 30, https://edition.cnn.com/travel/article/chinese-travelers-to-us-gun-violence-intl-hnk-mic/index.html

Medical Tourism Association (2022) "About Us," www.medicaltourismassociation.com/about-us

Ministry of Business, Innovation and Employment (New Zealand) (2022) "International Visitor Survey (IVS)," www.mbie.govt.nz/immigration-and-tourism/tourism-research-and-data/tourism-data-releases/international-visitor-survey-ivs/

Ministry of Culture and Tourism (Türkiye) (2022) "Yearly Bulletins," www.ktb.gov.tr/EN-249299/yearly-bulletins.html

Morrison, A. M. (2022) *Hospitality and Travel Marketing*, 5th edn, London and New York: Routledge.

National Statistics Institute (Spain) (2022) "Tourist Movement on Borders," www.ine.es/jaxiT3/Tabla.htm?t=10822

Newland, K., and Taylor, C. (2010) "Heritage Tourism and Nostalgia Trade: A Diaspora Niche in the Development Landscape," United States Agency for International Development, www.migrationpolicy.org/pubs/diasporas-tradetourism.pdf

O'Connor, D. (2022) "Macau Casino Revenue Climbs 44 Percent in 2021, but Industry Remains Unsettled," Casino.org, January 1, www.casino.org/news/macau-casino-revenue-climbs-44-percent-in-2021/

Office for National Statistics (UK) (2022) "International Passenger Survey," www.ons.gov.uk/surveys/informationforhouseholdsandindividuals/householdandindividualsurveys/internationalpassengersurvey

Ontario Culinary Tourism Alliance (2022) "Ontario Culinary," https://ontarioculinary.com/

Partners for Livable Communities (2014) "Cultural Heritage Tourism," http://livable.nonprofitsoapbox.com/storage/documents/reports/CBC/culturalheritagetourism.pdf

Rinschede, G. (1992) "Forms of Religious Tourism," *Annals of Tourism Research*, 19 (1): 51–67.

Shen, Y., Kokkranikal, J., Christensen, C. P., and Morrison, A. M. (2023) "Perceived Importance of and Satisfaction with Marina Attributes in Sailing Tourism Experiences: A Kano Model Approach," *Journal of Outdoor Recreation and Tourism*, 48 (1): 30–42.

Slovenian Tourist Board (2018) "Taste Slovenia: Action Plan for the Development and Marketing of Gastronomy Tourism 2019–2023," www.europeanregionofgastronomy.org/wp-content/uploads/2019/04/Slovenia-Gastronomy-Tourism-Plan.pdf

Smith, M., and Puczkó, L. (2014) *Health and Wellness Tourism*, 2nd edn, London and New York: Routledge.

Solotravel.365 (2022) "What Does Solo Travel Actually Mean?" www.solotravel365.com/travel-guide/solo-travel/what-does-solo-travel-actually-mean/

Statistics New Zealand (2022) "International travel," https://www.stats.govt.nz/indicators/international-travel-provisional

Stone, P. R. (2006) "A Dark Tourism Spectrum: Towards a Typology of Death and Macabre Related Tourist Sites, Attractions and Exhibitions," *Tourism*, 54 (2): 145–160.

Tang, J. (2022) "Nevada Sets All-Time Gambling Revenue Records as Casinos End 2021 on a High," January 28, https://gamblingindustrynews.com/news/las-vegas/nevada-gambling-revenue-2021/

Tarlow, P. (2005) "Dark Tourism: The Appealing 'Dark' Side of Tourism and More," in M. Novelli (ed.), *Niche Tourism*, pp. 47–58.

The International Ecotourism Society (2015) "What Is Ecotourism?" https://ecotourism.org/what-is-ecotourism/

Timothy, D. J. (2005) *Shopping Tourism, Retailing and Leisure*, Bristol: Channel View.

Tourism Australia (2021) "Tourism Australia Relaunches Aussie Specialist Program," www.tourism.australia.com/en/news-and-events/news-stories/tourism-australia-relaunches-aussie-specialist-program.html

Tourism Research Australia (2022) "International Visitor Survey results June 2022," www.tra.gov.au/data-and-research/reports/international-visitor-survey-results/international-visitor-survey-results

Tourism Malaysia (2022a) "Tourist Arrivals to Malaysia by Country of Nationality December 2021," http://mytourismdata.tourism.gov.my/?page_id=14#!from=2021&to=2022&destination=34MY

——— (2022b) "About Shopping," www.tourism.gov.my/niche/shopping

Tourisme Charlevoix (2022) "Route des Saveurs," www.tourisme-charlevoix.com/quoi-faire/routes-et-circuits/route-des-saveurs/

Tourwriter (2022) "Why Bike Tourism Ticks All the Boxes for Travellers in 2021," www.tourwriter.com/future-bike-tourism-2021/

United Nations Educational, Scientific and Cultural Organization (2022a) "World Heritage List," https://whc.unesco.org/en/list/

——— (2022b) "What Is Intangible Heritage?" https://ich.unesco.org/en/what-is-intangible-heritage-00003

University of Las Vegas Gaming Research Center (2022) "Nevada Gaming Revenues, 1984–2021, https://gaming.library.unlv.edu/reports/NV_1984_present.pdf

United Nations World Tourism Organization (2014) "Shopping Tourism," www.unwto.org/shopping-tourism

——— (2016) "UNWTO Tourism International Conference on Tourism and Sports, Danang, Vietnam: Technical Note," https://webunwto.s3-eu-west-1.amazonaws.com/imported_images/45930/technical_note_8.pdf

——— (2020a) "International Tourism Highlights 2020 edition," www.e-unwto.org/doi/pdf/10.18111/9789284422456

——— (2020b) "International Tourism Growth Continues to Outpace the Global Economy," www.unwto.org/international-tourism-growth-continues-to-outpace-the-economy

——— (2022a) "International Tourism Back to 60% of Pre-Pandemic Levels in January–July 2022," September 26, www.unwto.org/taxonomy/term/347

——— (2022b) "Tourism and Culture," www.unwto.org/tourism-and-culture

US Department of Commerce (2022) "National Travel and Tourism Office: International Visitation to and from the United States," www.trade.gov/sites/default/files/2021-03/Fact%20Sheet%20International%20Visitation%20FINAL.pdf

US Department of State (2022) "Russia Travel Advisory," https://travel.state.gov/content/travel/en/traveladvisories/traveladvisories/russia-travel-advisory.html

Vietnam Investment Review (2022) "Thailand Targets Central Asia to Boost Inbound Tourism," October 5, https://vir.com.vn/thailand-targets-central-asia-to-boost-inbound-tourism-96875.html

VisitBritain (2022a) "Quarterly Inbound Update and Full Year 2021," www.visitbritain.org/sites/default/files/vb-corporate/2021_ips_summary_16th_august_2022.pdf

——— (2022b) "Inbound Trends by UK Nation, Region and County," www.visitbritain.org/inbound-trends-uk-nation-region-county

——— (2022c) "Brazil," www.visitbritain.org/markets/brazil

——— (2022d) "Russia," www.visitbritain.org/markets/russia

———— (2022e) "India," www.visitbritain.org/markets/india

———— (2022f) "China," www.visitbritain.org/markets/china

Weed, M. and Bull, C. (2004) *Sports Tourism: Participants, Policy and Providers*. London: Routledge.

Wong, D. (2022) "Great Singapore Sale 2022: Everything You Need to Know About It," *Truly Singapore*, July 7, https://trulysingapore.com/great-singapore-sale/

World Bank (2022) "Is a Global Recession Imminent?" www.worldbank.org/en/research/brief/global-recession

World Monuments Fund (2017) "Fundidora Park," www.wmf.org/project/fundidora-park/

Xploreasia.org (2022) "Amazing Thailand Homestay Program," https://xploreasia.org/amazing-thailand-homestay-program/

19

Business Travel and Business Event Markets

Taking care of business

DOI: 10.4324/9781003343356-23

Warming Up

You have learned in Chapters 17 and 18 that the COVID-19 pandemic had a profound (and negative) effect on domestic and international travel. More domestic travel was reported in Chapter 17 and the collapse of international tourism featured in Chapter 18. Then what happened to business travel and business events? The answer is that traditional business travel and business events declined precipitously and were mainly replaced by virtual communications.

The business travel and business event markets are the backbone of the client base for many city destinations around the world. For some DMOs, they are the main focus, and pleasure and leisure travelers are of secondary concern. For example, this is true for hundreds of CVBs in North America and convention bureaus in Europe and elsewhere as well as for many other larger DMOs in other parts of the world.

Although DMOs cannot directly influence regular business travel (except perhaps blended travel trips), they play a major role in attracting business events to their destinations. Regular business travel motivations are quite different from the motivations of leisure and VFR travelers, which were discussed in Chapters 16 to 18. Unlike regular business travel, where the destination is fixed, business event organizers have a choice of potential destinations, and tourism products play a role in their site selection decision-making.

Business travel and business events represent a significant proportion of domestic and international tourism in many destinations around the world. The global economic crisis in 2007 to 2009 had a major adverse impact on these markets, and there was a disastrous influence as a result of the COVID-19 pandemic.

DMOs are very professional in their marketing approaches to business events, and this is required because of the high level of competition and bidding situations. This chapter introduces some outstanding examples of marketing, branding, and communications approaches for business events markets.

Your author has been involved in organizing several conferences and webinars, and exhibiting at trade shows. His experience is reflected in this chapter.

Definitions of Market Segments

One of the toughest challenges in this chapter is how to define the market segments of business travel and business events. You might ask, why is this so? The answer is because people use terminology interchangeably and definitions tend to vary from region to region and even by country. For example, there was a period when the term MICE was used quite widely and particularly in Asia. However, there has now been a movement in the tourism sector not to use this term anymore and instead use business events (e.g., Business Events Australia 2022).

Before providing the definitions, you should know that an alternative collective term for all of them is "business tourism" (International Congress and Convention Association [ICCA] 2022). In this book, the preferred terminology is business travel and business events because this term is more descriptive of the two major components of this form of tourism.

Regular Business Travel

The types of business-related travel tend to fall into the following seven categories:

1. customer visits;
2. sales and marketing;

3. internal meetings;
4. employee training;
5. conferences and conventions;
6. trade shows and exhibitions;
7. incentive and reward (Fig. 19.1).

For the purposes of this book, the first four categories are included in regular business travel, and the last three are within business events.

- Customer visits
- Sales and marketing
- Internal meetings
- Employee training
- Conferences and conventions
- Trade shows and exhibitions
- Incentive and reward

Categories of business-related travel

Figure 19.1 Categories of business-related travel.

Business Events

There is a huge variety of definitions of business events, and it is really confusing to try to make sense out of them. This chapter will attempt to remove the confusion for you and the following is a set of definitions for the most commonly held business events.

The USTA (2012) says that business events include meetings, conventions, conferences, trade shows, exhibitions, and incentive travel. They last at least four hours, include a minimum of ten participants and take place at a contracted venue. This definition is useful because it specifies a minimum duration and a number of participants (four hours; ten participants). The other useful part of this definition is that it specifies that events must be held at contracted venues, and this means that the events are held at places where there is a contract between the organizers and the facility owners (e.g., convention center, hotel or resort, cruise ship). The following definition from Australia is more comprehensive in specifying the types of business events.

> **DEFINITION**
>
> **Business events**
>
> Any public or private activity consisting of a minimum of fifteen persons with a common interest or vocation, held in a specific venue or venues, and hosted by an organization (or organizations). This may include (but not limited to): conferences, conventions, symposia, congresses, incentive group events, marketing events, special celebrations, seminars, courses, public or trade shows, product launches, exhibitions, company general meetings, corporate retreats, study tours, or training programs (Business Events Council of Australia 2022).

CITYWIDE

A citywide is an event that requires the use of a convention center or event complex and multiple hotels in the host city (Events Industry Council 2022a). Thus, this is a very large business event held in an urban setting.

CONFERENCE

This is one of the major categories of business events. The International Association of Professional Congress Organizers (IAPCO) defines a conference as:

> **DEFINITION**
>
> **Conference**
>
> A participatory meeting designed for discussion, fact-finding, problem solving and consultation. As compared with a congress, a conference is normally smaller in scale and more select in character—features which tend to facilitate the exchange of information. The term conference carries no special connotation as to frequency. Though not inherently limited in time, conferences are usually of limited duration with specific objectives (IAPCO 2022).

CONGRESS

IAPCO (2022) defines a congress as the regular coming together on a representational basis of several hundred, or even thousands, of individuals belonging to a single professional, cultural, religious or other group. One example is the World Vaccine Congress (Europe) held in Barcelona in October 2022. This event can attract more than 1,000 vaccine experts, when held in Europe or North America.

CONVENTION

This is usually taken as the "C" in MICE although some prefer to use conference. A convention is typically organized by an association with a membership base. For example, Destinations

International holds an annual convention for its DMO members (Destinations International 2022) (Fig. 19.2). Unlike with meetings, there may be an exhibit component at conventions, but they are a secondary part of the event.

Figure 19.2 Destinations International Annual Convention in Toronto 2022.

Here is the definition of a convention:

Exhibition

Exhibition is the "E" in the MICE acronym and these events are significant in destination marketing, branding, and communications. The World Travel Market (WTM) held in London in November is a great example of a key tourism sector exhibition (RX 2022) (Fig. 19.3), as is ITB that is held in Berlin (Messe Berlin 2022).

Figure 19.3 The World Travel Market in London, 2022.

Here is the definition of an exhibition:

> **DEFINITION**
>
> ## Exhibition
>
> An event at which products, services or promotional materials are displayed to attendees visiting exhibits on the show floor. These events focus primarily on business-to-business (B2B) relationships, but consumers are also allowed to attend on certain days (Events Industry Council 2022a).

EXPOSITION

An exposition or expo for short is a large-scale event with a global appeal and participation. Here is the official definition:

Exposition

Expos are global events dedicated to finding solutions to fundamental challenges facing humanity by offering a journey inside a chosen theme through engaging and immersive activities. Organized and facilitated by governments and bringing together countries and international organizations (Official Participants), these major public events are unrivaled in their ability to gather millions of visitors, create new dynamics, and catalyze change in their host cities. Four types of Expo are organized under the auspices of the Bureau International des Expositions (BIE): World Expos, Specialized Expos, Horticultural Expos, and the Triennale di Milano (BIE 2022).

INCENTIVE TRAVEL

The "I" in MICE stands for incentive travel which is a business event with a motivational component for participants. You should note that these are commonly called incentives. Here is a definition of the concept:

Incentive travel

Incentive travel is defined as a trip designed to motivate, incentivize, and reward employees or business associates. This type of trip could range from being given to one individual, all the way up to large group awards made available only after certain targets have been met throughout the year (Celebrity Cruises 2022).

MEETING

This is the "M" in MICE. At a meeting the primary activity of the participants is to attend educational sessions, participate in discussions, social functions, or attend other organized events (Events Industry Council 2022a). Meetings do not have an exhibit component according to this definition.

TRADE SHOW

A trade show is a business-to-business (B2B) event. They are exhibitions of products and/or services held for members of common or related industries (Events Industry Council 2022a). Trade shows are not usually open to the public.

You may be a little confused because there seems to be overlap among some of these definitions, and some further explanation is in order. The main issue is because of differences in terminology between North America and Europe. The term convention is more of a North American term and encompasses the ideas of congresses and conferences. The term "congress" is more of a European concept, and you might think of it as being synonymous with convention although the two are not exactly the same.

The terms "exhibition" and "trade show" are quite similar, but the difference in meaning is that trade shows are exclusively B2B. Exhibitions have a consumer component as well and those components are often referred to as consumer shows.

The terms that are used for meetings include "forums," "seminars," "webinars," "symposia," and "workshops." For the sake of keeping things simple, this chapter will not define these additional terms. However, there are some further definitions about the participants of business events that you need to know about.

DEFINITION

Attendees

Attendees (or participants) are a combination of delegates, exhibitors, media, speakers, and guests and their companions attending an event; basically, this term includes everybody who participates in business events.

Delegates

Delegates attend an event to primarily visit the exhibits or attend meetings and/or conference sessions. It can mean a person that is chosen or authorized to attend a given business event.

Exhibitors

The people who attend trade shows and exhibitions and staff the exhibits at these events are referred to as exhibitors.

Site inspections

A site inspection is an in-person and detailed inspection of a hotel/resort, convention/exhibition center, or other proposed venue for a business event, by a meeting planner and other representatives of the event organizers.

Size and Importance of Business Travel and Business Event Markets

Tourism sector advocates usually argue that business travel and business events are large markets with high daily spending in destinations. In the following materials, you will see that these claims are valid.

Business Travel and Business Events

Business travel and business event markets are substantial in both domestic and international tourism. You learned in Chapter 18 that for 2019, UNWTO estimated that business and professional trip purposes accounted for 11 percent of all international tourist arrivals (UNWTO 2020).

Figure 19.4 shows the breakdown between leisure and business spending in the world's top destinations as defined by UNWTO (2020); the percentages shown in the table are from the respective country reports by the WTTC (2022). As you can see, the business spending proportions vary from a high of 34 percent for Canada to a low of 4 percent for Mexico. However, most of the business spending proportions are in the range of 15 percent to 30 percent.

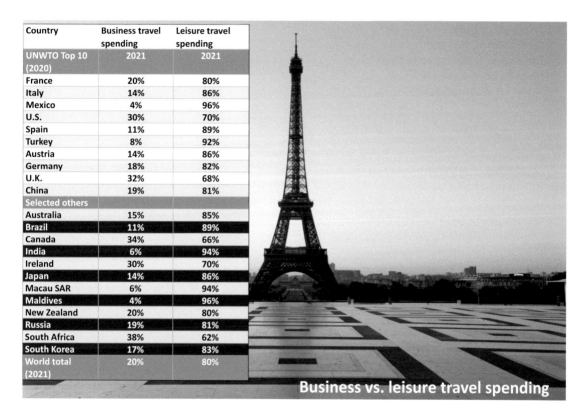

Country	Business travel spending	Leisure travel spending
UNWTO Top 10 (2020)	2021	2021
France	20%	80%
Italy	14%	86%
Mexico	4%	96%
U.S.	30%	70%
Spain	11%	89%
Turkey	8%	92%
Austria	14%	86%
Germany	18%	82%
U.K.	32%	68%
China	19%	81%
Selected others		
Australia	15%	85%
Brazil	11%	89%
Canada	34%	66%
India	6%	94%
Ireland	30%	70%
Japan	14%	86%
Macau SAR	6%	94%
Maldives	4%	96%
New Zealand	20%	80%
Russia	19%	81%
South Africa	38%	62%
South Korea	17%	83%
World total (2021)	20%	80%

Business vs. leisure travel spending

Figure 19.4 Business vs. leisure spending (WTTC 2022).

The following is a selection of indicators on the size of the business travel and business event markets for a set of countries based upon their national travel surveys and statistics:

UK

There were 15.6 million domestic business trips in 2019 in Great Britain. This 2019 figure of business trips was 12.7 percent of all domestic trips in Great Britain; however, business travel spending represented a higher 18.5 percent of the total spending for trips (VisitBritain and Kantar 2022).

USA

The USTA reported that business travel declined rapidly in 2020, and improved slightly in 2021 although total business travel spending remained at 41 percent of the 2019 figure (USTA 2022b). There were 464 million domestic business trips taken in the USA in 2019 (Condor Ferries 2022).

Australia

There were 15.9 million domestic business overnight visitors in Australia, and they generated 63 million visitor nights in all accommodations for the year ending June 2022. These figures were slightly above the comparable period of 2020–2021. Business travelers represented 18.5 percent of all domestic overnight visitors and 19.3 percent of total visitor nights (Tourism Research Australia 2022).

Business Events

There are many statistics published on the size and importance of business events but none at a worldwide level that are truly comprehensive of all business events in every country. The Union of International Associations (UIA) and the ICCA publish worldwide business event statistics, but they are only for international association events and domestic business events and some international business events are not included. Most of the complete sets of business event statistics are produced individually by country.

Union of International Associations

UIA is based in Brussels, Belgium, and has been publishing statistics on business events for more than sixty years. UIA (2016) reported that approximately 12,350 association international meetings took place worldwide in 2015. The top ten countries for these international meetings in 2016 were: (1) South Korea, (2) Belgium, (3) Singapore, (4) USA, (5) France (tied), (5) Japan (tied), (7) Spain, (8) Austria, (9) Germany, and (10) the Netherlands. The top ten cities were (1) Brussels, (2) Singapore, (3) Seoul, (4) Paris, (5) Vienna, (6) Tokyo, (7) Bangkok, (8) Berlin, (9) Barcelona, and (10) Geneva (UIA 2017). Not included in these figures from UIA are purely national meetings, meetings with an exclusively religious, didactic, political, commercial or sporting nature, and corporate and incentive meetings. The numbers of meetings maintained at over 12,000 per year until 2019, then declined in 2020 (to less than 5,000) and 2021 (just above 5,000) (UIA 2022).

International Congress and Convention Association

According to the ICCA (2020), based in Amsterdam, approximately 13,254 rotating international association meetings were held around the world in 2019. By the ICCA's definition, an international association meeting must have at least 300 participants, of whom at least 40 percent must be from countries other than the host country, and at least five nationalities must be represented. ICCA also requires that international association meetings must rotate among at least three countries (UIA does not have this requirement).

ICCA also produces a list of international association meetings by country, and the top twenty countries are shown in Figure 19.5. It is noteworthy that seven of the top ten destinations for international association meetings (US, Germany, Spain, UK, France, Italy, and China) are usually also in the top ten destinations for international tourist arrivals according to UNWTO.

ICCA country rankings

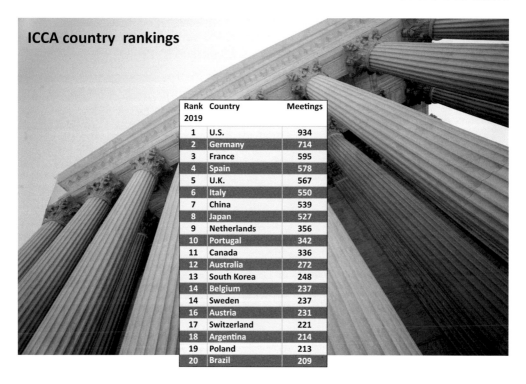

Rank 2019	Country	Meetings
1	U.S.	934
2	Germany	714
3	France	595
4	Spain	578
5	U.K.	567
6	Italy	550
7	China	539
8	Japan	527
9	Netherlands	356
10	Portugal	342
11	Canada	336
12	Australia	272
13	South Korea	248
14	Belgium	237
14	Sweden	237
16	Austria	231
17	Switzerland	221
18	Argentina	214
19	Poland	213
20	Brazil	209

Figure 19.5 The ICCA top twenty ranking country destinations for international association meetings (ICCA 2020).

EXAMPLE 19.1

Importance of Business Events in Germany

This example underlines the importance of business events and their contribution to business health in general. It explains the ranking and extent of business events in Germany.

> Meetings, conferences, and congresses are platforms for the exchange of know-how, experiences, and ideas. They provide essential input for political, economic, scientific, and social processes and thus promote innovation and generate solutions. In Germany, meetings and congresses play an important economic role: in the 2019 ranking of the ICCA, Germany was ranked first among European meeting and congress destinations, a position it has been holding for many years. Worldwide, Germany ranks second behind the USA. In 2019, almost three million events with over 420 million attendees took place in Germany. Business events are important for Germany as a business location.
>
> (Dienes et al. 2022)

Learning Point

Germany is a key player in business events in Europe and globally. Business events are critical to overall business success in a country.

The ICCA also tracks the number of international association meetings by city, and for 2019, the top ten cities were (1) Barcelona, (2) Paris, (3) Madrid, (4) Lisbon, (5) Vienna, (6) Berlin, (7) London, (8) Milan, (9) Copenhagen, and (10) Amsterdam (Fig. 19.6).

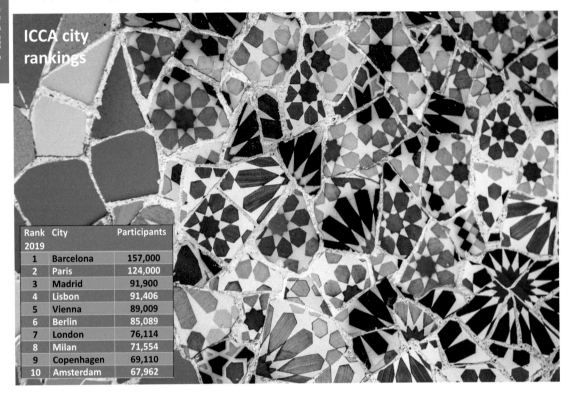

ICCA city rankings

Rank 2019	City	Participants
1	Barcelona	157,000
2	Paris	124,000
3	Madrid	91,900
4	Lisbon	91,406
5	Vienna	89,009
6	Berlin	85,089
7	London	76,114
8	Milan	71,554
9	Copenhagen	69,110
10	Amsterdam	67,962

Figure 19.6 The ICCA top ten ranking city destinations for international association meetings (ICCA 2020).

Benefits of Business Travel and Business Event Markets

This is an interesting topic because of the differences between regular business travel and business events. The benefits of business events are typically expressed in economic terms and particularly in total expenditures and expenditures per capita. The advantages of regular business travel trips that are not associated with a business event are often expressed through the benefits that accrue to the companies rather than to the destinations. More recently, however, groups such as the USTA, Global Business Travel Association, and the ICCA have put greater emphasis on researching and disseminating data on the economic and broader impacts of business travel as a whole.

EXAMPLE 19.2

Economic Importance of Business Travel

This example argues that business travel is good for business and if business travel is reduced by a company, it will suffer negative consequences.

Total direct travel spending recovered to 75 percent of 2019 levels in 2021. However, total business travel remained at just 53 percent of 2019 levels in 2021—and group meetings and events were at a meager 36 percent of 2019 levels. But a return to a thriving travel industry—and American economy—is dependent on the swift return of business travel and open international travel market.

Our research shows that over half of large-company executives agree that reducing business travel will lead to long-term losses.

(USTA 2022a)

Learning Point

Business success is related to business travel.

Benefits of Business Travel

An interesting study was conducted by Oxford Economics on behalf of the USTA and published in 2009. It was called "The Return on Investment of US Business Travel" and was a unique perspective on business travel and its benefits. The study pinpointed four benefits of business travel: (1) keeping customers (2) converting prospects (3) building relational networks and (4) investing in people (Oxford Economics and USTA 2009). The study was conducted during the economic recession of 2009 in the USA, and companies were already cutting back on business travel to reduce their costs. However, the research study concluded that cutting back on business travel could reduce a company's profits for several years. On average, a company would give up 17 percent of its profits in the first year of eliminating business travel, and then it would take more than three years for profits to recover.

EXAMPLE 19.3

How Less Business Travel Influences Economic Development

This example reports on significant research by the Mastercard Center for Inclusive Growth. It estimates the impacts on global GDP from the cessation of business travel.

If Germany stopped business travel, global GDP could decline by an estimated 4.8 percent. The researchers' predictions suggest that Austria would likely be most affected by the stoppage, followed by South Africa, Switzerland, Nigeria, Czech Republic, and Türkiye.

If the USA ceased all business travel, global GDP could decline by an estimated 1 percent. Canada and Mexico would likely be most affected, but so too would Haiti, Jamaica, El Salvador, Rwanda, and Peru.

Not only does business travel account for one-fifth of the global travel and hospitality sectors, but as this research shows, it drives economic growth and diversification. Yet, a recent McKinsey report shows that historically business travel rebounds from crises more slowly than leisure travel. They also predict

> that domestic business travel will return first, which risks setting emerging markets farther behind, given that these markets are already poorly connected and risk becoming completely cut off from the world's global body of know-how.
>
> (Mastercard 2020)

Learning Point

Business travel levels are directly related to global GDP.

There are also costs to regular business travel that need to be controlled by companies in the same way as other costs. These are often called T&E, or travel and entertainment, expenses. T&E costs are difficult to control because many individuals incur travel expenses and companies must rely on their honesty and integrity in reporting T&E expenses accurately. In fact, a survey of financial decision-makers conducted by Forrester Research found that T&E expenses were thought to be among the most difficult to control (DeLuna 2014). It is strongly recommended that every company should develop, implement and enforce a T&E policy for all their travelers. Policy compliance is the name companies give to the steps and procedures used to encourage employees to adhere to T&E guidelines.

Benefits of Business Events

The benefits of business events tend to be quoted in terms of delegate expenditures. The strongest argument is often that business event participants spend more than other tourists on a per capita daily basis. According to the Vienna Convention Bureau (2021), business event participants spent €541 per capita per day in 2018 compared to an average of €276 for other visitors. VisitBritain (2021) reported that a business visitor spent 41 percent more per night than a leisure visitor in 2019. The Vancouver Convention Centre (2022) in British Columbia, Canada, estimates that its non-resident delegates are in British Columbia for 4.2 nights and spend C$1,400 in the province.

The USTA (2017) divides the economic benefits of meetings and business events into four categories: spending, payroll, jobs, and tax receipts. The USTA definition of benefits tends to be more economic and short-term in measurement; however, business events have impacts that may spread over several years. The Association of Australian Convention Bureaux (2022) provides another perspective of the benefits of business events because they emphasize the longer term beyond tourism benefits to communities.

EXAMPLE 19.4

Beyond Tourism Benefits of Business Events

The benefits of business events go well beyond direct spending with tourism sector stakeholders. This example is an expression of an industry association in Australia about the "beyond tourism" benefits of business events.

> International business events play a significant role in building a stronger, more productive and more diverse Australian economy. Around the world, business

events are being used as strategic tools for attracting trade and investment as well as global talent. For Australia, hosting international business events offers high-yield and long-term benefits accruing from growth in the visitor and knowledge-based economies.

The "beyond tourism benefits" are:

- attracting global talent
- transferring knowledge
- encouraging foreign investment
- stimulating trade
- fostering innovation
- boosting productivity
- nurturing research collaboration
- promoting cultural exchange
- delivering community benefits.

(Association of Australian Convention Bureaux 2022)

Learning Point

The benefits of business events are extensive and can be long-lasting for communities.

Therefore, business events have both short-term economic benefits and long-term community and company benefits. Their strongest economic benefit is the above-average daily spending rates of participants.

EXAMPLE 19.5

Meeting Legacies

A meeting legacy represents a long-term impact of a business event on a destination. This example describes ways of measuring meeting legacies based upon research by the BestCities Global Alliance, GainingEdge, and MeetDenmark.

Meeting legacies are the long-term impacts which a meeting has on wider society. Meeting legacy goals can be defined for both the destination in which the meeting is held as well as for the association.

- Environmental legacies: Green energy transition; carbon neutrality; protection of ecosystems.
- Political legacies: Policy reform; enhanced state regulations; improved governmental services.
- Economic legacies: Business growth; increased exports; national economic growth.
- Sectoral legacies: HR capacity development; advances in research, technology, and practice; industry adaptation and mitigation.
- Social legacies: Highly skilled workforce; new medical treatment discoveries; improved access to health services.

(BestCities Global Alliance 2020)

> **Learning Point**
>
> It is crucial for destinations to determine the long-term legacies of individual business events.

However, business travel and business events are not without challenges, and there are important issues as well. Chapter 19 now reviews the most significant of these challenges and issues for destination marketing, branding, and communications, and product development.

Challenges for Business Travel and Business Events

Business travel and business events passed through a very challenging phase in 2007 to 2009 because of the adverse global economic conditions and their after-effects in the following years. During that time, companies cut back on their business travel costs, and fewer people attended business events. Since then, up until the global pandemic, a recovery took place until COVID arrived. The challenges facing business travel and business events are not just economic and can be classified into:

1. recovery from pandemic;
2. sustainability and climate change;
3. market transformation;
4. technological innovation and adoption;
5. competitive intensity;
6. economic downturns;
7. safety and security;
8. interdependency;
9. policy compliance and cost control;
10. reputation and credibility (Fig. 19.7).

Each of the challenges in Figure 19.7 is now briefly discussed:

Challenges for business travel and business events

- Pandemic recovery
- Sustainability and climate change
- Market transformation
- Technological innovation and adoption
- Competitive intensity
- Economic downturns
- Safety and security concerns
- Supply chain interdependency
- Policy compliance and cost control
- Reputation and credibility

Figure 19.7 Challenges for business travel and business events.

PANDEMIC RECOVERY

The impacts of COVID-19 on business travel and business events were enormous and are still being felt. While a partial recovery is happening, there is uncertainty about the long-term effects of three years of business disruption.

EXAMPLE 19.6

Business Travel Has Changed Forever

Business travel is a critical component of the market for many destinations. Since 2019, this trip-purpose segment has experienced disruptions and changes. This example describes some of the changes.

> At a *New York Times* event back in November 2020, Bill Gates sent a chill through the travel industry when he predicted that more than 50 percent of business travel and more than 30 percent of days worked in offices would go away permanently.
>
> Flash forward sixteen months and Gates' assessment is now accepted, more or less, both inside and outside the travel industry. "The pandemic has led to extensive use of videoconferencing and virtual meetings, and many companies expect virtual work to persist over the long term," concluded the US Bureau of Labor Statistics in a February 2022 report forecasting employment demand in various industries. The labor bureau predicted that many types of business trips would be replaced by virtual meetings, though some in-person trips—for instance, sales pitches and trade conferences—would return to pre-pandemic normal.
>
> (Kelleher 2022)

Learning Point

Some destinations will have to consider what to do to compensate for less business travel.

SUSTAINABILITY AND CLIMATE CHANGE

Business travel and business events contribute to greenhouse gas emissions as a result of air travel and the use of non-reusable materials. It is necessary for the sector to limit its impacts on climate change in the future. Later in Chapter 19, you will hear about the movement toward green or sustainable meetings.

These challenges are not just the result of societal changes and calls for greater social responsibility (Chapter 2), they are being required by business travelers. Sixty percent of business travelers indicate that the pandemic has made them more socially and environmentally conscious about their impact on the world when traveling (Crowne Plaza Hotels and Resorts/IHG Hotels and Resorts 2022).

MARKET TRANSFORMATION

The customer profile for business travel and business events is undergoing fundamental changes as the impacts of generational and other social and economic trends are felt. The increased attention to Millennials is one of the major of these trends. Contemporary business travelers are much more challenging and complex than their predecessors (Association of Corporate Travel Executives (ACTE)/American Express Global Business Travel 2017). They demand more flexibility in travel and expect instant service at the press of a key on a smartphone, tablet, or laptop. These travelers are more concerned with work–life balance and quality of life.

Examples of the need for greater flexibility are the blended travel and bleisure trend and increasing use of sharing economy providers. A recent study found that 45 percent of travelers in the UK, planned to add leisure days to future business trips, and the figure was higher for US travelers, at 60 percent (Crowne Plaza Hotels and Resorts/IHG Hotels and Resorts 2022).

Technological Innovation and Adoption

New technologies and technological changes are having a profound effect on business travel and business events. You learned about many of these technologies in Chapter 15. Here are just a few of the technological adaptation challenges.

Incorporating Use of Social Media Platforms

Chapters 13 to 15 highlighted the explosion in consumer use of social media platforms, and these so-called Web 2.0 tools are presenting a host of new challenges as well as opportunities for business travel and business events. Is the use of social media platforms a help or hindrance to business travel and business events? Does using social media platforms distract business people from doing their real work? These are good questions indeed, but most observers believe that the use of social media is a positive development for corporations and NPOs.

Technology as a Substitute for Travel

ICTs were discussed in Chapter 15, and they are having a very positive impact on destination management and marketing, by providing DMOs with many new tools and channels. But is it possible that ICTs could be both friend and foe for tourism destinations? Virtual travel (through virtual reality) and virtual meetings (through platforms like Zoom and Teams) are on a strong upward growth trend and may lead to less business travel for destinations.

EXAMPLE 19.7

Airlines Struggling to Replace Lucrative Business Travelers

This example describes how airlines are having difficulties due to declines in business travel.

> Corporations have recognized that they can get their business done with fewer flights taken. Leisure traffic has rebounded strongly, but airlines cannot make up the revenue from the loss of even a small amount of business travel. That's why you see airlines labeling long-time trends like bundling business and leisure trips or leisure customers willing to pay for a nicer experience as new, post-pandemic realities. Some airline CEOs are still clinging to the myth that

business traffic has not really changed and it's just a matter of time until things go back to the way they were.

(Baldanza 2022)

Learning Point

Companies and destinations should not be over-reliant on one source of business.

ICTs are getting much better and will improve further in the future. Two-way video and audio are now available in many more ICTs, including laptops, smartphones and tablets as well as the dedicated video conferencing platforms. Webinars are very popular because of their convenience and the comfort of attending in a person's own office or even at home. It is noteworthy that several tourism sector associations and businesses are themselves making extensive use of webinars, including PATA headquartered in Bangkok.

Although older generations (Baby Boomers) tend to favor face-to-face meetings over technology-assisted get-togethers, this may not be so strong a sentiment in the future when Millennials and Generation Z move into the decision-making positions. These tech-savvy, Internet generation business travelers will make greater use of ICTs for all types of business communications. After all, this is not just an issue of whether or not to travel, but these ICTs can greatly improve business communications at a global level while also boosting productivity and profitability.

Adding Corporate Travel Apps

With almost all business travelers using smartphone apps, it makes sense for companies to issue their own corporate travel apps to their travelers. Some 89 percent of corporate travel managers in 2017 provided and planned to provide apps for travel bookings (Association of Corporate Travel Executives/American Express Global Business Travel 2017).

Introducing AI

Artificial intelligence will have a significant impact on business travel and business events in the future (Flight Centre Travel Group Limited 2022). Generally, AI is getting machines to simulate aspects of human intelligence, and this is demonstrated in voice recognition applications.

EXAMPLE 19.8

AI to Play a Greater Role in Business Travel

This example advocates for greater use of AI in business travel, especially by travel management companies (TMCs), airlines, hotels, and other tourism sector stakeholders.

AI is playing an ever-increasing role in our private and business lives. The huge popularity of messaging platforms like WhatsApp and digital assistants like Amazon's Alexa, Google's Siri and Cortana has propelled AI into the mainstream, where corporates are generating new business value by integrating voice into their technology, thanks to AI.

> Essentially, artificial intelligence performs computing tasks that previously required human assistance, enabling computers to make relevant responses to specific questions or requests. AI and travel are the perfect fit because of the volume and depth of information travel companies—TMCs in particular—hold on travelers, their travel patterns and preferences. In a travel world where personalization and big data are the megatrends, artificial intelligence is the great enabler.
>
> (Flight Centre Travel Group Limited 2022)

Learning Point

Artificial intelligence and big data can be aligned to provide better service for business travelers.

COMPETITIVE INTENSITY

The competition for many major business events is global and intense. Most events are bidding situations where competing destinations must vie against each other to try to find the edge that will allow them to win. Prices are always a major factor in site selection decisions, and some destinations can offer larger price incentives and sponsorship packages than others to secure events. Some call this buying the business but in fact financial support from host destinations to event organizers has become more common. The Busan Tourism Organization Convention Bureau in South Korea offers a variety of financial assistance for companies or organizations that want to attract and hold corporate meetings and incentive events that exceed the internally stipulated standards (Busan Tourism Organization 2022).

ECONOMIC DOWNTURNS

Government agencies and private companies are cutting back on business-related travel because of COVID-19 and the accompanying negative economic conditions that have adversely affected many of the major developed countries. This has particularly been true in 2020 to 2022. Many government agencies are operating with reduced budgets, and the private sector has been cost cutting to maintain profitability of operations.

Unfortunately, when unfavorable economic conditions are encountered, travel is one of the first candidates considered for cost cutting. This is unfortunate for destinations, but as yet the value of business-related travel is still considered inferior to other cost centers.

EXAMPLE 19.9

Google Tries to Limit Business Travel

This example reports on large, iconic technology companies that are trimming business travel costs. These may be bellwethers (predictors) of what more companies will be doing in the near future.

Google has told its senior managers to limit employee travel only to "business critical" trips, according to a leaked internal email seen by *The Information*.

No more team off-sites or social functions, and no more in-person meetings when a virtual option is available.

Last month, Microsoft asked employees to cut back on business travel and company events in an effort to keep costs under control, *The Wall Street Journal* reported. Taken on their own, these are simply tales of corporations trimming expenses during inflationary times. But viewed through a macro lens, Google's new policy is emblematic of a travel trend that could pose a longer-term challenge to airlines.

(Kelleher 2022)

Learning Point

In tougher economic times, companies may choose virtual travel/meeting options rather than incurring the high costs associated with business travel.

SAFETY AND SECURITY CONCERNS

Business and business event travelers are becoming increasingly concerned about their safety, especially because of COVID-19 and the escalation of terrorist attacks at tourism sites and transportation systems and terminals.

Meeting planners are becoming more aware of safety concerns and the need for planning risk assessment (Palmer 2016). Part of the meeting planner's responsibility is making delegates aware of potential risks, and here DMOs can also lend a hand.

SUPPLY CHAIN INTERDEPENDENCY

DMOs usually do not control and operate the facilities that are used by the business travel and business event markets; they must rely on the performance of tourism sector stakeholders. DMOs market, brand, and communicate about the hotels/resorts and convention/exhibition centers within their destinations, but it is the performance levels of these facilities that ultimately determine customer satisfaction. This is challenging for DMOs because they make the promises but it is up to others to deliver on these promises. Therefore, it is very important that DMOs conduct post-event audits of participant and event planner satisfaction levels.

POLICY COMPLIANCE AND COST CONTROL

Particularly for regular business travel, the control of travel expenses and having employees comply with corporate travel policies is a major challenge. Cost control is also a major issue for meeting planners. This may not at first glance seem to be of direct concern to DMOs, but they should do what they can to assist the organizations involved to control their costs.

REPUTATION AND CREDIBILITY

There is an ever-lingering perk perception of business travel and business events. Fear of adverse public relations in difficult economic times is another issue that governments and companies have had to contemplate. The USTA (2018) argues that business travel has been inaccurately portrayed as an unnecessary perk rather than a critical component of job creation and innovation.

These challenges and issues are putting greater pressure on those who coordinate business travel and those who plan business events to become more professional and accountable.

Trends for Business Travel and Business Events

As the discussion of challenges suggests, there is no doubt that business travel and business events are undergoing some fundamental shifts and the future will see even more change occurring. Business travel and business events are not immune from the economic, political, social and cultural, technological, and natural environments surrounding them, and they need to adapt accordingly.

The following are short discussions of just some selected trends and emerging concepts in these markets, including:

1. blended travel and bleisure;
2. virtual meetings;
3. hybrid meetings;
4. webinars;
5. green or sustainable meetings;
6. meaningful and healthy meetings;
7. festivalization of events;
8. unique event venues (Fig. 19.8).

Figure 19.8 Trends for business travel and business events.

Blended Travel and Bleisure

DEFINITION

Blended travel

Blended travel is any type of travel that blends work and leisure time, including adding extra days to a business trip or working remotely from a different location. This type of travel has risen in popularity since the COVID-19 pandemic began thanks to the widespread adoption of remote and hybrid working formats (Zay 2022).

This market trend applies to both regular business travel and business events, and it is the combination of business and leisure while traveling (Fig. 19.9). Although this book treats leisure and VFR (Chapters 17 and 18) as being different from business travel, companies and travelers are increasingly combining them. Why are business travelers multi-purposing their trips? As you can imagine, it is a combination of factors contributing to blended travel and bleisure, including generational, social, economic, technological and other changes. Figure 19.11 supplies some potential influencing factors along with reasons people are taking more blended travel and bleisure trips.

Blended travel and bleisure

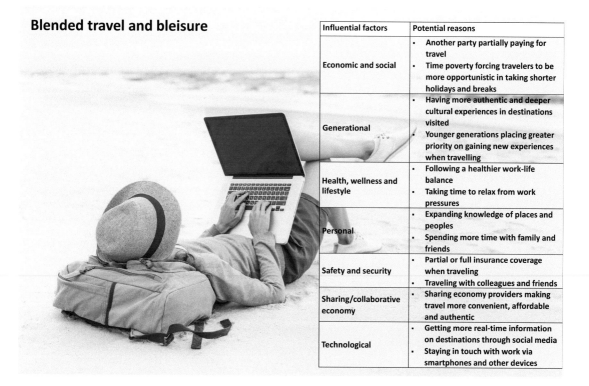

Influential factors	Potential reasons
Economic and social	• Another party partially paying for travel • Time poverty forcing travelers to be more opportunistic in taking shorter holidays and breaks
Generational	• Having more authentic and deeper cultural experiences in destinations visited • Younger generations placing greater priority on gaining new experiences when travelling
Health, wellness and lifestyle	• Following a healthier work-life balance • Taking time to relax from work pressures
Personal	• Expanding knowledge of places and peoples • Spending more time with family and friends
Safety and security	• Partial or full insurance coverage when traveling • Traveling with colleagues and friends
Sharing/collaborative economy	• Sharing economy providers making travel more convenient, affordable and authentic
Technological	• Getting more real-time information on destinations through social media • Staying in touch with work via smartphones and other devices

Figure 19.9 Keeping up with work while at the beach: an example of blended travel and bleisure and influential factors of and potential reasons.

EXAMPLE 19.10

Blended Travel Replaces Bleisure

The term "bleisure" is now being replaced with the concept of blended travel. This example reports on a survey in the UK and USA about this new idea in the post-pandemic era.

> In our 2022 Crowne Plaza survey of travelers, two-thirds of UK respondents and 80 percent in the USA say they love the idea of traveling while working remotely. And there is more interest in blended travel than before the pandemic. 45 percent of UK respondents say they plan to add leisure days to future business trips. In the USA, this is 60 percent. It's clear that the next generation of blended travelers are looking to make far-reaching changes to the way in which they combine work and travel.
>
> Equally apparent is the fact that the experience of remote working for millions of formerly office-bound staff has had a transformative effect on where and how they will expect to work in the future. In fact, around half of respondents say they would turn down a job that did not offer flexible or remote working.
> (Crowne Plaza Hotels and Resorts/IHG Hotels and Resorts 2022)

Learning Point

Business travelers are expecting greater flexibility in the balance between office time and that spent remotely working.

Virtual Meetings

DEFINITION

Virtual meeting

A virtual meeting is a form of communication that enables people in different physical locations to use their mobile or Internet connected devices to meet in the same virtual room (Webex 2022).

During 2020 and 2021, many business events were canceled or postponed due the COVID-19 pandemic and the resulting travel restrictions and social distancing rules. Still others were converted to hybrid meetings, which are discussed next. This trend was continuing in 2022, although not to the same level as in the previous two years.

EXAMPLE 19.11

Two Opposing Views of Virtual Meetings

Many experts scoffed at what was called teleconferencing before COVID-19 became a reality. They said that virtual meetings would never replace the face-to-face variety of business events. This example contrasts two viewpoints on virtual meetings—one skeptical and the other praiseworthy.

> One of the biggest criticisms we heard was that face-to-face meetings were going to die out—that digital meetings would take over and the need for meeting venues would dissipate as people could now meet virtually from the comfort of their living room. Nearly a decade later, here we are—and the meetings industry is bigger than ever. What happened? How did the prognosticators get it so wrong?
>
> (Convene 2019)

> It is fair to say the vast majority of businesses and employees were oblivious to the benefits of virtual meetings until it was thrust upon them by necessity and virtually overnight. The move to virtual meetings as a business norm is an exciting development that is hopefully here to stay as we witness it leading to changes in meeting dynamics as well as providing a much-needed tool to help boost workplace inclusion, diversity and work–life balance.
>
> (Ferguson 2020)

Learning Point

Major crises can disrupt how business is done and that applies to business events as well.

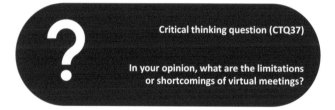

Critical thinking question (CTQ37)

In your opinion, what are the limitations or shortcomings of virtual meetings?

Hybrid Meetings

DEFINITION

Hybrid meeting

A hybrid meeting refers to the physical location of participants. In a hybrid meeting, a subset of the people attending the meeting is located together in the same place. Other participants join the meeting by conference call or web conference (Lucid 2022).

Hybrid meetings may be a win-win for associations, companies and other event organizers. These are meetings that combine traditional meetings with ICTs; some attendees meet in the traditional way, but others are connected by ICTs to the event. By livestreaming a conference or convention and allowing two-way communication, organizations may be able to expand the reach and influence of their events.

Webinars

Webinars are seminars on the Web, hence the combination of the two terms. They existed well before COVID-19; however, the pandemic led to their increased use.

EXAMPLE 19.12

Increasing Popularity and Use of Webinars

Webinars are being used by companies for marketing purposes as well as by many other types of organizations to deliver training, educational, and other contents. They are flexible for their creators and participants; they can be watched live or on-demand later. This example highlights the growth in popularity of webinars.

> It reflects the potential of webinars and their huge impact on the business world today. A recent 2021 global report shows the use of webinars increased by 162 percent and attendance quadrupled to 60 million people. The popularity of webinars can be attributed to the recent pandemic and the package of benefits these events offer.
>
> (Mittal 2022)

> Companies are using webinars to deliver dynamic digital experiences that engage their prospects and customers, with more marketers using video to increase audience engagement and viewing times during their events.
>
> (ON24 2021)

Learning Point

The COVID-19 pandemic created more demand for webinars with video content and opportunities to engage, participate, and network.

Green or Sustainable Meetings

DEFINITION

Green meeting

A green meeting is one that is organized and implemented in such a way as to minimize negative impacts on the environment and promote a positive social impact for the host community (United States Environmental Protection Agency 2022).

EXAMPLE 19.13

What Makes an Event Sustainable?

This example outlines how sustainability can be built into business events.

There are many different definitions of sustainability. However, a more sustainable approach to event management will typically:

- provide an accessible and inclusive setting for all;
- have minimal negative impacts on the environment;
- provide a safe and secure atmosphere;
- encourage healthy living;
- promote responsible sourcing;
- deliver excellent customer experience;
- encourage more sustainable behavior;
- leave a positive legacy.

(BSI Group, n.d.)

Learning Point

There are several criteria that a business event must satisfy to be considered sustainable.

There is increasing concern around the world about the potential adverse effects on the environment that can be caused by business travel and events. Green or sustainable meetings is a movement designed to have environmental considerations in mind when planning and implementing business events, and so it is another trend coming from the event sector. The UN Environmental Programme (2022) published *The Green Meeting Guide* 2009, which provides guidelines for organizers and hosts. This was followed up in 2012 with *The Sustainable Events Guide*. The Sustainable Events Guide makes three recommendations for implementing sustainable events:

1. Reduce the negative impacts of your event.
2. Include social aspects in your event.
3. Integrate sustainability in your event.

The UN Environmental Programme's Green Meeting Guide suggests the environmental targets for meetings shown in Figure 19.10.

A Centre for Sustainability and Social Impact has been established by the Events Industry Council. This unit is dedicated to providing globally relevant resources that champion the adoption of sustainable and socially impactful practices (Events Industry Council 2022b). The International Organization for Standardization (2022) has created standards for sustainable events with the code of ISO 20121. This standard requires that events develop and operate an event sustainability management system. A Sustainable Event Alliance organization has been established to promote the sustainability of events. They have prepared a ISO 20121 registry (Sustainable Event Alliance 2022).

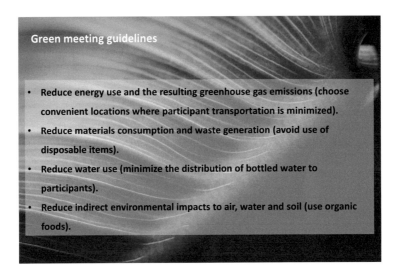

Figure 19.10 Green meeting guidelines.

Some individual DMOs have developed their own green meeting initiatives. Vienna, Austria, is a place that is serious about green meetings. The Vienna Convention Bureau also has a green meeting certification process (Vienna Convention Bureau 2022a). The bureau provides a checklist of sustainable actions for meeting planners on its website (Vienna Convention Bureau 2022b).

EXAMPLE 19.14

Vienna Austria Is a Capital for Green Meetings

This example highlights the steps taken by Vienna to make it a recognized destination for green and sustainable meetings.

Vienna welcomes its visitors with fresh air—no other city in Europe has a higher proportion of green spaces. Sustainability is a major topic so it comes with no surprise that the city offers the best conditions for green meetings. Parks and gardens make up almost half of the city, which gives your participants plenty of opportunity to enjoy nature. At the Vienna Convention Bureau, we can give you all the support and advice you need for certifying your meeting with the Austrian Ecolabel for Green Meetings and Green Events once it meets all the necessary criteria.

- Vienna is the internationally recognized capital of environmental protection, setting an example in water supply, wastewater management, waste disposal, and air quality management.
- In Vienna, pure spring water comes directly out of the city's drinking water taps.
- Close to 50 percent of the city is accounted for by green spaces.

The Vienna Convention Bureau offers guidance on sustainability and can certify your meeting in accordance with the Austrian Ecolabel.

(Vienna Convention Bureau 2022c)

Learning Point

Vienna Austria is a great model for other destinations for promoting and supporting sustainable practices in business events.

Meaningful and Healthy Meetings

The market transformation that has occurred includes the changing expectations of business event attendees. They expect events to have more meaningful outcomes and to place greater emphasis on health and wellness.

EXAMPLE 19.15

Mindfulness at Business Events

Meetings can be quite stressful for some people. It is suggested that meditation sessions or other mindfulness activities can enhance meeting participation experiences.

If you're considering the possibility of including optional mindfulness sessions into your program, you should first be clear about your intentions and what you hope to accomplish, such as:

- Offering a new and different way to elevate the virtual attendee experience.
- Helping your attendees overcome meeting or screen fatigue and stay connected to the content you have worked so hard to deliver.
- Giving participants the opportunity to learn about and experience the benefits of mindfulness in an engaging format, particularly if you have personally benefited from the practice.
- Providing attendees with tools to reduce stress, recharge, and refocus that will transcend the life of your program.
- Incorporating well-being activities into your event aligns with your core organizational values.

(Brown 2020)

Learning Point

Event organizers should consider introducing mindfulness activities into programs.

Festivalization of Events

Festivalization has been flagged as one of the hottest trends in events (Oates 2017; Peterson 2017). It is a blending of tourism and the creative industries and involves multiple programming formats. This can be achieved by making business events more "festive," or coinciding business events with festivals and other events. Festivalization is a trend initiated by the event sector to expand the range of experiences that delegates gain from attendance. TED, South by Southwest and C2 Montreal are often used as examples of the fusion of business and commerce with creative arts (Oates 2017).

EXAMPLE 19.16

Event Festivalization

The new crop of business event attendees want them to be memorable and meaningful experiences. This example highlights how festivalization can achieve these objectives.

> Festivalization, therefore, attempts to harness the emphasis on engagement and togetherness by using elements commonly associated with festivals to make other types of events more dynamic, interactive, and memorable. It exploits the ideas that information should pop and events should be "experiences," and it is one of the most worthwhile trends currently influencing the events industry, even—or perhaps especially—given the recent shift to online platforms.
>
> The "new normal" has made it more difficult, but also more essential, to create these enjoyable, memorable shared experiences, and festivalization offers useful tools to achieve this in both off and online scenarios. In a world where many face-to-face interactions have been replaced by virtual ones, it's an idea that might be more important than ever.
>
> (Event Industry News 2021)

Learning Point

Event festivalization aligns well with the expectations of business event attendees.

Unique Event Venues

Business event planners are increasingly choosing unique event venues to create more varied and interesting experiences for participants. Normally, events are held in corporate offices, hotels, convention centers, or conference resorts. There are too many of these unique or non-traditional venues to list here, but they include castles, caves, museums, ships and theme parks to name but a few. For example, 2B UK and Maritz Travel used the Natural History Museum in London for an event (Fig. 19.11).

Figure 19.11 The Natural History Museum in London, England, is a unique venue for an event.

EXAMPLE 19.17

Having a Conference Dinner in a Cave

This example describes a unique event venue in Western Australia that is truly memorable and a very different experience. Your author can testify to that as he had a conference dinner there in Cabaret Cave. This unique experience of Cabaret Cave is within Yanchep National Park near Perth, Western Australia.

> Why not consider the stunning Cabaret Cave for your next function or event. Originally used in the 1930s to provide a secret dinner and dance location for Perth's rich and famous, Cabaret Cave is Perth's only venue cave for hire. It has been beautifully modified to accommodate up to 120 guests sit-down style, or 200 guests cocktail style. The cave's natural air conditioning makes it the perfect location all year around. Extraordinarily unique, visually amazing and acoustically sensational, Cabaret Cave is a perfect location for your upcoming event.
> (Parks and Wildlife Service, Western Australia 2022)

Learning Point

Destinations, DMOs, and tourism sector stakeholders need to think creatively about new and memorable venues for business events.

These ten challenges and eight trends for business travel and business events are not the only ones, but they give you a good sample of the change that is occurring. All challenges and trends should be concerns to destination managers and not just to meeting planners and corporate travel managers. As these clients are adapting their travel policies and offers to better meet traveler needs, DMOs too must expand and enrich the experiences they provide. Like leisure travel, a greater emphasis must be placed on providing unique and novel destination experiences for business travelers and for those who are multi-purposing trips. DMOs also need to understand that much convergence and consolidation are happening with business travel and business events.

Professional Congress or Conference Organizers (PCOs)

Companies and associations that are holding business events must make one very fundamental decision: Do we plan and implement the event ourselves, or should we outsource the tasks to professional event planners? You can call this a make or buy decision. If you ever get involved with an event in the future, you will soon realize how complex and complicated they are to plan and operate. This is not something to take on without much previous experience.

Therefore, before delving into DMO business event marketing, branding, and communications, you need to know a little about PCOs and their roles. PCOs are called either professional congress organizers or professional conference organizers. In Continental Europe, congress is preferred, whereas in the UK conference will more likely be used. The term PCO is not used much in the USA, and people performing similar functions tend to be called independent meeting planners. In Canada, they are called event planners.

A PCO is a company that focuses mainly on conferences, events and meetings (Visit Bruges Convention Bureau 2022). PCOs are expert professionals at planning, organizing, and implementing business events. Although not called PCOs, the functions of independent meeting or event planners in North America are much the same.

Incentive Travel Planners

Incentive travel planners are companies that specialize in designing and operating incentives, and they primarily serve corporate clients. The main trade association for incentive travel planning companies is the Society for Incentive Travel Excellence (SITE), which has chapters around the world. The separation between incentive travel and other business events is becoming increasingly blurred as organizations seek to multipurpose these for economic and performance management reasons.

The trips arranged by incentive travel planning companies are given to employees or dealers of their clients as a reward for outstanding sales or work performance. Companies pay for the incentive travel planner's services through a mark-up on the incentive trip costs or pay an agreed-upon fixed fee.

Maritz Global Events (2022) identifies different aspects of the incentive planning services, and these provide a good outline for the roles played by incentive travel planning companies:

Event Design

Incentive travel planners design customized travel trips for the winners from their client companies. They suggest the destinations for trips as well as the activities and events program. They operate these trips, and this may be done with or without destination management companies (DMCs) within specific destinations. Events are designed strategically to meet organizational and traveler needs.

Event Sourcing

These companies find the best suppliers in destinations and negotiate the most favorable prices.

Event Management and Meeting Logistics

They operate the incentive trips to ensure that all goes as planned, especially in the detailed logistics of trips and any meetings that are included. Project management and technology applications are important for monitoring and delivering services.

Event Promotion and Communications

Incentive travel companies design and implement programs to promote incentive trips to the pool of potential winners within the client company.

Corporate Flight Management

They negotiate with airlines and book flights as well as monitor and assist travelers if flight problems occur.

Registration and Event Housing

Incentive travel planners provide online, integrated and one-stop registration and booking services for their travelers.

Event Technology

Incentive travel planners use many types of technological applications to operate trip programs and for communicating with potential participants and winners. These include customized websites, online registration and booking systems, app design, and using social media platforms for communication and discussions.

On-site Event Support

They provide the people and other resources on-site within the destinations to make sure everything goes as planned and runs smoothly.

Event Measurement, Analysis and Reporting

They develop metrics to measure and evaluate the performance outcomes of incentives. For example, they may do surveys of trip winners' satisfaction and the elements of the trip they liked most. They also estimate the benefits and ROI of the incentive trip to the company.

Part IV

Corporate Events and Incentives in Buenos Aires

Destinations must provide highly memorable experiences for incentives and other major corporate events. The DMO in Buenos Aires, Argentina identifies a creative set of ideas for these business events.

> Enjoy unique experiences in the City of Buenos Aires and its surrounds. The vibrant city offers plenty of unique and creative opportunities for corporate events and incentive trips, both by day and night.

- Tango classes
- Farmstead days
- Polo days and polo clinics
- Cookery classes and wine tasting
- Sailing on the Río de La Plata
- Bicycle tours
- Attending a football game

(Turismo Buenos Aires 2022)

Learning Point

The DMO should be proactive in suggesting creative activities to incentive travel planners that will create highly memorable experiences for participants.

Before leaving the topic of incentive travel, one more predominant trend needs to be mentioned. This is usually referred to as the convergence of meetings and incentives, or in other words, a combination of business meetings and incentive travel. Business meetings are being scheduled during incentive trips more frequently as companies try to eke out the greatest value and ROI from their investments in travel.

Requests for Proposals (RFPs)

RFPs are used frequently in the planning and organizing of business events, and you should know about them. Basically, RFPs are forms that meeting and incentive planners complete to request proposals for their events from DMOs, hotels, and convention centers. DMOs now have these posted on their websites to make it easier for meeting planners to complete them than the traditional hard-copy versions. Completed RFPs represent leads that DMOs can pass along to hotels and meeting venues that satisfy the meeting planner's needs and requirements. Most good RFPs ask for nine categories of information about planned events (Fig. 19.12).

You can see that RFPs are very useful tools for all parties involved with business events. For DMOs, they provide an assured way of demonstrating their value to tourism sector stakeholders by passing along these leads; for meeting planners, they represent a convenient way of expressing event requirements; and for hotels, resorts and meeting venues, they provide the basic information for developing proposals and sales approaches.

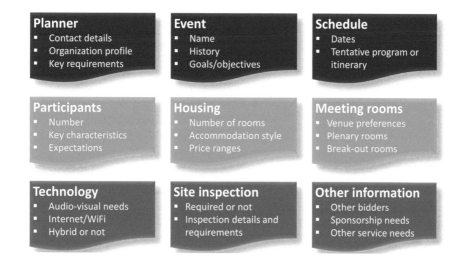

Figure 19.12 Requests for proposals: required categories of information.

Business Event Marketing, Branding, and Communications

Generally, DMOs do not specifically target individual regular business travelers, assuming that this type of travel cannot be influenced. Tourism sector stakeholders and particularly local hotels aggressively sell to locally based companies, government agencies and nonprofits to accommodate their so-called transient guests.

However, this does not mean that DMOs should completely ignore the companies and government agencies located within their destinations, especially knowing about the trend for blended travel. Soft sell approaches should be used, including supplying companies with brochures and other information on the local destination, that can be given out to their visitors and prospective employees.

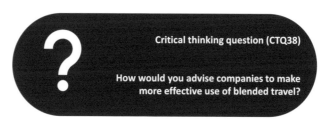

Additionally, local organizations may be very helpful in assisting the DMO in attracting business events to the destinations. For example, there may be local chapters of state/provincial, national or international associations in the destination. Additionally, there may be local people who are holding executive positions on associations or other nonprofit groups. Striking up partnerships with local chapters and the officers of nonprofits is a worthwhile effort for DMOs to initiate.

For business events, DMOs must develop a dedicated set of approaches to destination marketing, branding, and communications. In contrast to the pleasure and leisure markets, potential business event customers and primary competitors are easier to identify. Many DMOs have developed highly professional approaches to business event marketing, branding, and communications. This is partly because of the relative ease of market and competitor identification but mainly because there is intense competition for business events and DMOs have in-depth experience in business event sales and servicing.

Before getting started on this topic, you need to know a little more about the types of organizations that get involved in business event marketing, branding, and communications because it is not just DMOs. Some countries have established business event divisions or convention bureaus at the national and administrative area levels. For example, Business Events Australia is one of these cases, as are the Singapore Exhibition and Convention Bureau, South Africa National Convention Bureau, and Meeting and Exhibitions Hong Kong (Meetings and Exhibitions Hong Kong 2022; Singapore Tourism Board 2022; South Africa National Convention Bureau 2022). Most city DMOs also are actively marketing toward business event organizers.

Another important player is convention and exhibition center facilities. Sometimes, these are under the direct jurisdiction of city DMOs (as in Las Vegas), but more often they are independent entities with their own marketing programs. Many local governments themselves operate convention/exhibition centers, but in other situations they are contracted out to private companies that specialize in managing these types of venues. For example, ASM Global (2022) is a company headquartered in Los Angeles that operates 350 event venues worldwide, including several convention centers. ASM Global is aggressively marketing the centers that they are operating, as are other facility-operating companies.

Companies that specialize in organizing large events are another important player in business event marketing. RX is a good example and has a portfolio of 400 events in twenty-two countries, across forty-three industry sectors (RX Global 2022).

There are also numerous trade associations serving different aspects of business events, and they are too many to mention here. There are associations for meeting planners, incentive planning companies, PCOs, DMCs, trade shows, conference centers, and several other categories. All these associations are advocating on behalf of business events and marketing the business event concept to multiple audiences.

The individual organizers of business events are also very much involved in promoting their events to potential participants and to the media. This marketing is of course beneficial to the event destinations. Now, you know that there are many different parties involved in business event marketing, branding, and communications. However, the materials that follow focus solely on DMOs and their marketing, branding, and communications for business event markets.

Where Are We Now?

The completion of a situation analysis based upon facilities, clients, and competitors is the starting point for the DMO's business event marketing efforts. As shown in Figure 12.10, the business event situation analysis must cover six topics: (1) destination, (2) competitors, (3) business event visitor market, (4) position and image, (5) marketing plan, and (6) community residents. The results of these six areas of analysis should be an identification of the destination's strengths and weaknesses and unique selling propositions (USPs) related to business event markets.

The site selection criteria used by meeting and event planners are the key to assessing the strengths and weaknesses of a destination for business events. Academic scholars have conducted many research studies on site-selection criteria, and other experts have also offered their opinions on this topic. Eight categories of convention site selection factors are shown in Figure 19.13.

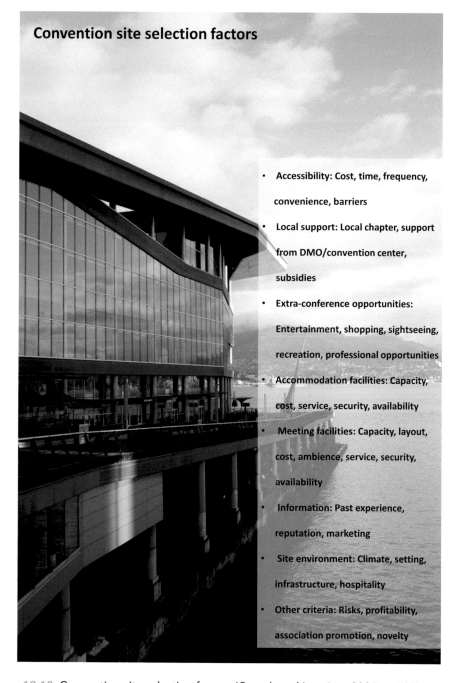

Convention site selection factors

- Accessibility: Cost, time, frequency, convenience, barriers
- Local support: Local chapter, support from DMO/convention center, subsidies
- Extra-conference opportunities: Entertainment, shopping, sightseeing, recreation, professional opportunities
- Accommodation facilities: Capacity, cost, service, security, availability
- Meeting facilities: Capacity, layout, cost, ambience, service, security, availability
- Information: Past experience, reputation, marketing
- Site environment: Climate, setting, infrastructure, hospitality
- Other criteria: Risks, profitability, association promotion, novelty

Figure 19.13 Convention site selection factors (Crouch and Louviere 2004, p. 120).

Pinpointing and assessing the relative strengths of competitive business event destinations is crucial in this type of marketing, branding, and communications. The DMO must therefore identify its principal competitors for business events. For example, MyCEB (Malaysia Convention and Exhibition Bureau 2018) pinpointed Thailand, Singapore and Indonesia as being its strongest competitors for business events. Determining the destination's USPs for business events is also a key here. With this knowledge in hand, many destinations suggest top reasons to meet.

EXAMPLE 19.19

Why Meet in Hong Kong?

Hong Kong is a very appealing destination for all types of business events. Meetings and Exhibitions Hong Kong (MEHK) identifies the reasons to meet there in this example.

> Meetings and Exhibitions Hong Kong provides eight reasons to hold business events there:
>
> 1. Strategic location
> 2. Gateway to Mainland China
> 3. Superb infrastructure
> 4. World-leading venues
> 5. Business-friendly environment
> 6. Professional support
> 7. Endless variety
> 8. Proven track record.
>
> (Meetings and Exhibitions Hong Kong 2022)

Learning Point

It is essential that destinations identify convincing reasons to meet there.

It is important that destinations gather detailed statistics on their business events and the characteristics of these events. This is not only important for guiding marketing decisions but also for demonstrating the DMO's performance accountability.

Because of the scale and potential impact of business events on local communities, it is advisable for DMOs to periodically survey residents about their perceptions of these events. In practice, this is seldom done, but that does not mean that such an analysis should not be conducted.

Where Would We Like to Be?

Next, the DMO needs to develop a business events marketing strategy comprising the target markets and the PIB approach. For business events, the typical approach is to divide up potential targets by organizational type (association vs. corporate), geography (international, national, regional, state/province/territory), and type of event (e.g., convention/conference/congress/meeting vs. trade show/exhibition vs. incentive travel).

The DMO should develop a PIB approach for business events, but this should be linked in some way to the approach used for leisure travel markets. The earlier example from the Vienna

Convention Bureau in Austria is a good case study of positioning cities as a business event destination. As you will remember, the Vienna Convention Bureau is communicating portraying the city as a great place for green or sustainable meetings, and so part of their positioning is based on the sustainable use of resources at business events.

The DMO must also develop a vision and a specific set of marketing goals and objectives for business-related markets, as in the case of Malaysia.

EXAMPLE 19.20

Malaysia Business Events Strategic Marketing Plan

It is great to find a country that articulates such a clear plan for marketing business events. In this example, the vision and goals in the Business Events Strategic Marketing Plan for Malaysia are identified.

Vision:
  To position Malaysia as one of the world's preferred business and international sporting events destinations.

Goals:

1. Malaysia to increase significant share of hosting business and international sporting events taking place in Asia.
2. Malaysia will become Asia's top five business events powerhouse by 2030.
3. The business events industry will contribute significant economic impact, direct contribution to the economy and national GDP.
4. Malaysia business and international sporting events industry will be yield-driven.
5. Business events as key element in ministries and government agencies by 2030.
6. Business events to connect and boost investment opportunities.
                              (Malaysia Convention and Exhibition Bureau 2021)

Learning Point

It is critical that a destination and DMO have clearly identified goals for business event marketing, branding, and communications.

The objectives should be expressed according to KRAs and as KPIs. These KRAs and KPIs can be built upon the Standard DMO Performance Reporting System from Destinations International, which is discussed in more detail in Chapter 20.

How Do We Get There?

DMOs need to develop specific marketing plans directed toward business travelers and particularly for business events. Often, these are included in DMOs' overall marketing plans, with special sections devoted to business travel or business events.

Personal selling or sales is the most important IMC component in pursuing business events, and as such, larger DMOs maintain substantial sales forces. These sales efforts need to be placed within a carefully orchestrated business event IMC campaign. There are many great business event marketing plans and campaigns around the world, but only a few can be mentioned. Some DMOs, for example, actively help event organizers to market their events to potential delegates, and Vancouver, British Columbia provides a great example. The Metro Vancouver Convention and Visitors Bureau has developed an Attendance Marketing Toolkit that can be accessed online. The toolkit includes images, Vancouver postcards, videos, conference landing pages, destination marketing copy, destination PowerPoint presentation, ad templates, and airport welcome support (Metro Vancouver Convention and Visitors Bureau 2022).

How Do We Make Sure We Get There?

Control and evaluation procedures are essential tools for DMOs in demonstrating accountability. Destinations International has developed a standard performance reporting system for DMOs, and this system is particularly detailed for business event marketing performance reporting. Included in the system are three components: (1) activity measures (2) performance measures and (3) productivity metrics.

For convention sales (business event sales), Destinations International (2011) created the following very important definitions.

LEAD

The forwarding by the DMO of a request for a minimum of ten sleeping rooms per night (peak rooms) over a specific set or range of dates. The request is related to an event being organized by a corporation, an association, an organization or an independent meeting planner. The DMO sales staff sends the lead only to those local hotels that satisfy the event planner's event criteria. A lead is not just a DMO passing business cards along to local hotels.

BID

A proposal submitted by the DMO (with or without a local hotel) to an event planner that includes defined dates and room blocks. Destinations International emphasizes that a bid is an activity and not a performance measure.

TENTATIVE

A bid that has been submitted to an event planner and the DMO is awaiting the decision. This is not a performance measure.

BOOKING

1. Hotel event: A future event where a written contract has been signed between the hotel and the event organizer.
2. Citywide/convention center event:
   - confirmed booking: a future event confirmed in writing;
   - contracted booking: a future event where a written contract has been signed between the event organizer and the event facility.

Lost Opportunity

A potential event that has been classified as a lead or a tentative but the destination subsequently loses the event. The reasons for losing the business may include:

- dates not available at hotels;
- hotel room rates too high;
- lack of hotel interest;
- dates not available at the convention center;
- convention center costs too high;
- no hotel adjacent to convention center;
- safety concerns;
- meeting canceled or postponed;
- union or labor costs;
- transportation or access issues;
- national or international incidents;
- board preference or internal politics.

Canceled Business

An event that was booked (contracted or confirmed) that subsequently does not take place because of cancelation by the event organizer.

How Do We Know If We Got There?

The fifth step in applying the DMS to business events marketing, branding, and communications is to evaluate the success or performance in implementing the marketing strategy and plan. You have seen a description in this chapter of how Destinations International recommends that DMOs report their performance for business events marketing. The main yardstick to be applied here is to answer the question, "Did we achieve our marketing objectives?" Also, as you already know, this involves the results for the KPIs that the DMO has set for business event marketing.

SUMMING UP

The business travel and business event markets are the backbone of tourism for many cities around the world. Business events are of different types, and these include conferences, congresses, conventions, exhibitions, incentives, meetings, and trade shows. Unfortunately, there are no universally accepted definitions of these terms, and different usages can cause confusion.

Business travel and business events are significant in size and have a major beneficial economic impact on many countries and individual communities. The higher-than-average yield of these markets makes them very appealing to destinations.

The major challenges and issues facing business travel and business events are the pandemic recovery, sustainability and climate change, market transformation, technology innovation and adoption, competitive intensity, economic downturns, safety and security concerns, supply-chain interdependency, policy compliance and cost control, and reputation and credibility.

Some of the major trends that are being felt in business travel and business events are blended travel and bleisure, virtual meetings, hybrid meetings, webinars, green or sustainable meetings, meaningful and healthy meetings, festivalization of events, and unique event venues. All these challenges and trends impacting on business travel and business events are forcing planners and managers to become more professional, comprehensive and integrated in their planning and implementation efforts.

There has been a definite movement toward greater professionalism in business travel and meeting management. New standards are being developed, including professional skill competencies, and these will undoubtedly benefit DMOs and destinations in the future. DMOs should not be silent partners in this process but should do all that they can to assist their client partners to achieve their goals.

PCOs are specialists in planning, organizing and implementing meetings and other events. These are highly qualified and experienced meeting professionals who can take care of all aspects of an event on behalf of companies and nonprofits.

Incentive travel planning companies are specialists in arranging motivation-oriented trips for companies. Their services typically include program design, communications, operations and measurement, and they apply various technologies in so doing. Because of the tighter economic conditions and the desire for companies to get a greater ROI from incentive travel, there has been a movement toward converging business meetings and incentive travel.

RFPs are forms that meeting planners complete and submit to DMOs or hotels and meeting venues. Now, most DMOs provide online versions of RFPs. Completed RFPs summarize the meeting planner's requirements for an upcoming event. RFPs are beneficial to all the parties involved, including the meeting planners, DMOs, as well as hotels, resorts and meeting venues.

The DMO's marketing, branding, and communications for business events are usually the most scrutinized areas of its operations. Therefore, it is vitally important that the DMO's performance reporting be thorough and cover all the relevant activity measures and productivity metrics. It is particularly important that a DMO demonstrate its contributions to the hotels and resorts within the destination, and so it must measure room nights generated through its business event marketing, branding, and communications.

KEYWORDS

attendees
beyond tourism benefits
bidding
bleisure
blended travel
business events
business tourism
corporate travel policy
citywide
conference
consumer shows
convention
convergence
delegates
exhibition

exhibitors
exposition
festivalization of events
green or sustainable
    meeting
hybrid meeting
incentive travel
leads
livestreaming
meeting
meeting legacies
MICE
Millennials
motivation
policy compliance

professional congress (or
    conference) organizer
    (PCO)
regular business travel
remote work
sharing economy providers
site inspection
T&E (travel and entertain-
    ment) costs
T&E policy
trade show
unique event venues
virtual meeting
voice recognition
webinar

REVIEW QUESTIONS

1. How would you define regular business travel?
2. What are the different business event markets, and how is each of them defined?
3. What are the benefits of regular business travel and business events?
4. Business travel and business events are facing which major challenges now?
5. Which trends are impacting upon business travel and business events?
6. What is a PCO, and what services do these specialists provide?
7. What are the roles played by incentive travel planning companies, and what is the meaning of convergence?
8. Why are RFPs convenient for meeting planners and at the same time a good marketing tool for DMOs, hotels and meeting venues?
9. Why is it important for a DMO to gather research data on the business events held within its jurisdiction, and what types of statistics should be collected?
10. How should a DMO demonstrate its accountability with respect to its marketing, branding, and communications aimed at business events?

REFERENCES

ASM Global (2022) "The Preeminent Venue and Live Experiences Company," www.asmglobal.com/

Association of Australian Convention Bureaux (2022) "Benefits of Business Events," http://aacb.org.au/benefitsofbusinessevents

Association of Corporate Travel Executives and American Express Global Business Travel (2017) "Managing the Modern Business Traveller: An Acte Corporate Travel Study," www.amexglobalbusinesstravel.com/content/uploads/2017/10/ACTE-LONDON-Managing-Modern-Business-Traveller-.pdf

Baldanza, B. (2022) "Five Reasons Why Airline Business Travel Has Permanently Changed," *Forbes*, October 7, www.forbes.com/sites/benbaldanza/2022/10/07/five-reasons-why-airline-business-travel-has-permanently-changed/?sh=418b43ee7416

BestCities Global Alliance (2020) "Advancing Event Legacies through Impact Measurement," www.bestcities.net/wp-content/uploads/2020/10/20200820_BestCities_Legacy-Impact-Measurement-FINAL.pdf?utm_source=legacy-download&utm_medium=website&utm_campaign=Legacy-impact-downloads

Brown, S. (2020) "5 Reasons Why and 5 Ways to Bring Meditation into Your Virtual Event," PCMA, www.pcma.org/5-reasons-why-5-ways-bring-meditation-your-virtual-event/

BSI Group (undated) "Sustainable Events Guide," www.bsigroup.com/Sustainability/Sustainable-events-guide.pdf

Bureau International des Expositions (2022) "What Is an Expo?" www.bie-paris.org/site/en/what-is-an-expo

Busan Tourism Organization (2022) "MICE Support," https://bto.or.kr/cvbeng/CMS/Contents/Contents.do? mCode=MN025

Business Events Australia (2022) "Choose Australia for Your Next Business Event," https://businessevents.australia.com/en

Business Events Council of Australia (2022) "What Is a Business Event?" www.businesseventscouncil.org.au/page/about_business_events.html

Celebrity Cruises (2022) "What Is Incentive Travel?" www.celebritycorporatekit.com/our-blog/what-is-incentive-travel/

Condor Ferries (2022) "US Tourism and Travel Statistics 2020–2021," www.condorferries.co.uk/us-tourism-travel-statistics

Convene (2019) "Five Trends Shaping the Corporate Meetings Industry," https://convene.com/catalyst/meeting-event-planning/five-trends-shaping-the-corporate-meetings-industry/

Crouch, G. I., and Louviere, J. J. (2004) "The Determinants of Convention Site Selection: A Logistic Choice Model from Experimental Data," *Journal of Travel Research*, 43 (2): 118–130.

Crowne Plaza Hotels and Resorts and IHG Hotels and Resorts (2022) "The Future of Blended Travel," https://digital.ihg.com/is/content/ihg/CP-Blended-Travel-White-Paper

DeLuna, J. (2014) "Survey: T&E Second Most Difficult Operating Expense to Control," *Business Travel News*, June 25, www.businesstravelnews.com/more-news/survey-t-e-second-most-difficult-operating-expense-to-control

Destination Marketing Association International (2011) *Standard DMO Performance Reporting. A Handbook for Destination Marketing Organizations (DMOs)*. Washington, DC: DMAI.

Destinations International (2022) "Annual Convention," https://destinationsinternational.org/annual-convention

Dienes, K., Naujoks, T., and Rief, S. (2022) "Changing Ecosystems: Future Scenarios for Business Events in the Age of Borderless Communication," Fraunhofer IAO and GCB German Convention Bureau eV, https://publica.fraunhofer.de/entities/publication/52404ad1-34e4-45b8-8eda-71fea34de24f/details

Event Industry News (2021) "Festivalisation and the 'New Normal': Creating Multi-sensory Event Experiences Both Off and Online," January 13, www.eventindustrynews.com/news/festivalisation-and-the-new-normal-creating-multi-sensory-event-experiences-both-off-and-online

Events Industry Council (2022a) "Insights: Glossary," https://insights.eventscouncil.org/Industry-glossary

——— (2022b) "Centre for Sustainability and Social Impact," www.eventscouncil.org/Sustainability/CSE

Ferguson, K. (2020) "Ten Reasons Why Virtual Meetings Are the Best Thing to Happen in 2020," *Forbes*, July 21, www.forbes.com/sites/kirstinferguson/2020/07/21/ten-reasons-why-virtual-meetings-are-the-best-thing-to-happen-in-2020/?sh=267ceab77cd0

Flight Centre Travel Group Limited (2022) "The Impact of Artificial Intelligence on Business Travel," www.fcmtravel.com/en-us/resources/insights/impact-artificial-intelligence-business-travel

International Congress and Convention Association (2020) "ICCA Statistics Report: Country and City Rankings—Public Abstract," www.iccaworld.org/knowledge/article.cfm?artid=701

——— (2022) "FAQs: Definition of Business Tourism," www.iccaworld.org/aeps/aeitem.cfm?aeid=107

International Association of Professional Congress Organisers (2022) "On-line Dictionary," www.iapco.org/publications/on-line-dictionary/

International Organization for Standardization (2022) "ISO 20121 Sustainable Events," www.iso.org/iso-20121-sustainable-events.html

Kelleher, S. R. (2022) "Google's Crackdown on Employee Trips Is Another Blow to Business Travel Recovery," Forbes, September 8, www.forbes.com/sites/suzannerowankelleher/2022/09/08/googles-crackdown-on-employee-trips-is-another-blow-to-business-travel-recovery/?sh=662592d71943

Lucid (2022) "Hybrid Meeting," www.lucidmeetings.com/glossary/hybrid-meeting#

Malaysia Convention and Exhibition Bureau (2021) "Malaysia Business Events Strategic Marketing Plan, 2021–2030," www.myceb.com.my/about-us/malaysia-be-smp-2021-2030#

Maritz Global Events (2022) "Meeting Logistics," www.maritzglobalevents.com/how-we-help/event-services/

Mastercard (2020) "How the Shutdown of Business Travel Impacts Economic Development," www.mastercardcenter.org/insights/how-the-shutdown-of-business-travel-impacts-economic-development

Meetings and Exhibitions Hong Kong (2022) "Why Hong Kong?" https://mehongkong.com/eng/why-hong-kong.html

Messe Berlin (2022) "The World of ITB," www.itb.com/en/

Metro Vancouver Convention and Visitors Bureau (2022) "Attendance Marketing Toolkit," www.destinationvancouver.com/meeting/our-services/attendance-marketing-toolkit/

Mittal, N. (2022) "8 Benefits of Webinars and Why They Are Important," Nunify.com, August 25, www.nunify.com/blogs/benefits-of-webinars/

MyCEB (Malaysia Convention and Exhibition Bureau) (2018) "Malaysia's Business Events Roadmap," www.myceb.com.my/about-us/malaysias-business-events-roadmap

Oates, G. (2017) "Travel Megatrends 2017: Festivalization of Meetings and Events," *Skift*, January 16, https://skift.com/2017/01/16/travel-megatrends-2017-festivalization-of-meetings-and-events/

ON24 (2021) "Webinars Triple, Driving Digital-First Engagement across Industries," www.on24.com/press-releases/global-report-shows-use-of-webinars-triples-driving-digital-first-engagement-across-industries/

Oxford Economics and US Travel Association (2009) "The Return on Investment of US Business Travel, https://treasureisland.com/uploads/prod/public/pdf/56df17fe78f6b_23917.pdf

Palmer, A. (2016) "Meeting Planners Hone Their Risk Assessment Plans," *Successful Meetings*, March 22, www.successfulmeetings.com/Strategy/Meeting-Strategies/Meeting-Planners-Risk-Assessment-Plans-International-Meetings/

Parks and Wildlife Service, Western Australia (2022) "Cabaret Cave," https://exploreparks.dbca.wa.gov.au/site/cabaret-cave

Peterson, B. (2017) "The 'Festivalization' of Events: How Mega-gatherings Have Transformed Cities and Redefined the Conference Model," *Meetings and Conventions*, July 1, www.meetings-conventions.com/News/Features/Conference-trends-festivals-special-event-citywide/

RX (2022) "The Ultimate Destination for Travel and Tourism," www.wtm.com/

RX Global (2022) "About Us," https://rxglobal.com/

Singapore Tourism Board (2022) "About Singapore Exhibition and Convention Bureau," www.stb.gov.sg/content/stb/en/industries/meetings-incentive-travel-conventions-exhibitions/about-singapore-exhibition-and-convention-bureau-secb.html

South Africa National Convention Bureau (2022) "Welcome," www.southafrica.net/gl/en/business

Sustainable Event Alliance (2022) "Welcome to the Sustainable Event Alliance," https://sustainable-event-alliance.org/

Tourism Research Australia (2022) "National Visitor Survey Results, June 2022," www.tra.gov.au/data-and-research/reports/national-visitor-survey-results/national-visitor-survey-results

Turismo Buenos Aires (2022) "Corporate Events and Incentive Trips," https://turismo.buenosaires.gob.ar/en/article/corporate-events-and-incentive-trips

Union of International Associations (2016) "International Meeting Statistics Report," 57th edn, https://uia.org/publications/meetings-stats

———— (2022) "Union of International Associations Releases 63rd International Meetings Statistics Report," https://uia.org/sites/uia.org/files/misc_pdfs/pubs/press_release_uia_statistics_report_ed_63_en_fr_es.pdf

United Nations Environment Programme (2022) "Greening the Blue," www.greeningtheblue.org/reports/green-meeting-guide-2009

United States Environmental Protection Agency (2022) "Green Meetings," www.epa.gov/p2/green-meetings#

United Nations World Tourism Organization (2020) "International Tourism Highlights 2020 Edition," www.e-unwto.org/doi/pdf/10.18111/9789284422456

US Travel Association (2012) "Keep America Meeting: Securing the Future of Meetings Industry," www.meetingsmeanbusiness.com/sites/default/files/LVCVA_Keep_America_Meeting_white_paper_0.pdf

———— (2017) "Meetings Mean Business: Economic Impact of Meetings and Business Events," www.ustravel.org/sites/default/files/media_root/document/06.%20MMB%20Economic%20Page%202016.pdf

———— (2018) "Meetings Mean Business Coalition," www.ustravel.org/programs/meetings-mean-business-coalition

———— (2022a) "Reignite In-Person Meetings and Events," www.ustravel.org/issues/reignite-person-meetings-and-events

———— (2022b) "US Travel Answer Sheet," www.ustravel.org/sites/default/files/2022-05/ust-data-master.pdf

Vienna Convention Bureau (2021) "Facts and Figures: Vienna—Austria's Second Most Important Visitor Economy," https://b2b.wien.info/en/statistics/data/vienna-austria-s-second-most-important-visitor-economy-418846

———— (2022a). "Certification Process," www.vienna.convention.at/en/sustainability/certification/certification-process-415312

———— (2022b). "Checklist of Sustainable Actions," www.vienna.convention.at/en/sustainability/green-meetings/checklist

———— (2022c) "Green Meetings and Sustainable Planning," www.vienna.convention.at/en/sustainability

VisitBritain (2021) "Understanding Business Visits Foresight," www.visitbritain.org/sites/default/files/vb-corporate/Documents-Library/documents/foresight_178_-_understanding_business_visits.pdf

VisitBritain and Kantar (2022) "The GB Tourist 2019 Annual Report," www.visitbritain.org/sites/default/files/vb-corporate/gb_tourist_annual_report_2019_final.pdf

Visit Bruges Convention Bureau (2022) "What Role Does a Professional Conference Organizer Play?" www.visitbrugesconventionbureau.be/en/what-role-does-a-professional-conference-organizer-play

Webex (2022) "What Is a Virtual Meeting?" www.webex.com/virtual-meetings-guide.html

World Travel and Tourism Council (2022) "Country Reports," https://wttc.org/research/economic-impact/economic-research/economic-impact-analysis/country-reports

Zay, L. (2022) "Business, Leisure, and Blended Travel Explained," TripActions, September 26, https://tripactions.com/blog/what-is-the-difference-between-leisure-and-business-travel

Part V

Destination Management Performance Measurement and the Future of Destination Management

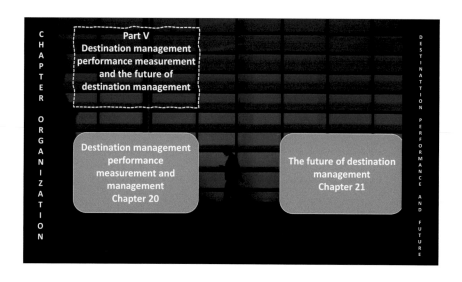

Destination Management Performance Measurement and Management

Assessing success

LEARNING OBJECTIVES

Having read this chapter, you should be able to:

1. define performance measurement and performance management;
2. explain the reasons for performance measurement in destination management;
3. elaborate on the role of performance metrics;
4. describe performance measurement systems;
5. discuss the performance measurement process;
6. elaborate on the issues with the funding of DMOs;
7. describe DMO funding sources and levels;
8. describe control and evaluation;
9. explain how DMOs accomplish performance reporting.

DOI: 10.4324/9781003343356-25

Warming Up

You learned about the many ups and downs of tourism in Chapters 17 to 19. The period of 2019 to 2022 was full of changes, some expected and some not even imagined. This has placed greater pressures on destinations and DMOs, making it even more vital for them to prove their worth and performance.

Chapter 20 is about measuring and managing destination management performance.

The chapter begins by discussing the uniqueness of destination management and DMOs and how this affects performance measurement. Then, performance measurement and management and their underlying reasons are defined. Measurement is connected with the destination management roles that you learned about in Chapter 1. Accountability, transparency, and benchmarking are discussed, as are ROI and performance improvement. The key role of performance metrics is explained and various levels for performance measurement are identified.

Performance measurement systems are reviewed including "off-the-shelf" ones such as the BSC and the Performance Prism, and DIY (do it yourself) approaches that tailor-make performance measurement for specific DMOs. Having clear metrics to measure performance is crucial and these are often called KPIs that accompany objectives.

Chapter 20 outlines a process for developing a performance measurement system and puts forward the general PRICE-R model. DMO performance reporting is critical and you can think of it as a specialized form of IMC in which DMOs tell their stakeholders what and how they have done. You will see how selected DMOs accomplish this reporting.

DMO funding sources and levels are described, along with relevant examples. You will learn that funding is a major issue for many DMOs.

Your author had the honor of serving on the 2004/2005 Performance Measurement Team for Destination Marketing Association International that helped develop the first version of the Standard DMO Performance Reporting system. He has also been active in developing website evaluation tools for destinations and DMOs.

The Uniqueness of Destination Management Performance Measurement

You learned in Chapter 1 that DMOs are unique entities due to the lack of control over the quality and quantity of services and products, the lack of a pricing function, the need to serve the requirements of many organizations, the need to build consensus among stakeholders, the need to be sensitive to the interests of local residents, the need to demonstrate broad economic benefits, and the difficulty in measuring performance. On the last point, that relates directly to this chapter, it was said that DMOs have no direct sales figures at their disposal because they do not sell products and services directly to visitors. You know already then that destination management performance is difficult to measure. However, perhaps a greater dilemma is what to measure. What do you think is the answer to this dilemma?

Here is a set of eight factors that can be assessed in destination management and DMO performance measurement:

1. The overall success of the destination: Is the destination vision being achieved?
2. The overall performance of the DMO: Is the DMO fulfilling its mandate and satisfying the DMO vision?
3. The performance of the DMO against strategies, plans, goals, and objectives: Is the DMO meeting the goals and objectives set out in various strategies and plans?

4. DMO financial performance: Are there adequate financial controls in place within the DMO? Is funding being used effectively?
5. DMO departmental performance: Are departments achieving their goals and objectives?
6. DMO management and staff performance: Are management and staff being productive and efficient? Are they meeting their individual goals and targets?
7. DMO vendor performance: Are vendors delivering what they promised? Are vendors being efficient and effective?
8. DMO social responsibility and sustainability performance: Are DMOs satisfying their goals for social responsibility and sustainable tourism? Are DMOs functioning ethically?

This surely is a rather a long list of factors to measure and in this chapter you will hear about all of them. Before starting, however, it is worth mentioning that observers say that performance measurement in tourism and hospitality has not been given enough attention by academics and practitioners (e.g., d'Angella and Go 2009; Altin et al. 2018). Research indicates that performance measurement assists destinations in being agile and able to transform, if necessary (McLennan et al. 2013) and this also applies to DMOs. This book suggests that performance measurement be assigned a high priority by DMOs.

The discussion starts with definitions of performance measurement and performance management.

Definitions of Performance Measurement and Performance Management

DEFINITION

Performance measurement

Performance measurement is a process that tracks the outcomes of destination management and how they reflect the organization's performance.

Performance management

Information, systems, and processes applied to optimally use the DMO's resources to achieve goals and objectives efficiently and effectively.

Efficiently means doing things at the lowest cost or with the least effort. Effectively means that the DMO is successful in achieving its objectives.

These definitions imply that performance needs to be tracked and that means that the DMO does not wait until the end of the year to tally the results. You already know that destinations are different from other products and DMOs are unique types of organizations. DMOs are typically either nonprofit or governmental organizations. They are not required to make profits; they have stakeholders rather than shareholders. Next, we need to discuss the outcomes for DMOs to track.

Destination Management Roles Performance (8 + 3D Platform)

The overall performance of DMOs should be assessed. However, what outcomes you might ask are to be tracked? Going back to Chapter 1, these are the outcomes of implementing all destination management roles (Fig. 20.1). In this figure you can see the eight DMO roles sitting on a

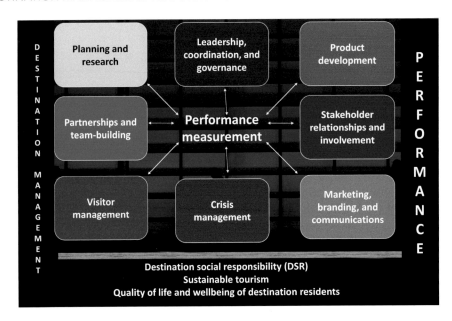

Figure 20.1 Performance measurement of destination management roles: 8 + 3D platform.

EXAMPLE 20.1

DMO Performance on Sustainability

DMOs should state what they have achieved in following sustainable tourism guidelines. This example describes Tourism Australia's sustainable tourism initiatives in 2020/2021.

> Driving awareness of, and capability for, a sustainable tourism industry is a priority for Tourism Australia and is enshrined in our corporate values. Our focus in 2020/21 concentrated on: Advocacy—showcasing sustainable and purpose-driven tourism experiences; Leadership—educating and enabling greater capacity for sustainability in our industry; Brand integration—highlighting sustainability in our marketing activities and driving uptake of sustainable tourism experiences; Industry support—encouraging industry best practice and raising awareness of Australian tourism's sustainability credentials; and Operational initiatives—including reducing our office and event footprint, sourcing from sustainable providers and establishing sustainable credentials for our partners and suppliers as outlined in Tourism Australia's Modern Slavery Statement.
>
> (Tourism Australia 2021)

Learning Point

DMOs should report on their sustainable tourism performance.

three-dimensional (3D) platform of destination social responsibility, sustainable tourism, and quality of life and well-being of destination residents.

Reasons for Performance Measurement

Effective governance is part of the reason for the performance tracking and you learned about accountability and transparency in Chapter 6. Improving performance in the future by learning from the past is another reason.

Tourism is rapidly changing and the competition is intense. Performance measurement in such a dynamic environment is not a luxury; it is a necessity. It must be in every tool-box of professional DMOs. There are five main reasons for measuring performance (Fig. 20.2):

1. Accountability: DMOs need to prove to others that they are being effective. Are they meeting their goals and objectives?
2. Benchmarking: DMOs should compare their performance with that of other DMOs and destination management best practices. What are other DMOs doing that they can emulate?
3. Performance improvement: DMOs as professional organizations should want to constantly improve their practices, strategies, programs, and activities. What should the DMO improve upon in the future?
4. Performance measurement: DMOs must measure performance for all roles. How effective was the DMO in performing each role?
5. ROI: DMOs should determine the ROI on all activities and on specific individual initiatives and campaigns. What did the DMO produce for the amount of resources used?

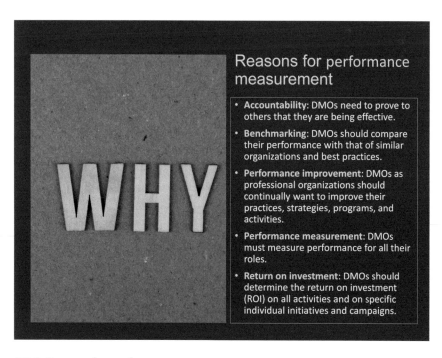

Figure 20.2 Reasons for performance measurement.

These reasons are now explored in greater detail, so you have a better understanding of what is involved with each of them. You already have heard about performance measurement.

Accountability

You learned in Chapter 6 that DMOs need to be accountable, and this is a major reason for performance measurement. The following is a definition of accountability:

DEFINITION

Accountability

Accountability is the obligation of a DMO to justify the roles, programs, and activities that it selects, and to accept the responsibility for the results from implementing these programs and activities. Performance results must be disclosed in a transparent manner and responsibility must be assumed for all resources used.

The following is a more detailed explanation of the components of accountability.

DISCLOSURE OF RESULTS

DMOs cannot keep results secret but must disclose them in the way that it is required by policies or legal constitution. If the organization is governmental, it may be subject to open public records and thus any resident can request to see all of its records. Many developed countries have enacted Freedom of Information (FOI) laws that apply to national, state, provincial, and territorial government agencies and give the public access to documents, data, and other information from governments. Disclosure is related to the concept of transparency which is a dimension of governance. By disclosing details on its decision-making and program results, an organization is demonstrating its transparency.

DEFINITION

Transparency

Transparency means openness in operations and communications.

MEASUREMENT OF RESULTS

DMOs must first specify the results they intend to achieve from particular roles, programs, and activities. Here is where goals and objectives along with KRAs and KPIs are used. Results must be measured during and after the implementation of the programs and activities.

EXAMPLE 20.2

Accountability Statement: Tourism Nova Scotia

This example from Nova Scotia provides a clear connection between accountability and DMO business planning.

> The Accountability Report of Tourism Nova Scotia for the year ended March 31, 2021 is prepared pursuant to the Finance Act and government policies and guidelines. These authorities require the reporting of outcomes against the Tourism Nova Scotia Business Plan for the fiscal year just ended. The reporting of Tourism Nova Scotia outcomes necessarily includes estimates, judgments, and opinions by Tourism Nova Scotia management.
>
> We acknowledge that this Accountability Report is the responsibility of Tourism Nova Scotia management. The report is, to the extent possible, a complete and accurate representation of outcomes relative to the goals and priorities set out in the Tourism Nova Scotia 2020–21 Business Plan.
>
> (Tourism Nova Scotia 2021a)

Learning Point

DMO should connect accountability with performance of their business plans.

PROGRAM JUSTIFICATION

DMOs must explain why they are proposing to implement specific programs and activities for an upcoming cycle of business operations. Assumptions and facts based upon completed research must be revealed in the rationale for plans. Typically, this is accomplished by making presentations of the strategies and plans to a broader audience and then seeking approval to proceed with them.

EXAMPLE 20.3

A DMO Business Plan Outline

Several DMOs prepare corporate or business plans that are comprehensive statements of what they plan to do in the next one to three years. This is an example of such a plan by the Greater Raleigh Convention and Visitors Bureau (GRCVB) in North Carolina, USA. You will notice that the plan states what each department will be doing.

> About the Greater Raleigh Convention and Visitors Bureau
> Visitor Profile for Raleigh and Wake County, NC
> Talking Points for the 2022–2023 Fiscal Year

Destination Strategic Plan and Implementation for Destination 2028
Business Planning for Post-Pandemic Tourism
Marketing and Communications Department
Public Relations and International Tourism Department
Convention Sales Department
Destination Services Department
Greater Raleigh Sports Alliance
Destination Technology Department
Administration Department
GRCVB Community Engagement Strategy
Summary of GRCVB Measurable Performance Objectives
Industry Leadership Positions Held by GRCVB Staff.

(GRCVB 2022)

Learning Point

Business or corporate plans go beyond marketing plans and are comprehensive statements of what DMOs are planning to do and why.

RESPONSIBILITY FOR USE OF RESOURCES

DMOs must account for the use of all resources and especially for the financial budget and staff
allocated to them. The accounting for the use of funding is done through the preparation of
audited financial statements. Many organizations prepare annual reports that provide an overall summary of results, as well as looking ahead to future operating cycles. For governmental
organizations, periodic financial audits may be conducted on the expenditures and on procedures used in contracting with vendors.

RESPONSIBILITY FOR RESULTS

DMOs must take full responsibility for the actual results for particular roles, programs, and
activities. If the expected results were not achieved, explanations are needed as to why performance did not meet the expected standards.

It is tough to say this, but it cannot be ignored—there are some people who feel that DMOs
are unnecessary. For example, they argue why do you need to market places like Paris and
Venice or Disney parks; don't they market themselves? Good question indeed. Another view
of marketers is that they love to spend money and hate to assess the results of that spending
(Adler 1967). Whether that is true or not, it is a fact that DMOs generally have come under
greater scrutiny since the early 2000s (da Gama 2011; O'Sullivan and Abela 2007; Webster,
Malter, and Ganesan 2005). In these circumstances, demonstrating accountability is essential
for DMOs.

Benchmarking

From the late 1990s onward there has been a growing interest in the concept of benchmarking
(Bosetti et al. 2006; Fuchs and Weiermair 2004; Kozak 2002; Kozak and Rimmington 1998;
Xiang et al. 2007; Wöber 2001). Based on the recommendations of these previous scholars, the
following is a working definition of benchmarking (Fig. 20.3).

Benchmarking

Benchmarking is continually measuring and improving performance against the best in destination management as well as relative to competitors. The goal is to obtain information about new and successful programs and activities, and to gather data on comparable results.

Figure 20.3 Benchmarking.

DEFINITION

Benchmarking

Benchmarking is continually measuring and improving performance against the best in destination management as well as relative to competitors. The goal is to obtain information about new and successful programs and activities, and to gather data on comparable results.

DMOs need to pinpoint who are the best at destination management and especially within their own regions. They also need to have standards and criteria to judge what is effective and successful in destination management. Honestly, this is a very difficult task as there are no worldwide standards; they are only partial. For example, Destination Marketing Association International (DMAI, now Destinations International) is one important source for suggested criteria for evaluating DMO marketing performance.

In order to benchmark successfully, the units of measurement must be the same and that is exactly what DMAI has been advocating. In the case of e-marketing, it is fortunate that there are standard measurement units that can be applied for benchmarking (Hua 2016; Plaza 2011; Stepchenkova et al. 2010; Wang 2008). You will remember the performance metrics for e-marketing that were discussed in Chapter 14 and shown in Figure 14.10.

Performance Improvement

A major benefit of performance measurement is that it has the potential to indicate where improvements can be made in strategies, programs, and activities. Here is a definition of performance improvement:

DEFINITION

Performance improvement

Measuring the outcomes of the roles, strategies and plans, programs, and activities used in destination management and then modifying these roles, strategies and plans, programs, and activities to enhance or increase the outcomes.

The evidence for motivating performance improvements may come through benchmarking or be a result of internal short-term assessments of strategies or plans or based on the recommendations of DMO audits.

Return on Investment

Calculating the financial ROI on the funds used is important in demonstrating the value of destination management. This may be a requirement within a DMO, and is an aspect of showing accountability for the resources used.

DEFINITION

Return on investment (ROI)

The ROI in destination management is how much revenues or profits are realized as a result of a given investment in a program or activity.

EXAMPLE 20.4

Traditional DMO Performance Measures Are Insufficient

This example based on a book chapter by Tyrell and Johnston argues that DMO performance measures do not adequately reflect all of the contributions to their communities. They were referring to the ROI measures in DMAI's Standard DMO Reporting System.

These (traditional) measures, while reflecting dollar flows at least arguably generated by convention and visitors bureau (CVB) investments, do not reflect the net benefits that CVB activities provide to the public.

When considering both return and investment, each should reflect a more comprehensive, total value perspective including environmental, social, and economic benefits and costs to each stakeholder. The purpose of this chapter is to provide a theoretical basis for performance measures based on total values. For simplicity, we consider benefits realized by three major stakeholders: the tourism industry, tourists, and local residents.

(Tyrell and Johnston 2013)

Learning Point

DMOs must more comprehensively measure all the benefits they create for their communities.

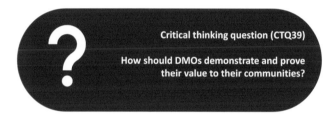

Critical thinking question (CTQ39)

How should DMOs demonstrate and prove their value to their communities?

Performance Metrics

Metrics are measures of performance and in Chapter 6 you learned that these are often called KPIs. KPIs are set for KRAs and these are the destination management roles (Fig. 20.4).

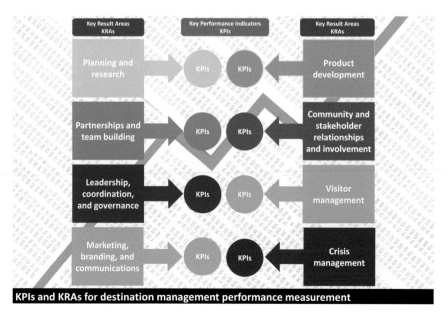

Figure 20.4 KPIs and KRAs for destination management performance measurement.

EXAMPLE 20.5

KPIs of Tourism Western Australia

It is important that DMOs set targets to achieve for upcoming planning periods and then measure actual results against these targets. This example lists the KPIs set by the state tourism agency for Western Australia.

> Key Effectiveness Indicators: Key Effectiveness Indicators assist with the assessment of agency (Tourism Western Australia) performance in the achievement of government desired outcomes.
> KPI 1. Total dollar amount spent by visitors in Western Australia.
> Target: $8.8 billion Actual: $7.6 billion
> KPI 2. Total overnight visitors to/within Western Australia.
> Target: 11.4 million Actual: 9.0 million
> KPI 3. Western Australia's market share of international visitor spend in Australia. Target: 7.7 percent Actual: 7.2 percent
> KPI 4. Number of persons employed directly or indirectly by tourism in Western Australia.
> Target: 118,200 Actual 94,800
> KPI 5. Percentage of visitors very likely to recommend visiting Western Australia. Target: 86 percent Actual: 90 percent
> KPI 6. Ratio of funds provided by the tourism industry to Tourism WA's investment in cooperative marketing.
> Target: 0.9:1 Actual: 1.7:1
> KPI 7. Direct economic impact of major events sponsorship.
> Target: $47.3 million Actual: Not applicable
> KPI 8. Ratio of Tourism WA's total cost of services to total visitor spend in Western Australia.
> Target 1:78 Actual 1:88.
>
> (Tourism Western Australia 2021)

Learning Point

KPIs are instrumental to measuring the performance of DMOs.

With such a great variety of DMOs worldwide, it is difficult to be highly specific about performance metrics. However, based upon the coordinative functions of DMOs supplied in Chapter 6 (Fig. 6.9), samples of metrics can be suggested for each role. Overall metrics are listed in Figure 20.5, and these are broader-reaching measures of performance, e.g., having shared ownership of the destination vision, uniform adoption of the destination brand. These metrics are not necessarily quantitative; however, they can be checked if satisfied or not.

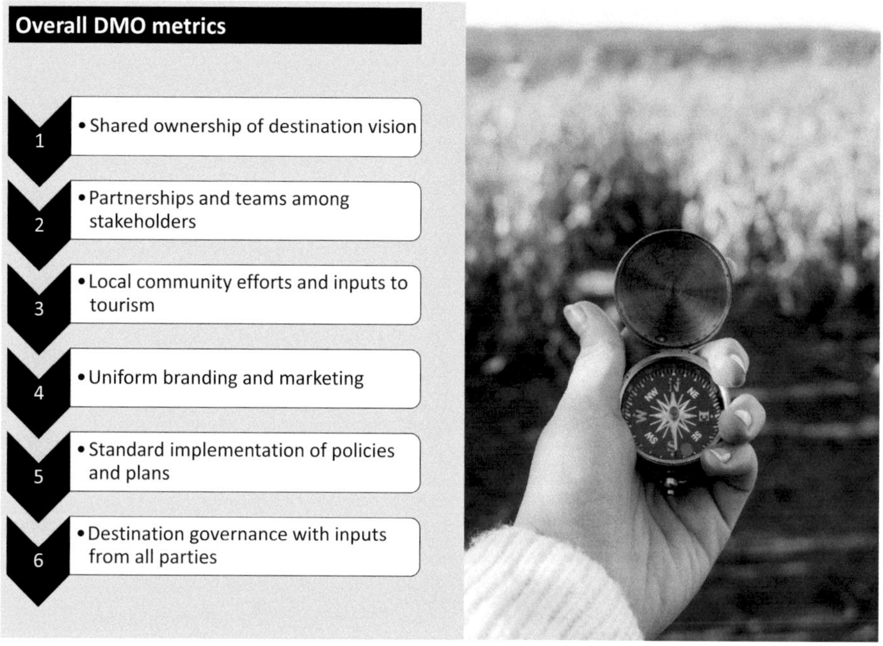

Overall DMO metrics	
1	• Shared ownership of destination vision
2	• Partnerships and teams among stakeholders
3	• Local community efforts and inputs to tourism
4	• Uniform branding and marketing
5	• Standard implementation of policies and plans
6	• Destination governance with inputs from all parties

Figure 20.5 Sample of overall DMO metrics.

EXAMPLE 20.6

Wonderful Copenhagen and Tourism for Good

This is an outstanding example of a DMO that is taking sustainability very seriously. Wonderful Copenhagen has undertaken an initiative known as Tourism for Good.

Focus area 1: Broadening tourism:
KPI: Continued growth in tourism is supported by at least 80 percent of local residents
KPI: Creating regular opportunities for locals to be involved in tourism development
KPI: Developing a method to measure broader tourism in terms of geography, interests and time
Focus area 2: Tourism choices matter:
KPI: 77 percent of visitors intend to recommend the destination
KPI: 100 percent of large convention venues and 90 percent of large hotels have third-party sustainability certification
KPI: To develop a detailed content strategy, that will nudge travelers to more diverse experiences in term of geography, season, time and interests
Focus area 3: Partnerships for good

KPI: Sustainability must be considered a core element in all of Wonderful Copenhagen's new projects and partnerships

KPI: Copenhagen maintains a score of over 90 percent and a top three ranking in the global destination sustainability index of the world's most sustainable meeting and conference destinations

KPI: Wonderful Copenhagen has established itself as the primary source for updated knowledge on sustainable tourism and destination development

Focus area 4: Leading by example

KPI: Having a third-party environmental certification of own operations in 2018 2021

KPI: An organic conversion of own food and beverage procurement: 30 percent in 2019, 60 percent in 2020 and 90 percent in 2021

KPI: Being an organization that considers social inclusion in its recruitment.

(Wonderful Copenhagen 2020)

Learning Point

DMOs can and should establish KPIs for sustainable development and sustainable tourism.

Figure 20.6 shows samples of metrics for the planning and research and leadership, coordination, and governance roles.

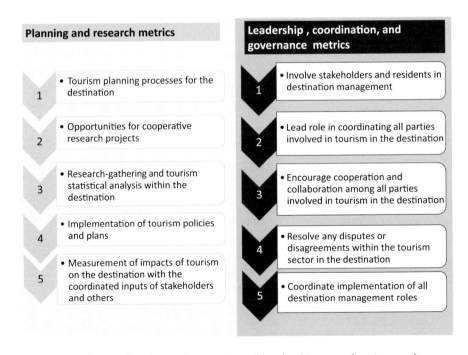

Figure 20.6 Samples of planning and research and leadership, coordination, and governance metrics.

Destination Canada Data and Analytics Performance

Destination Canada, in this example, reports on the results of implementing its research role.

> Destination Canada plays a significant role in supplying industry, governments, partners, media and our own organization with useful and reliable information. Throughout 2021, we continued to supply a torrent of data, research and analysis—including business intelligence, competitive insights, industry trends, market analysis and revenue forecasts—to governments, industry associations and businesses to assist them with navigating the pandemic and its challenges.
> (Destination Canada 2022: 33)

Learning Point

DMOs should report the results for each of their destination management roles.

Figure 20.7 supplies a sample of metrics for measuring performance of the product development and partnership and team-building roles.

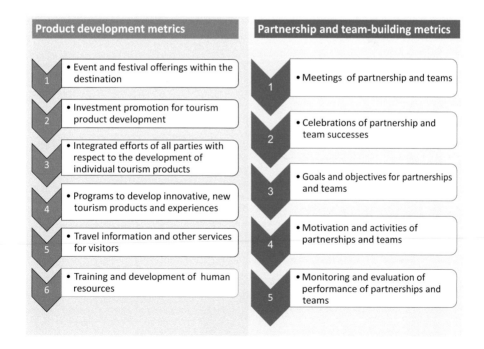

Product development metrics	Partnership and team-building metrics
1 • Event and festival offerings within the destination	1 • Meetings of partnership and teams
2 • Investment promotion for tourism product development	2 • Celebrations of partnership and team successes
3 • Integrated efforts of all parties with respect to the development of individual tourism products	3 • Goals and objectives for partnerships and teams
4 • Programs to develop innovative, new tourism products and experiences	4 • Motivation and activities of partnerships and teams
5 • Travel information and other services for visitors	5 • Monitoring and evaluation of performance of partnerships and teams
6 • Training and development of human resources	

Figure 20.7 Samples of product development and partnership and team-building metrics.

Potential metrics for the stakeholder relationships and involvement and visitor management roles are listed in Figure 20.8.

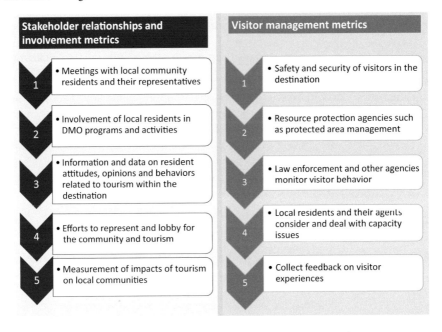

Figure 20.8 Samples of stakeholder relationships and involvement and visitor management metrics.

Figure 20.9 provides a set of metrics for the crisis management and marketing, branding, and communications roles.

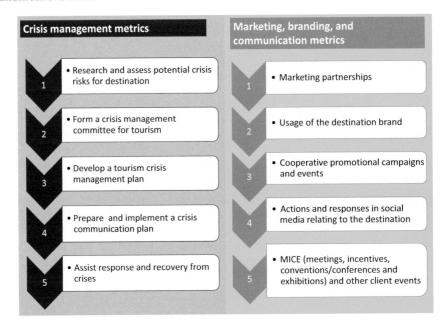

Figure 20.9 Samples of crisis management and marketing, branding, and communications metrics.

The example for Fredericksburg (Texas) shows how one city DMO sets up its marketing role metrics.

EXAMPLE 20.8

Fredericksburg CVB Metrics

DMOs should select metrics that reflect key aspects of their performance. This example lists the metrics used by the DMO in Fredericksburg, Texas: Fredericksburg CVB (FCVB). These metrics are mainly related to marketing, branding, and communications.

> In this annual report, we are providing statistical data to show where we were in 2019, the negative effects of COVID in 2020 and the recovery in 2021.
> Unique visitors to VisitFredericksburgTX.com
> Visitors welcomed at Visitor Information Center
> Packets mailed or distributed
> Phone calls answered
> People watched DVD
> Millions in media value
> Future group room nights booked by FCVB sales team
> Media professionals hosted by FCVB communications team
> Group planners visited Fredericksburg.
>
> (FCVB 2022)

Learning Point

Without specific metrics, performance cannot be effectively and accurately measured.

Levels of Performance Measurement for Destination Management

Before going any further, you should know about the different levels at which performance is conducted. There are eight major levels:

1. Customers;
2. Residents;
3. Competitive and peer;
4. Campaign;
5. IMC component or sub-component;
6. Plans;
7. Strategies;
8. Organization.

CUSTOMERS

Visitors and potential visitors are a top priority for destination management. The author argues that it is crucial to include visitor evaluations of destinations and destination management. The factors to be measured include awareness, image, satisfaction, and loyalty (Eccleston and

MacMillan 2012). MacMillan et al. (2017) and others recommend that evaluation should be done over the entire consumer journey in travel, a concept that was covered in Chapter 15 (Fig. 15.1).

RESIDENTS

How do local residents evaluate the destination and destination management? This was a topic discussed in Chapter 3. The need for resident sentiment analysis is being accentuated by the overtourism phenomenon and local people are questioning whether more marketing, branding, and communications are required to produce greater volumes of visitors.

COMPETITIVE AND PEER

DMOs can benefit from assessing their programs and activities against competitors and peers. This should be part of the situation analyses (Chapter 12) conducted to support planning. The most basic level is to compare budgets with competitors or peers (if these figures are available). For example, the Survey of US State Tourism Office Budgets allows US STOs to compare their total budgets with those of other states (USTA 2022).

EXAMPLE 20.9

State Tourism Office Funding in the USA

This example reviews useful budget and staff level data for the state-level DMOs in the USA. These statistics have been gathered for many years, providing useful benchmarking information for STOs.

The fact sheet provides an overview of state tourism offices (STOs) total funding, funding dedicated to marketing/promotion, other revenue, funding sources and staff breakdowns for FY 2021–2022. Includes changes in funding compared to the prior fiscal year."

Some of the highlights are:
The mean average total budget was $22.36 million (FY 2021/2022).
The mean average budget for marketing was $12.5 million.
Other funding sources included COVID-19 relief funding (twenty-three states), pass through funds (sixteen states), and grants and/or co-ops (thirty states).
The staff distribution breakdown was: 1–10 staff = 25 percent (of forty STOs); 11–20 = 17 percent; 21–30 = 20 percent; 31–50 = 15 percent; more than 50 = 23 percent
State tourism funding has increased 20 percent during the past five years.

(USTA 2022)

Learning Point

Budget and staff level data assist DMOs in performance measurement and benchmarking.

It is also possible to do comparisons by analyzing best practices. This was made possible for city DMOs when UNWTO and the WTCF published a success factor report for city tourism (UNWTO/WTCF 2019).

EXAMPLE 20.10

Success Factors for City Tourism Performance

DMOs need to have critical success factors (CSFs) to guide in the implementation of various roles. UNWTO and the WTCF benchmarked the success of tourism in fifteen cities (Antwerp, Beijing, Berlin, Bogota, Buenos Aires, Cape Town, Copenhagen, Hangzhou, Linz, Marrakech, Sapporo, Seoul, Tianjin, Tokyo, and Turin). The resulting success factors in this example should be useful to all DMOs.

> Based on an analysis and evaluation of the case studies, the following success factors for city tourism performance have been identified:

> - Long-term vision and strategic planning
> - Public and private sector involvement
> - Economic support
> - Authenticity
> - Community engagement
> - Cultural-heritage investments
> - Product development
> - Events
> - Policy for sustainable development and management
> - Technology.
>
> (UNWTO/WTCF 2019)

Learning Point

CSFs provide guidelines for implementing destination management roles.

The remaining five levels are internal measures from an organizational perspective.

CAMPAIGN

This is the most basic level of evaluation with the focus being on a single campaign.

IMC COMPONENT OR SUB-COMPONENT

Here, the individual components of IMC are evaluated. This can be critical in guiding how to prioritize the spending on the IMC components. For example, an evaluation was made of Ireland's social media marketing for tourism (Barcoe and Whelan 2018). Sometimes, evaluations probe deeper into the components; for example, there are evaluations of social media influencers (Gräve 2019).

PLANS

The focus is on the evaluation of an entire business or marketing plan (or strategic business or marketing plan) usually covering one year. This is part of the situation analysis (i.e., marketing plan analysis) as you learned in Chapter 12.

STRATEGIES

This evaluation takes a three- to five-year perspective on the implementation of a strategy. In Chapters 12 and 13, a marketing strategy is defined as consisting of target markets and PIB. The evaluation can focus on the choice of target markets by the destination; the image among consumers; or on the branding approach that has been used. Chapter 5 reviewed how destination image analysis is conducted. Chapter 13 discussed brand evaluation which is also recommended by industry experts (Pike 2014).

ORGANIZATION

There is more to destination management than just having a focus on external programming, and a more holistic evaluation is also needed of a DMO and its human and non-human resources.

The 80–20 Principle and the Iceberg Effect

You should know about one common problem with destination management. This can best be described as the 80–20 principle, or putting 80 percent of the effort or resources into capturing only 20 percent of the roles or targets. For example, there is a tendency to put too much effort and budget into attracting certain types of customers and too little into others. Although the actual percentages may not be 80 percent and 20 percent, the important point is that many DMOs are unaware of the problem in the first place.

Some also refer to this as the iceberg effect, meaning that managers often make decisions based on superficial information (they see only the tip of the iceberg). As every captain knows, it is the larger section of the iceberg under the water that can sink a ship. A wide course must be steered around this navigational obstacle. Likewise, a manager must take an in-depth look at a broad range of information to ensure that activities and programs are as effective as possible. How can the 80–20 principle or the iceberg effect be avoided? The answer is by carefully controlling and comprehensively evaluating plan results.

EXAMPLE 20.11

The 80–20 Principle

This principle highlights an issue of putting too much effort into certain programs and activities, while there are others that are contributing more to overall DMO performance.

The 80–20 principle asserts that a minority of causes, inputs or effort usually lead to a majority of the results, outputs or rewards. Taken literally, this means that, for example, 80 percent of what you achieve in your job comes from 20 percent of time spent. Thus, for all practical purposes, four-fifths of the effort—a dominant part of it—is largely irrelevant. This is contrary to what people normally expect. So, the 80–20 Principle states that there is an inbuilt imbalance between causes and results, inputs and outputs, and effort and reward.

(Koch 1998)

Learning Point

DMOs need to carefully assess the contributions to performance of all programs and activities.

Performance Measurement Systems

Performance measurement is a popular management topic and a number of performance measurement systems are in use. You will now get a brief review of the most prominent of these systems.

Balanced Scorecard

The BSC is one of the most recognized performance measurement systems in management. The BSC was introduced in Chapter 4 as a potential planning approach. It was introduced by Kaplan and Norton in 1992 (Kaplan and Norton 1992, 1993; Kaplan 2010). The basic idea behind the BSC is that performance measurement must be multidimensional and not just based on financial success. The model brought more balance in financial versus non-financial objectives, long-term versus short-term, and external versus internal factors (Star et al. 2016). The original model measures performance from four perspectives—financial, customer, learning and growth, and internal processes (Fig. 20.10).

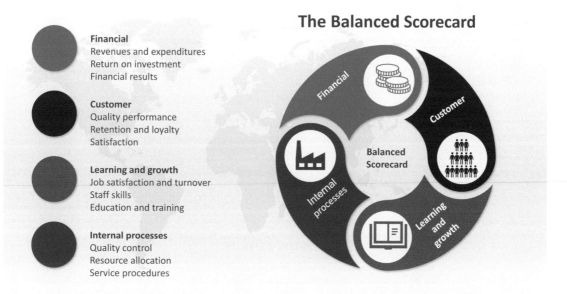

Financial
Revenues and expenditures
Return on investment
Financial results

Customer
Quality performance
Retention and loyalty
Satisfaction

Learning and growth
Job satisfaction and turnover
Staff skills
Education and training

Internal processes
Quality control
Resource allocation
Service procedures

Figure 20.10 The Balanced Scorecard.

The BSC approach has not been widely applied in hospitality and tourism (Fatima and Elbanna 2020; Phillips and Louvieris 2005). Some BSC users have added sustainability as a fifth perspective. However, it can be modified and applied to destinations and DMOs, as you saw in Chapter 15 with the WebEVAL system (Fig. 15.10) that was based on a modified BSC. There is a major lesson as well from the BSC and it is that performance measurement must be multidimensional (Aureli and Del Baldo 2019) and that no single perspective should dominate the others.

Performance Prism

The development of the Performance Prism is attributed to Neely (Neely et al. 2001; Najmi et al. 2012). These authors believed it was an enhancement on the BSC since it considered all stakeholders' wants, needs, and potential contributions. The system contemplates stakeholders including management and staff, customers, employees, local communities, suppliers, regulatory agencies, and other interested parties (Star et al. 2016). This seems to be a good fit with destinations and DMOs. The five facets of the Prism (Fig. 20.11) are:

1. Stakeholder satisfaction: Who are the DMO's stakeholders and what do they want and need?
2. Strategies: What are the strategies the DMO requires to make sure the wants and needs of its stakeholders are satisfied?
3. Processes: What are the processes that the DMO has to put in place to allow its strategies to be delivered?
4. Capabilities: What are the capabilities the DMO needs to operate its processes?

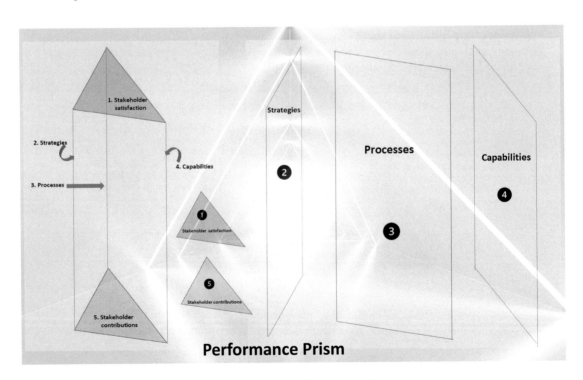

Figure 20.11 The Performance Prism (Neely et al. 2001, p. 12).

5. Stakeholder contributions: What are and can stakeholders contribute to the DMO's strategies, processes, and capabilities?

Dashboards

A dashboard is "a graphical display, ideally suited to share the status of the various performance measures that make up the scorecard. Dashboards use familiar objects such as gauges, stoplights, and [other] graphs to make the performance information more intuitive to a wider audience" (Schiff 2008: 29).

Dashboards are being used by several DMOs on their websites. Just a small sampling of these are the Asheville Convention and Visitors Bureau (North Carolina, USA), Belize Tourism Board, Destination Greater Victoria (Canada), Dubai Tourism, Hawai'i Department of Business, Economic Development and Tourism, Ministry of Tourism Republic of Maldives, Myrtle Beach Area CVB (South Carolina, USA), and Qatar Tourism (see References for links to these dashboards). It should be mentioned that these dashboards tend to measure the destination's tourism performance and results for hotels (Fig. 20.12). They do not usually measure the performance of the DMOs.

Destination Performance Report — ASHEVILLE

Lodging & Visitor Overview - August 2022

	Lodging Sales	Hotel Occupancy*	Hotel Demand*	Hotel ADR*	Hotel RevPAR*
	$64,545,050	76.9%	214,862	$192.34	$147.83
(July)	↓ -2.8% (July)	↓ -7.5% (July)	↓ -4.7% (July)	↓ -1.1% (July)	↓ -8.5%

	Airport Passengers	Asheville Visitor Center	Pack Sq Visitor Center	Black Mtn Visitor Center	Travel Guide Requests
	196,393	15,425	0	3,930	2,595
(July)	↕ 7.6%	↓ -5.3%	N/A	↓ -25.1%	↕ 15.8%

Lodging & Visitor Overview - Fiscal Year 22-23

	Lodging Sales	Hotel Occupancy*	Hotel Demand*	Hotel ADR*	Hotel RevPAR*
	$64,545,050	76.9%	214,862	$192.34	$147.83
	↓ -2.8%	↓ -7.5%	↓ -4.7%	↓ -1.1%	↓ -8.5%

	Airport Passengers	Asheville Visitor Center	Pack Sq Visitor Center	Black Mtn Visitor Center	Travel Guide Requests
	196,393	33,726	0	8,027	5,060
	↕ 7.6%	↓ -9.3%	N/A	↓ -25.8%	↕ 5.5%

Figure 20.12 Asheville Convention and Visitors Bureau Destination Performance Report dashboard.

EXAMPLE 20.12

What Should DMO Dashboards Measure?

This example tries to provide guidance to DMOs on the metrics to include in their online dashboards. This book does not treat individual attractions as destinations; however, apart from that, gathering data on economic impact and expenditures are good suggestions.

Not surprisingly though, like most marketers, DMOs are under pressure to prove their performance. We'd like to lend them a hand uncovering the top KPIs and charts to include in their performance dashboard in order to be able to not only justify, but also optimize their efforts.

What KPIs should DMO dashboards measure?

DMOs define their objectives around their top priorities: awareness and economic impact, if they are a tourism board, and revenue if they are a paid attraction. Depending on which objectives are most crucial to their business success, they may include some of the following KPIs in their dashboard— awareness, economic impact, revenue.

(McKendry 2015)

Learning Point

DMOs should choose dashboard metrics that are connected with their missions, visions, goals, strategies, and plans.

Custom-Designed Performance Measurement Systems

Many DMOs design custom performance measurement systems because "off-the-shelf" approaches to not completely fit their unique circumstances. The Standard DMO Performance Reporting system that was developed by Destinations International is an example of a system specifically designed for destinations and DMOs.

Performance Measurement Process

A general performance measurement process is illustrated in Figure 20.13. You can think of this as the PRICE-R process: planning, research, implementation, control, and evaluation, followed by reporting.

Specific steps have been recommended for establishing performance measurement systems for public and NPOs (e.g., Poister et al. 2015). Your author recommends the following steps:

- Identify the purposes of the performance measurement system: Articulate the reasons for having the system and the system's objectives.
- Identify and engage stakeholders: Select and engage with the stakeholders who will advise on the system design and metrics.
- Design system development process: Detail the procedure for developing the system.
- Define the system components: Identify what is to be measured, e.g., destination management roles.
- Define metrics: Select the metrics or KPIs to be measured.

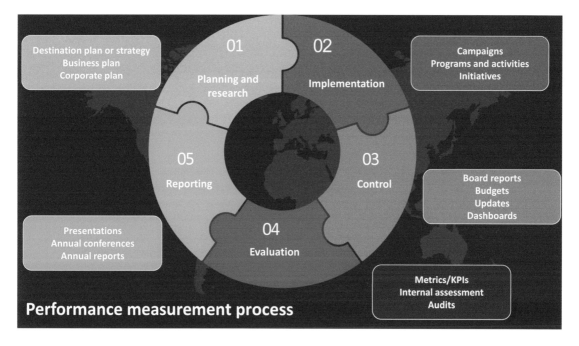

Figure 20.13 Performance measurement process: PRICE-R.

- Develop data collection procedures: Specify how the information or data for each metric is to be gathered.
- Specify system design: Define the reporting frequencies and communication channels; specify formats for reporting; identify any software needs; assign responsibilities for system maintenance.
- Conduct a test run and implement the full-scale system: Try out the system in a beta version and, after any needed adjustments, fully implement the system.
- Monitor, modify, and evaluate the system: Check the progress with system implementation; modify when and if necessary; assess system success against objectives.
- Share results with stakeholders: Report to shareholders the performance results and receive feedback.

Standard DMO Reporting System

It was mentioned in Chapter 19 that Destinations International (then DMAI) developed a standard performance reporting system for DMOs, and this system is particularly detailed for business event marketing performance reporting. The system has three components: (1) activity measures, (2) performance measures, and (3) productivity metrics. This could be classified as a custom-designed performance measurement system.

EXAMPLE 20.13

The Need for Standard DMO Performance Measurement

This example highlights that some DMOs are in danger of being audited by people who are not knowledgeable and skilled in destination management. The author agrees with this suggestion as destination management is a specialized field different from others.

> In addition to internally reviewing their operations, DMOs are often required, due to their unique funding sources, to undergo external performance reviews by various stakeholders within their local communities. At times, these external audits/reviews may be done by firms lacking DMO knowledge and experience. In the past, the DMO community had no uniform approach to reporting performance to these audiences. As a result, DMOs would sometimes find themselves limited in their ability to articulate their contribution systematically and credibly to the destination. This Handbook will serve as a basis for standards and best practices among DMOs.
>
> (DMAI 2011)

Learning Point

A uniform system of performance measurement for DMOs is needed. This Handbook was a good start but now more must be done and the scope of performance needs to be expanded.

The system identified six areas for performance measurement:

1. DMO Convention Sales Performance Reporting;
2. DMO Travel Trade Sales Performance Reporting;
3. DMO Marketing and Communications Performance Reporting;
4. DMO Membership Performance Reporting;
5. Visitor Information Center Performance Reporting;
6. DMO ROI.

Examples for convention sales performance are shown in Figures 20.14 (convention sales activities and activity measures) and 20.15 (convention sales performance and performance measures).

You can see that the measures in this system are very detailed, yet it did not cover all of the destination management roles identified in this book. It was a system to mainly measure destination marketing performance.

	Convention Sales Activities	Convention Sales Activity Measures
1.	Number of bids	
2.	Trade shows attended/exhibited	a. Number of trade shows b. Number of co-op partners attending c. Co-op monies generated
3.	Sales missions (with sector partners)	a. Number of sales missions b. Number of co-op partners participating c. Co-op monies generated
4.	Familiarization tours	a. Number of familiarization tours b. Number of participants (event organizers only) c. Number of accounts d. Number of co-op partners participating e. Co-op monies generated
5.	Number of sales calls	
6.	Number of client site inspections	
7.	Client events	a. Number of client events b. Number of participants (event organizers only) c. Number of accounts d. Number of co-op partners participating e. Co-op monies generated
8.	Sponsorships	a. Number of client events b. Trade show elements/sessions c. Monies spent d. Number of people at sponsored events ('customer-exposed impressions)
9.	Number of accounts with activity	

Figures 20.14 Convention sales activities and measures (DMAI 2011, p. 7).

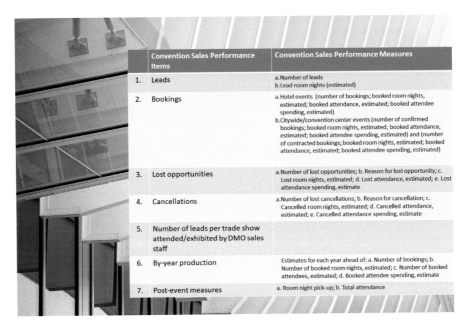

Convention Sales Performance Items	Convention Sales Performance Measures
1. Leads	a. Number of leads b. Lead room nights (estimated)
2. Bookings	a. Hotel events (number of bookings; booked room nights, estimated; booked attendance, estimated; booked attendee spending, estimated) b. Citywide/convention center events (number of confirmed bookings; booked room nights, estimated; booked attendance, estimated; booked attendee spending, estimated) and (number of contracted bookings; booked room nights, estimated; booked attendance, estimated; booked attendee spending, estimated)
3. Lost opportunities	a. Number of lost opportunities; b. Reason for lost opportunity; c. Lost room nights, estimated; d. Lost attendance, estimated; e. Lost attendance spending, estimate
4. Cancellations	a. Number of lost cancellations; b. Reason for cancellation; c. Cancelled room nights, estimated; d. Cancelled attendance, estimated; e. Cancelled attendance spending, estimate
5. Number of leads per trade show attended/exhibited by DMO sales staff	
6. By-year production	Estimates for each year ahead of: a. Number of bookings; b. Number of booked room nights, estimated; c. Number of booked attendees, estimated; d. Booked attendee spending, estimate
7. Post-event measures	a. Room night pick-up; b. Total attendance

Figures 20.15 Convention sales performance items and measures (DMAI 2011, p. 8).

DMO Funding and Budgets

An important function of performance management and evaluation is budgeting—allocating human resources and money toward the implementation of strategies and plans. However, for DMOs the discussion about budgeting must first consider funding. DMO budgets are constrained by the funding that they receive, as they do not generate their own incomes. While some DMOs can request certain budgets, many have to take the funding they are given and then allocate amounts to each role and department.

EXAMPLE 20.14

DMO Funding Is a Big Problem in England

Finding adequate operational funding has been a perennial problem for DMOs. This example highlights the DMO funding problem in England and how COVID-19 made things worse.

> Funding is a big problem. The pandemic has led to a huge drop in commercial revenues, but this comes against the backdrop of a decade of funding being withdrawn by the public sector starting in 2012 when the government somewhat brutally cut loose DMOs from core grant funding via the old Regional Development Agencies. The DMO response was resourceful and they looked elsewhere for money by becoming more commercially minded and reliant on private sector membership. In some senses this is a good

thing, but it has also meant DMOs focusing inwards on the marketing desires of their members and has led to a huge amount of time spent constantly chasing for money.

(Department for Digital, Culture, Media and Sport 2021)

Learning Point

DMOs must diversify funding sources in the future.

Funding Sources

DMOs receive funding from a variety of sources that include the public (government) and private (commercial) sectors. Government agencies provide money to DMOs through budgetary allocations (more long-term) or grants (more short-term); they also collect and redistribute user tax collections (e.g., room taxes) to DMOs. Commercial income is mainly through memberships, sponsorships, and cooperative marketing contributions. Four models of DMO funding are now reviewed:

GOVERNMENTAL MODELS

The government allocates part of its overall budget to public-sector-operated DMOs at the national, state or territorial levels. For example, the Indonesian government allocated approximately $313 million to the Ministry of Tourism and Creative Economy for 2021.

EXAMPLE 20.15

Ministry of Tourism and Creative Economy Budget (Indonesia)

Government-run DMOs receive budgetary allocations from higher levels of government, as in Indonesia's case.

The House of Representatives" Commission XI has approved a budget ceiling of Rp 4.9 trillion for the Ministry of Tourism and Creative Economy in the 2021 budget year. The approved amount is 19.4 percent higher than the ministry's indicative ceiling of Rp 4,111,437,568,000 for the 2021 budget year.

According to Tourism and Creative Economy Minister Wishnutama Kusubandio, the budget reflects the House's support to the government to revive tourism and creative economy as the sectors struggle with the impact of the coronavirus (COVID-19) pandemic.

(IDN Financials 2020)

Learning Point

The funding of government-operated DMOs depends on the budgets allocated to them by senior government levels.

USER-PAY TAX MODELS

Visitors to destinations are required to pay taxes (user-pay taxes) that are typically added as a percentage of room charges in accommodations. These are referred to as room, bed, lodging, or transient accommodation taxes. These taxes are collected by government agencies and thereafter all or a portion of the tax collections are distributed to DMOs. In some cases, short-term accommodation operators remit the taxes directly to DMOs. In Puerto Rico, collections of a 7 percent room tax are sent each month by operators to the Puerto Rico Tourism Company (Puerto Rico Tourism Company 2022).

EXAMPLE 20.16

DMO Staff Reductions Due to COVID-19

The COVID-19 pandemic had a huge detrimental impact on many DMOs. This was especially true for DMOs relying on room or other visitor taxes, which fell drastically. This example highlights the issue in the USA where room taxes are a common method of DMO funding.

> Here we are five months into it and the situation has not improved from a financial standpoint. On average, you can probably assume 70 percent to 80 percent in staffing reductions from where we were in March, so all of our members have been having to do much more with less, with much fewer people on the sales and services side.
>
> (Davidson 2020)

> Restaurants and hotels were among the first industry segments to close their doors and reduce staffing due to coronavirus. Now, CVBs are facing the same difficult decisions. Across the nation, CVBs are being forced to furlough or lay off employees as the travel and events industries remain on hold.
>
> (Schoening 2020)

Learning Point

There are situations in DMOs where staff are laid off or furloughed not due to issues with their own performance. Alternative funding sources should be considered.

If there are casinos in the destination, DMOs may receive a portion of the taxes collected on casino gaming revenues. This is the case in Las Vegas (LVCVA 2021). Some destinations also collect food and beverage taxes.

BUSINESS IMPROVEMENT DISTRICT MODELS

A third funding model is more of a partnership approach. Here businesses in specific geographic areas fund a collective effort to market their destinations. The funds are principally spent on marketing, branding, and communications.

EXAMPLE 20.17

Tourism Improvement Districts

Historically, DMOs have been reliant on government funding. This is changing and new business models with greater commercial funding have emerged. These go by different names including Tourism Improvement Districts (TIDs), Tourism Business Improvement Districts (TBIDs), and Business Improvement Districts (BIDs).

> A TID is formed when a group of local businesses get together and invest collectively to support the growth and development of their area's tourism industry. Improvement Districts with a focus on tourism exist to give businesses a voice and financial stake in the future direction of tourism in their area.
>
> (VisitScotland 2022)

> A Tourism Improvement District (TID) is a revolutionary way to fund destination marketing programs. They are typically run by local businesses that collaborate and invest collectively to support the growth and development of their destination's tourism industry. Depending on where you are in the world, the concept of a TIDs has several different names. The USA first started using this term in West Hollywood in 1989. The UK and other destinations soon followed, by developing similar public–private partnerships sometimes called "Business Improvement Districts" or "Tourism Marketing Districts." Though they have different names, the goal is the same—increase the number of overnight visitors using businesses and services.
>
> (O'Hare 2021)

Learning Point

New models for DMO funding are needed and are emerging.

MEMBERSHIP MODELS

You learned about DMO membership programs in Chapter 8 as being a form of partnering. Many non-governmental DMOs have these programs and set up special departments to handle them. In general, membership fees are not sufficient to fund the entire operations of a DMO.

EXAMPLE 20.18

DMOs Are Dependent on Public Money

The Destinations International Advocacy Team provided recommendations to DMOs on diversifying funding sources beyond the public sector. This example suggests that DMOs are over-reliant on monies coming through government agencies and should seek more commercial funding from sources within their communities.

> According to our data, over 90 percent of destination organization funding comes from public sector sources. Let's break this down further: The mainstay of every destination organization is the hotel, transient occupancy, or room-night tax. This "heads in beds" levy is collected at the hotel and remitted to the government to allocate in its entirety or some percentage to the destination organization. This "transaction" through government, no matter the level, makes the destination organization the recipient of public money.
>
> (Destinations International 2020)

Learning Point

DMOs need to diversify funding sources and not be so dependent on government funding.

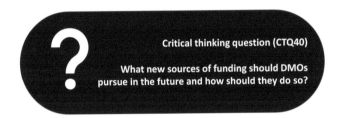

Critical thinking question (CTQ40)

What new sources of funding should DMOs pursue in the future and how should they do so?

Funding Levels

There are wide variations in DMO budget levels, even within individual countries. Earlier in this chapter, you saw information on the funding levels of state DMOs in the USA. The mean average total budget for Fiscal Year 2021/2022 was $22.36 million and, on average, $12.5 million was spent on marketing. At more of the city and county level, approximately 600 of the larger DMOs belong to Destinations International, which reports that 43 percent of its members have budgets less than $5 million, 29 percent have from $5 to $15 million, and 28 percent have budgets greater than $15 million (Destinations International 2022).

Figure 20.16 shows the income and expenses for Australian state and territorial tourism offices for 2020–2021. The table in Figure 20.16 shows that DMO income ranges from a low of AUD 37.7 million for Tasmania to a high of AUD 197.6 million for New South Wales. Total expenses vary from a high of AUD 190 million for New South Wales to a low of AUD 38.3 million for Tasmania. You will notice that income and expenses are almost equal, meaning that the DMOs tend to spend their budgets.

Figure 20.17 shows similar information for Canadian provincial-territorial DMOs for 2021.

Australian State-Territorial DMOs	Income	Expenses
Destination New South Wales	$197.6	$190.0
South Australian Tourism Commission	$94.1	$88.1
Tourism & Events Queensland	$143.3	$143.6
Tourism Northern Territory	$57.8	$58.9
Tourism Tasmania	$37.7	$38.3
Tourism Western Australia	$97.1	$85.8
Visit Victoria	$112.4	$112.4
Means	$105.7	$102.4

Australian state-territorial DMO income and expenses, 2020-2021

Figure 20.16 Australian state-territorial DMO income and expenses, 2020–2021. Information from annual reports (ACT not available). Figures in millions of Australian dollars.

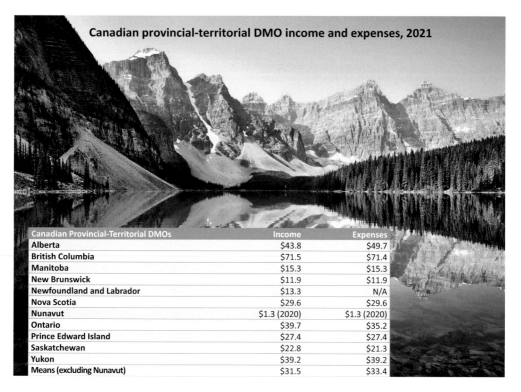

Canadian provincial-territorial DMO income and expenses, 2021

Canadian Provincial-Territorial DMOs	Income	Expenses
Alberta	$43.8	$49.7
British Columbia	$71.5	$71.4
Manitoba	$15.3	$15.3
New Brunswick	$11.9	$11.9
Newfoundland and Labrador	$13.3	N/A
Nova Scotia	$29.6	$29.6
Nunavut	$1.3 (2020)	$1.3 (2020)
Ontario	$39.7	$35.2
Prince Edward Island	$27.4	$27.4
Saskatchewan	$22.8	$21.3
Yukon	$39.2	$39.2
Means (excluding Nunavut)	$31.5	$33.4

Figure 20.17 Canadian provincial-territorial DMO income and expenses, 2021. Information from annual reports (Northwest Territories and Quebec not available). Figures in millions of Canadian dollars.

You saw the budget earlier for Indonesia's national tourism office. It should be interesting to see a few more national DMO budget levels:

- Brand USA: $68.6 million income; $47.7 million expenses (Brand USA 2021).
- Department of Tourism, South Africa: ZAR 1,392.2 million income; ZAR 1,392.2 million expenses (Department of Tourism, South Africa 2021).
- Destination Canada: CAD 113.2 million income; CAD 137.5 million expenses (Destination Canada 2022).
- German National Tourist Board (DZT): €50 million income; €50 million expenses (German National Tourist Board 2021).
- HKTB: HKD 801.8 million income; HKD 731.5 million expenses (HKTB 2021).
- Singapore Tourism Board: SGD 295.7 million income; SGD 303.4 million expenses (Singapore Tourism Board 2021).
- Tourism Australia: AUD 197.4 million income; AUD 205.7 million expenses (Tourism Australia 2021).
- VisitBritain/VisitEngland: £56.9 million income; £49.5 million expenses (VisitBritain and VisitEngland 2022).

Figure 20.18 shows these statistics in US dollars for comparison purposes.

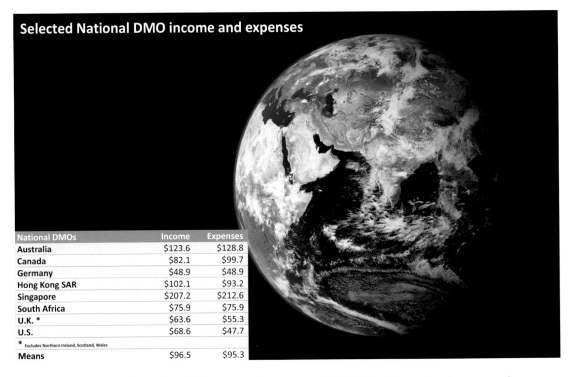

Selected National DMO income and expenses

National DMOs	Income	Expenses
Australia	$123.6	$128.8
Canada	$82.1	$99.7
Germany	$48.9	$48.9
Hong Kong SAR	$102.1	$93.2
Singapore	$207.2	$212.6
South Africa	$75.9	$75.9
U.K. *	$63.6	$55.3
U.S.	$68.6	$47.7
* Excludes Northern Ireland, Scotland, Wales		
Means	$96.5	$95.3

Figure 20.18 Selected DMO income and expenses, 2020–2021. Information from annual reports. Figures in millions of US dollars.

The major expenditure areas in most of these budgets are for marketing, branding, and communications, and DMO staff. For example, Tourism Australia stated that its costs included advertising expenses of AUD 89.7 million, promotion and publicity expenses of AUD 42.8 million, and digital and technology expenses of AUD 13.3 million. Together these three represented around 70 percent of its total expenditures. The German National Tourist Board allocated 68 percent of its budget to marketing spend. These are just two examples and should not be taken as indicative as other DMOs do not spend as much proportionately on marketing.

The author apologizes for giving you all these numbers. However, they provide you with an idea of what DMOs are spending and what they get to spend. It will be a bit difficult for you to gather this information on your own. Great care needs to be taken in using the budget figures supplied as DMO responsibilities vary. For example, in India and Indonesia, the Tourism Ministries operate tourism schools and colleges, and get part of their budget allocations for that.

Now that funding sources and levels have been reviewed, we can move to discussing evaluation.

Evaluation

You can assume that performance measurement and management are a form of destination management evaluation.

Formative and Summative Evaluation—Control and Evaluation

Destination management evaluation is completed in two parts: formative (control) and summative (evaluation). Control and evaluation are the two pillars of the overall management concept of performance measurement.

DEFINITIONS

Control

Control includes all the steps that a DMO takes to monitor and adjust its strategies and plans as they progress, as well as the procedures it selects to ensure implementation as planned. Control helps answer the question. "How do we make sure we get there?"

Evaluation

Evaluation involves analyzing results to determine the final performance of strategies and plans. Evaluation satisfies the "How do we know if we got there?" question.

Control

Controlling what goes on in a DMO is a key management function. All systems of control include three steps:

1. establishing performance standards or metrics based on strategies and plans and the objectives contained in these strategies and plans;
2. periodically monitoring actual performance against these standards;
3. adjusting procedures or activities accordingly.

What do DMOs need to control? The answer is partly to monitor the implementation of plans and strategies to ensure they are proceeding according to objectives. The other part is that funds and major cost centers must be controlled including vendors and DMO staff.

How then do DMOs control their strategies and plans? What are their standards or metrics? The two key measurement tools are objectives and budgets. Budgets assist with the financial control of plans. Periodic checks are made to see whether the budget is being spent according to the plan. Additionally, results are monitored periodically to determine progress toward achieving individual objectives. Objective-and-task budgeting is the recommended approach for DMOs. The name given to this method aptly describes what is involved. The DMO sets objectives, figures out what must be done to achieve them (the tasks), and then estimates the costs of completing the tasks (or activities).

Cost center controls include the following:

- vendor appraisals;
- staff and management appraisals;
- departmental appraisals.

Vendor Appraisals

DMOs work with a wide variety of vendors in support of their operations and marketing, branding, and communications. These include marketing, advertising, and PR agencies, research suppliers, content management system and other software firms, designers and graphic artists, and more. There must be a process in place to carefully select vendors—you will remember in Chapter 5 the discussion on selecting research vendors and the RESPECT-U process in Figure 5.17. The use of requests for proposals is a critical part of vendor selection.

Staff and Management Appraisals

It is essential that DMOs continuously conduct performance appraisals of individual staff and managers. For nonprofit DMOs, DMO executives are evaluated annually by their boards of directors. Staff appraisals are normally conducted by the heads of respective DMO departments.

Departmental Appraisals

DMOs typically evaluate the performance of all their departments each year. The appraisals are done internally by senior DMO executives, with departments submitting formal reports of performance against goals and objectives. Later, these reports may be used as part of the contents of annual reports.

Evaluation

Formal or summative evaluation takes place at the end of a DMO planning period. It focuses on effectiveness, meaning the DMO's success in achieving its predetermined objectives. You already have heard much on this already in this chapter in the discussions on how performance is measured. You also learned about evaluation research in Chapter 5 with the reasons for performance measurement shown in Figure 5.15 and the measurement of DMO roles highlighted in Figure 5.16. There you also learned about destination audits that are a formation of external evaluation research.

Before leaving the topic of evaluation, you should be aware that performance measurement and evaluation is affected by the type of DMO organization. Nonprofit DMOs are usually evaluated internally by their boards of directors and periodically may be subject to external audits. Public sector DMOs are continuously scrutinized by government audit agencies and ombudsman offices.

There will in future be more DMOs that are established as social enterprises and these types of organizations have different performance standards than traditional DMO organizational formats. For example, strong leadership and awareness of market conditions are two CSFs for social enterprises in tourism and hospitality (von der Weppen and Cochrane 2012).

Some experts suggest that performance measurement be extended to the DMO's entire value chain (d'Angella and Go 2009; Yilmaz and Bititci 2006a, 2006b). This chapter has primarily focused on performance measurement of the DMO itself, although vendor evaluations were recommended.

Performance Reporting

The last step in the PRICE-R process is reporting. For performance measurement to be effective, reporting procedures must be highly effective and carefully developed. The procedures are divided into formative (interim) and summative (final) reporting. DMOs that are nonprofits have boards of directors and the interim reporting will be to them on a monthly, bi-monthly, or quarterly basis. You also heard earlier about DMO dashboards that keep a running tally of metric results; they are an example of interim reporting.

Annual Reports and Contents

The summative reporting is at calendar or fiscal year end and the communications is much broader. Annual reports are the main tool for summative reporting. Many DMOs put their annual reports online and they can be accessed by anyone.

EXAMPLE 20.19

Functions of South Australian Commission's Annual Report

Annual reports from DMOs are a key tool for performance reporting. This example identifies the contents of the South Australian Tourism Commission's annual report and why it is prepared.

> Our annual report provides an evaluation of our agency against the KPIs agreed between our Board and the Premier with responsibility for tourism. They are published online and are publicly accessible. What does the annual report contain?
>
> - Report on the state of tourism and the tourism industry in South Australia
> - Evaluation of agency programs and initiatives
> - Financial statements
> - Human resource information.
>
> (South Australian Tourism Commission 2021)

Learning Point

The DMO annual report should include information on destination and DMO performance, and provide financial and staffing data.

The typical contents of DMO annual reports are:

- Statements from DMO executives and board chairs: Most annual reports open with broad statements about performance and intentions from senior DMO officials and political leaders.
- Highlights of recent tourism performance within the destination. Most annual reports quote visitor arrival and expenditure data.
- Discussion of recent trends in tourism. Trends are discussed at an overall and destination level.
- Review of performance either by department, initiatives, or roles. Many annual reports include sections by DMO departments and/or major initiatives.
- Comments about future plans and initiatives: There is usually some coverage in annual reports about DMO future intentions and plans.
- Financial statements: Many annual reports contain financial statements that are audited by CPAs or chartered accountants. These usually include balance sheets, income statements, cash flow statements, and accompanying support data.

Designing and Theming of Annual Reports

Presenting themselves professionally should be the goal for all DMOs when reporting. This can be thought of as a special form of IMC (Chapter 14) where the audience is composed of the DMO's stakeholders. Annual reports should be well organized with convincing and useful information. Some DMOs go to great lengths to produce eye-catching report designs. They also may attach a special annual theme to each report, as in the following cases:

- Destination Canada: *Building the Tourism of Tomorrow* (2021), 84 pages digital.
- German National Tourist Board: *Taking Opportunities* (2021), 119 pages digital.
- HKTB: *Rediscover Hong Kong* (2020/2021), 133 pages digital.
- Singapore Tourism Board: *A Year of Rediscoveries and Reimagination* (2020/2021), 129 pages digital.
- Tourism Promotion Board Philippines: *Transforming Together* (2021), 13 pages digital.
- Tourism Tasmania: *The Off Season* (2020/2021), 78 pages digital.
- Travel Manitoba: *Leading Tourism Recovery* (2021/2022), 56 pages digital.

As you can see, some of these documents are extensive, being over 100 pages in length. For example, the annual report of the Ministry of Tourism, Government of India reaches to 175 pages (Ministry of Tourism, [India] 2021).

Presentation and Distribution of Annual Reports

The release of annual reports is commonly accompanied by PR efforts that include public presentations and news releases. Annual reports are made available through DMO websites and it is a normal practice to provide archived copies of previous annual reports online.

EXAMPLE 20.20

Macao Government Tourism Office (MGTO) Annual Press Conference

An effective way to communicate performance information and future plans is to hold a press conference. This example is from Macao where the MGTO holds an excellent event each year. Your author has attended one of these conferences and was impressed.

> The Macao Government Tourism Office (MGTO) is to host its Annual Press Conference on 10 February. During the event, officials from MGTO will give a summary of last year's activities and of the 2020 performance of Macao's tourism sector, which was negatively impacted by the COVID-19 pandemic. The office will also announce during the press conference the marketing and promotional programs for 2021.
>
> According to the Macao SAR Government Policy Address for the Fiscal Year 2021 announced last November, the local authorities plan to foster efforts to expedite recovery and development of the tourism industry in order to accelerate economic revitalization following the impact of the COVID-19 pandemic.
>
> (MGTO 2021)

Learning Point

Press conferences are a great way to disseminate DMO performance information.

SUMMING UP

The COVID-19 pandemic shook destination management and DMOs. In DMO parlance, many organizations had to pivot, meaning they had to change direction. Above all, this crisis proved that having strategies and plans does not guarantee success. Major changes have taken place in destination management and DMOs in the past ten years and these were accelerated by the COVID-19 pandemic in 2020 to 2022. This has accentuated the need for performance measurement.

Destination management performance measurement should track the DMO's progress and success in achieving its roles. A performance measurement system and process should be carefully designed and implemented. Performance metrics are integral to performance measurement. It is recommended that metrics (or KPIs) be set for all destination management roles. DMOs should also prepare business or corporate plans.

Consistency and adequacy of funding are major issues for many DMOs around the globe. DMOs have a variety of potential funding sources from government and commercial entities. DMO funding levels vary greatly and even within specific countries.

Reporting is a highly important function within performance management. Some of the reporting is interim and dashboards are a good example here. Annual reports are the major tool of summative reporting and are crucial for many DMOs. DMOs put considerable effort into designing annual reports.

Some of the themes emerging in this chapter will be mentioned in Chapter 21, which looks at the future of destination management.

KEYWORDS

accountability
annual reports
audits
balanced scorecard (BSC)
benchmarking
best practices
budgeting
business improvement districts (BIDs)
business plan
capabilities
corporate plan
critical success factors (CSFs)
customer perspective
dashboards
destination audits
destination governance

destination management roles
effectiveness
efficiency
evaluation research
formative evaluation
freedom of information (FOI)
funding
interim reporting
key performance indicator (KPI)
internal processes
learning and growth
metrics
objective-and-task budgeting
performance appraisals
performance improvement

performance management
performance measurement
performance prism
pivot
PRICE-R
processes
requests for proposals (RFPs)
return on investment (ROI)
stakeholders
strategies
summative evaluation
summative reporting
tourism business improvement districts (TBIDs)
transparency
user-pay taxes
vendor evaluations

REVIEW QUESTIONS

1. Review how the uniqueness of destinations and DMOs influences performance measurement.
2. Define performance measurement and performance management.
3. Identify the reasons for performance measurement.
4. Explain the role of performance metrics.
5. Elaborate on performance measurement systems.
6. Discuss the performance measurement process.
7. Identify the issues with DMO funding.
8. Describe DMO funding sources and levels.
9. Explain control and evaluation in destination management.
10. Explain how DMOs report on their performance.

REFERENCES

Adler, L. (1967) "Systems approach to marketing," *Harvard Business Review*, 45(3), 105–118.

Altin, M., Koseoglu, M. A., Yu, X., and Riasi, A. (2018) "Performance Measurement and Management Research in the Hospitality and Tourism Industry," *International Journal of Contemporary Hospitality Management*, 30 (2): 1172–1189.

d'Angella, F., and Go, F. M. (2007) "Tale of Two Cities' Collaborative Tourism Marketing: Towards a Theory of Destination Stakeholder Assessment," *Tourism Management*, 30 (3): 429–440.

Asheville Convention and Visitors Bureau (2022) "Destination Dashboard and Performance Index," www.ashevillecvb.com/monthly-indexes/

Aureli, S., and Del Baldo, M. (2019) "Performance Measurement in the Networked Context of Convention and Visitors Bureaus (CVBs)," *Annals of Tourism Research*, 75: 92–105.

Barcoe, C., and Whelan, G. (2018) "A Proposed Framework for Measuring the Effectiveness of Social Media: A Study of Irish Tourism," *WIT Transactions on Ecology and The Environment*, 227. doi:10.2495/ST180151

Belize Tourism Board (2022) "Tourism Performance Dashboard," www.belizetourismboard.org/belize-tourism/statistics/

Bosetti, V., Cassinelli, M., and Lanza, A. (2006) "Benchmarking in Tourism Destination, Keeping in Mind the Sustainable Paradigm," Nota di Lavoro, Fondazione Eni Enrico Mattei, No. 12.2006.

Brand USA (2021) "Annual Report FY 2021," www.thebrandusa.com/about/reports?tab-order=0

da Gama, A. P. (2011) "An Expanded Model of Marketing Performance," *Marketing Intelligence and Planning*, 29 (7): 643–661.

Davidson, T. (2020) "CVBs Enter Triage Mode in the Wake of COVID-19 Staff Reductions," *Meetings Today*, August 10, www.meetingstoday.com/articles/142399/cvbs-enter-triage-mode-wake-covid-19-staff-reductions

Department for Digital, Culture, Media and Sport (UK) (2021) "The de Bois Review: An Independent Review of Destination Management Organisations in England," https://assets.publishing.service.gov.uk/government/uploads/system/uploads/attachment_data/file/1011664/2585-C_The_de_Bois_Review_ACCESSIBLE__for_publication_.pdf

Department of Tourism (South Africa) "Annual Report 2020/2021," www.gov.za/sites/default/files/gcis_document/202110/tourism-annual-report-202021.pdf

Destination British Columbia (2021) "Destination BC Corp.: Statements of Financial Information," www.destinationbc.ca/who-we-are/corporate-documents/

Destination Canada (2022) "Building the Tourism of Tomorrow: 2021 Annual Report," www.destinationcanada.com/sites/default/files/archive/1613-Destination%20Canada%20Annual%20Report%20-%202021/2021%20Annual%20Report.pdf

Destination Greater Victoria (Canada) (2022) "Tourism Industry indicators and COVID-19 Impacts Dashboard," www.tourismvictoria.com/covid-19/tourism-industry-indicators-dashboard

Destination Marketing Association International (2011) *Standard DMO Performance Reporting. A Handbook for Destination Marketing Organizations (DMOs)*, Washington, DC: DMAI.

Destinations International (2020) "The Community Benefit Funding Model: If They Value You, They Will Fund You," https://destinationsinternational.org/sites/default/master/files/IfTheyValueYouTheyWillFundYou.pdf

——— (2022) "Compensation and Benefits Reporting Platform," https://destinationsinternational.org/compensation-and-benefits-study

Dubai Tourism (2022) "The Latest Research and Insights," www.dubaitourism.gov.ae/en/research-and-insights

Eccleston, J., and MacMillan, K. (2012) "Evaluating Tourism Marketing: Overview of Key Themes," TNS, http://docplayer.net/11225367-Evaluating-tourism-marketing-overview-of-key-themes-september-2012-kpis-for-tourism-marketing-evaluation-2012-handbook.html

Fatima, T., and Elbanna, S. (2020) "Balanced Scorecard in the Hospitality and Tourism Industry: Past, Present and Future," *International Journal of Hospitality Management*, 91. https://doi.org/10.1016/j.ijhm.2020.102656.

Fredericksburg CVB. (2022) "The future of travel," https://assets.simpleviewinc.com/simpleview/image/upload/v1/clients/fredericksburgtx/FCVB_1517_Annual_Report_2021_r8_WEB_86bafda9-b4f1-444d-b685-a01e70d5c6c6.pdf

Fuchs, M., and Weiermair, K. (2004) "Destination Benchmarking: An Indicator-System's Potential for Exploring Guest Satisfaction," *Journal of Travel Research*, 42 (3): 212–225.

German National Tourist Board (2021) "Taking Opportunities: Annual Report 2021," www.germany.travel/media/redaktion/pdf/ueber_uns/2022/DZT_Jahresbericht2021_EN_WEB79.pdf

Gräve, J.-F. (2019) "What KPIs Are Key? Evaluating Performance Metrics for Social Media Influencers," *Social Media + Society*, July–September: 1–9, https://doi.org/10.1177/2056305119865475

Greater Raleigh Convention and Visitors Bureau (2022) "2022–2023 Business Plan," www.visitraleigh.com/partners/business-plan/

Hawaii Department of Business, Economic Development and Tourism (2022) "Tourism Dashboard," https://dbedt.hawaii.gov/visitor/tourism-dashboard/

Hong Kong Tourism Board (2021) "Rediscover Hong Kong: Annual Report 2020/2021," www.discoverhongkong.com/eng/hktb/about/annual-report.html

Hua, N. (2016) "E-commerce Performance in Hospitality and Tourism," *International Journal of Contemporary Hospitality Management*, 28 (9): 2052–2079.

IDN Financials (2020) "House Approves Rp 4.9 Trillion Budget for Ministry of Tourism and Creative Economy in 2021," September 24, www.idnfinancials.com/news/36328/house-approves-budget-ministry-tourism-creative-economy

Kaplan, R. S. (2010) "Conceptual Foundations of the Balanced Scorecard," Working Paper 10–074, Harvard Business School.

Kaplan, R. S., and Norton, D. P. (1992) "The Balanced Scorecard: Measures That Drive Performance," *Harvard Business Review*, 70 (1): 71–79.

——— (1993) "Putting the Balanced Scorecard to Work," *Harvard Business Review*, 71 (5): 134–147.

Koch, R. (1998) *The 80–20 Principle: The Secret of Achieving More with Less*, London: Nicholas Brealey.

Kozak, M. (2002) "Destination Benchmarking," *Annals of Tourism Research*, 29 (2): 497–519.

Kozak, M., and Rimmington, M. (1998) "Benchmarking: Destination Attractiveness and Small Hospitality Business Performance," *International Journal of Contemporary Hospitality Management*, 10 (5): 184–188.

Las Vegas Convention and Visitors Authority (2021) "Comprehensive Annual Financial Report," https://assets.simpleviewcms.com/simpleview/image/upload/v1/clients/lasvegas/ACFR_FY_2021_71844e23-87b3-4465-be14-c4496e04cbaa.pdf

McKendry, H. (2015) "Travel Industry: Top Metrics and Charts for DMO Dashboards," www.sweetspot.com/en/2015/06/25/prove-performance-destination-marketing/

McLennan, C.-L. J., Moyle, B. D., Ruhanen, L. M., and Ritchie, B. W. (2013) "Developing and Testing a Suite of Institutional Indices to Underpin the Measurement and Management of Tourism Destination Transformation," *Tourism Analysis*, 18: 157–171.

MacMillan, K., Eccleston, J., and Munro, J. (2017) *Handbook on Key Performance Indicators for Tourism Marketing Evaluation*, Madrid: UNWTO.

Macao Government Tourism Office (2021) "MGTO to Hold Annual Press Conference This Month," https://mtt.macaotourism.gov.mo/2021/02/mgto-to-hold-annual-press-conference-this-month/

Ministry of Tourism (India) (2021) "Annual Report 2021–2022," https://tourism.gov.in/media/annual-reports

Ministry of Tourism (Republic of Maldives) (2022) "Statistics: Maldives Tourism Key Indicators," www.tourism.gov.mv/en/statistics/dashboard

Morrison, A. M. (2022) *Hospitality and Travel Marketing*, 5th edn, London and New York, NY: Routledge.

Myrtle Beach Area CVB (2022) "Myrtle Beach Area Lodging Metrics Update," www.myrtlebeachareacvb.com/lodging-dashboard

Najmi, M., Etebari, M., and Emami, S. (2012) "A Framework to Review Performance Prism," *International Journal of Operations and Production Management*, 32 (10): 1124–1146.

Neely, A., Adams, C., and Crowe, P. (2001) "The Performance Prism in Practice," *Measuring Business Excellence*, 5 (2): 6–12.

O'Hare, A. W. (2021) "Tourism Improvement District: A Funding Model Case Study," *Solimar International*, www.solimarinternational.com/tourism-improvement-district-funding/

O'Sullivan, D., and Abela, A. V. (2007) "Marketing Performance Measurement Ability and Firm Performance," *Journal of Marketing*, 71 (2): 79–93.

Phillips, P., and Louvieris, P. (2005) "Performance Measurement Systems in Tourism, Hospitality, and Leisure Small Medium-Sized Enterprises: A Balanced Scorecard Perspective," *Journal of Travel Research*, 44 (2): 201–211.

Pike, S. (2014) "Destination Brand Performance Measurement over Time," in *Tourists' Perceptions and Assessments: Advances in Culture, Tourism and Hospitality Research*, vol. VIII, Bingley: Emerald, pp. 111–120.

Plaza, B. (2011) "Google Analytics for Measuring Website Performance," *Tourism Management*, 32: 477–481.

Poister, T. H., Aristigueta, M. P., and Hall, J. L. (2015) *Managing and Measuring Performance in Public and Nonprofit Organizations: An Integrated Approach*, 2nd edn, San Francisco, Calif.: John Wiley & Sons.

Puerto Rico Tourism Company (2022) "Room Tax," https://prtourism.com/room-tax/

Qatar Tourism (2022) "Tourism Dashboards," www.qatartourism.com/en/news-and-media/sector-statistics/tourism-dashboards

Schiff, C. (2008) "Three Things You Should Know About Dashboards," *DM Review*, 18, 29.

Schoening Singapore Tourism Board (2021) "A Year of Rediscoveries and Reimagination," www.stb.gov.sg/content/stb/en/media-centre/corporate-publications/annual-reports.html

South Australian Tourism Commission (2021) "South Australian Tourism Commission, 2020–21 Annual Report," https://tourism.sa.gov.au/media/i3ecuhja/2020-21-satc-annual-report-final.pdf

Star, S., Russ-Eft, D., Braverman, M. T., and Levine, R. (2016) "Performance Measurement and Performance Indicators: A Literature Review and a Proposed Model for Practical Adoption," *Human Resource Development Review*, 15 (2): 151–181.

Stepchenkova, S., Tang, L., Jang, S. C. S., Kirilenko, A. P., and Morrison, A. M. (2010) "Benchmarking CVB Website Performance: Spatial and Structural Patterns," *Tourism Management*, 31: 611–620.

Tourism Australia (2021) "Annual Report 2020/2021," www.tourism.australia.com/content/dam/digital/corporate/documents/ta-annual-report-fy21.pdf

Tourism Nova Scotia (2021a) "Accountability Report, 2020–2021," https://tourismns.ca/plans-and-reports/financial-statements-and-reports

—— (2021b) "Financial Statements Tourism Nova Scotia," Grant Thornton, https://tourismns.ca/plans-and-reports/financial-statements-and-reports

Tourism Saskatchewan (2022) "Tourism Saskatchewan Annual Report for 2021–22," https://business.tourismsaskatchewan.com/en/about/annual-report

Tourism Tasmania (2021) "The Off Season: Tourism Tasmania Annual Report 2020–2021," www.tourismtasmania.com.au/about/publications/annual_report/

Tourism Western Australia (2021) "Tourism Western Australia Annual Report 2020–2021," www.tourism.wa.gov.au/Publications%20Library/About%20us/020496TWA%20Annual%20Report%202020-21.pdf

Travel Manitoba (2021) "Leading Tourism Recovery: 2021/2022 Annual Report," www.travelmanitoba.com/tourism-industry/industry-resources/reports-and-publications/

Tyrrell, T. J., and Johnston, R. J. (2013) "Measuring the Performance of Convention and Visitors Bureaus," in L. Mook (ed.), *Accounting for Social Value*, Toronto: University of Toronto Press, pp. 167–187.

United Nations World Tourism Organization and World Tourism Cities Federation (2019) "City Tourism Performance Research," www.unwto.org/city-tourism-performance-research

US Travel Association (2022) "State Tourism Office Budget Dashboard (FY 2021–22)," www.ustravel.org/research/state-tourism-office-budget-dashboard-fy-2020-21

VisitBritain and VisitEngland (2022) "Annual Report and Accounts for the Year Ended 31 March 2022," www.visitbritain.org/our-performance-reporting

VisitScotland (2022) "Tourism Business Improvement Districts," www.visitscotland.org/supporting-your-business/funding/business-improvement-districts#

von der Weppen, J., and Cochrane, J. (2012) "Social Enterprises in Tourism: An Exploratory Study of Operational Models and Success Factors," *Journal of Sustainable Tourism*, 20 (3): 497–511.

Wang, Y. (2008) "Web-Based Destination Marketing Systems: Assessing the Critical Factors for Management and Implementation," *International Journal of Tourism Research*, 10: 55–70.

Webster, F. E., Malter, A. J., and Ganesan, S. (2005) "The Decline and Dispersion of Marketing," *MIT Sloan Management Review*, 46 (4): 35–43.

Wöber, K. W. (2001) "Benchmarking for Tourism Organizations: An E-guide for Tourism Managers," Urbana-Champaign, Ill.: National Laboratory for Tourism and eCommerce.

Wonderful Copenhagen (2020) "TOURISM FOR GOOD follow up 2020," www.wonderfulcopenhagen.com/wonderful-copenhagen/analyses-insights/reports-and-insights

Xiang, Z., Kothari, T., Hu, C., and Fesenmaier, D. R. (2007) "Benchmarking as a Strategic Tool for Destination Management Organizations," *Journal of Travel and Tourism Marketing*, 22 (1): 81–93.

Yilmaz, Y., and Bititci, U. (2006a) "Performance Measurement in Tourism: A Value Chain Model," *International Journal of Contemporary Hospitality Management*, 18 (4): 341–349.

———— (2006b) "Performance Measurement in the Value Chain: Manufacturing V. Tourism," *International Journal of Productivity and Performance Management*, 55 (5): 371–389.

Chapter **21**

The Future of Destination Management

Foreseeing

LEARNING OBJECTIVES

Having read this chapter, you should be able to:

1. explain the challenges and issues affecting destination management pre-COVID;
2. describe the expected changes in destination management post-COVID;
3. pinpoint future trends and potential challenges for destinations and DMOs;
4. suggest some of the characteristics of future DMOs.

Warming Up

What does the future hold for destination management? Will DMOs survive all the challenges and issues with which they are faced? Chapter 21 addresses these questions by reviewing the major challenges, issues, and trends that are impacting upon destinations and DMOs now and that are expected to have an effect in the future. You heard in Chapter 20 that continuous funding was one of these major issues, as was the recovery from the COVID-19 pandemic.

DOI: 10.4324/9781003343356-26

DMOs have been around for more than 100 years, but they have never felt the impact of the winds of change as they are experiencing now, especially the devastating effects of COVID-19. In this chapter, several authoritative sources are reviewed that identify the key challenges, issues, and trends affecting destination management and DMOs. As you will see, these sources are unanimous in their opinion that DMOs need to significantly adapt their ways of operating in the future.

The chapter is divided into two parts. The first part provides you with viewpoints pre-COVID-19 and the second includes opinions and forecasts during and after COVID-19. The author chose to do this because DMOs had serious challenges and issues before the pandemic; COVID-19 if anything made these more prominent and added a new set of difficulties.

Destination management is an emerging professional field in tourism. It will have to become even more professional in the future, and this book suggests what needs to be done to achieve this outcome. A summary of the main challenges, issues and trends noted in the previous twenty chapters is provided. Chapter 21 also previews the expected future trends and potential challenges for destinations and DMOs and provides some ideas on the future characteristics of DMOs.

Pre-COVID Issues in Destination Management

Earlier chapters have identified various challenges and issues that destinations and DMOs are encountering. These included funding sources and levels, competition, overtourism, changes in technology, economic and other crises, and several others. In the materials that follow, you will learn about the issues that have been identified by one DMO professional association and several company and individual experts in destination management. The following ten sources of information are reviewed for the first part on the pre-COVID situation:

1. Fifteen Cs framework (Fyall and Leask 2006);
2. Destination Marketing Association International (DMAI) Futures Study (Destinations International 2008);
3. *Managing Destination Marketing Organizations* (Ford and Peeper 2008);
4. The PhoCusWright destination marketing study (Schetzina 2009);
5. "The Future of Destination Marketing" (Pollock 2009);
6. DestiCorp conceptual discussion paper (DestiCorp 2010);
7. DestinationNEXT Phase 1 (Destinations International 2014);
8. DestinationNEXT Phase 2 (Destinations International 2017);
9. TrekkSoft survey of DMO marketing (TrekkSoft 2017).
10. Destination Think! Survey of international tourism offices (Destination Think! 2017).

Fifteen Cs Framework (Fyall and Leask 2006)

Fyall and Leask (2006) suggested a fifteen Cs framework (Fig. 21.1) for describing the strategic challenges in destination marketing. These two authors examined the application of the fifteen Cs in terms of the DMOs in London and Edinburgh in the UK.

These fifteen Cs—complexity, control, change, crisis, complacency, customers, culture, competition, commodification, creativity, communication, channels, cyberspace, consolidation, and collaboration are briefly explained below.

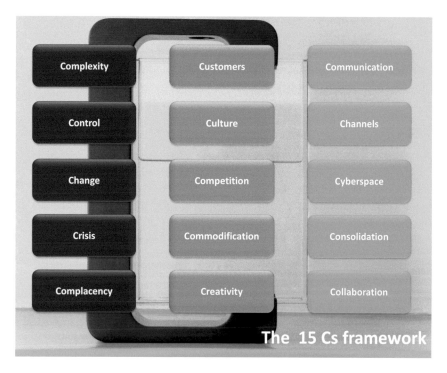

Figure 21.1   Fifteen Cs framework (Fyall and Leask 2006, pp. 53–61).

COMPLEXITY

The destination product is very complex and therefore extremely difficult to manage. DMOs must build positive relationships with multiple stakeholders within their destinations and form collaborative relationships outside. Moreover, DMOs must perform multiple roles at a time they are adapting to new technologies and shrinking government funding.

CONTROL

DMOs do not have direct control over the product within their destinations, and this has been mentioned several times already in this book. Additionally, there is a danger that tourism sector stakeholders might launch their own communication programs that do not support the overall destination branding approach.

CHANGE

The winds of change are buffeting DMOs from several directions. You have heard that many DMOs have moved away from being purely government-run to being PPPs. In addition, DMOs have been transforming from being promotional agencies only and are becoming destination-management organizations with greater responsibilities for product development, tourism planning, community involvement, visitor management, and crisis management.

CRISIS

Many destinations have had to deal with major crises that have caused great trauma in their tourism sectors. These crises have been caused by economic difficulties, natural disasters, civil disturbances, acts of terrorism, onsets of diseases and so on. They have undermined tourists' confidence in traveling to certain destinations. Nowadays, DMOs must be proactive and have crisis management plans. Moreover, they need to avoid having too many eggs in one basket market-wise, and they must expand their portfolios of target markets and collaborations. DMOs should never neglect their nearby regional and domestic markets because these can become critical business sources amidst a period of crisis, as you learned in Chapter 17.

COMPLACENCY

"Nothing lasts forever" is a phrase that DMOs need to remember so they do not become complacent in today's dynamic external environments. DMO complacency can set in when the organization has enjoyed long-running success and the destinations' market demand and funding sources have been steady for many years. DMOs must guard against becoming complacent in this era of global competition, and one of the best ways to do this is with zero-based planning, which means that no program or market is sacred and each one is constantly being re-evaluated.

CUSTOMERS

Customers are constantly changing, and for DMOs, it is worthwhile to remember that no two customers are exactly alike. People from even the same markets go to destinations with differing motives and expectations. Although market segmentation analysis is essential in destination marketing, it is still an approximation of reality, and even within distinct market segments there is considerable diversity.

CULTURE

Many destinations rely on their unique cultural and heritage resources to attract tourists. These resources tend to be a destination's key point of differentiation (USPs). Many of these buildings and sites are owned and operated by government agencies and are therefore reliant on government support. They are often among the most popular tourism attractions in a destination, and so the issue becomes who should pay for their upkeep. Should governments pay and use residents' tax contributions in so doing, or should the predominant users (tourists) be required to pay through admission fees? This is becoming a delicate issue, particularly in Europe, when governments want to operate such buildings and sites on a free-admission basis, to provide greater educational and cultural experiences for local people.

COMPETITION

Most DMOs are facing new competitors. Fyall and Leask (2006) suggest that the expansion of LCCs has opened many new destinations for Europeans and that the same can be said about the Asia-Pacific region, where LCCs have started many new routes plus offering better deals for passengers on well-established routes.

COMMODIFICATION

Globalization has blurred the differences among places and even between destinations that are geographically far apart. For example, almost everywhere you travel, you can find McDonald's, Starbucks and KFC, and downtowns, shopping centers, and airports look increasingly alike. Commodification is the process of taking a resource that is truly unique and turning it into a commodity that can be consumed by many people. In the transformation, the true meaning of the resource is lost. In tourism, the commercialization of resources means they often lose their intrinsic authenticity and uniqueness.

Although commodification makes tourism resources such as culture and heritage more consumable for some people, it is not a favorable trend for destinations in terms of their uniqueness and sustainability. DMOs must constantly try to find and communicate what is truly unique about their destinations and not what makes them like competitors.

CREATIVITY

DMOs must be creative in their destination-management approaches in the face of intensifying competition. Having a highly creative approach to positioning-image-branding is certainly part of this requirement, but it is not enough. This creativity also must be present in the experiences and products that tourists can have within destinations. Earlier in this book, you learned about several creative approaches by DMOs, and you may remember the Canadian Signature Experiences example from Destination Canada (2022). Based upon thorough market research, Destination Canada responded with uniquely Canadian experiences that are desired by people within its target markets.

COMMUNICATION

DMOs must be outstanding at communications, both within their destinations and externally. DMOs need to listen to their various publics and then respond with the initiatives, services and programs that these publics need and expect. You have heard about many clever DMO IMC campaigns in this book.

CHANNELS

DMOs need to adopt a multi-channel approach to communications, and in most cases, this includes both traditional media and travel trade channels and the newer e-marketing channels, particularly DMO websites, social media platforms and smartphones (Fig. 21.2).

Figure 21.2   Smartphones are becoming an increasingly important channel for DMOs.

CYBERSPACE

DMOs need to become more active and sophisticated in their use of ICTs. OTAs and travel review websites are increasingly offering more detailed information, features and services related to destinations.

CONSOLIDATION

Consolidation is a trend in many sub-sectors of tourism, including, for example, among airlines, hotels and resorts, travel agencies, and tour companies. Interestingly, this is also happening, perhaps more quietly, in the management of convention centers, arenas and sports stadiums, and other public performance venues. This is putting more marketing power and political clout in fewer hands. This is not a trend that DMOs should ignore or view as outside of their domain.

COLLABORATION

According to Fyall and Leask (2006), greater collaboration by DMOs is a necessity and not a luxury.

Fyall and Leask (2006) did an outstanding job of pinpointing many issues and challenges for DMOs, and in this case, the examples were drawn mainly from the UK. In many ways, the issues defined by these two authors were mirrored in the DMAI Futures Study, although Fyall and Leask identified issues that were not in the US study, such as crisis, complacency, culture, and consolidation.

DMAI Futures Study 2008

In 2007 to 2008, Destinations International (then DMAI) and Karl Albrecht International conducted a landmark study that was called the DMAI Futures Study 2008 with the sub-title "The Future of Destination Marketing." Although this research is most relevant for DMOs based in North America, it does have broader implications for DMOs in other countries.

Three high-level strategic themes emerged from this study related to DMOs: (1) relevance, (2) value proposition, and (3) visibility.

RELEVANCE

DMOs operate in a space between tourism sector stakeholders and potential visitors. That space is becoming increasingly crowded with other players and this is eroding the traditional and unique position that DMOs once held. According to Destinations International and Karl Albrecht International and the DMO executives they interviewed; this is challenging the relevancy of DMOs.

EXAMPLE 21.1

The Challenges to Relevancy

This example argues that DMOs are facing stiff new competition, externally and internally. They must change to maintain their relevancy.

> The increasing disintermediation of the visitor services marketplace, the rise of new business entities contending for the attention of visitors and meeting organizers, the wealth of free information made available online, and

increasing local competition for funds formerly earmarked for destination marketing all conspire to erode or marginalize the traditional role of the DMO as the "marketing department" of a particular locality.

(Destinations International 2008)

Learning Point

DMOs need to change to continue to be relevant in the marketplace.

VALUE PROPOSITION

What is the unique contribution of DMOs, or stated another way, what is their core value proposition? According to the DMAI Futures Study, new players have been nibbling away at the traditional value package offered to local tourism sector stakeholders and their communities in general.

VISIBILITY

DMO executives interviewed for the DMAI Futures Study were extremely concerned about their organizations' visibility and consumer recognition. This concern was especially about visibility on the Internet, where competing sources of destination information were judged to be doing a superior job to many DMOs.

EXAMPLE 21.2

Consumers Know Little about DMOs

This example uncovers a worrying fact that not many consumers know about DMOs. They need to have greater online presence to be better recognized.

DMAI's branding research indicates that consumers typically know very little about CVBs and have little inclination to seek them out. Valid measures are difficult to find as of the publication of this report, but it appears that many DMOs rely on statistical good fortune in search engine listings, as an adjunct to whatever population of "loyal" visitors they may have who go directly to their websites for information.

Relatively few DMO websites demonstrate the level of sophistication, user-friendly design and interactiveness needed to compete with other sources. City-operated websites, sites operated by city-specific magazines, and sites of individual local attractions all compete with the DMO site for visitor attention. Some DMOs, particularly small ones, have merely moved their print brochures online, so to speak.

(Destinations International 2008)

Learning Point

The general public needs to know more about what DMOs are and what they do.

The DMAI Futures Study identified the following eight super-trends that were impacting destination marketing:

1. Customer: Called proliferating preferences, this trend was about pleasure/leisure and business travelers constantly seeking new products and experiences at destinations.
2. Competitor: Termed the battle for attention, this trend concerned the increasing competitive intensity in travel and tourism and the movement toward online travel purchases.
3. Economic: Dodging asteroids was about DMOs becoming increasingly vulnerable to economic downturns and other types of global crises (terrorism, political unrest, pandemics, rising energy prices).
4. Technological: This trend stressed the increasing importance of information and communication technologies (ICTs) and particularly the Internet. It was named smart and friendly websites.
5. Social: The electronic society was the trend toward much greater use of social media platforms and the creation of UGC about destinations.
6. Political: This trend was about the funding of DMOs from local government agencies. Billed as the quest for relevance, this trend concerned the greater difficulties that DMOs were

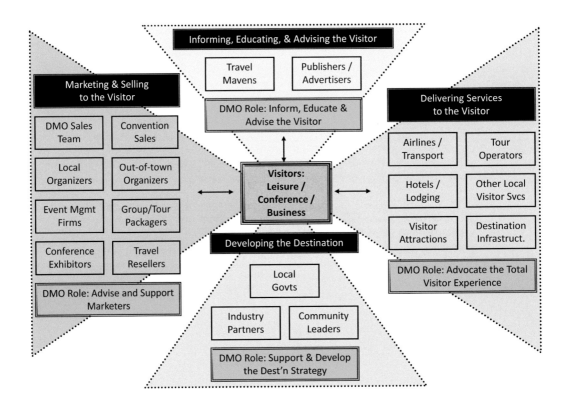

Figure 21.3   New strategic map for destination marketing from DMAI and Karl Albrecht International (Destinations International 2008).

having convincing stakeholders of their value. There was also a growing trend for governments to use more of room tax collections for non-tourism purposes.

7. Legal: Under the title of mixed signals from government, this trend concerned how tourism organizations were constantly being affected by changes in government policies, legislation, and regulations.

8. Geophysical: Going green was the eighth super-trend and related to the increasing emphasis on sustainable tourism development and green practices.

Based upon eight super-trends and twenty DMO-specific trends, Destinations International and Karl Albrecht International recommended a new strategic map for destination marketing, which is shown in Figure 21.3.

The core part of this new strategic map was the four key roles for DMOs:

1. Informing, educating, and advising the visitor: The key contribution here is serving as the official face and voice of the tourism sector within a destination.

2. Advising and supporting marketers: The DMO should perform the role of a matchmaker, bringing those together who buy and sell the destination's services and products.

3. Advocating the total visitor experience: The DMO needs to convince tourism sector stakeholders to focus on all aspects of the visitor experience within the destination.

4. Supporting and developing the destination strategy: The DMO needs to take a strategic perspective on destination development and insist on the master planning of tourism.

Overall, the DMAI Futures Study was a realistic portrayal of the current issues affecting DMOs, albeit with a strong US orientation. This research study emphasized the changes among customers as well as in ICTs and funding sources. However, perhaps more importantly, it carried a serious warning for DMOs: increase relevancy, value, and visibility or slowly be replaced by a variety of other entities performing similar roles.

The recommendations of the DMAI Futures Study very much reflect an expansion of the role from just destination marketing to the broader perspective of destination management. Throughout this book, this transformation of roles has been strongly advocated, and you have learned about all aspects of destination management and not just destination marketing.

Managing Destination Marketing Organizations (Ford and Peeper 2008)

Robert C. Ford is a professor at the University of Central Florida, and William C. Peeper is a former president of the Orlando/Orange County CVB and worked at that bureau for more than twenty-five years. They wrote a book, *Managing Destination Marketing Organizations*, which was published in 2008. This book focused mainly on the tasks, roles, and responsibilities of CVB executives. They conducted twenty-four in-depth interviews with the CEOs of large, medium and small DMOs, and most of these were based in the USA.

In the final chapter, Ford and Peeper identified five future challenges for CVB executives:

1. Funding and governance.
2. Job responsibilities.
3. Technological change.
4. Information.
5. Competition.

Funding and Governance

The CEOs who were interviewed highlighted the continuing difficulties in securing funding for their DMOs. In the USA, this was because other community agencies were vying for shares of the hotel room tax. As shown by the following example, this meant that the DMOs had to do a more effective job of proving their economic contributions to their communities.

EXAMPLE 21.3

Values of DMOs Not Yet Fully Understood

This example emphasizes the importance of DMOs to proving their value in their own communities.

> The CVB leaders interviewed recognized that the increased competition for funding required them to market their value more aggressively and effectively to their own communities and local stakeholders. They felt a strong need to do a better job of telling their communities about their contributions to its economic health. But most of the interviewed believed that their stakeholders did not understand either what they did or the value of their work to the community.
>
> (Ford and Peeper 2008)

Learning Point

DMOs must build strong local support at their home bases.

These two authors also pointed out that local hotels exerted the greatest power in DMO governance but they tended to have a "heads in beds" and short-term outlook on DMO objectives and performance.

Job Responsibilities

DMO executives' job responsibilities are rapidly expanding, and this is to be expected in the shift from destination marketing to destination management. Ford and Peeper pointed out that in addition to marketing, DMO CEOs have similar responsibilities to those who run companies, including financial management and human resource management. They are also playing a much greater role in the brand management of their destinations than before. However, they tend to be evaluated solely on the results from their sales and marketing responsibilities.

Technological Change

DMOs are experiencing competition from online providers of destination information, and they need to adapt to these changes. These two authors viewed technology not only as a great opportunity for DMOs but also as a huge threat. The availability of lower hotel room rates on these and other OTA sites meant that business event participants were booking their rooms there and not within the block of rooms that the hotels and meeting planners had contracted for. This was causing a serious problem for the hotels, meeting planners, and DMOs.

INFORMATION

Providing destination information in a variety of different ways has been a traditional DMO role. In addition, in North America, Destinations International and its forerunner, International Association of Convention and Visitor Bureaus, have maintained a databank of information about meeting resources and venues for many years, called MINT+ (Destinations International 2022b). However, other online providers have come along in recent years and now offer comparable and sometimes more complete information for meeting planners. Other online providers, such as Google Maps and MapQuest, also offer great map and direction information that was traditionally given out by DMOs. So, the traditional information role of DMOs is rapidly being undermined by for-profit online companies.

COMPETITION

Ford and Peeper argued that many cities have greatly expanded their convention center and hotel capacities and this was placing greater pressure on DMOs to bring in even more business events. They pointed out that in the USA, there was more supply of meeting space than there was demand and this was leading to a high level of discounting on meeting space and even giving convention center space away for free as an incentive.

The increased competition from a variety of online information providers has already been mentioned. These two authors, also through their CEO interviews, found two further sources of new competition. The first source was an internal one and was from city-owned convention/exhibition centers. These venues in many cases were desperately seeking any business to cover their operating costs, and the deals they were making were undermining the DMOs' efforts to attract high-yielding business events for hotels that met the room tax goals of their communities. The second source of competition was from large meeting planning services companies, including American Express Global Business Travel (2022), Maritz Global Events (2022), ConferenceDirect (2022), Helms Briscoe (2022), and others. These companies now provided many similar services for business events that were traditionally performed by DMOs. However, they have a much different funding model than DMOs, getting their revenues via commissions from business event suppliers such as hotels. They can offer these planning and meeting logistics services to meeting planners free of charge.

The Ford and Peeper book paints a highly challenging future picture for DMOs, particularly in the USA. The issues they raise are in many ways quite like those that you have heard about earlier in this chapter. However, they draw specific attention to the problems and challenges that US CVBs have related to the system of hotel room taxes. These two authors predicted the following future directions for DMOs:

FINANCING

DMOs, and especially the North American style CVBs, will have to aggressively compete for commission incomes and reduce their reliance on hotel room tax revenues.

SPOKESPERSON

DMOs not only need to assume the role of marketing their communities; they must also become more involved in managing their destination's resources. They must ensure that the promises made in marketing are delivered to tourists. DMOs must also act as the spokespersons for tourism in their communities.

COOPERATION

DMOs need to form new partnerships and collaborative models, sometimes with other DMOs that previously were deemed to be competitors. The BestCities Global Alliance that was discussed in Chapter 19 is a great example of what needs to be done.

BUSINESS MODELS

Ford and Peeper predicted a very different future for CVBs. They recommended consideration of six alternative business models for the future:

1. outsource model;
2. RFP model;
3. national-consolidation model: privatization version;
4. national-consolidation model: cooperative version;
5. franchise model;
6. status quo.

The PhoCusWright Destination Marketing Study (Schetzina), 2009

The US online travel market research company PhoCusWright, Inc., published a research study titled "Destination Marketing: Understanding the Role and Impact of Destination Marketers" in 2009 (Schetzina 2009). This study had three main research objectives:

1. to analyze consumer trends;
2. to profile destination marketers and identify best practices;
3. to identify the opportunities to serve and/or partner with DMOs.

The research included a web-based consumer survey about using DMOs and their websites, a web-based survey of destination marketers, phone interviews with fifty destination marketers and partners/suppliers, an analysis of traffic to DMO websites, and an analysis of fifteen specific websites.

The key findings of this study were that DMO websites were most important to consumers and were the preferred way for potential tourists to interact with DMOs. They visited DMO websites at different times, including both before and after making their bookings. Some 57 percent of the users said the DMO websites influenced their activity selections at destinations. Deals, packages and promotions posted on websites were of special interest to tourists.

The study also concluded that DMOs were highly engaged online and had gradually been increasing their e-marketing spending. However, the DMOs reported spending just 37 percent of their marketing budgets online. It was also found that DMOs had been slow to integrate interactive features on their websites.

One of the sponsors of the PhoCusWright research study on destination marketing was usdm. net, an interactive agency and media company. In 2010, usdm.net produced the *Leadership Report: Are You a Revolutionary DMO?*, which summarized and commented upon the results of both the DMAI Futures Study and the PhoCusWright research study. The company drew many important conclusions and recommendations:

- Travelers view DMOs primarily as sources of information.
- DMOs can greatly enhance their visibility and relevancy by investing more in online content and interactivity (Fig. 21.4).

- DMOs should promote events, specials, and packages on their websites and across social media platforms and to mobile phones.

- DMOs should particularly focus on activity development and marketing because consumers look for these contents on DMO websites.

- It would be preferable to allow consumers to book online at DMO websites.

- DMOs are wasting their marketing budgets on newspaper, magazine, radio and outdoor advertising; they should divert more of their budgets online, including to search engines.

- The Internet offers immediate and detailed tracking of consumer and meeting planner responses. This enhanced measurability quantifies and validates the DMO's value proposition and relevance.

Figure 21.4   Online content creation about destinations is now a key priority for DMOs.

Overall, the PhoCusWright research study and the follow-up recommendations by usdm. net emphasized that DMOs should be making much greater use of ICTs and especially the Internet. They suggested, however, that DMOs were not moving rapidly enough in that direction and so other parties were entering that space. The implication here is that DMOs had been reluctant to give up their years-old practices, especially in using traditional media advertising.

"The Future of Destination Marketing" (Pollock 2009)

Figure 21.5 shows a diagram based on a presentation by Anna Pollock from DestiCorp that was delivered in Norway in 2009. The main idea within the diagram is that DMOs must move more from pushing (or promoting) their destinations to potential tourists toward pulling (or attracting) people to destinations. The five Ps must change into the five Cs:

1. Customer: DMOs need to focus more on the experiences that customers want rather than on the features of their products. Customers have the greatest power now in the digital content era.
2. Connections: DMOs must find the most appropriate ways of connecting with customers and not worry so much about positioning their products.
3. Conversations: Markets have become conversations, and DMOs must engage others to have good conversations about their destinations.
4. Content: Traditional types of promotion need to give way to the creation of digital content.
5. Community: DMOs need to build online communities and then engage others (residents, suppliers, tourists) to have conversations about their destinations.

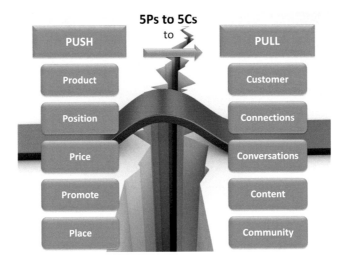

Figure 21.5   From 5 Ps to 5 Cs (Pollock 2009).

These ideas from DestiCorp and Anna Pollock about how destination marketing needed to adapt were very thought-provoking and again strongly advocated a move toward greater integration and use of ICTs by DMOs. However, the ideas were not just about using technologies; they were as much about adapting new DMO business models that involved much higher levels of collaboration and networking. Overall, the implication was that the old model for DMOs was unlikely to be successful in the future.

"Destination and Enterprise Management for a Tourism Future" (Dwyer et al. 2009)

Dwyer et al. (2009) published an article in *Tourism Management*, "Destination and Enterprise Management for a Tourism Future," which, among other things, outlined the implications of five global trends for destination management. The research team conducted tourism sector workshops in Brisbane, Melbourne and Sydney, Australia, as well as reviewing all the published forecasts on tourism until 2020. Six drivers of change in tourism were identified as: (1)

economic, (2) political, (3) environmental, (4) technological, (5) demographic, and (6) social. The five global trends and a brief statement of their implications are provided below:

Sustainable Tourism Development

DMOs should focus on the yield per capita rather than on just growth in visitor numbers. They should adopt sustainability principles as a foundation for tourism development. Community residents should be more involved in determining the directions for future tourism development.

Climate Change

DMOs should encourage tourism sector stakeholders to minimize their impacts on climate change.

Target Marketing

Destination product development and marketing in the future will be increasingly targeted and theme based. Emotional benefits of tourism products should be emphasized more than their functional benefits. Once again, this group of authors emphasized the use of technologies in achieving this new emphasis in destination marketing.

Risk Management

DMOs along with their stakeholders must introduce risk management strategies that make sure that tourists feel safe and secure in their destinations.

Education for Tourism Management

The tourism sector needs to increase its knowledge and skill base to improve its innovative capabilities.

The contributions from Dwyer et al. were valuable and offered some additional issues and challenges that deserve careful consideration by DMOs. For example, the concept of tourist safety and security, and with it the destination's risk management strategy, is extremely important in an era of frequent crises and acts of terrorism. These authors also raised the topics of sustainable development and education to a higher level than the previous works.

DestiCorp Conceptual Development Paper, 2010

Anna Pollock of DestiCorp in the UK is a well-known expert on destination management. In 2010, her company released a conceptual discussion paper under the title of "Speculation on the Future of Destination Marketing Organizations (DMOs)." This paper indicated that there were seven main drivers of change that were affecting destination marketing:

1. Information technology enables global connectivity and digital platforms that mirror reality.
2. Marketing is being turned upside down, from push to pull and promotion to attraction.
3. Emergence of the creative/experience economy.
4. Changing economic realities.
5. Biophysical realities.
6. Fiscal realities.
7. Changing models and mindsets.

INFORMATION TECHNOLOGY ENABLES GLOBAL CONNECTIVITY AND DIGITAL PLATFORMS THAT MIRROR REALITY

ICTs and particularly the Internet have completely removed the barrier of distance and offer consumers instant and continuous information about destinations. However, although the digitization of content has been pervasive for more than a decade, DestiCorp felt that DMOs had changed relatively little and only some DMO websites are interactive. This needed to change in the future as DMOs become "orchestrators of DMO experiences" rather than "promoters of tourism products."

EXAMPLE 21.4

The DMO as an Orchestrator

This example argues that DMOs must use online platforms differently to offer greater value to consumers and tourism sector stakeholders.

> If a destination is to convince visitors it can offer a unique set of distinctive experiences that reflect a specific place, the DMO will need to think of itself as less of a marketer in the promotion sense and more of an orchestrator. Creation of an agile, flexible, electronic platform that enables collaboration, distribution, cross selling, intelligence gathering and exchange to occur will be essential.
>
> (DestiCorp 2010)

Learning Point

DMOs must become conductors of the local tourism orchestra.

MARKETING IS BEING TURNED UPSIDE DOWN, FROM PUSH TO PULL AND PROMOTION TO ATTRACTION

DMOs have traditionally been promoters of the tourism products within their destinations. This worked when the supply of information was more limited, but it is not that way anymore. Now, consumers are in the driver's seat, and they want to be involved in designing their own tourism experience products. DestiCorp argued that DMOs need to put less emphasis on promotion and give a much greater priority to creating and staging the types of experiences that tourists want within destinations.

EMERGENCE OF THE CREATIVE/EXPERIENCE ECONOMY

Tourists are buying experiences at their destinations and not products. DestiCorp suggests, therefore, that DMOs need "to recognize their role is more of a stage manager and conductor than promoter."

CHANGING ECONOMIC REALITIES

There are two trends that are going in different directions at the same time: globalization versus localization. The world has become more globalized in the past twenty to twenty-five years.

There is a greater need for places to stand out in this global environment and not only for tourism but also in attracting more inward investment, talented workforces and students. However, economic downturns and rising energy costs are forcing more people not to travel so far and to discover more things locally.

BIOPHYSICAL REALITIES

DMOs need to pay more attention to environmental considerations and play their part in the low-carbon economy. This is because of global warming as well as the steadily increasing world demand for energy, food and water.

FISCAL REALITIES

There are increasing pressures on governments to deal with huge national debt situations plus funding major infrastructure improvements and greater demand for social and health services for aging populations. In these testing circumstances for governments, it is very likely that the funds available for destination management will dwindle and DMOs will be required to look elsewhere for support.

CHANGING MODELS AND MINDSETS

Today's society and business require a network model and mindset where there is collaboration and transparency among DMOs, partners, suppliers, and customers. This is a change from the traditional command-and-control model and mindset that many DMOs have become accustomed to over many decades.

Based upon these seven drivers of change, DestiCorp recommended that DMOs respond and adapt in the following eight ways:

1. DMOs need to change their perceptions and mindsets: The main point here is that DMOs were formed many decades ago and have maintained a similar model since then. This model views destinations as value chains with linear relationships. However, this model does not fit with today's realities, and DMOs must view destinations as a network of self-organizing agents that need to collaborate and offer tourists some level of consistency.
2. DMOs should do less and enable more: DMOs need to focus on developing an enabling digital infrastructure. DestiCorp calls this a "destination web," which is an electronically connected community of autonomous interdependent users in the destination.
3. DMOs should promote less and attract more: The DMO needs to engage all parts of the host community, including tourists, in conversations about the destination.
4. DMOs need to align and integrate with other organizations: In most communities, economic development and other agencies charged with attracting inward investment usually have much greater resources than DMOs. Rather than fearing the competition from these agencies, DMOs need to find new ways to align and integrate their efforts with these bodies.
5. DMOs should engage suppliers and visitors during and after experiences: DMOs should enlist the help of suppliers and tourists in assisting with destination marketing. DestiCorp recommended that DMOs put more emphasis on becoming platform builders for others and less emphasis on being purely one-dimensional promoters. Crowdsourcing within the context of e-marketing is a good example of recruiting the help of residents and/or visitors in engaging in conversations about destinations and posting content on social media.
6. DMOs should nurture the intelligence of destinations: DMOs need to find new and quicker ways for gathering research on what is happening within their destinations. This intelligence needs to be real time, and it can be gathered by using smartphones and social media platforms.

7. DMOs should rationalize to a higher degree: There tends to be some overlapping and redundancy among the various levels of DMOs in given countries, from the national to the community level. DMOs need to collaborate and make use of new technologies to rationalize their efforts to a higher degree.

8. The "M" in DMO should become management: This has been a predominant and recurring theme throughout your book. DMOs must be engaged in many more activities than just purely promotion and sales. For example, the biophysical realities mentioned earlier require DMOs to get more involved in sustainable tourism. They must also be more involved in quality assurance and visitor management programs.

DestinationNEXT Phases 1 and 2 (Destinations International, 2014–2017)

The DestinationNEXT effort was launched by Destinations International in 2014 with a survey of DMO leaders. The survey was conducted by the InterVISTAS Consulting Group, Inc., and had 361 responses from thirty-six countries (Ouimet 2014). Sixty-four major trends were identified, and they were classified into eight categories (customer, competitor, economic, technological, social, political, legal, and geophysical). Forty-nine potential strategies for DMOs were defined. Many of the top priority trends according to DMO leaders were related to technology and customer expectations (Fig. 21.6).

DestinationNEXT Phase 1 top priority trends

1. Prominence of social media
5. Experiences personalized
2. Mobile platforms for primary engagement
7. Meeting planners prefer value and experience
4. Smart technology innovations
8. Experience local way of life
6. Geotargeting and localization
9. Quicker travel decision making
12. Big data
10. Online booking

Technology and Social Media   Customers

Figure 21.6   DestinationNEXT Phase 1 top priority trends (Ouimet 2014).

The first phase of DestinationNEXT suggested three major opportunities for DMOs:

1. Dealing with the new marketplace: Engaging more with travelers rather than just one-way (DMO-generated) communication, especially via social media. Becoming more strategic rather than tactical in planning and making greater use of big data (Fig. 21.7).
2. Building and protecting destination brand: Becoming more of a champion for the community and being more concerned with resident quality of life. Playing a stronger role in destination product development.
3. Evolving the DMO business model: Being more collaborative and having broader involvement in community. Building more partnerships.

Figure 21.7   DMOs must grasp the potential of big data.

Phase 2 of DestinationNEXT was conducted in early 2017 with a view to identifying new trends and potential strategies for DMOs. The top ten trends from DMO leaders were like those from 2014, and there was again a strong emphasis on technology, especially social media, smartphones and other smart applications. Once again, there was a strong emphasis on engaging with customers through two-way communications (Fig. 21.8).

Based upon the combination of the trends found in 2017, DestinationNEXT suggested a newly re-engineered DMO model with these five roles (Destinations International 2017):

1. Curators: Preparing and gathering content on the destination.
2. Adopters: Collecting and analyzing data, including big data analysis.
3. Catalysts: Being active participants in destination economic development.
4. Activists: Placemaking advocates in developing distinctive sense of place.
5. Collaborators: Building partnership networks.

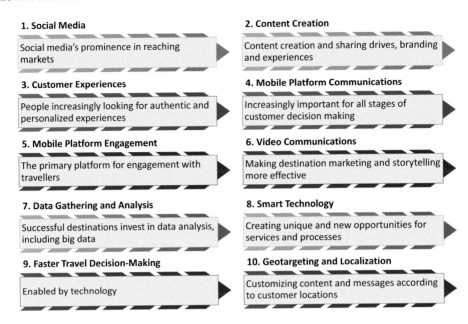

1. Social Media
Social media's prominence in reaching markets

2. Content Creation
Content creation and sharing drives, branding and experiences

3. Customer Experiences
People increasingly looking for authentic and personalized experiences

4. Mobile Platform Communications
Increasingly important for all stages of customer decision making

5. Mobile Platform Engagement
The primary platform for engagement with travellers

6. Video Communications
Making destination marketing and storytelling more effective

7. Data Gathering and Analysis
Successful destinations invest in data analysis, including big data

8. Smart Technology
Creating unique and new opportunities for services and processes

9. Faster Travel Decision-Making
Enabled by technology

10. Geotargeting and Localization
Customizing content and messages according to customer locations

Top ten trends in Phase 2 of DestinationNEXT

Figure 21.8   Top ten trends in Phase 2 of DestinationNEXT (Destinations International 2017).

TrekkSoft Survey of DMO Marketing

TrekkSoft is a software provider for tourism with its headquarters in Switzerland. In 2017, the company conducted a survey of sixty-one DMOs on their destination marketing activities. They found that DMOs in North America were spending 60 percent of their budgets on e-marketing and 40 percent offline. European DMOs were spending less online, at 53 percent. Most organizations (56 percent) believed that experiences were a vital part of their marketing (TrekkSoft 2017).

The TrekkSoft survey demonstrated that DMOs were finding it difficult to stay relevant for travelers among all the online competitors.

EXAMPLE 21.5

Staying Relevant Online Is Challenging for DMOs

This example suggests that it is increasingly difficult for DMOs to compete with online travel giants.

Organizations investing most in the planning stage find themselves directly in competition with big-budget giants (e.g., Tripadvisor, Google Trips). Similarly, at the booking stage, the majority of activity bookings are happening on the OTAs and supplier sites. While organizations shouldn't ignore the planning and booking stages, they must acknowledge that they simply cannot compete with the likes of Tripadvisor and Booking.com who have much larger budgets.

(TrekkSoft 2017)

Learning Point

DMOs must find an online niche that delivers value to consumers.

Destination Think! Survey of International Tourism Offices

Destination Think! is a consultancy and marketing agency for DMOs with its headquarters in Vancouver, Canada. During 2017, the company did a survey of seventy-one international tourism offices of DMOs located in the USA, Canada, the UK, Australia and The Netherlands. They found that the marketing done by these overseas offices of DMOs had changed from a main emphasis on the travel trade and media to more customer-direct activities, especially online. The offices were finding it challenging to adapt to the new circumstances (Destination Think! 2017).

EXAMPLE 21.6

Are DMOs Going to Become Obsolete?

This short quote questions whether some DMOs will become obsolete.

As traditional marketing tactics become less effective, and some international offices are closing, DMOs are under pressure to find new approaches that can compete in a global market. The need to remain relevant is leading DMO staff to embrace new technologies and adopt new tactics.

(Destination Think! 2017)

Learning Point

DMOs must increase their value to consumers and the tourism sector.

As a postscript to this first part of Chapter 21, you should realize that many DMOs are already transforming from the old to the new model of destination management. Additionally, although many of the foregoing comments and ideas have been about pleasure and leisure travel, the same applies to business travel and business events. The ten sources comprehensively reviewed the issues in destination management. They provide a wide variety of perspectives on the operation of DMOs and from different geographic regions and types of professionals and span from 2006 to 2018. There were many similarities in the opinions expressed in the ten sources, although each of them offered certain unique views on important issues.

Summary of Issues and Trends from Previous Chapters

Before beginning the second part and the future trends and potential challenges, it is worth reviewing the issues and trends that have been cited in this book. Some of these reinforce the sentiments from the ten sources, whereas others were not covered in these sources:

Destination Management

The success of a DMO is at least in part measured by how well it communicates and interacts with its stakeholders (Chapter 1). The field of destination management is receiving greater recognition and becoming more professional (Chapter 1).

Destination Sustainability and Social Responsibility

Destinations and DMOs must become more socially responsible and give a higher priority to sustainable tourism (Chapter 2).

Quality of Life and Well-Being of Destination Residents

Local resident quality of life and well-being require greater care and attention from DMOs (Chapter 3).

EXAMPLE 21.7

DMOs Becoming a Community Asset: Community Shared Value

Destinations International advocates that DMOs must get more involved in their local communities and become a more valuable force therein.

Becoming a community asset focusing on residents as your customers:

We can no longer count on blind government support; we can no longer solely rely on ROI statistics and we can no longer rely on visitation numbers to be the measure of our success. As our elected officials, the media and our communities are asking for transparency and taking a closer look at our budgets and operations, it is our job to make sure we are prepared to answer any questions by staying vigilant and proactive. We must realize that our local residents are our ultimate customers and make our efforts a shared value in our community and our teams a community asset.

(Destinations International 2022a)

Learning Point

Making a greater contribution to local communities should be a future focus for DMOs.

Destination Planning

Tourism planning for destinations is still maturing, and there remain many destinations around the world that are without long-term tourism plans. It is difficult to contemplate professional destination management without long-term planning (Chapter 4).

There is not enough investment in various forms of consumer and product research by DMOs (Chapter 5).

Destination Leadership, Coordination, and Governance

Destination governance is a concept that is receiving increasing attention. This is how a DMO is administered and who does the administering. Governance involves the policies, systems and processes to ensure that all stakeholders are involved and that the DMO is accountable for its results and resource usage and has a high level of transparency (Chapter 6).

The funding of DMOs in many places in the world has been under threat because of government budget deficits and downturns in tourism business levels. Several DMOs are looking for new ways to earn revenues in the face of significant cost cutting (Chapter 6).

EXAMPLE 21.8

New DMO Organizational Structures Needed

This example, based on research in The Netherlands, recommends that DMOs need to explore new organizational structures. This supports what many experts have been saying for the past fifteen to twenty years.

> New, alternative organizational structures and models for destination management and governance are emerging, as is discussed in this trends paper based on a set of observations made in The Netherlands. Forces driving change include the overall growth of the tourism industry, competition is increasing, visitors become experienced and more demanding, the negative impacts of tourism are openly debated and solutions to manage emerging issues involve the actions and capacities of many (and new) stakeholders, across different (policy) domains and governance levels. Clearly, a focus exclusively on destination marketing is insufficient and DMOs and NTOs shift their focus en masse from marketing to management.
>
> (Hartman et al. 2020)

Learning Point

DMOs need to expand their roles and find novel ways to structure themselves.

Destination Product Development

DMOs are generally becoming more involved in destination product development as the competition for tourists intensifies. There is also greater recognition that destination marketing and product development are closely intertwined and that those involved in destination marketing should have an interest and involvement in product development (Chapter 7).

Quality is important for destinations, and all the dimensions of quality (hardware, software and environment) need to be managed. Significant benefits accrue to those destinations that make a concerted effort to manage quality (Chapter 7).

All destinations are facing serious challenges with respect to human resource availability and quality (Chapter 7).

Destination Partnership and Team-Building

Although the potential benefits from destination partnerships are substantial, there are many barriers and challenges to setting up such cooperation and collaborations. Lack of adequate financial resources, communication problems, uneven benefit distribution and unwillingness to cooperate are just a few of the roadblocks to destination partnerships (Chapter 8).

Destination Stakeholder and Community Relationships and Involvement

Community relationships and involvement are becoming a more important role of destination management as DMOs increasingly recognize that they must have the support of local community residents and tourism sector stakeholders. This is putting much more pressure on DMOs not only to perform at a high level in external markets but also to be outstanding at building and maintaining relationships at home (Chapter 9).

Visitor Management

DMOs must play a more active role in visitor management. Some destinations are suffering from having too many visitors (overtourism). DMOs must have greater concern for visitor safety and security. DMOs must have crisis management plans. DMOs should use yield management to increase the positive economic benefits of tourism (Chapter 10).

Destination Crisis Management

Destinations and DMOs are not yet well prepared for crises (Chapter 11).

Destination Marketing Planning

Many DMOs are not yet following a long-term and systematic, step-by-step approach to destination marketing, branding, and communications (Chapter 12).

Destination PIB

Branding tourism destinations is challenging given the diversity of destination products and the experience good characteristic of tourism. Destination branding often requires time to be successful, and so patience is required as well as continual investment in the brand (Chapter 13).

Destination IMC

E-marketing using ICTs is now being given much greater emphasis by DMOs (Chapter 14).

E-marketing and ICTs

E-marketing is becoming the most important way to communicate about destinations. Content creation to support e-marketing is now a critical activity for DMOs (Chapter 15).

For the past thirty years, ICTs have had a major impact on tourism in general. They have revolutionized how DMOs share destination information and engage with people. It is very likely that they will be even more important for destination management in the future (Chapter 15).

Consumer Behavior, Market Segmentation and Trends

DMOs need to constantly stay on top of market trends because customers and their behaviors are changing more quickly than before (Chapter 16).

EXAMPLE 21.9

What Destinations Should Communicate Post-COVID

A group of researchers from Purdue University in the USA conducted a research study on which communication messages would be best to use in post-COVID recovery. The features of the messages are highlighted in this example.

> Three rounds of conventional Delphi research delivered fifteen message features, eight of which attained panel consensus. These included COVID-related features such as safety, accurate pandemic information, a show of open outdoor spaces, and building visitor confidence along with destination-related features including positive destination attributes, authentic local experience, locals support, and reminder of joys of travel.
>
> (Singh et al. 2022)

Learning Point

Safety and authenticity are among the most appropriate messages for destinations to communicate.

Domestic Pleasure and Leisure Travel Markets

Domestic tourism is a mainstay of the tourism sectors in many parts of the world, particularly in the developed nations. Unfortunately, domestic tourism often is given second-class status compared to international tourism. However, this changed during the COVID-19 pandemic (Chapter 17).

International Pleasure and Leisure Travel Markets

International tourism remains highly susceptible to negative impacts from various types of crises, as exemplified by COVID-19 (Chapter 18).

Business Travel and Business Event Markets

The major challenges and issues facing business travel and business events are market, technology, competition, economic, safety and security, interdependency, policy compliance and cost control, and reputation and credibility (Chapter 19).

Destination-Management Performance Measurement and Management

DMOs need to do a more thorough job of performance measurement. New systems and processes are needed (Chapter 20).

As well as providing a good summary of some of the main recommendations of this book, these points bring out some additional issues regarding DMOs and destination management. For example, this book emphasizes that the professionalization of destination management is under way but this still requires greater recognition and attention. Programs such as Destination International's Certified Destination Management Executive have done much to focus attention on this issue, as also have its Standard DMO Performance Reporting system and Destination Marketing Accreditation Program. These truly have been visionary initiatives to improve the professionalism in destination management.

The ten sources described earlier seem to assume that DMOs were or are doing a good job of destination marketing and promotion but needed to focus more attention elsewhere. However, if we take more of a global focus, this is not entirely accurate because the destination marketing, IMC, and research practices in many countries still require great improvement.

Another issue that was not heavily touched upon by the ten sources is how DMOs need to allocate priorities among different markets (domestic vs. international, pleasure/leisure vs. visiting friends and relatives vs. business travel/business events). Too many experts are quick to say that DMOs must get more engaged online, but exactly where is still a practical question that they leave unanswered.

One must also wonder whether the issues being experienced by DMOs and destination management are in fact a symptom of a lack of understanding and respect for tourism in general in many nations of the world. The late American comedian Rodney Dangerfield always used the line "I don't get no respect." In many ways, tourism is a "don't get no respect" economic sector that is not given the priority that it deserves. In the bigger picture, the issues that face destination management are also issues faced by tourism in general.

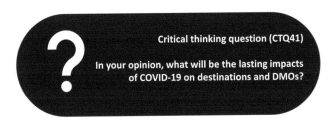

? Critical thinking question (CTQ41)

In your opinion, what will be the lasting impacts of COVID-19 on destinations and DMOs?

Destination Management Issues in the COVID-19 Years

EXAMPLE 21.10

From Overtourism to Industry Survival

The priority for several destinations has switched from battling overtourism to just surviving the ravages caused by COVID, as expressed in this example.

The COVID-19 pandemic represents an unprecedent shock to the tourism industry's growth model since World War II, challenging tourism stakeholders

Part V

(destinations and companies) with several threats and opportunities to their future competitiveness. In addition to the massive impacts in terms of business development, the abrupt reduction of tourism demand and the significative loss of jobs, the pandemic also caused significant disruption in terms of destination-management models. In less than four months, the focus of governments and DMOs shifted from defining development models compatible with improving the quality of life of residents due to the emergence of the so-called overtourism phenomenon, to the urgent need to support the industry's survival, to preserve jobs and ensure conditions of safety for tourists and workers.

(Guerreiro 2022)

Learning Point

Visitor safety and job retention in tourism have earned a higher priority due to COVID.

There was a flood of opinions about what DMOs should be doing during and after the COVID-19 pandemic. At the time of writing, there were still COVID cases in several countries and China was enforcing a zero-COVID policy that was restricting international travel departures. Just to give you a snapshot of what was being said, the author has summarized ten of the major suggestions along with their sources, which were from practitioners and academics (Fig. 21.9).

Post-COVID recommendations for destination management

- Need to change
- Shift from destination marketing to destination management
- Put greater emphasis on sustainable tourism
- Do more to halt climate change
- Have more of a local focus
- Have a greater focus on visitor needs
- Prioritize authenticity and experiences
- Diversify funding sources
- Give greater attention to partnering
- Use new technologies and platforms

Figure 21.9   Post-COVID recommendations for destination management.

DMOs Need to Change

This is definitely the strongest collective sentiment being expressed in the wake of the pandemic. You might say this is a "no brainer" after all you have read already in this chapter—and your author agrees. COVID-19 made the need to change more obvious, however.

From Destination Marketing to Destination Management

Your author thinks it is time to stop calling DMOs destination marketing organizations and to get completely rid of the DMMO moniker (destination marketing and management organizations) that some use. More people are now agreeing with him (e.g., PGAV Destinations 2022). Narrowing down what DMOs do to just marketing is dangerous and is one of the reasons why they receive significant criticism. A broader set of roles should be assumed by DMOs in the future, as advocated throughout this book.

DMOs Must Put Greater Emphasis on Sustainable Tourism

The absence of visitors from famous destinations was illuminating for many people and showed that environmental conditions improved. There is strong agreement among the prognosticators that DMOs must get more serious about sustainable tourism (e.g., Anderson and Bolger 2021; Babii and Nadeem 2021; Fromm 2022; Masiga 2022).

EXAMPLE 21.11

A "Do Better" Future

This example makes the point that travelers should do their best to improve the destinations that they visit—making a positive contribution to communities.

> Marketers should now measure success not only by how many people it booked to a particular destination, but in what condition those visitors left that destination—both ecologically and economically—after the trip was over. Many signs are telling us that the future of travel is sustainable, but also that the definition of sustainability is evolving from "do no harm" to "do better." Those that lead the way will create thriving destinations for travelers and local communities alike, benefiting both the economy and the environment.
>
> (Butera 2021)

Learning Point

Tourists must enrich rather than damage the places they go to.

Destinations and DMOs Must Do More to Halt Climate Change

Picking up on what was said in Chapter 2, destinations must do more individually to deal with the climate change issue (Gössling and Higham 2021).

DMOs Must Have More of a Local Focus

You learned in Chapter 3 that DMOs need to put a high priority on resident quality and life and well-being. Several of the forecasters agree that DMOs must put more focus on local communities (e.g., Becker and Hanft 2021; Kaefer 2021).

DMOs need to have a greater focus on visitor needs

Destinations are being urged toward the "marketing of care" or a holistic set of benefits for visitors (Becker and Hanft 2021). DMOs must be more diligent in following and responding to long-term changes in what visitors need (Lahood 2020). A greater emphasis on mindfulness and more conscious travelers is recommended by some observers (e.g., Hussain 2021; Stankov et al. 2020).

EXAMPLE 21.12

Tourism Taxes Can Have Visitor and Resident Support

User-pay taxes will be accepted if visitors and residents agree with how they are applied; that is the message in this example.

> It is evident that revenues from tourism taxes can make a positive difference for destinations' work in nature preservation, restoration of cultural heritage, and help fund social and community projects. While tourism taxes are often a hot topic of debate and strongly opposed by industry stakeholders, there is also evidence that the willingness to pay among consumers is comparatively higher if the purpose of taxation and the use of revenue is transparent and meaningful. Also, tourism taxes are often favored by residents and can provide a platform for stronger destination collaboration.
>
> (Group NAO 2020)

Learning Point

Devote part of the taxes to causes with which visitors and residents agree, and be transparent about how the funds are used.

Destinations and DMOs Must Prioritize Authenticity and Experiences

There is a consensus among the predictions that destinations and DMOs should be putting more focus on visitor experiences rather than on product features (Globo Drew 2022; Gulf Business 2022). In so doing, the emphasis should be on making experiences as authentic as possible.

DMOs Need to Diversify Funding Sources

This was a recommendation that you heard about in Chapter 20. Several of the expert sources support the notion that in future DMOs must have a broader portfolio of funding sources than at present (Girma 2020; Group NAO 2020; Miles Partnership 2021).

Partnering Requires Greater Attention

Some expert sources note that destination rivals became friends when faced with similar challenges resulting from the pandemic (Girma 2021). There are many untapped partnering opportunities for DMOs.

New Technologies and Platforms Will Increase in Importance

DMOs were expected to make even greater use of technology in the future including metaverse (Auslander 2022) and TikTok (Simpleview Europe 2021). Destinations and DMOs will also be making more use of mixed reality (augmented and virtual) and artificial intelligence in the years to come (EDGventures 2020; Egger and Neuburger 2022).

EXAMPLE 21.13

Welcome the Metaverse to Destination Management

The metaverse offers great future potential for destination management. This example explains how it will provide an exciting new venue for DMOs.

> This new application of the web allows marketers to reach travelers through immersive technologies that offer physical and digital experiences and blur the boundaries between virtual and physical spaces. In the metaverse, a destination's attractions: museums, botanical gardens, heritage sites, restaurants, hotels, and national parks can reach travelers through a virtual tour miles away. While it cannot recreate travel, the new web can serve as a source of inspiration and storytelling for travelers. In the immersive reality of the virtual setting, destination marketers can feed users with sight, sound, hearing, and even smell.
>
> (Auslander 2021)

Learning Point

DMOs need to embrace the metaverse quickly and make it work for them.

Expected Future Trends and Potential Challenges for Destinations and DMOs

It is difficult to predict exactly what will happen with DMOs in the next ten years, but in all probability, many of the current issues and trends will continue into the foreseeable future. However, the following eight future trends and potential challenges are anticipated:

1. Consolidation of place marketing and branding entities.
2. Digitalization of content continues.
3. Funding sources remain troublesome.
4. Greater investment in technology-enabled marketing.
5. More collaboration among DMOs and associations.
6. New DMO business models appear.
7. Professionalization of destination management gains pace.
8. Sustainable tourism development gets a higher priority.

Consolidation of Place Marketing and Branding Entities

There has been a strong movement toward place marketing and branding in recent times, and this has been extended to all economic sectors of nations, states/provinces/territories and cities. Places are becoming increasingly aggressive in trying to attract inward investment, human talent, university and other students, and major events. DMOs have shown other sectors how to be successful at place branding, but ironically the greater visibility gained from these efforts may make them targets for consolidation into more comprehensive and integrated economic development agencies. In the continuing fragile economic times ahead and tight public-sector funding, this consolidation or rationalization of place marketing and branding entities seems inevitable.

Digitalization of Content Continues

Everyone expects that DMOs will continue to digitalize content and that the primary way to communicate with all audiences will be through ICTs, especially social media and smartphone platforms. DMOs have made great strides in this respect since around 1995, but other for-profit entities have innovated more rapidly. DMOs need to quickly catch up with these other entities, or else they will eventually be overlooked online by consumers and meeting planners.

EXAMPLE 21.14

DMO Staff Need to Become More Digital Savvy

This example suggests that DMO staff skill sets need to change as their organizations evolve and put greater emphasis on e-marketing. The integration of more use of AI will be part of this trend.

> With digitalization comes the need for a workforce prepared to take on the challenges that AI integration presents. In particular, T&H (tourism and hospitality) organizations require a highly skilled workforce with both technical and non-technical skill sets. DMOs should also consider providing training to improve workers' AI knowledge, resilience, and flexibility in the swiftly changing labor market. In addition, the workforce needs to have advanced communication and critical thinking soft skills to provide consumer- and stakeholder-oriented services. DMO staff need to be well versed in digital tools and be capable of understanding the pros and cons of various AI applications in destination marketing. Given the richness of insights that can be extracted from user-generated data, DMOs need knowledgeable and skilled staff to administer destinations' massive databases, apply data mining and data scraping procedures, and integrate data analytics into decision-making processes.
>
> (Huang et al. 2022)

Learning Point

The trend toward e-marketing in DMOs will continue into the future.

Funding Sources Remain Troublesome

The funding of DMOs will continue to be a very troubling issue in many countries, and it is very likely that many DMOs will have to make do with lower budgets than they have been accustomed to. Retail travel agencies have been able to survive by changing their revenue source models, and so too must DMOs in the future.

Greater Investment in Technology-Enabled Marketing

As suggested by several of the sources pre- and post-COVID described earlier, DMOs need to make a much heavier investment in technology-enabled marketing, probably by diverting funds away from the expensive traditional media that they have been using for decades.

More Collaboration among DMOs and Associations

Greater collaboration and more partnerships among DMOs and other entities seem to be highly likely and needed. DMOs will increasingly be sharing resources to achieve common goals and desired outcomes. Also, and as suggested by Ford and Peeper (2008), associations that are active in destination management will need to work more collaboratively in the future to support the efforts of DMO practitioners.

EXAMPLE 21.15

DMOs Need to Find New Partnership Models

This example recommends that DMOs should develop new partnerships within their own destinations.

> Most immediately, a range of DMOs have successfully built a model as community-marketing leaders or are currently building connections with a wide range of partners in their destination around "Community Shared Values" (championed by Destinations International). This envisages building relationships, services and funding with "unusual" suspects from airports to universities, major public facilities to employers and commercial property owners.
>
> (Miles Partnership 2021)

Learning Point

DMOs must reach out to new partners locally.

New DMO Business Models Appear

As Ford and Peeper (2008) and DestinationNEXT have suggested, many DMOs will have to make radical changes in their business models in the future. For example, the USA, for a long time the sleeping giant of world tourism, finally awoke in May 2012 because of a new business model and launched its first-ever global tourism marketing campaign through Brand USA.

Professionalization of Destination Management Gains Pace

Undoubtedly these past twenty to twenty-five years have witnessed increasing professionalism in destination management. Destination-management associations have been pioneering this movement to better prepare DMO professionals for the future. In the future, it is anticipated that academic institutions will join in this effort by offering degree programs in destination management.

Sustainable Tourism Development Gets a Higher Priority

In some parts of the world, such as Australia and New Zealand, DMOs are placing a high priority on environmental concerns as well as on the social-cultural impacts of tourism. However, many DMOs have still to fully engage in this movement and seem to be giving it lip service rather than allocating resources to it. This will change in the future, and DMOs will generally give sustainable tourism development a much higher priority.

EXAMPLE 21.16

What Is Revenge Travel?

This example highlights the new consumer trend of revenge travel. It means that people are more keen to travel post-COVID after having their trips so restricted.

> Revenge travel is a slang term for leisure travel that follows a period of being unable to travel. Specifically, the term originated as a way to refer to vacationing following the lessening of COVID-19 restrictions (which had greatly reduced travel). As such restrictions lessened in 2021 and 2022, leisure travel and particularly air travel increased significantly. This trend has been explained, particularly by travel marketers and in media reports, as being the result of revenge travel—people taking "revenge" on COVID-19 by taking the trips that the pandemic prevented them from taking earlier.
>
> (*Pop Culture Dictionary* 2022)

Learning Point

Revenge travel will be beneficial for destinations.

?

Critical thinking question (CTQ42)

How do you think that DMOs will look in the future?

The DMO of the Future

What will the future DMOs look like? One could say that the writing is already on the wall for DMOs to see how they must change to be more responsive to consumer and external environmental trends. Many DMOs need to change from being mainly sales organizations to becoming well-rounded and officially endorsed destination-management organizations. The following eight future DMO characteristics are likely (Fig. 21.10):

1. Professional destination managers.
2. Tourism network hubs.
3. Collaboration experts.
4. Digital content masters and facilitators.
5. Experience brokers.
6. Environmental and cultural champions.
7. Official consumer and tourism advocates.
8. Supporters of residents.

Professional Destination Managers

The DMO of the future is operated by professional destination managers who have attended universities and obtained degrees in this field. The universities have worked closely with destination-management associations in creating curricula and sit on the advisory boards for these programs.

Tourism Network Hubs

The DMO of the future is a hub of many networked organizations. Local sector stakeholders go to DMOs for market and industry intelligence and research. DMOs coach local tourism sector stakeholders on how to make their products and services have greater appeal in the marketplace.

Collaboration Experts

DMOs are experts in collaborations and partnership and team-building. DMO staff members are tasked with reaching out to other organizations and are rewarded for establishing effective collaborative models. Collaborative models are established at all geographic levels, from international to local, across markets and tourism sub-sectors, and according to major issues (e.g., the environment, professional education and training, crisis/risk management, quality assurance).

Digital Content Masters and Facilitators

DMOs are masters at managing digital content. They encourage residents, tourism sector stakeholders, and tourists to develop content and to engage in discussions and conversations about the destination. They teach tourism sector stakeholders how to put content online.

Experience Brokers

DMOs arrange experiences for tourists within their destinations. They find out what experiences consumers want and work with tourism sector stakeholders to design these experiences. They stay in touch with tourists to ensure that their experiences go well and meet their expectations. DMOs encourage tourists to write and develop digital content about their experiences. DMOs provide feedback to tourism sector stakeholders and coach them to make necessary improvements in the experiences they offer.

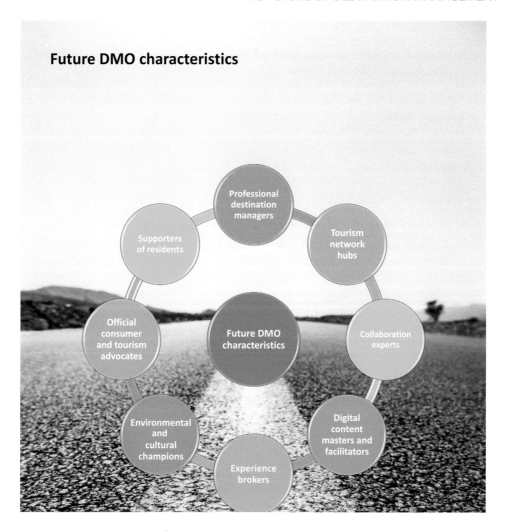

Future DMO characteristics

Figure 21.10   Future DMO characteristics.

EXAMPLE 21.17

Immersive Experiences for Conscious Travelers

This example suggests that Indigenous tourism will increase (in Australia) as travelers become more conscious of their surroundings and have a greater willingness to learn about local cultures.

When asked why a keener focus has been placed on Indigenous tourism experiences in this particular campaign, Anderson shared that the segment has "been growing," and is an "immersive experience" sought after by today's conscious travelers.

"Prior to the pandemic in 2019, around 1.4 million international visitors participated in an Indigenous tourism experience in Australia, a six per cent year-on-year increase since 2010. Our Aboriginal and Torres Strait Islander stories are rich and diverse, and have the potential to be a point of difference and an area of competitive advantage for Australian tourism," he said.

(Lee 2022)

Learning Point

More conscious travelers will seek immersive destination experiences including Indigenous tourism.

Environmental and Cultural Champions

DMOs are at the forefront in promoting sustainable tourism and other initiatives designed to protect the environment. They champion all efforts in their communities to conserve and protect heritage resources and insist on the authentic portrayal of local culture.

EXAMPLE 21.18

Tourism to Get Greener Post-COVID

This example from the International Monetary Fund highlights the expectation that destinations will put greater emphasis on ecotourism and health and wellness post-COVID.

Post-pandemic, a continuing shift toward ecotourism—a fast-growing industry focused on conservation and local job creation—could give an additional boost to the industry. This is already a key element of Costa Rica's tourism strategy. Thailand too is trying to shift to niche markets, including adventure travel and health and wellness tours.

(Babii and Nadeem 2021)

Learning Point

Destinations and DMOs will pursue more niche markets in the future including nature-based tourism and ecotourism, and health and wellness tourism.

Official Consumer and Tourism Advocates

Official is the word that separates DMOs from all other players in destination management. DMOs have been ratified by local government policies to serve the best interests of tourists and of the local tourism sector. Consumers deeply trust DMOs because they are truthful, honest, and ethical in all that they do.

Supporters of Residents

DMOs view community residents as vitally important to tourism and place identity. They accept that managing visitor volumes and their dispersion within the destination are part of their responsibility. DMOs seek out smart destination solutions to avoid overcrowding and to enhance visitor and resident satisfaction.

EXAMPLE 21.19

Localhood by Copenhagen

Many commentators suggest that DMOs must have more of a local focus in the future. Wonderful Copenhagen, the DMO for Denmark's capital, is a strong advocate of this strategy, as evidenced in this example.

> Localhood is a long-term vision that supports the inclusive co-creation of our future destination. A future destination where human relations are the focal point. Where locals and visitors not only co-exist, but interact around shared experiences of localhood. Where our global competitiveness is underpinned by our very own localhood. And where tourism growth is co-created responsibly across industries and geographies, between new and existing stakeholders, with localhood as our shared identity and common starting point.
>
> (Wonderful Copenhagen 2017)

Learning Point

Visitors and residents can co-create new destination experiences.

Many experts predicted that the days of brick-and-mortar travel agencies were over when airlines, particularly in North America, removed the commissions to which they had become accustomed. However, although fewer in numbers than in their heyday, traditional travel agencies are still around. DMOs similarly are very likely to survive because they can play an essential role in tourism.

EXAMPLE 21.20

Putin Abolishes Rostourism

This example demonstrates how politics and political leaders can upset the good work of DMOs over decades.

> Russian President Vladimir Putin on Thursday signed a decree abolishing Rostourism, Russia's federal tourism agency, and handing its remit to the Economic Development Ministry. The Economic Ministry said in a statement that the decision to dissolve Rostourism and to give its responsibilities to the ministry would help Russia meet its tourism objectives more effectively. Rostourism had overseen the provision of state services related to tourism across Russia since it was established in 2004, overseeing big-ticket events such as the 2018 FIFA World Cup.
>
> The decision to abolish the agency comes at a time of turmoil for Russia's tourism industry, with strict Western sanctions imposed on Moscow for its invasion of Ukraine and the suspension of flights from most European countries.

> Over the past three years, the number of foreign tourists arriving in Russia has continued to decrease, according to Dmitry Gorin, the vice president of the Russian Union of Travel Industry, Izvestia reported in August.
>
> (*Moscow Times* 2022)

Learning Point

Politics and tourism often do not mix well.

SUMMING UP

Destination management is an emerging field in tourism, and it is not yet well understood by political decision-makers and the public. At the same time, DMOs are struggling for recognition while doing much more in proving their worth to their communities. Additionally, DMOs are experiencing new and intensifying competition from across the globe to within their own destinations. Their traditional exclusive space as information providers for tourists and meeting planners has been invaded by many new online, for-profit providers.

In the pre-COVID part, this chapter comprehensively reviewed ten authoritative sources providing expert commentary and ideas on the future of destination management and DMOs. Although drawn from different parts of the world, there was a strong consensus among these sources that DMOs need to change fundamentally if they are to survive.

The arrival of the COVID-19 pandemic worsened the plight of destinations and DMOs. The second part of Chapter 21 discussed the changes suggested by multiple sources. Several of these changes are similar to those suggested pre-COVID.

Many issues are affecting destination management and DMOs at the current time. These include the availability of funding for operations, increasing importance of ICTs, emergence of new competitors, global environmental problems, resident backlash because of overtourism, continual economic and other crises, growing concerns for personal safety and security, expanding market fragmentation, changing consumer expectations, requirements for more community resident involvement, and tightening controls on DMO operations and accountability. The broad scope of these issues and dealing with all of their implications mean that DMOs cannot just be sales offices or community megaphones for their tourism sectors; they must become strategic champions for their destinations, involved in all aspects of planning, research, development, and marketing.

The DMO of the future will probably look quite different from the one of today. It is envisaged that future DMOs will be professional destination managers, tourism network hubs, collaboration masters, digital content masters and facilitators, experience brokers, environmental and cultural champions, official consumer and tourism advocates, and supporters of residents. DMO executives and managers will have to have a much broader skill set in the future to deal with all the issues and challenges that they will undoubtedly face. It is incumbent on industry associations, DMO practitioners, and academic institutions to work together to prepare future professionals for these challenges.

KEYWORDS

artificial intelligence (AI)

big data

climate change

commodification

crowdsourcing

experiences

funding

low-carbon economy

metaverse

mindfulness

mixed reality

pivoting

place identity

place marketing and branding

public–private partnerships (PPPs)

recognition

recovery

relevancy

resilience

revenge travel

risk management

smart destination

value

virtual tourism

visibility

zero-based planning

REVIEW QUESTIONS

1. What were the challenges and issues affecting destination management pre-COVID?
2. What are the expected changes in destination management post-COVID?
3. What are the expected future trends and potential challenges for destinations and DMOs?
4. What might be some of the characteristics of future DMOs.

REFERENCES

American Express Global Business Travel (2022) "Corporate Meetings and Events," www.amexglobalbusinesstravel.com/meetings-events/

Anderson, K., and Bolger, L. (2021) "How to Evolve Destination Marketing for the Future of Travel," *PhocusWire*, June 28, www.phocuswire.com/How-to-evolve-destination-marketing-for-the-future-of-travel

Auslander, S. (2022) "The Future of Destination Marketing: Welcome to the Metaverse Generation," *Destinations International*, https://destinationsinternational.org/future-destination-marketing-welcome-metaverse

Babii, A., and Nadeem, S. (2021) "Tourism in a Post-Pandemic World," International Monetary Fund, February 26, www.imf.org/en/News/Articles/2021/02/24/na022521-how-to-save-travel-and-tourism-in-a-post-pandemic-world

Becker, M., and Hanft, A. (2021) "'Marketing of Care' and the Future of Tourism," *PhocusWire*, April 5, www.phocuswire.com/marketing-of-care-and-the-future-of-tourism-marketing

Butera, S. (2021) "The Future of Destination Marketing," June 29, https://sethbutera.com/the-future-of-destination-marketing/

ConferenceDirect (2022) "ConferenceDirect®," https://conferencedirect.com/

DestiCorp (2010) "Speculation on the future of destination marketing organizations (DMOs): A conceptual discussion paper." DestiCorp UK.

Destination Canada (2022) "Canadian Signature Experiences," https://travel.destinationcanada.com/canadian-signature-experiences

Destinations International (2008) "DMAI Futures Study 2008: The Future of Destination Marketing."

——— (2017) "DestinationNEXT: A Strategic Road Map for the NEXT Generation of Global Destination Organizations," *2017 Futures Study Update*, https://destinationsinternational.org/sites/default/master/files/Destinations_International_DestinationNEXT_2017_Futures_Study.pdf

——— (2022a) "Community Shared Value," https://destinationsinternational.org/community-shared-value

——— (2022b) "MINT+," https://destinationsinternational.org/mint

Destinations International and Inter VISTAS Consulting (2014) "DestinationNEXT: A Strategic Road Map for the NEXT Generation of Global Destination Marketing—Phase 1," http://mktg.destinationmarketing.org/acton/attachment/9856/f-06c0/1/-/-/-/-/DMAI_DestinationNEXT_2014_Report.pdf

Destinations Marketing Association International (2008) *DMAI Futures Study 2008: The Future of Destination Marketing*. Washington, DC: DMAI.

Destination Think! (2017) "Will International Tourism Offices Remain Relevant? Your Roadmap for the Future," https://destinationthink.com/white-paper-international-tourism-offices/

Dwyer, L., Edwards, D., Mistilis, N., Roman, C., and Scott, N. (2009) "Destination and Enterprise Management for a Tourism Future," *Tourism Management*, 30 (1): 63–74.

EDGventures (2020) "Transforming Destinations with Artificial Intelligence (AI)," www.edgventures.com/blog/transforming-destinations-with-artificial-intelligence-ai

Egger, R., and Neuburger, L. (2022) "Augmented, Virtual, and Mixed Reality in Tourism," in Z. Xiang, M. Fuchs, U. Gretzel, and W. Höpken (eds), *Handbook of E-tourism*, Cham: Springer, pp. 317–341.

Ford, R. C., and Peeper, W. C. (2008) *Managing Destination Marketing Organizations*, Orlando, Fla.: ForPer Publications.

Fromm, J. (2022) "CEO Shares Insights into the Future of Sustainable Travel: Brand Actions Are Critical," *Forbes*, September 29, www.forbes.com/sites/jefffromm/2022/09/29/ceo-shares-insights-into-the-future-of-sustainable-travel-brand-actions-are-critical/

Fyall, A., and Leask, A. (2006) "Destination Marketing: Future Issues, Strategic Challenges," *Tourism and Hospitality Research*, 7 (1): 50–63.

Girma, L. L. (2020) "A Funding Crisis at DMOs Spurs New Tourism Marketing Models," *Skift*, December 1, https://skift.com/2020/12/01/funding-crisis-facing-destinations-forces-rethinking-for-tourism-marketing/

——— (2021) "Destinations Put Aside Old Rivalries with New Combined Marketing," *Skift*, September 2, https://skift.com/2021/09/02/destinations-put-aside-old-rivalries-with-new-combined-marketing/

Globo Drew (2022) "The Long-Term Successful Future of Destination Tourism Marketing Must Include Authentic Community Tourism + Micro-Branding," *Grey Journal*, https://greyjournal.net/play/learn-culture/the-long-term-successful-future-of-destination-tourism-marketing-must-include-authentic-community-tourism-micro-branding/amp/

Gössling, S., and Higham, J. (2021) "The Low-Carbon Imperative: Destination Management under Urgent Climate Change," *Journal of Travel Research*, 60 (6): 1167–1179.

Group NAO (2020) "Tourism Taxes by Design," https://groupnao.com/tourism-taxes-by-design/

Guerreiro, S. (2022) "Destination Management in a Post-Covid Environment," *Worldwide Hospitality and Tourism Themes*, 14 (1): 48–55.

Gulf Business (2022) "ATM 2022: In-Destination Experiences to Shape the Future of Global Travel and Tourism," *Gulf Business*, May 10, https://gulfbusiness.com/atm-2022-in-destination-experiences-to-shape-the-future-of-global-travel-and-tourism/

Hartman, S., Wielenga, B., and Heslinga, J. H. (2020) "The Future of Tourism Destination Management: Building Productive Coalitions of Actor Networks for Complex Destination Development," *Journal of Tourism Futures*, 6 (3): 213–218.

Helms Briscoe (2022) "The Global Leader in Meetings Procurement and Site Selection," www.helmsbriscoe.com/

Huang, A., De la Mora Velasco, E., Haney, A., and Alvarez, S. (2022) "The Future of Destination Marketing Organizations in the Insight Era," *Tourism and Hospitality*, 3: 803–808.

Hussain, A. (2021) "A Future of Tourism Industry: Conscious Travel, Destination Recovery and Regenerative Tourism," *Journal of Sustainability and Resilience*, 1 (1), https://digitalcommons.usf.edu/jsr/vol1/iss1/5

Kaefer, F. (2021) "Bill Geist on the Future of Destination Marketing and DMOs," in F. Kaefer, *An Insider's Guide to Place Branding*, Cham: Springer, pp. 81–85.

Lahood, D. (2020) "Destination Marketing Is Not Just About the Recovery—It's Now a Long Game," *PhocusWire*, June 10, www.phocuswire.com/Destination-marketing-coronavirus-long-game

Lee, R. A. J. (2022) "Tourism Australia Gets Cute and Serious in Latest Destination Marketing," *TTG Asia*, October 20, www.ttgasia.com/2022/10/20/tourism-australia-gets-cute-and-serious-in-latest-destination-marketing/

Maritz Global Events (2022) "Like No Other," www.maritzglobalevents.com/

Masiga, J. (2022) "What's Next for the Future of Travel and Tourism? Here's What the Experts Say," World Economic Forum, June 30, www.weforum.org/agenda/2022/06/what-next-for-travel-and-tourism-industry-experts-explain/

Miles Partnership (2021) "Funding Futures: Executive Summary and Recommendations," https://ss-usa.s3.amazonaws.com/c/308483931/media/15766183f6386855739468076744659/2021_FundingFutures_ExecSummary.pdf

Moscow Times (2022) "Putin Abolishes Russia's Federal Tourism Agency," October 20, www.themoscowtimes.com/2022/10/20/putin-dissolves-russias-federal-tourism-agency-a79143

Ouimet, P. (2014) "Destination NEXT. A Strategic Road Map for the NEXT Generation of Destination Marketing," https://destinationsinternational.org/sites/default/files/DestinationNEXT_2021FuturesStudy_FINAL2.pdf

PGAV Destinations (2022) "Destination Marketing Becomes Destination Management," https://pgavdestinations.com/quarterly-publications/destination-marketing-becomes-destination-management/

Pollock, A. (2009) "The Future of Destination Marketing: Why All Marketing Is Social Marketing," Presentation to BIT Reiseliv, Oslo, Norway.

——— (2010) "Speculation on the Future of Destination Marketing Organizations (DMOs): A Conceptual Discussion Paper."

Pop Culture Dictionary (2022) "What Is Revenge Travel?" July 26, www.dictionary.com/e/pop-culture/revenge-travel/

Schetzina, C. (2009) "Destination Marketing: Understanding the Role and Impact of Destination Marketers," PhoCusWright Inc. White paper. New York.

Simpleview Europe (2021) "Is TikTok the Future of Destination Marketing?" February 24, www.simplevieweurope.com/blog/read/2021/02/is-tiktok-the-future-of-destination-marketing-b126

Singh, S., Nicely, A., Day, J., and Cai, L. A. (2022) "Marketing Messages for Post-pandemic Destination Recovery: A Delphi Study," *Journal of Destination Marketing and Management*, 23. https://doi.org/10.1016/j.jdmm.2021.100676

Stankov, U., Filimonau, V., and Vujičić, M. D. (2020) "A Mindful Shift: An Opportunity for Mindfulness-Driven Tourism in a Post-pandemic World," *Tourism Geographies*, 22 (3): 703–712.

TrekkSoft (2017) "Making Experiences the Cornerstone of Destination Marketing Organisations Remaining Relevant in 2017," www.trekksoft.com/en/blog/how-dmos-are-remaining-relevant-with-experiences-report

usdm.net (2010) "Leadership Report: Are You a Revolutionary DMO?"

Wonderful Copenhagen (2017) "The End of Tourism as We Know It," http://localhood.wonderful-copenhagen.dk/

Index

Note: **Bold** page numbers refer to tables; *italic* page numbers refer to figures.